The Complete

Chi's Sweet Home

Part 1

Konami Kanata

contents
homemade 1~56 + 🐱 + 🐾

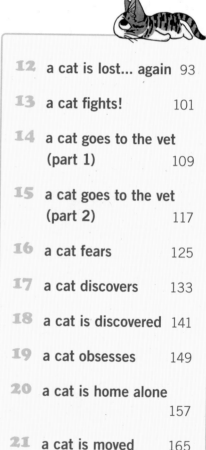

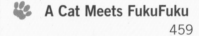

homemade 1: a cat is lost

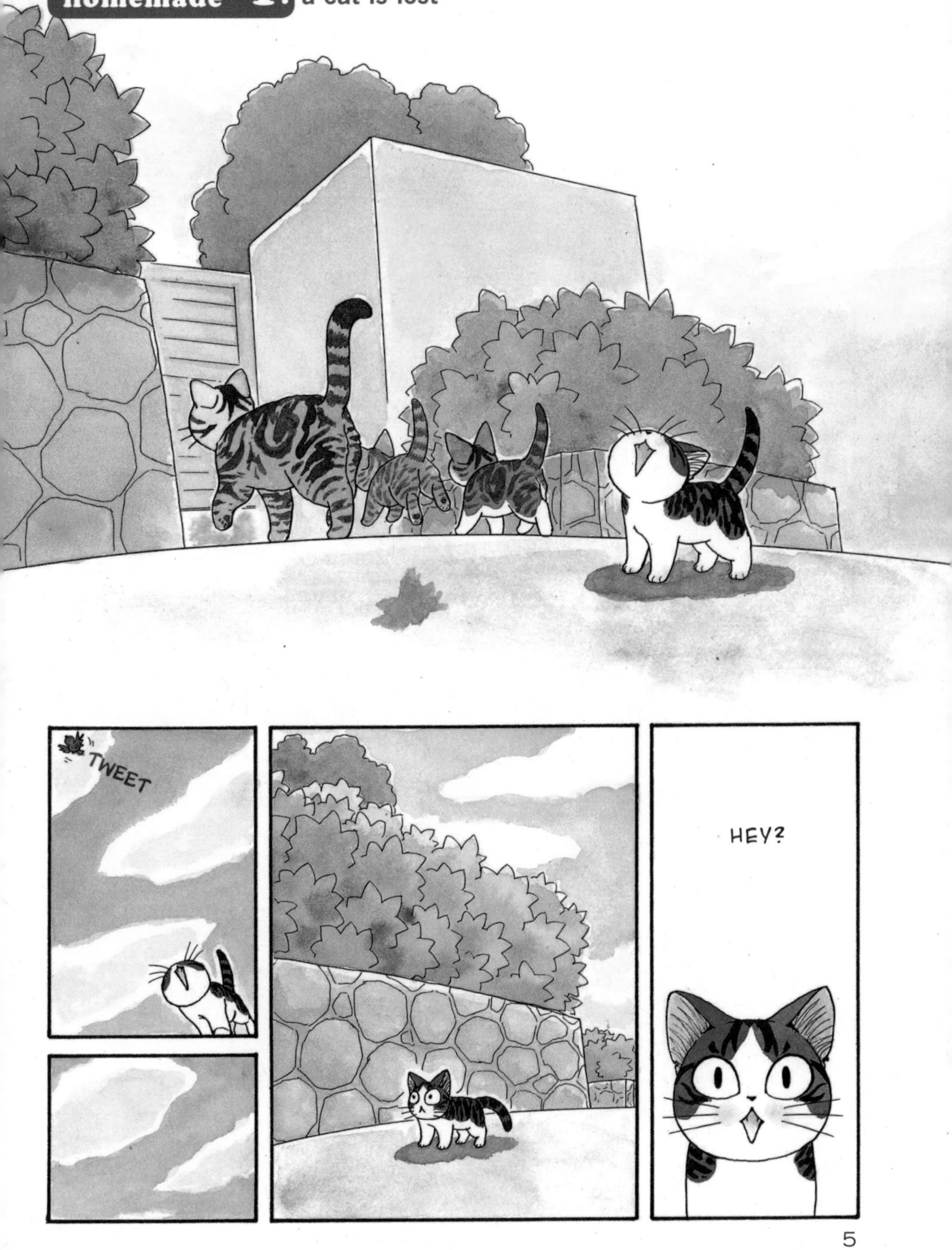
TWEET
HEY?

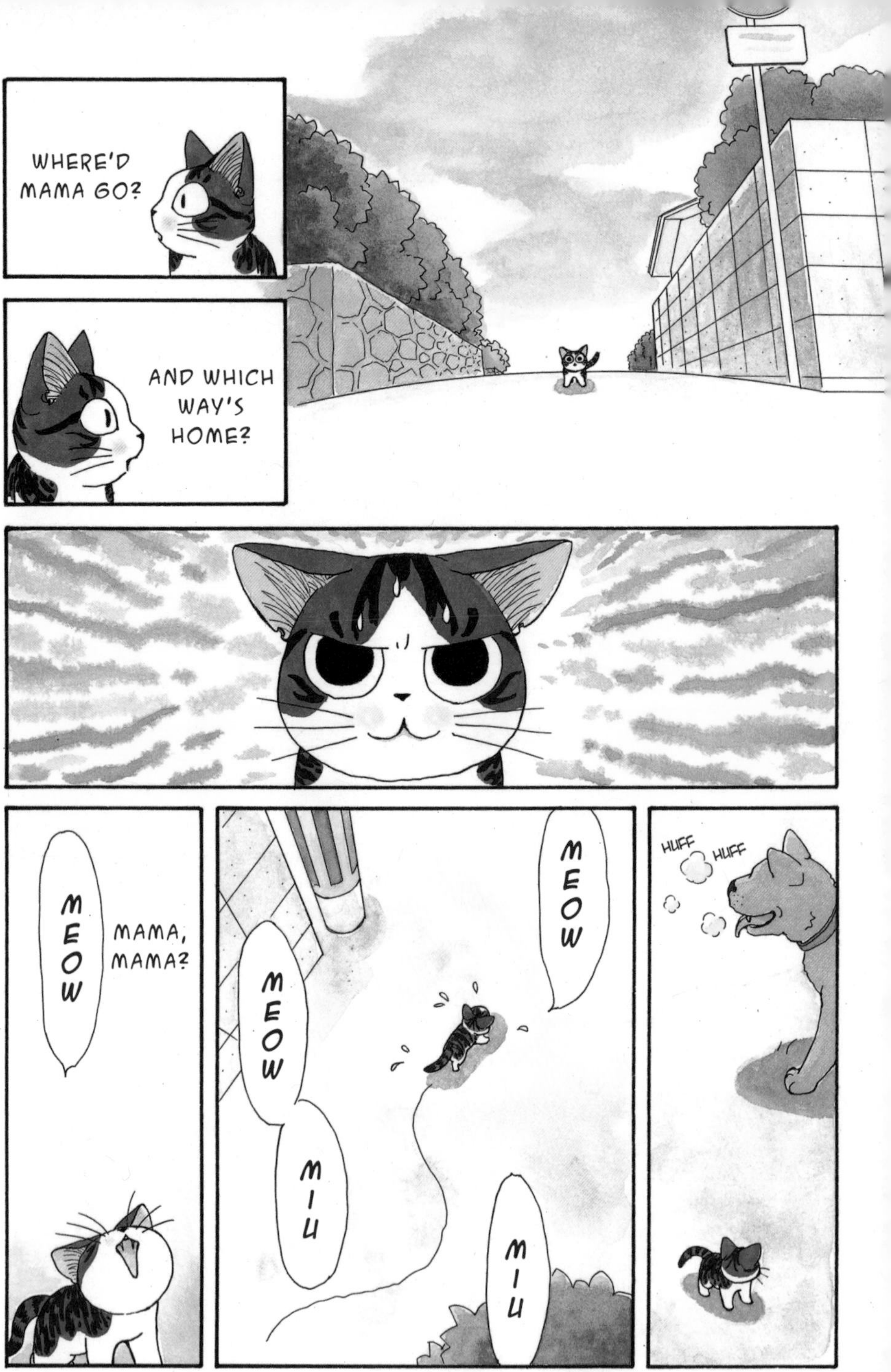
WHERE'D MAMA GO?
AND WHICH WAY'S HOME?
MEOW
MAMA, MAMA?
MEOW
MEOW
MIU
MIU
HUFF HUFF

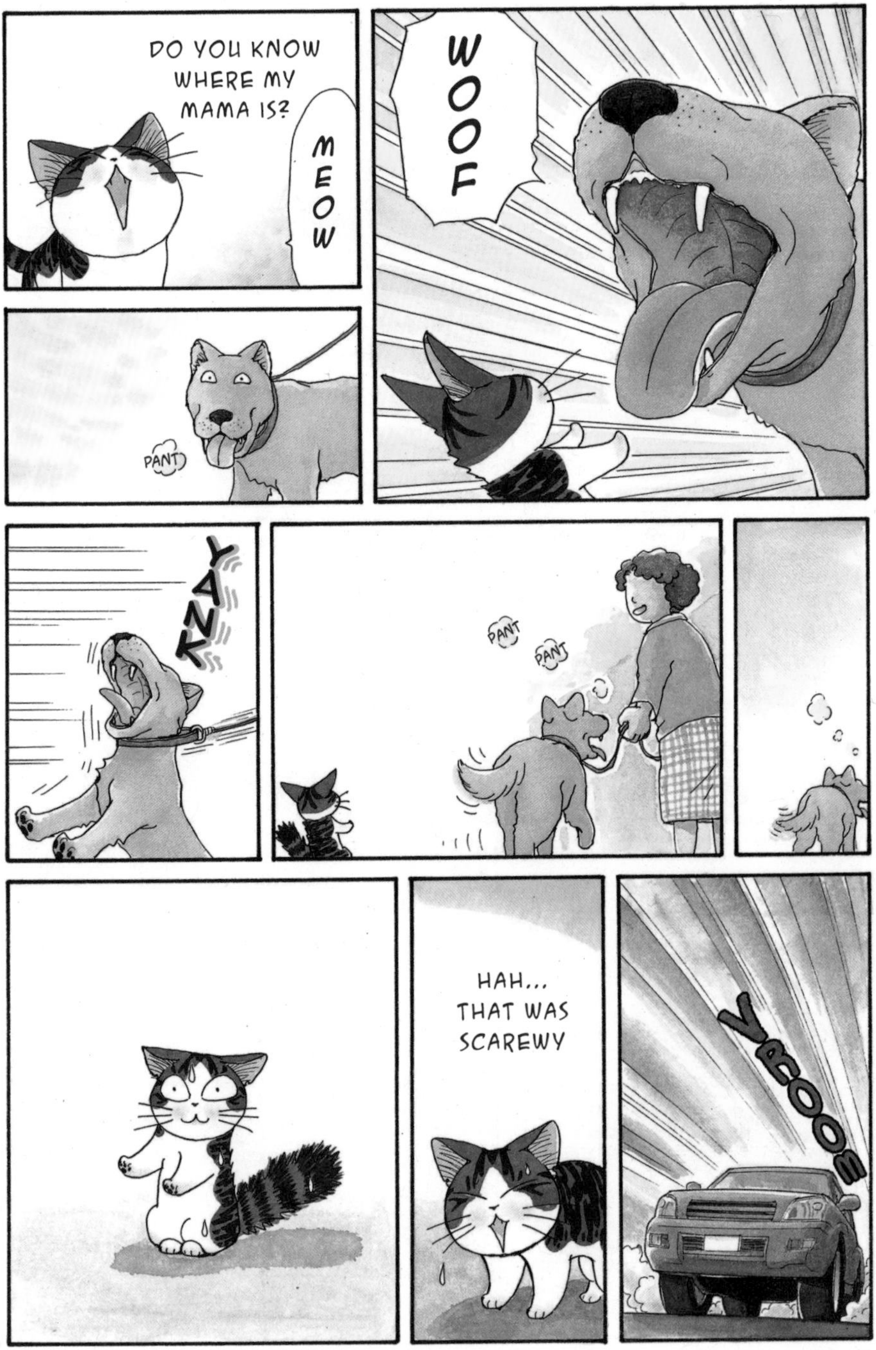
DO YOU KNOW WHERE MY MAMA IS?
MEOW
WOOF
PANT
YANK
PANT
PANT
HAH... THAT WAS SCAREWY
VROOOM

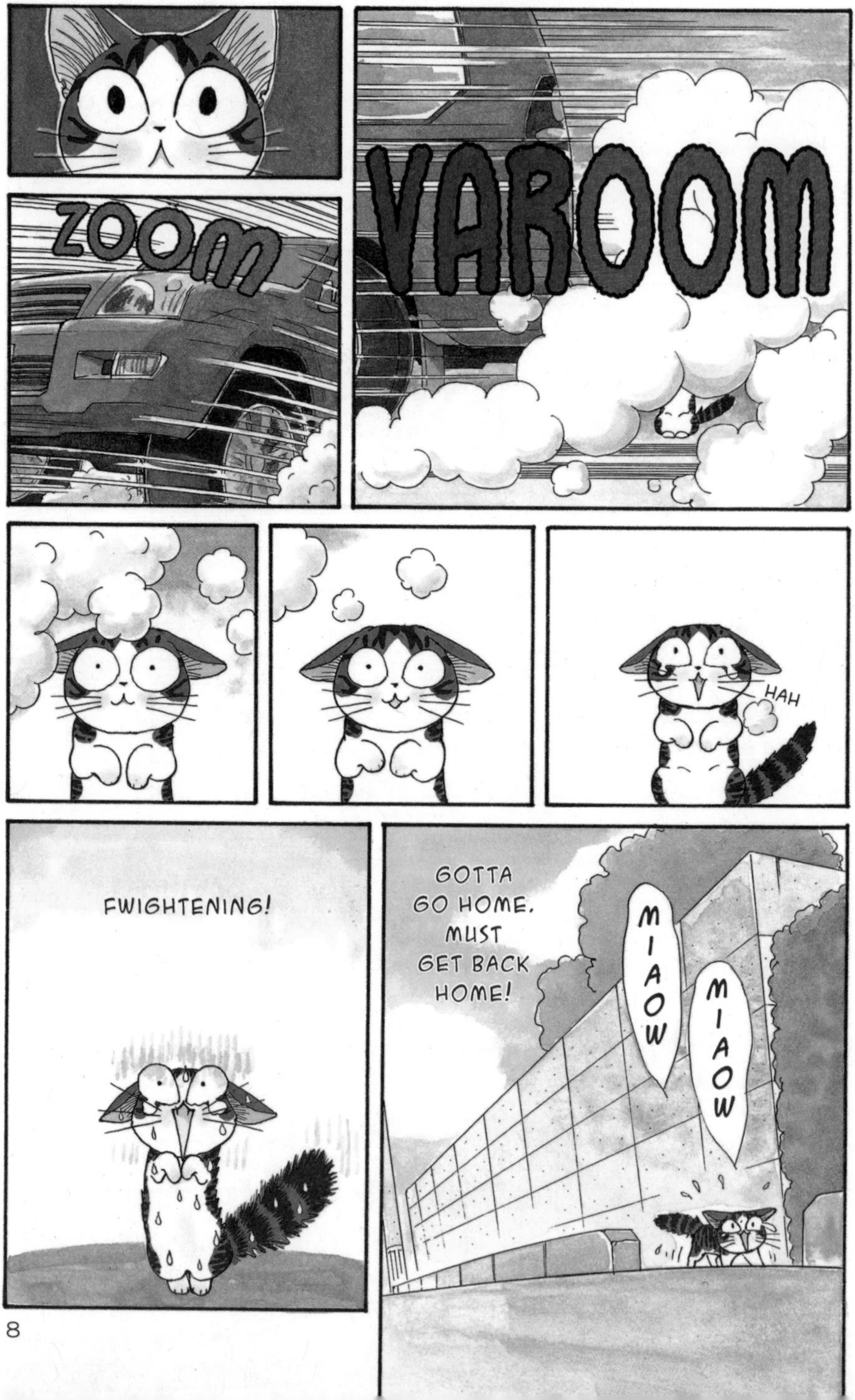
ZOOM
VAROOM
HAH
FWIGHTENING!
GOTTA GO HOME. MUST GET BACK HOME!
MIAOW
MIAOW

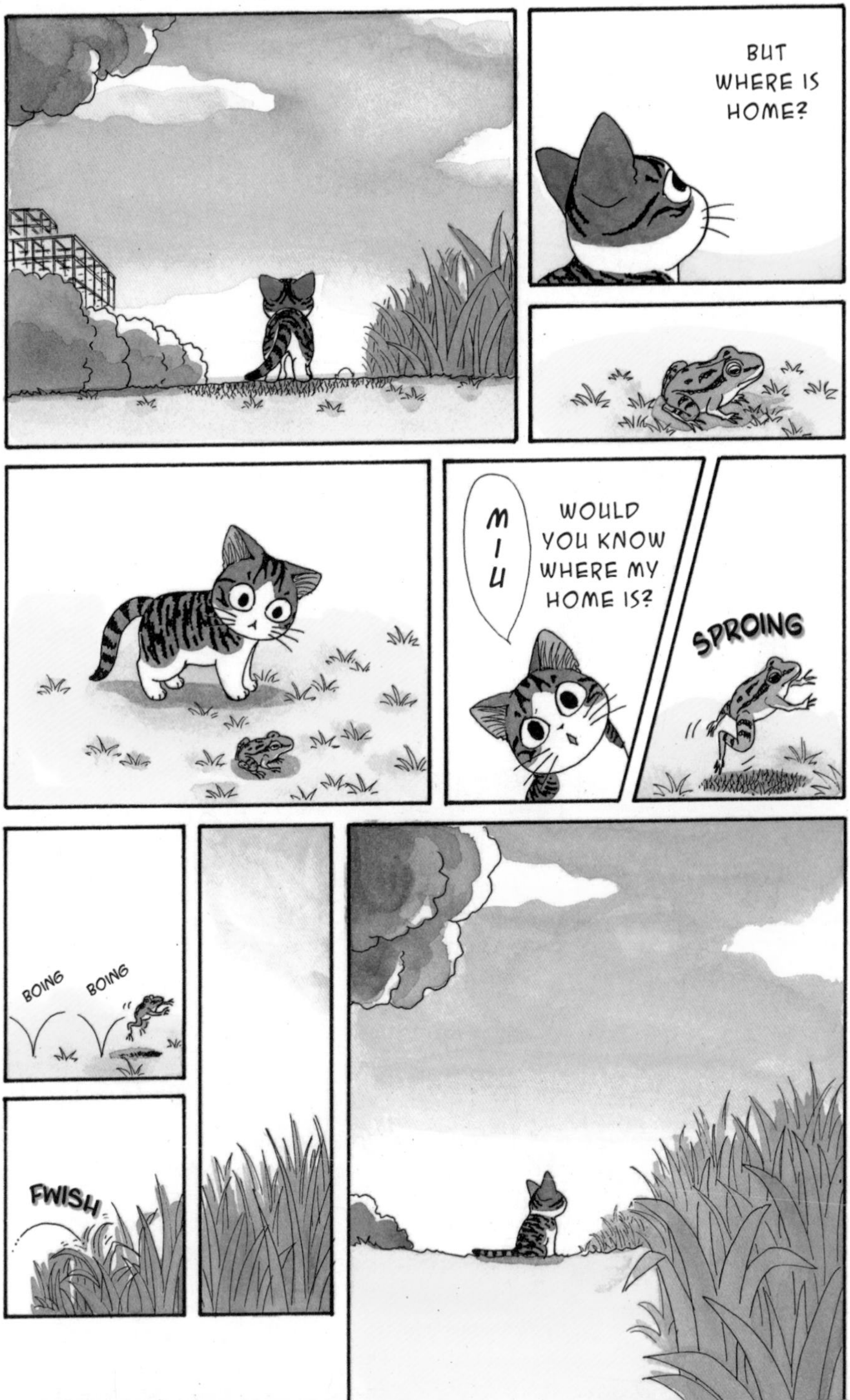
BUT WHERE IS HOME?
MIU
WOULD YOU KNOW WHERE MY HOME IS?
SPROING
BOING
BOING
FWISH

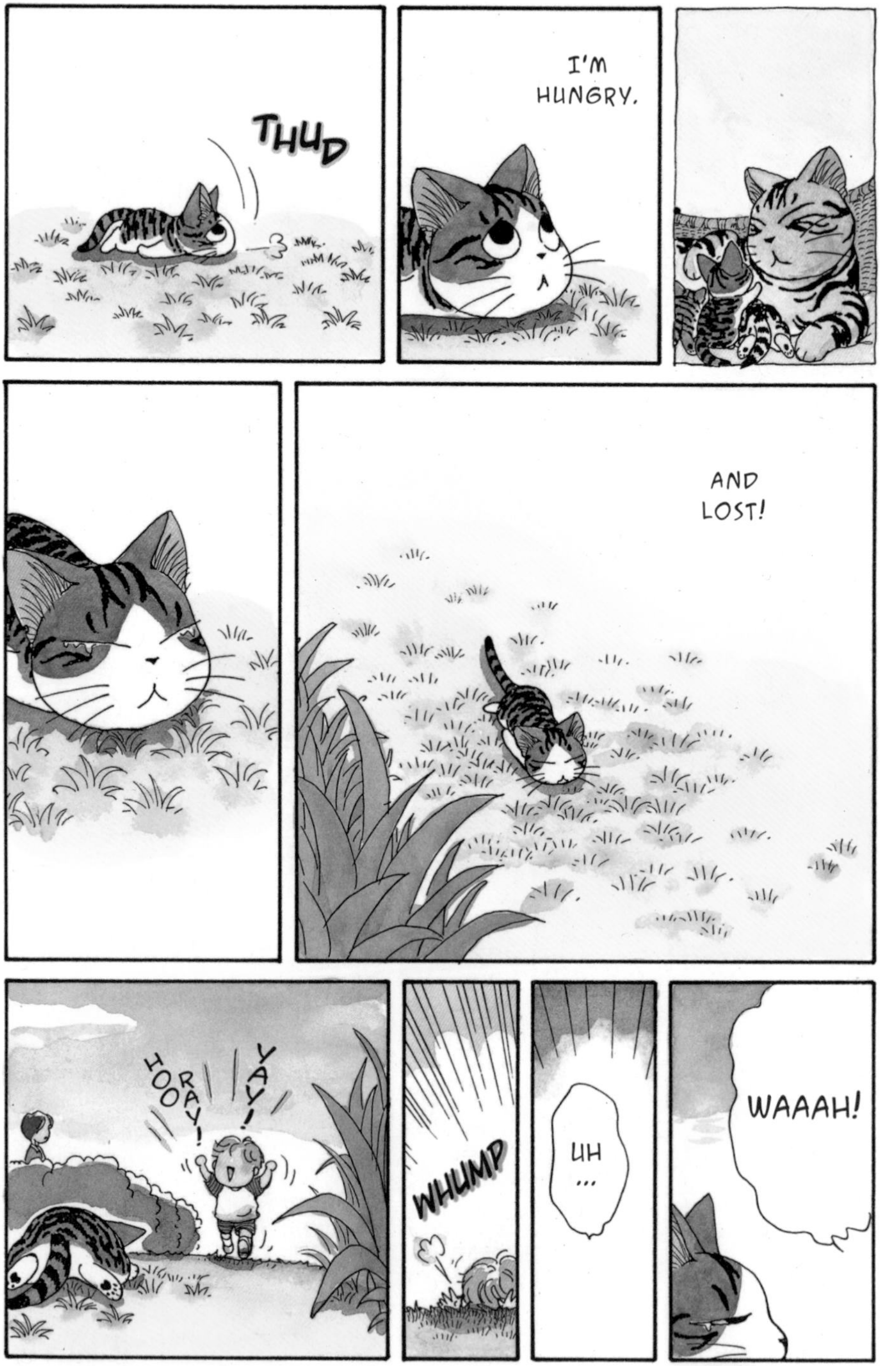
THUD
I'M HUNGRY.
AND LOST!
HOORAY!
YAY!
WHUMP
UH ...
WAAAH!

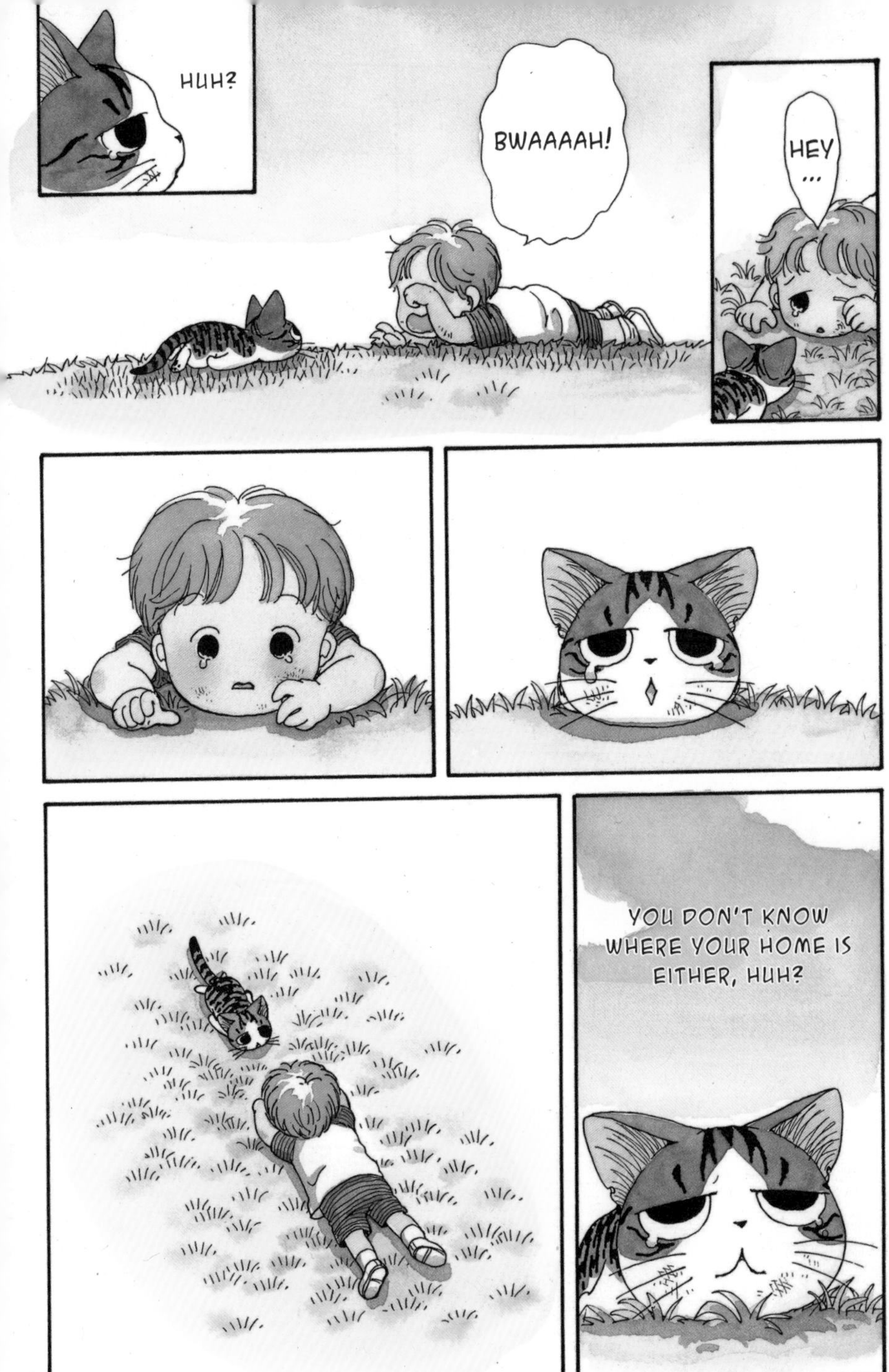
HUH?
BWAAAAH!
HEY ...
YOU DON'T KNOW WHERE YOUR HOME IS EITHER, HUH?

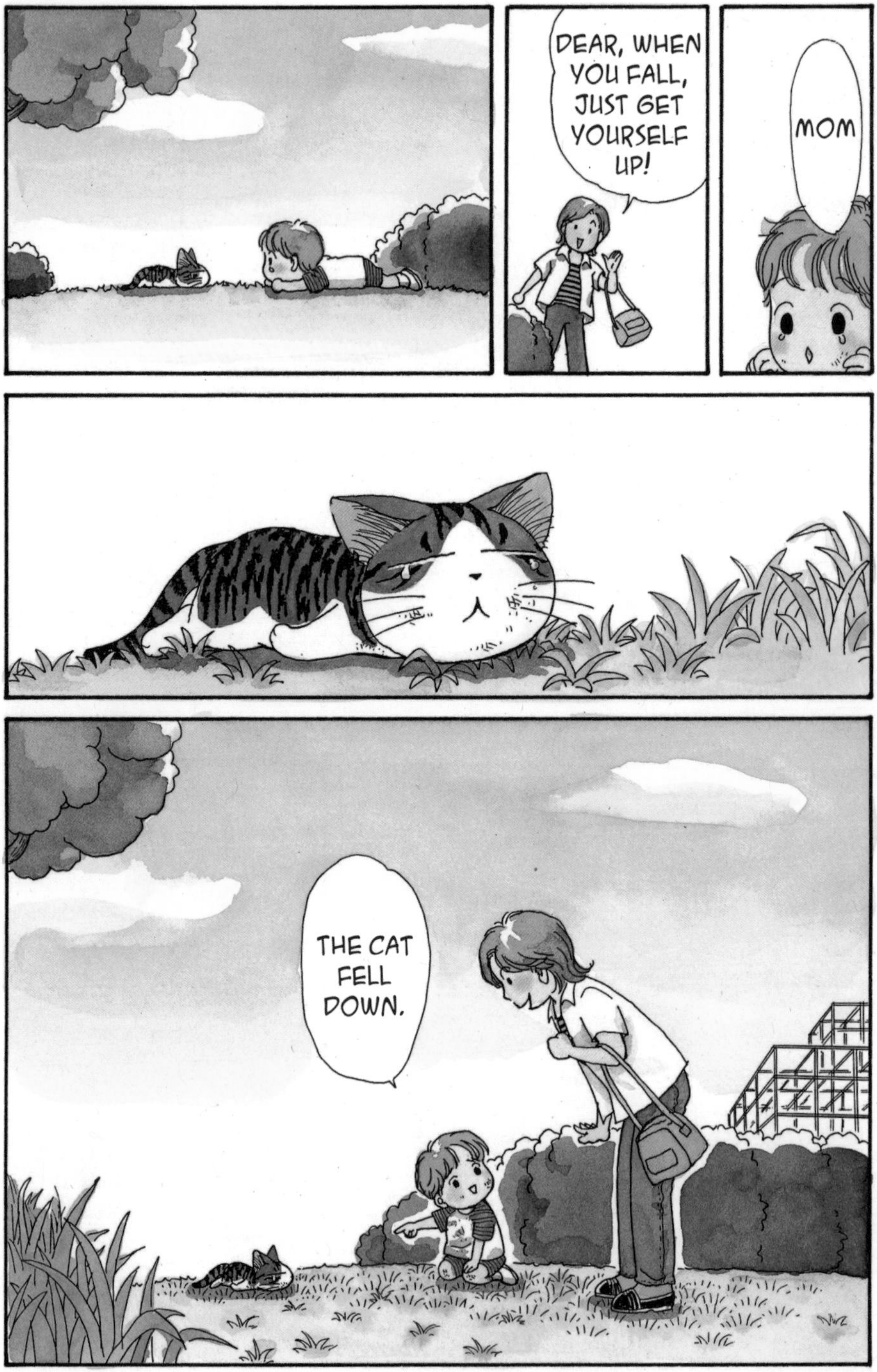
DEAR, WHEN YOU FALL, JUST GET YOURSELF UP!
MOM
THE CAT FELL DOWN.

the end

homemade 2: a cat is found

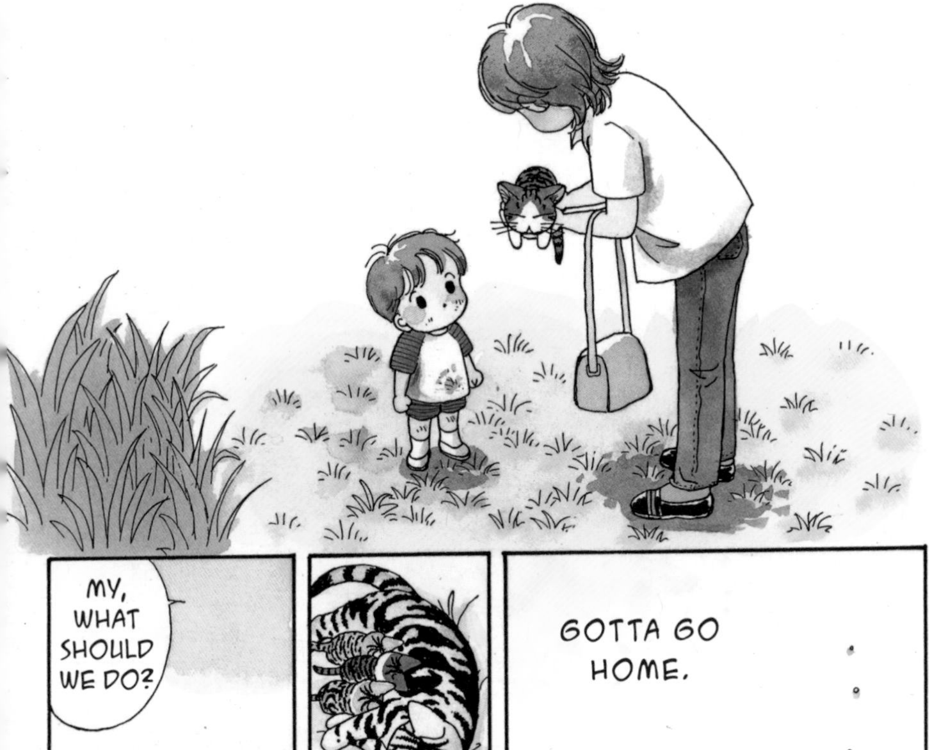

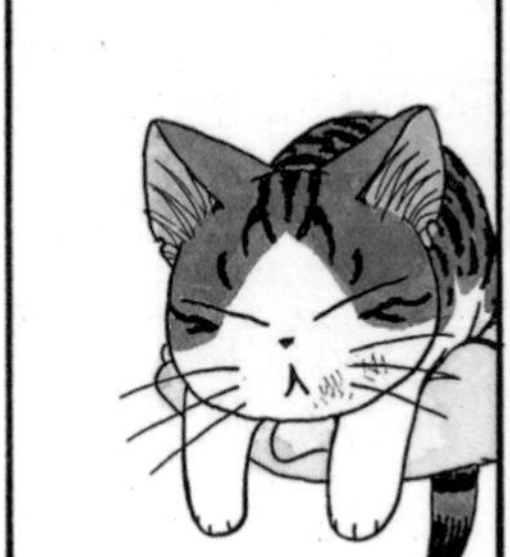
MY, WHAT SHOULD WE DO?

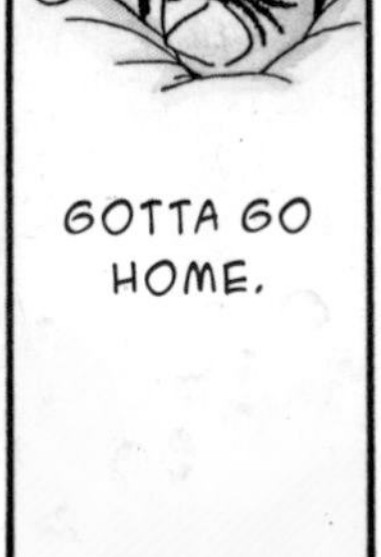
GOTTA GO HOME.

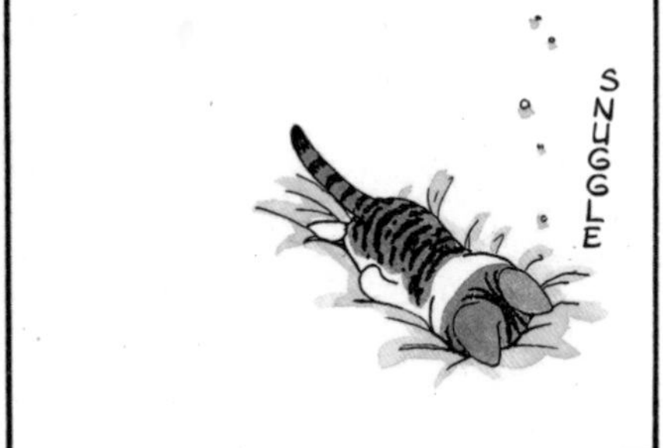
GOTTA GO HOME.
SNUGGLE

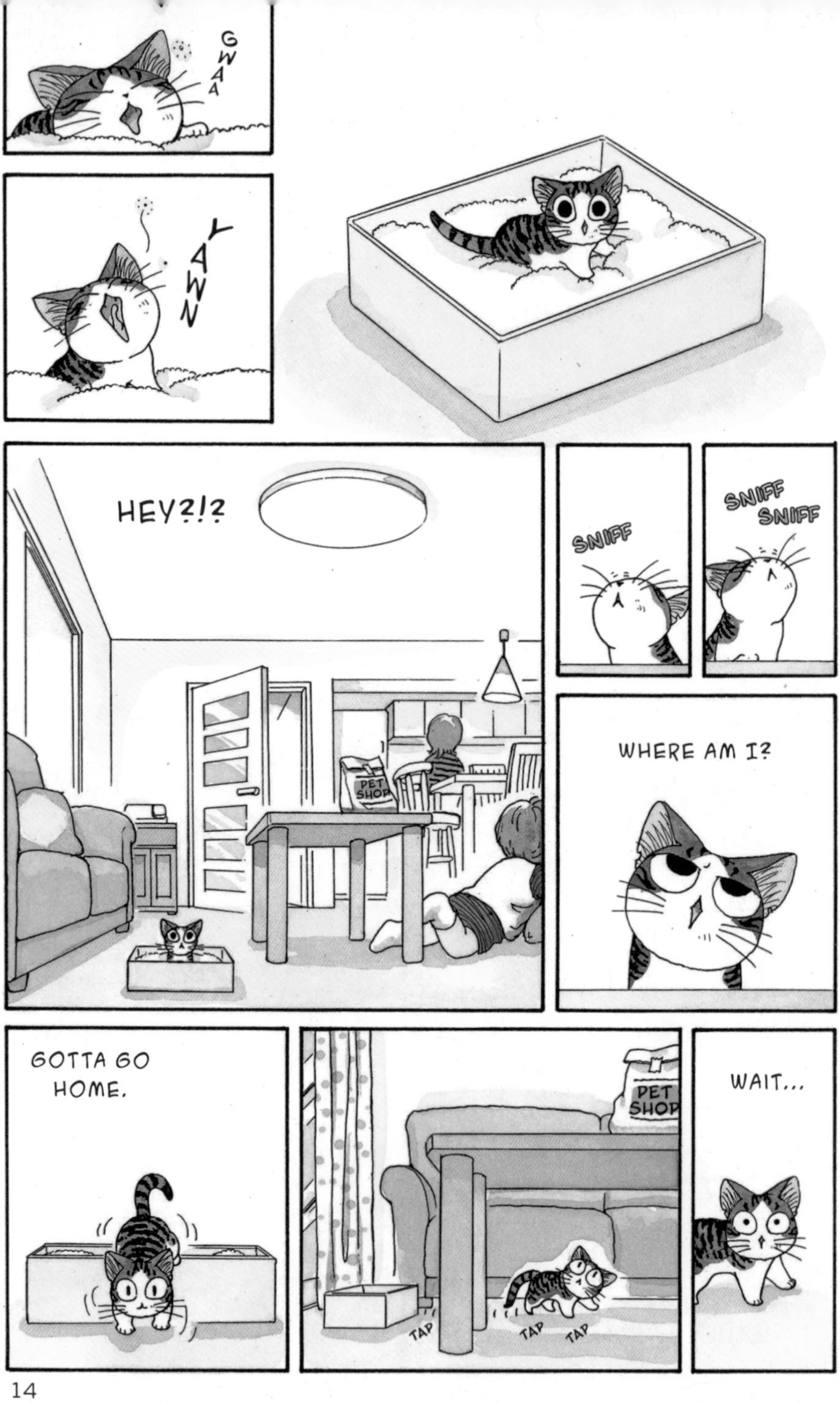
GWAA
YAWN
HEY?!?
PET SHOP
SNIFF
SNIFF SNIFF
WHERE AM I?
GOTTA GO HOME.
PET SHOP
TAP
TAP
TAP
WAIT...

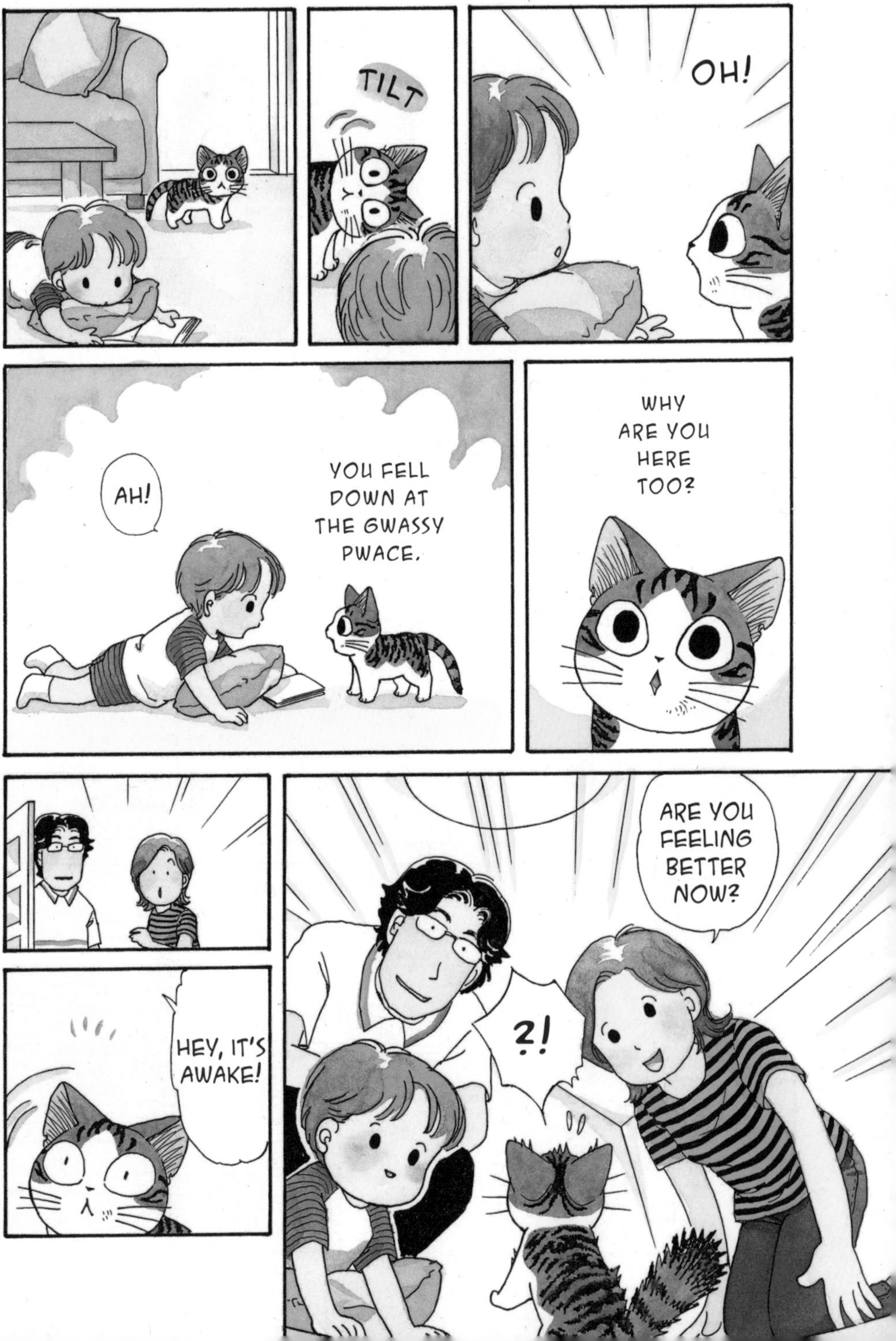
TILT
OH!
AH!
YOU FELL DOWN AT THE GWASSY PWACE.
WHY ARE YOU HERE TOO?
HEY, IT'S AWAKE!
ARE YOU FEELING BETTER NOW?
?!

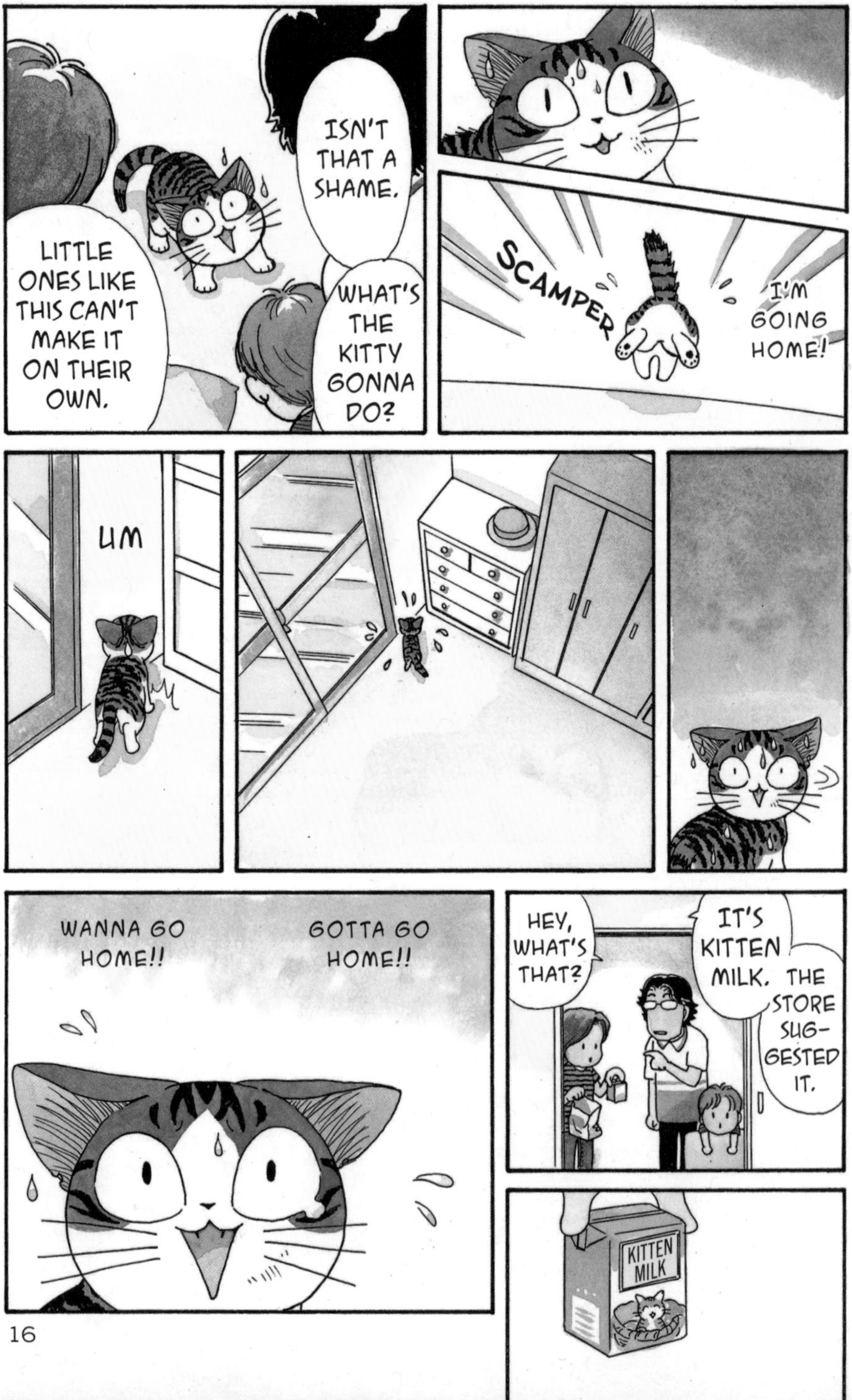
ISN'T THAT A SHAME.
LITTLE ONES LIKE THIS CAN'T MAKE IT ON THEIR OWN.
WHAT'S THE KITTY GONNA DO?
SCAMPER
I'M GOING HOME!
UM
WANNA GO HOME!!
GOTTA GO HOME!!
HEY, WHAT'S THAT?
IT'S KITTEN MILK.
THE STORE SUG-GESTED IT.
KITTEN MILK

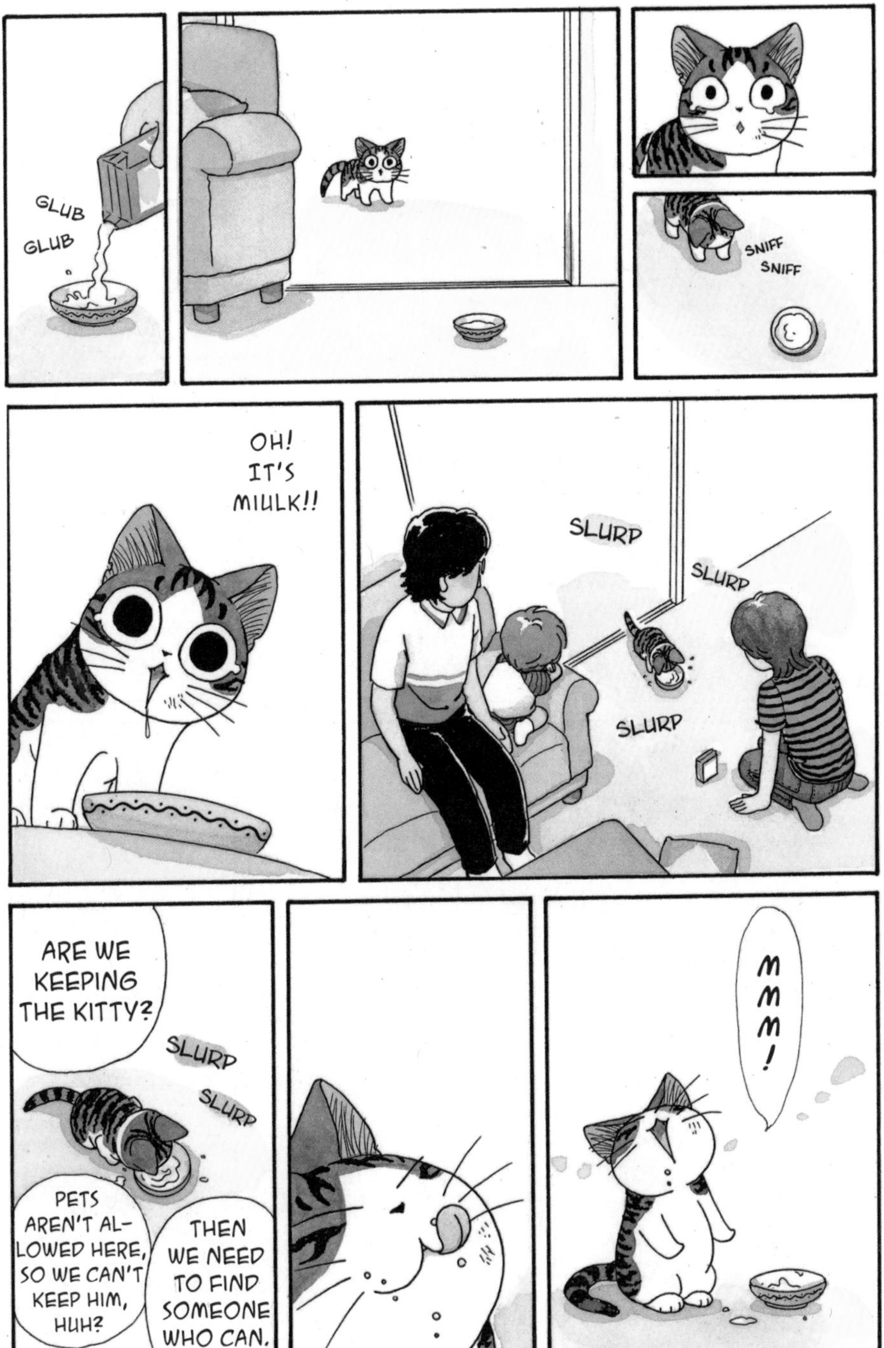
GLUB
GLUB
SNIFF
SNIFF
OH! IT'S MIULK!!
SLURP
SLURP
SLURP
ARE WE KEEPING THE KITTY?
SLURP
SLURP
PETS AREN'T AL-LOWED HERE, SO WE CAN'T KEEP HIM, HUH?
THEN WE NEED TO FIND SOMEONE WHO CAN.
MMM!

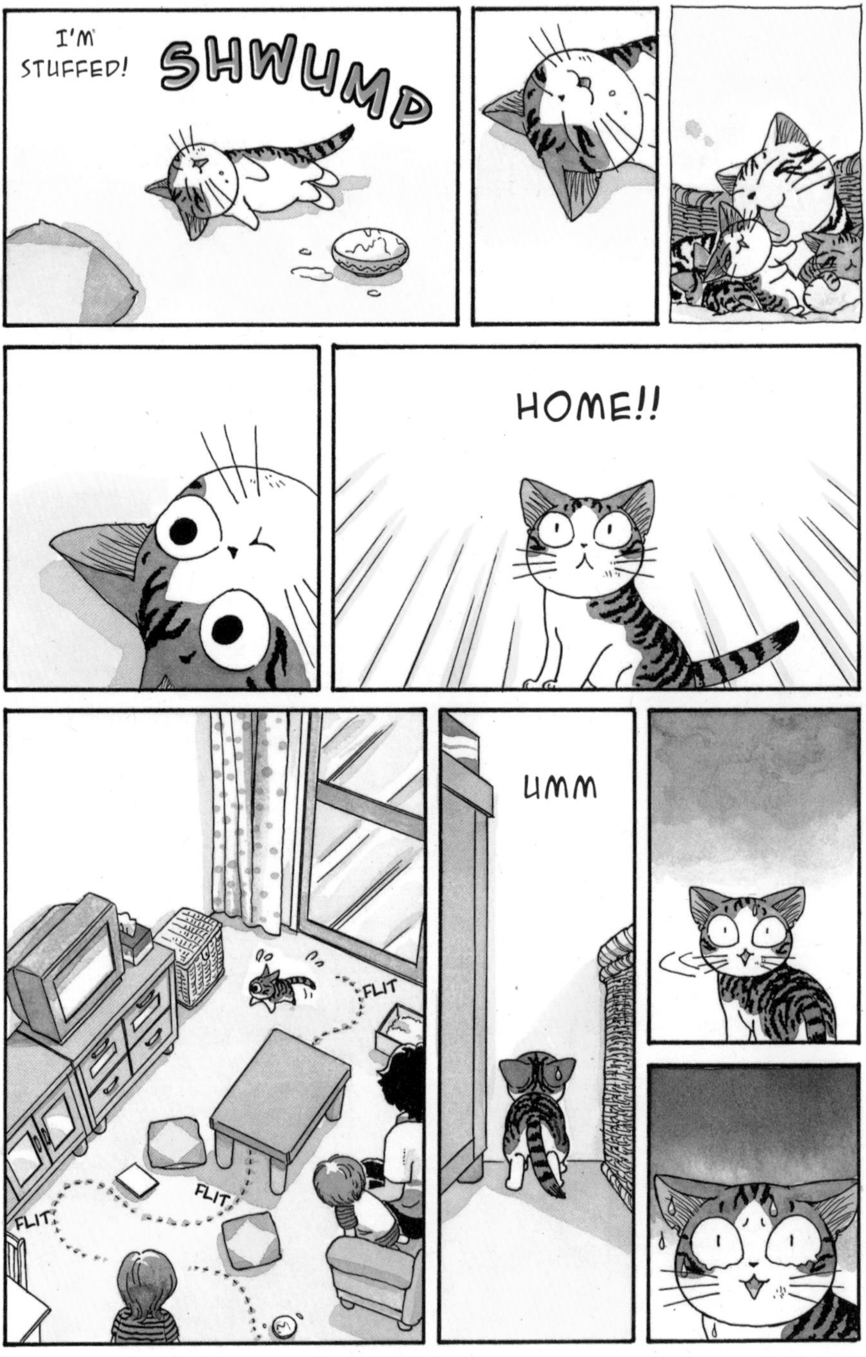
I'M STUFFED!
SHWUMP
HOME!!
FLIT
FLIT
FLIT
UMM

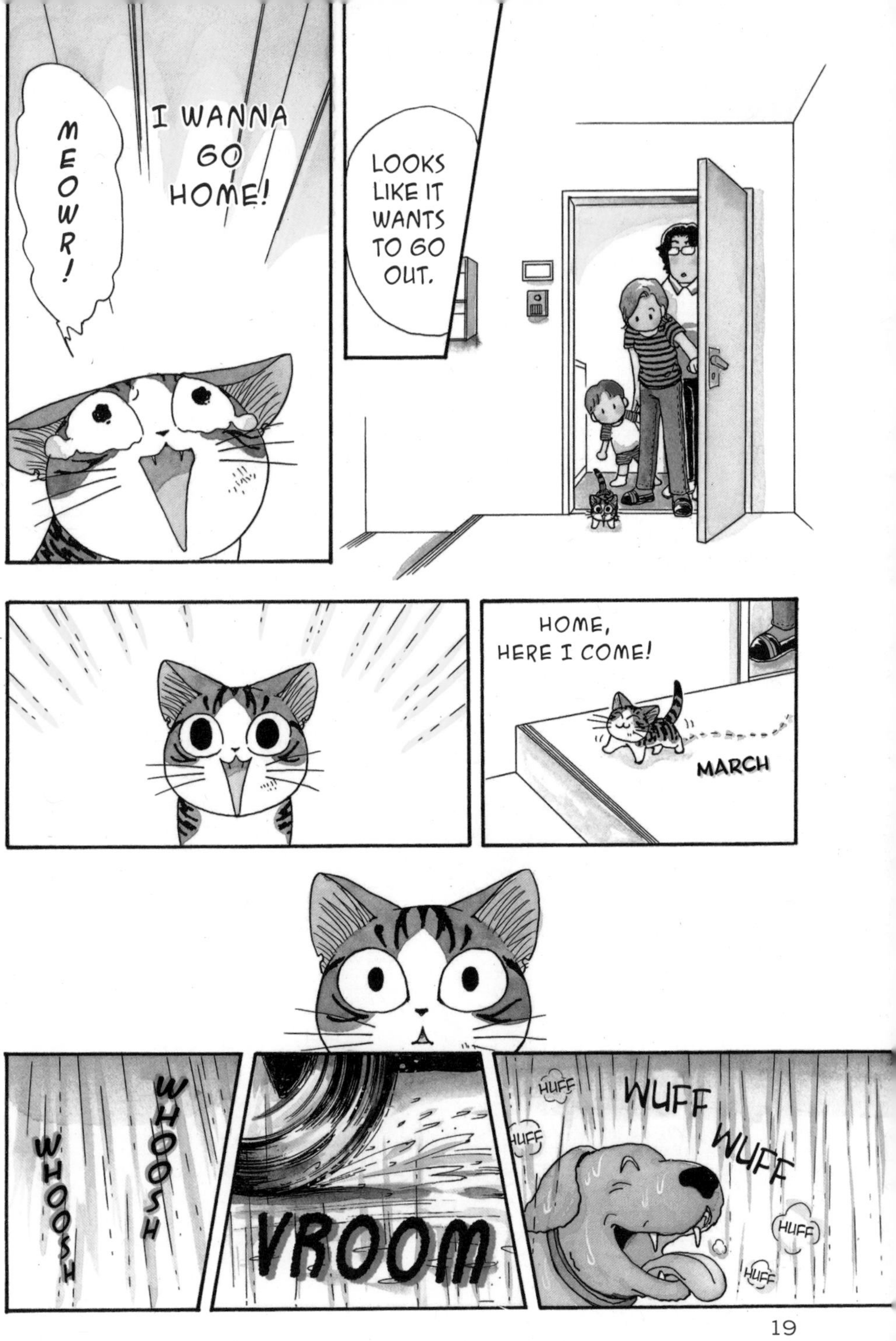
MEOWR!
I WANNA GO HOME!
LOOKS LIKE IT WANTS TO GO OUT.
HOME, HERE I COME!
MARCH
WHOOSH
WHOOSH
VROOM
HUFF
WUFF
HUFF
WUFF
HUFF
HUFF

VROOM

...

YAMADA

I WONDER WHAT'S THE MATTER?

DASH

POOF

I THINK I'LL SHTAY HERE FOR A WITTLE WHILE MORE.

the end

homemade 3: a cat is given a hard time

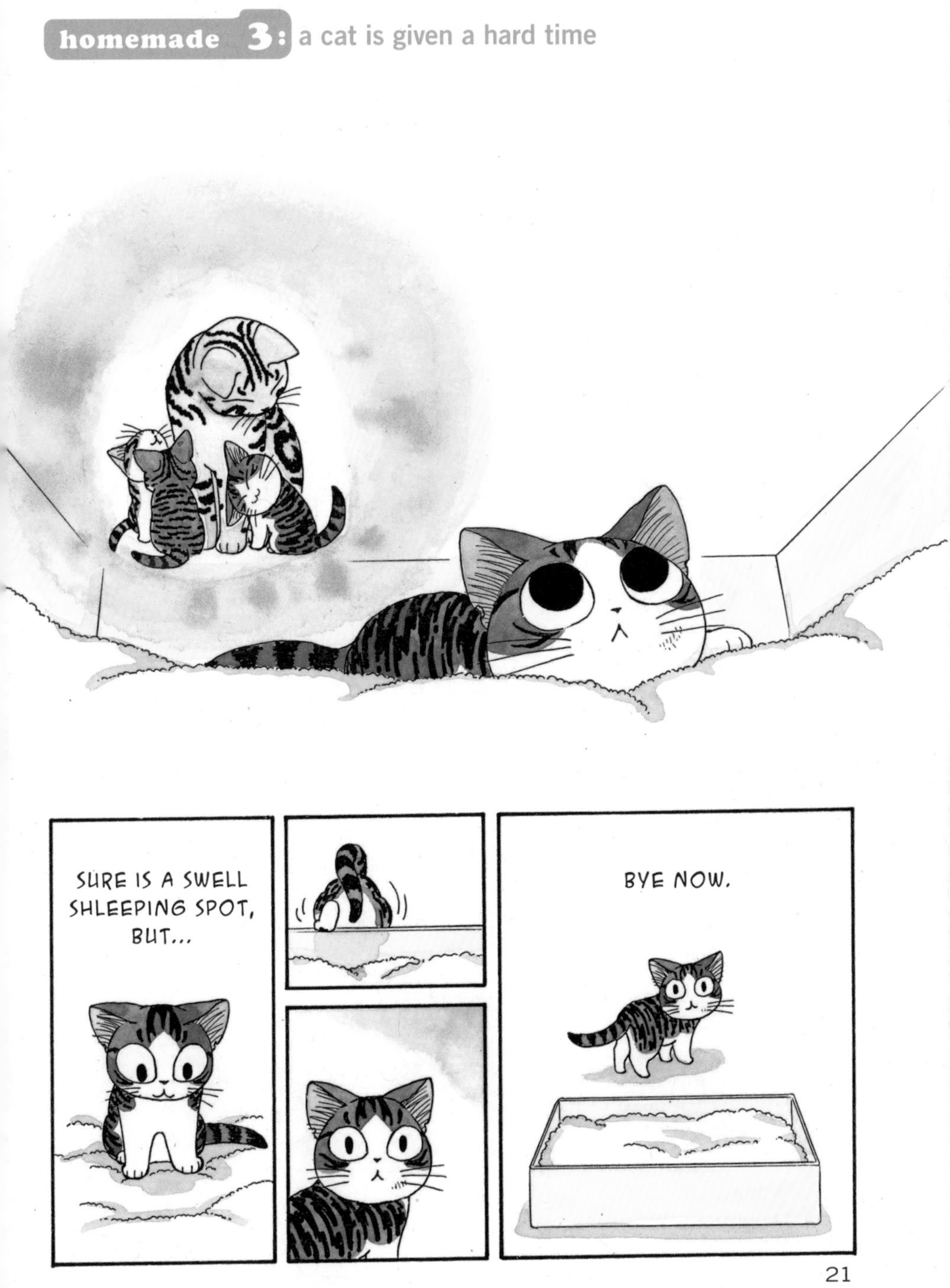
SURE IS A SWELL SHLEEPING SPOT, BUT...
BYE NOW.

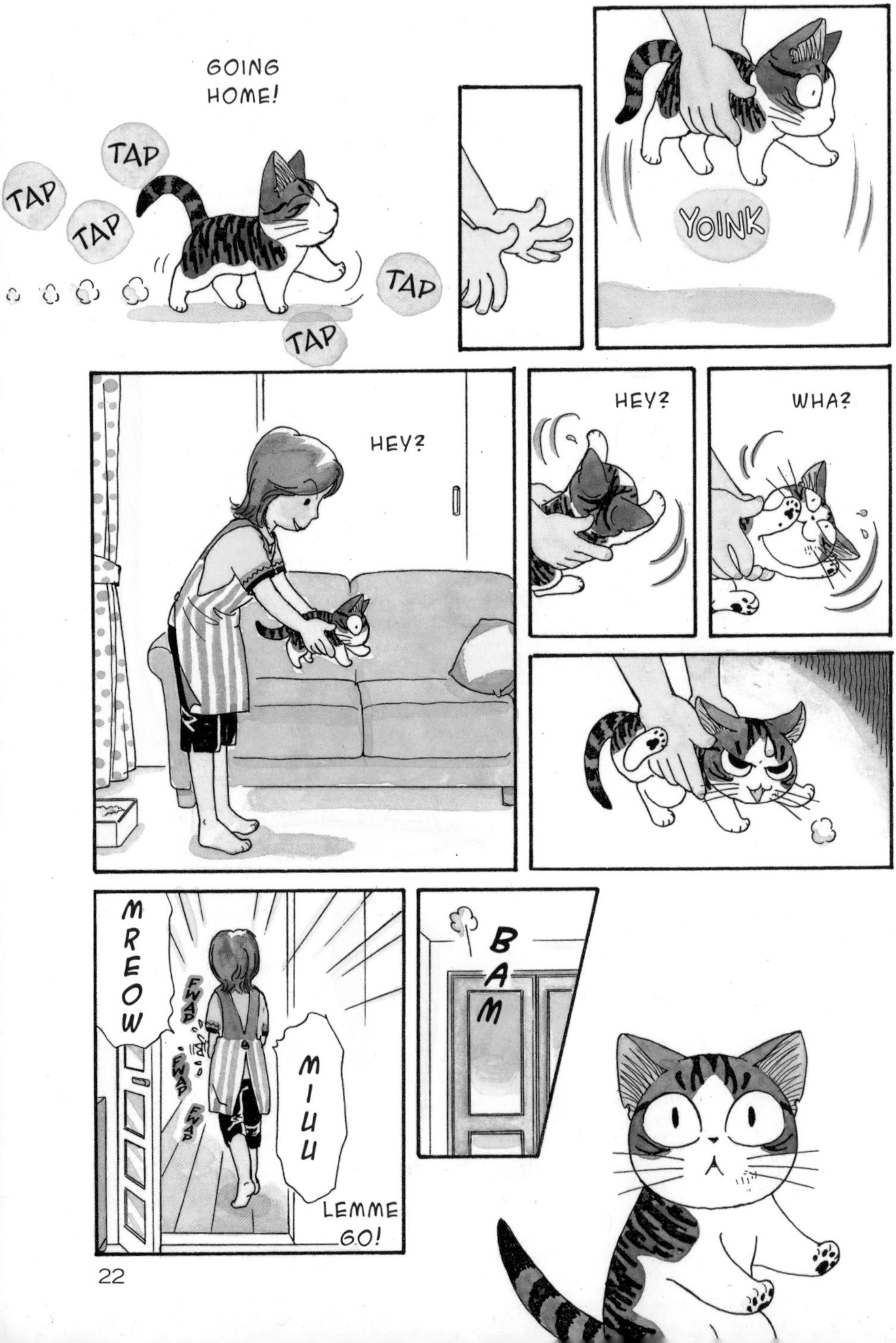
GOING HOME!
TAP
TAP
TAP
TAP
TAP
YOINK
HEY?
HEY?
WHA?
MREOW
FWAP
FWAP
FWAP
MIUU
LEMME GO!
BAM

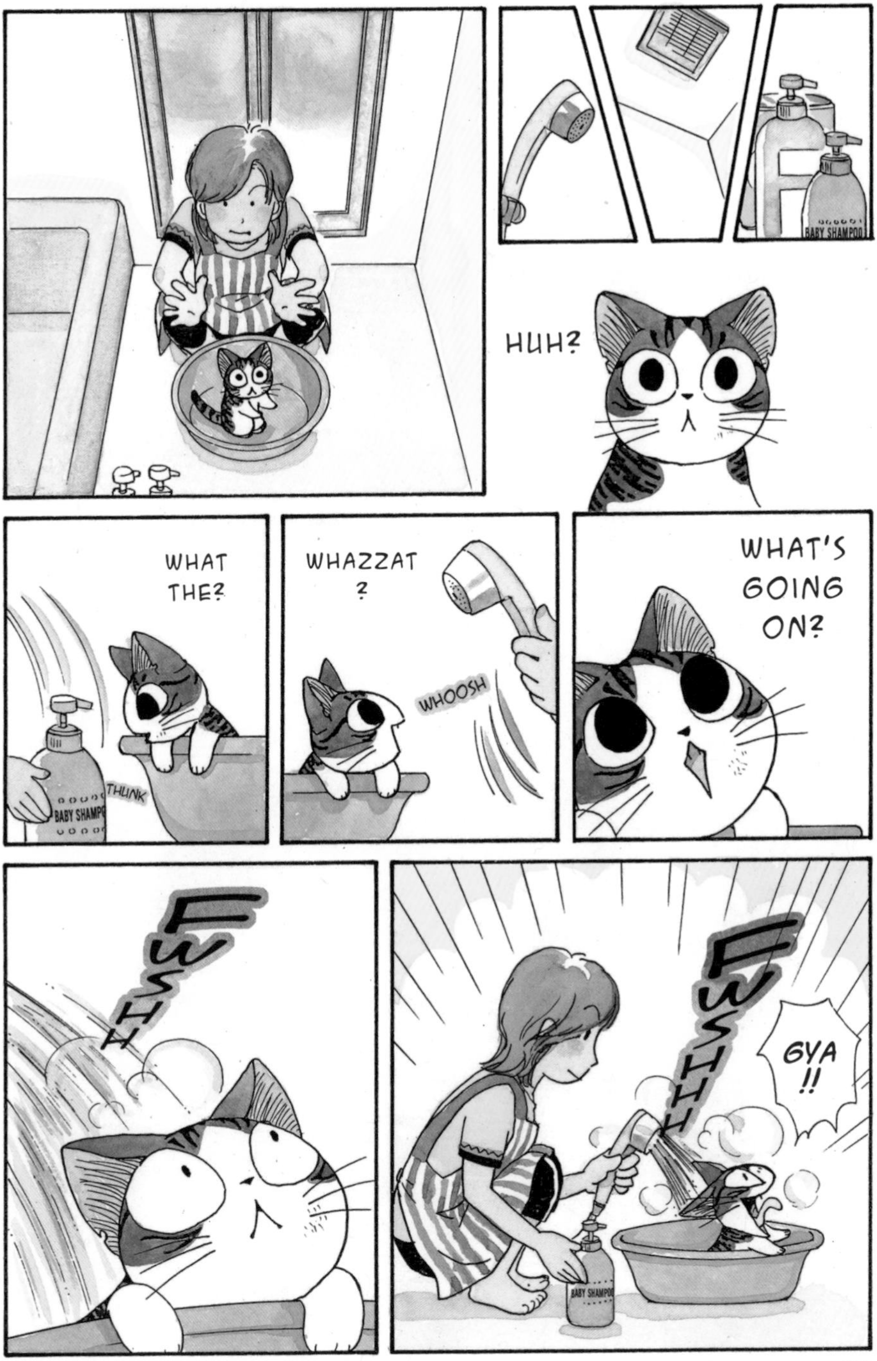
BABY SHAMPOO
HUH?
WHAT THE?
BABY SHAMPOO
THUNK
WHAZZAT ?
WHOOSH
WHAT'S GOING ON?
FWSHH
FWSHHH
GYA !!
BABY SHAMPOO

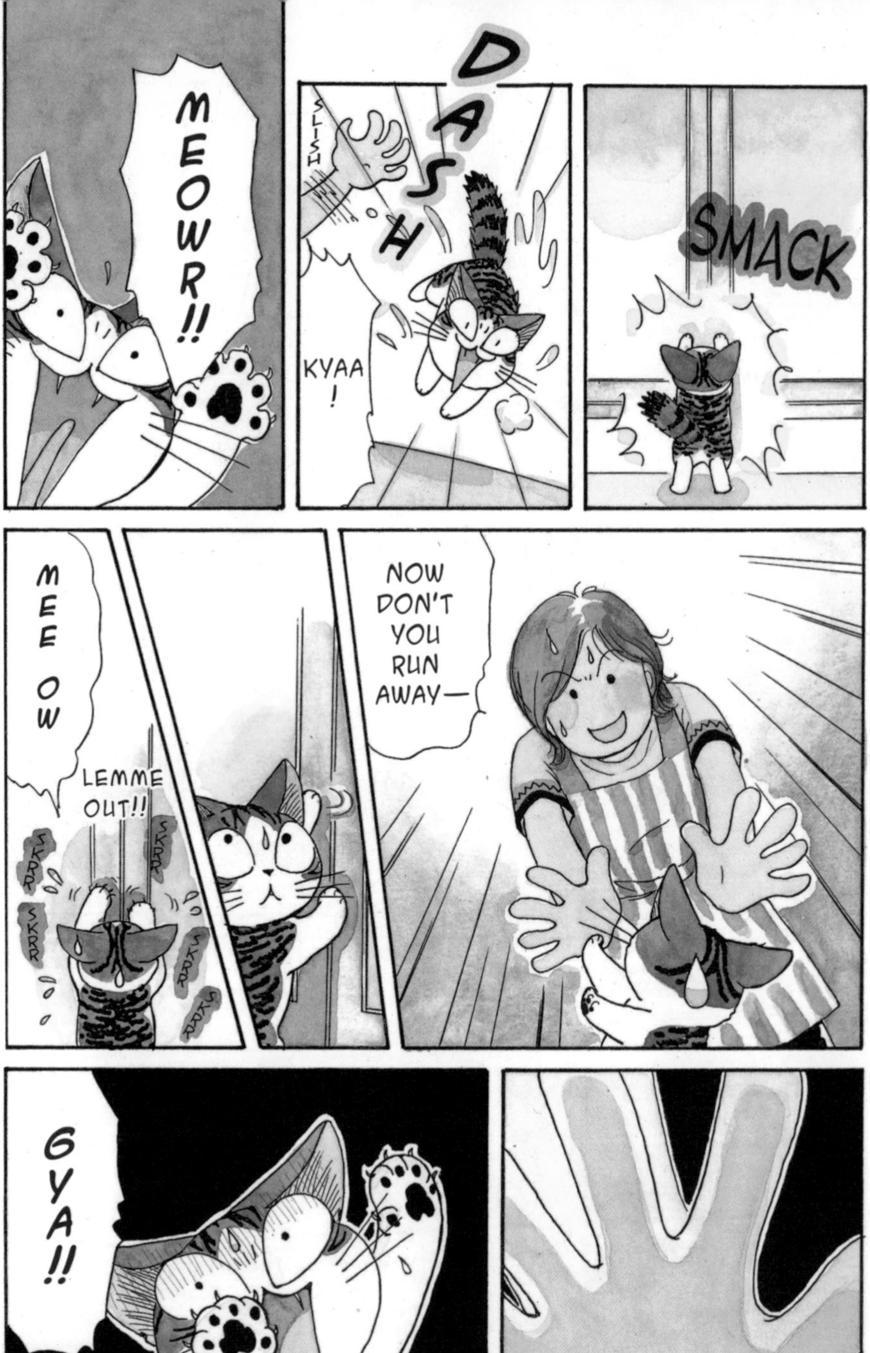
MEOWR!!
DASH
SLISH
KYAA!
SMACK
MEE OW
LEMME OUT!!
SKRR
SKRR
SKRR
SKRR
SKRR
NOW DON'T YOU RUN AWAY—
GYA!!

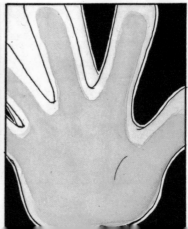

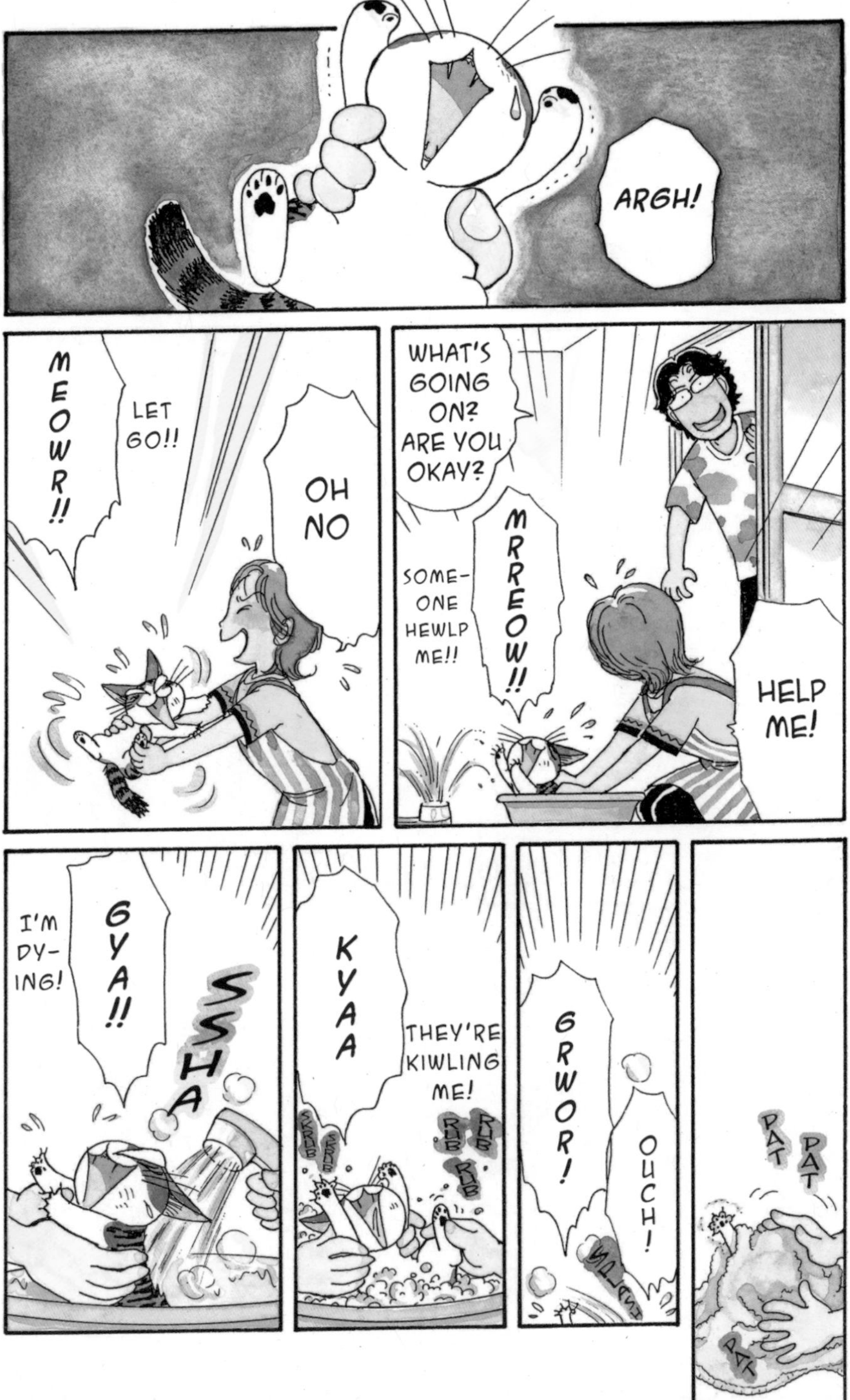
ARGH!
MEOWR!!
LET GO!!
OH NO
WHAT'S GOING ON? ARE YOU OKAY?
MRREOW!!
SOME-ONE HEWLP ME!!
HELP ME!
I'M DY-ING!
GYA!!
SSHA
KYAA
THEY'RE KIWLING ME!
SCRUB SCRUB
RUB RUB RUB
GRWOR!
OUCH!
PAT PAT
PAT

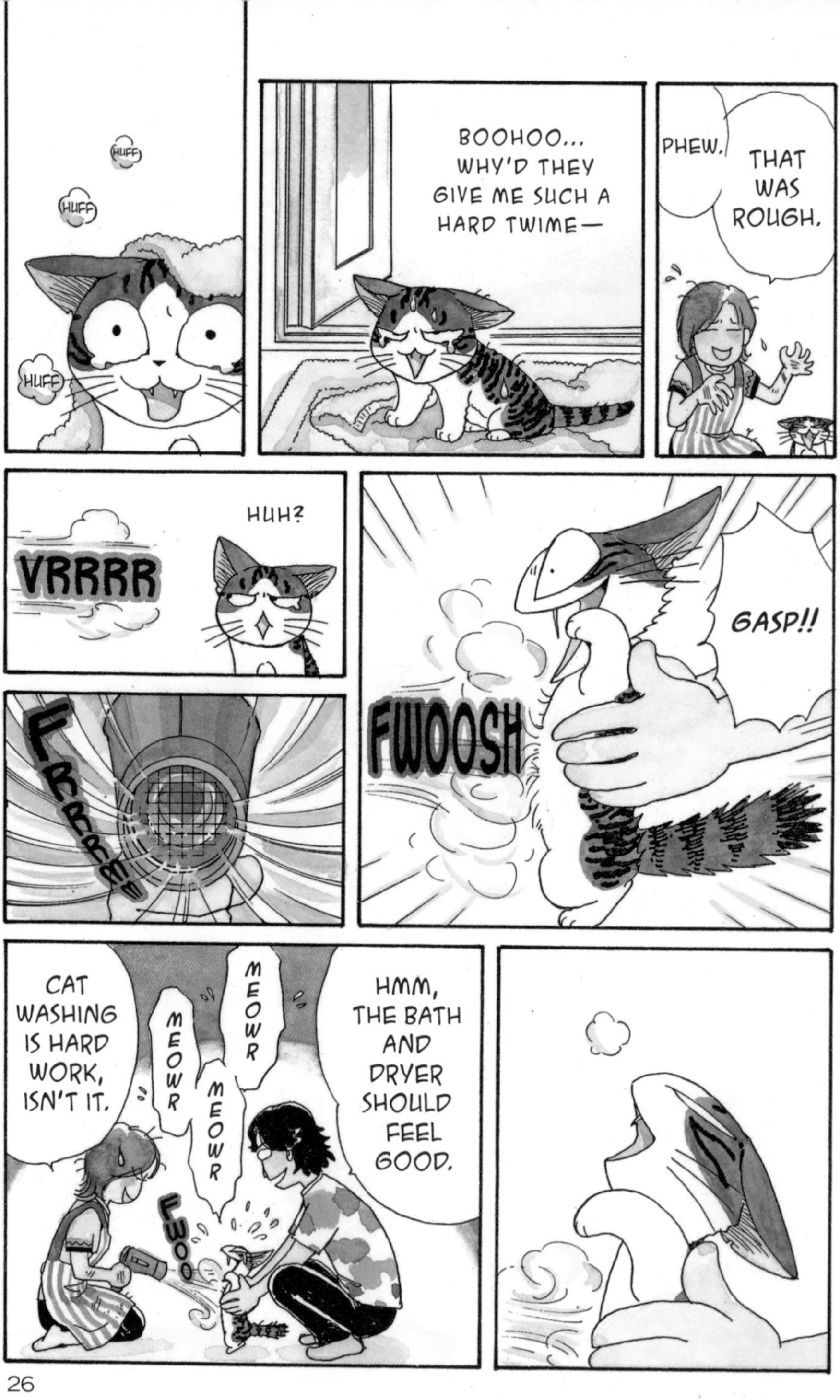
HUFF
HUFF
HUFF
BOOHOO... WHY'D THEY GIVE ME SUCH A HARD TWIME—
PHEW.
THAT WAS ROUGH.
HUH?
VRRRR
FRRRRM
GASP!!
FWOOSH
CAT WASHING IS HARD WORK, ISN'T IT.
MEOWR
MEOWR
MEOWR
HMM, THE BATH AND DRYER SHOULD FEEL GOOD.
FWOO

WOBBL
WOBBL
WOBBL
WOBBL
STUMBLE
FWUMP
I'M GWAD
I DIDN'T DIE.
BUT...

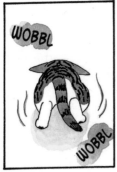

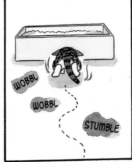

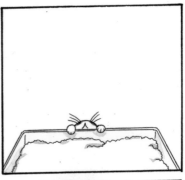

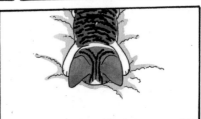

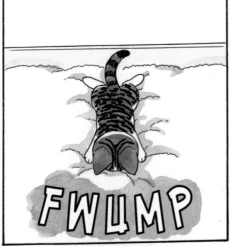

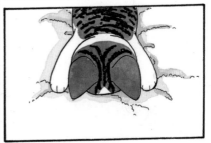

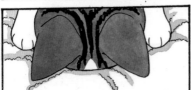

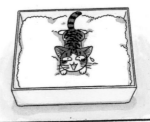

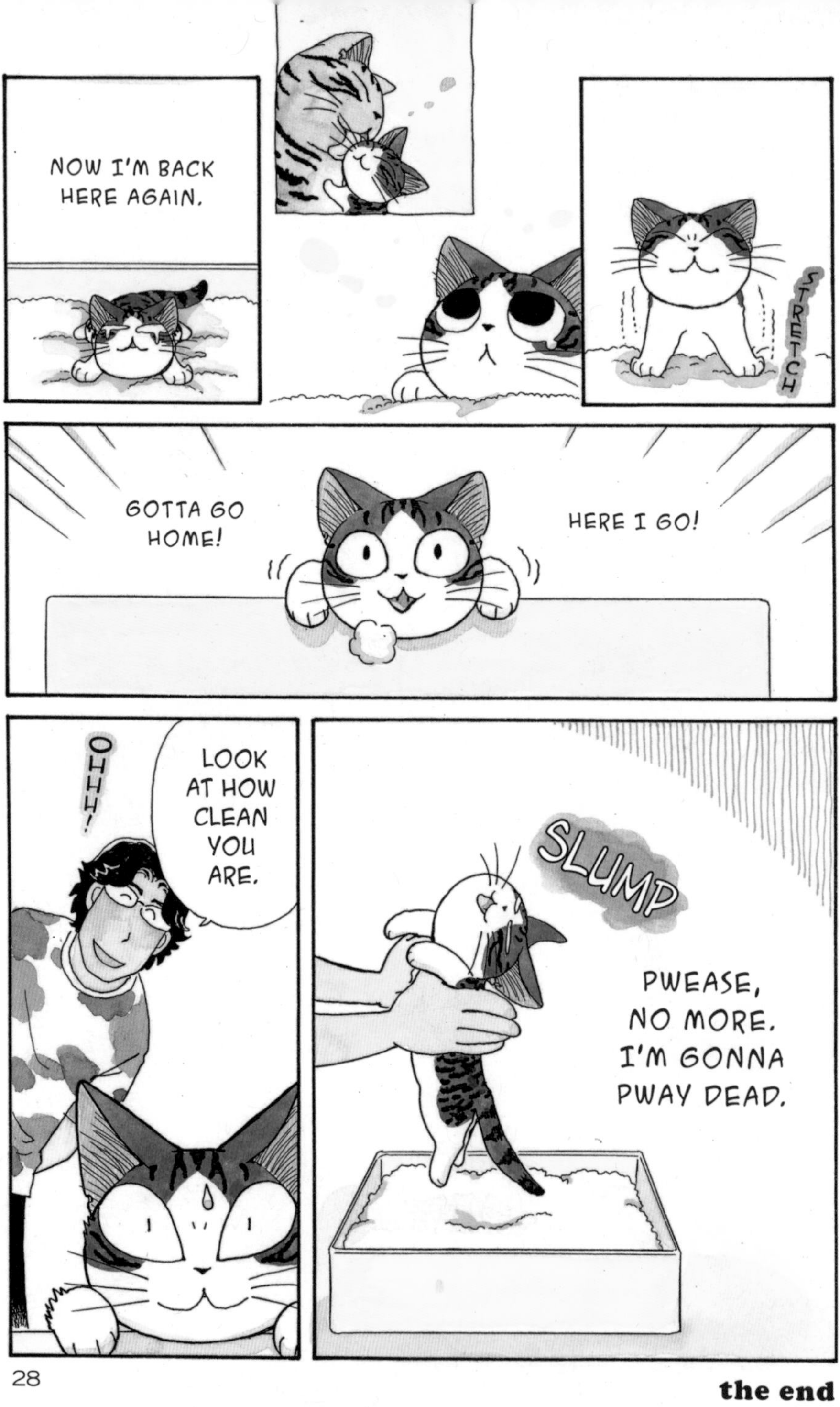
NOW I'M BACK HERE AGAIN.
STRETCH
GOTTA GO HOME!
HERE I GO!
OHHH!
LOOK AT HOW CLEAN YOU ARE.
SLUMP
PWEASE, NO MORE. I'M GONNA PWAY DEAD.

the end

homemade 4: a cat forgets

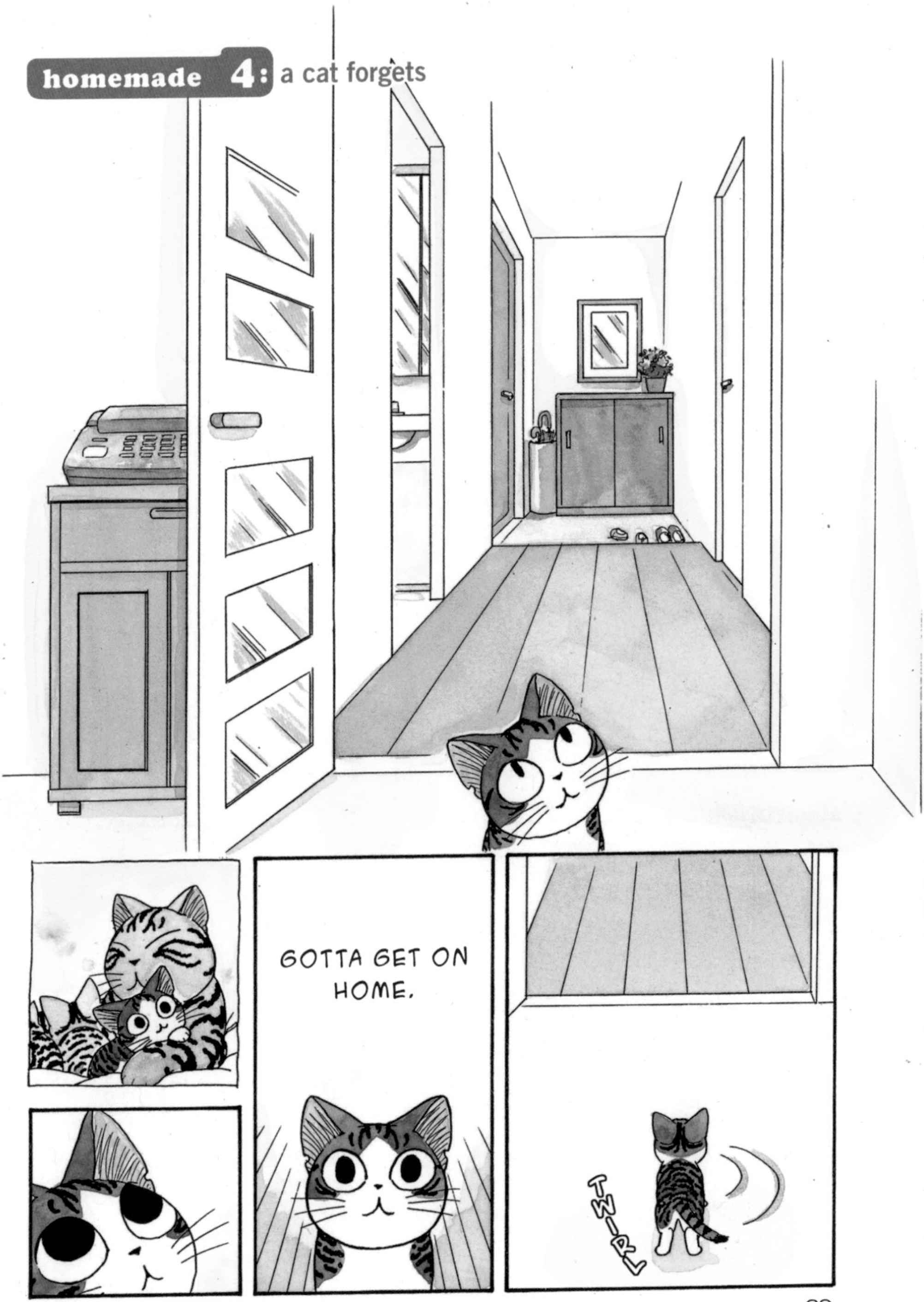
GOTTA GET ON HOME.
TWIRL

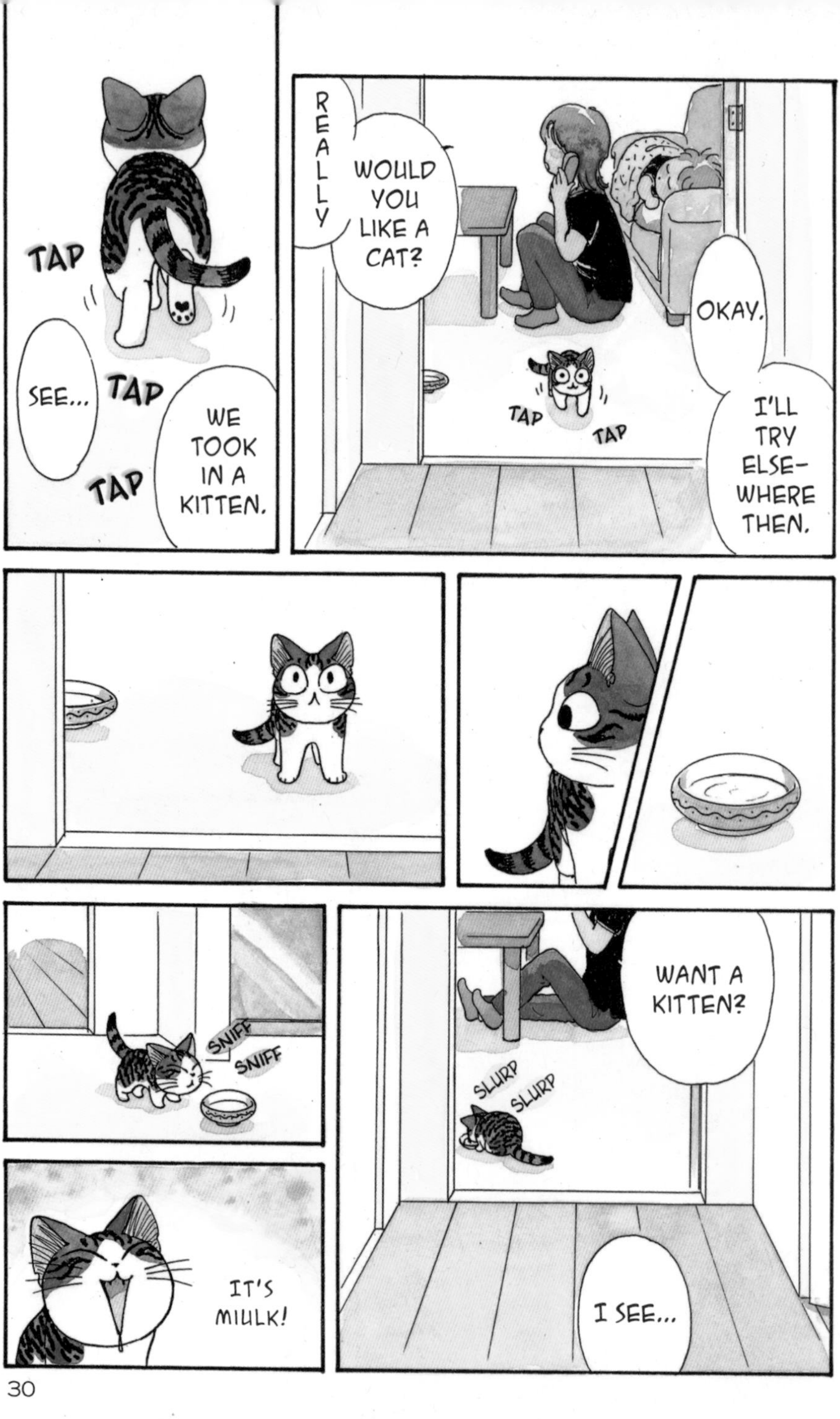
TAP
SEE...
TAP
TAP
WE TOOK IN A KITTEN.
REALLY
WOULD YOU LIKE A CAT?
OKAY.
TAP
TAP
I'LL TRY ELSE-WHERE THEN.
SNIFF
SNIFF
IT'S MIULK!
WANT A KITTEN?
SLURP
SLURP
I SEE...

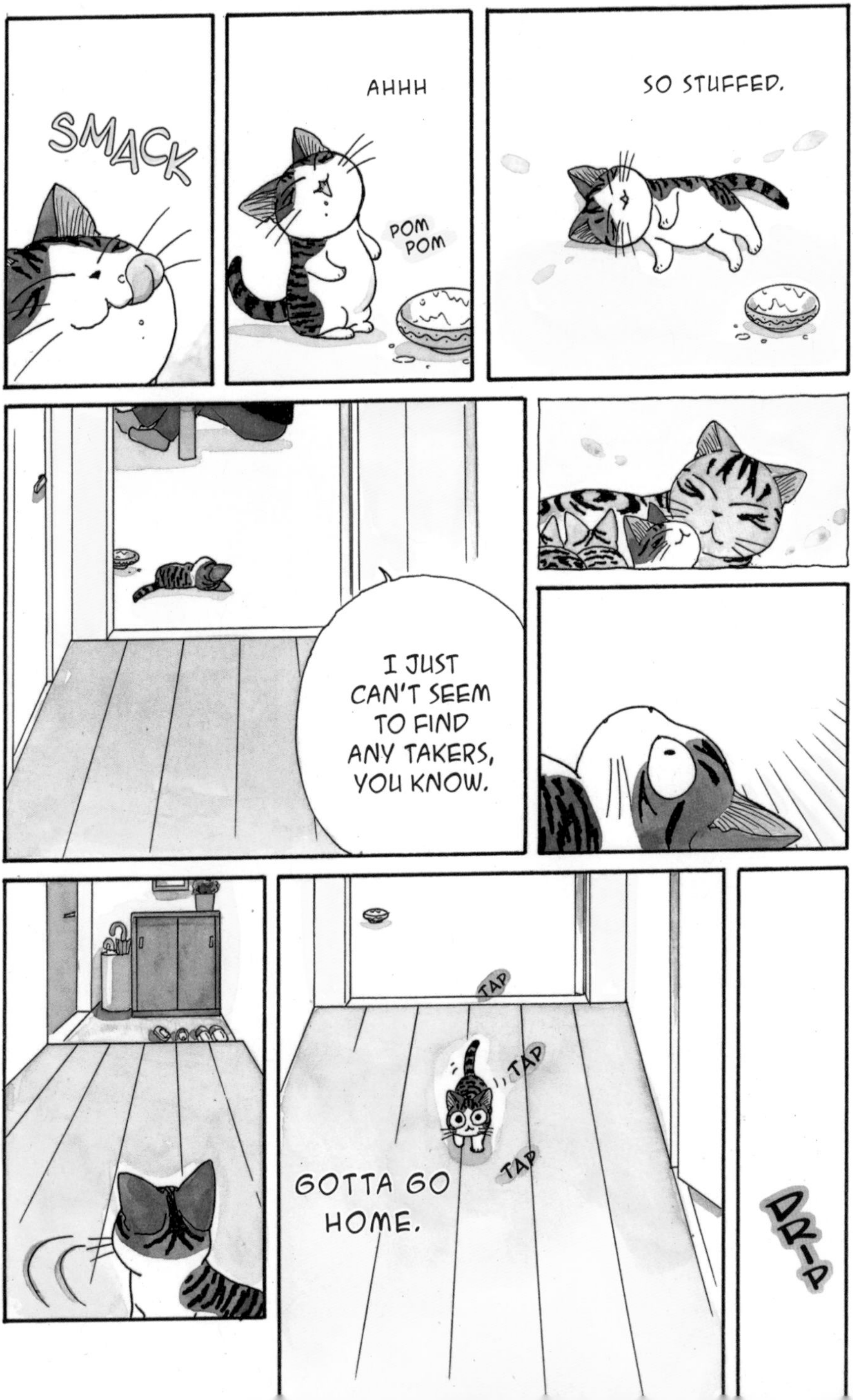
SMACK
AHHH
POM POM
SO STUFFED.
I JUST CAN'T SEEM TO FIND ANY TAKERS, YOU KNOW.
GOTTA GO HOME.
TAP
TAP
TAP
DRIP

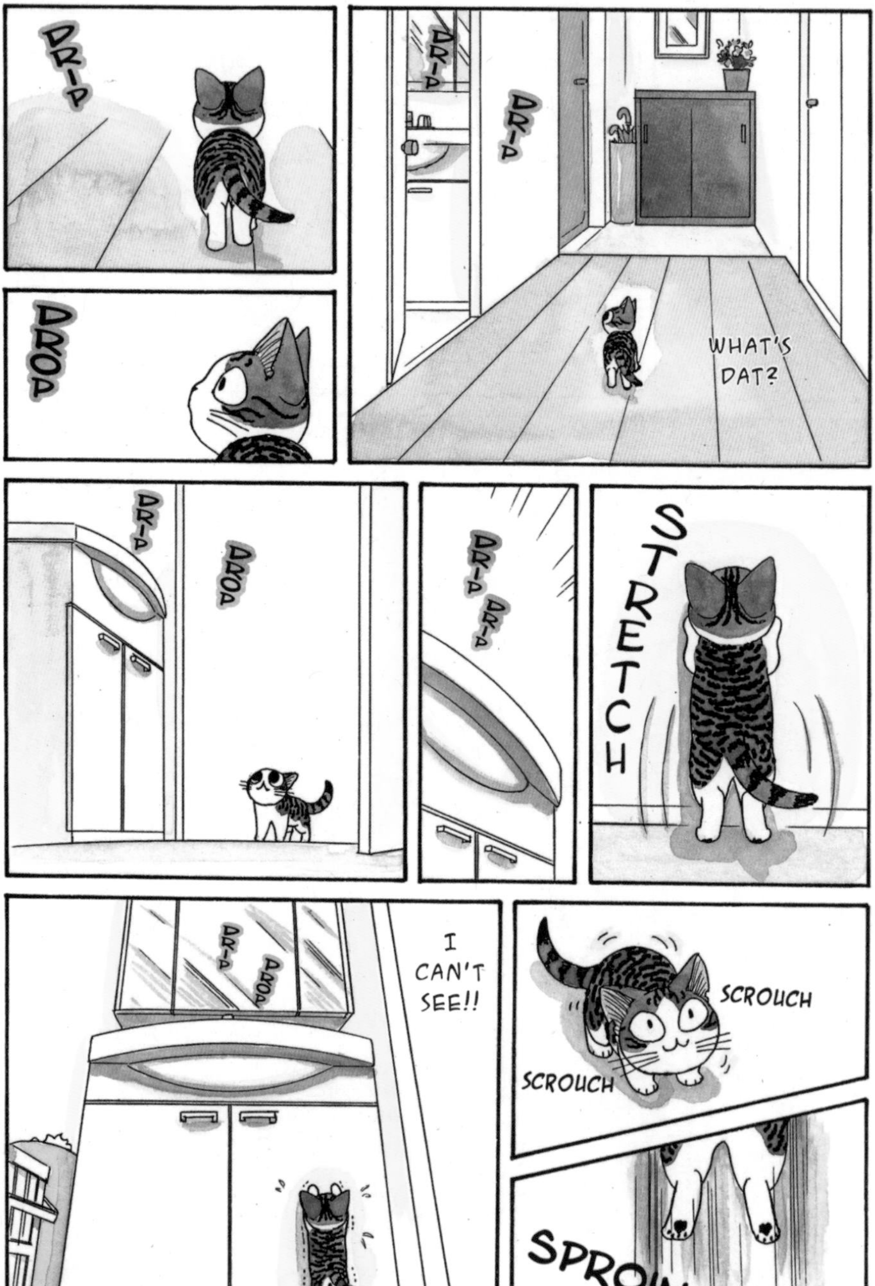
DRIP
DROP
DRIP
DRIP
WHAT'S DAT?
DRIP
DROP
DRIP
DRIP
STRETCH
DRIP
DROP
I CAN'T SEE!!
SCROUCH
SCROUCH
SPROING

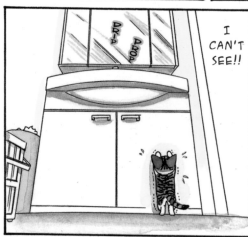

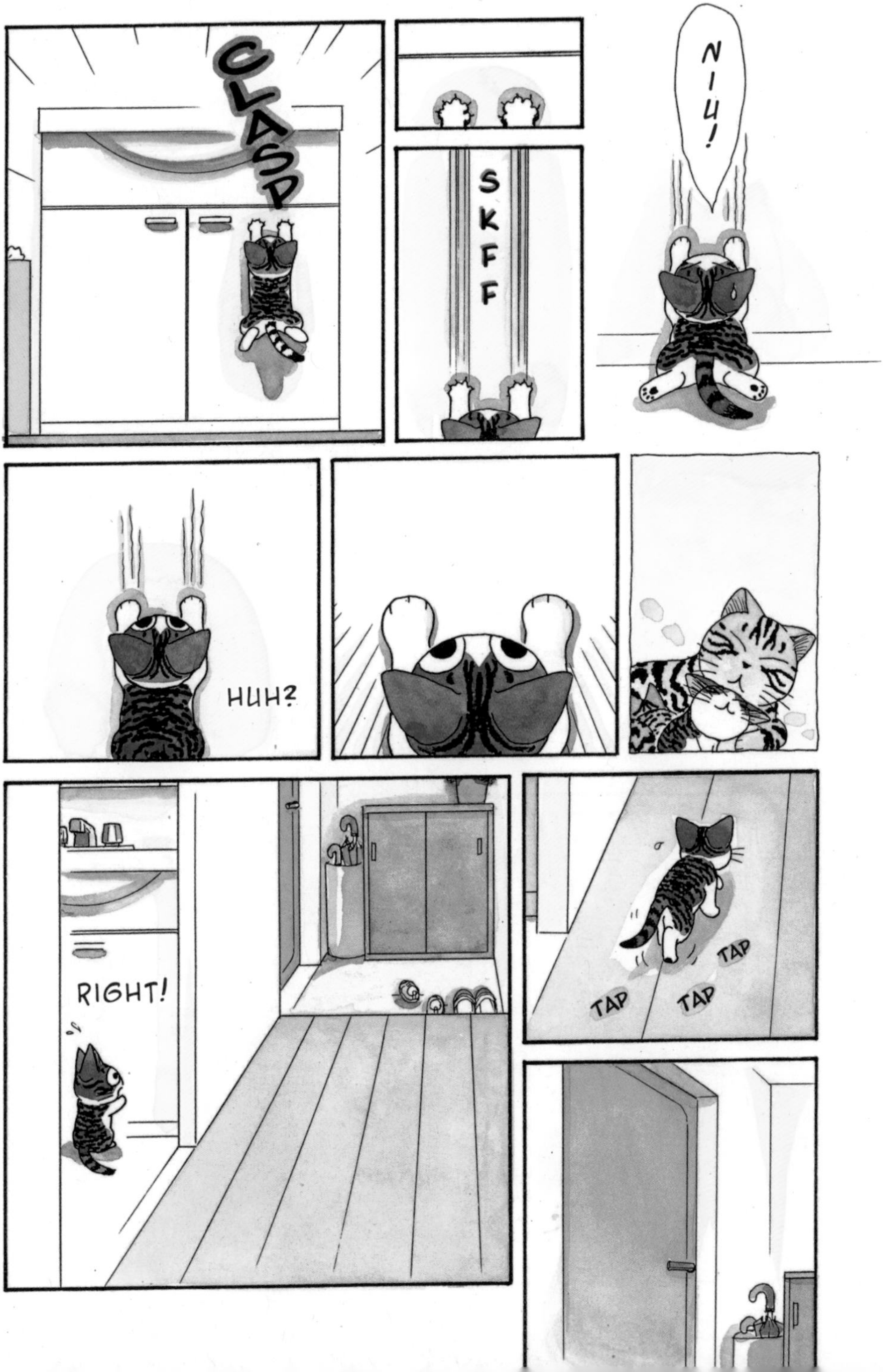
CLASP
SKFF
NIU!
HUH?
RIGHT!
TAP
TAP
TAP

I'M GOWING HOME!

HOP

OH?

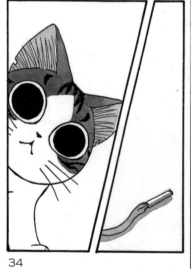

SPROING!

MEOWR

34

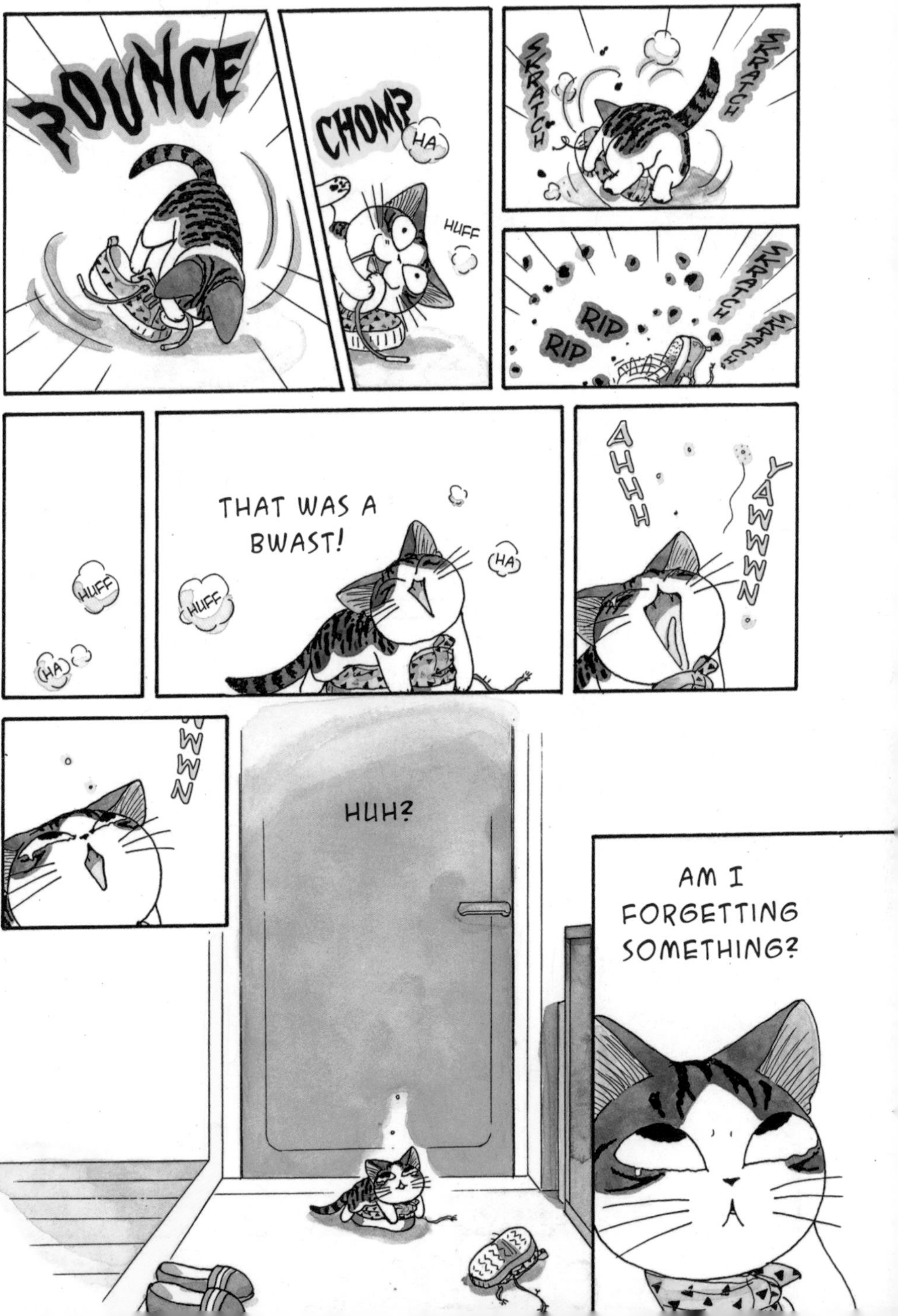
POUNCE
CHOMP
HA
HUFF
SKRATCH
SKRATCH
SKRATCH
RIP
RIP
SKRATCH
HUFF
HUFF
HA
THAT WAS A BWAST!
HUFF
HUFF
HA
AHHHH
YAWWWN
WWWN
HUH?
AM I FORGETTING SOMETHING?

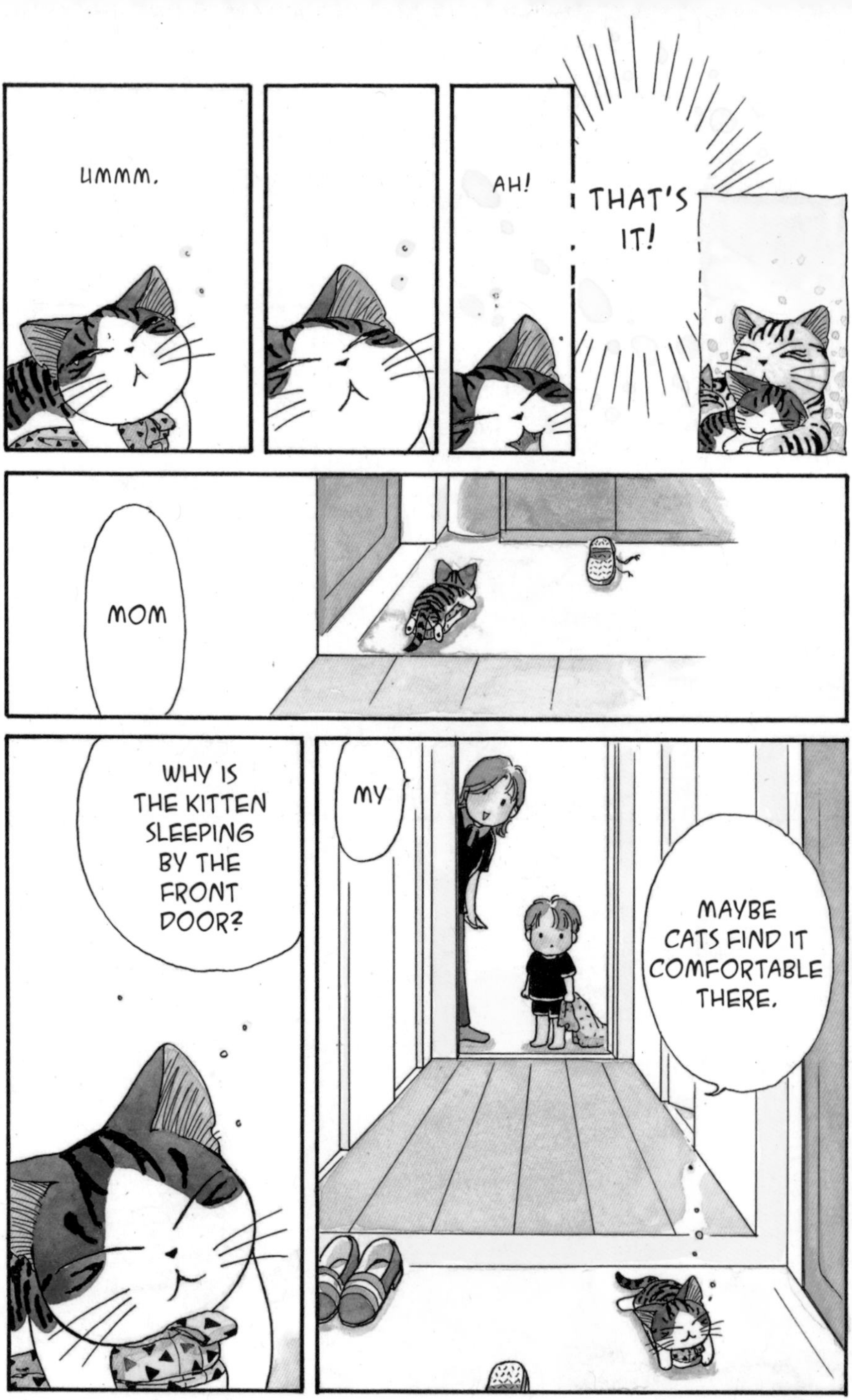
UMMM.
AH!
THAT'S IT!
MOM
WHY IS THE KITTEN SLEEPING BY THE FRONT DOOR?
MY
MAYBE CATS FIND IT COMFORTABLE THERE.

the end

homemade 5: a cat begins

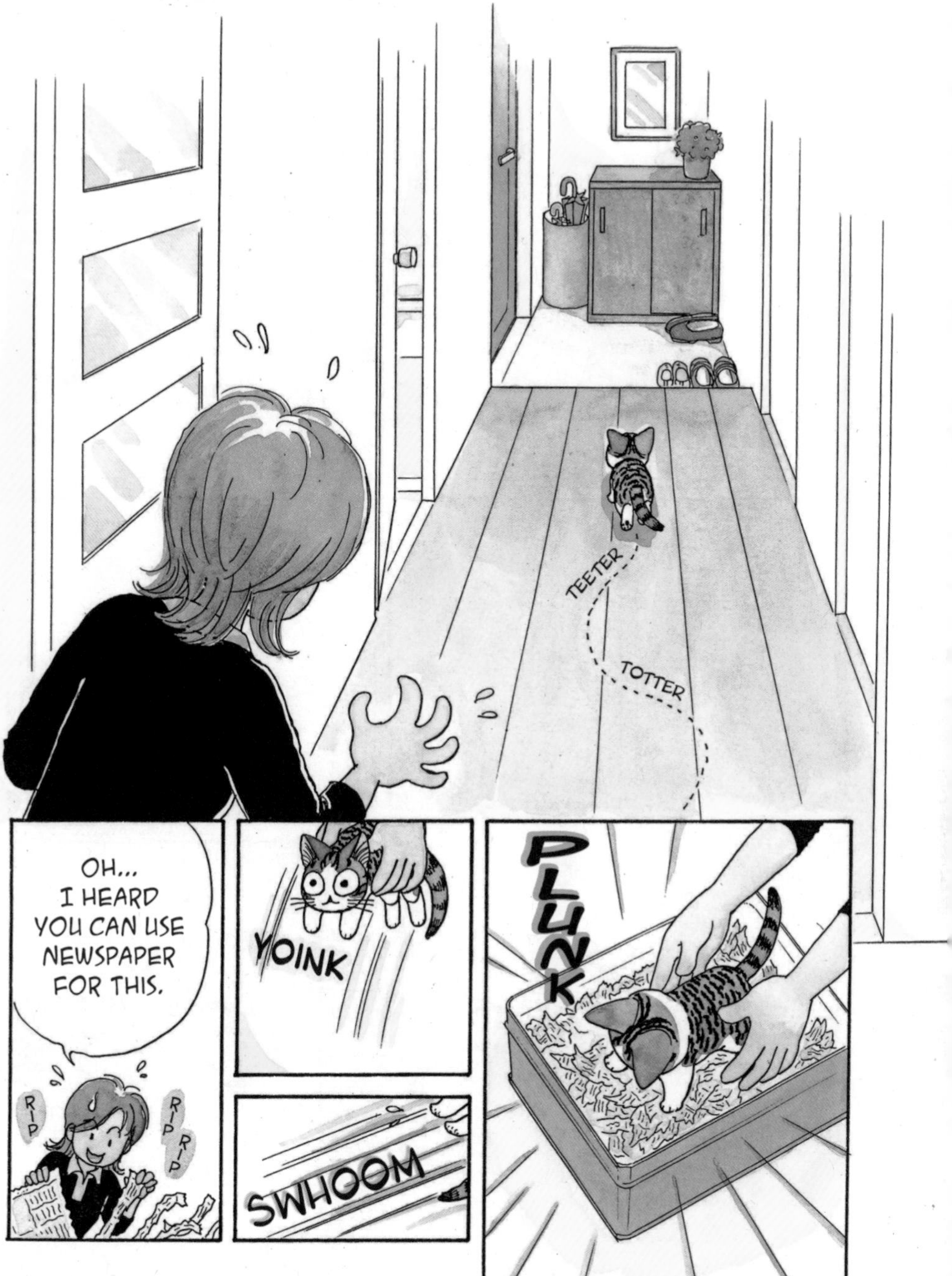
TEETER
TOTTER
OH... I HEARD YOU CAN USE NEWSPAPER FOR THIS.
RIP
RIP RIP
YOINK
SWHOOM
PLUNK

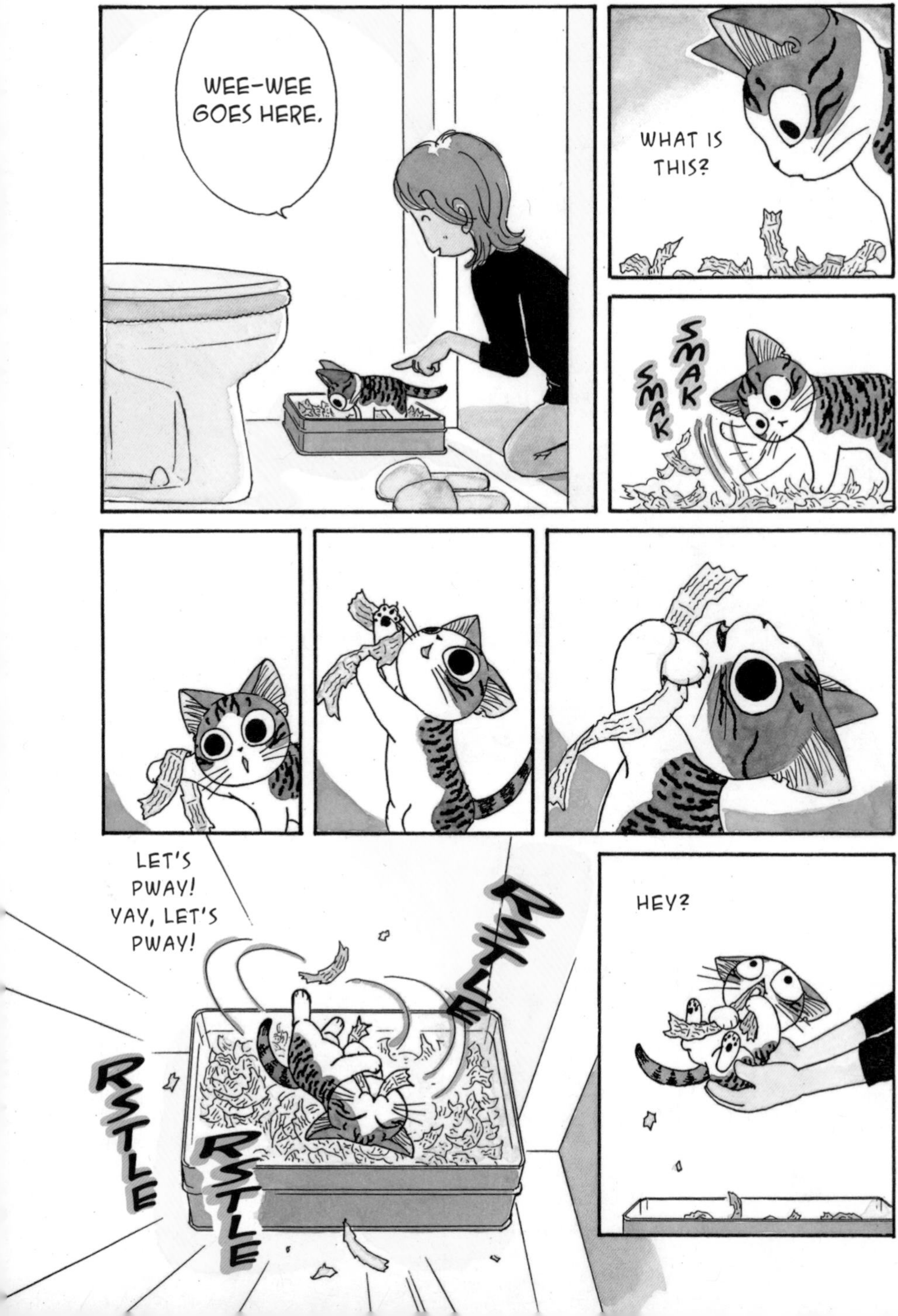
WEE-WEE GOES HERE.
WHAT IS THIS?
SMAK SMAK
LET'S PWAY! YAY, LET'S PWAY!
RSTLE
RSTLE
RSTLE
HEY?

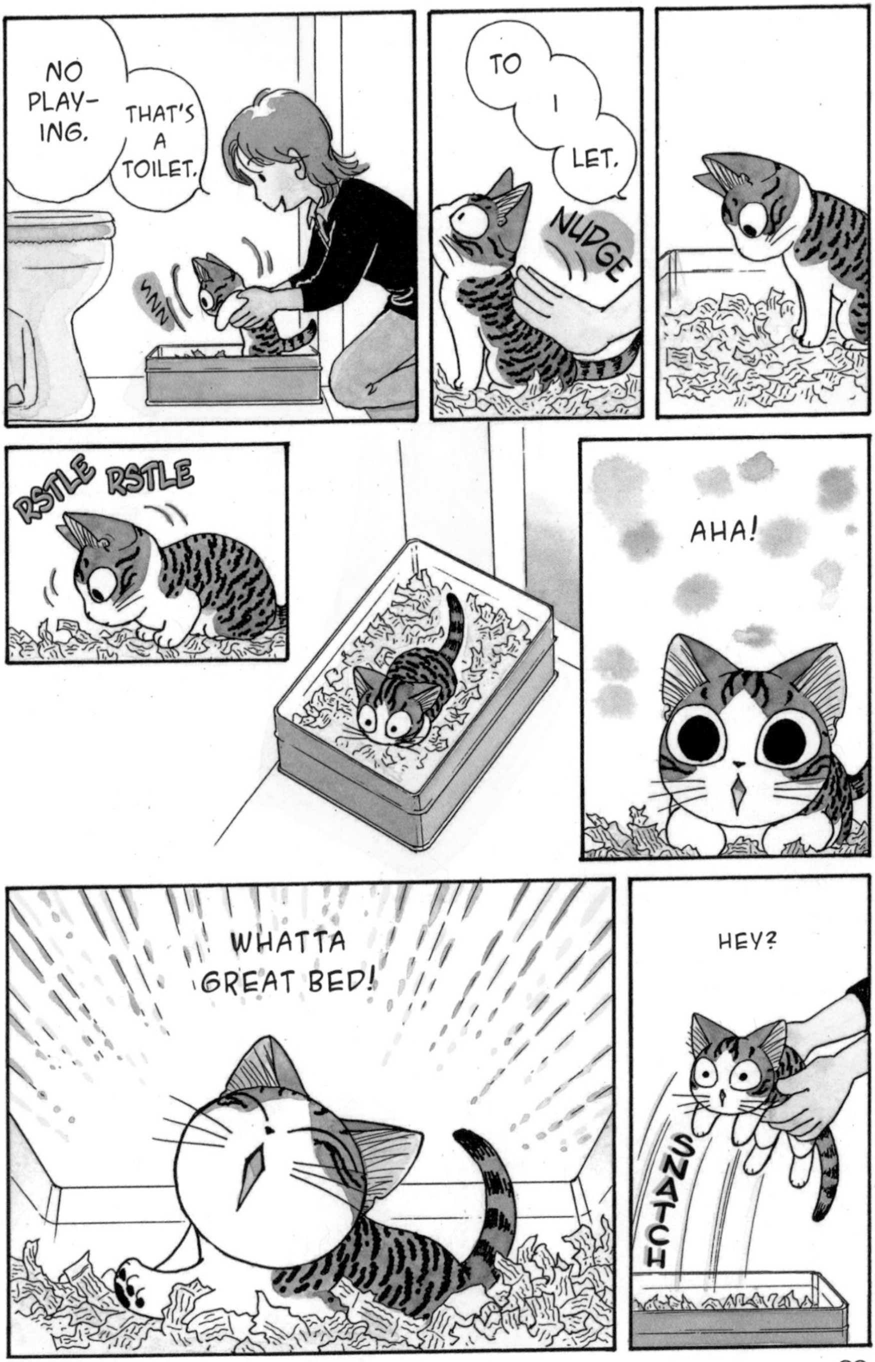
NO PLAY-ING.
THAT'S A TOILET.
SNN
TO I LET.
NUDGE
RSTLE RSTLE
AHA!
WHATTA GREAT BED!
HEY?
SNATCH

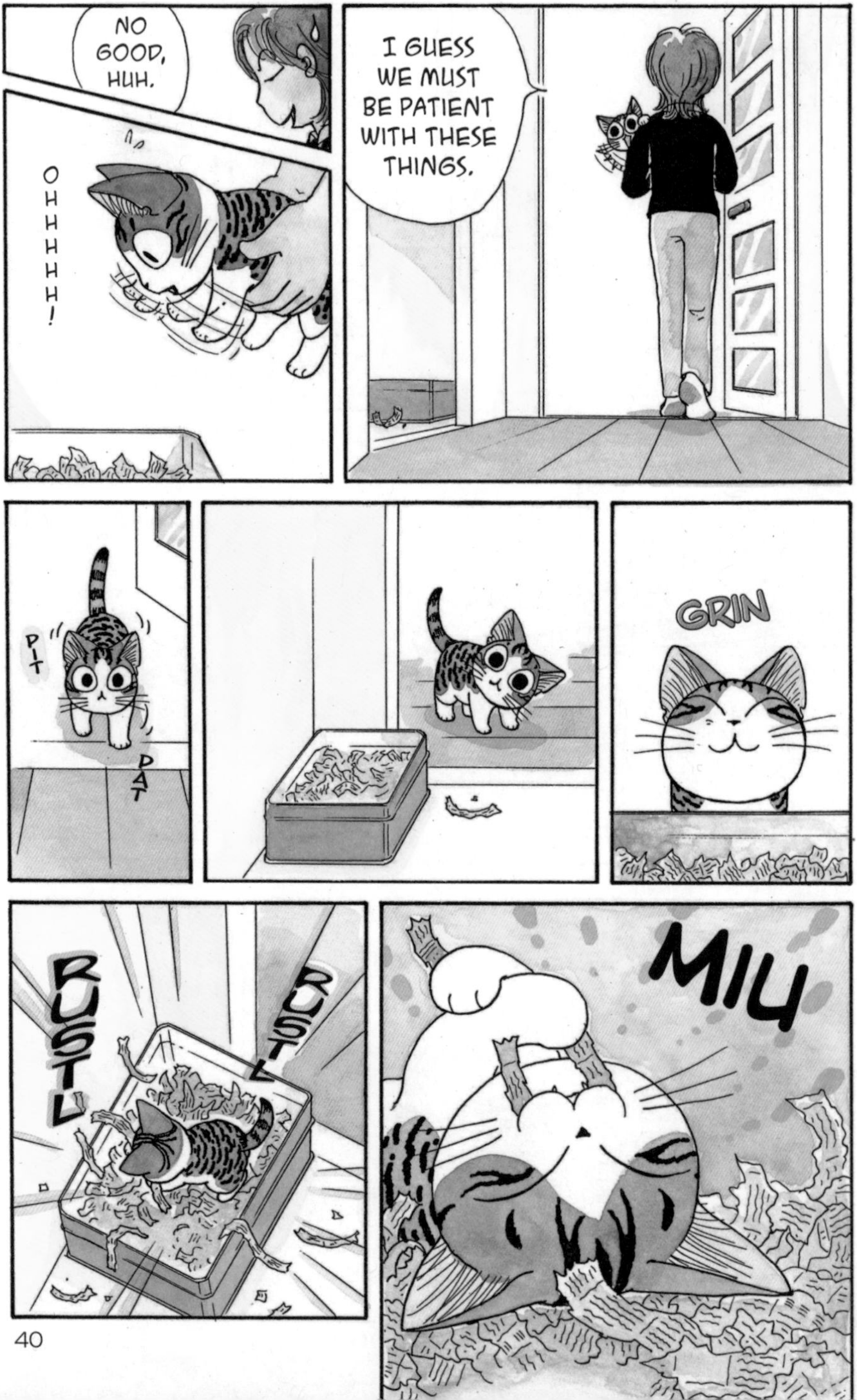
NO GOOD, HUH.
OHHHHHH!
I GUESS WE MUST BE PATIENT WITH THESE THINGS.
PIT
PAT
GRIN
RUSTL
RUSTL
MIU

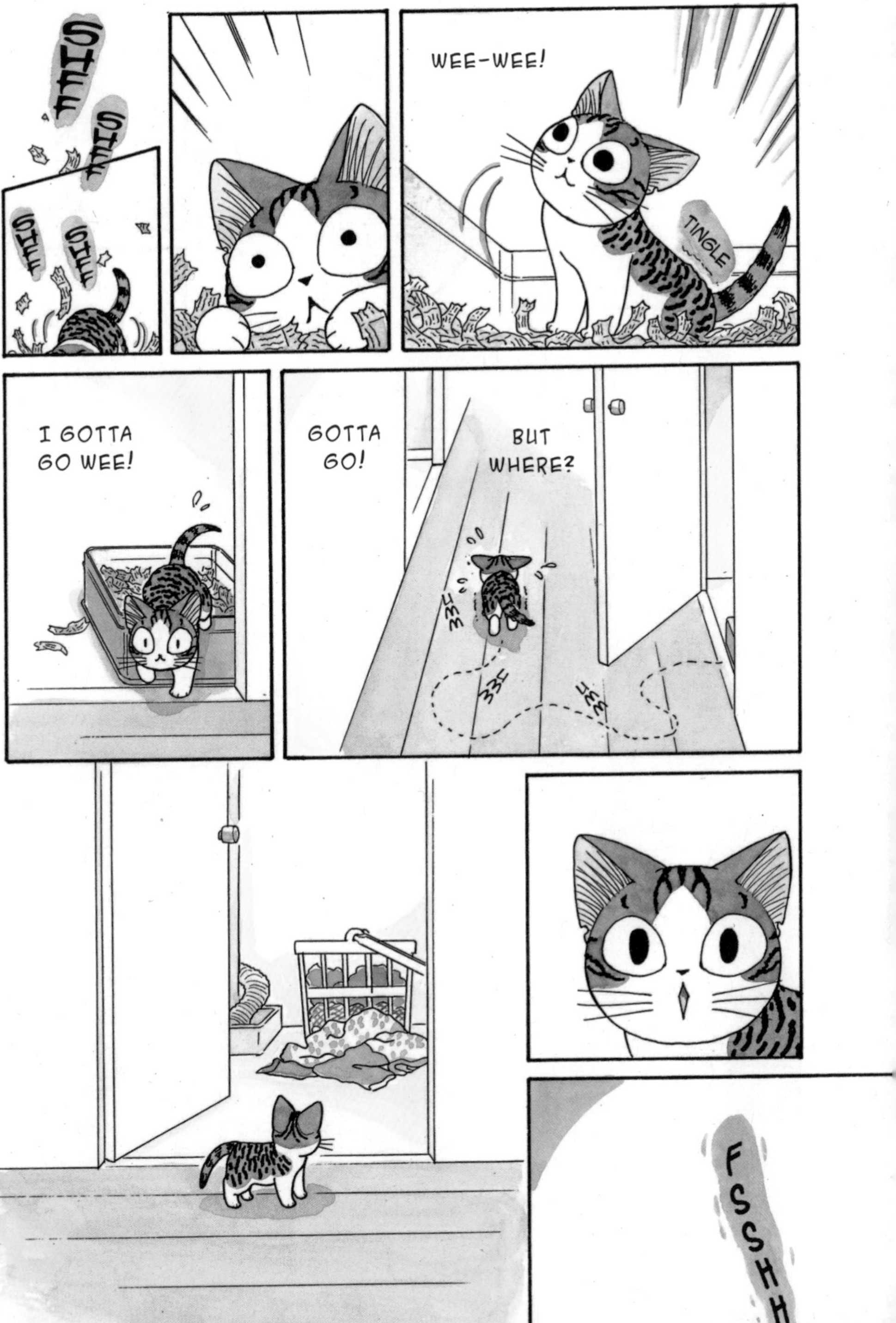
SHFF SHFF
SHFF SHFF
WEE-WEE!
TINGLE
I GOTTA GO WEE!
GOTTA GO!
BUT WHERE?
FSSHH

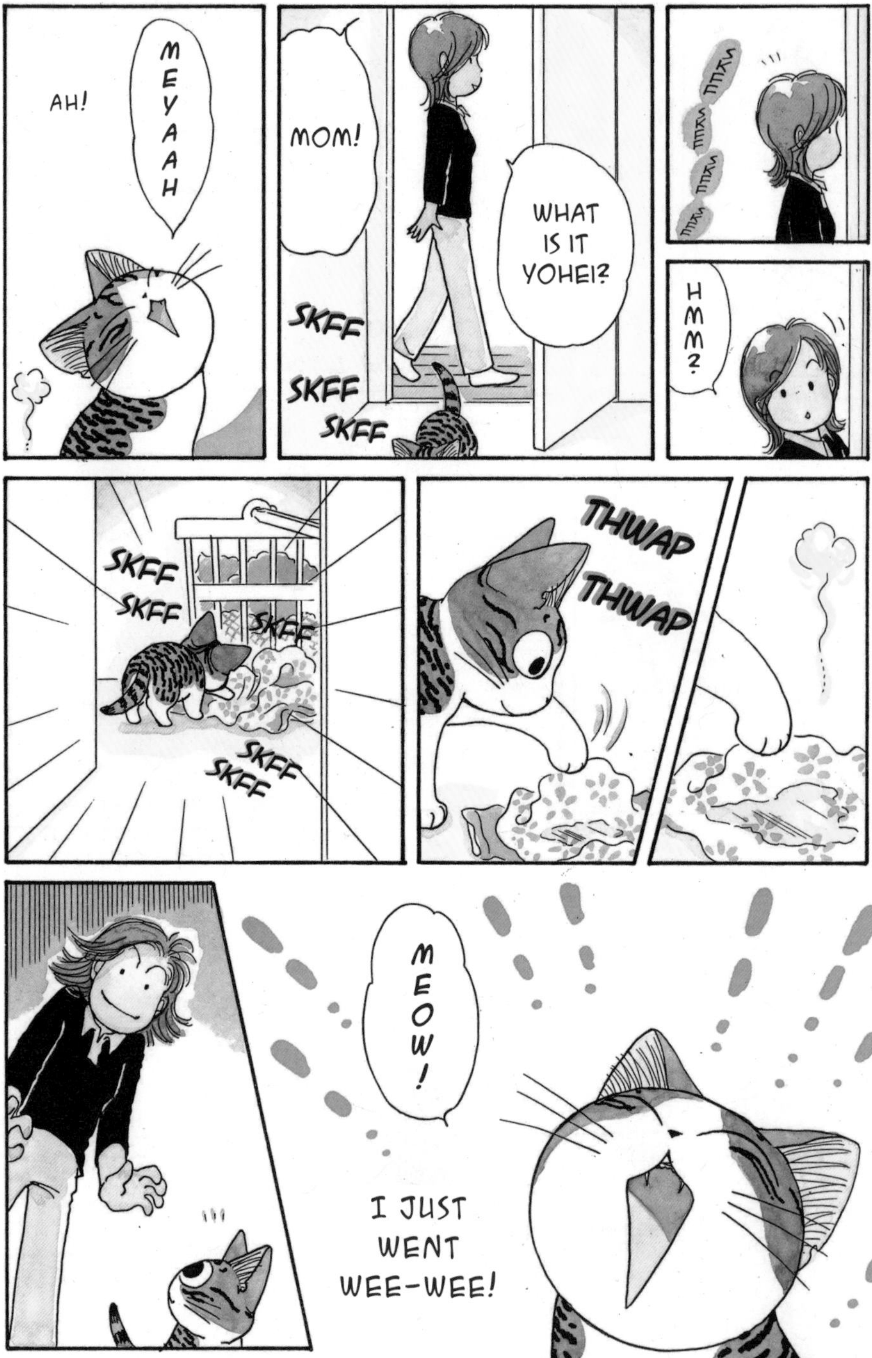
AH!
MEYAAAH
MOM!
SKFF
SKFF
SKFF
WHAT IS IT YOHEI!?
SKFF SKFF SKFF SKFF
HMM?
SKFF
SKFF
SKFF
SKFF
SKFF
THWAP
THWAP
MEOW!
I JUST WENT WEE-WEE!

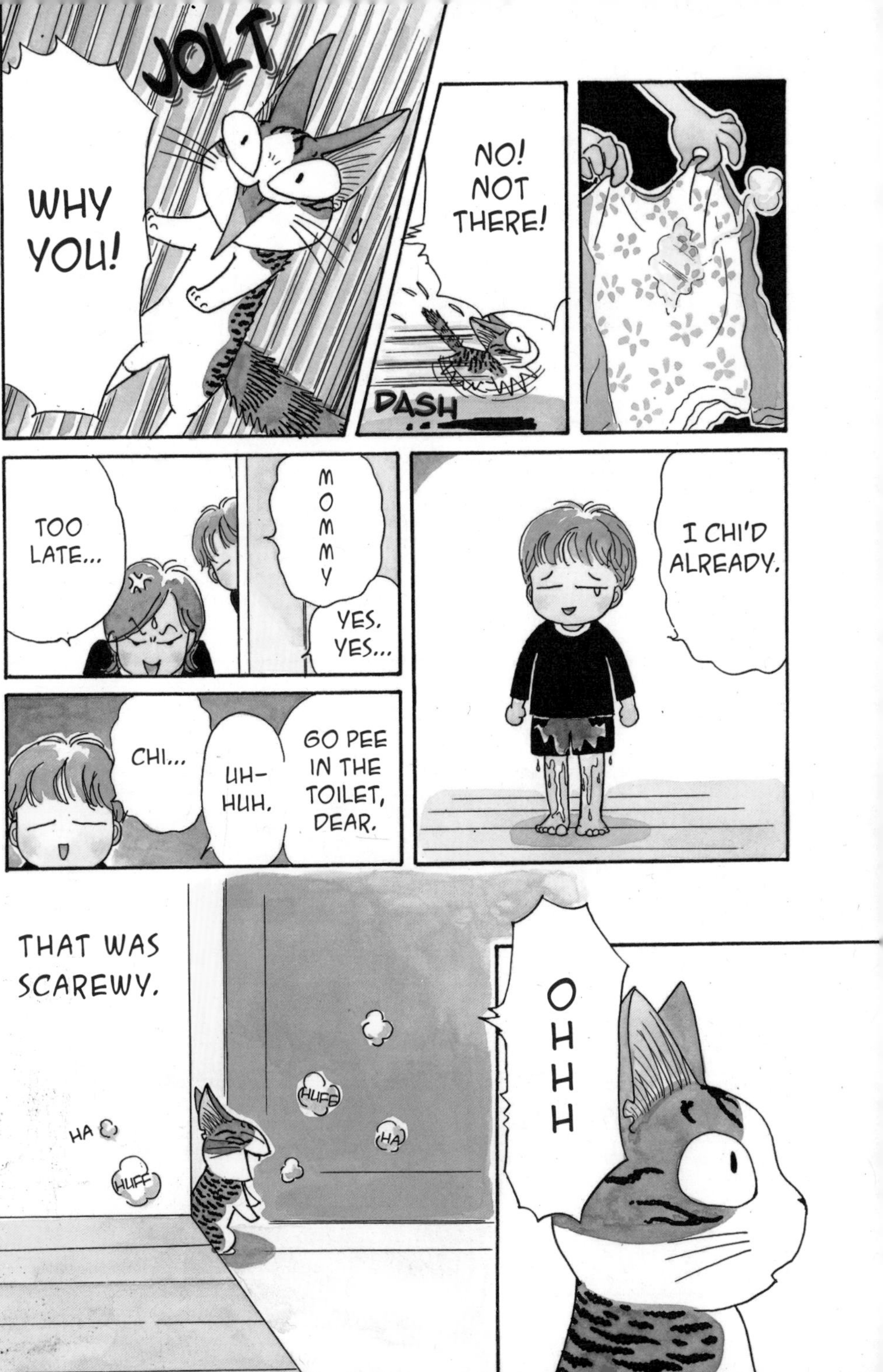
JOLT
WHY YOU!
NO! NOT THERE!
DASH
TOO LATE...
MOMMY
YES. YES...
CHI...
UH-HUH.
GO PEE IN THE TOILET, DEAR.
I CHI'D ALREADY.
THAT WAS SCAREWY.
HA
HUFF
HUFF
HA
OHHH

THAT'S NO GOOD.

PEAK

THMP THMP

YOU HAVE TO GO TO THE TOILET BEFORE YOU WEE-WEE.

?

SNIFF SNIFF

SNIFF

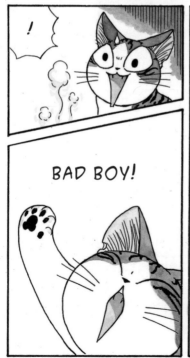

!

BAD BOY!

DON'T FORGET TO COVER UP YOUR WEE-WEE WITH SAND OR DIRT.

SKEE SKEE SKEE SKEE

the end

homemade 6: a cat is disappointed

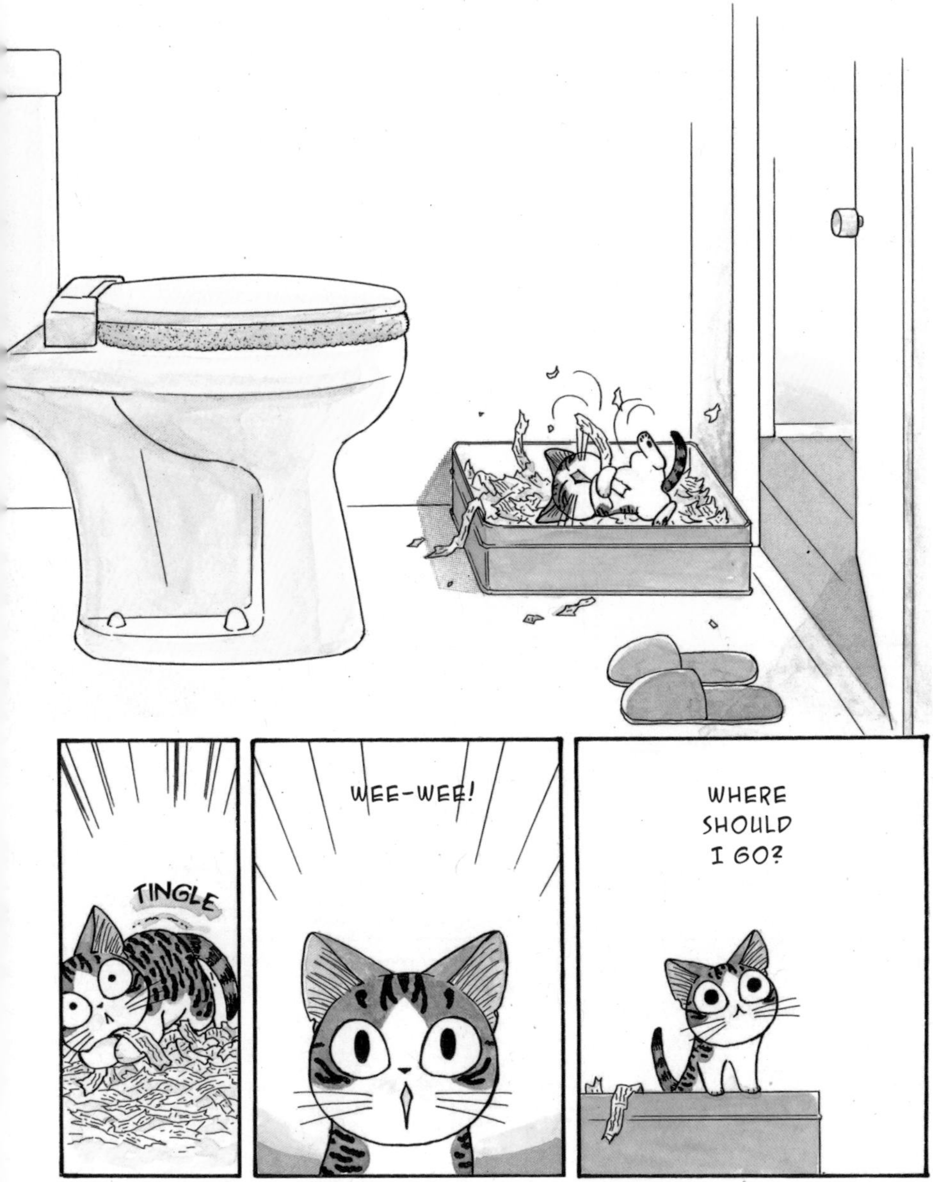
TINGLE
WEE-WEE!
WHERE SHOULD I GO?

WANDER

WANDER

THIS LOOKS LIKE A GOOD SPOT.

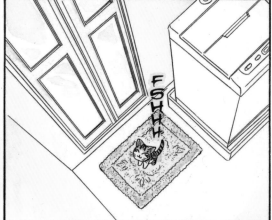

FSHHH

AH!

SKEE SKEE SKEE

TUMP TUMP

ARGH!

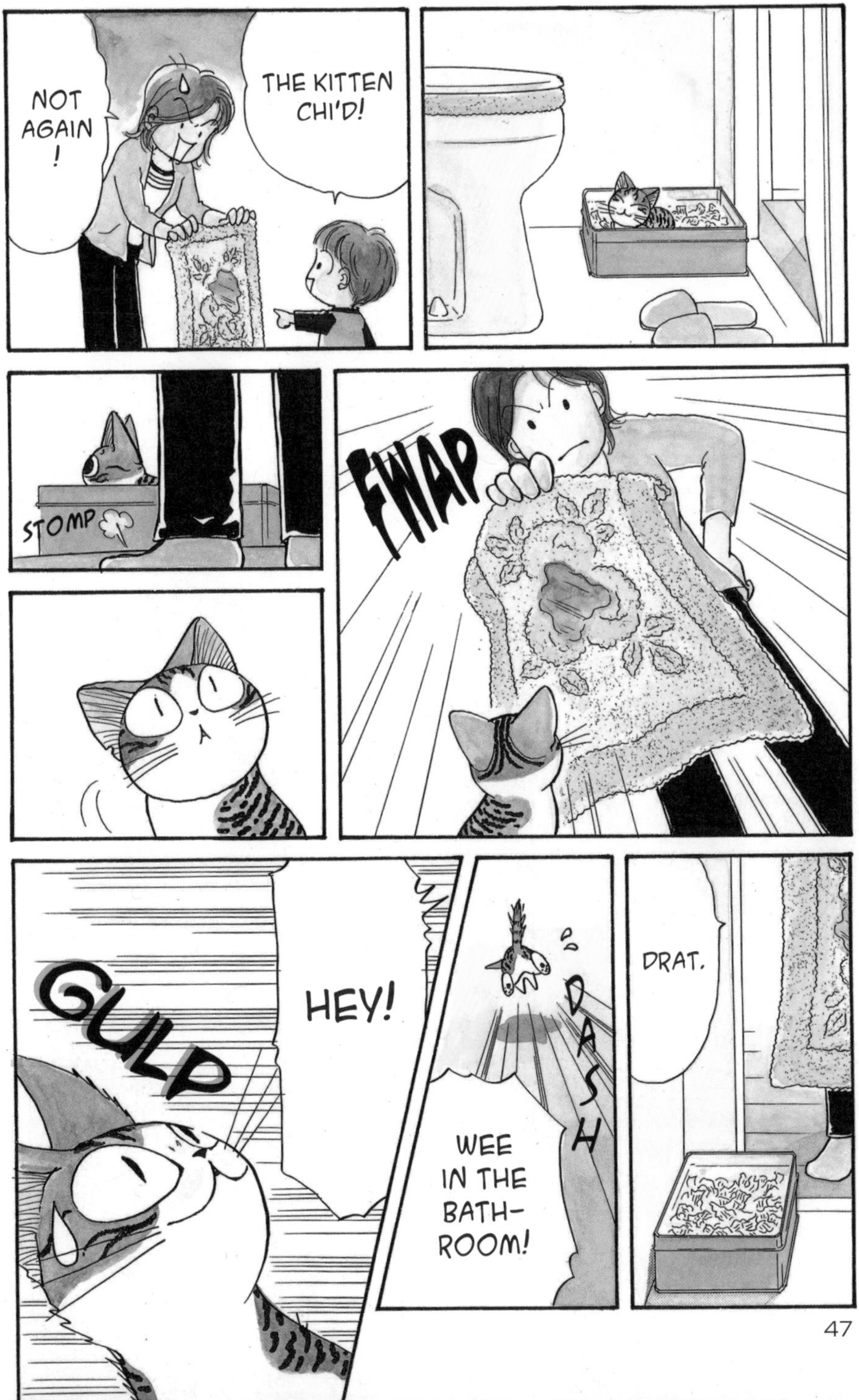
NOT AGAIN!
THE KITTEN CHI'D!
STOMP
FWAP
GULP
HEY!
DASH
WEE IN THE BATH-ROOM!
DRAT.

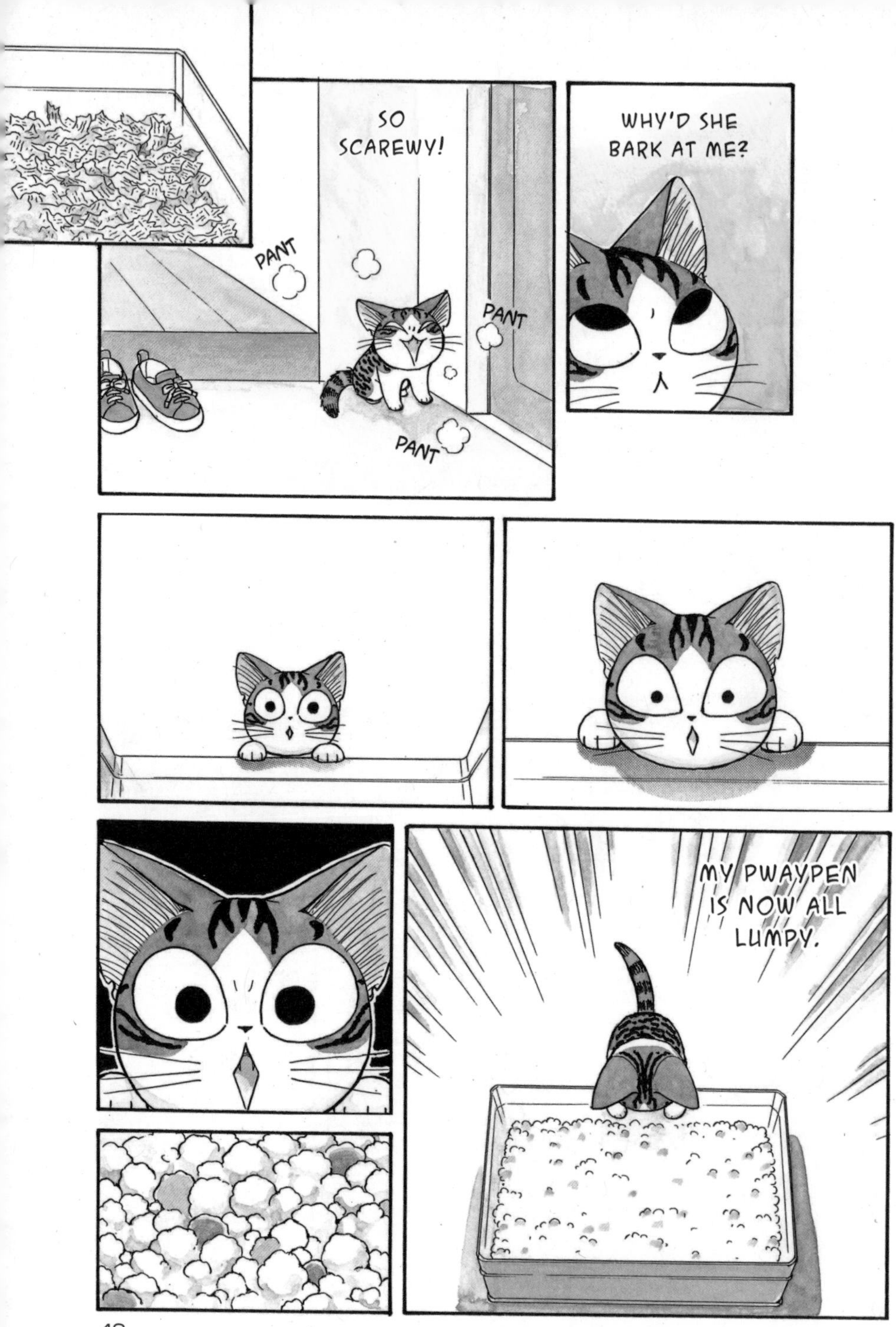
SO SCAREWY!
PANT
PANT
PANT
WHY'D SHE BARK AT ME?
MY PWAYPEN IS NOW ALL LUMPY.

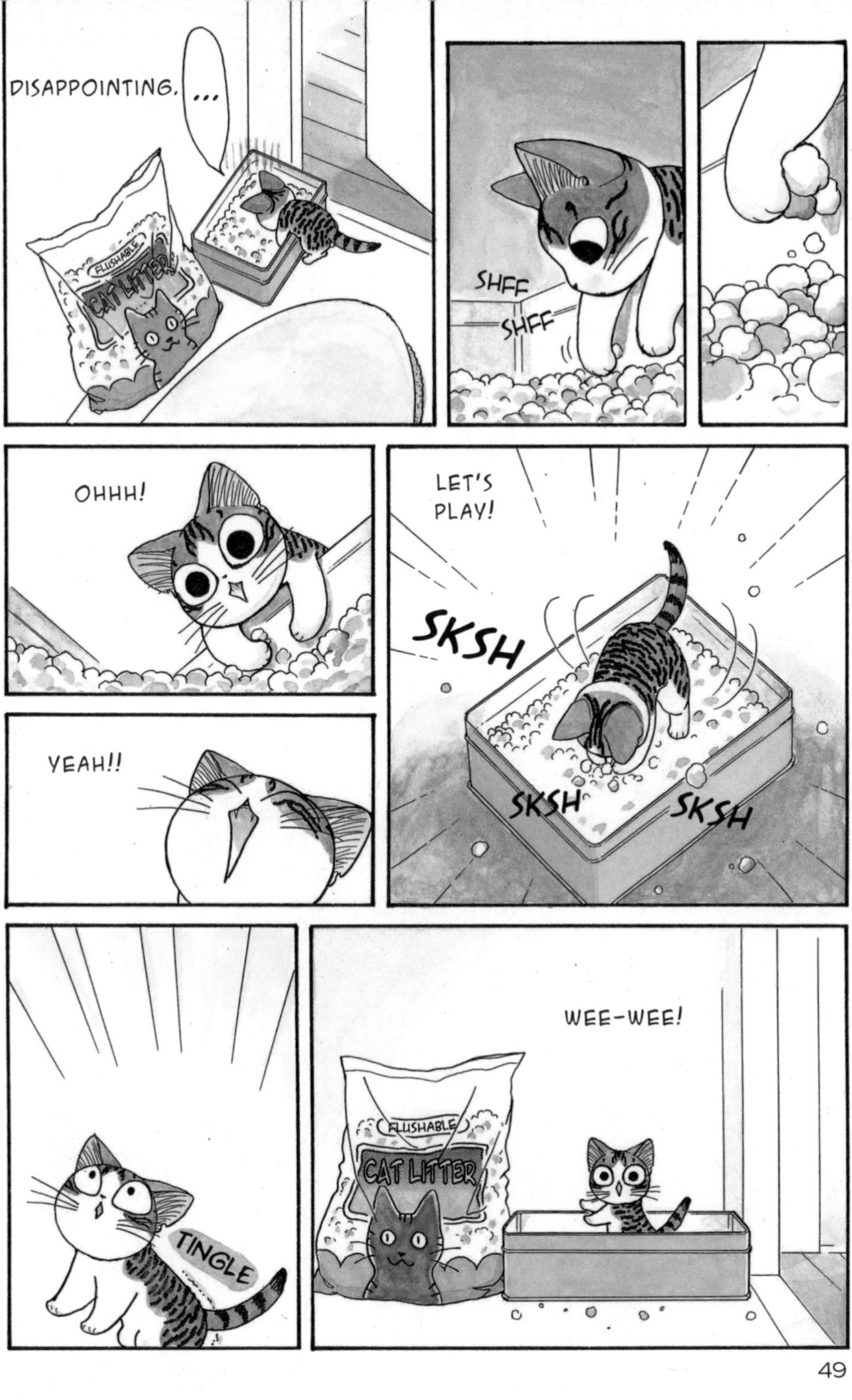
DISAPPOINTING.
...
FLUSHABLE
CAT LITTER
SHFF
SHFF
OHHH!
LET'S PLAY!
SKSH
SKSH
SKSH
YEAH!!
TINGLE
WEE-WEE!
FLUSHABLE
CAT LITTER

WEE-WEE! WEE-WEE!

SCAMPER

OH! NOT AGAIN!

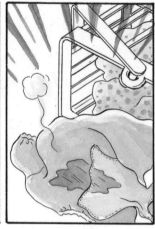

WHAT A PLACE TO GO WEE IN.

SHOOT!

IT'S CHI! CHI, MOMMY!

WE SHOULD CHI IN THE TOILET, RIGHT?

RIGHT!

CHI GOES IN THE TOILET!

CHI GOES IN THE TOILET!

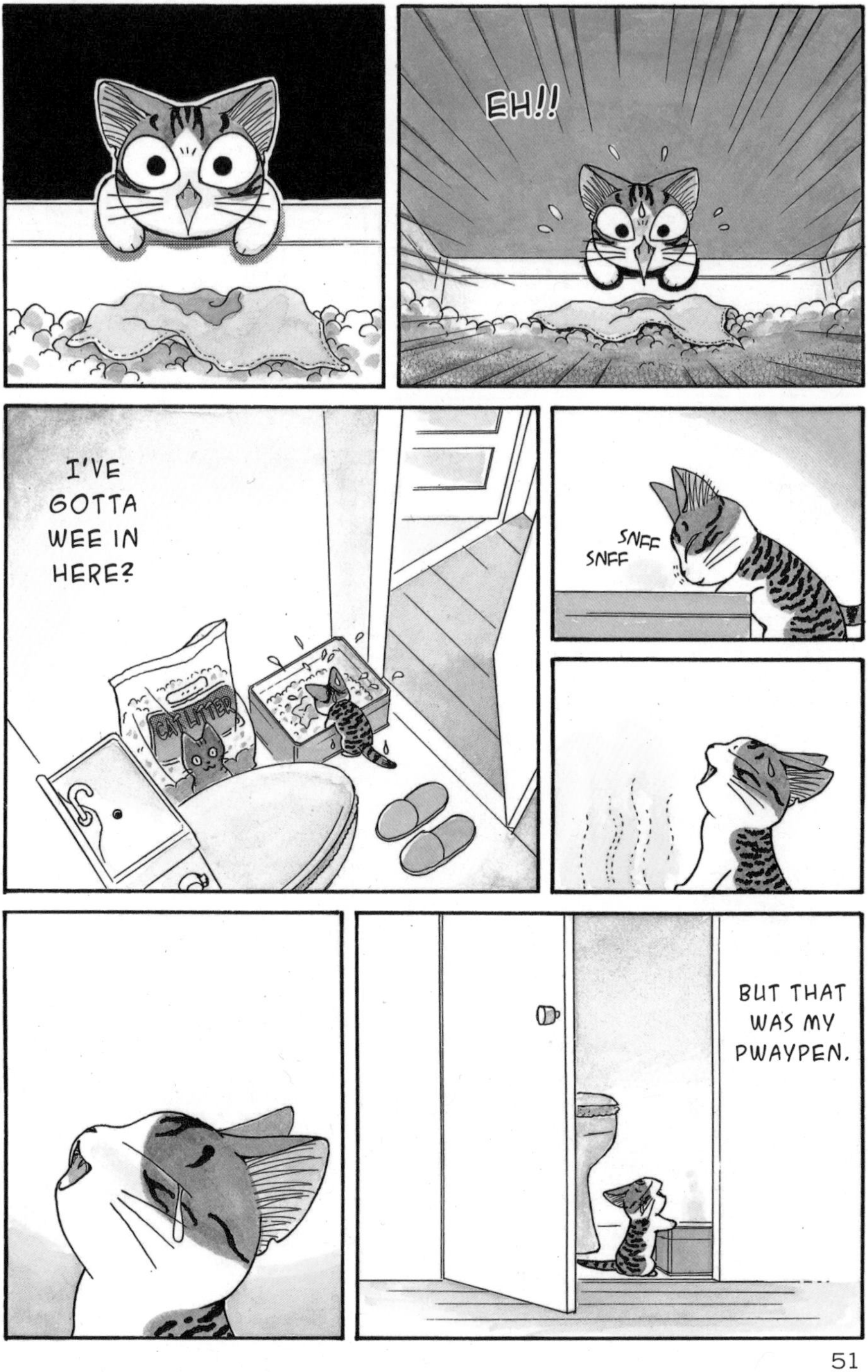
EH!!
I'VE GOTTA WEE IN HERE?
CAT LITTER
SNFF
SNFF
BUT THAT WAS MY PWAYPEN.

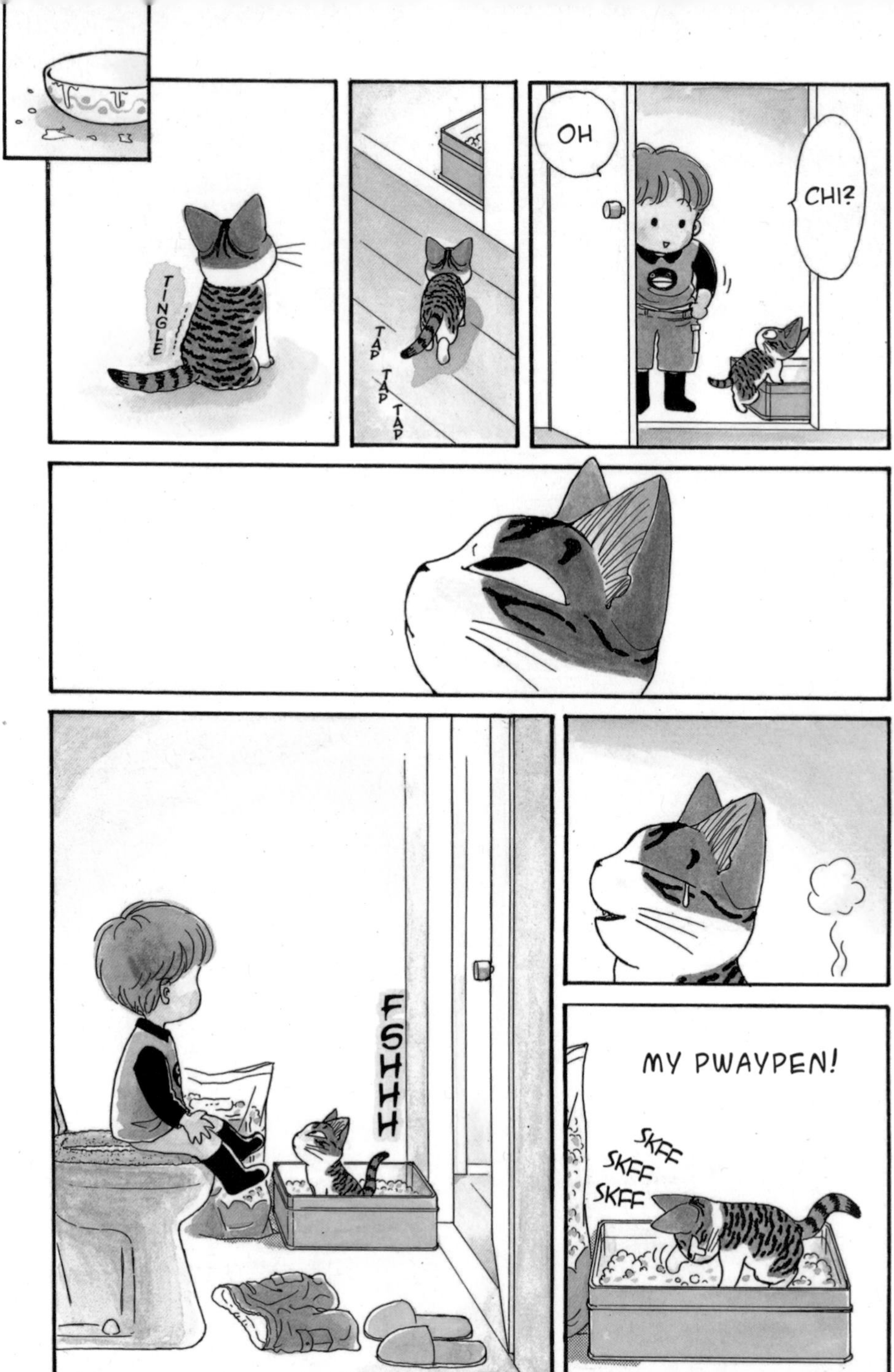
TINGLE
TAP TAP TAP TAP
OH
CHI?
FSHHH
MY PWAYPEN!
SKFF SKFF SKFF

the end

homemade 7: a cat understands

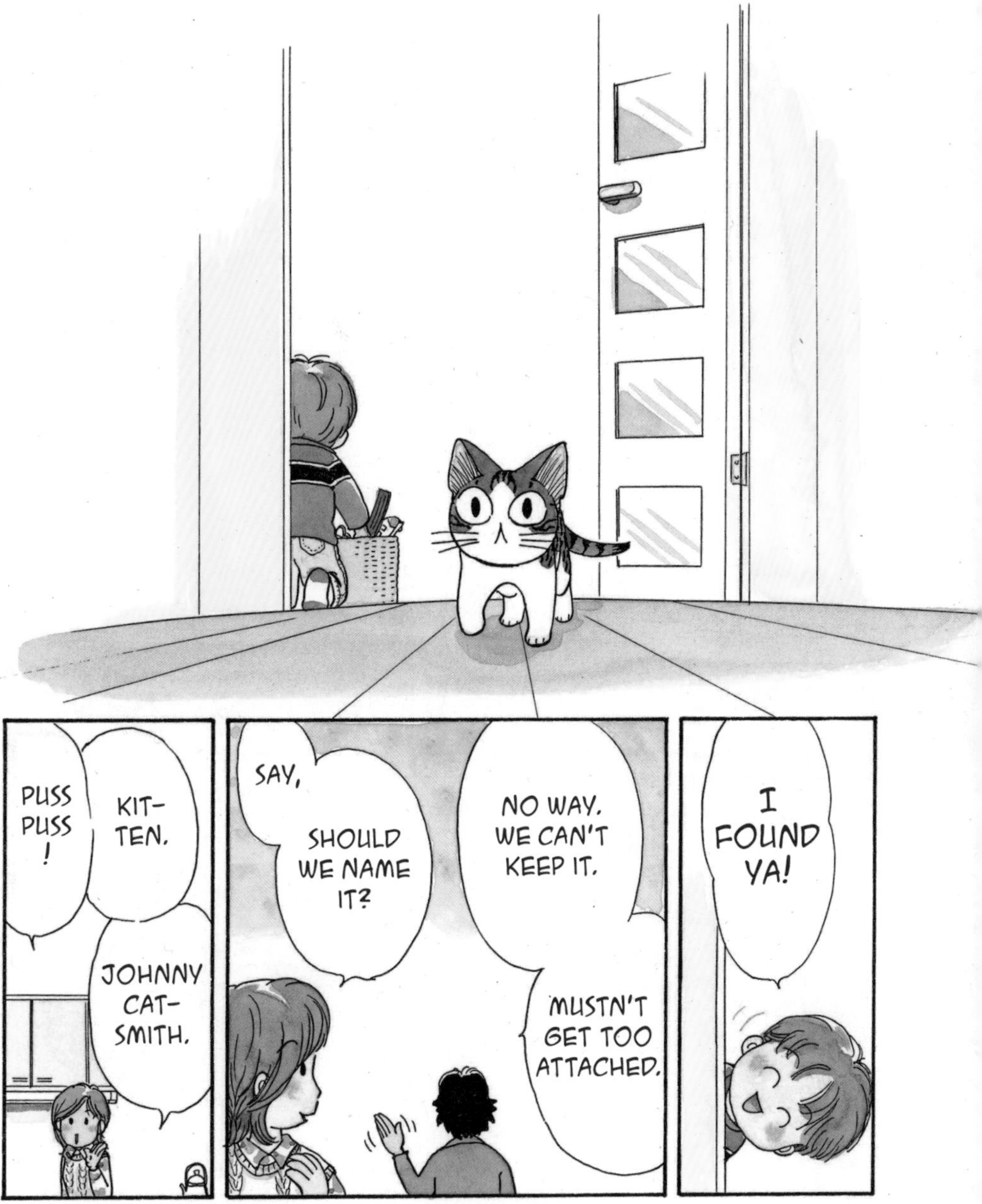
PUSS PUSS!
KIT-TEN.
JOHNNY CAT-SMITH.
SAY, SHOULD WE NAME IT?
NO WAY. WE CAN'T KEEP IT.
MUSTN'T GET TOO ATTACHED.
I FOUND YA!

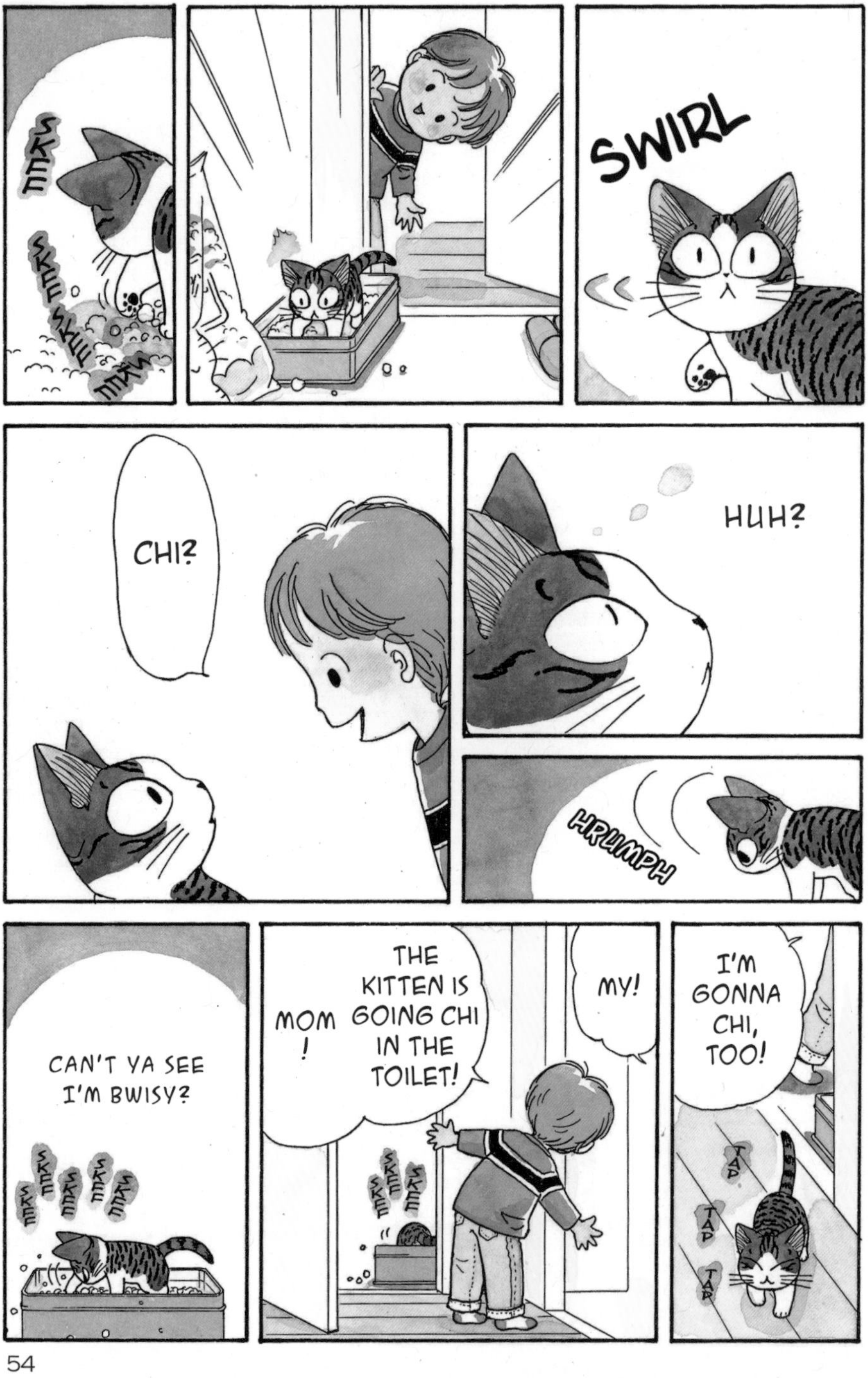
SKEE
SKEE
SKEE
SKEE
SWIRL
CHI?
HUH?
HRUMPH
CAN'T YA SEE I'M BWISY?
SKEE SKEE SKEE SKEE
MOM!
THE KITTEN IS GOING CHI IN THE TOILET!
SKEE SKEE
MY!
I'M GONNA CHI, TOO!
TAP TAP TAP

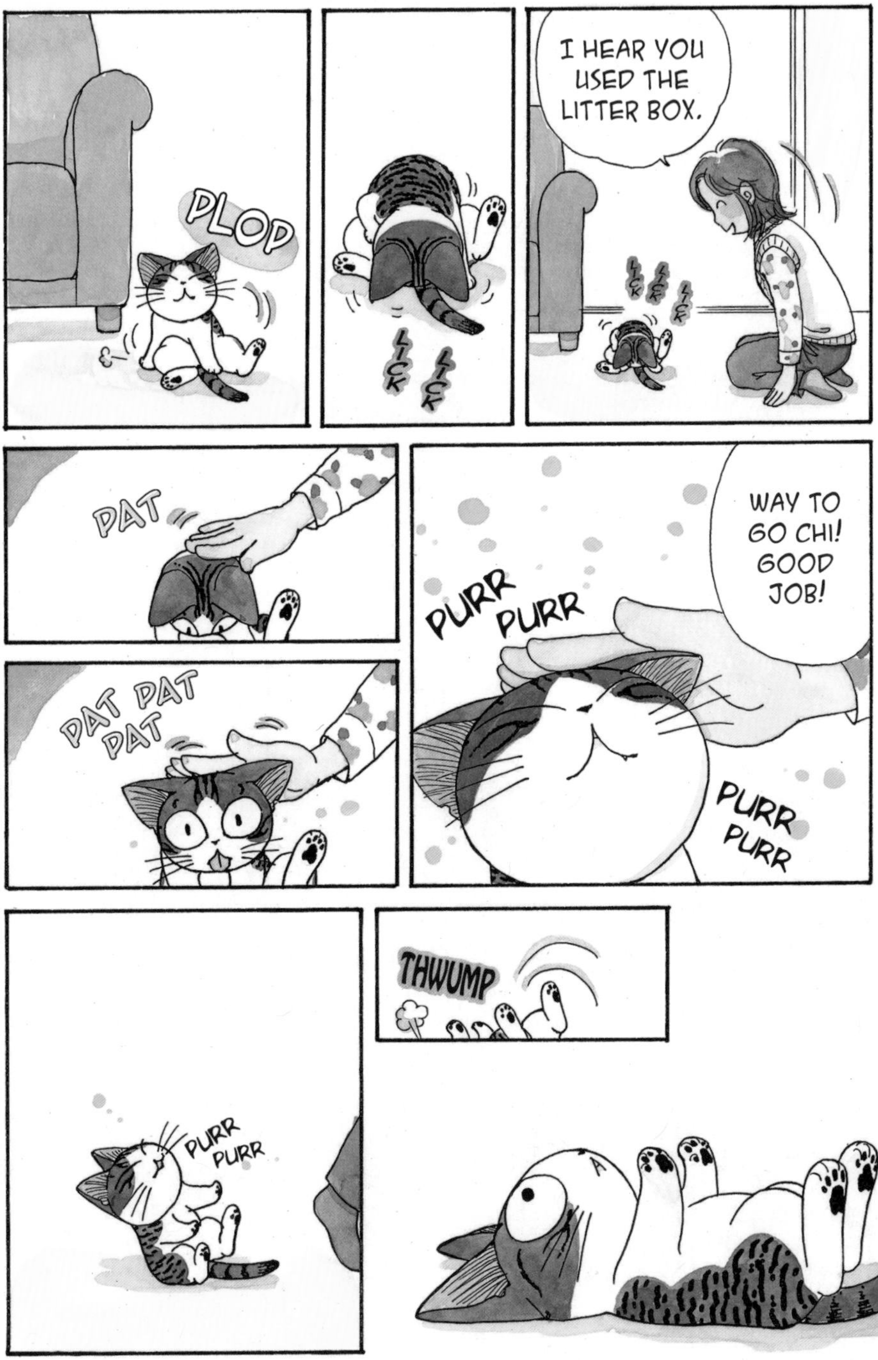
PLOP
LICK LICK
I HEAR YOU USED THE LITTER BOX.
LICK LICK LICK
PAT
PAT PAT PAT
WAY TO GO CHI! GOOD JOB!
PURR PURR
PURR PURR
THWUMP
PURR PURR

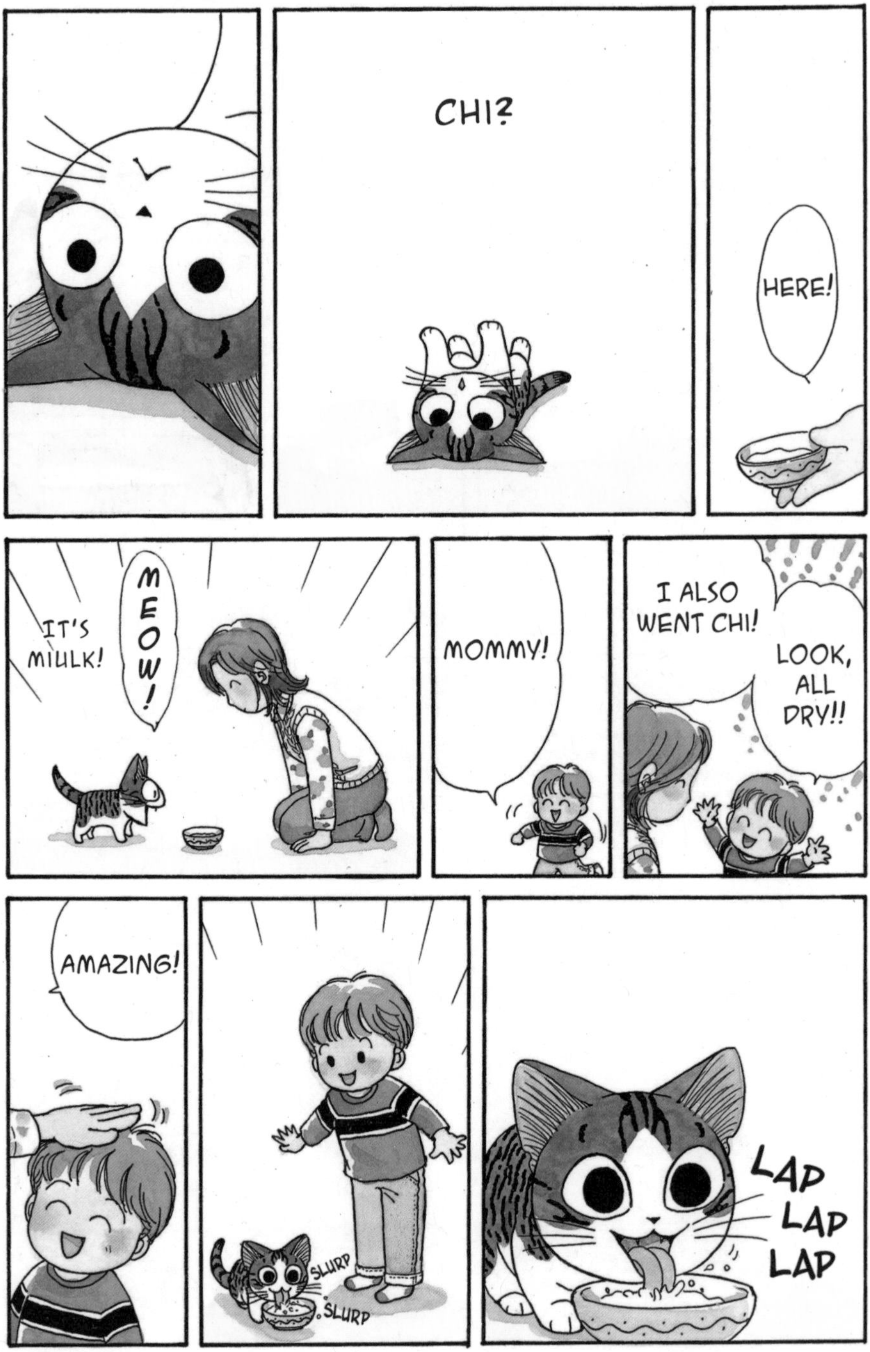
CHI?
HERE!
IT'S MIULK!
MEOW!
MOMMY!
I ALSO WENT CHI!
LOOK, ALL DRY!!
AMAZING!
SLURP
SLURP
LAP
LAP
LAP

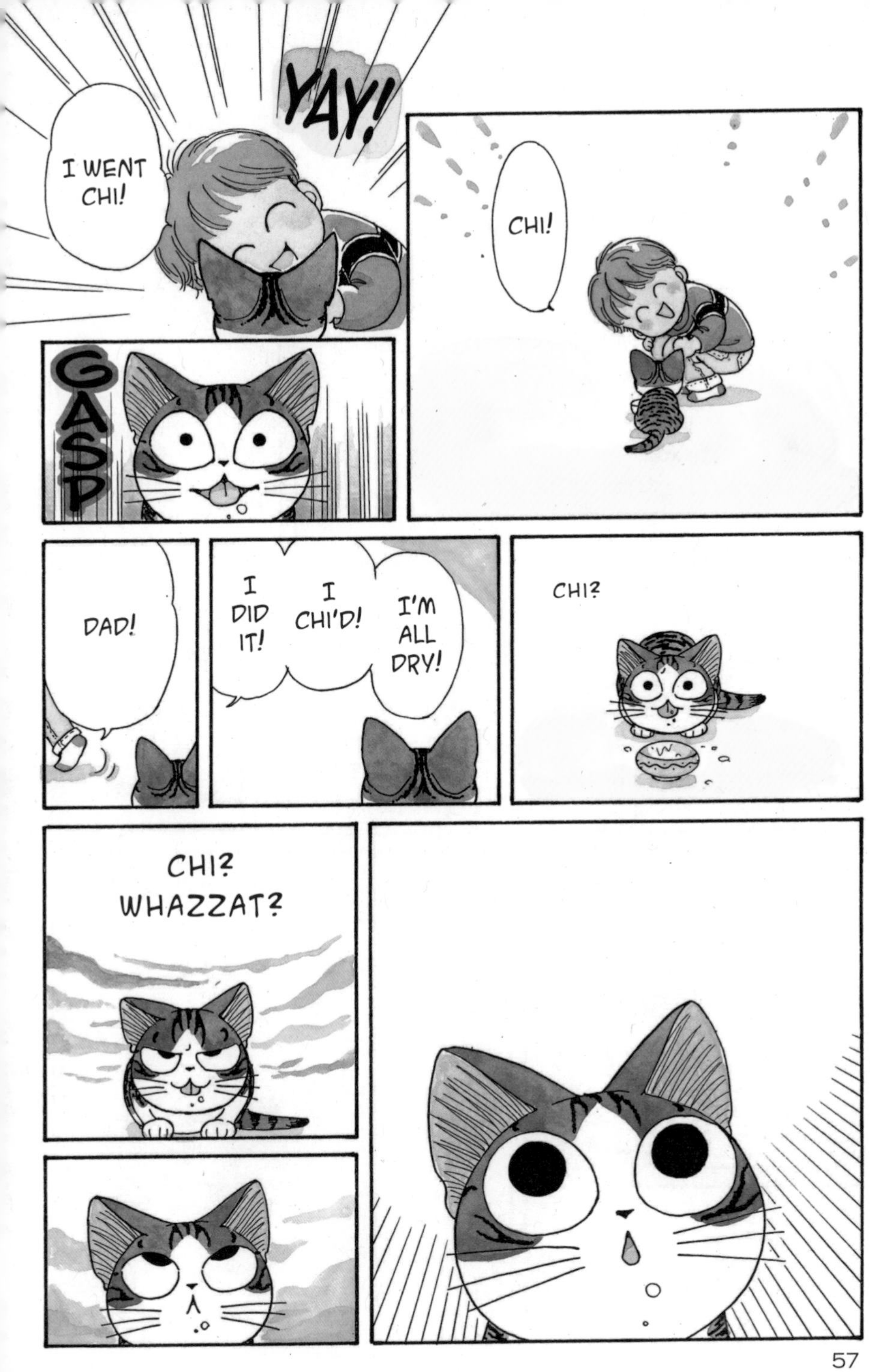

I WENT CHI!
YAY!
CHI!
GASP
DAD!
I DID IT!
I CHI'D!
I'M ALL DRY!
CHI?
CHI? WHAZZAT?

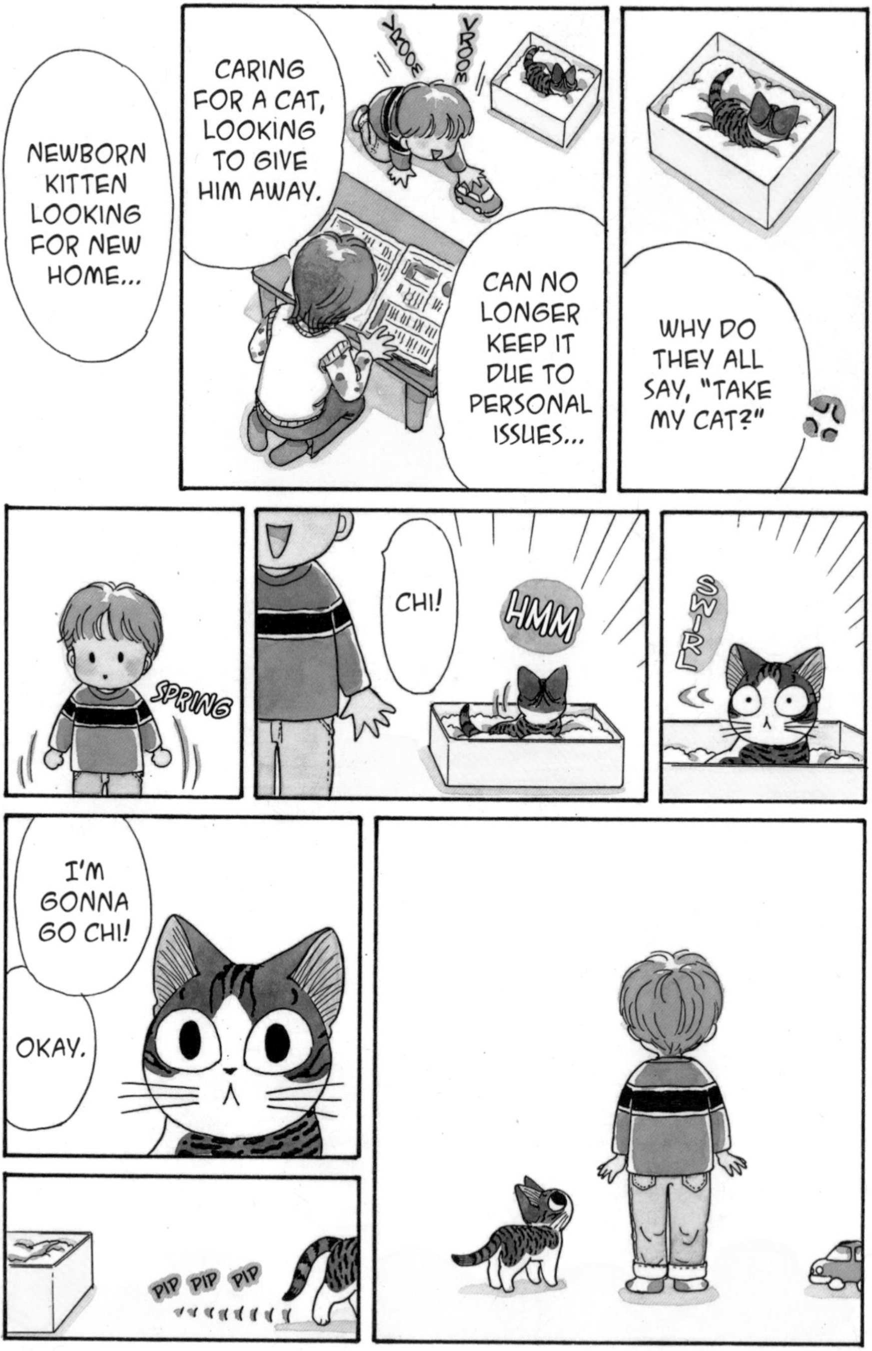
NEWBORN KITTEN LOOKING FOR NEW HOME...
VROOM
VROOM
CARING FOR A CAT, LOOKING TO GIVE HIM AWAY.
CAN NO LONGER KEEP IT DUE TO PERSONAL ISSUES...
WHY DO THEY ALL SAY, "TAKE MY CAT?"
SPRING
CHI!
HMM
SWIRL
I'M GONNA GO CHI!
OKAY.
PIP PIP PIP

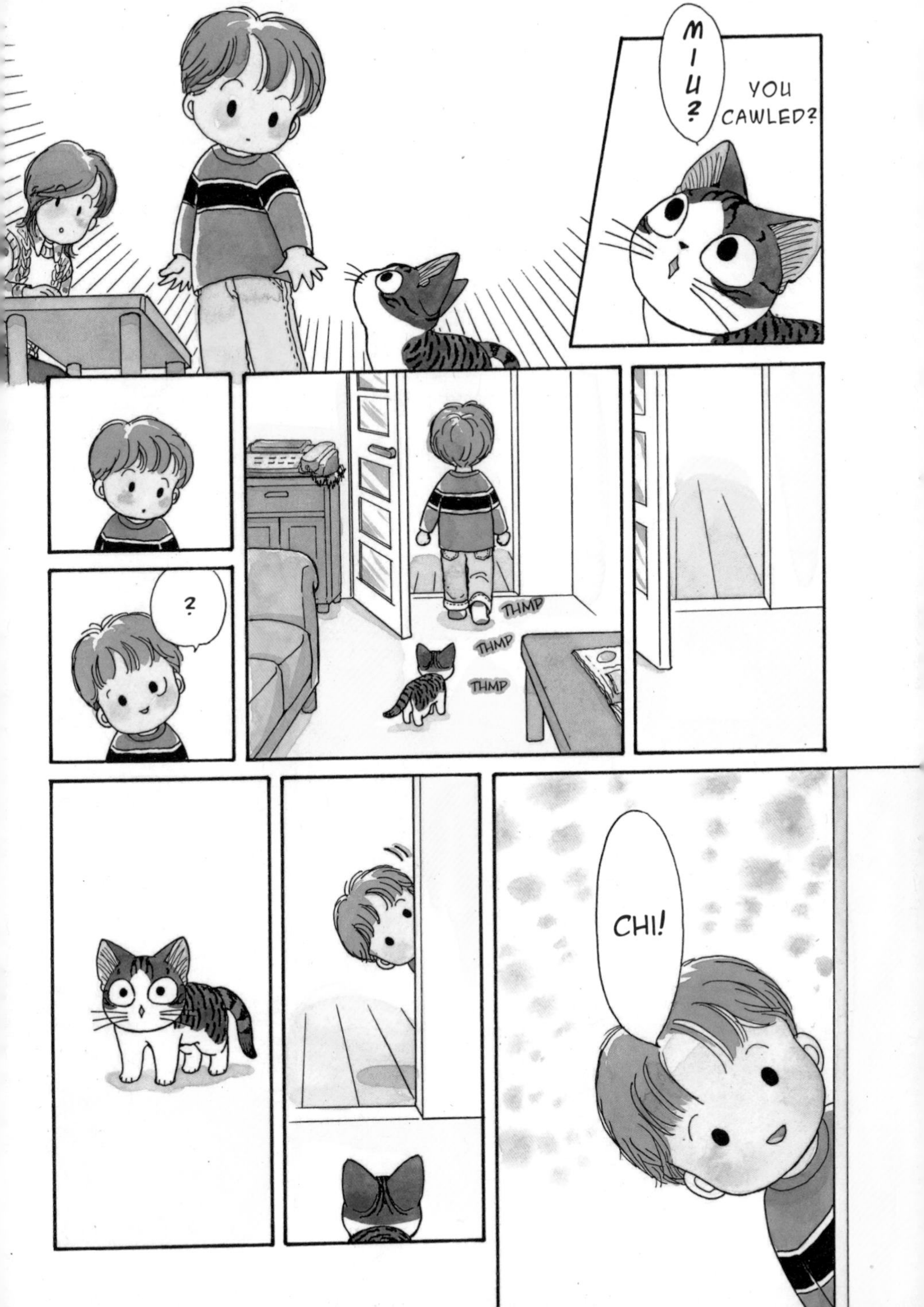
MIU?
YOU CAWLED?
?
THMP
THMP
THMP
CHI!

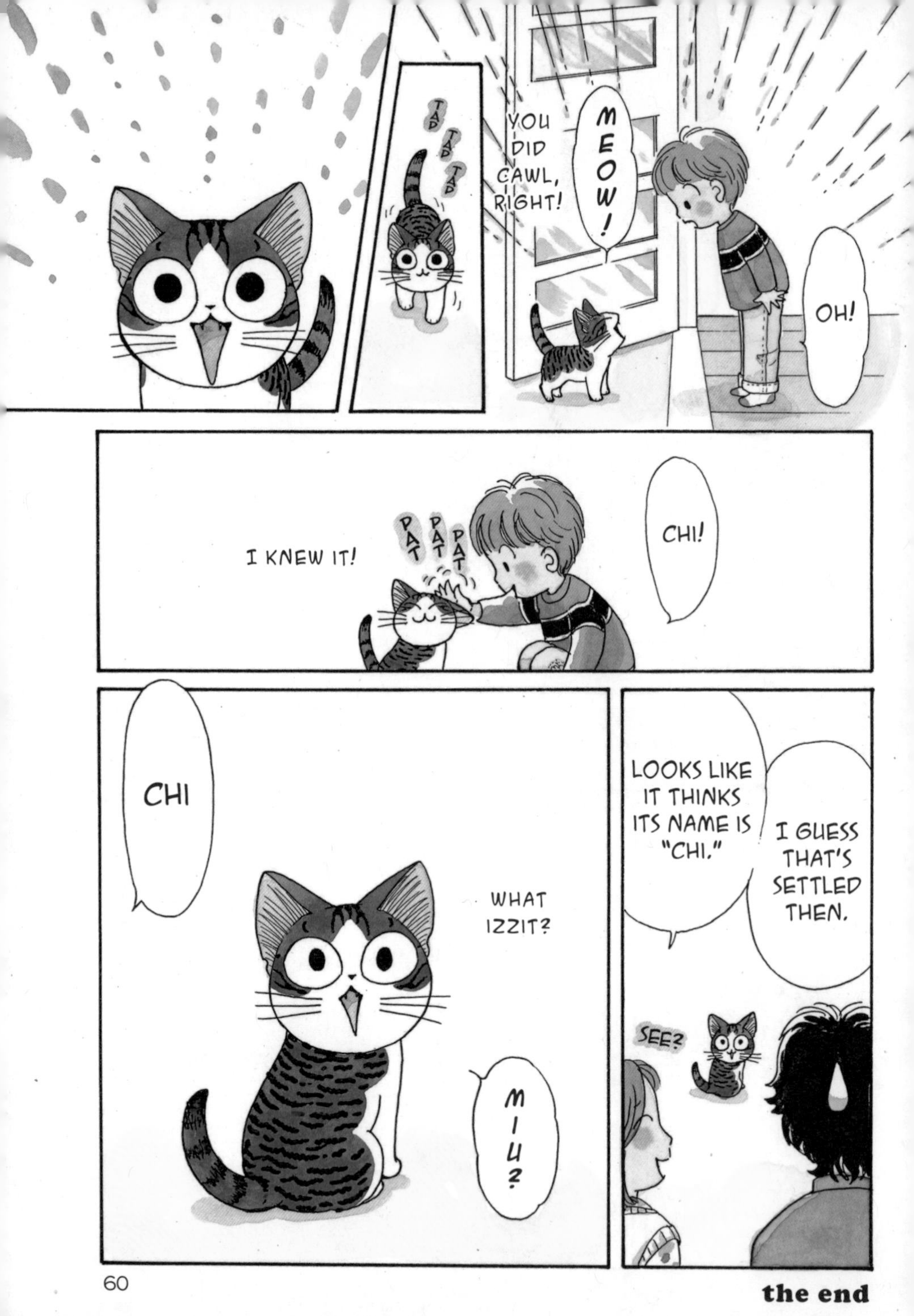
TAP TAP TAP
YOU DID CAWL, RIGHT!
MEOW!
OH!
I KNEW IT!
PAT PAT PAT
CHI!
CHI
WHAT IZZIT?
MIU?
LOOKS LIKE IT THINKS ITS NAME IS "CHI."
I GUESS THAT'S SETTLED THEN.
SEE?

the end

homemade 8: a cat remembers

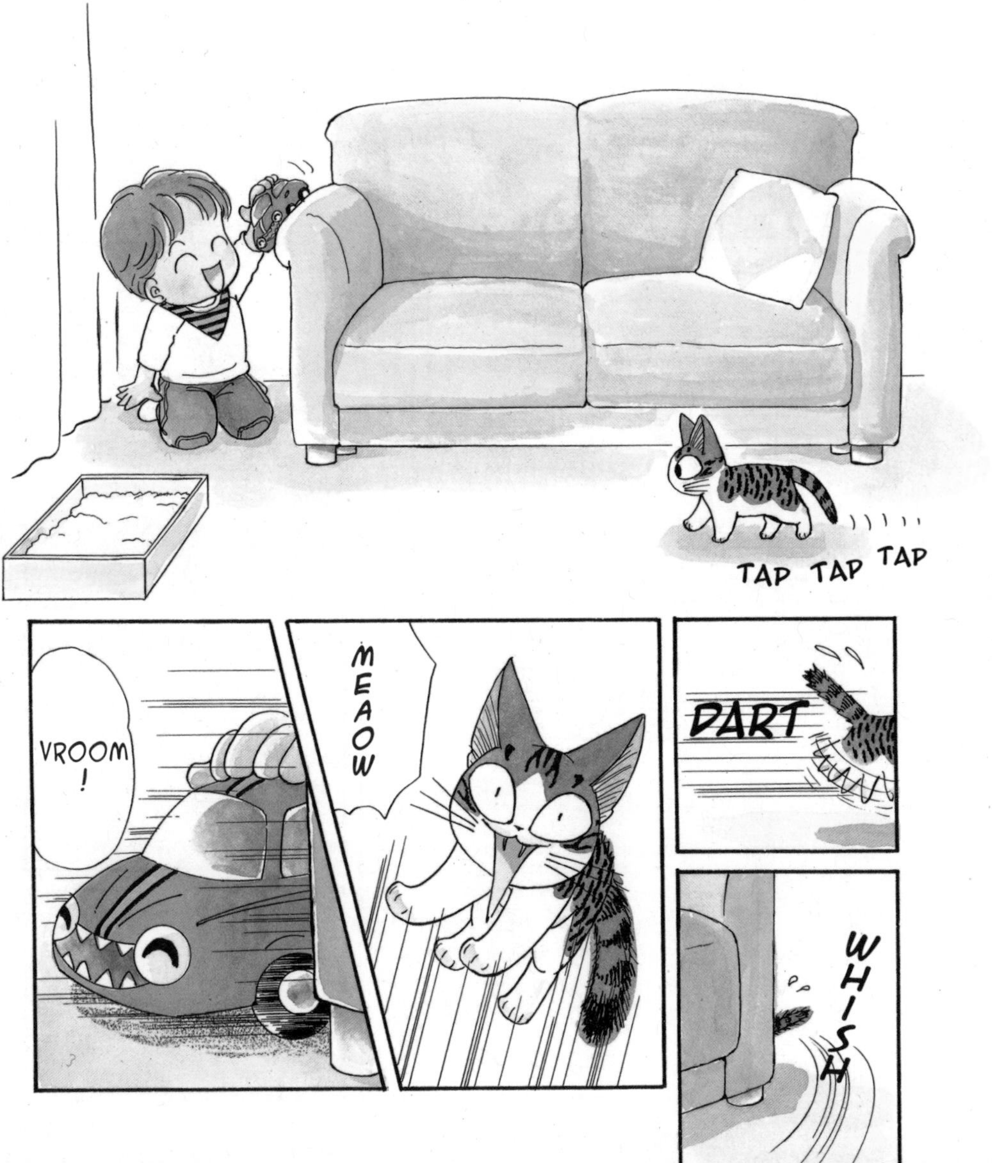
TAP TAP TAP
VROOM!
MEAOW
DART
WHISH

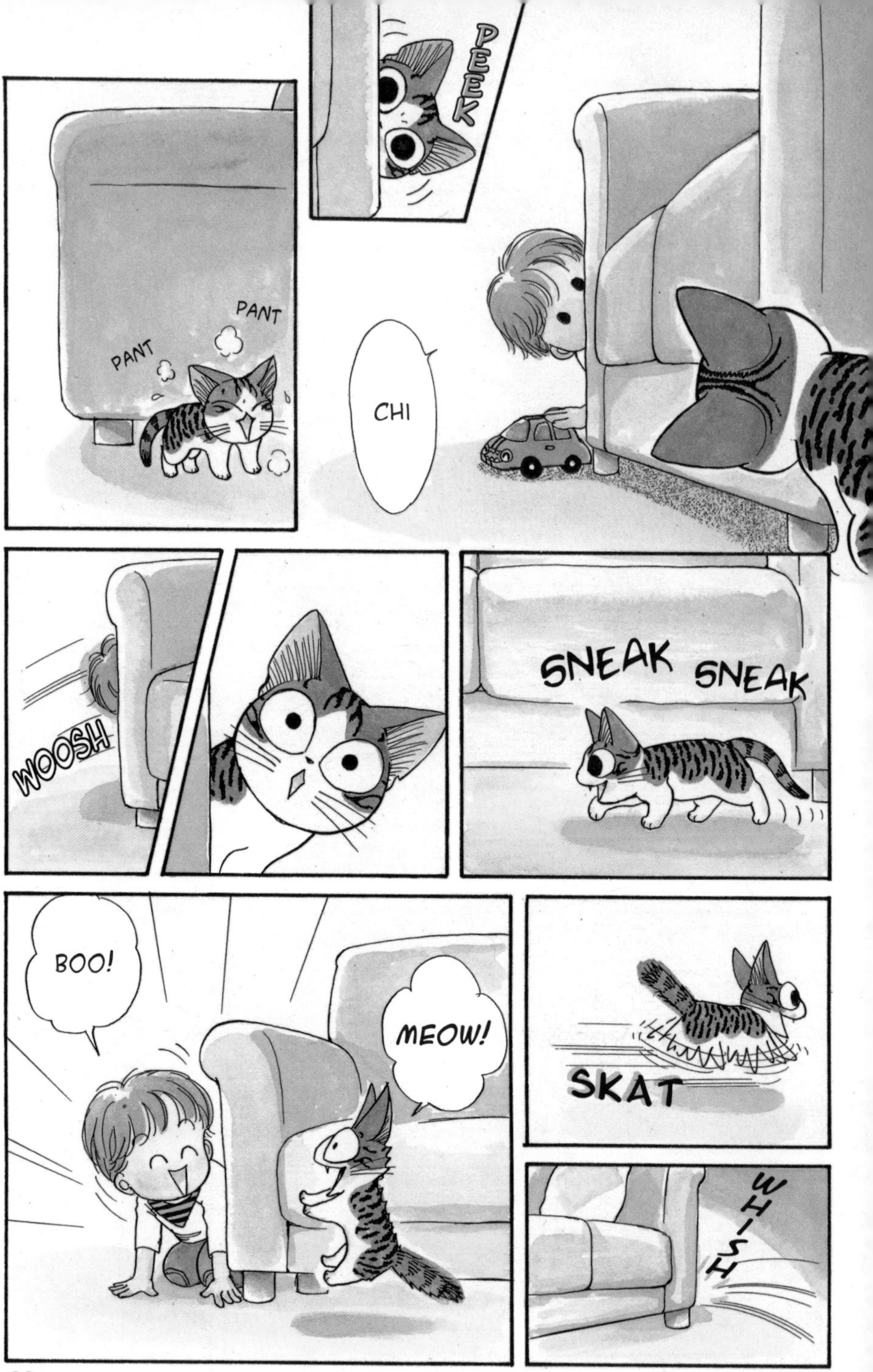
PANT
PANT
PEEK
CHI
WOOSH
SNEAK
SNEAK
BOO!
MEOW!
SKAT
WHISH

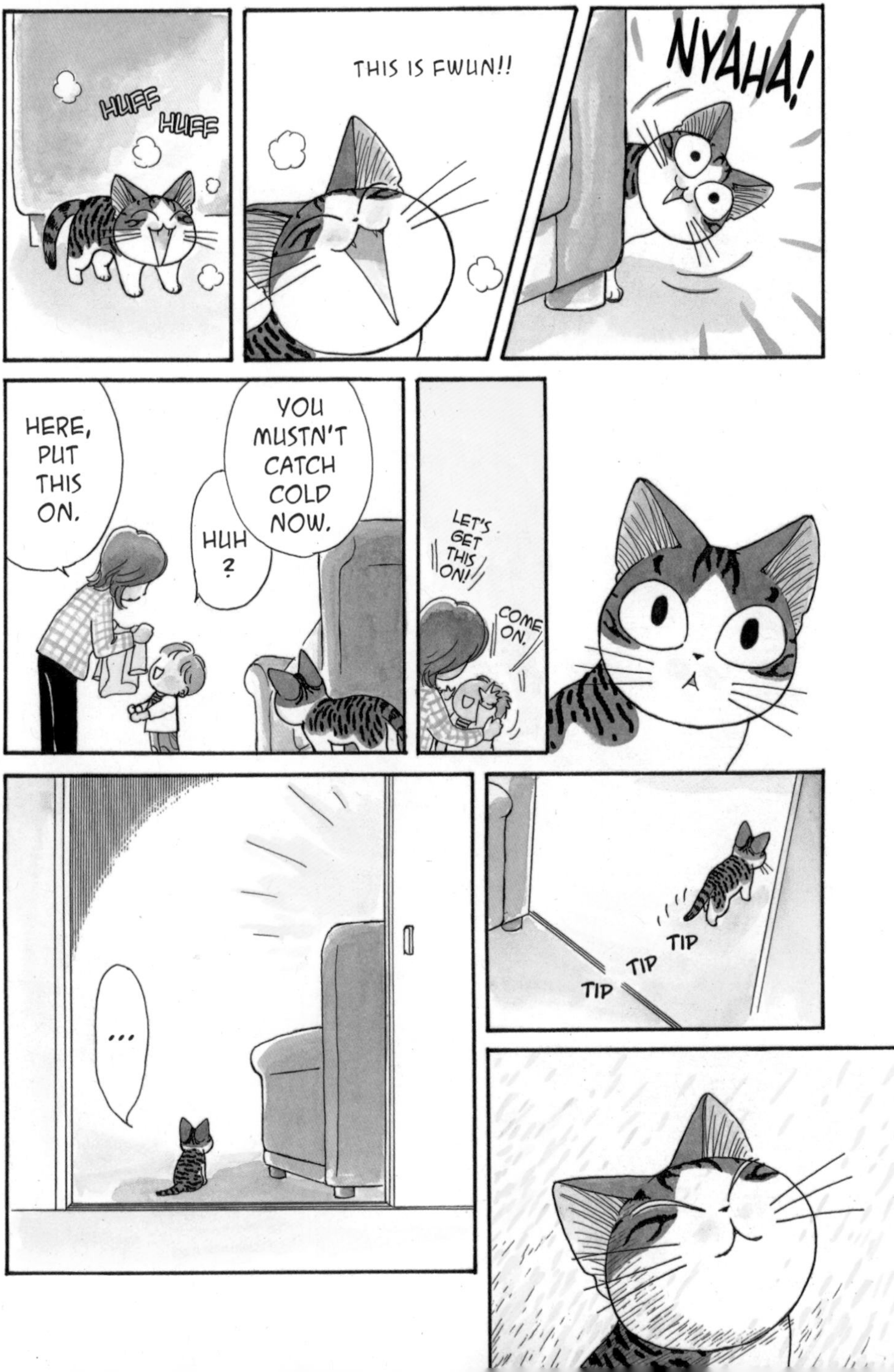
HUFF
HUFF
THIS IS FWUN!!
NYAHA!
HERE, PUT THIS ON.
YOU MUSTN'T CATCH COLD NOW.
HUH?
LET'S GET THIS ON!
COME ON.
...
TIP
TIP
TIP

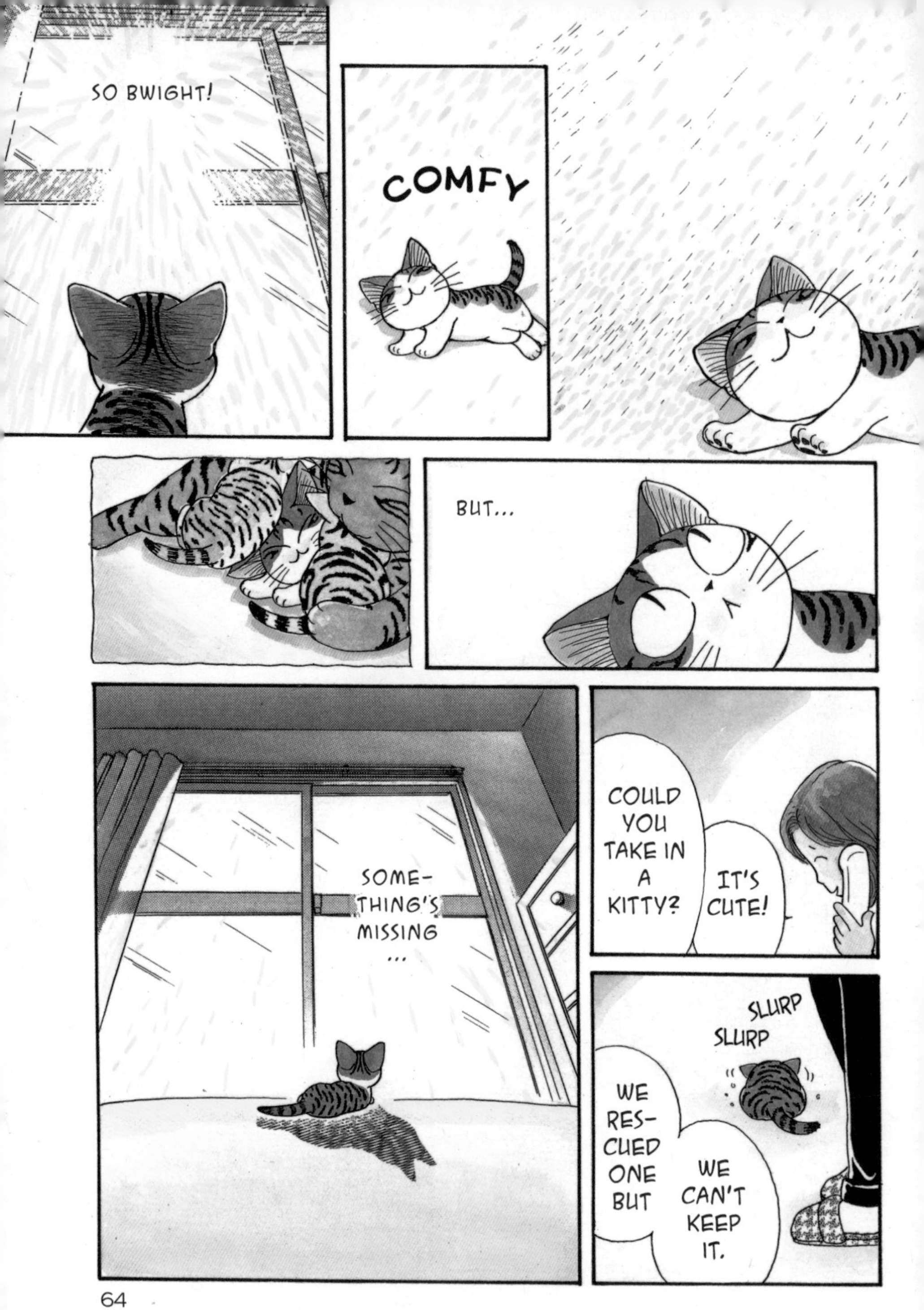
SO BWIGHT!
COMFY
BUT...
SOME-THING'S MISSING ...
COULD YOU TAKE IN A KITTY?
IT'S CUTE!
SLURP
SLURP
WE RES-CUED ONE BUT
WE CAN'T KEEP IT.

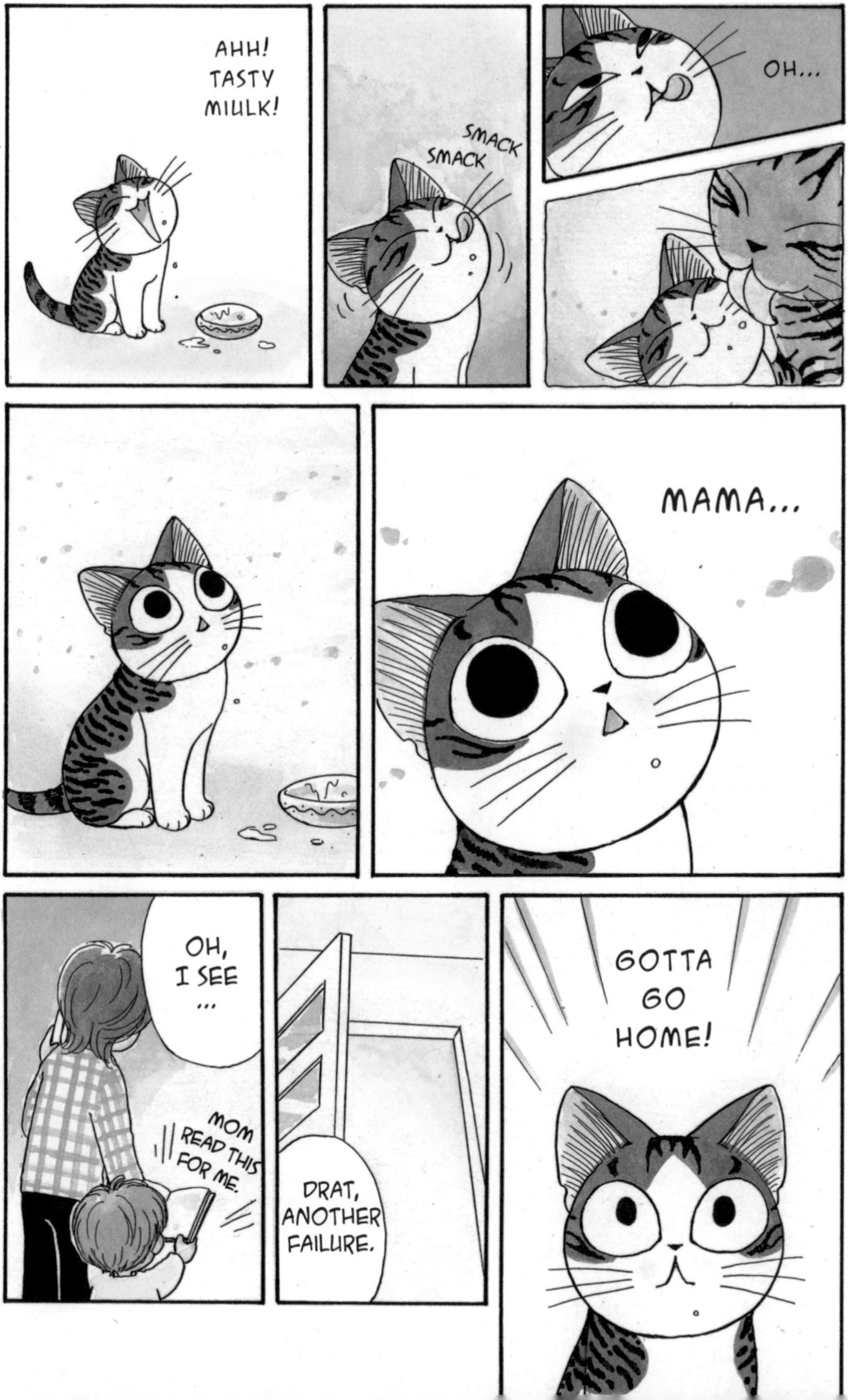
AHH! TASTY MIULK!
SMACK SMACK
OH...
MAMA...
OH, I SEE ...
MOM READ THIS FOR ME.
DRAT, ANOTHER FAILURE.
GOTTA GO HOME!

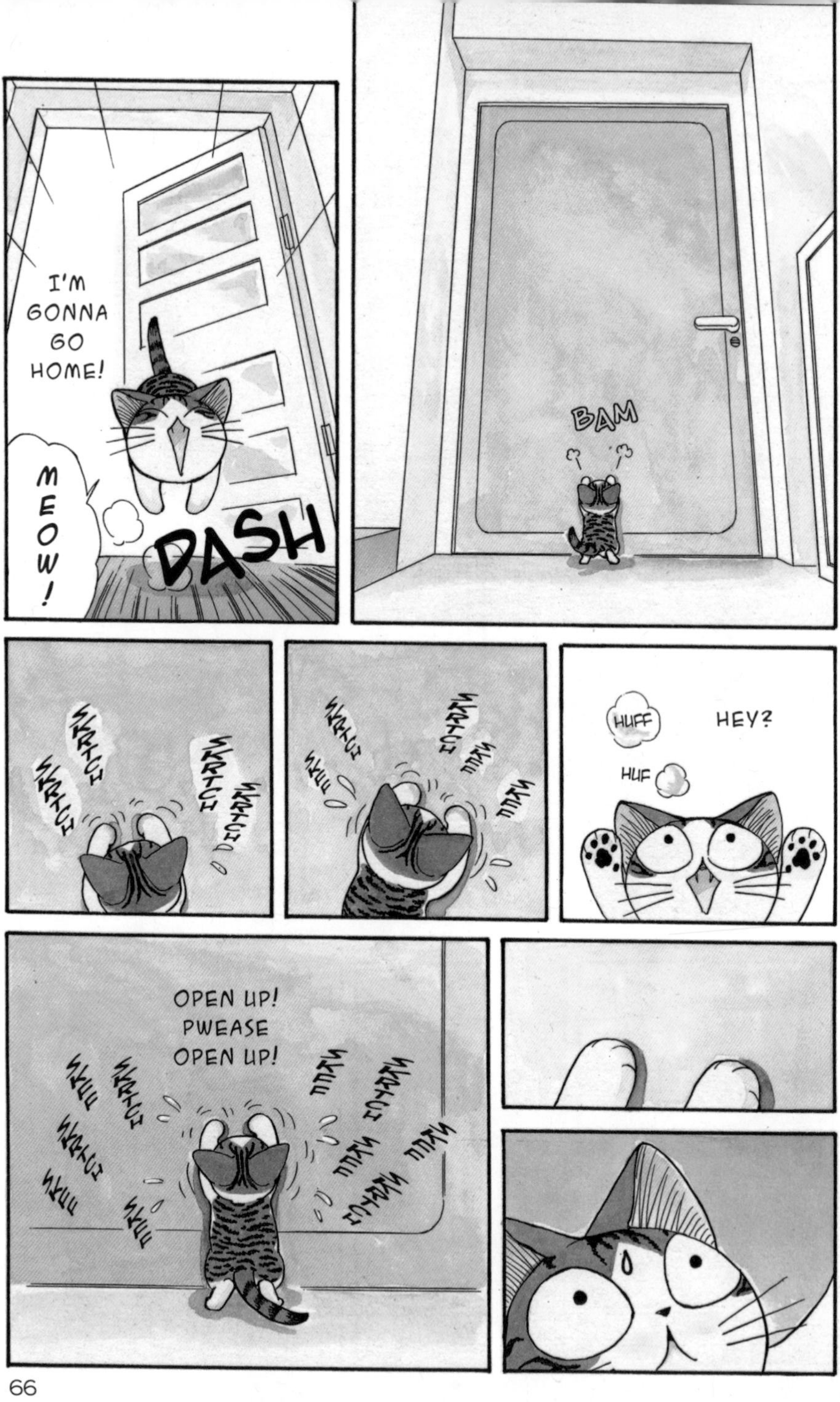
I'M GONNA GO HOME!
MEOW!
DASH
BAM
SKRITCH
SKRITCH
SKRITCH
SKRITCH
SKRITCH
SKREE
SKREE
SKREE
HUFF
HEY?
HUF
OPEN UP! PWEASE OPEN UP!

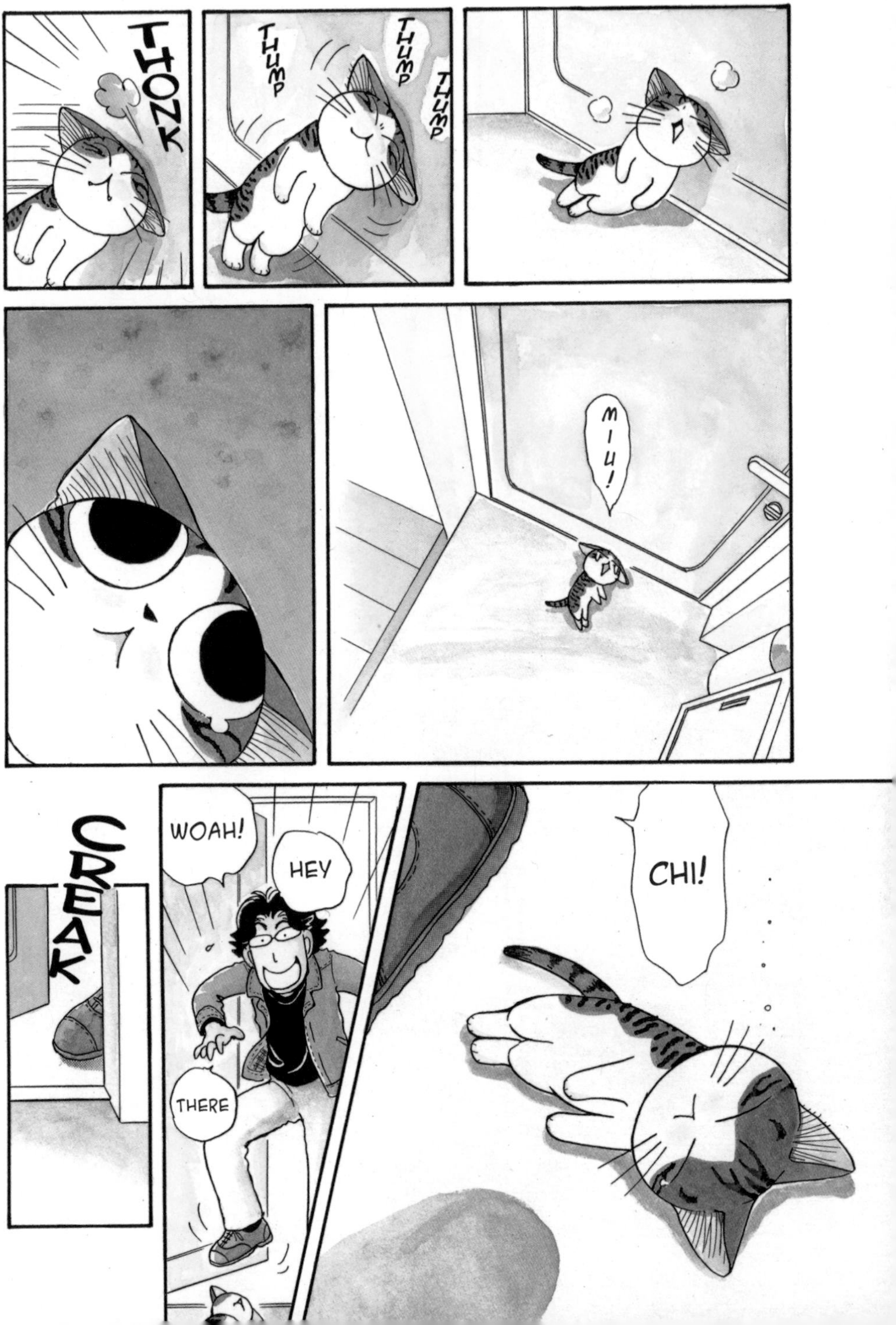
THONK
THUMP
THUMP
THUMP
MIU!
CREAK
WOAH!
HEY
THERE
CHI!

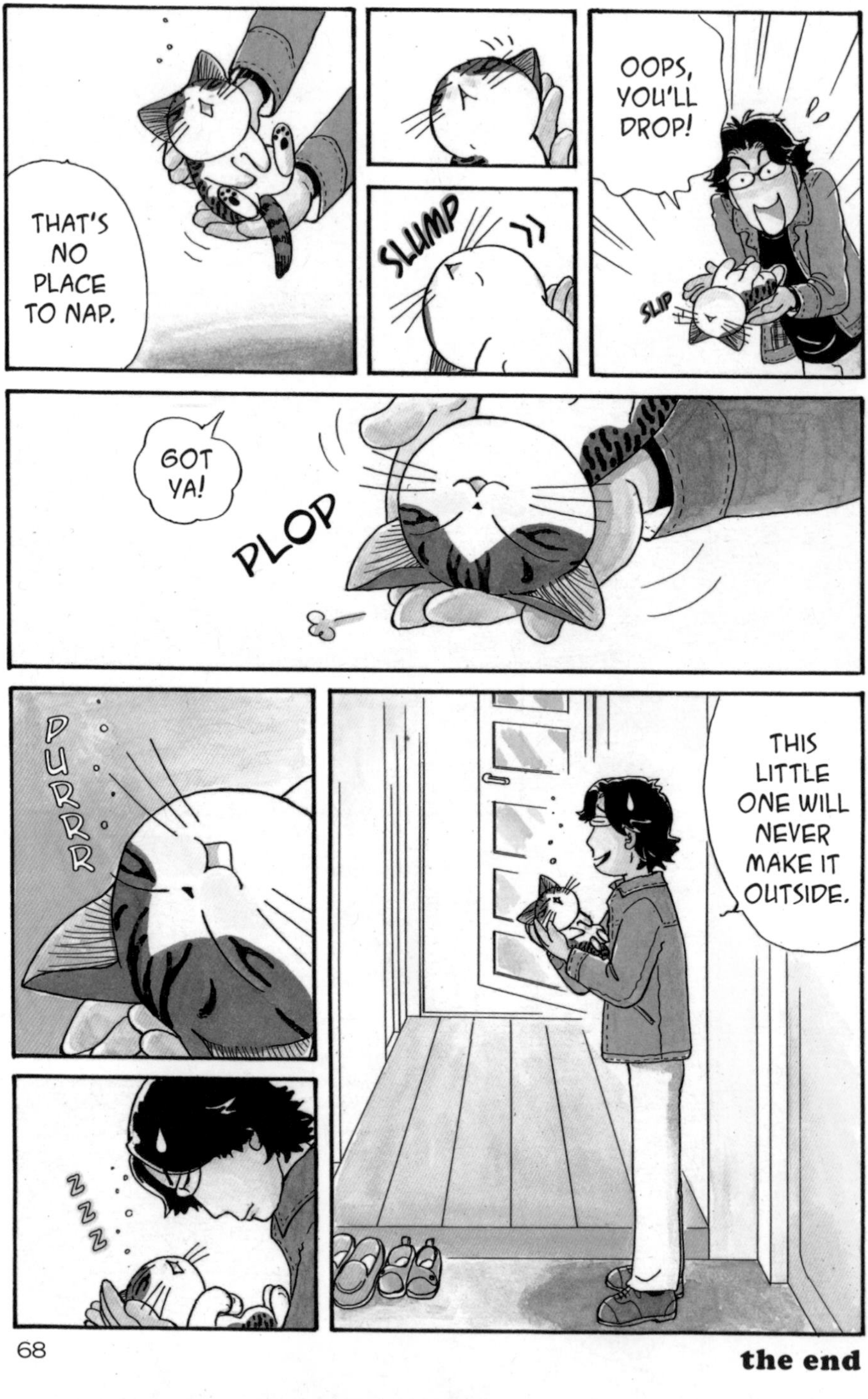

THAT'S NO PLACE TO NAP.
OOPS, YOU'LL DROP!
SLUMP
SLIP
GOT YA!
PLOP
PURRR
ZZZ
THIS LITTLE ONE WILL NEVER MAKE IT OUTSIDE.

the end

homemade 9: a cat dreams

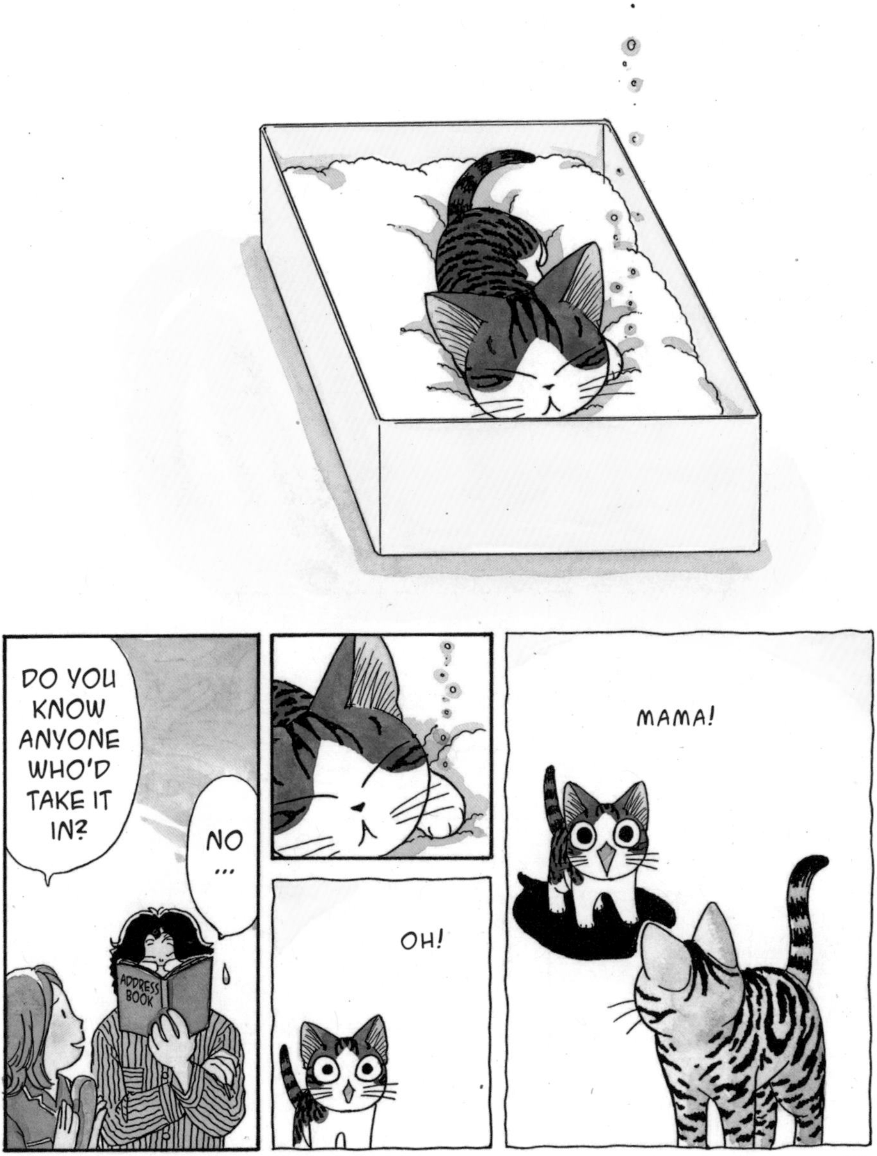
DO YOU KNOW ANYONE WHO'D TAKE IT IN?
NO ...
ADDRESS BOOK
OH!
MAMA!

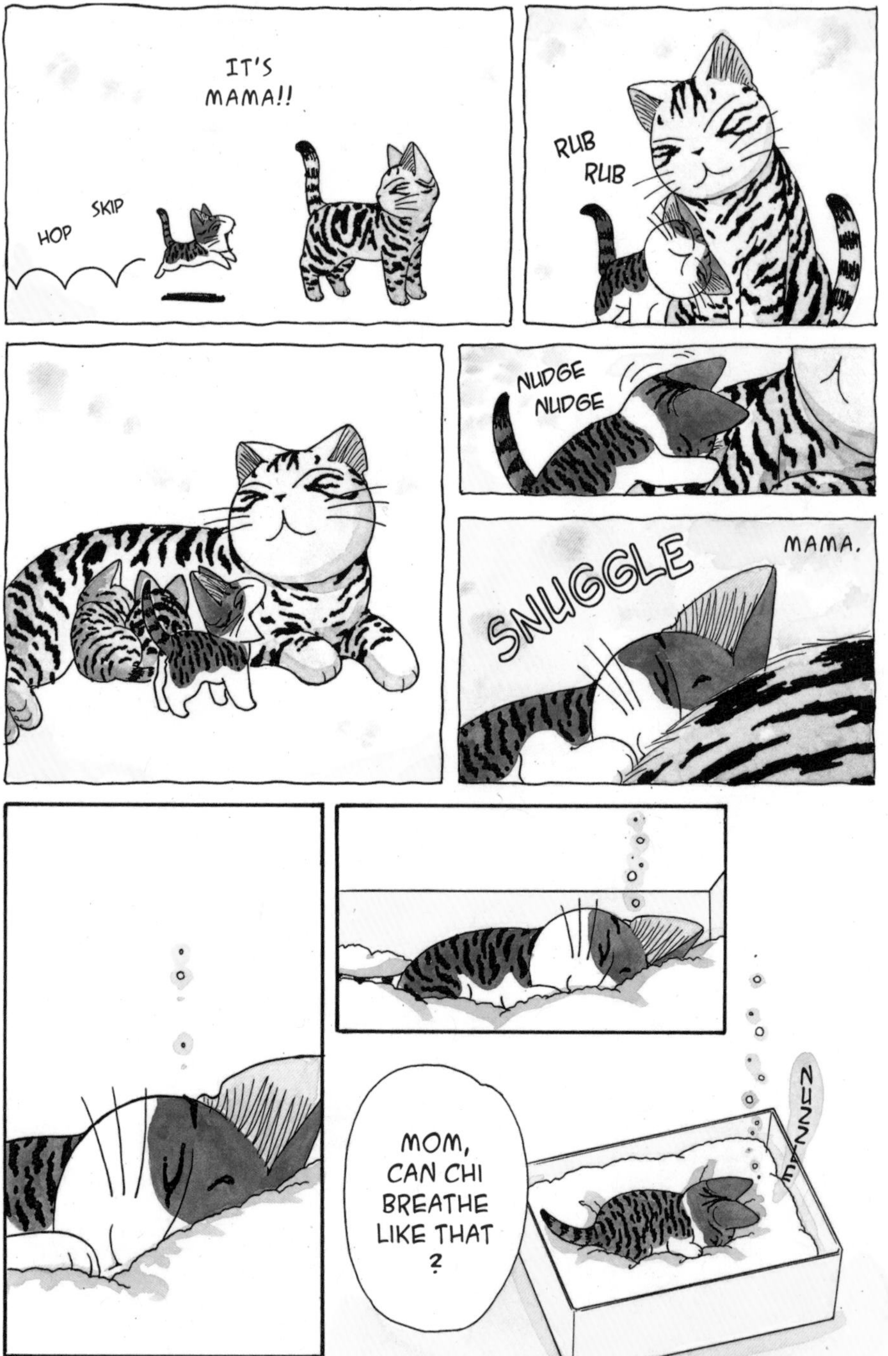
IT'S MAMA!!
HOP
SKIP
RUB RUB
NUDGE NUDGE
SNUGGLE
MAMA.
MOM, CAN CHI BREATHE LIKE THAT?
NUZZLE

WELL,

IT'S SOUND ASLEEP.

AND BABIES SLEEP A LOT.

WE'RE SURE IN A BIND. WE NEED TO FIND IT A HOME.

BED-TIME, YOHEI!

GOOD NIGHT DAD.

NIGHT!

CAN I SLEEP WITH YOU MOM?

CAN'T YOU SLEEP BY YOUR-SELF YET?

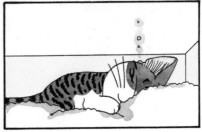

TWITCH TWITCH

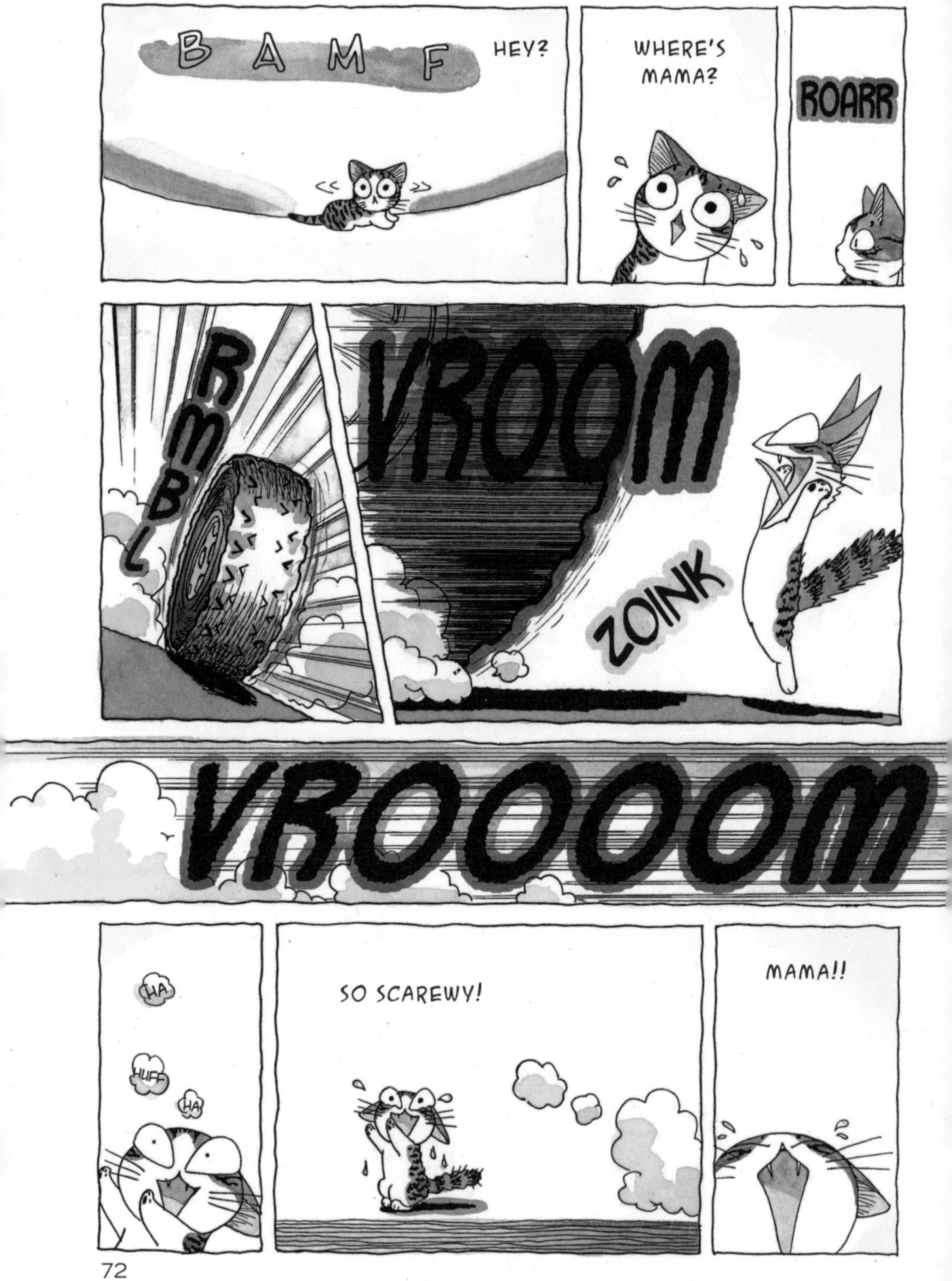
BAMF
HEY?
WHERE'S MAMA?
ROARR
RMBL
VROOM
ZOINK
VROOOOM
HA
HUFF
HA
SO SCAREWY!
MAMA!!

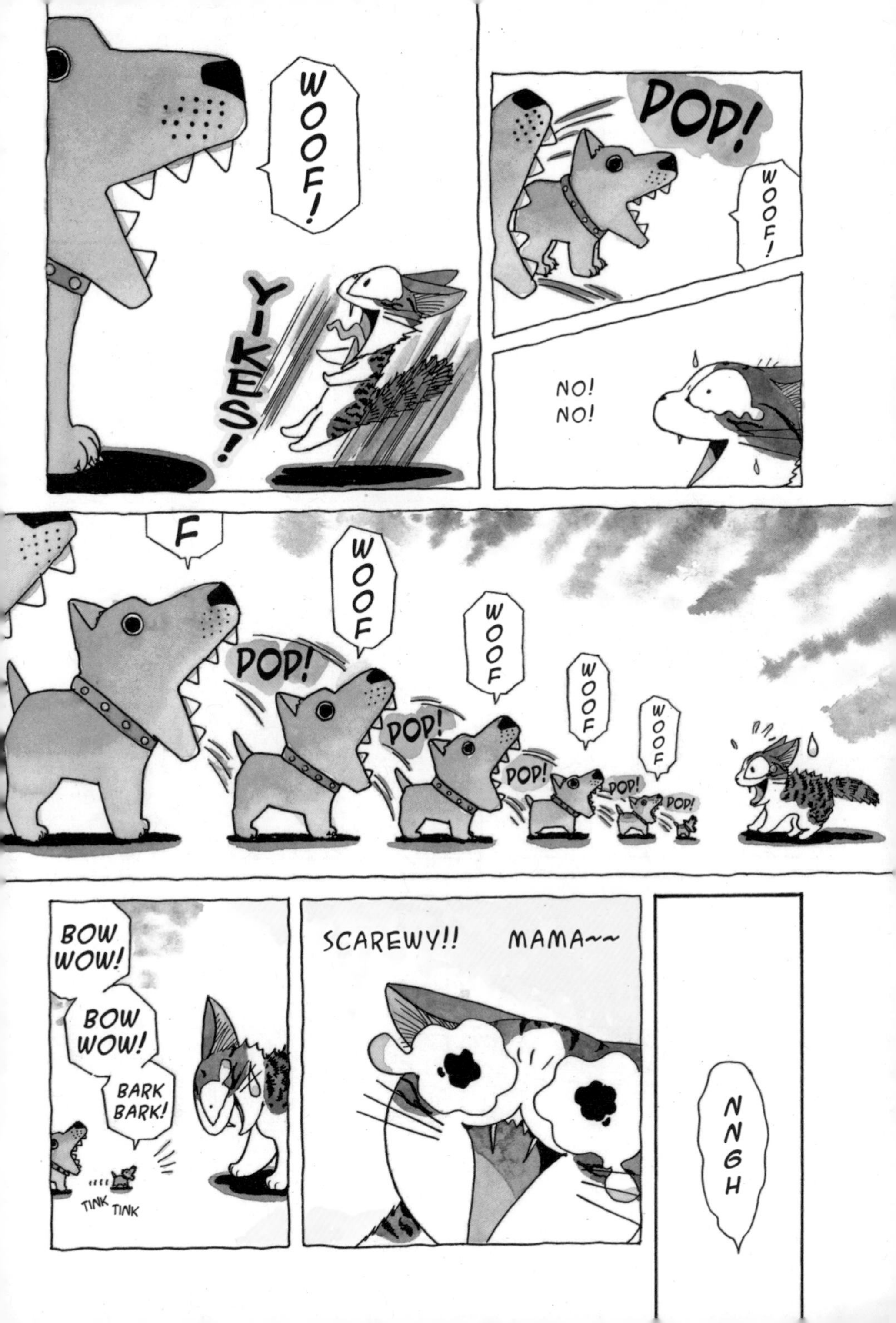
WOOF!
YIKES!
POP!
WOOF!
NO!
NO!
F
WOOF
POP!
WOOF
POP!
WOOF
POP!
WOOF
POP!
POP!
BOW WOW!
BOW WOW!
BARK BARK!
TINK TINK
SCAREWY!!
MAMA~~
NNGH

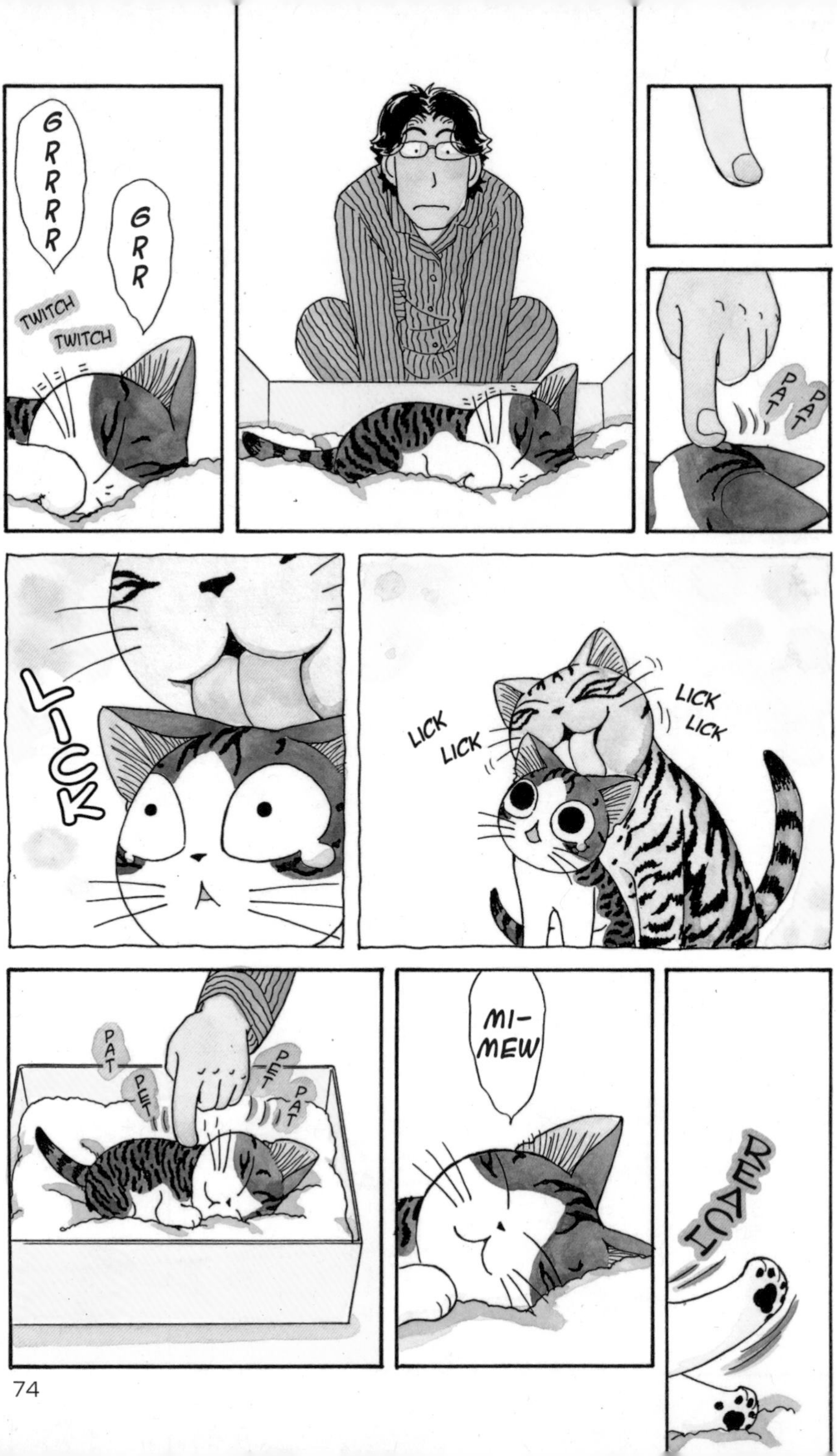
GRRRR
GRR
TWITCH
TWITCH
PAT PAT
LICK
LICK LICK
LICK LICK
PAT PET PET PAT
MI-MEW
REACT

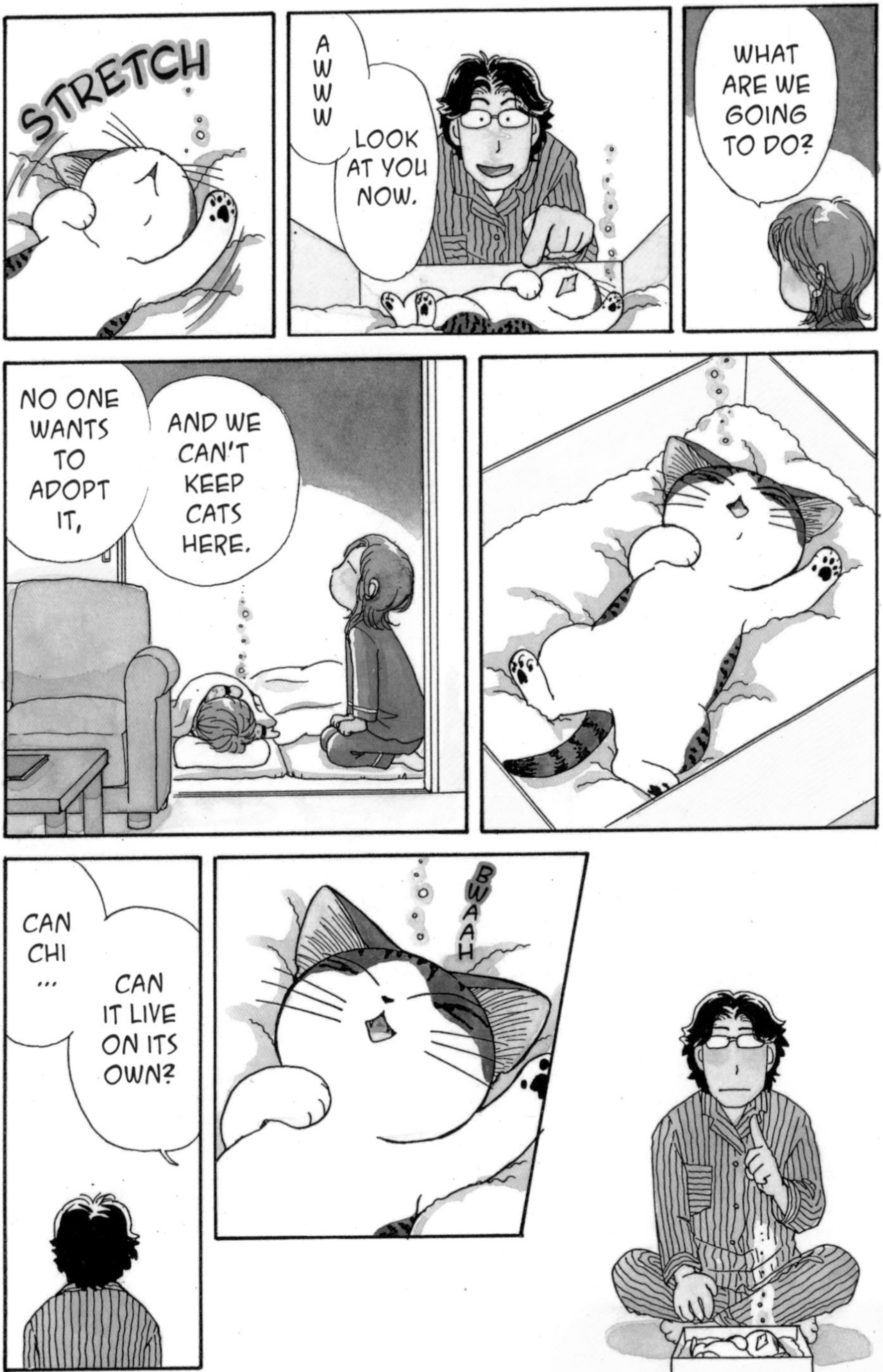
STRETCH
AWWW
LOOK AT YOU NOW.
WHAT ARE WE GOING TO DO?
NO ONE WANTS TO ADOPT IT,
AND WE CAN'T KEEP CATS HERE.
CAN CHI ...
CAN IT LIVE ON ITS OWN?
BWAAH

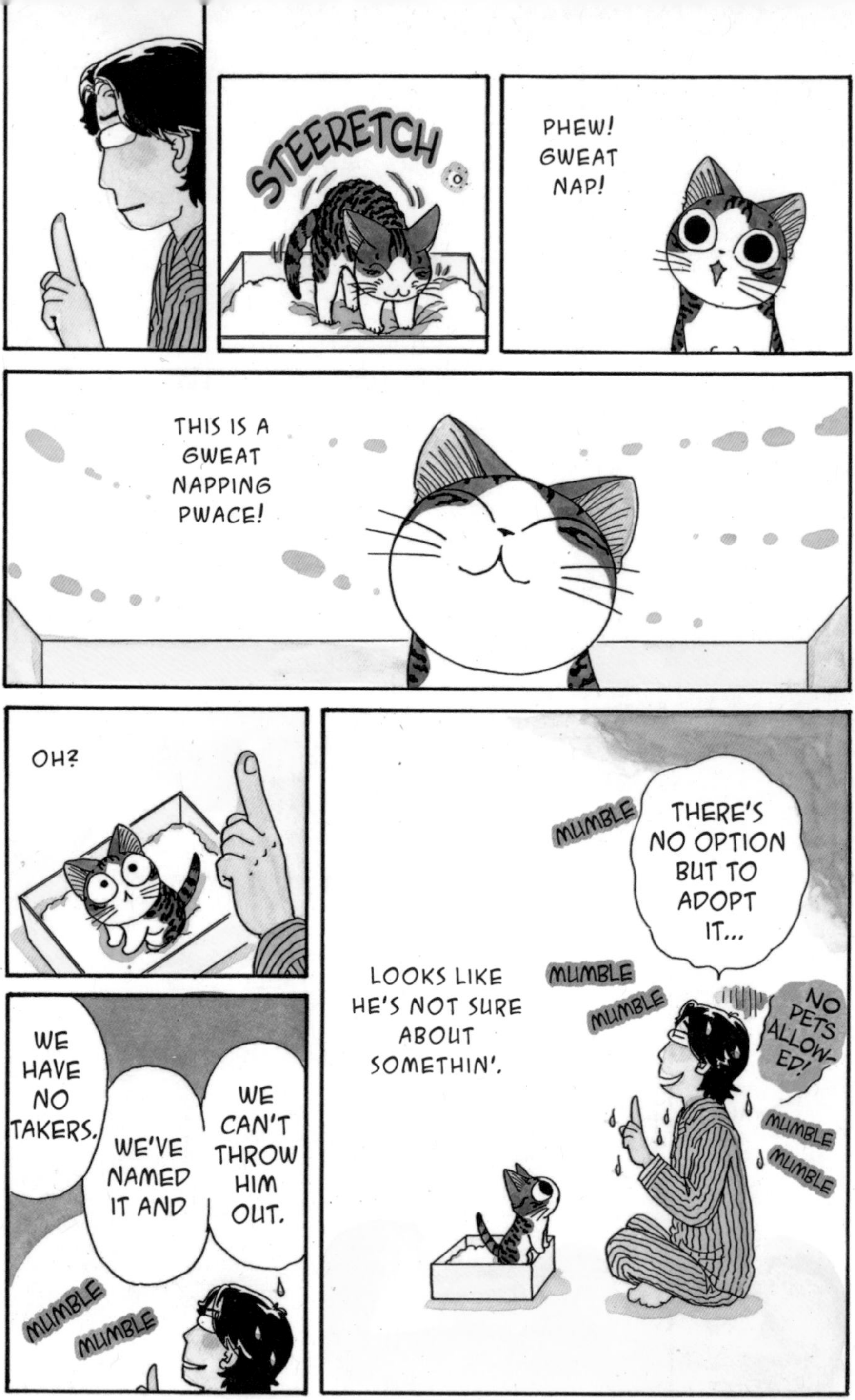
STEERETCH
PHEW! GWEAT NAP!
THIS IS A GWEAT NAPPING PWACE!
OH?
WE HAVE NO TAKERS.
WE'VE NAMED IT AND
WE CAN'T THROW HIM OUT.
MUMBLE
MUMBLE
MUMBLE
THERE'S NO OPTION BUT TO ADOPT IT...
LOOKS LIKE HE'S NOT SURE ABOUT SOMETHIN'.
MUMBLE
MUMBLE
NO PETS ALLOW-ED!
MUMBLE
MUMBLE

the end

homemade 10: a cat is fired up

YOHEI
YOHEI
YOHEI.

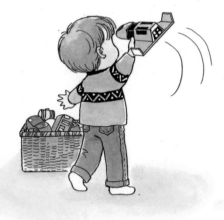

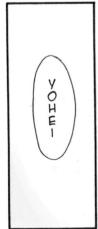

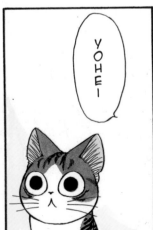

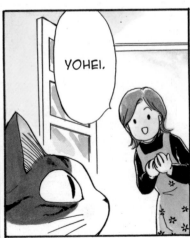

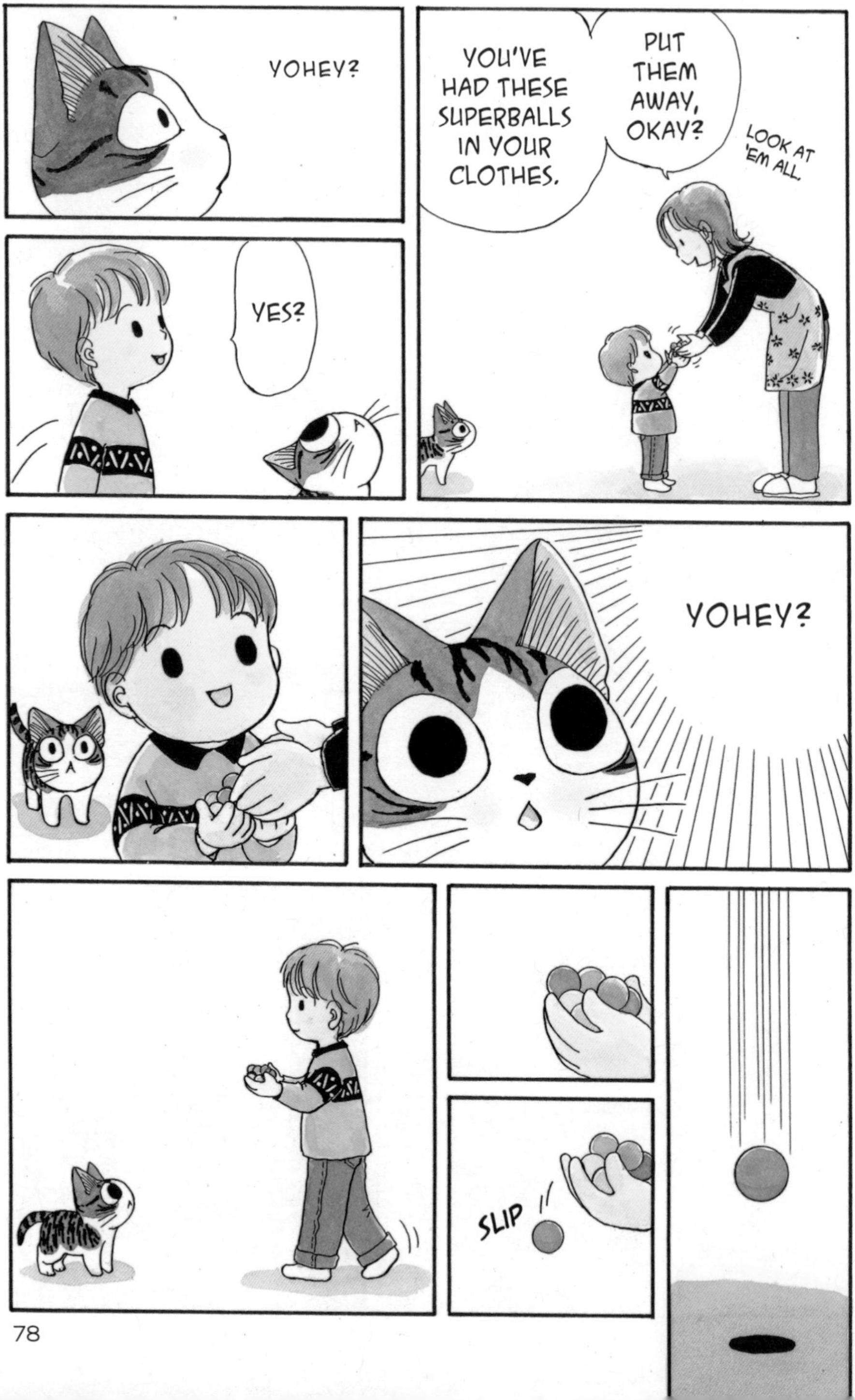

YOHEY?
YES?
YOU'VE HAD THESE SUPERBALLS IN YOUR CLOTHES.
PUT THEM AWAY, OKAY?
LOOK AT 'EM ALL.
YOHEY?
SLIP

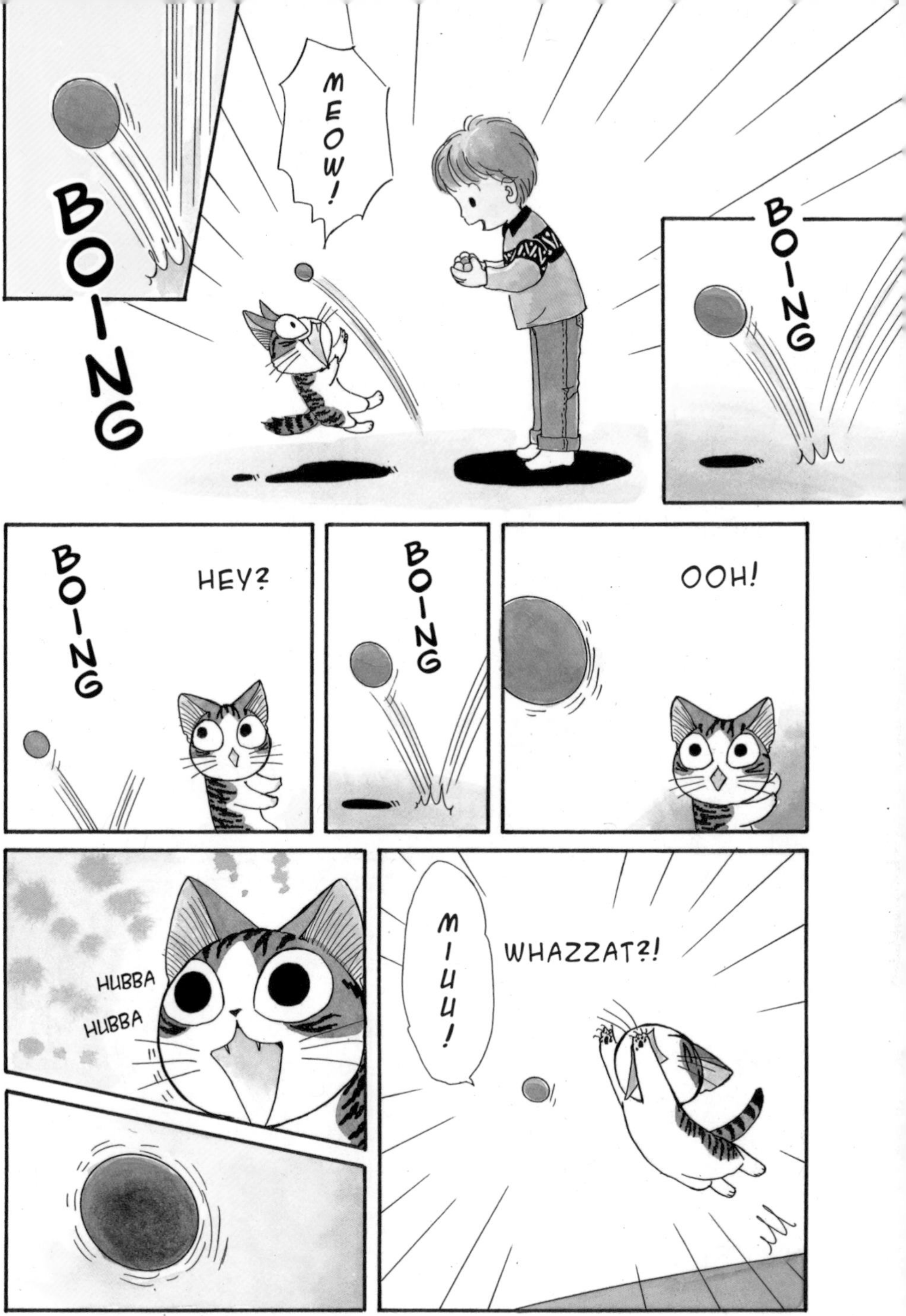
BOING
MEOW!
BOING
BOING
HEY?
BOING
OOH!
HUBBA
HUBBA
MIUU!
WHAZZAT?!

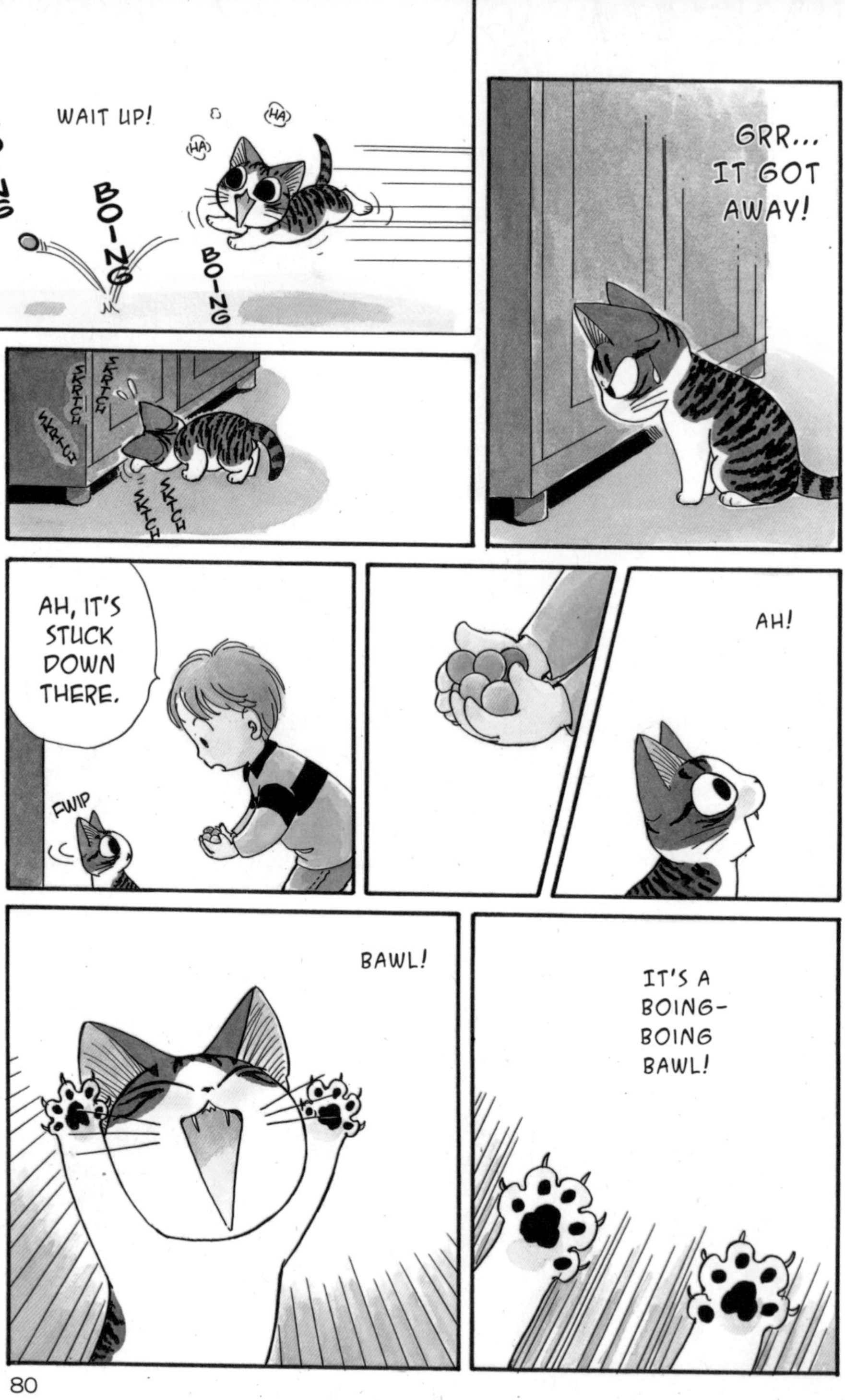
BOING
WAIT UP!
HA
HA
BOING
BOING
SKRATCH
SKRATCH
SKTCH
SKTCH
GRR... IT GOT AWAY!
AH, IT'S STUCK DOWN THERE.
FWIP
AH!
BAWL!
IT'S A BOING-BOING BAWL!

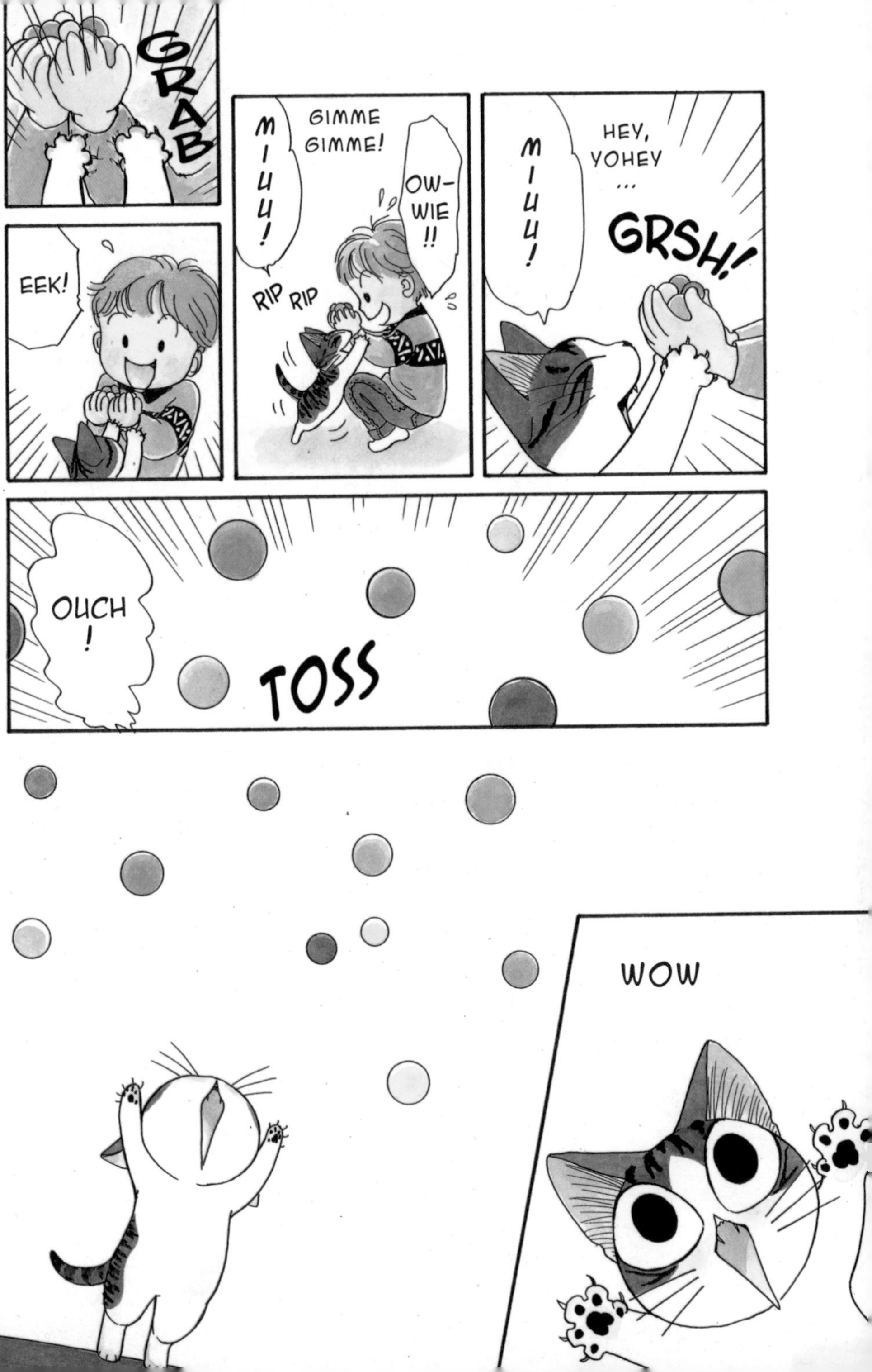
GRAB
EEK!
MIUU!
GIMME GIMME!
OW-WIE!!
RIP RIP
MIUU!
HEY, YOHEY ...
GRSH!
OUCH!
TOSS
WOW

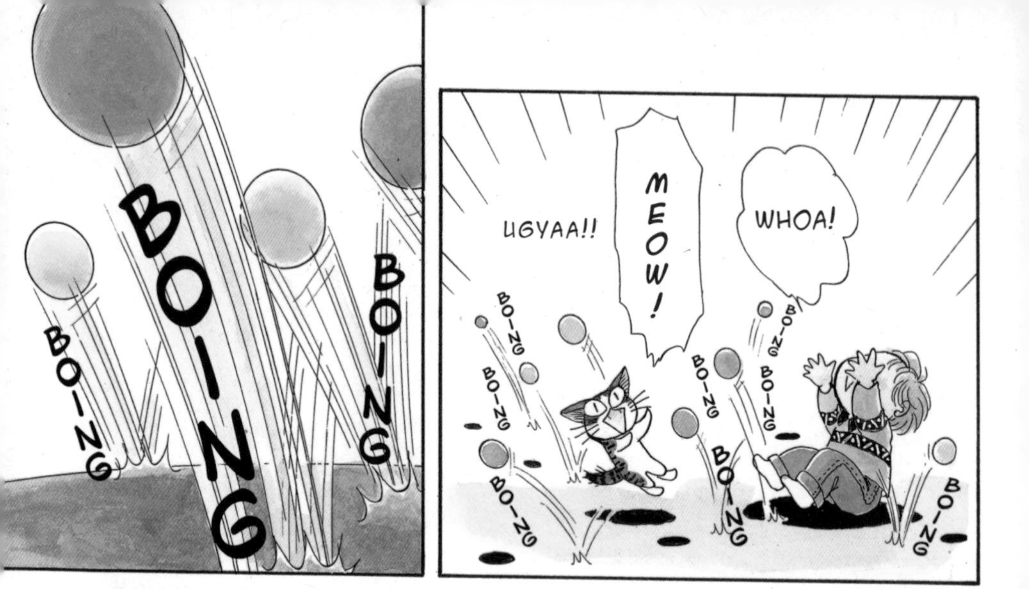
BOING
BOING
BOING
UGYAA!!
MEOW!
WHOA!
BOING
BOING
BOING
BOING
BOING
BOING
BOING
BOING
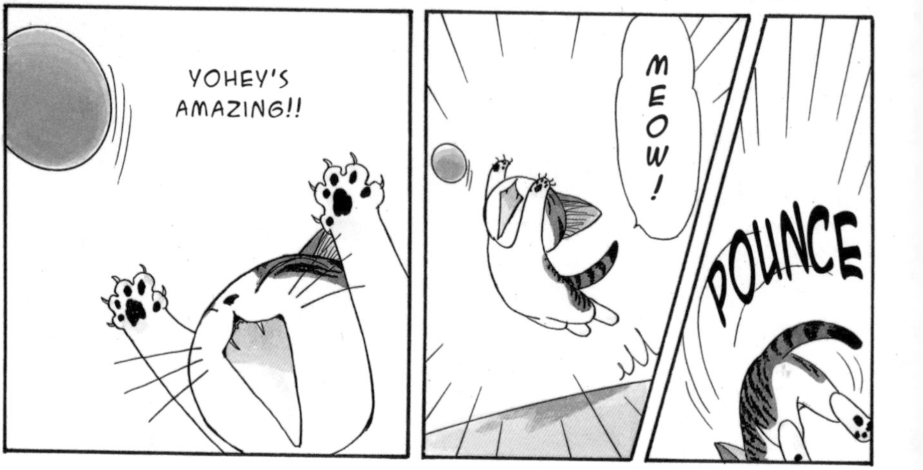
YOHEY'S AMAZING!!
MEOW!
POUNCE
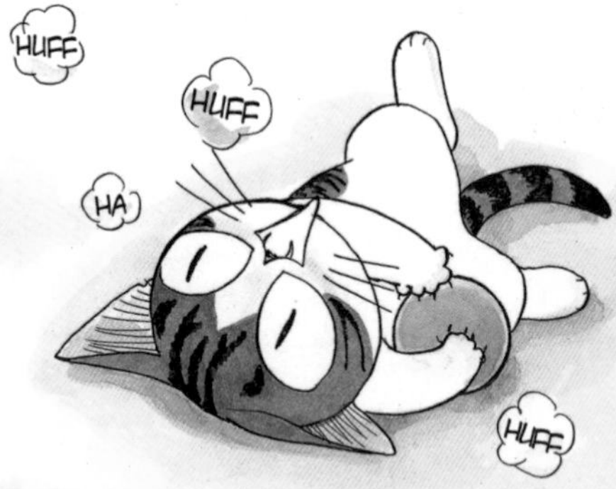
HUFF
HUFF
HA
HUFF
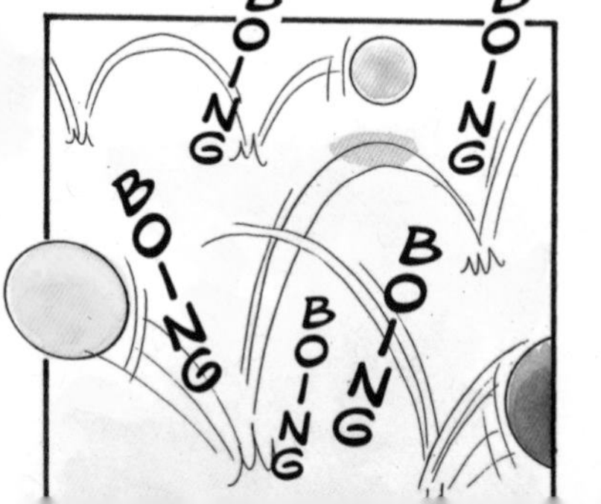
BOING
BOING
BOING
BOING
BOING

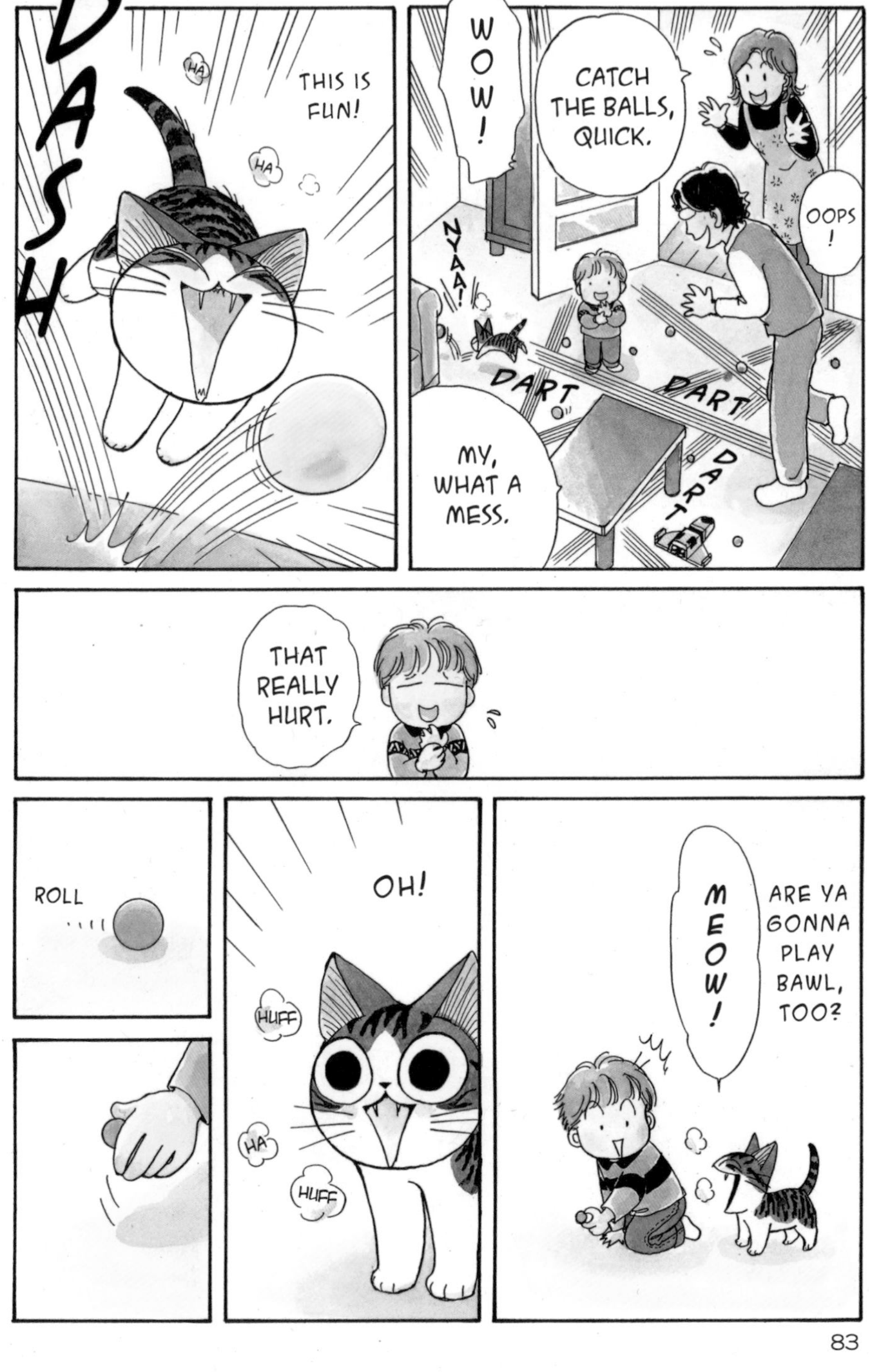
DASH
HA
THIS IS FUN!
HA
WOW!
CATCH THE BALLS, QUICK.
NYAA!
OOPS!
DART
DART
DART
MY, WHAT A MESS.
THAT REALLY HURT.
ROLL
OH!
HUFF
HA
HUFF
MEOW!
ARE YA GONNA PLAY BAWL, TOO?

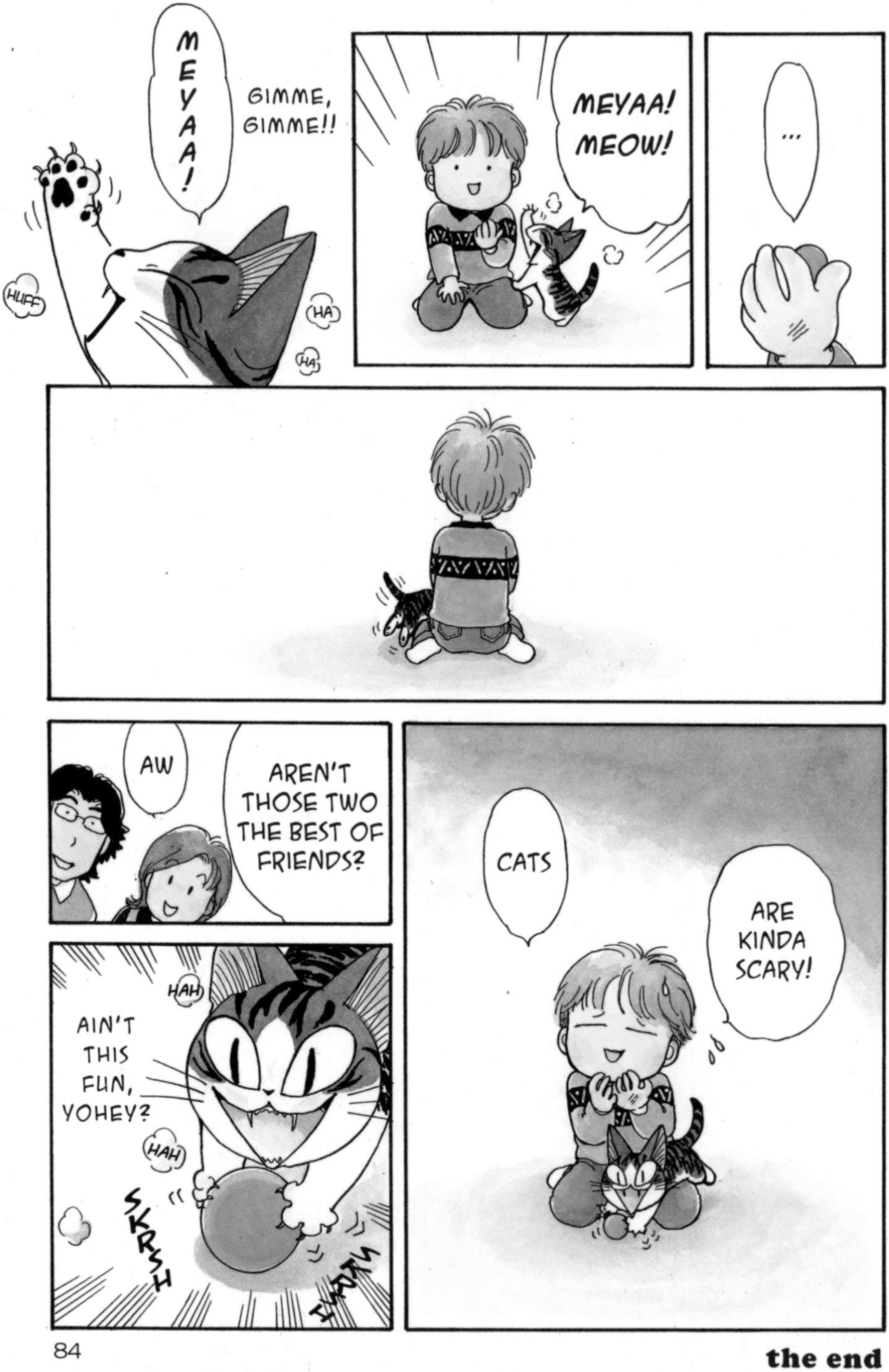
MEYAA!
GIMME, GIMME!!
HUFF
HA
HA
MEYAA! MEOW!
...
AW
AREN'T THOSE TWO THE BEST OF FRIENDS?
HAH
AIN'T THIS FUN, YOHEY?
HAH
SKRSH
CATS
ARE KINDA SCARY!

the end

homemade 11: a cat plays

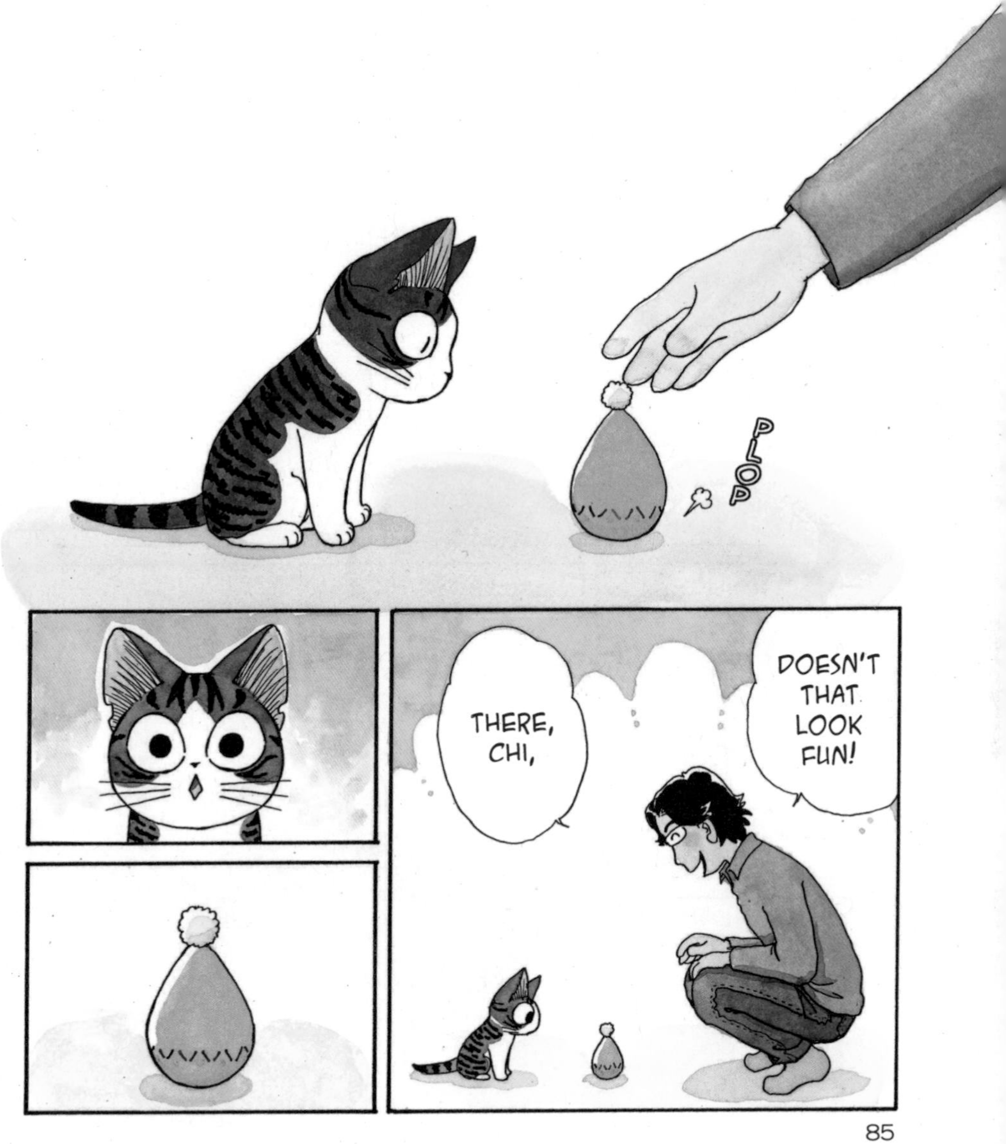
PLOP
THERE, CHI,
DOESN'T THAT LOOK FUN!

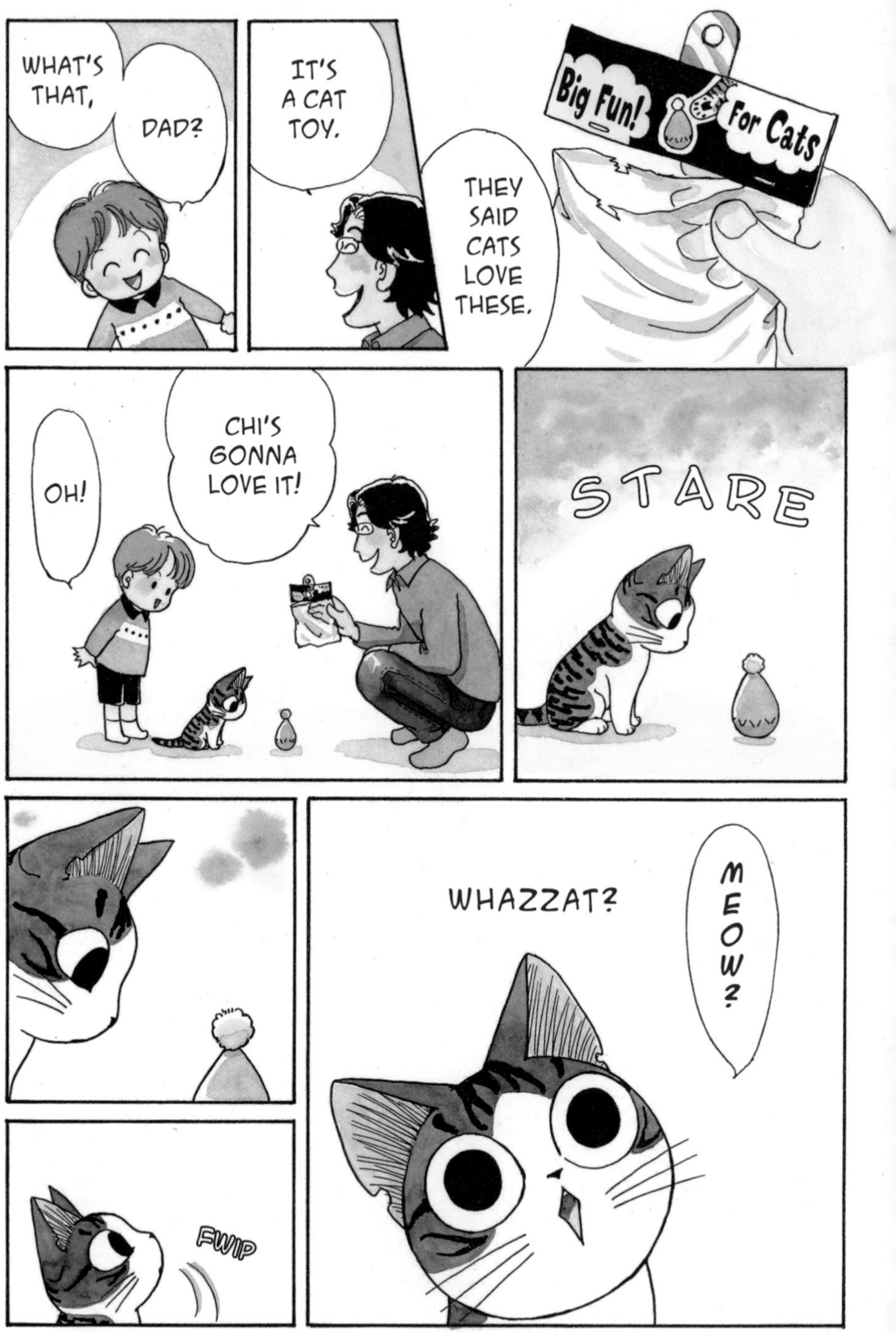
WHAT'S THAT,
DAD?
IT'S A CAT TOY.
Big Fun!
For Cats
THEY SAID CATS LOVE THESE.
OH!
CHI'S GONNA LOVE IT!
STARE
WHAZZAT?
MEOW?
FWIP

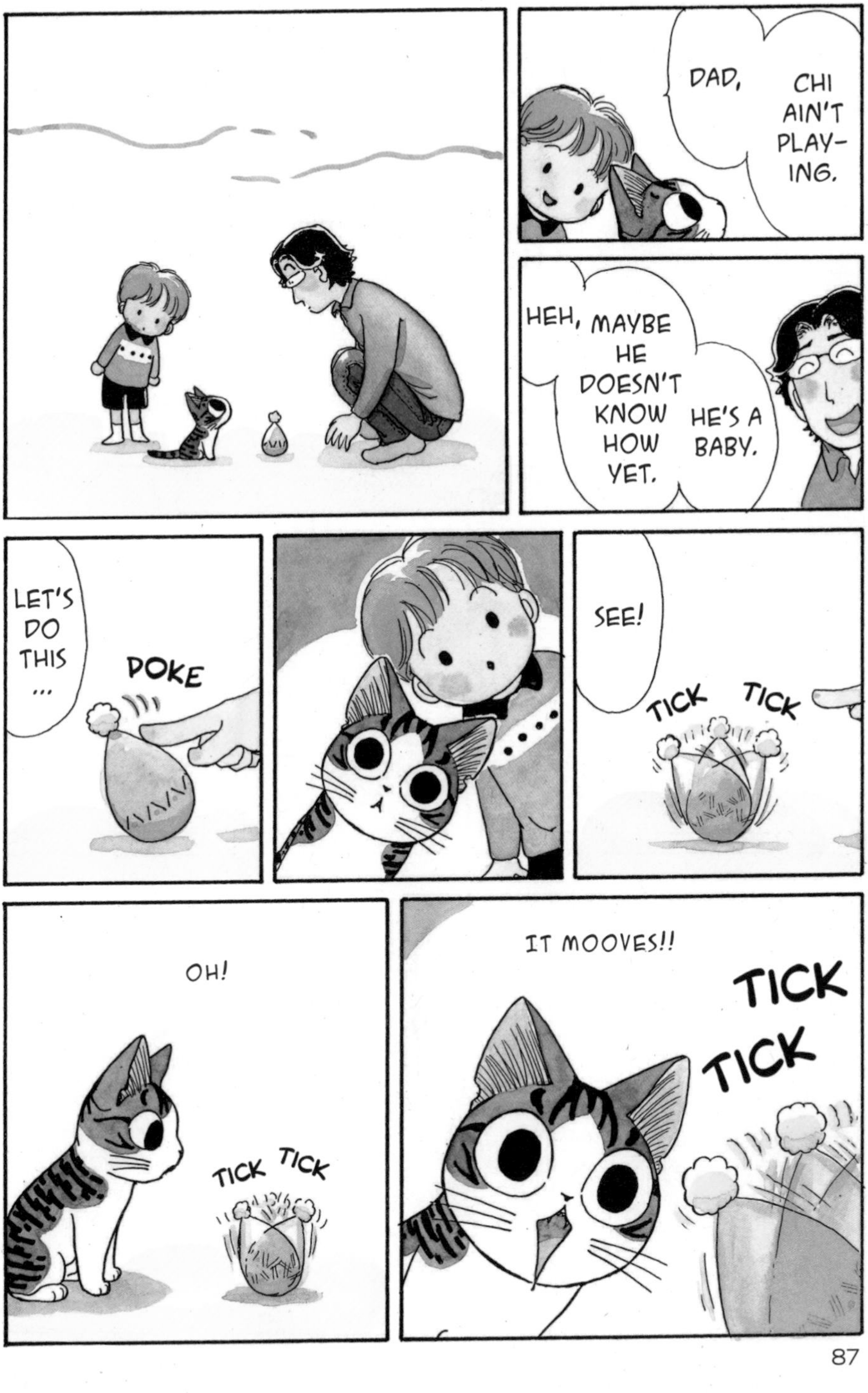
DAD,
CHI AIN'T PLAY-ING.
HEH, MAYBE HE DOESN'T KNOW HOW YET.
HE'S A BABY.
LET'S DO THIS ...
POKE
SEE!
TICK TICK
OH!
TICK TICK
IT MOOVES!!
TICK
TICK

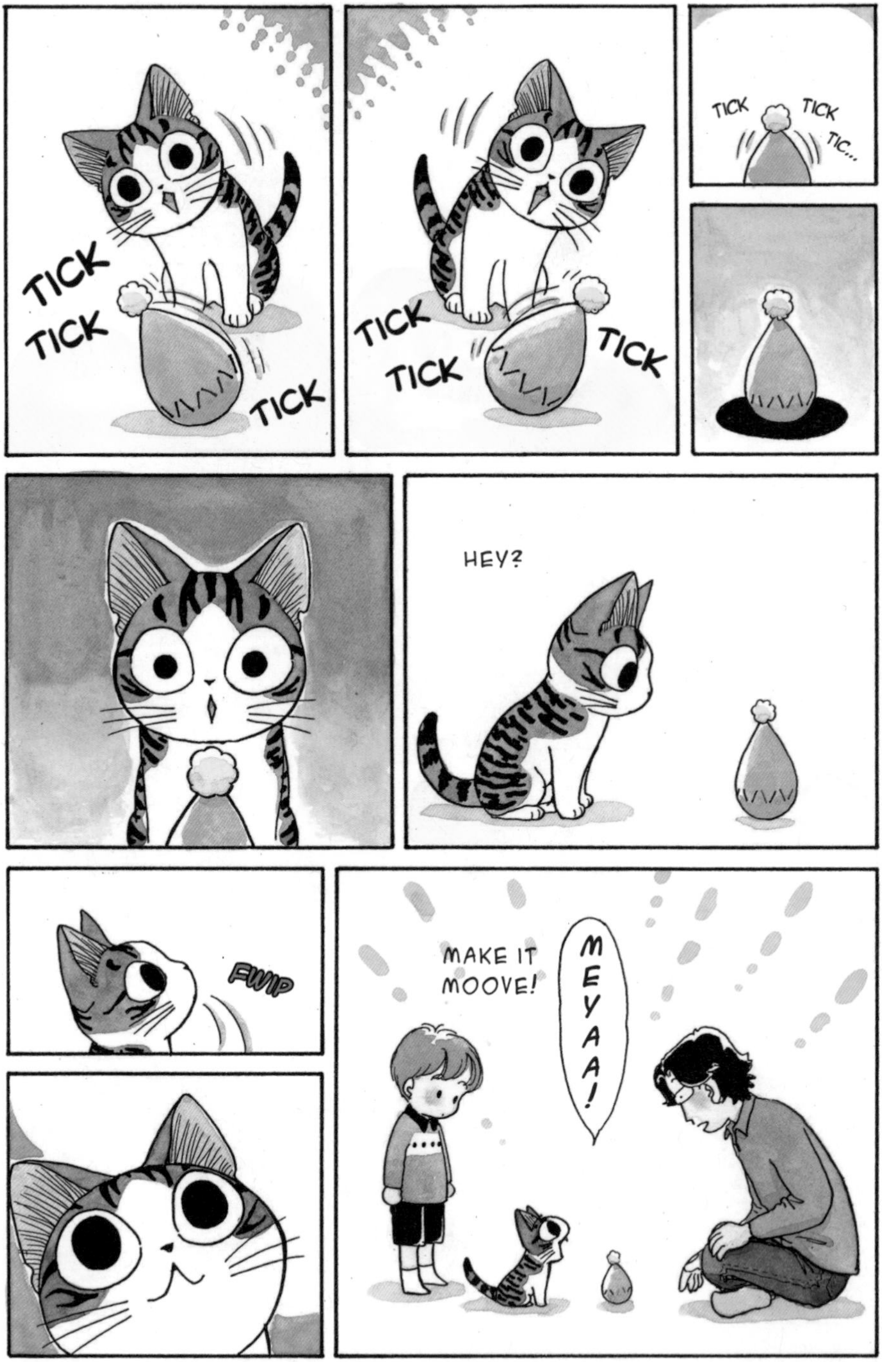
TICK
TICK
TICK
TICK
TICK
TICK
TICK
TICK
TIC...
HEY?
FWIP
MAKE IT MOOVE!
MEYAA!

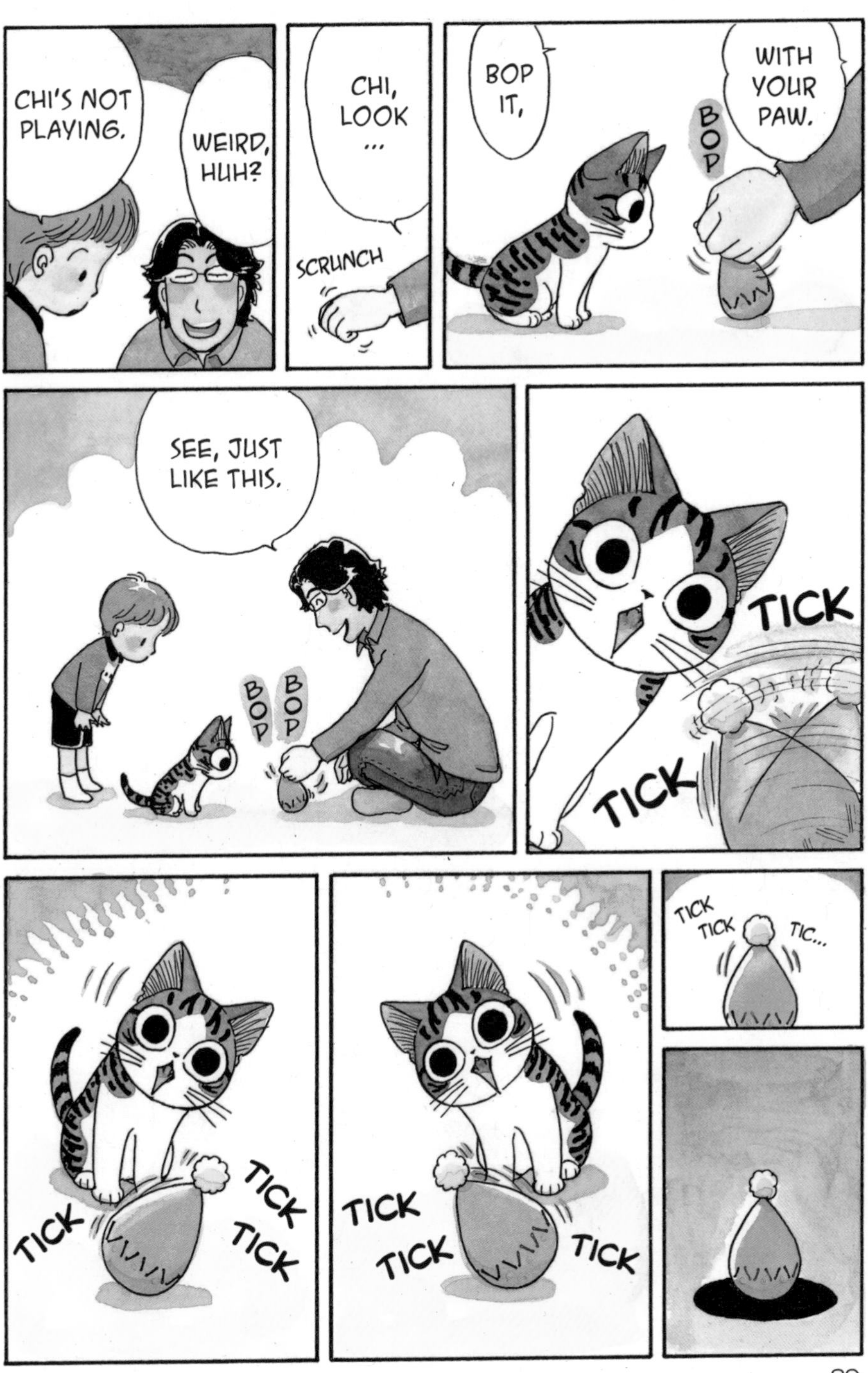
CHI'S NOT PLAYING.
WEIRD, HUH?
CHI, LOOK ...
SCRUNCH
BOP IT,
WITH YOUR PAW.
BOP
SEE, JUST LIKE THIS.
BOP
BOP
TICK
TICK
TICK
TICK
TICK
TICK
TICK
TICK
TICK
TICK
TIC...

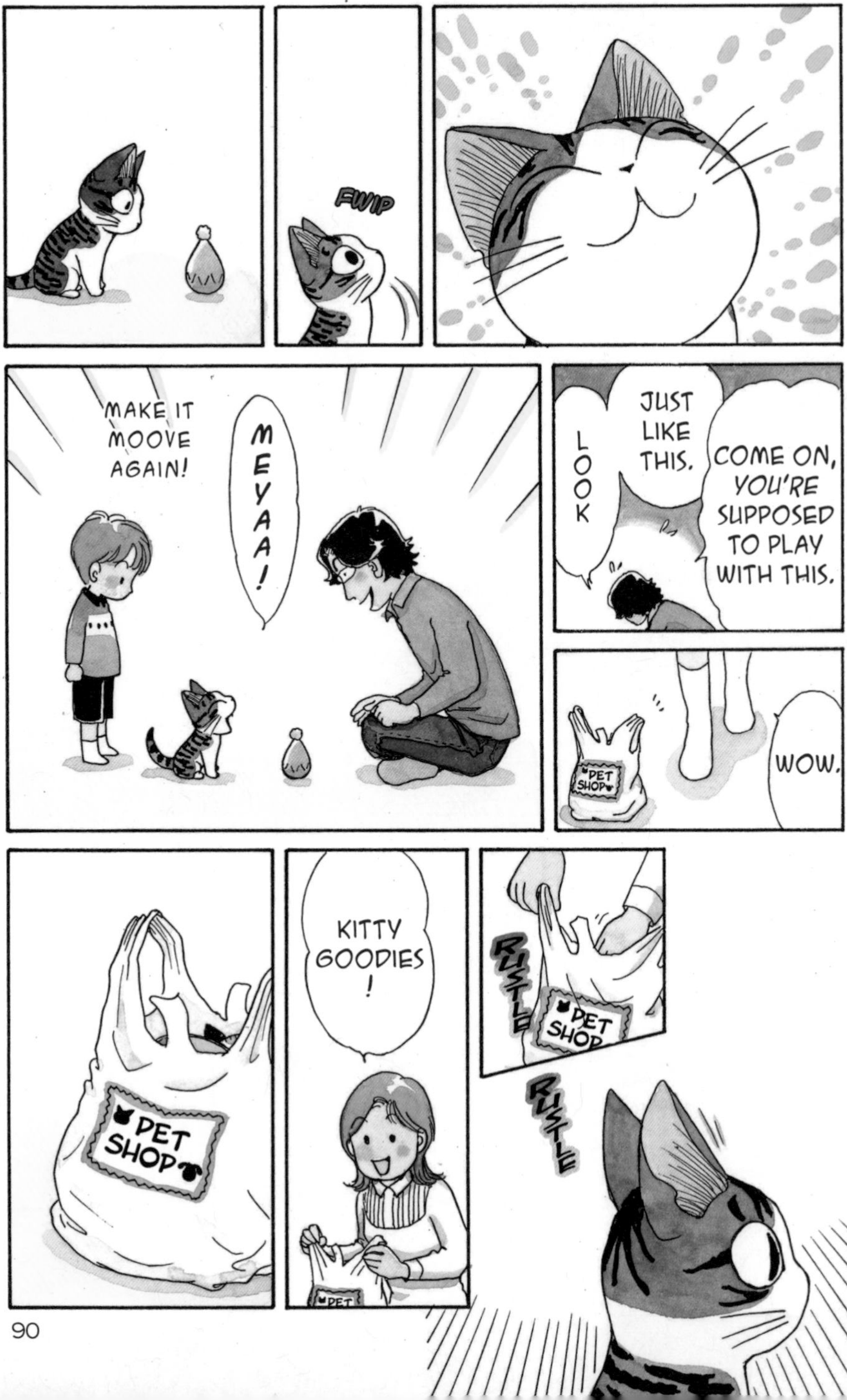
FWIP
MAKE IT MOOVE AGAIN!
MEYAAA!
LOOK
JUST LIKE THIS.
COME ON, YOU'RE SUPPOSED TO PLAY WITH THIS.
PET SHOP
WOW.
PET SHOP
KITTY GOODIES!
RUSTLE
PET SHOP
RUSTLE

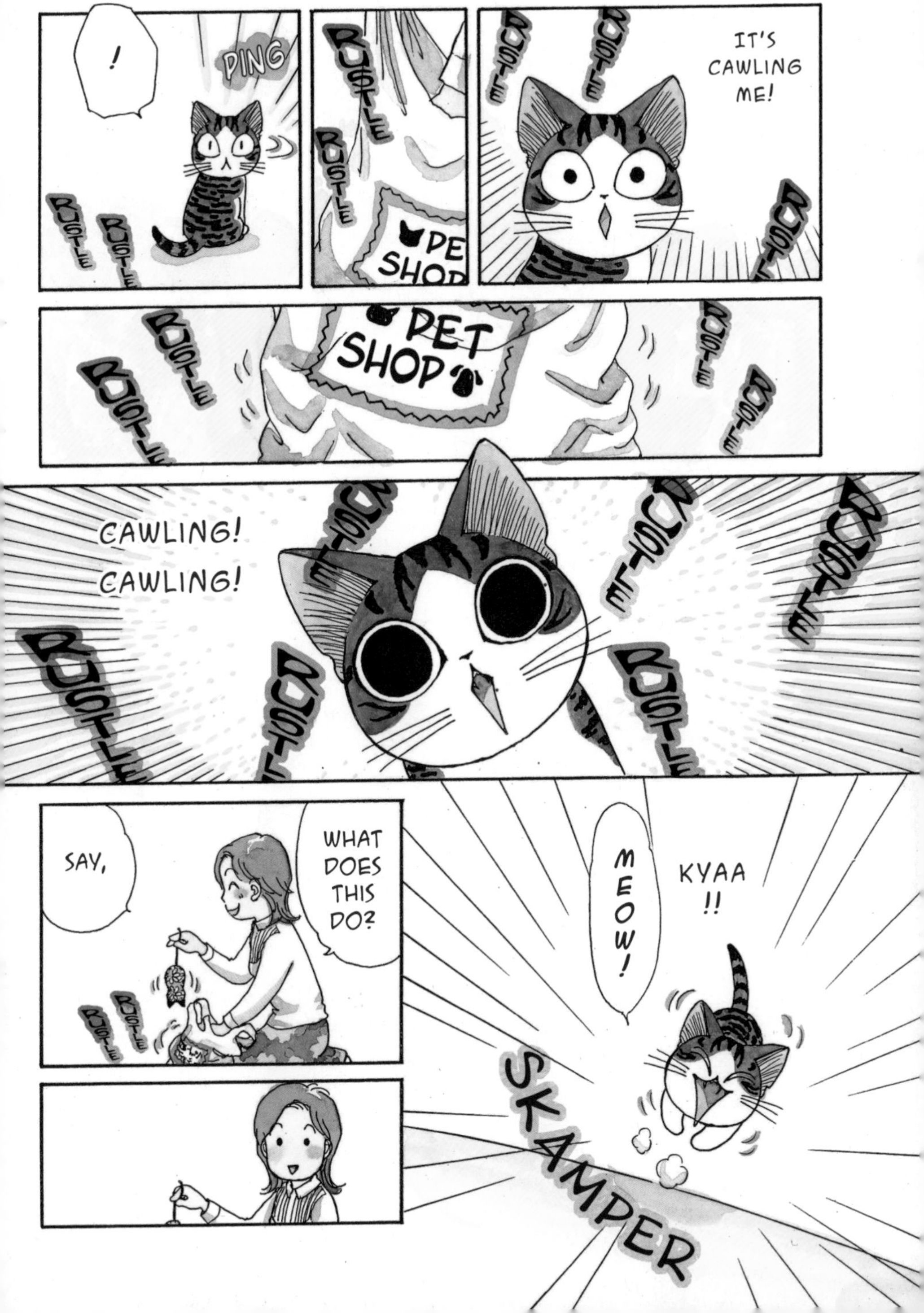
!
PING
RUSTLE
RUSTLE
RUSTLE
RUSTLE
PET SHOP
RUSTLE
RUSTLE
IT'S CAWLING ME!
RUSTLE
RUSTLE
RUSTLE
PET SHOP
RUSTLE
RUSTLE
CAWLING!
CAWLING!
RUSTLE
RUSTLE
RUSTLE
RUSTLE
RUSTLE
RUSTLE
SAY,
WHAT DOES THIS DO?
RUSTLE
RUSTLE
MEOW!
KYAA !!
SKAMPER

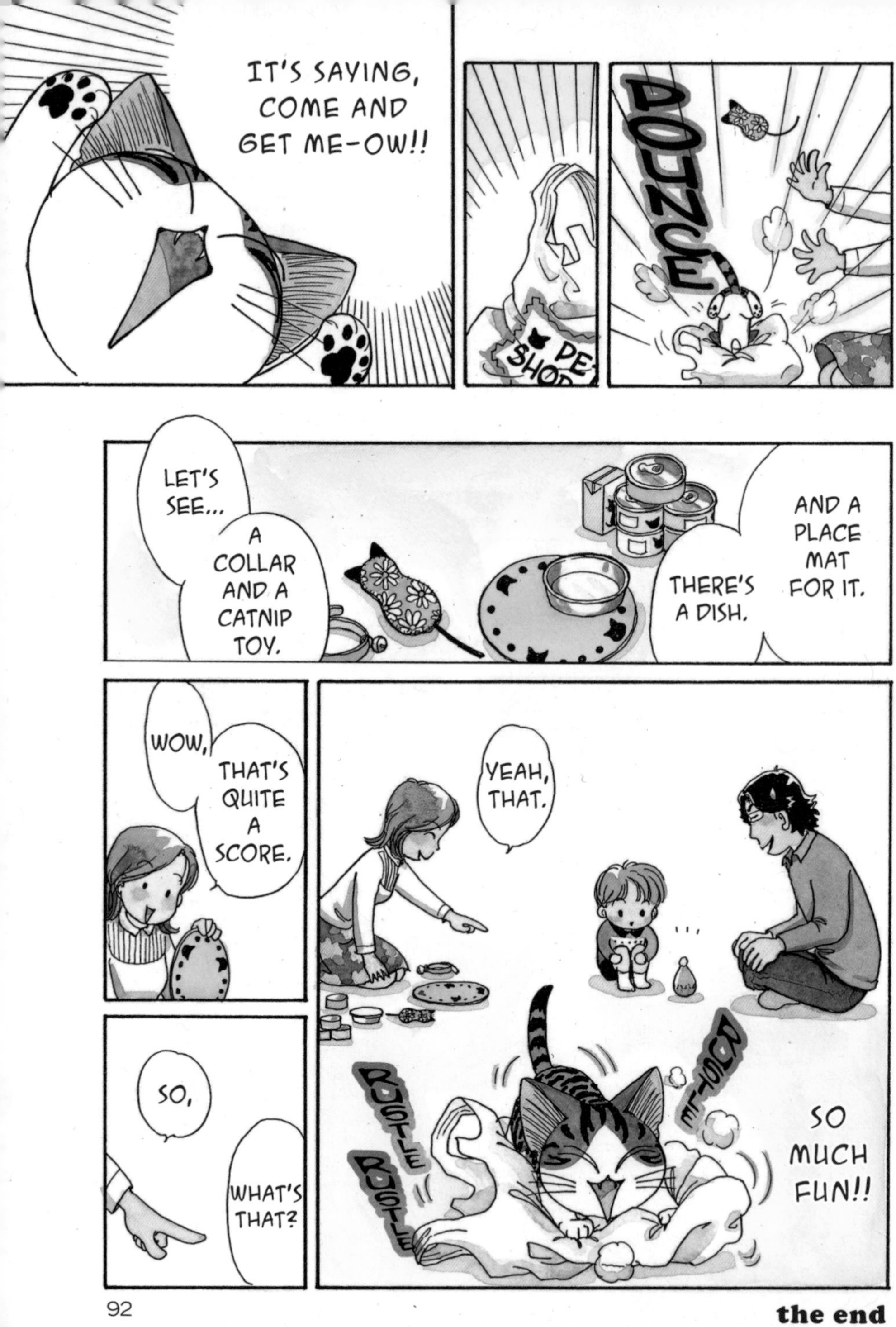

IT'S SAYING, COME AND GET ME-OW!!
POUNCE
LET'S SEE...
A COLLAR AND A CATNIP TOY.
THERE'S A DISH.
AND A PLACE MAT FOR IT.
WOW,
THAT'S QUITE A SCORE.
SO,
WHAT'S THAT?
YEAH, THAT.
RUSTLE RUSTLE
SO MUCH FUN!!

the end

homemade 12: a cat is lost... again

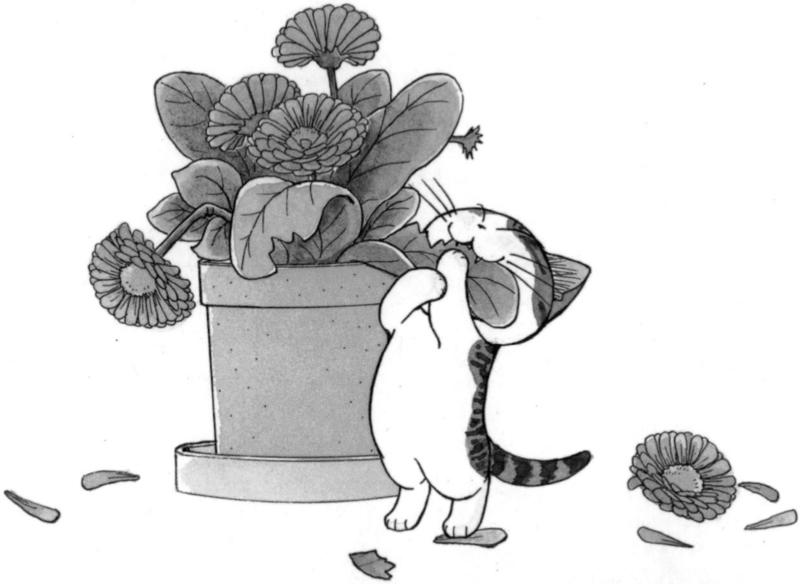

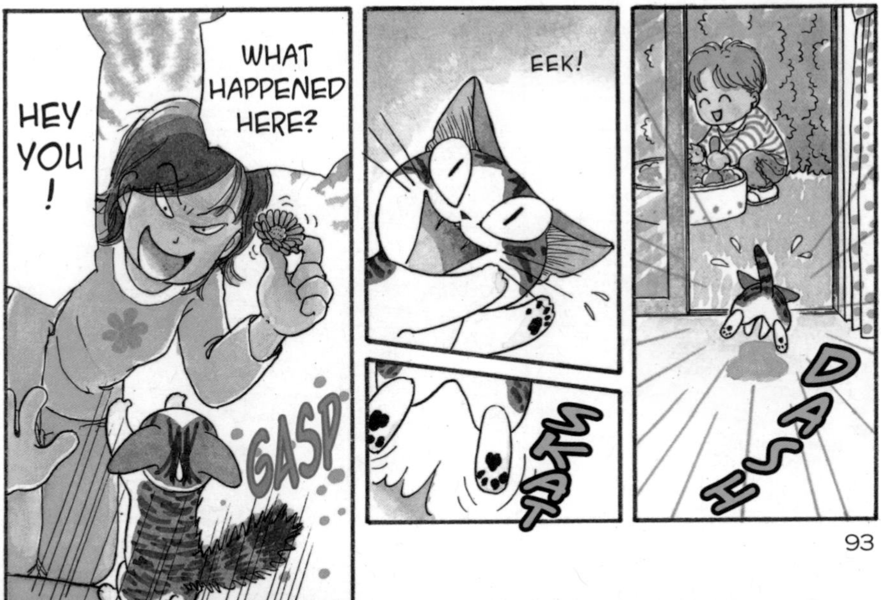
HEY YOU!
WHAT HAPPENED HERE?
GASP
EEK!
SKAT
DASH

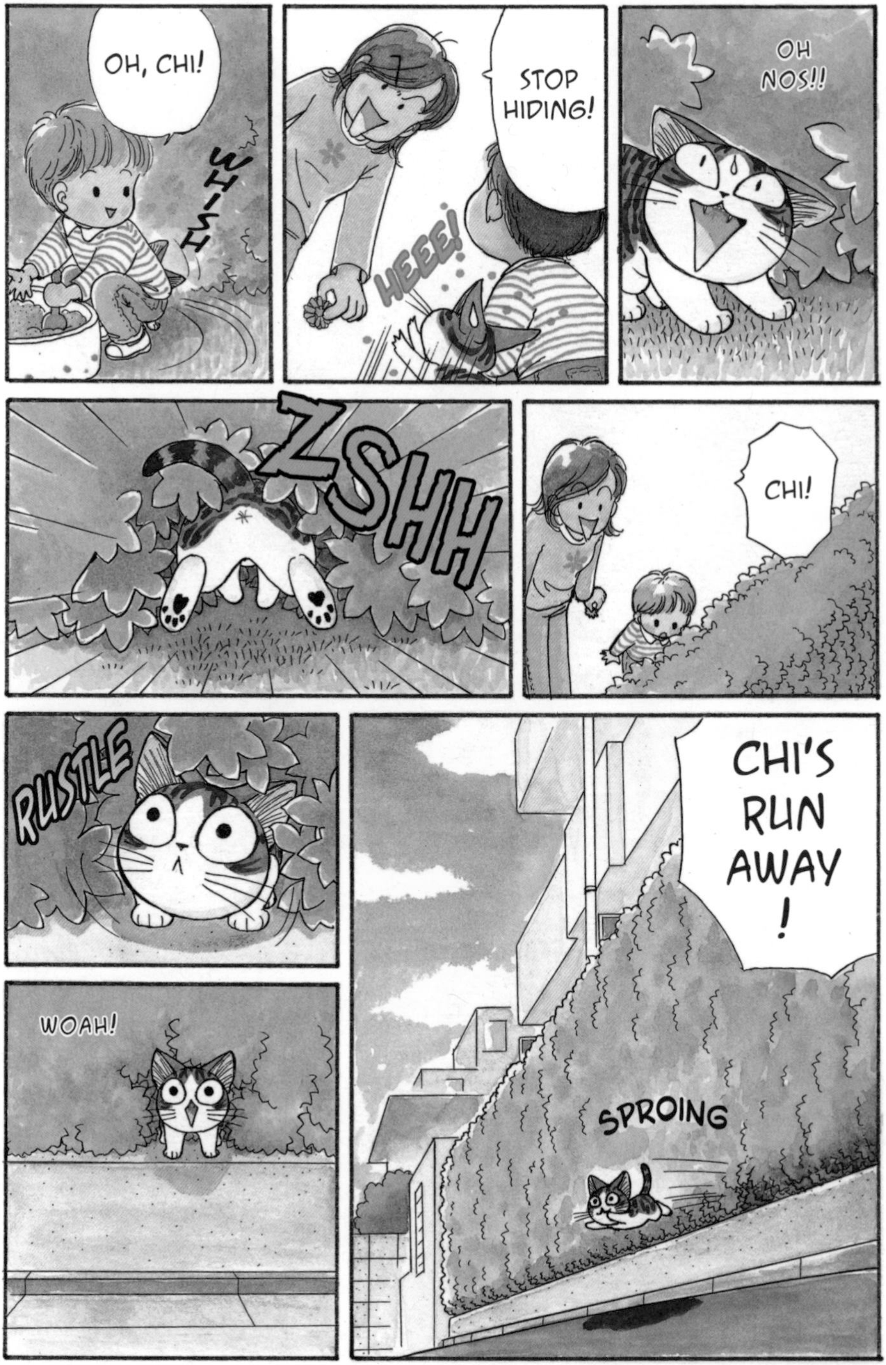
OH, CHI!
WHISH
STOP HIDING!
HEEE!
OH NOS!!
ZSHH
CHI!
RUSTLE
WOAH!
CHI'S RUN AWAY !
SPROING

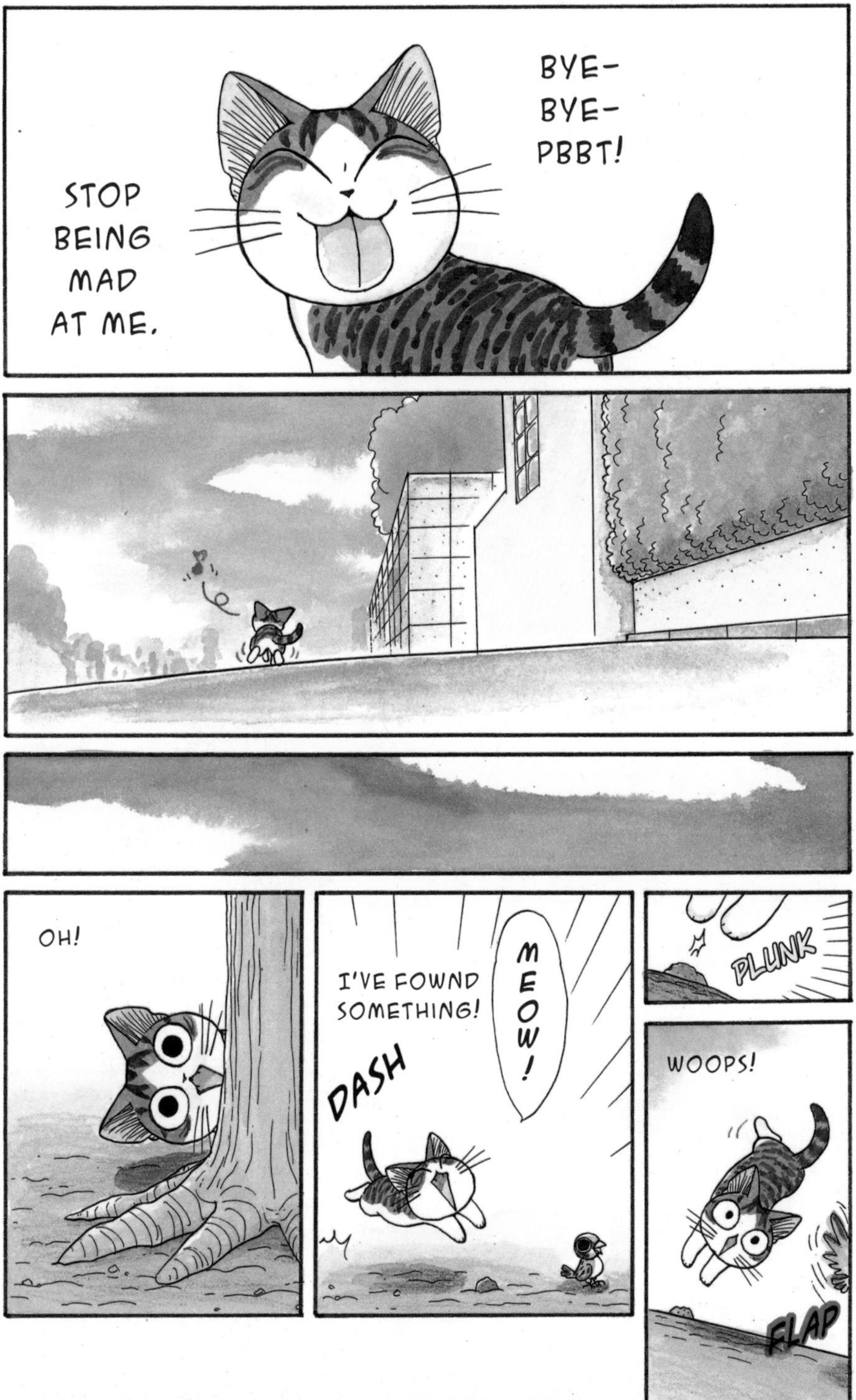
STOP BEING MAD AT ME.
BYE-BYE-PBBT!
OH!
I'VE FOWND SOMETHING!
MEOW!
DASH
PLUNK
WOOPS!
FLAP

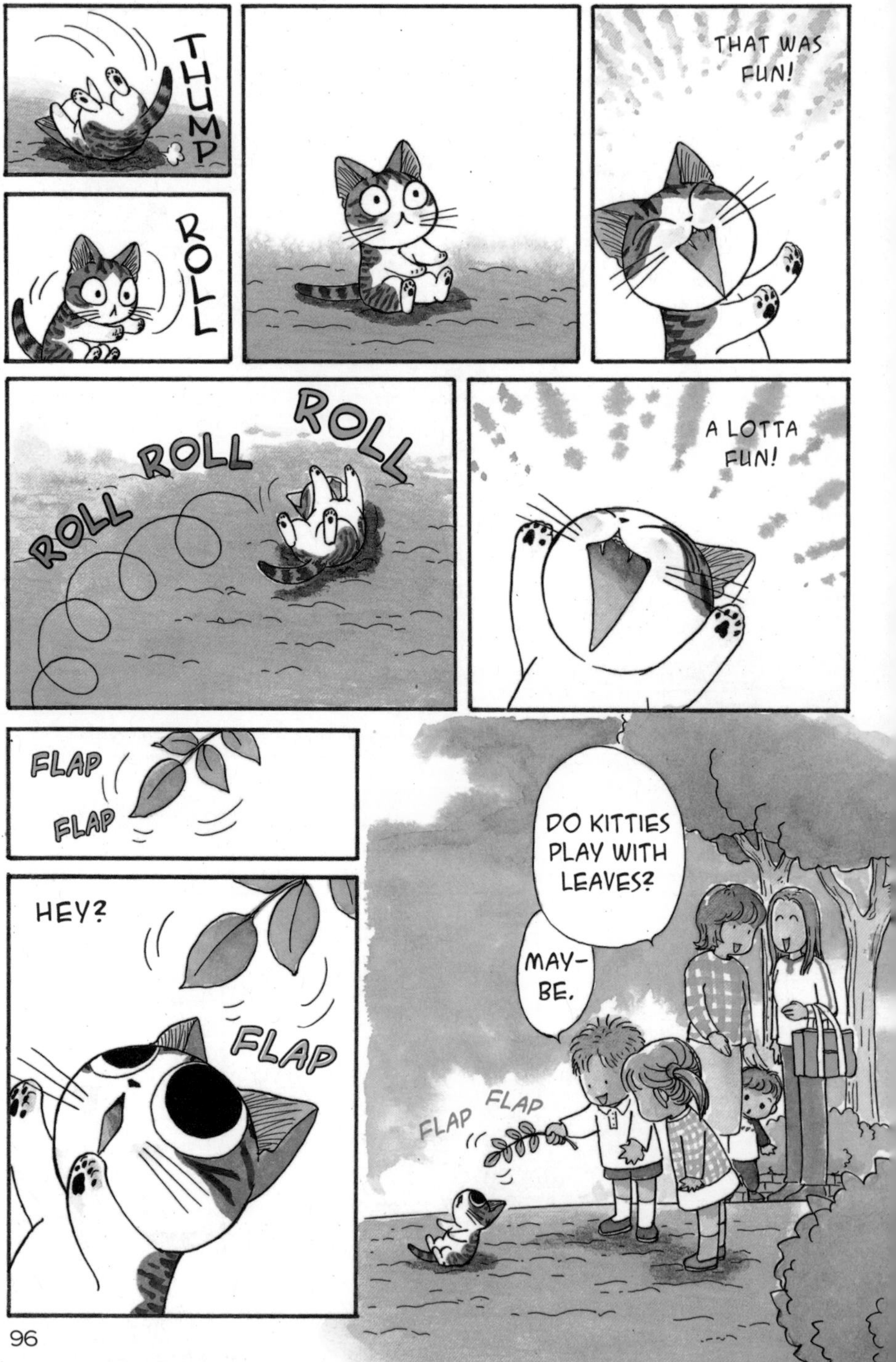
THUMP
ROLL
THAT WAS FUN!
ROLL ROLL ROLL
A LOTTA FUN!
FLAP FLAP
HEY?
FLAP
DO KITTIES PLAY WITH LEAVES?
MAY-BE.
FLAP FLAP

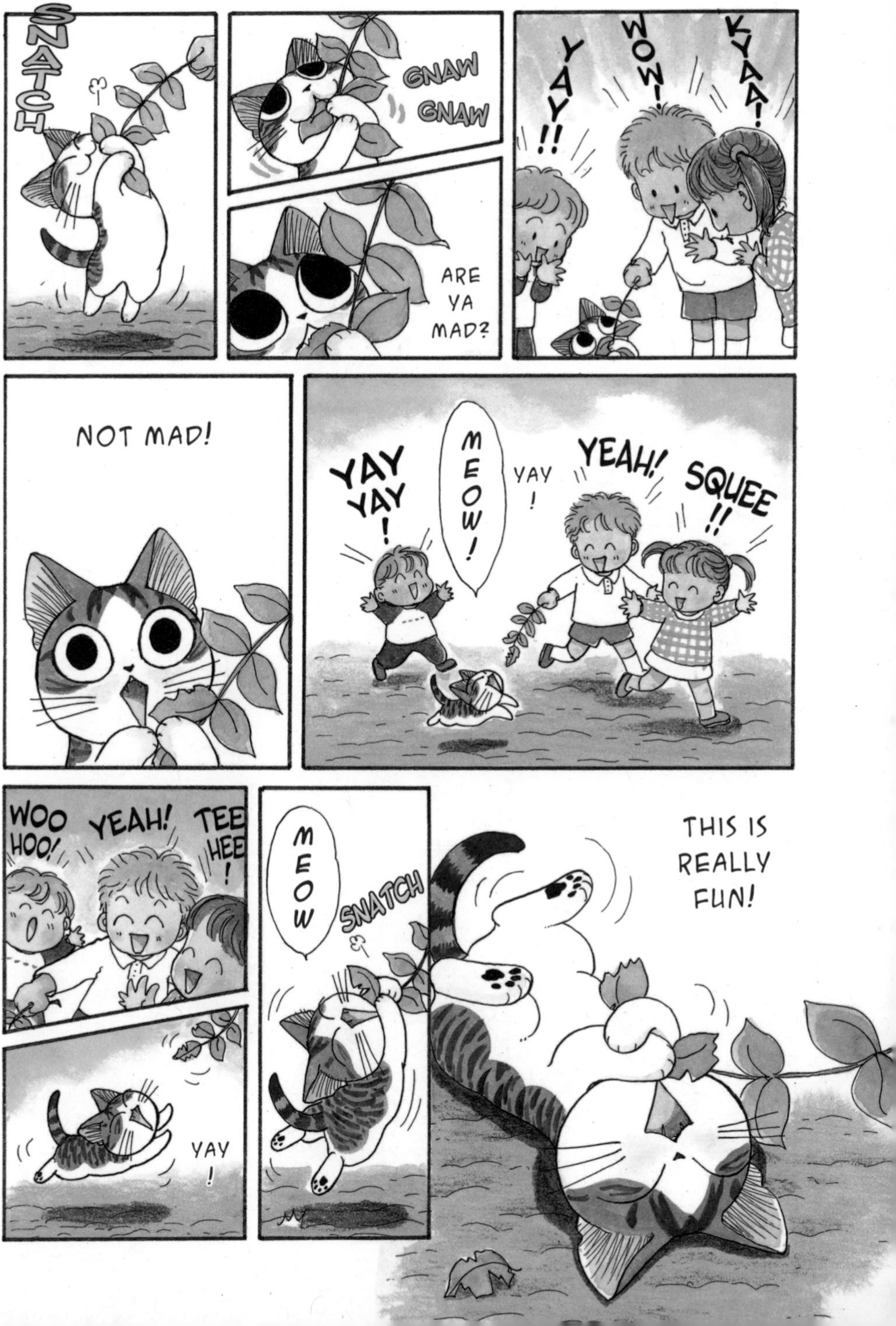
SNATCH
GNAW GNAW
ARE YA MAD?
YAY!!
WOW!
KYAA!
NOT MAD!
YAY YAY!
MEOW!
YAY!
YEAH!
SQUEE!!
WOO HOO!
YEAH!
TEE HEE!
YAY!
MEOW
SNATCH
THIS IS REALLY FUN!

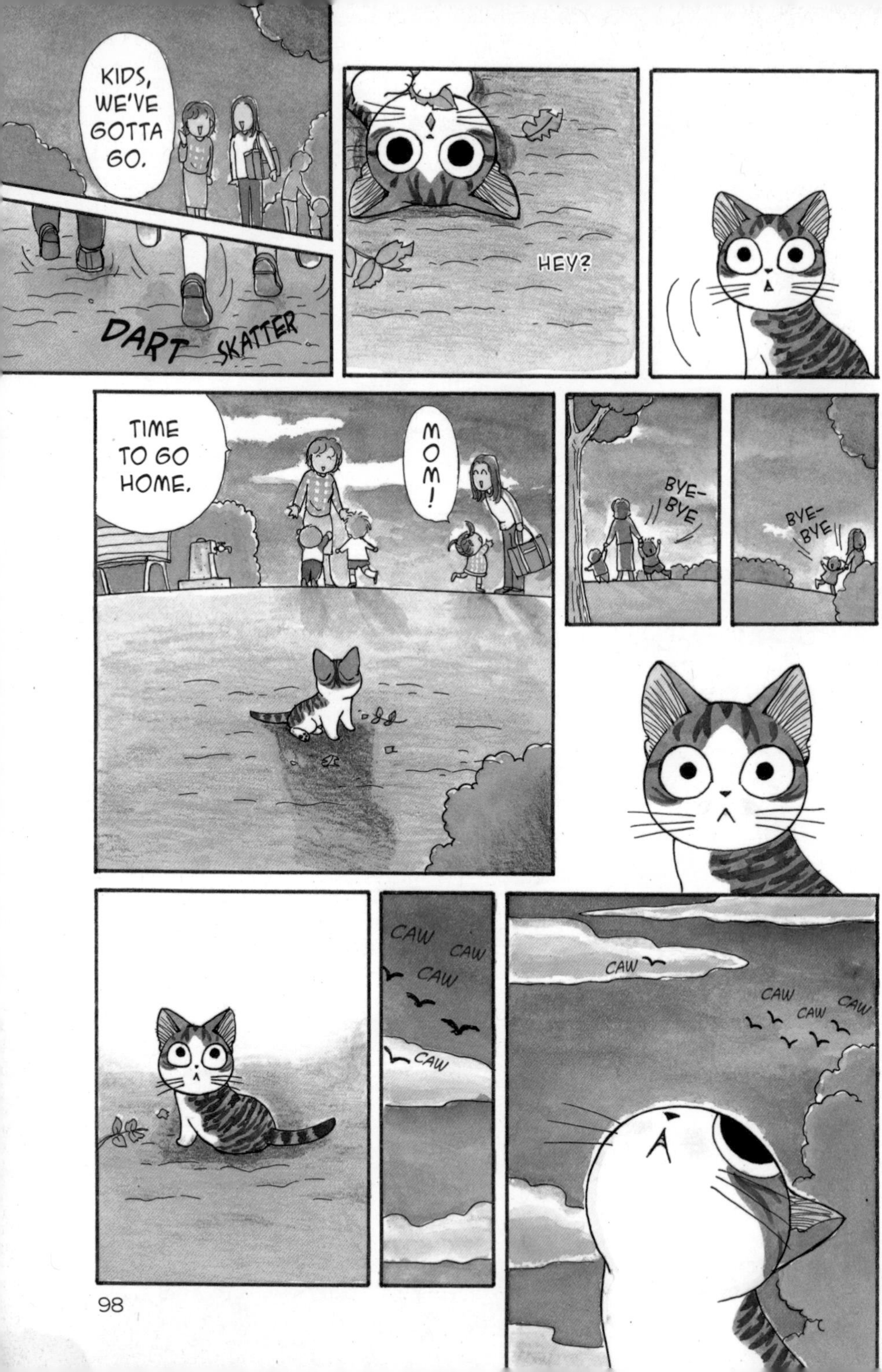
KIDS, WE'VE GOTTA GO.
DART
SKATTER
HEY?
TIME TO GO HOME.
MOM!
BYE-BYE
BYE-BYE
CAW
CAW
CAW
CAW
CAW
CAW
CAW
CAW

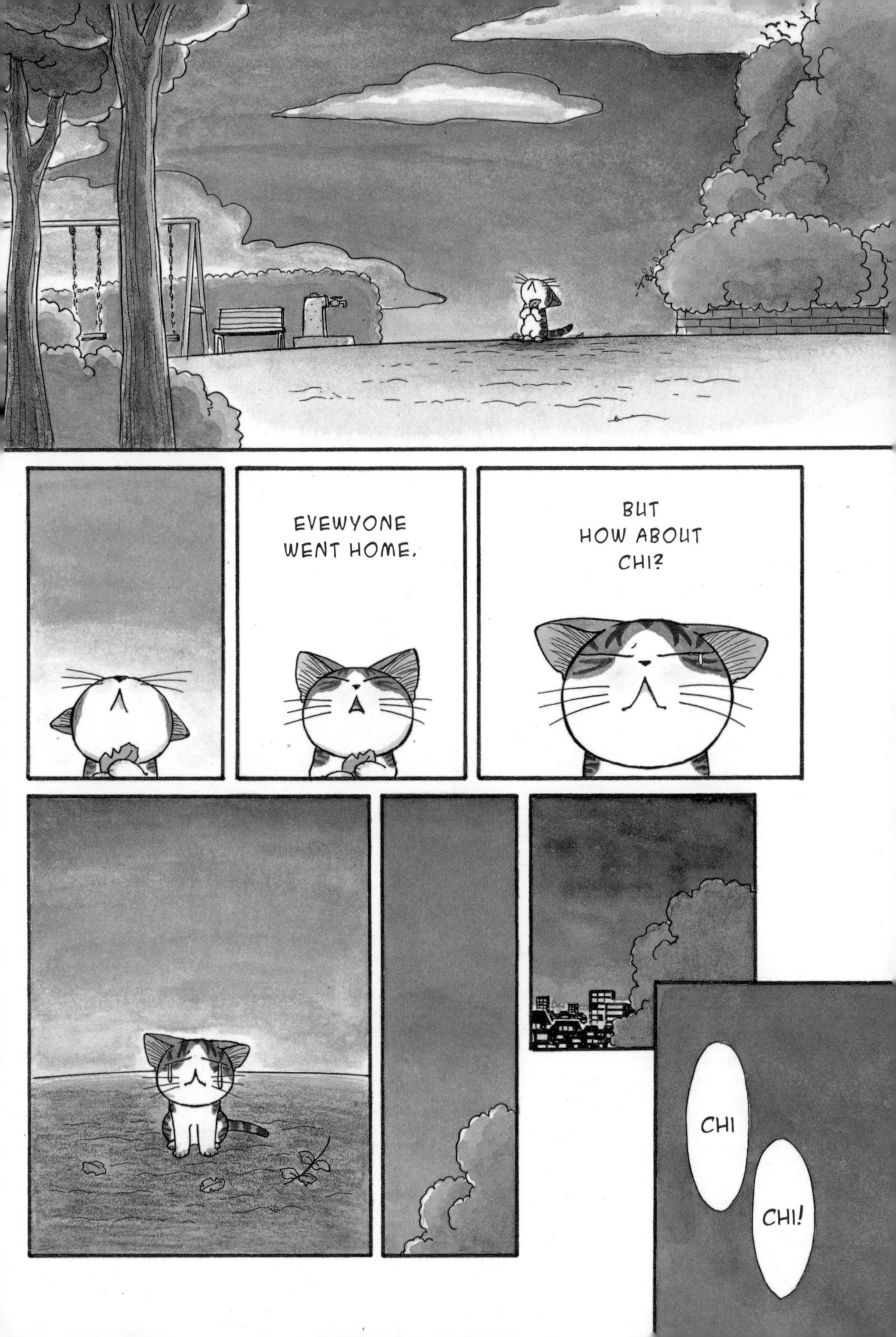
EVEWYONE WENT HOME.
BUT HOW ABOUT CHI?
CHI
CHI!

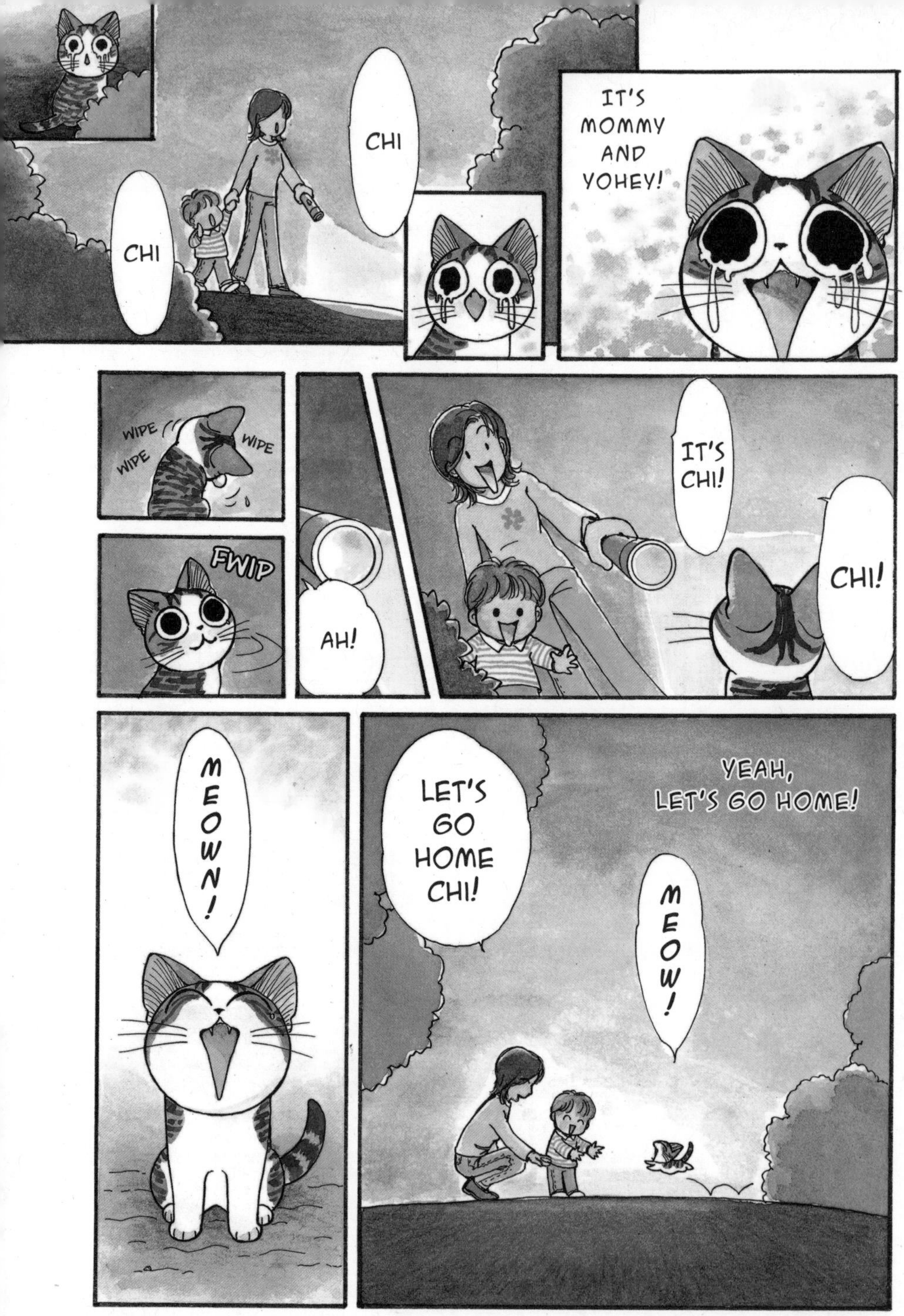
CHI
CHI
IT'S MOMMY AND YOHEY!
WIPE WIPE WIPE
FWIP
AH!
IT'S CHI!
CHI!
MEOWN!
LET'S GO HOME CHI!
YEAH, LET'S GO HOME!
MEOW!

the end

homemade 13: a cat fights!

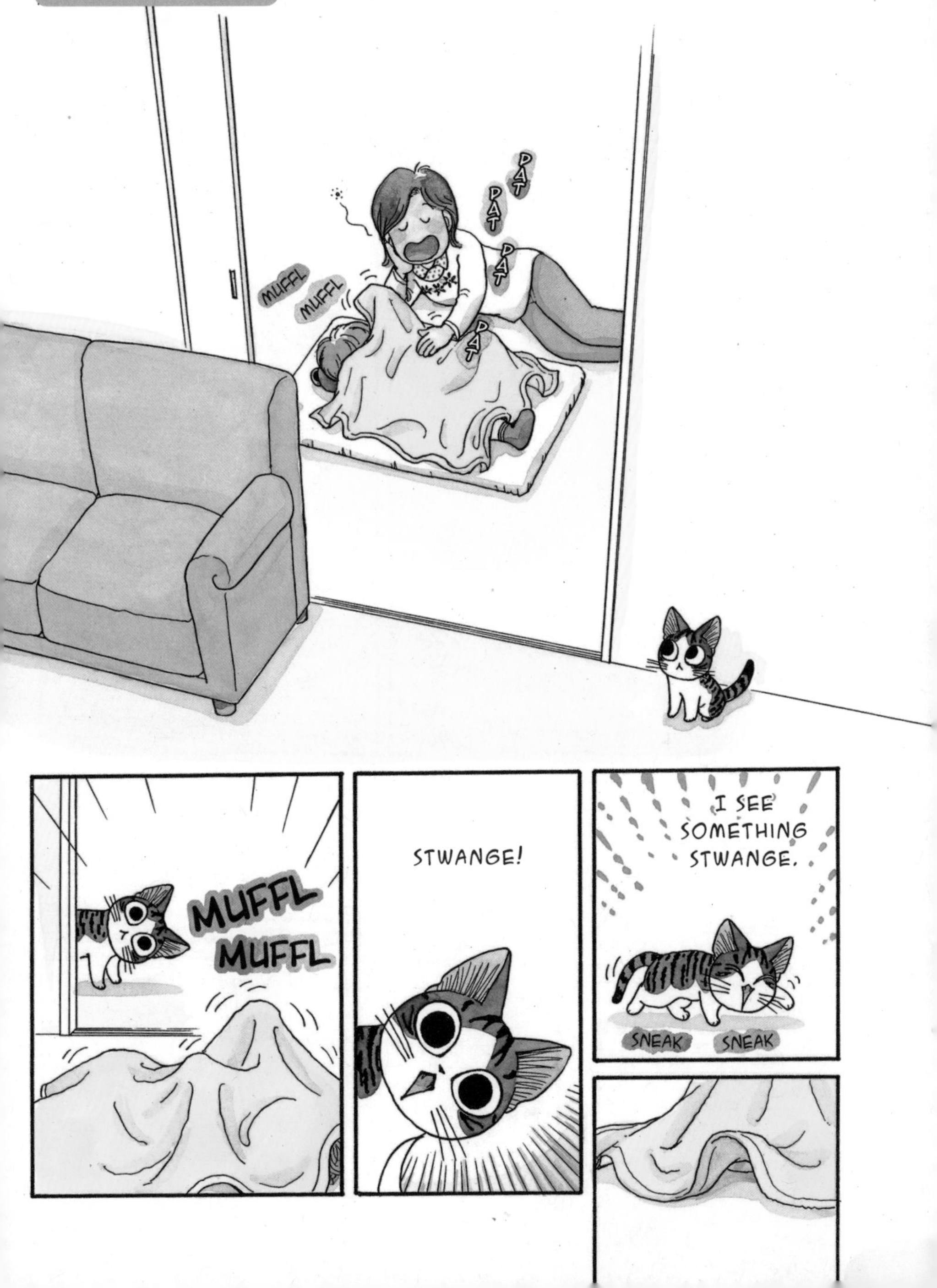
PAT
PAT
PAT
MUFFL
MUFFL
PAT
MUFFL
MUFFL
STWANGE!
I SEE SOMETHING STWANGE.
SNEAK
SNEAK

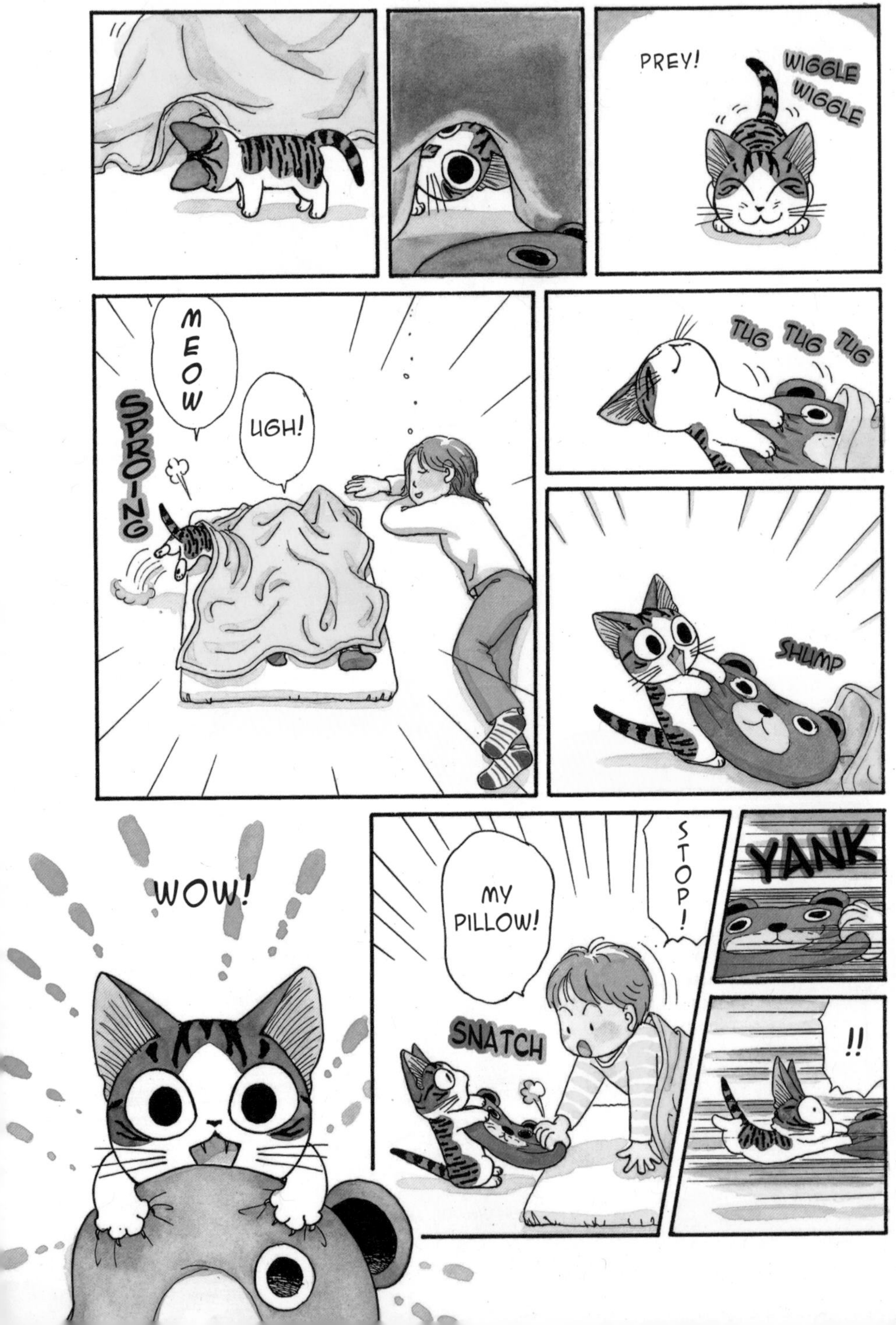
PREY!
WIGGLE WIGGLE
MEOW
SPROING
UGH!
TUG TUG TUG
SHUMP
WOW!
MY PILLOW!
STOP!
SNATCH
YANK
!!

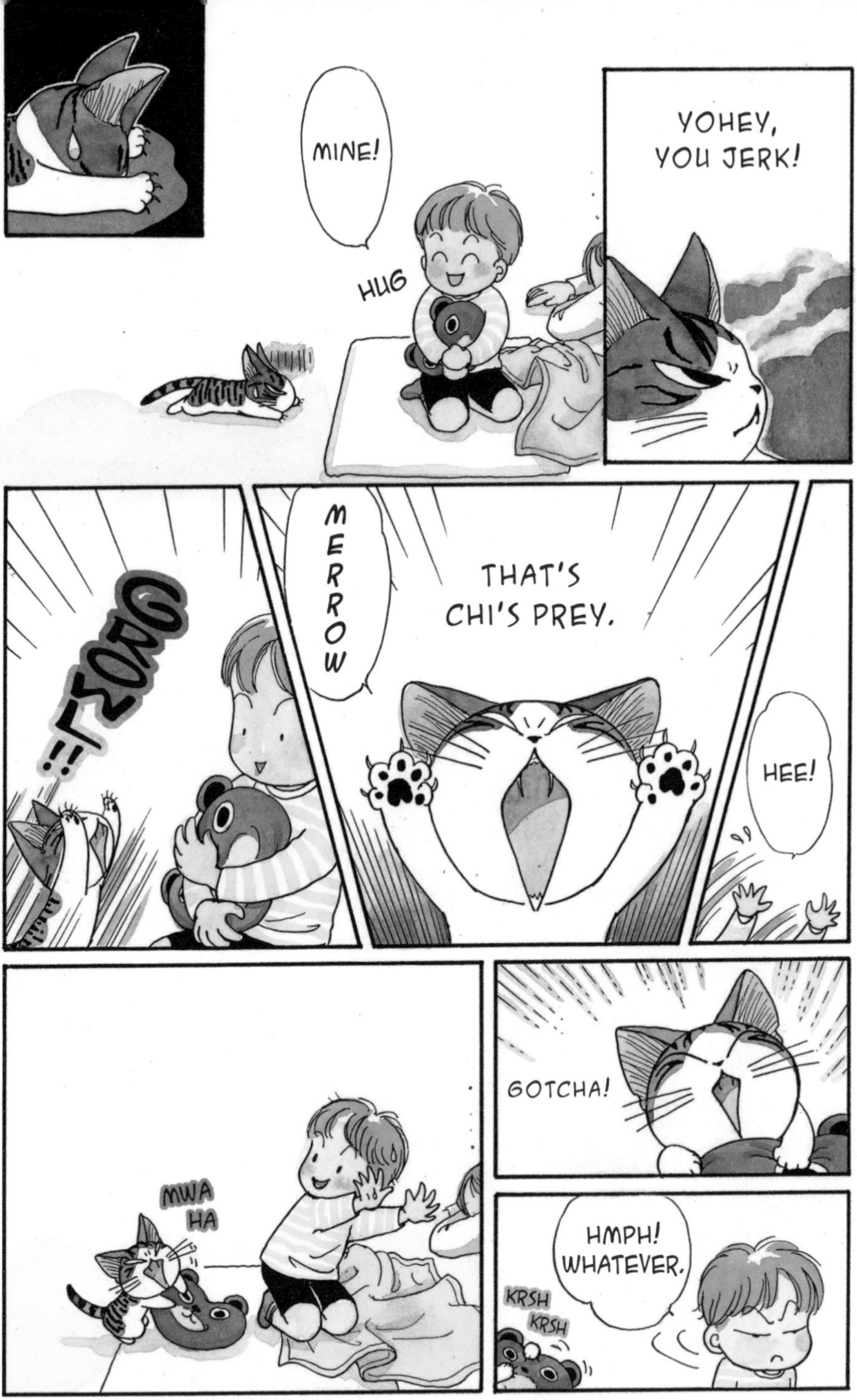
MINE!
HUG
YOHEY, YOU JERK!
GROWL!!
MERROW
THAT'S CHI'S PREY.
HEE!
MWA HA
GOTCHA!
HMPH! WHATEVER.
KRSH KRSH

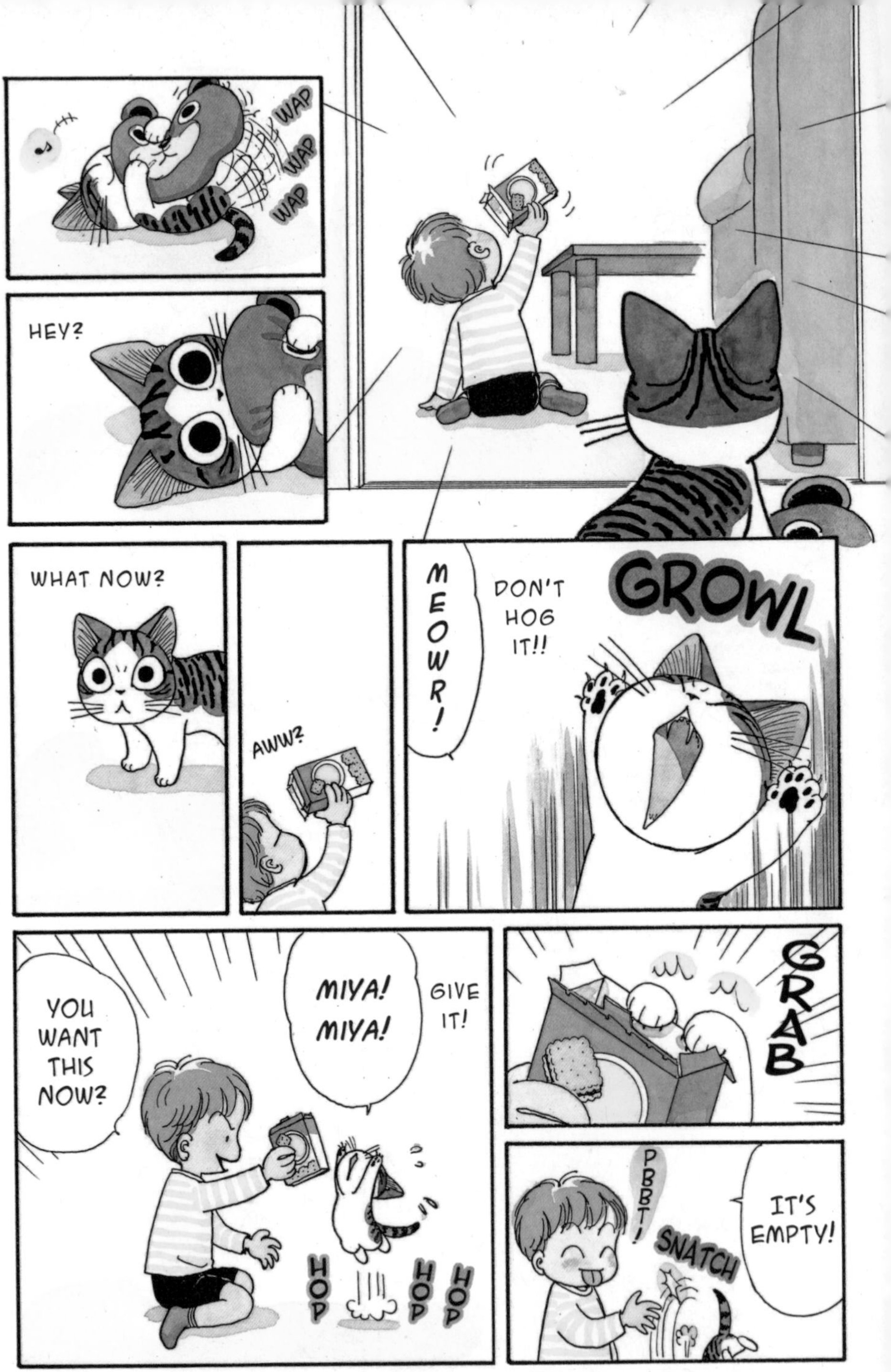
WAP
WAP
WAP
HEY?
WHAT NOW?
AWW?
MEOWR!
DON'T HOG IT!!
GROWL
YOU WANT THIS NOW?
MIYA! MIYA!
GIVE IT!
HOP
HOP
HOP
GRAB
PBBBT!
SNATCH
IT'S EMPTY!

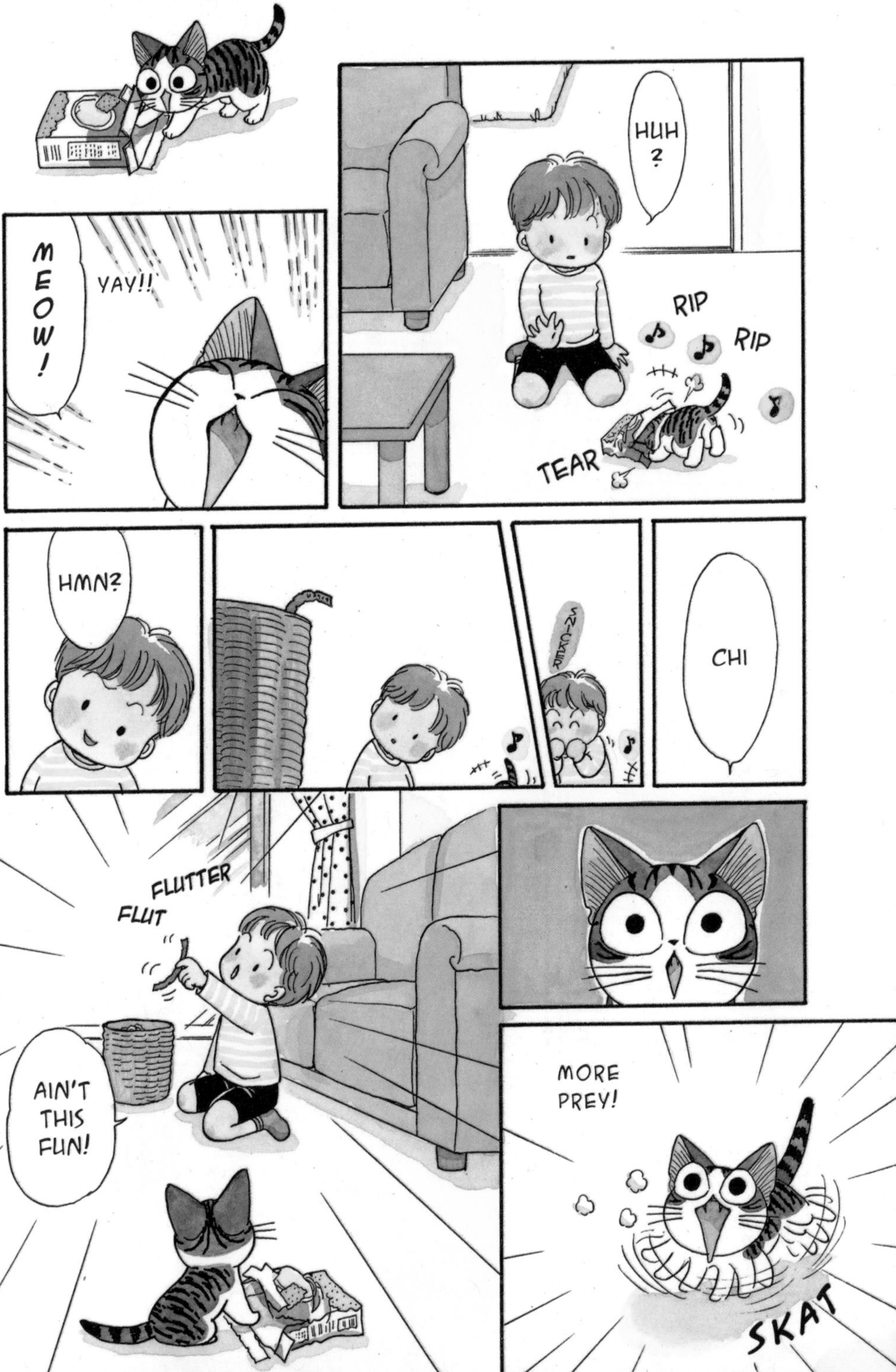
MEOW!
YAY!!
HUH?
RIP
RIP
TEAR
HMN?
SNICKER
CHI
FLUTTER
FLUT
AIN'T THIS FUN!
MORE PREY!
SKAT

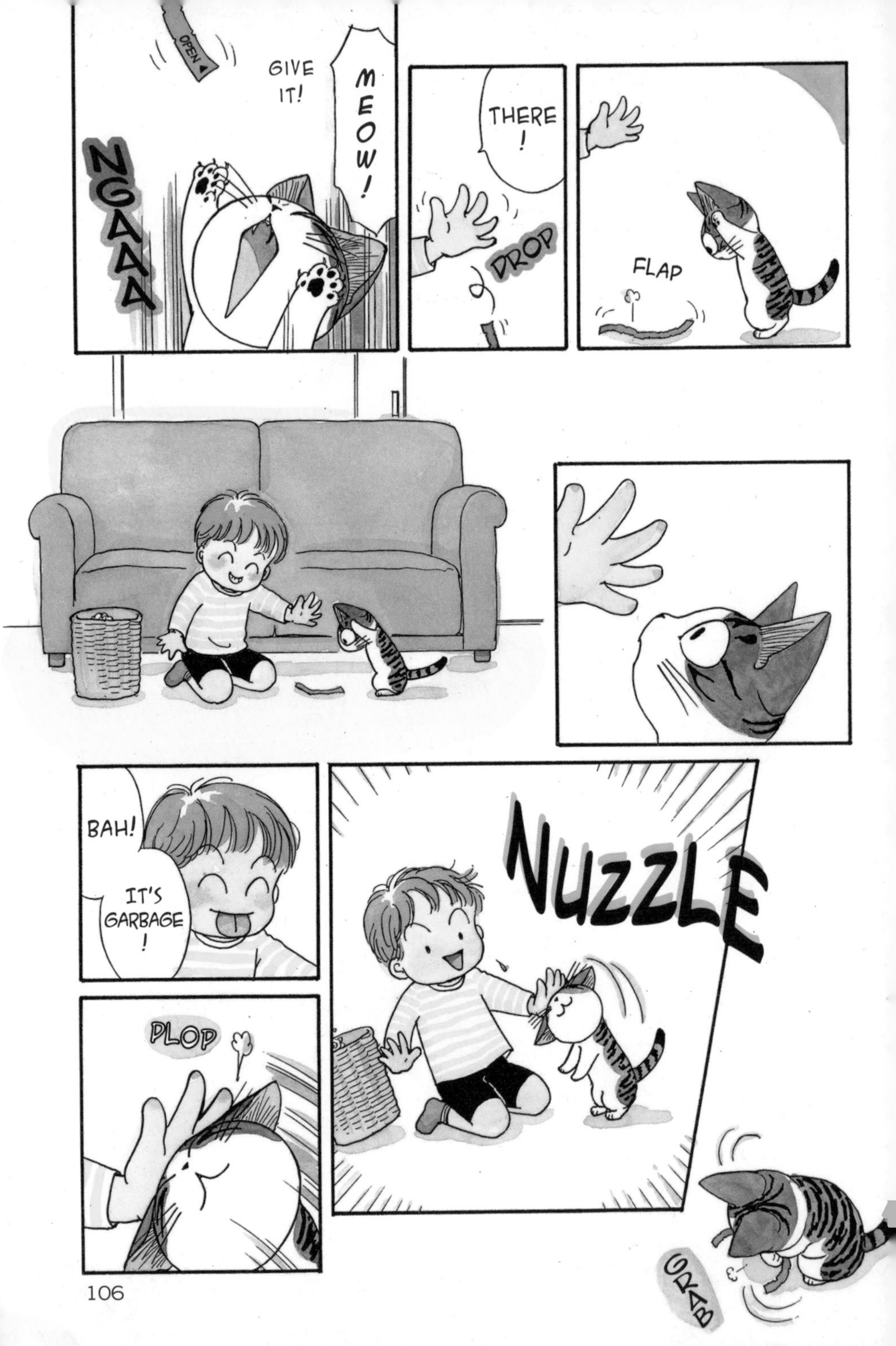

OPEN
GIVE IT!
MEOW!
NGAAA
THERE!
DROP
FLAP
BAH!
IT'S GARBAGE!
PLOP
NUZZLE
GRAB

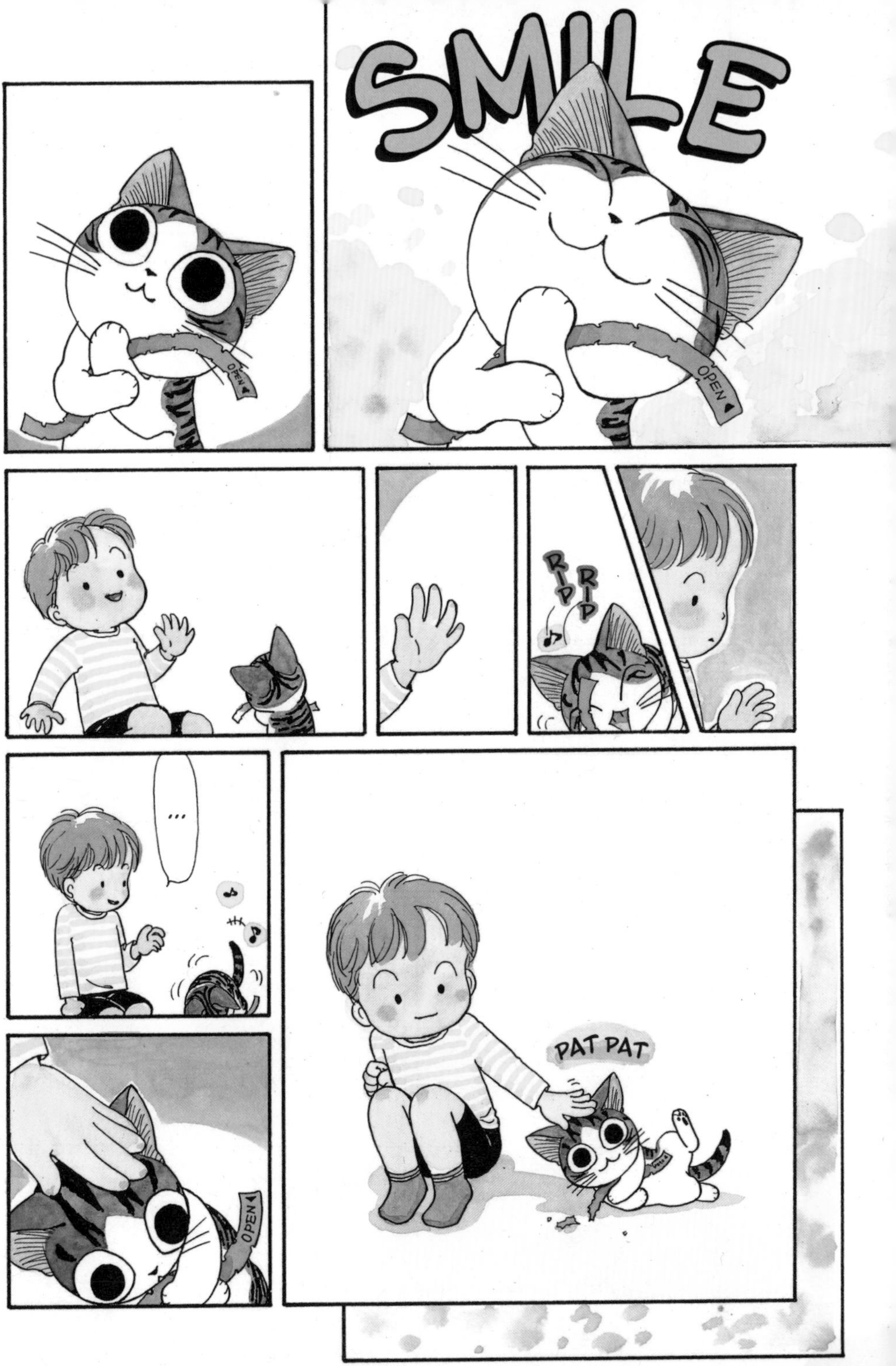
SMILE
OPEN
OPEN
RIP RIP
...
PAT PAT
OPEN

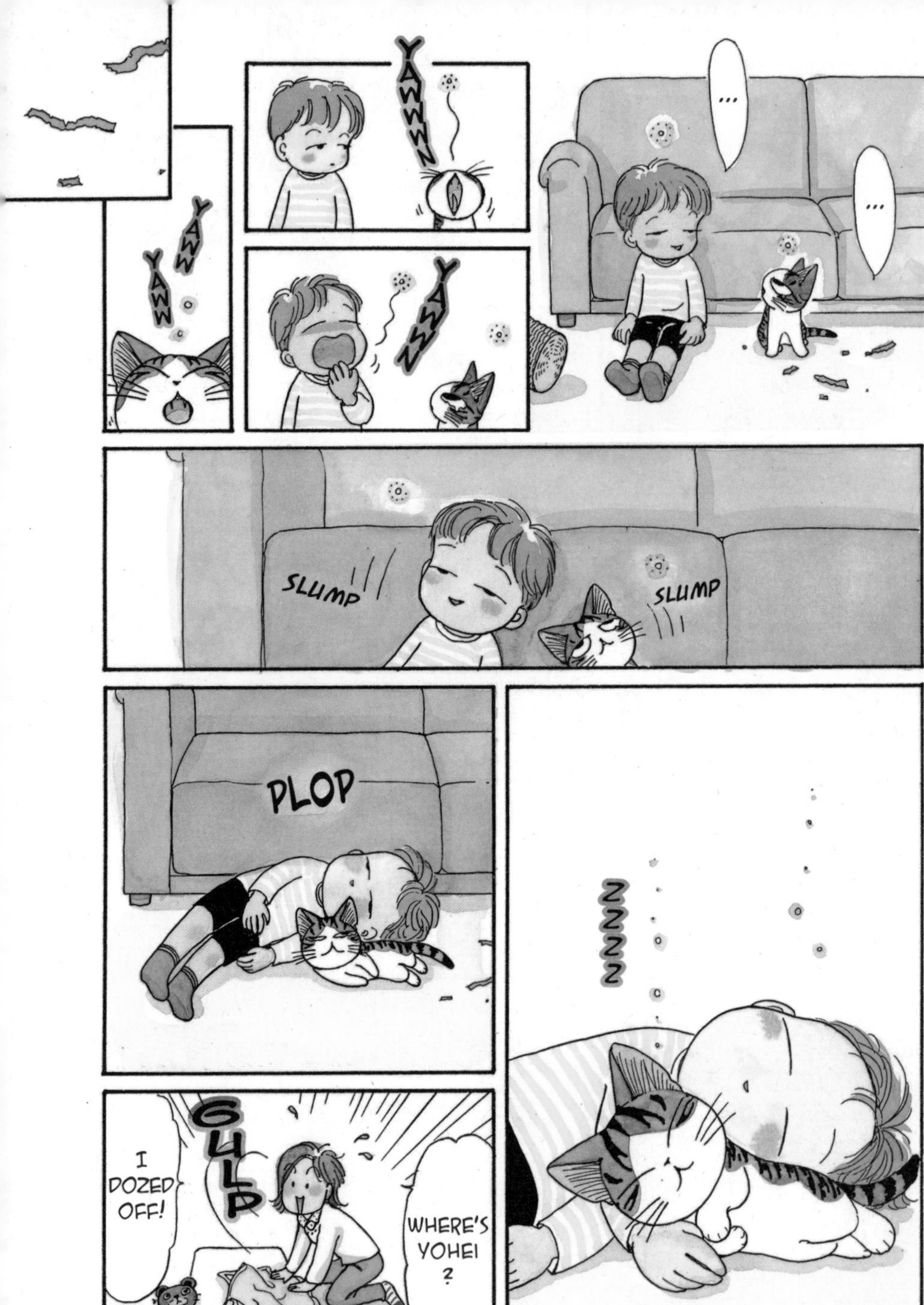

YAWN
YAWN
YAWWWN
YAWWN
...
...
SLUMP
SLUMP
PLOP
ZZZZ
GULP
I DOZED OFF!
WHERE'S YOHEI?

the end

homemade 14: a cat goes to the vet (part 1)

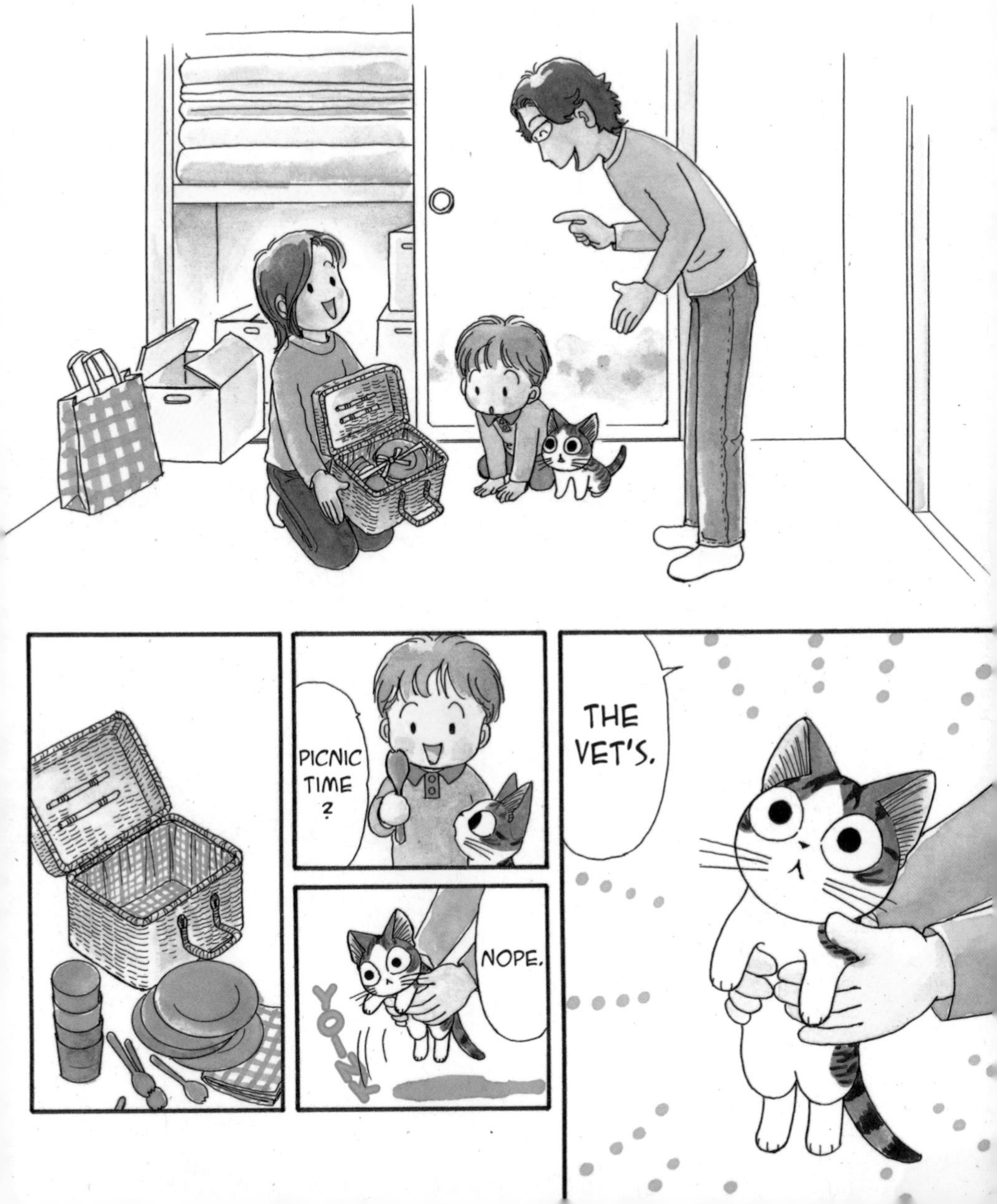
PICNIC TIME ?
NOPE.
YOINK
THE VET'S.

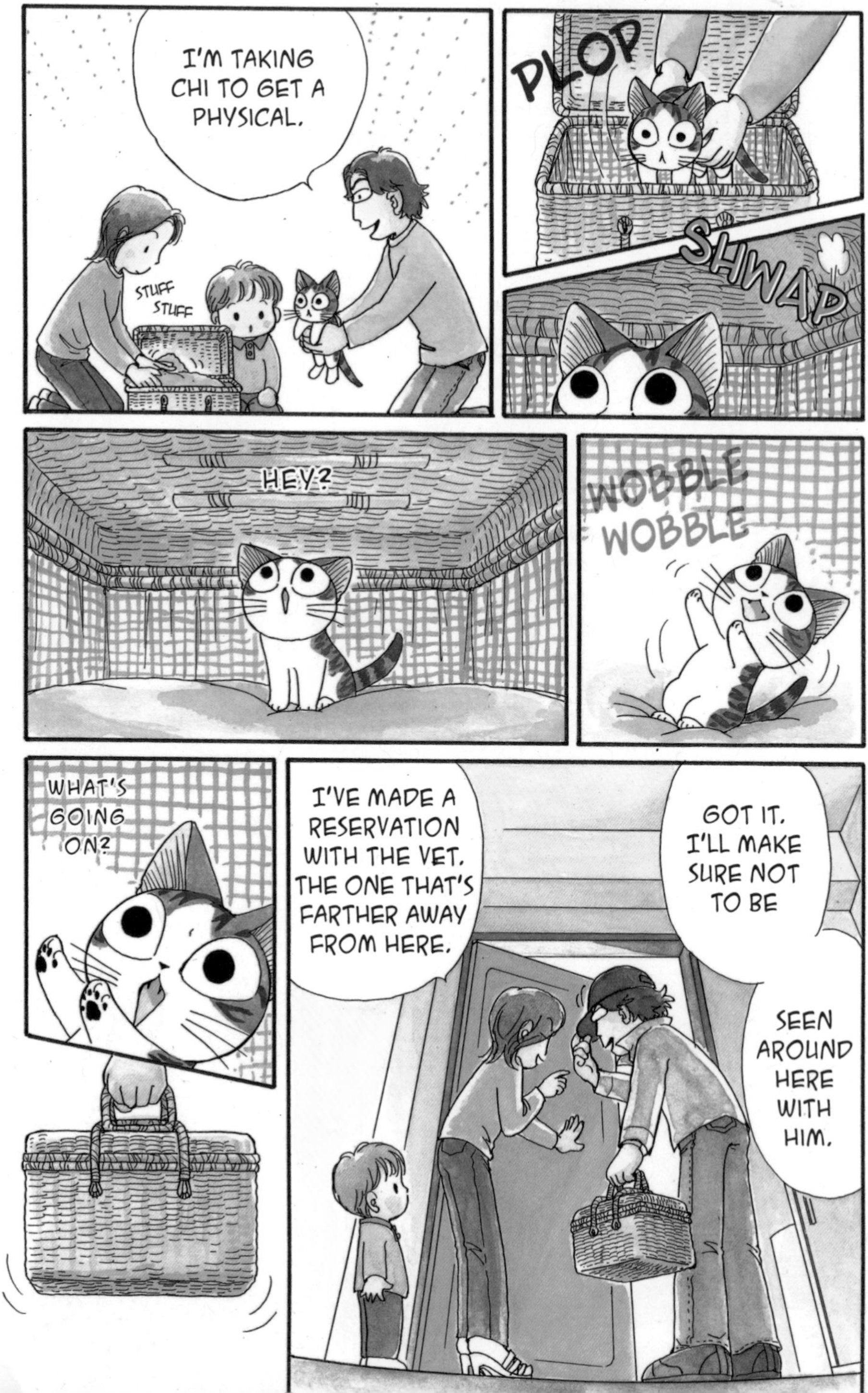
I'M TAKING CHI TO GET A PHYSICAL.
STUFF STUFF
PLOP
SHWAP
HEY?
WOBBLE WOBBLE
WHAT'S GOING ON?
I'VE MADE A RESERVATION WITH THE VET. THE ONE THAT'S FARTHER AWAY FROM HERE.
GOT IT. I'LL MAKE SURE NOT TO BE
SEEN AROUND HERE WITH HIM.

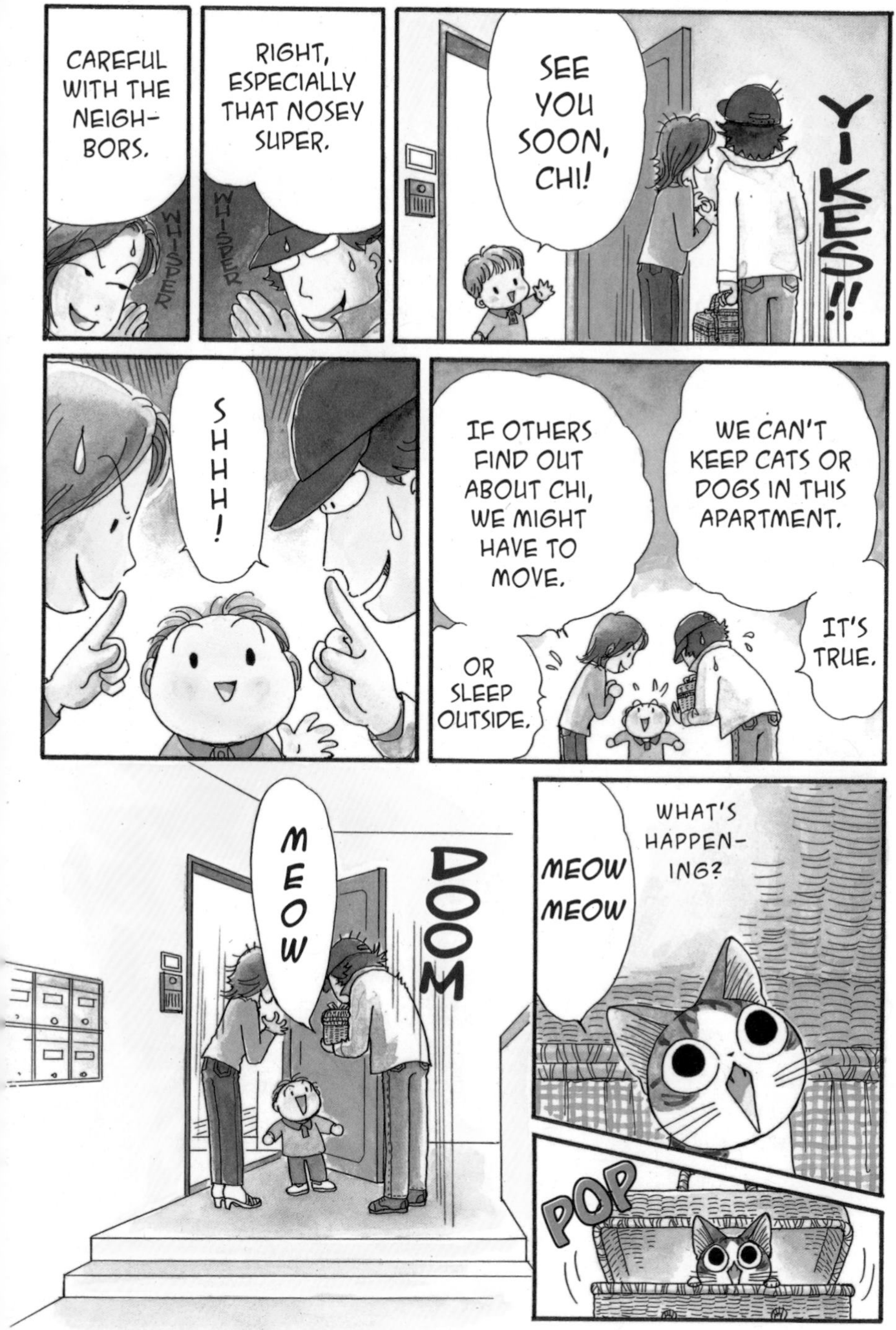
CAREFUL WITH THE NEIGH-BORS.
WHISPER
RIGHT, ESPECIALLY THAT NOSEY SUPER.
WHISPER
SEE YOU SOON, CHI!
YIKES!!
SHHH!
WE CAN'T KEEP CATS OR DOGS IN THIS APARTMENT.
IF OTHERS FIND OUT ABOUT CHI, WE MIGHT HAVE TO MOVE.
OR SLEEP OUTSIDE.
IT'S TRUE.
MEOW
DOOM
MEOW MEOW
WHAT'S HAPPEN-ING?
POP

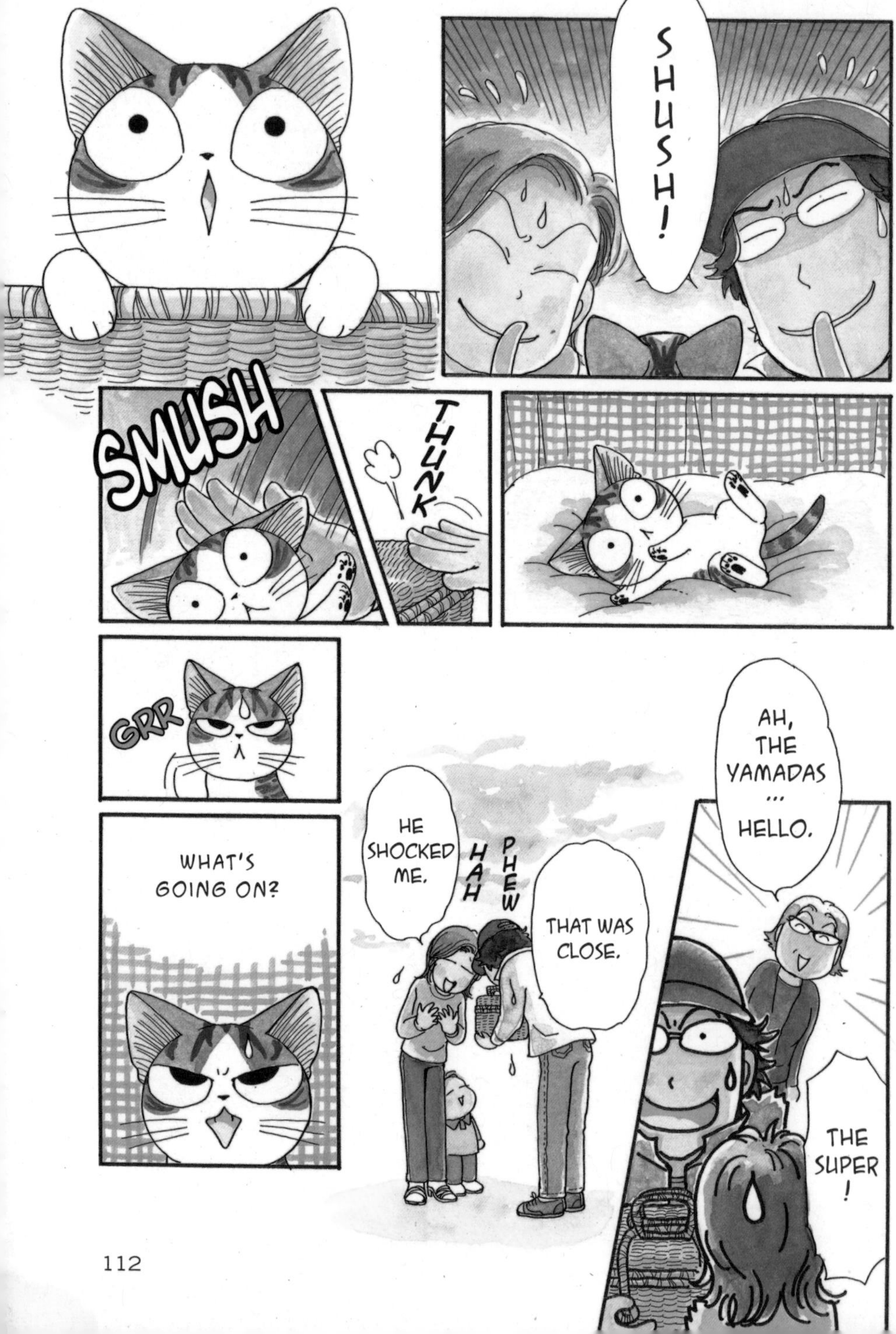
SHUSH!
SMUSH
THUNK
GRR
WHAT'S GOING ON?
HE SHOCKED ME.
HAH
PHEW
THAT WAS CLOSE.
AH, THE YAMADAS ... HELLO.
THE SUPER!

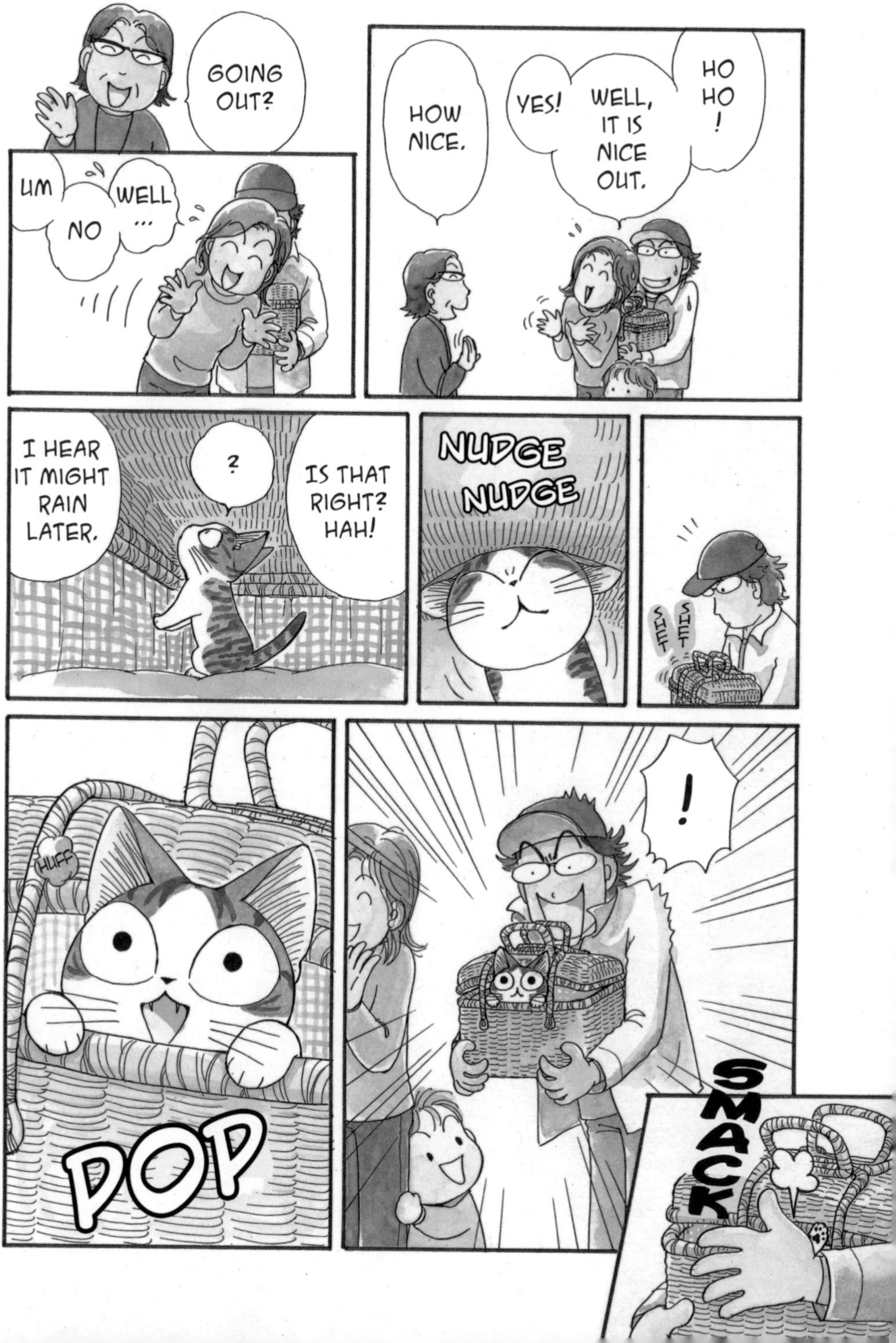
GOING OUT?
UM
NO
WELL ...
HOW NICE.
YES!
WELL, IT IS NICE OUT.
HO HO!
I HEAR IT MIGHT RAIN LATER.
?
IS THAT RIGHT? HAH!
NUDGE
NUDGE
SHFT
SHFT
HUFF
DOP
!
SMACK

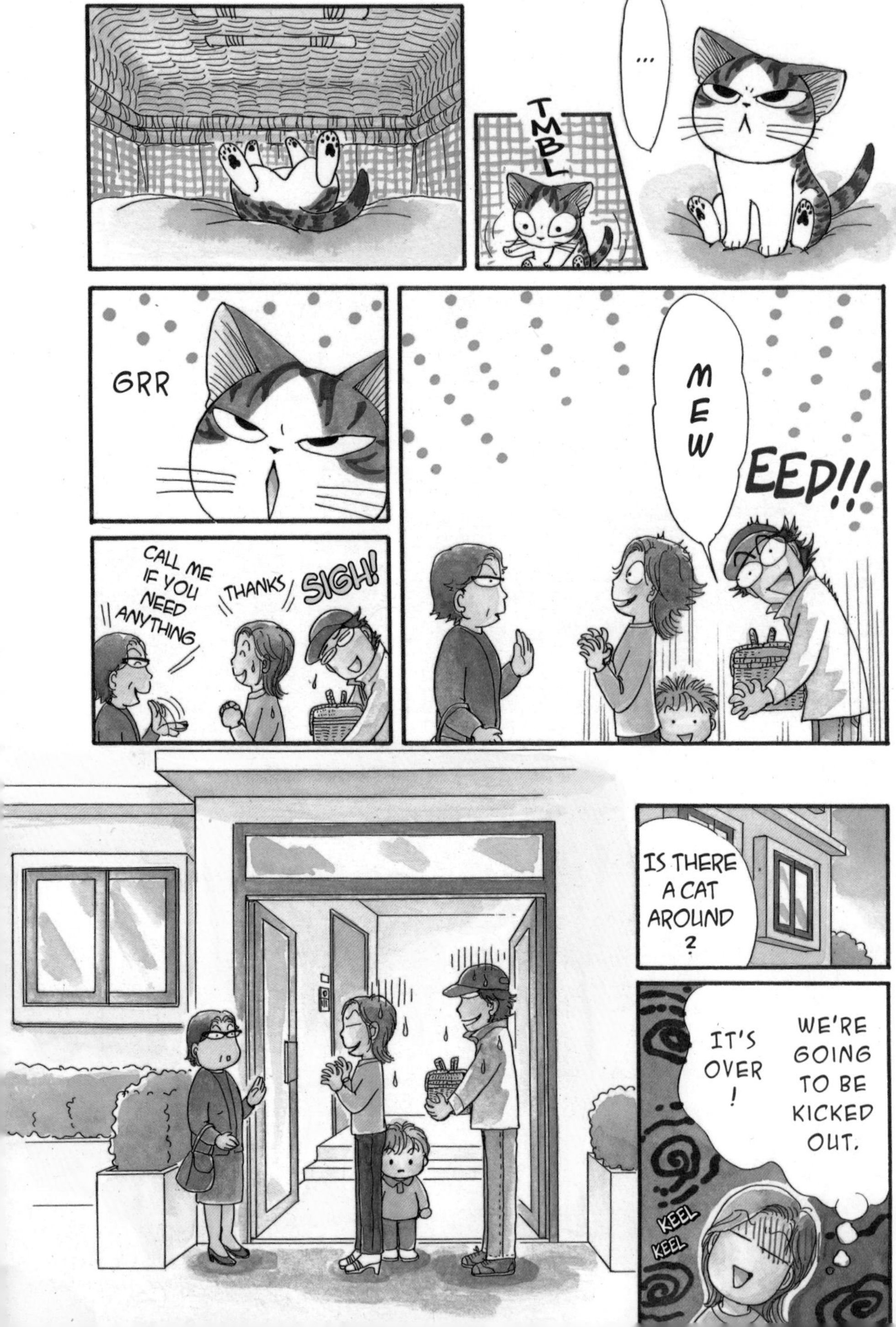

TMBL
...
GRR
MEW
EED!!
CALL ME IF YOU NEED ANYTHING
THANKS
SIGH!
IS THERE A CAT AROUND?
IT'S OVER!
WE'RE GOING TO BE KICKED OUT.
KEEL KEEL

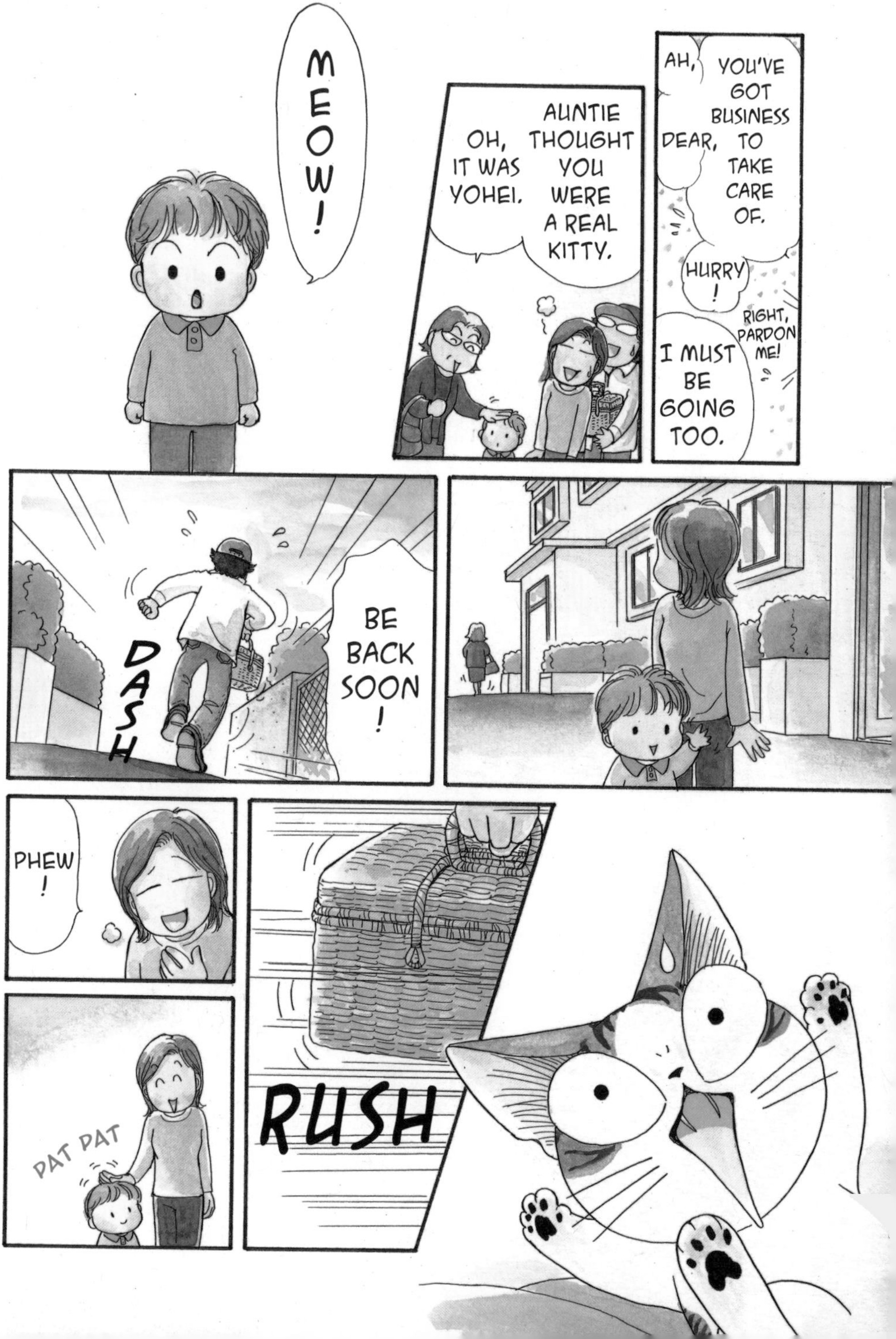
MEOW!
OH, IT WAS YOHEI.
AUNTIE THOUGHT YOU WERE A REAL KITTY.
AH, DEAR,
YOU'VE GOT BUSINESS TO TAKE CARE OF.
HURRY!
RIGHT, PARDON ME!
I MUST BE GOING TOO.
DASH
BE BACK SOON!
PHEW!
PAT PAT
RUSH

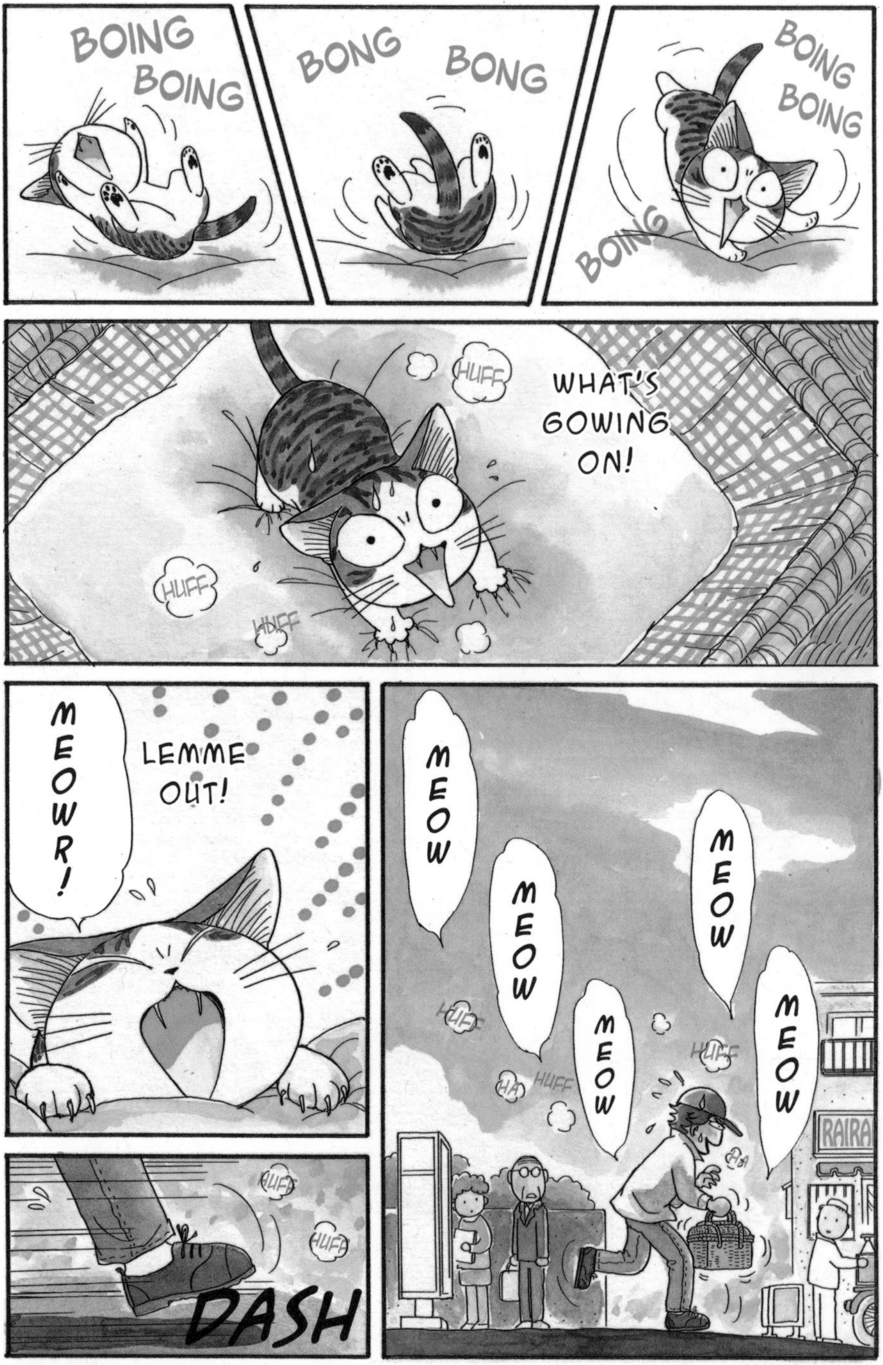
BOING
BOING
BONG
BONG
BOING
BOING
BOING
HUFF
WHAT'S GOWING ON!
HUFF
HUFF
MEOWR!
LEMME OUT!
HUFF
HUFF
DASH
MEOW
MEOW
HUFF
MEOW
MEOW
MEOW
HA
HUFF
HUFF
HA
RAIRA

the end

homemade 15: a cat goes to the vet (part 2)

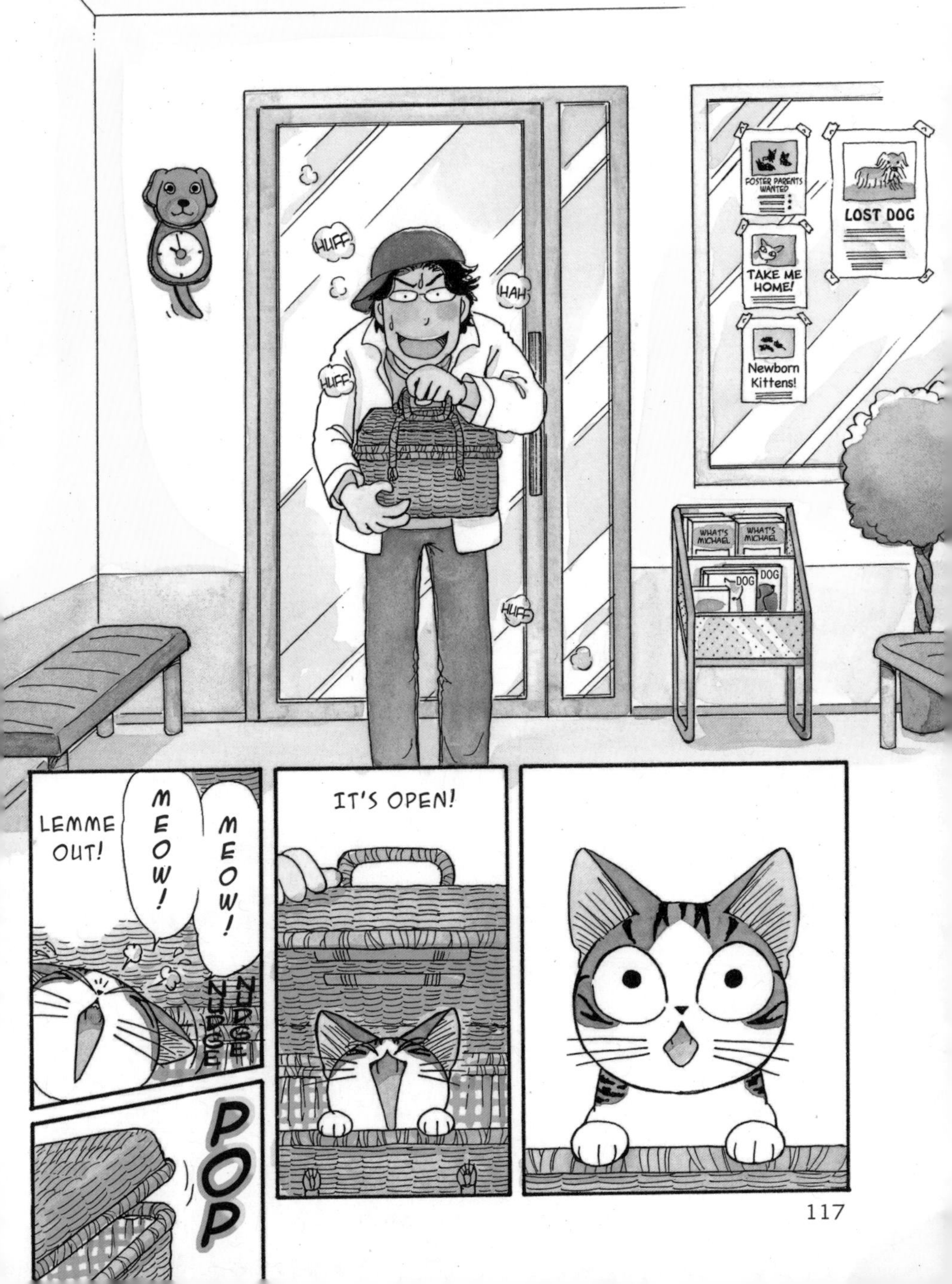
HUFF
HAH
HUFF
HUFF
FOSTER PARENTS WANTED
LOST DOG
TAKE ME HOME!
Newborn Kittens!
WHAT'S MICHAEL
WHAT'S MICHAEL
DOG
DOG
LEMME OUT!
MEOW!
MEOW!
NUDGE
NUDGE
POP
IT'S OPEN!

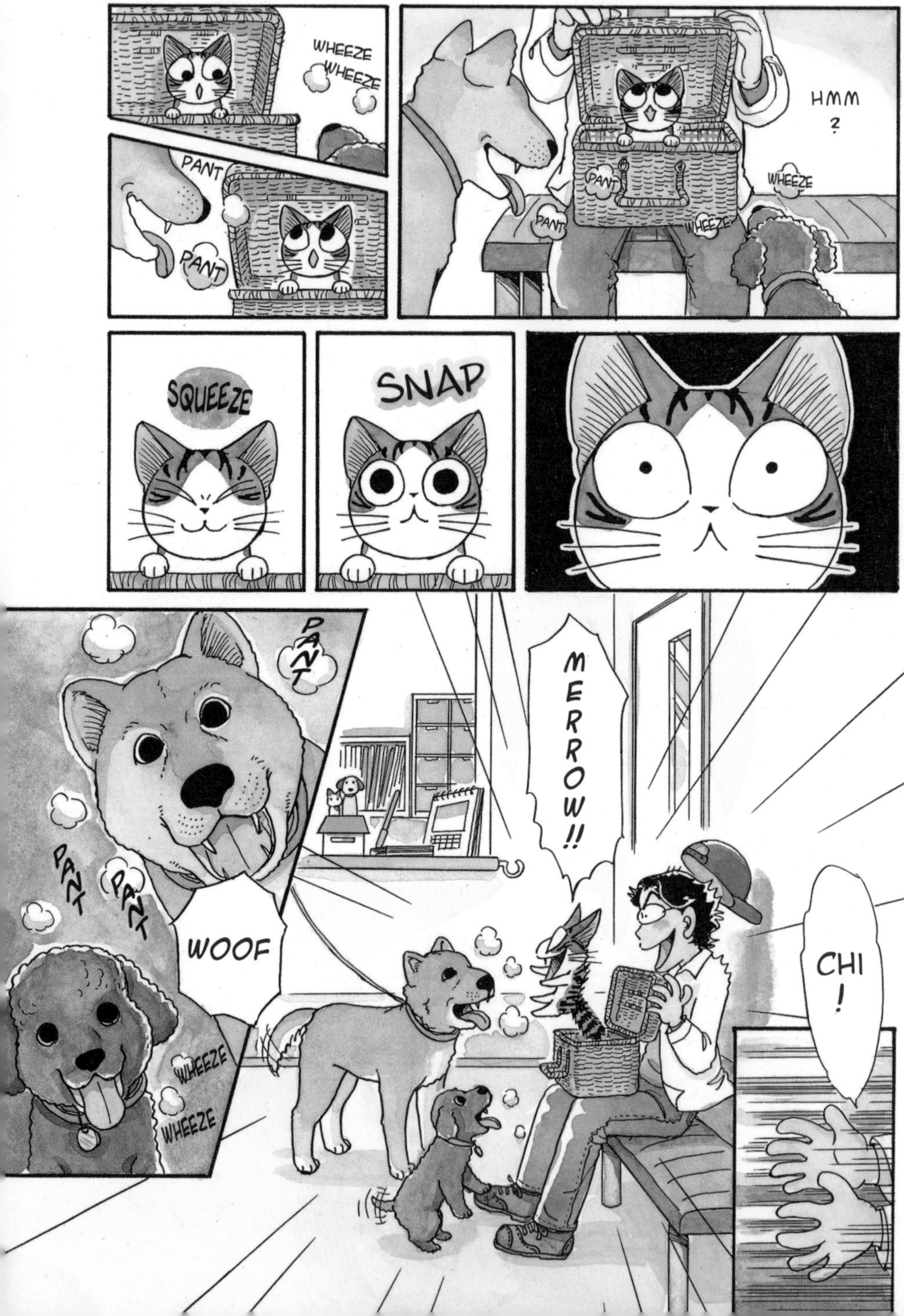
WHEEZE
WHEEZE
PANT
PANT
HMM ?
PANT
PANT
WHEEZE
WHEEZE
SQUEEZE
SNAP
PANT
PANT
PANT
WOOF
WHEEZE
WHEEZE
MERROW!!
CHI!

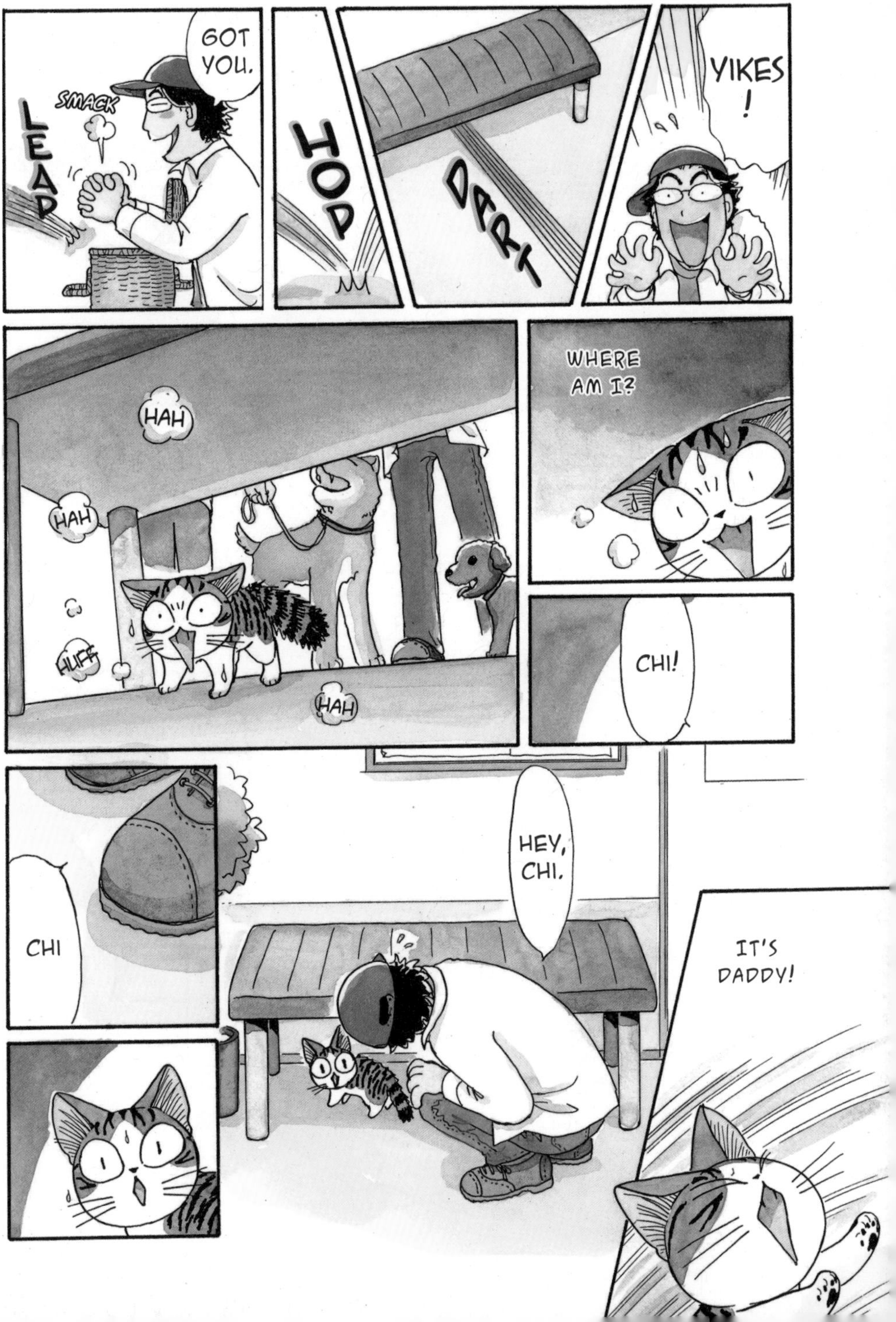
LEAD
SMACK
GOT YOU.
HOP
DART
YIKES!
HAH
HAH
HUFF
HAH
WHERE AM I?
CHI!
CHI
HEY, CHI.
IT'S DADDY!

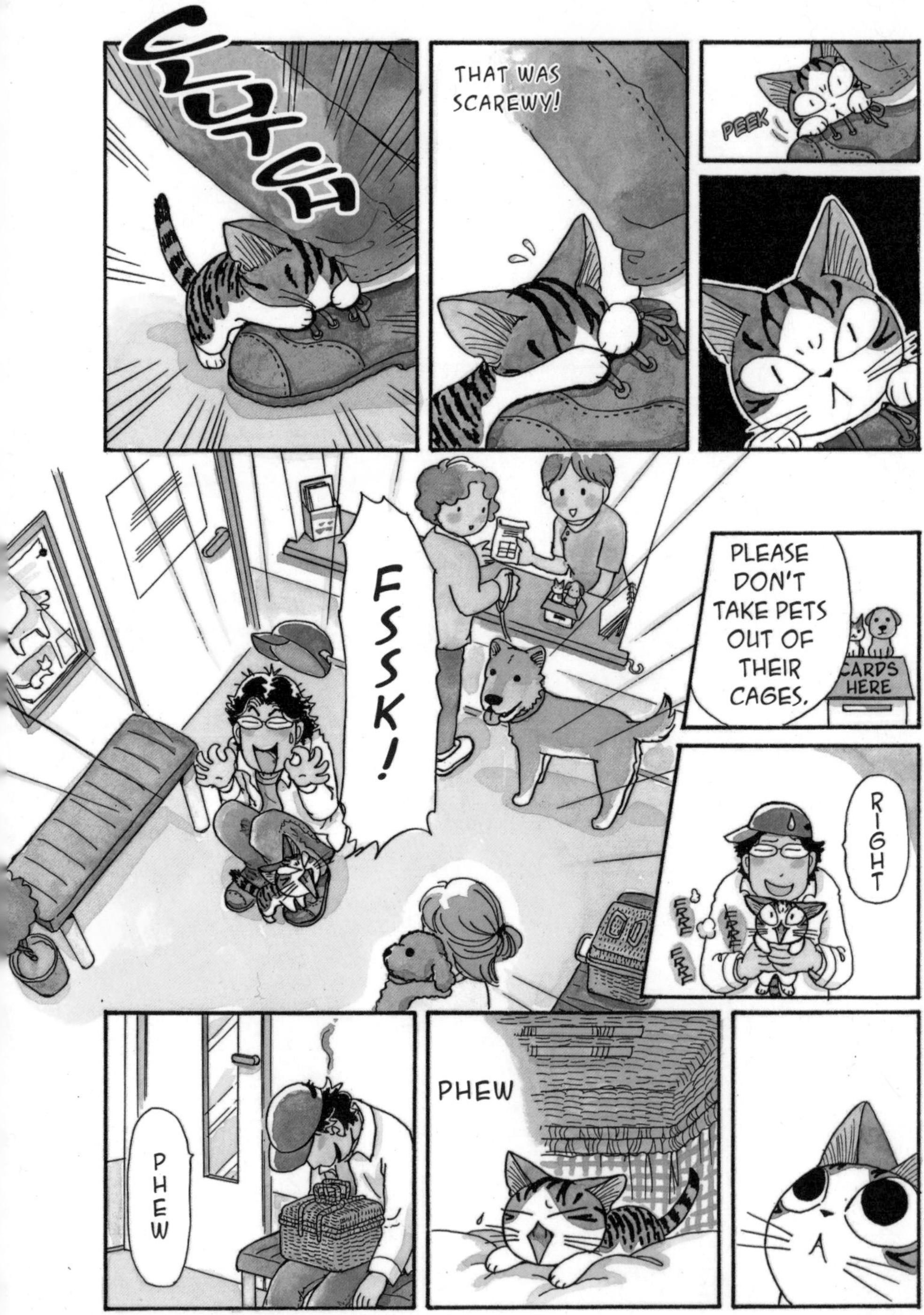
CLUTCH
THAT WAS SCAREWY!
PEEK
FSSK!
PLEASE DON'T TAKE PETS OUT OF THEIR CAGES.
CARDS HERE
RIGHT
PHEW
PHEW

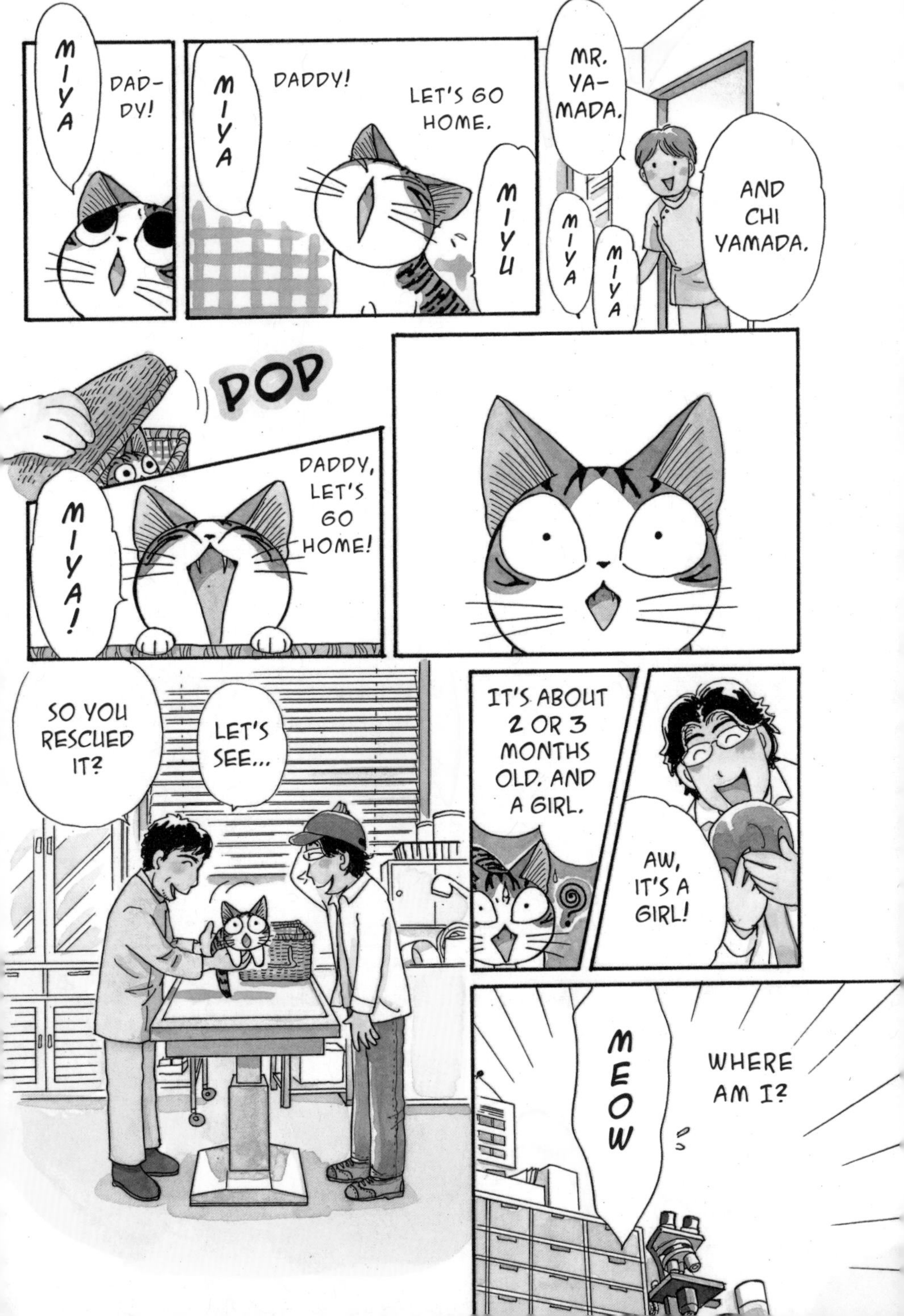
MIYA
DADDY!
MIYA
DADDY!
LET'S GO HOME.
MIYU
MR. YAMADA.
MIYA
MIYA
AND CHI YAMADA.
POP
DADDY, LET'S GO HOME!
MIYA!
SO YOU RESCUED IT?
LET'S SEE...
IT'S ABOUT 2 OR 3 MONTHS OLD. AND A GIRL.
AW, IT'S A GIRL!
MEOW
WHERE AM I?

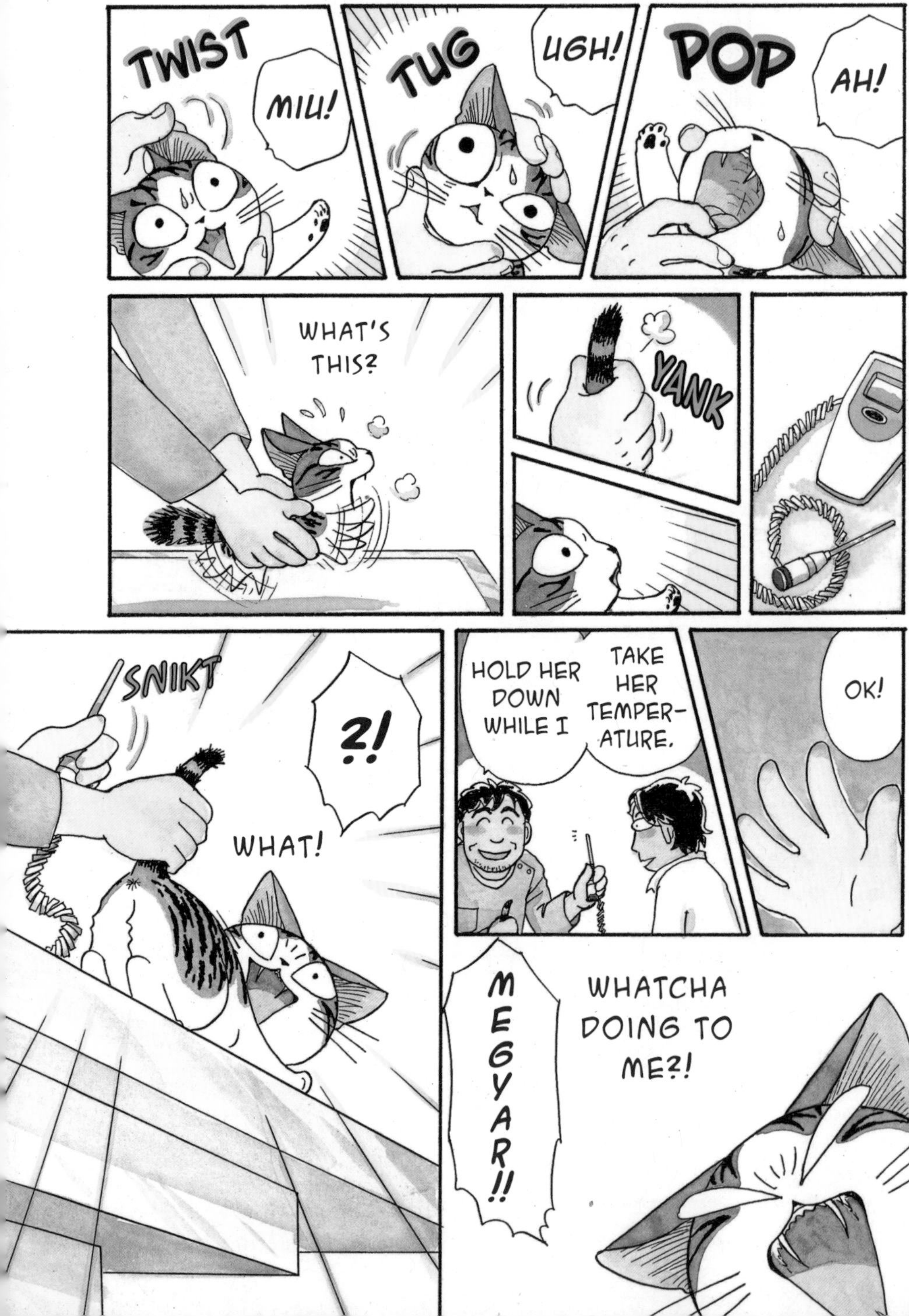
TWIST
MIU!
TUG
UGH!
POP
AH!
WHAT'S THIS?
YANK
SNIKT
?!
WHAT!
HOLD HER DOWN WHILE I
TAKE HER TEMPER-ATURE.
OK!
MEGYAR!!
WHATCHA DOING TO ME?!

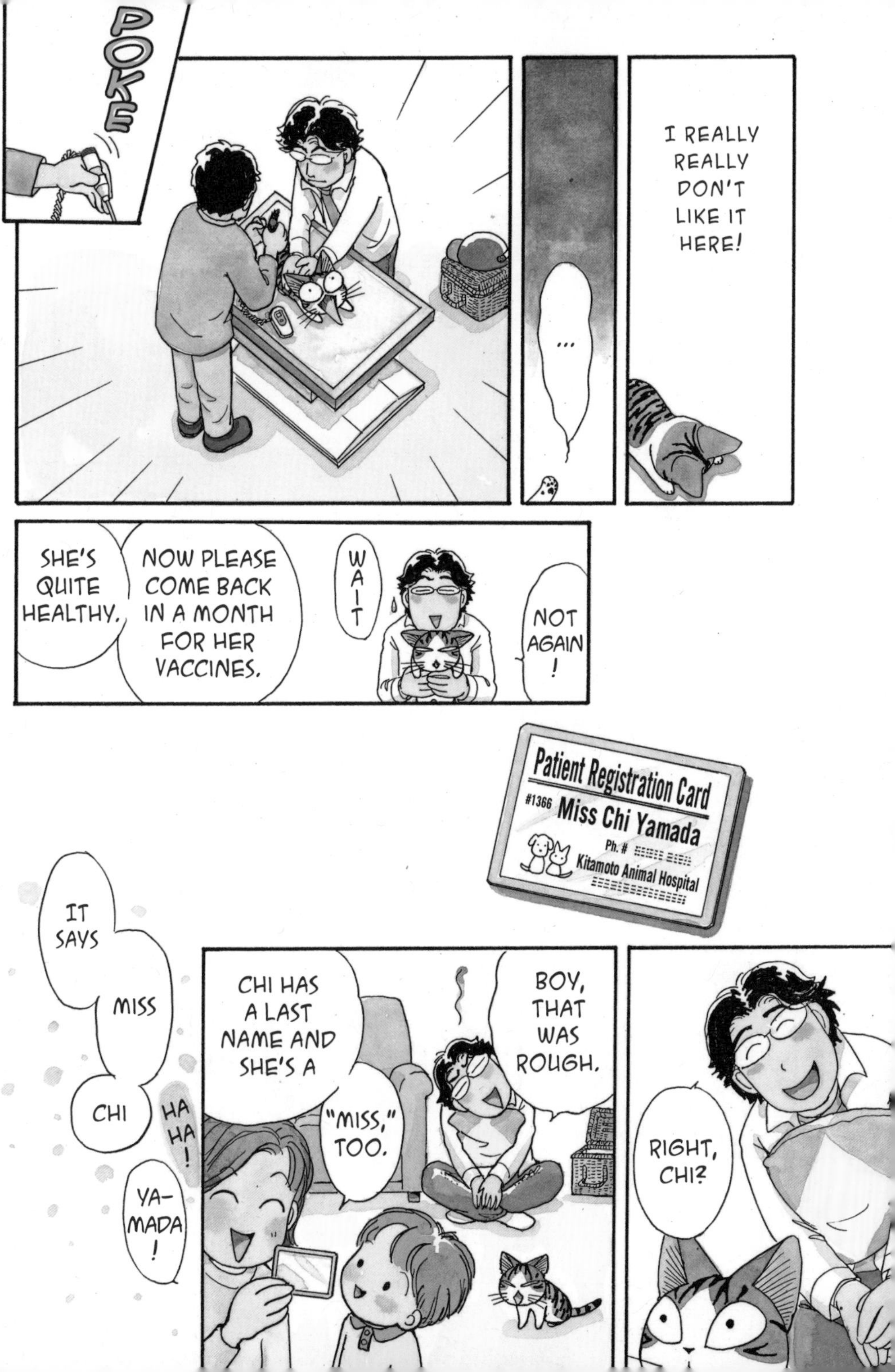
POKE
...
I REALLY REALLY DON'T LIKE IT HERE!
SHE'S QUITE HEALTHY.
NOW PLEASE COME BACK IN A MONTH FOR HER VACCINES.
WAIT
NOT AGAIN!
Patient Registration Card
#1366 Miss Chi Yamada
Ph. #
Kitamoto Animal Hospital
IT SAYS
MISS
CHI
YA-MADA!
HA HA!
CHI HAS A LAST NAME AND SHE'S A
"MISS," TOO.
BOY, THAT WAS ROUGH.
RIGHT, CHI?

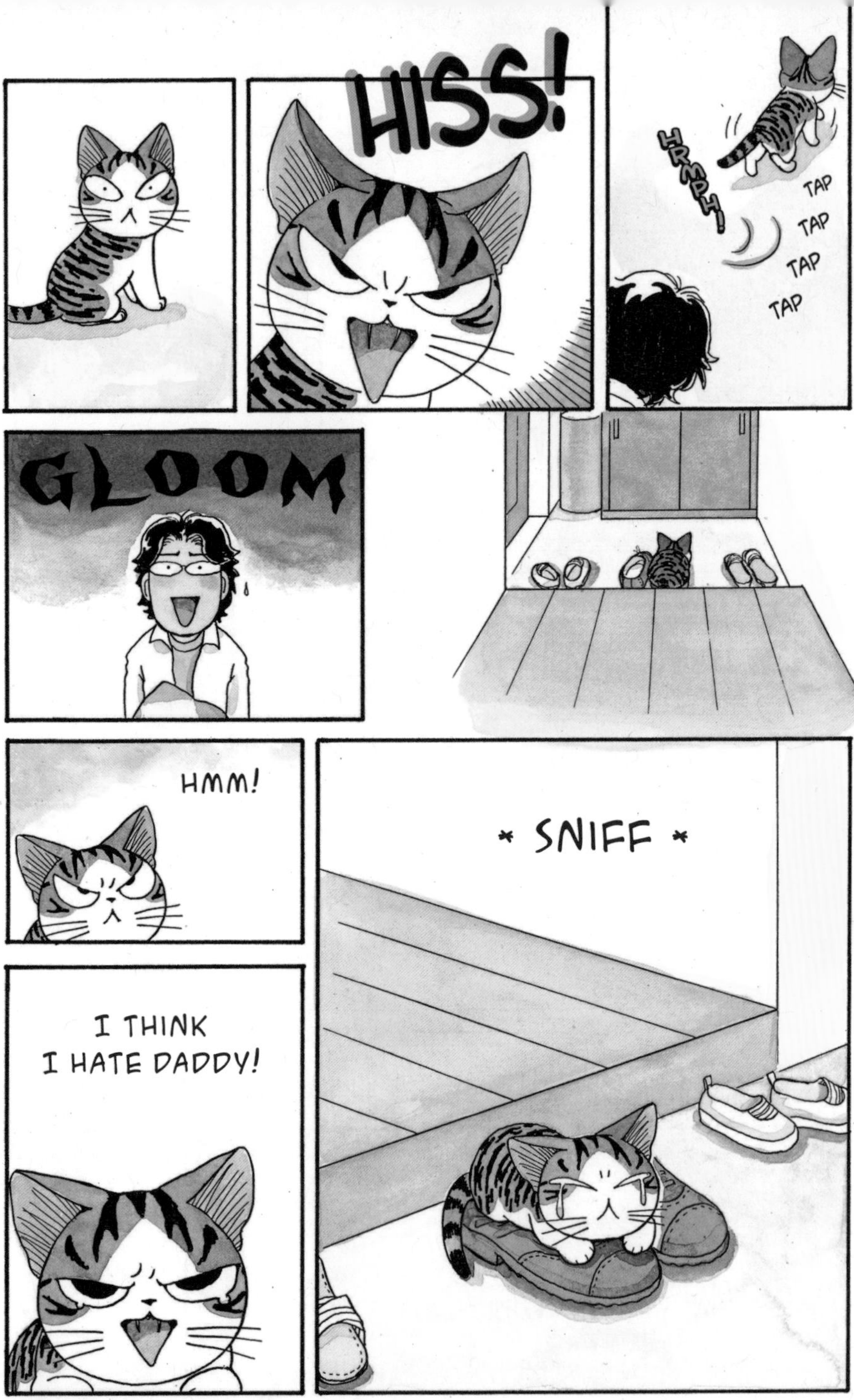
HISS!
HRMPH!
TAP
TAP
TAP
TAP
GLOOM
HMM!
I THINK
I HATE DADDY!
* SNIFF *

the end

homemade 16: a cat fears

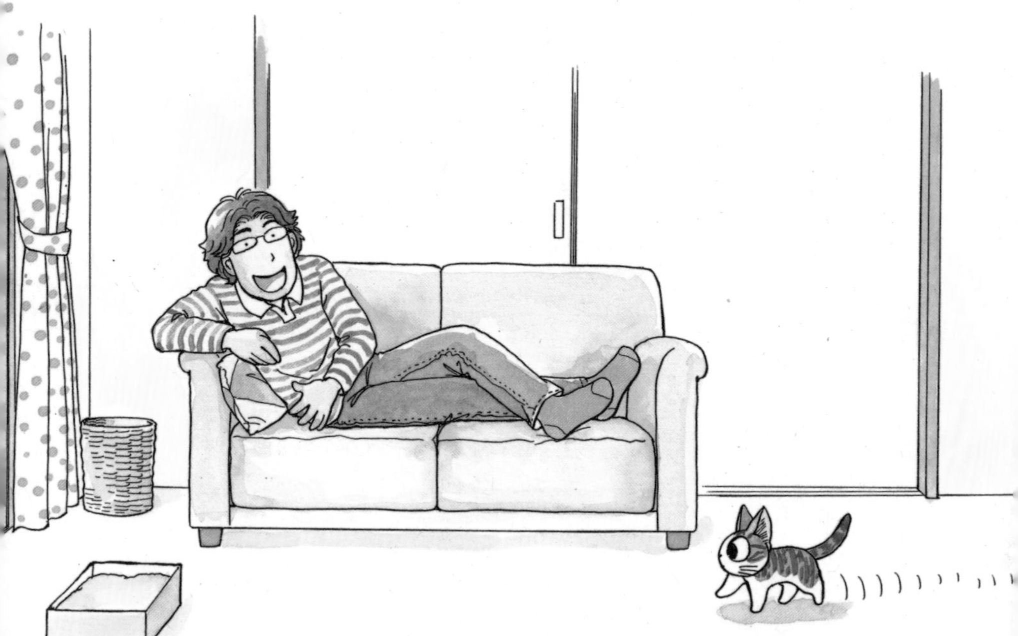

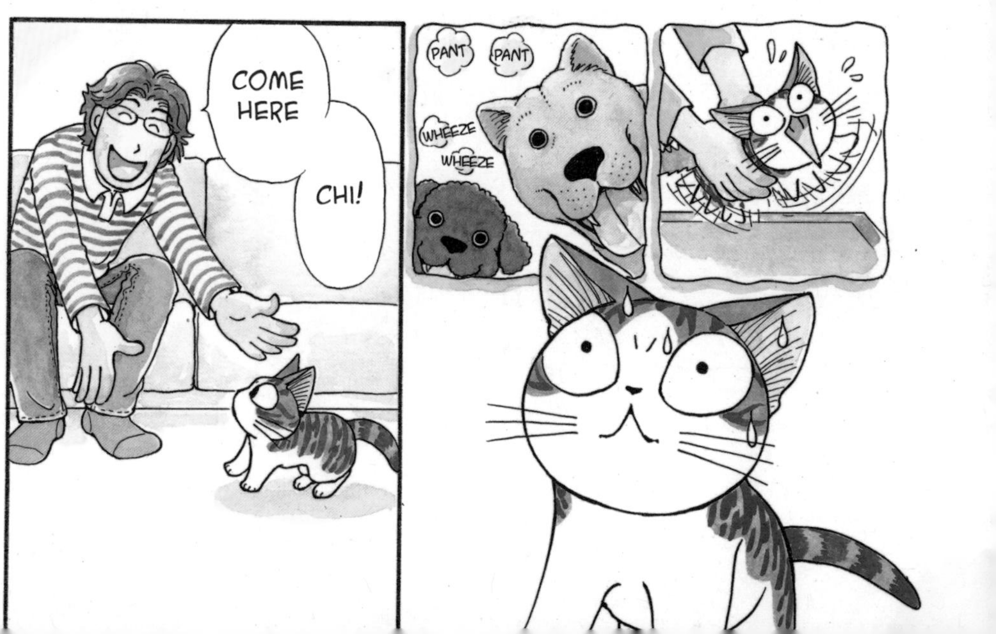
COME HERE
CHI!
PANT
PANT
WHEEZE
WHEEZE

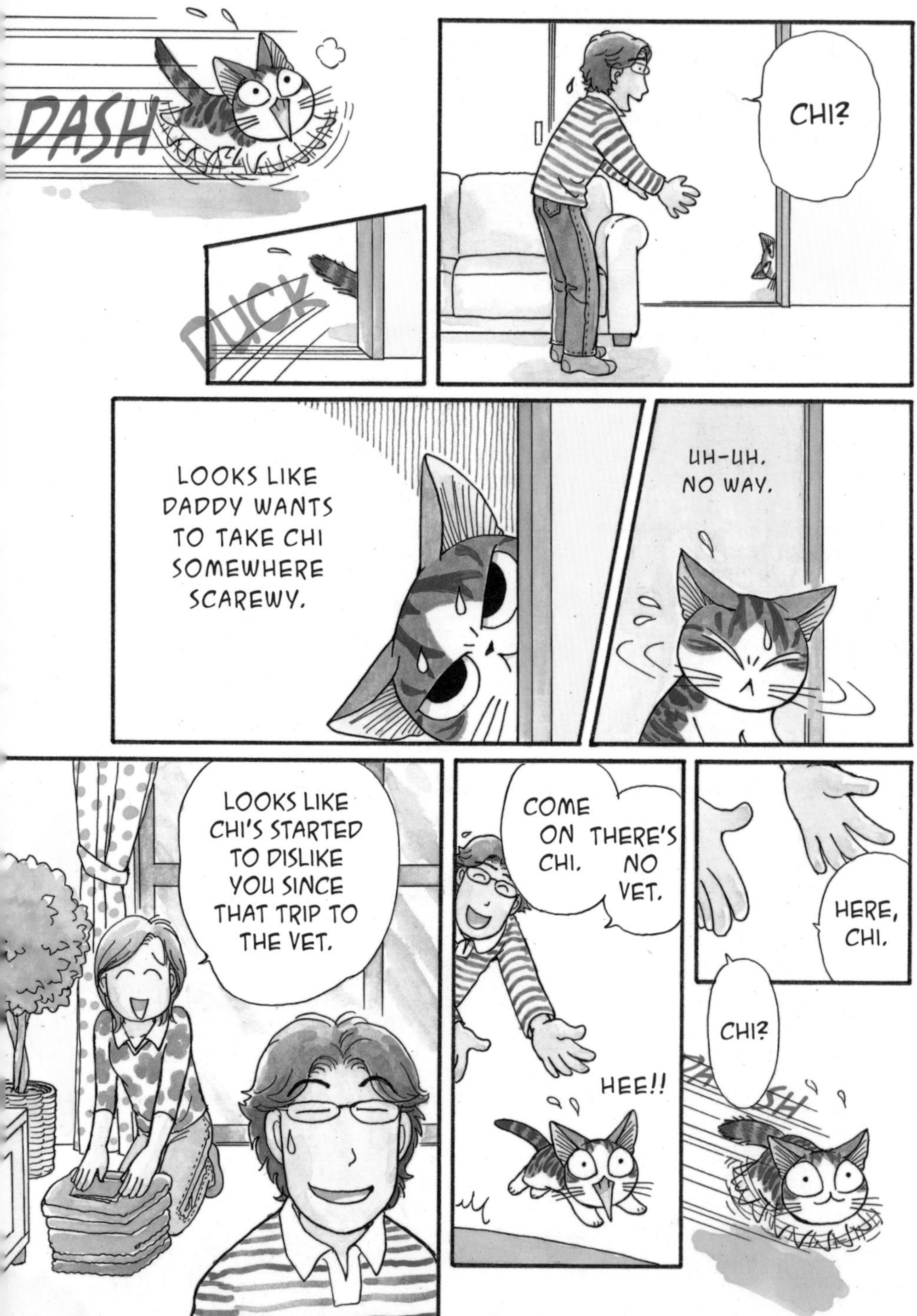
DASH
DUCK
CHI?
LOOKS LIKE DADDY WANTS TO TAKE CHI SOMEWHERE SCAREWY.
UH-UH. NO WAY.
LOOKS LIKE CHI'S STARTED TO DISLIKE YOU SINCE THAT TRIP TO THE VET.
COME ON CHI.
THERE'S NO VET.
HEE!!
HERE, CHI.
CHI?

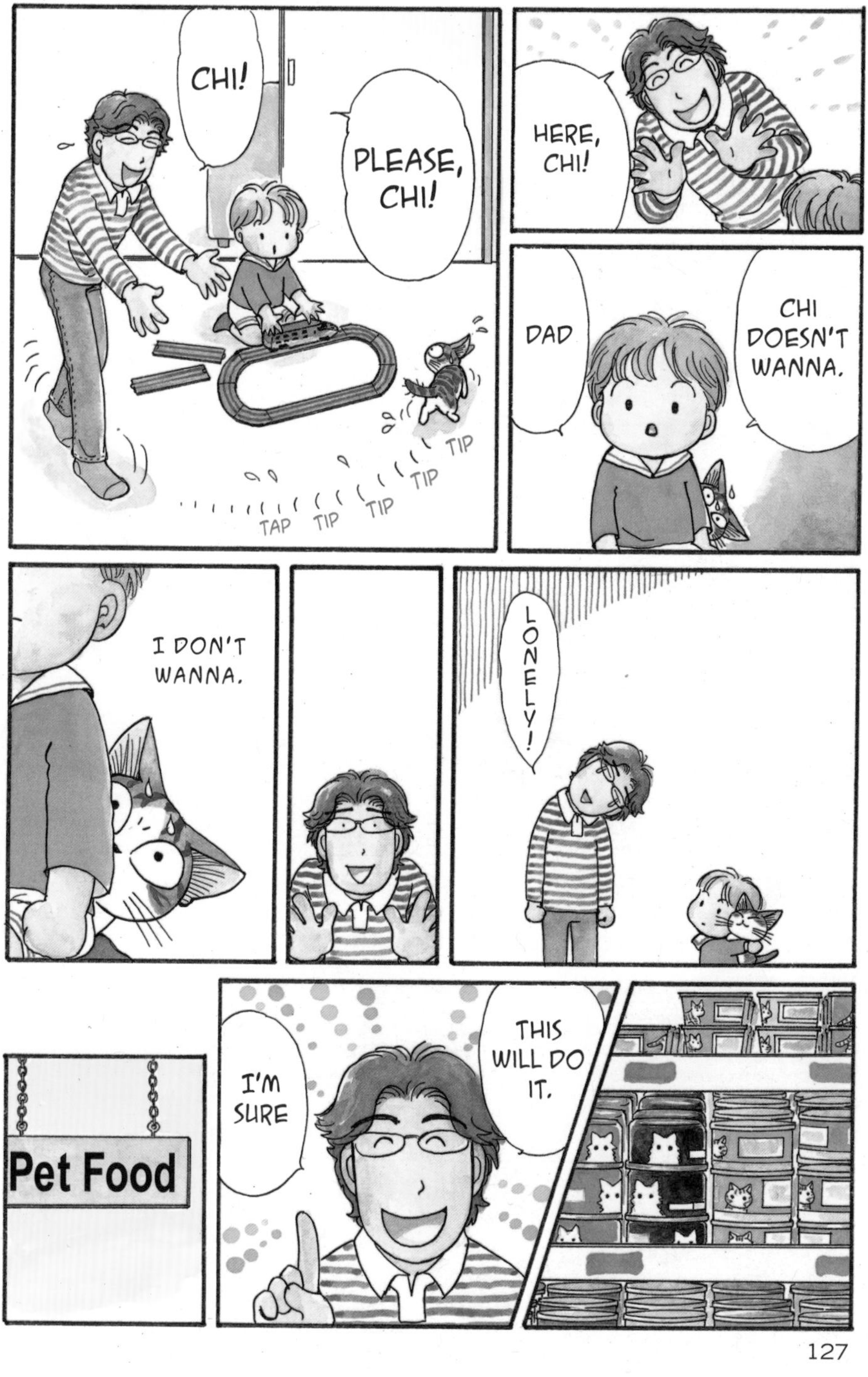
CHI!
PLEASE, CHI!
TAP TIP TIP TIP TIP
HERE, CHI!
DAD
CHI DOESN'T WANNA.
I DON'T WANNA.
LONELY!
Pet Food
I'M SURE
THIS WILL DO IT.

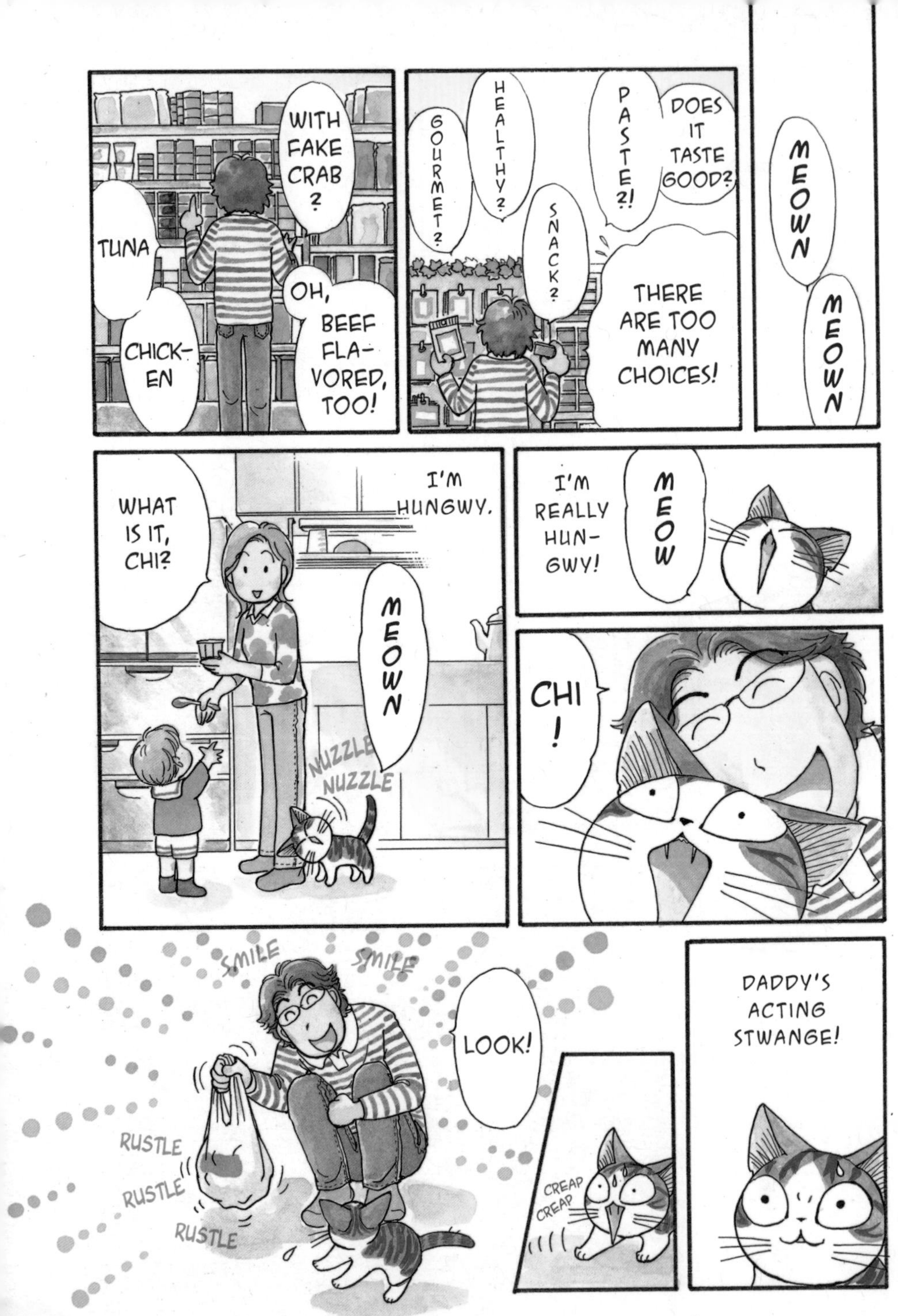
WITH FAKE CRAB?
TUNA
OH, BEEF FLA-VORED, TOO!
CHICK-EN
GOURMET?
HEALTHY?
PASTE?!
DOES IT TASTE GOOD?
SNACK?
THERE ARE TOO MANY CHOICES!
MEOWN
MEOWN
WHAT IS IT, CHI?
I'M HUNGWY.
MEOWN
NUZZLE NUZZLE
I'M REALLY HUN-GWY!
MEOW
CHI!
SMILE
SMILE
LOOK!
RUSTLE
RUSTLE
RUSTLE
CREAP CREAP
DADDY'S ACTING STWANGE!

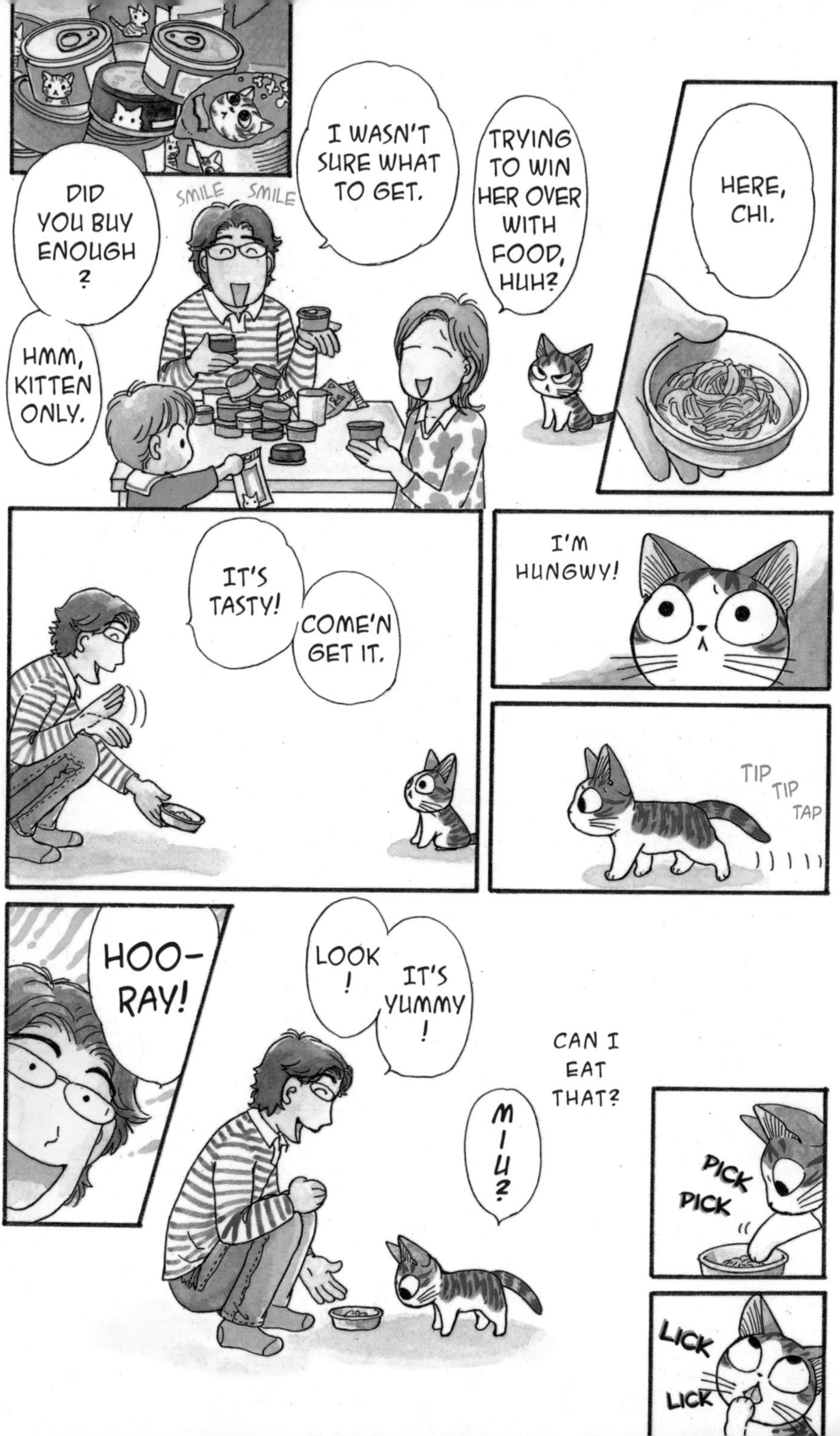
DID YOU BUY ENOUGH?
HMM, KITTEN ONLY.
SMILE SMILE
I WASN'T SURE WHAT TO GET.
TRYING TO WIN HER OVER WITH FOOD, HUH?
HERE, CHI.
IT'S TASTY!
COME'N GET IT.
I'M HUNGWY!
TIP TIP TAP
HOO-RAY!
LOOK!
IT'S YUMMY!
MIU?
CAN I EAT THAT?
PICK PICK
LICK LICK

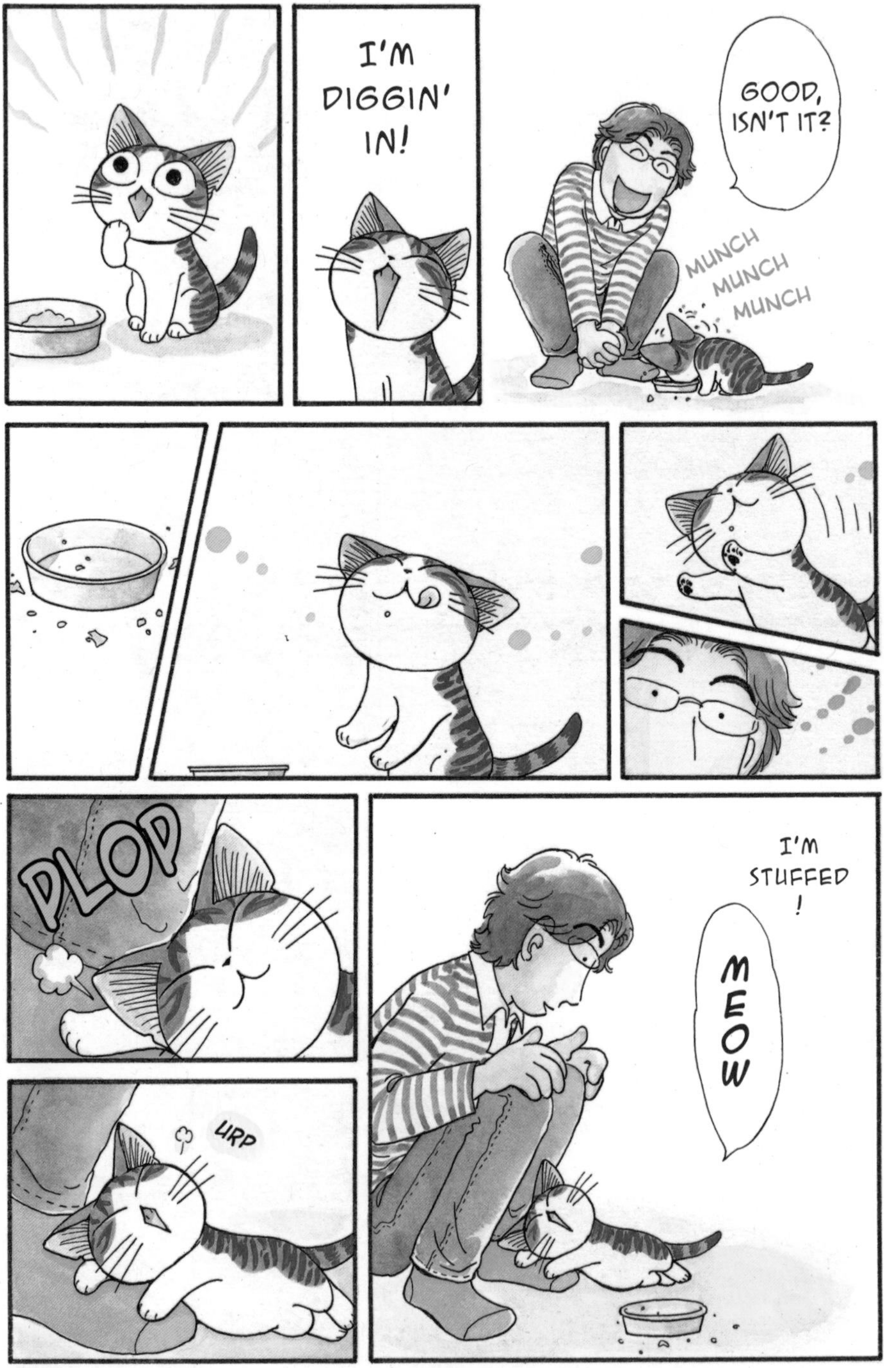
I'M DIGGIN' IN!
GOOD, ISN'T IT?
MUNCH MUNCH MUNCH
PLOP
I'M STUFFED!
MEOW
URP

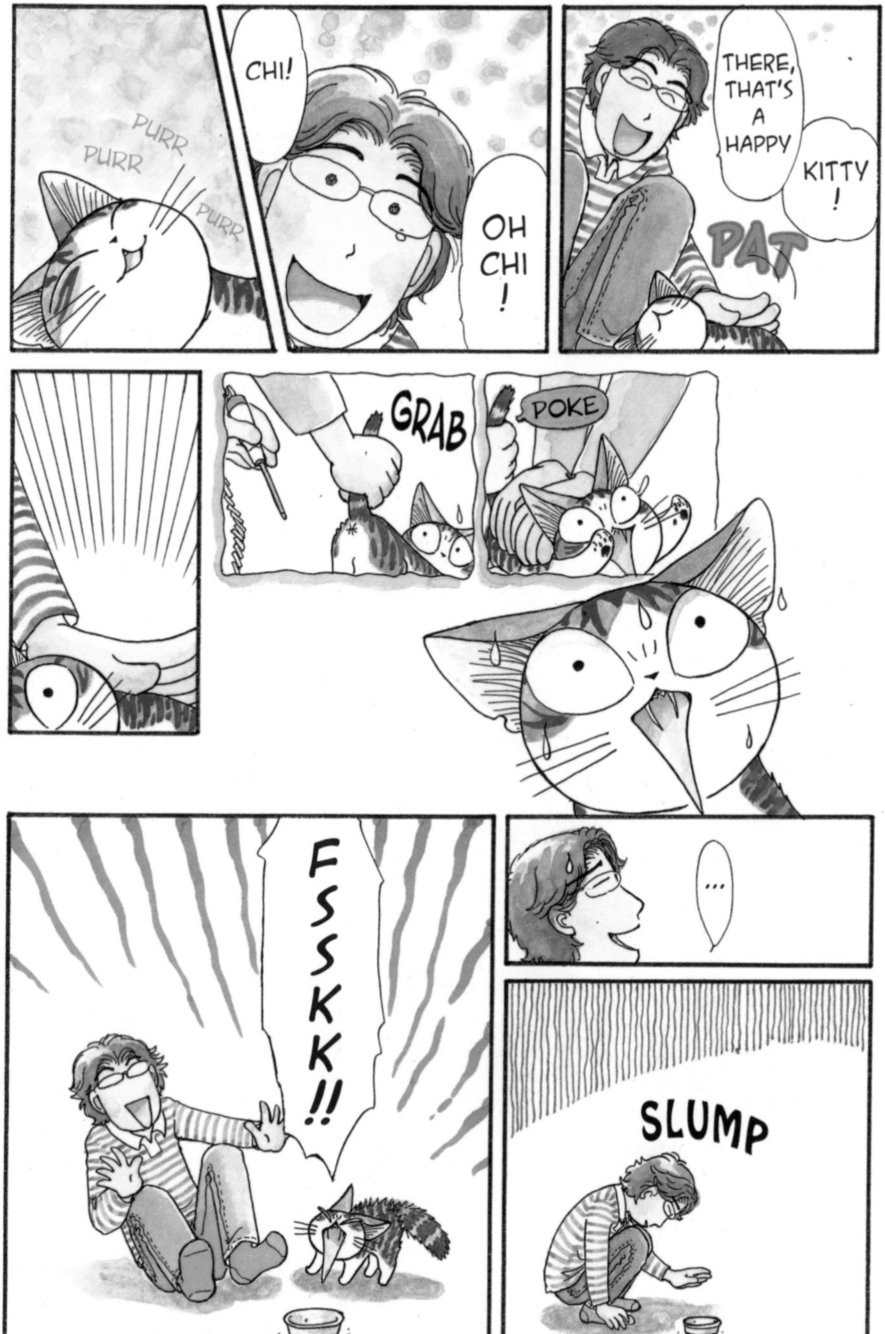
PURR
PURR
PURR
CHI!
OH CHI!
THERE, THAT'S A HAPPY
KITTY!
PAT
GRAB
POKE
FSSKK!!
...
SLUMP

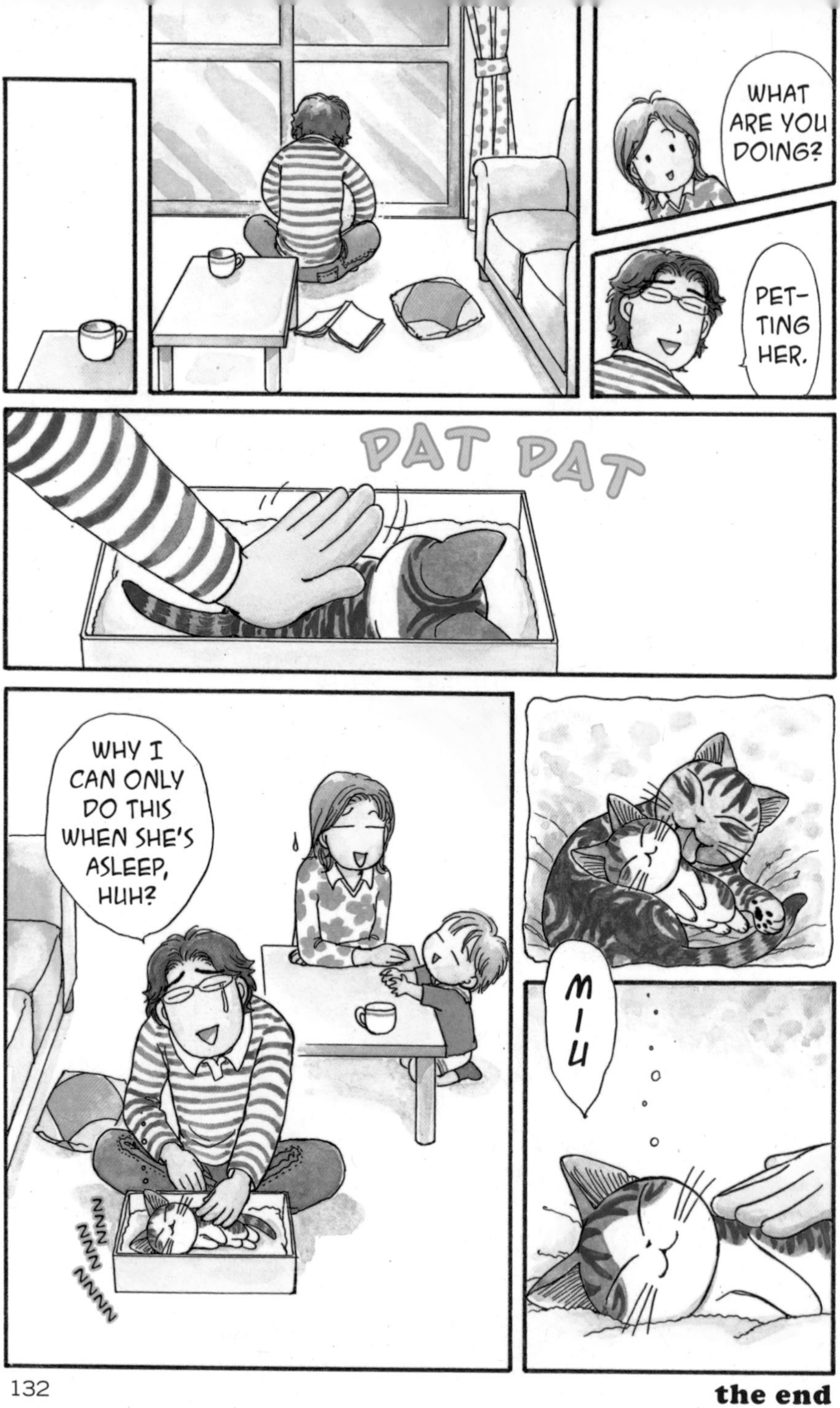
WHAT ARE YOU DOING?
PET-TING HER.
PAT PAT
WHY I CAN ONLY DO THIS WHEN SHE'S ASLEEP, HUH?
NNN NNN NNNN
MIU

the end

homemade 17: a cat discovers

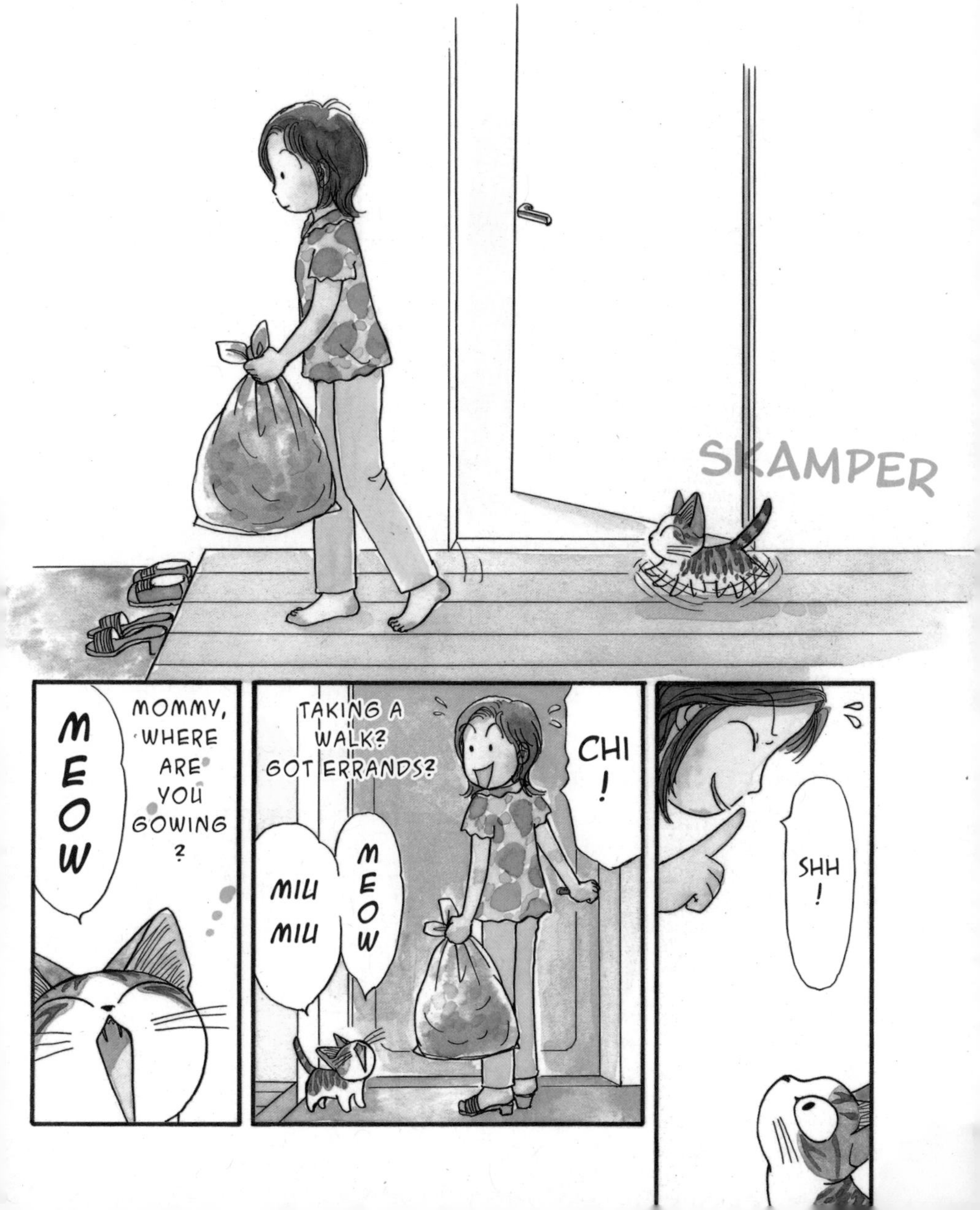

SKAMPER
MEOW
MOMMY, WHERE ARE YOU GOWING?
TAKING A WALK? GOT ERRANDS?
CHI!
MIU MIU
MEOW
SHH!

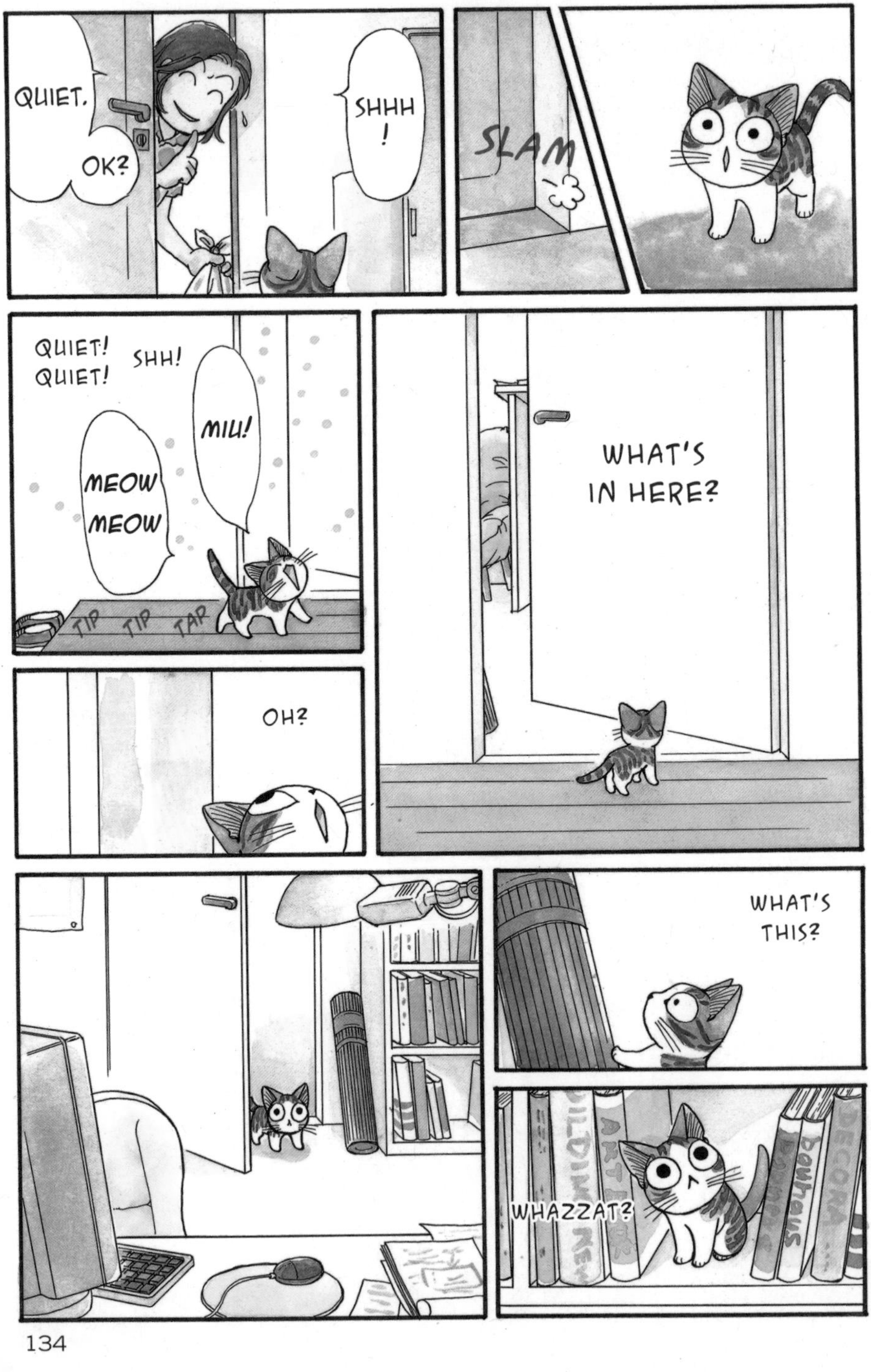
QUIET.
OK?
SHHH!
SLAM
QUIET! QUIET!
SHH!
MEOW MEOW
MIU!
TIP TIP TAP
OH?
WHAT'S IN HERE?
WHAT'S THIS?
WHAZZAT?

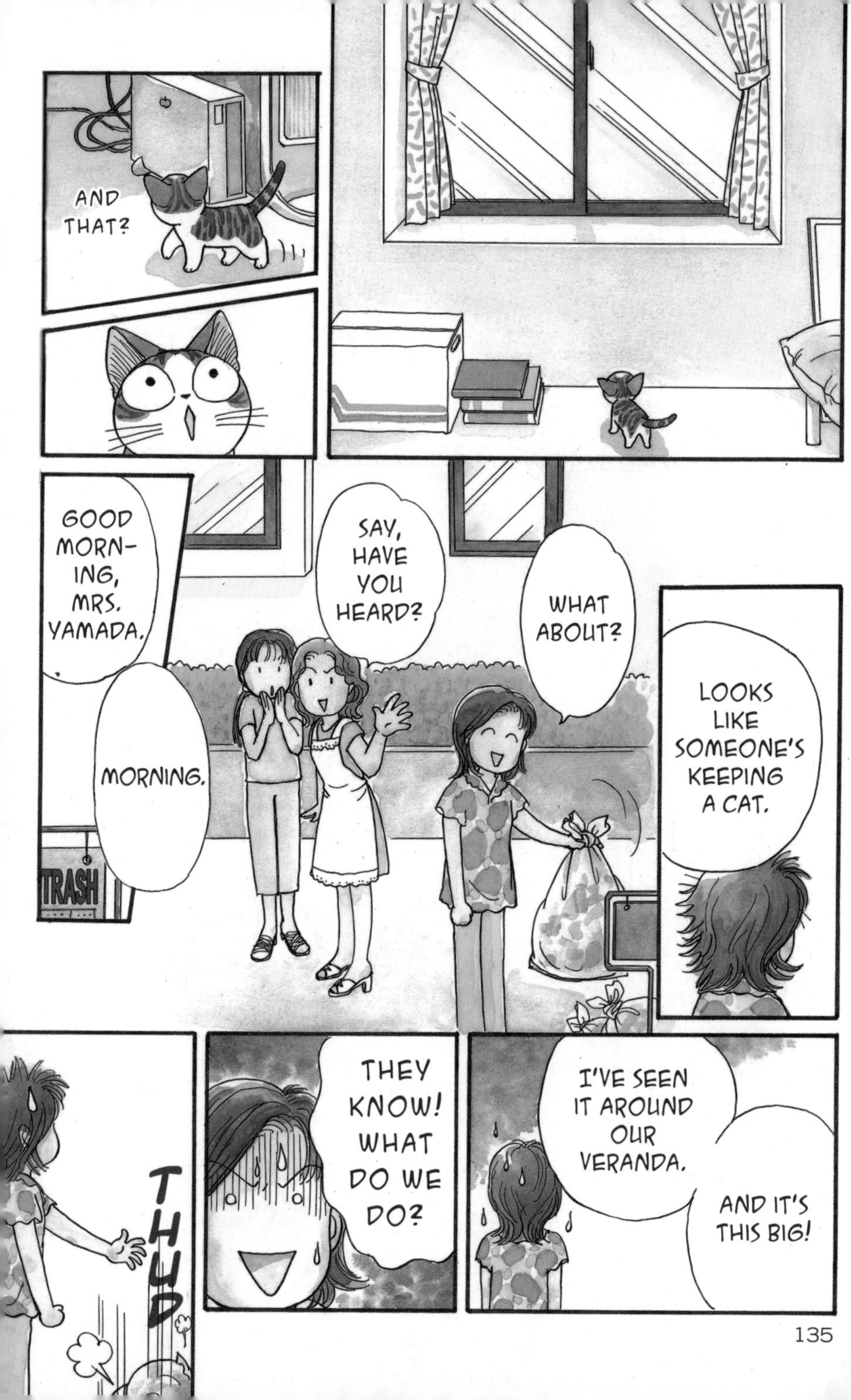

AND THAT?
GOOD MORNING, MRS. YAMADA.
MORNING.
SAY, HAVE YOU HEARD?
WHAT ABOUT?
LOOKS LIKE SOMEONE'S KEEPING A CAT.
TRASH
THUD
THEY KNOW! WHAT DO WE DO?
I'VE SEEN IT AROUND OUR VERANDA.
AND IT'S THIS BIG!

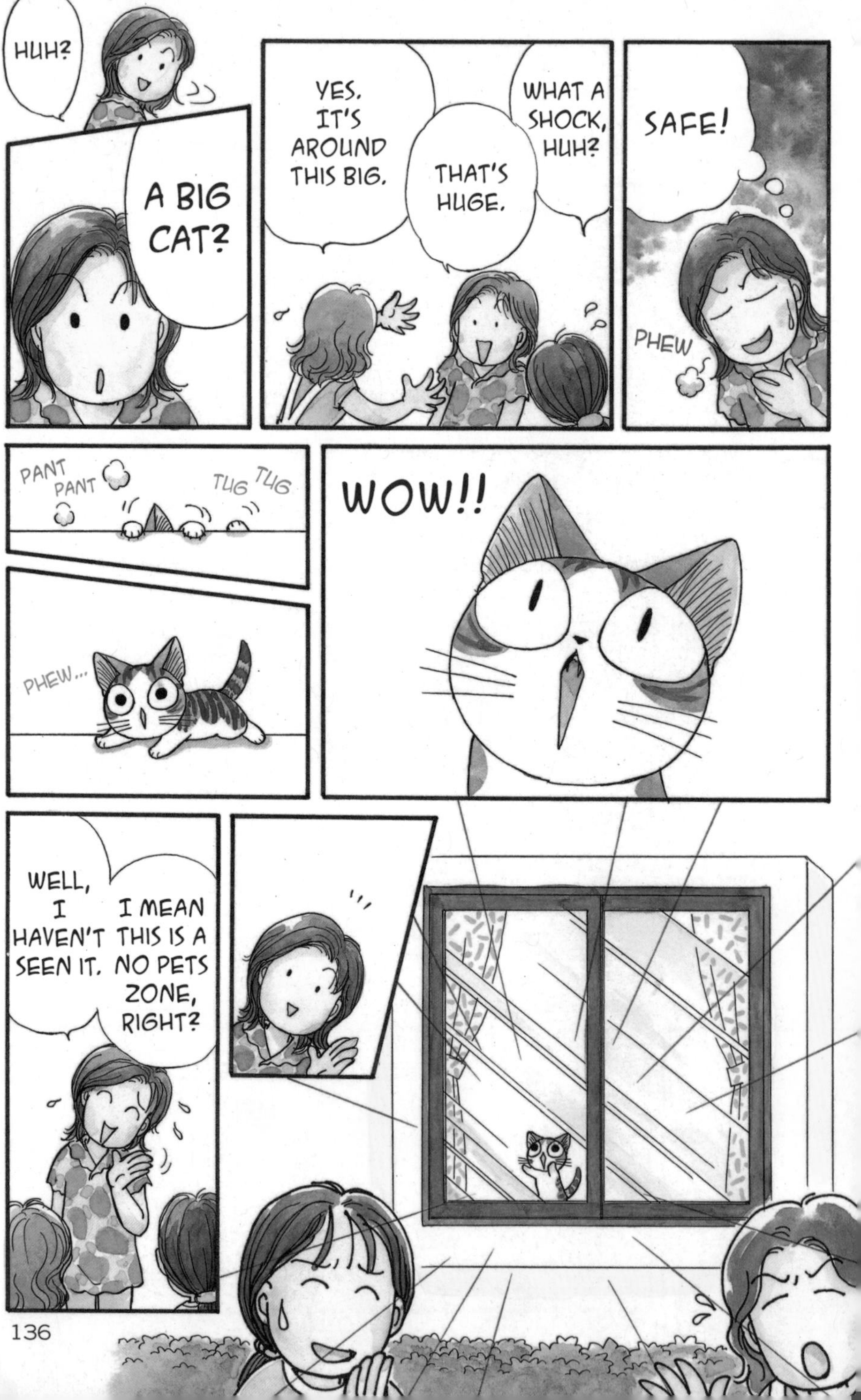
HUH?
A BIG CAT?
YES. IT'S AROUND THIS BIG.
WHAT A SHOCK, HUH?
THAT'S HUGE.
SAFE!
PHEW
PANT PANT
TUG TUG
PHEW...
WOW!!
WELL, I HAVEN'T SEEN IT.
I MEAN THIS IS A NO PETS ZONE, RIGHT?

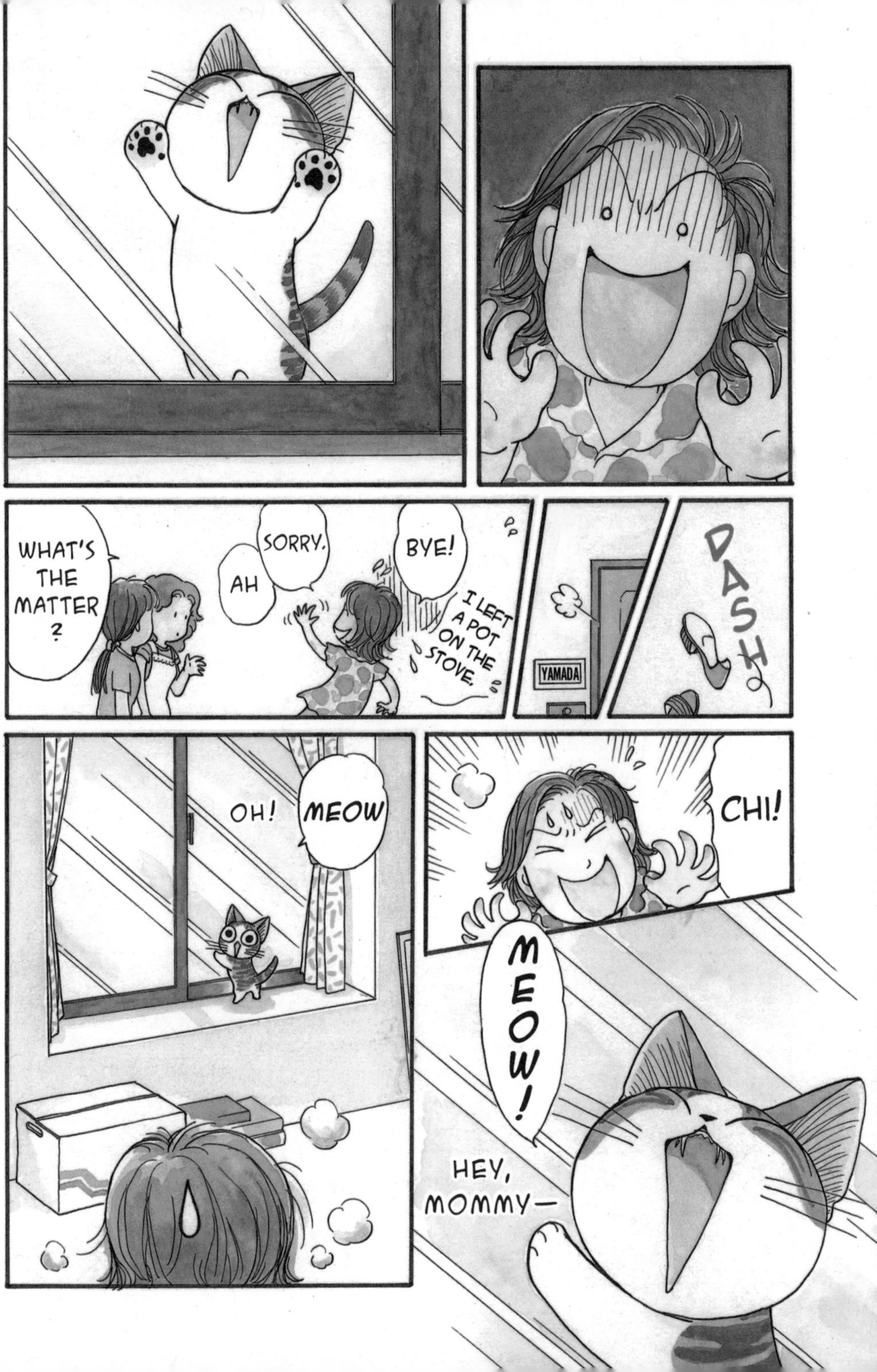
WHAT'S THE MATTER?
AH
SORRY.
BYE!
I LEFT A POT ON THE STOVE.
YAMADA
DASH
OH!
MEOW
CHI!
MEOW!
HEY, MOMMY—

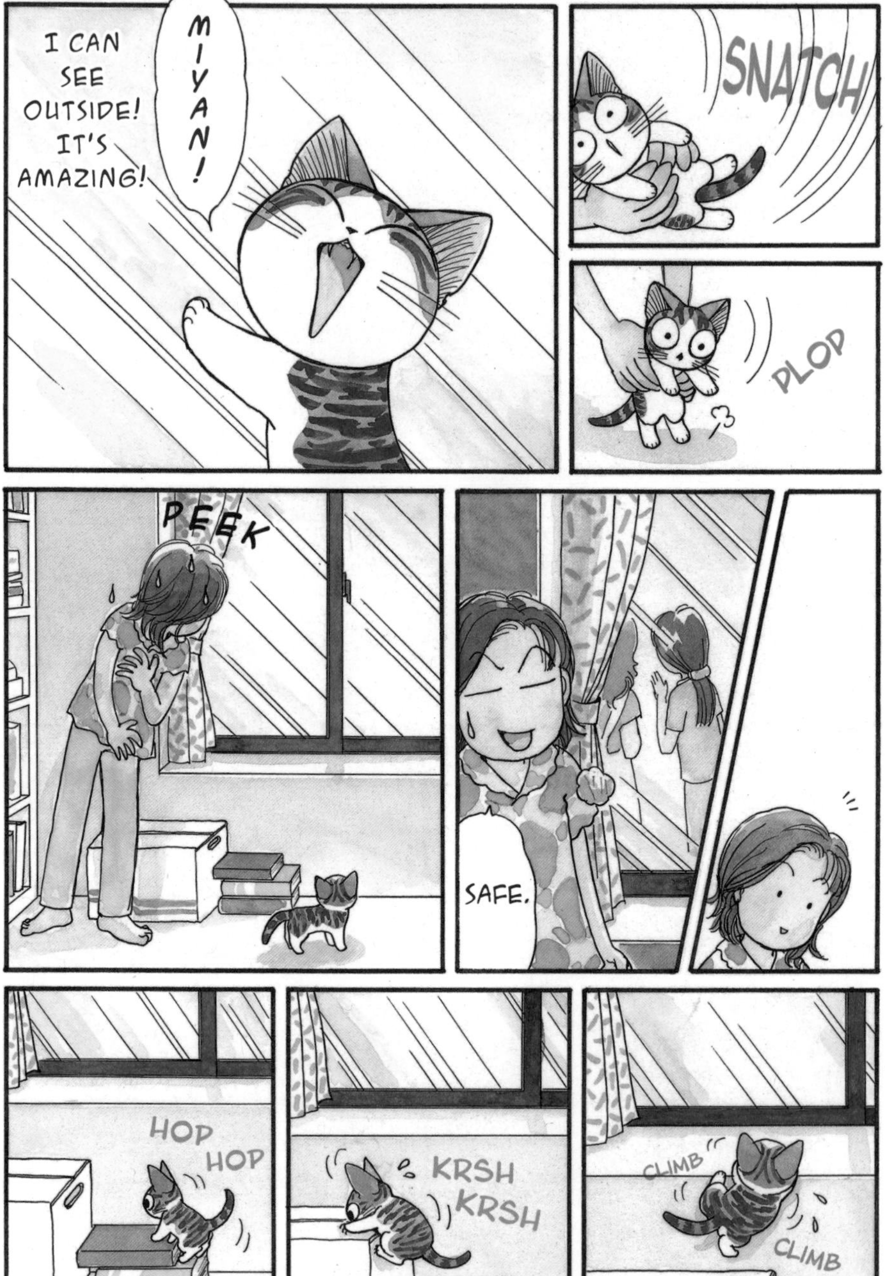

I CAN SEE OUTSIDE! IT'S AMAZING!
MIYAN!
SNATCH
PLOP
PEEK
SAFE.
HOP HOP
KRSH KRSH
CLIMB
CLIMB

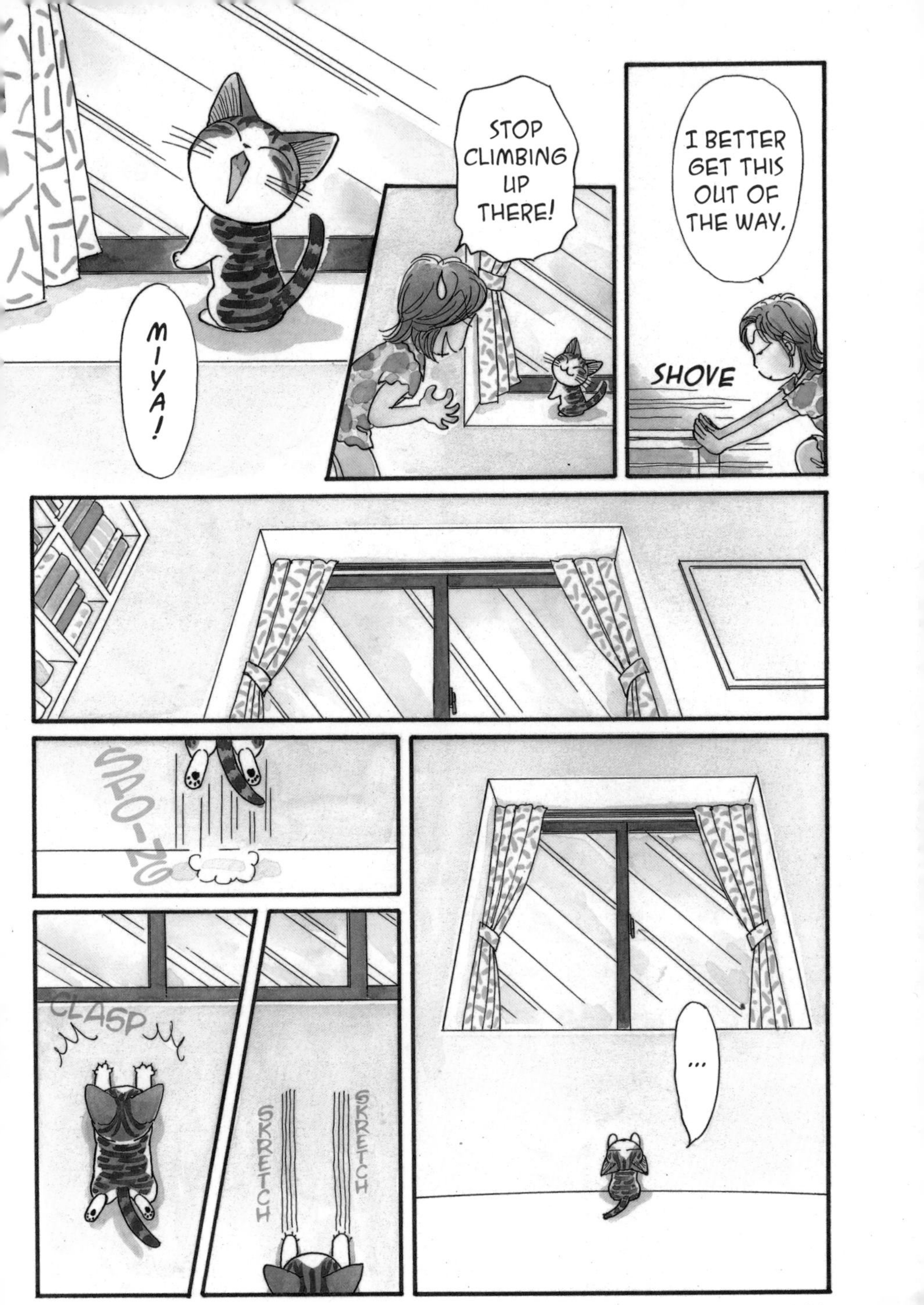
MIYA!
STOP CLIMBING UP THERE!
I BETTER GET THIS OUT OF THE WAY.
SHOVE
SPOING
CLASP
SKRETCH
SKRETCH
...

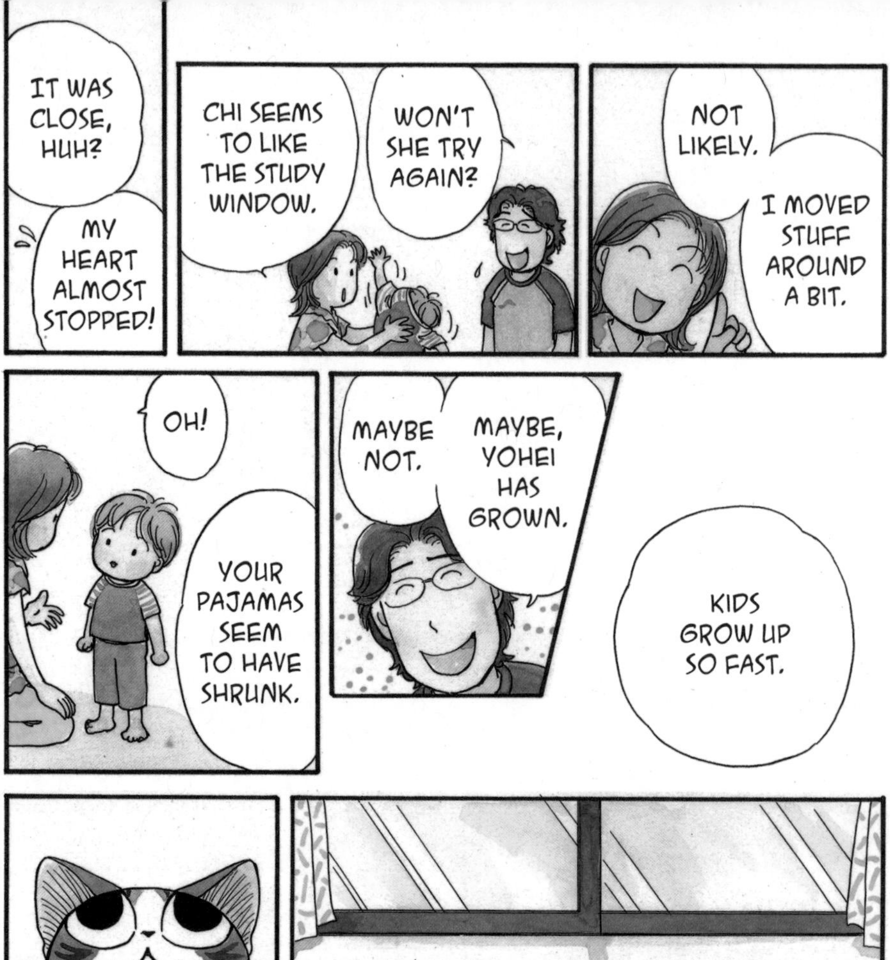
IT WAS CLOSE, HUH?
MY HEART ALMOST STOPPED!
CHI SEEMS TO LIKE THE STUDY WINDOW.
WON'T SHE TRY AGAIN?
NOT LIKELY.
I MOVED STUFF AROUND A BIT.
OH!
YOUR PAJAMAS SEEM TO HAVE SHRUNK.
MAYBE NOT.
MAYBE, YOHEI HAS GROWN.
KIDS GROW UP SO FAST.
SPROING
CLASP
A WITTLE MORE!

the end

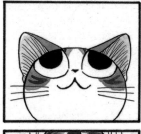

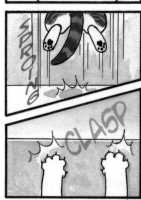

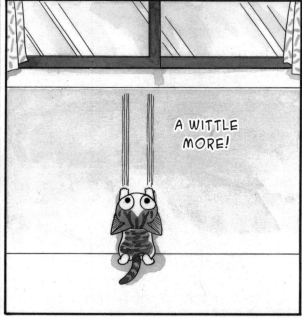

homemade 18: a cat is discovered

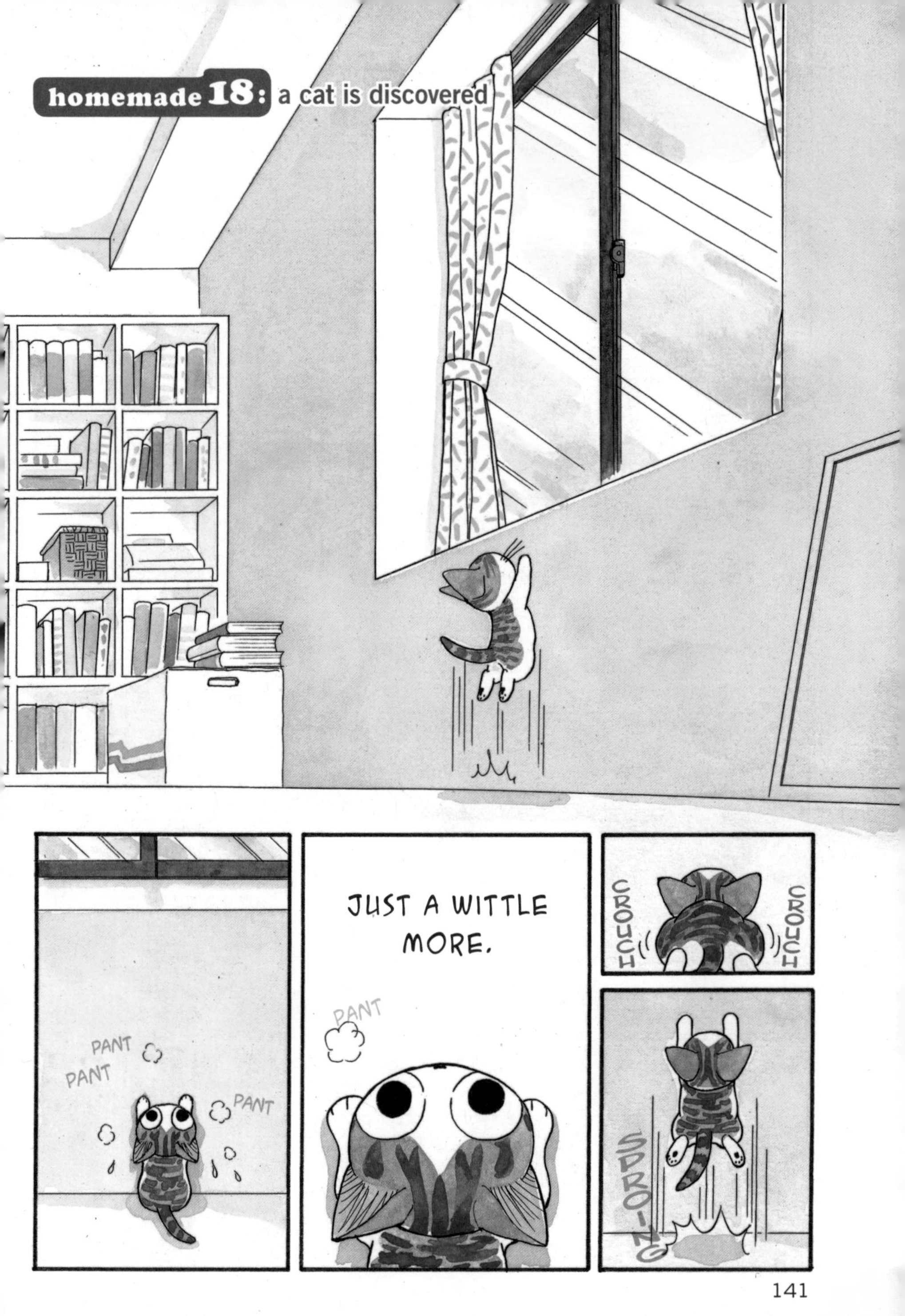
PANT
PANT
PANT
PANT
JUST A WITTLE MORE.
CROUCH
CROUCH
SPROING

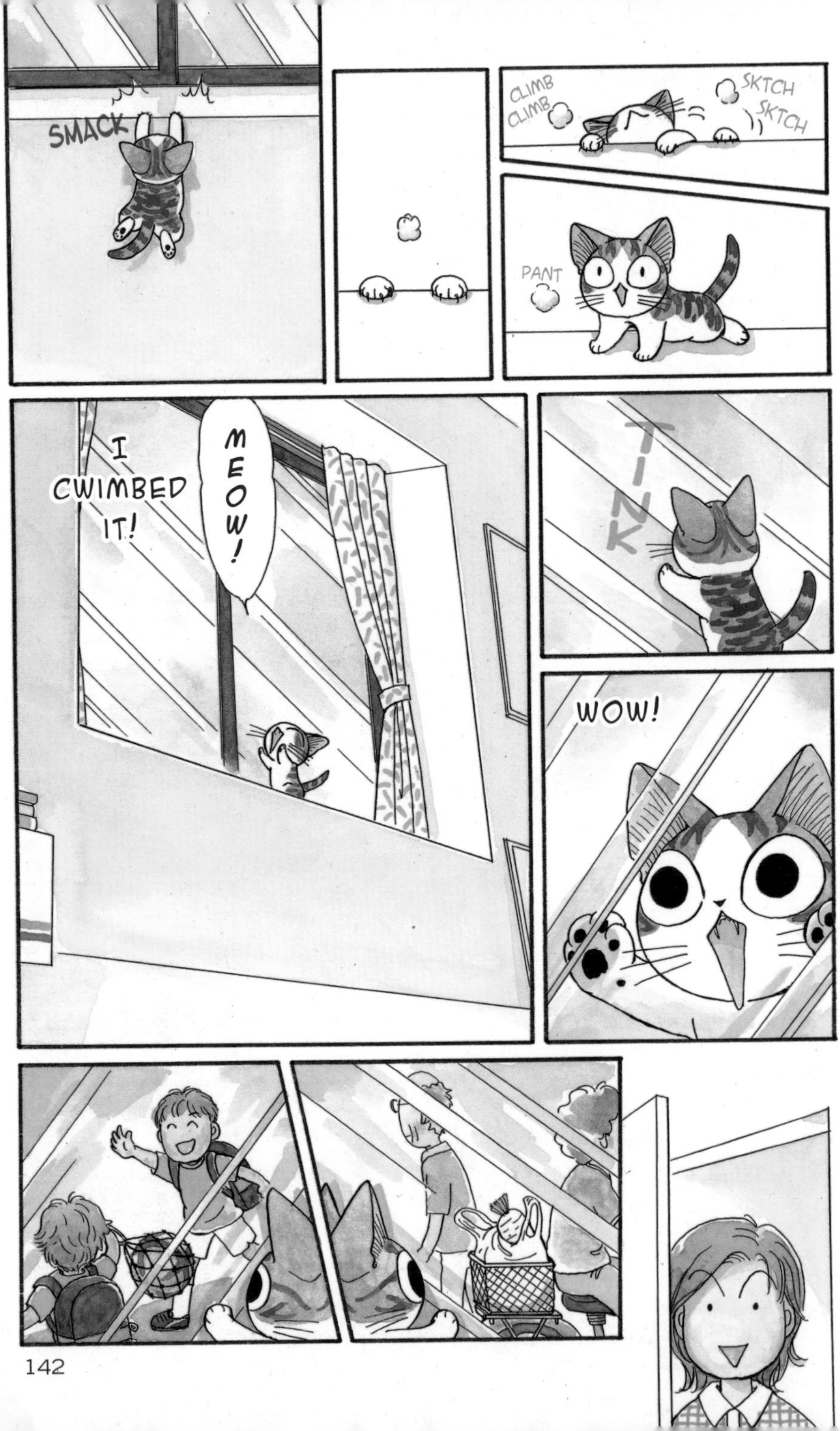
SMACK
CLIMB CLIMB
SKTCH SKTCH
PANT
I CWIMBED IT!
MEOW!
TINK
WOW!

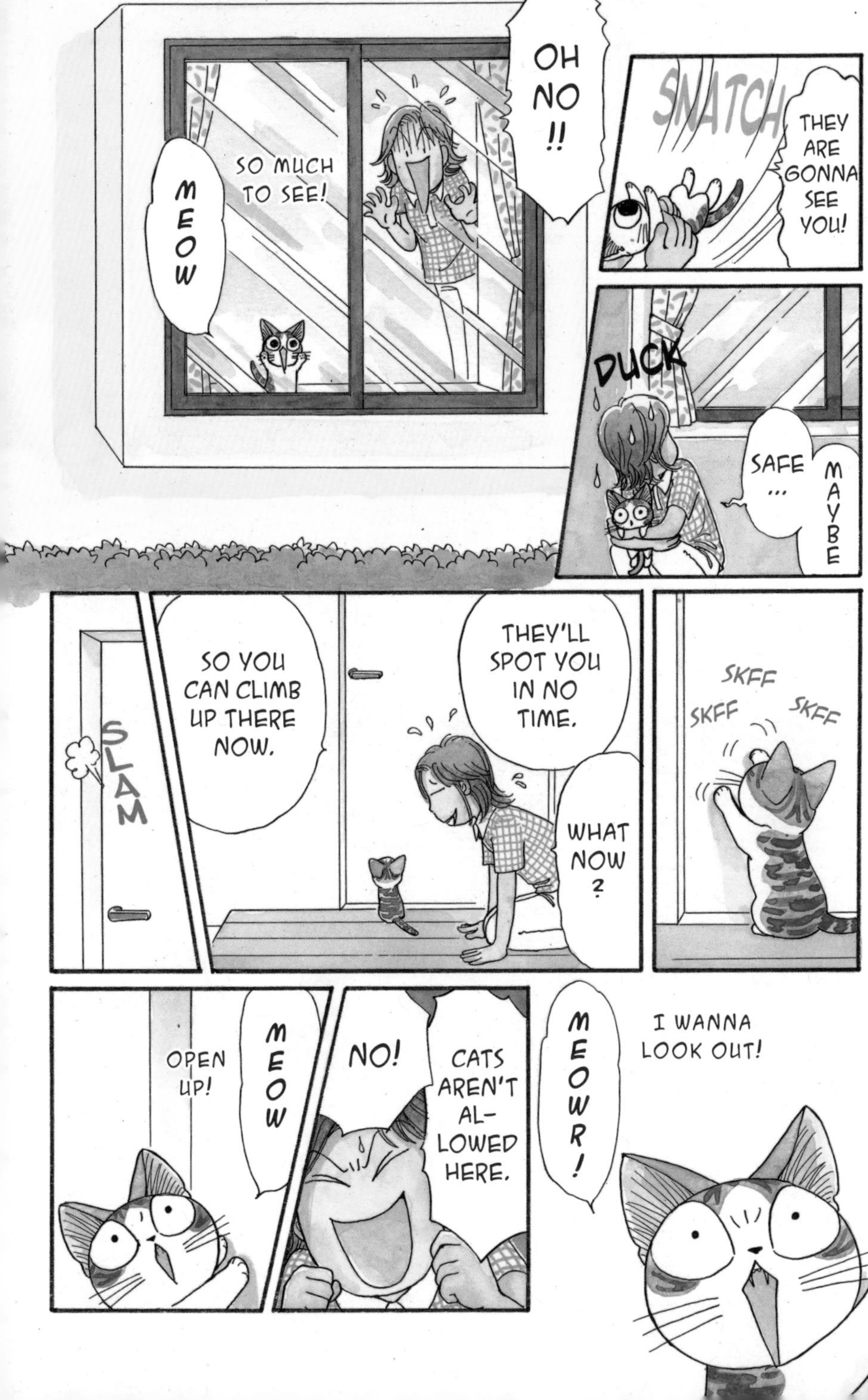
MEOW
SO MUCH TO SEE!
OH NO !!
SNATCH
THEY ARE GONNA SEE YOU!
DUCK
SAFE ...
MAYBE
SLAM
SO YOU CAN CLIMB UP THERE NOW.
THEY'LL SPOT YOU IN NO TIME.
WHAT NOW ?
SKFF
SKFF
SKFF
OPEN UP!
MEOW
NO!
CATS AREN'T AL- LOWED HERE.
MEOWR!
I WANNA LOOK OUT!

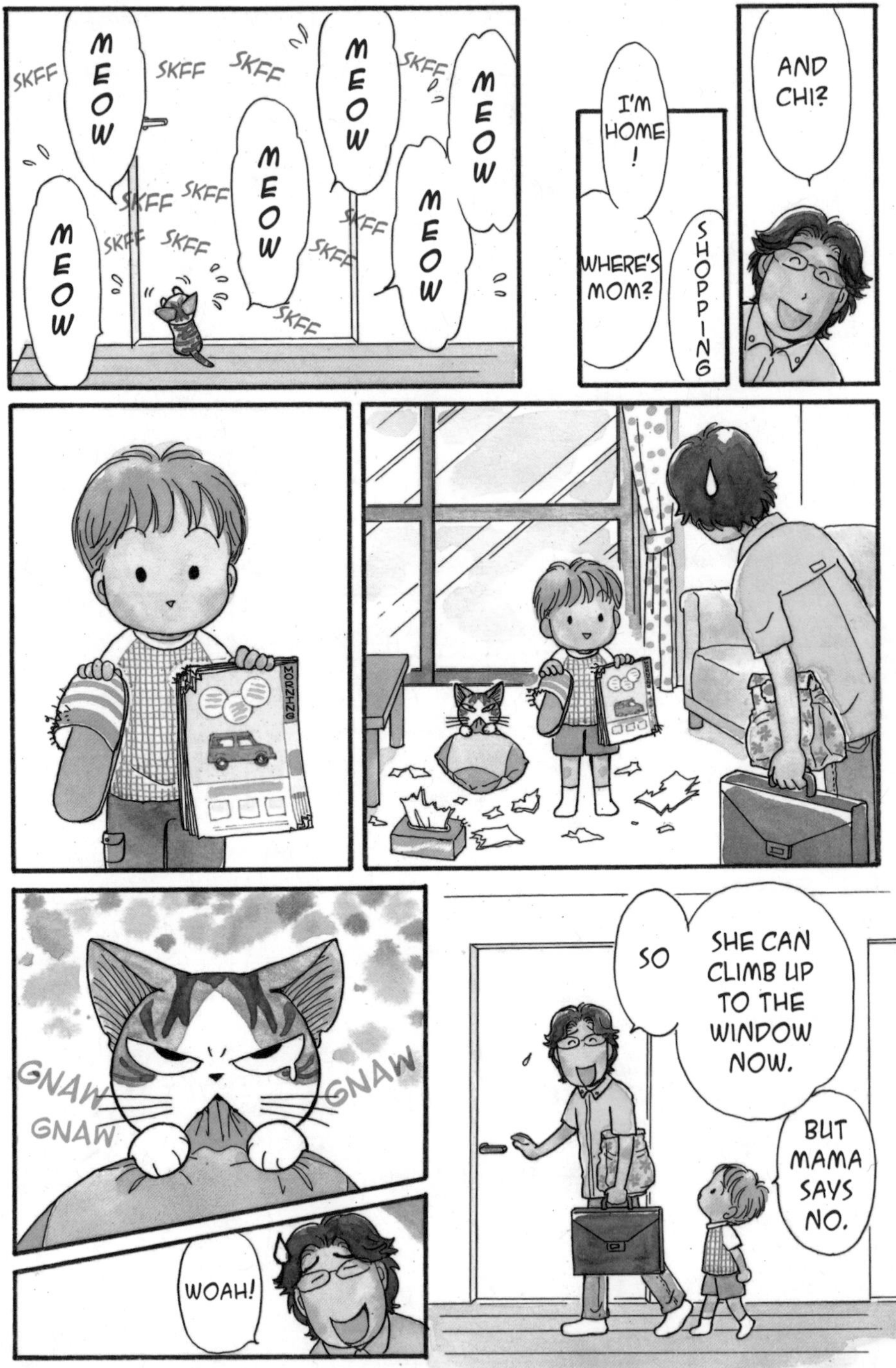
MEOW
SKFF
SKFF
SKFF
MEOW
SKFF
MEOW
MEOW
SKFF
SKFF
SKFF
SKFF
MEOW
MEOW
SKFF
SKFF
MEOW
SKFF
I'M HOME!
WHERE'S MOM?
SHOPPING
AND CHI?
MORNING
GNAW
GNAW
GNAW
WOAH!
SO
SHE CAN CLIMB UP TO THE WINDOW NOW.
BUT MAMA SAYS NO.

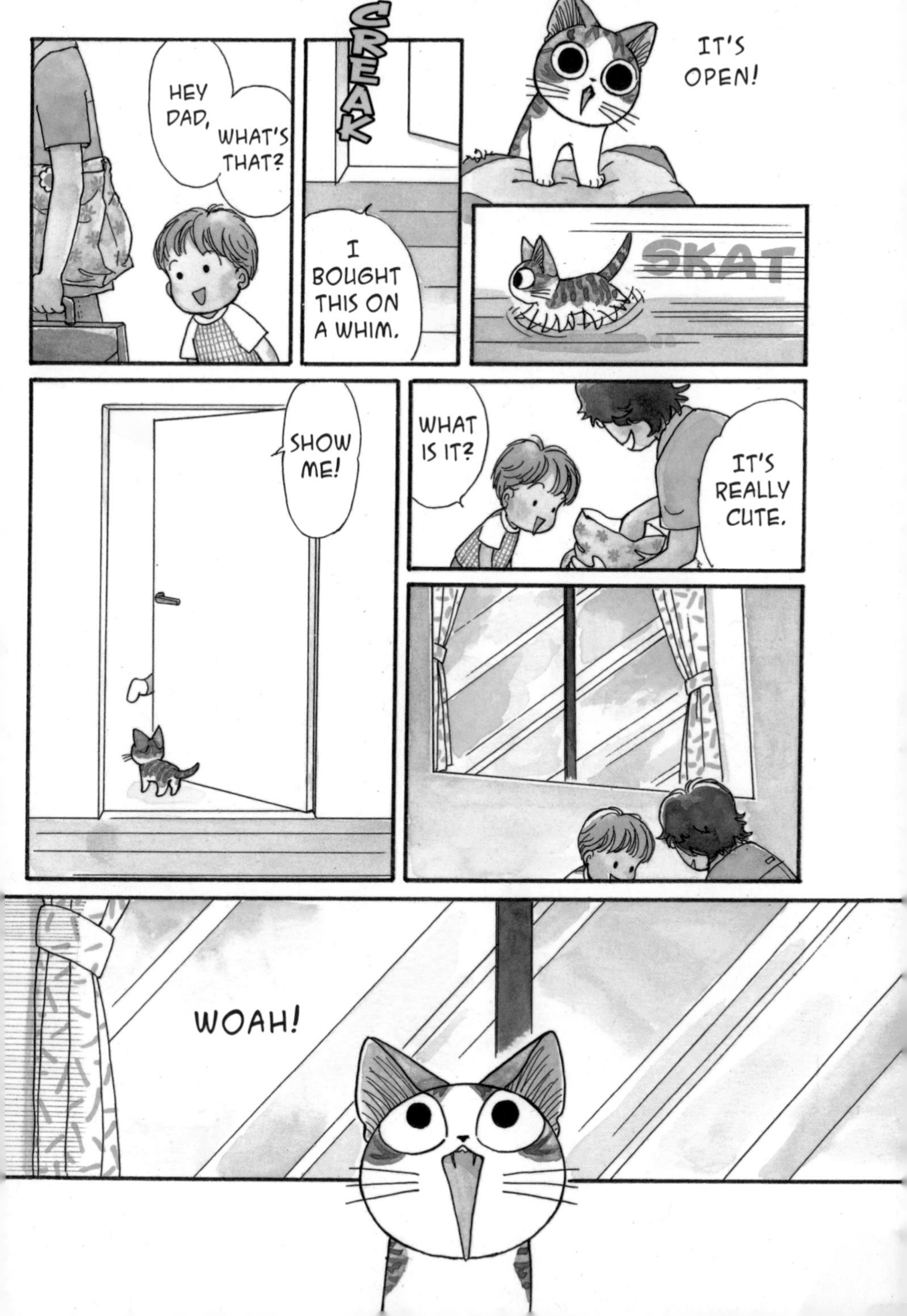
HEY DAD, WHAT'S THAT?
CREAK
I BOUGHT THIS ON A WHIM.
IT'S OPEN!
SKAT
SHOW ME!
WHAT IS IT?
IT'S REALLY CUTE.
WOAH!

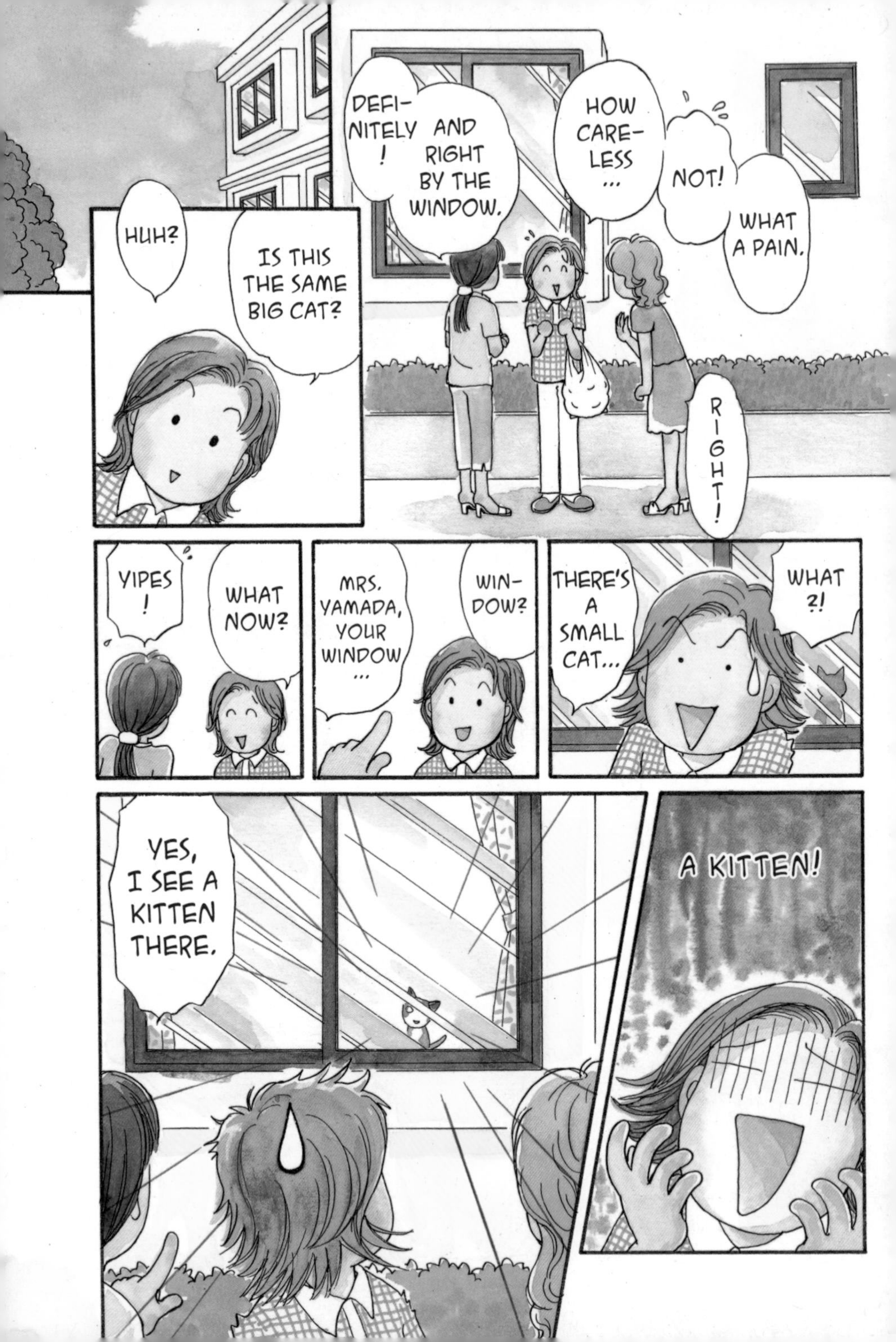
DEFINITELY!
AND RIGHT BY THE WINDOW.
HOW CARELESS...
NOT!
WHAT A PAIN.
RIGHT!
HUH?
IS THIS THE SAME BIG CAT?
YIPES!
WHAT NOW?
MRS. YAMADA, YOUR WINDOW...
WINDOW?
THERE'S A SMALL CAT...
WHAT?!
YES, I SEE A KITTEN THERE.
A KITTEN!

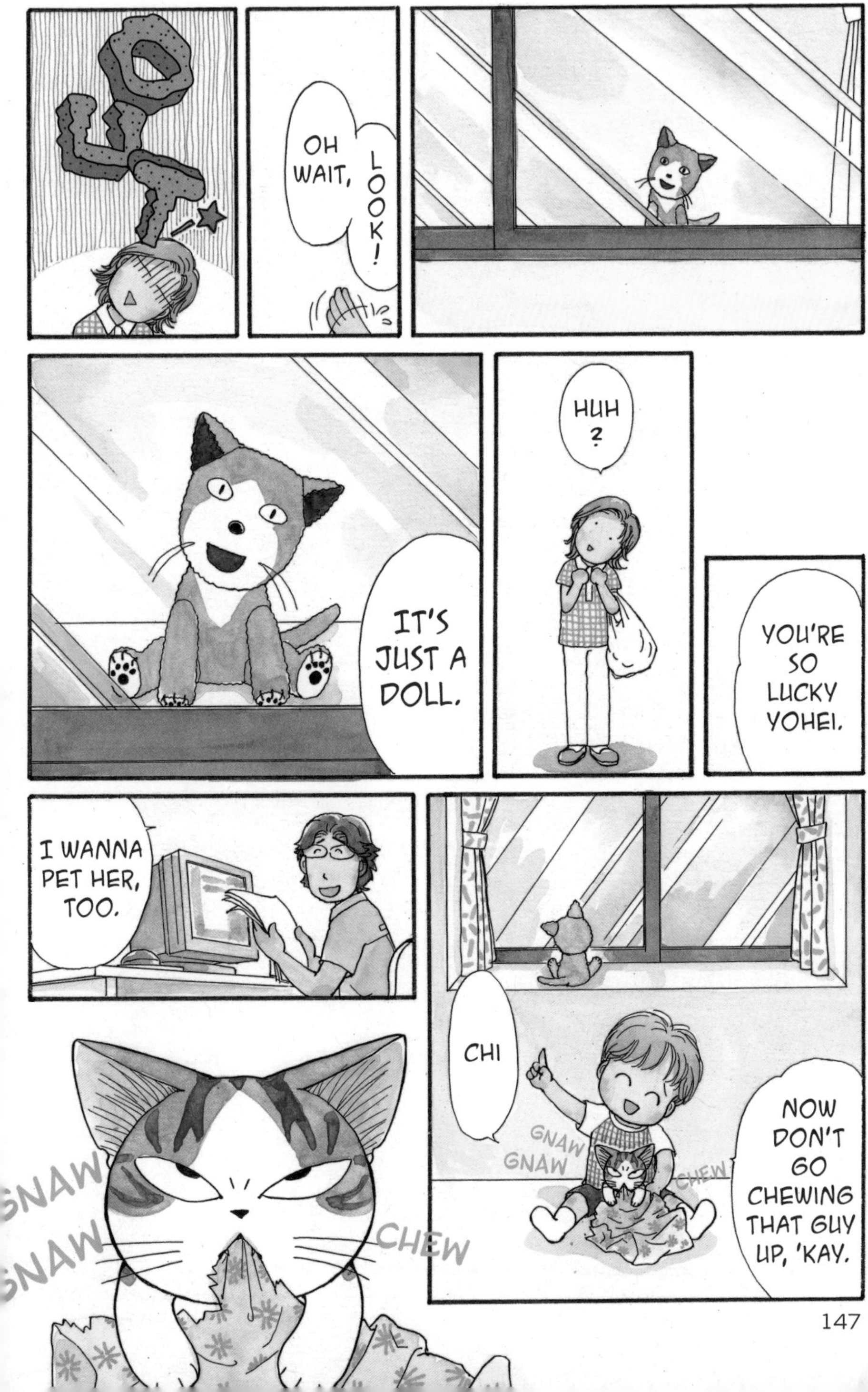
OH WAIT,
LOOK!
IT'S JUST A DOLL.
HUH?
YOU'RE SO LUCKY YOHEI.
I WANNA PET HER, TOO.
GNAW GNAW
CHEW
CHI
GNAW GNAW
CHEW
NOW DON'T GO CHEWING THAT GUY UP, 'KAY.

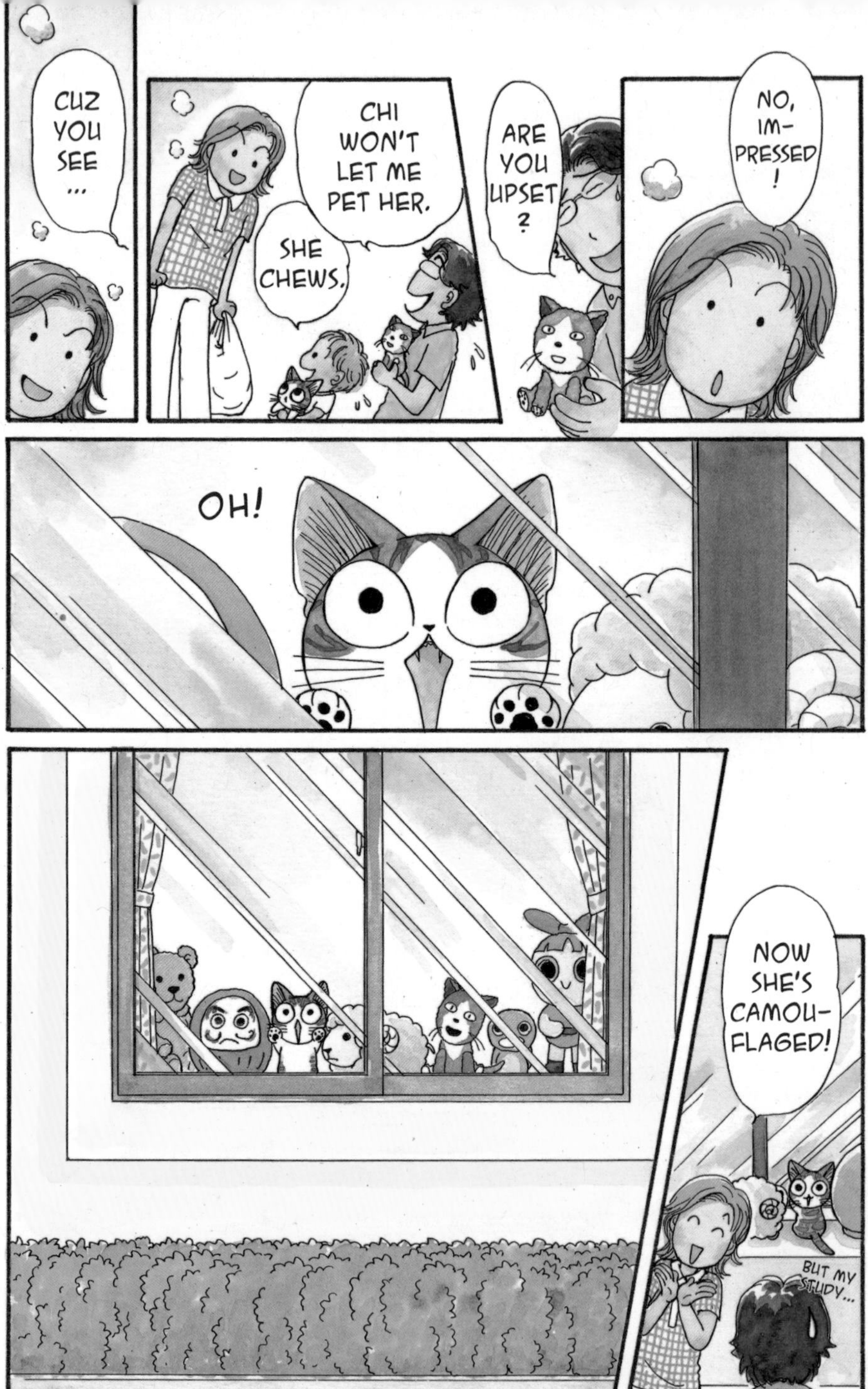
CUZ YOU SEE ...
CHI WON'T LET ME PET HER.
SHE CHEWS.
ARE YOU UPSET?
NO, IM-PRESSED!
OH!
NOW SHE'S CAMOU-FLAGED!
BUT MY STUDY...

the end

homemade 19: a cat obsesses

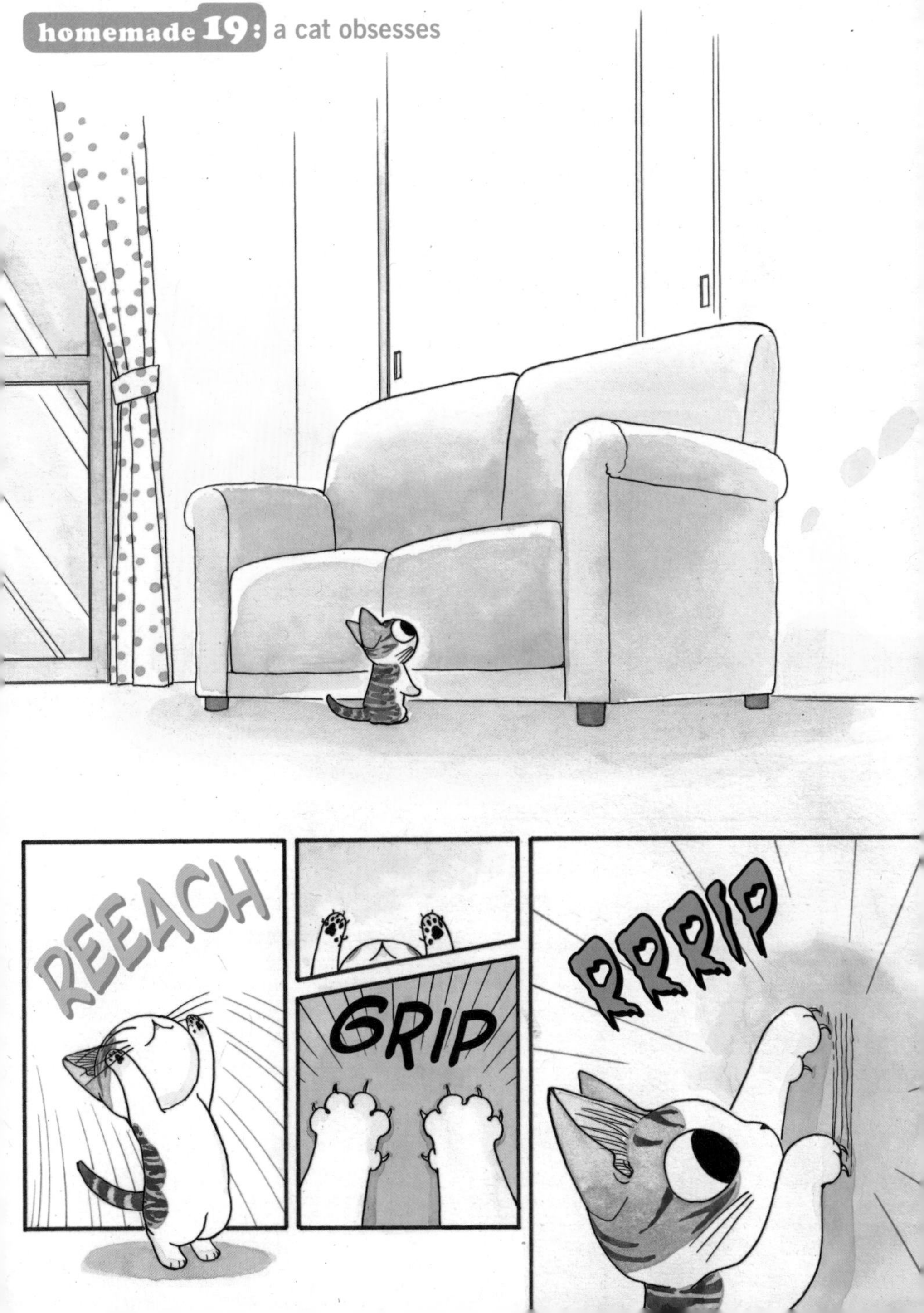

REEACH
GRIP
RRRIP

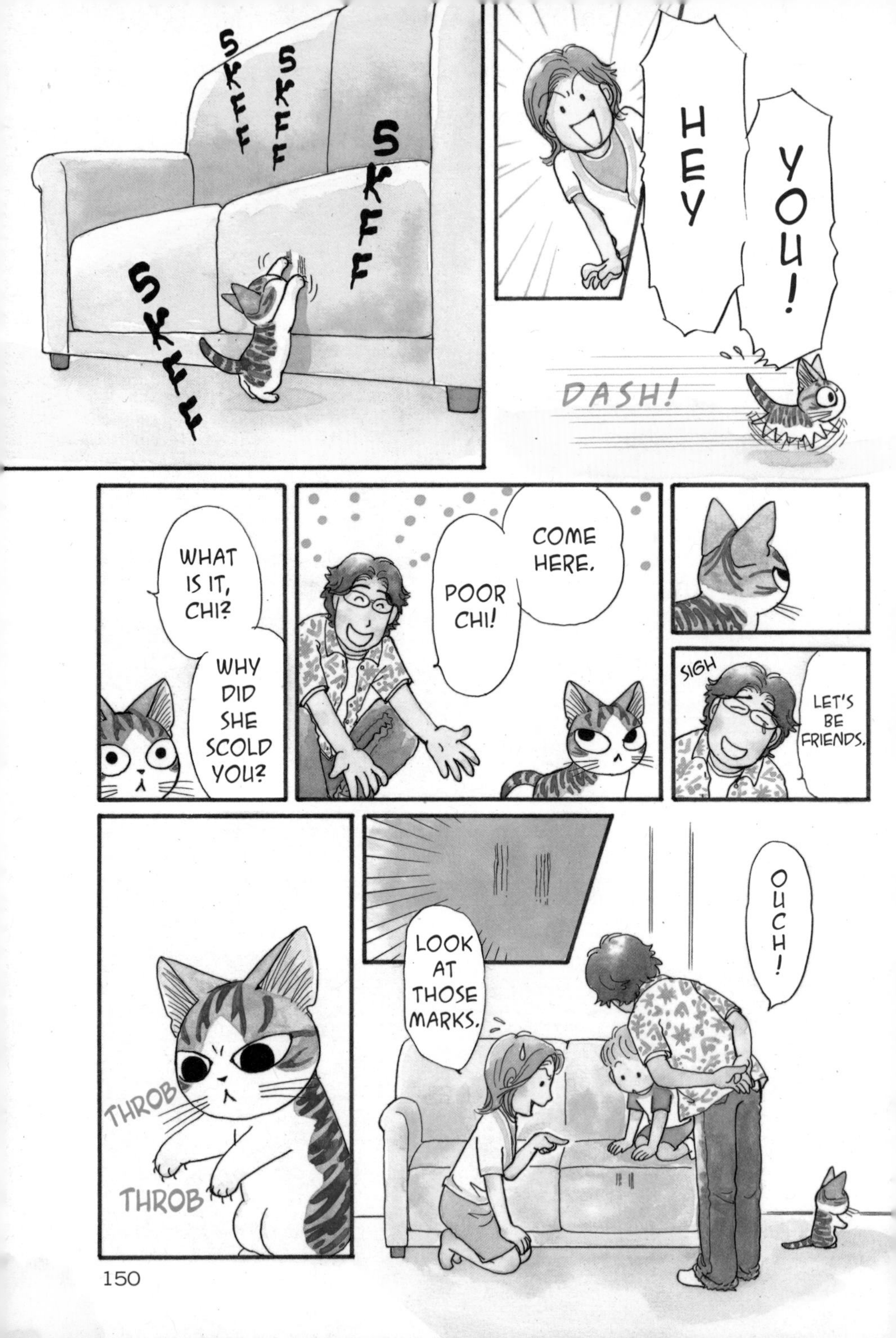
SKFF
SKFF
SKFF
SKFF
HEY
YOU!
DASH!
WHAT IS IT, CHI?
WHY DID SHE SCOLD YOU?
POOR CHI!
COME HERE.
SIGH
LET'S BE FRIENDS.
THROB
THROB
LOOK AT THOSE MARKS.
OUCH!

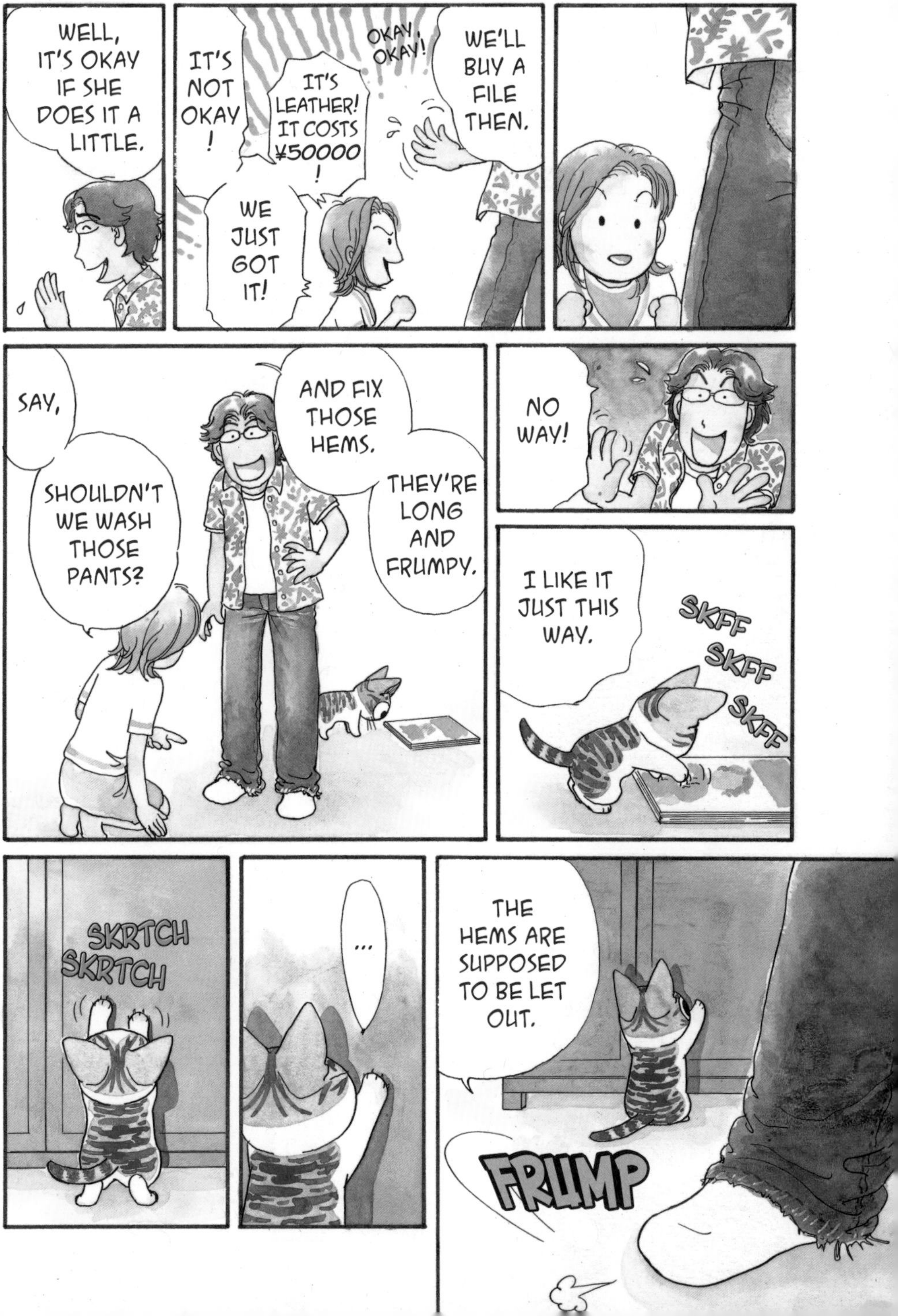
WELL, IT'S OKAY IF SHE DOES IT A LITTLE.
IT'S NOT OKAY!
IT'S LEATHER! IT COSTS ¥50000!
WE JUST GOT IT!
OKAY, OKAY!
WE'LL BUY A FILE THEN.
SAY,
SHOULDN'T WE WASH THOSE PANTS?
AND FIX THOSE HEMS.
THEY'RE LONG AND FRUMPY.
NO WAY!
I LIKE IT JUST THIS WAY.
SKFF SKFF SKFF
SKRTCH SKRTCH
...
THE HEMS ARE SUPPOSED TO BE LET OUT.
FRUMP

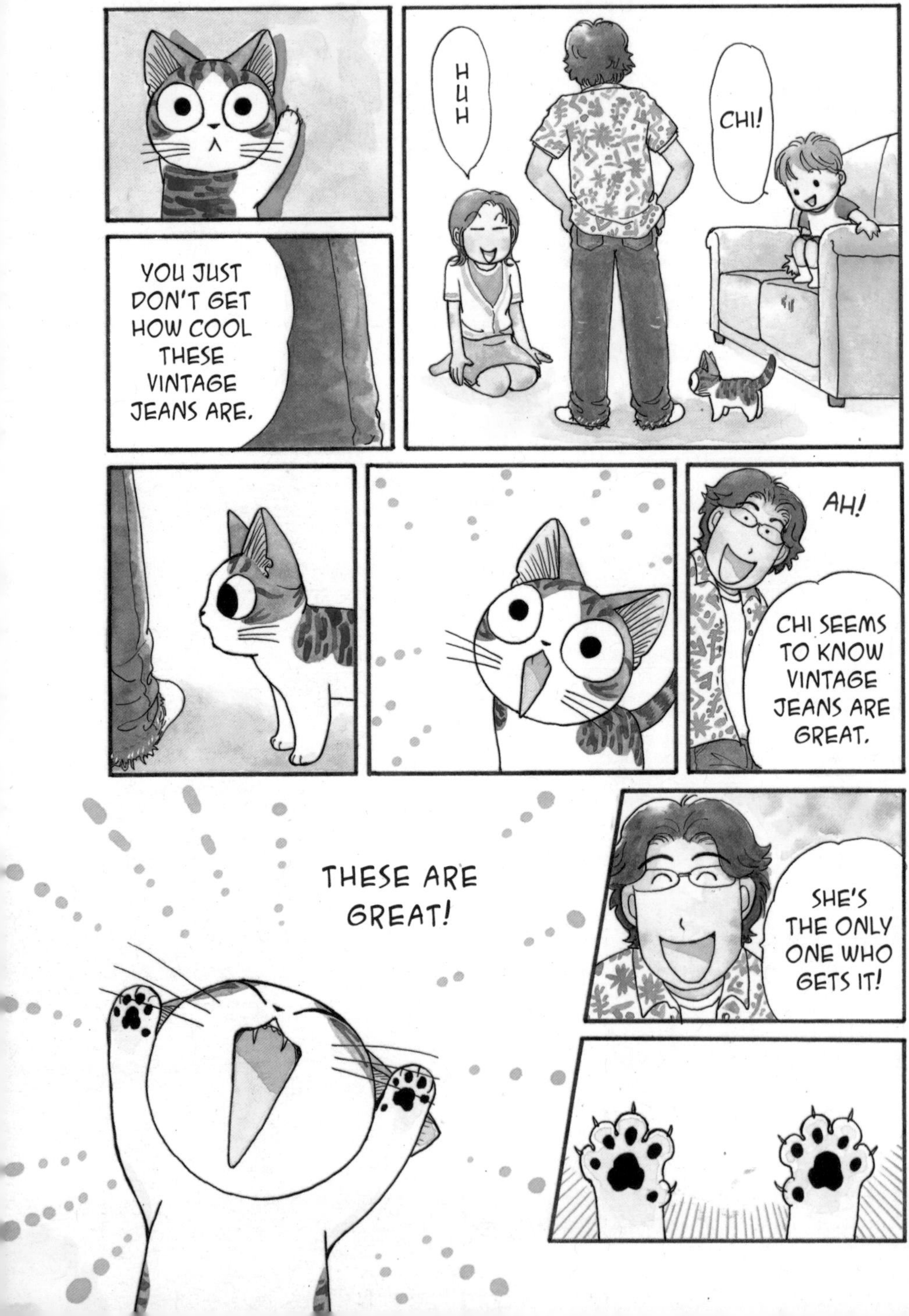
YOU JUST DON'T GET HOW COOL THESE VINTAGE JEANS ARE.
HUH
CHI!
AH!
CHI SEEMS TO KNOW VINTAGE JEANS ARE GREAT.
THESE ARE GREAT!
SHE'S THE ONLY ONE WHO GETS IT!

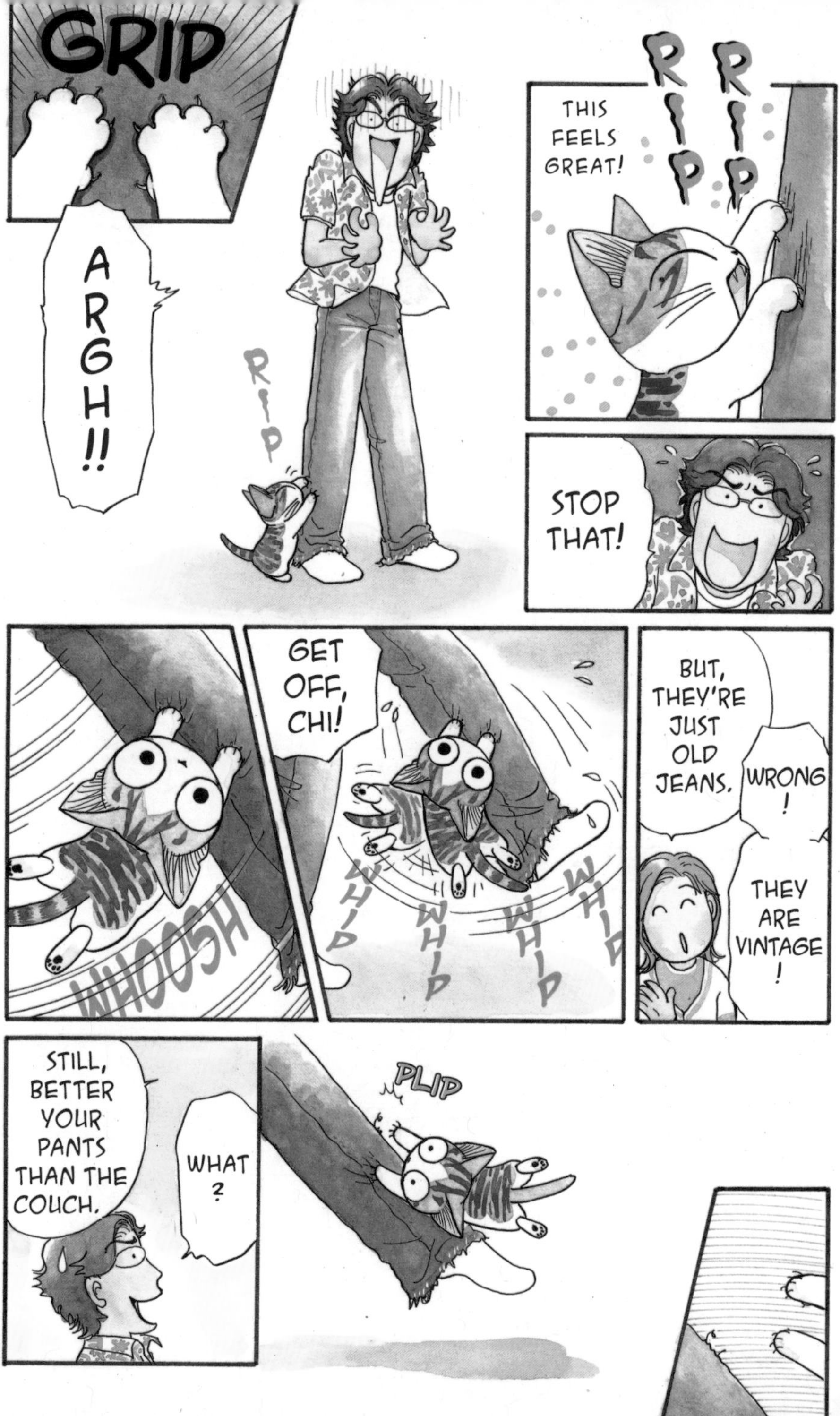
GRIP
ARGH!!
RIP
RIP RIP
THIS FEELS GREAT!
STOP THAT!
WHOOSH
GET OFF, CHI!
WHIP WHIP WHIP WHIP
BUT, THEY'RE JUST OLD JEANS.
WRONG!
THEY ARE VINTAGE!
STILL, BETTER YOUR PANTS THAN THE COUCH.
WHAT?
PLIP

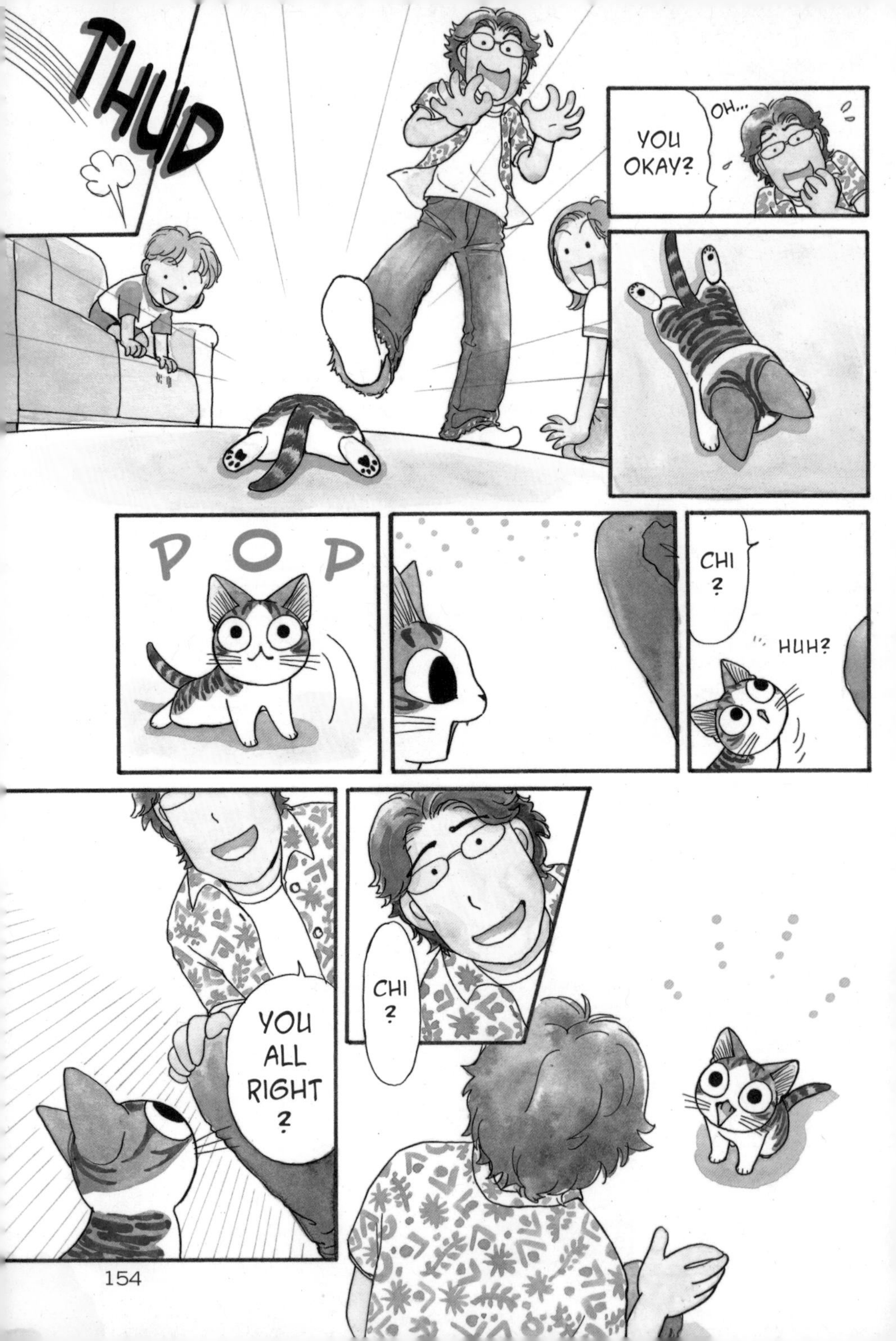
THUD
YOU OKAY?
OH...
POP
CHI?
HUH?
YOU ALL RIGHT?
CHI?

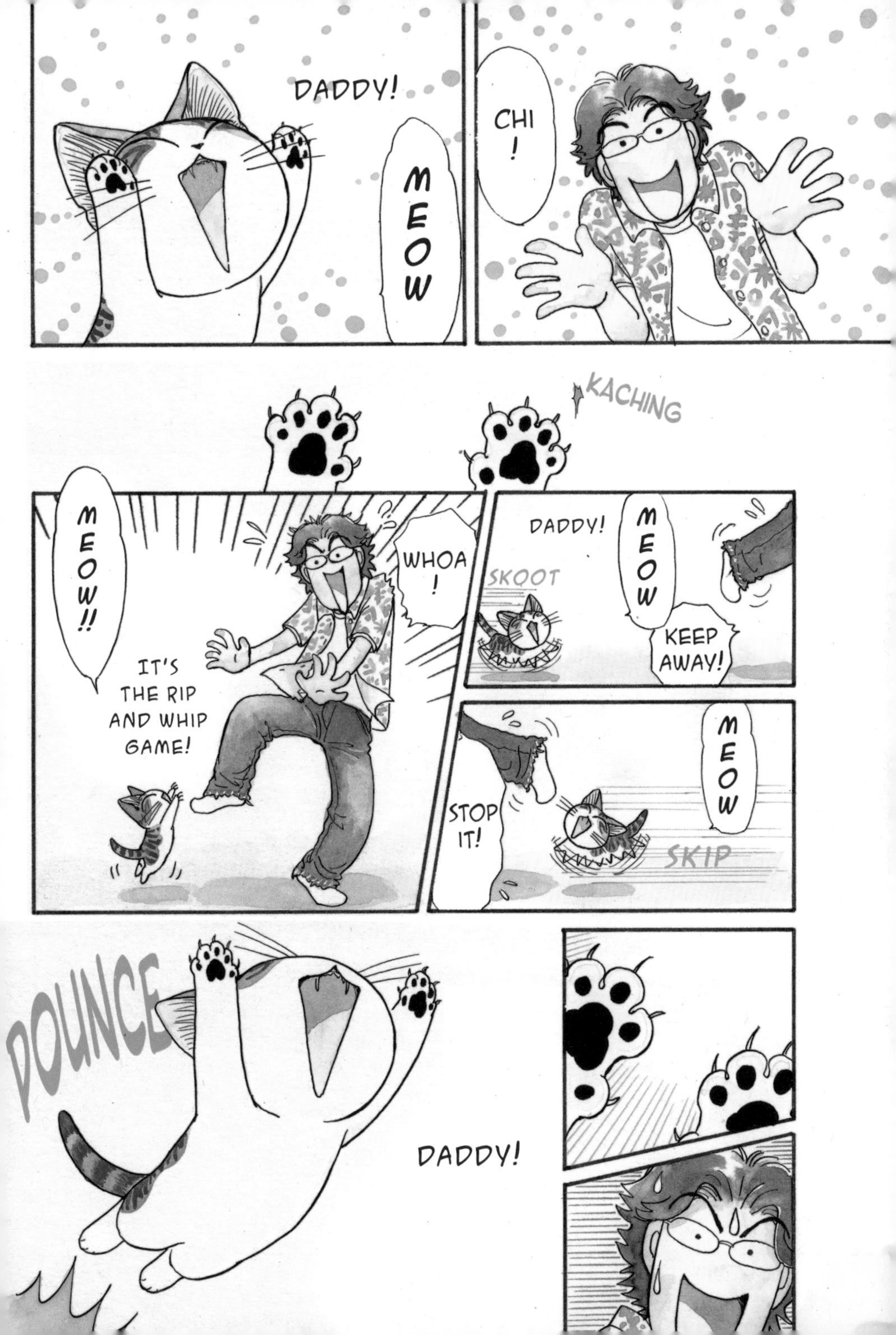
DADDY!
MEOW
CHI!
KACHING
MEOW!!
WHOA!
IT'S THE RIP AND WHIP GAME!
DADDY!
MEOW
SKOOT
KEEP AWAY!
MEOW
STOP IT!
SKIP
POUNCE
DADDY!

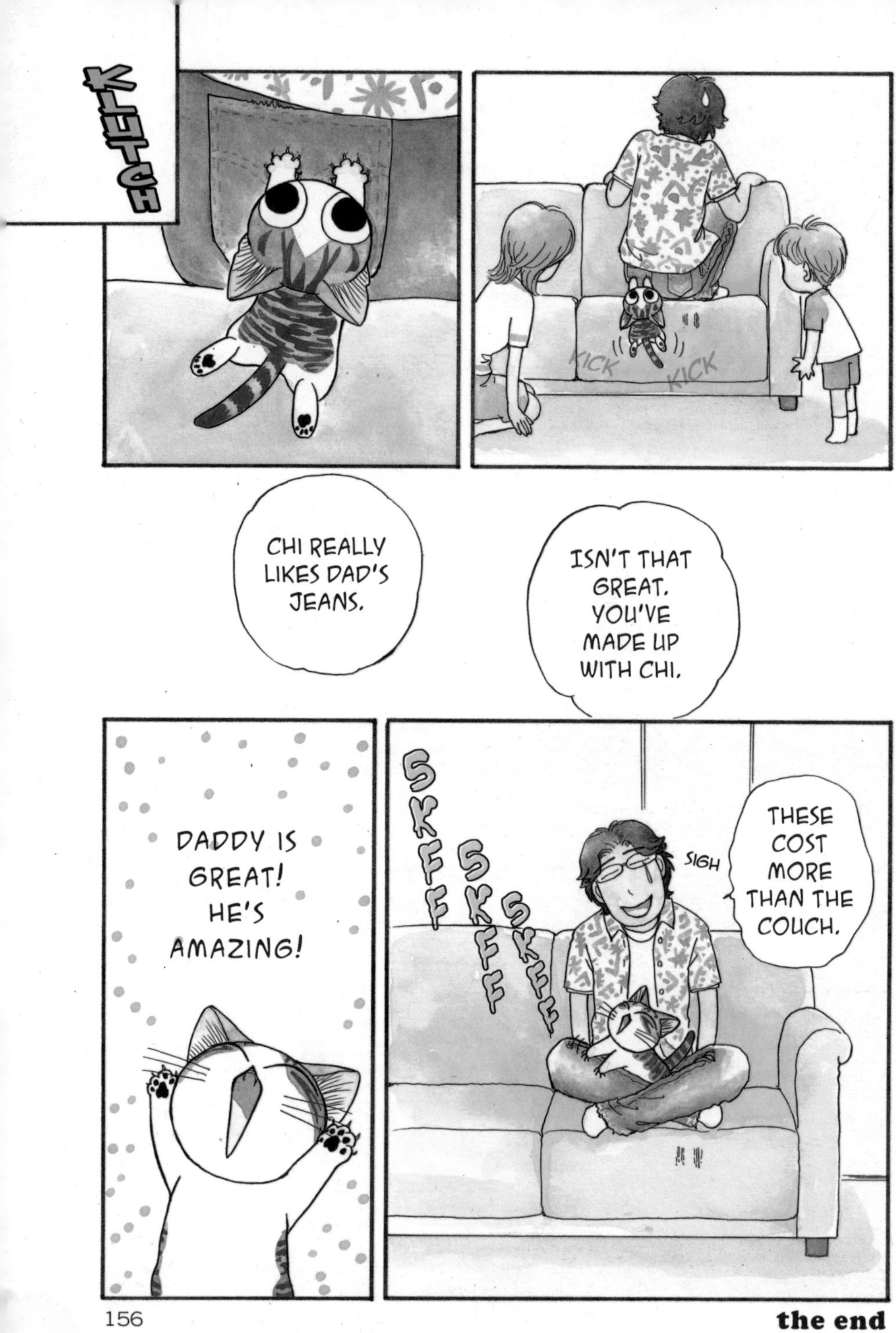
KLUTCH
KICK
KICK
CHI REALLY LIKES DAD'S JEANS.
ISN'T THAT GREAT. YOU'VE MADE UP WITH CHI.
DADDY IS GREAT! HE'S AMAZING!
SKFF
SKFF
SKFF
SIGH
THESE COST MORE THAN THE COUCH.

the end

homemade 20: a cat is home alone

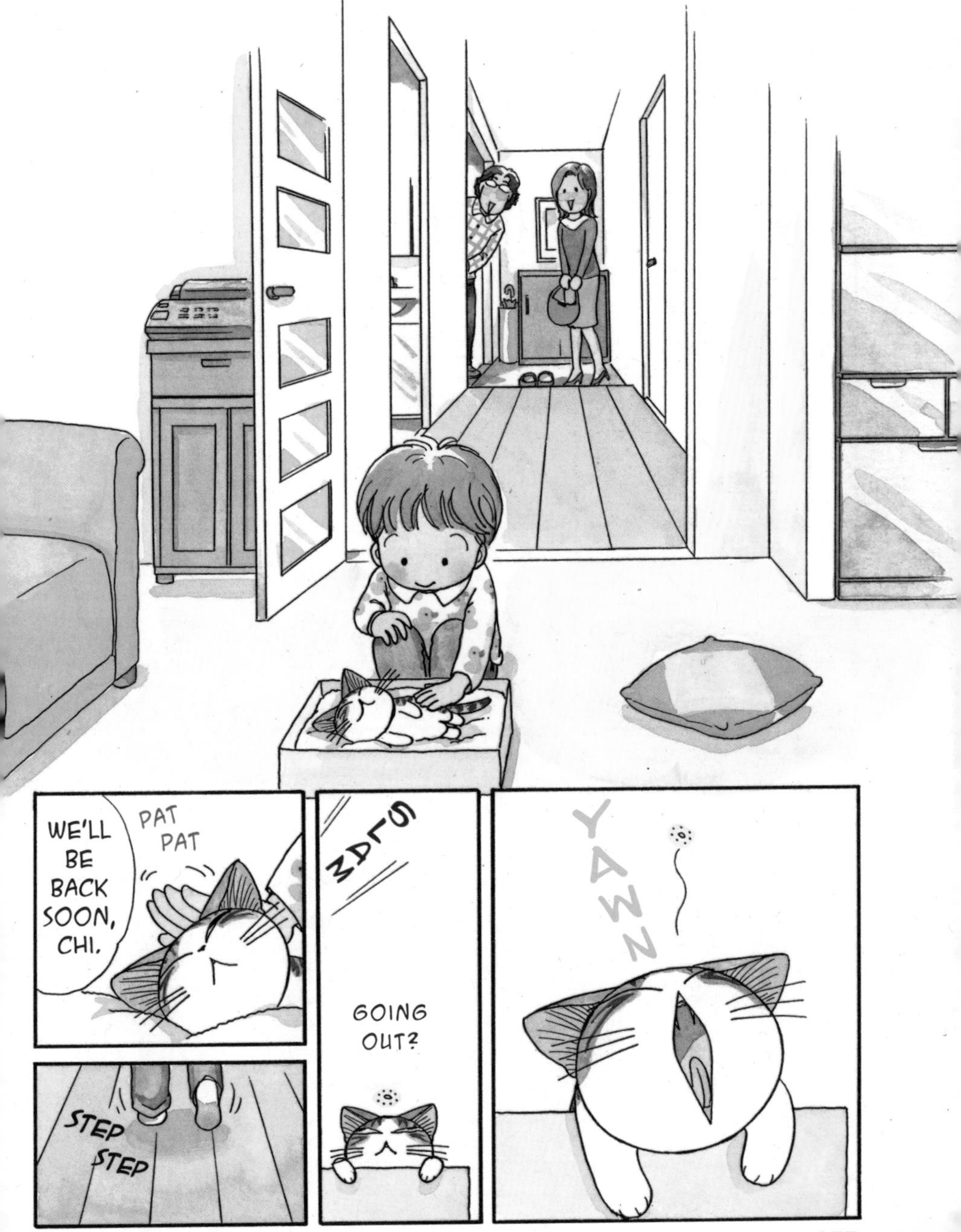
WE'LL BE BACK SOON, CHI.
PAT PAT
STEP STEP
SLAM
GOING OUT?
YAWN

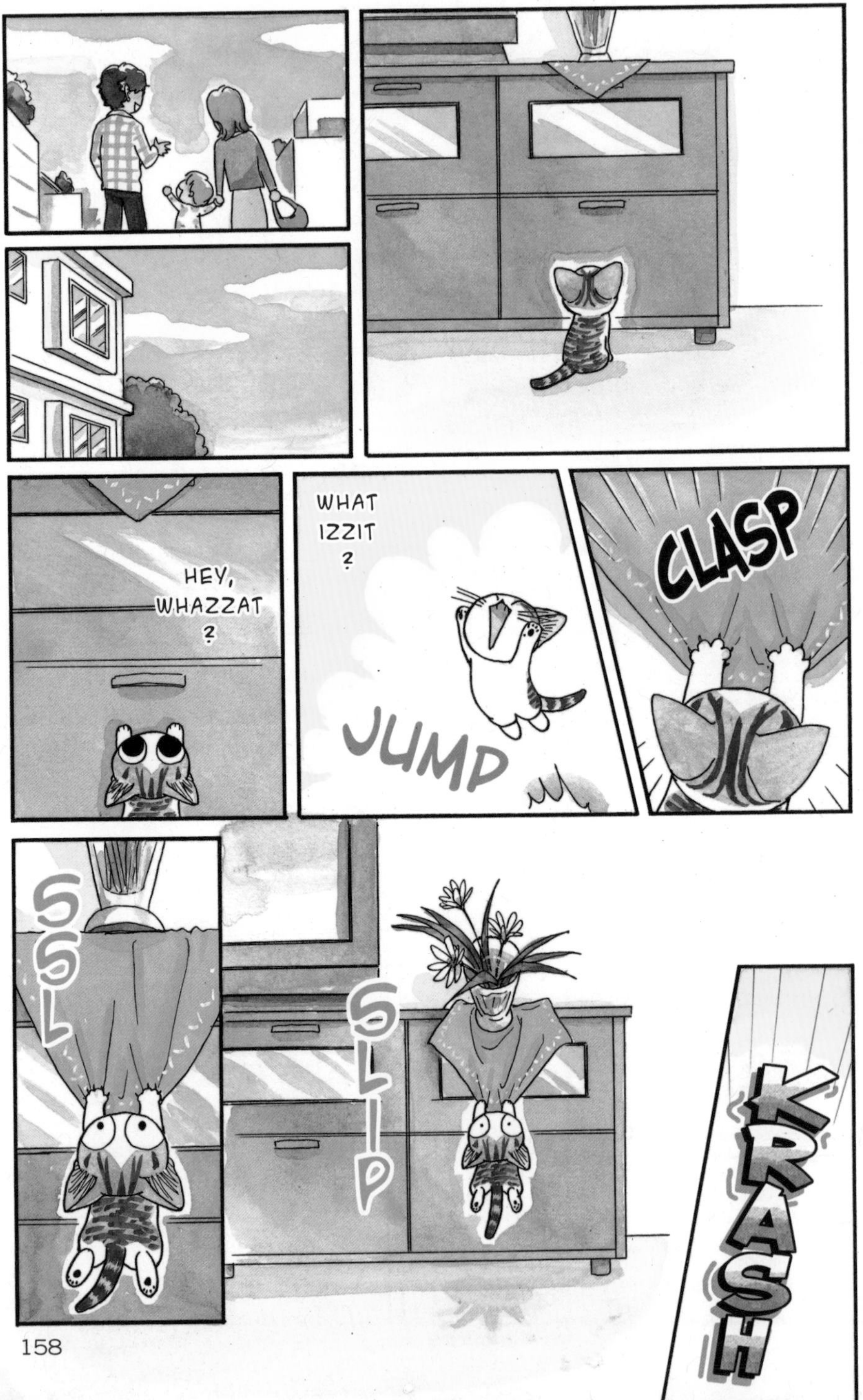
HEY, WHAZZAT?
WHAT IZZIT?
JUMP
CLASP
SSL
SLIP
KRASH

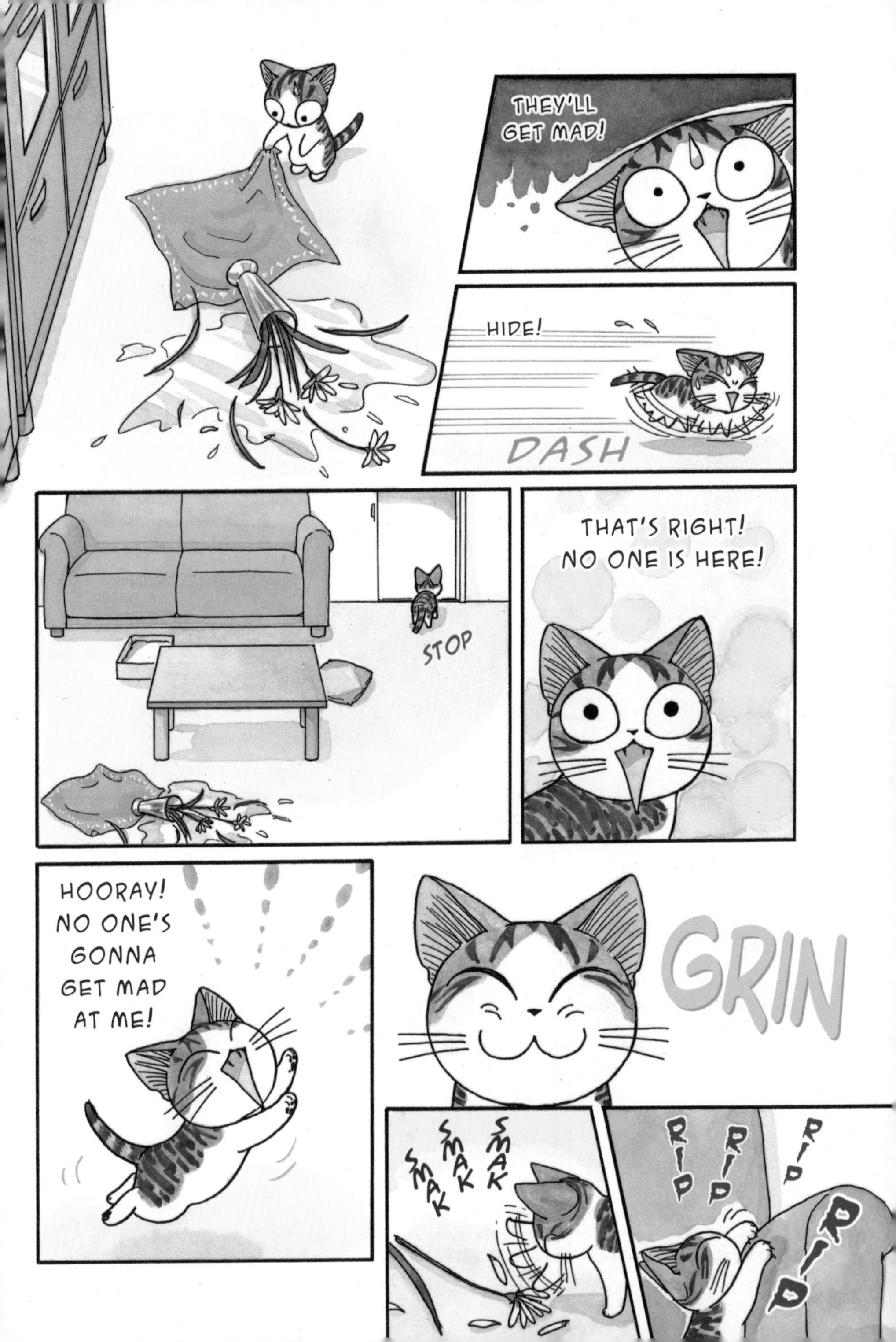
THEY'LL GET MAD!
HIDE!
DASH
STOP
THAT'S RIGHT! NO ONE IS HERE!
HOORAY! NO ONE'S GONNA GET MAD AT ME!
GRIN
SMAK
SMAK
SMAK
RIP
RIP
RIP
RIP

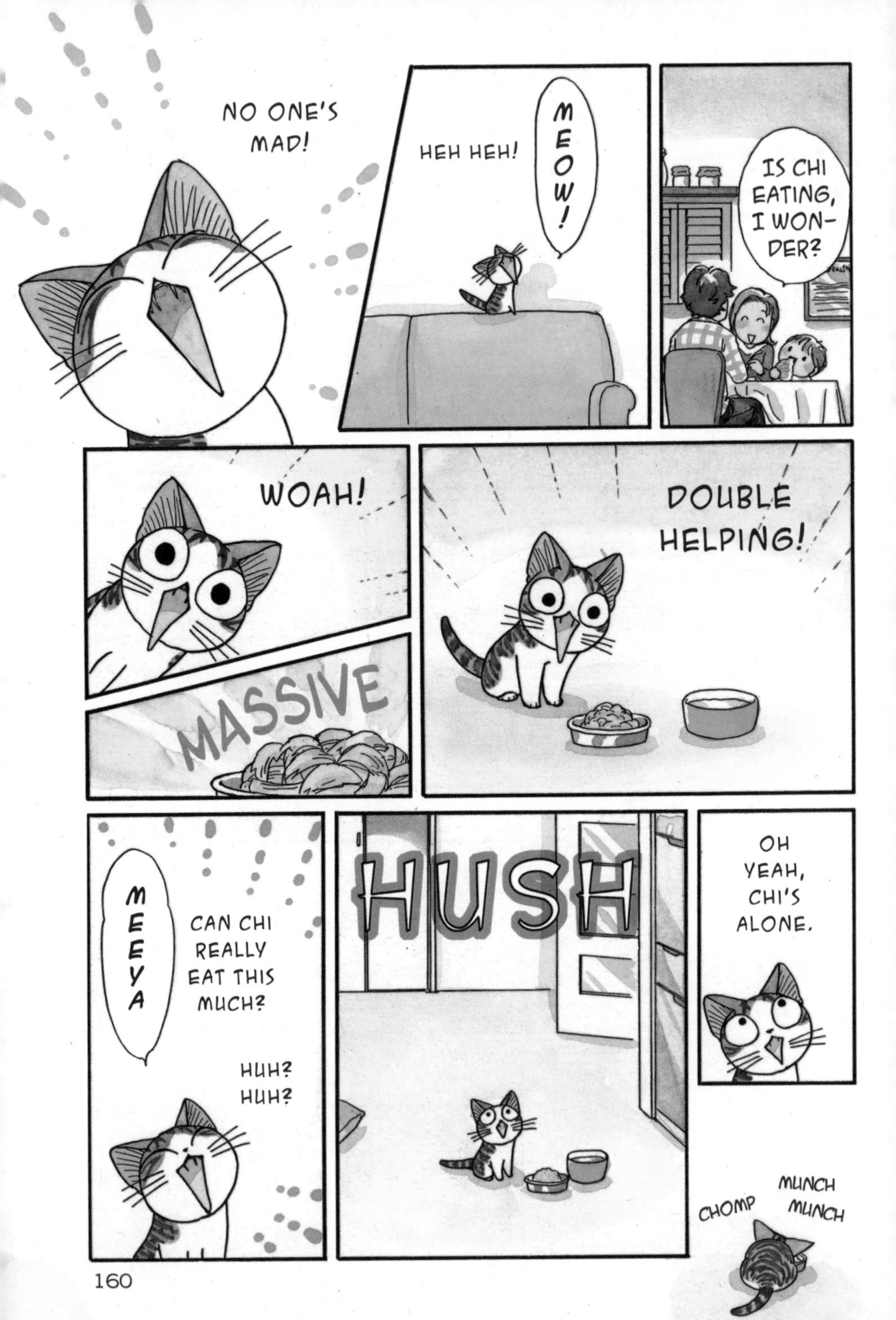
NO ONE'S MAD!
HEH HEH!
MEOW!
IS CHI EATING, I WONDER?
WOAH!
MASSIVE
DOUBLE HELPING!
MEEYA
CAN CHI REALLY EAT THIS MUCH?
HUH? HUH?
HUSH
OH YEAH, CHI'S ALONE.
CHOMP
MUNCH MUNCH

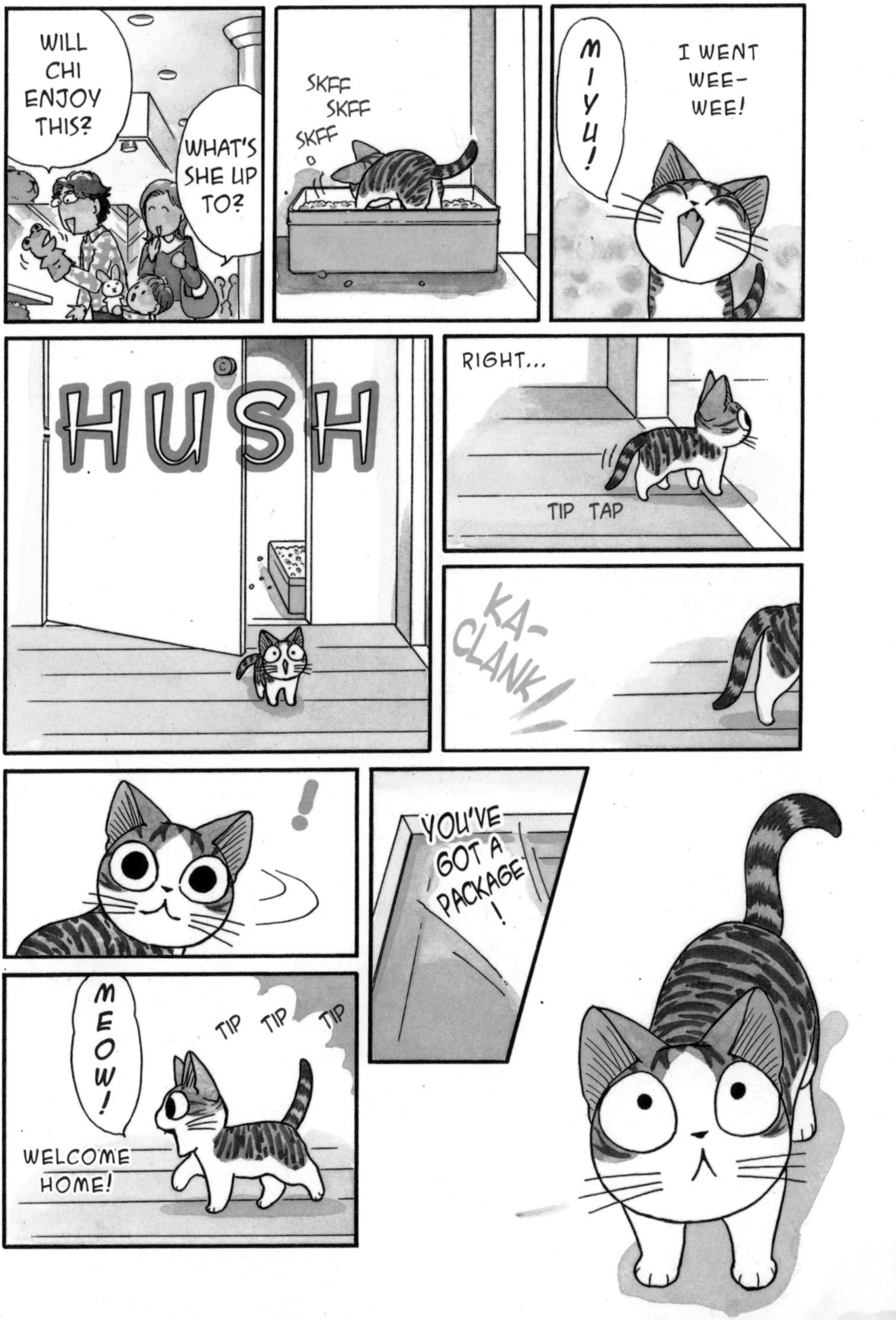
WILL CHI ENJOY THIS?
WHAT'S SHE UP TO?
SKFF SKFF SKFF
MIYU!
I WENT WEE-WEE!
HUSH
RIGHT...
TIP TAP
KA-CLANK
!
YOU'VE GOT A PACKAGE!
MEOW!
TIP TIP TIP
WELCOME HOME!

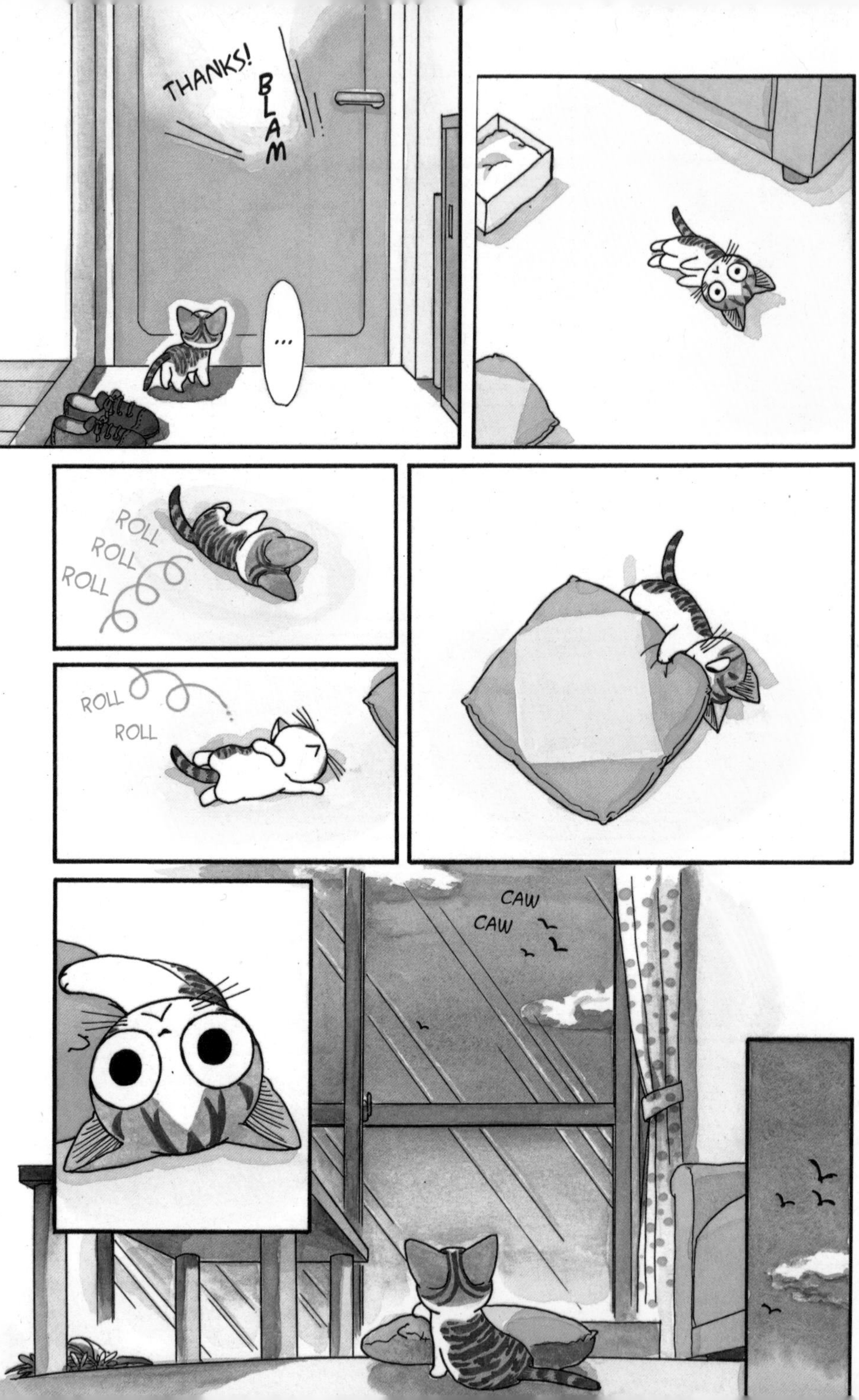
THANKS!
BLAM
...
ROLL
ROLL
ROLL
ROLL
ROLL
CAW
CAW

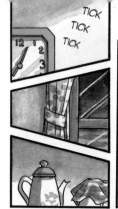

TICK
TICK
TICK

THEY ARE
COMING BACK,
WIGHT?

WIGHT?

GNAW
GNAW

GNAW
GNAW

TIP TIP TIP

BUT...

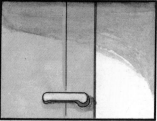

WHAT
IF...

SHAKE SHAKE

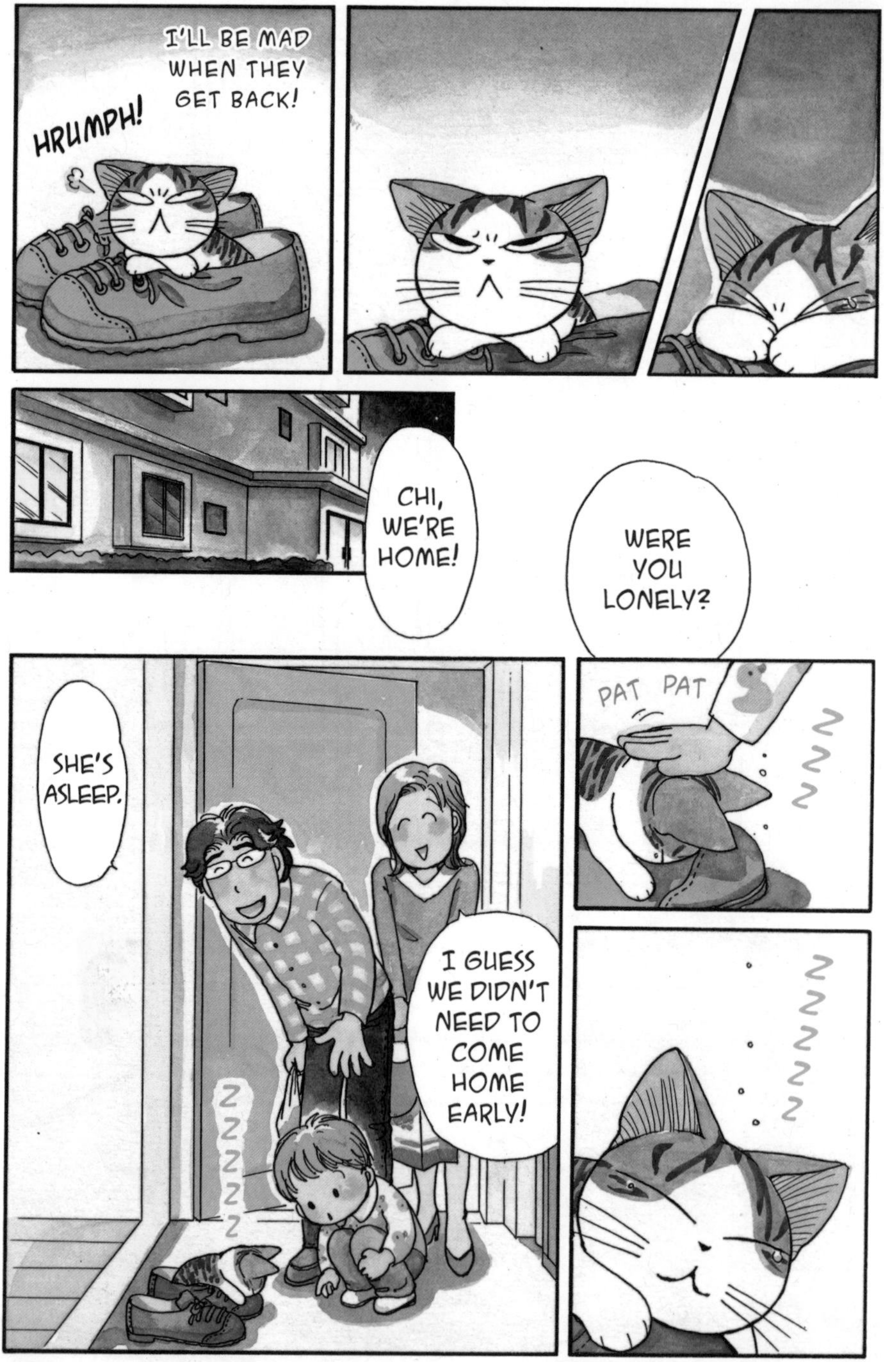
I'LL BE MAD WHEN THEY GET BACK!
HRUMPH!
CHI, WE'RE HOME!
WERE YOU LONELY?
SHE'S ASLEEP.
I GUESS WE DIDN'T NEED TO COME HOME EARLY!
PAT PAT
ZZZZ
ZZZZZ
ZZZZZ

the end

homemade 21: a cat is moved

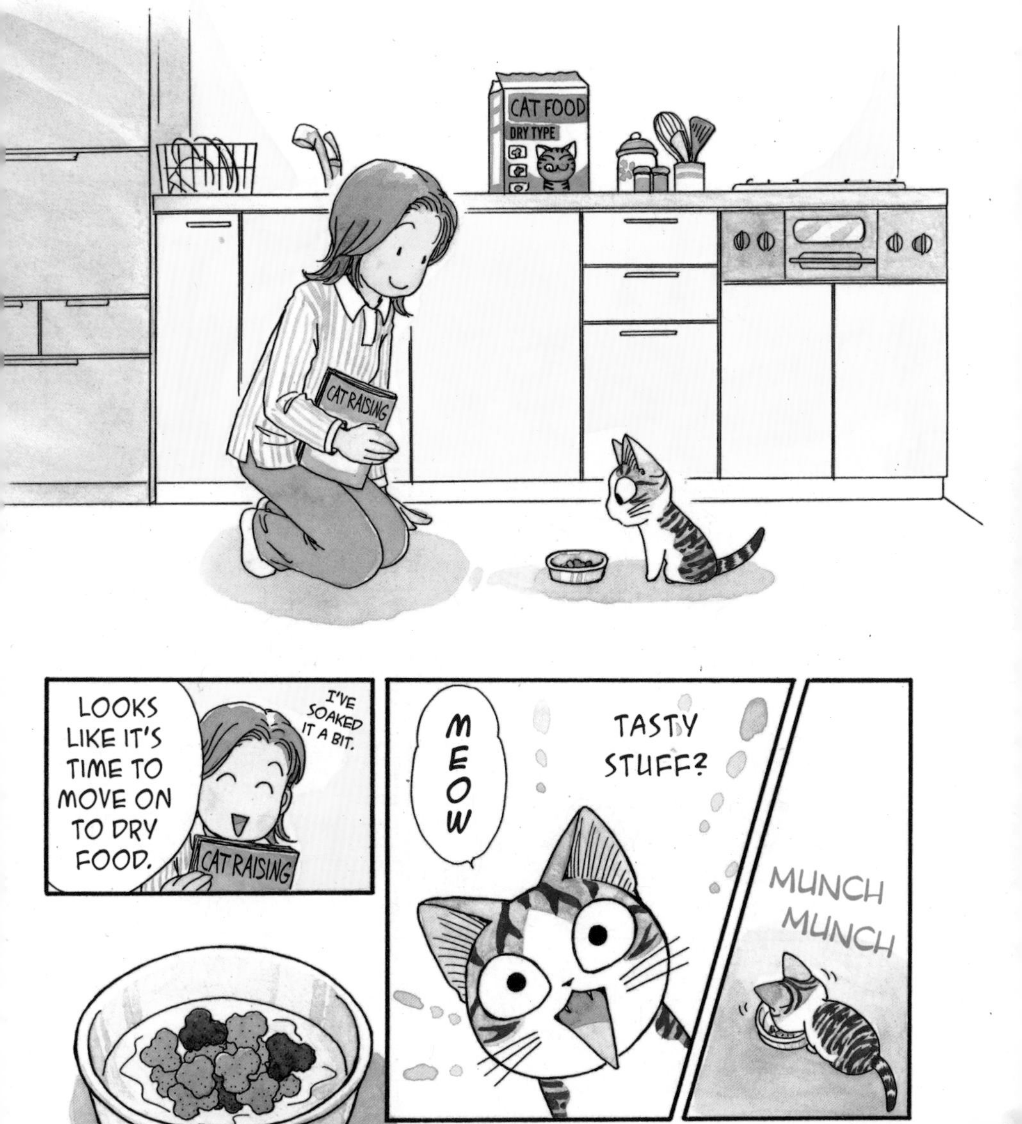
CAT FOOD
DRY TYPE
CAT RAISING
LOOKS LIKE IT'S TIME TO MOVE ON TO DRY FOOD.
I'VE SOAKED IT A BIT.
CAT RAISING
MEOW
TASTY STUFF?
MUNCH MUNCH

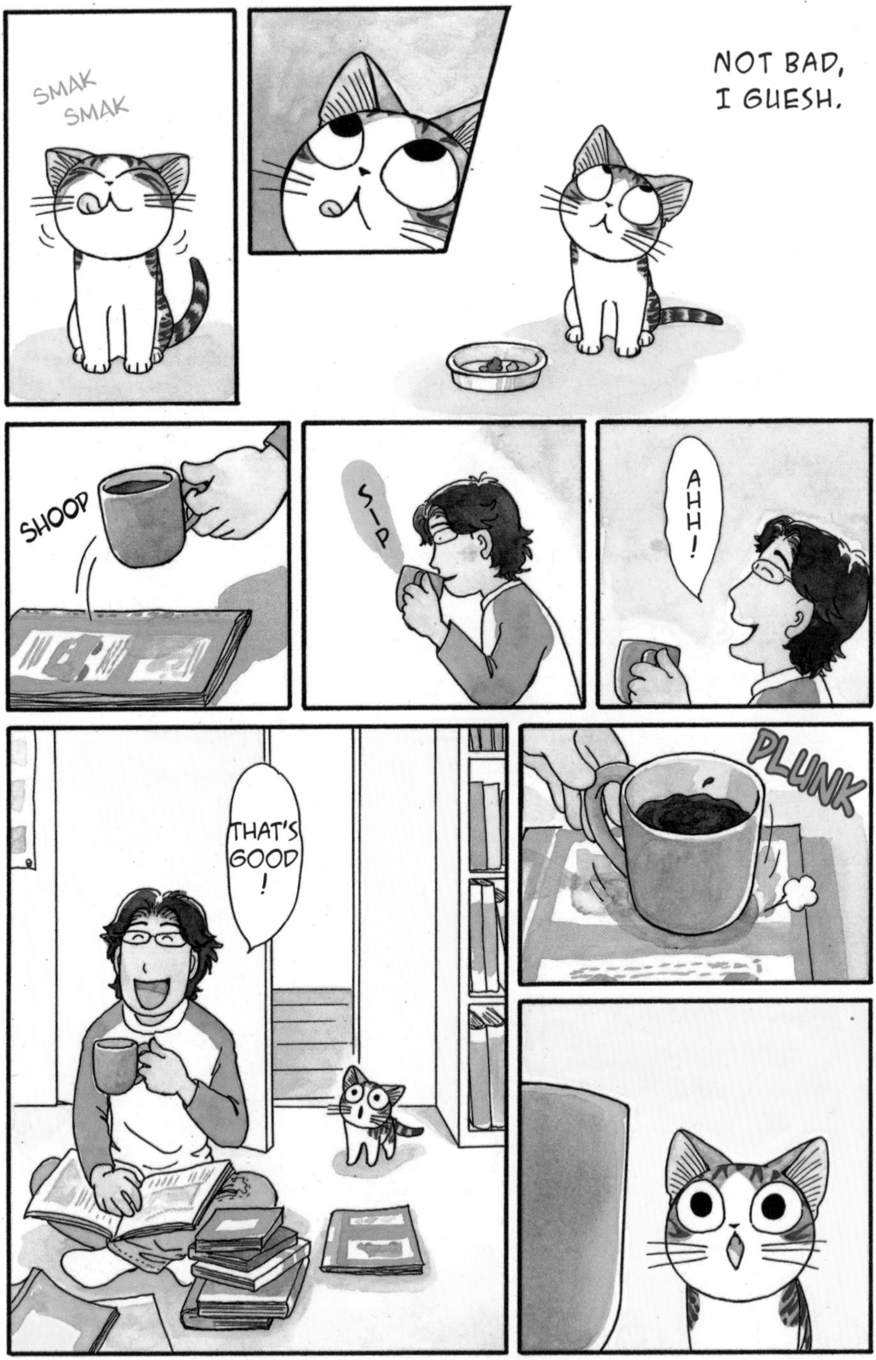
SMAK
SMAK
NOT BAD, I GUESH.
SHOOP
SIP
AHH!
THAT'S GOOD!
PLUNK

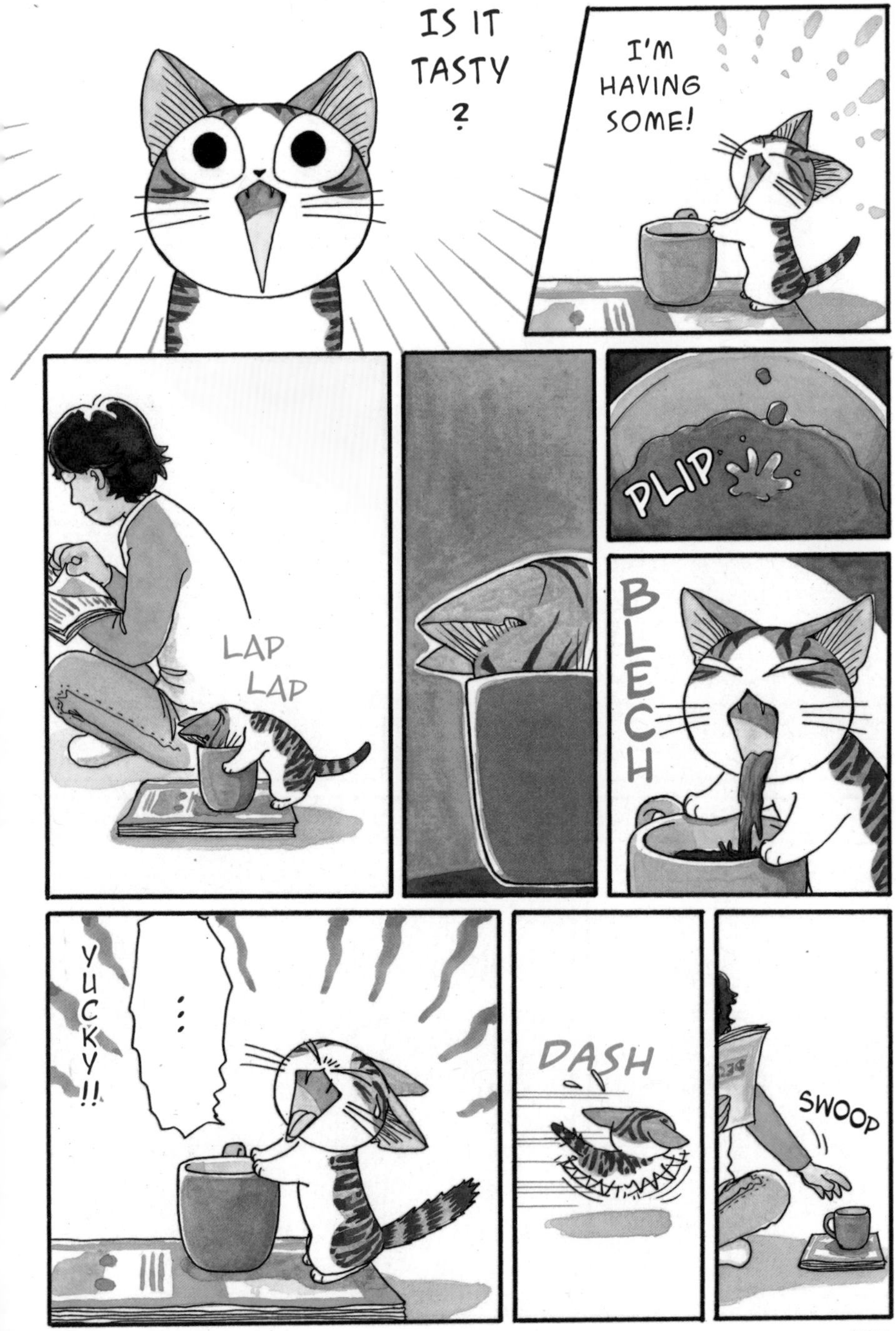
IS IT TASTY ?
I'M HAVING SOME!
LAP LAP
PLIP
BLECH
YUCKY!!
...
DASH
SWOOP

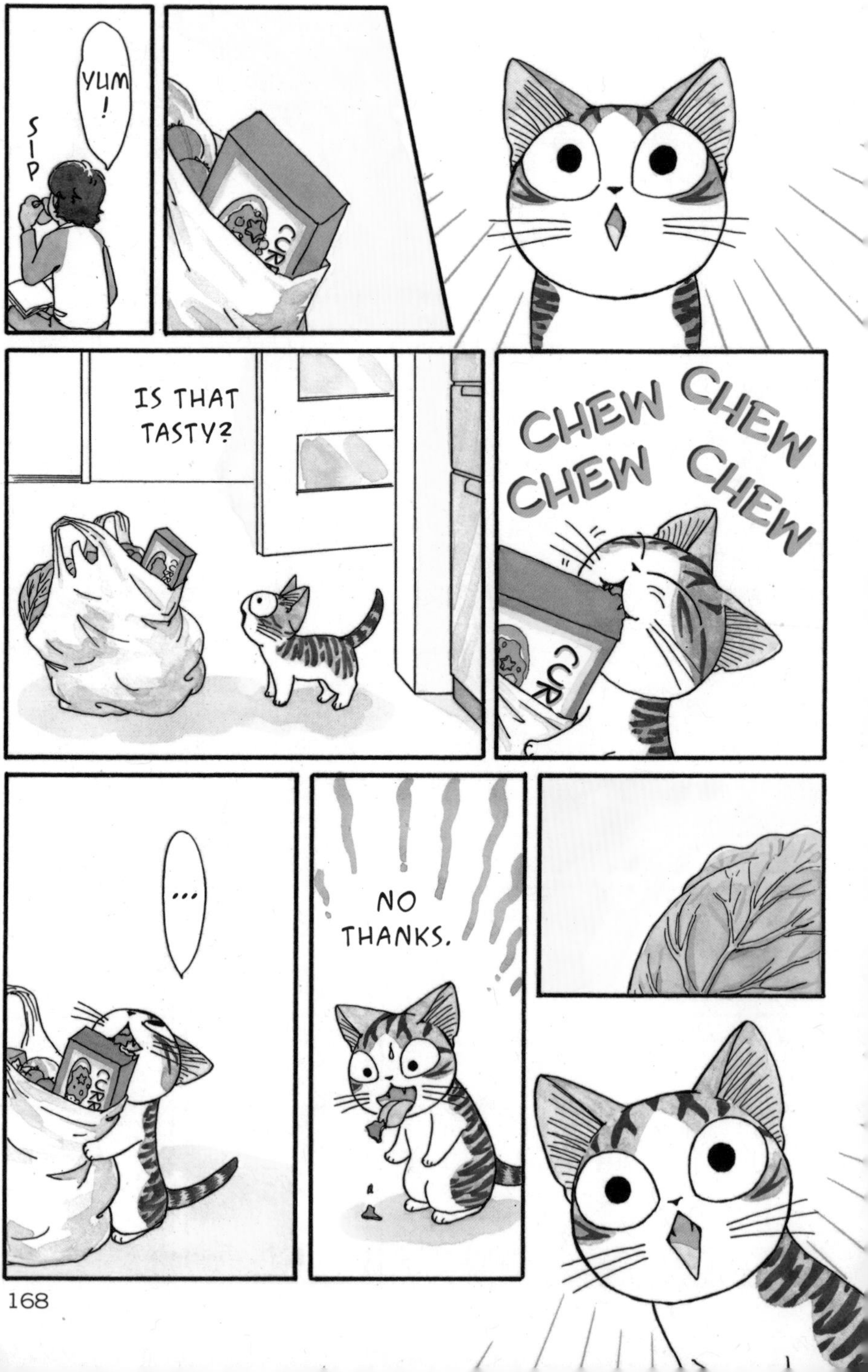
YUM!
SIP
IS THAT TASTY?
CHEW CHEW CHEW CHEW
...
NO THANKS.

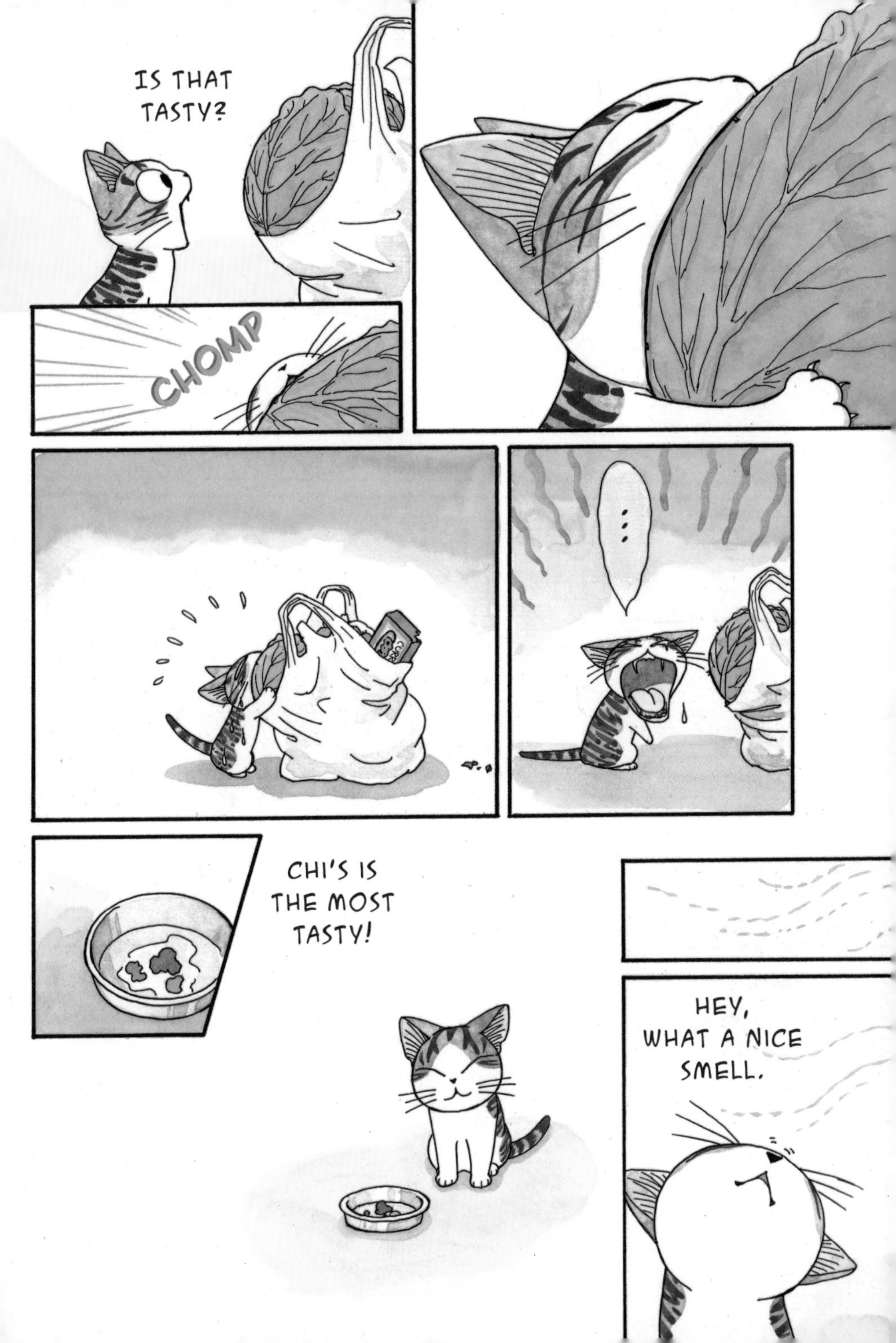
IS THAT TASTY?
CHOMP
...
CHI'S IS THE MOST TASTY!
HEY, WHAT A NICE SMELL.

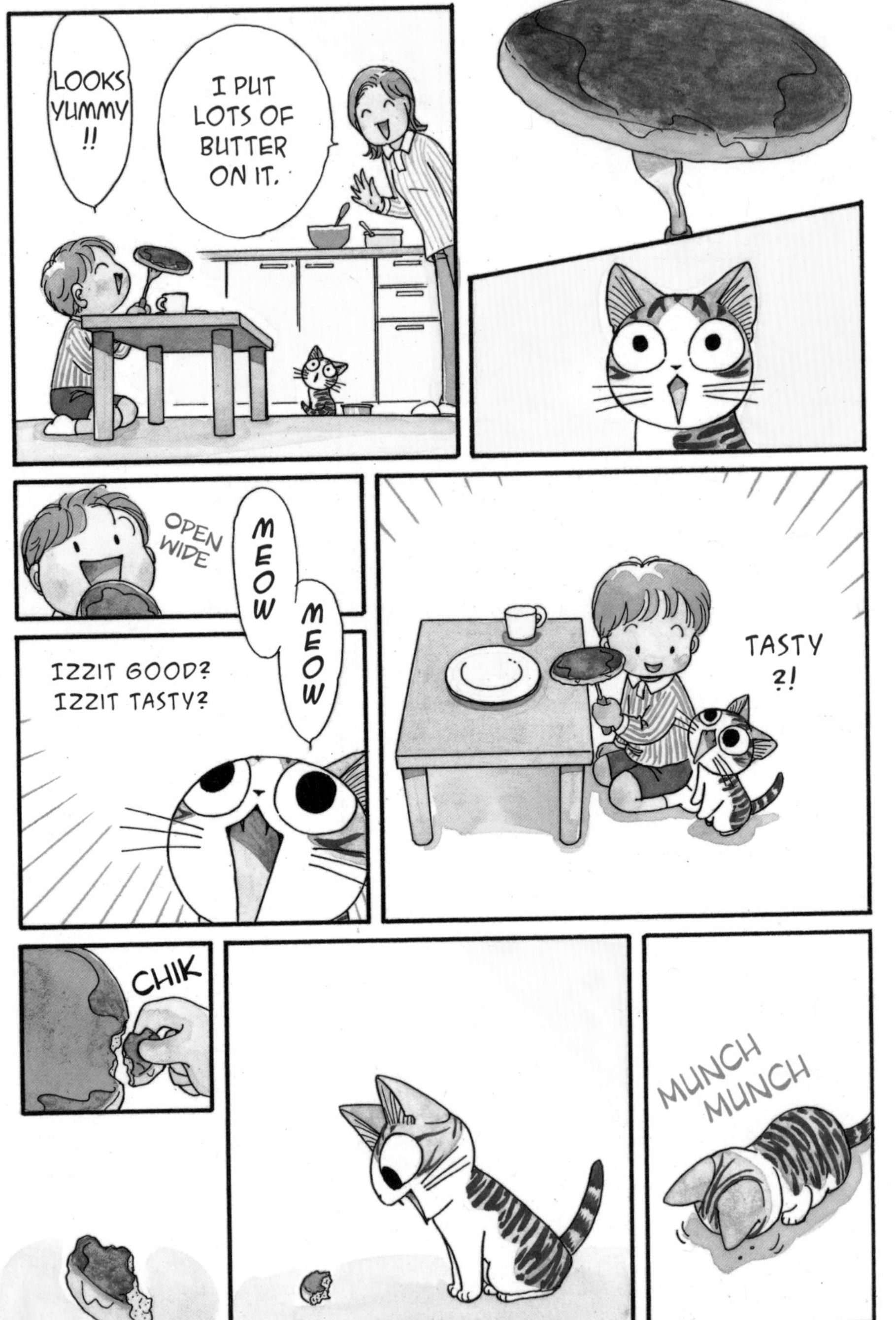
LOOKS YUMMY !!
I PUT LOTS OF BUTTER ON IT.
OPEN WIDE
MEOW
MEOW
IZZIT GOOD? IZZIT TASTY?
TASTY ?!
CHIK
MUNCH MUNCH

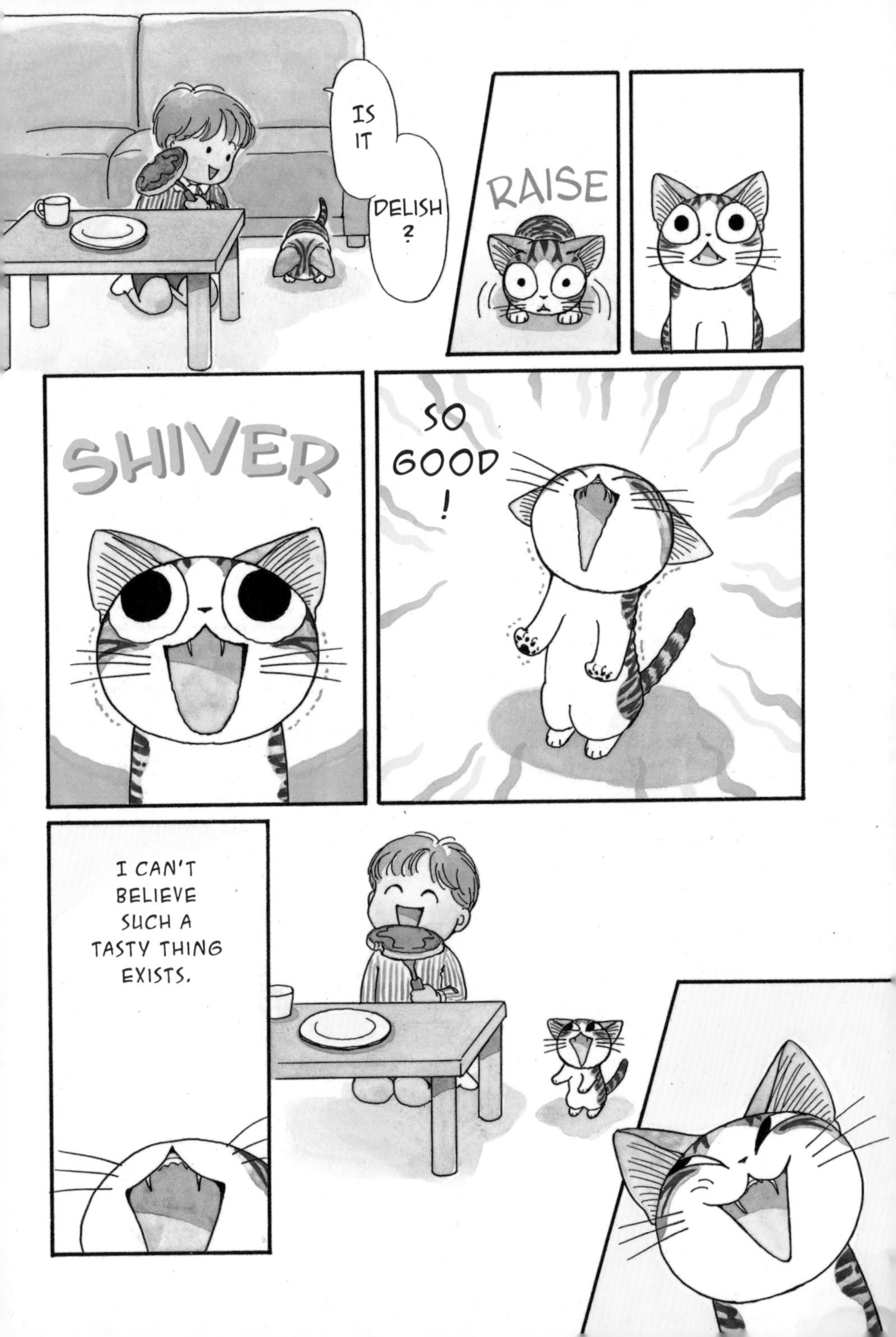
IS IT DELISH?
RAISE
SHIVER
SO GOOD!
I CAN'T BELIEVE SUCH A TASTY THING EXISTS.

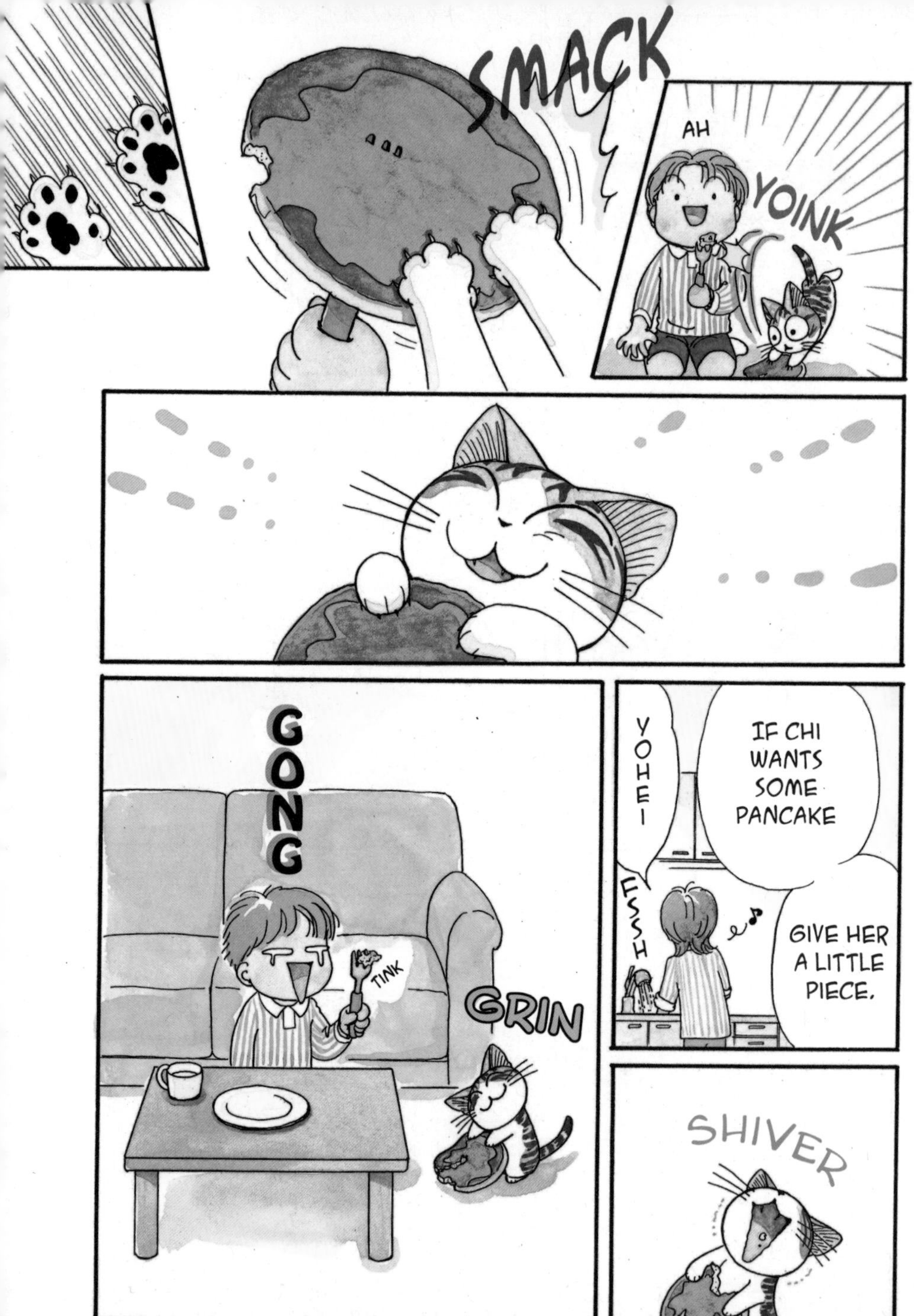
SMACK
AH
YOINK
GONG
TINK
GRIN
YOHEI
IF CHI WANTS SOME PANCAKE
FSSH
GIVE HER A LITTLE PIECE.
SHIVER

the end

homemade 22: a cat takes a bath

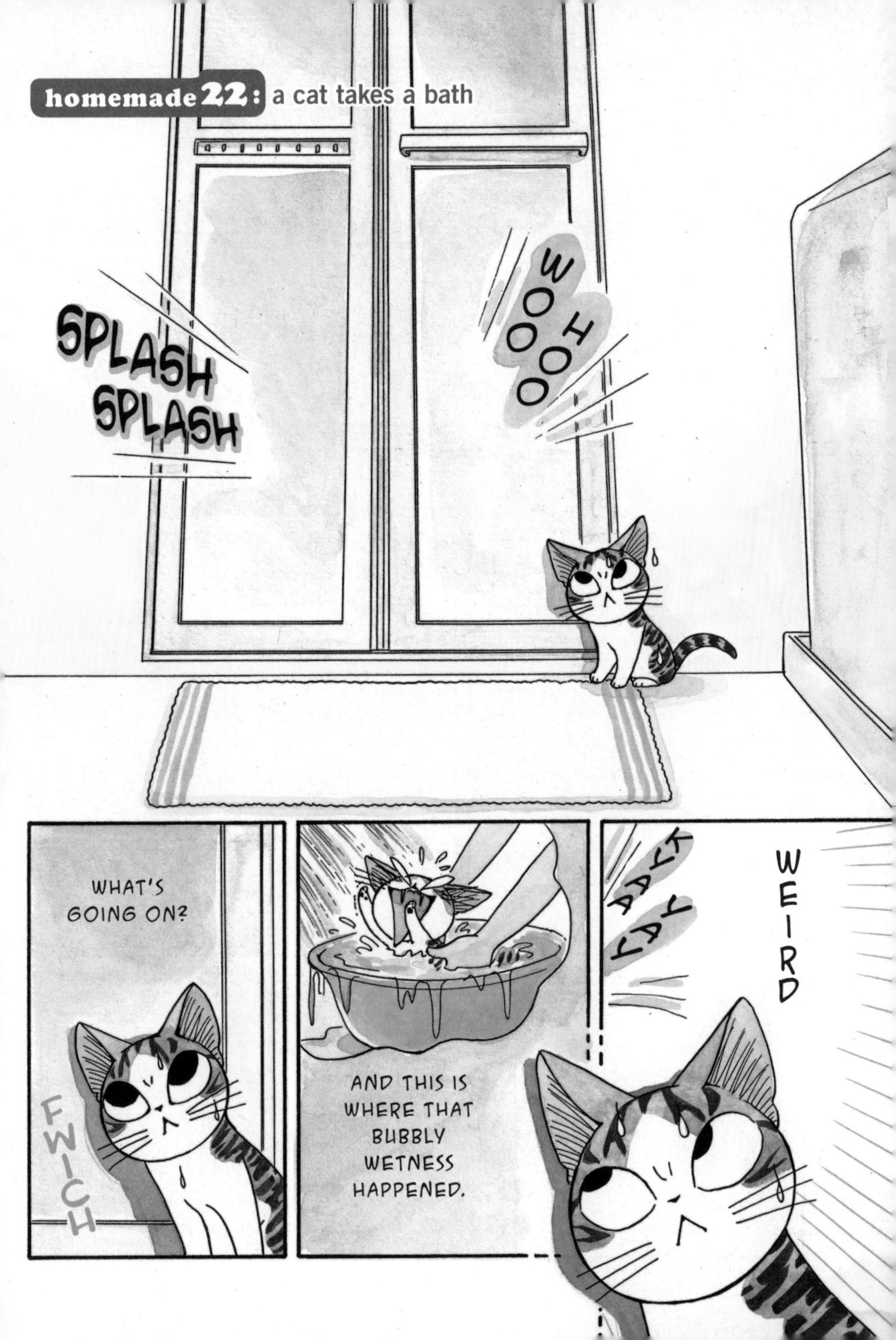
SPLASH
SPLASH
WOOHOO
WHAT'S GOING ON?
FWICH
AND THIS IS WHERE THAT BUBBLY WETNESS HAPPENED.
YAY
AAYK
WEIRD

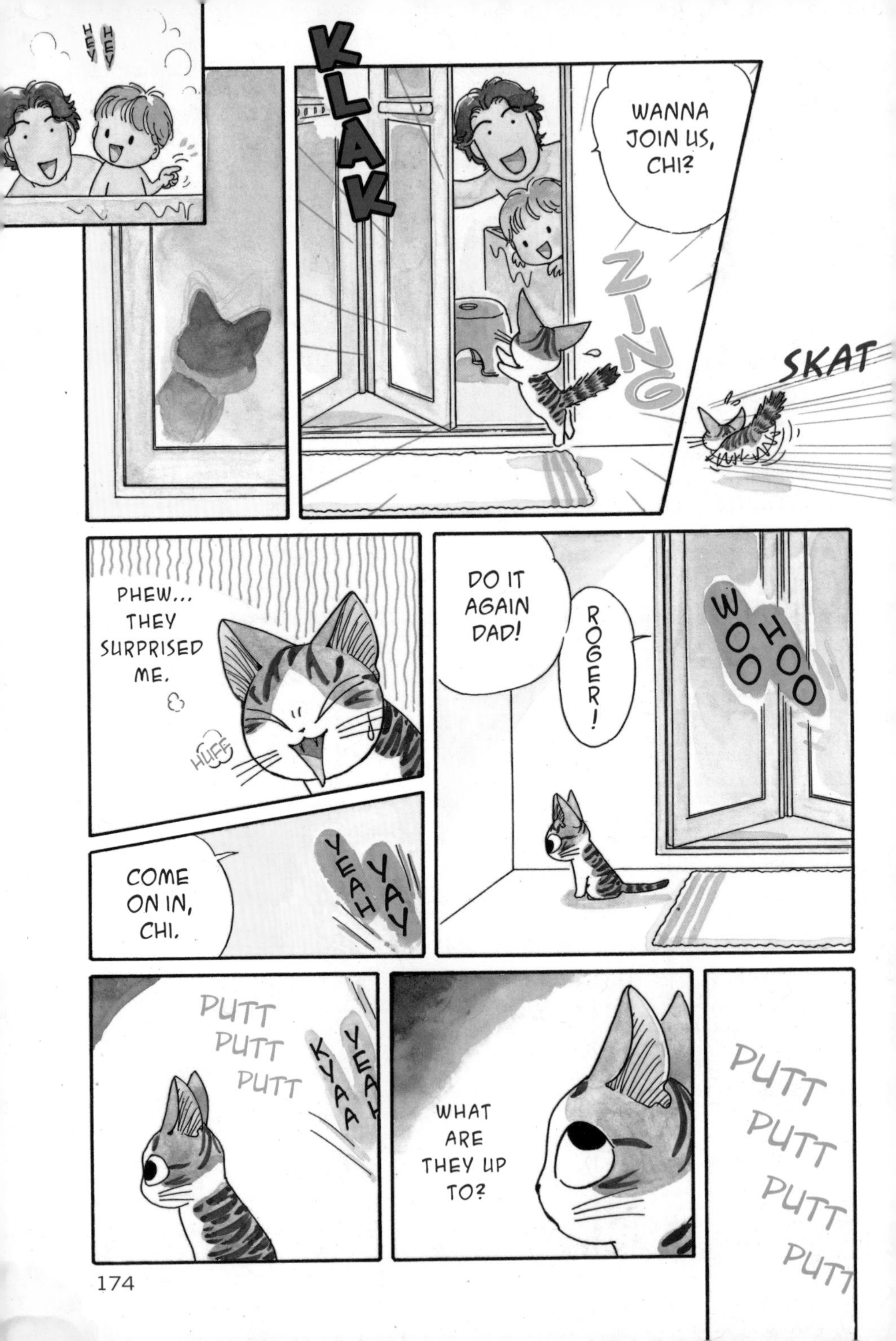
HEY HEY
KLAK
WANNA JOIN US, CHI?
ZING
SKAT
PHEW... THEY SURPRISED ME.
HUFF
COME ON IN, CHI.
YEAH YAY
DO IT AGAIN DAD!
ROGER!
WOO HOO
PUTT PUTT PUTT
KYAA YEAH
WHAT ARE THEY UP TO?
PUTT PUTT PUTT PUTT

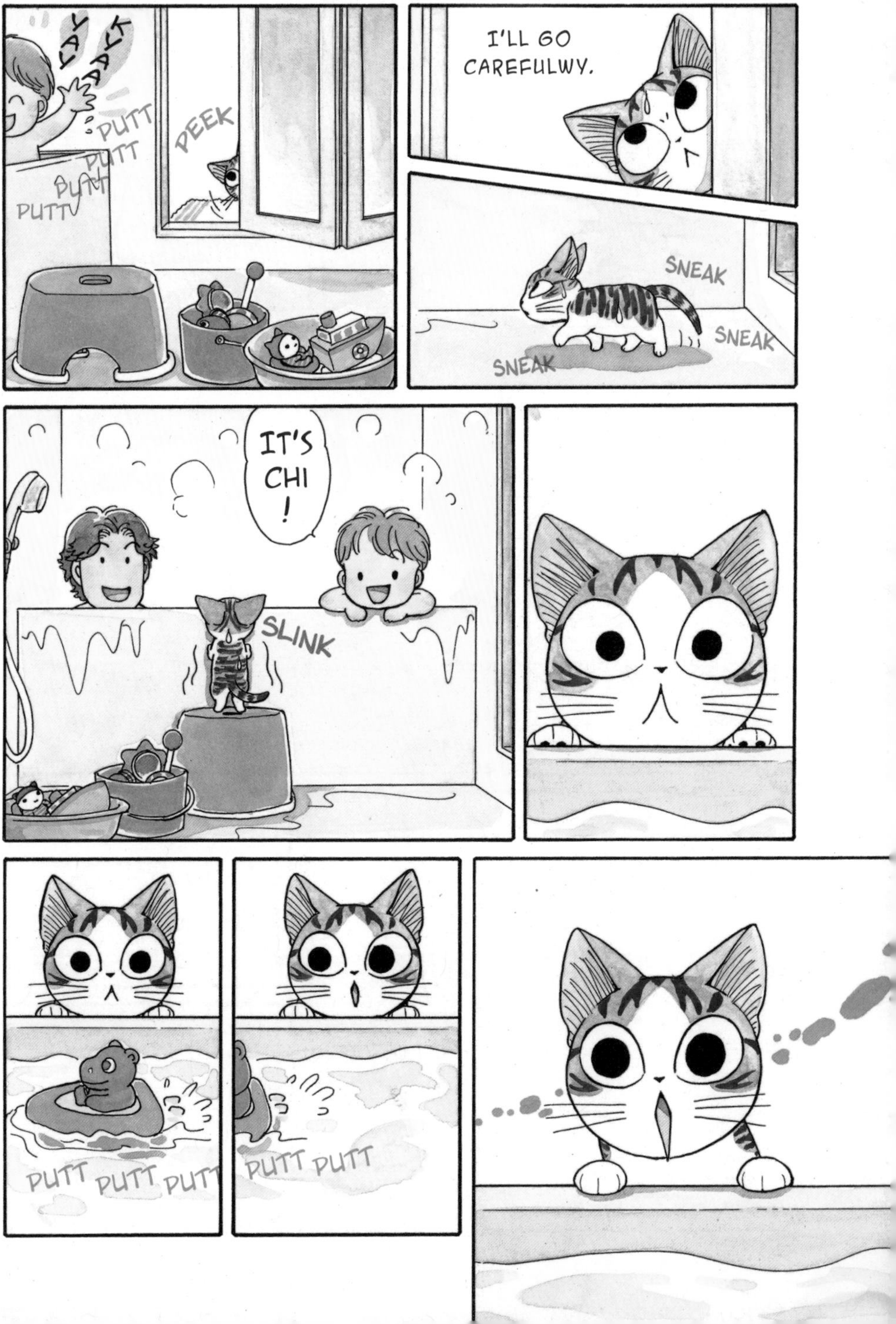
YAY
KYAAA
PUTT
PUTT
PUTT
PUTT
PEEK
I'LL GO CAREFULWY.
SNEAK
SNEAK
SNEAK
IT'S CHI!
SLINK
PUTT
PUTT
PUTT
PUTT PUTT

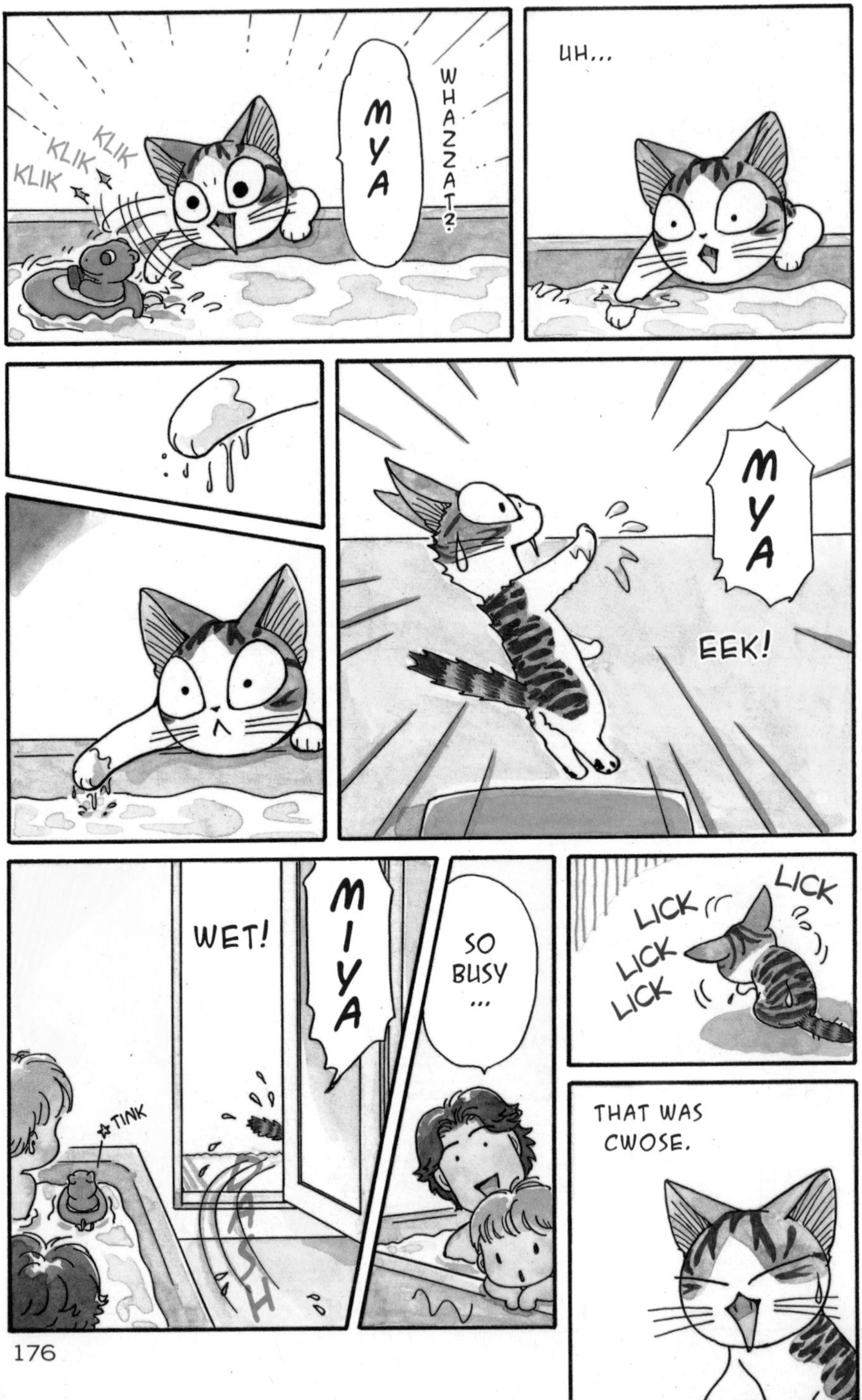
KLIK
KLIK
KLIK
MYA
WHAZZAT?
UH...
MYA
EEK!
WET!
MIYA
TINK
SO BUSY ...
LICK
LICK
LICK
LICK
THAT WAS CWOSE.

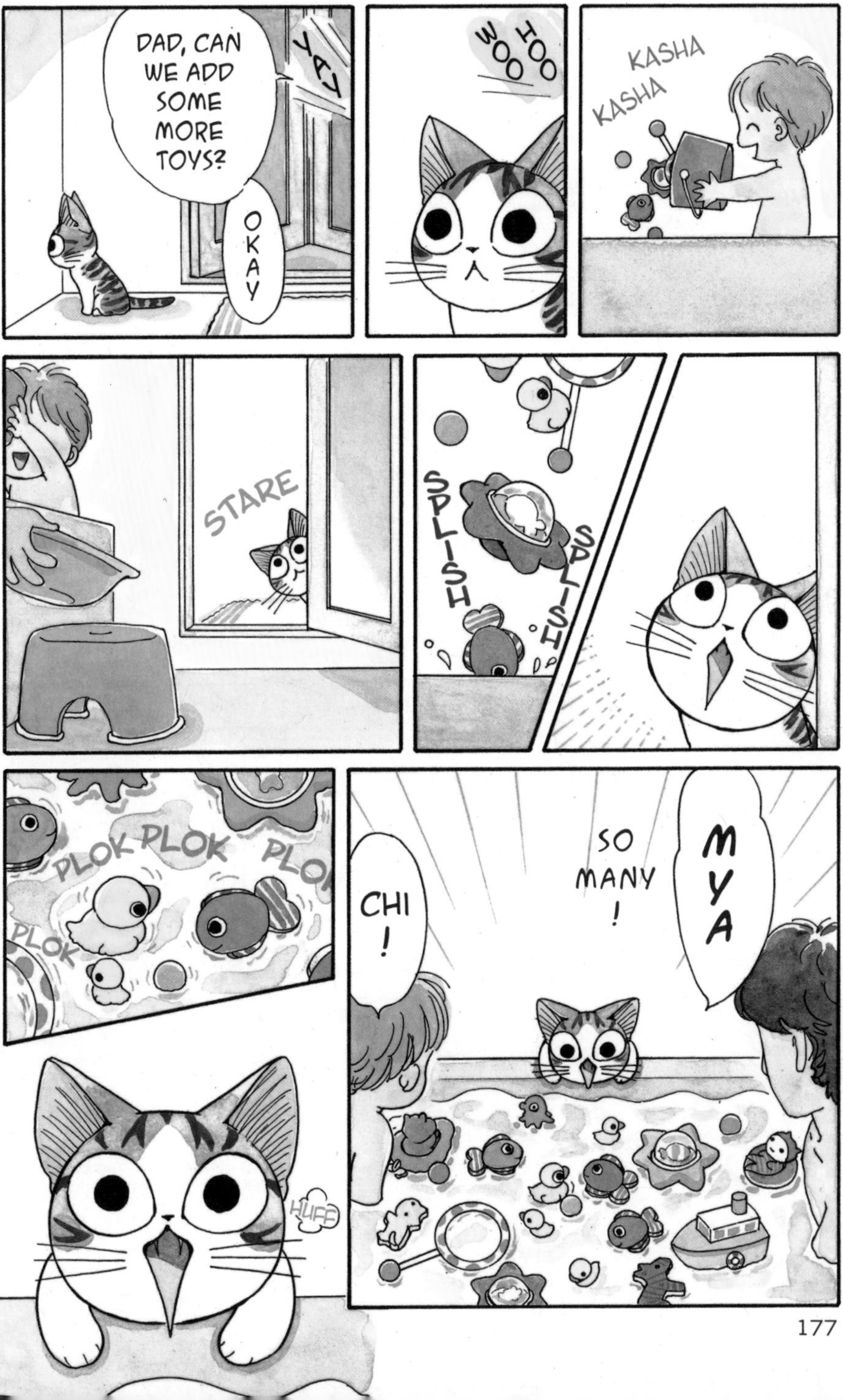
DAD, CAN WE ADD SOME MORE TOYS?
OKAY
WOO HOO
KASHA KASHA
STARE
SPLISH SPLISH
PLOK PLOK PLOK
PLOK
HUFF
CHI!
SO MANY!
MYA

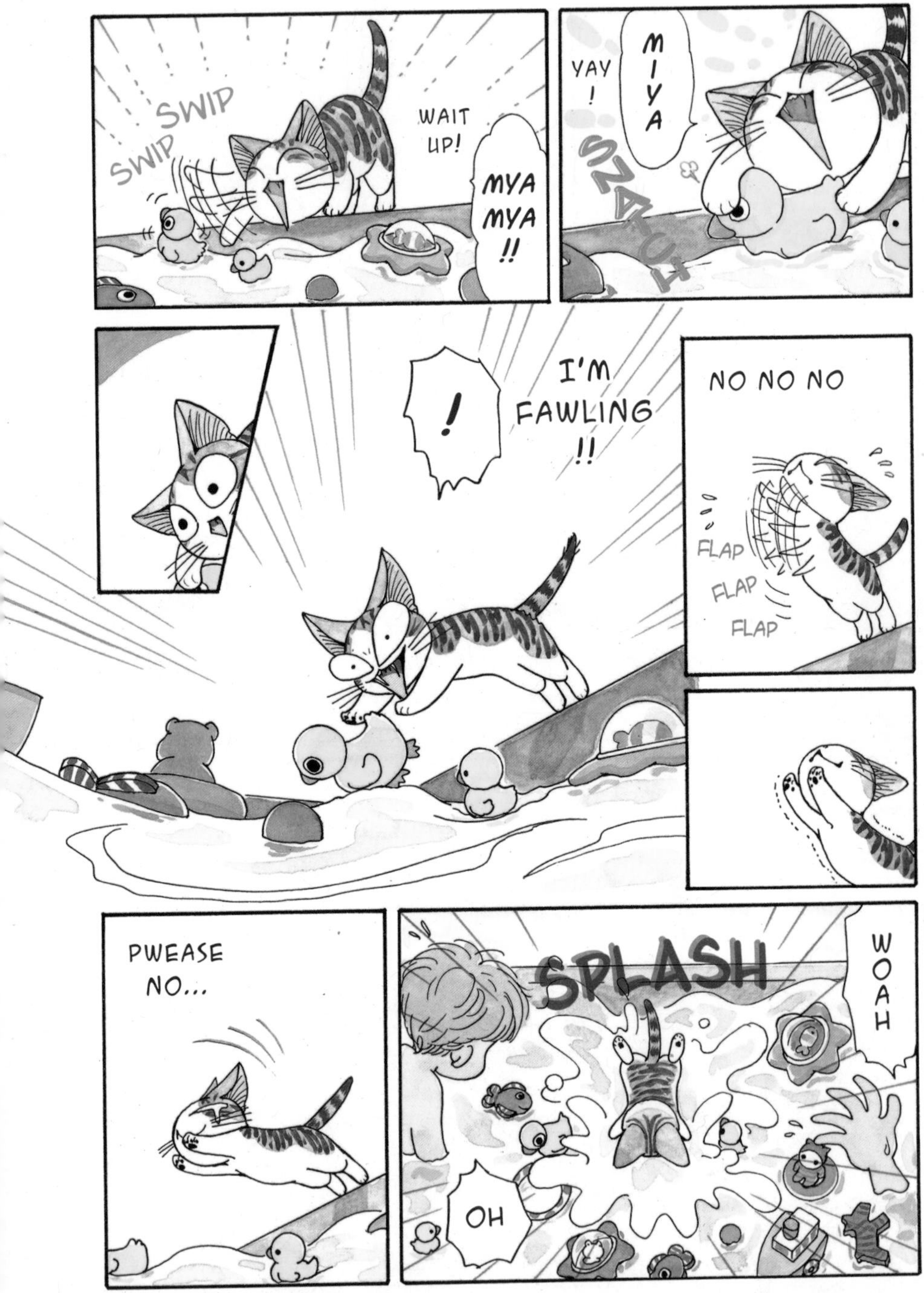
SWIP
SWIP
WAIT UP!
MYA MYA !!
YAY!
MIYA
SNATCH
!
I'M FAWLING !!
NO NO NO
FLAP
FLAP
FLAP
PWEASE NO...
SPLASH
WOAH
OH

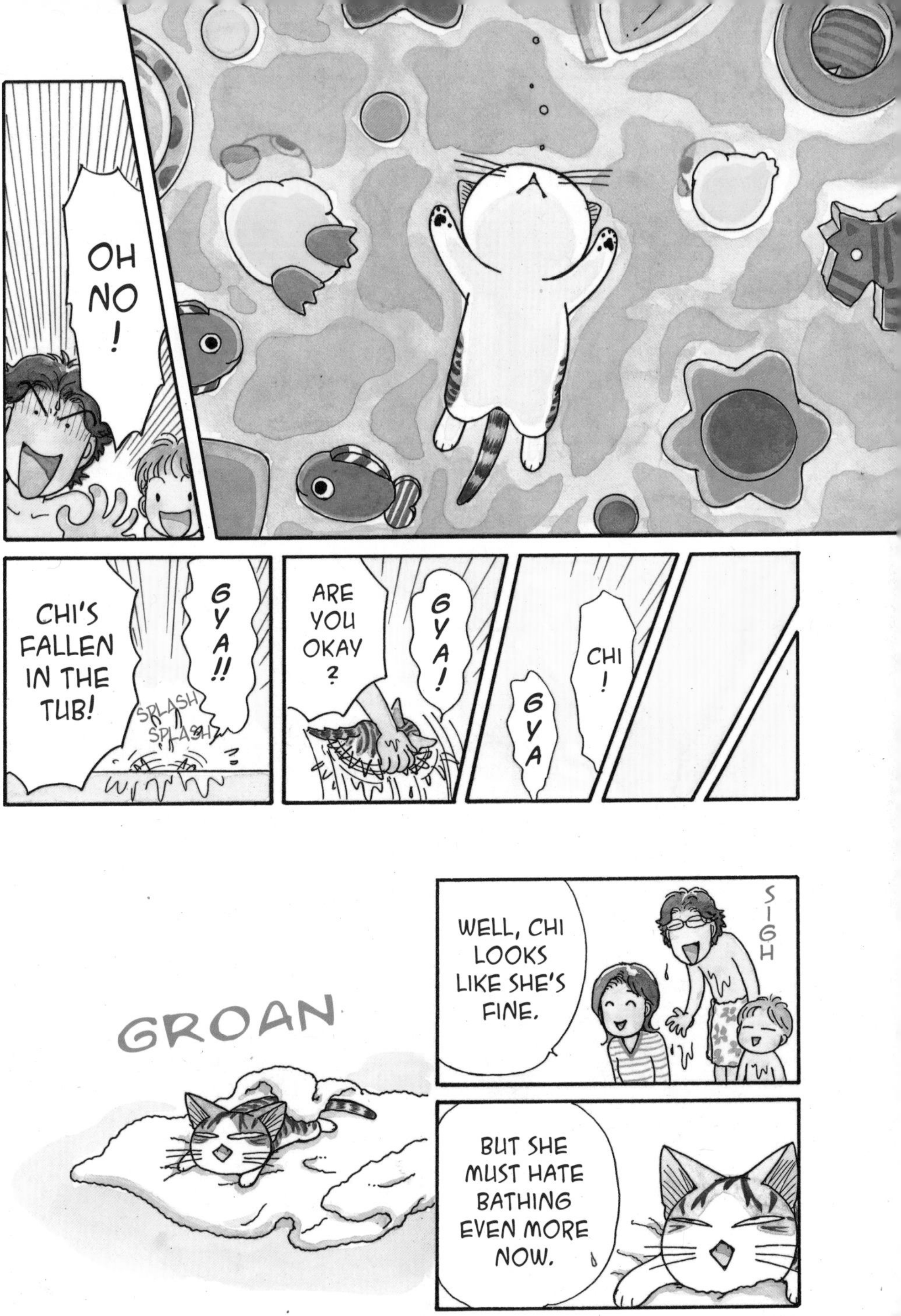

OH NO!
CHI'S FALLEN IN THE TUB!
GYA!!
SPLASH SPLASH
ARE YOU OKAY?
GYA!
CHI!
GYA
GROAN
WELL, CHI LOOKS LIKE SHE'S FINE.
SIGH
BUT SHE MUST HATE BATHING EVEN MORE NOW.

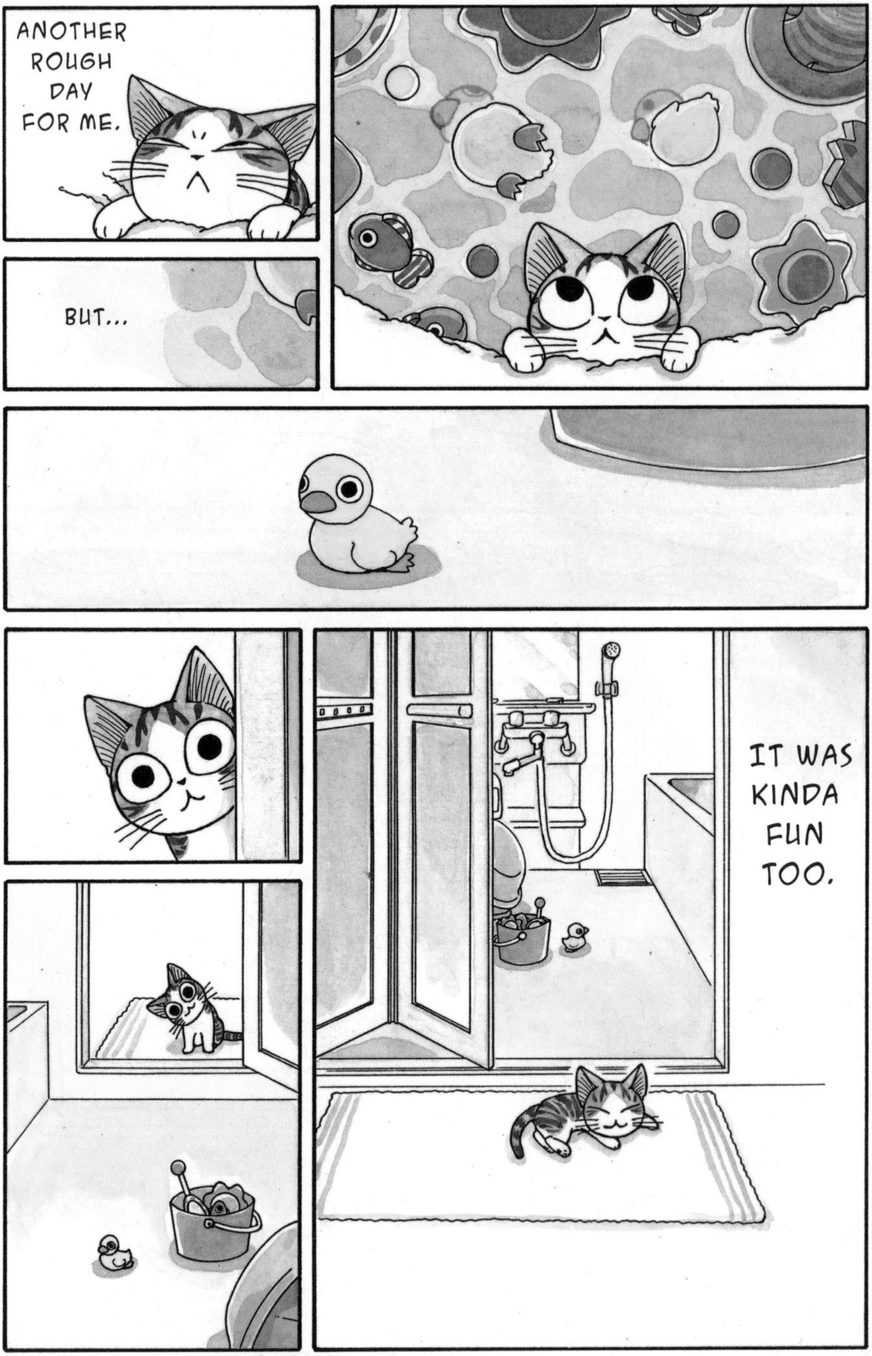
ANOTHER ROUGH DAY FOR ME.
BUT...
IT WAS KINDA FUN TOO.

the end

homemade 23: a cat throws down

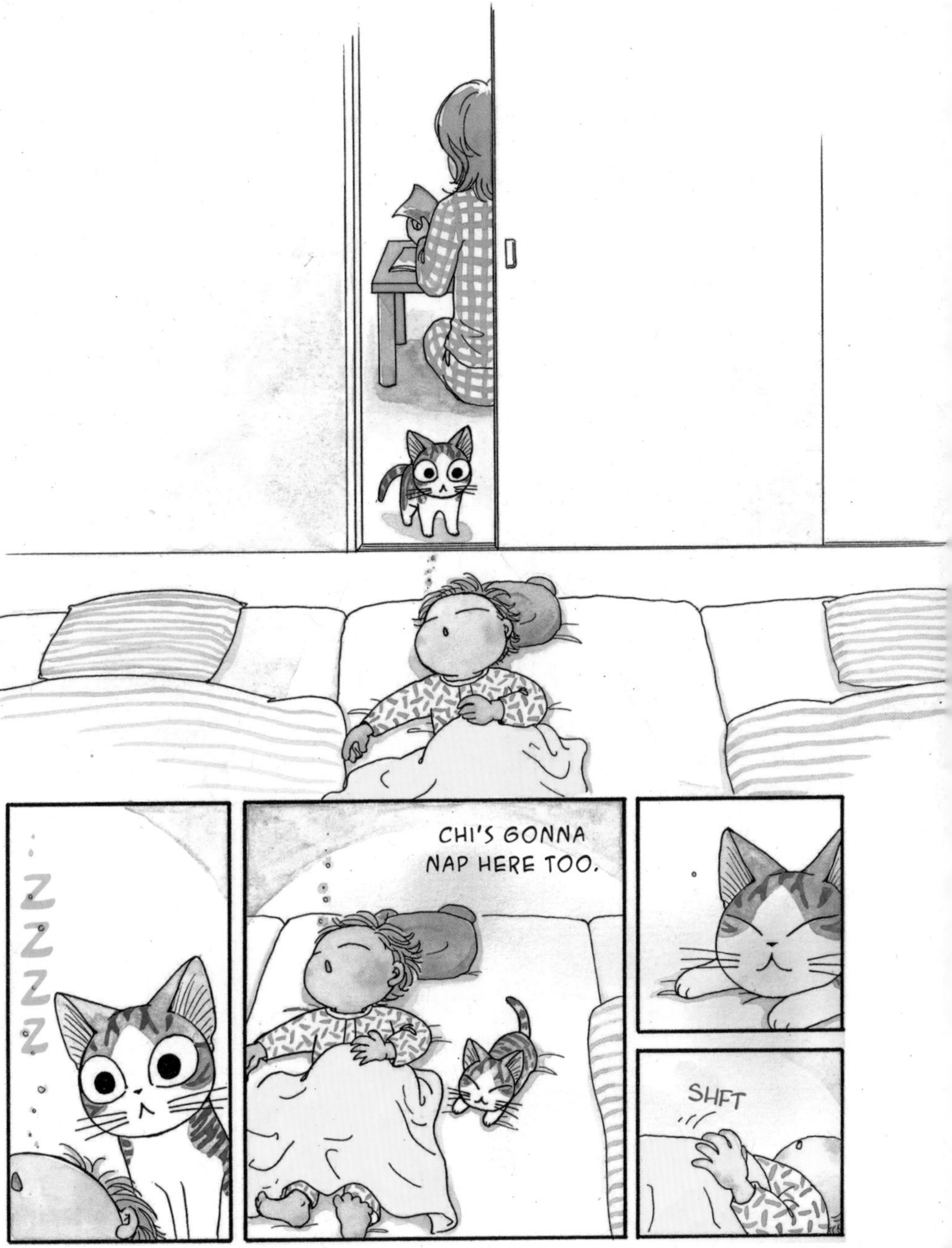
ZZZZ
CHI'S GONNA NAP HERE TOO.
SHFT

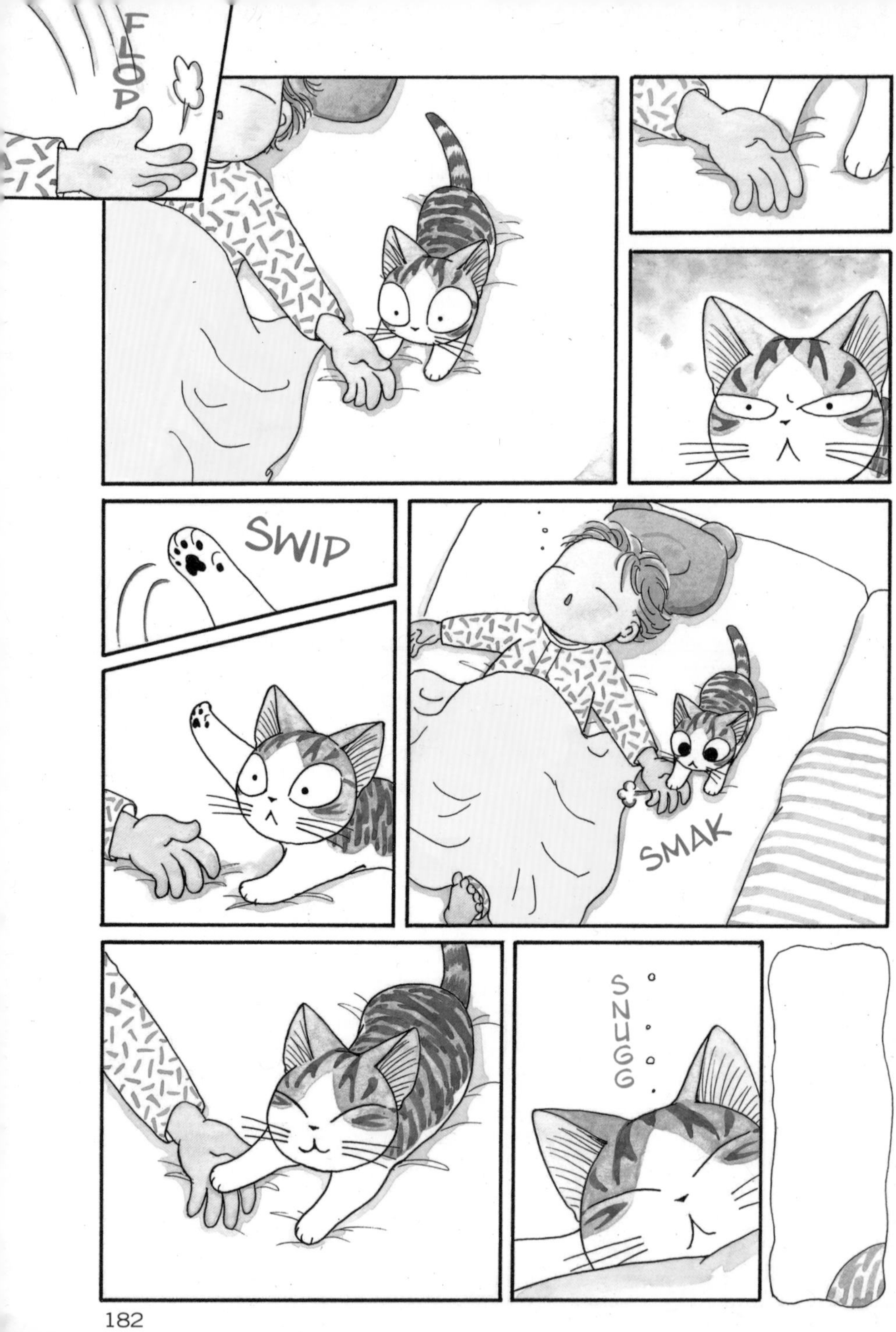
FLOP
SWIP
SMAK
SNUGG

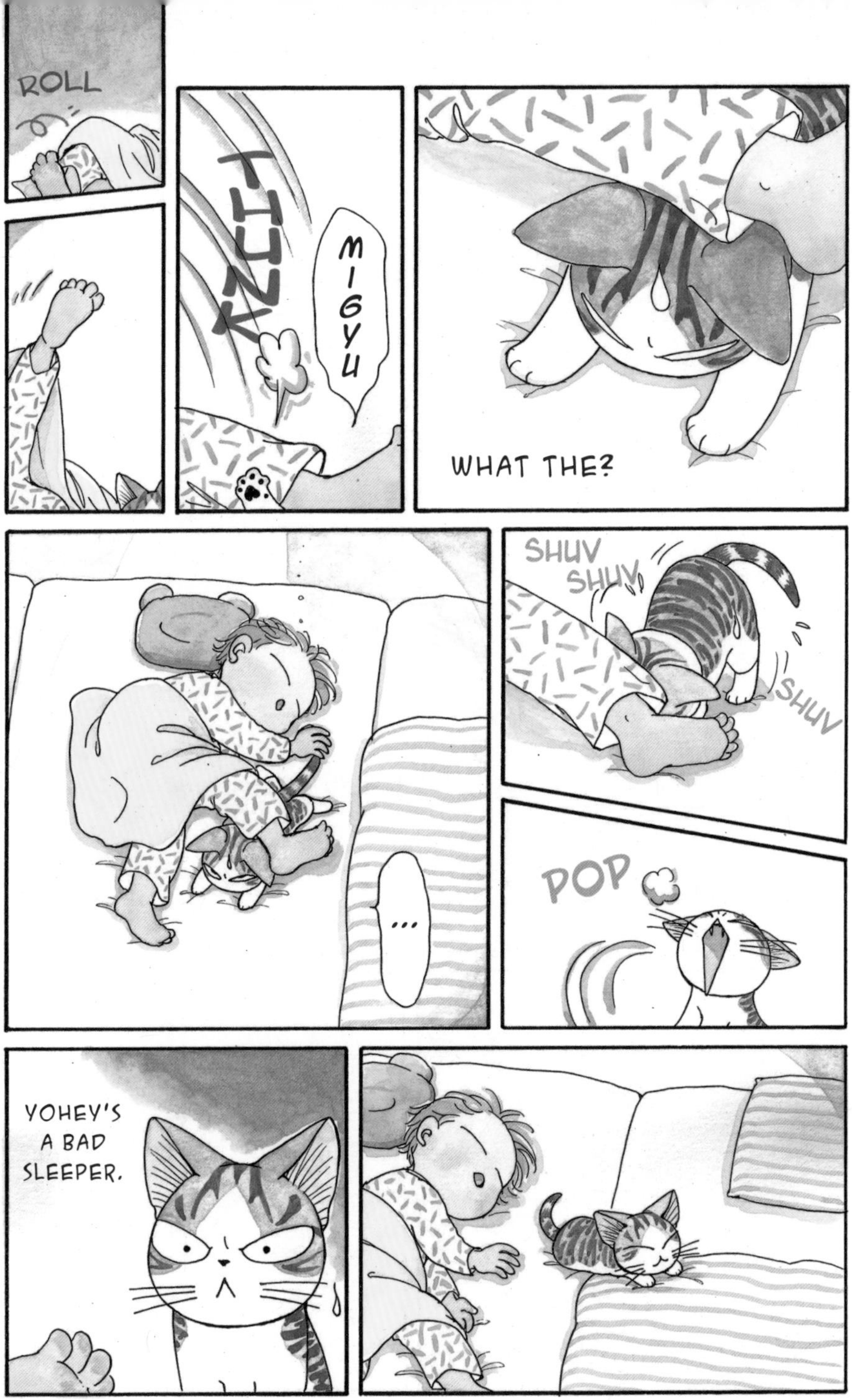
ROLL
THUNK
MIGYU
WHAT THE?
...
SHUV
SHUV
SHUV
POP
YOHEY'S A BAD SLEEPER.

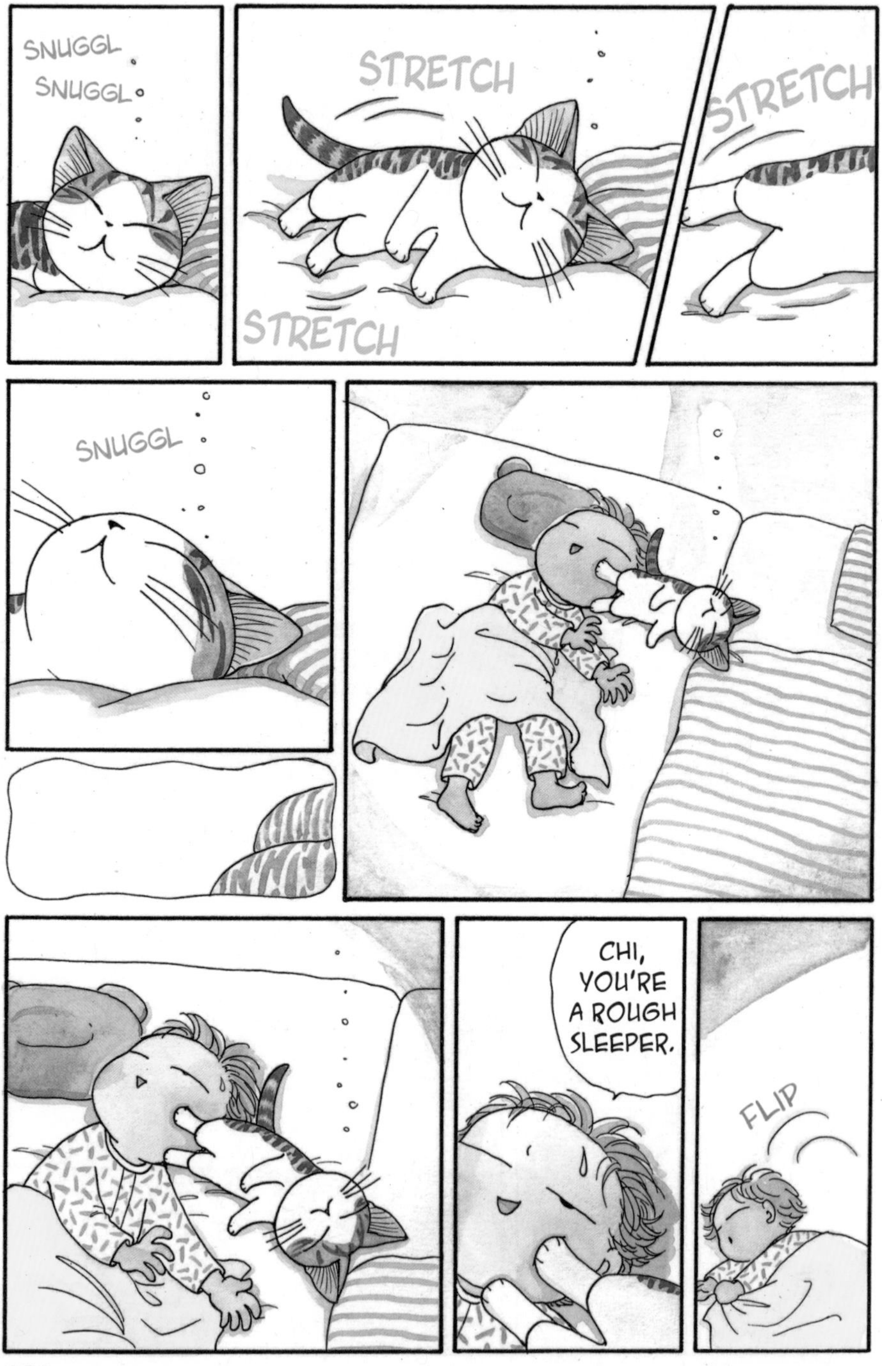
SNUGGL
SNUGGL
STRETCH
STRETCH
STRETCH
SNUGGL
CHI, YOU'RE A ROUGH SLEEPER.
FLIP

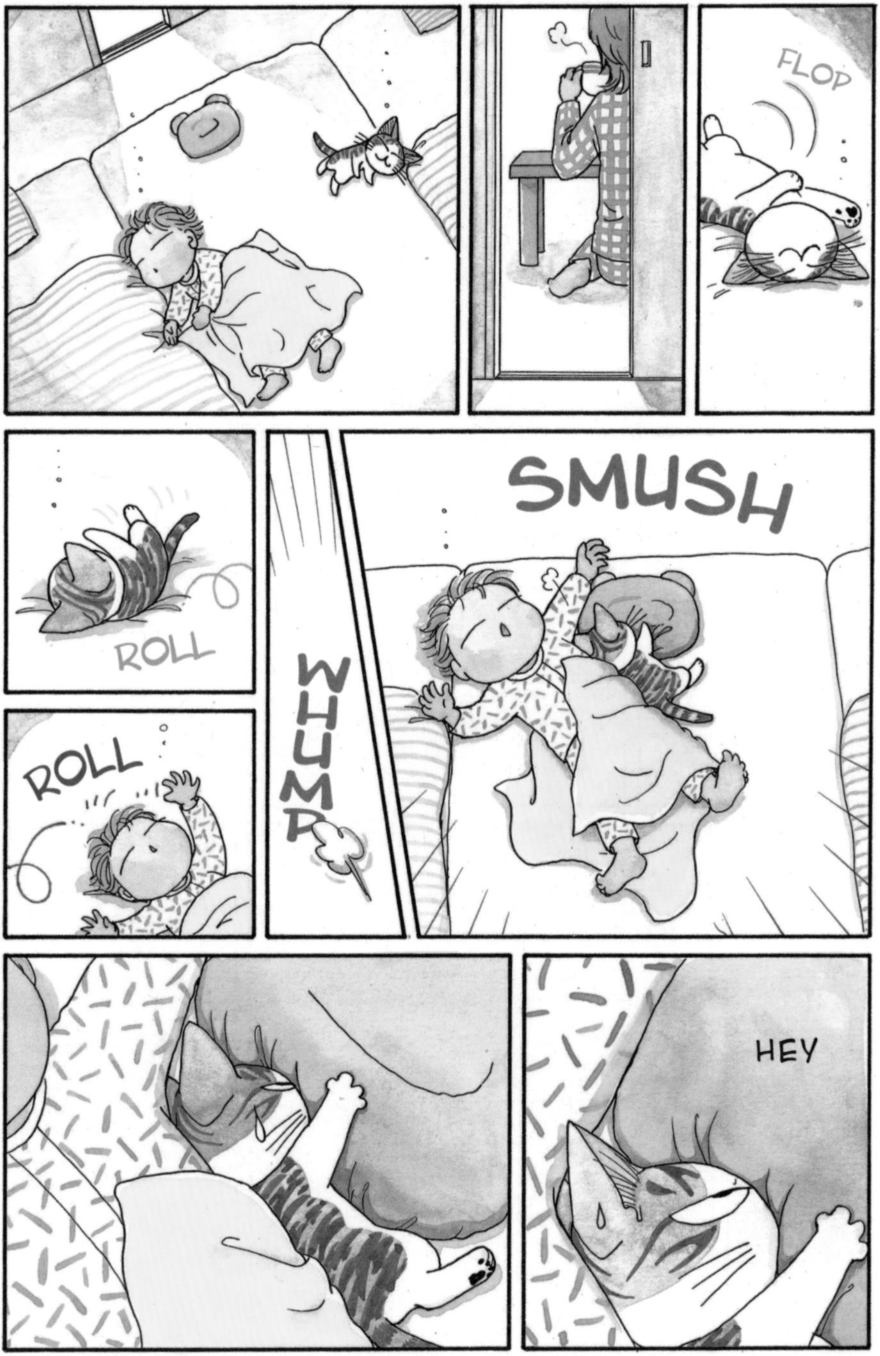
FLOP
ROLL
ROLL
WHUMP
SMUSH
HEY

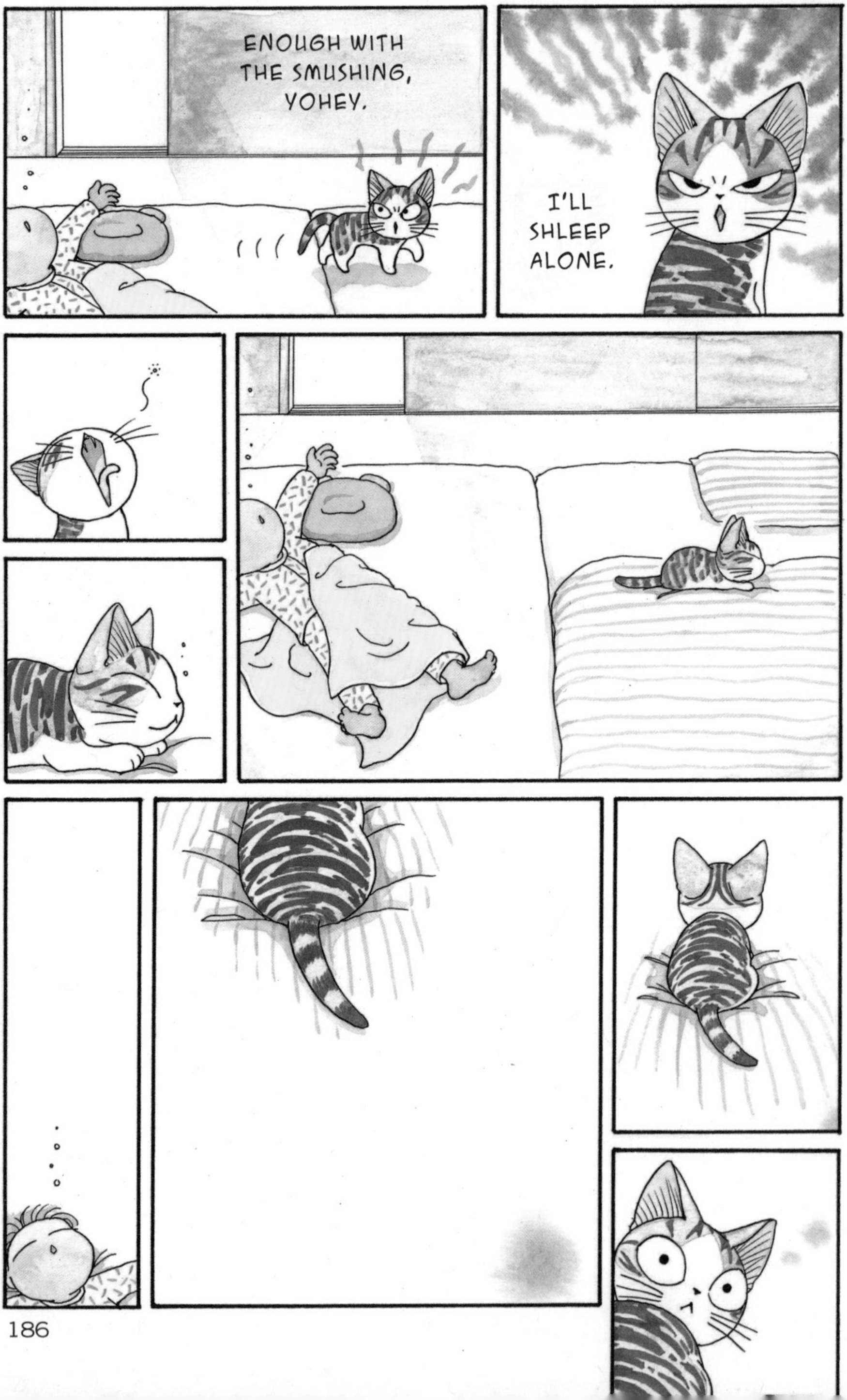
ENOUGH WITH THE SMUSHING, YOHEY.
I'LL SHLEEP ALONE.

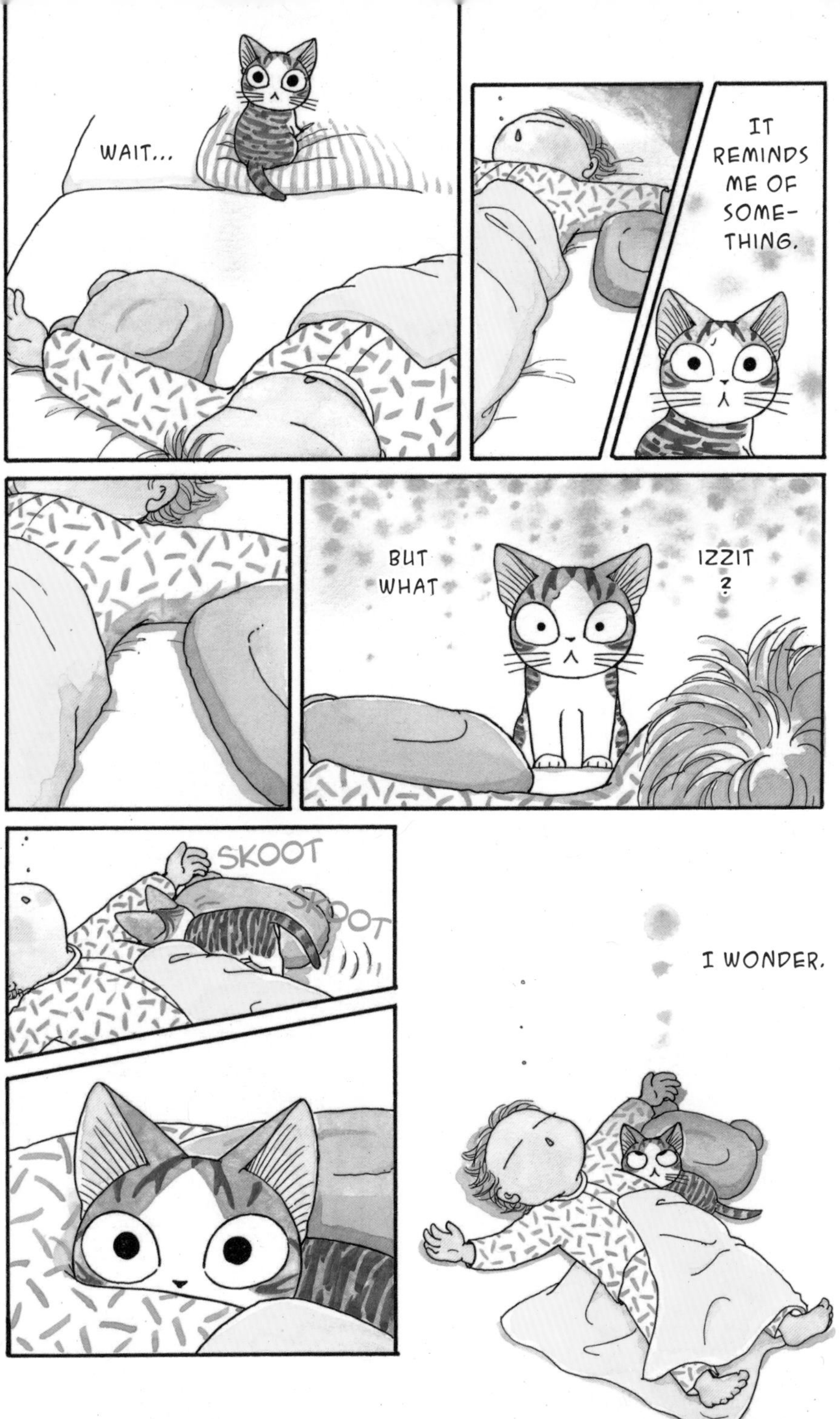
WAIT...
IT REMINDS ME OF SOME-THING.
BUT WHAT
IZZIT?
SKOOT
SKOOT
I WONDER.

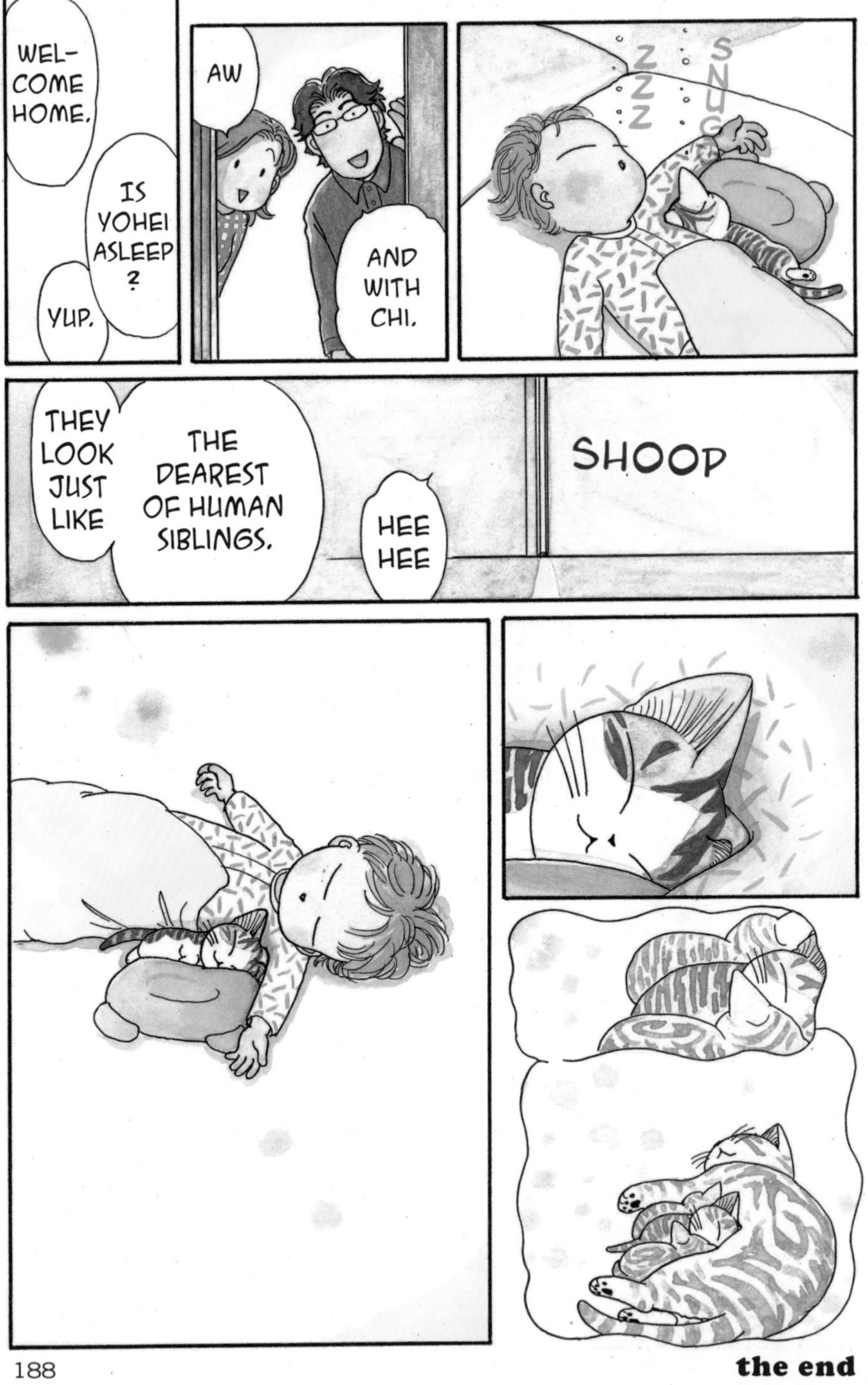
WEL-COME HOME.
IS YOHEI ASLEEP?
YUP.
AW
AND WITH CHI.
ZZZ
SNUG
THEY LOOK JUST LIKE
THE DEAREST OF HUMAN SIBLINGS.
HEE HEE
SHOOP

the end

homemade 24: a cat asserts itself

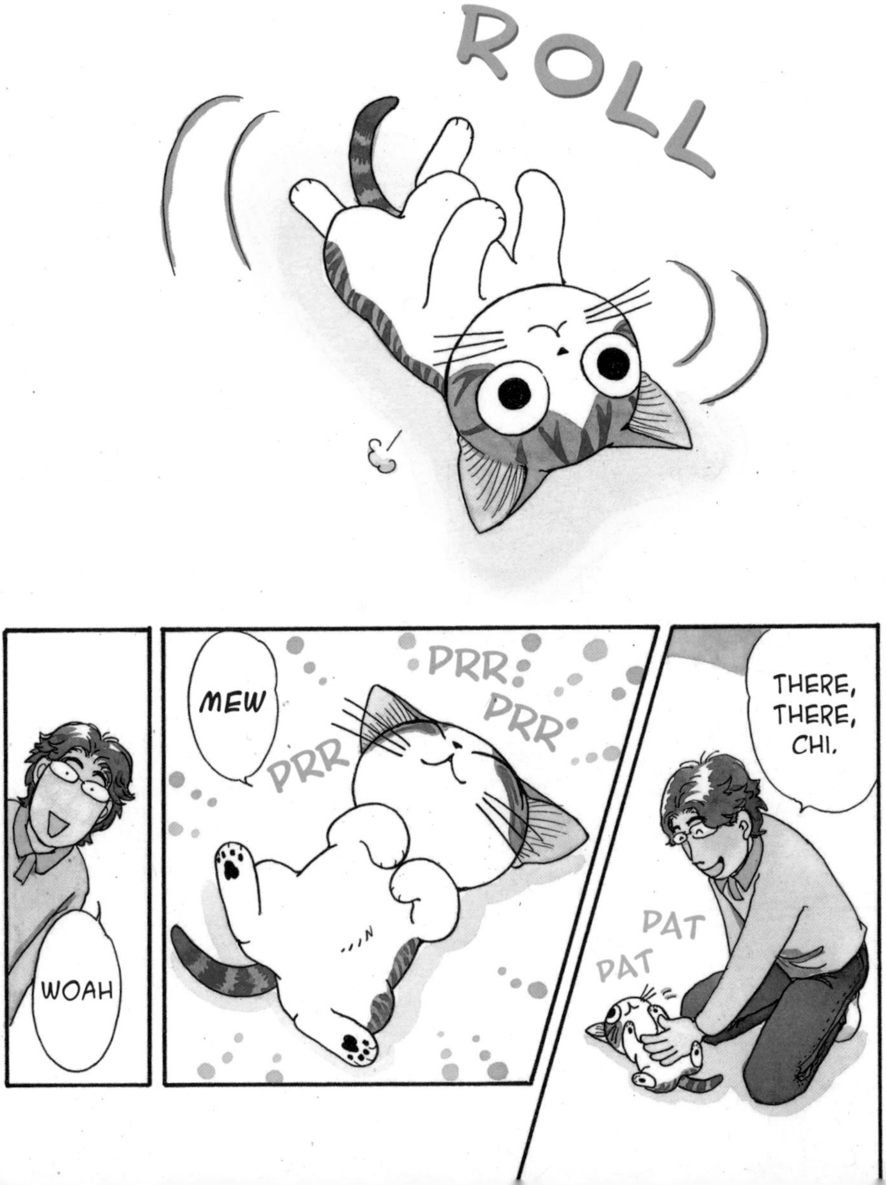

ROLL
WOAH
MEW
PRR
PRR
PRR
THERE, THERE, CHI.
PAT
PAT

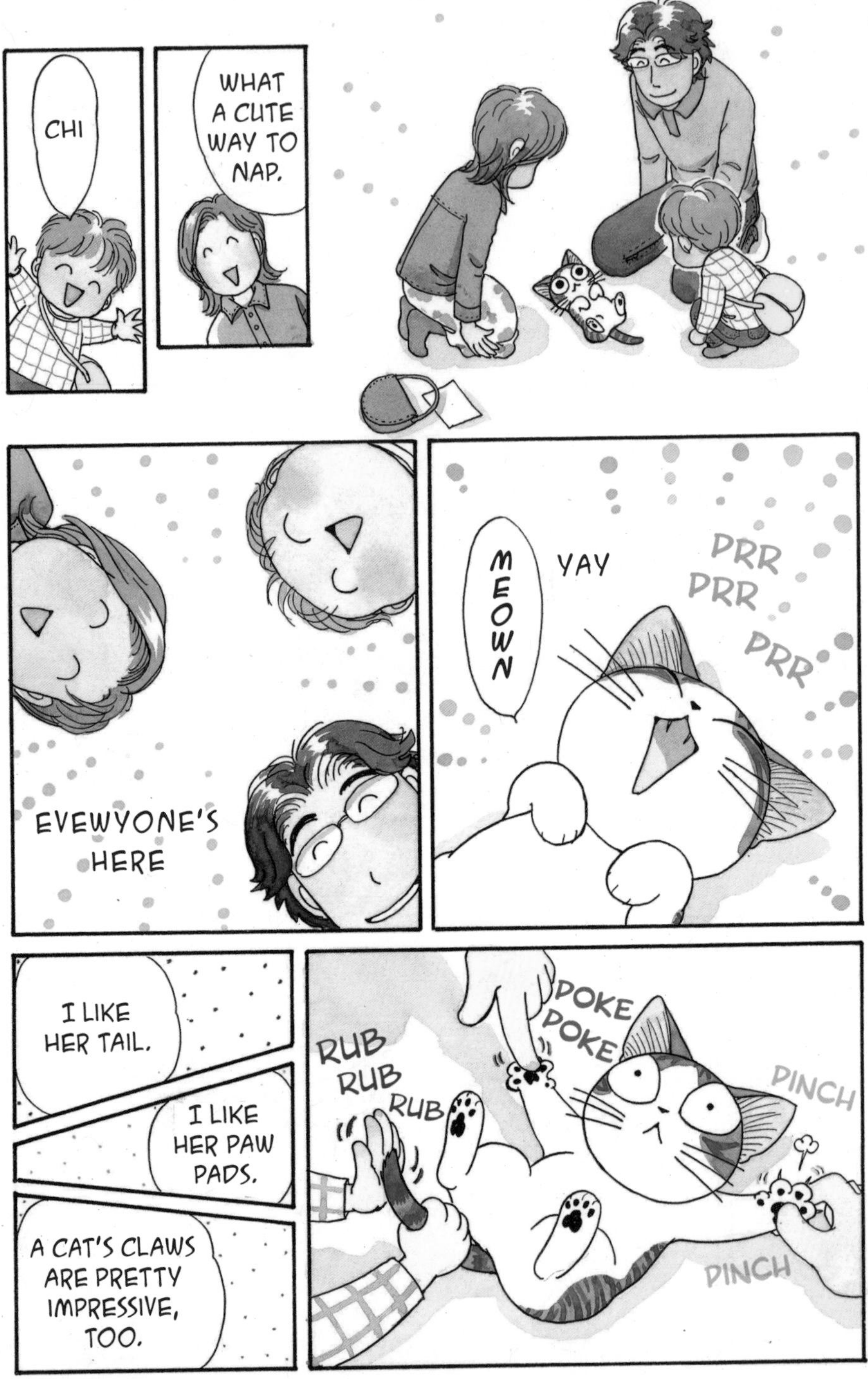
CHI
WHAT A CUTE WAY TO NAP.
EVEWYONE'S HERE
MEOWN
YAY
PRR PRR PRR
I LIKE HER TAIL.
I LIKE HER PAW PADS.
A CAT'S CLAWS ARE PRETTY IMPRESSIVE, TOO.
POKE POKE
RUB RUB RUB
PINCH
PINCH

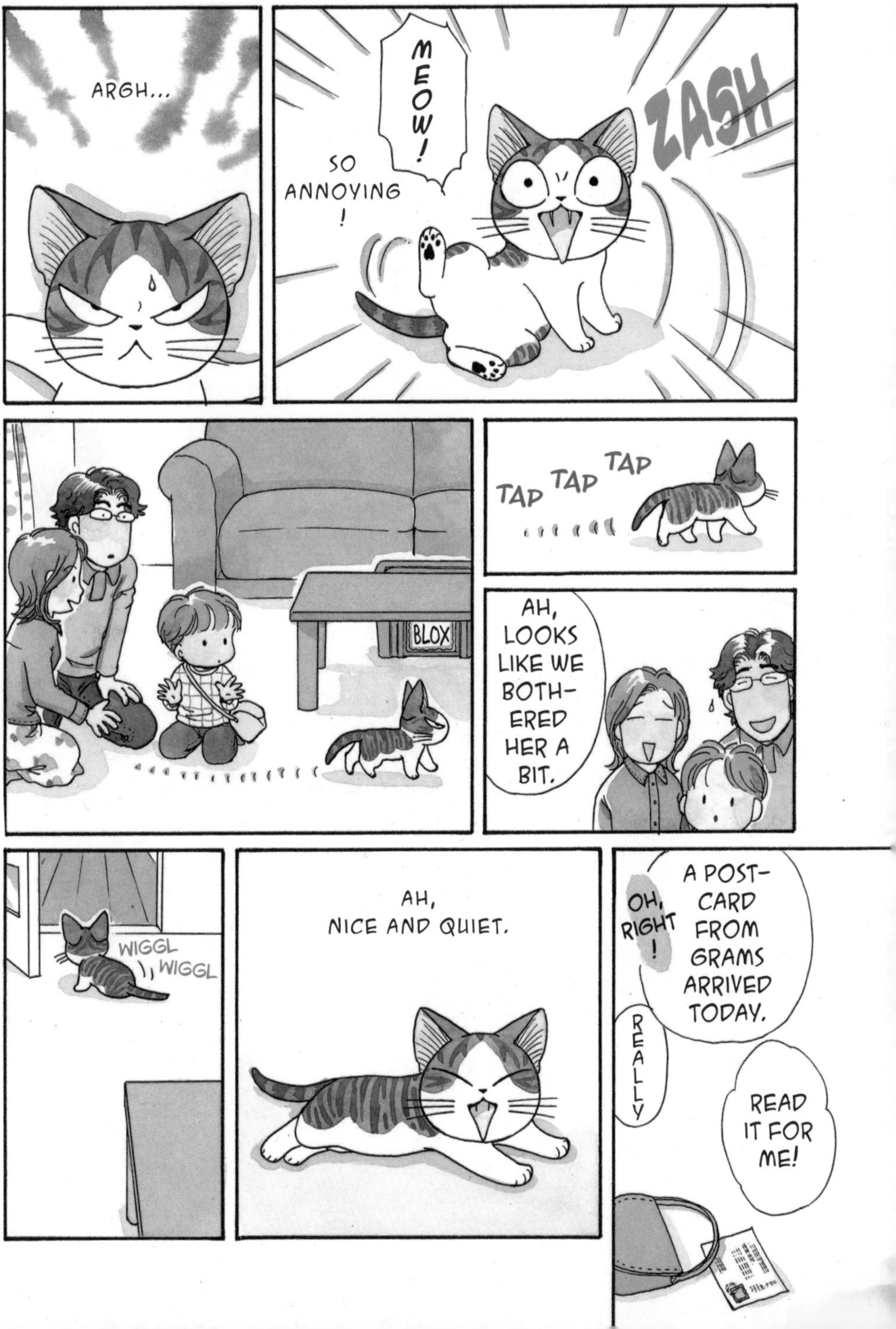
ARGH...
SO ANNOYING!
MEOW!
ZASH
TAP TAP TAP
AH, LOOKS LIKE WE BOTHERED HER A BIT.
BLOX
WIGGL WIGGL
AH, NICE AND QUIET.
OH, RIGHT!
A POSTCARD FROM GRAMS ARRIVED TODAY.
REALLY
READ IT FOR ME!

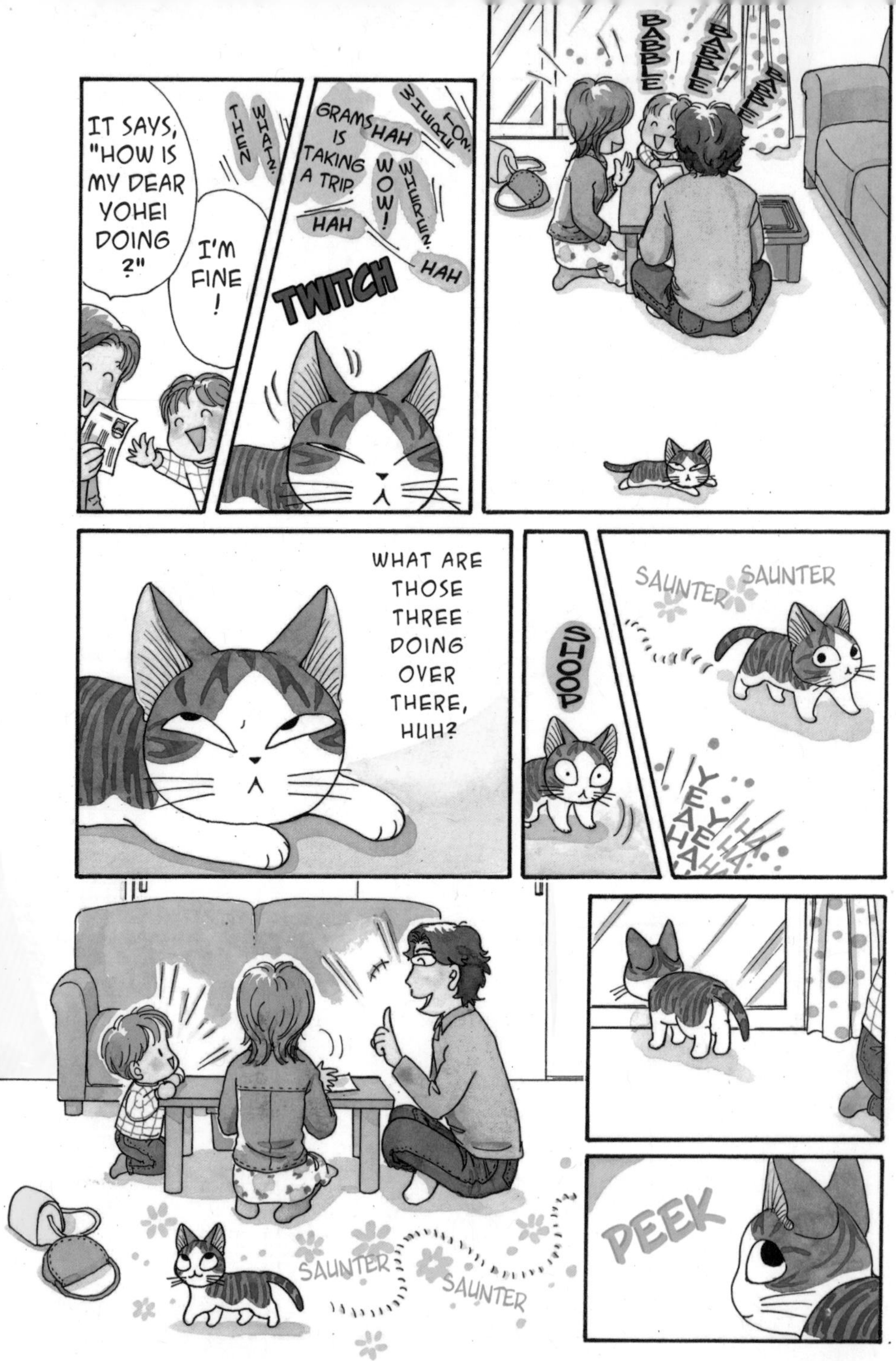
IT SAYS, "HOW IS MY DEAR YOHEI DOING?"
THEN WHAT?
I'M FINE!
GRAMS IS TAKING A TRIP.
HAH
HAH
WOW!
WHERE?
HAH
TWITCH
BABBLE
BABBLE
BABBLE
WHAT ARE THOSE THREE DOING OVER THERE, HUH?
SHOOP
SAUNTER
SAUNTER
SAUNTER
SAUNTER
PEEK

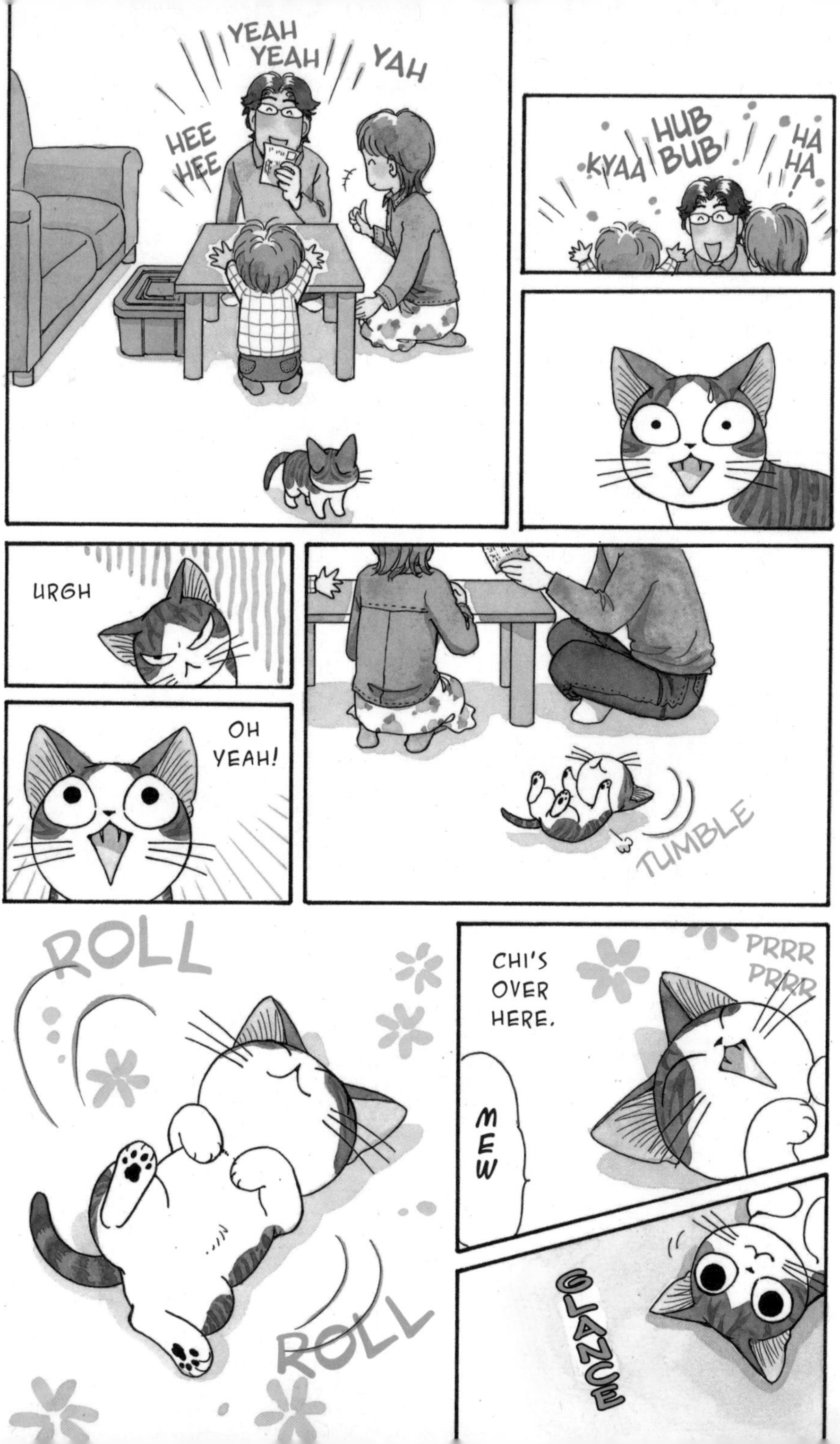
YEAH YEAH
YAH
HEE HEE
KYAA
HUB BUB
HA HA!
URGH
OH YEAH!
TUMBLE
ROLL
ROLL
CHI'S OVER HERE.
PRRR PRRR
MEW
GLANCE

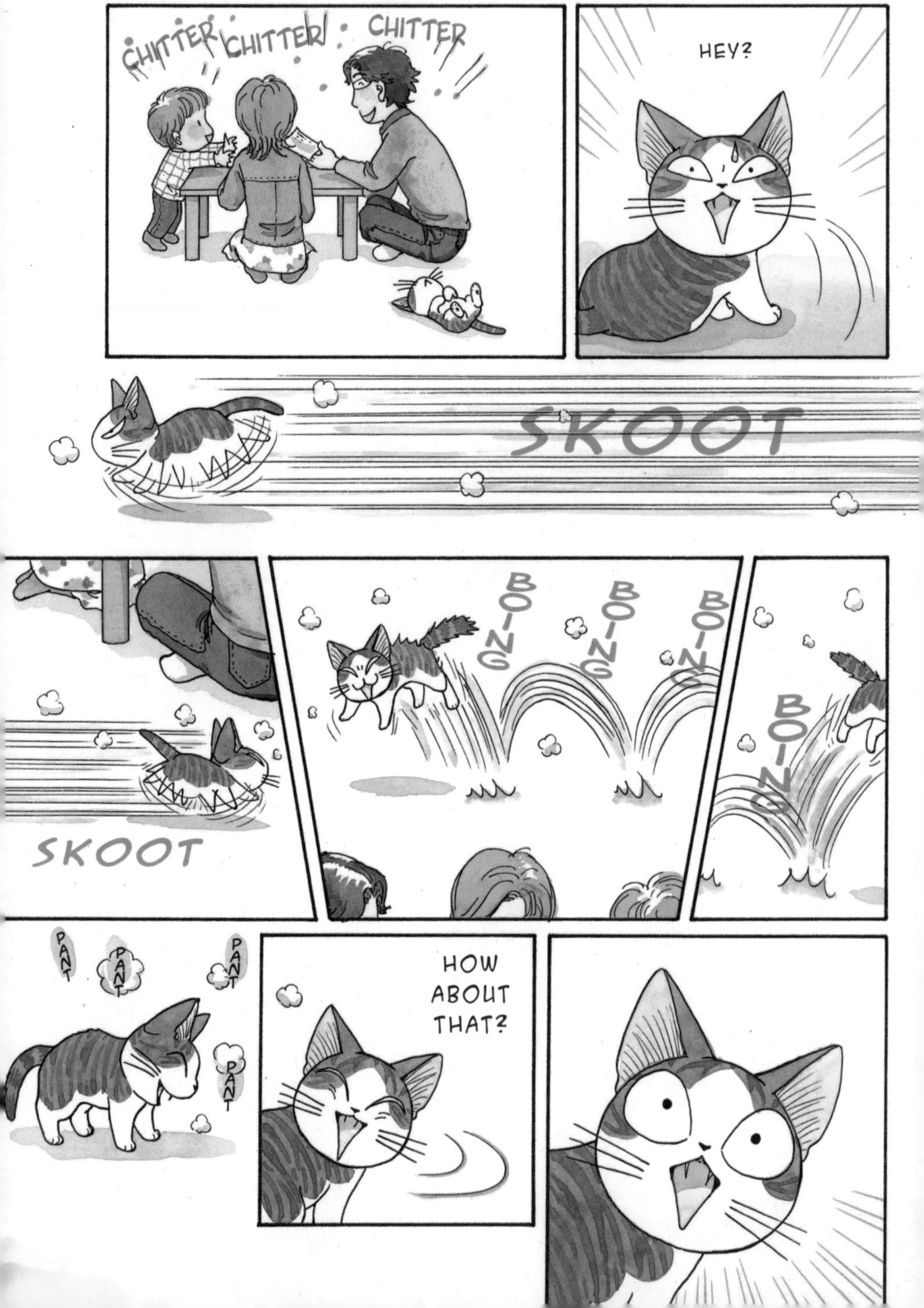
CHITTER CHITTER CHITTER
HEY?
SKOOT
SKOOT
BOING BOING BOING
BOING
PANT PANT PANT PANT
HOW ABOUT THAT?

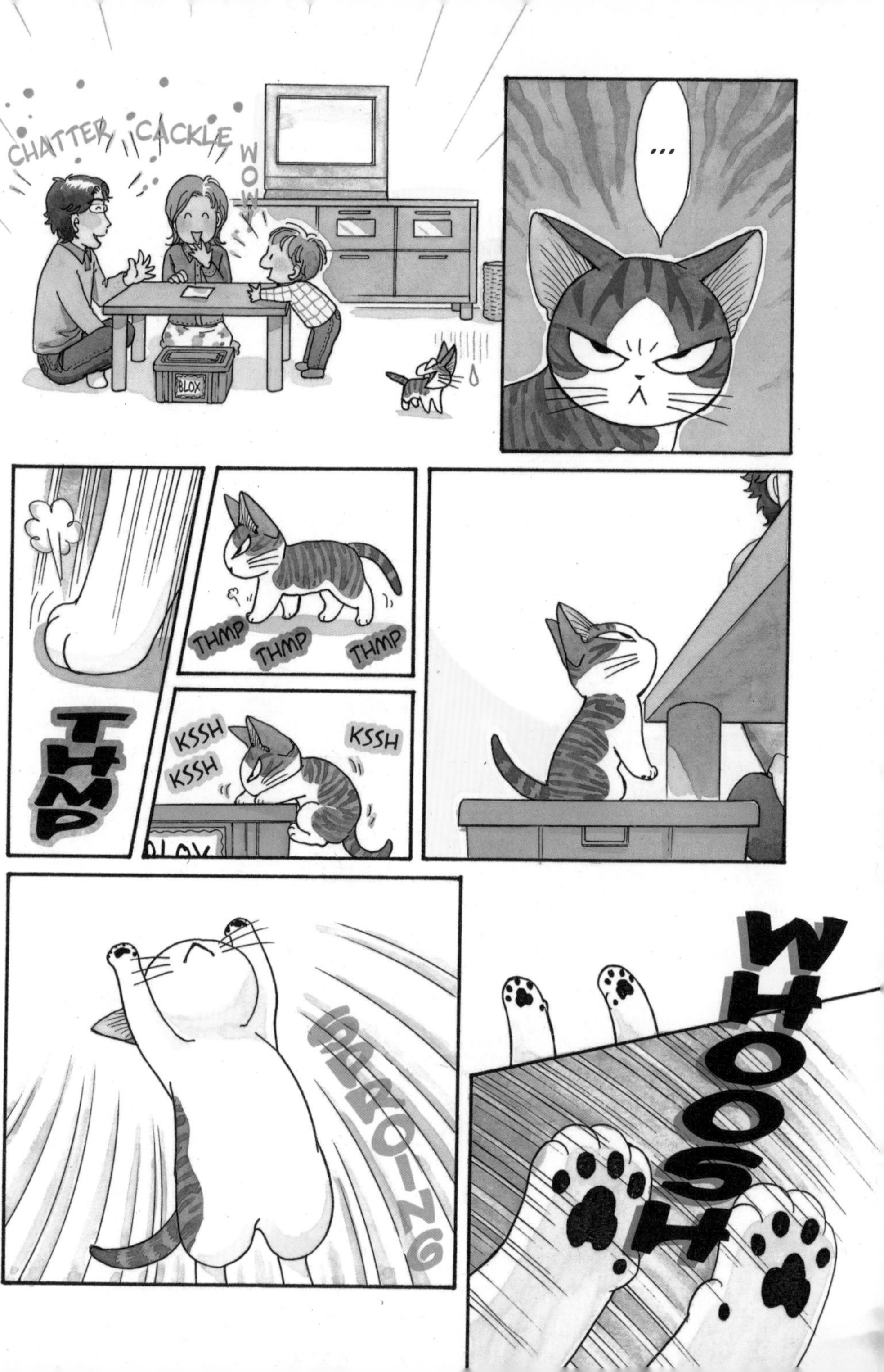
CHATTER
CACKLE
WOW
BLOX
...
THMP
THMP
THMP
THMP
KSSH
KSSH
KSSH
SPROING
WHOOSH

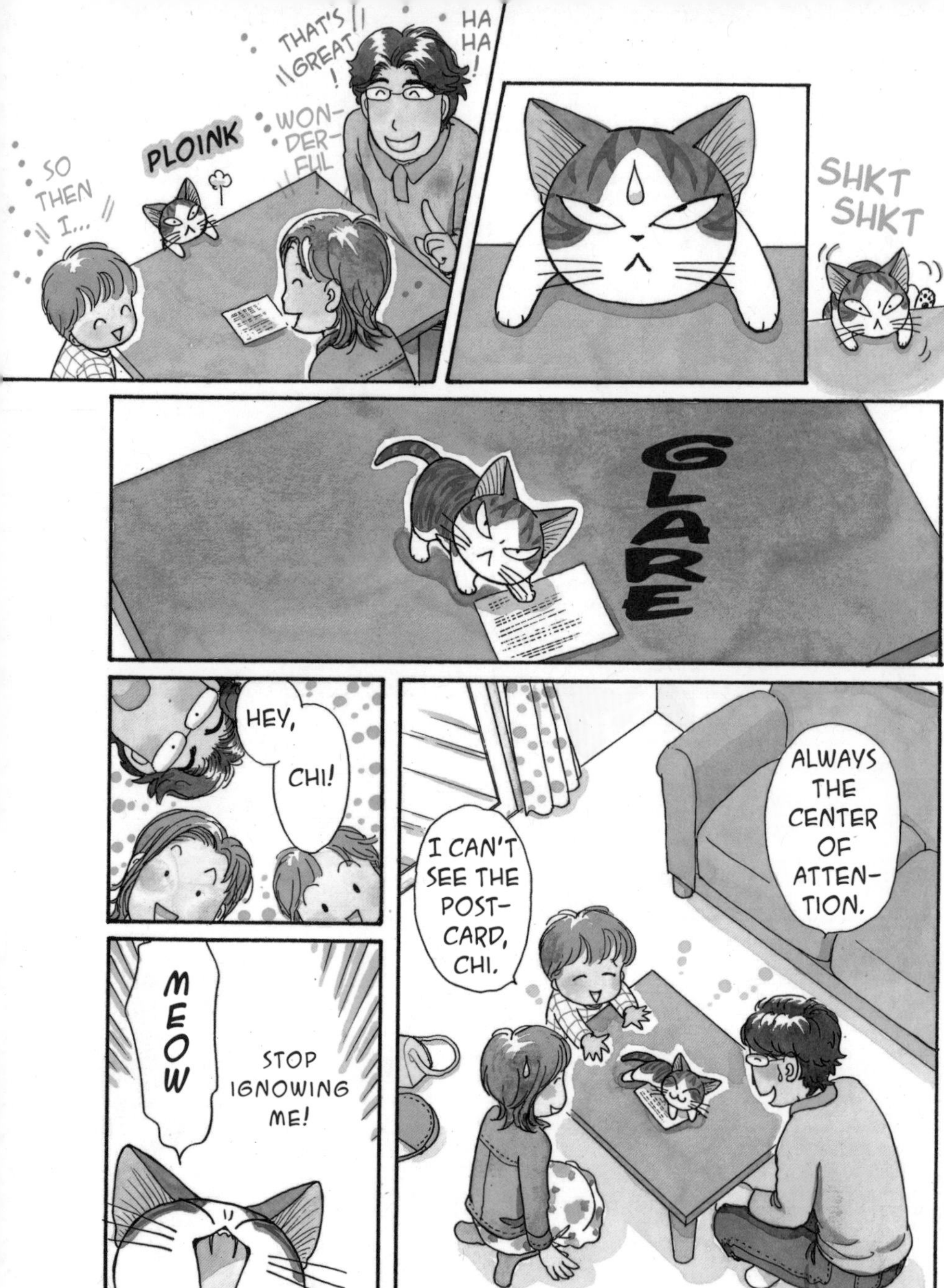

SO THEN I...
PLOINK
WON-DER-FUL!
THAT'S GREAT!
HA HA!
SHKT SHKT
GLARE
HEY,
CHI!
I CAN'T SEE THE POST-CARD, CHI.
ALWAYS THE CENTER OF ATTEN-TION.
MEOW
STOP IGNOWING ME!

the end

homemade 25: a cat stands firm

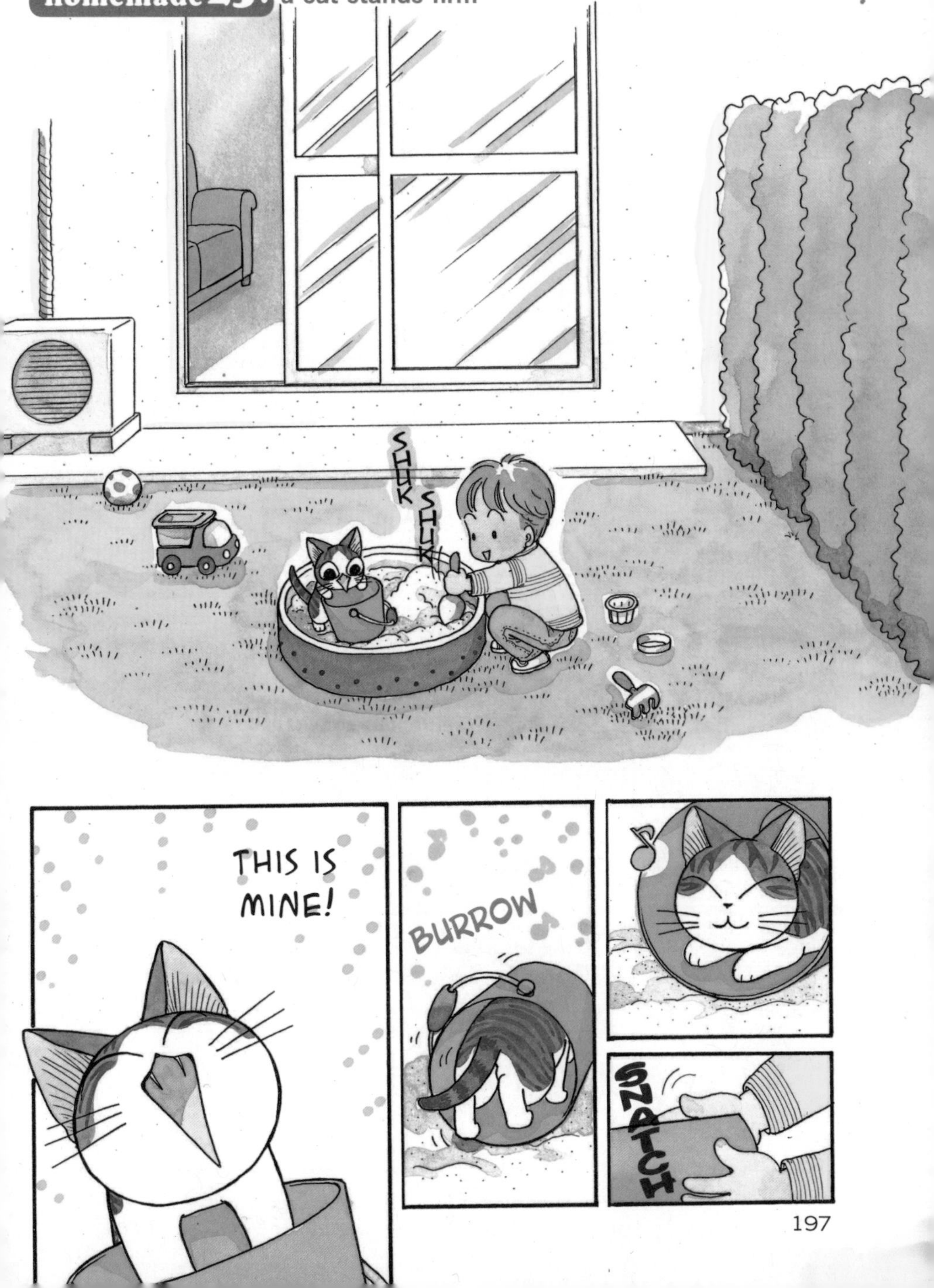
SHUK
SHUK
THIS IS MINE!
BURROW
SNATCH

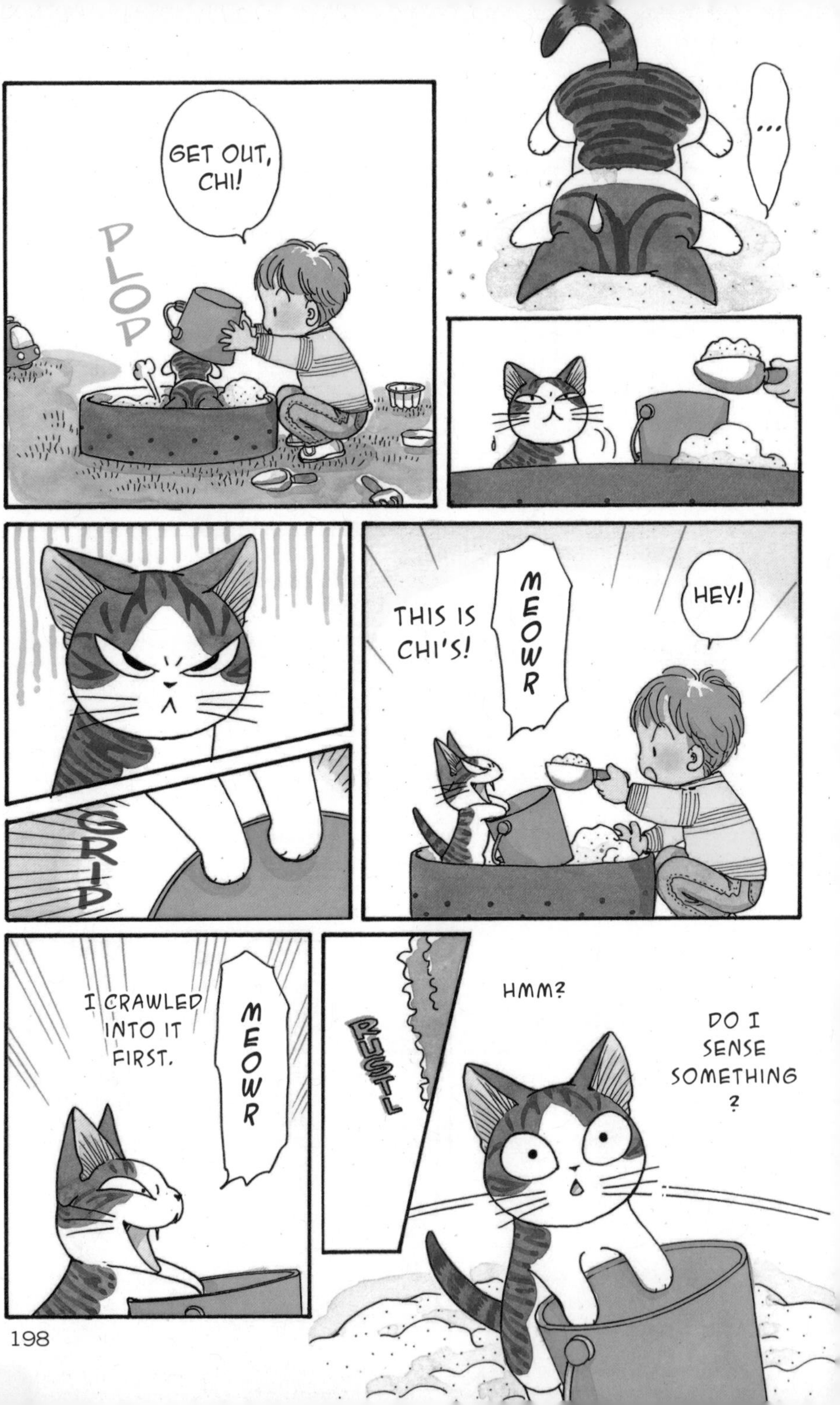
GET OUT, CHI!
PLOP
...
GRIP
THIS IS CHI'S!
MEOWR
HEY!
I CRAWLED INTO IT FIRST.
MEOWR
RUSTL
HMM?
DO I SENSE SOMETHING?

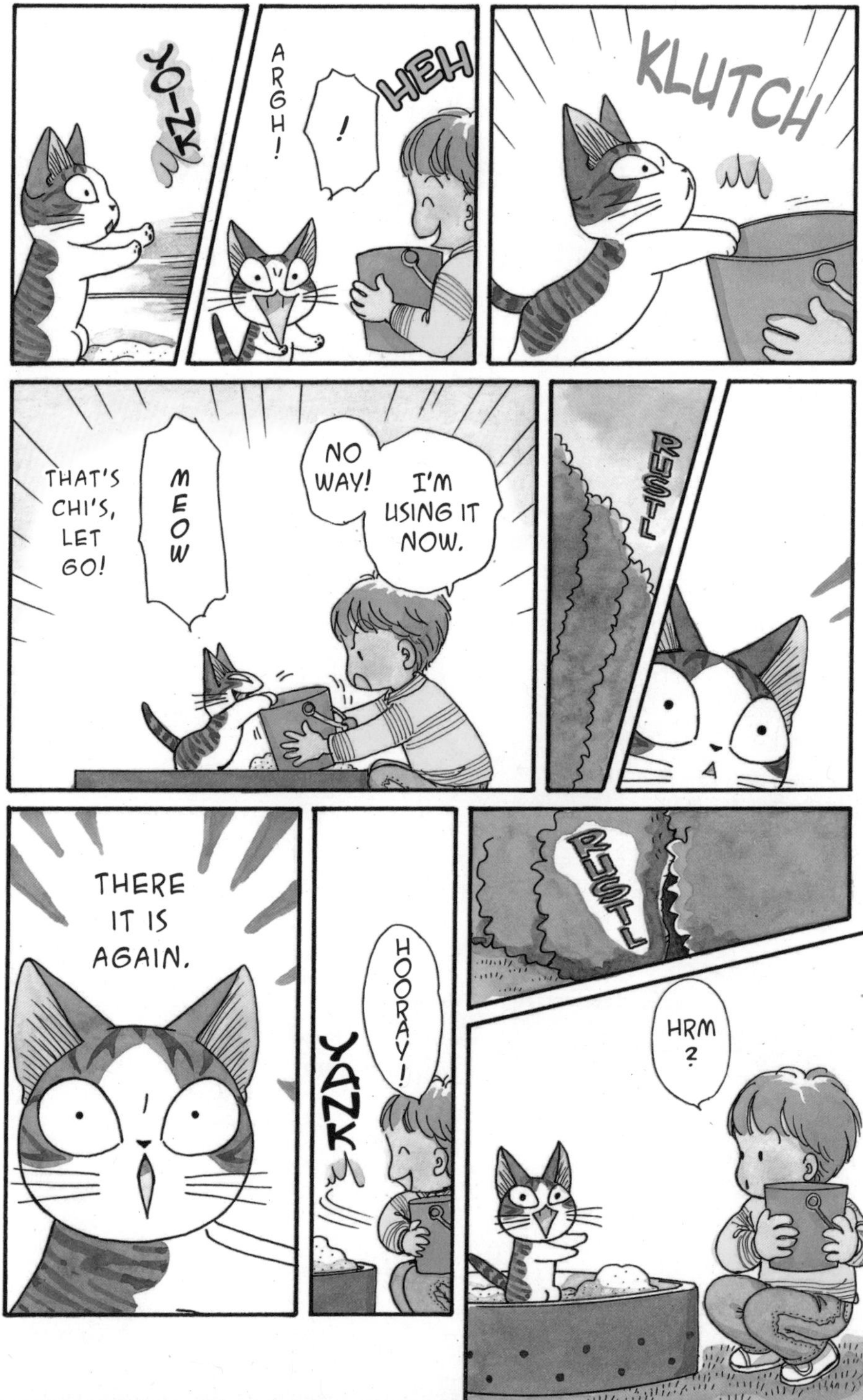
YOINK
ARGH!
!
HEH
KLUTCH
THAT'S CHI'S, LET GO!
MEOW
NO WAY!
I'M USING IT NOW.
RUSTL
THERE IT IS AGAIN.
HOORAY!
YANK
RUSTL
HRM ?

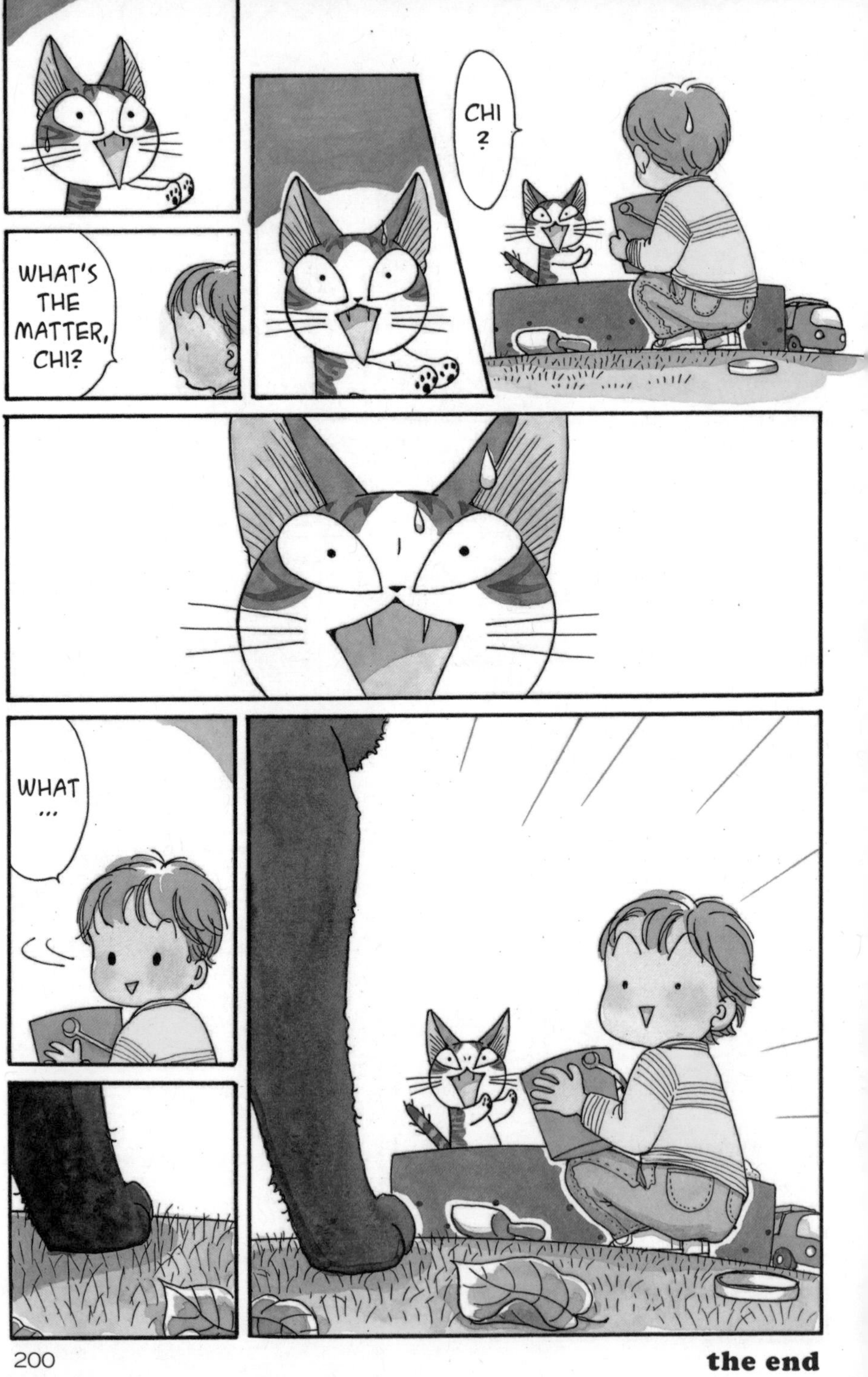
WHAT'S THE MATTER, CHI?
CHI?
WHAT ...

the end

homemade 26: a cat encounters

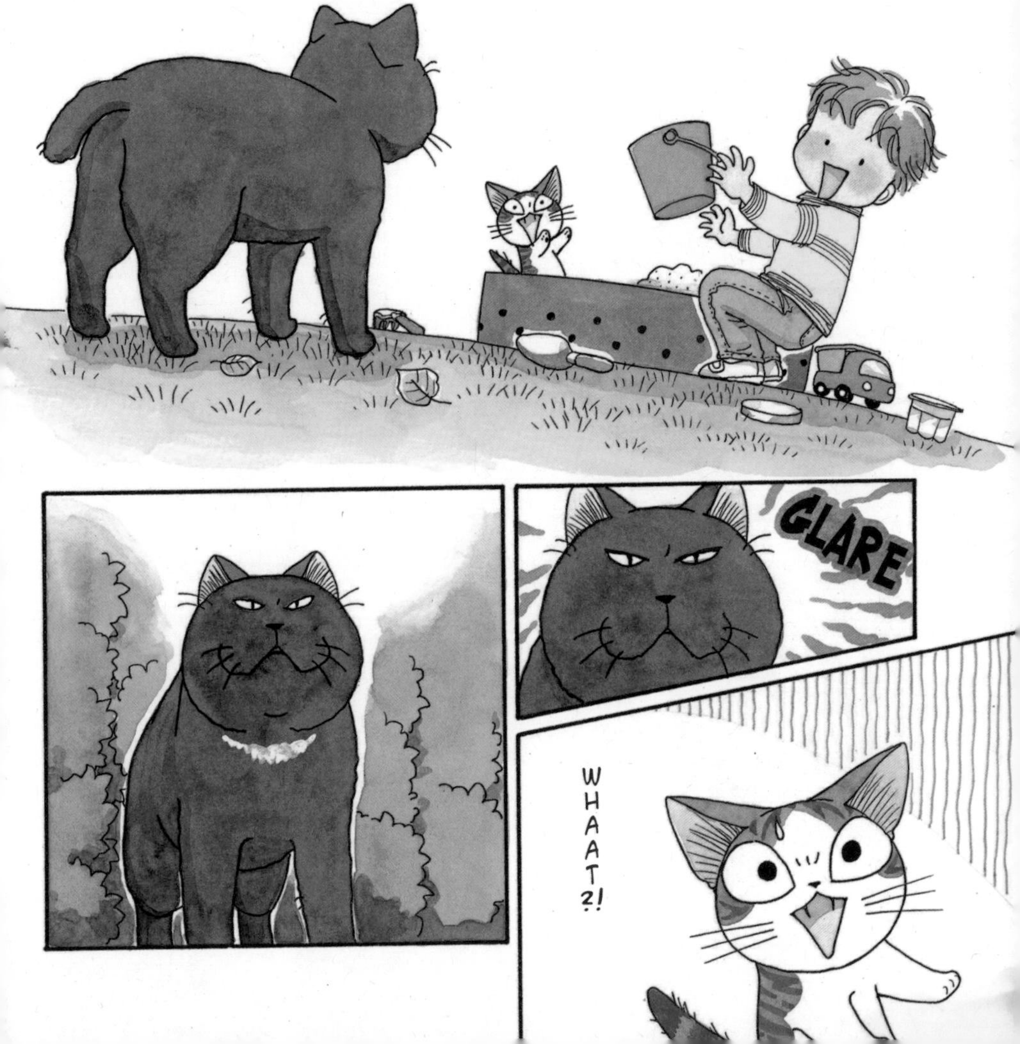
GLARE
WHAAAT?!

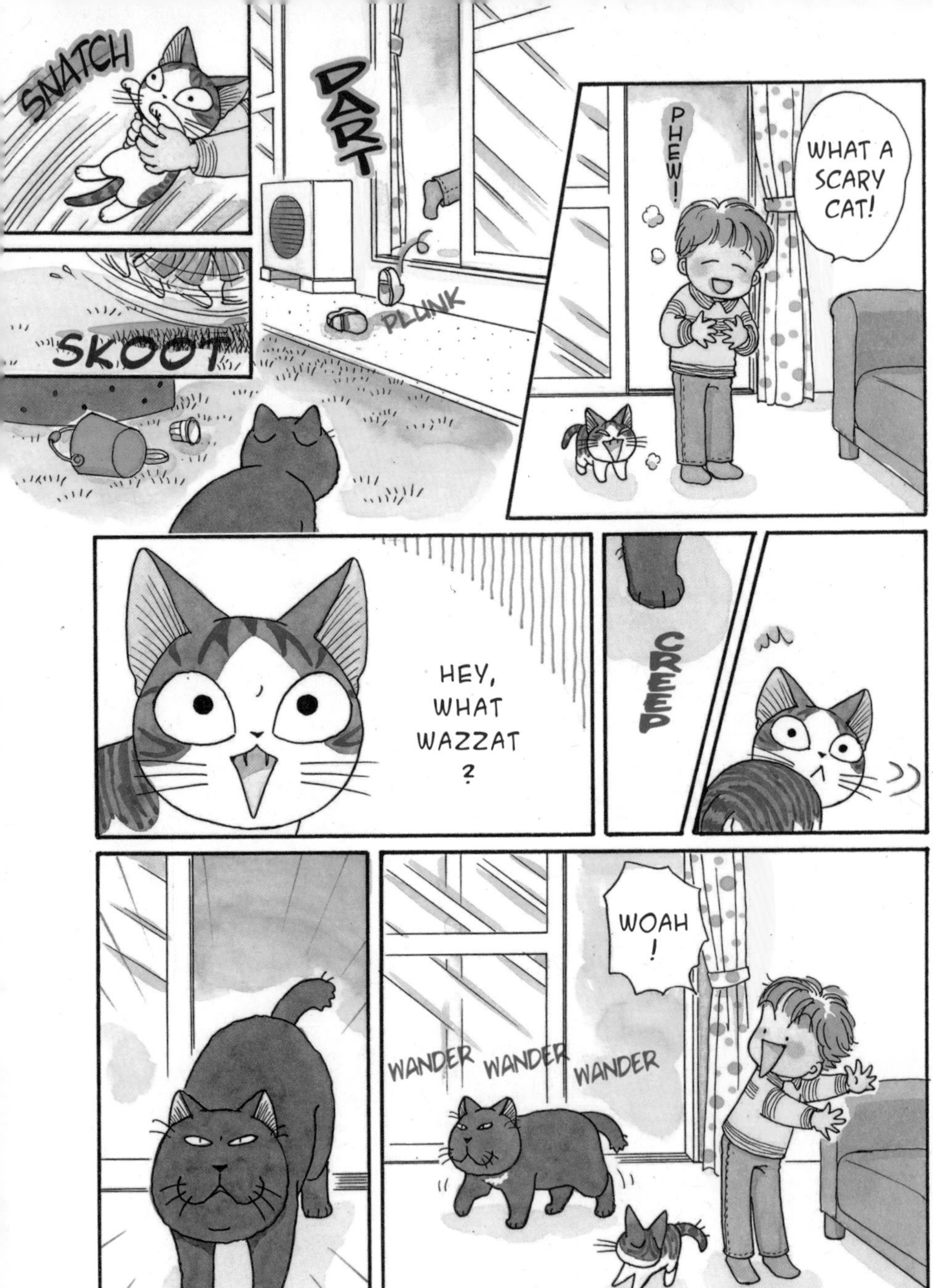
SNATCH
SKOOT
DART
PLUNK
PHEW!
WHAT A SCARY CAT!
HEY, WHAT WAZZAT?
CREEP
WANDER WANDER WANDER
WOAH!

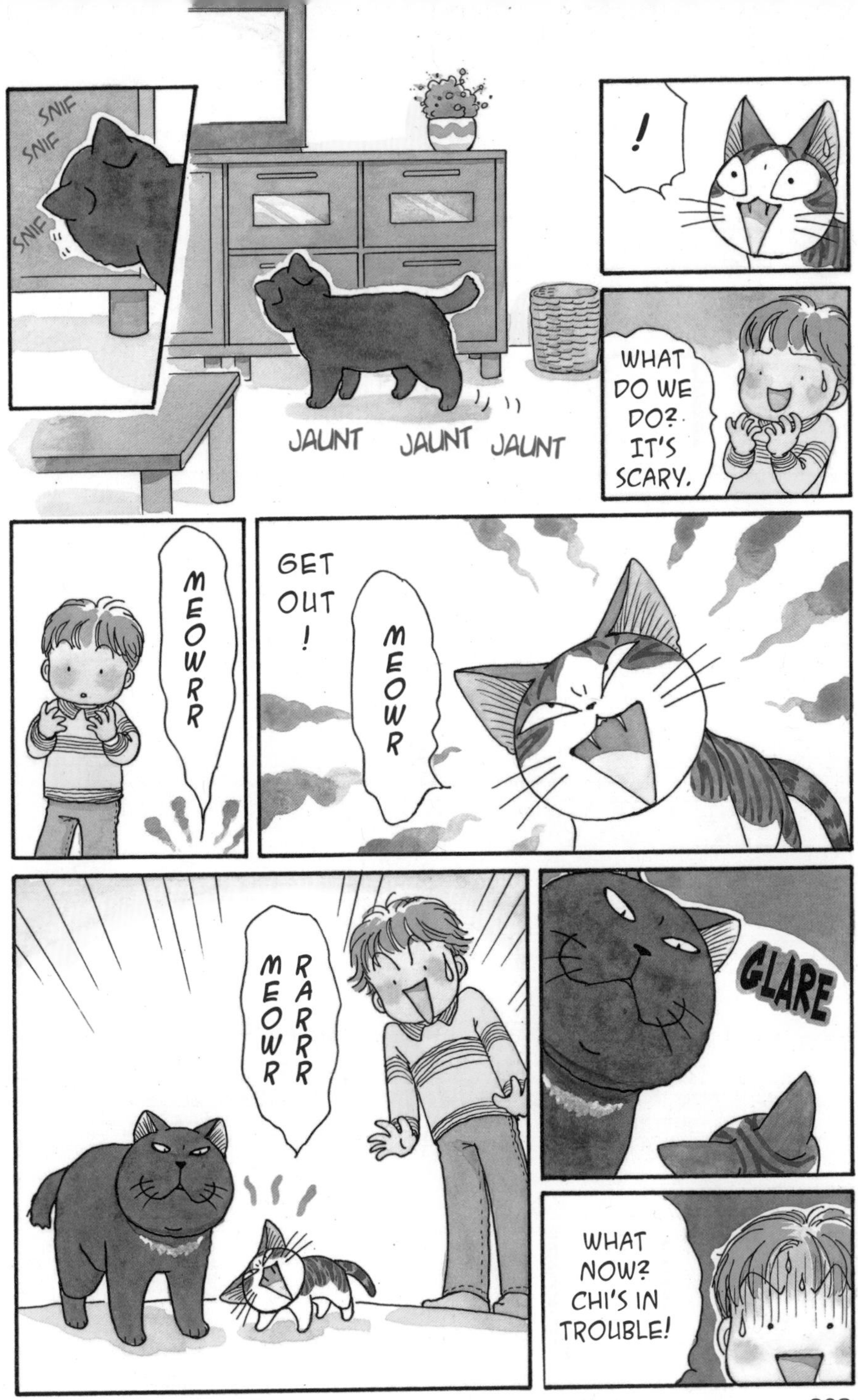
SNIF
SNIF
SNIF
JAUNT
JAUNT
JAUNT
!
WHAT DO WE DO? IT'S SCARY.
MEOWRR
GET OUT!
MEOWR
RARRR
MEOWR
GLARE
WHAT NOW? CHI'S IN TROUBLE!

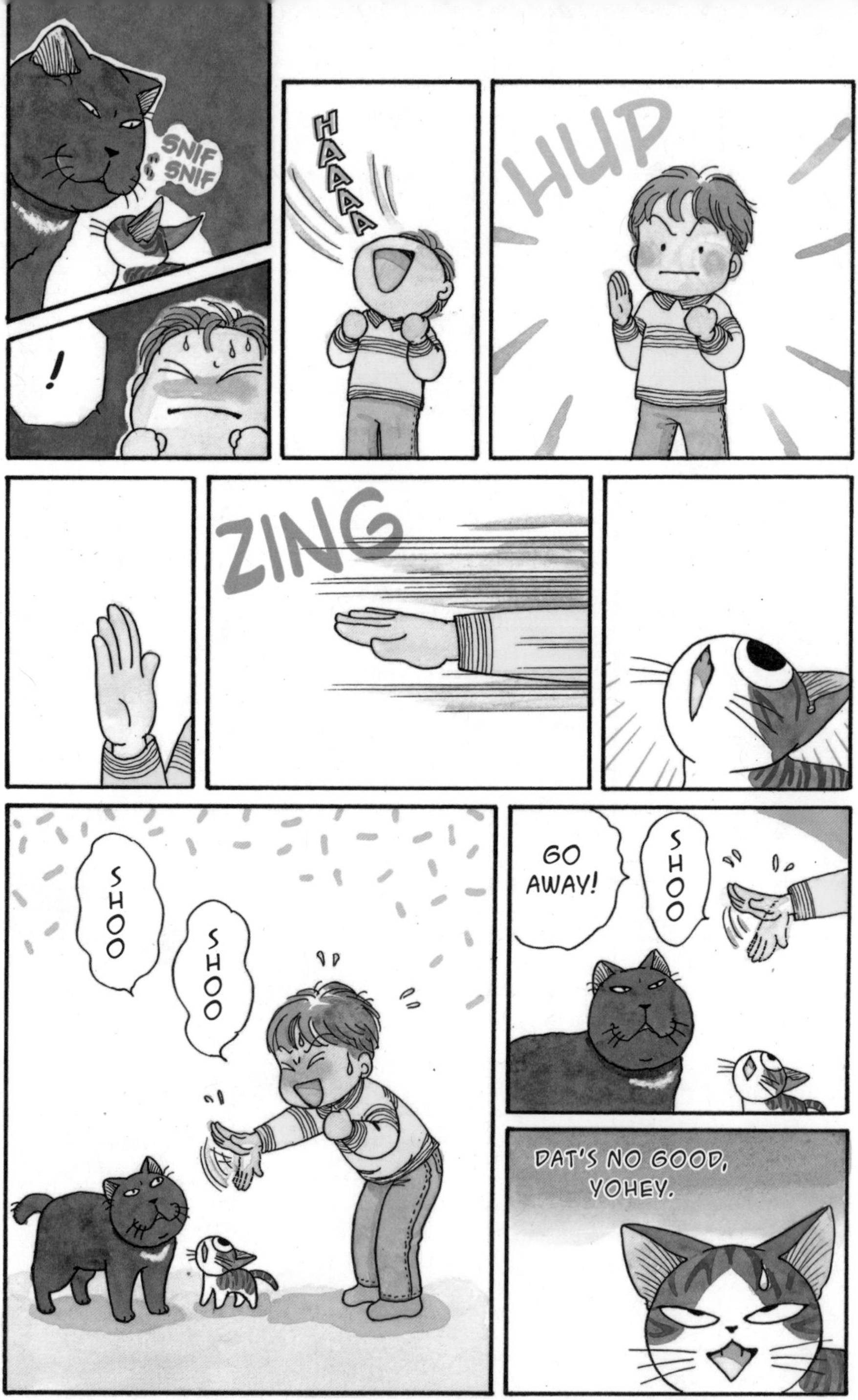
SNIF SNIF
!
HAAAAA
HUP
ZING
SHOO
SHOO
GO AWAY!
SHOO
DAT'S NO GOOD, YOHEY.

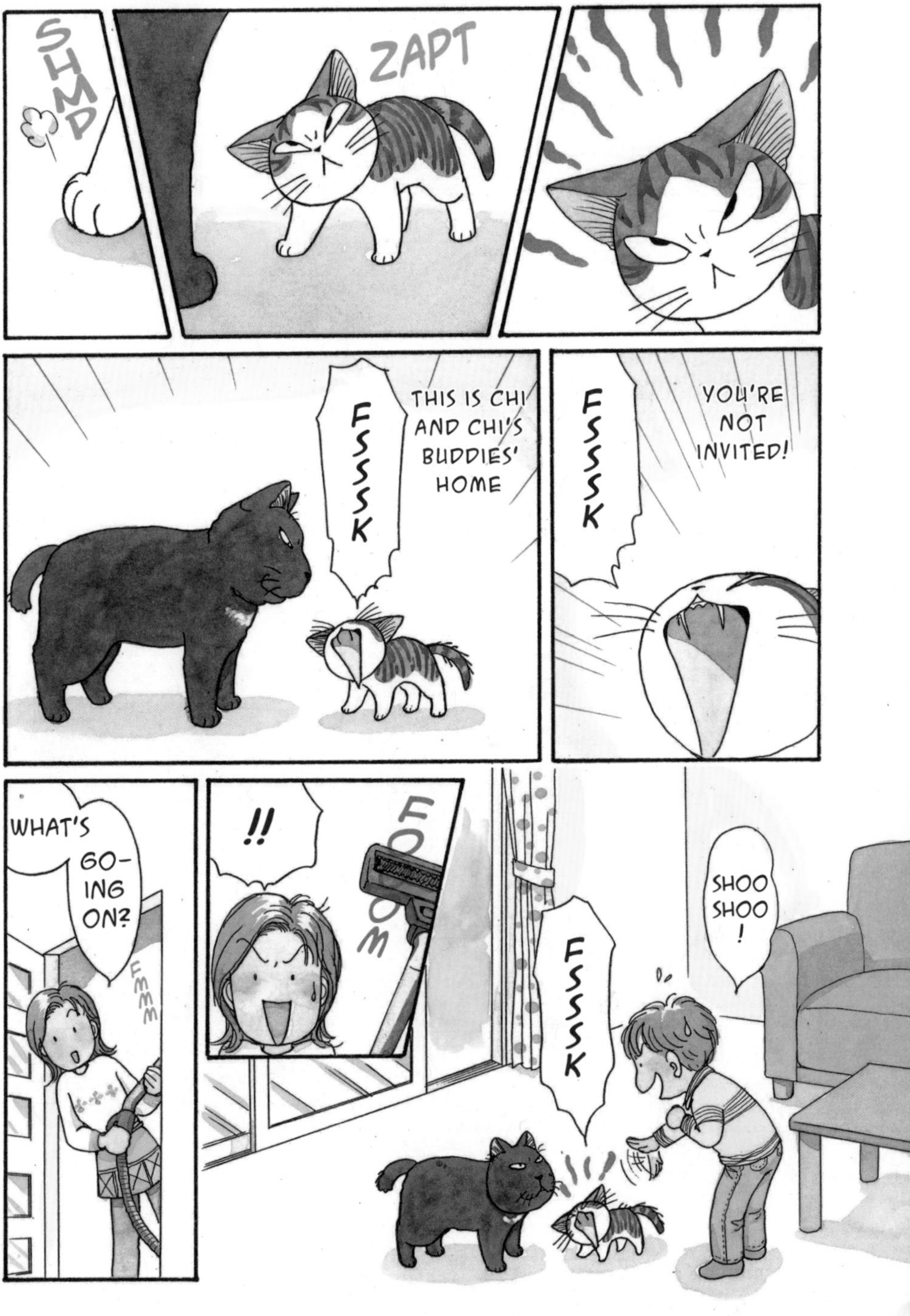

SHMP
ZAPT
FSSSK
THIS IS CHI AND CHI'S BUDDIES' HOME
FSSSK
YOU'RE NOT INVITED!
WHAT'S GO-ING ON?
FMMM
!!
FOOOM
FSSSK
SHOO SHOO!

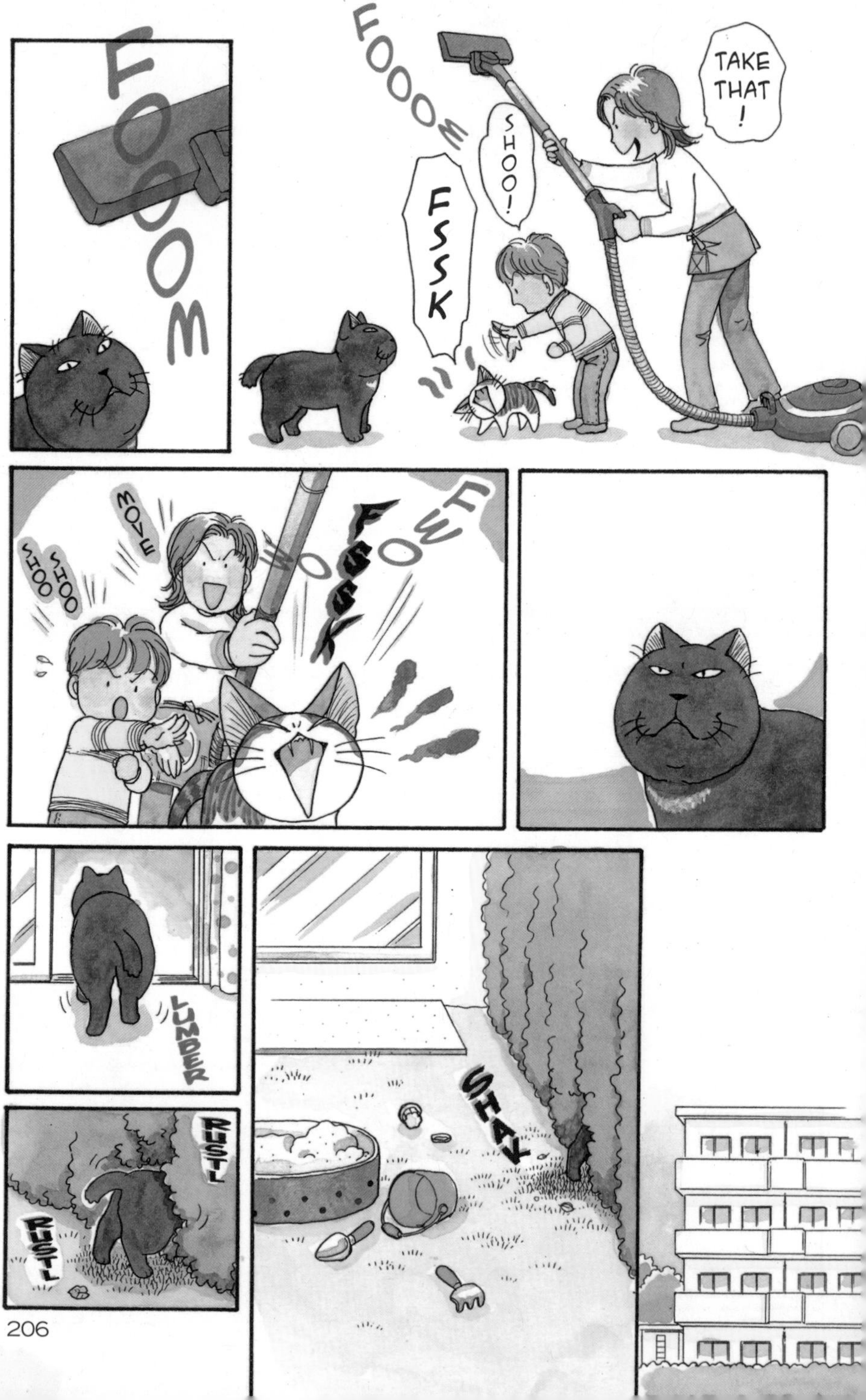
FOOOM
FOOOE
FSSK
SHOO!
TAKE THAT!
SHOO SHOO
MOVE
FSSK
FWOOSH
LUMBER
RUSTL
RUSTL
SHAK

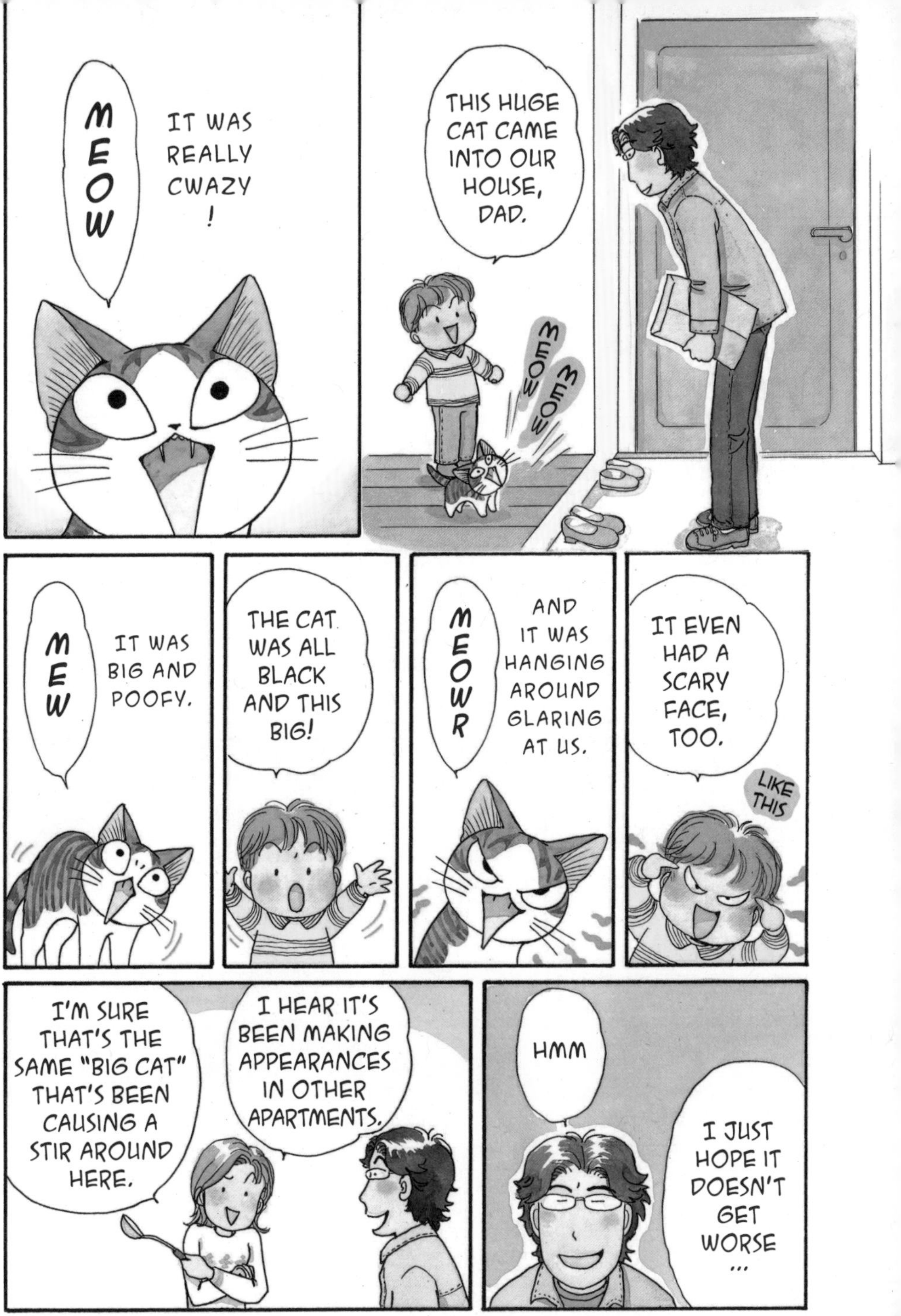
MEOW
IT WAS REALLY CWAZY!
THIS HUGE CAT CAME INTO OUR HOUSE, DAD.
MEOW MEOW
MEW
IT WAS BIG AND POOFY.
THE CAT WAS ALL BLACK AND THIS BIG!
MEOWR
AND IT WAS HANGING AROUND GLARING AT US.
IT EVEN HAD A SCARY FACE, TOO.
LIKE THIS
I'M SURE THAT'S THE SAME "BIG CAT" THAT'S BEEN CAUSING A STIR AROUND HERE.
I HEAR IT'S BEEN MAKING APPEARANCES IN OTHER APARTMENTS.
HMM
I JUST HOPE IT DOESN'T GET WORSE...

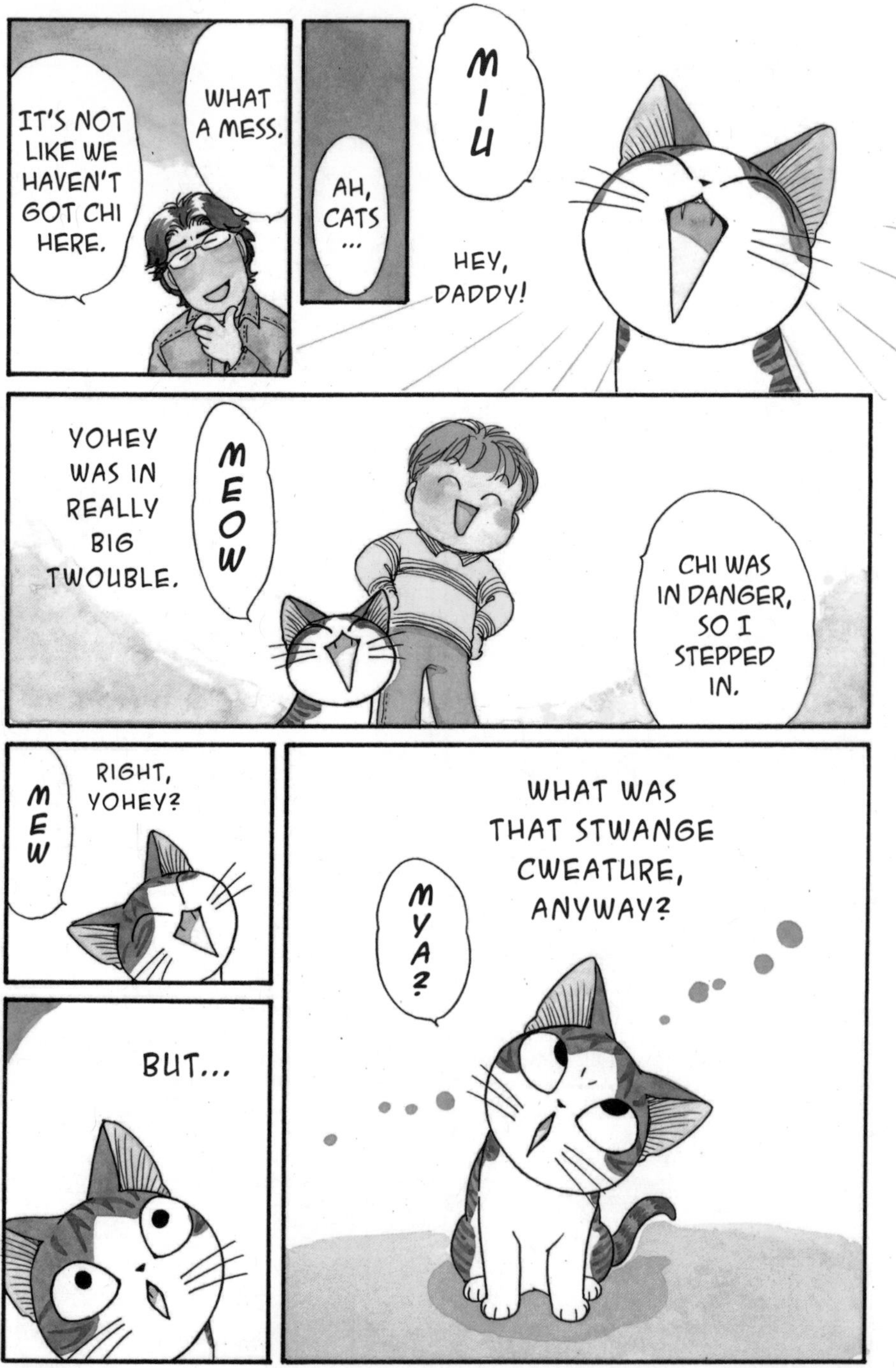
WHAT A MESS.
IT'S NOT LIKE WE HAVEN'T GOT CHI HERE.
AH, CATS ...
MIU
HEY, DADDY!
YOHEY WAS IN REALLY BIG TWOUBLE.
MEOW
CHI WAS IN DANGER, SO I STEPPED IN.
MEW
RIGHT, YOHEY?
BUT...
WHAT WAS THAT STWANGE CWEATURE, ANYWAY?
MYA?

the end

homemade 27: a cat intrudes

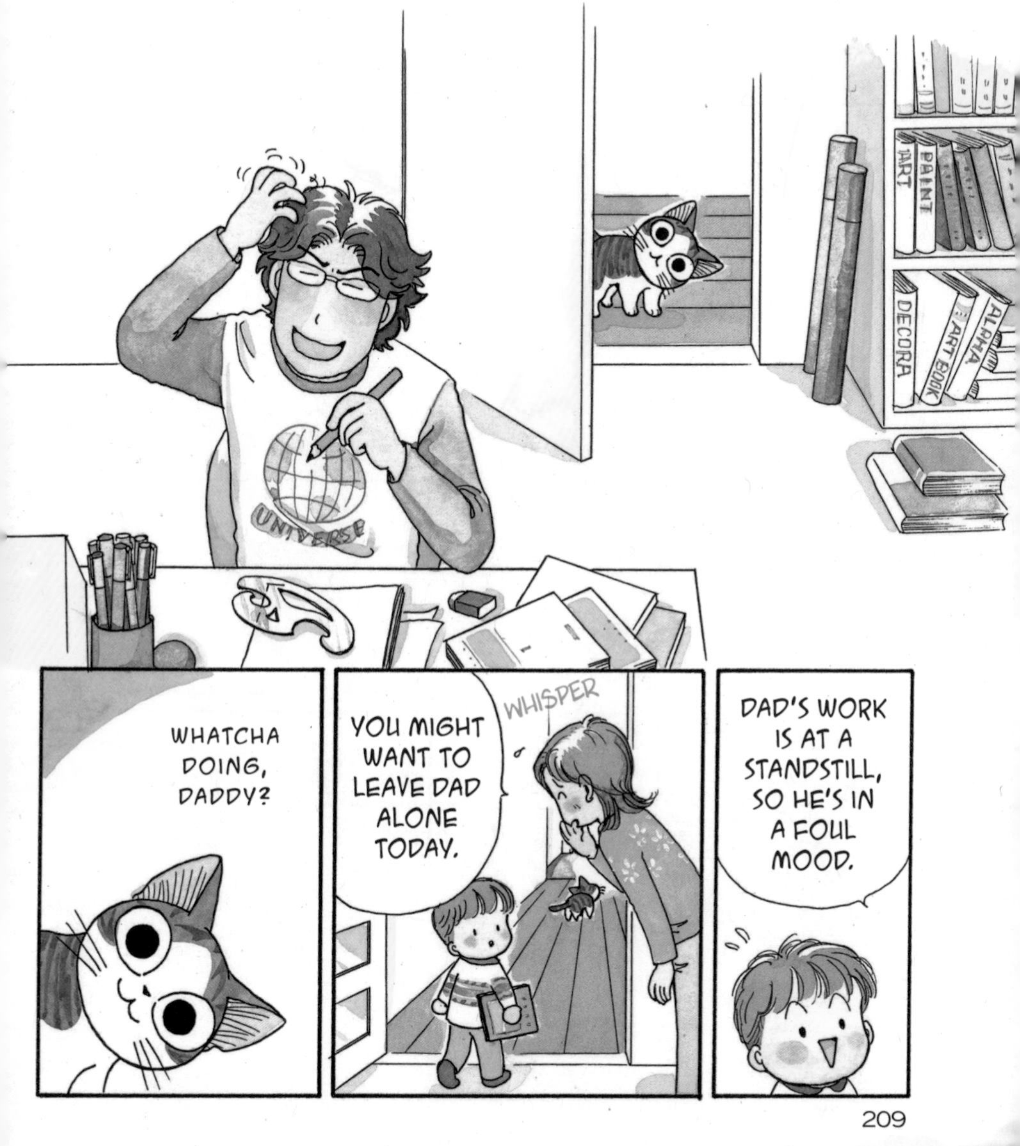
ART
PAINT
DECORA
ART BOOK
ALPHA
UNIVERSE
WHATCHA DOING, DADDY?
YOU MIGHT WANT TO LEAVE DAD ALONE TODAY.
WHISPER
DAD'S WORK IS AT A STANDSTILL, SO HE'S IN A FOUL MOOD.

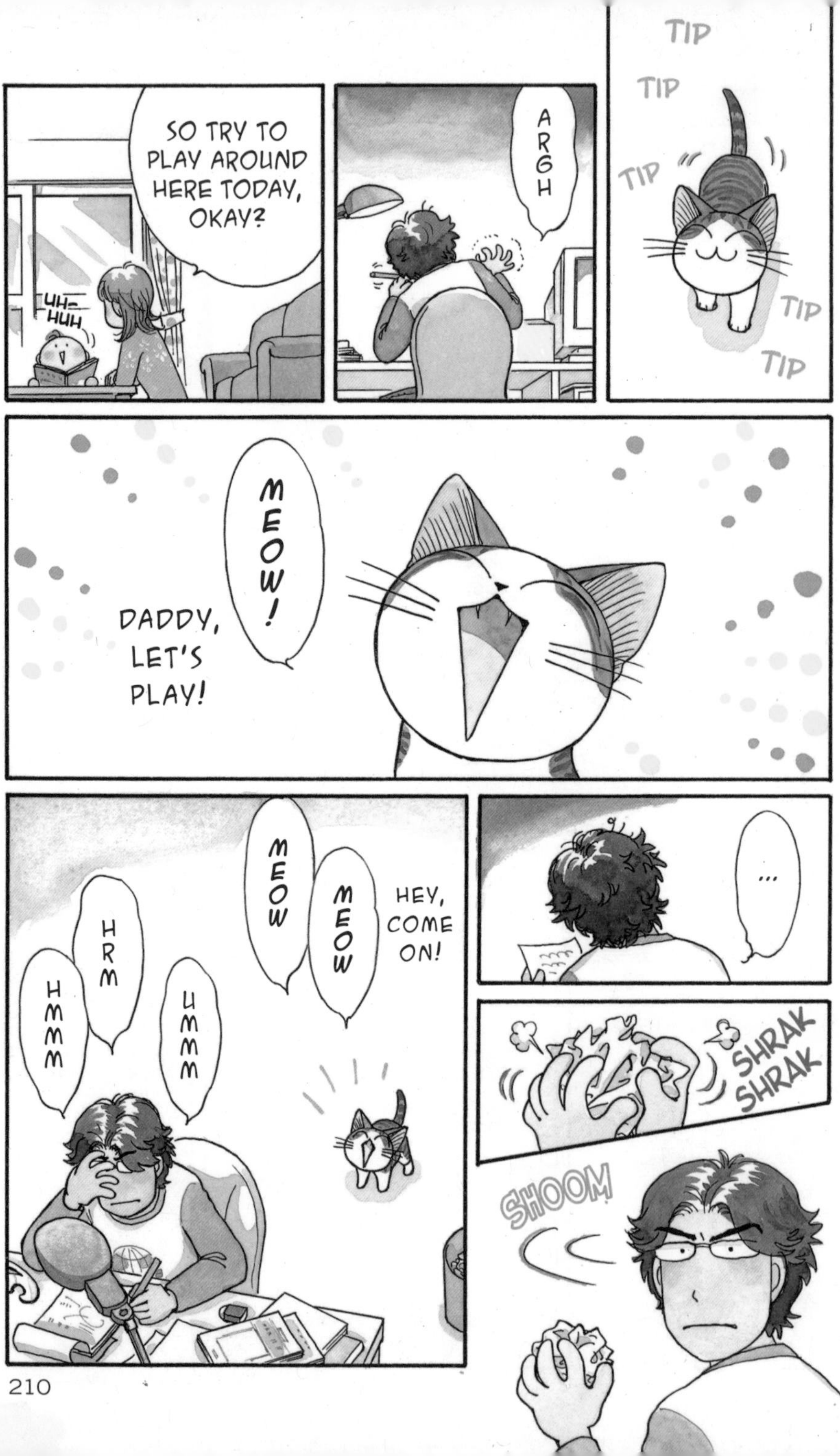
SO TRY TO PLAY AROUND HERE TODAY, OKAY?
UH-HUH
ARGH
TIP
TIP
TIP
TIP
TIP
MEOW!
DADDY, LET'S PLAY!
HMMM
HRM
UMMM
MEOW
MEOW
HEY, COME ON!
...
SHRAK SHRAK
SHOOM

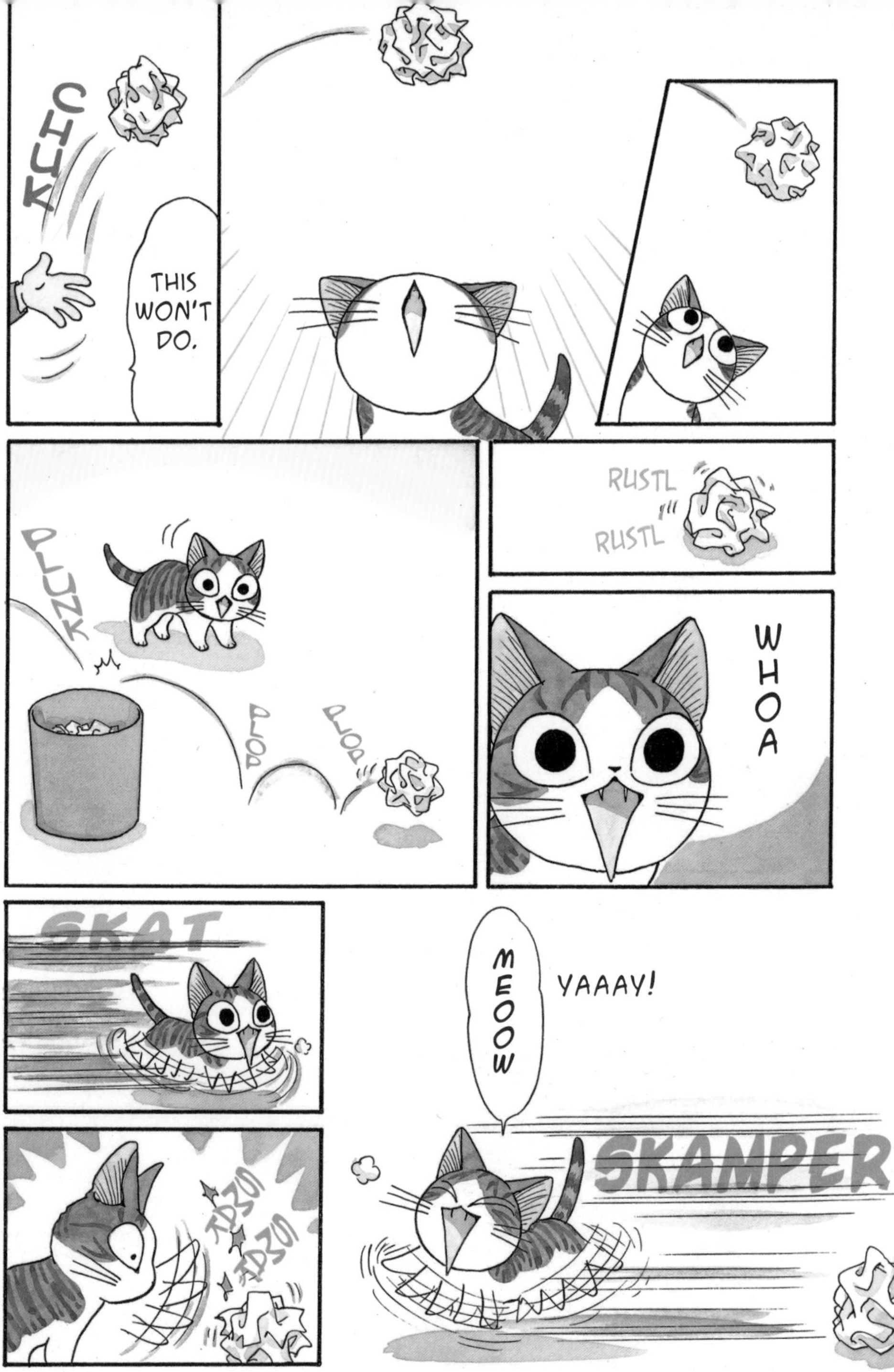
CHUK
THIS WON'T DO.
PLUNK
PLOP
PLOP
RUSTL
RUSTL
WHOA
SKAT
MEOOW
YAAAY!
SKAMPER

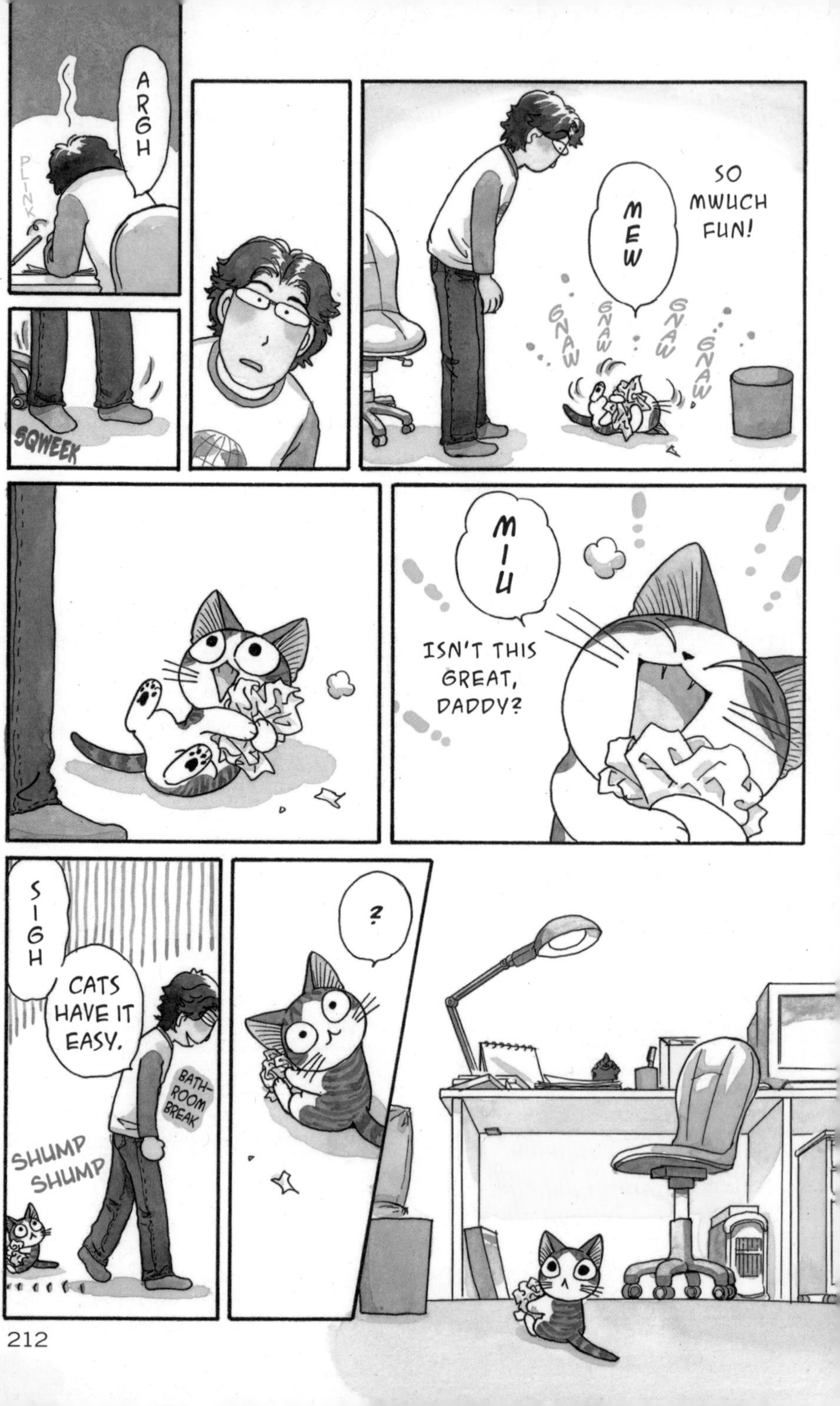
ARGH
PLINK
SQWEEK
MEW
SO MWUCH FUN!
GNAW GNAW GNAW GNAW
MIU
ISN'T THIS GREAT, DADDY?
SIGH
CATS HAVE IT EASY.
BATH-ROOM BREAK
SHUMP SHUMP
?

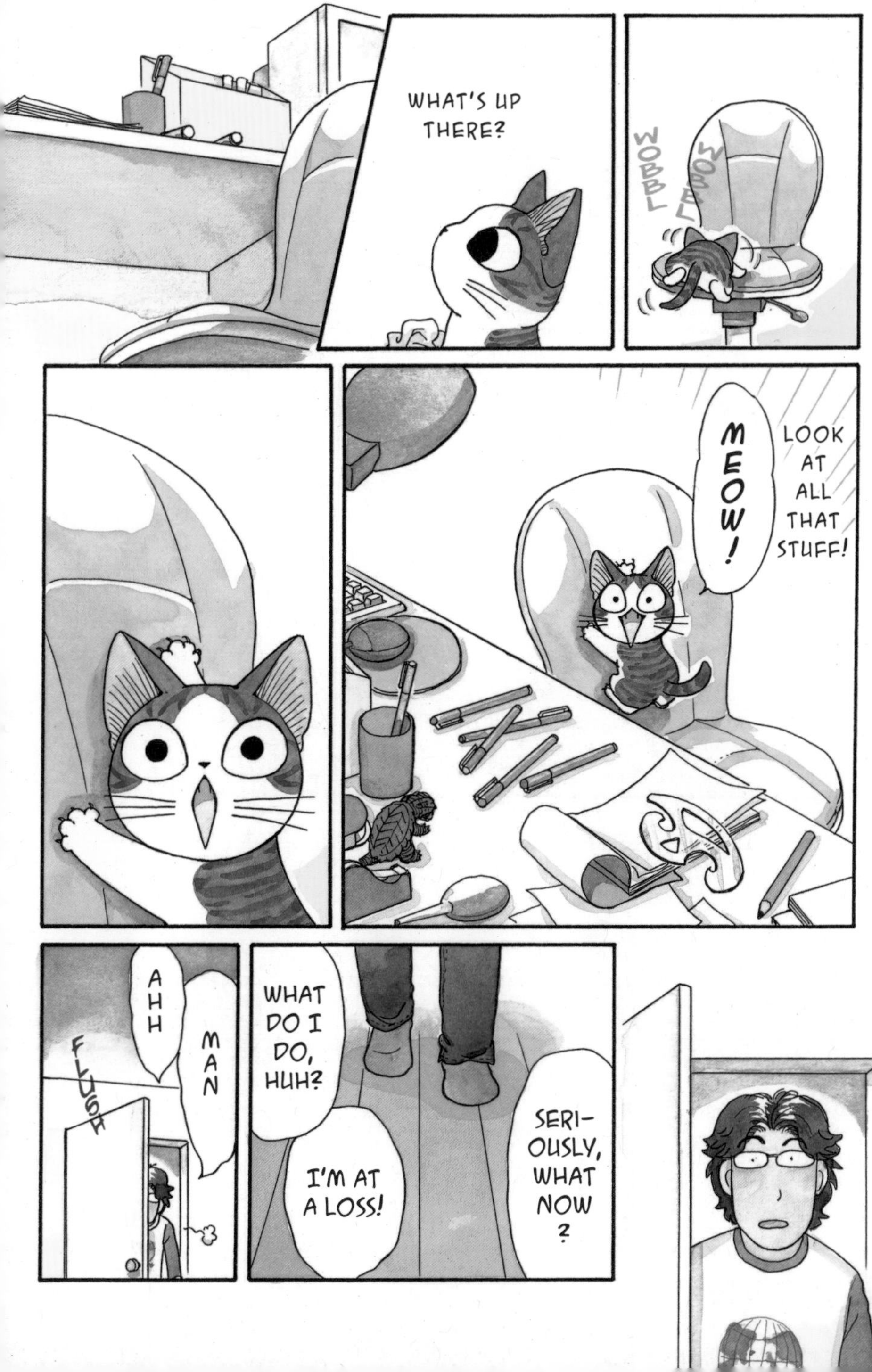
WHAT'S UP THERE?
WOBBL
WOBBL
MEOW!
LOOK AT ALL THAT STUFF!
AHH
MAN
FLUSH
WHAT DO I DO, HUH?
I'M AT A LOSS!
SERI-OUSLY, WHAT NOW ?

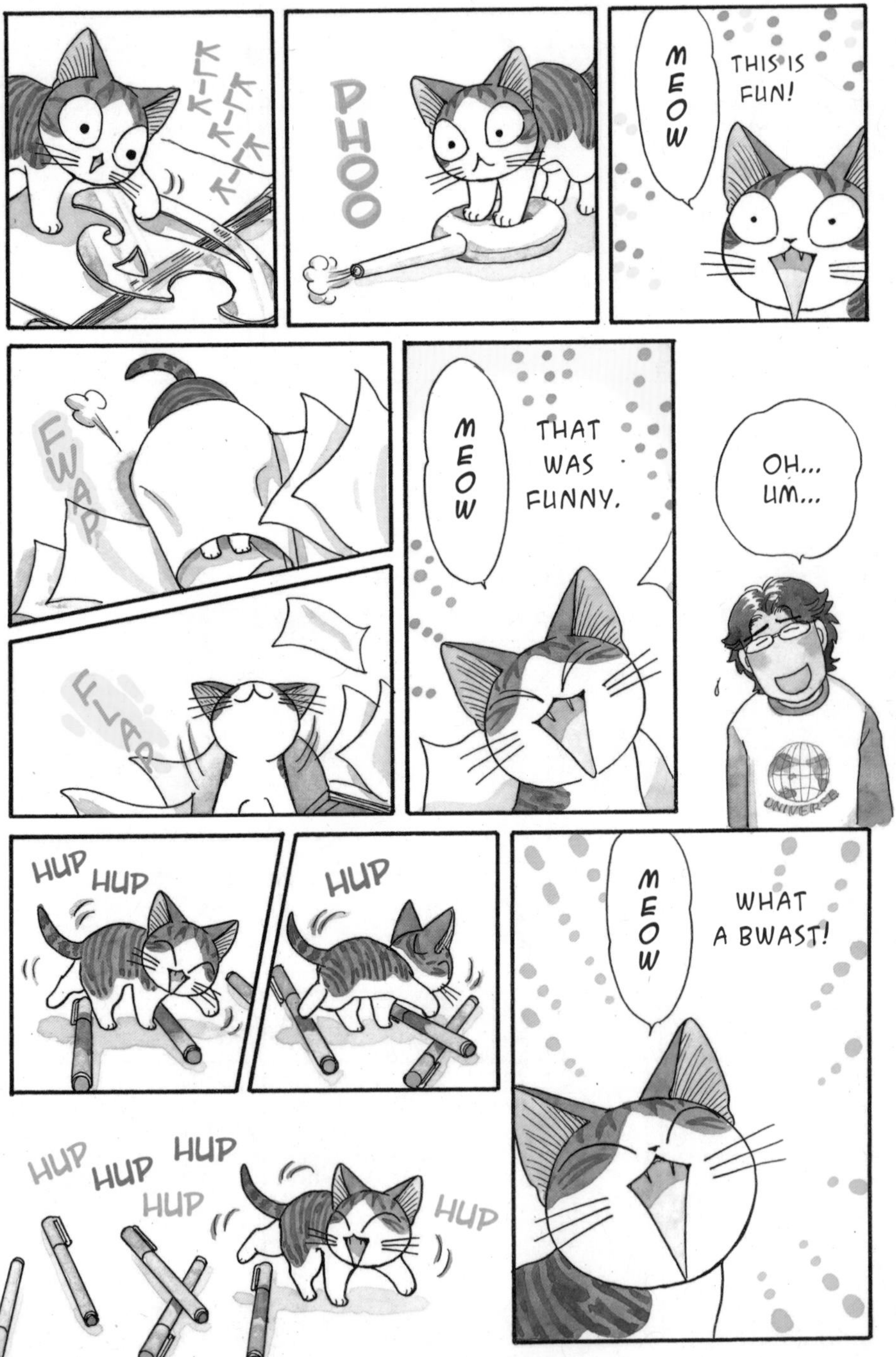
KLIK KLIK
PHOO
MEOW
THIS IS FUN!
FWAP
FLAP
MEOW
THAT WAS FUNNY.
OH... UM...
UNIVERSE
HUP HUP
HUP
HUP HUP HUP HUP HUP
MEOW
WHAT A BWAST!

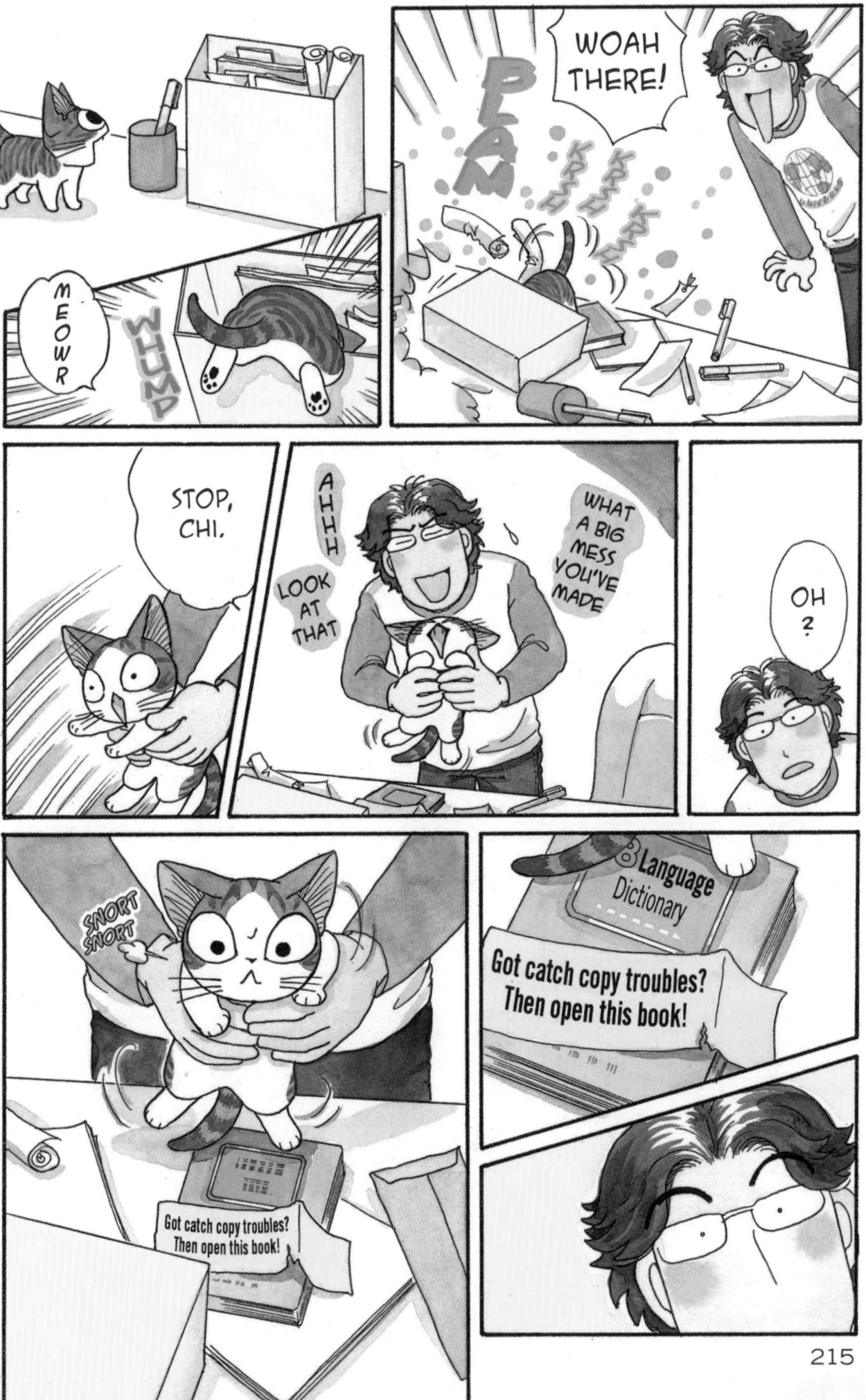
MEOWR
WHUMP
WOAH THERE!
PLAM
KRSH
KRSH
KRSH
STOP, CHI.
AHHH
LOOK AT THAT
WHAT A BIG MESS YOU'VE MADE
OH ?
SNORT SNORT
Got catch copy troubles? Then open this book!
Language Dictionary
Got catch copy troubles? Then open this book!

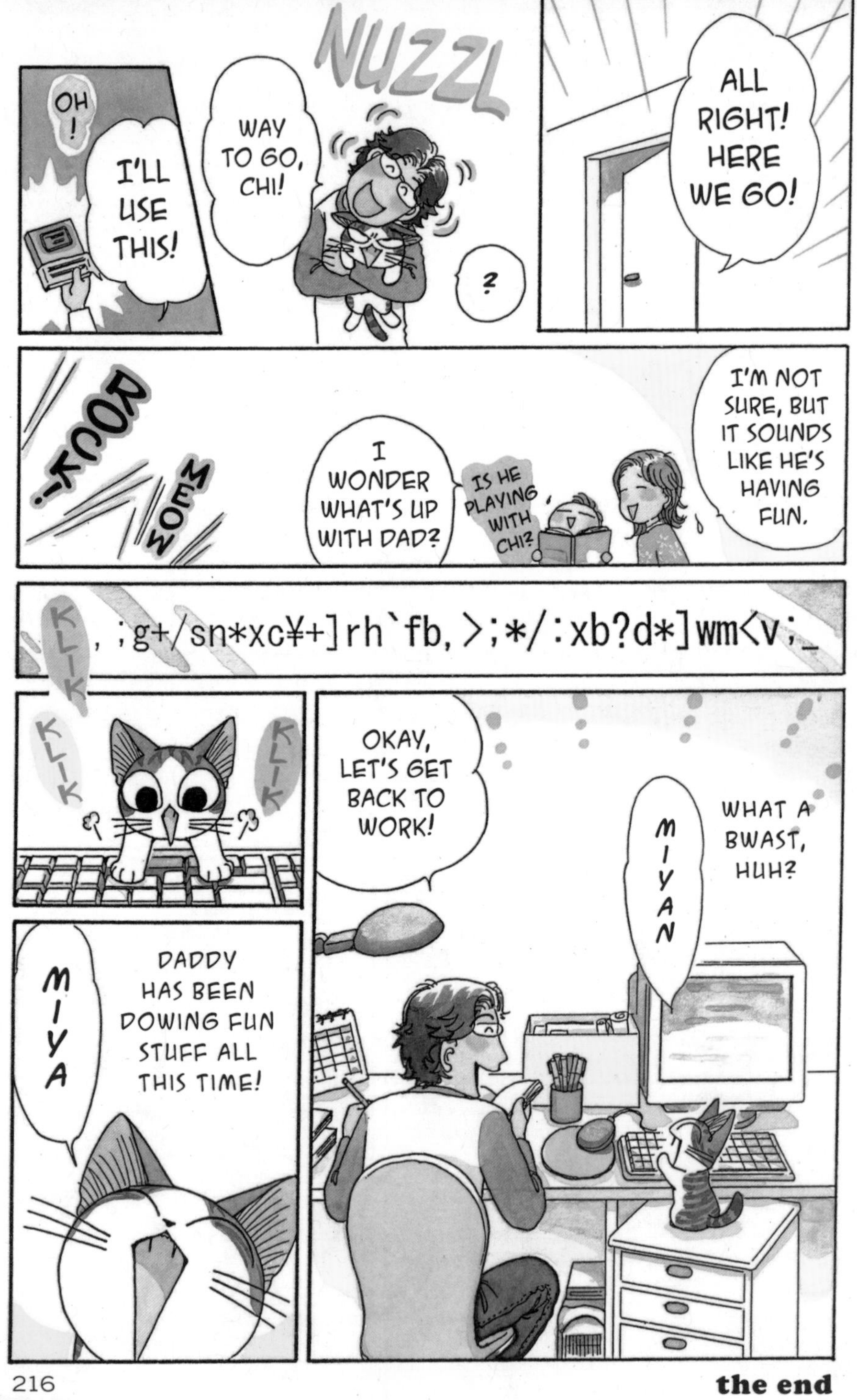
OH!
I'LL USE THIS!
NUZZL
WAY TO GO, CHI!
?
ALL RIGHT! HERE WE GO!
KROOR-!
MEOW
I WONDER WHAT'S UP WITH DAD?
IS HE PLAYING WITH CHI?
I'M NOT SURE, BUT IT SOUNDS LIKE HE'S HAVING FUN.
, ;g+/sn*xc¥+]rh`fb,>;*/:xb?d*]wm<v;_
KLIK
KLIK
KLIK
DADDY HAS BEEN DOWING FUN STUFF ALL THIS TIME!
MIYA
OKAY, LET'S GET BACK TO WORK!
MIYAN
WHAT A BWAST, HUH?

the end

homemade 28: a cat is robbed

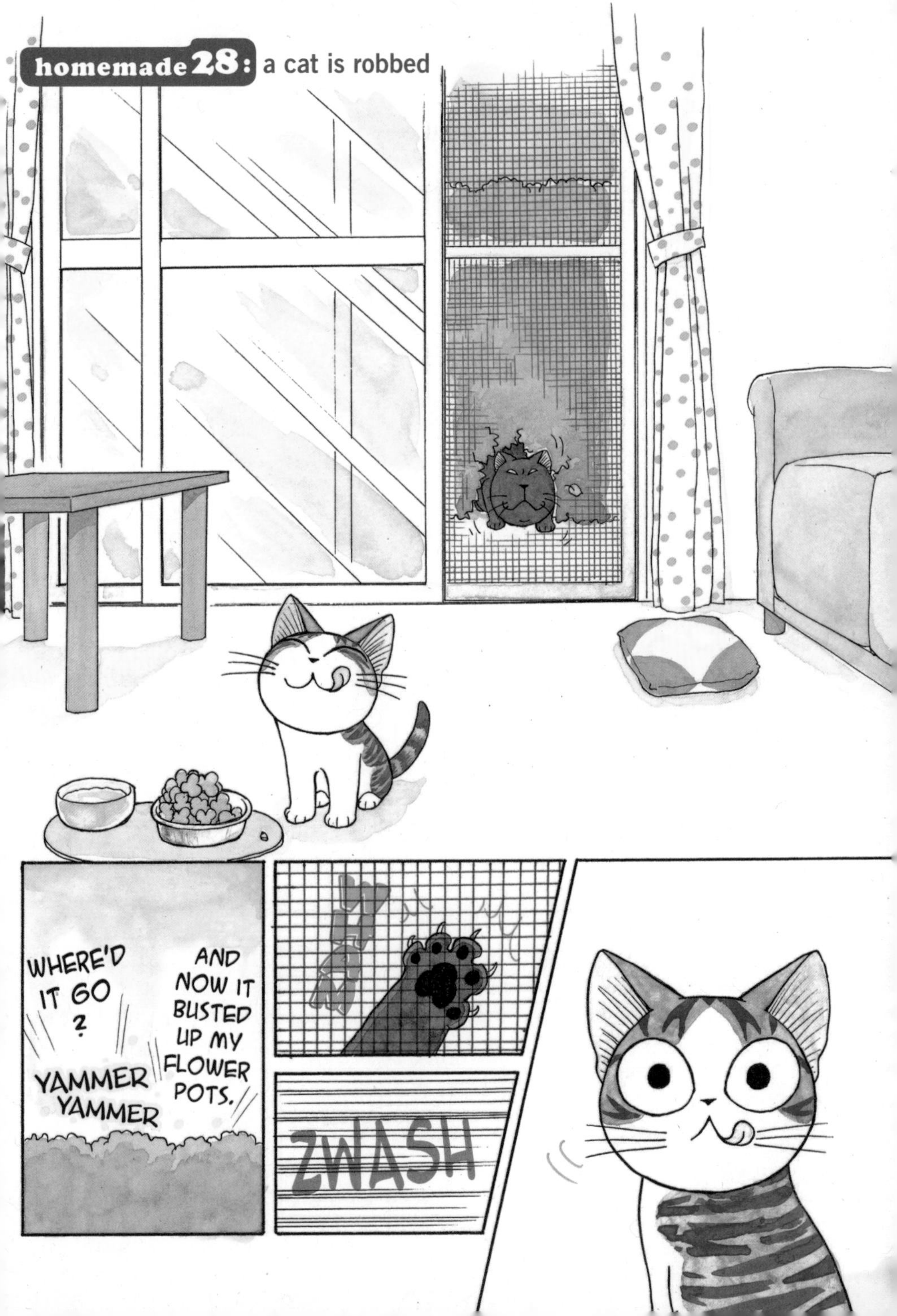
WHERE'D IT GO ?
AND NOW IT BUSTED UP MY FLOWER POTS.
YAMMER YAMMER
ZWASH

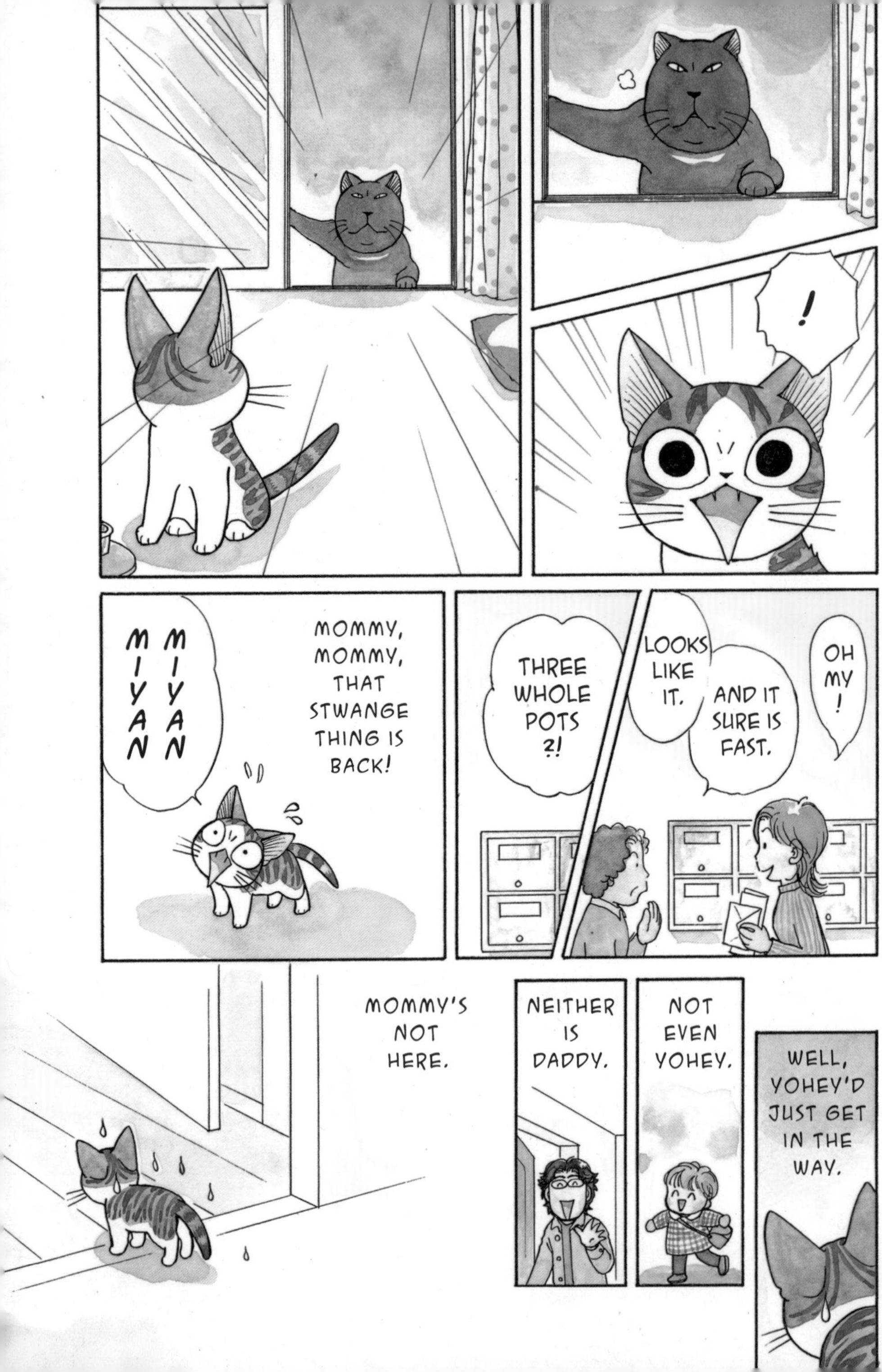
!
MIYAN MIYAN
MOMMY, MOMMY, THAT STWANGE THING IS BACK!
THREE WHOLE POTS?!
LOOKS LIKE IT.
OH MY!
AND IT SURE IS FAST.
MOMMY'S NOT HERE.
NEITHER IS DADDY.
NOT EVEN YOHEY.
WELL, YOHEY'D JUST GET IN THE WAY.

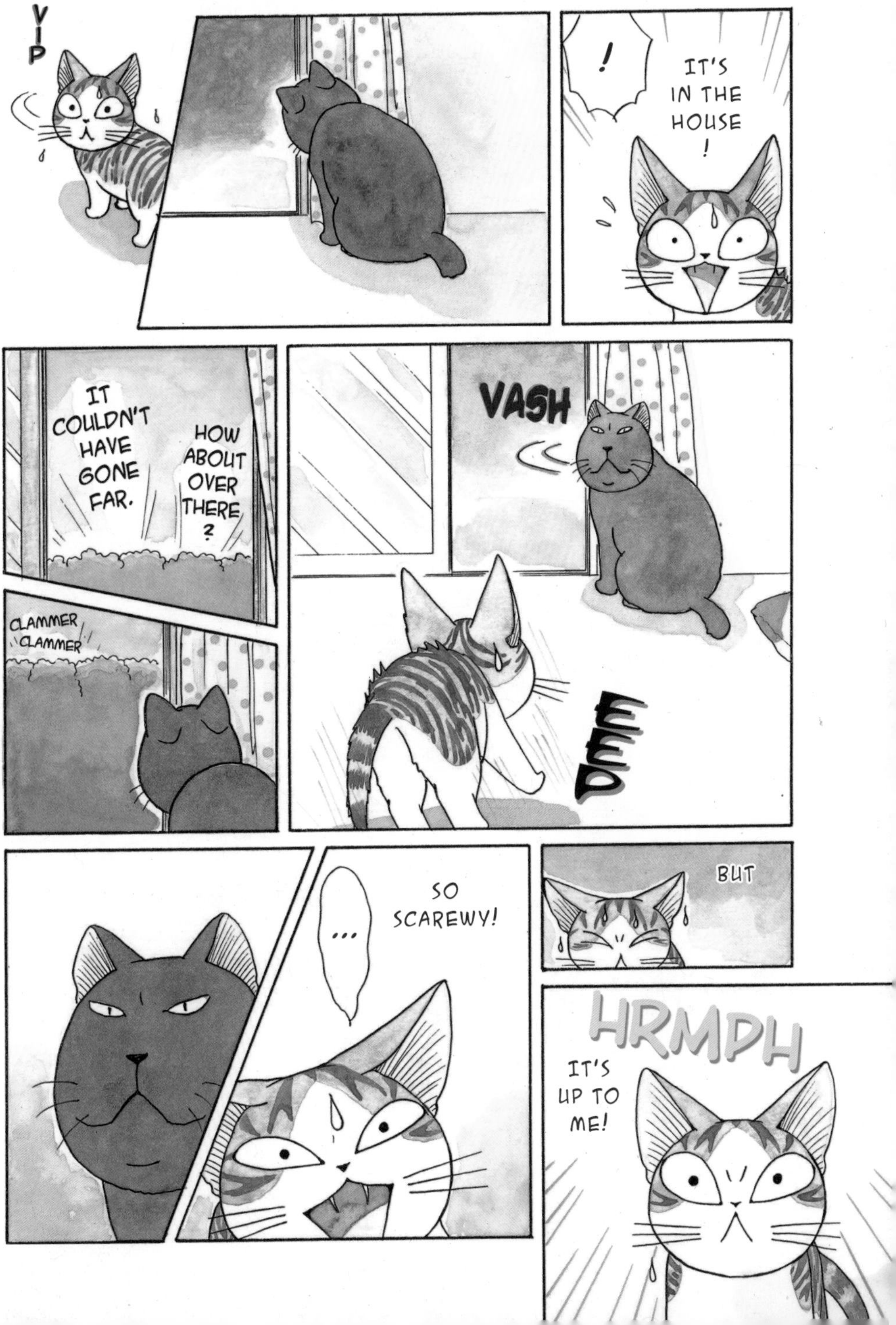

VIP
!
IT'S IN THE HOUSE !
IT COULDN'T HAVE GONE FAR.
HOW ABOUT OVER THERE ?
CLAMMER CLAMMER
VASH
...
SO SCAREWY!
BUT
HRMPH
IT'S UP TO ME!

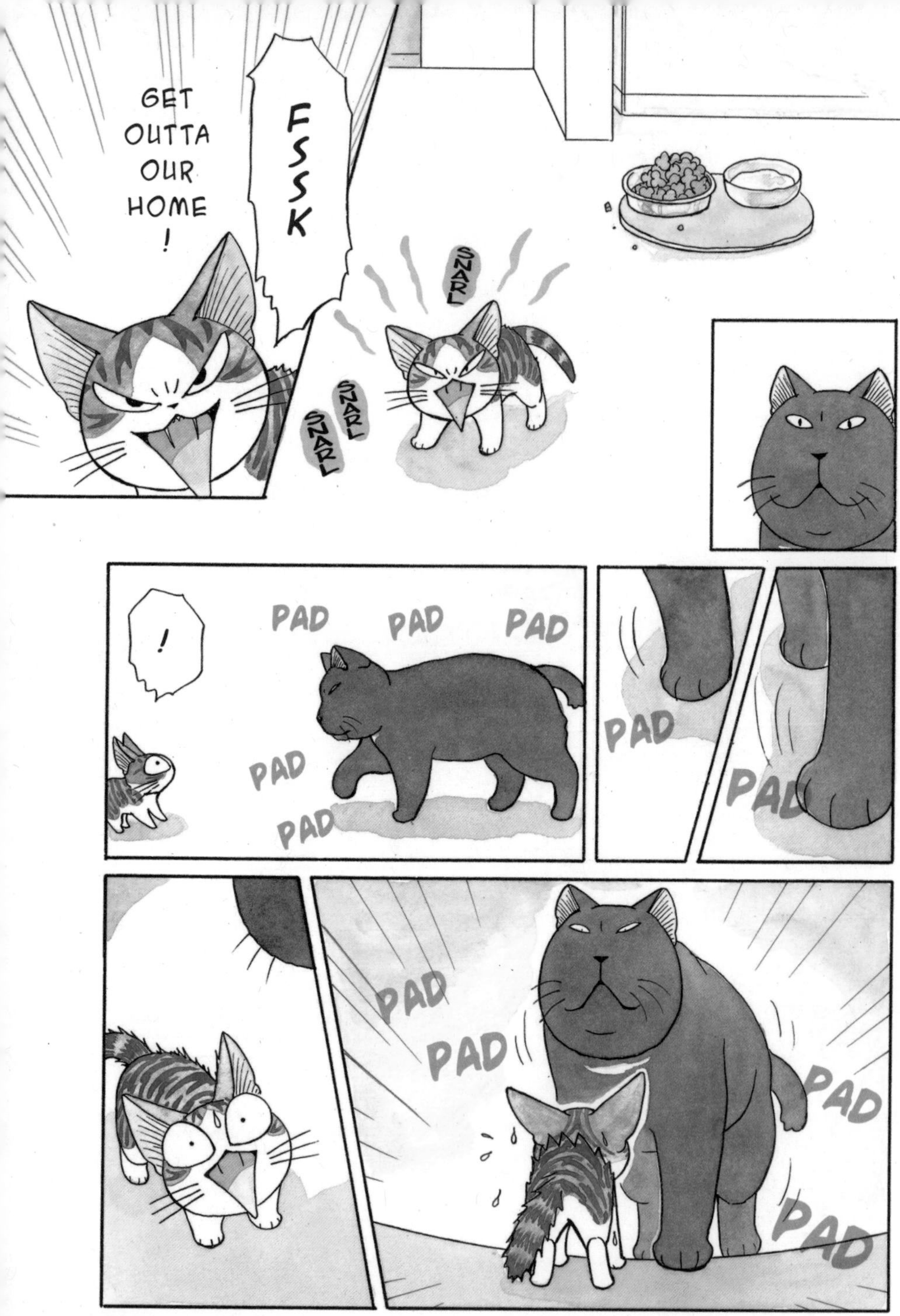
GET OUTTA OUR HOME !
FSSK
SNARL
SNARL
SNARL
!
PAD
PAD
PAD
PAD
PAD
PAD
PAD
PAD
PAD
PAD
PAD

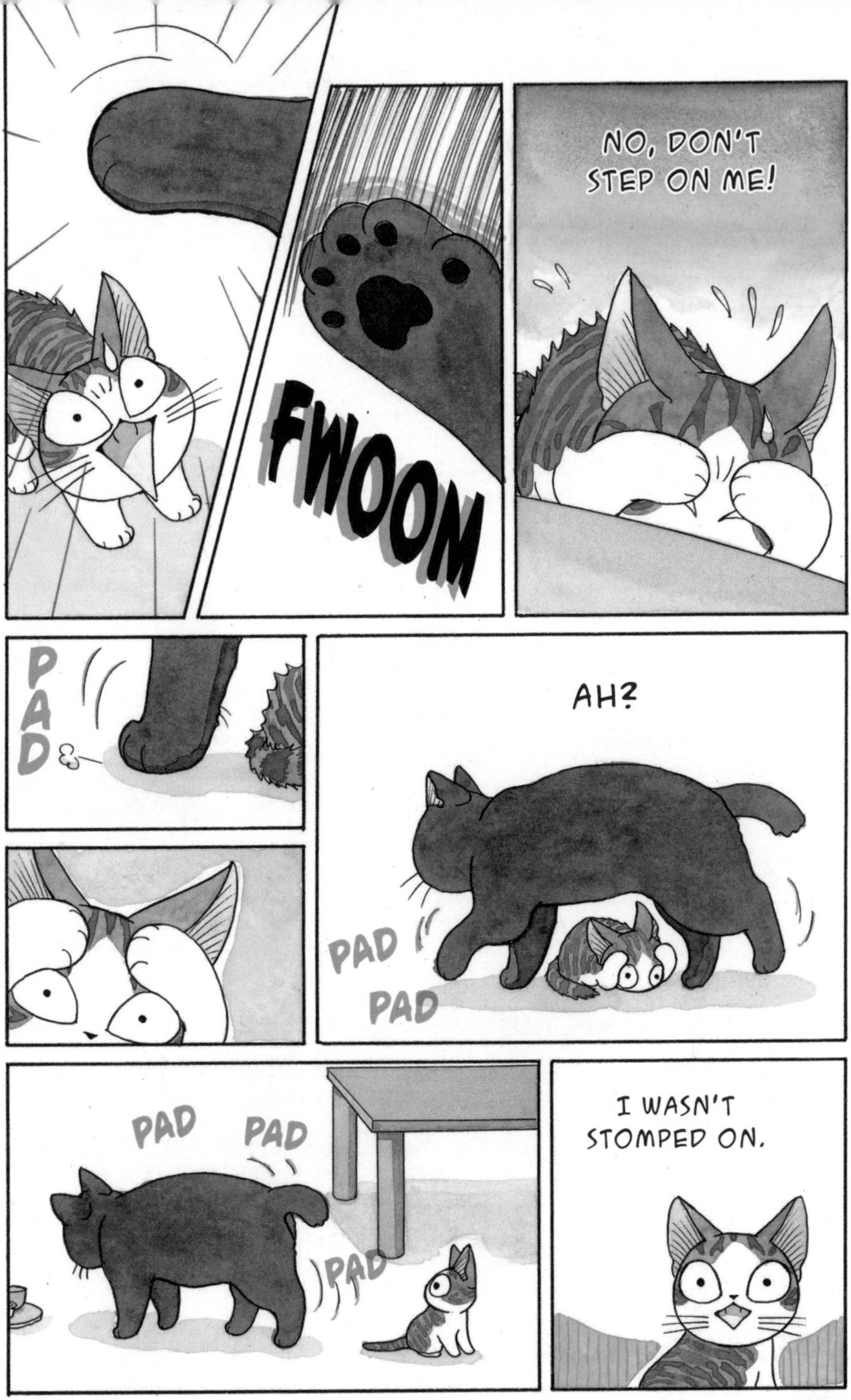
FWOOM
NO, DON'T STEP ON ME!
PAD PAD
AH?
PAD PAD
PAD PAD
PAD
I WASN'T STOMPED ON.

MUNCH
MUNCH
MUNCH
MUNCH
MUNCH
MUNCH
CHOMP
CHOMP
!
MY FOOD!
HSSS
STOP THAT! IT'S CHI'S FOOD!
SHFT
KRUNCH
KRUNCH
KRUNCH
KRUNCH
!!

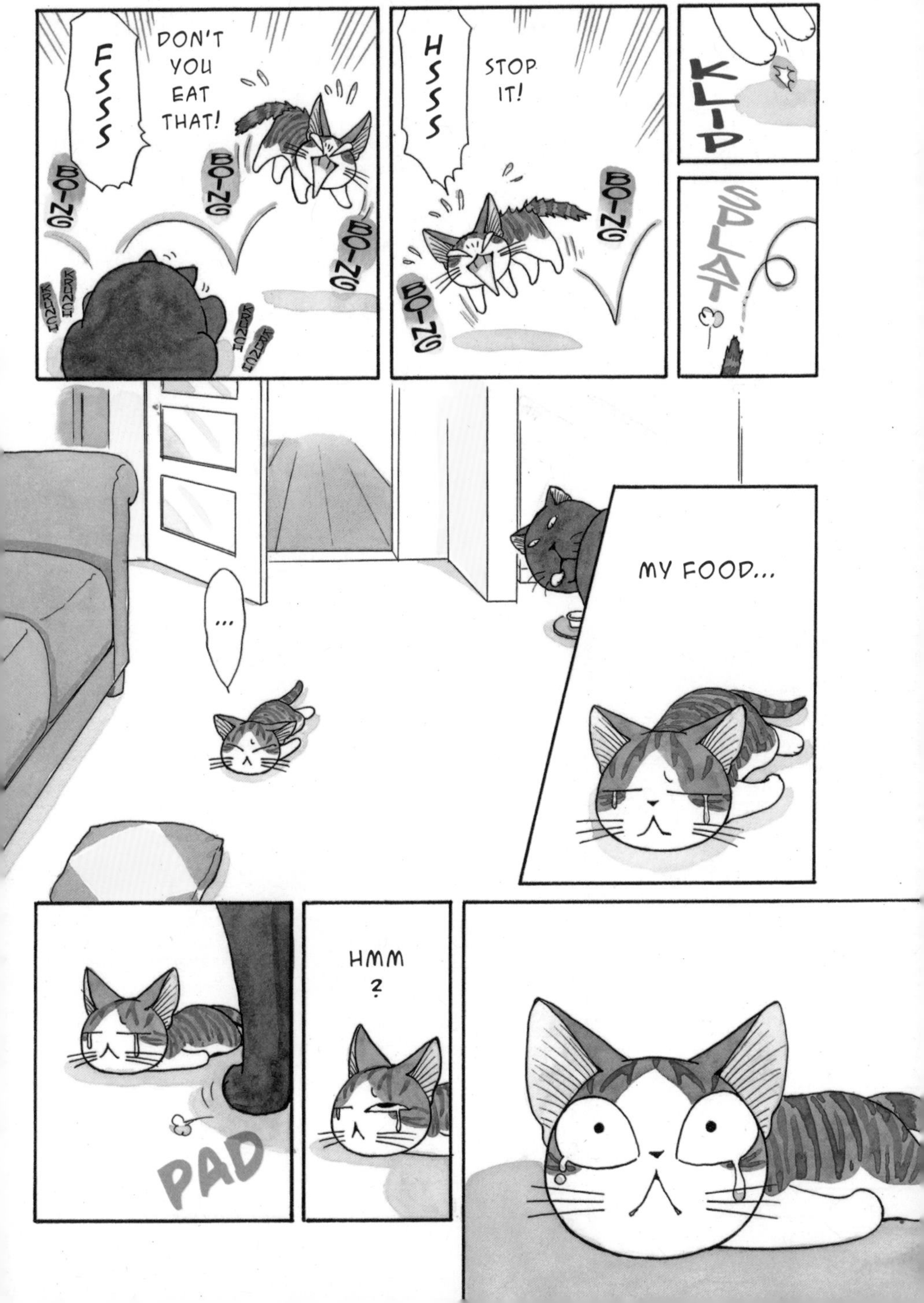
FSSS
DON'T YOU EAT THAT!
BOING
BOING
BOING
KRUNCH KRUNCH
KRUNCH KRUNCH
HSSS
STOP IT!
BOING
BOING
KLIP
SPLAT
...
MY FOOD...
PAD
HMM?

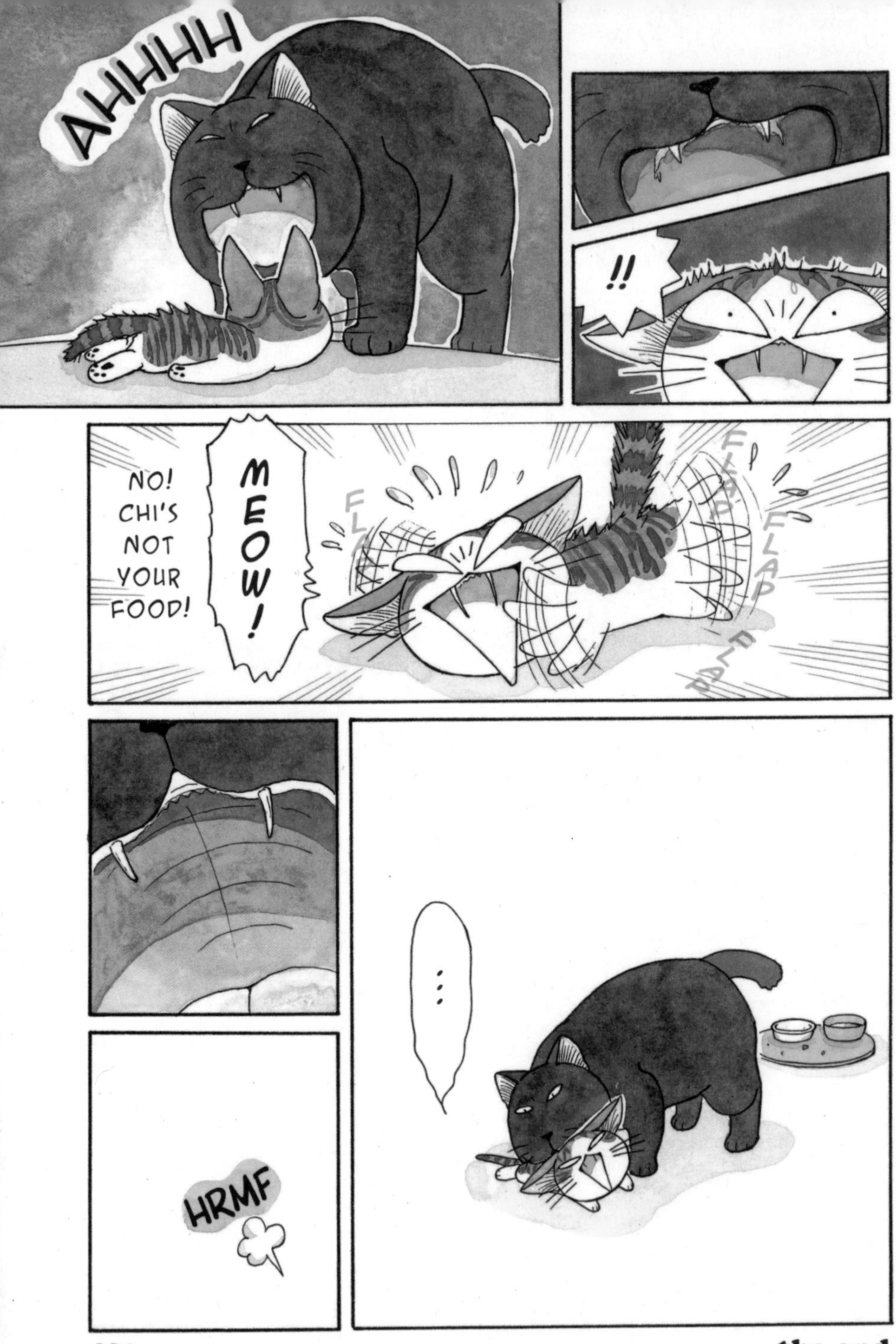
AHHHH
!!
MEOW!
NO! CHI'S NOT YOUR FOOD!
FLA
FLAP
FLAP
FLAP
HRMF
...

the end

homemade 29: a cat considers

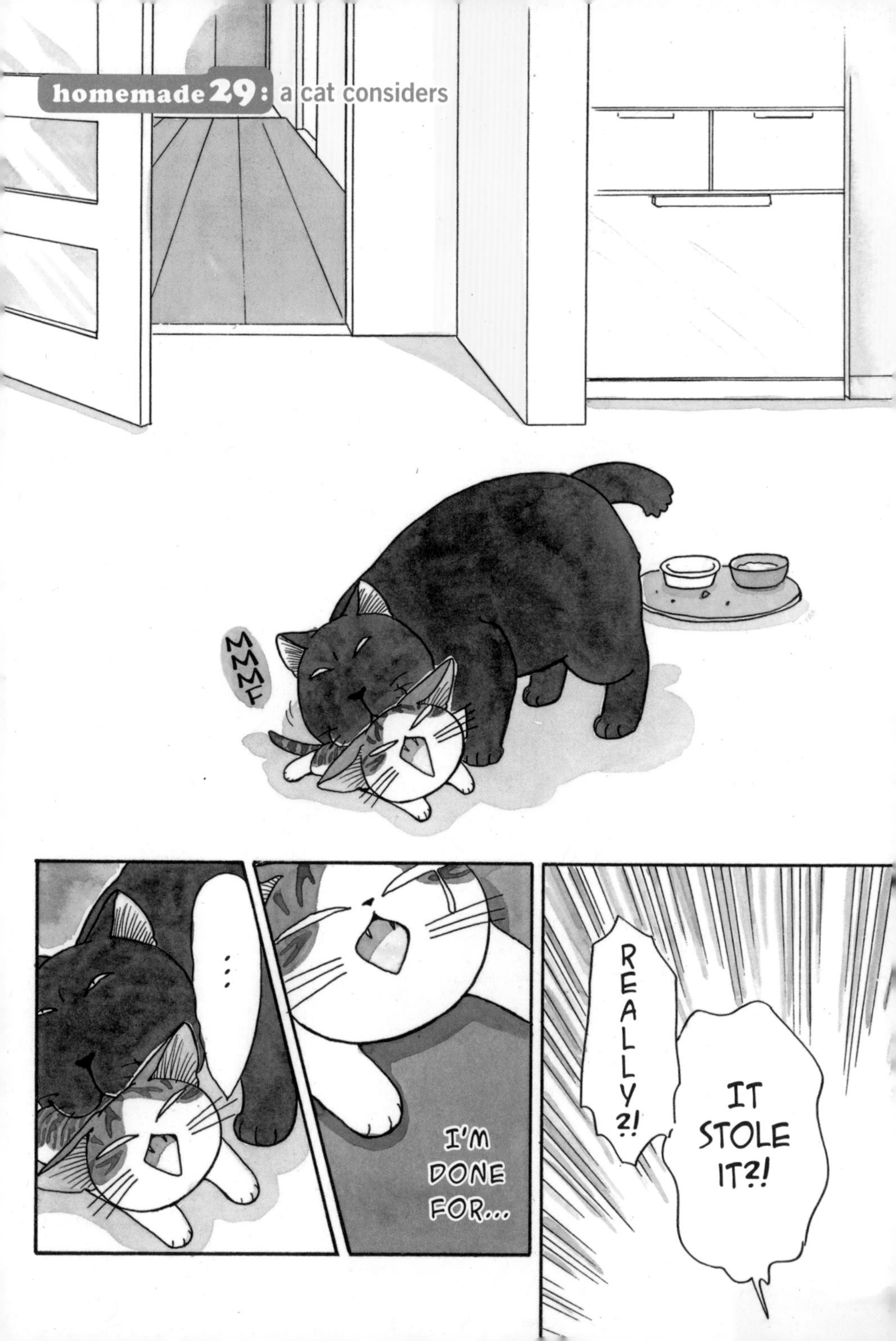
MMMF
...
I'M DONE FOR...
REALLY?!
IT STOLE IT?!

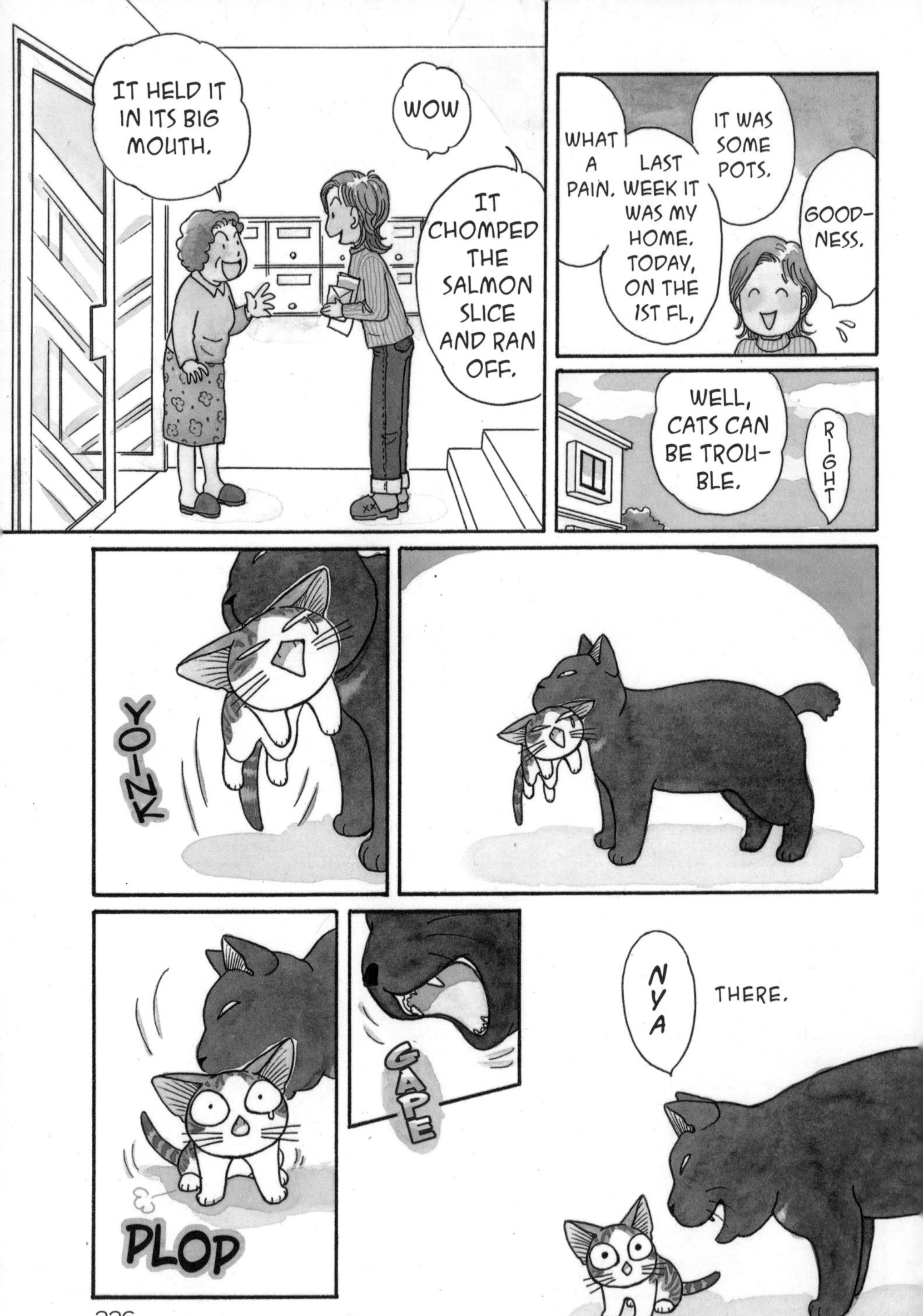
IT HELD IT IN ITS BIG MOUTH.
WOW
IT CHOMPED THE SALMON SLICE AND RAN OFF.
WHAT A PAIN.
LAST WEEK IT WAS MY HOME. TODAY, ON THE 1ST FL,
IT WAS SOME POTS.
GOOD-NESS.
WELL, CATS CAN BE TROU-BLE.
RIGHT
YOINK
PLOP
GAPE
NYA
THERE.

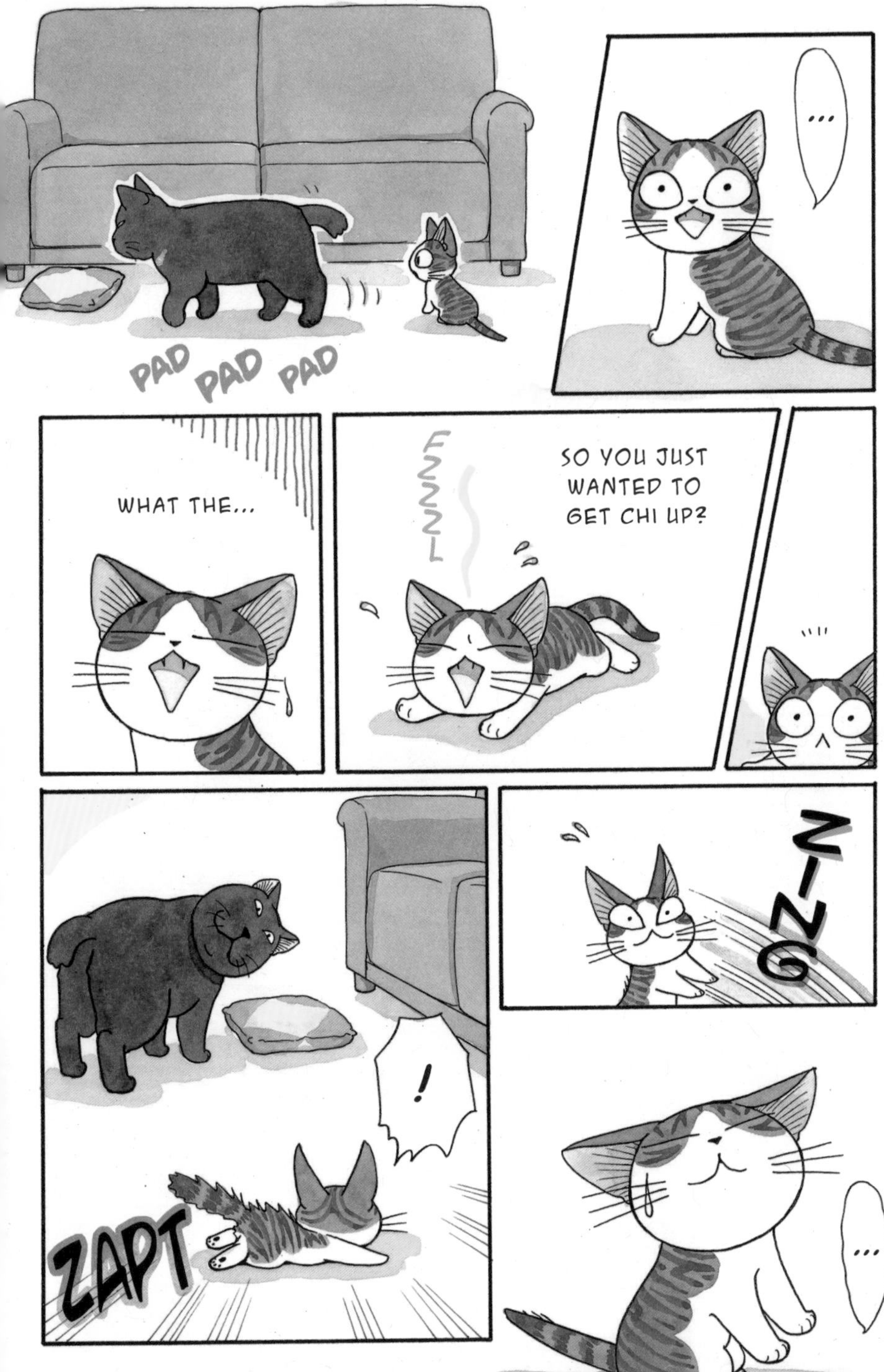
PAD PAD PAD
...
WHAT THE...
FZZZL
SO YOU JUST WANTED TO GET CHI UP?
ZAPT
!
ZING
...

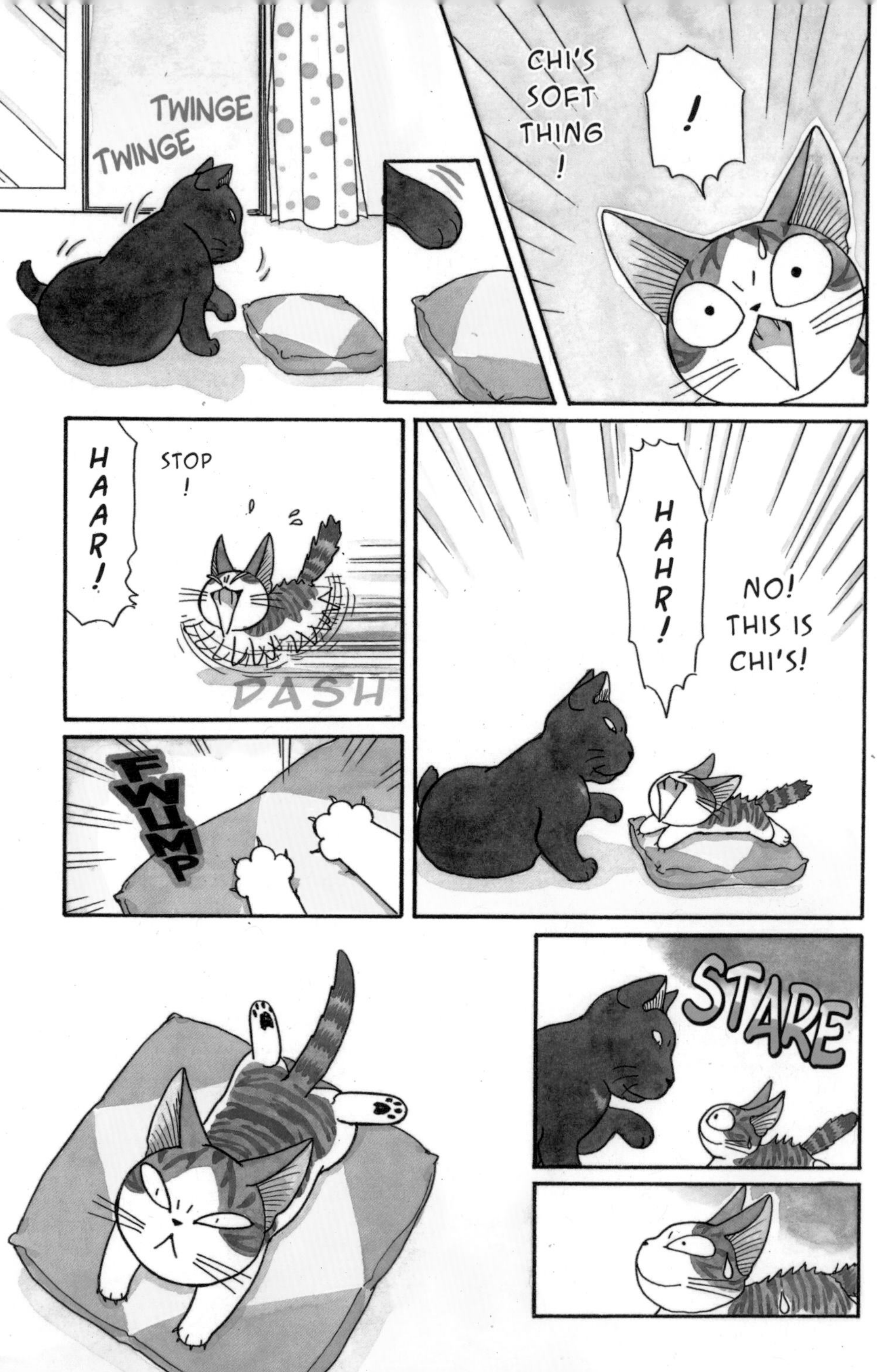
TWINGE
TWINGE
CHI'S SOFT THING!
!
HAAR!
STOP!
DASH
FWUMP
HAHR!
NO! THIS IS CHI'S!
STARE

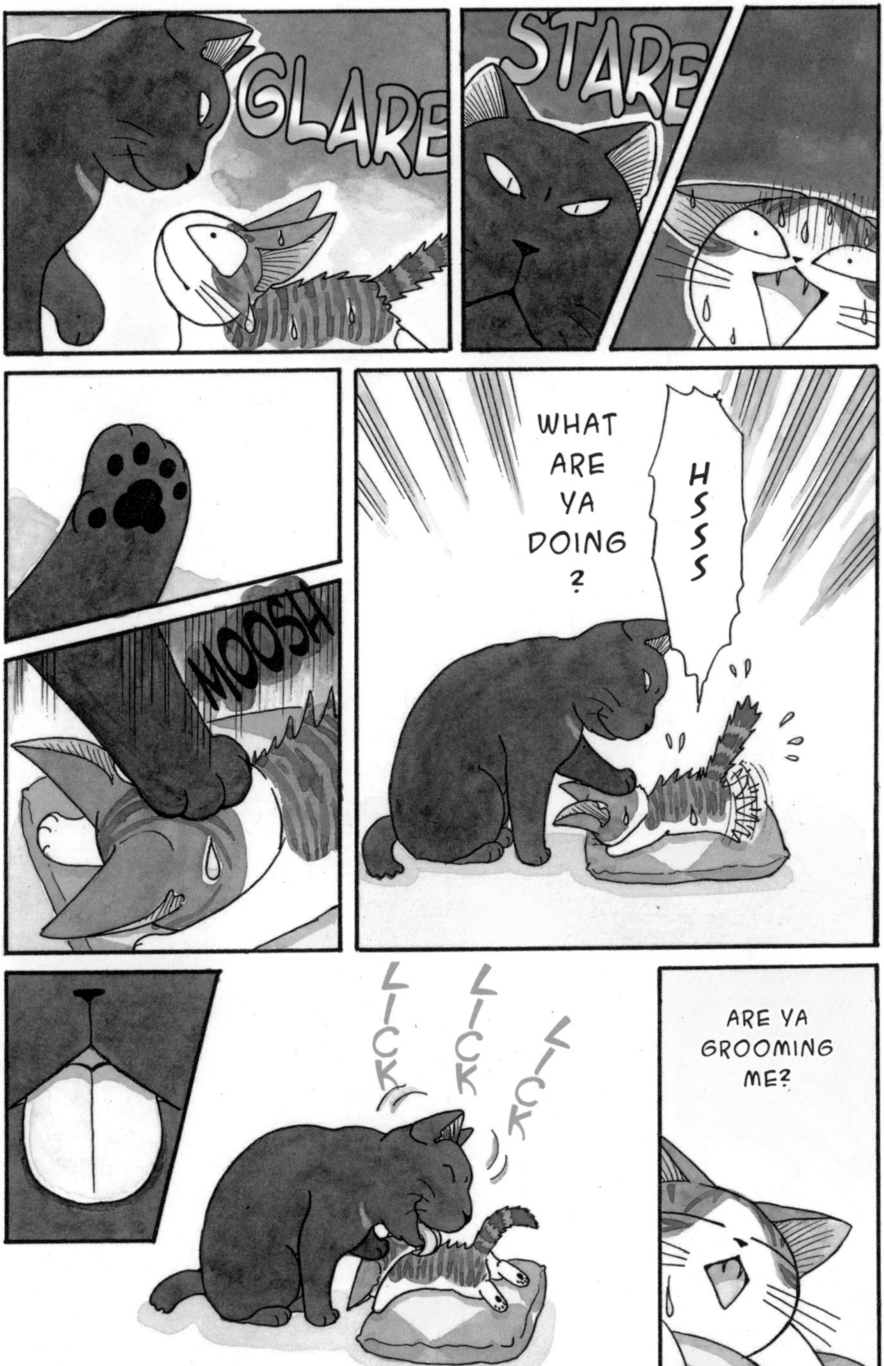
GLARE
STARE
MOOSH
WHAT ARE YA DOING?
HSSS
LICK LICK LICK
ARE YA GROOMING ME?

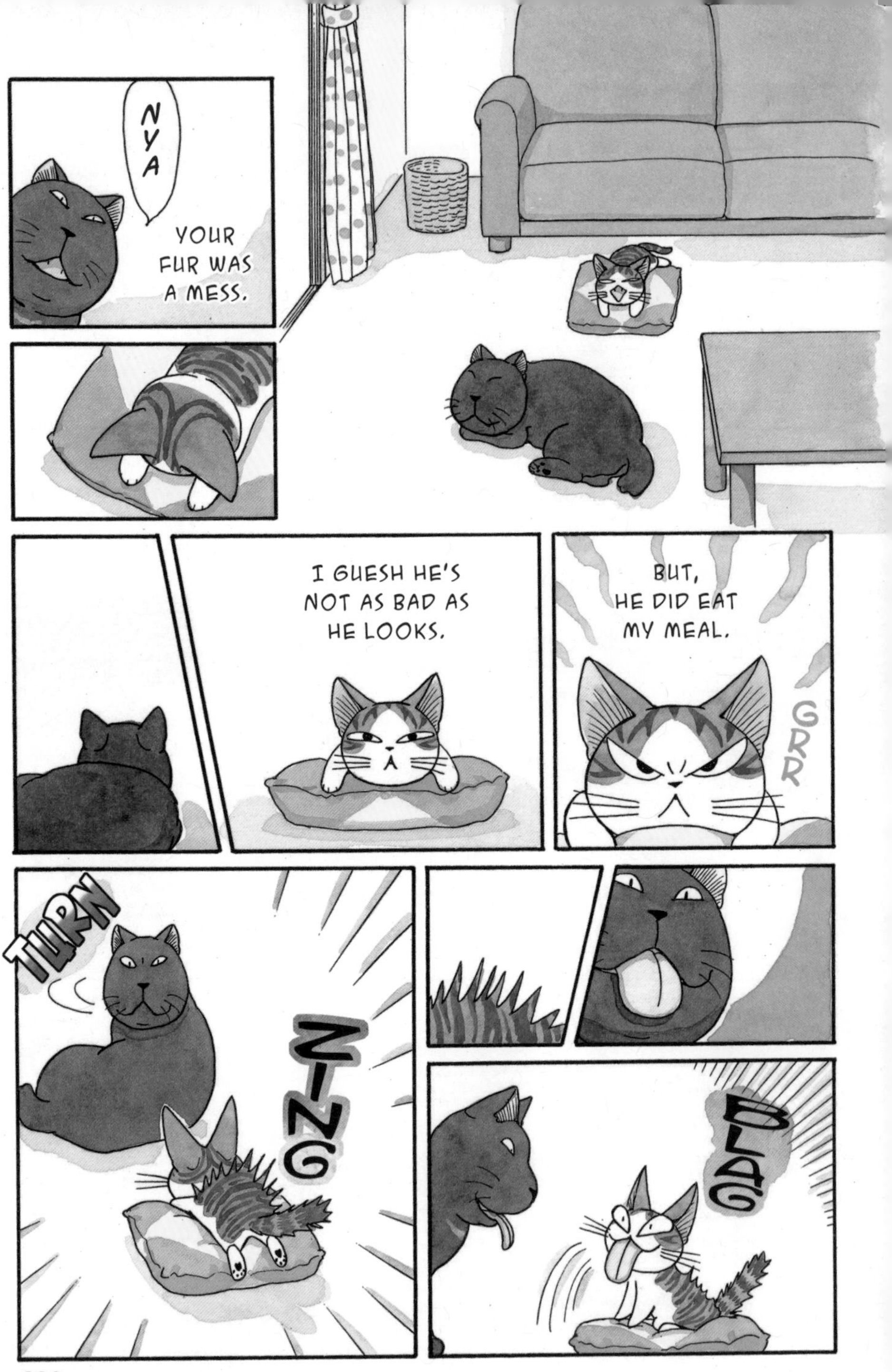
NYA
YOUR FUR WAS A MESS.
I GUESH HE'S NOT AS BAD AS HE LOOKS.
BUT, HE DID EAT MY MEAL.
GRR
TURN
ZING
BLAG

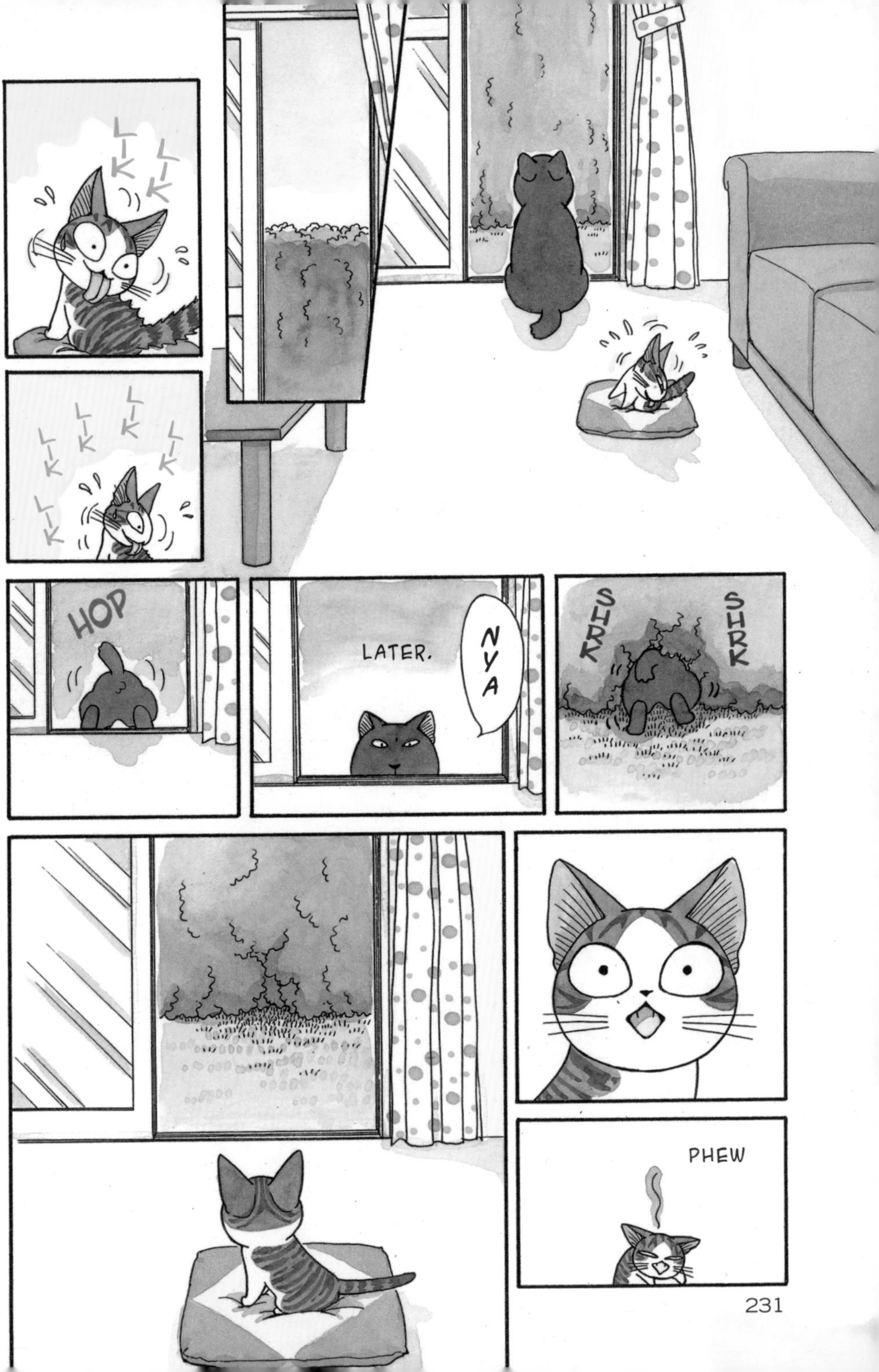
LIK
LIK
LIK
LIK
LIK
LIK
LIK
HOP
LATER.
NYA
SHRK
SHRK
PHEW

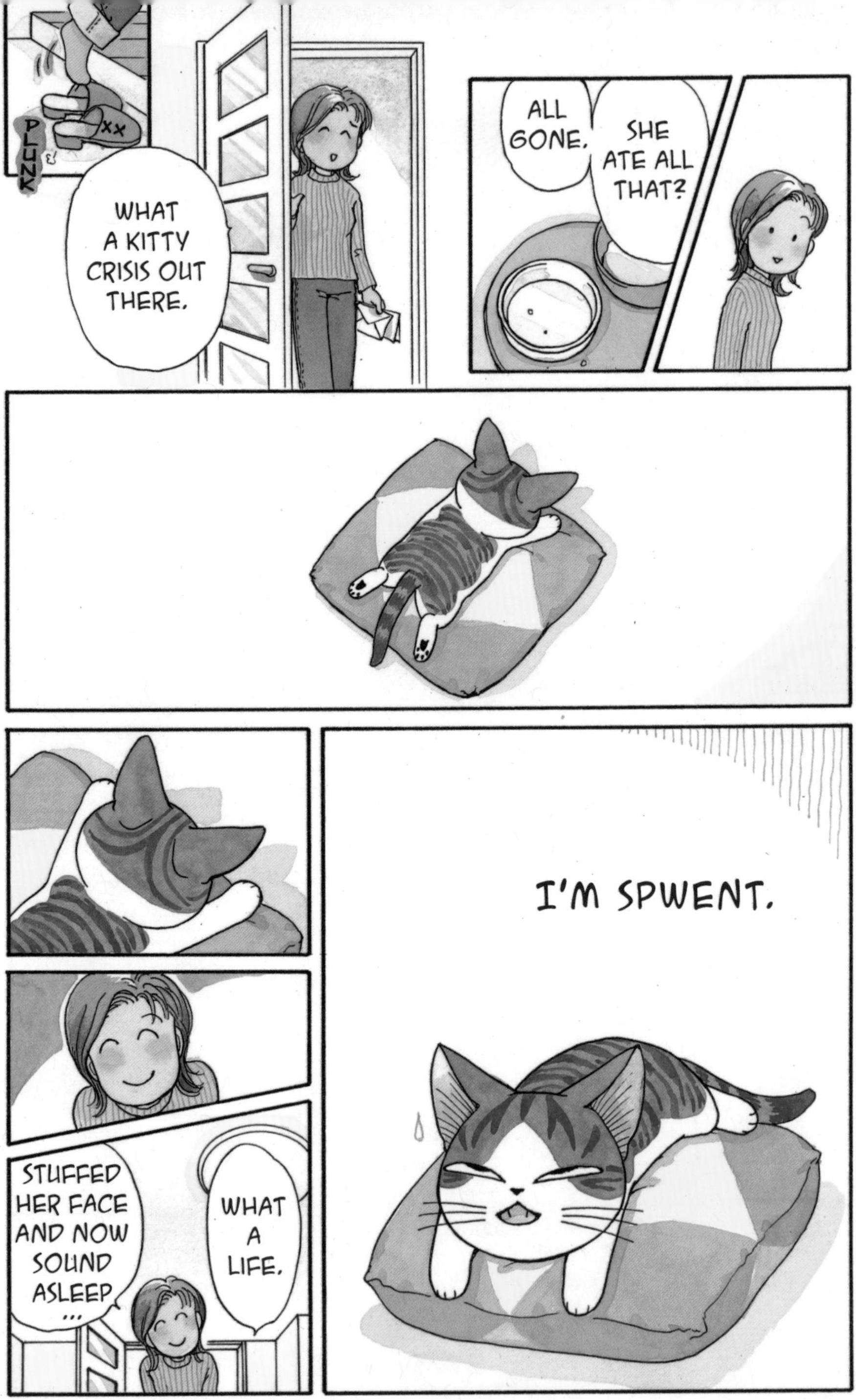
PLUNK
WHAT A KITTY CRISIS OUT THERE.
ALL GONE.
SHE ATE ALL THAT?
STUFFED HER FACE AND NOW SOUND ASLEEP...
WHAT A LIFE.
I'M SPWENT.

the end

homemade 30: a cat reports

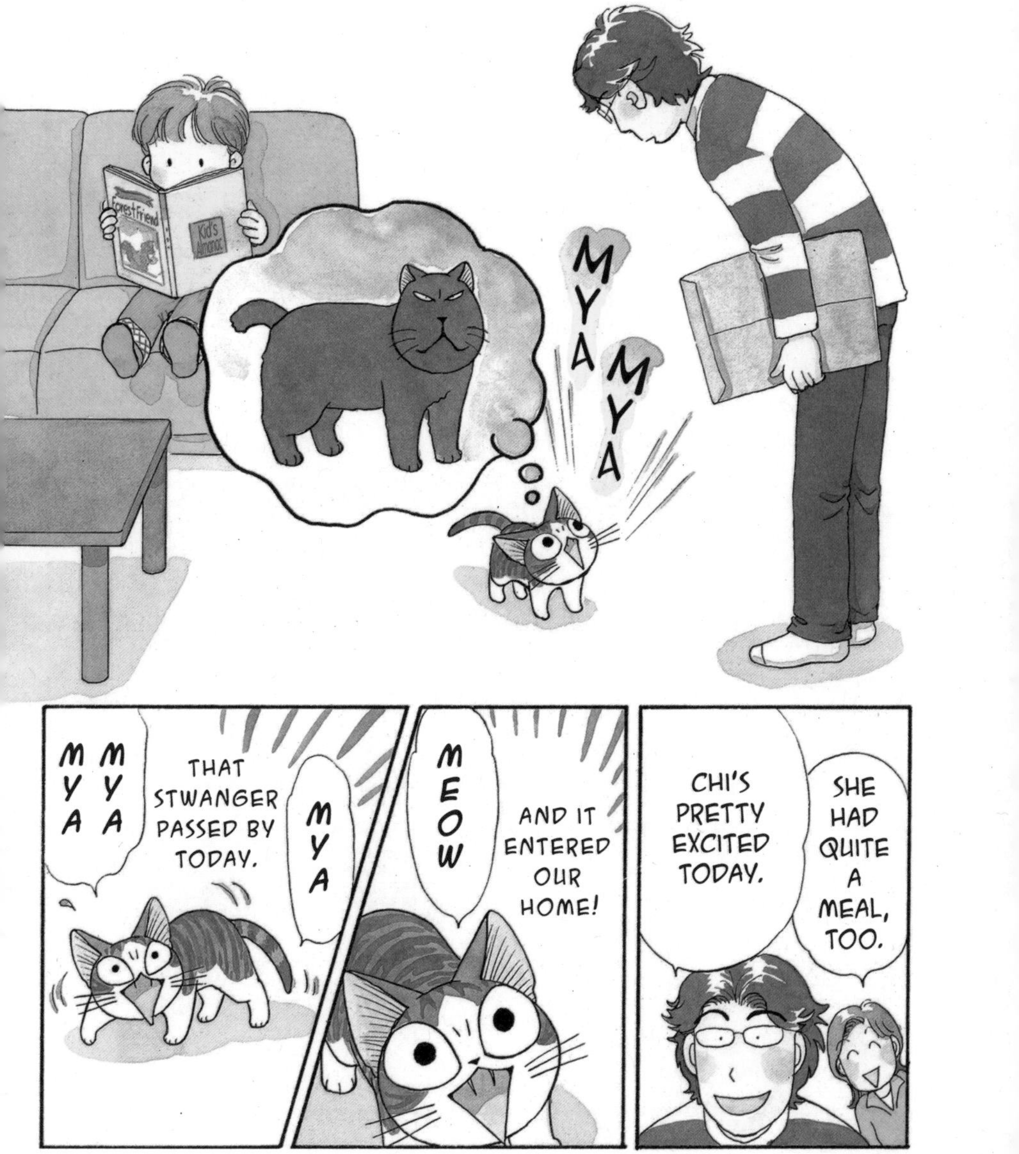
Forest Friend
Kid's Almanac
MYA
MYA
MYA
MYA MYA
THAT STWANGER PASSED BY TODAY.
MYA
MEOW
AND IT ENTERED OUR HOME!
CHI'S PRETTY EXCITED TODAY.
SHE HAD QUITE A MEAL, TOO.

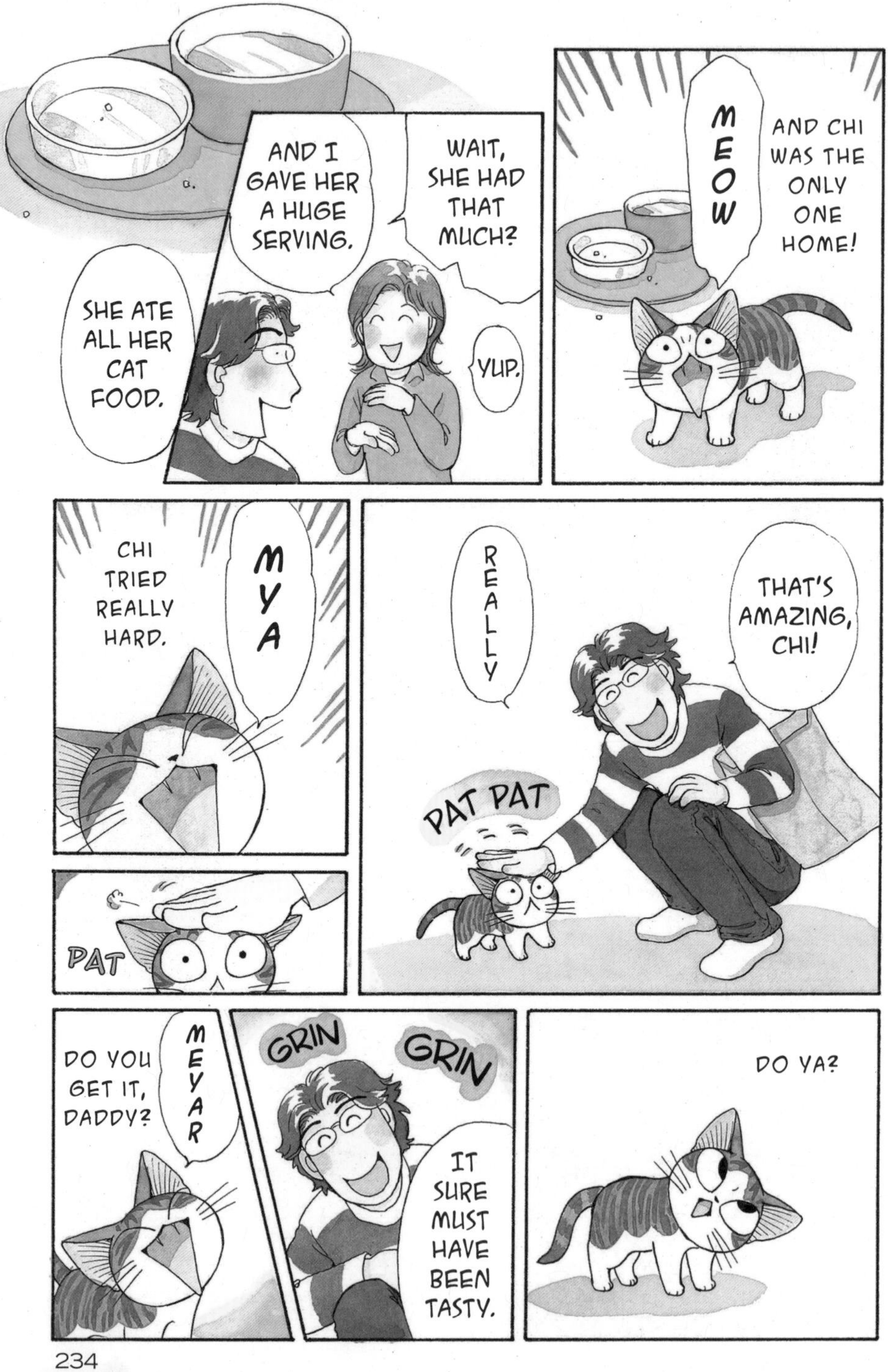
SHE ATE ALL HER CAT FOOD.
AND I GAVE HER A HUGE SERVING.
WAIT, SHE HAD THAT MUCH?
YUP.
MEOW
AND CHI WAS THE ONLY ONE HOME!
CHI TRIED REALLY HARD.
MYA
PAT
REALLY
THAT'S AMAZING, CHI!
PAT PAT
DO YOU GET IT, DADDY?
MEYAR
GRIN GRIN
IT SURE MUST HAVE BEEN TASTY.
DO YA?

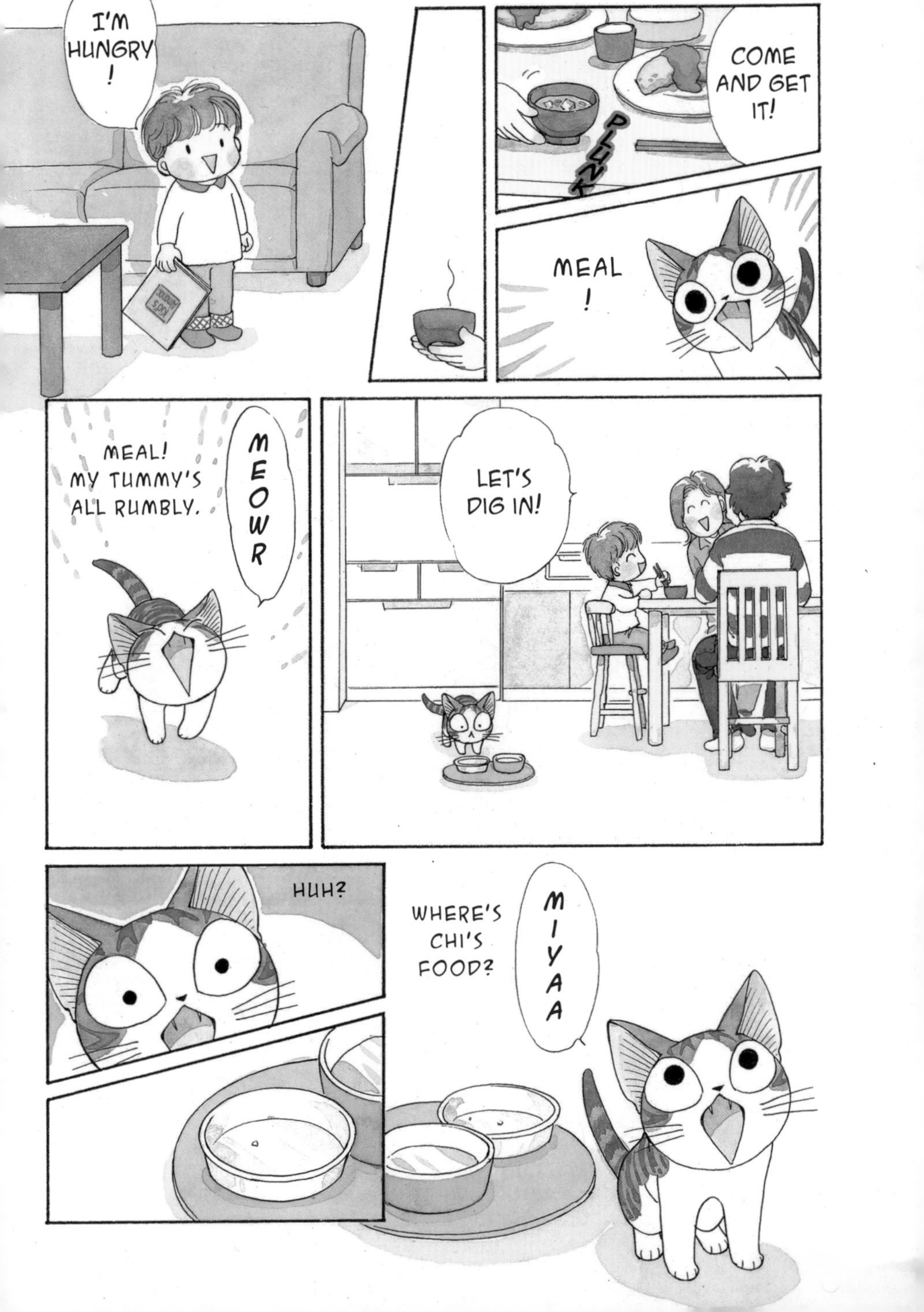
I'M HUNGRY!
COME AND GET IT!
PLUNK
MEAL!
MEAL! MY TUMMY'S ALL RUMBLY.
MEOWR
LET'S DIG IN!
HUH?
WHERE'S CHI'S FOOD?
MIYAA

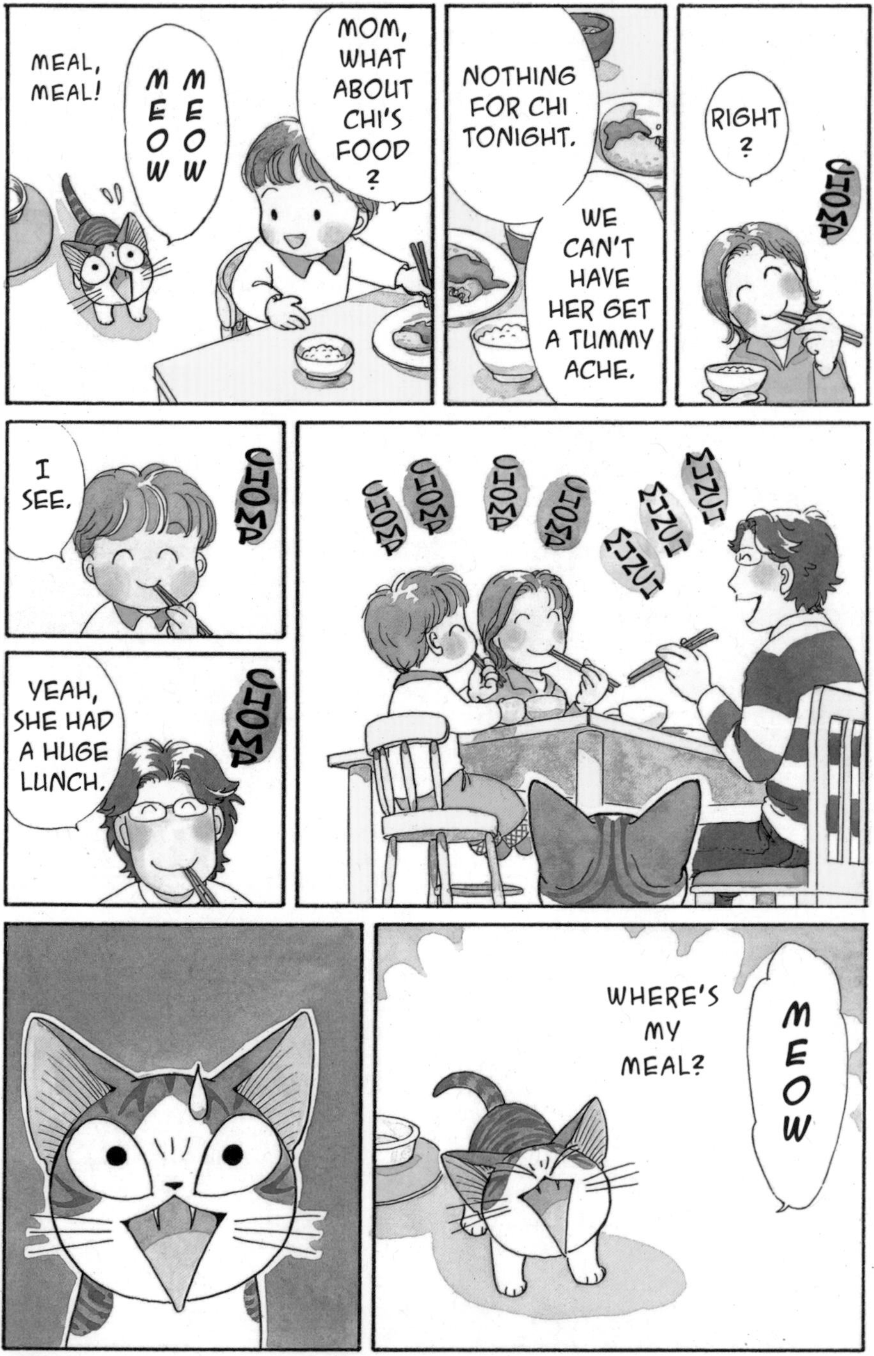
MEAL, MEAL!
MEOW MEOW
MOM, WHAT ABOUT CHI'S FOOD?
NOTHING FOR CHI TONIGHT.
WE CAN'T HAVE HER GET A TUMMY ACHE.
RIGHT?
CHOMP
I SEE.
CHOMP
YEAH, SHE HAD A HUGE LUNCH.
CHOMP
CHOMP
CHOMP
CHOMP
CHOMP
MUNCH
MUNCH
MUNCH
WHERE'S MY MEAL?
MEOW

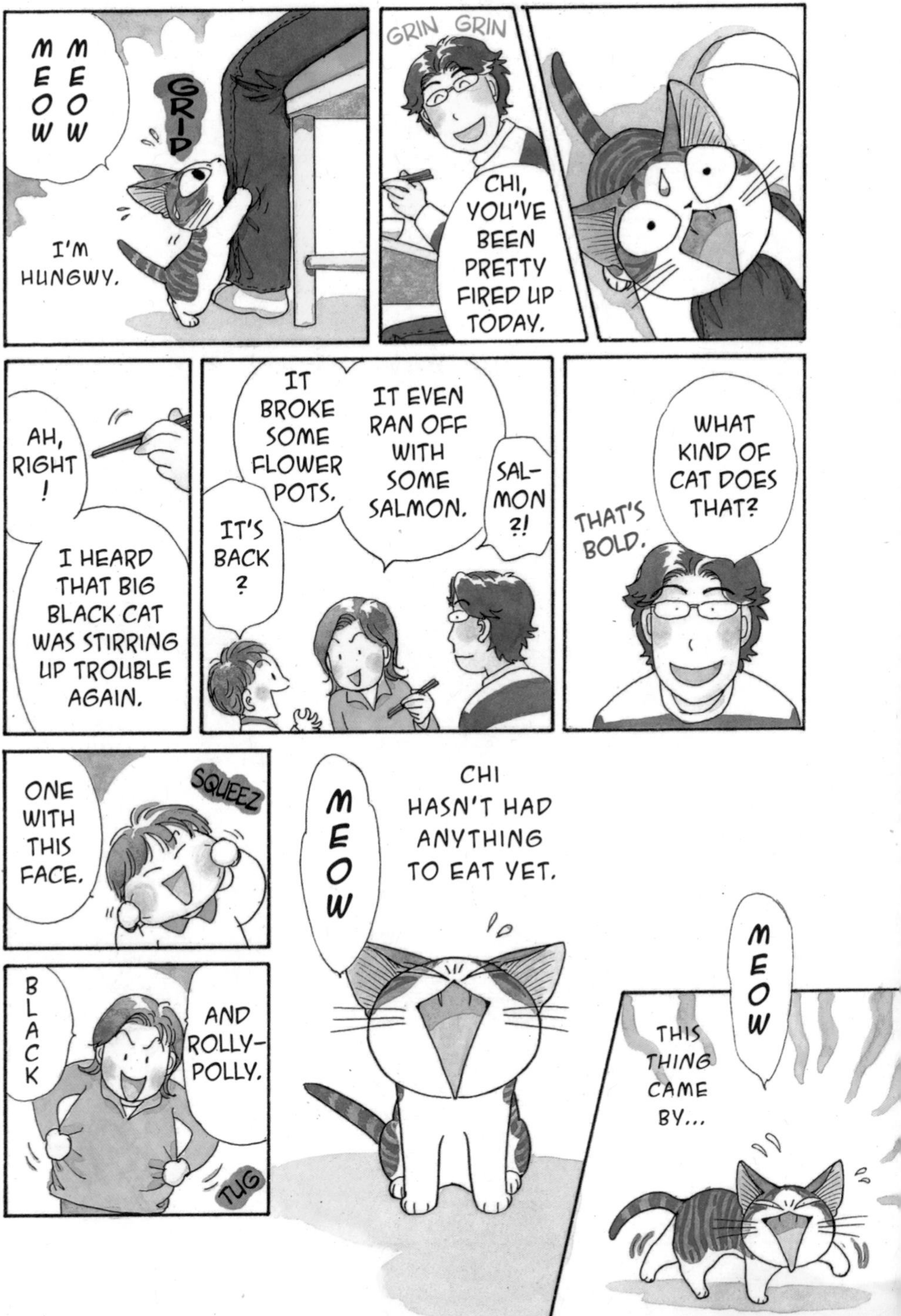
MEOW MEOW
GRID
I'M HUNGWY.
GRIN GRIN
CHI, YOU'VE BEEN PRETTY FIRED UP TODAY.
AH, RIGHT!
I HEARD THAT BIG BLACK CAT WAS STIRRING UP TROUBLE AGAIN.
IT BROKE SOME FLOWER POTS.
IT EVEN RAN OFF WITH SOME SALMON.
IT'S BACK?
SAL-MON?!
THAT'S BOLD.
WHAT KIND OF CAT DOES THAT?
ONE WITH THIS FACE.
SQUEEZ
BLACK
AND ROLLY-POLLY.
TUG
MEOW
CHI HASN'T HAD ANYTHING TO EAT YET.
THIS THING CAME BY...
MEOW

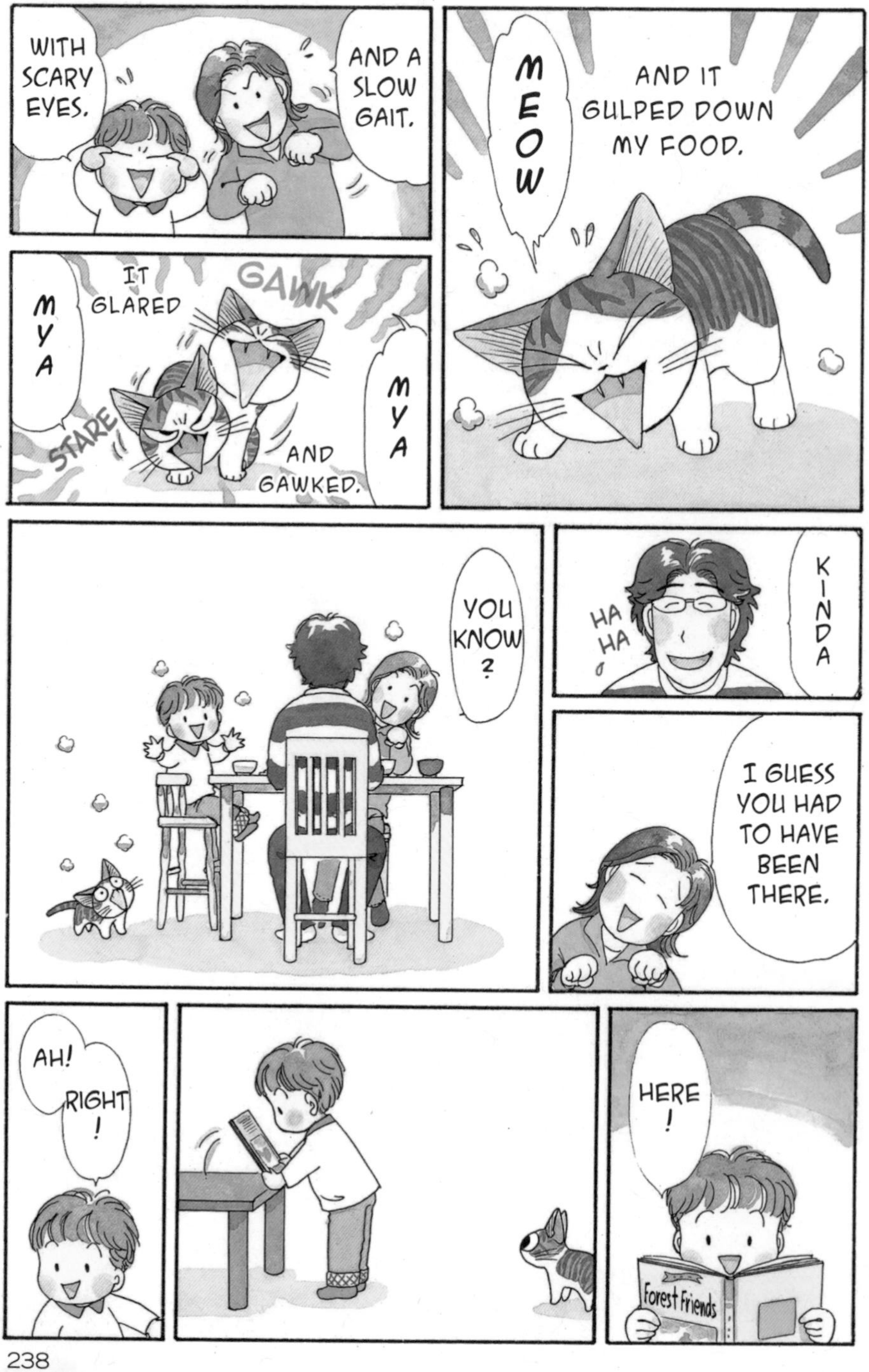
WITH SCARY EYES.
AND A SLOW GAIT.
MYA
IT GLARED
GAWK
STARE
AND GAWKED.
MYA
MEOW
AND IT GULPED DOWN MY FOOD.
YOU KNOW?
HA HA
KINDA
I GUESS YOU HAD TO HAVE BEEN THERE.
AH!
RIGHT!
HERE!
Forest Friends

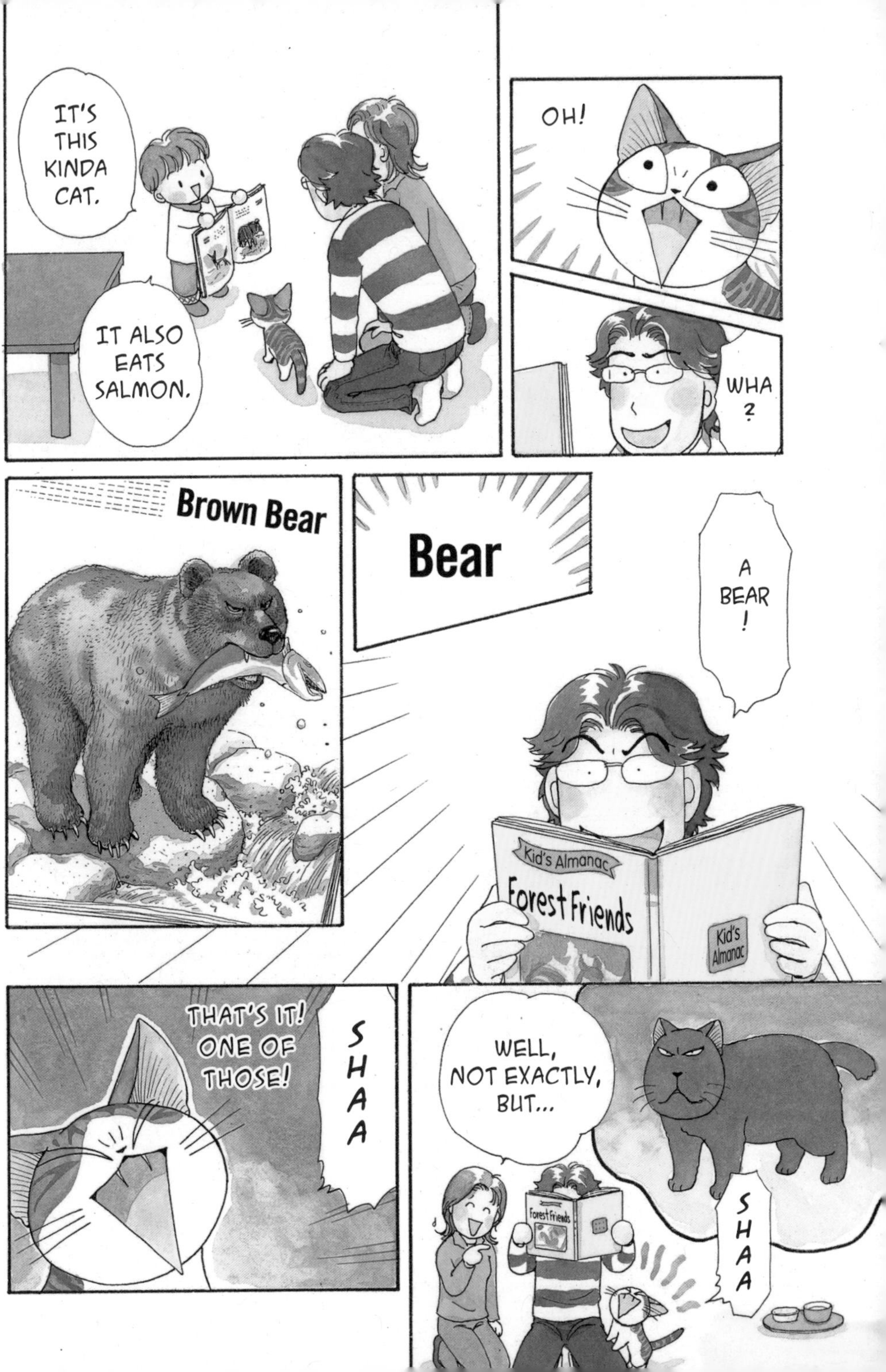
IT'S THIS KINDA CAT.
IT ALSO EATS SALMON.
OH!
WHA?
Brown Bear
Bear
A BEAR!
Kid's Almanac
Forest Friends
Kid's Almanac
THAT'S IT! ONE OF THOSE!
SHAA
WELL, NOT EXACTLY, BUT...
Forest Friends
SHAA

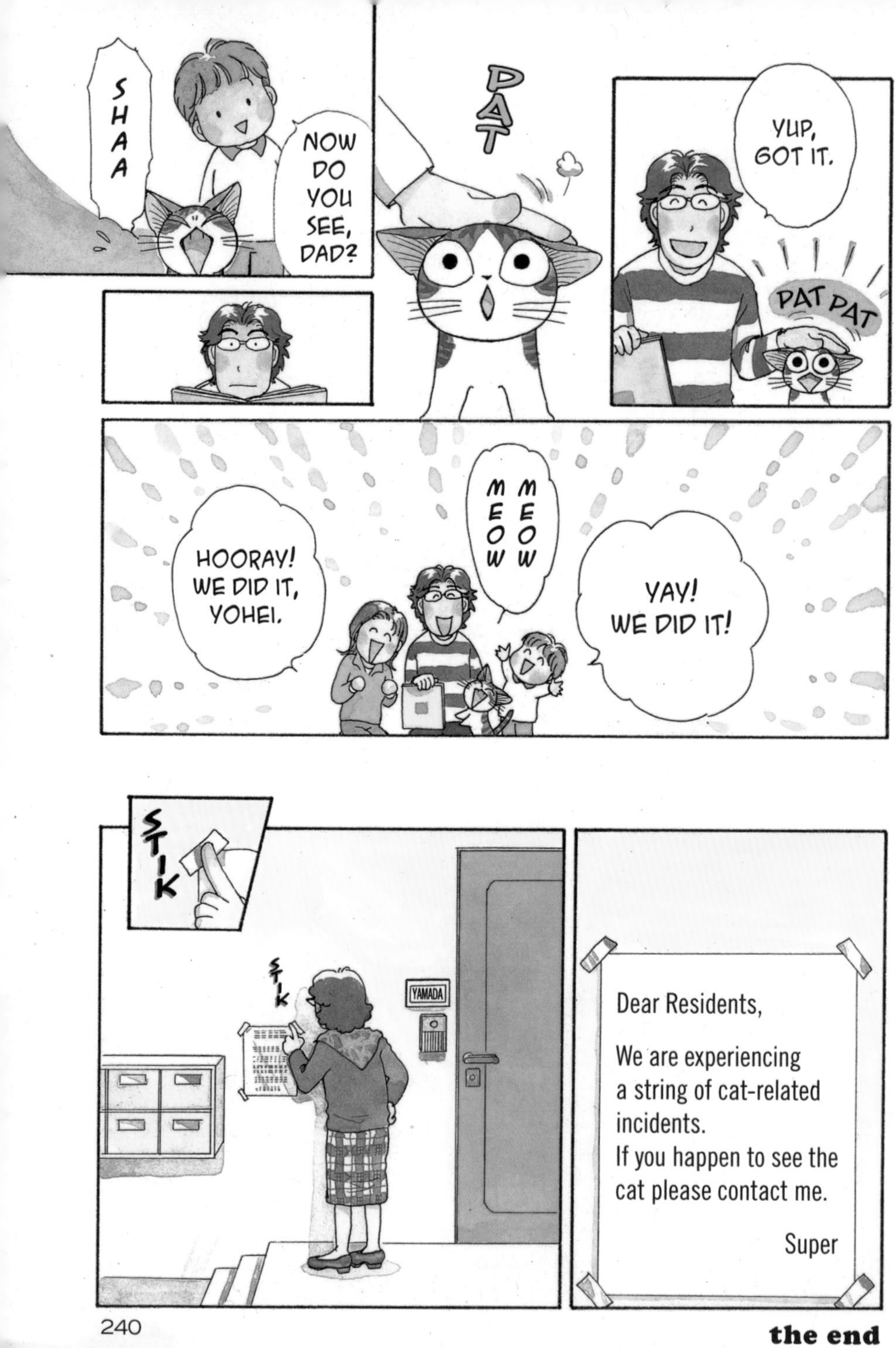
SHAA
NOW DO YOU SEE, DAD?
PAT
YUP, GOT IT.
PAT PAT
HOORAY! WE DID IT, YOHEI.
MEOW MEOW
YAY! WE DID IT!
STIK
STIK
YAMADA
Dear Residents,
We are experiencing a string of cat-related incidents.
If you happen to see the cat please contact me.
Super

the end

homemade 31: a cat uses her head

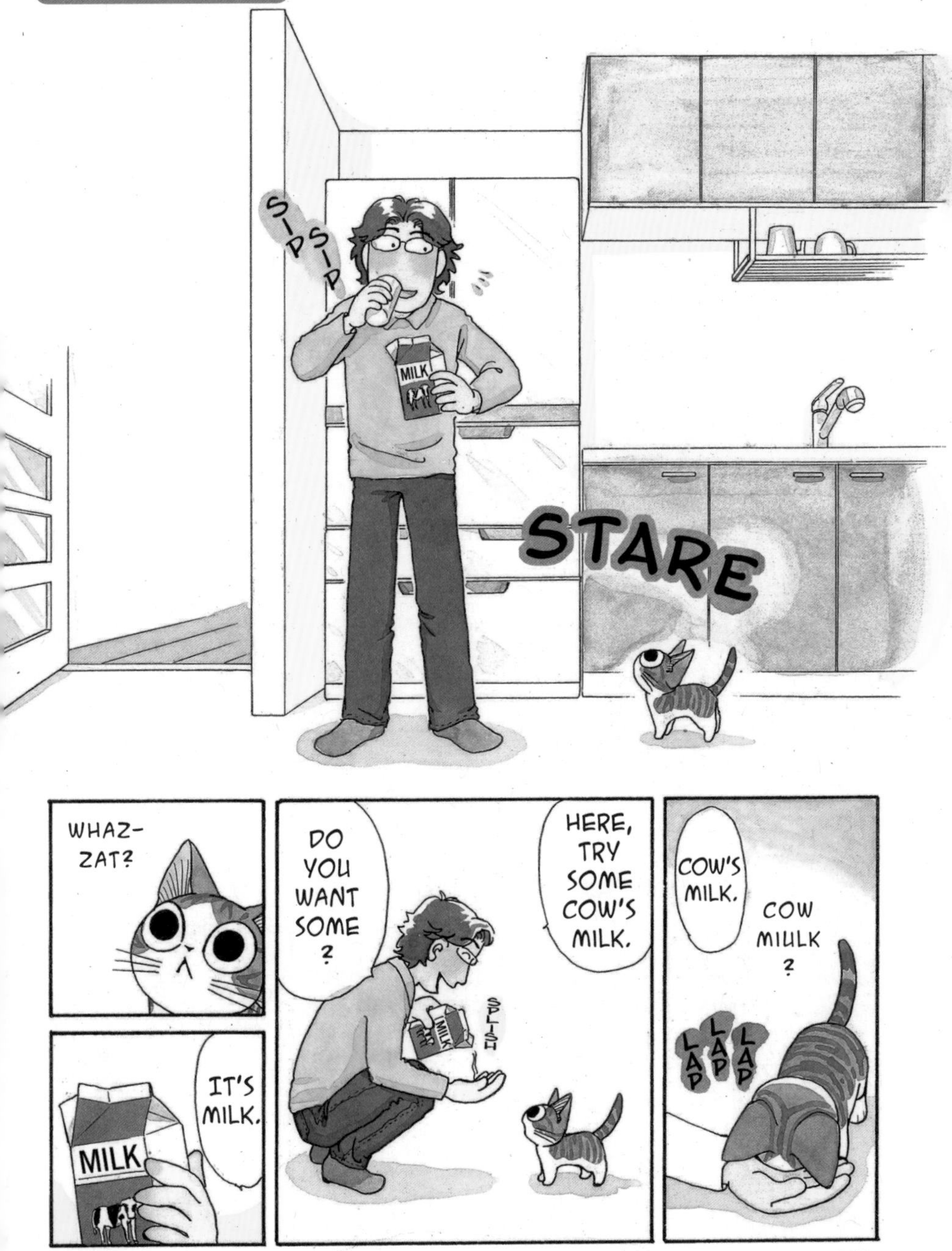
SIP SIP
STARE
WHAZ-ZAT?
IT'S MILK.
MILK
DO YOU WANT SOME?
HERE, TRY SOME COW'S MILK.
MILK
SPLISH
COW'S MILK.
COW MIULK?
LAP LAP LAP

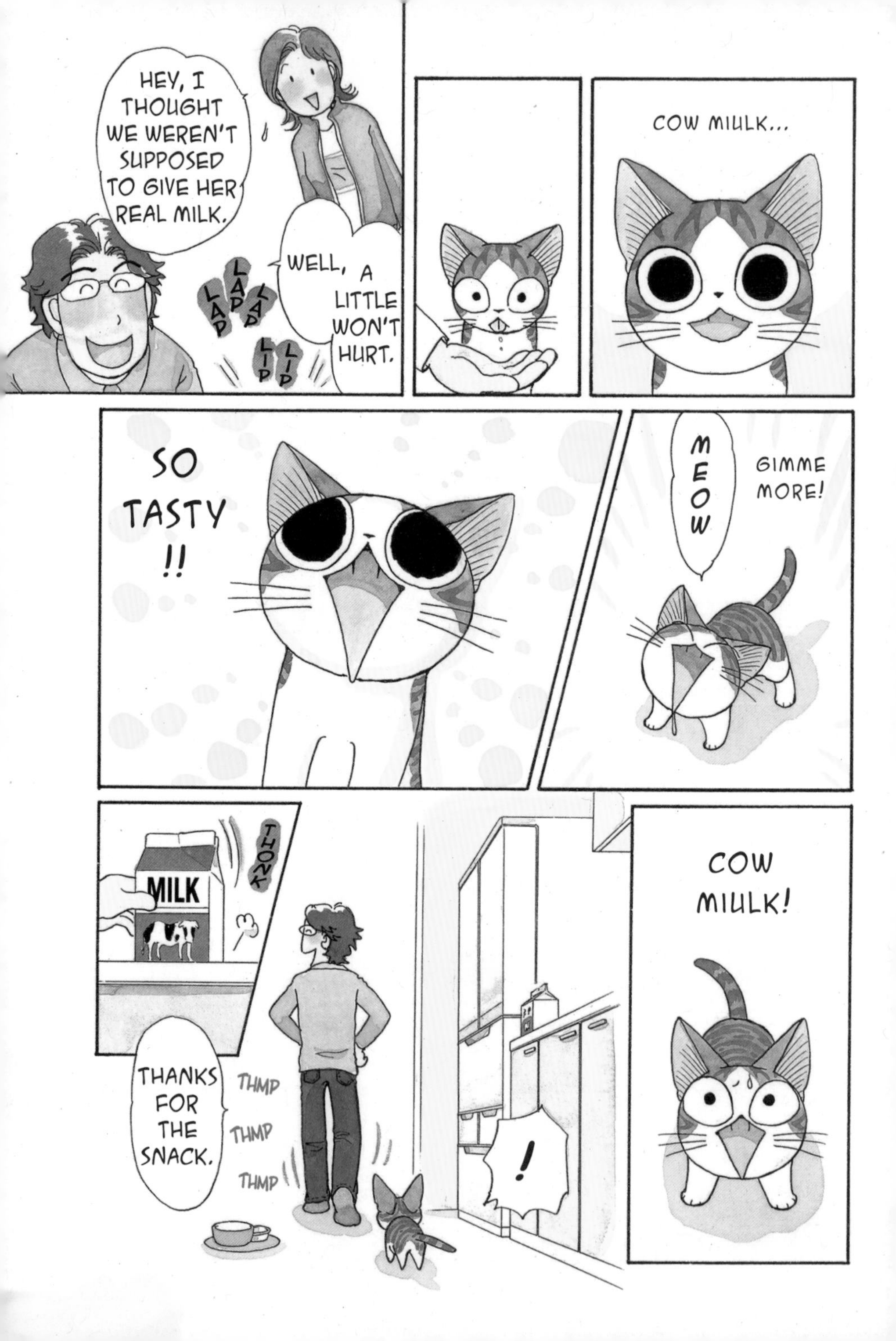
HEY, I THOUGHT WE WEREN'T SUPPOSED TO GIVE HER REAL MILK.
LAP LAP LAP
LIP LIP
WELL, A LITTLE WON'T HURT.
COW MIULK...
SO TASTY !!
MEOW
GIMME MORE!
MILK
THONK
THANKS FOR THE SNACK.
THMP
THMP
THMP
!
COW MIULK!

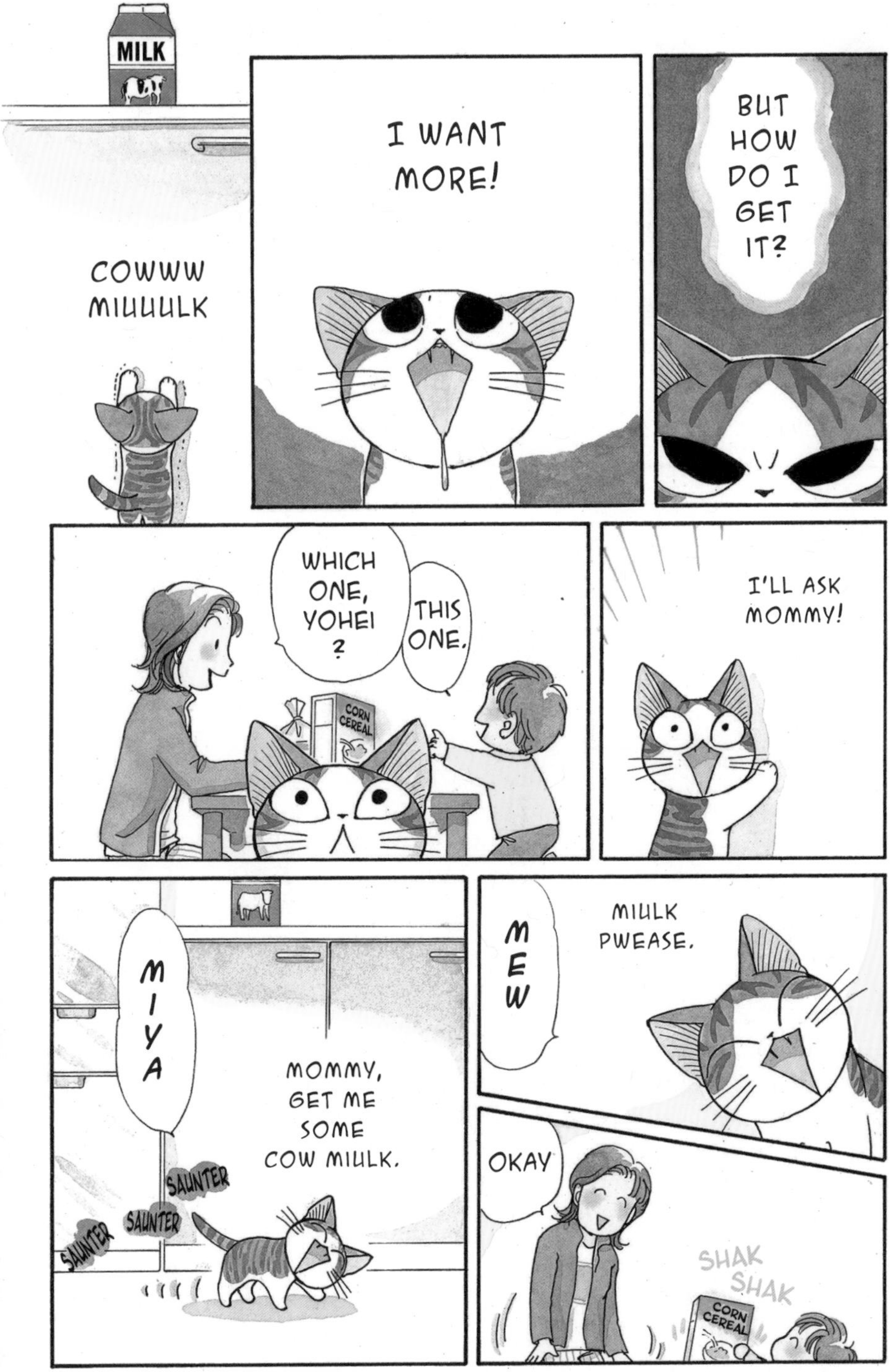
MILK
COWWW MIUUULK
I WANT MORE!
BUT HOW DO I GET IT?
WHICH ONE, YOHEI?
THIS ONE.
CORN CEREAL
I'LL ASK MOMMY!
MIYA
MOMMY, GET ME SOME COW MIULK.
SAUNTER
SAUNTER
SAUNTER
MEW
MIULK PWEASE.
OKAY
SHAK SHAK
CORN CEREAL

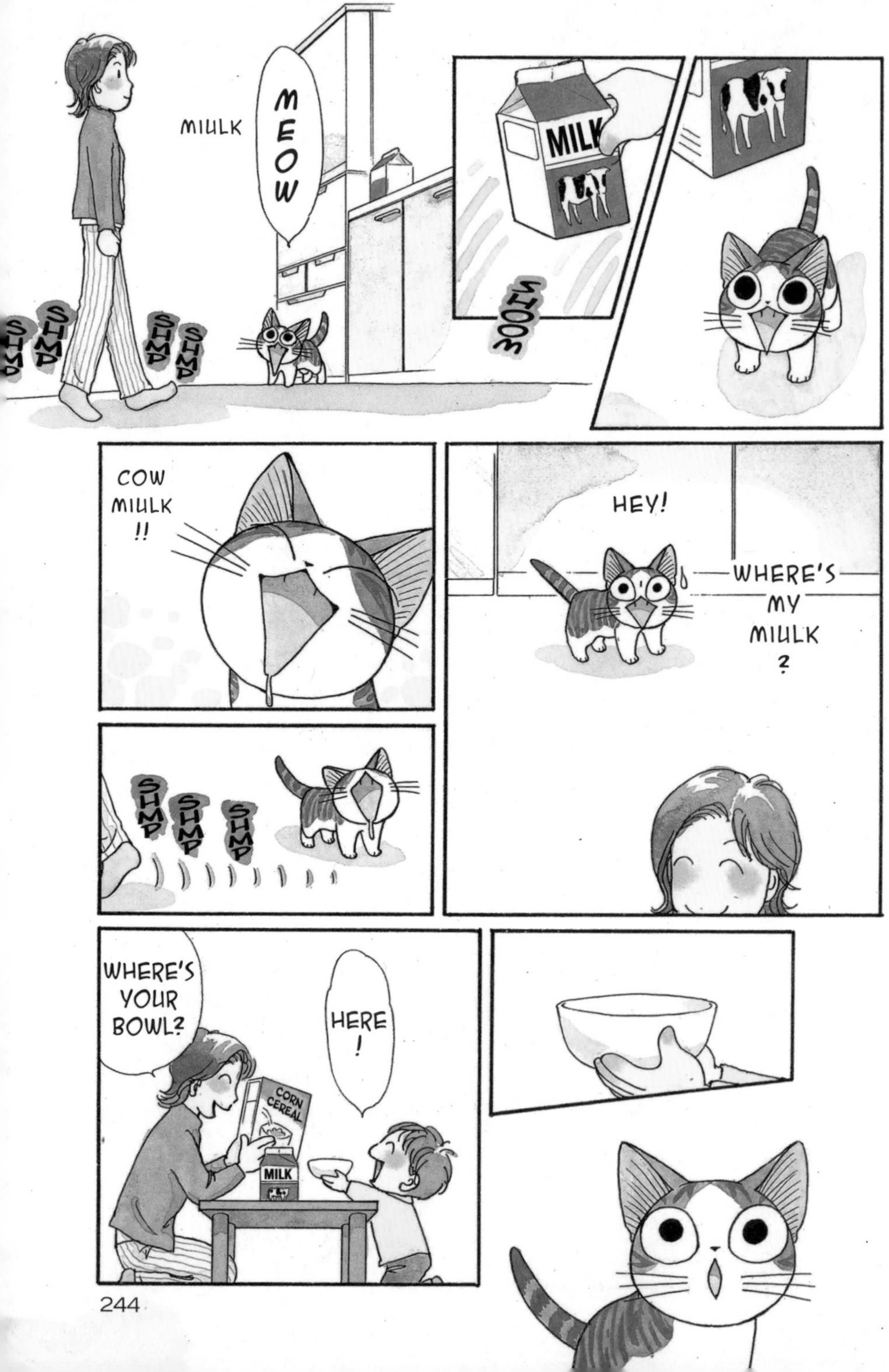
MIULK
MEOW
SHMP
SHMP
SHMP
SHMP
SWOOSH
COW MIULK !!
HEY!
WHERE'S MY MIULK ?
SHMP
SHMP
SHMP
WHERE'S YOUR BOWL?
HERE !
CORN CEREAL
MILK

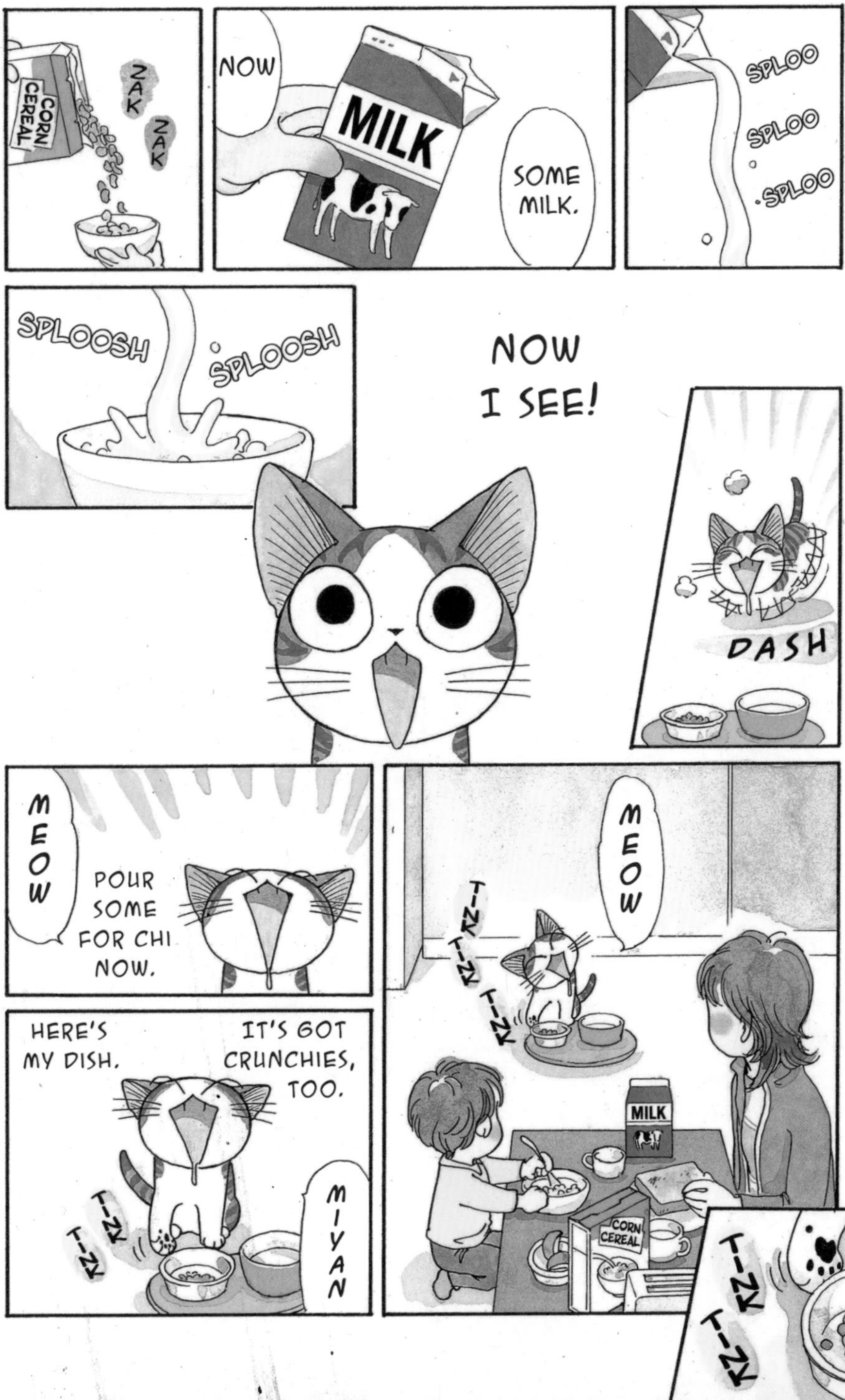
CORN CEREAL
ZAK
ZAK
NOW
MILK
SOME MILK.
SPLOO
SPLOO
SPLOO
SPLOOSH
SPLOOSH
NOW I SEE!
DASH
MEOW
POUR SOME FOR CHI NOW.
HERE'S MY DISH.
IT'S GOT CRUNCHIES, TOO.
TINK
TINK
MIYAN
MEOW
TINK
TINK
TINK
MILK
CORN CEREAL
TINK
TINK

COW MIULK!

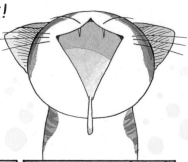

ALL RIGHT.

I'LL GIVE CHI SOME, TOO.

SLURP

LOOK, MORE OF YOUR FAVORITE.

SO CRUNCHY!

ZAK ZAK

CAT FOOD DRY

ZAK ZAK ZAK

THAT'S NOT WHAT I MEANT.

MILK

HUH ?

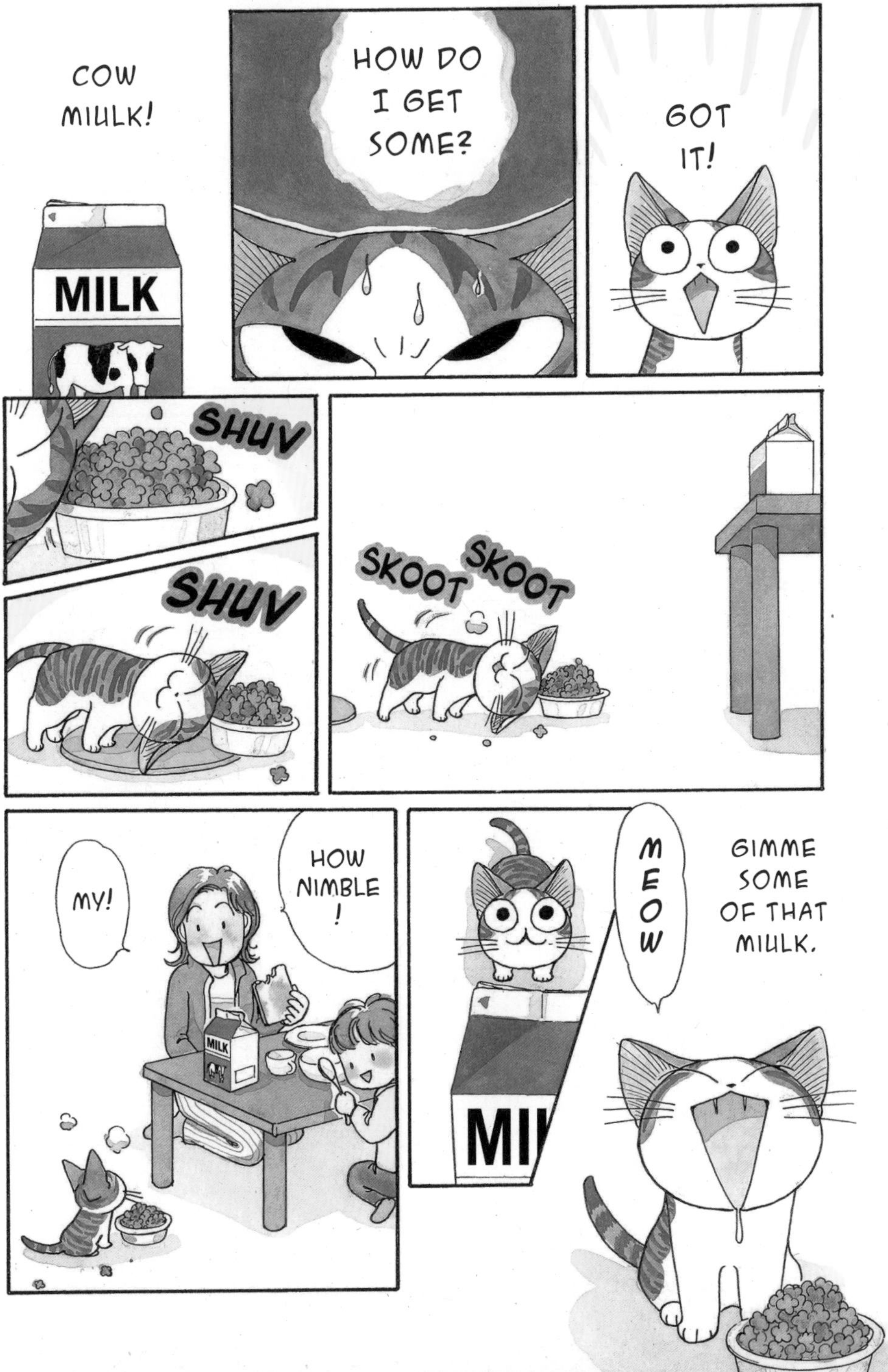
COW MIULK!
MILK
HOW DO I GET SOME?
GOT IT!
SHUV
SHUV
SKOOT
SKOOT
MY!
HOW NIMBLE!
MILK
MEOW
GIMME SOME OF THAT MIULK.
MIL

WANNA JOIN US, CHI?

YOU DROPPED SOME.

THERE

COW MIULK

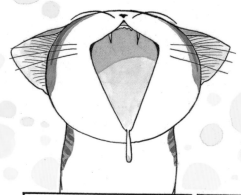

SHMP SHMP SHMP

HEY?!

POP

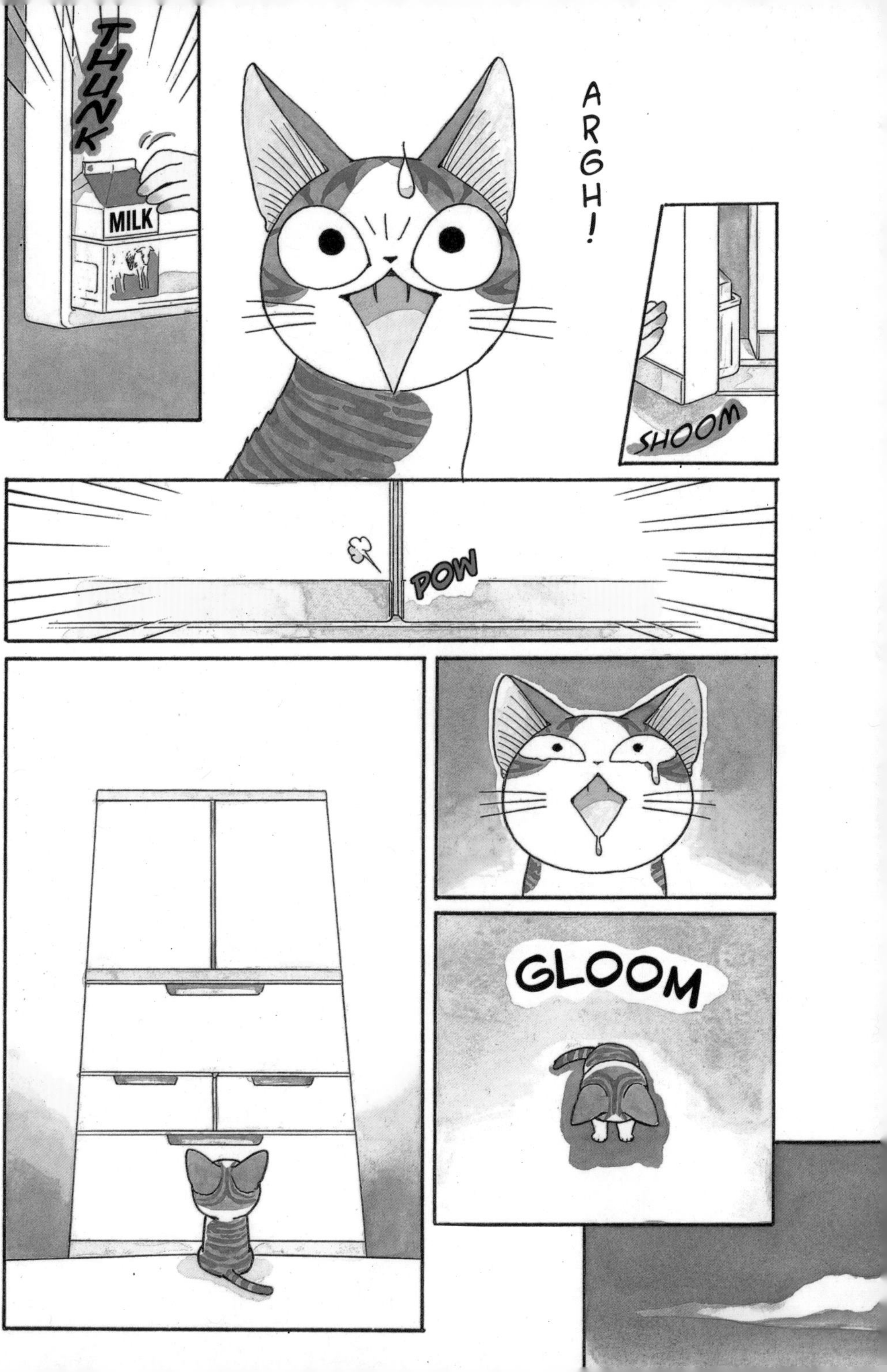
THUNK
MILK
ARGH!
SHOOM
POW
GLOOM

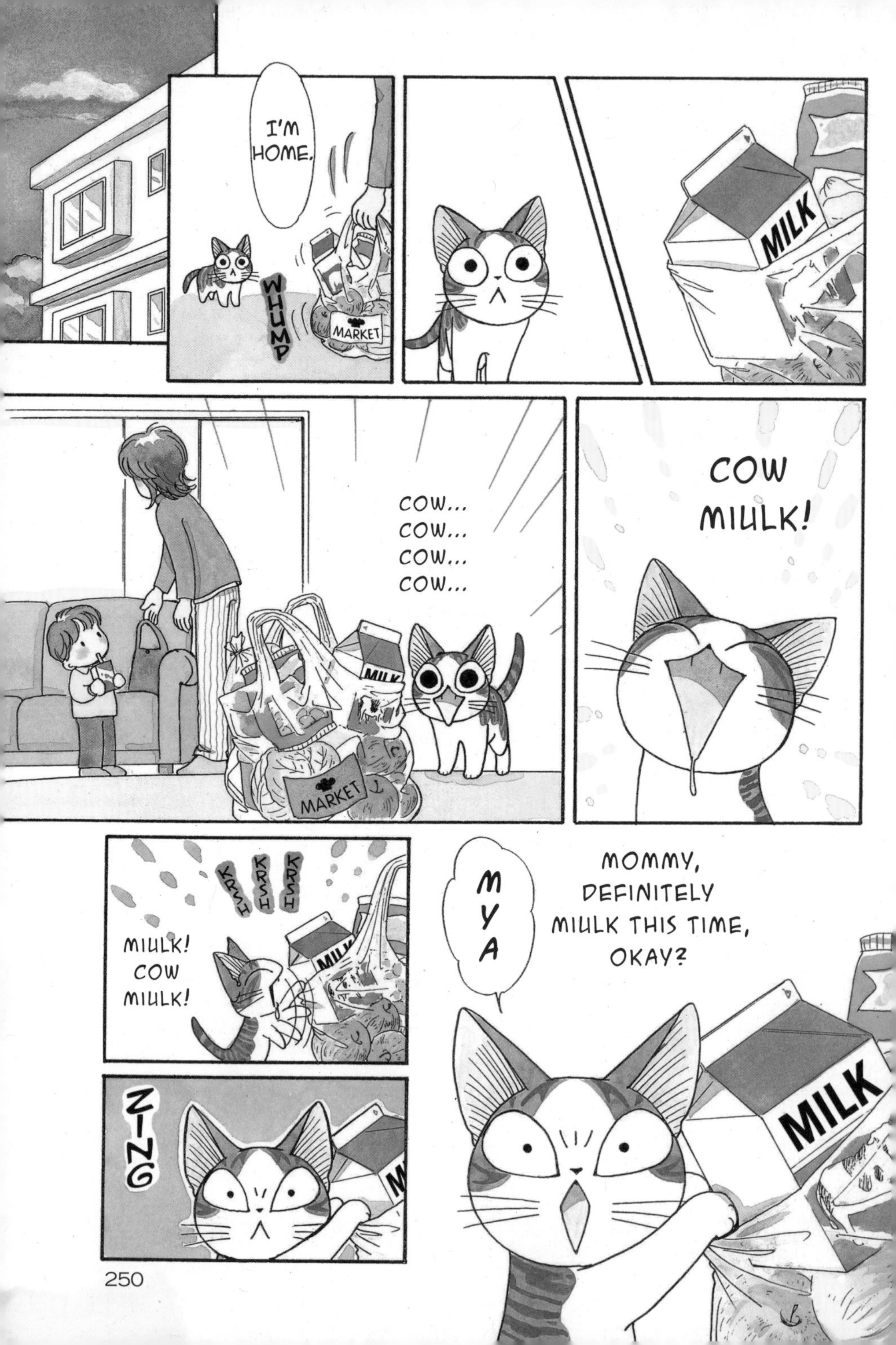
MILK
I'M HOME.
WHUMP
MARKET
COW MIULK!
COW... COW... COW... COW...
MILK
MARKET
MOMMY, DEFINITELY MIULK THIS TIME, OKAY?
MYA
MILK
KRSH KRSH KRSH
MIULK! COW MIULK!
ZING

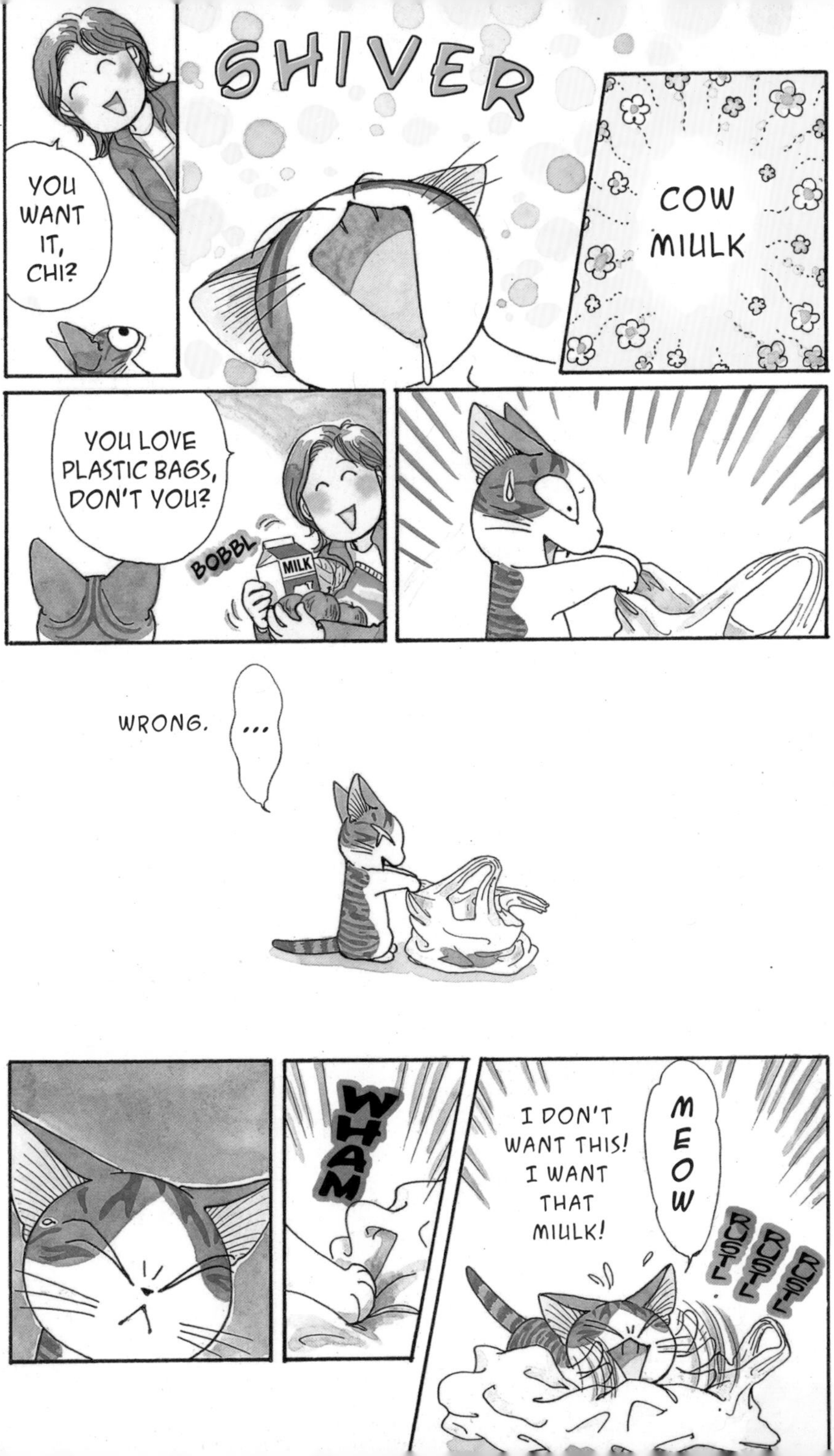
YOU WANT IT, CHI?
SHIVER
COW MIULK
YOU LOVE PLASTIC BAGS, DON'T YOU?
BOBBL
MILK
WRONG.
...
WHAM
I DON'T WANT THIS! I WANT THAT MIULK!
MEOW
RUSTL
RUSTL
RUSTL

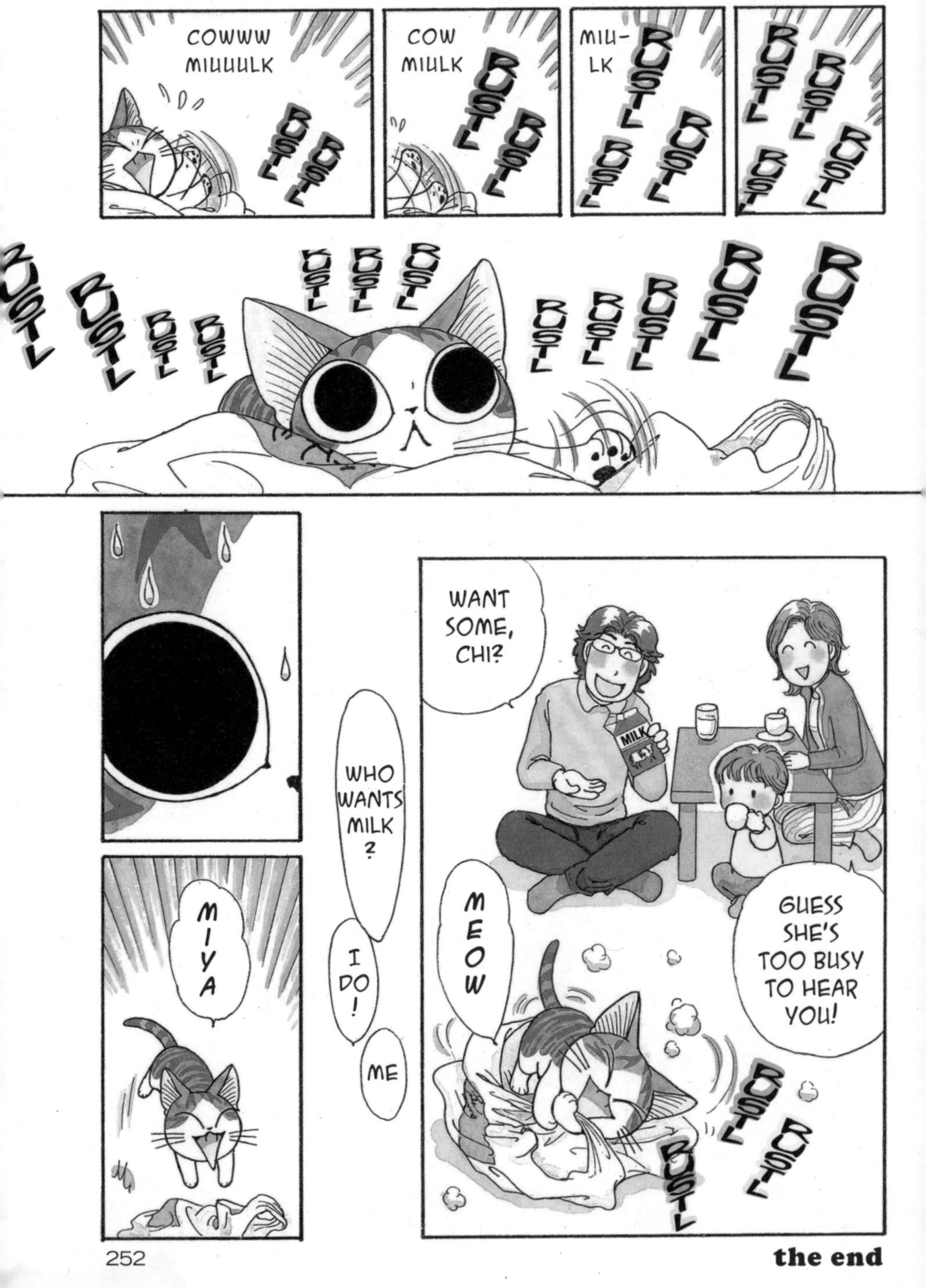
COWWW MIUUUULK
RUSTL RUSTL
COW MIULK
RUSTL RUSTL
MIU-LK
RUSTL RUSTL RUSTL
RUSTL RUSTL RUSTL RUSTL
RUSTL RUSTL RUSTL RUSTL RUSTL RUSTL RUSTL RUSTL RUSTL RUSTL RUSTL RUSTL
MIYA
WANT SOME, CHI?
MILK
WHO WANTS MILK?
I DO!
ME
MEOW
GUESS SHE'S TOO BUSY TO HEAR YOU!
RUSTL RUSTL RUSTL

the end

homemade 32: a cat aggravates

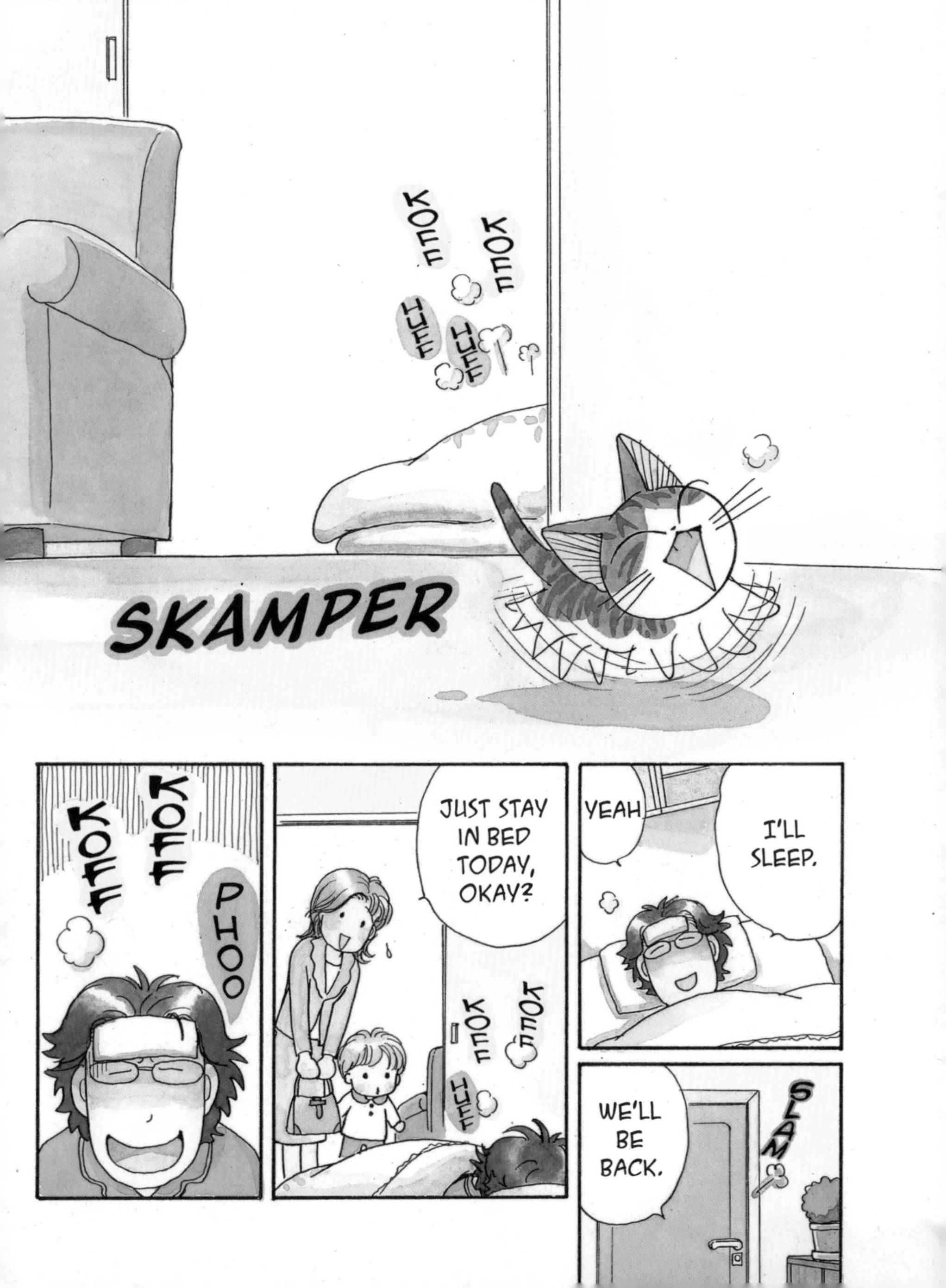
KOFF
KOFF
HUFF
HUFF
SKAMPER
KOFF
KOFF
PHOO
JUST STAY IN BED TODAY, OKAY?
KOFF
KOFF
HUFF
YEAH
I'LL SLEEP.
WE'LL BE BACK.
SLAM

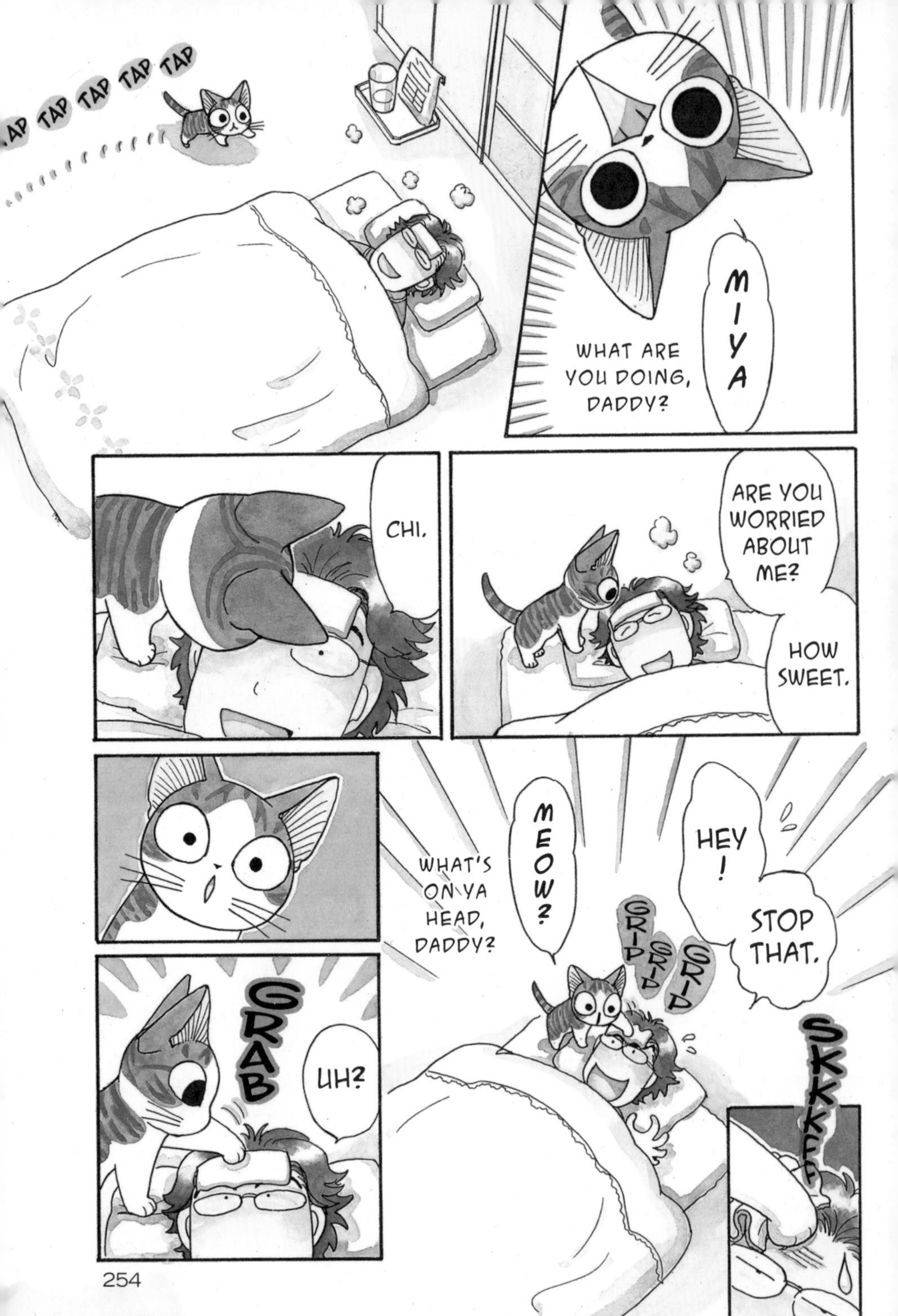
TAP TAP TAP TAP TAP
MIYA
WHAT ARE YOU DOING, DADDY?
CHI.
ARE YOU WORRIED ABOUT ME?
HOW SWEET.
MEOW?
WHAT'S ON YA HEAD, DADDY?
GRAB
UH?
HEY!
STOP THAT.
GRIP GRIP GRIP
SKKFF

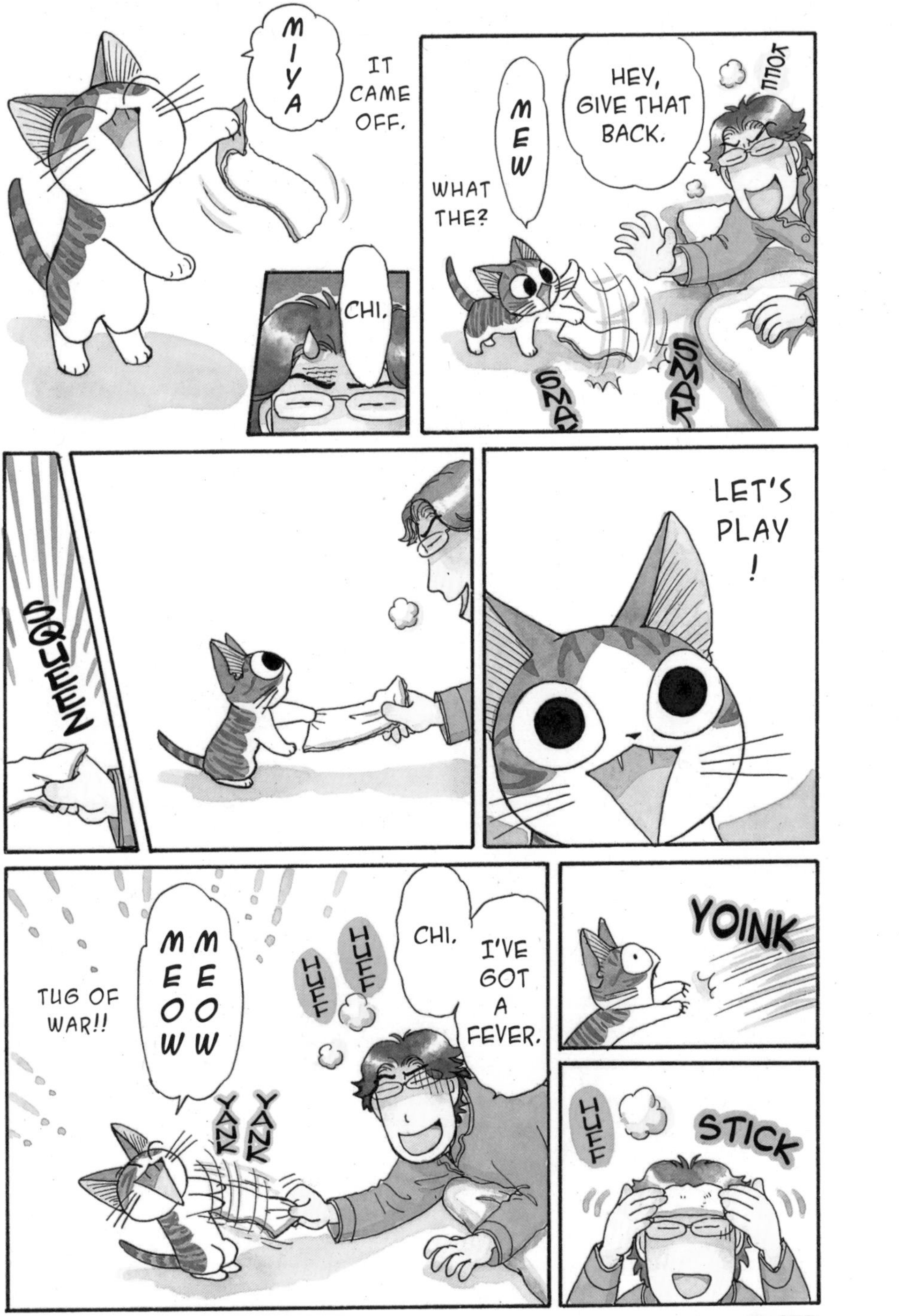

MIYA
IT CAME OFF.
CHI.
KOFF
HEY, GIVE THAT BACK.
MEW
WHAT THE?
SMAK
SQUEEZ
LET'S PLAY!
TUG OF WAR!!
MEOW MEOW
HUFF HUFF
CHI.
I'VE GOT A FEVER.
YANK YANK
YOINK
HUFF
STICK

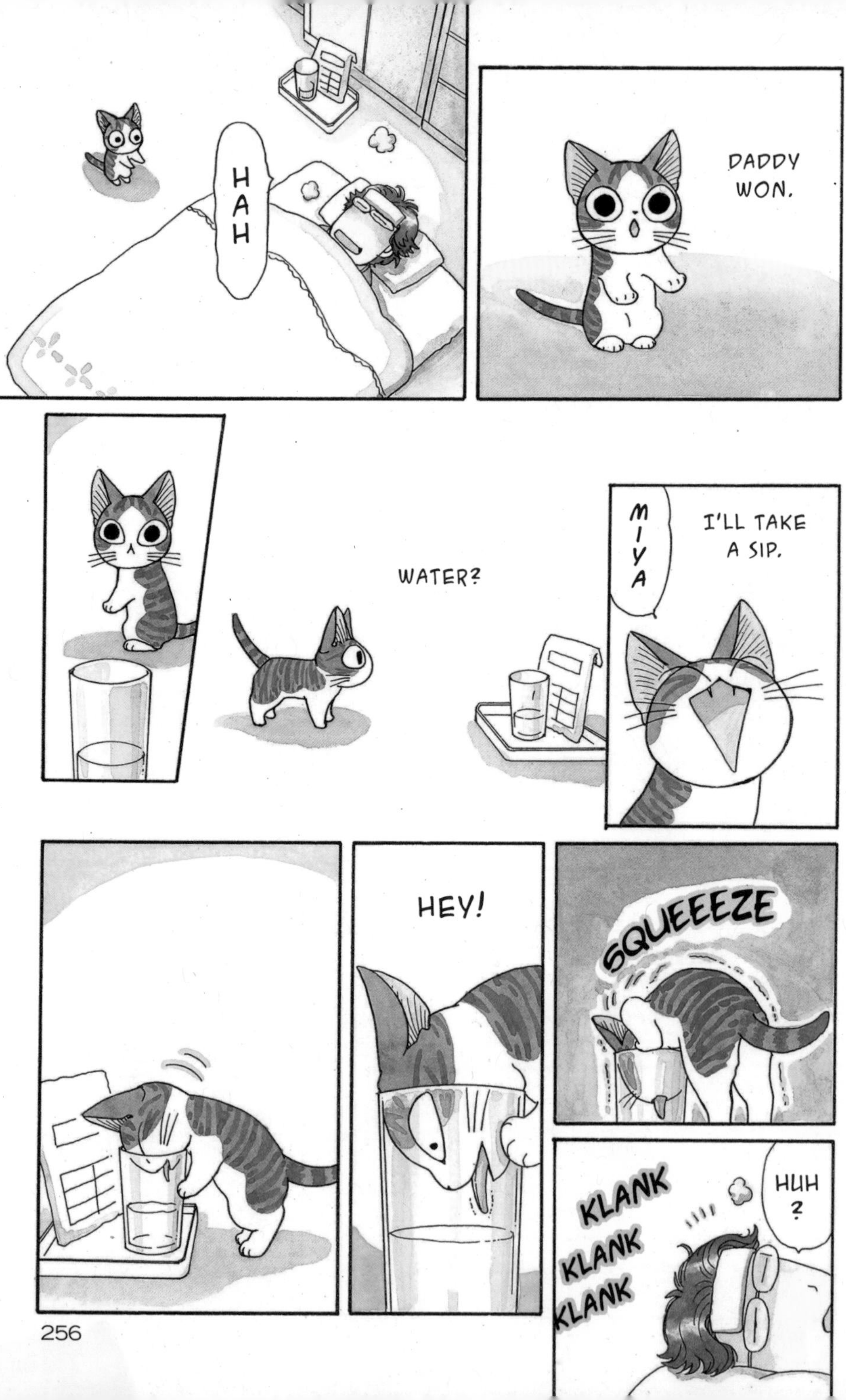
HAH
DADDY WON.
WATER?
MIYA
I'LL TAKE A SIP.
HEY!
SQUEEEZE
KLANK KLANK KLANK KLANK
HUH?

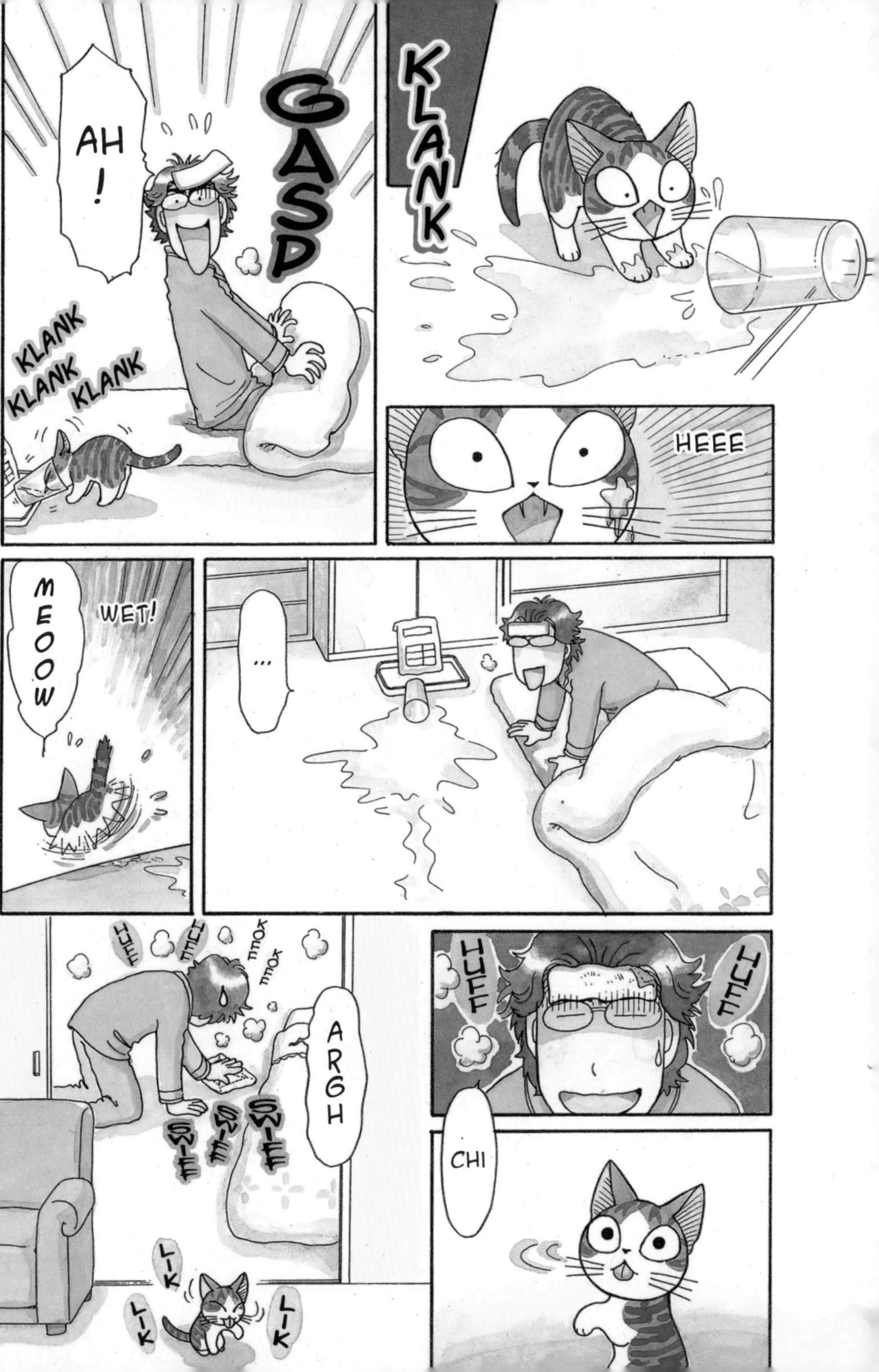
AH!
GASP
KLANK
KLANK
KLANK
KLANK
HEEE
MEOOOW
WET!
...
HUFF
HUFF
TTOK
TTOK
ARGH
SWIFF
SWIFF
SWIFF
LIK
LIK
LIK
HUFF
HUFF
CHI

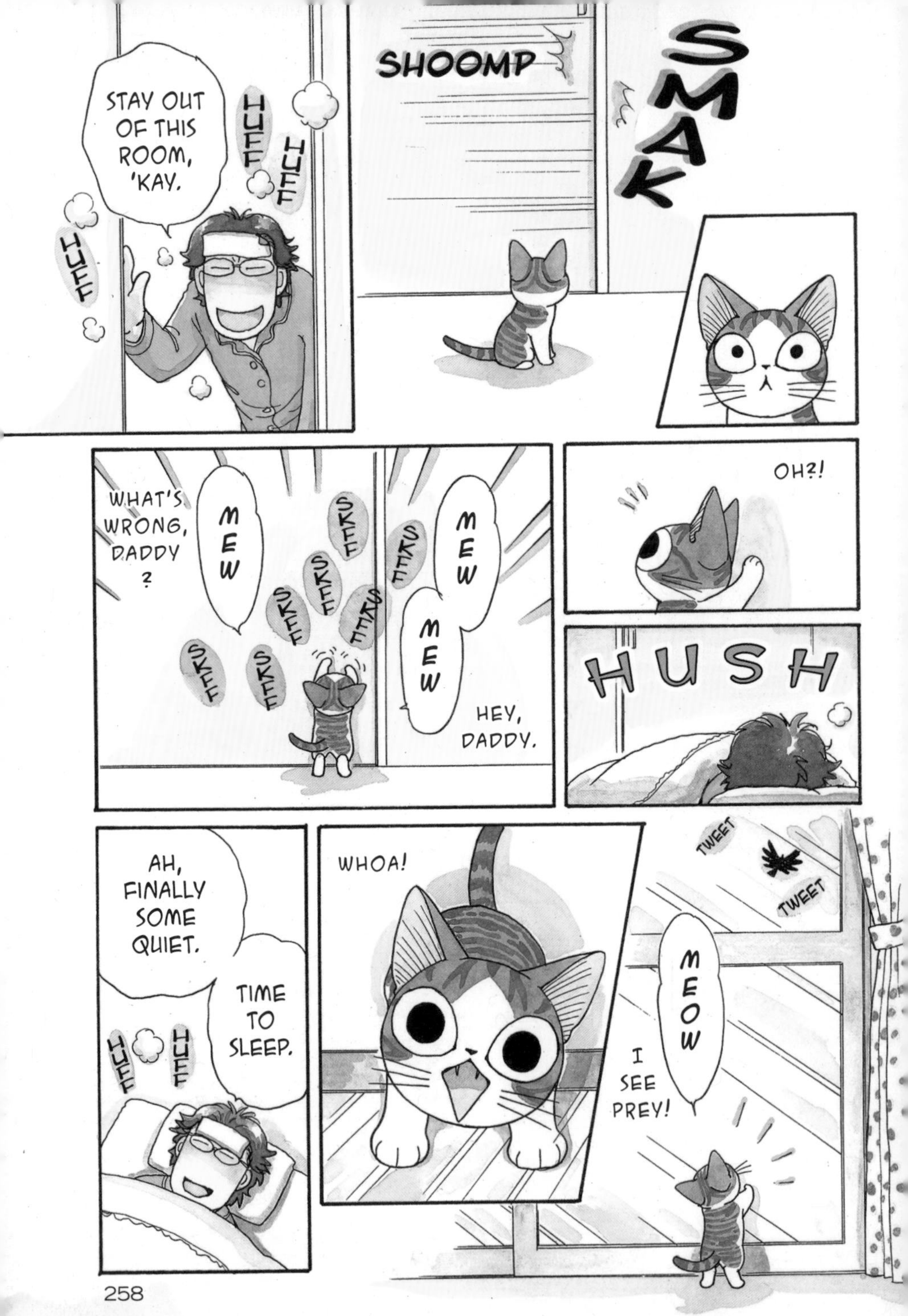
STAY OUT OF THIS ROOM, 'KAY.
HUFF
HUFF
HUFF
SHOOMP
SMAK
WHAT'S WRONG, DADDY?
MEW
SKFF
SKFF
SKFF
SKFF
SKFF
SKFF
SKFF
MEW
MEW
HEY, DADDY.
OH?!
HUSH
AH, FINALLY SOME QUIET.
TIME TO SLEEP.
HUFF
HUFF
WHOA!
TWEET
TWEET
MEOW
I SEE PREY!

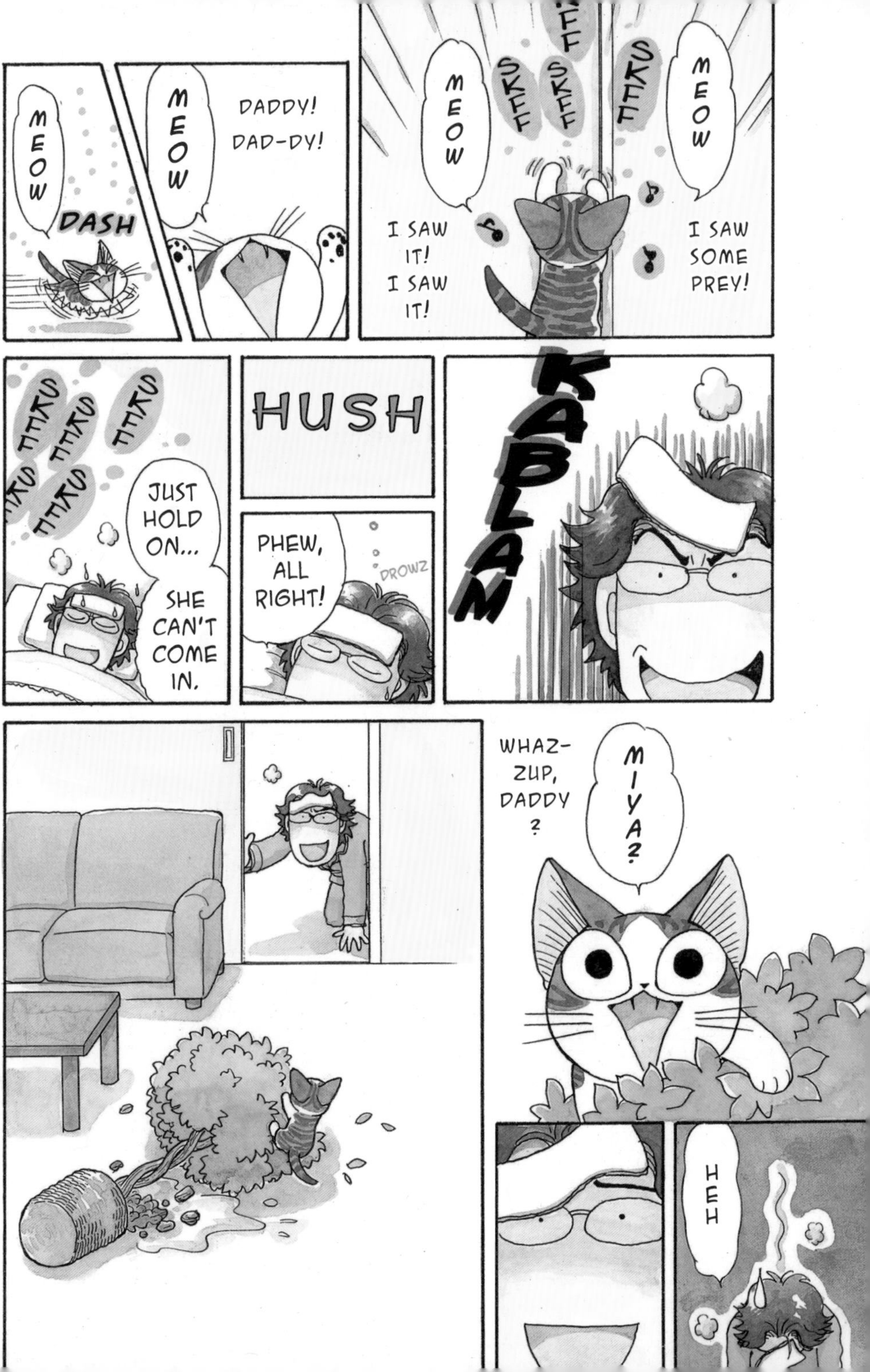
MEOW
DASH
MEOW
DADDY!
DAD-DY!
MEOW
SKFF
SKFF
SKFF
MEOW
I SAW IT! I SAW IT!
I SAW SOME PREY!
SKTTT SKTTT
SKTTT SKTTT
SKTTT
JUST HOLD ON...
SHE CAN'T COME IN.
HUSH
PHEW, ALL RIGHT!
DROWZ
KABLAM
WHAZ-ZUP, DADDY?
MIYA?
HEH

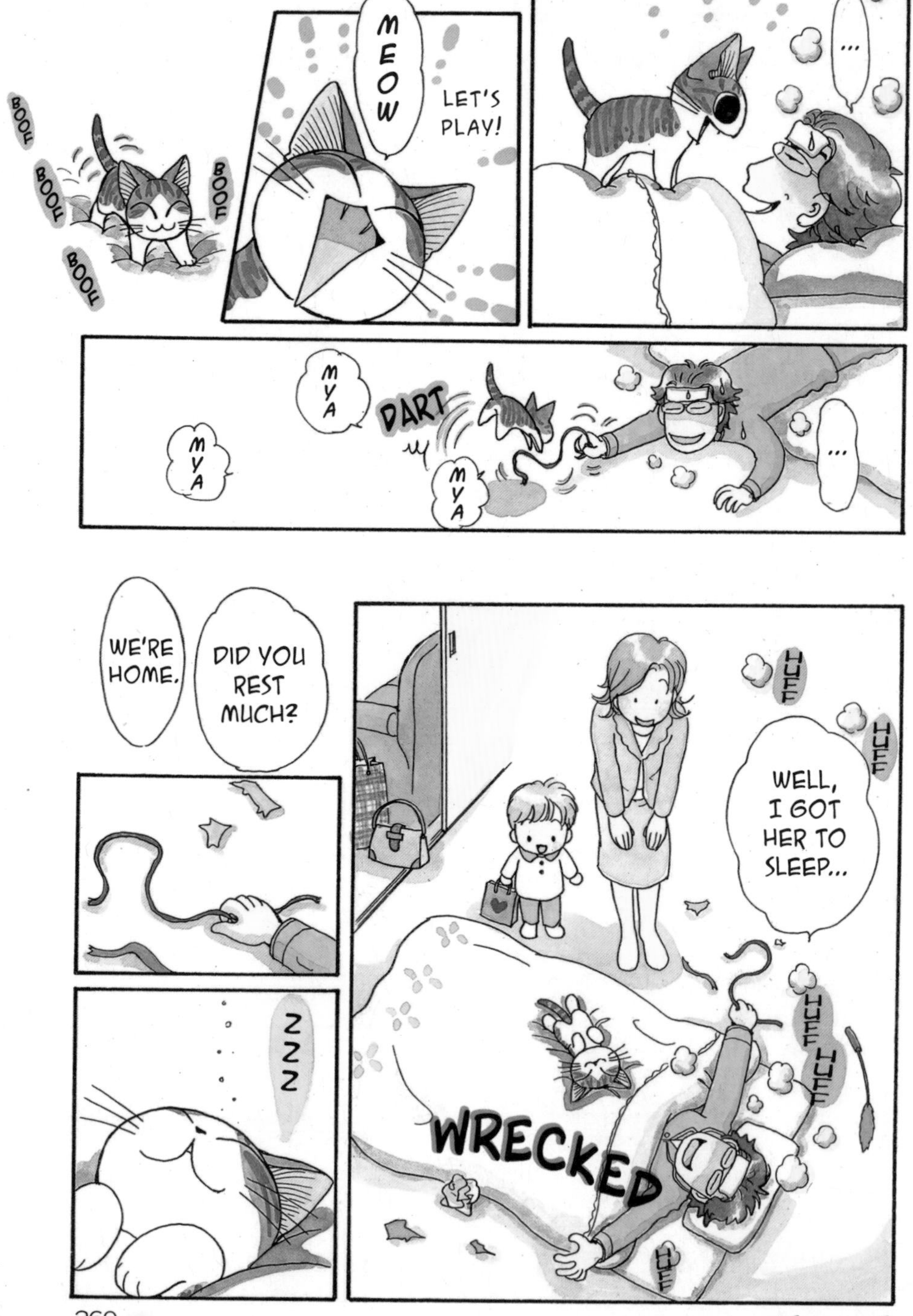
BOOF
BOOF
BOOF
BOOF
MEOW
LET'S PLAY!
...
MYA
MYA
DART
MYA
...
WE'RE HOME.
DID YOU REST MUCH?
ZZZ
HUFF
HUFF
WELL, I GOT HER TO SLEEP...
HUFF HUFF
WRECKED
HUFF

the end

homemade 33: a cat searches

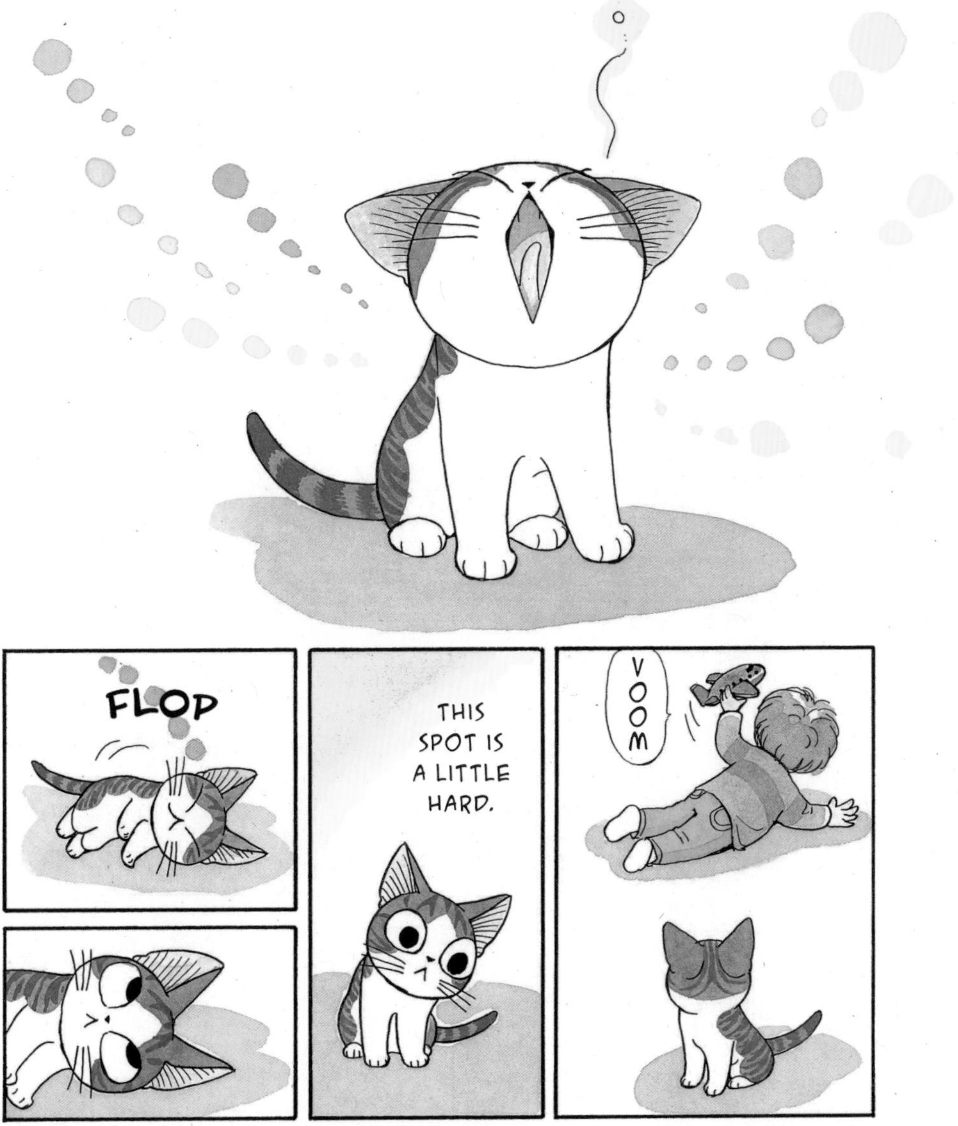
FLOP
THIS SPOT IS A LITTLE HARD.
VOOM

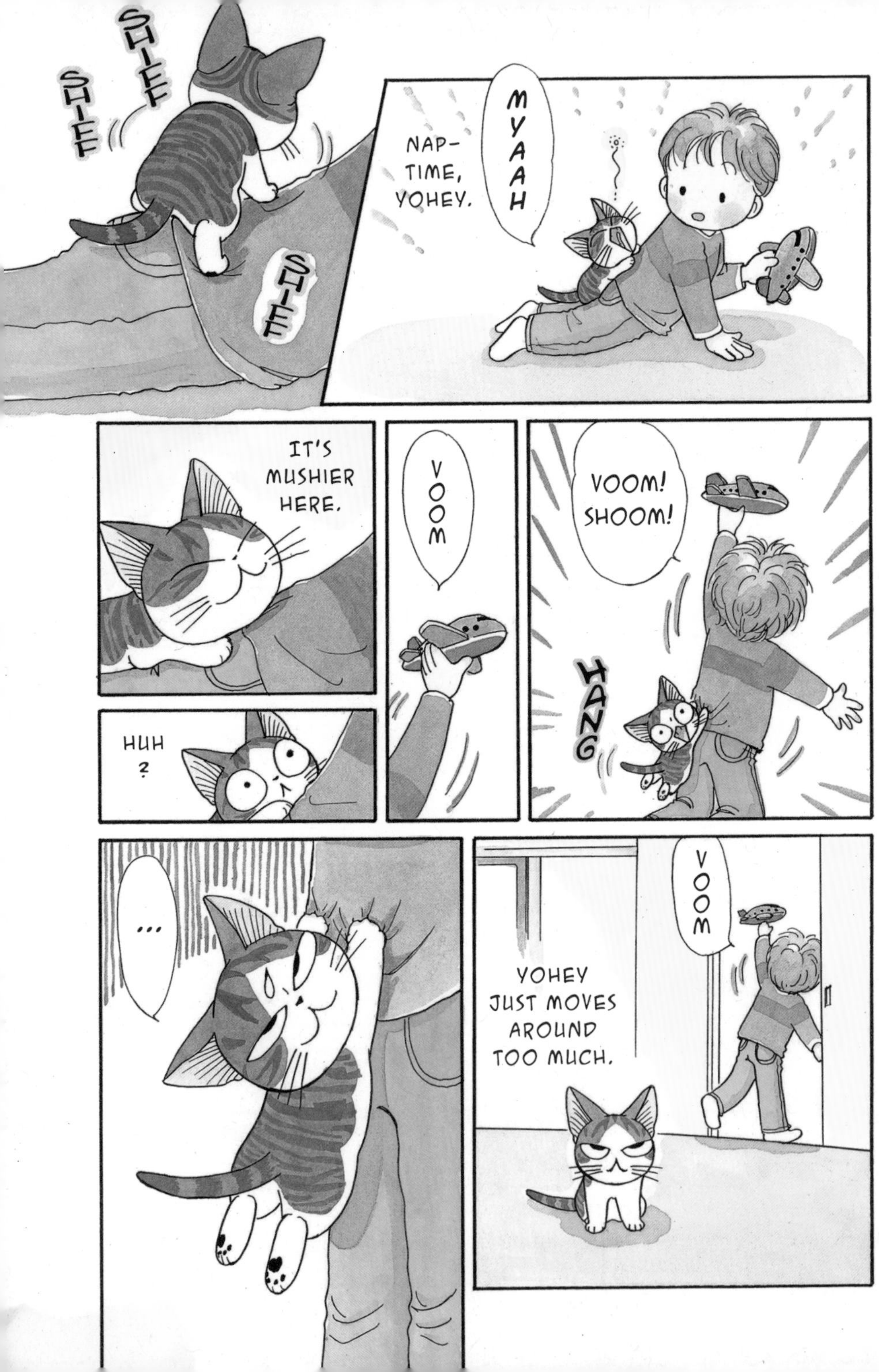
SHIFF
SHIFF
SHIFF
NAP-TIME, YOHEY.
MYAAH
IT'S MUSHIER HERE.
HUH?
VOOM
VOOM! SHOOM!
HANG
...
VOOM
YOHEY JUST MOVES AROUND TOO MUCH.

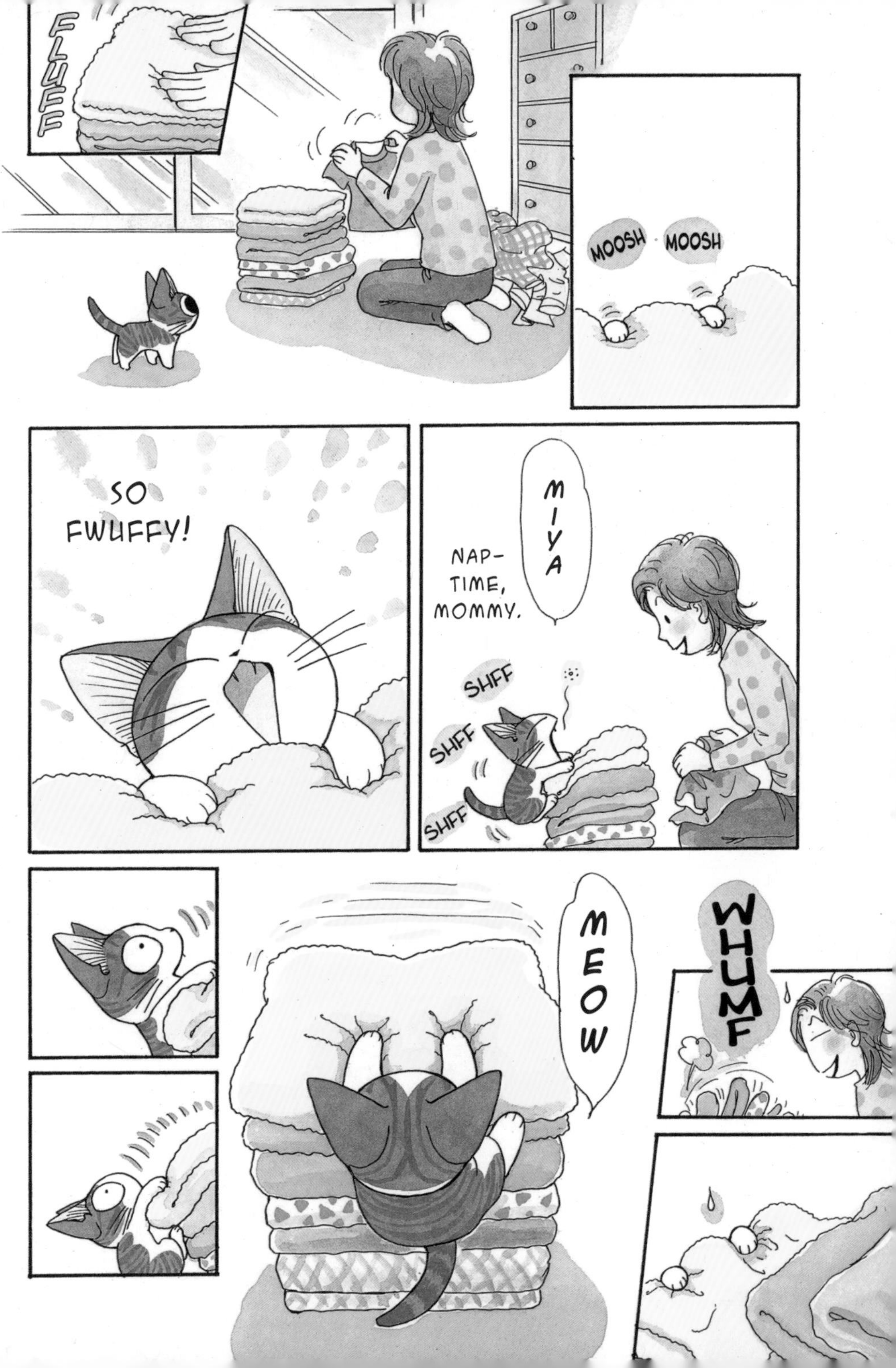
FLUFF
MOOSH MOOSH
SO FWUFFY!
NAP-TIME, MOMMY.
MIYA
SHFF
SHFF
SHFF
MEOW
WHUMF

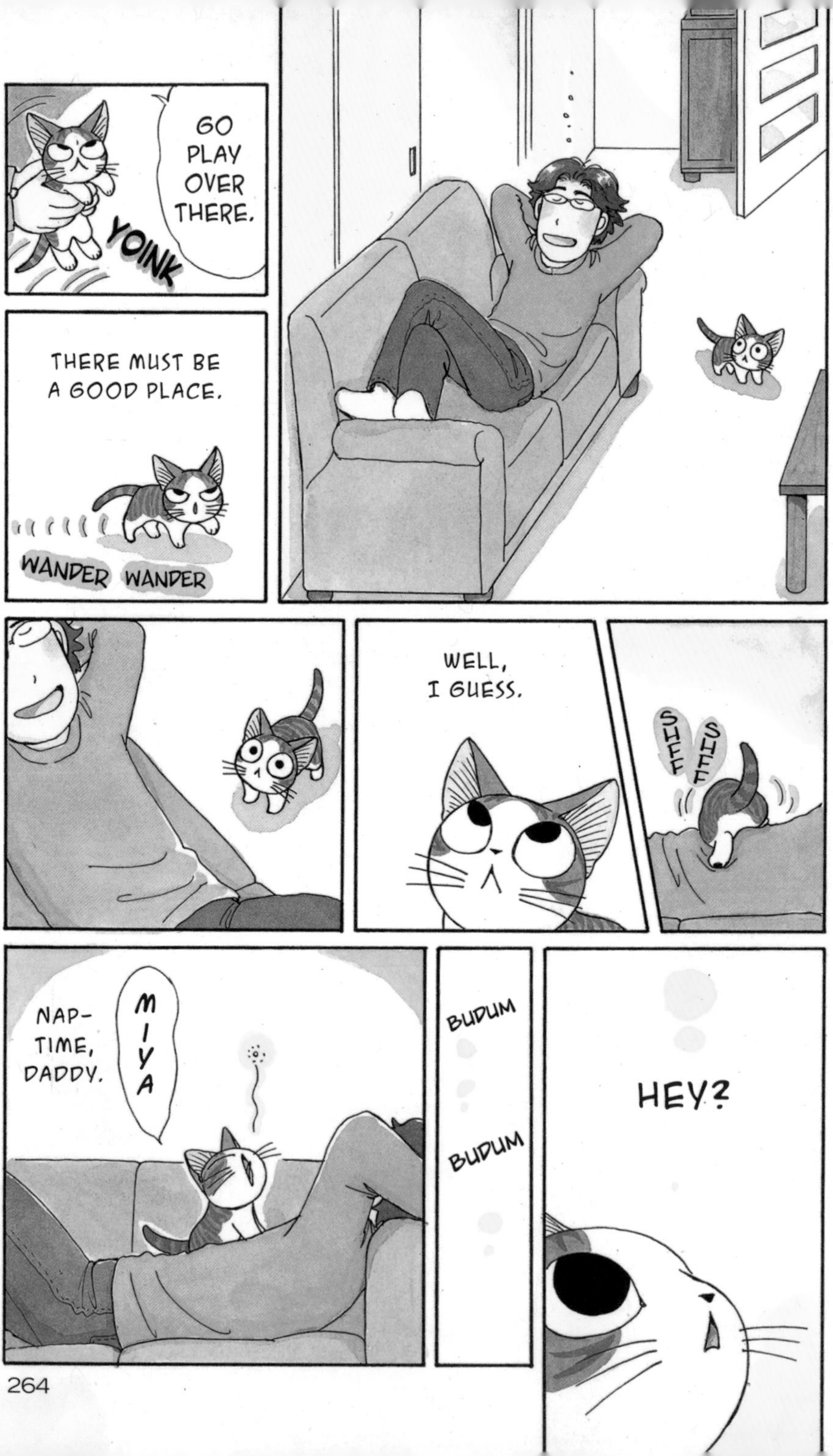
GO PLAY OVER THERE.
YOINK
THERE MUST BE A GOOD PLACE.
WANDER WANDER
WELL, I GUESS.
SHUFF SHUFF
NAP-TIME, DADDY.
MIYA
BUDUM
BUDUM
HEY?

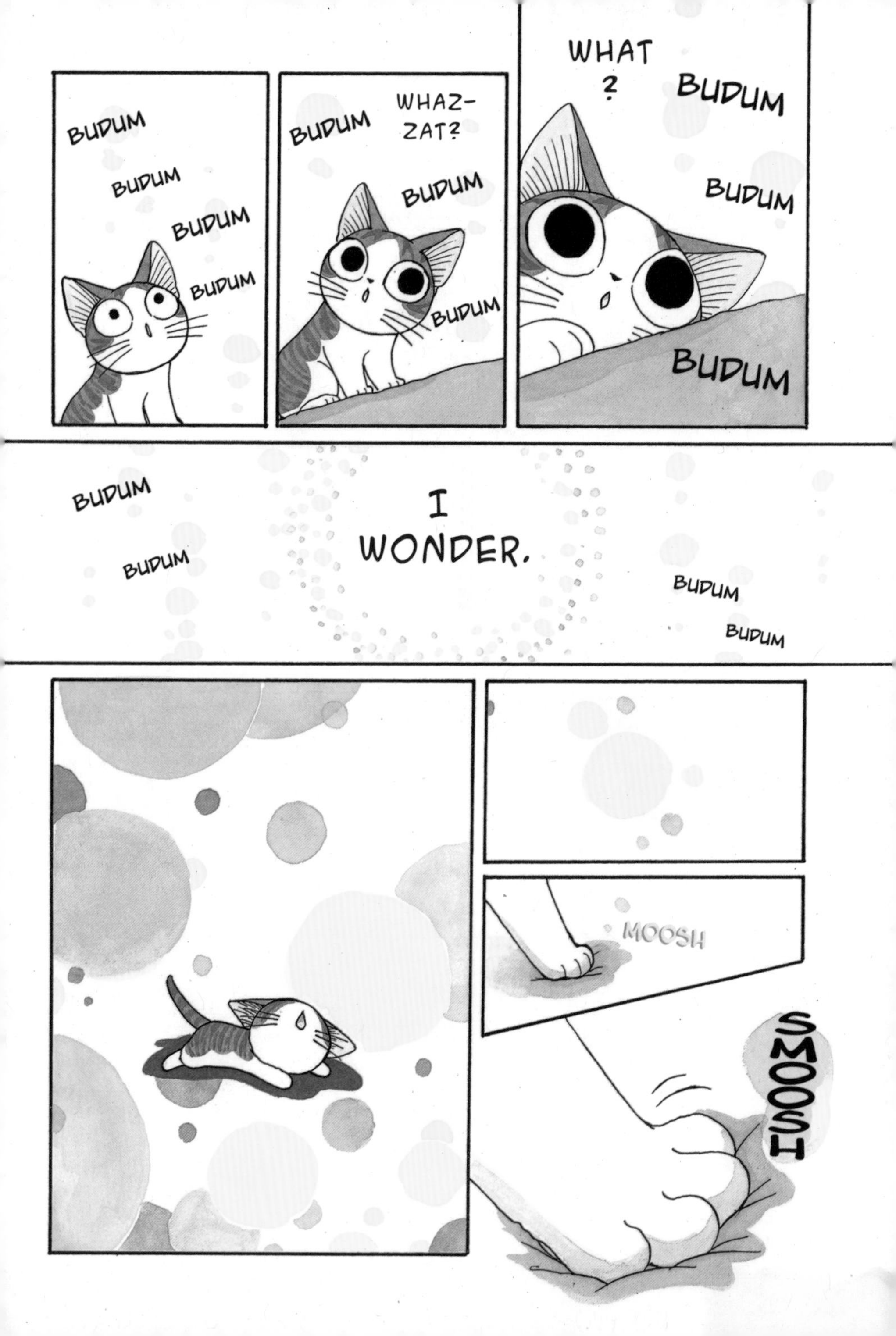
BUDUM
BUDUM
BUDUM
BUDUM
BUDUM
WHAZ-
ZAT?
BUDUM
BUDUM
WHAT
?
BUDUM
BUDUM
BUDUM
BUDUM
BUDUM
I
WONDER.
BUDUM
BUDUM
MOOSH
SMOOSH

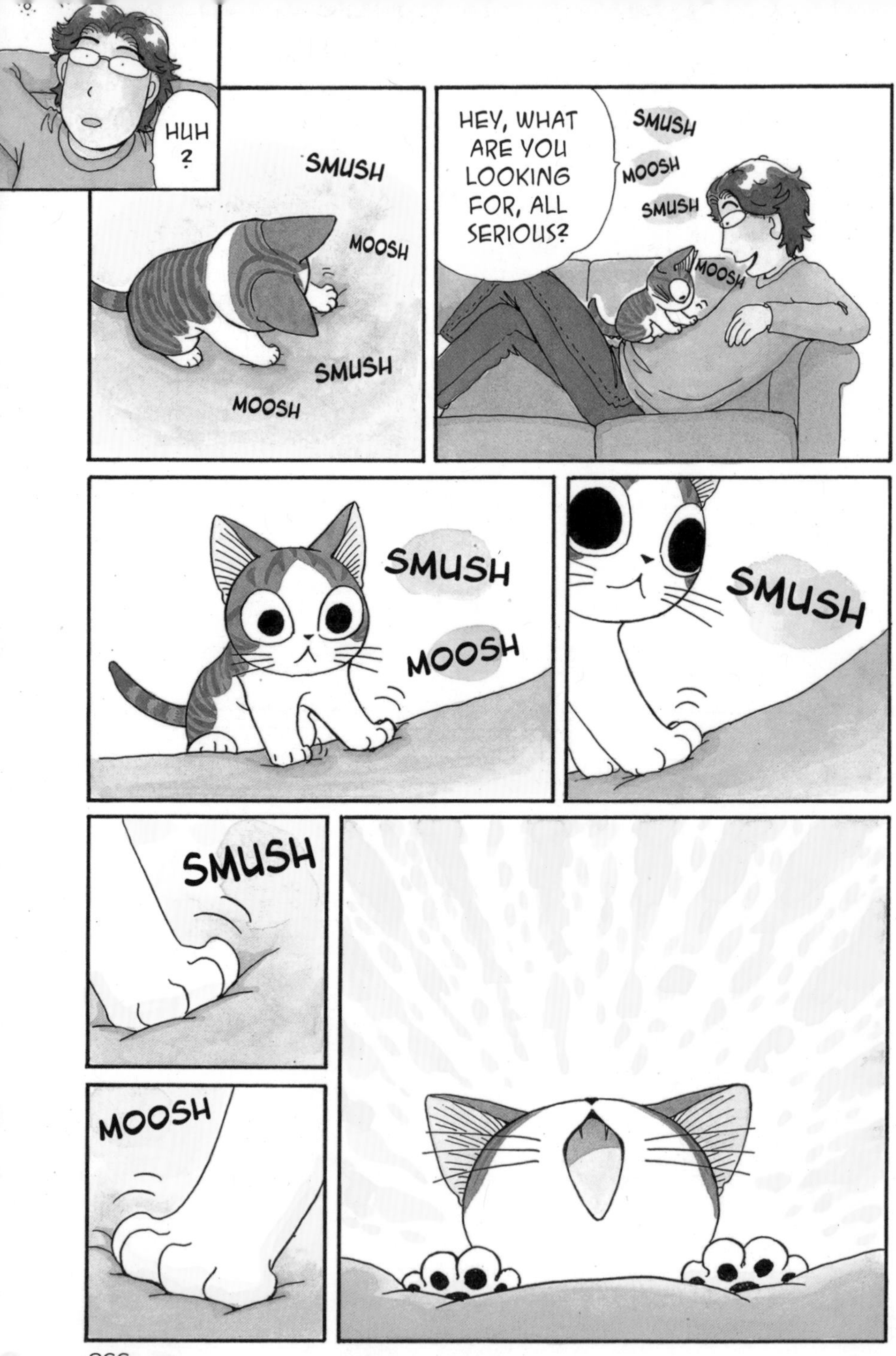
HUH?
SMUSH
MOOSH
SMUSH
MOOSH
HEY, WHAT ARE YOU LOOKING FOR, ALL SERIOUS?
SMUSH
MOOSH
SMUSH
MOOSH
SMUSH
MOOSH
SMUSH
SMUSH
MOOSH

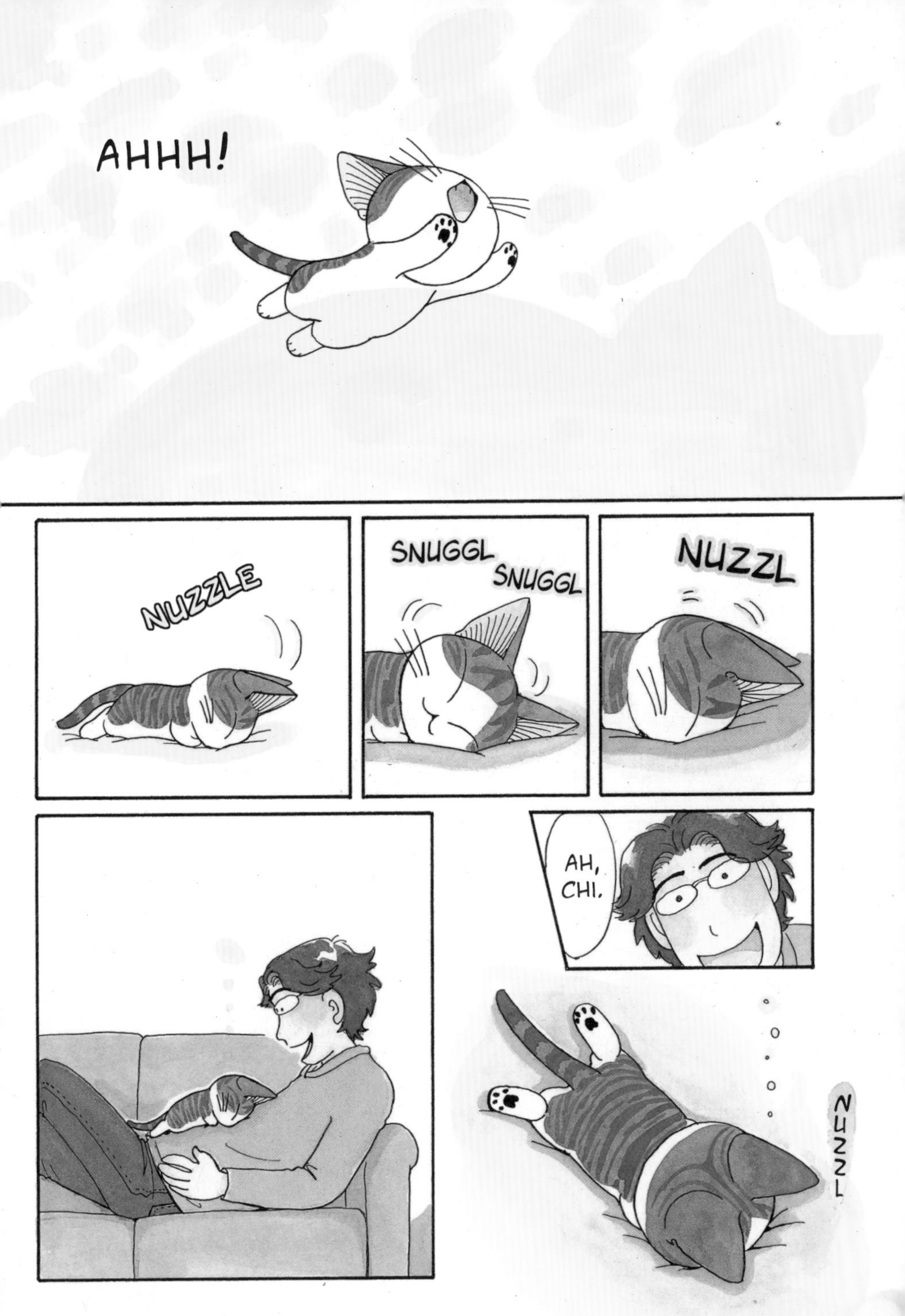
AHHH!
NUZZLE
SNUGGL
SNUGGL
NUZZL
AH, CHI.
NUZZL

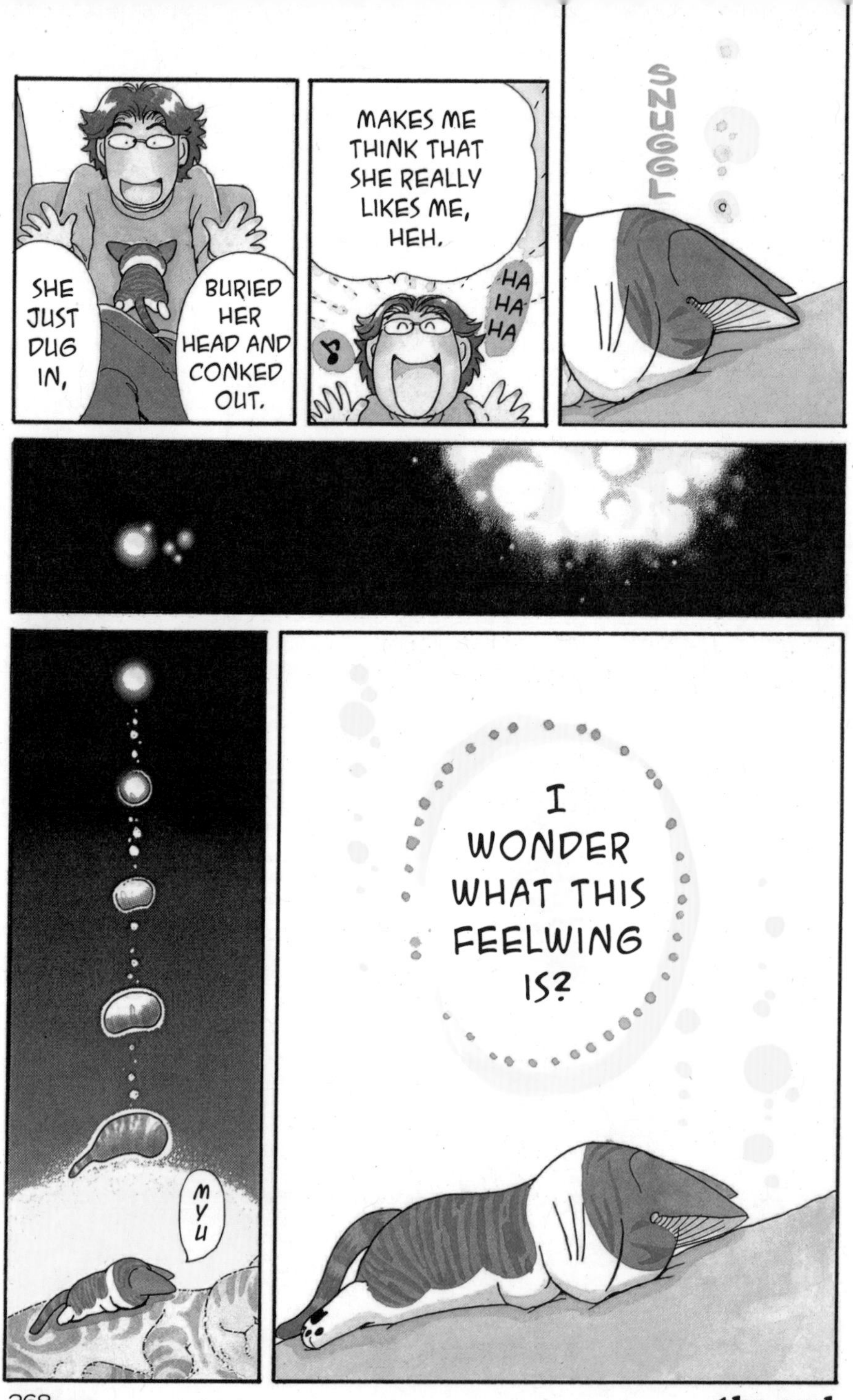
SHE JUST DUG IN,
BURIED HER HEAD AND CONKED OUT.
MAKES ME THINK THAT SHE REALLY LIKES ME, HEH.
HA HA HA
SNUGGL
MYU
I WONDER WHAT THIS FEELWING IS?

the end

homemade 34: a cat stalks

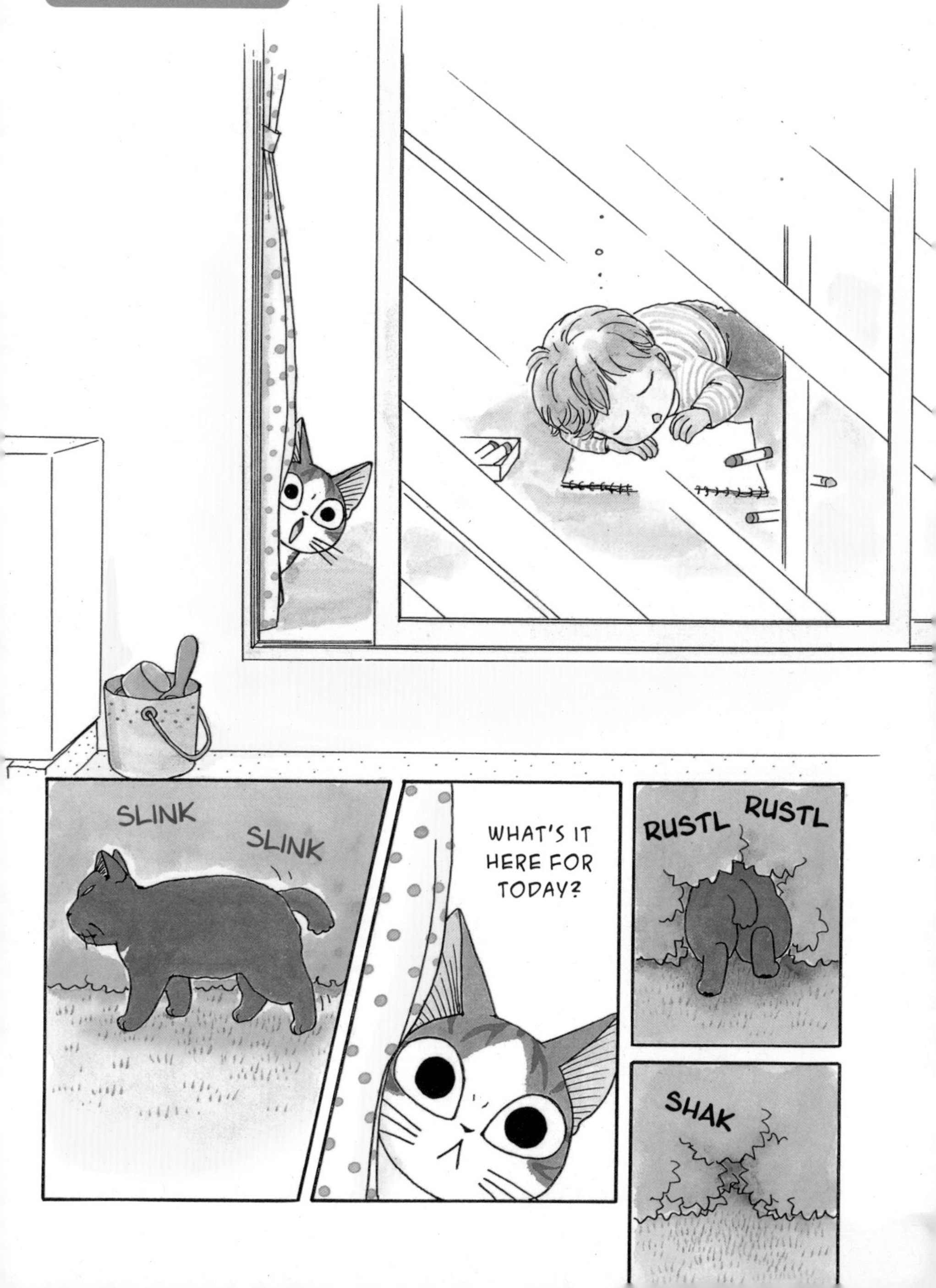
SLINK
SLINK
WHAT'S IT HERE FOR TODAY?
RUSTL
RUSTL
SHAK

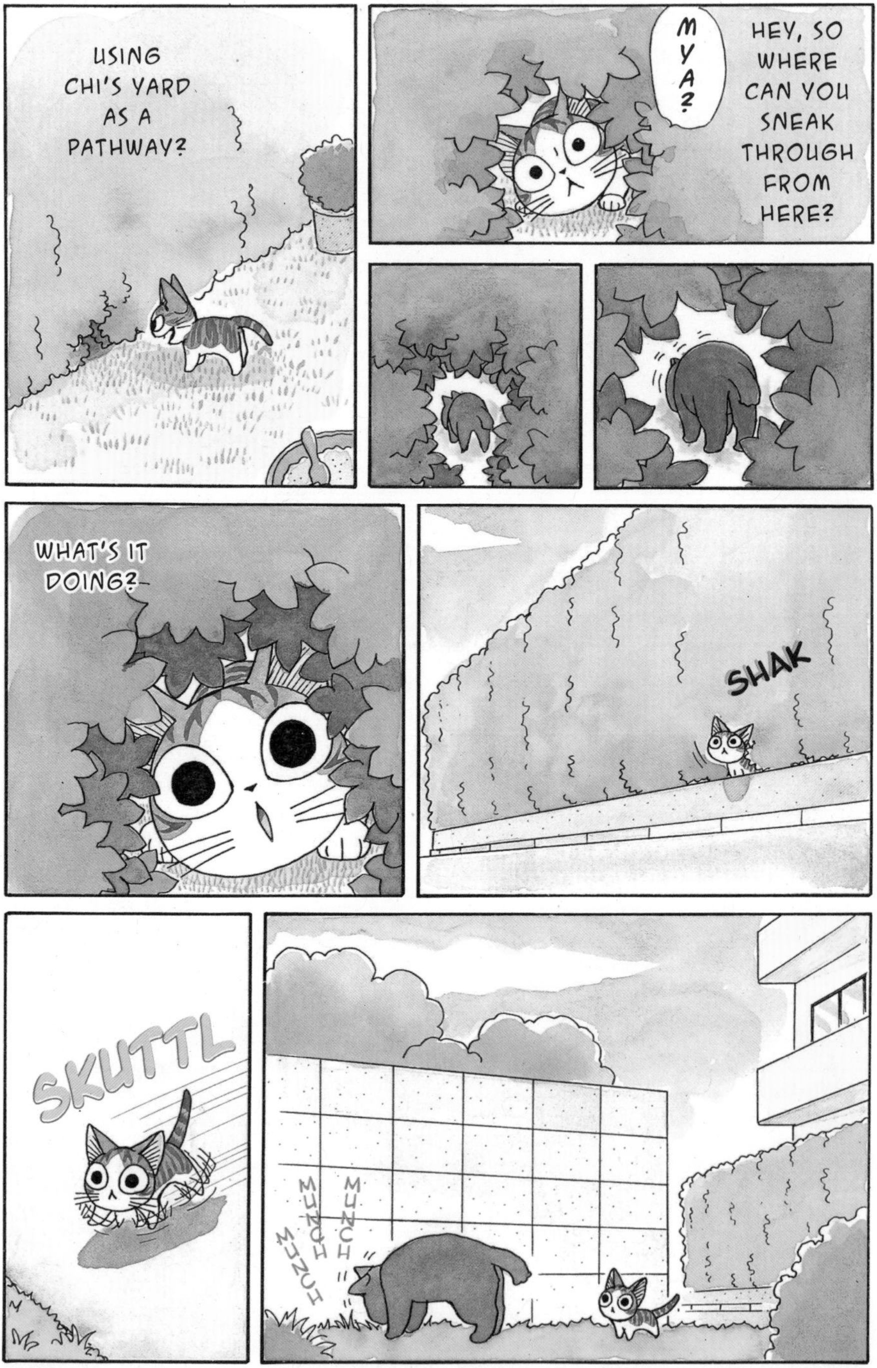
USING CHI'S YARD AS A PATHWAY?
MYA?
HEY, SO WHERE CAN YOU SNEAK THROUGH FROM HERE?
WHAT'S IT DOING?
SHAK
SKUTTL
MUNCH MUNCH
MUNCH

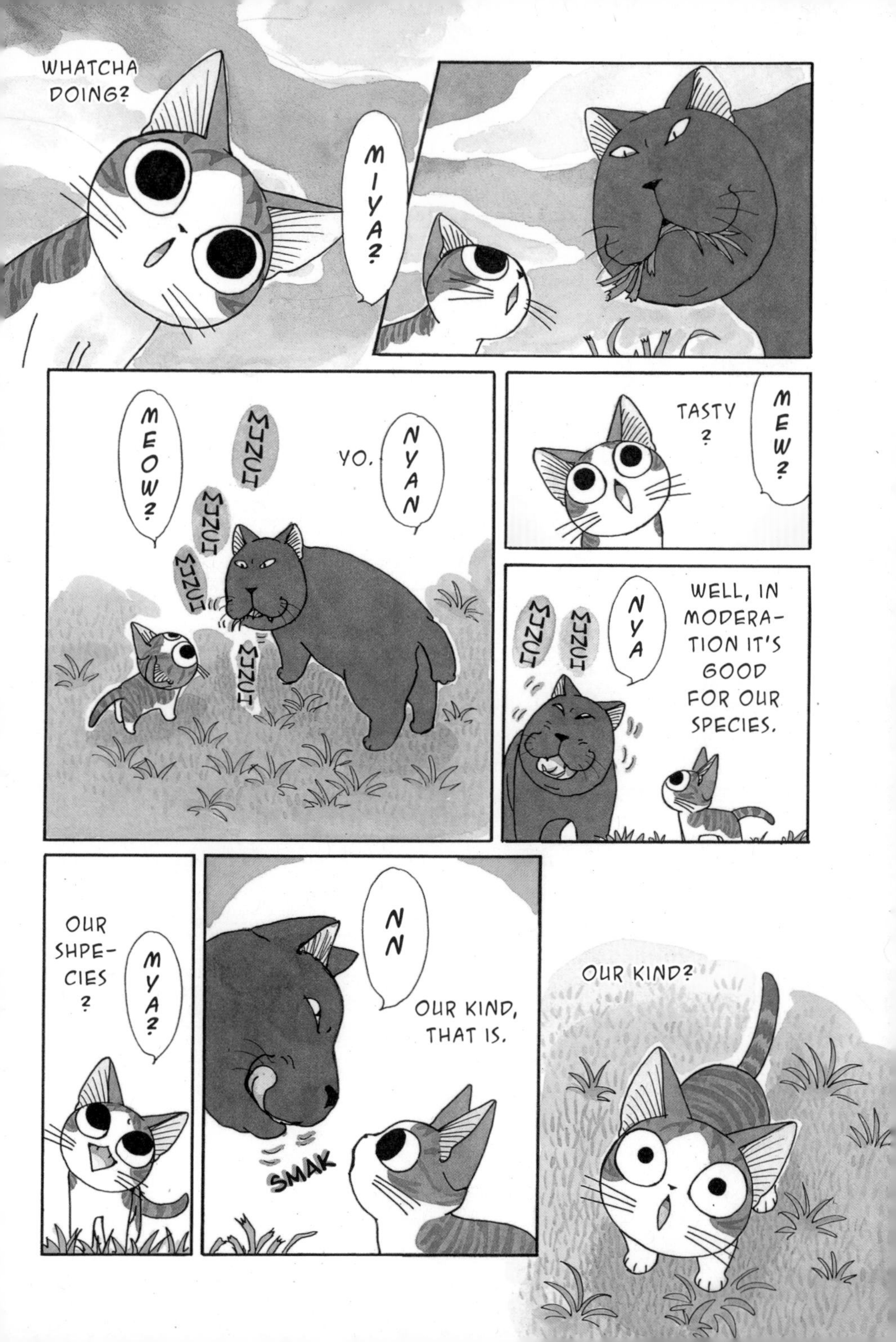
WHATCHA DOING?
MIYA?
MEOW?
MUNCH
MUNCH
MUNCH
YO.
NYAN
MUNCH
TASTY?
MEW?
MUNCH
MUNCH
NYA
WELL, IN MODERATION IT'S GOOD FOR OUR SPECIES.
OUR SHPE-CIES?
MYA?
NN
OUR KIND, THAT IS.
SMAK
OUR KIND?

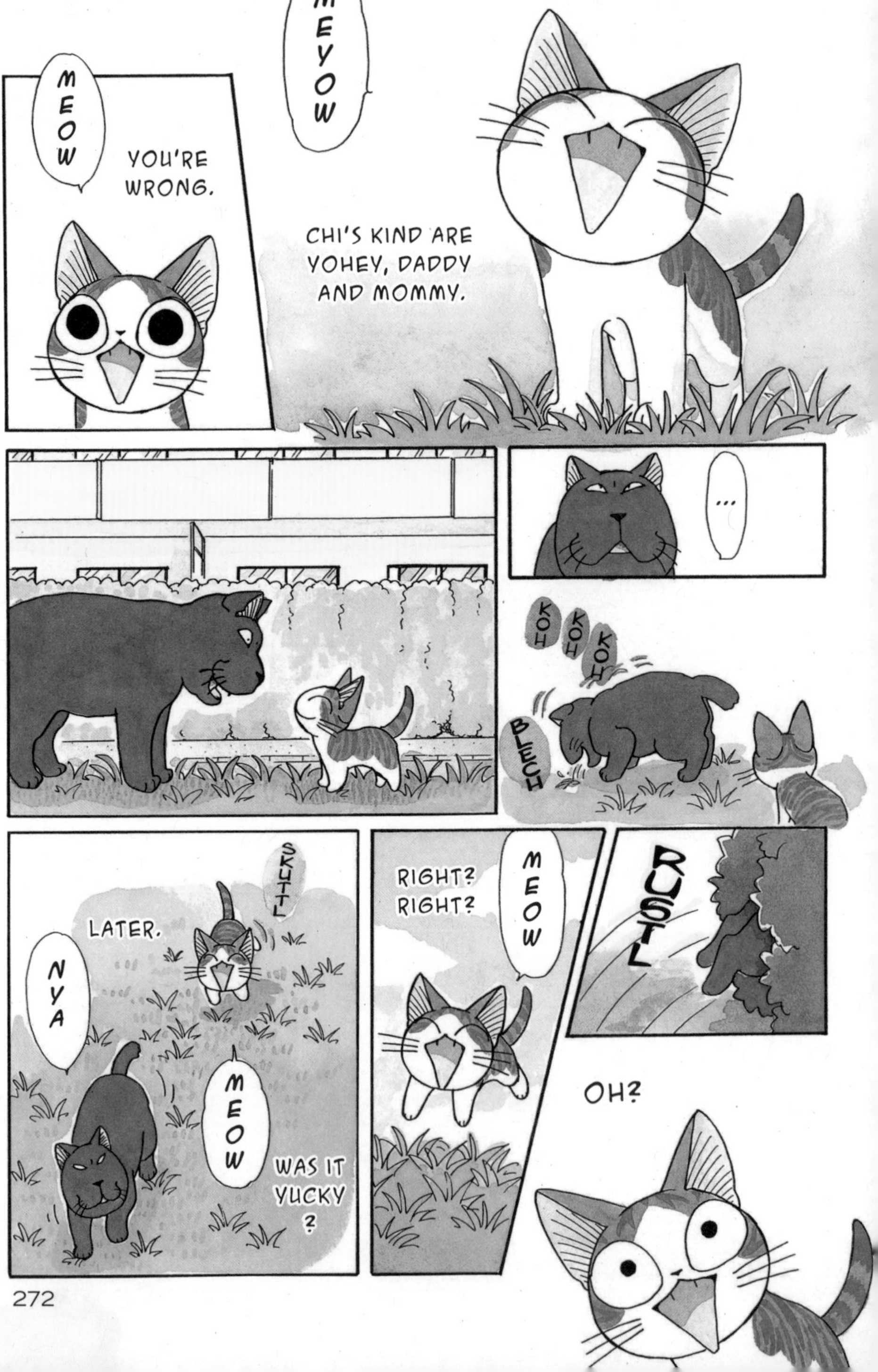
MEOW
YOU'RE WRONG.
MEYOW
CHI'S KIND ARE YOHEY, DADDY AND MOMMY.
...
KOH KOH KOH
BLECH
SKUTTL
LATER.
NYA
MEOW
WAS IT YUCKY?
RIGHT? RIGHT?
MEOW
RUSTL
OH?

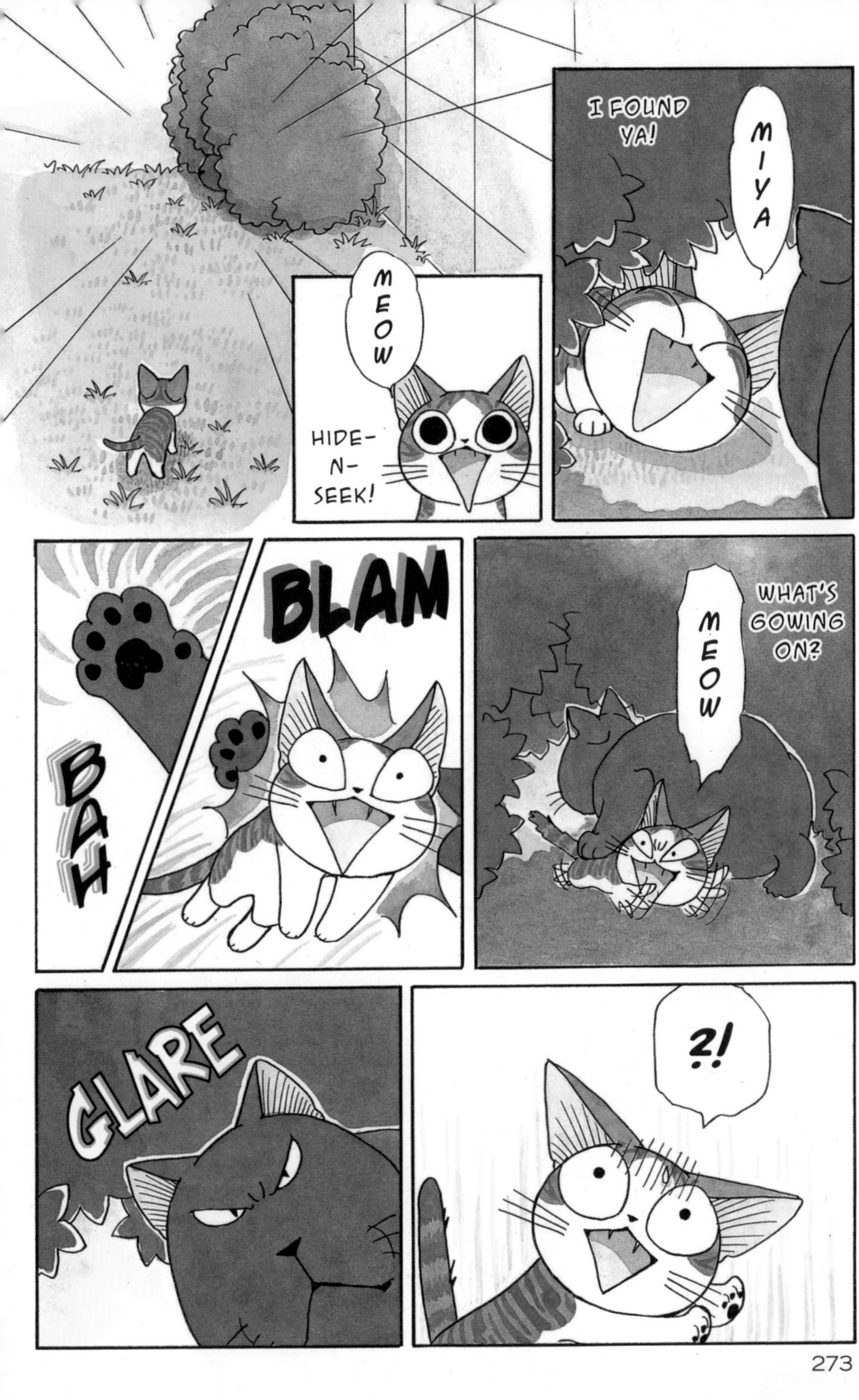
MEOW
HIDE-N-SEEK!
I FOUND YA!
MIYA
BAH
BLAM
MEOW
WHAT'S GOWING ON?
GLARE
?!

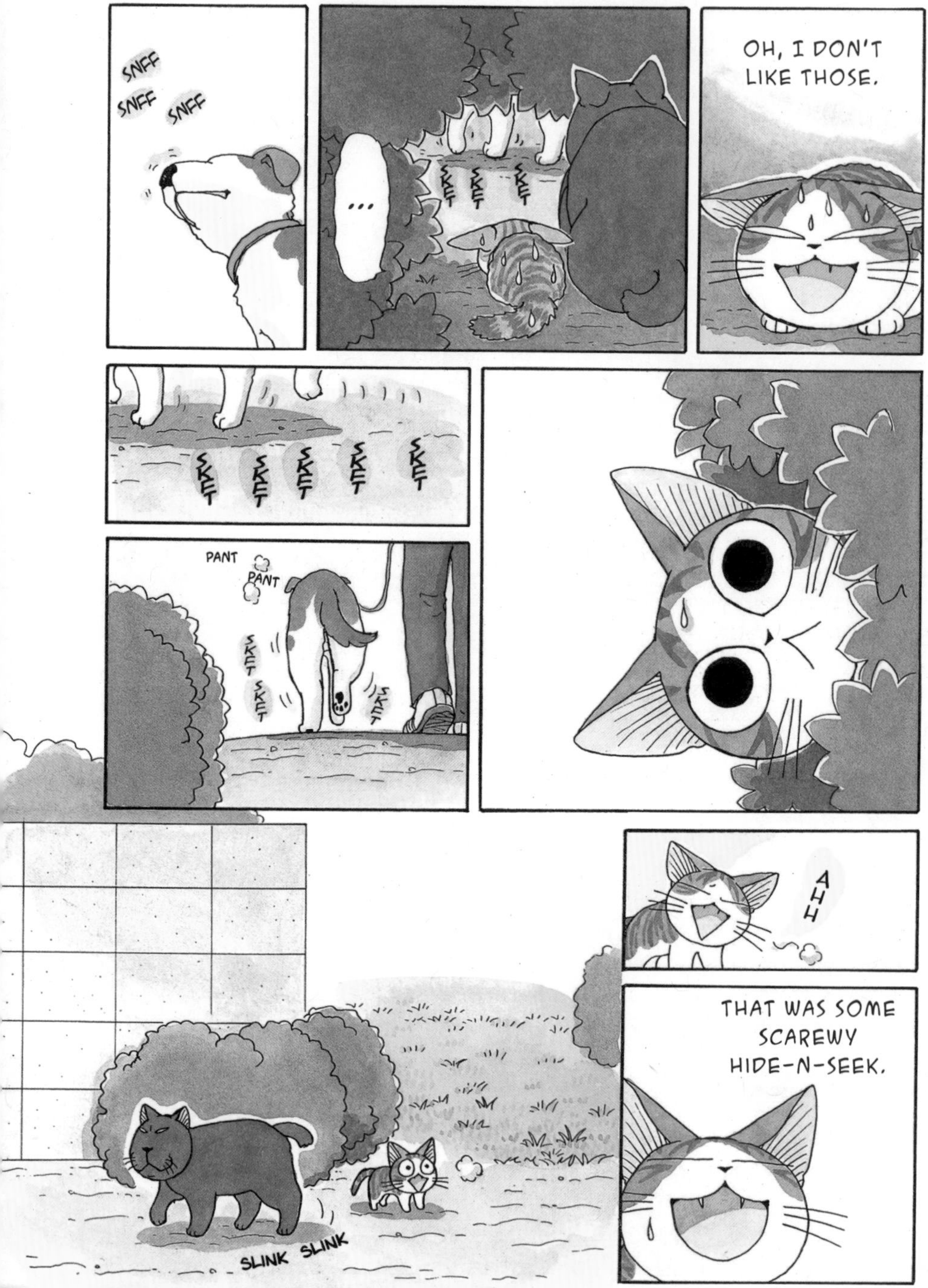
SNFF
SNFF
SNFF
...
SKET
SKET
SKET
OH, I DON'T LIKE THOSE.
SKET
SKET
SKET
SKET
SKET
PANT
PANT
SKET
SKET
SKET
AHH
SLINK SLINK
THAT WAS SOME SCAREWY HIDE-N-SEEK.

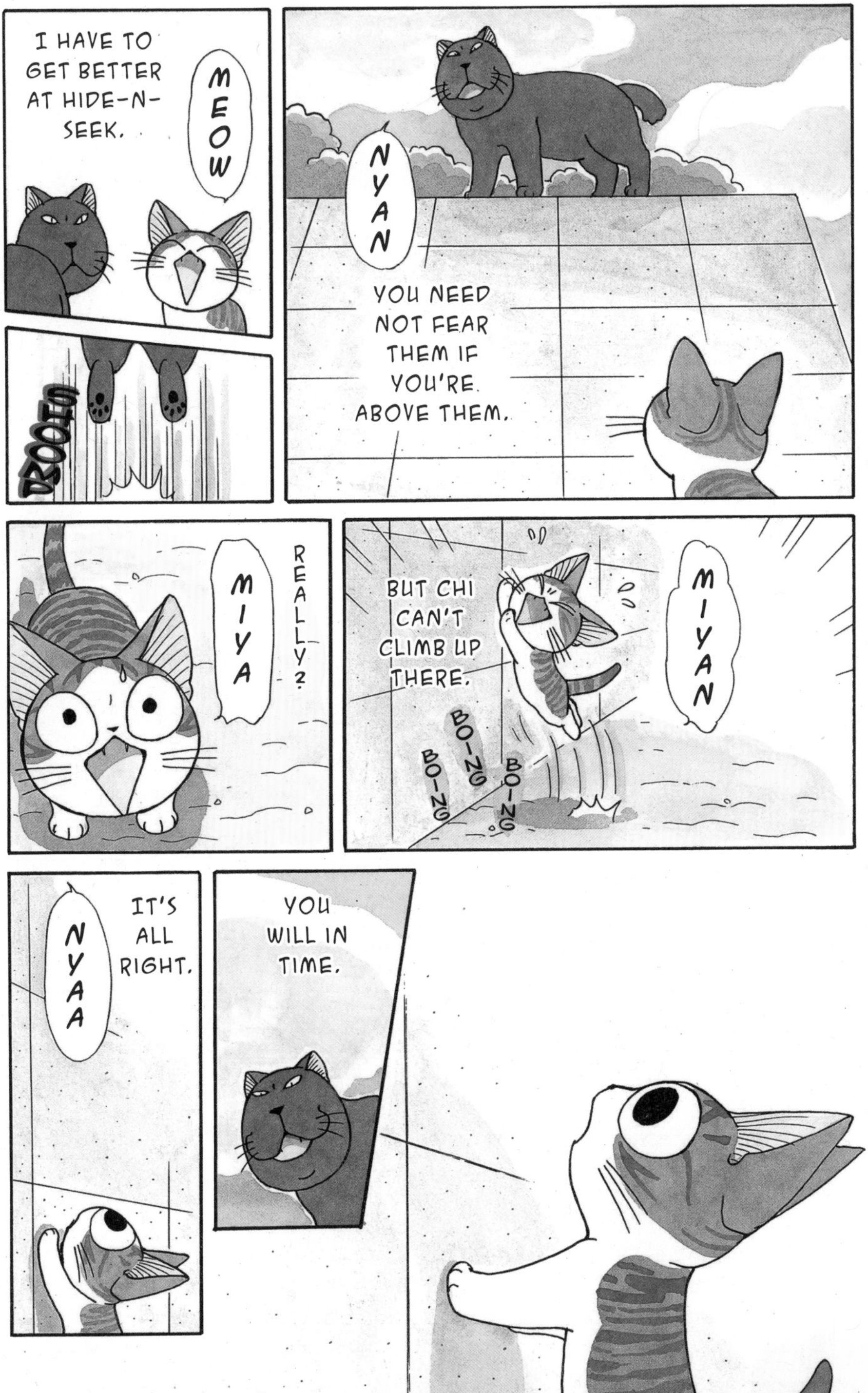

I HAVE TO GET BETTER AT HIDE-N-SEEK.
MEOW
DROOFS
NYAN
YOU NEED NOT FEAR THEM IF YOU'RE ABOVE THEM.
MIYA
REALLY?
BUT CHI CAN'T CLIMB UP THERE.
MIYAN
BOING
BOING
BOING
NYAA
IT'S ALL RIGHT.
YOU WILL IN TIME.

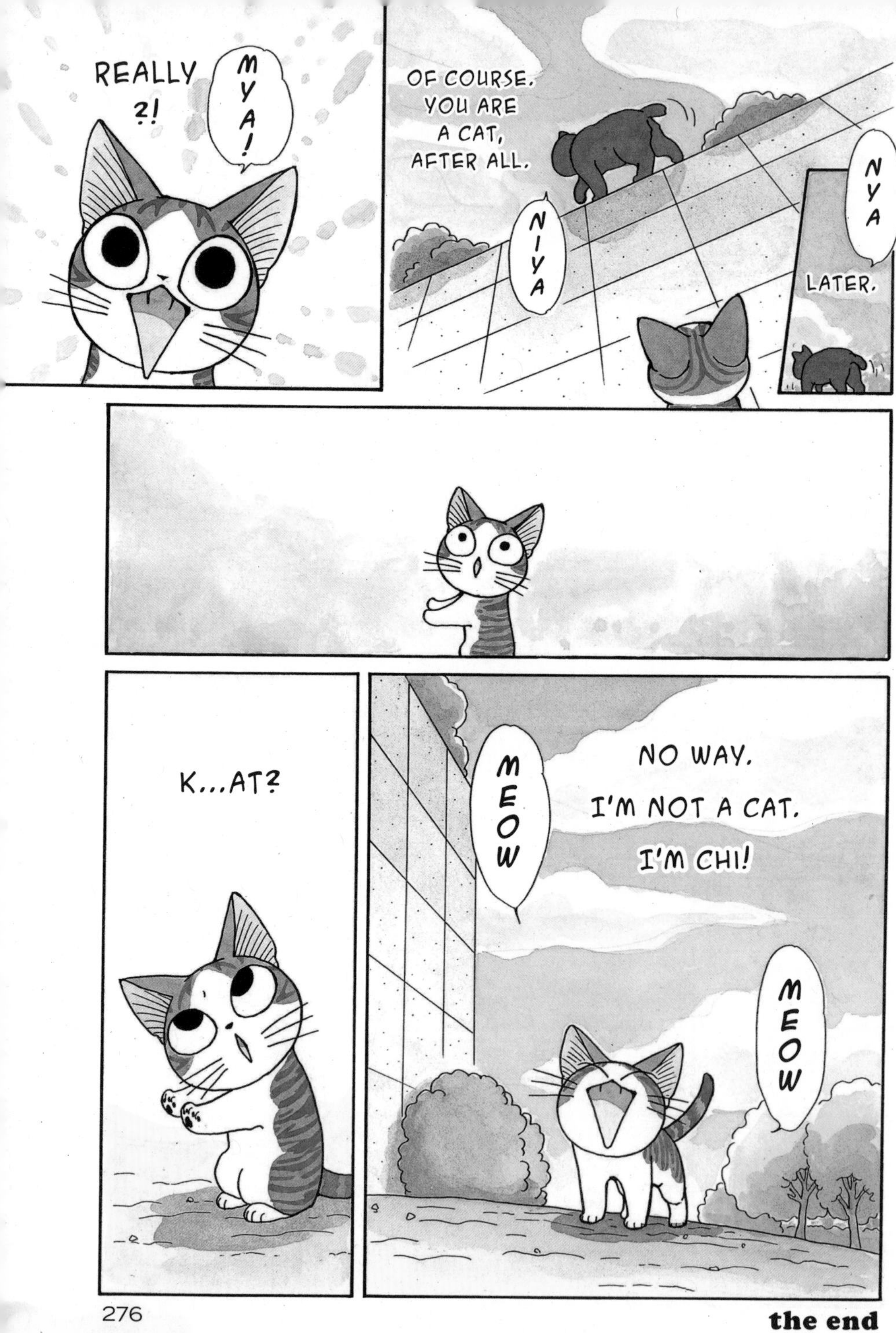
REALLY ?!
MYA!
OF COURSE. YOU ARE A CAT, AFTER ALL.
NIYA
NYA
LATER.
K...AT?
MEOW
NO WAY. I'M NOT A CAT. I'M CHI!
MEOW

the end

homemade 35: a cat goes home

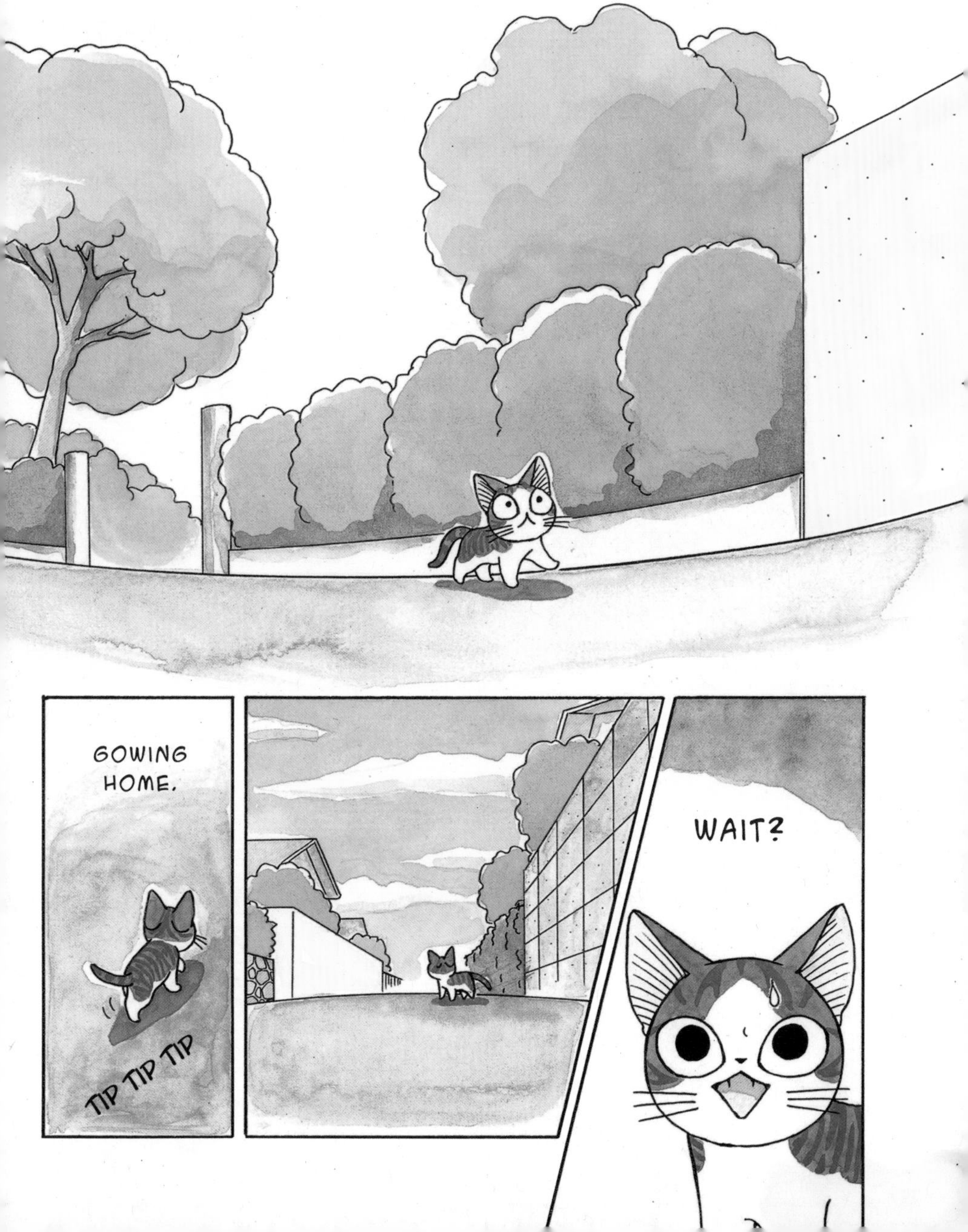
GOWING HOME.
TIP TIP TIP
WAIT?

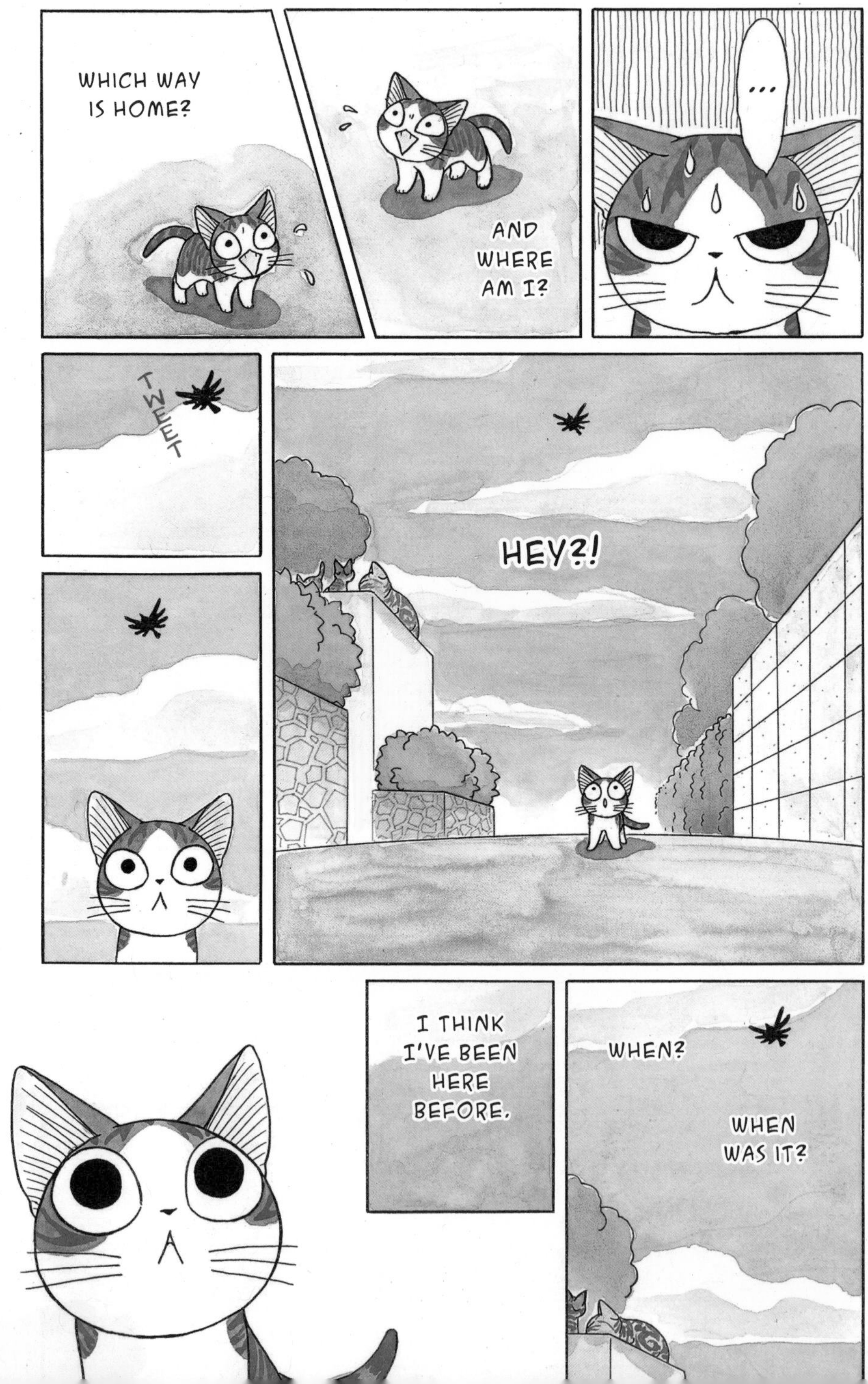
WHICH WAY IS HOME?
AND WHERE AM I?
...
TWEET
HEY?!
I THINK I'VE BEEN HERE BEFORE.
WHEN?
WHEN WAS IT?

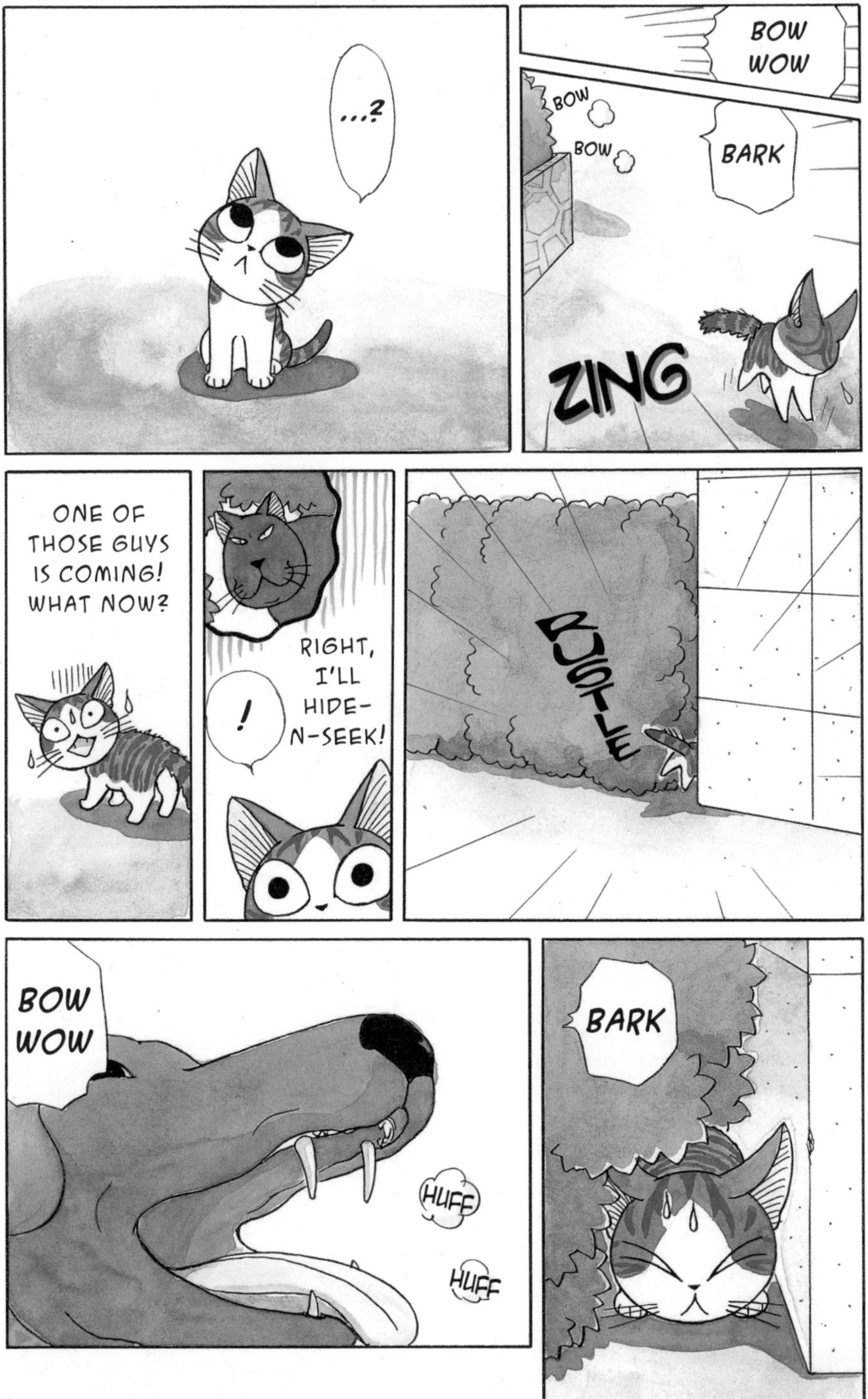
...?
BOW WOW
BOW
BOW
BARK
ZING
ONE OF THOSE GUYS IS COMING! WHAT NOW?
!
RIGHT, I'LL HIDE-N-SEEK!
RUSTLE
BOW WOW
HUFF
HUFF
BARK

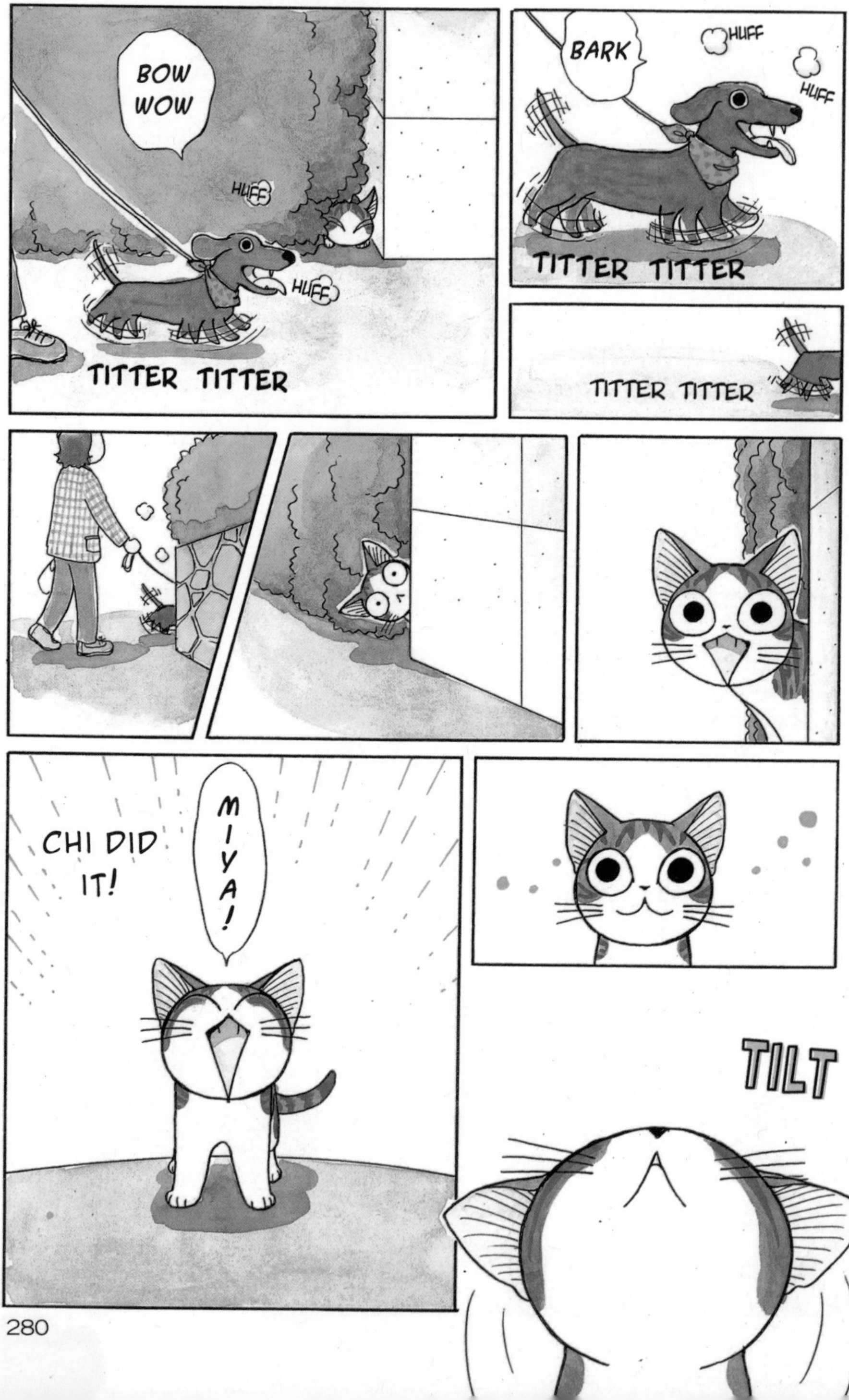

BOW WOW
HUFF
HUFF
TITTER TITTER
BARK
HUFF
HUFF
TITTER TITTER
TITTER TITTER
CHI DID IT!
MIYA!
TILT

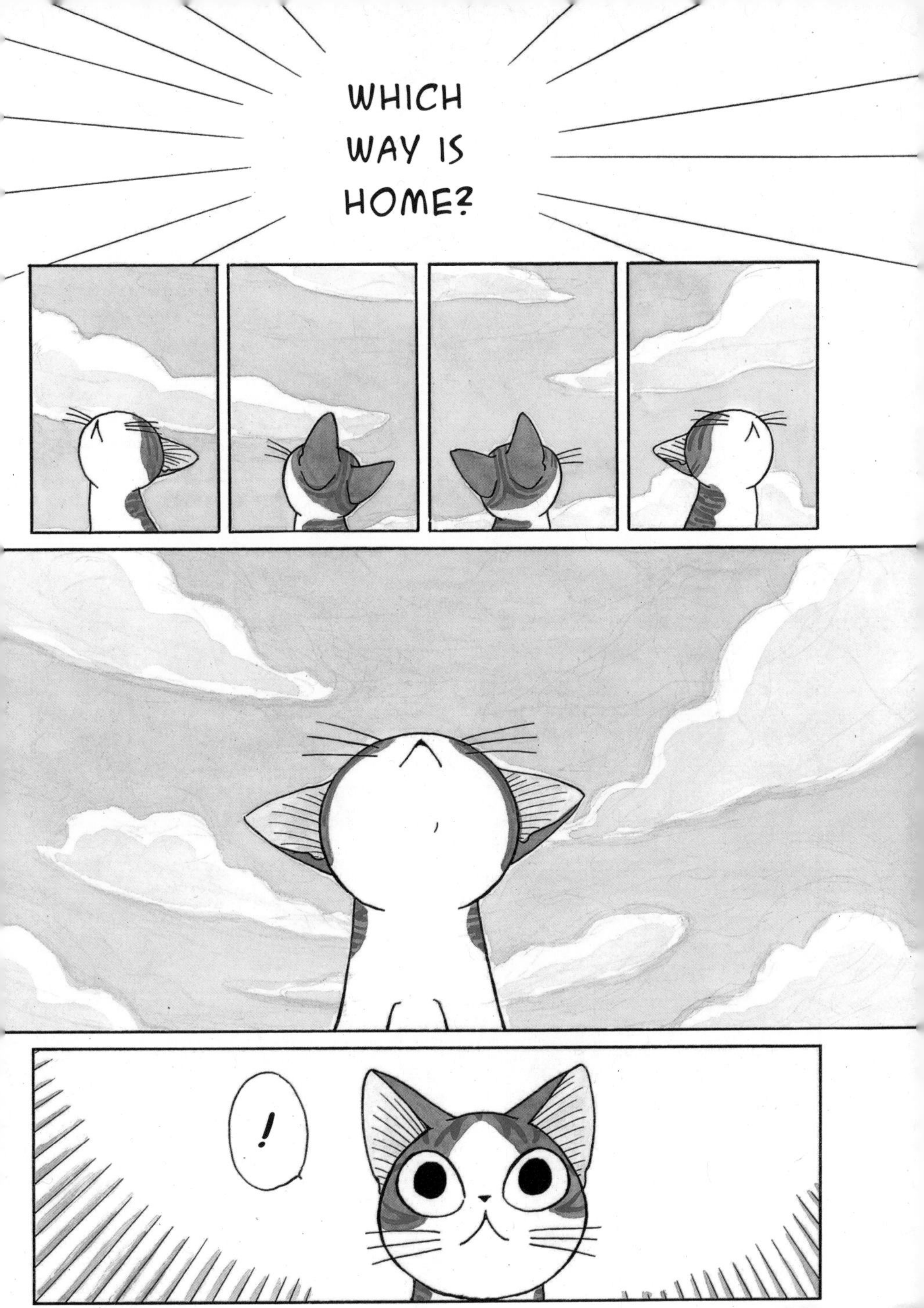
WHICH WAY IS HOME?
!

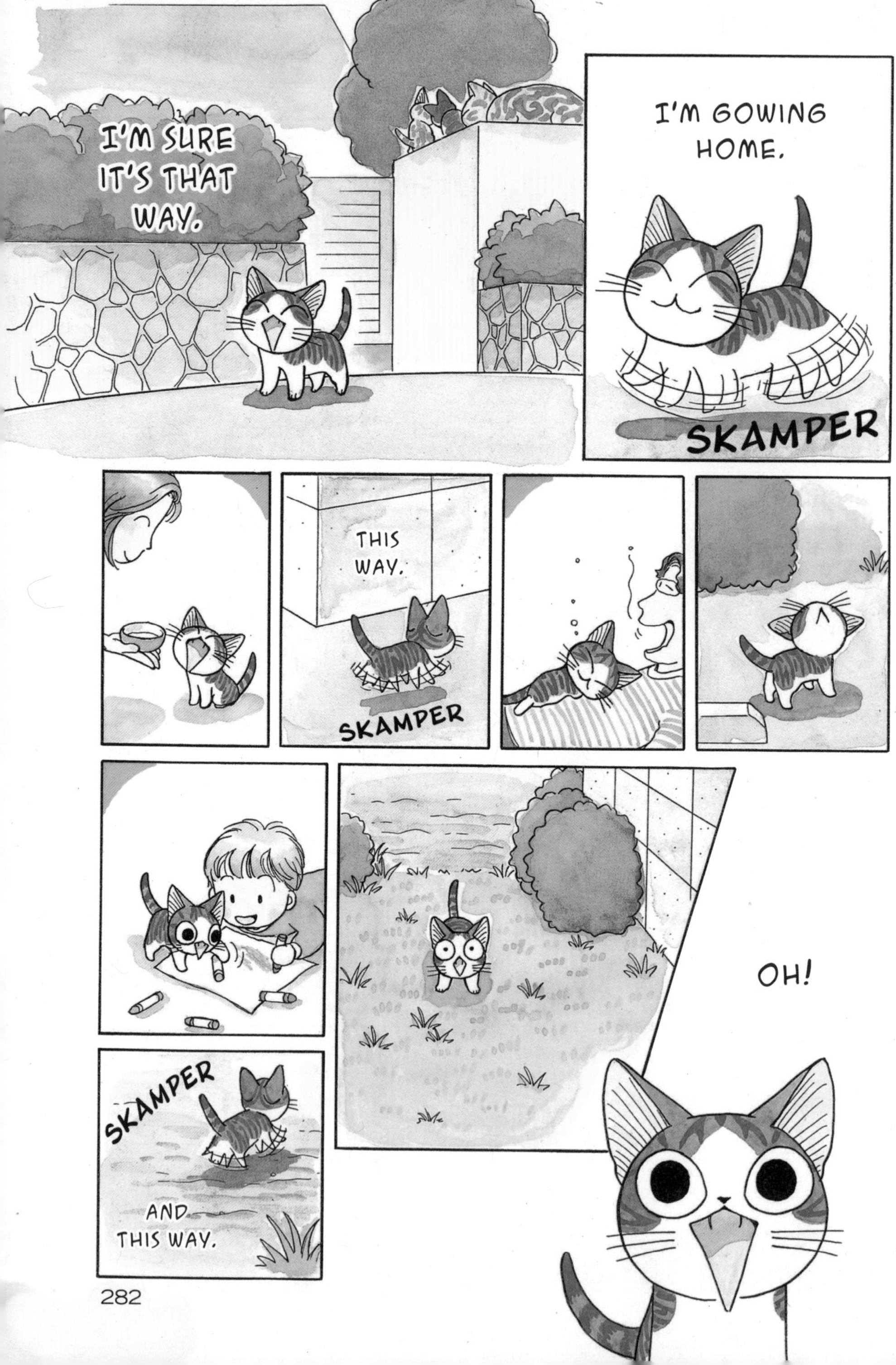
I'M SURE IT'S THAT WAY.
I'M GOWING HOME.
SKAMPER
THIS WAY.
SKAMPER
SKAMPER
AND THIS WAY.
OH!

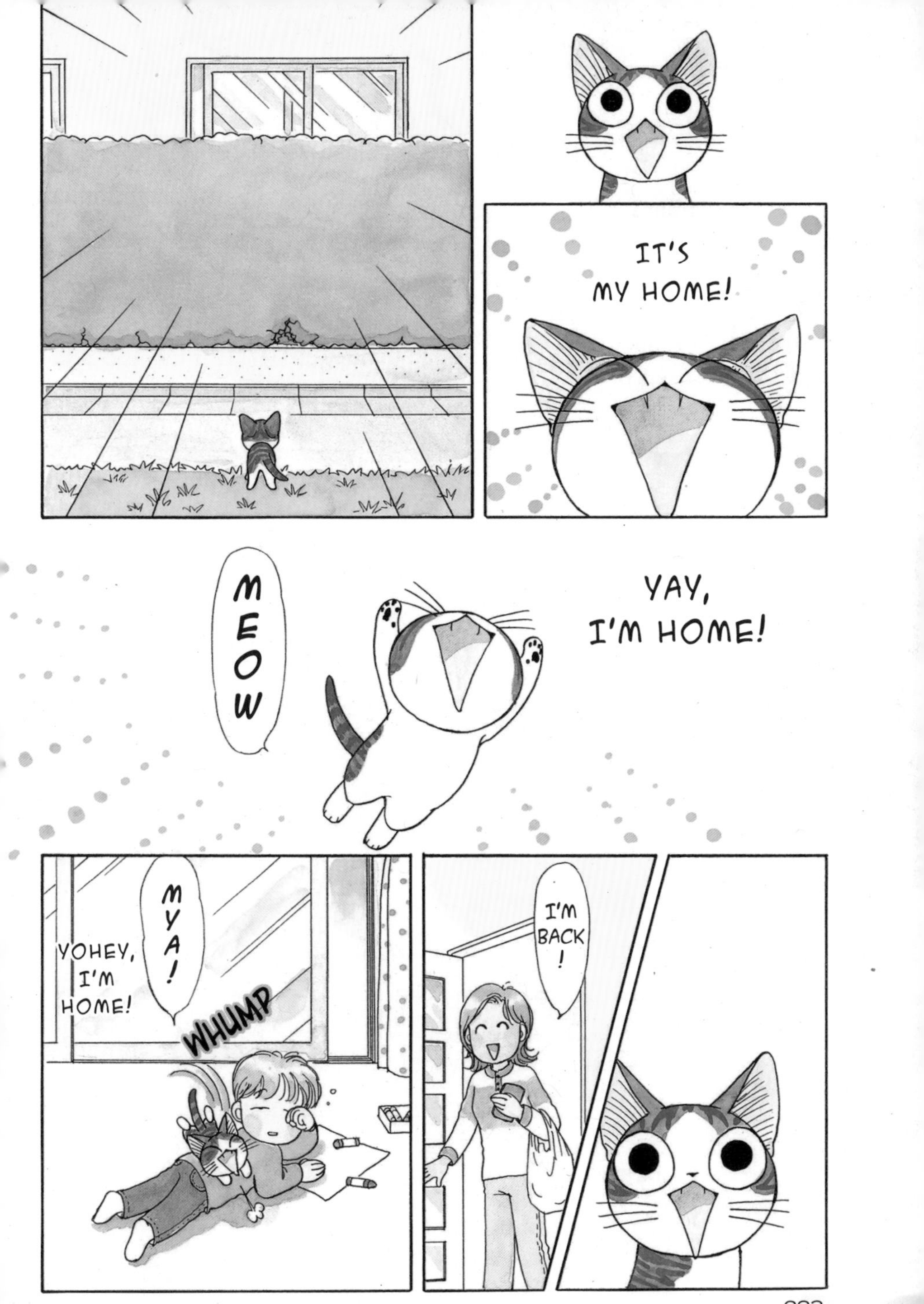
IT'S MY HOME!
MEOW
YAY, I'M HOME!
YOHEY, I'M HOME!
MYA!
WHUMP
I'M BACK!

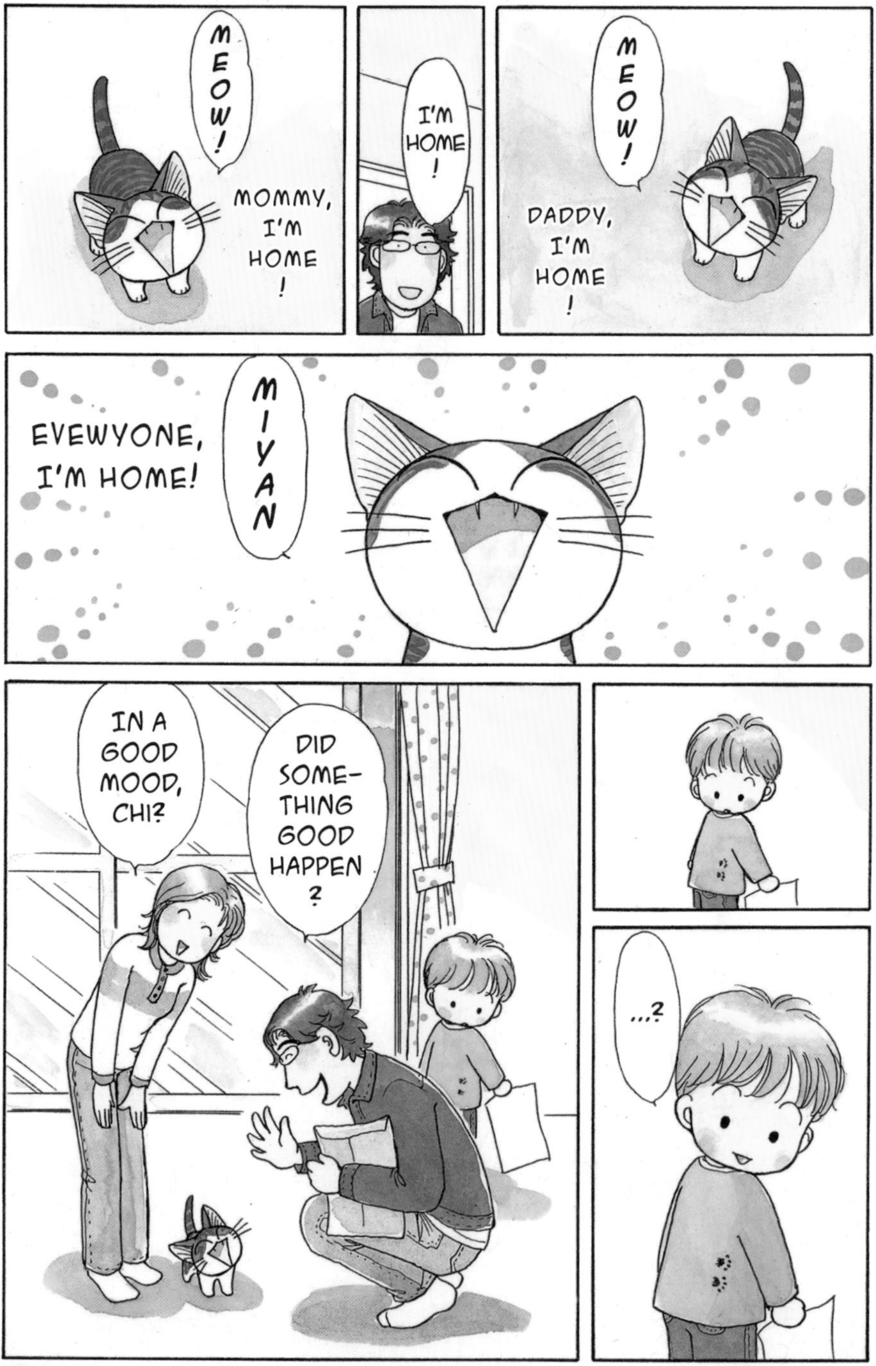
MEOW!
MOMMY, I'M HOME!
I'M HOME!
MEOW!
DADDY, I'M HOME!
EVEWYONE, I'M HOME!
MIYAN
IN A GOOD MOOD, CHI?
DID SOME-THING GOOD HAPPEN?
...?

the end

homemade 36: a cat resists

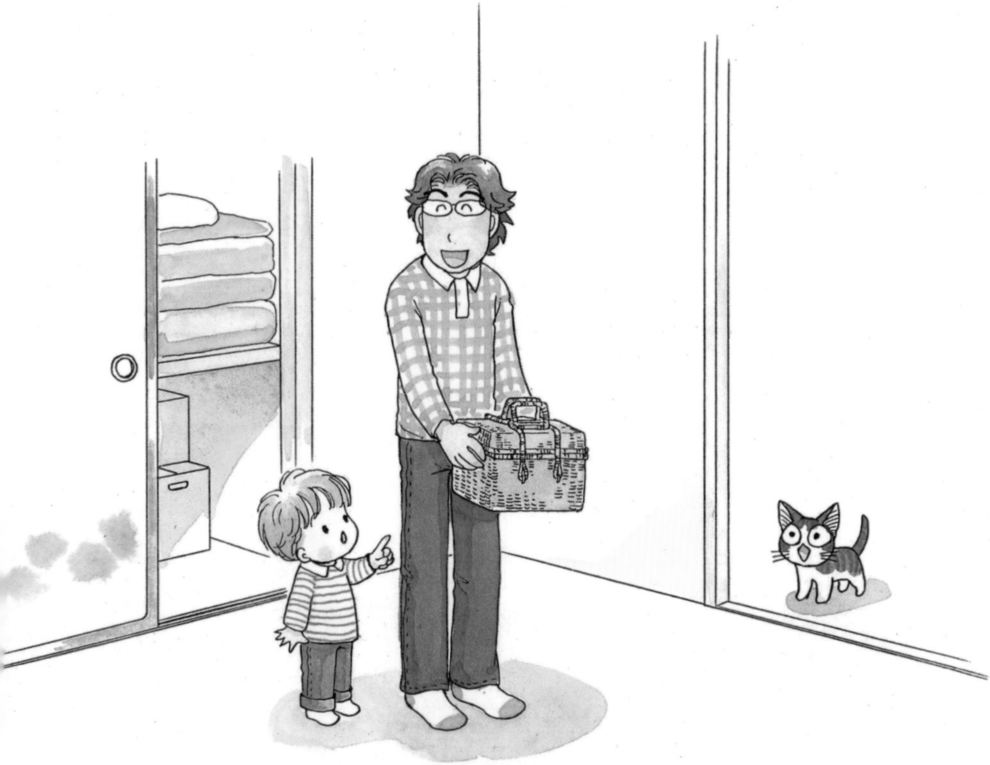

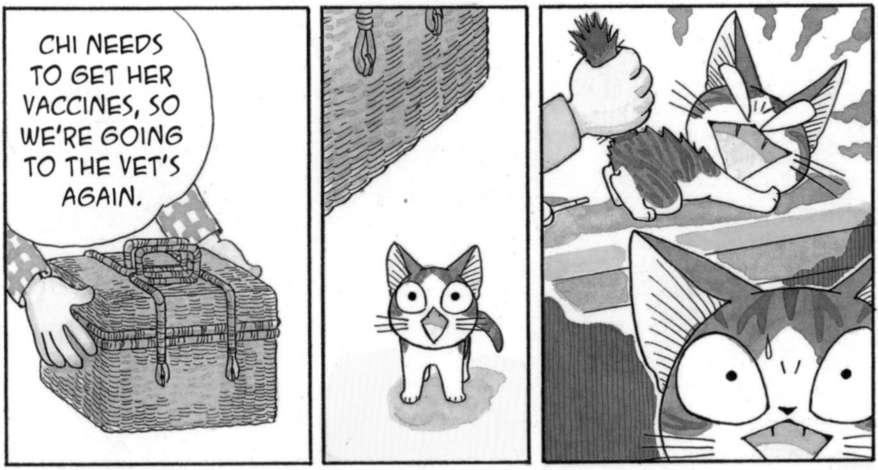
CHI NEEDS TO GET HER VACCINES, SO WE'RE GOING TO THE VET'S AGAIN.

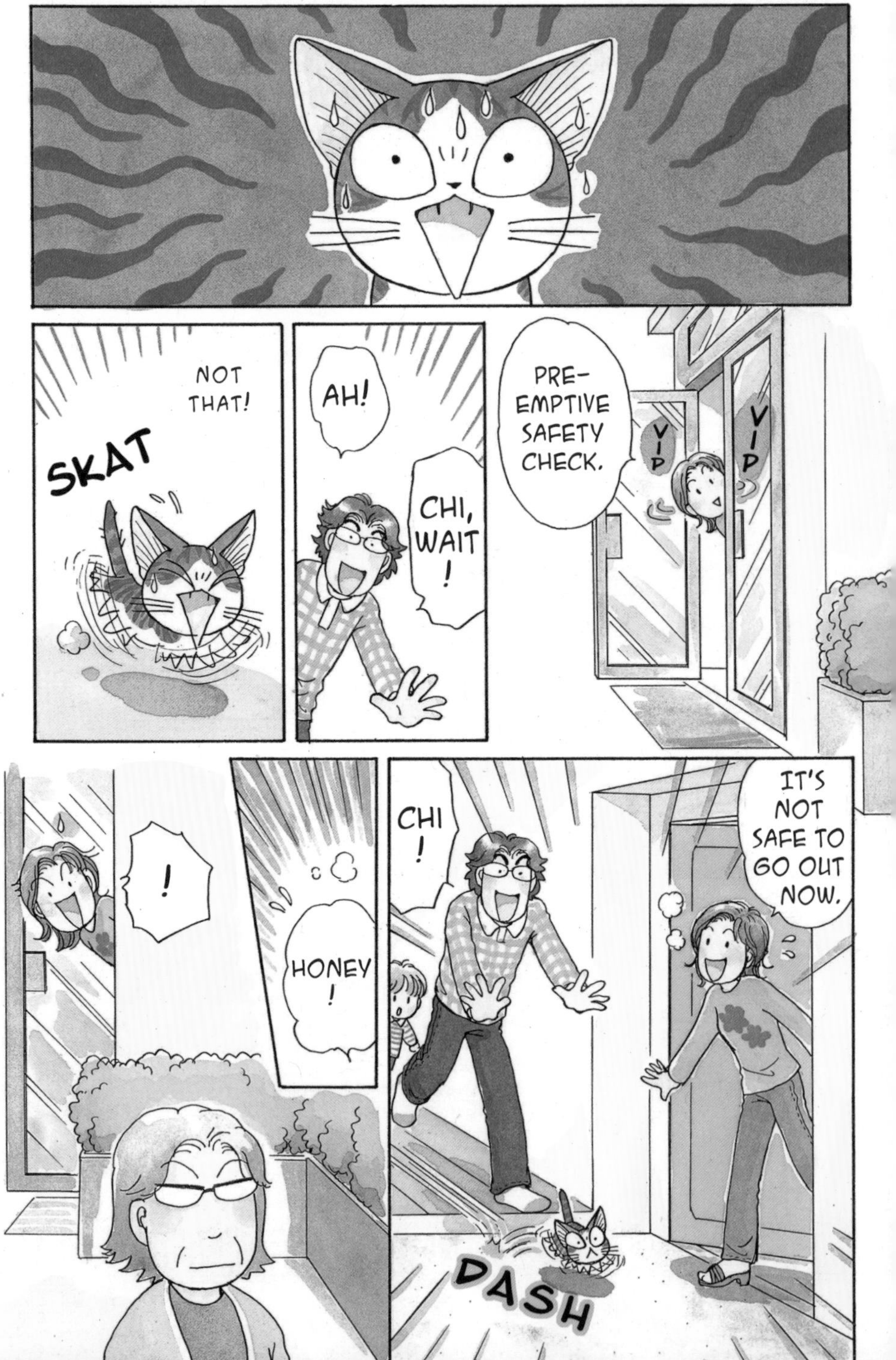
NOT THAT!
SKAT
AH!
CHI, WAIT!
PRE-EMPTIVE SAFETY CHECK.
VIP
VIP
!
HONEY!
CHI!
IT'S NOT SAFE TO GO OUT NOW.
DASH

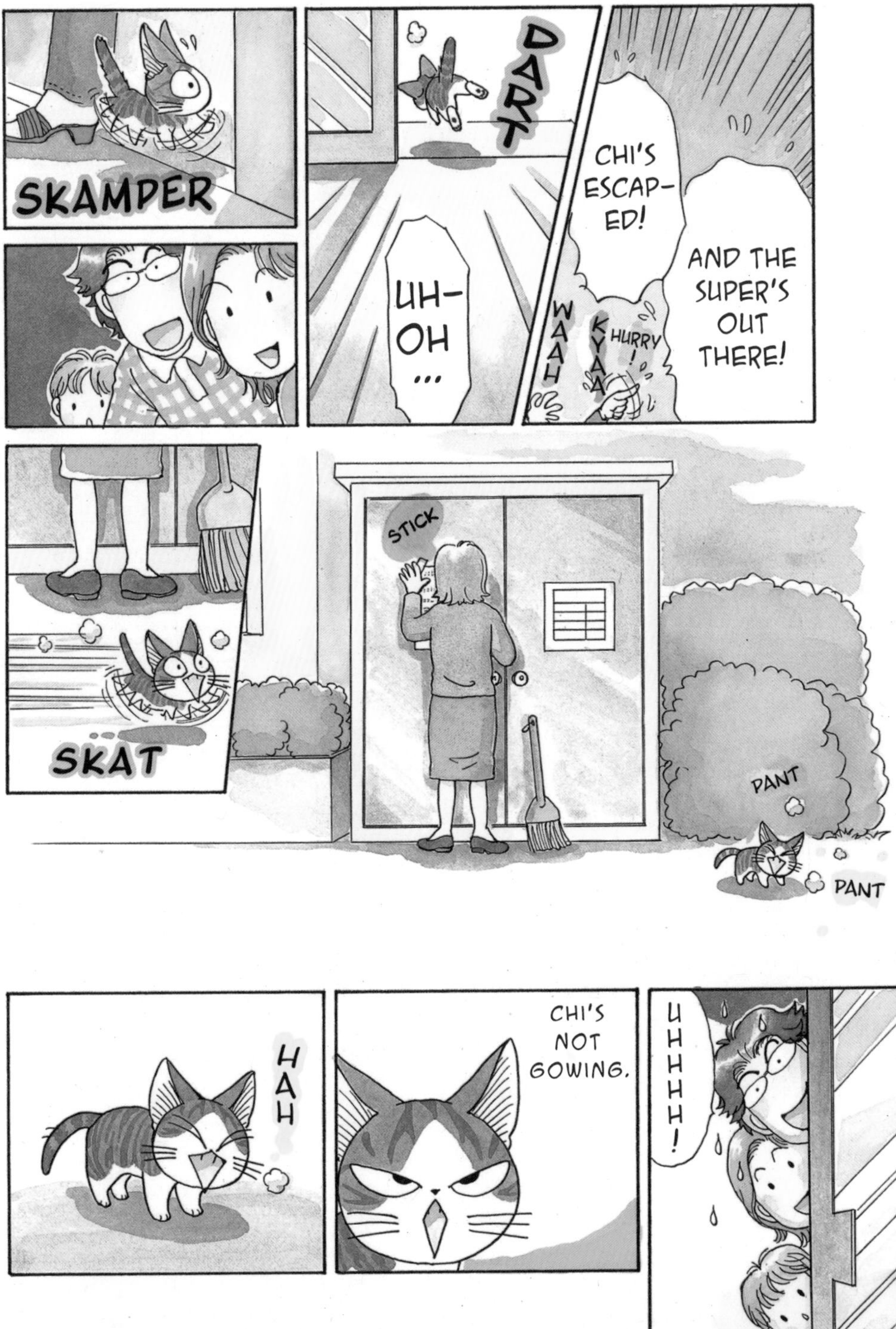
SKAMPER
DART
UH-OH ...
CHI'S ESCAPED!
WAAAH
KYAA
HURRY!
AND THE SUPER'S OUT THERE!
SKAT
STICK
PANT
PANT
HAH
CHI'S NOT GOWING.
UHHHHH!

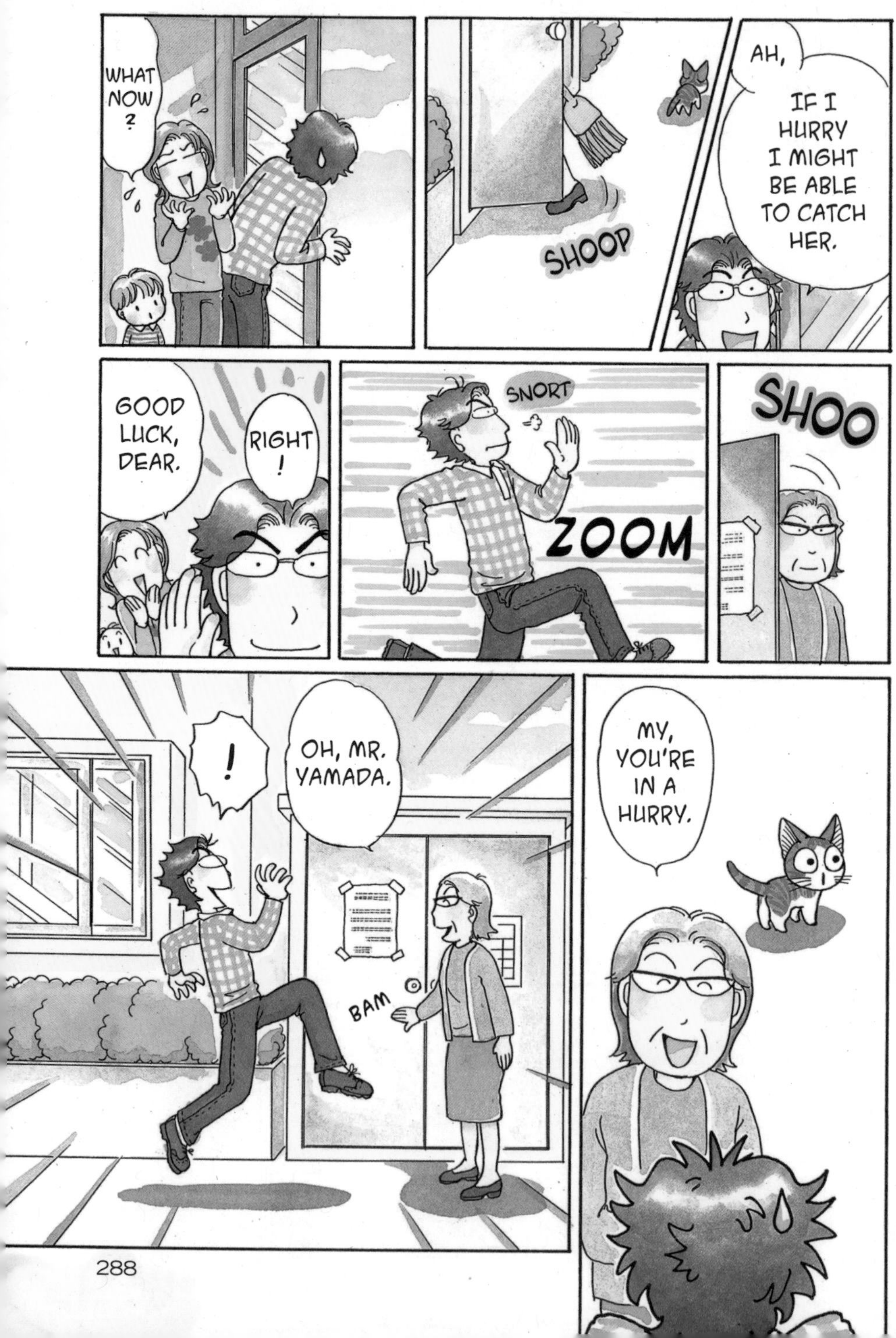
WHAT NOW ?
SHOOP
AH,
IF I HURRY I MIGHT BE ABLE TO CATCH HER.
GOOD LUCK, DEAR.
RIGHT !
SNORT
ZOOM
SHOO
!
OH, MR. YAMADA.
BAM
MY, YOU'RE IN A HURRY.

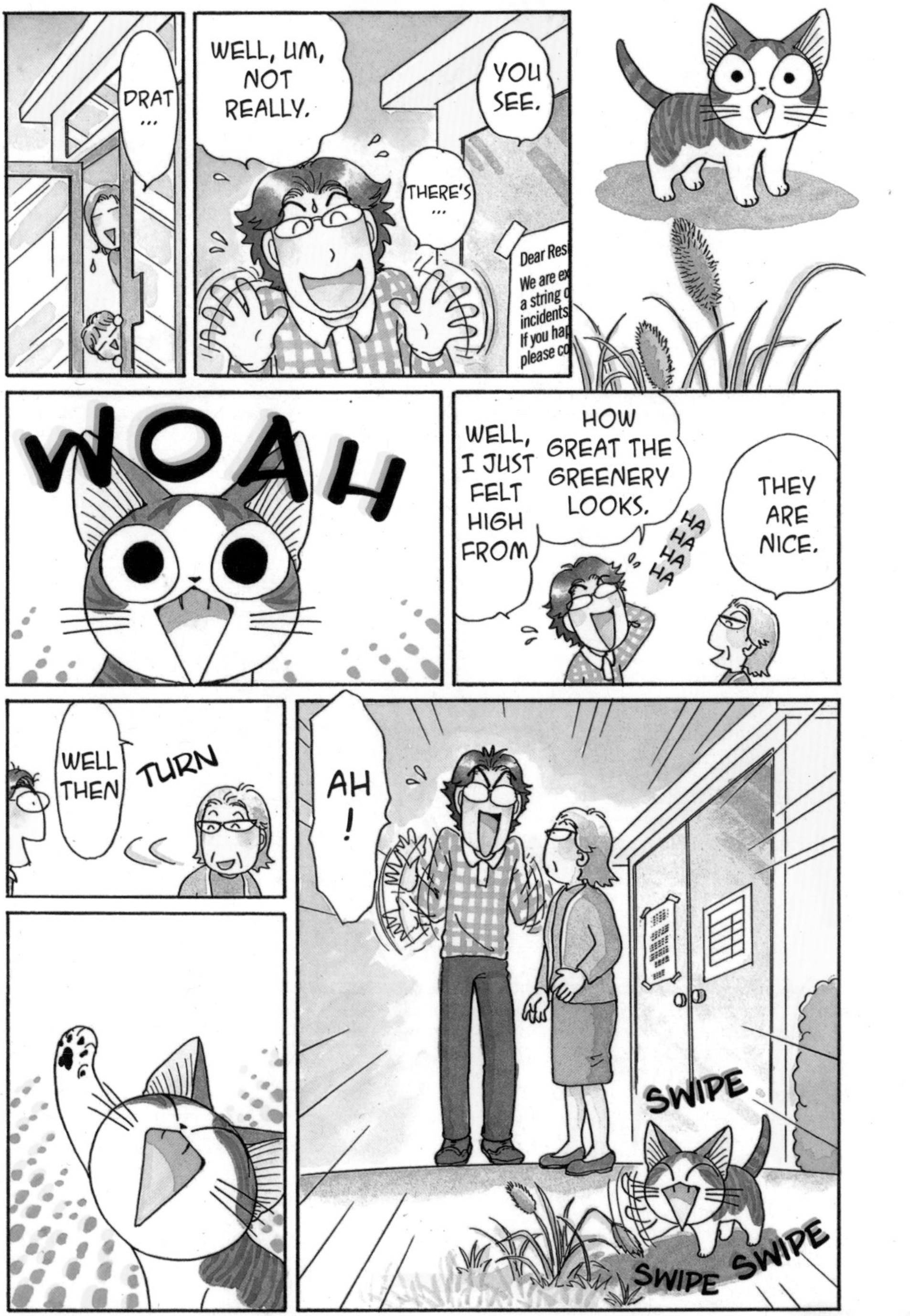
DRAT ...
WELL, UM, NOT REALLY.
YOU SEE.
THERE'S ...
Dear Res
We are ex
a string o
incidents
If you hap
please co
WOAH
WELL, I JUST FELT HIGH FROM
HOW GREAT THE GREENERY LOOKS.
HA HA HA HA
THEY ARE NICE.
WELL THEN
TURN
AH!
SWIPE
SWIPE SWIPE

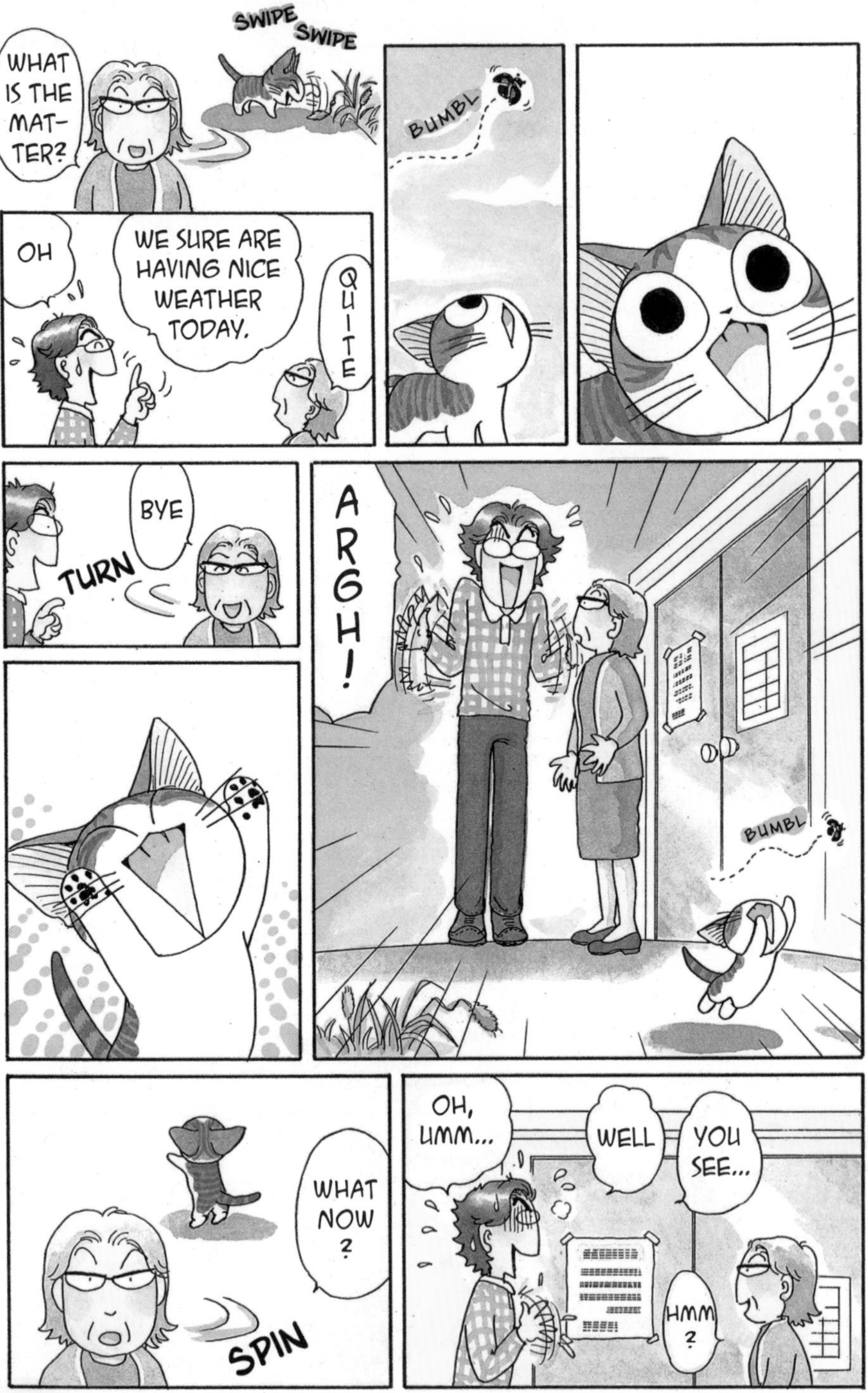
WHAT IS THE MATTER?
SWIPE SWIPE
BUMBL
OH
WE SURE ARE HAVING NICE WEATHER TODAY.
QUITE
BYE
TURN
ARGH!
BUMBL
WHAT NOW?
SPIN
OH, UMM...
WELL
YOU SEE...
HMM?

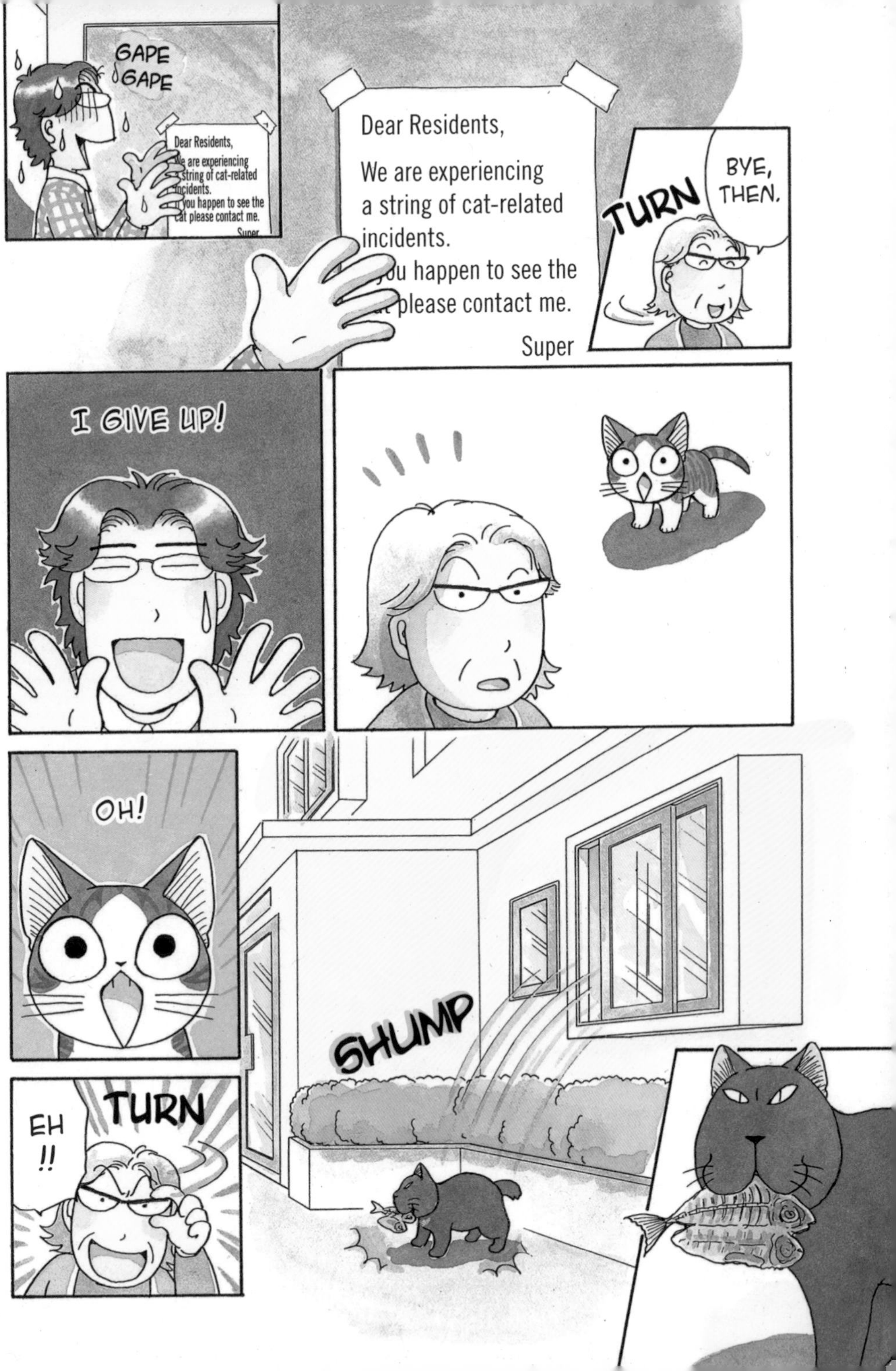
GAPE GAPE
Dear Residents,
e are experiencing
string of cat-related
ncidents.
you happen to see the
at please contact me.
Dear Residents,
We are experiencing
a string of cat-related
incidents.
ou happen to see the
please contact me.
Super
TURN
BYE, THEN.
I GIVE UP!
OH!
EH !!
TURN
SHUMP

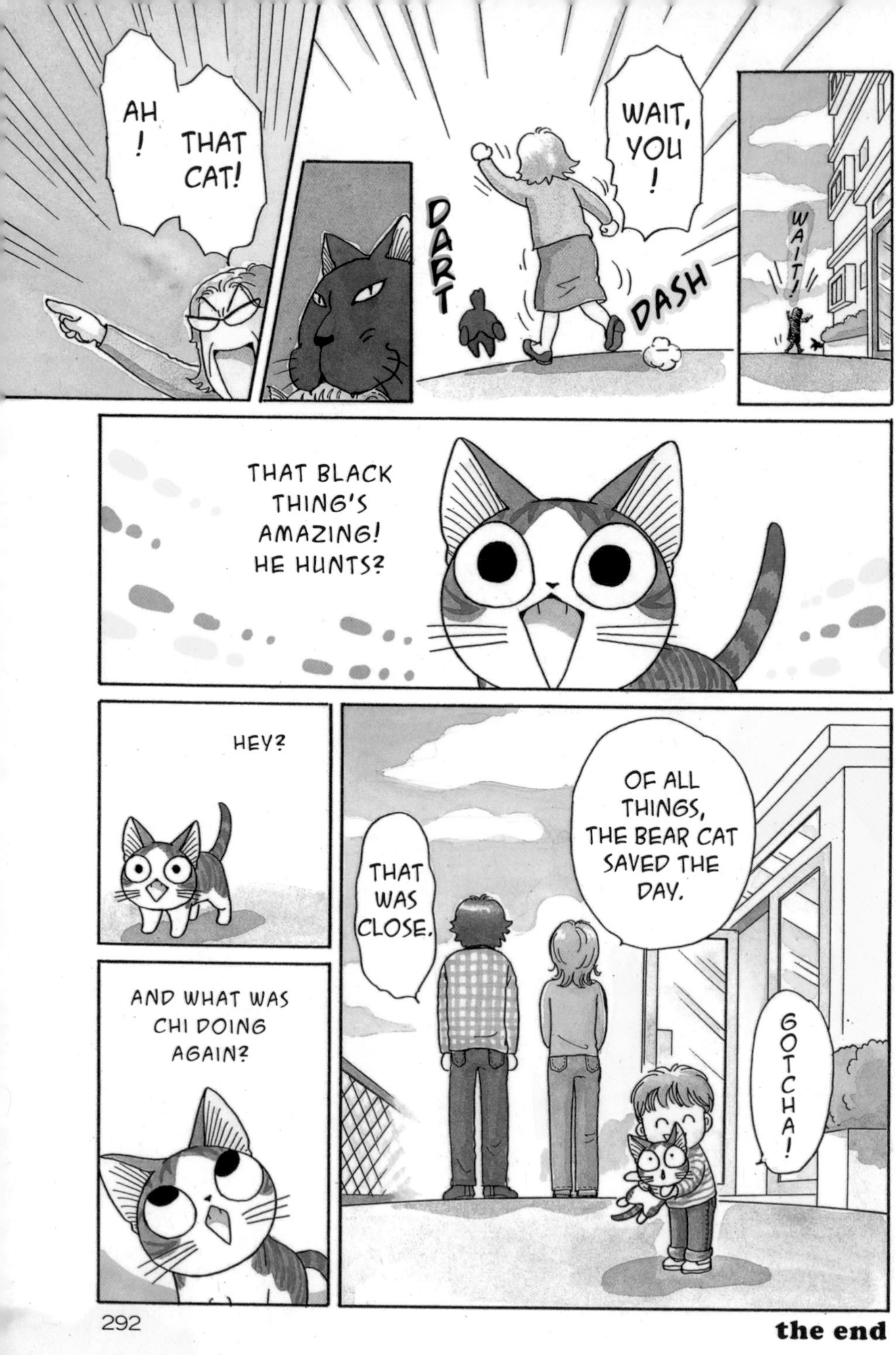
AH!
THAT CAT!
DART
WAIT, YOU!
DASH
WAIT!
THAT BLACK THING'S AMAZING! HE HUNTS?
HEY?
AND WHAT WAS CHI DOING AGAIN?
THAT WAS CLOSE.
OF ALL THINGS, THE BEAR CAT SAVED THE DAY.
GOTCHA!

the end

homemade 37: a cat is defiant

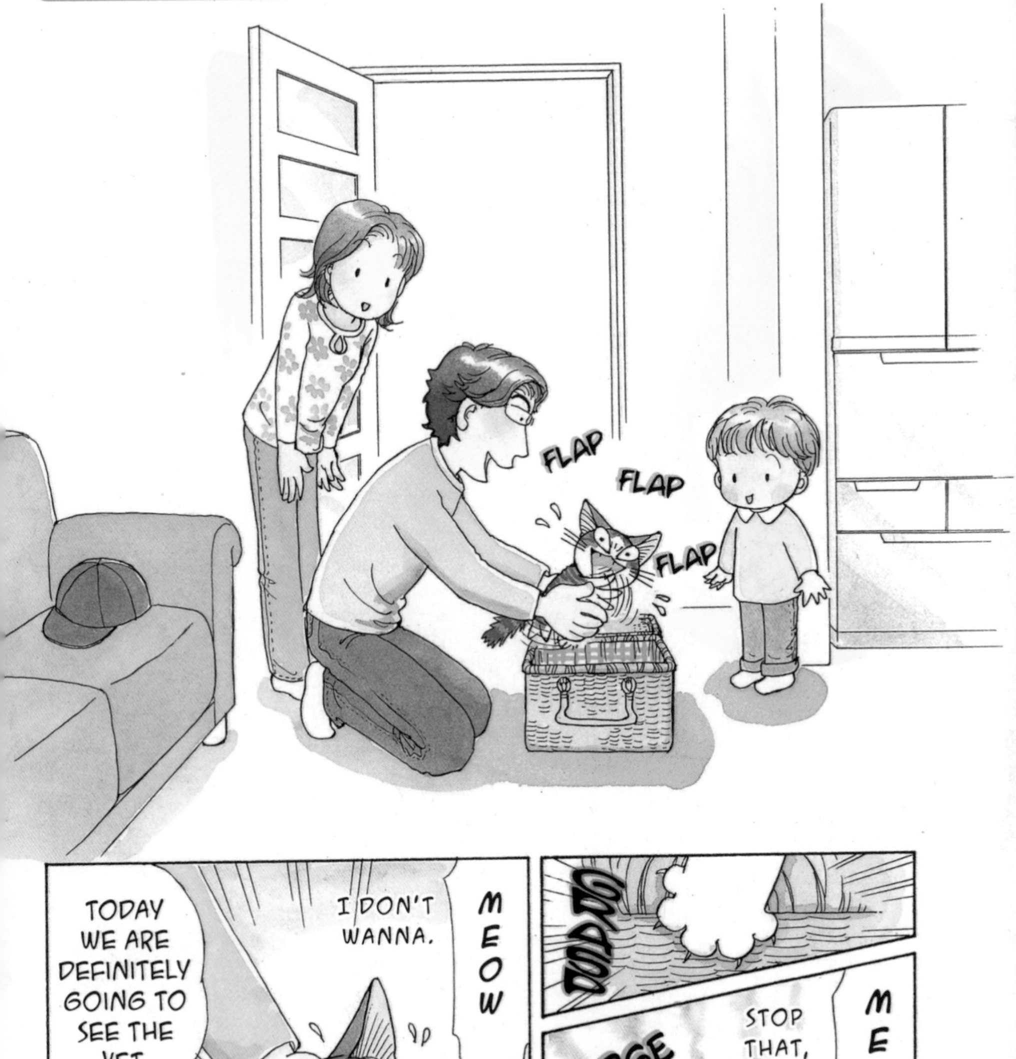
FLAP
FLAP
FLAP

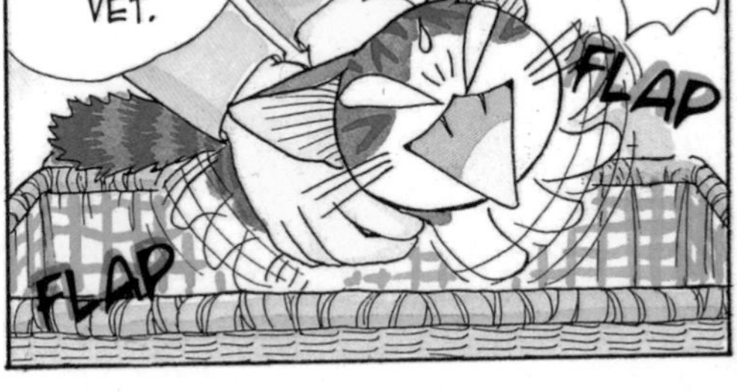
TODAY WE ARE DEFINITELY GOING TO SEE THE VET.
I DON'T WANNA.
MEOW
FLAP
FLAP

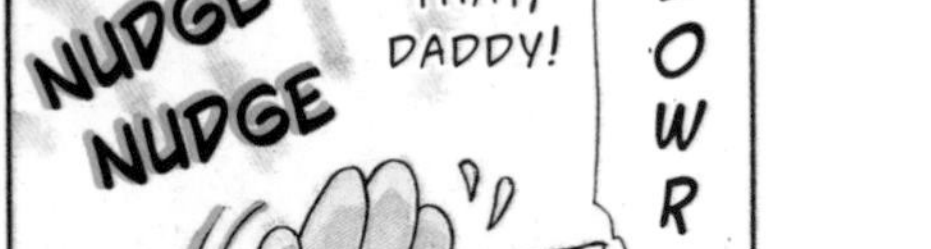

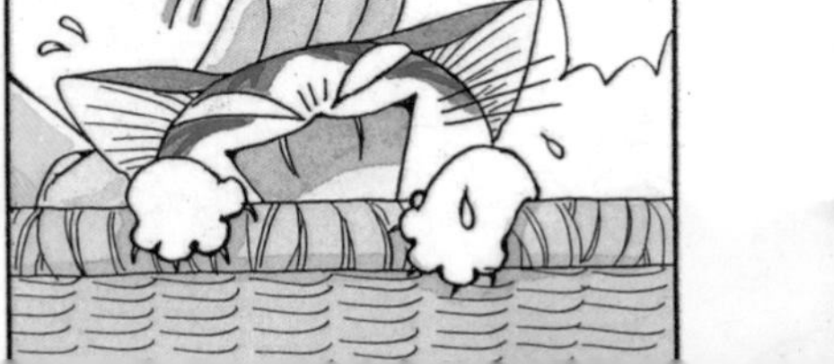
STOP THAT, DADDY!
MEOWR
NUDGE NUDGE

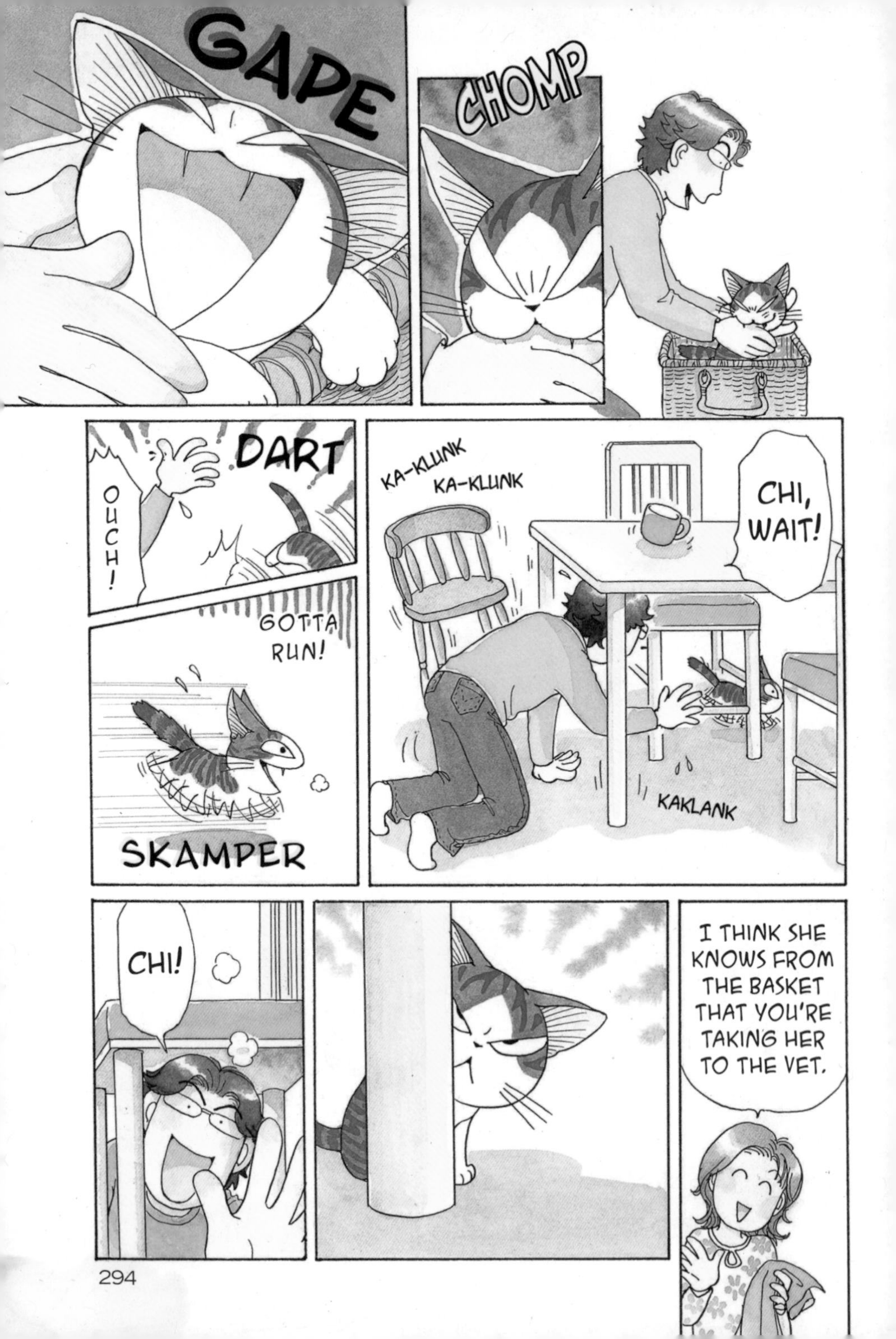
GAPE
CHOMP
OUCH!
DART
GOTTA RUN!
SKAMPER
KA-KLUNK
KA-KLUNK
CHI, WAIT!
KAKLANK
CHI!
I THINK SHE KNOWS FROM THE BASKET THAT YOU'RE TAKING HER TO THE VET.

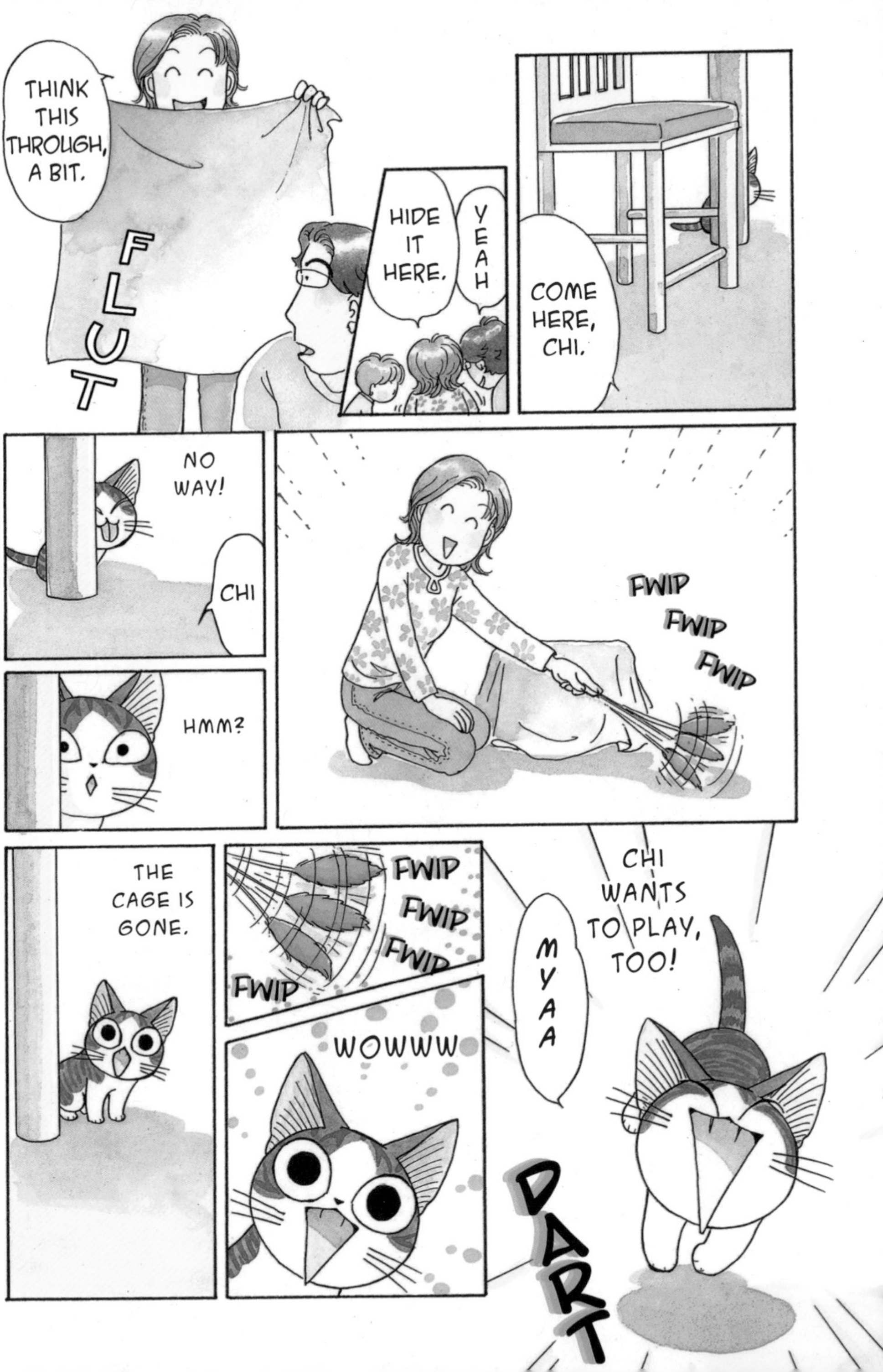
THINK THIS THROUGH, A BIT.
FLUT
HIDE IT HERE.
YEAH
COME HERE, CHI.
NO WAY!
CHI
HMM?
FWIP
FWIP
FWIP
THE CAGE IS GONE.
FWIP
FWIP
FWIP
FWIP
WOWWW
MYAA
CHI WANTS TO PLAY, TOO!
DART

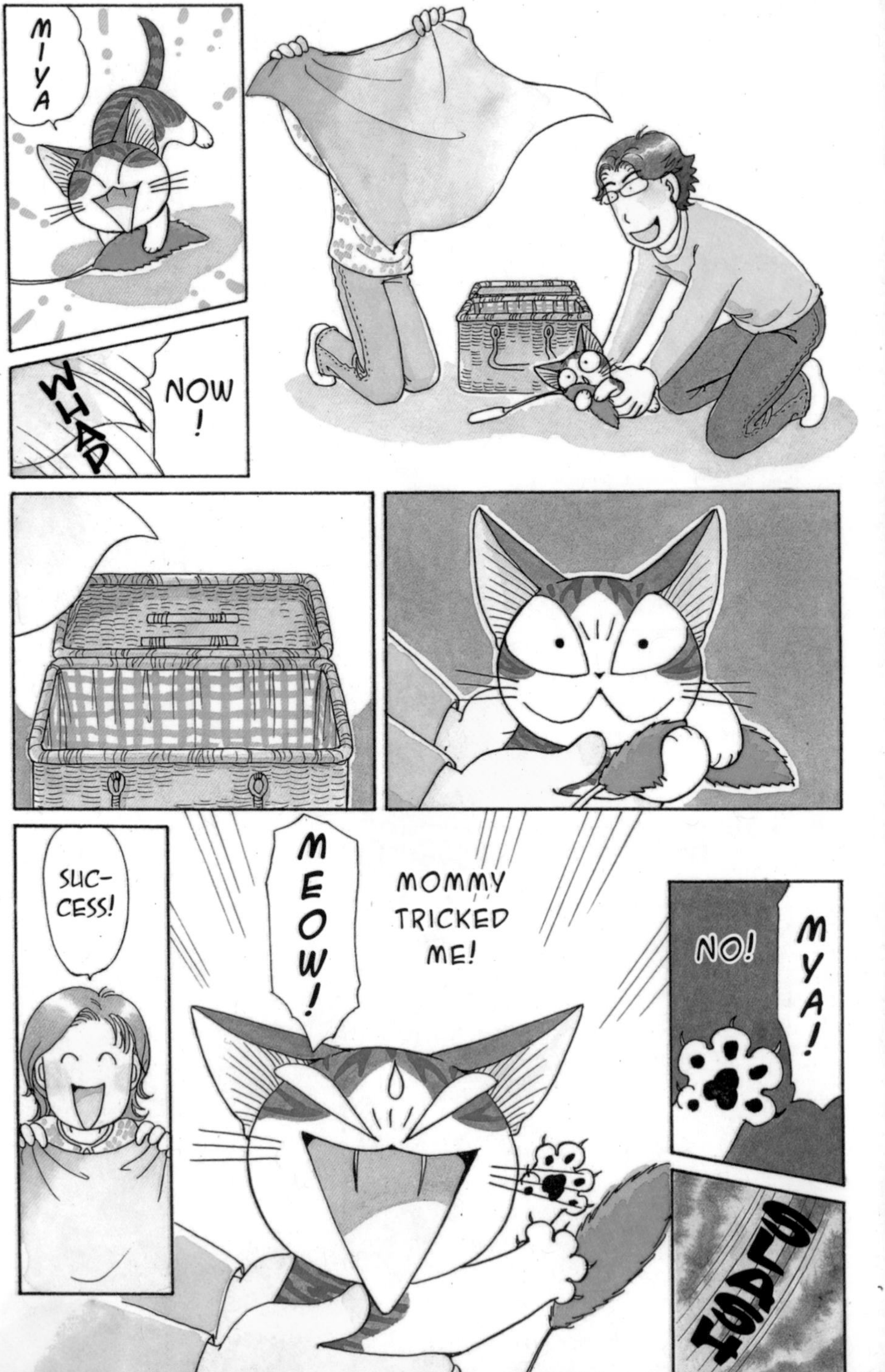
MIYA
NOW!
WHAP
MYA!
NO!
MEOW!
MOMMY TRICKED ME!
SUC-CESS!

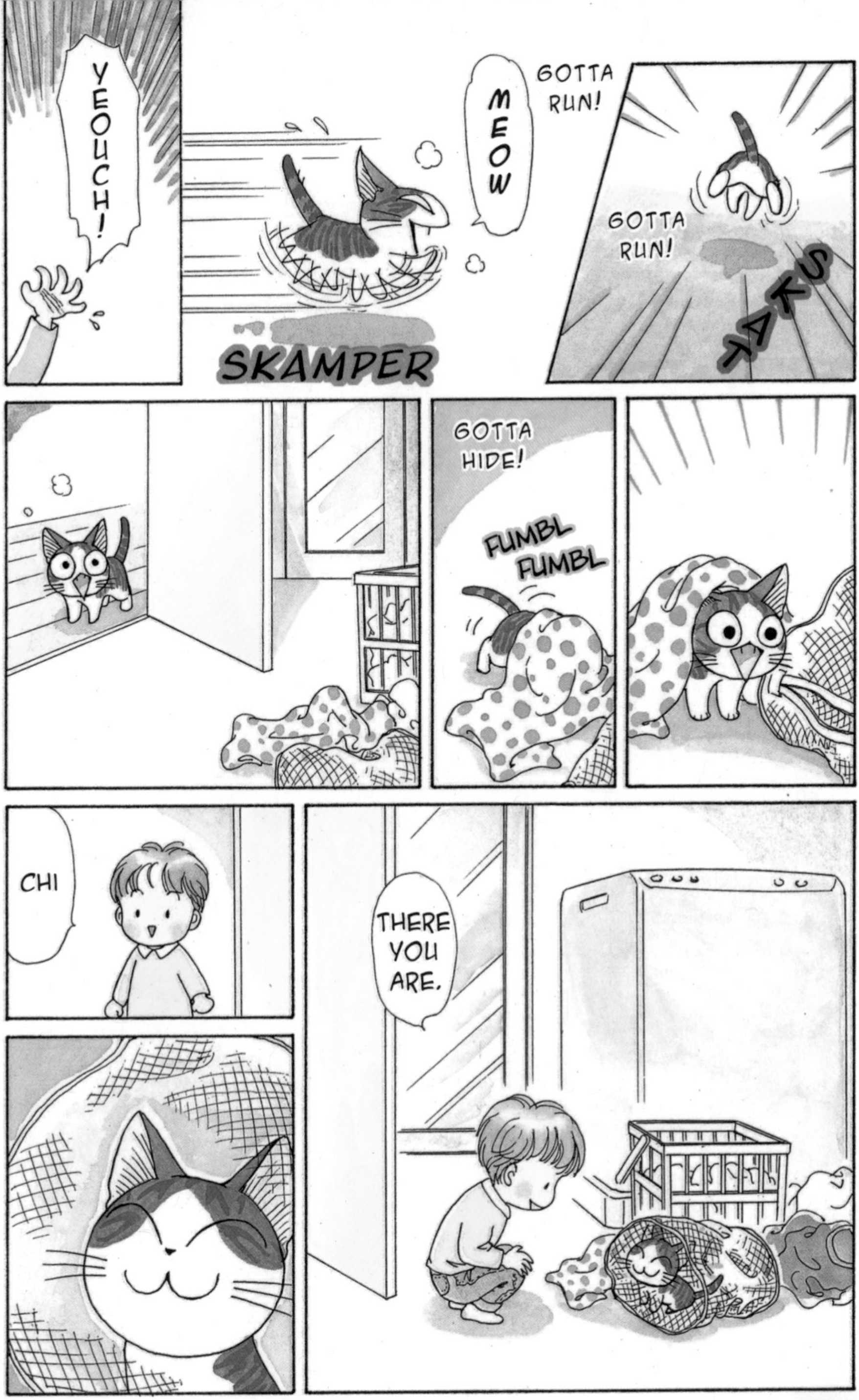

YEOUCH!
MEOW
SKAMPER
GOTTA RUN!
GOTTA RUN!
TAKS
GOTTA HIDE!
FUMBL FUMBL
CHI
THERE YOU ARE.

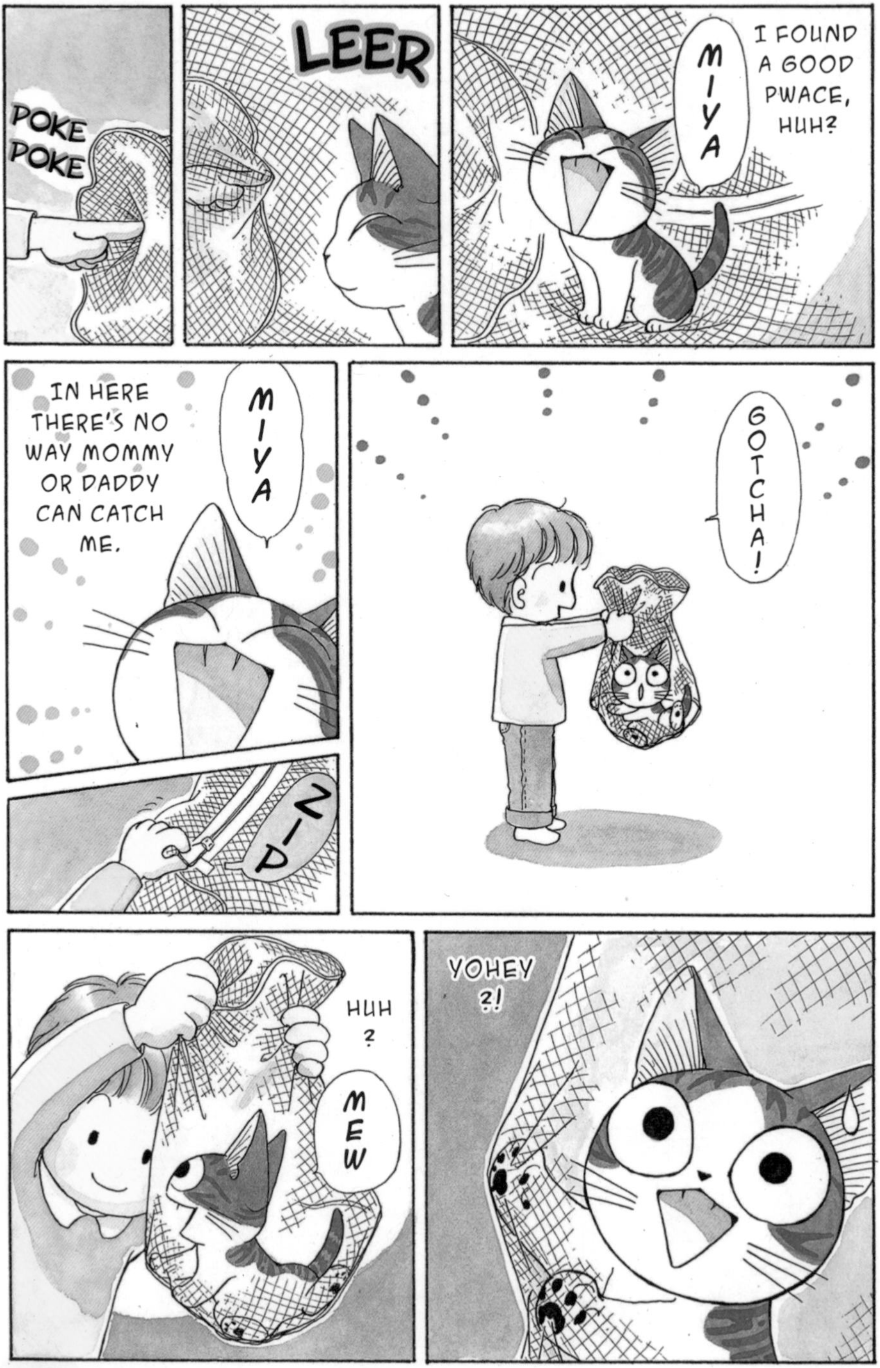
POKE POKE
LEER
MIYA
I FOUND A GOOD PWACE, HUH?
IN HERE THERE'S NO WAY MOMMY OR DADDY CAN CATCH ME.
MIYA
ZIP
GOTCHA!
HUH?
MEW
YOHEY?!

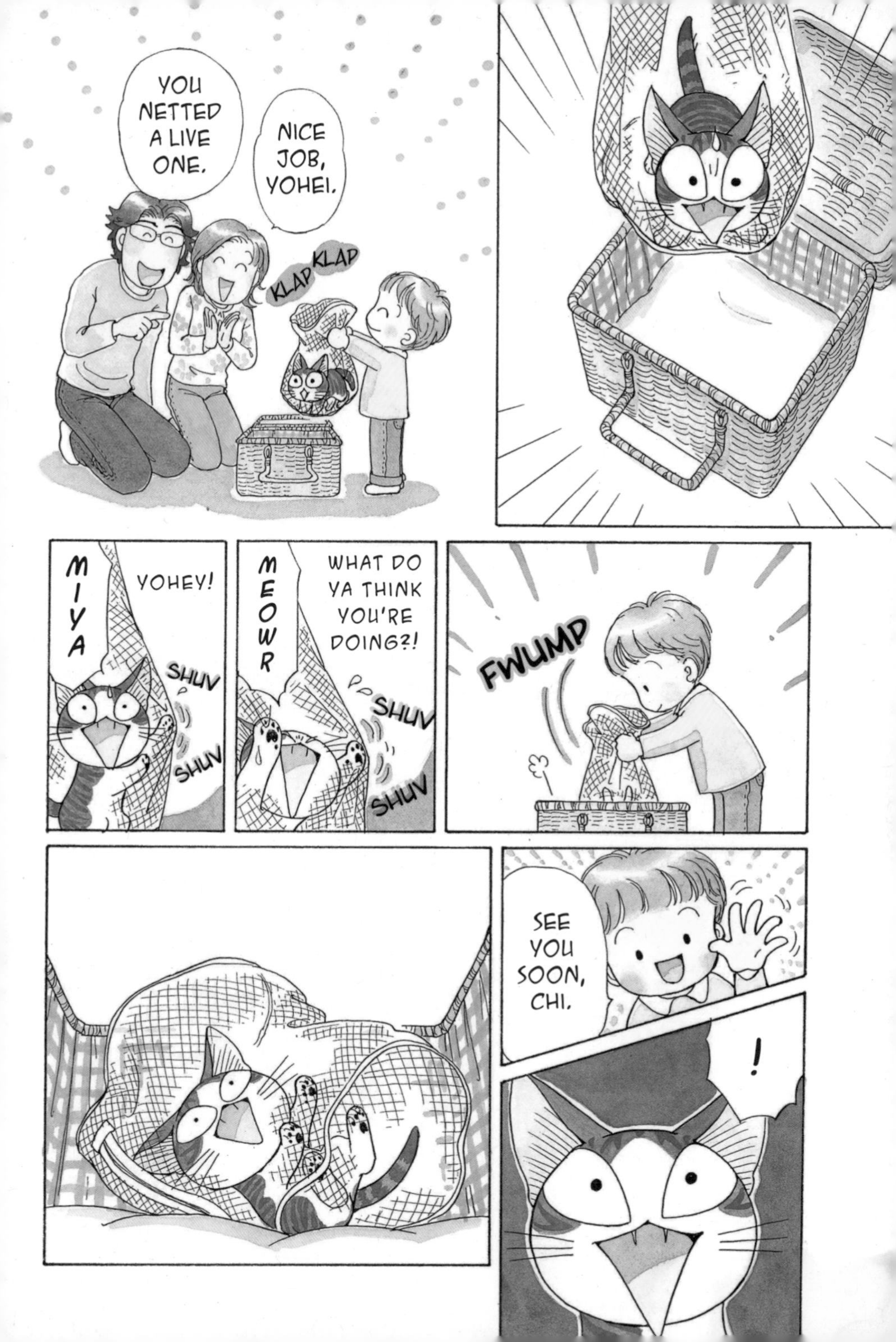
YOU NETTED A LIVE ONE.
NICE JOB, YOHEI.
KLAP KLAP
MIYA
YOHEY!
SHUV
SHUV
MEOWR
WHAT DO YA THINK YOU'RE DOING?!
SHUV
SHUV
FWUMP
SEE YOU SOON, CHI.
!

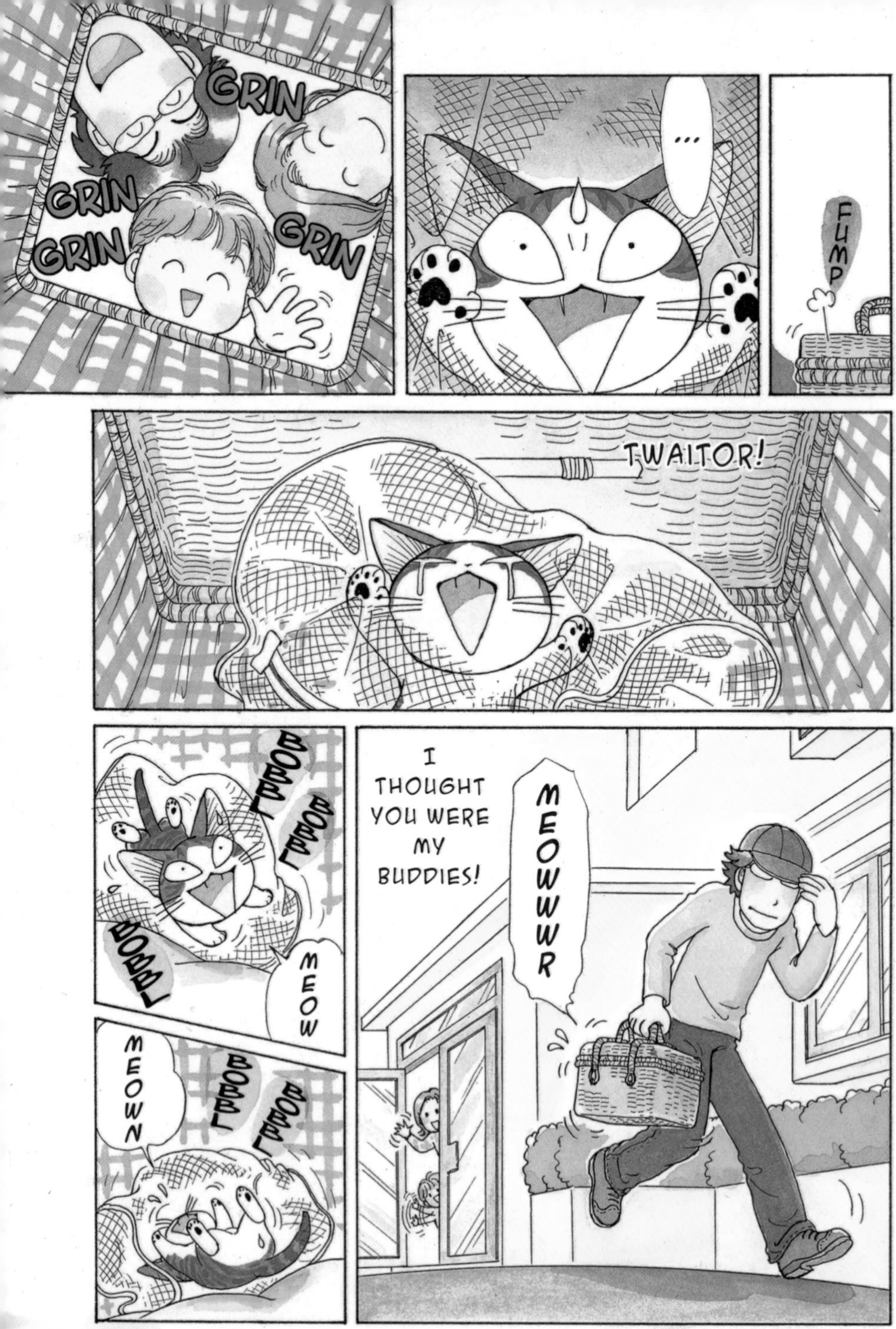
GRIN
GRIN
GRIN
GRIN
...
FUMP
TWAITOR!
BOBBL
BOBBL
BOBBL
MEOW
MEOWN
BOBBL
BOBBL
I THOUGHT YOU WERE MY BUDDIES!
MEOWWWWR

the end

homemade 38: a cat sulks

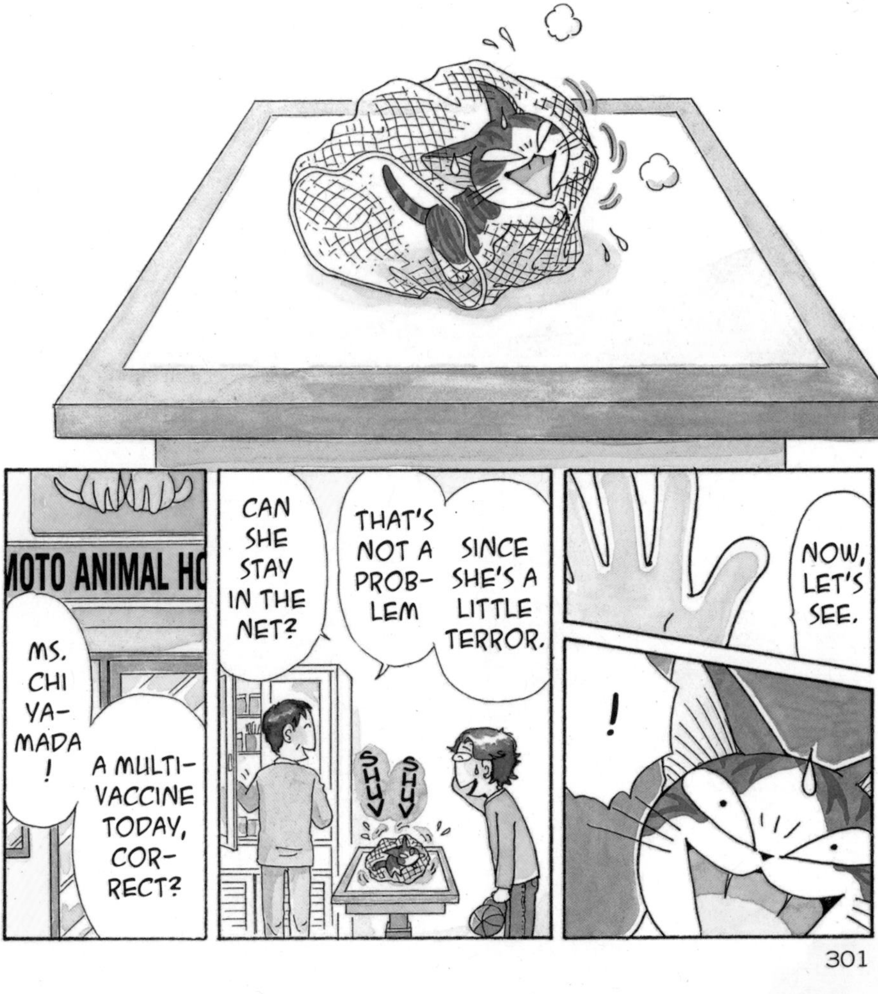

MOTO ANIMAL HO
MS. CHI YA-MADA!
A MULTI-VACCINE TODAY, COR-RECT?
CAN SHE STAY IN THE NET?
THAT'S NOT A PROB-LEM
SINCE SHE'S A LITTLE TERROR.
SHUV SHUV
NOW, LET'S SEE.
!

GWA

GAK

FSSSK

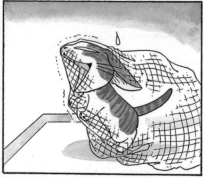

PINCH

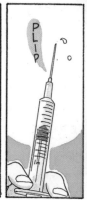

PLIP

?!

WHAT'S GOWING ON!

MREOW

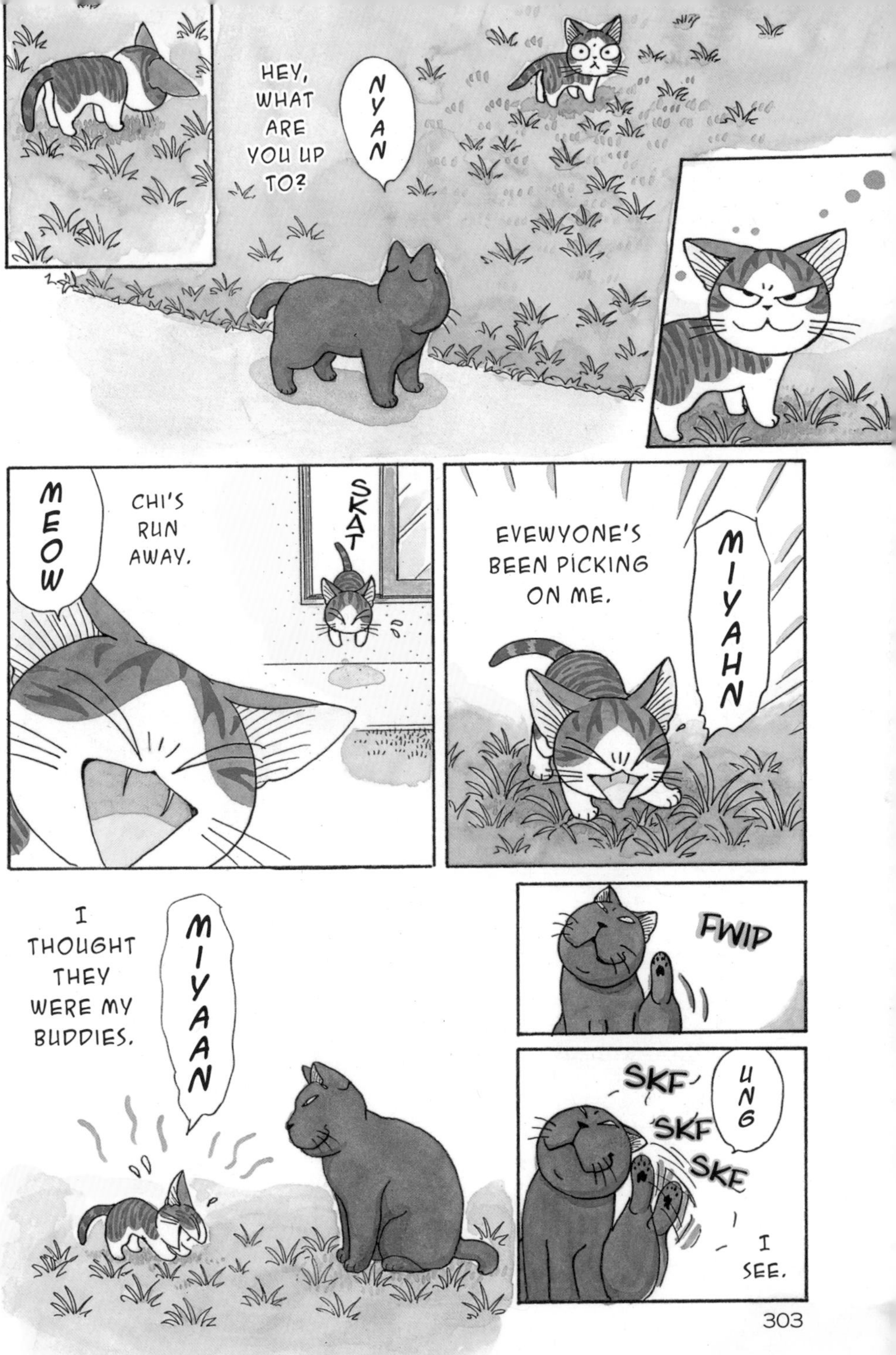
HEY, WHAT ARE YOU UP TO?
NYAN
MEOW
CHI'S RUN AWAY.
SKAT
EVEWYONE'S BEEN PICKING ON ME.
MIYAHN
I THOUGHT THEY WERE MY BUDDIES.
MIYAAN
FWIP
SKF
SKF
SKE
UNG
I SEE.

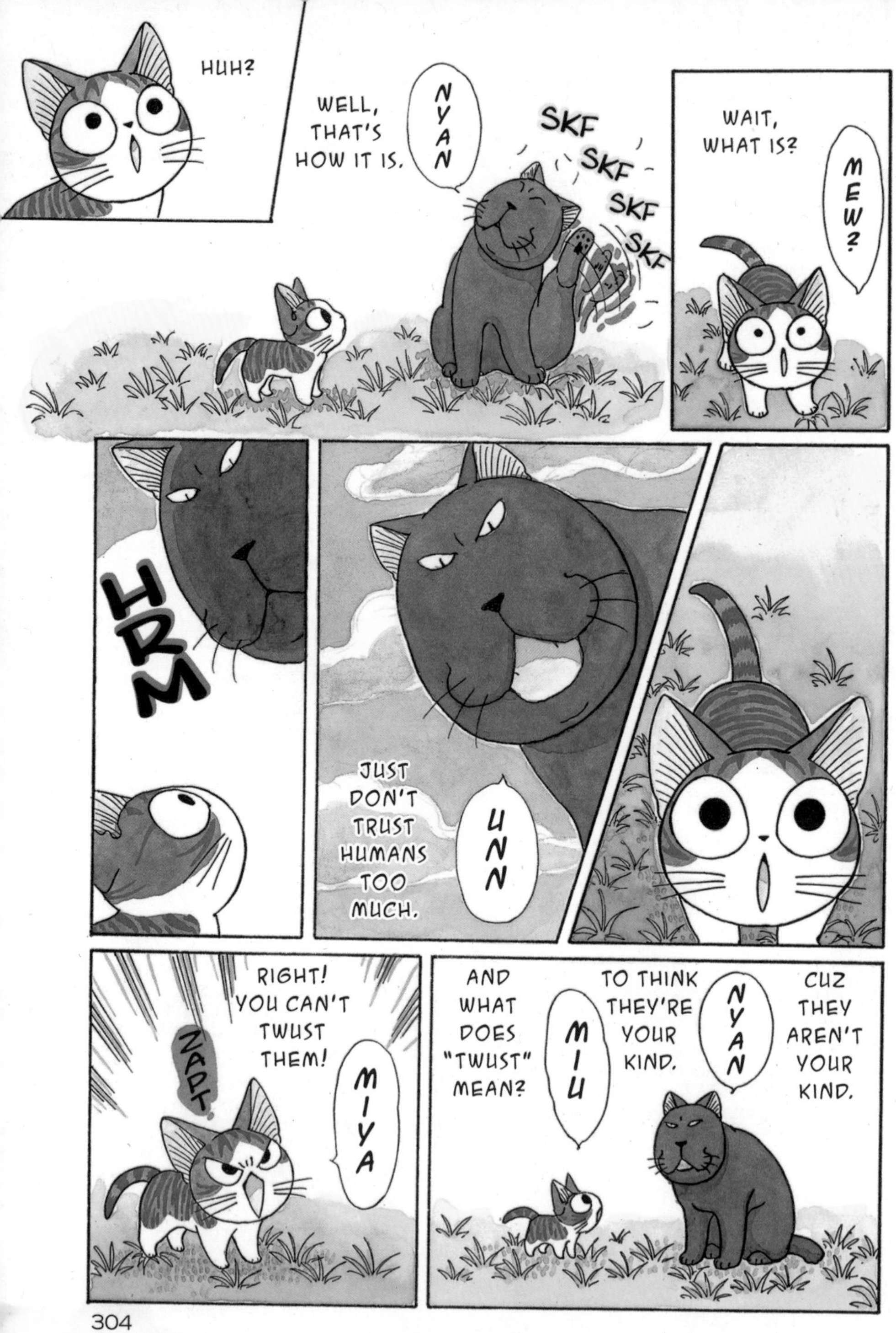
HUH?
WELL, THAT'S HOW IT IS.
NYAN
SKF
SKF
SKF
SKF
WAIT, WHAT IS?
MEW?
HRM
JUST DON'T TRUST HUMANS TOO MUCH.
UNN
RIGHT! YOU CAN'T TWUST THEM!
ZAPT
MIYA
AND WHAT DOES "TWUST" MEAN?
MIU
TO THINK THEY'RE YOUR KIND.
NYAN
CUZ THEY AREN'T YOUR KIND.

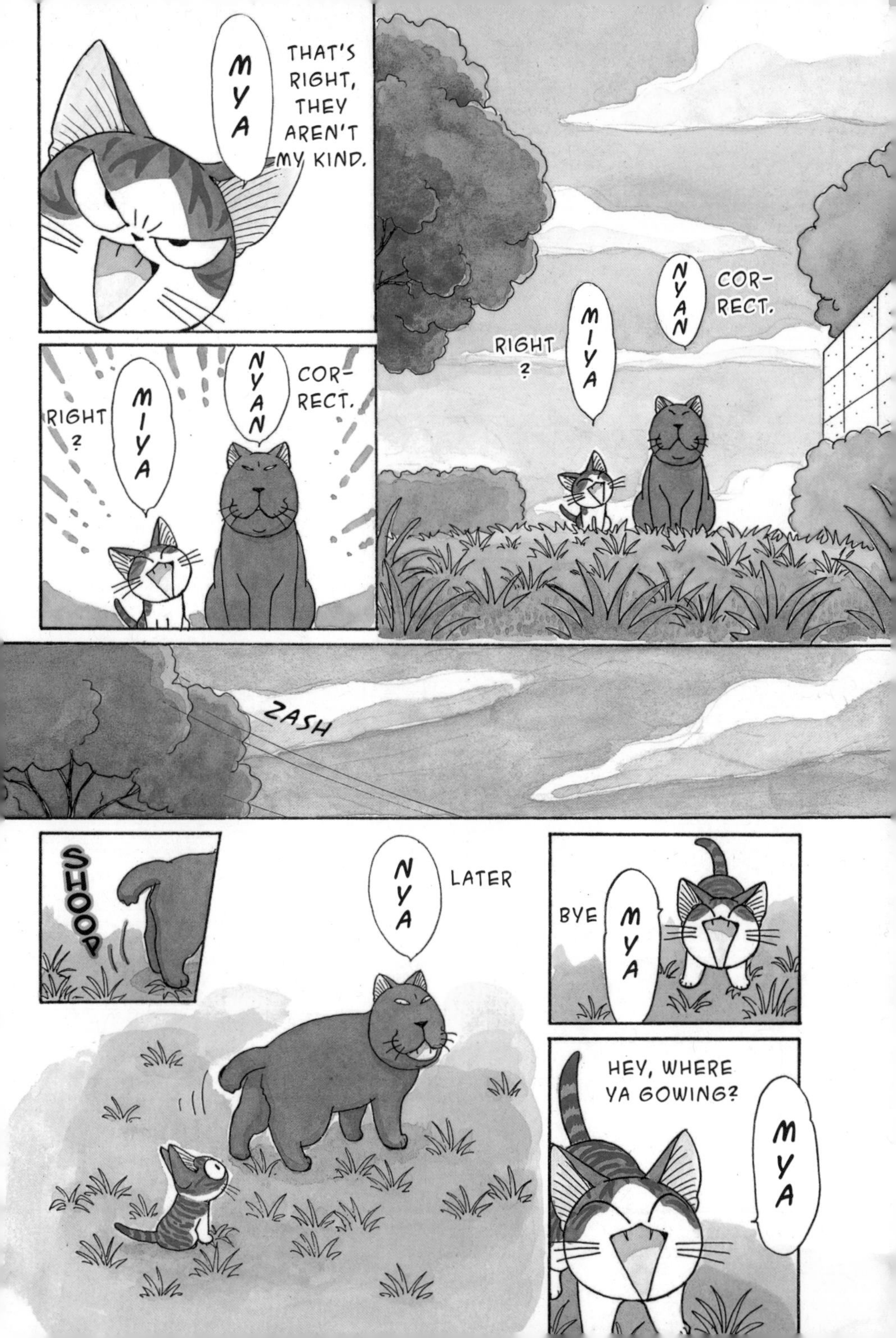
MYA
THAT'S RIGHT, THEY AREN'T MY KIND.
MIYA
RIGHT?
NYAN
CORRECT.
MIYA
RIGHT?
NYAN
CORRECT.
ZASH
SHOOP
NYA
LATER
MYA
BYE
HEY, WHERE YA GOWING?
MYA

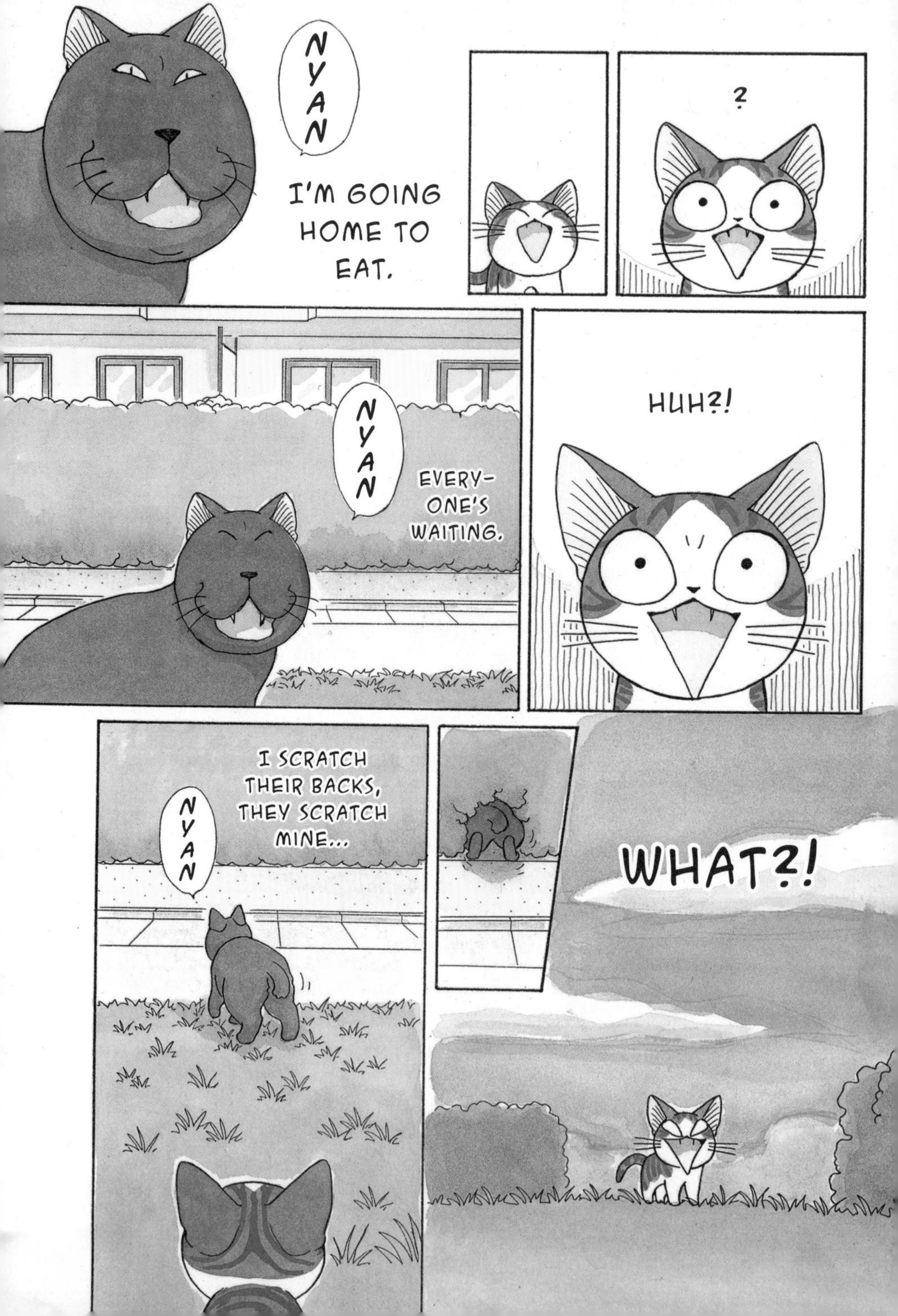
NYAN
I'M GOING HOME TO EAT.
?
NYAN
EVERY-ONE'S WAITING.
HUH?!
I SCRATCH THEIR BACKS, THEY SCRATCH MINE...
NYAN
WHAT?!

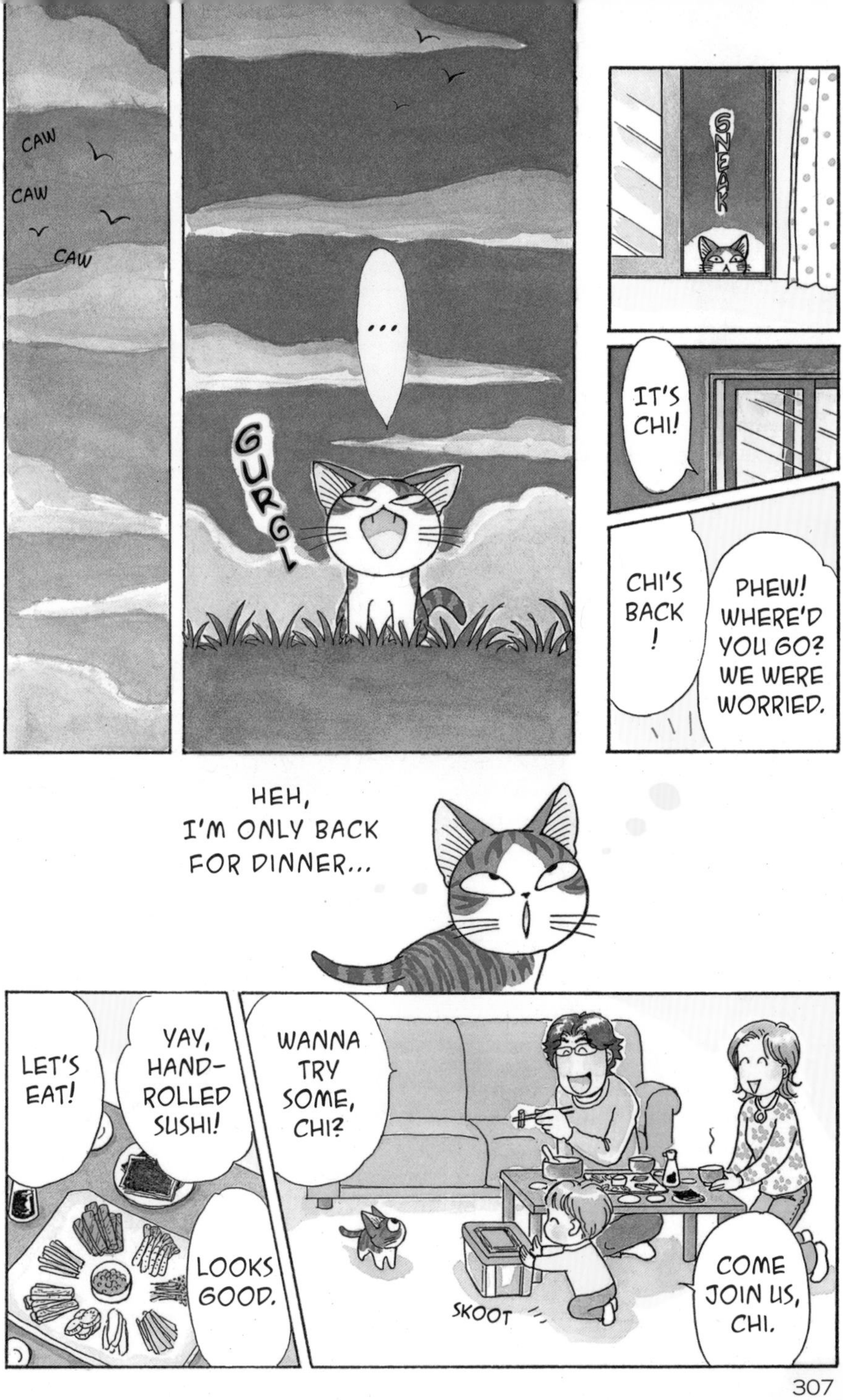
CAW
CAW
CAW
...
GURGL
SNEAK
IT'S CHI!
CHI'S BACK!
PHEW! WHERE'D YOU GO? WE WERE WORRIED.
HEH, I'M ONLY BACK FOR DINNER...
LET'S EAT!
YAY, HAND-ROLLED SUSHI!
LOOKS GOOD.
WANNA TRY SOME, CHI?
SKOOT
COME JOIN US, CHI.

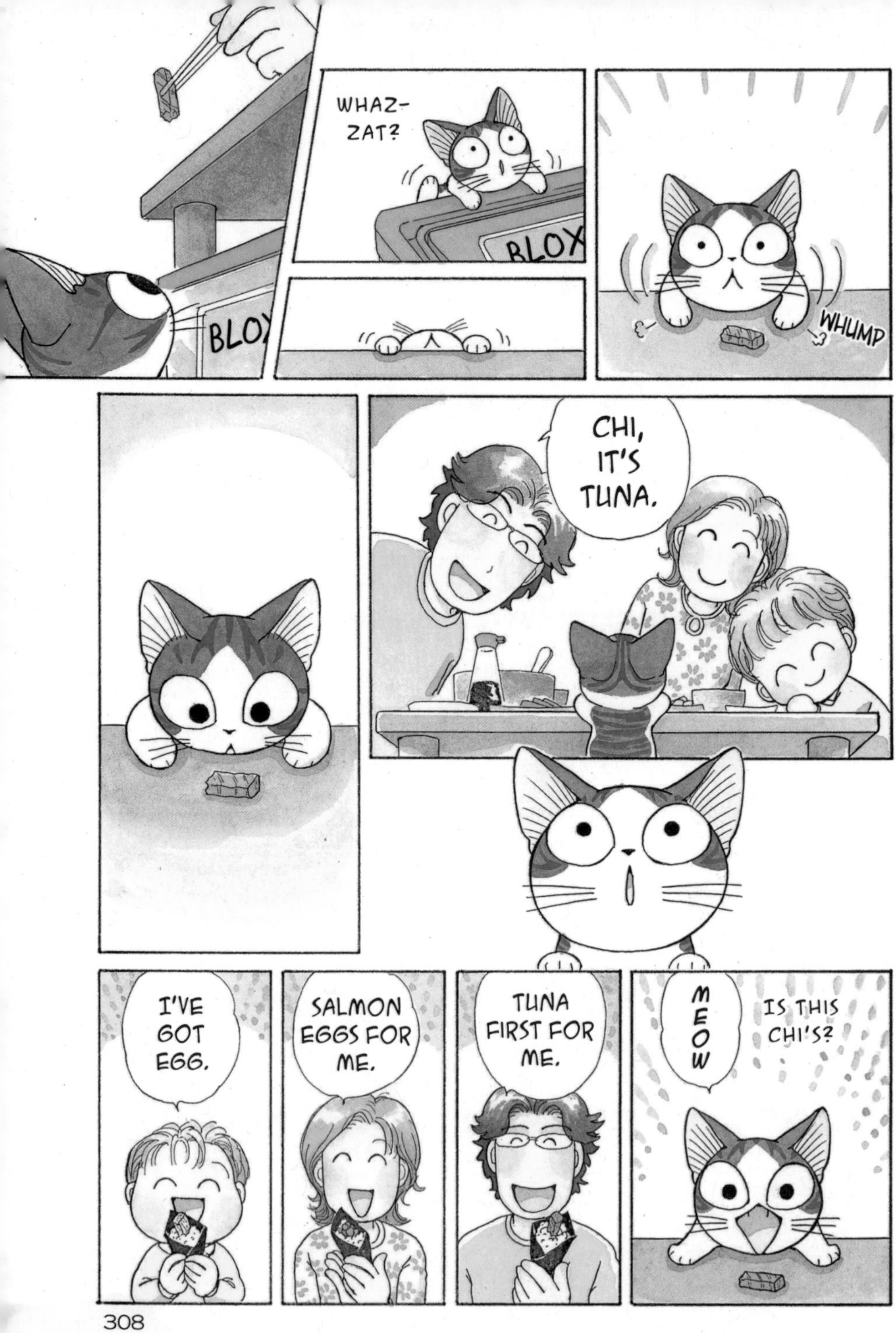
BLOX
WHAZ-ZAT?
BLOX
WHUMP
CHI, IT'S TUNA.
I'VE GOT EGG.
SALMON EGGS FOR ME.
TUNA FIRST FOR ME.
MEOW
IS THIS CHI'S?

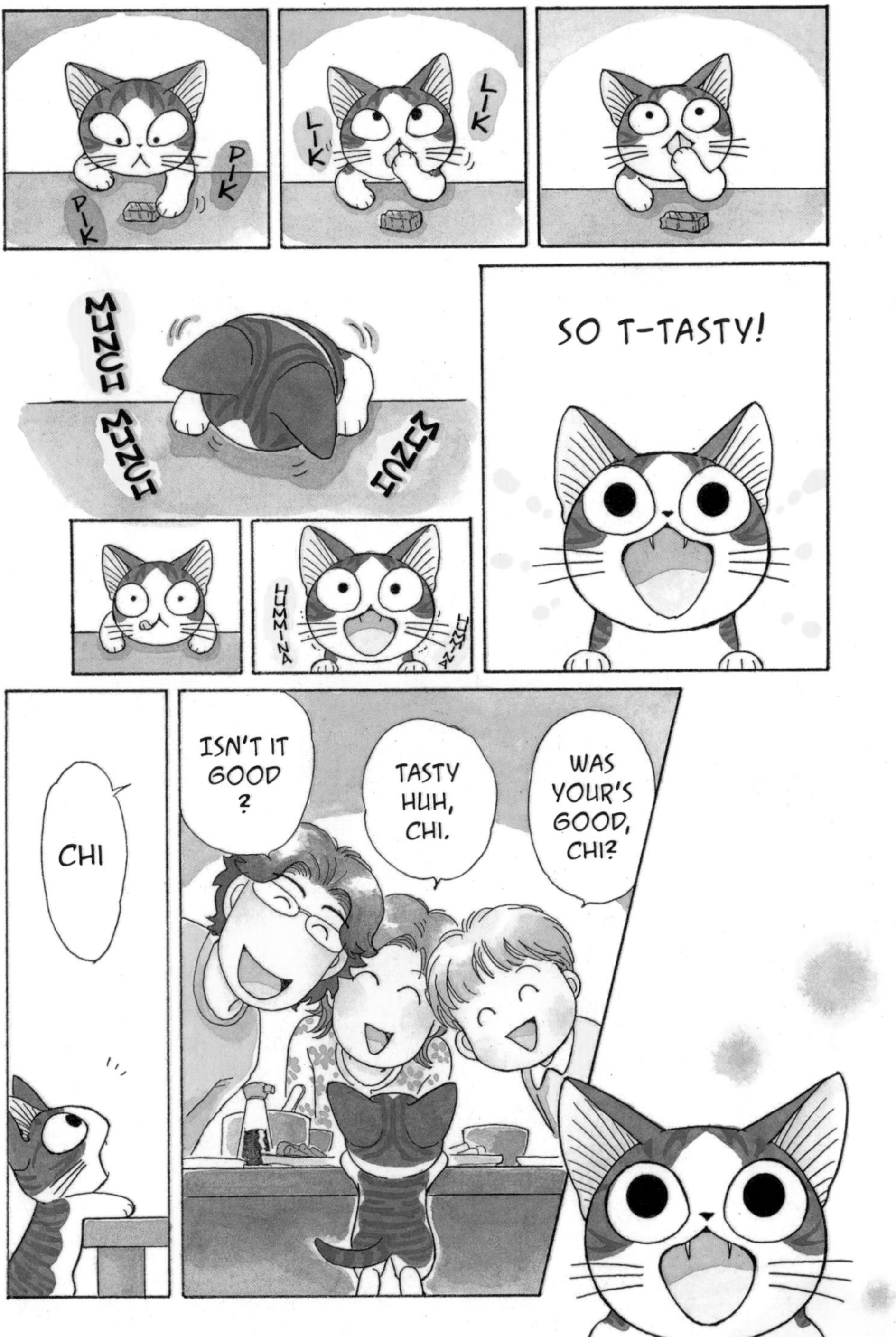
PIK
PIK
LIK
LIK
MUNCH
MUNCH
MUNCH
HUMMINA
HUMMINA
SO T-TASTY!
CHI
ISN'T IT GOOD?
TASTY HUH, CHI.
WAS YOUR'S GOOD, CHI?

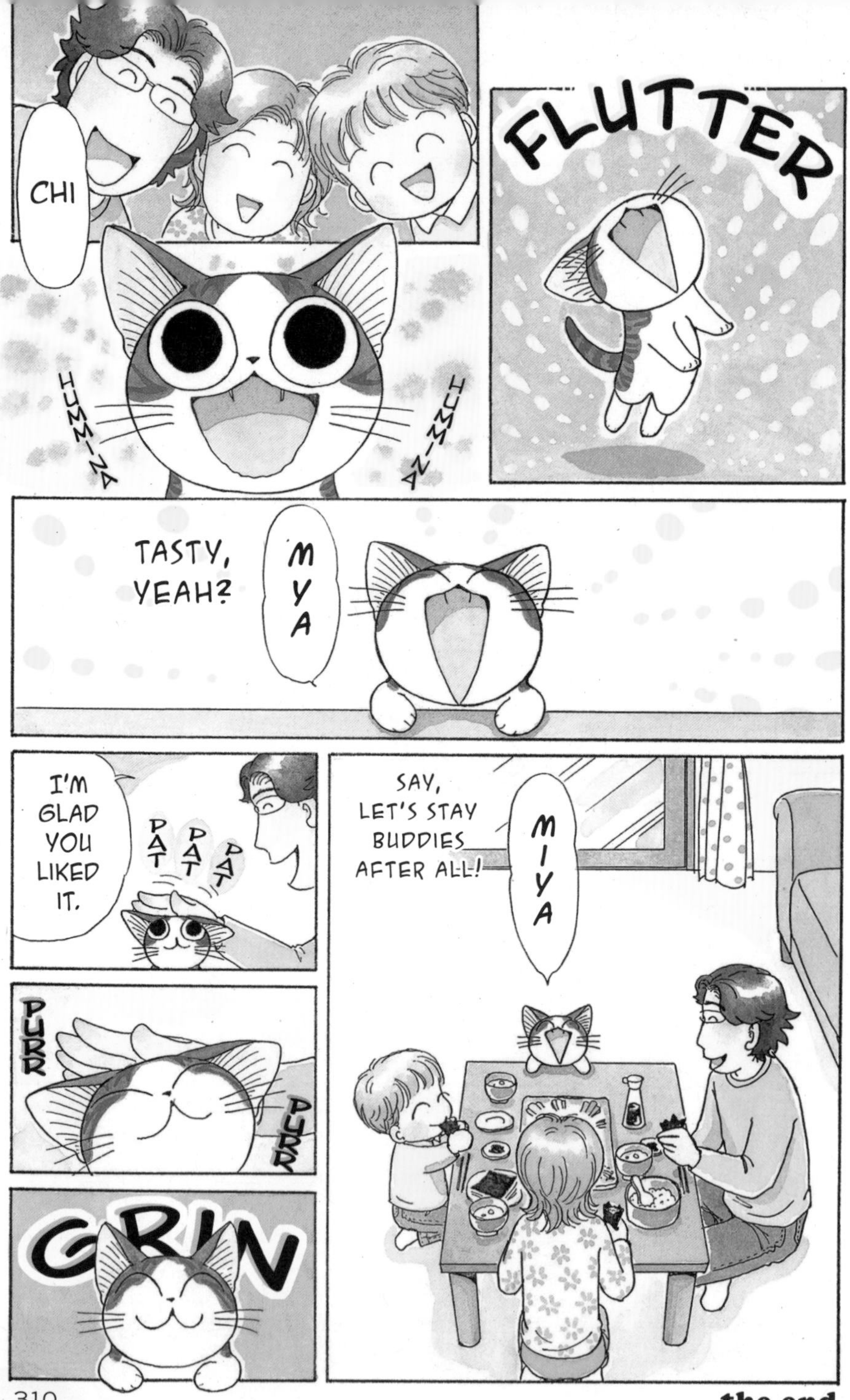
CHI
HUMM-INA
HUMM-INA
FLUTTER
TASTY, YEAH?
MYA
I'M GLAD YOU LIKED IT.
PAT PAT PAT
PURR
PURR
GRIN
SAY, LET'S STAY BUDDIES AFTER ALL!
MIYA

the end

homemade 39: a cat mimics

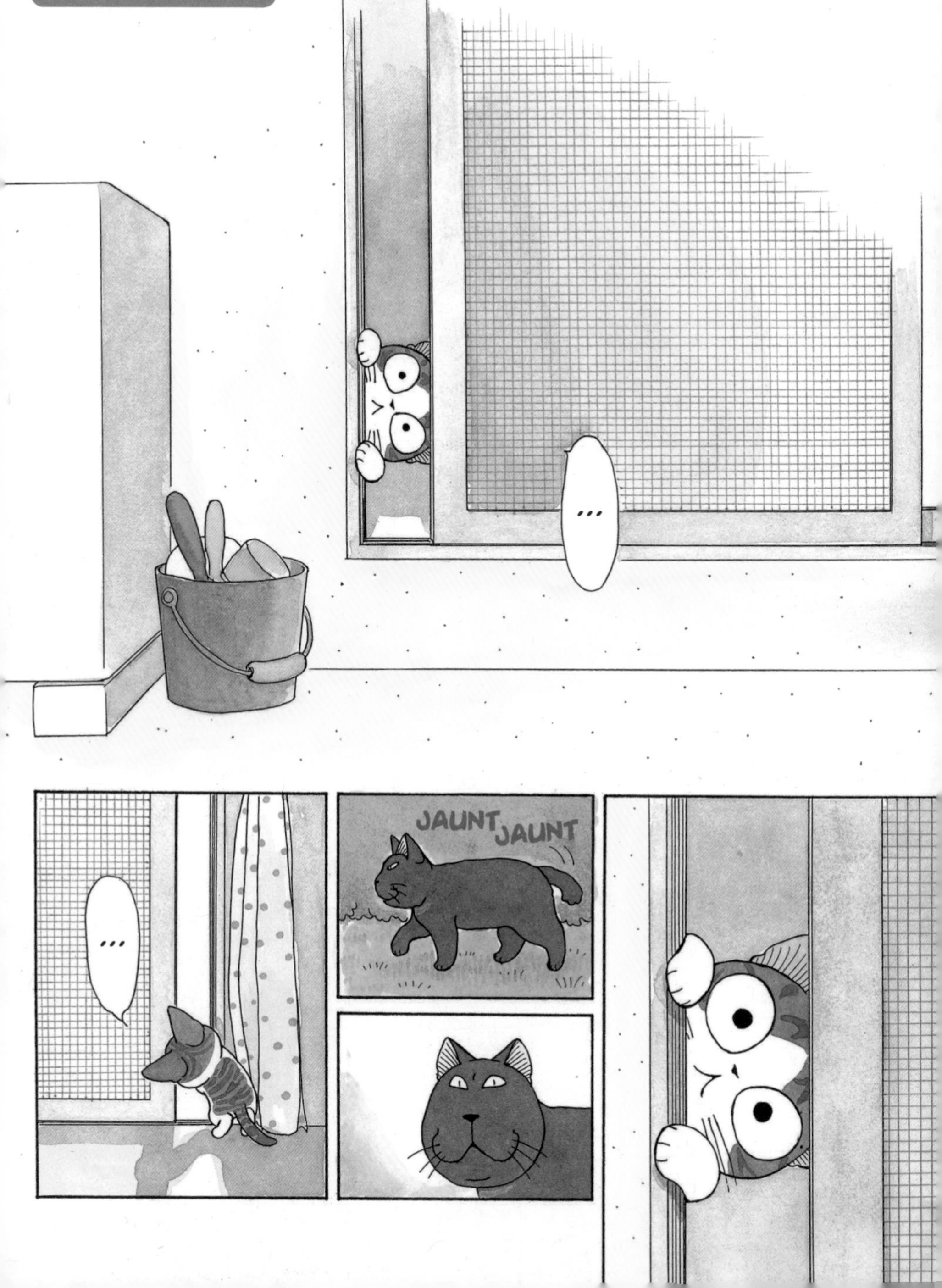
...
...
JAUNT JAUNT

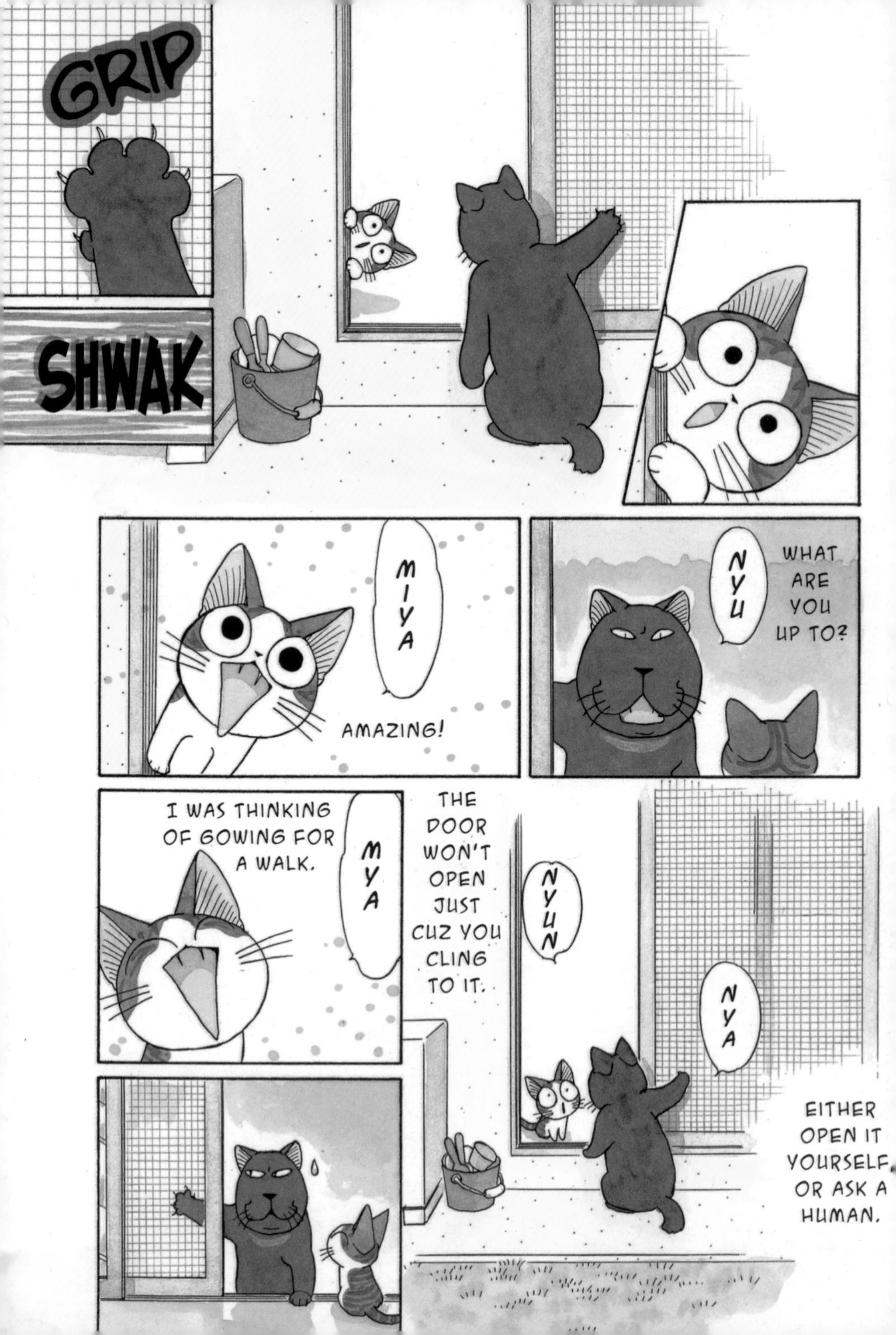
GRIP
SHWAK
MIYA
AMAZING!
NYU
WHAT ARE YOU UP TO?
I WAS THINKING OF GOWING FOR A WALK.
MYA
THE DOOR WON'T OPEN JUST CUZ YOU CLING TO IT.
NYUN
NYA
EITHER OPEN IT YOURSELF, OR ASK A HUMAN.

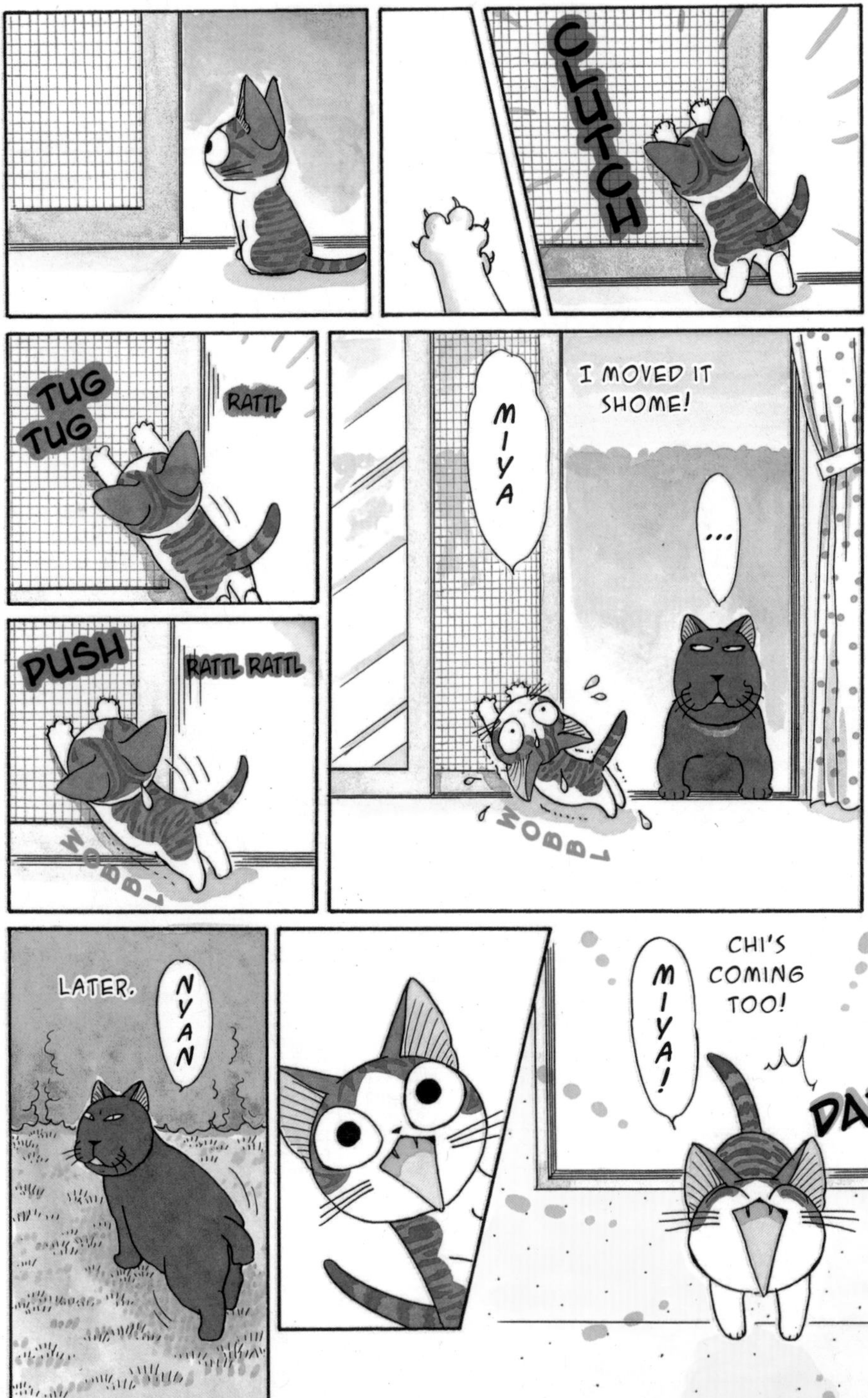
CLUTCH
TUG TUG
RATTL
PUSH
RATTL RATTL
WOBBL
MIYA
I MOVED IT SHOME!
...
WOBBL
LATER.
NYAN
MIYA!
CHI'S COMING TOO!
DART

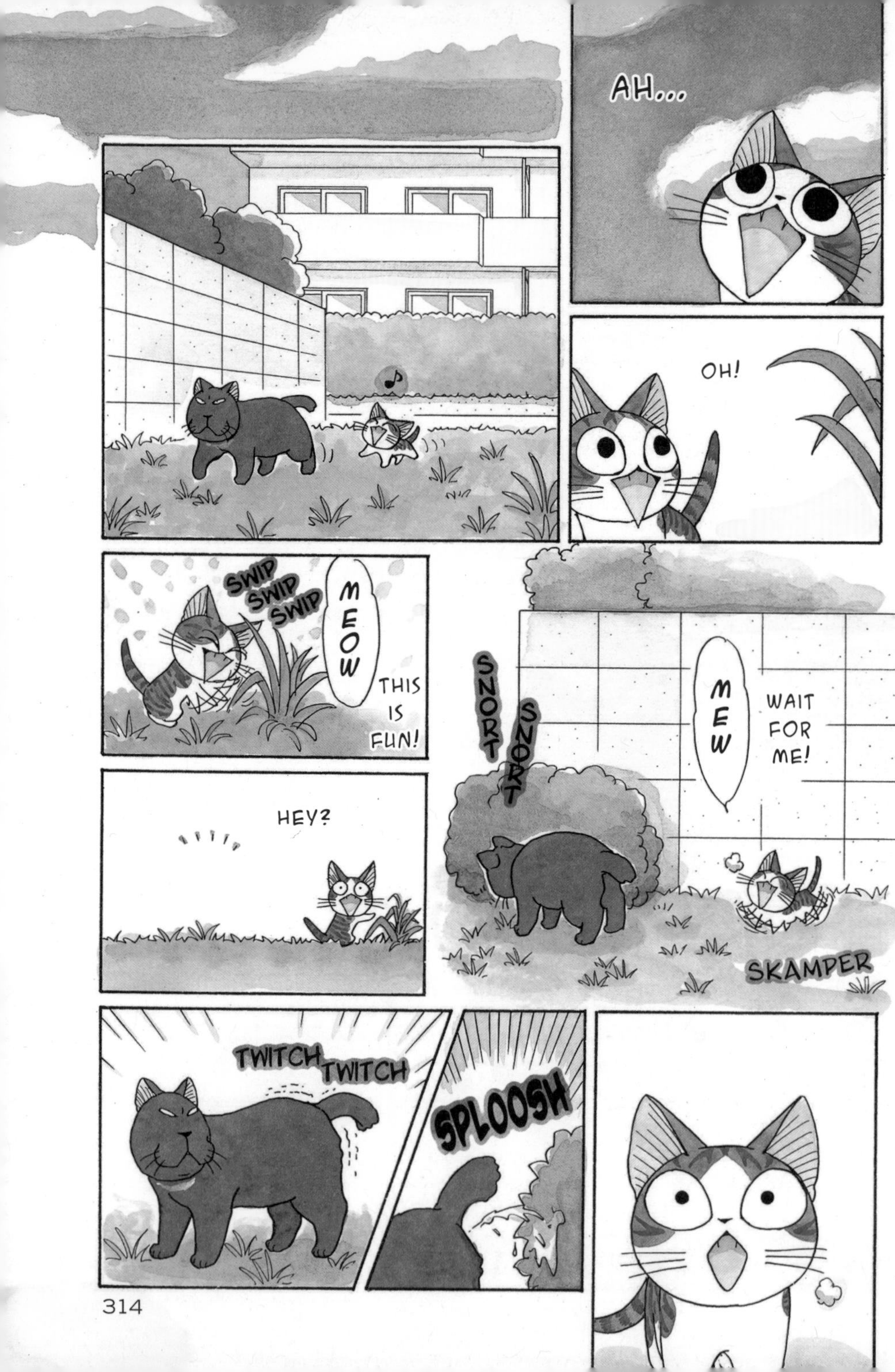
AH...
OH!
SWIP SWIP SWIP
MEOW
THIS IS FUN!
HEY?
SNORT SNORT
MEW
WAIT FOR ME!
SKAMPER
TWITCH TWITCH
SPLOOSH

HEY, WEE GOES IN THE SANDY BOX.

MEOW

MEOW

MOMMY'S GONNA BE MAD.

NGU

HOHO

THAT'S A MARK THAT MAKES THIS PLACE MINE.

MYA

I'M GONNA MAKE THIS MINE.

TWINGE

TWINGE

TWINGE

TWINGE

TWINGE

TWINGE

...

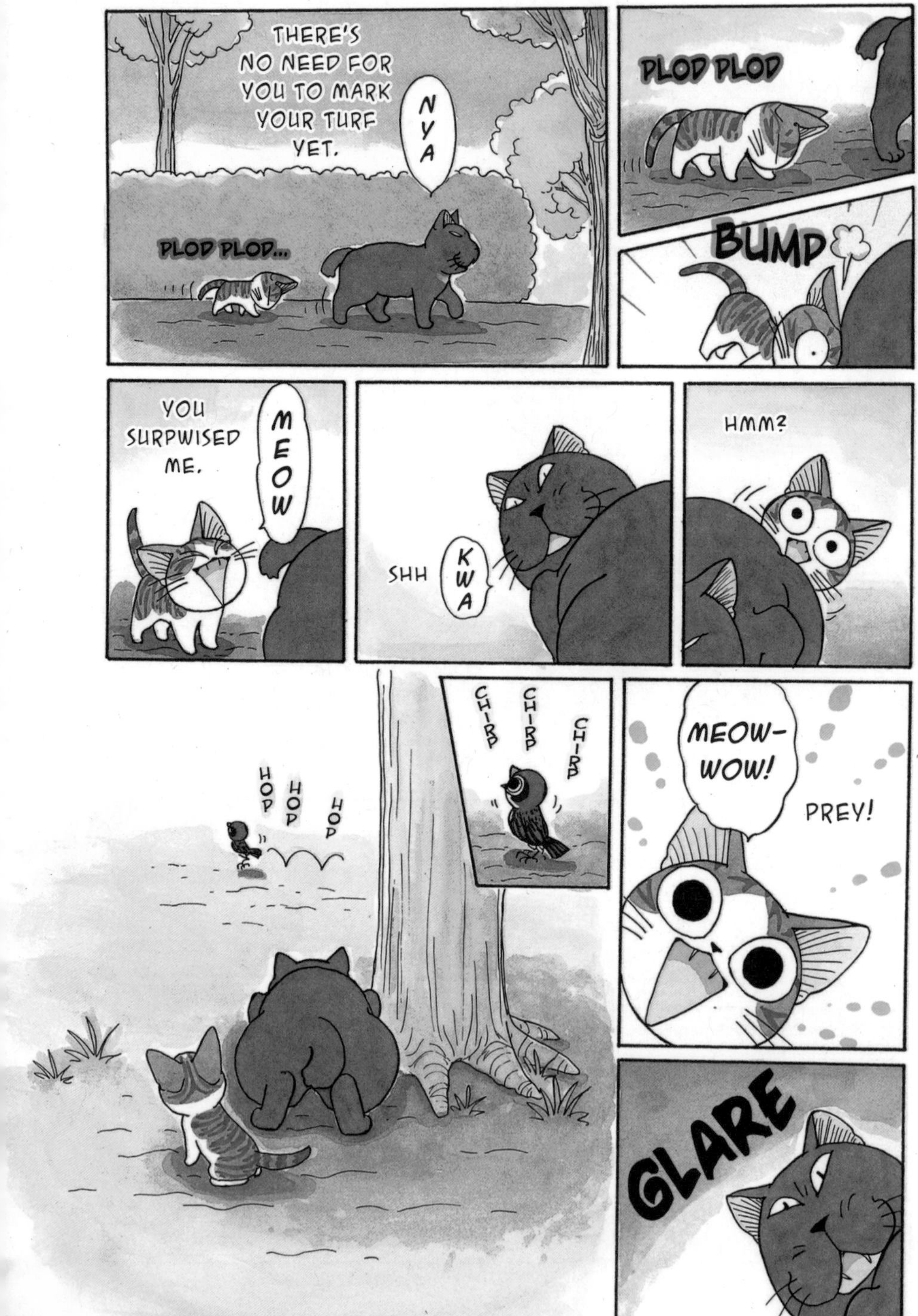
THERE'S NO NEED FOR YOU TO MARK YOUR TURF YET.
NYA
PLOD PLOD...
PLOD PLOD
BUMP
YOU SURPWISED ME.
MEOW
SHH
KWA
HMM?
HOP
HOP
HOP
CHIRP
CHIRP
CHIRP
MEOW-WOW!
PREY!
GLARE

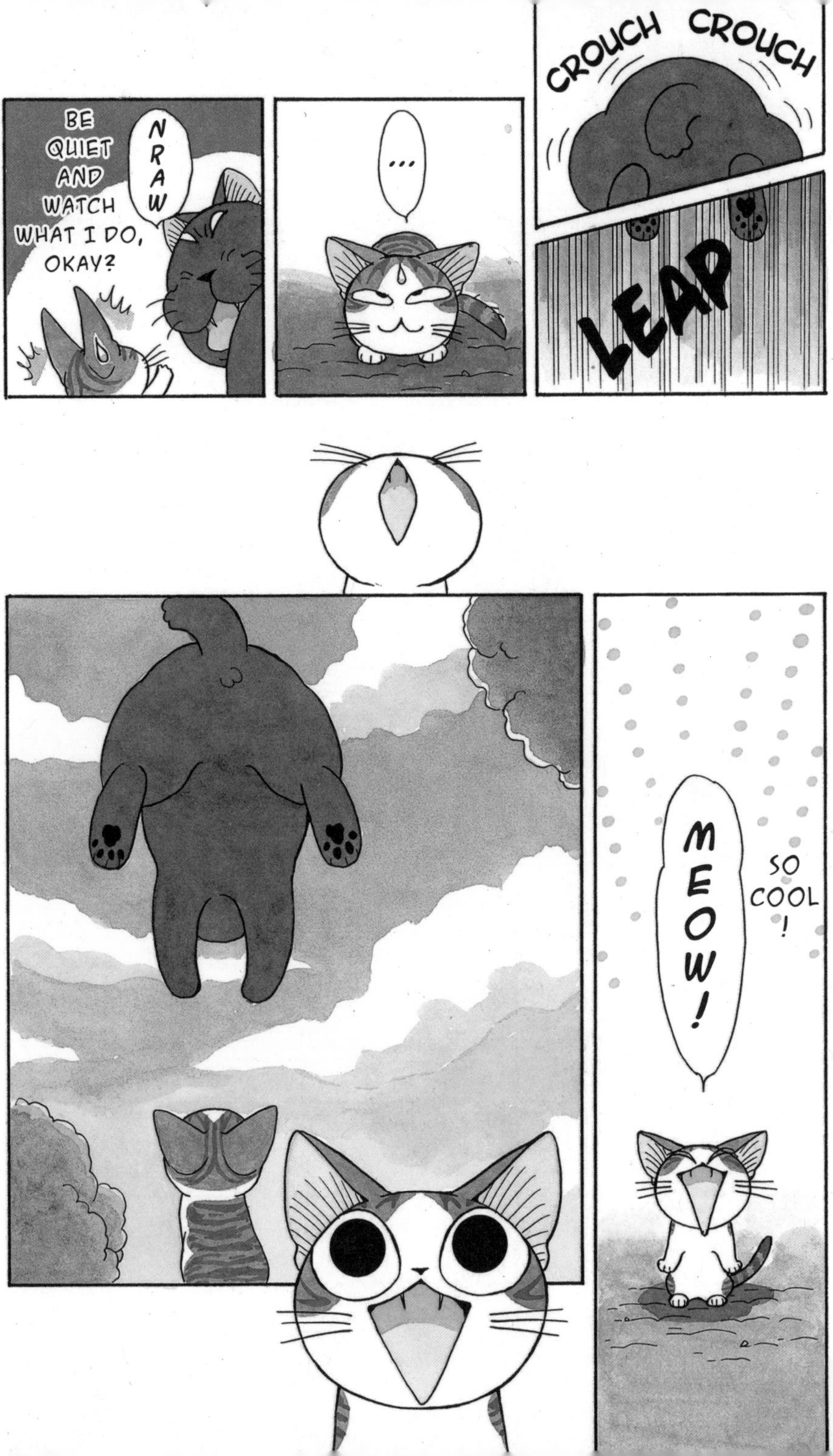
BE QUIET AND WATCH WHAT I DO, OKAY?
NRAW
...
CROUCH CROUCH
LEAP
MEOW!
SO COOL!

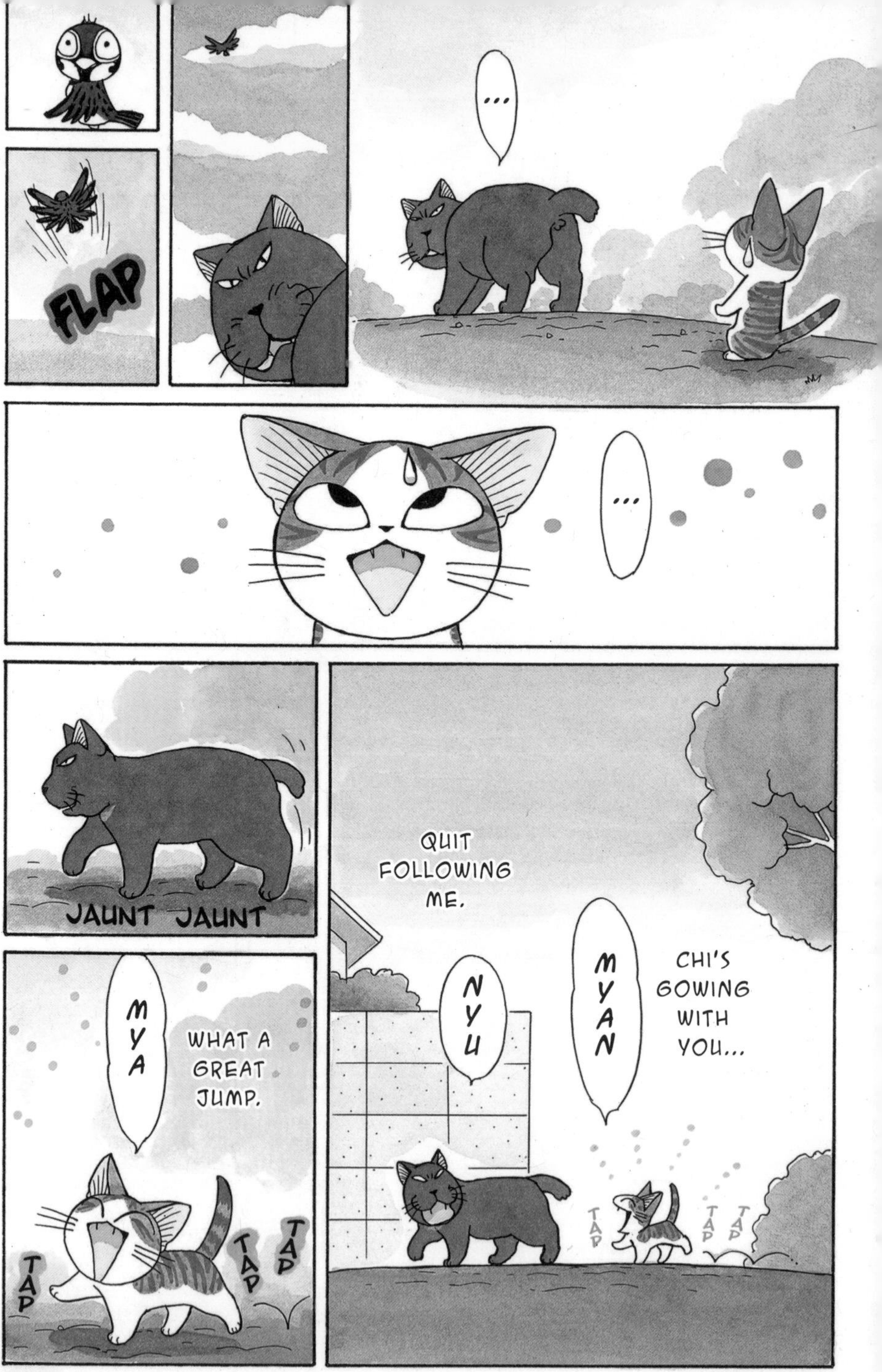
FLAP
...
...
JAUNT JAUNT
MYA
WHAT A GREAT JUMP.
TAP TAP TAP
QUIT FOLLOWING ME.
NYU
MYAN
CHI'S GOWING WITH YOU...
TAP TAP TAP

the end

homemade 40: a cat is photographed

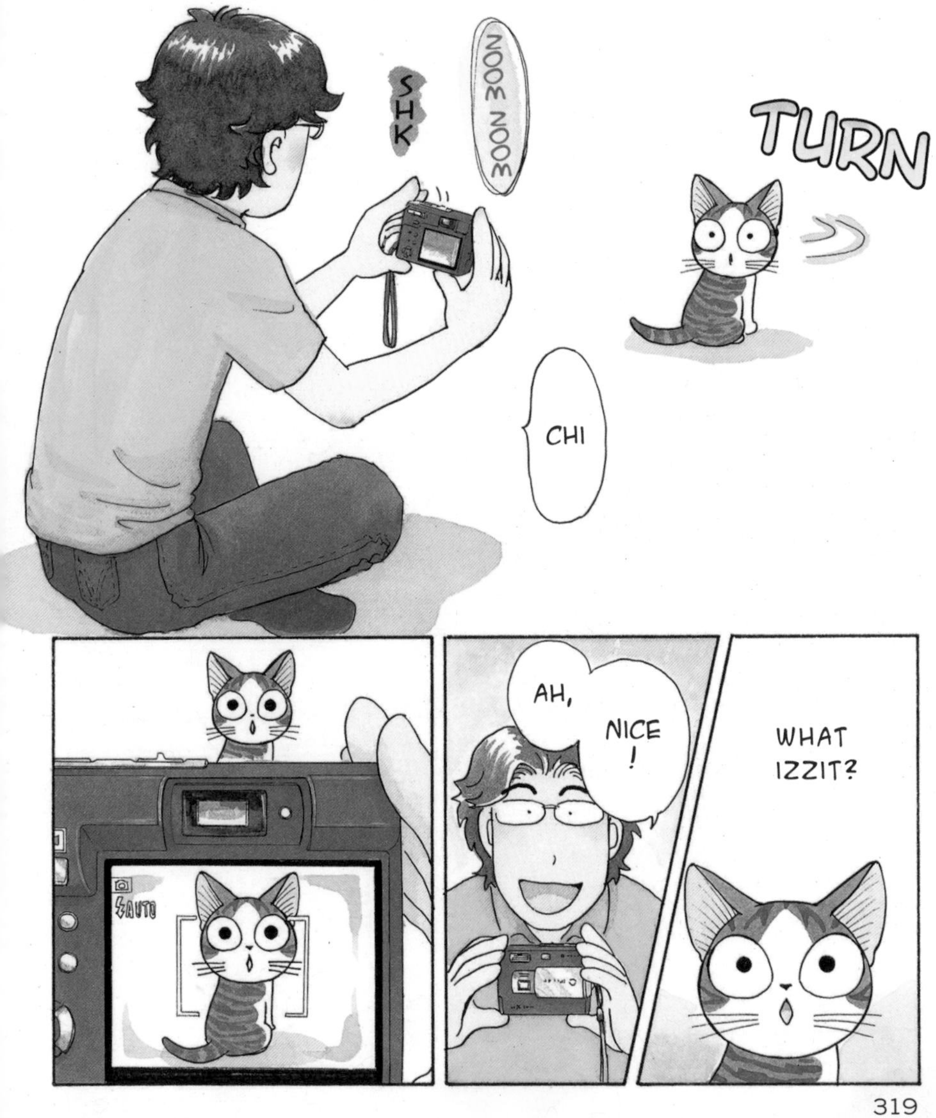
SHK
ZOOM ZOOM
TURN
CHI
AH,
NICE!
WHAT IZZIT?

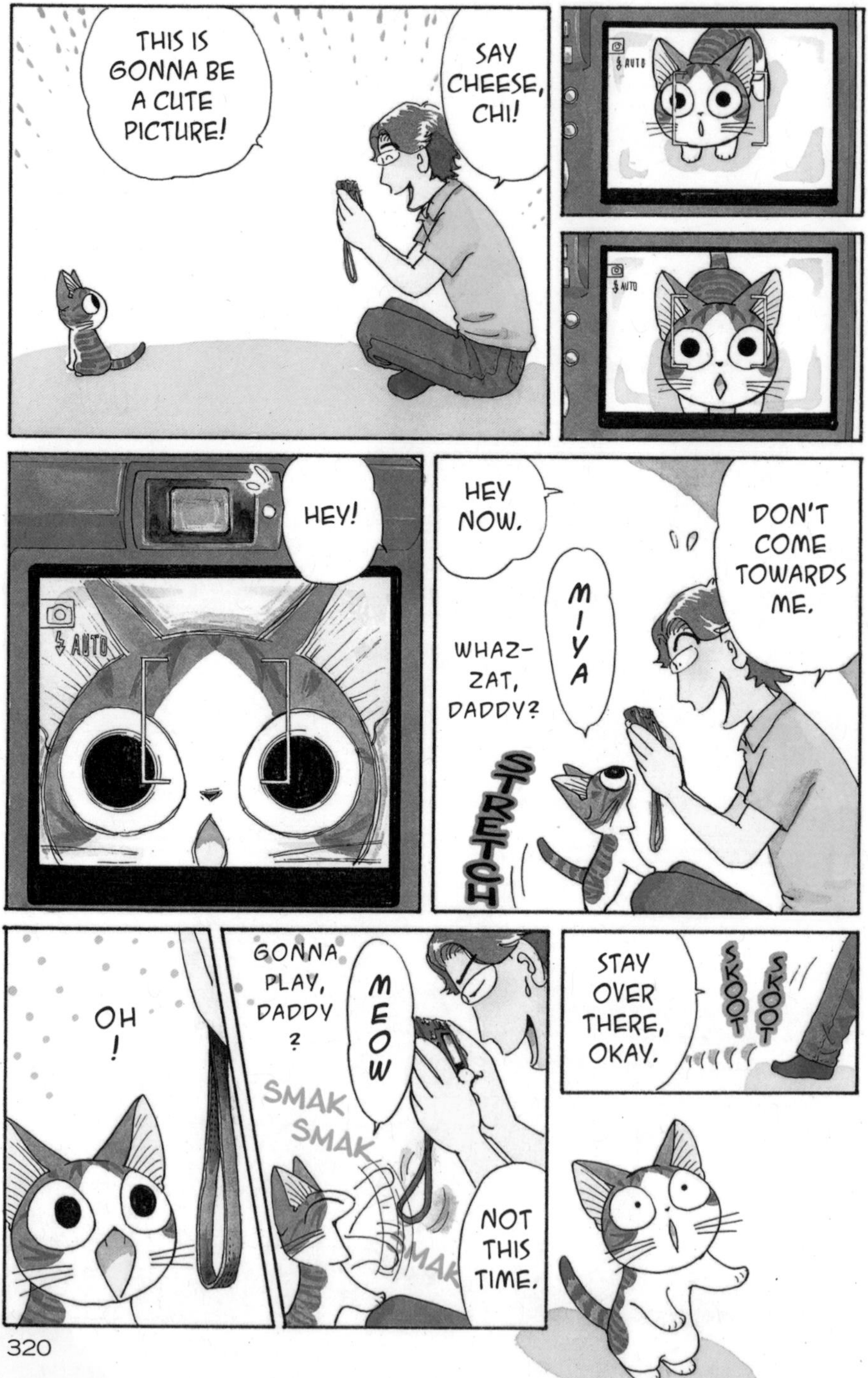
THIS IS GONNA BE A CUTE PICTURE!
SAY CHEESE, CHI!
AUTO
AUTO
AUTO
HEY!
HEY NOW.
DON'T COME TOWARDS ME.
WHAZ-ZAT, DADDY?
MIYA
STRETCH
OH!
GONNA PLAY, DADDY?
MEOW
SMAK SMAK
SMAK
NOT THIS TIME.
STAY OVER THERE, OKAY.
SKOOT SKOOT

OKAY, CHI! JUST STAY STILL.

HUH?

GOOD POSE.

OK!

KLIK

KASHH

TINK

SHAK

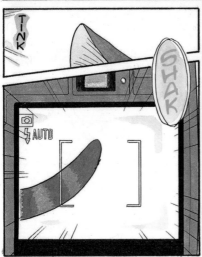

ARGH!

MEOW

WOAH!

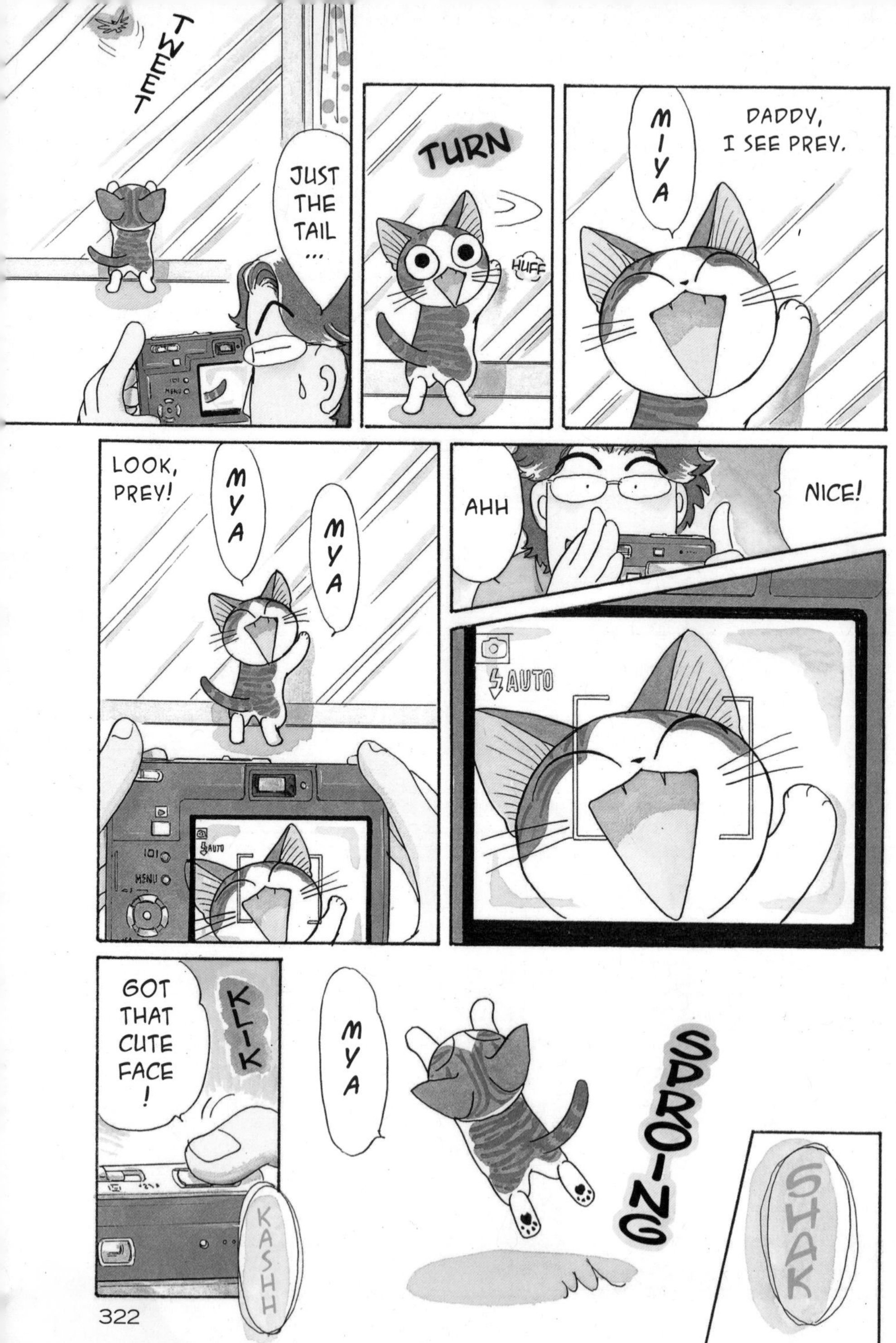
TWEET
JUST THE TAIL ...
TURN
HUFF
MIYA
DADDY, I SEE PREY.
LOOK, PREY!
MYA
MYA
AHH
NICE!
AUTO
GOT THAT CUTE FACE!
KLIK
KASHH
MYA
SPROING
SHAK

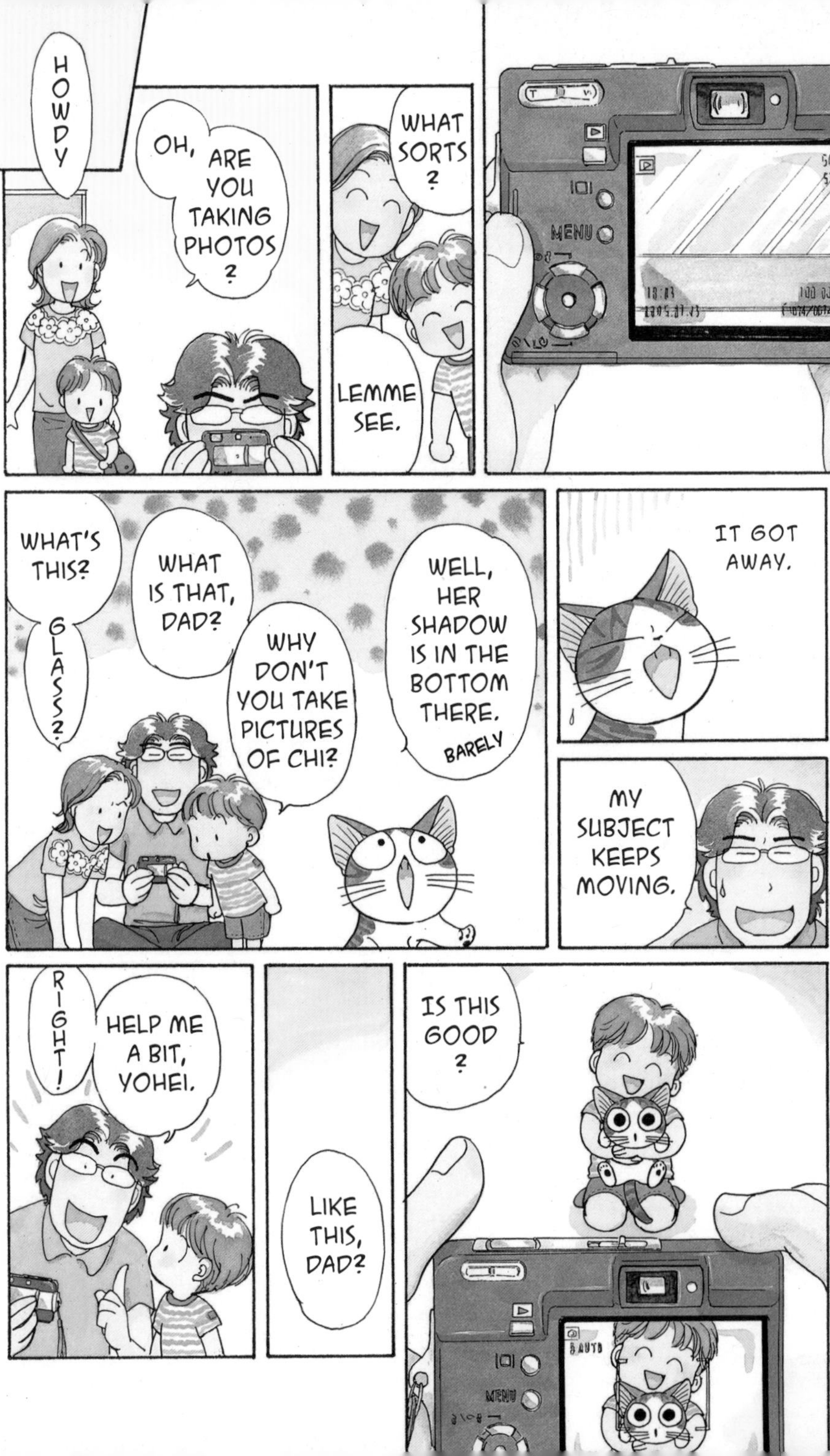
HOWDY
OH, ARE YOU TAKING PHOTOS?
WHAT SORTS?
LEMME SEE.
WHAT'S THIS?
WHAT IS THAT, DAD?
GLASS?
WHY DON'T YOU TAKE PICTURES OF CHI?
WELL, HER SHADOW IS IN THE BOTTOM THERE.
BARELY
IT GOT AWAY.
MY SUBJECT KEEPS MOVING.
RIGHT!
HELP ME A BIT, YOHEI.
LIKE THIS, DAD?
IS THIS GOOD?

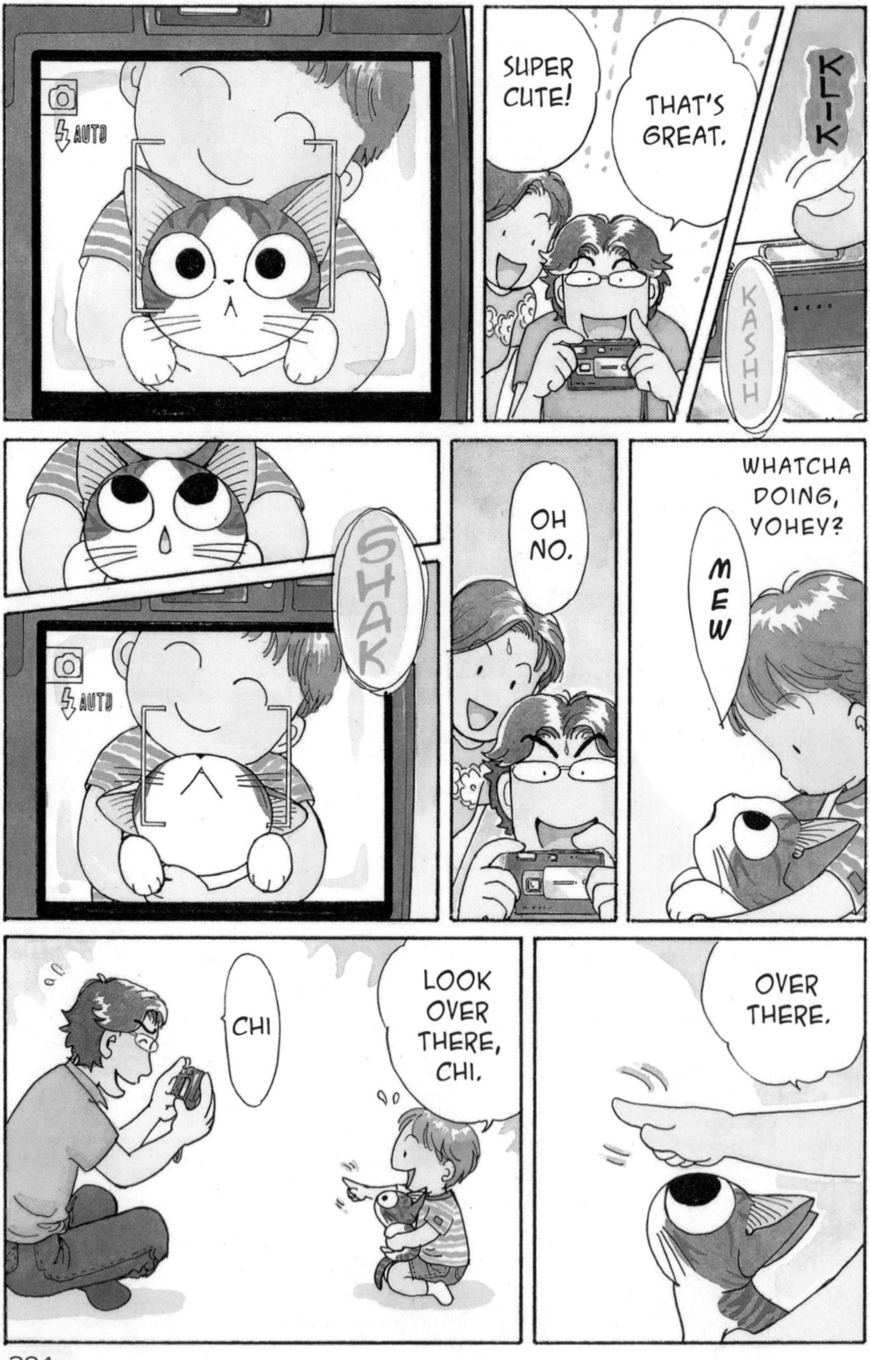
AUTO
SUPER CUTE!
THAT'S GREAT.
KLIK
KASHH
SHAK
AUTO
OH NO.
WHATCHA DOING, YOHEY?
MEW
CHI
LOOK OVER THERE, CHI.
OVER THERE.

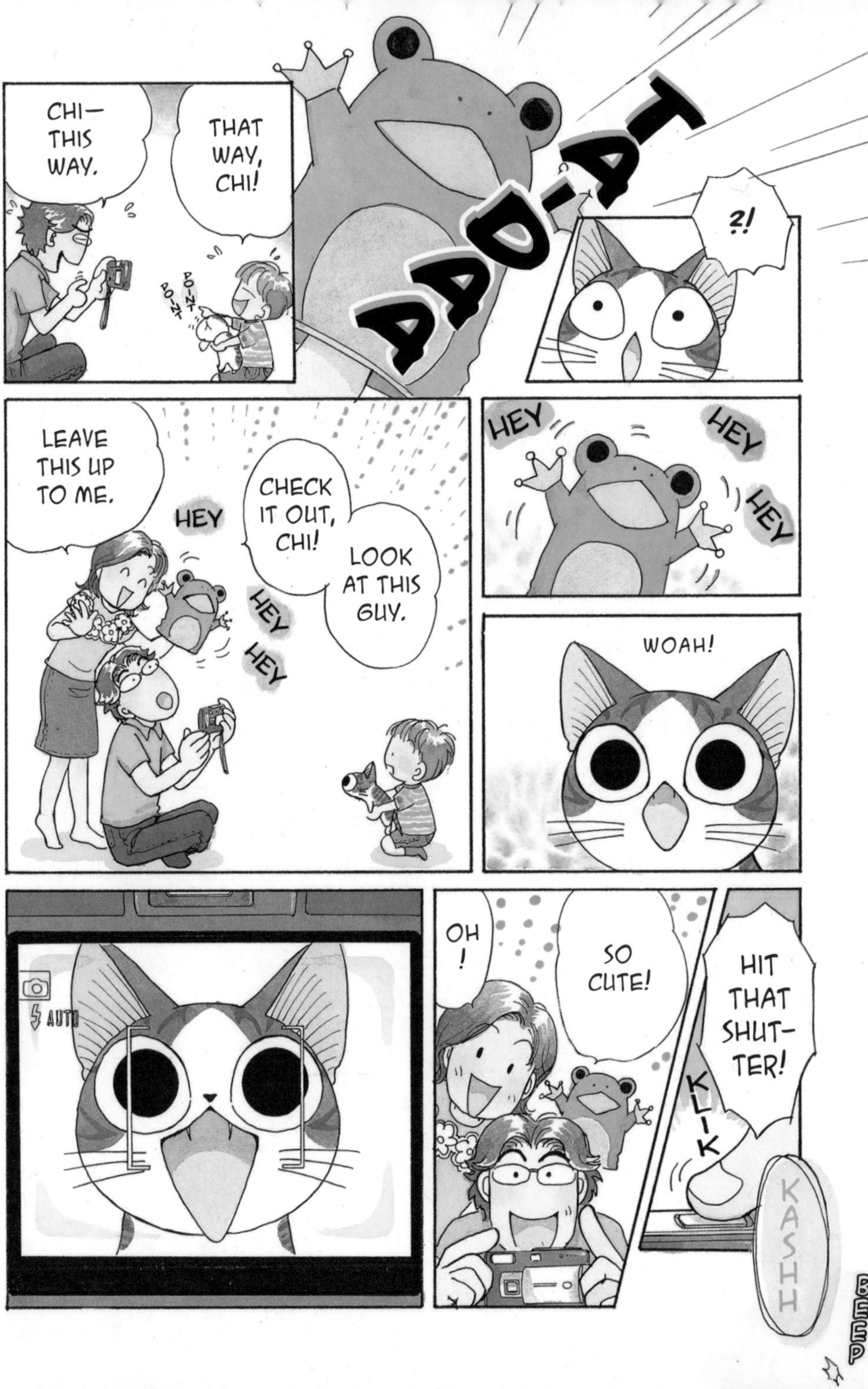
CHI—THIS WAY.
THAT WAY, CHI!
POINT POINT
AAD-AT
?!
LEAVE THIS UP TO ME.
HEY
CHECK IT OUT, CHI!
LOOK AT THIS GUY.
HEY
HEY
HEY
HEY
HEY
WOAH!
AUTO
OH!
SO CUTE!
HIT THAT SHUT-TER!
KLIK
KASHH
BEEP

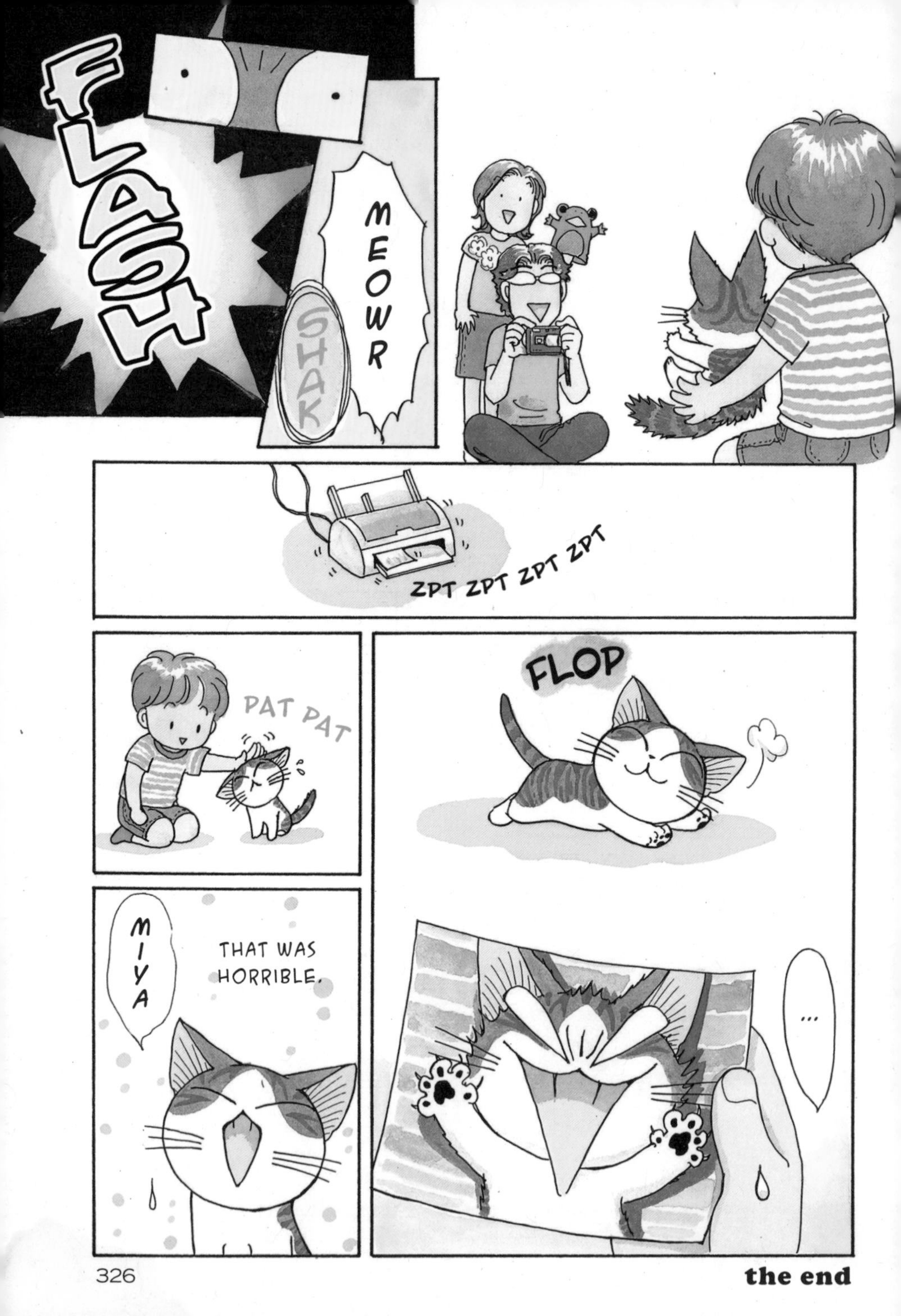
FLASH
MEOWR
SHAK
ZPT ZPT ZPT ZPT
PAT PAT
FLOP
MIYA
THAT WAS HORRIBLE.
...

the end

homemade 41: a cat is taught

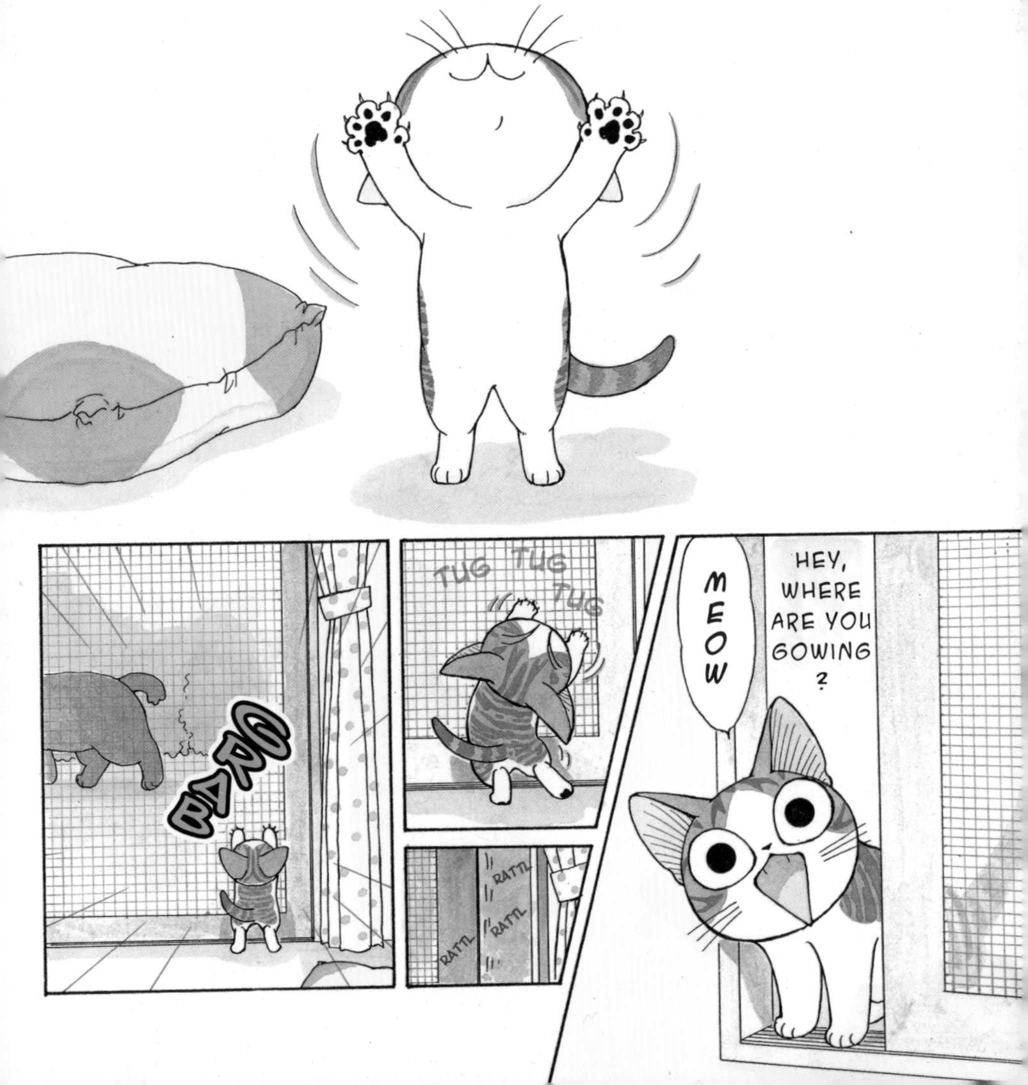
GRAB
TUG TUG TUG
RATTL
RATTL
RATTL
RATTL
MEOW
HEY, WHERE ARE YOU GOWING?

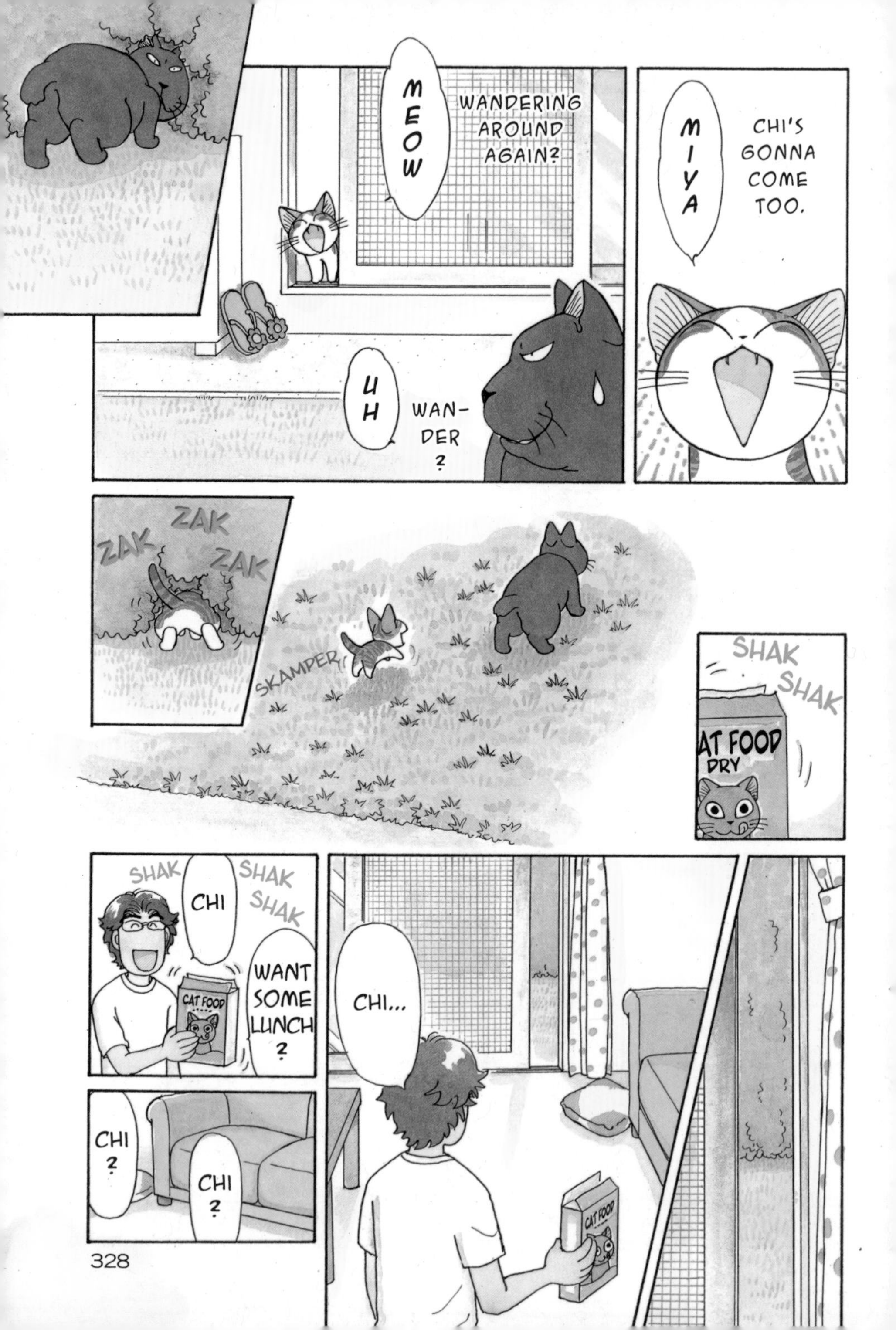
MEOW
WANDERING AROUND AGAIN?
UH
WAN-DER?
MIYA
CHI'S GONNA COME TOO.
ZAK
ZAK
ZAK
SKAMPER
SHAK
SHAK
CAT FOOD
DRY
SHAK
CHI
SHAK
SHAK
WANT SOME LUNCH?
CAT FOOD
CHI?
CHI?
CHI...
CAT FOOD

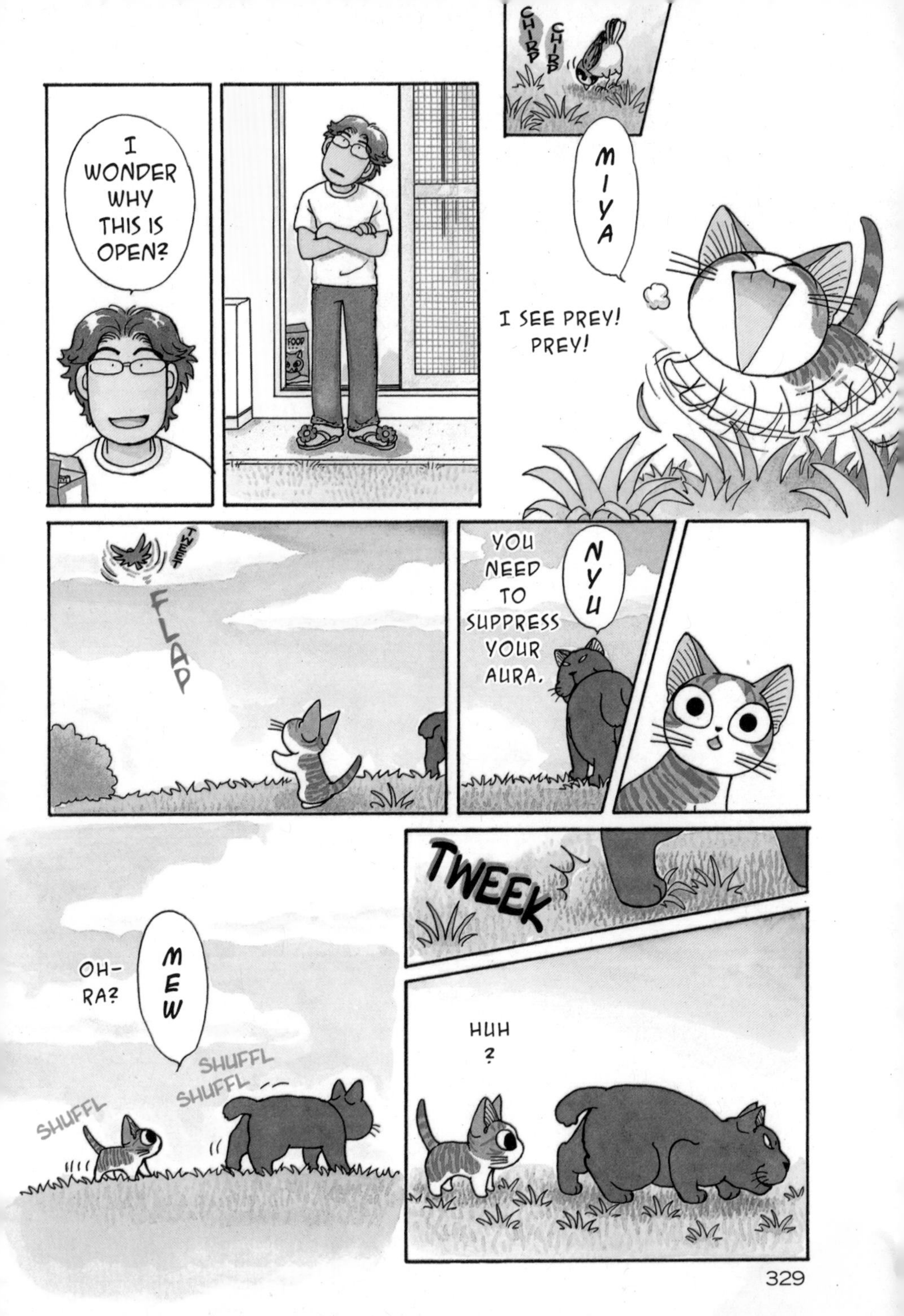
I WONDER WHY THIS IS OPEN?
FOOD
CHIRP
CHIRP
MIYA
I SEE PREY! PREY!
TWEET
FLAP
YOU NEED TO SUPPRESS YOUR AURA.
NYU
OH-RA?
MEW
SHUFFL
SHUFFL
SHUFFL
TWEEK
HUH?

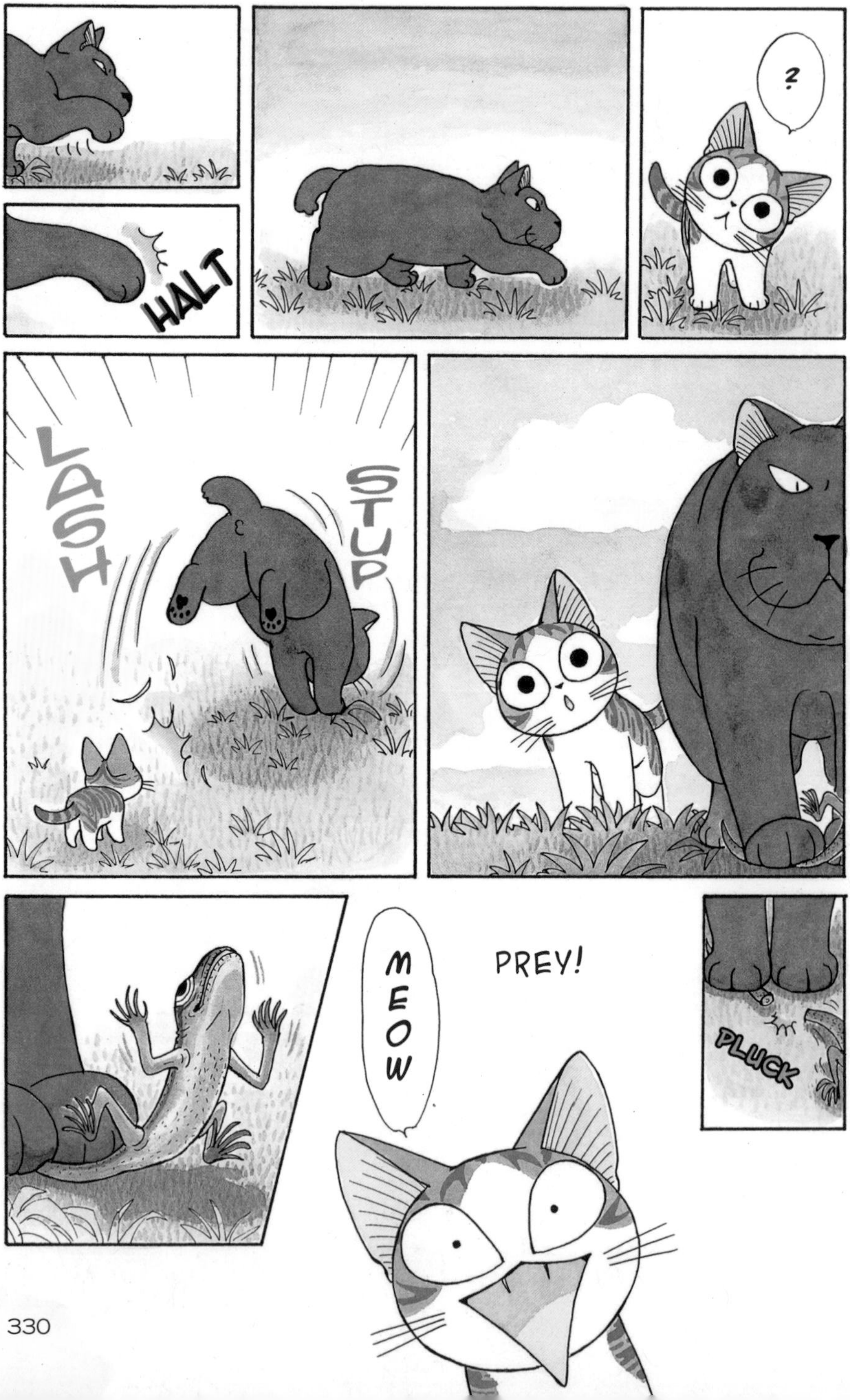
HALT
?
LASH
STUP
MEOW
PREY!
PLUCK

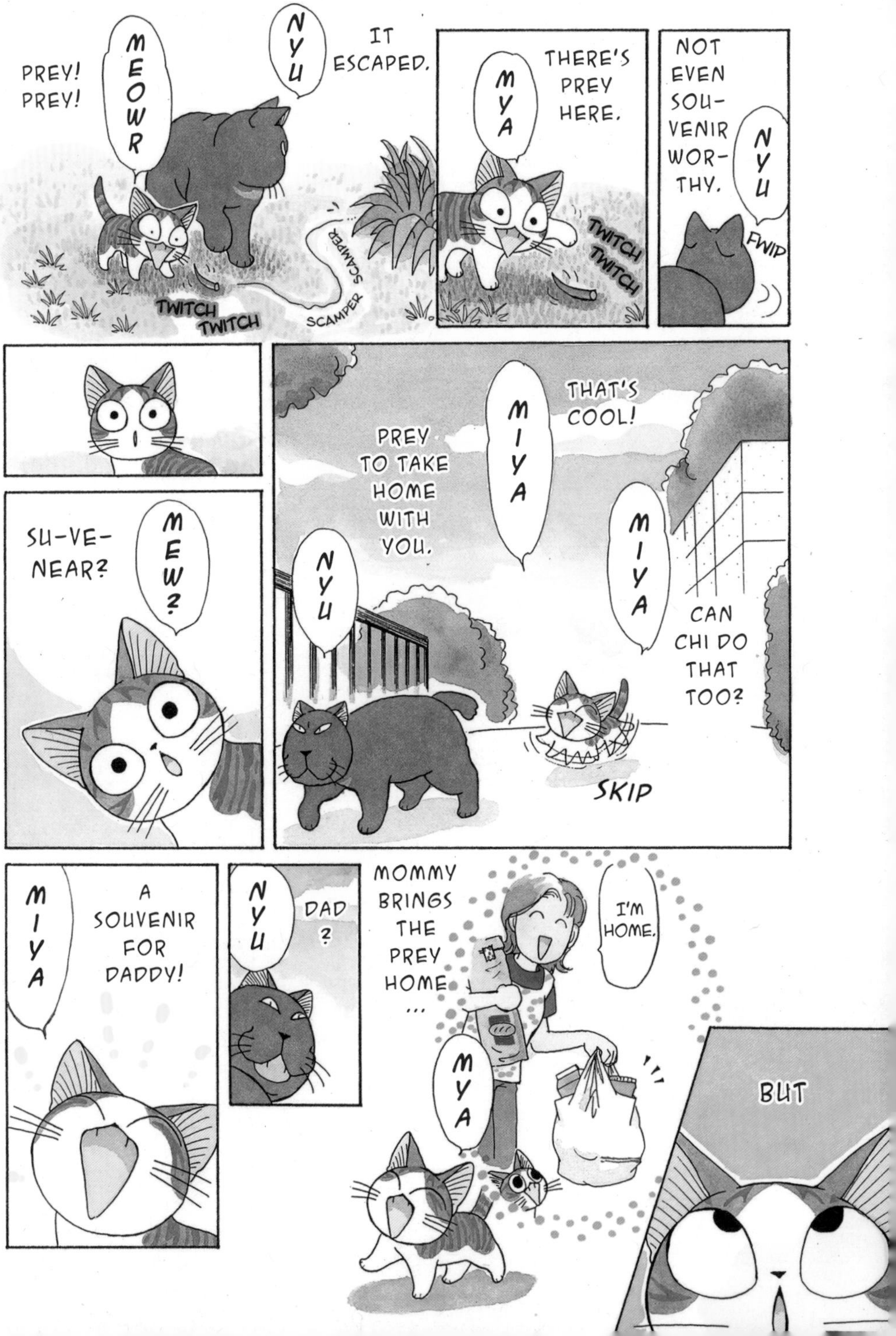
PREY! PREY!
MEOWR
NYU
IT ESCAPED.
TWITCH TWITCH
SCAMPER SCAMPER
MYA
THERE'S PREY HERE.
TWITCH TWITCH
NOT EVEN SOU-VENIR WOR-THY.
NYU
FWIP
SU-VE-NEAR?
MEW?
PREY TO TAKE HOME WITH YOU.
NYU
MIYA
THAT'S COOL!
MIYA
CAN CHI DO THAT TOO?
SKIP
MIYA
A SOUVENIR FOR DADDY!
NYU
DAD?
MOMMY BRINGS THE PREY HOME...
I'M HOME.
MYA
BUT

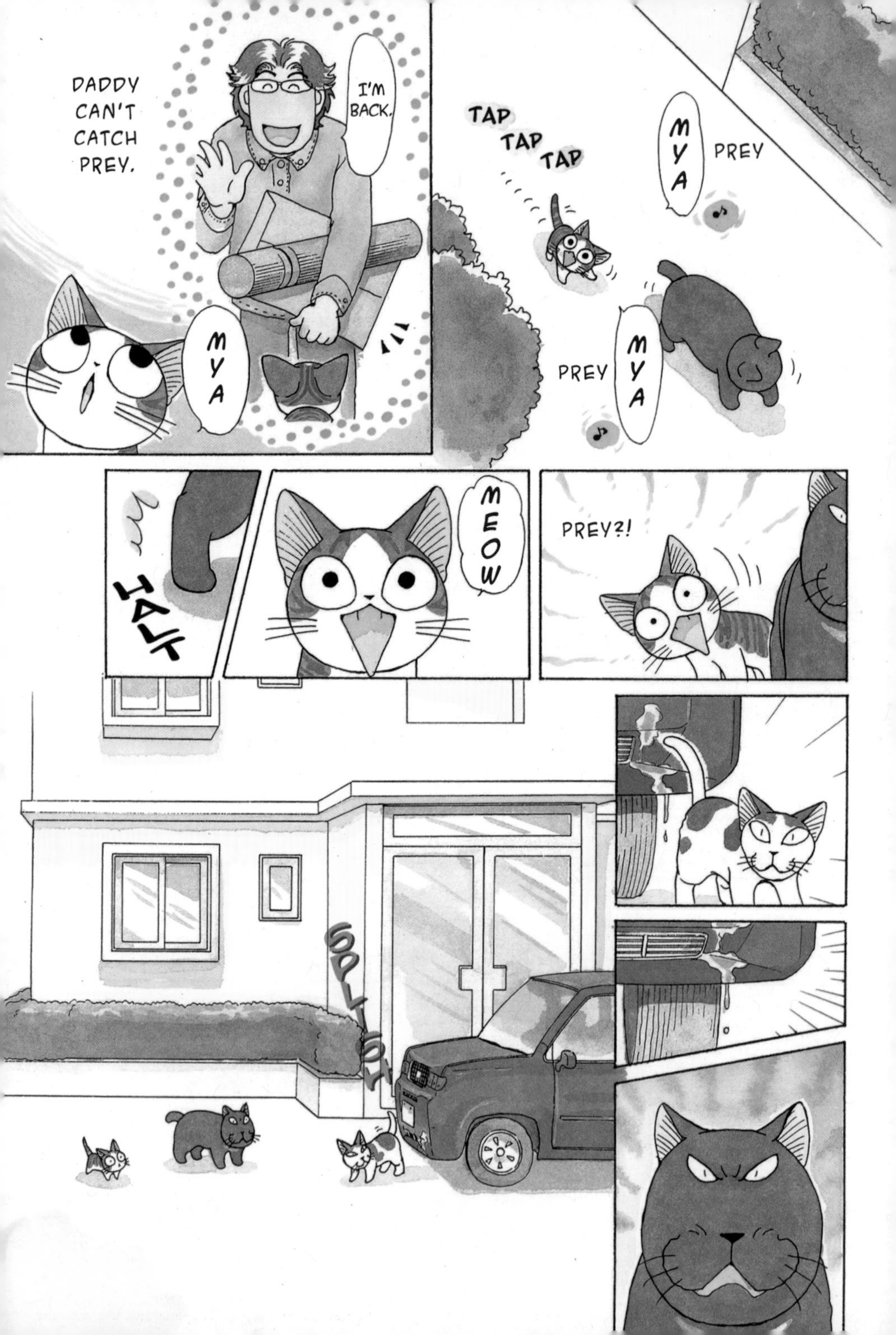
DADDY CAN'T CATCH PREY.
I'M BACK.
MYA
TAP TAP TAP
MYA
PREY
MYA
PREY
HALT
MEOW
PREY?!
SPLISH

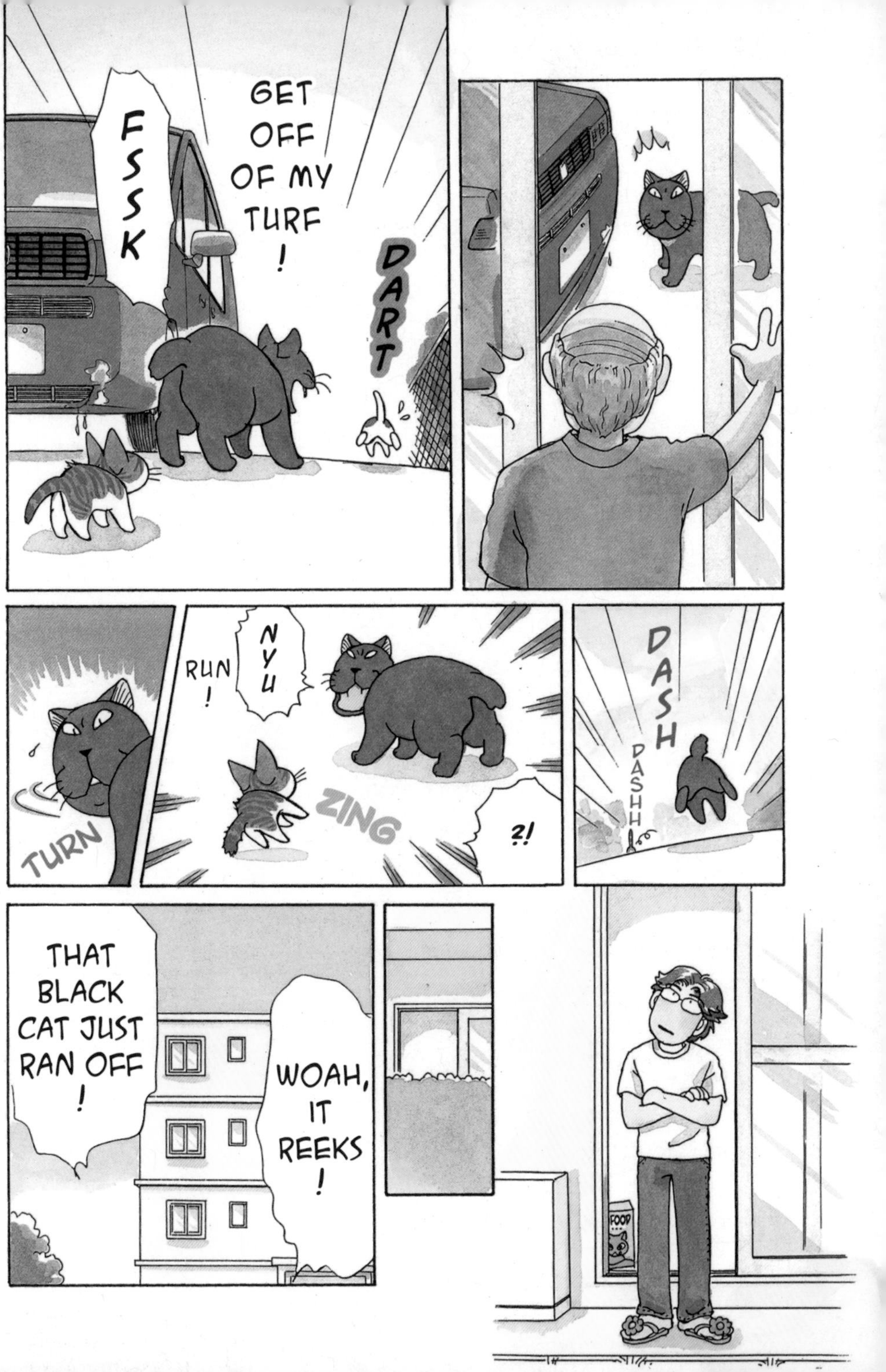
FSSK
GET OFF OF MY TURF!
DART
TURN
RUN!
NYU
ZING
?!
DASH
DASHH
THAT BLACK CAT JUST RAN OFF!
WOAH, IT REEKS!
FOOD

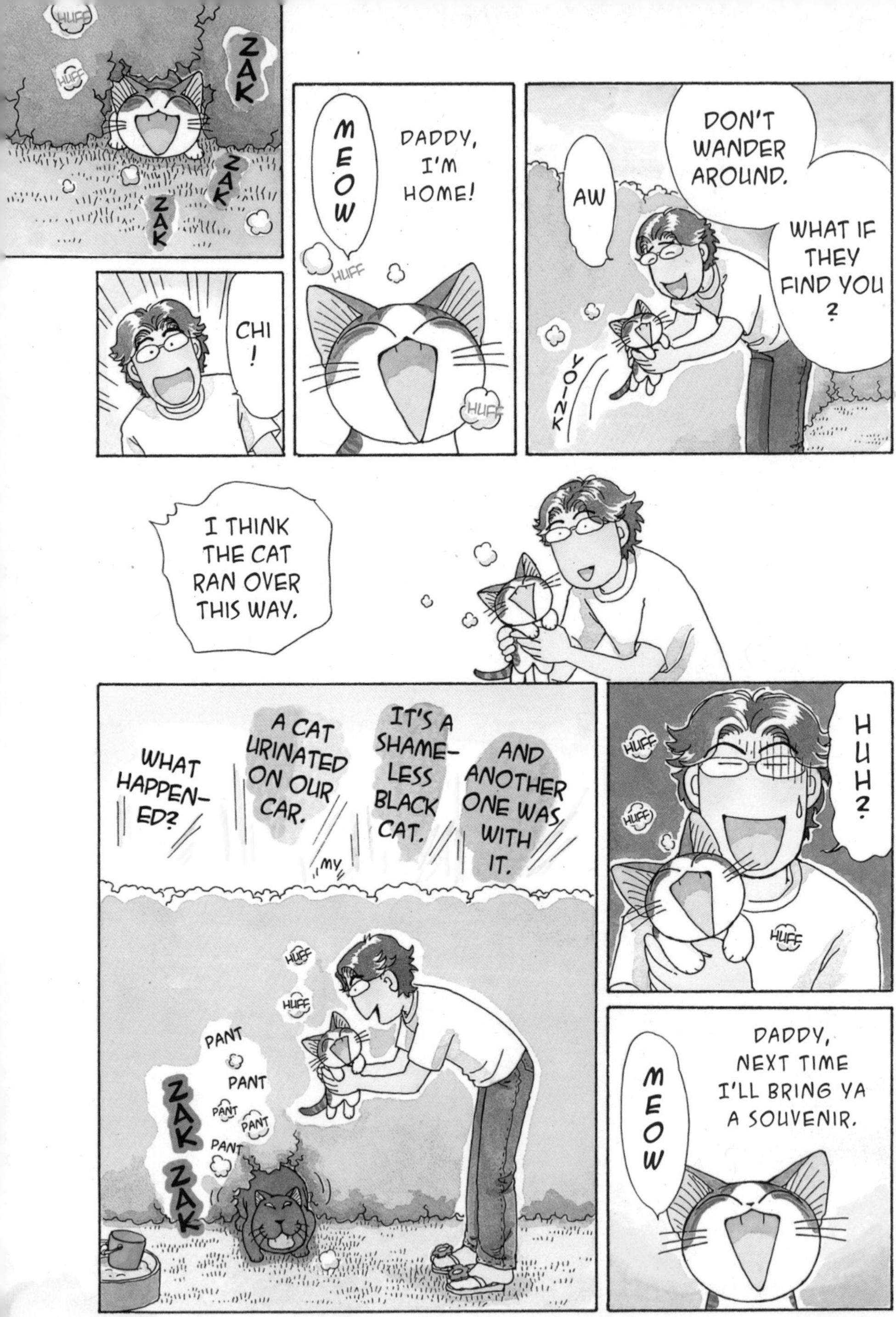
HUFF
HUFF
ZAK
ZAK
ZAK
CHI!
MEOW
DADDY, I'M HOME!
HUFF
HUFF
AW
DON'T WANDER AROUND.
WHAT IF THEY FIND YOU?
YOINK
I THINK THE CAT RAN OVER THIS WAY.
WHAT HAPPENED?
A CAT URINATED ON OUR CAR.
MY
IT'S A SHAMELESS BLACK CAT.
AND ANOTHER ONE WAS WITH IT.
HUFF
HUFF
PANT
PANT
PANT
PANT
PANT
ZAK
ZAK
HUFF
HUFF
HUH?
HUFF
MEOW
DADDY, NEXT TIME I'LL BRING YA A SOUVENIR.

the end

homemade 42: a cat hides

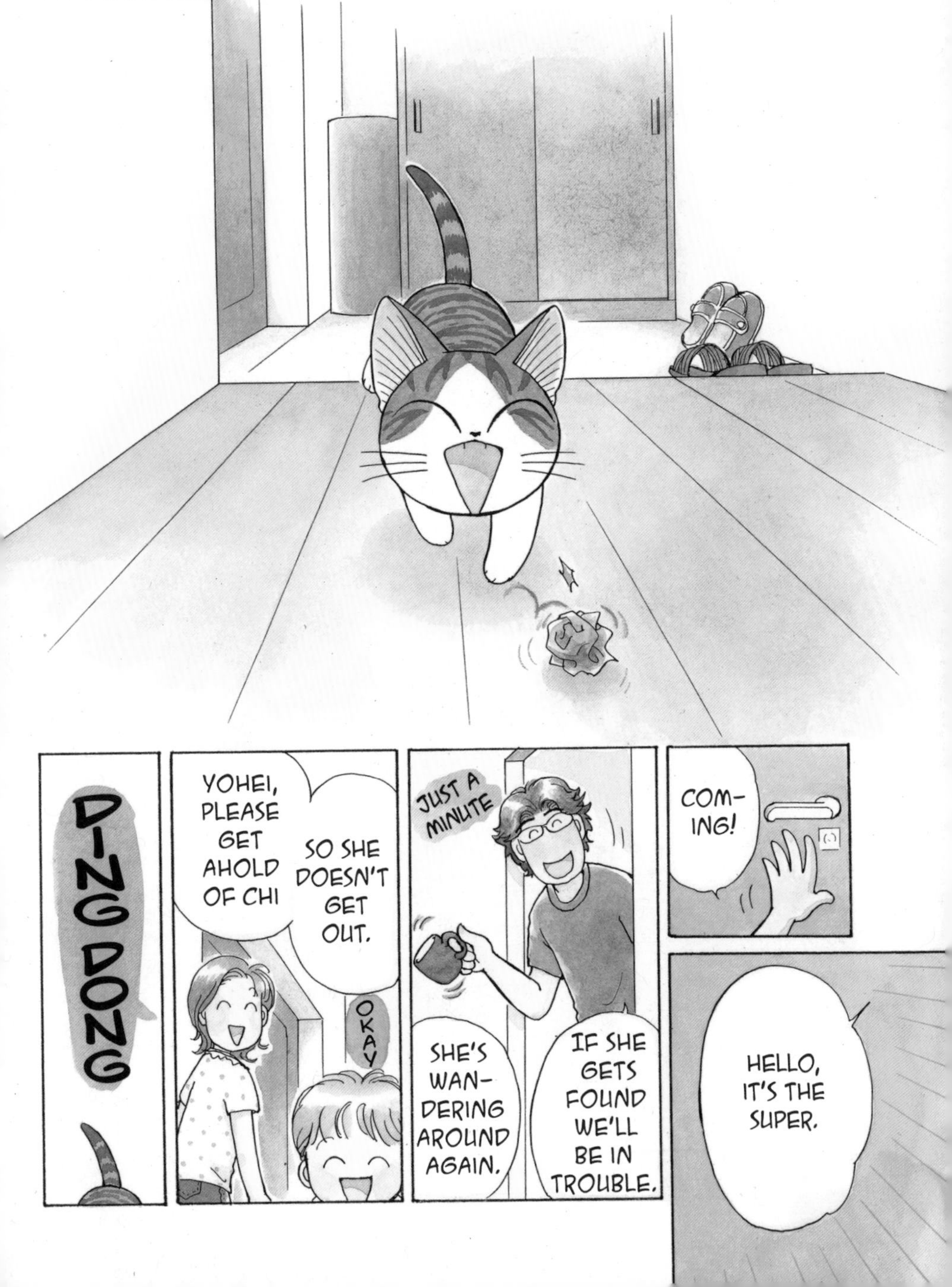
DING DONG
YOHEI, PLEASE GET AHOLD OF CHI
SO SHE DOESN'T GET OUT.
OKAY
JUST A MINUTE
SHE'S WAN-DERING AROUND AGAIN.
IF SHE GETS FOUND WE'LL BE IN TROUBLE.
COM-ING!
HELLO, IT'S THE SUPER.

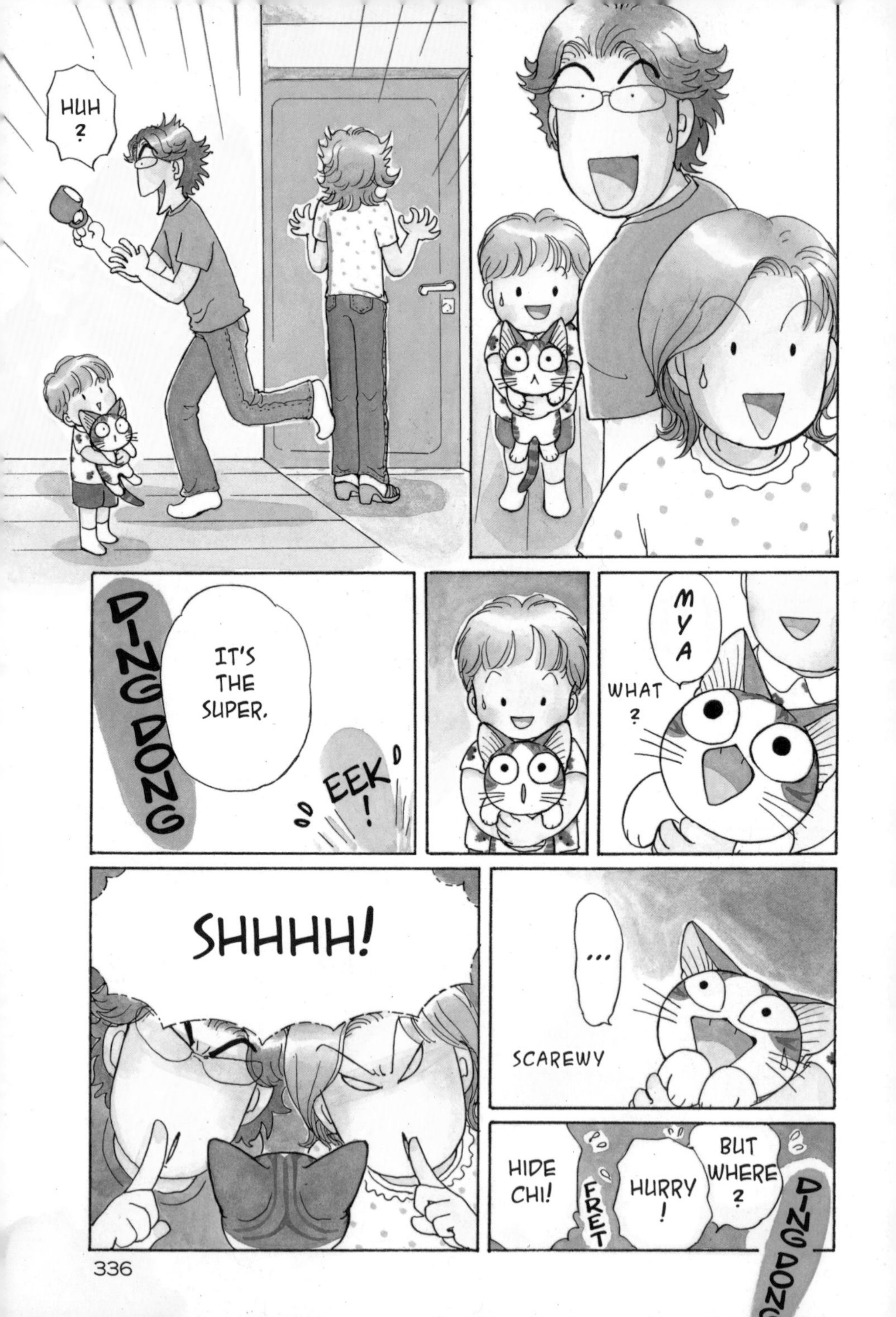
HUH?
DING DONG
IT'S THE SUPER.
EEK!
MYA
WHAT?
SHHHH!
...
SCAREWY
HIDE CHI!
FRET
HURRY!
BUT WHERE?
DING DONG

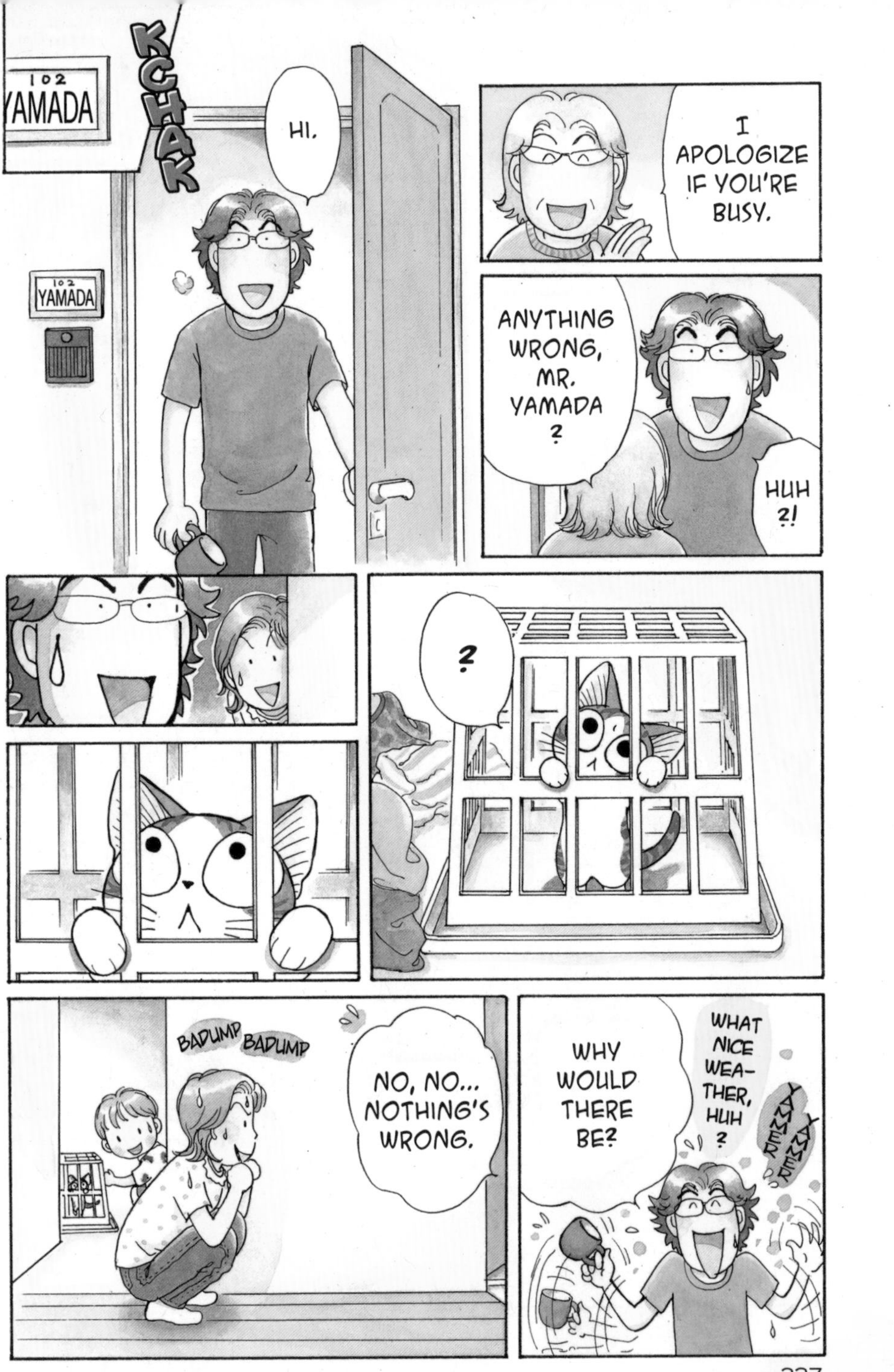
102 YAMADA
KCHAK
HI.
102 YAMADA
I APOLOGIZE IF YOU'RE BUSY.
ANYTHING WRONG, MR. YAMADA?
HUH?!
?
BADUMP BADUMP
NO, NO... NOTHING'S WRONG.
WHY WOULD THERE BE?
WHAT NICE WEATHER, HUH?
YAMMER YAMMER

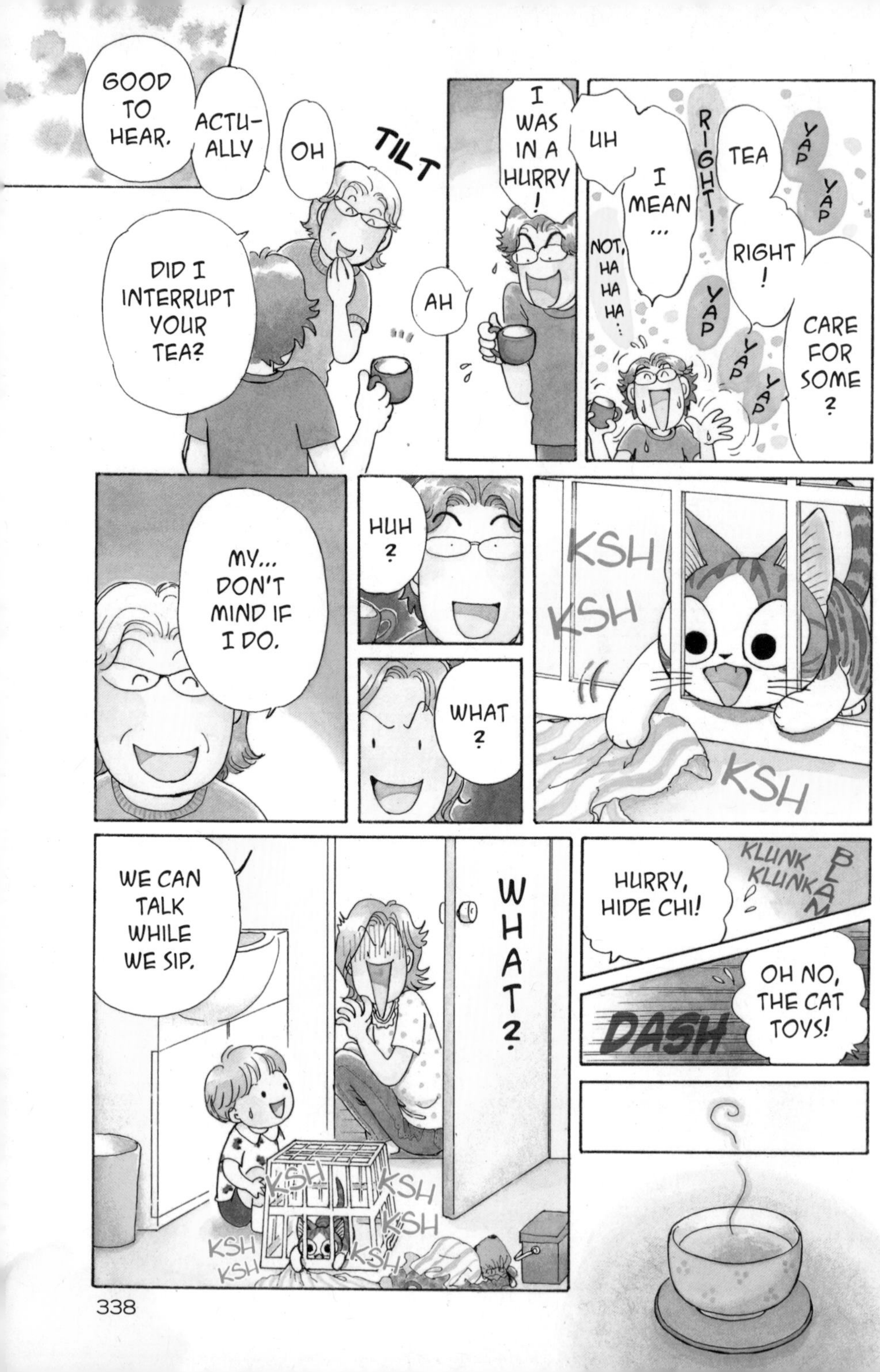
GOOD TO HEAR.
ACTU-ALLY
OH
TILT
DID I INTERRUPT YOUR TEA?
AH
I WAS IN A HURRY!
UH
I MEAN...
NOT, HA HA HA...
RIGHT!
TEA
RIGHT!
YAP YAP YAP
CARE FOR SOME?
YAP YAP YAP
MY... DON'T MIND IF I DO.
HUH?
WHAT?
KSH KSH
KSH
WE CAN TALK WHILE WE SIP.
WHAT?
KSH KSH KSH KSH KSH KSH
HURRY, HIDE CHI!
KLUNK KLUNK BLAM
DASH
OH NO, THE CAT TOYS!

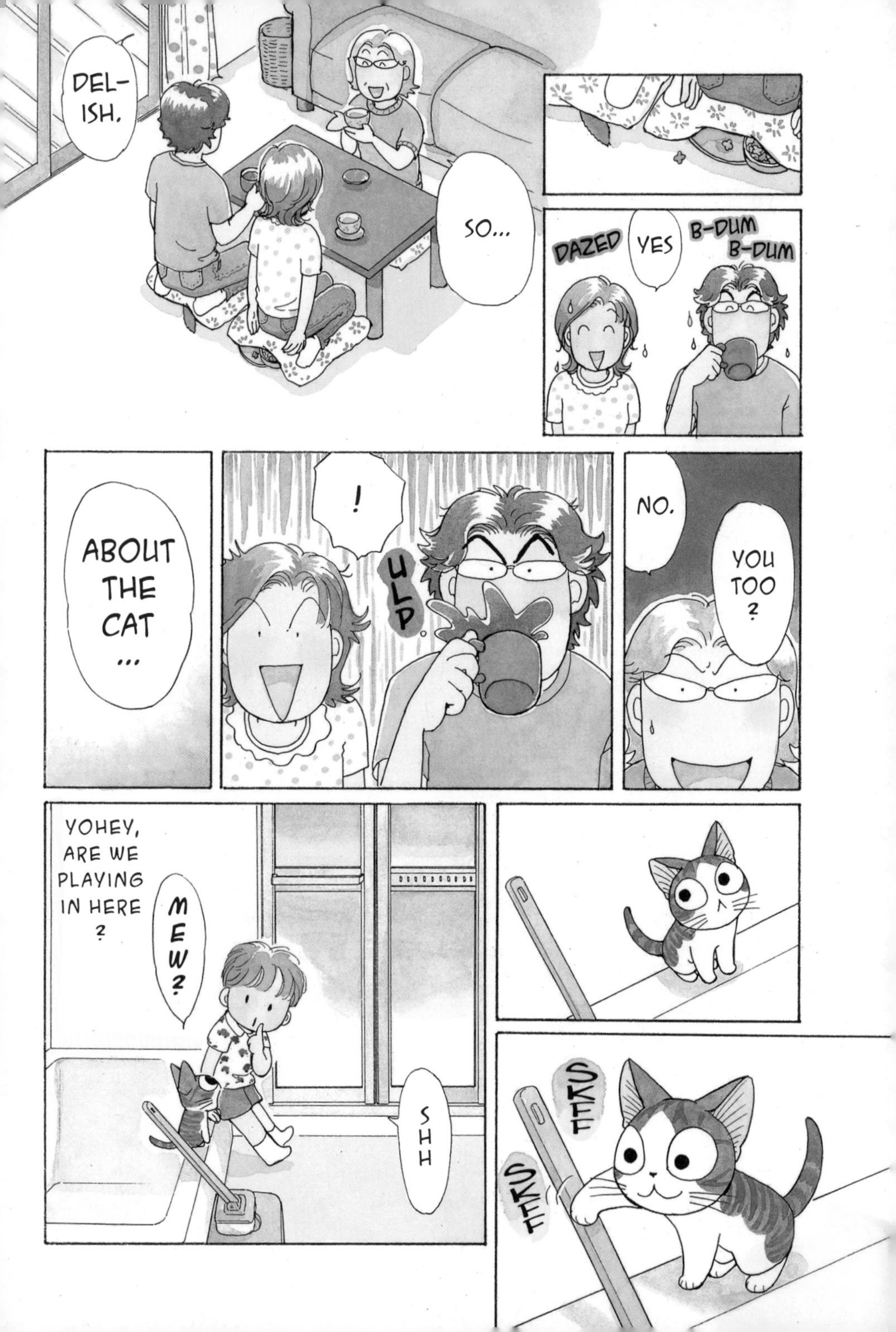
DEL-ISH.
SO...
DAZED
YES
B-DUM B-DUM
ABOUT THE CAT ...
!
ULP
NO.
YOU TOO?
YOHEY, ARE WE PLAYING IN HERE?
MEW?
SHH
SKFF
SKFF

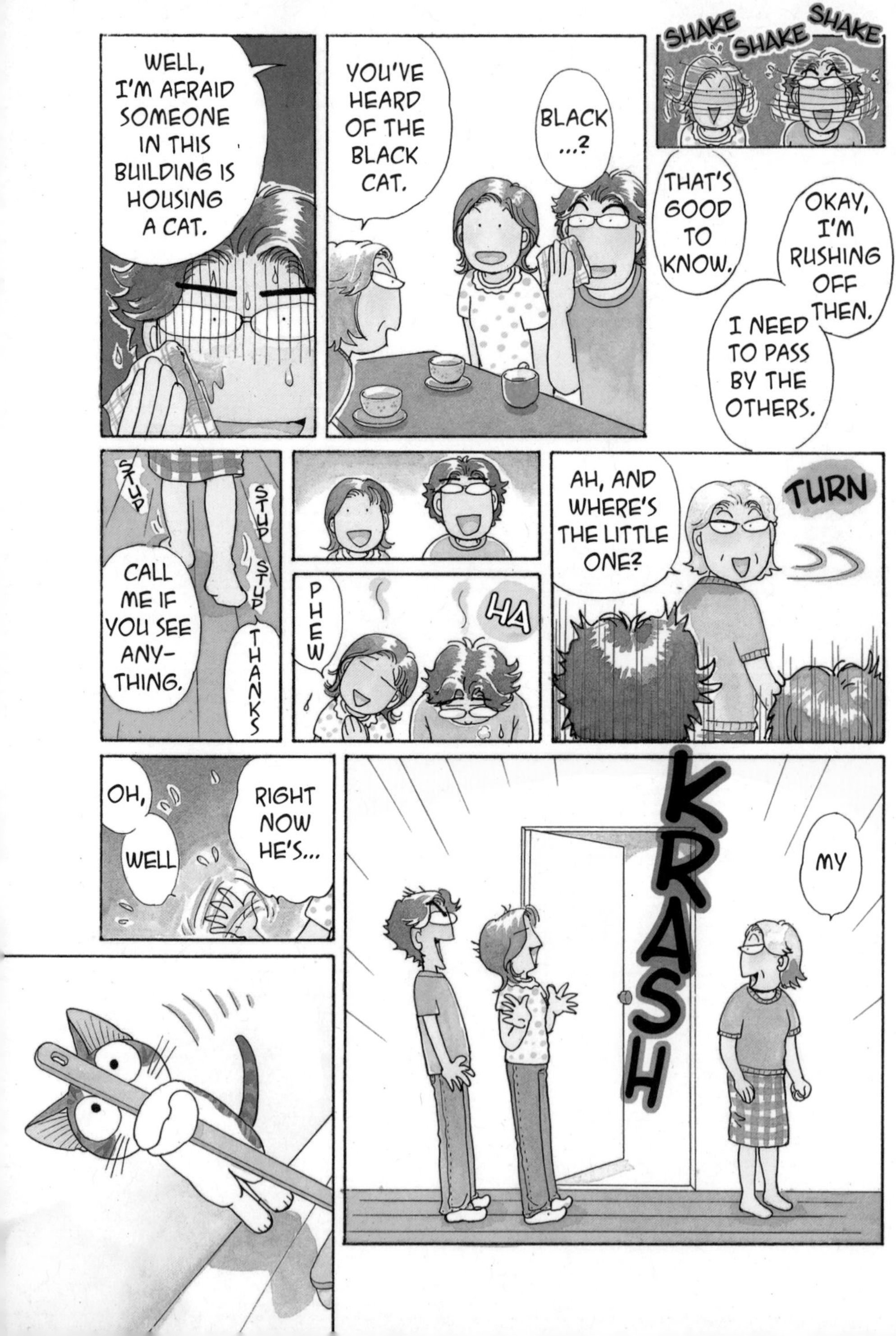

WELL, I'M AFRAID SOMEONE IN THIS BUILDING IS HOUSING A CAT.
YOU'VE HEARD OF THE BLACK CAT.
BLACK ...?
SHAKE
SHAKE
SHAKE
THAT'S GOOD TO KNOW.
OKAY, I'M RUSHING OFF THEN.
I NEED TO PASS BY THE OTHERS.
STUP
STUP
STUP
CALL ME IF YOU SEE ANY-THING.
THANKS
PHEW
HA
AH, AND WHERE'S THE LITTLE ONE?
TURN
OH,
WELL
RIGHT NOW HE'S...
KRASH
MY

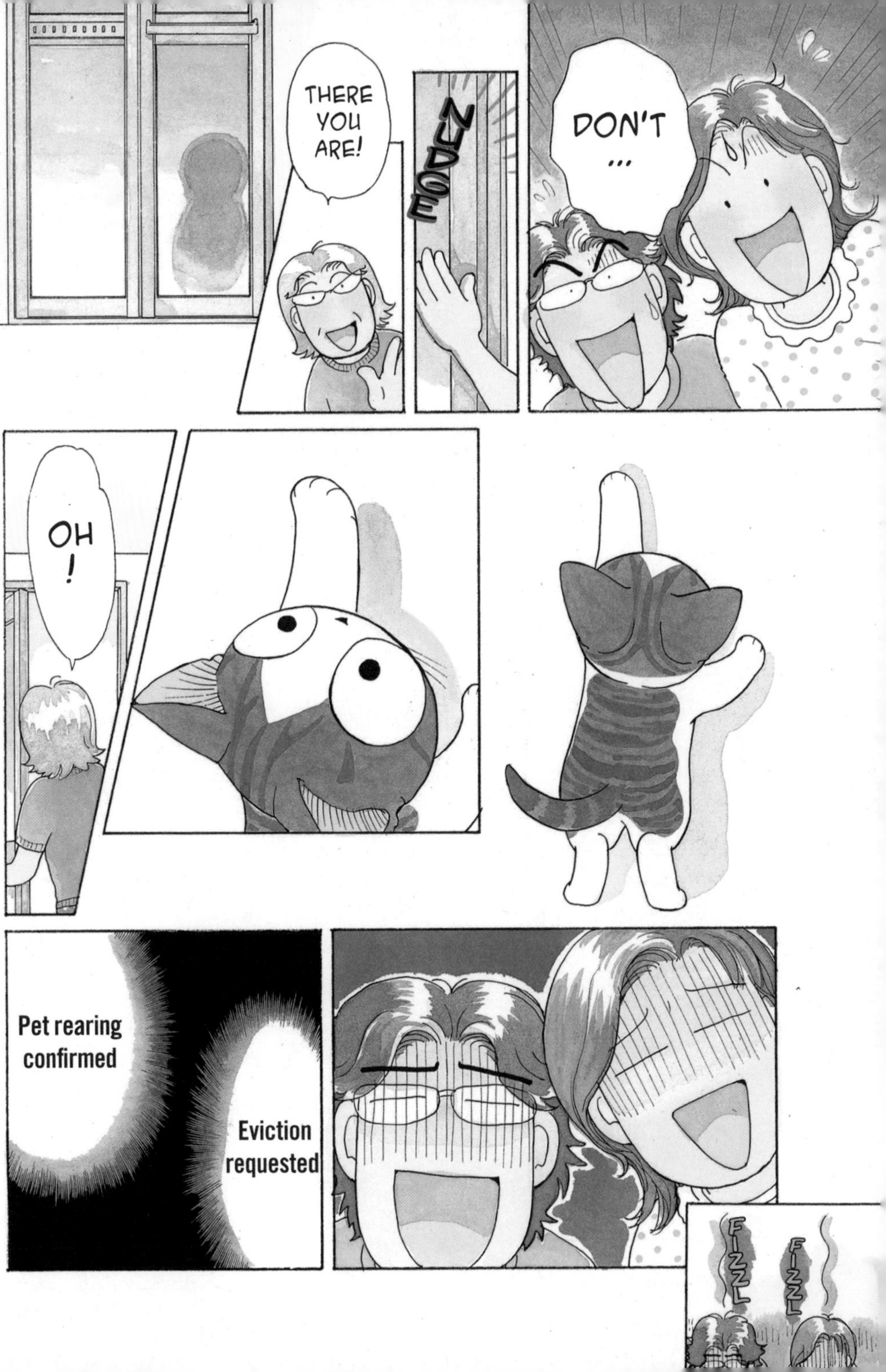
THERE YOU ARE!
NUDGE
DON'T ...
OH!
Pet rearing confirmed
Eviction requested
FIZZL
FIZZL

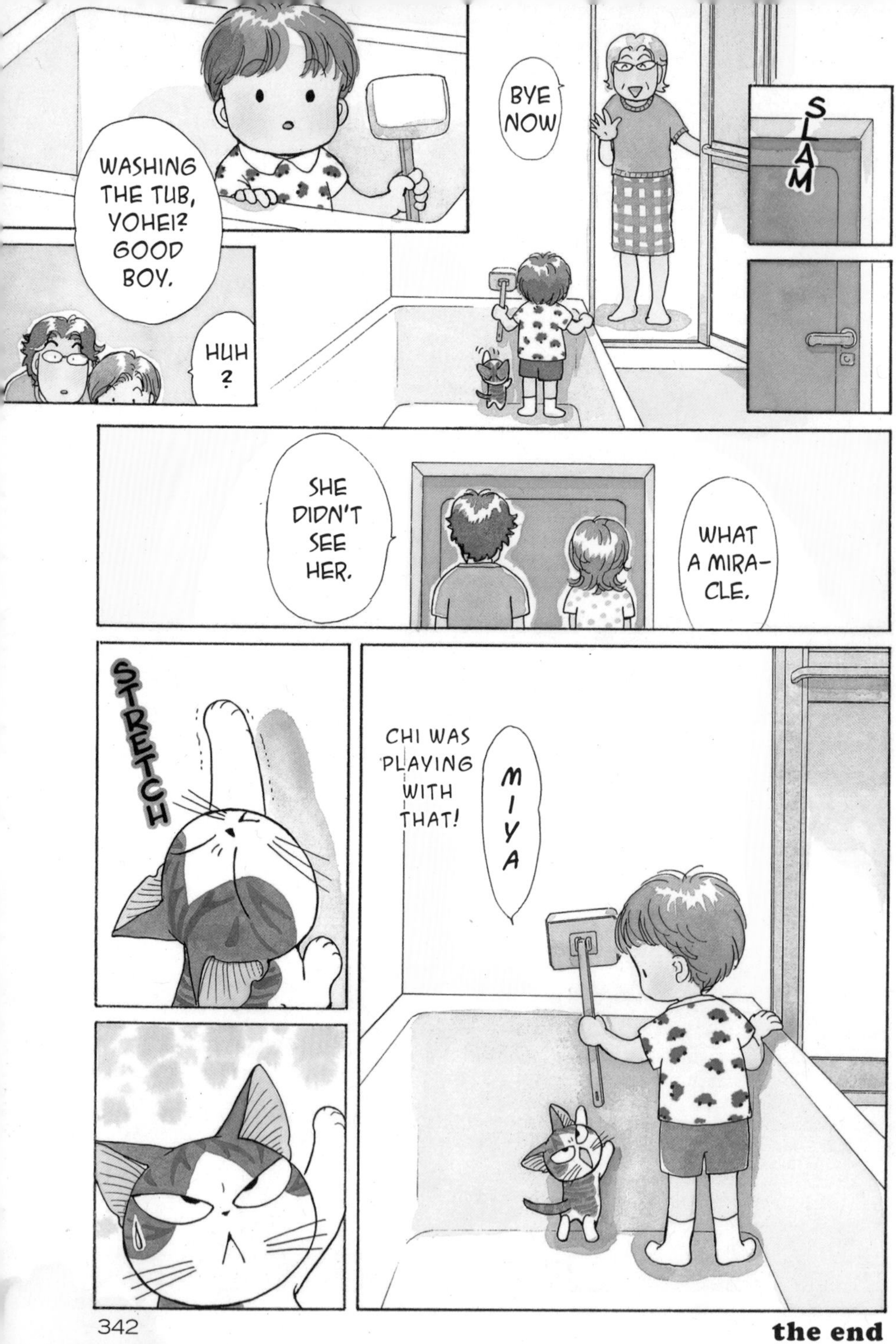
WASHING THE TUB, YOHEI? GOOD BOY.
HUH?
BYE NOW
SLAM
SHE DIDN'T SEE HER.
WHAT A MIRA-CLE.
STRETCH
CHI WAS PLAYING WITH THAT!
MIYA

the end

homemade 43: a cat mediates

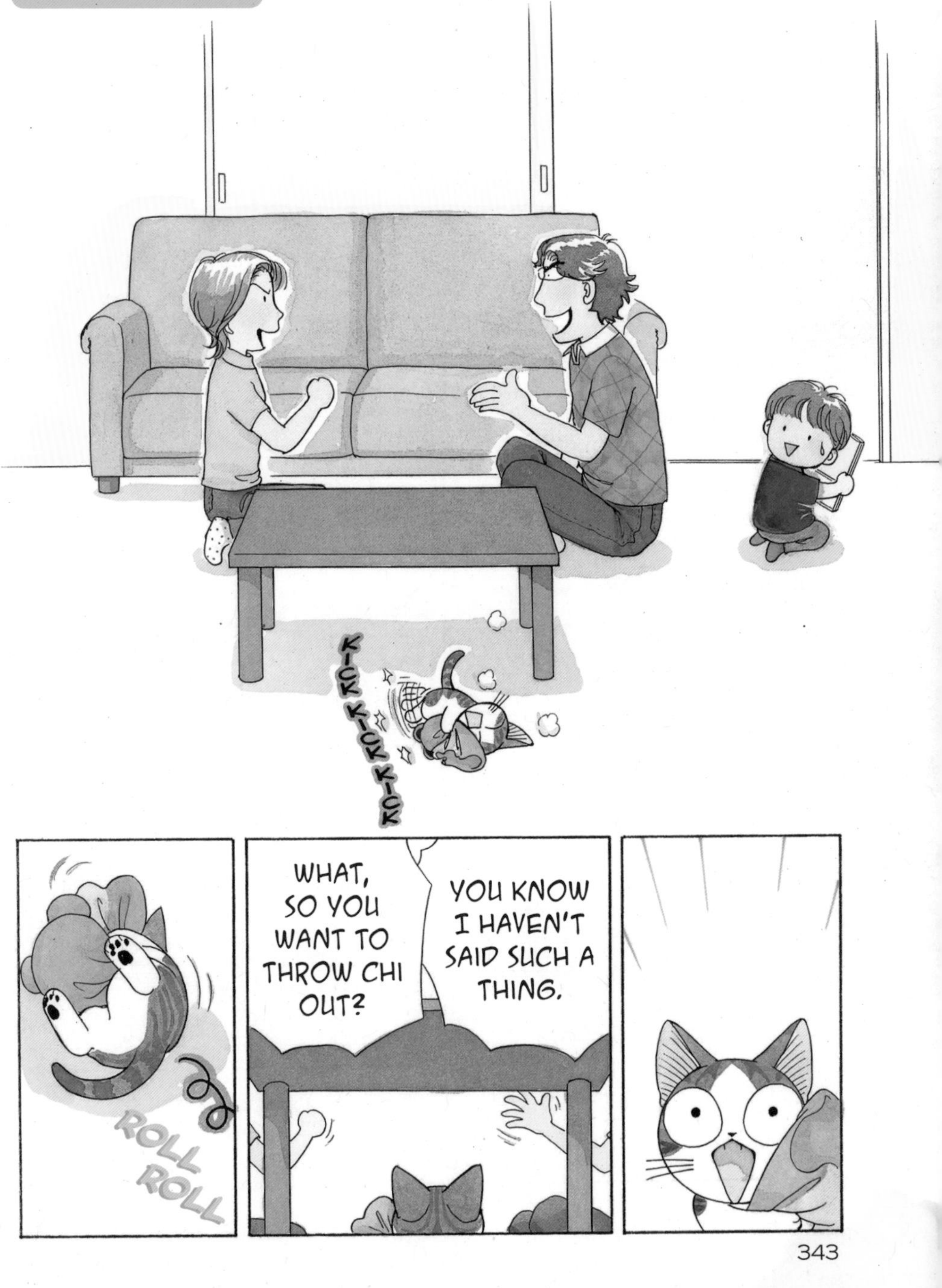

KICK KICK KICK
ROLL ROLL
WHAT, SO YOU WANT TO THROW CHI OUT?
YOU KNOW I HAVEN'T SAID SUCH A THING.

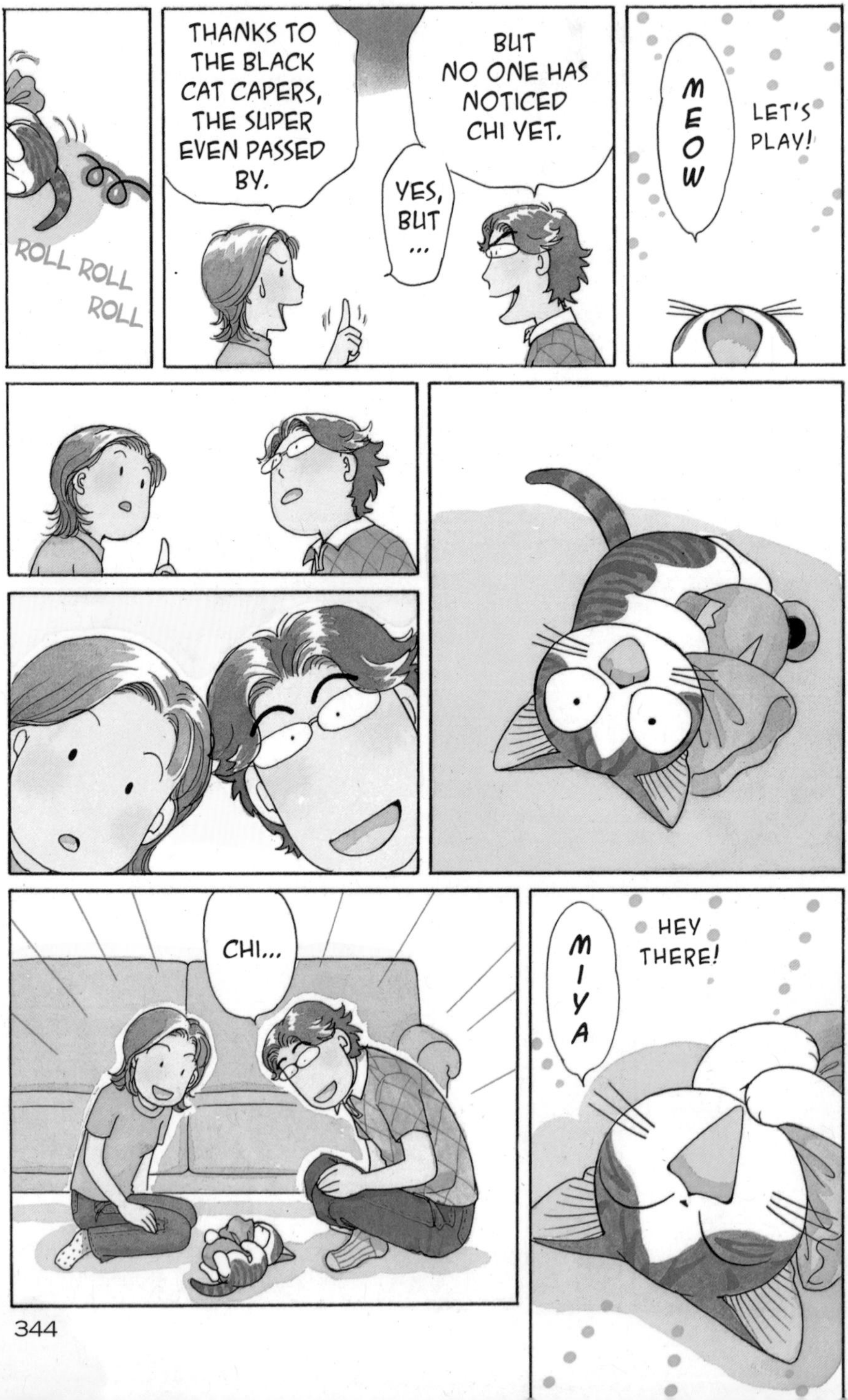
ROLL ROLL ROLL
THANKS TO THE BLACK CAT CAPERS, THE SUPER EVEN PASSED BY.
BUT NO ONE HAS NOTICED CHI YET.
YES, BUT ...
MEOW
LET'S PLAY!
CHI...
MIYA
HEY THERE!

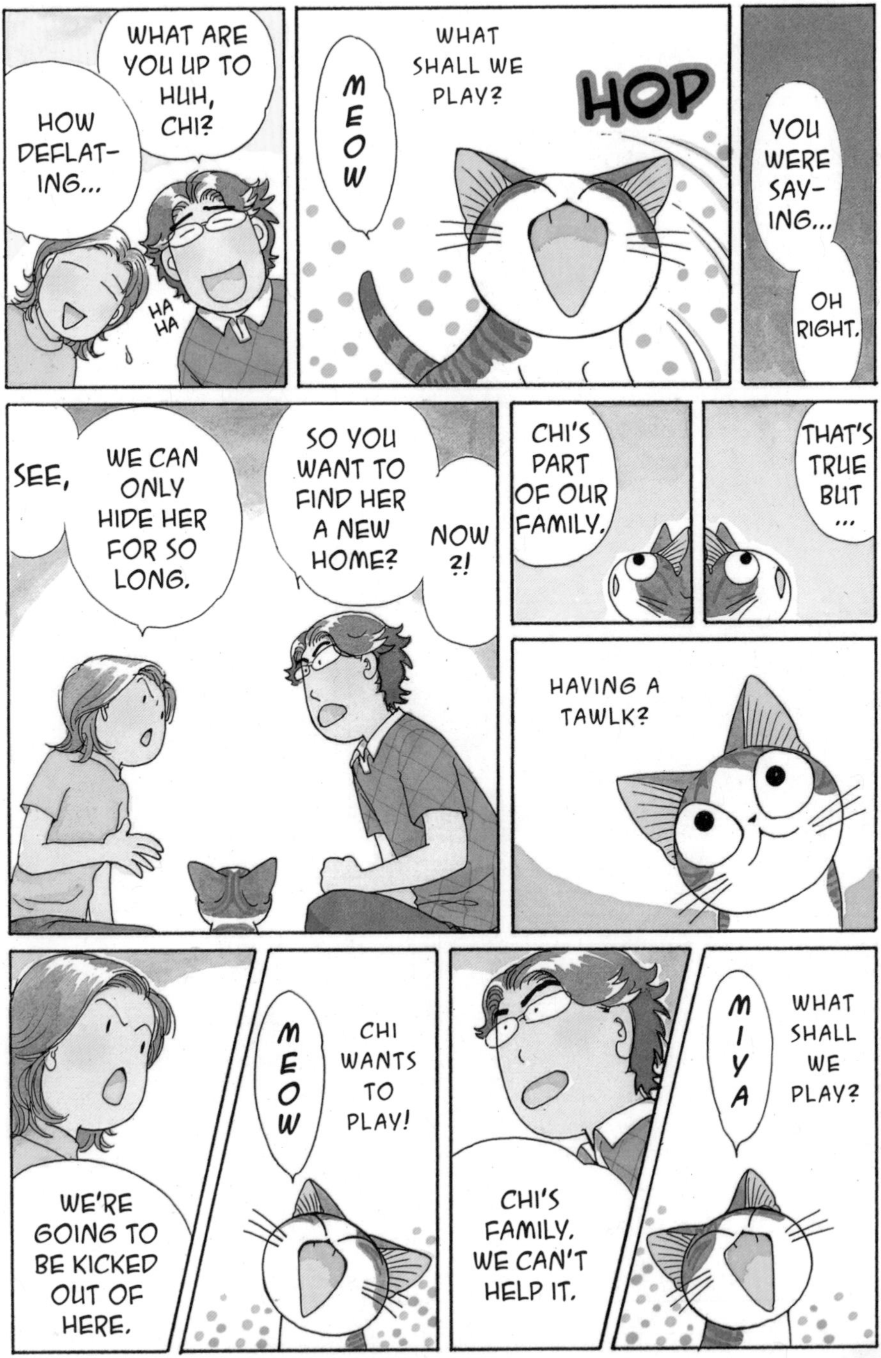
WHAT ARE YOU UP TO HUH, CHI?
HOW DEFLATING...
HA HA
MEOW
WHAT SHALL WE PLAY?
HOP
YOU WERE SAYING...
OH RIGHT.
SEE,
WE CAN ONLY HIDE HER FOR SO LONG.
SO YOU WANT TO FIND HER A NEW HOME?
NOW ?!
CHI'S PART OF OUR FAMILY.
THAT'S TRUE BUT ...
HAVING A TAWLK?
WE'RE GOING TO BE KICKED OUT OF HERE.
MEOW
CHI WANTS TO PLAY!
CHI'S FAMILY. WE CAN'T HELP IT.
MIYA
WHAT SHALL WE PLAY?

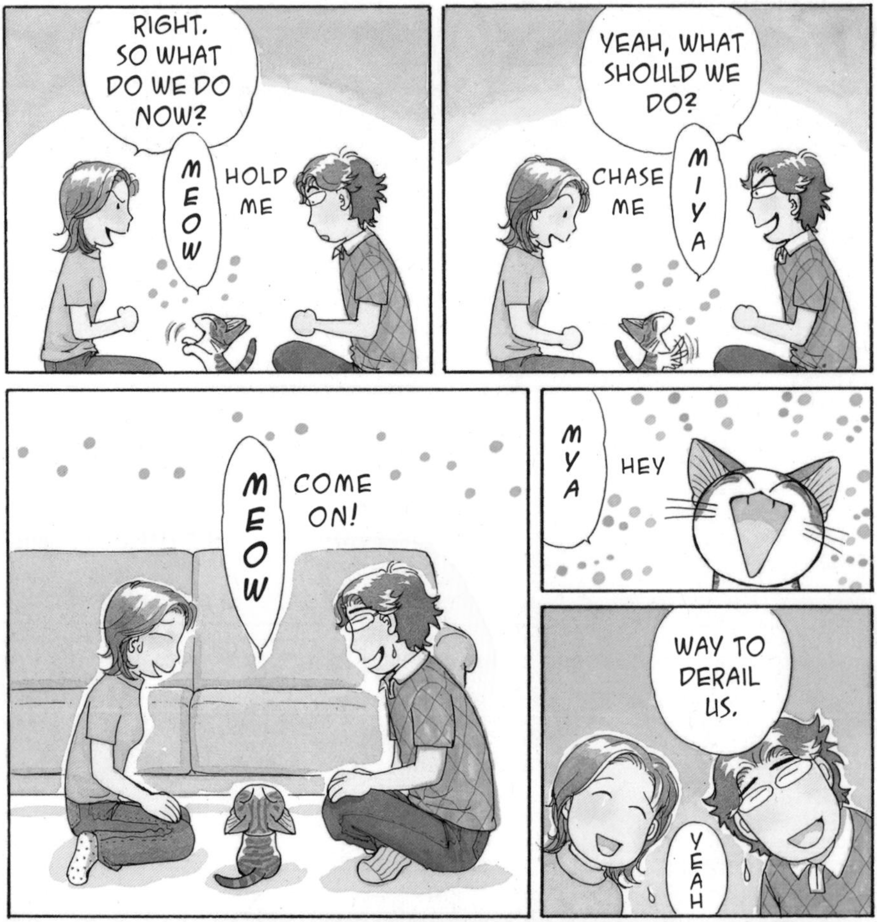
RIGHT. SO WHAT DO WE DO NOW?
MEOW
HOLD ME
YEAH, WHAT SHOULD WE DO?
CHASE ME
MIYA
MEOW
COME ON!
MYA
HEY
WAY TO DERAIL US.
YEAH
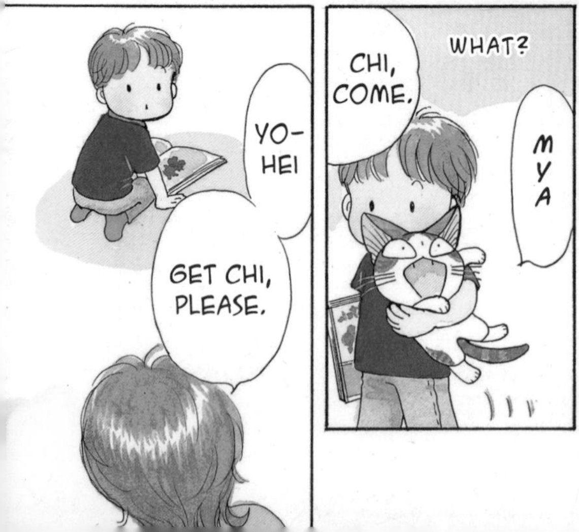
YO-HEI
GET CHI, PLEASE.
CHI, COME.
WHAT?
MYA
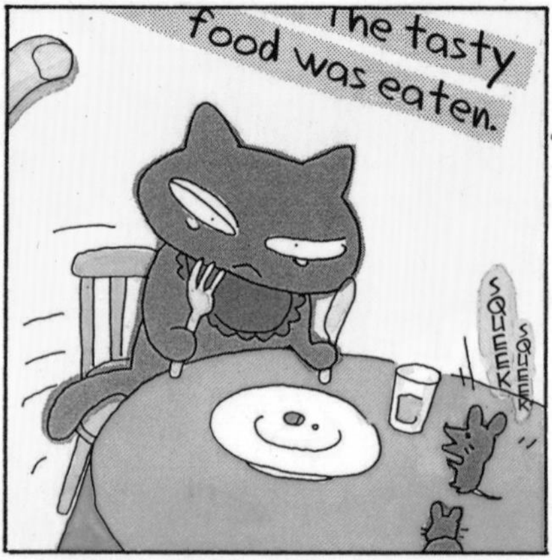
The tasty food was eaten.
SQUEEK
SQUEEK
THE FOLLOWING ILLUSTRATIONS WERE DRAWN BY ARTIST RISA ITO.

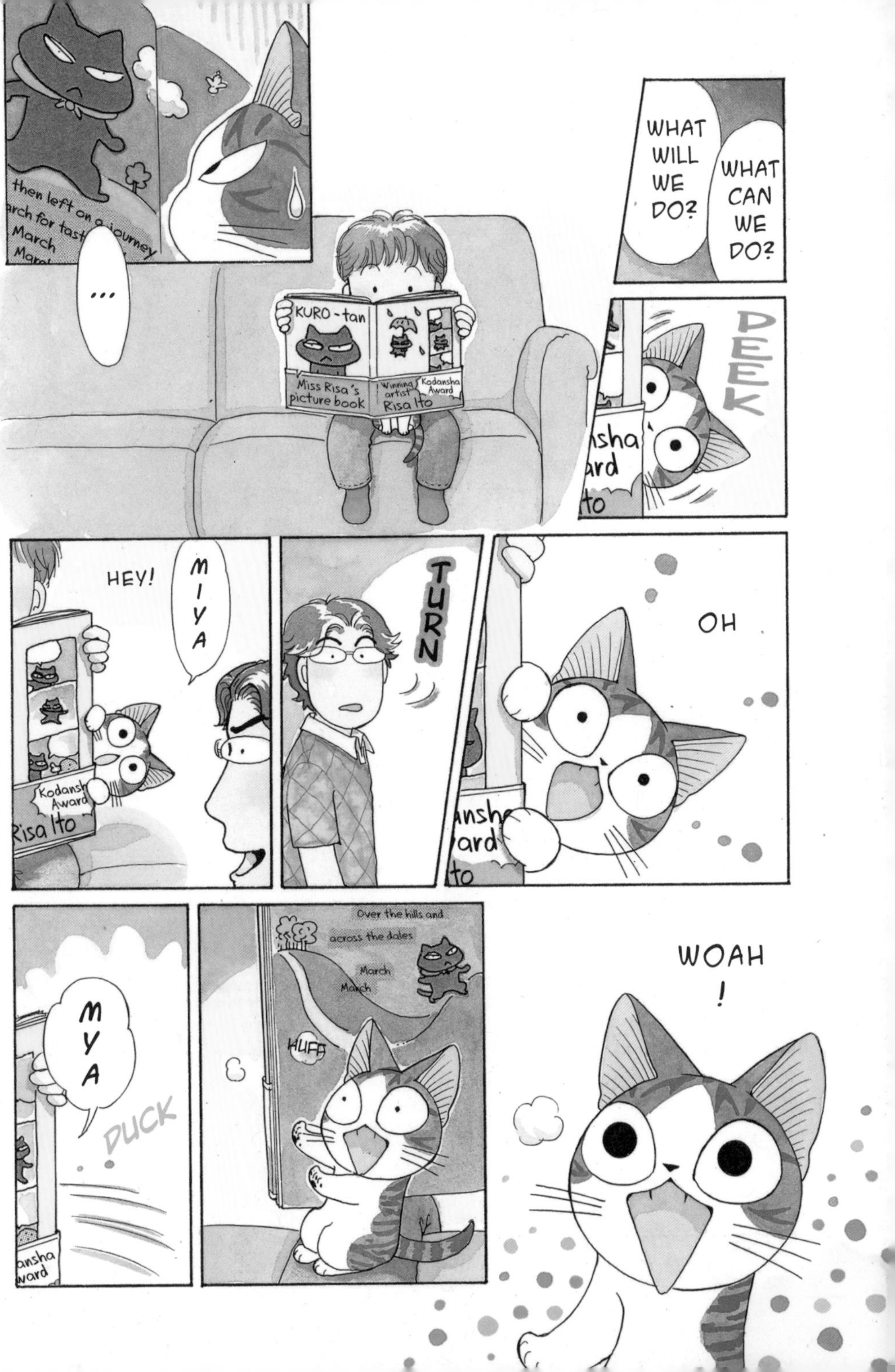

then left on a journey
March
...
KURO-tan
Miss Risa's picture book
Winning artist Risa Ito
Kodansha Award
WHAT WILL WE DO?
WHAT CAN WE DO?
DEEK
HEY!
MIYA
Kodansha Award
Risa Ito
TURN
OH
MYA
DUCK
Over the hills and
across the dales
March
March
HUFF
WOAH!

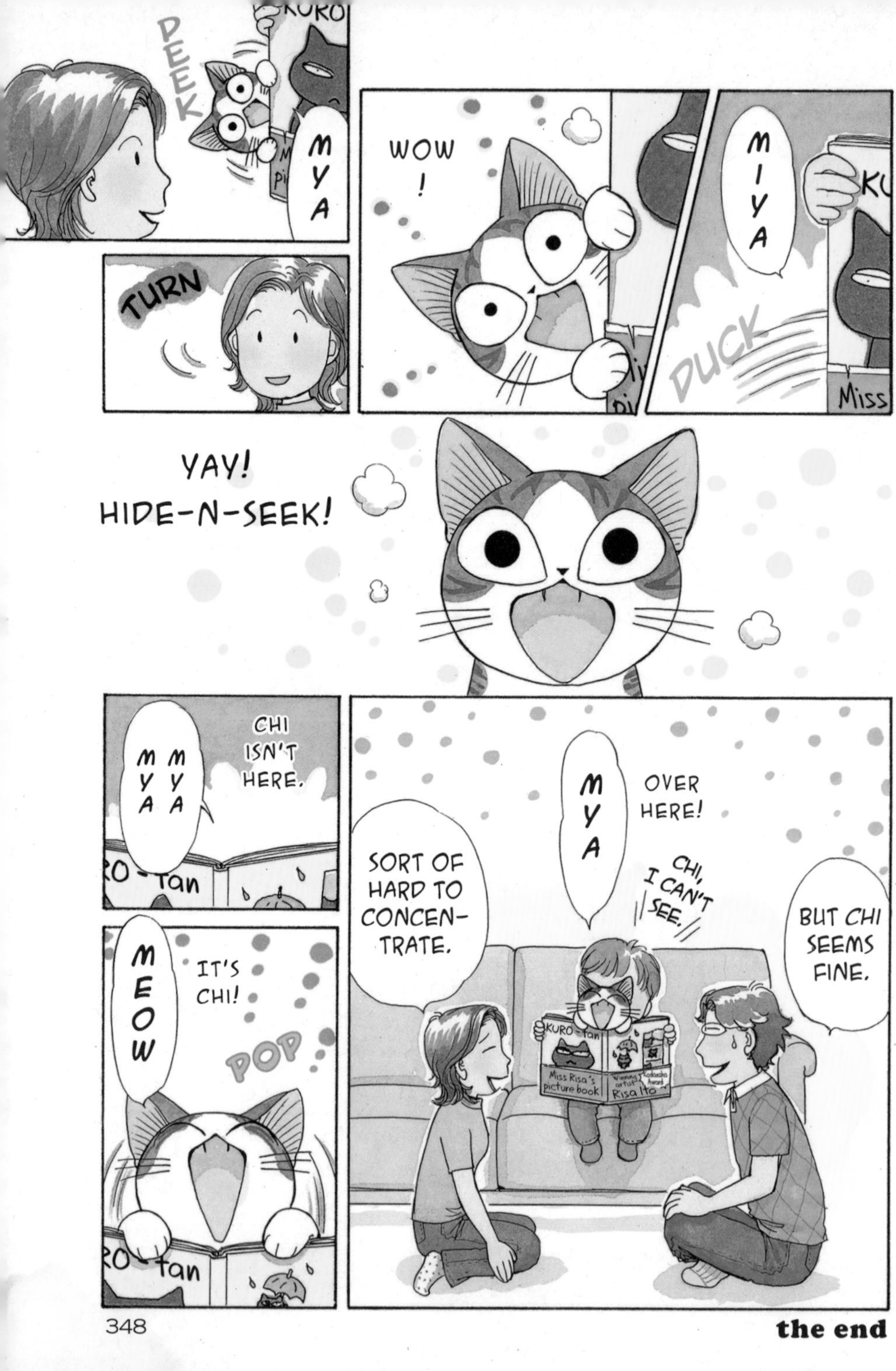
KURO
PEEK
MYA
TURN
WOW!
MIYA
KU
DUCK
Miss
YAY! HIDE-N-SEEK!
MYA MYA
CHI ISN'T HERE.
RO-tan
MEOW
IT'S CHI!
POP
RO-tan
SORT OF HARD TO CONCENTRATE.
MYA
OVER HERE!
CHI, I CAN'T SEE.
BUT CHI SEEMS FINE.
KURO-tan
Miss Risa's picture book
Winning artist Risa Ito
Kodansha Award

the end

homemade 44: a cat is attacked

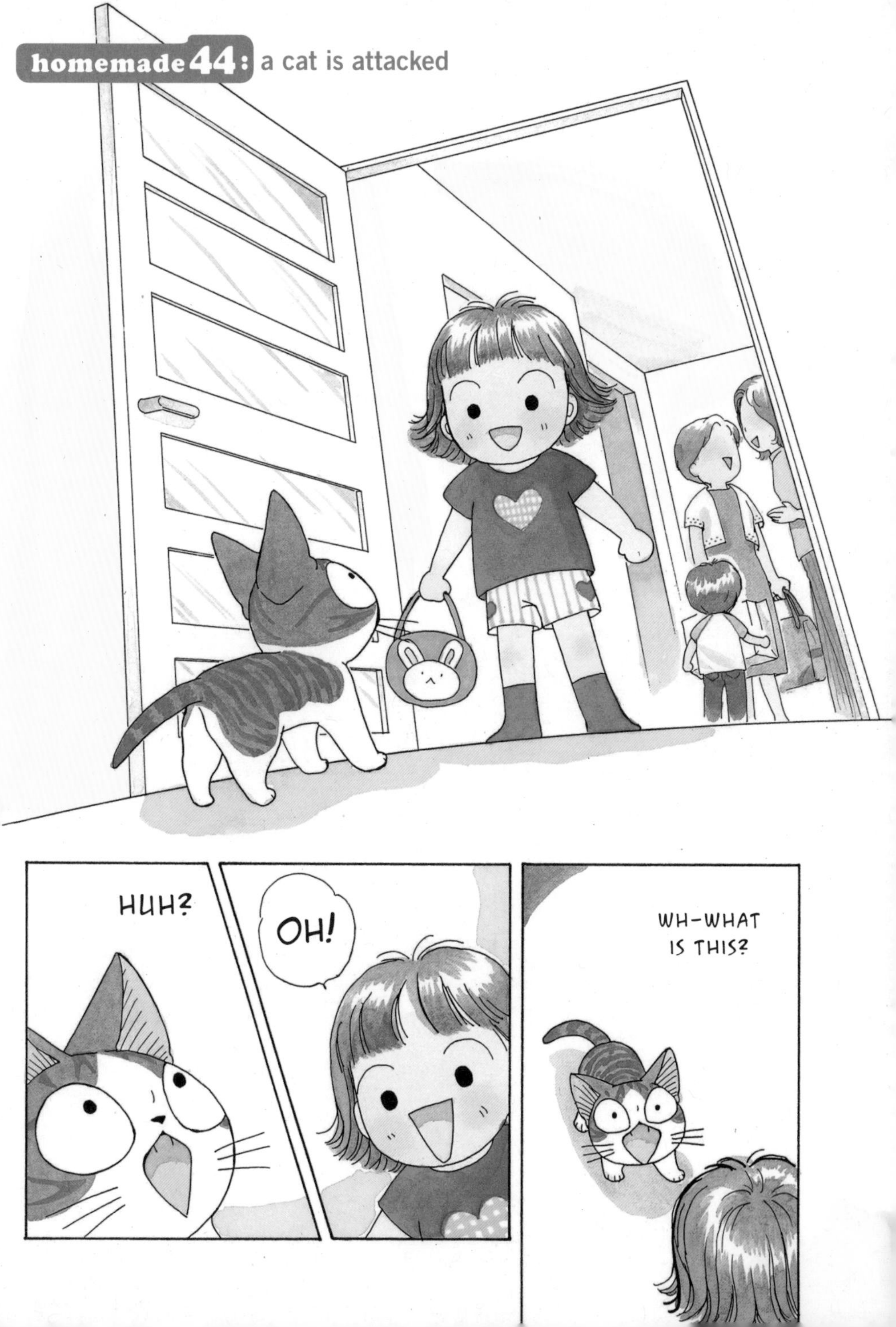
HUH?
OH!
WH-WHAT IS THIS?

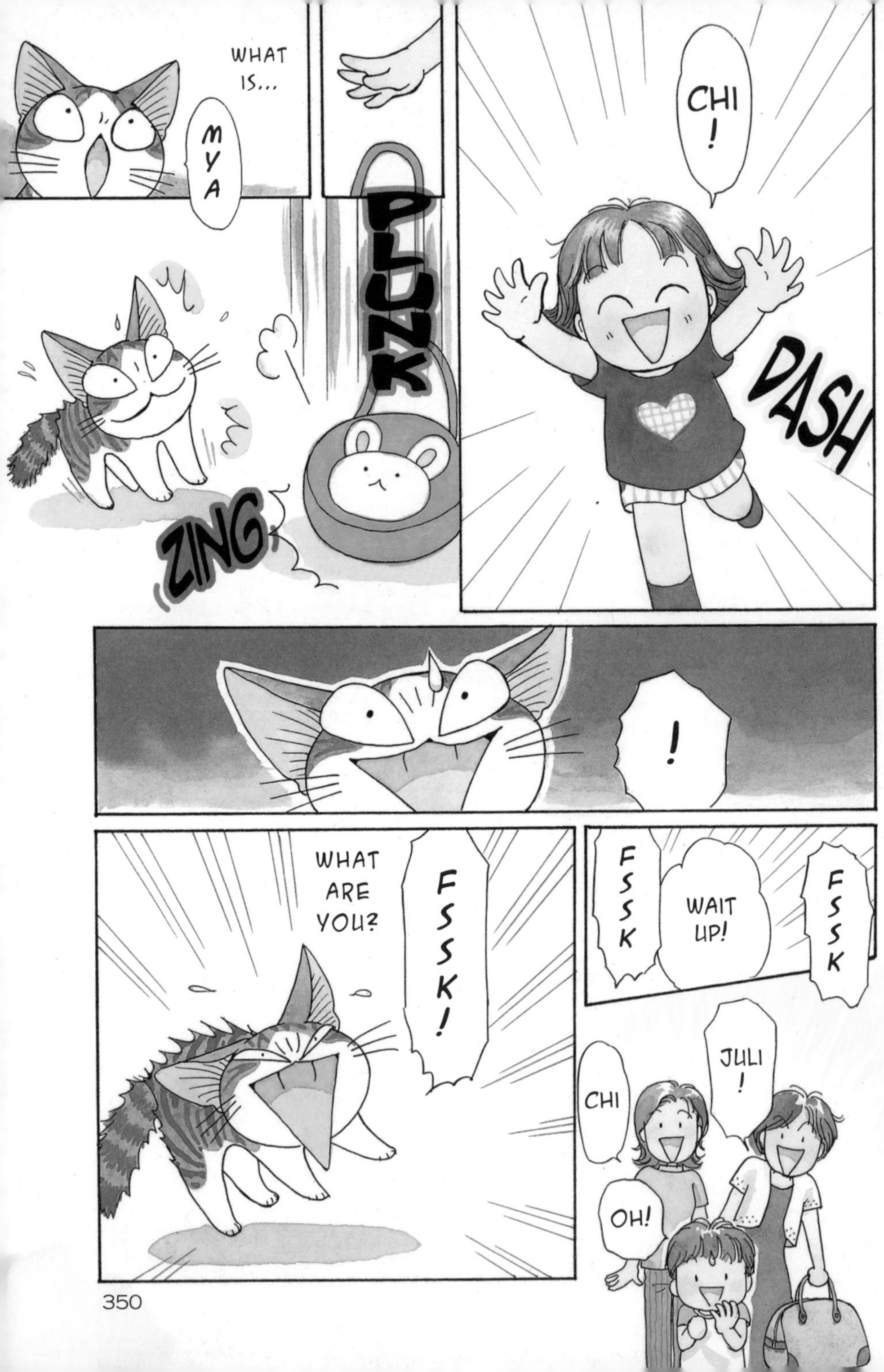
WHAT IS...
MYA
PLUNK
ZING
CHI!
DASH
!
WHAT ARE YOU?
FSSSK!
FSSK
WAIT UP!
FSSK
CHI
JULI!
OH!

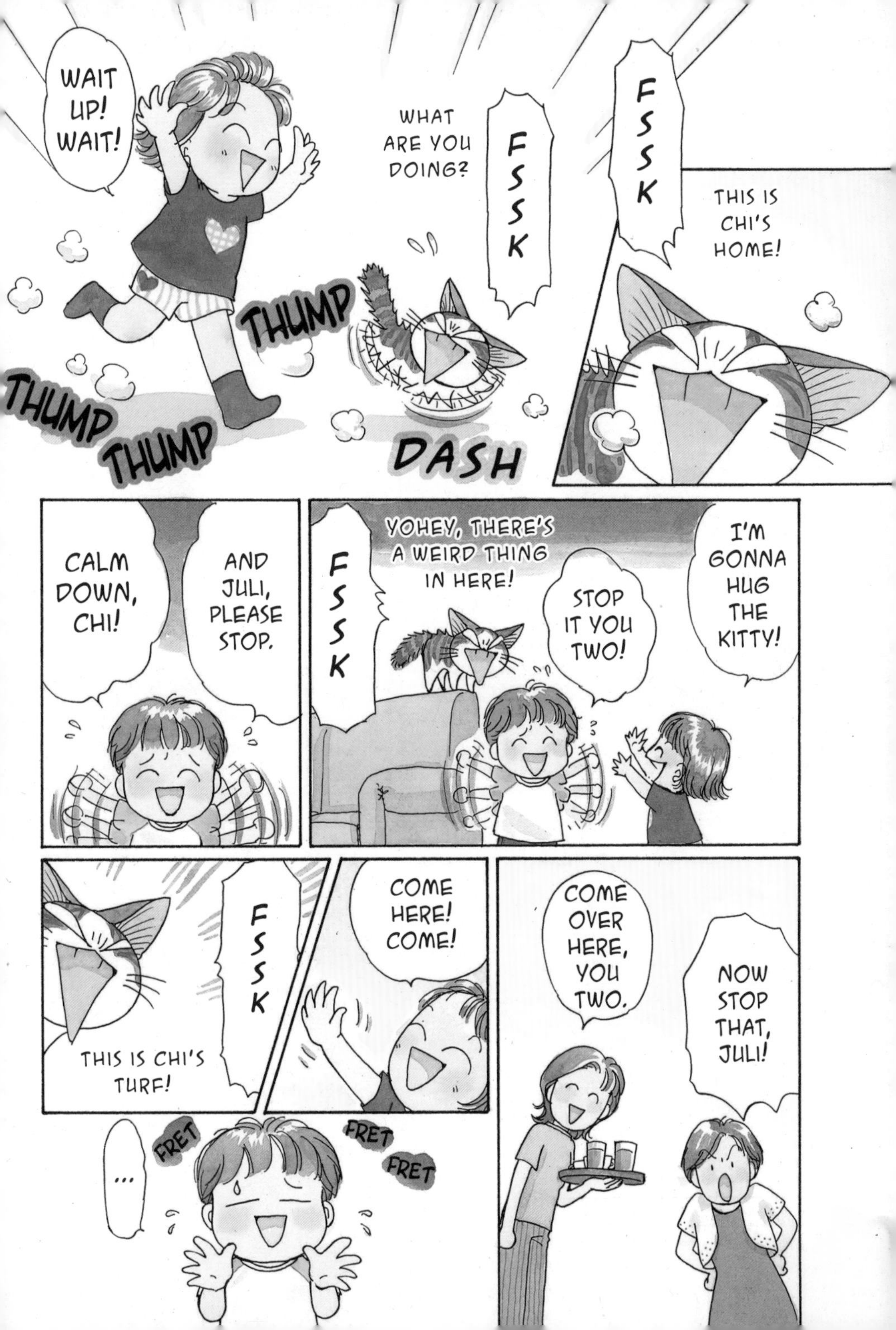
WAIT UP! WAIT!
THUMP
THUMP
THUMP
WHAT ARE YOU DOING?
FSSK
DASH
FSSK
THIS IS CHI'S HOME!
CALM DOWN, CHI!
AND JULI, PLEASE STOP.
FSSK
YOHEY, THERE'S A WEIRD THING IN HERE!
STOP IT YOU TWO!
I'M GONNA HUG THE KITTY!
FSSK
THIS IS CHI'S TURF!
COME HERE! COME!
...
FRET
FRET
FRET
COME OVER HERE, YOU TWO.
NOW STOP THAT, JULI!

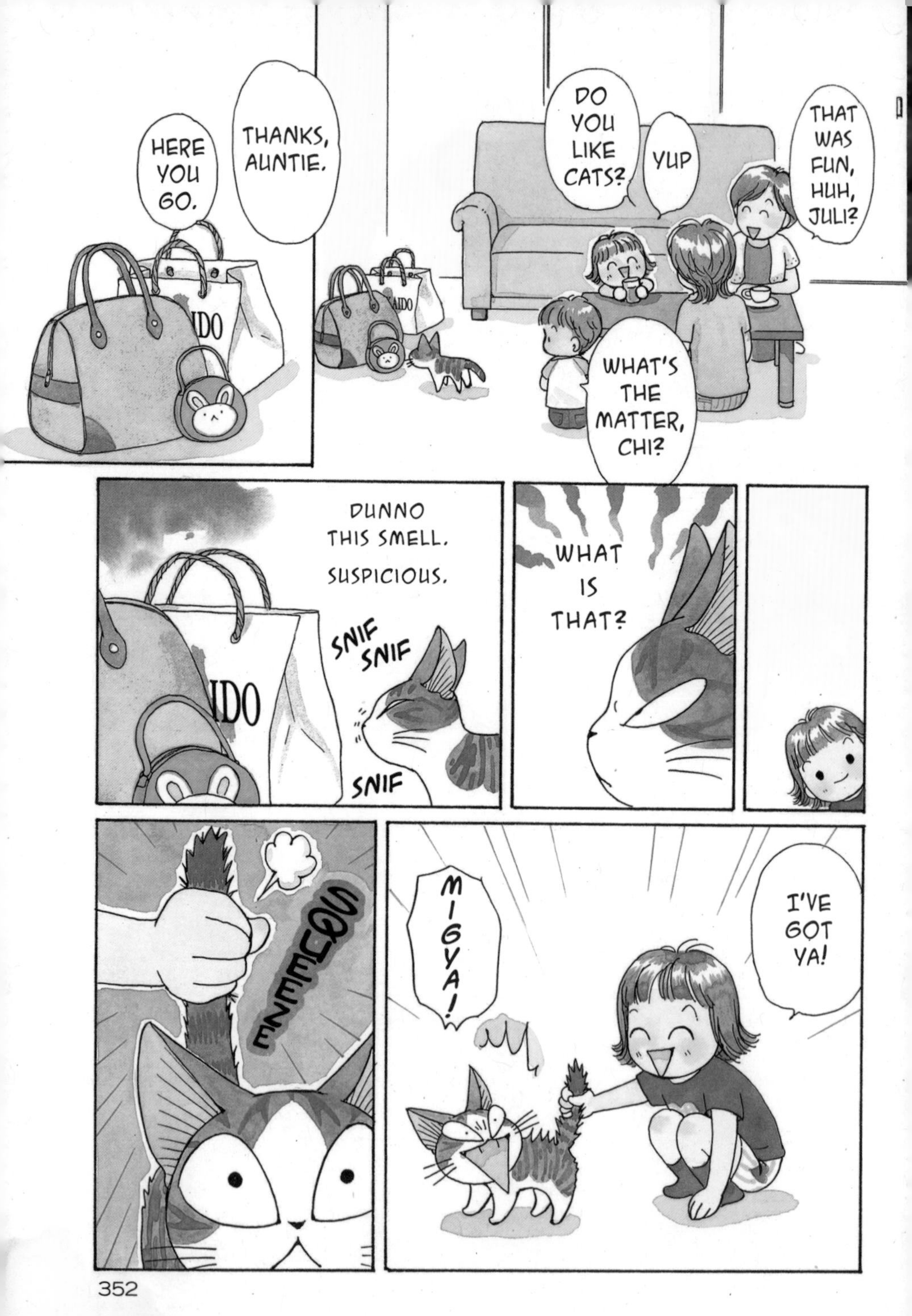
HERE YOU GO.
THANKS, AUNTIE.
DO YOU LIKE CATS?
YUP
THAT WAS FUN, HUH, JULI?
WHAT'S THE MATTER, CHI?
DUNNO THIS SMELL.
SUSPICIOUS.
SNIF SNIF
SNIF
WHAT IS THAT?
SQUEEEZE
MIGYA!
I'VE GOT YA!

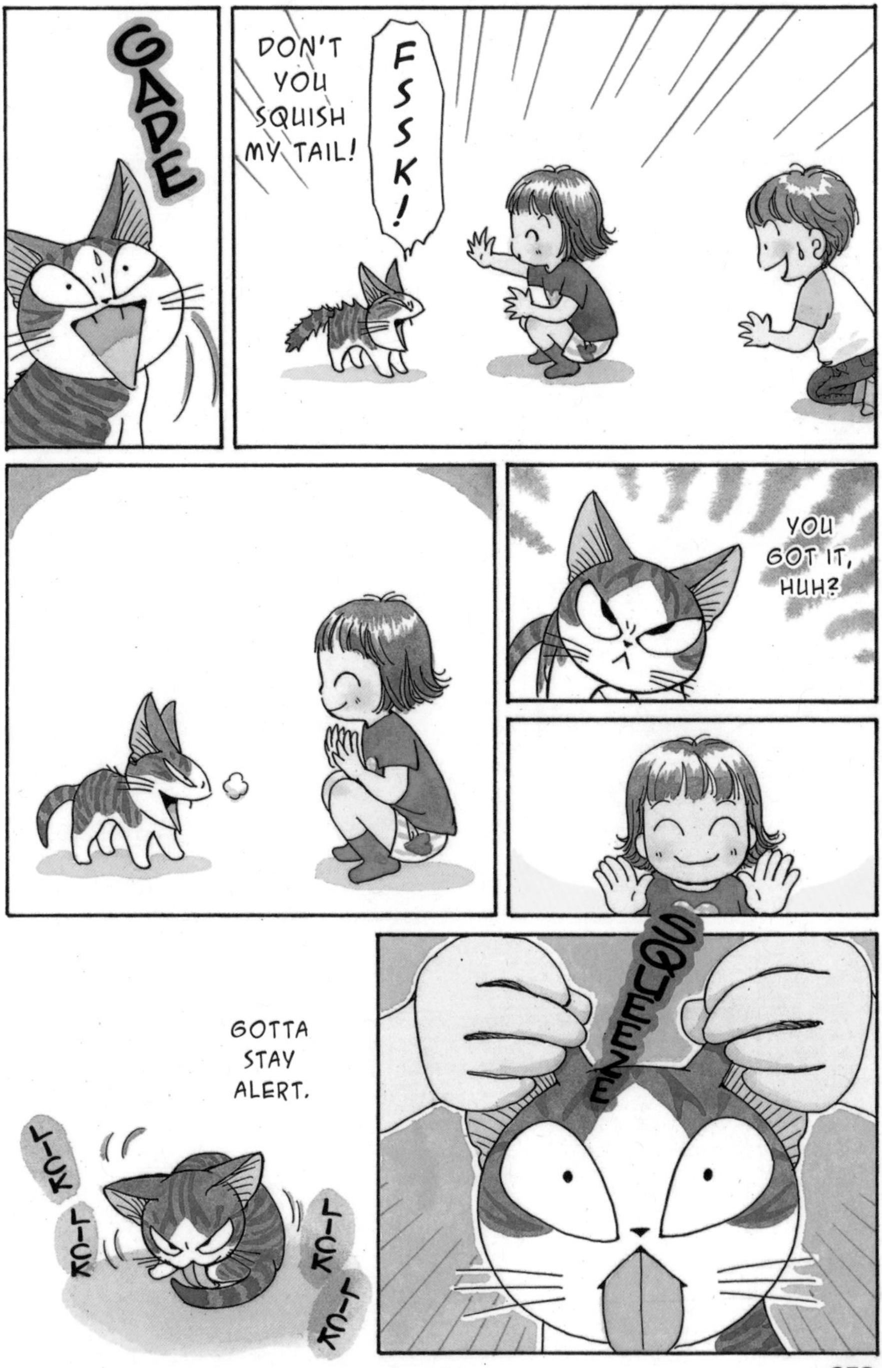
GAPE
DON'T YOU SQUISH MY TAIL!
FSSK!
YOU GOT IT, HUH?
SQUEEEEE
GOTTA STAY ALERT.
LICK LICK
LICK LICK

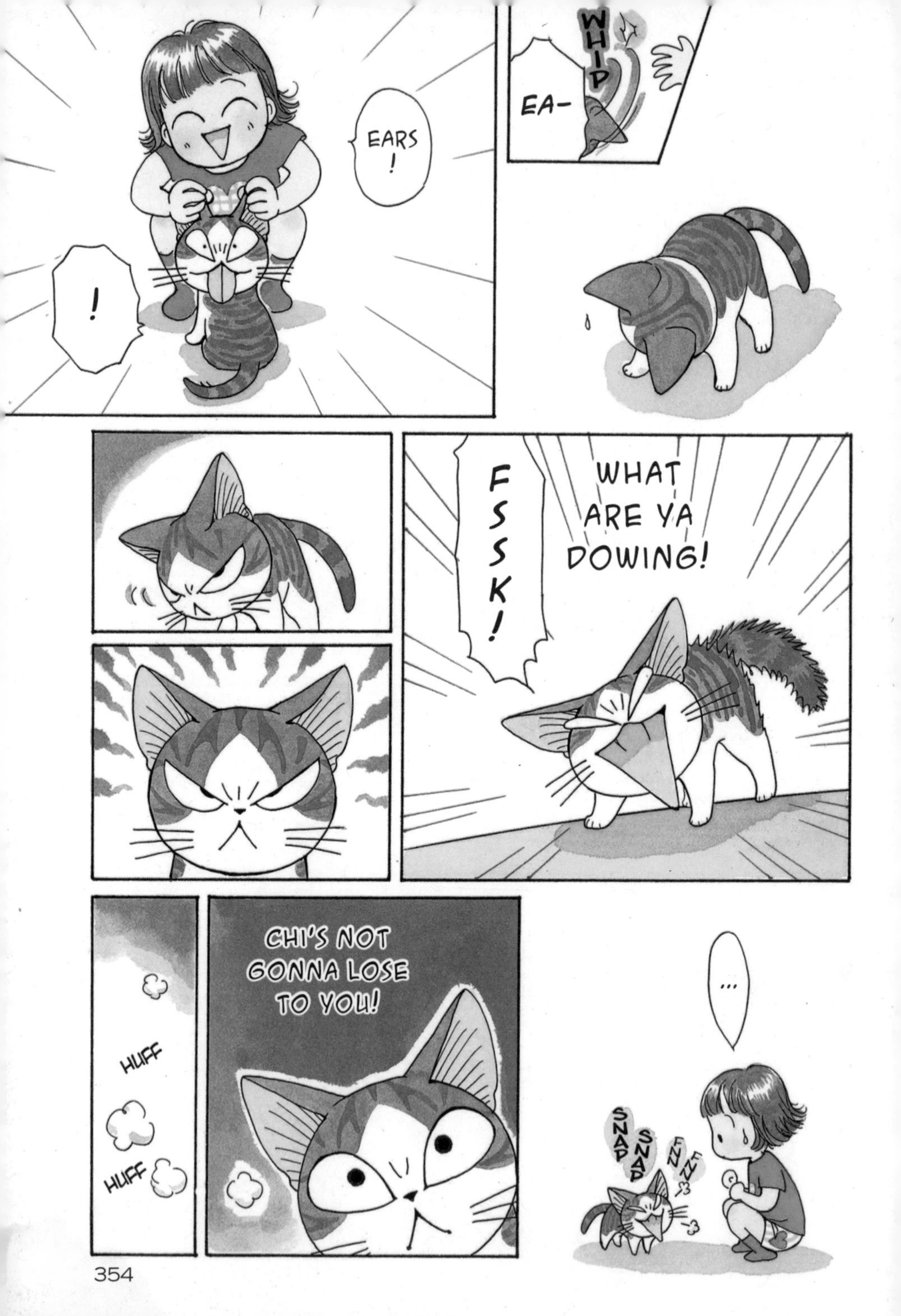
EARS!
!
WHIP
EA-
FSSK!
WHAT ARE YA DOWING!
HUFF
HUFF
CHI'S NOT GONNA LOSE TO YOU!
...
SNAP SNAP
FNN FNN

CHI'S TINY BUT SHE'S PRETTY SPUNKY.

YEAH.

YOU'RE A GOOD MATCH.

LET'S OPEN UP THE SOUVENIR, YES?

RIGHT

HOKKAIDO

WOAH, AWESOME!

YAMMER OOH AH

I'M TOO SCARED TO TOUCH IT.

WOW

WHEE

WHAT NOW?

KYAA!

PEEK

SKAMPER

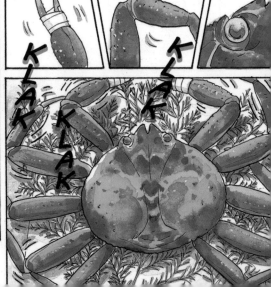

KLAK

KLAK

KLAK

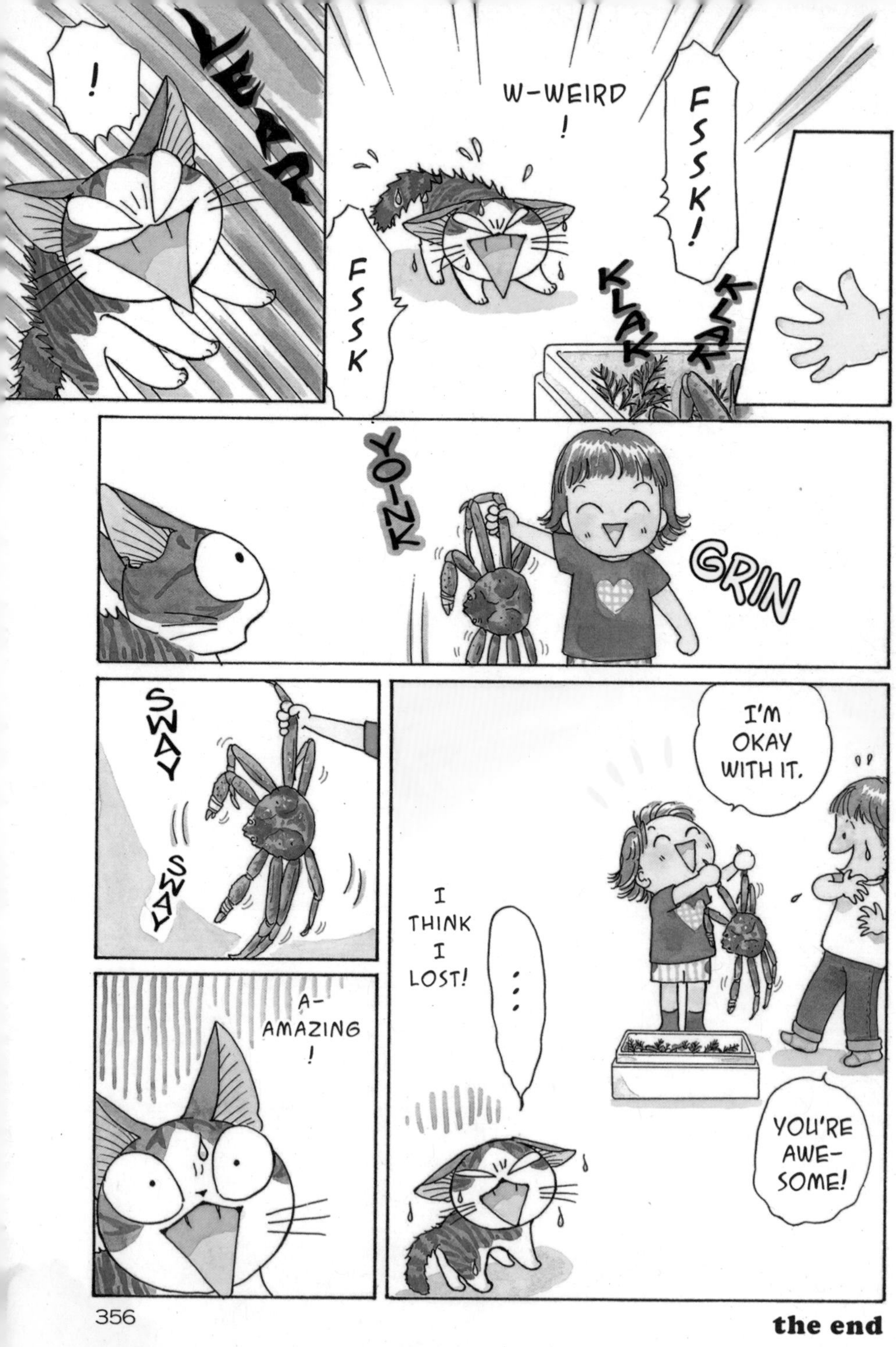
!
YEAR
W-WEIRD!
FSSK
FSSK!
KLAK
KLAK
YOINK
GRIN
SWAY
SWAY
A-AMAZING!
I'M OKAY WITH IT.
I THINK I LOST!
...
YOU'RE AWESOME!

the end

homemade 45: a cat gets along

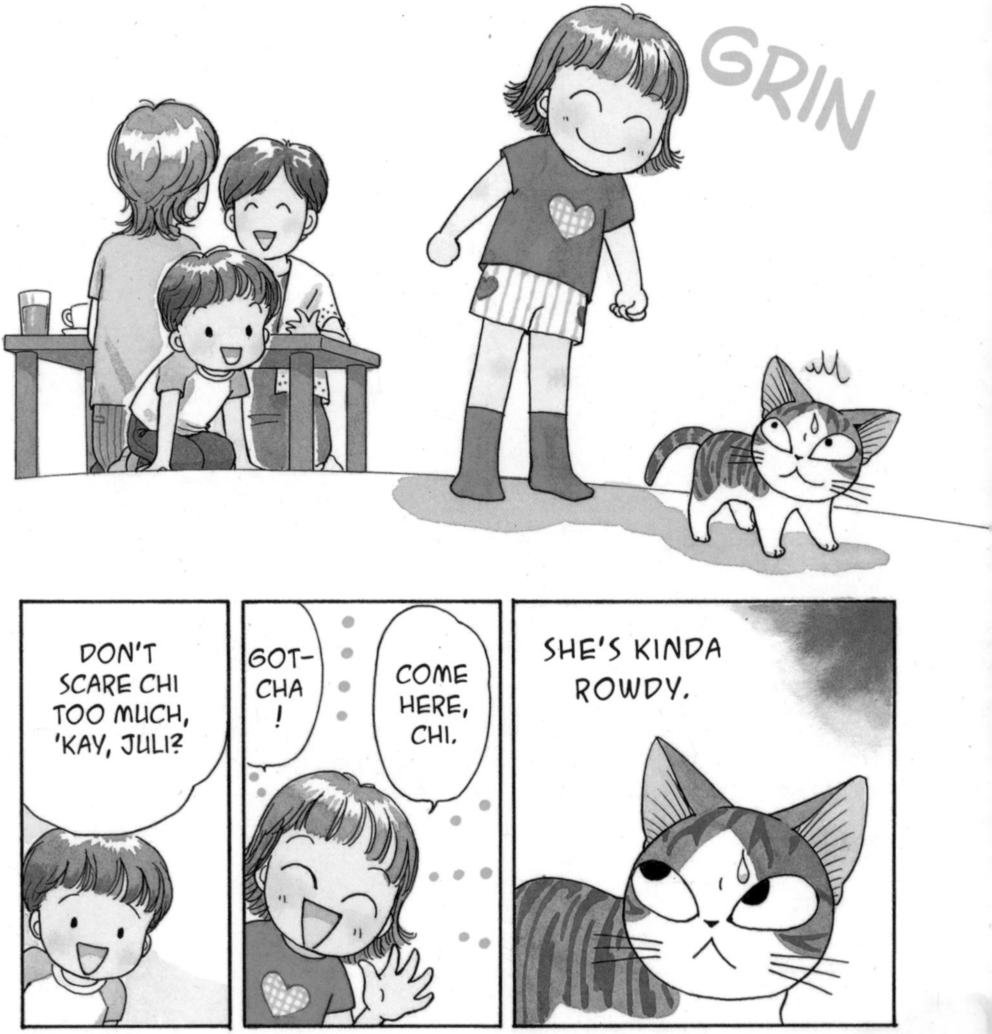
GRIN
DON'T SCARE CHI TOO MUCH, 'KAY, JULI?
GOT-CHA!
COME HERE, CHI.
SHE'S KINDA ROWDY.

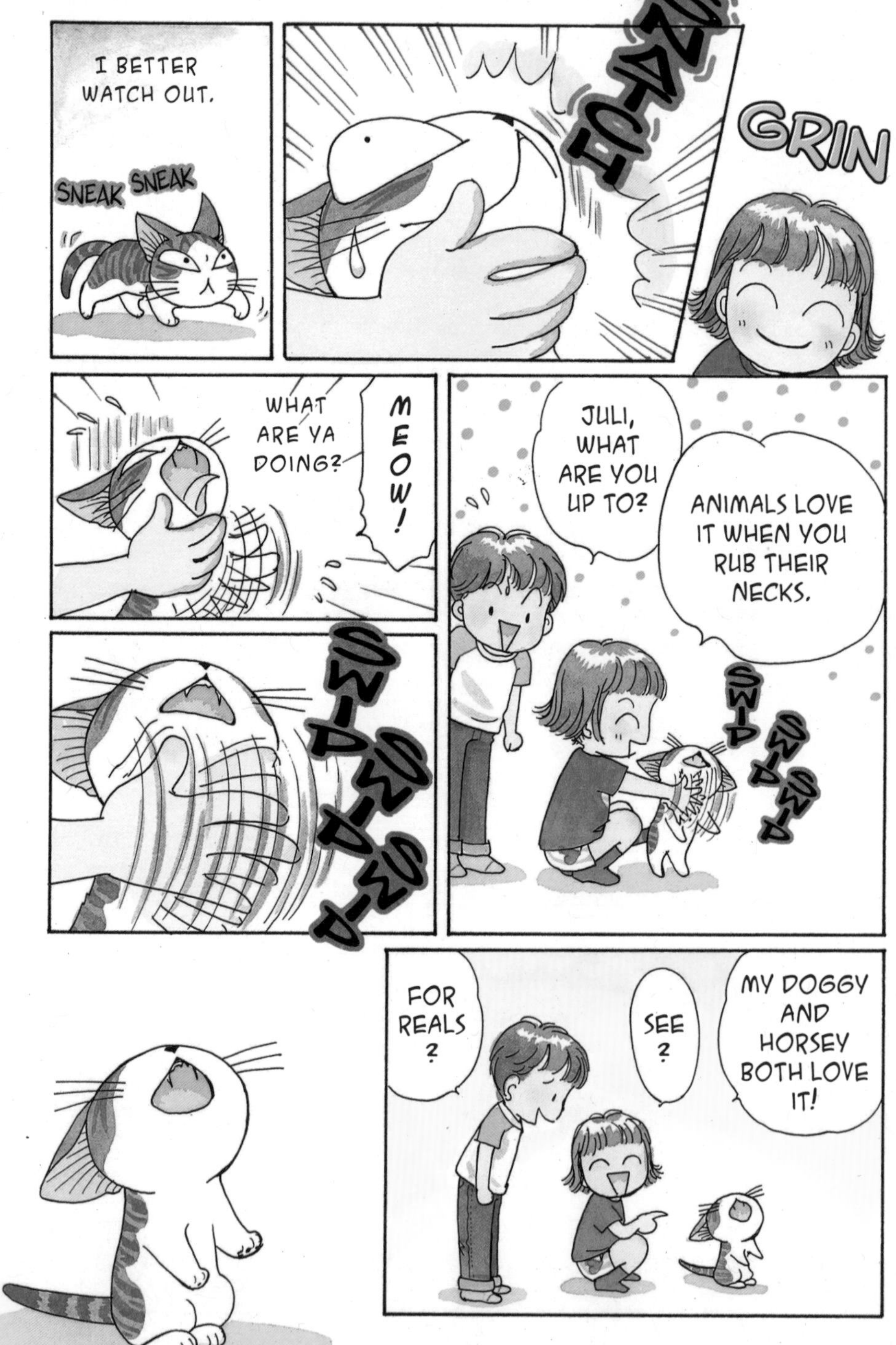
I BETTER WATCH OUT.
SNEAK SNEAK
SNATCH
GRIN
WHAT ARE YA DOING?
MEOW!
SWIP SWIP SWIP
JULI, WHAT ARE YOU UP TO?
ANIMALS LOVE IT WHEN YOU RUB THEIR NECKS.
SWIP SWIP SWIP
FOR REALS?
SEE?
MY DOGGY AND HORSEY BOTH LOVE IT!

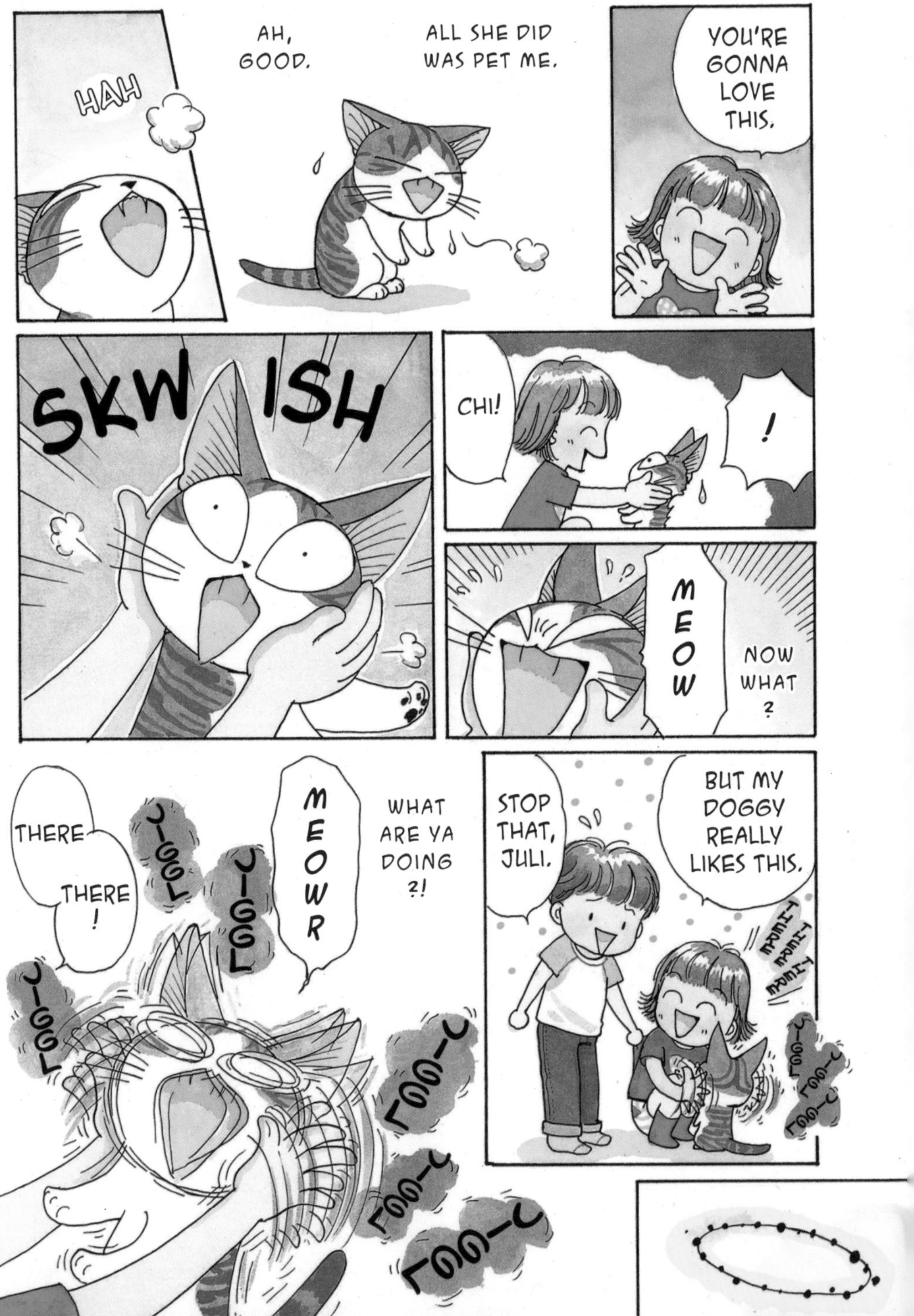
HAH
AH, GOOD.
ALL SHE DID WAS PET ME.
YOU'RE GONNA LOVE THIS.
SKWISH
CHI!
!
MEOW
NOW WHAT?
THERE
THERE!
JIGGL
JIGGL
JIGGL
MEOWR
WHAT ARE YA DOING?!
JIGGL
JIGGL
JIGGL
STOP THAT, JULI.
BUT MY DOGGY REALLY LIKES THIS.
JIGGL
JIGGL
JIGGL

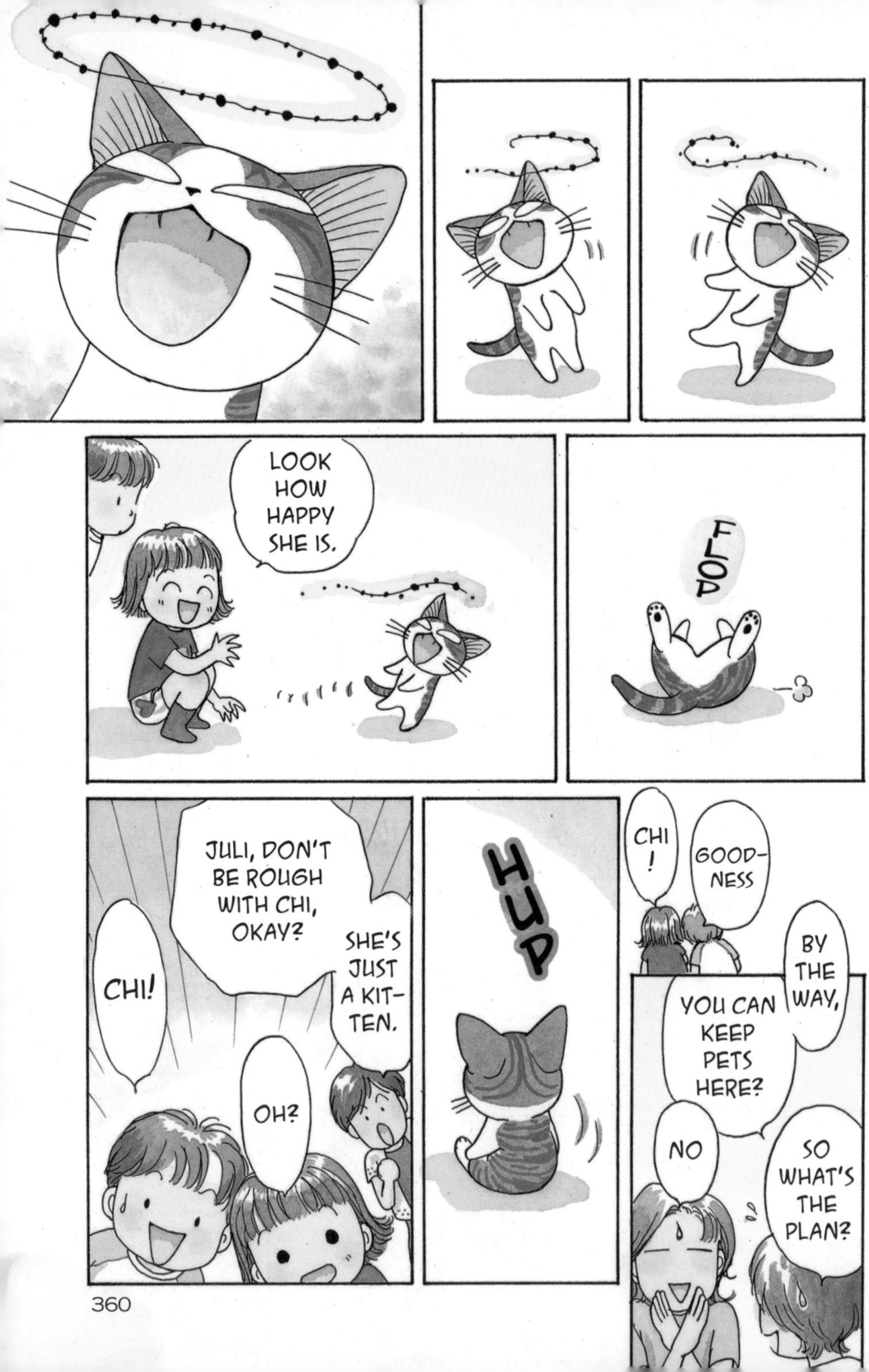
LOOK HOW HAPPY SHE IS.
FLOP
JULI, DON'T BE ROUGH WITH CHI, OKAY?
CHI!
SHE'S JUST A KIT-TEN.
OH?
HUP
CHI!
GOOD-NESS
BY THE WAY,
YOU CAN KEEP PETS HERE?
NO
SO WHAT'S THE PLAN?

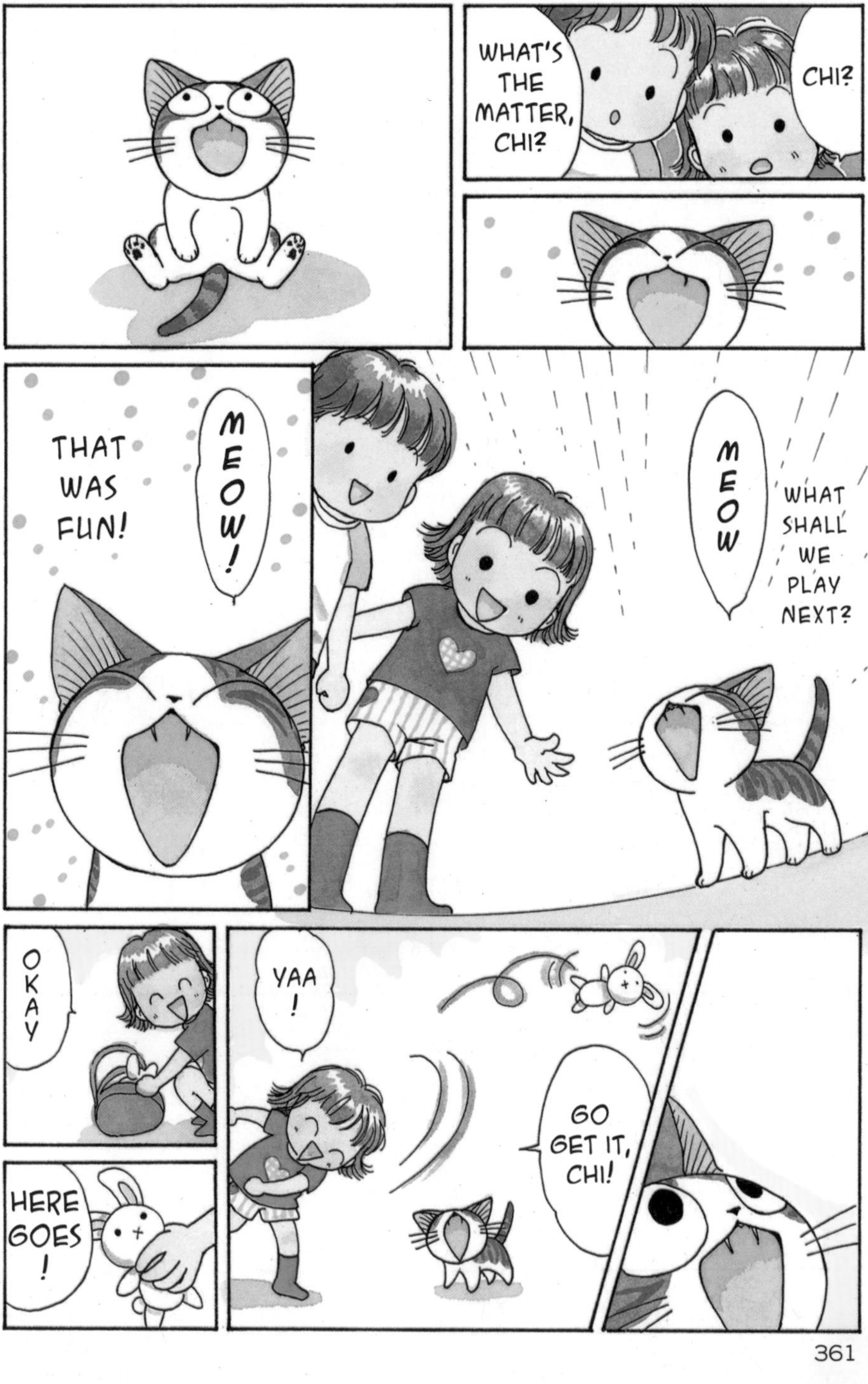
WHAT'S THE MATTER, CHI?
CHI?
THAT WAS FUN!
MEOW!
MEOW
WHAT SHALL WE PLAY NEXT?
OKAY
HERE GOES!
YAA!
GO GET IT, CHI!

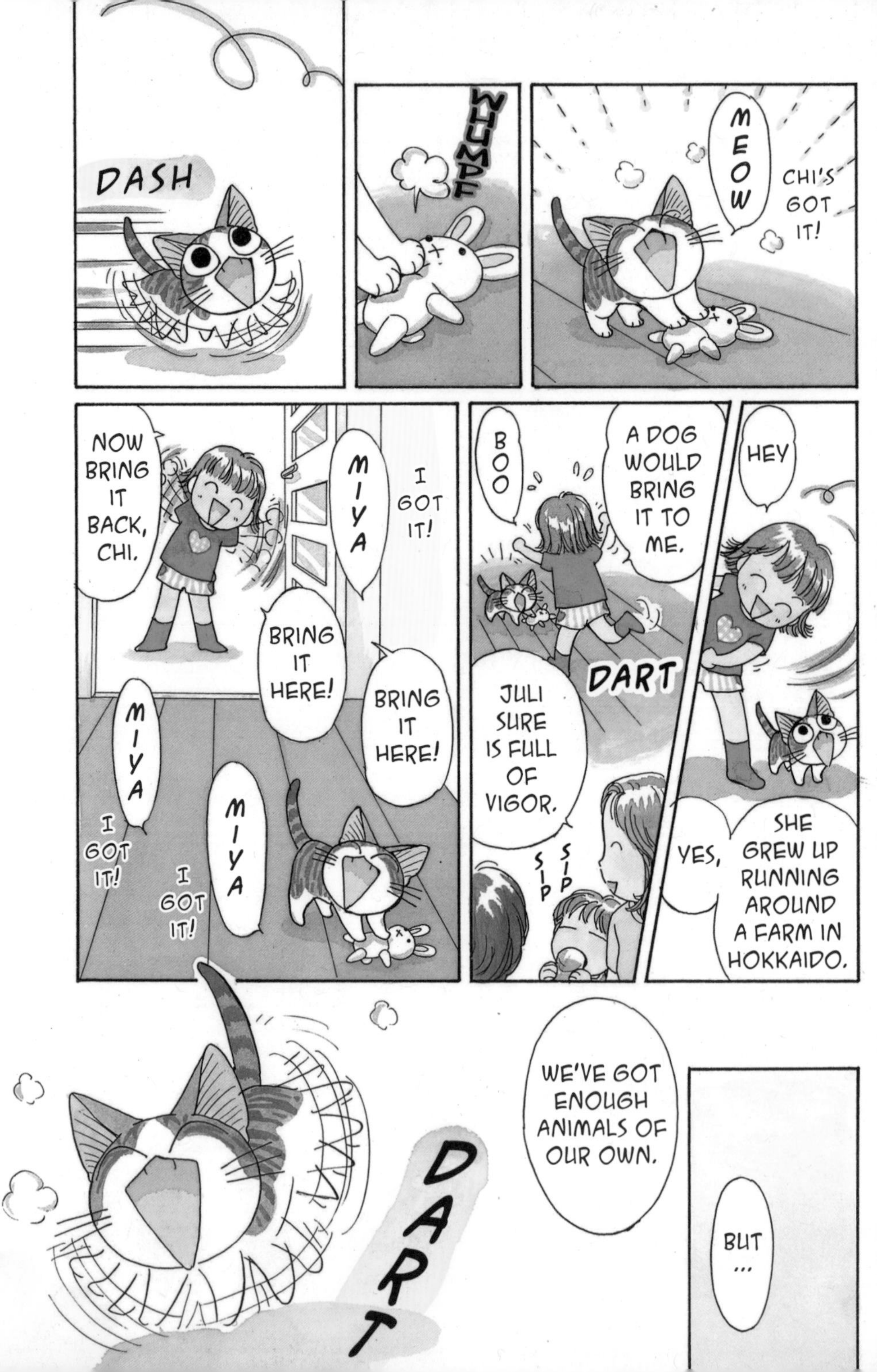
DASH
WHUMPF
MEOW
CHI'S GOT IT!
NOW BRING IT BACK, CHI.
MIYA
I GOT IT!
BRING IT HERE!
BRING IT HERE!
MIYA
I GOT IT!
MIYA
I GOT IT!
BOO
A DOG WOULD BRING IT TO ME.
DART
JULI SURE IS FULL OF VIGOR.
SIP SIP
HEY
YES,
SHE GREW UP RUNNING AROUND A FARM IN HOKKAIDO.
DART
WE'VE GOT ENOUGH ANIMALS OF OUR OWN.
BUT ...

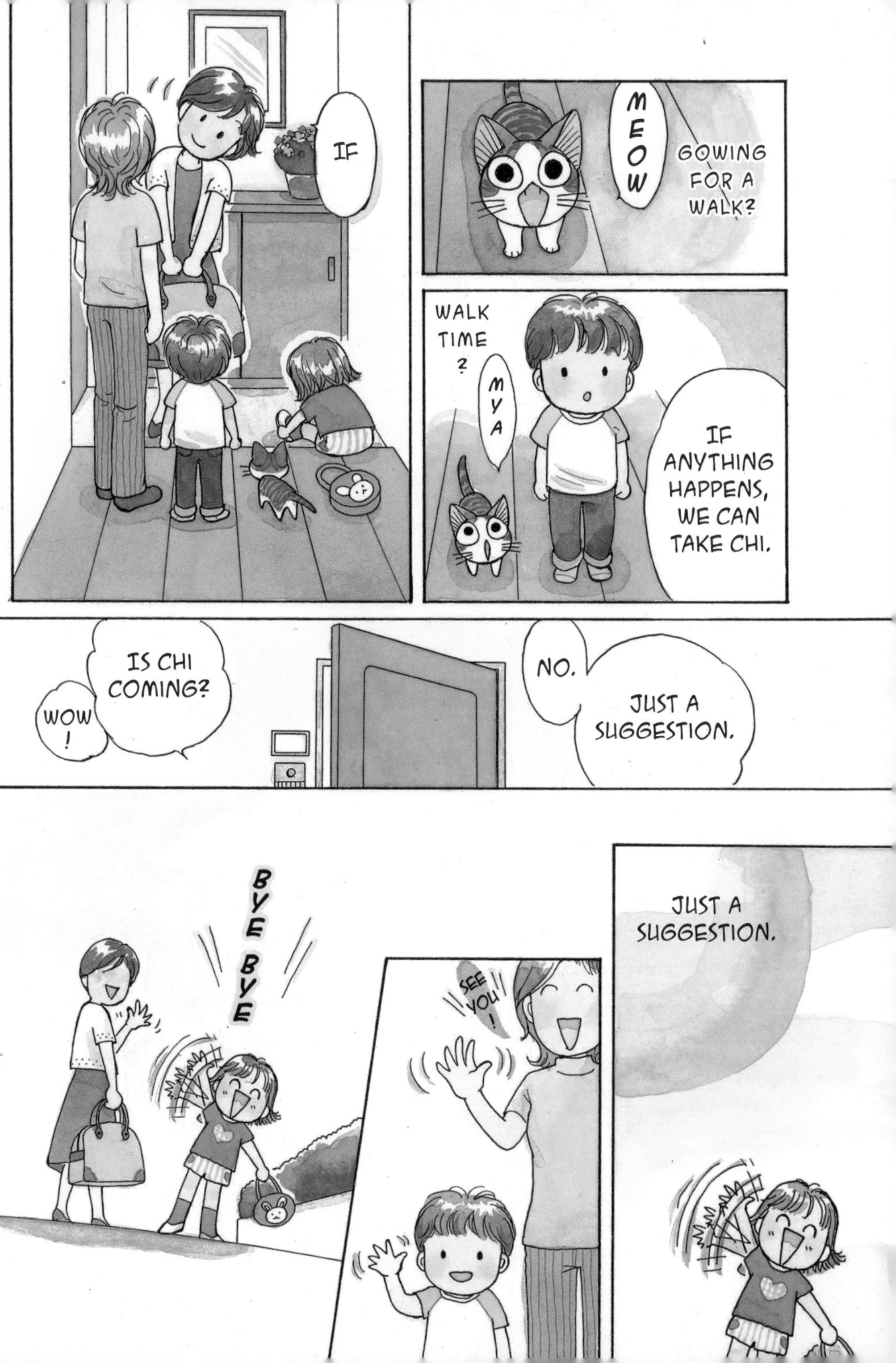
IF
MEOW
GOWING FOR A WALK?
WALK TIME?
MYA
IF ANYTHING HAPPENS, WE CAN TAKE CHI.
WOW!
IS CHI COMING?
NO.
JUST A SUGGESTION.
BYE BYE
SEE YOU!
JUST A SUGGESTION.

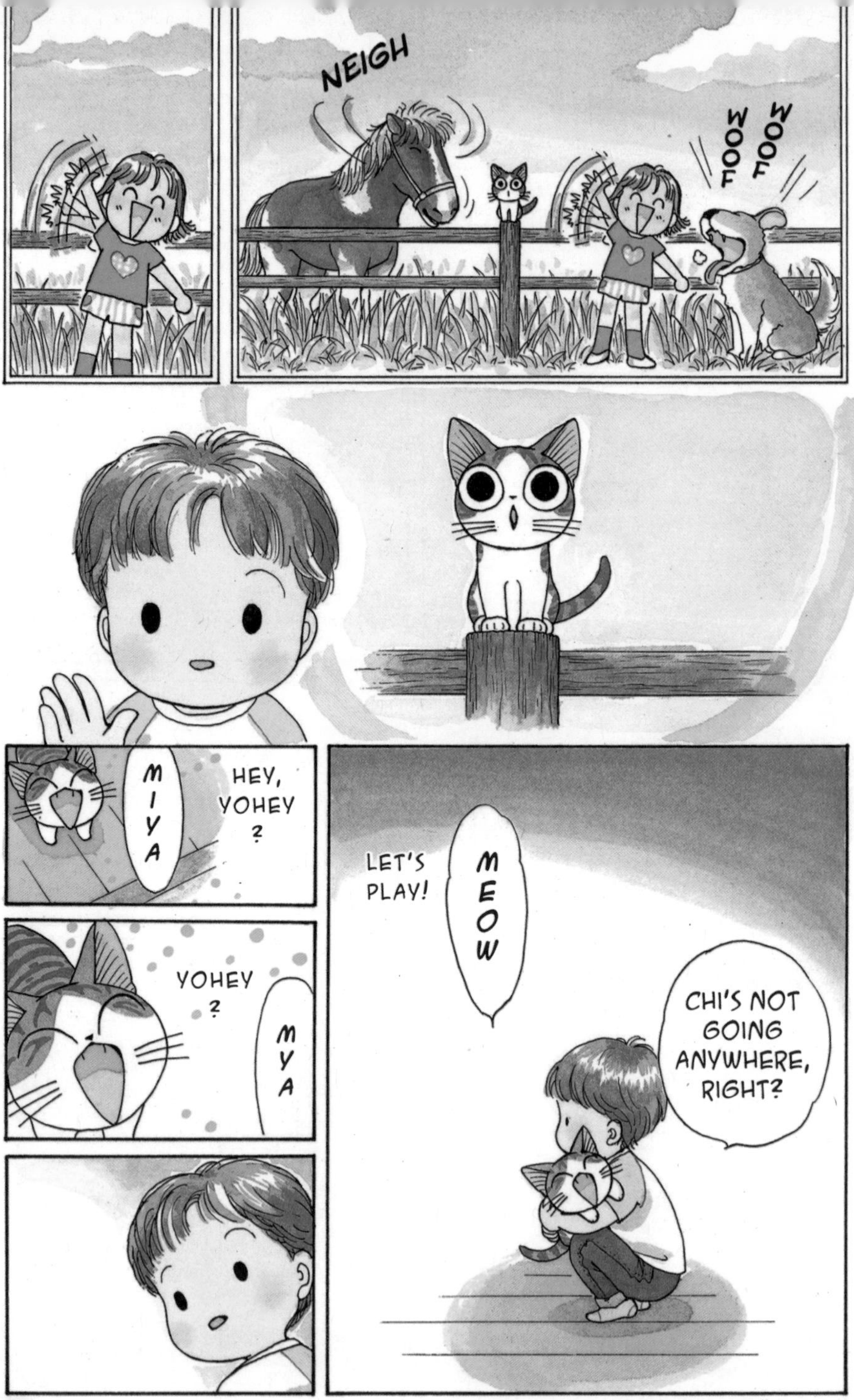
NEIGH
WOOF WOOF
MIYA
HEY, YOHEY?
YOHEY?
MYA
LET'S PLAY!
MEOW
CHI'S NOT GOING ANYWHERE, RIGHT?

the end

homemade 46: a-cat-learns

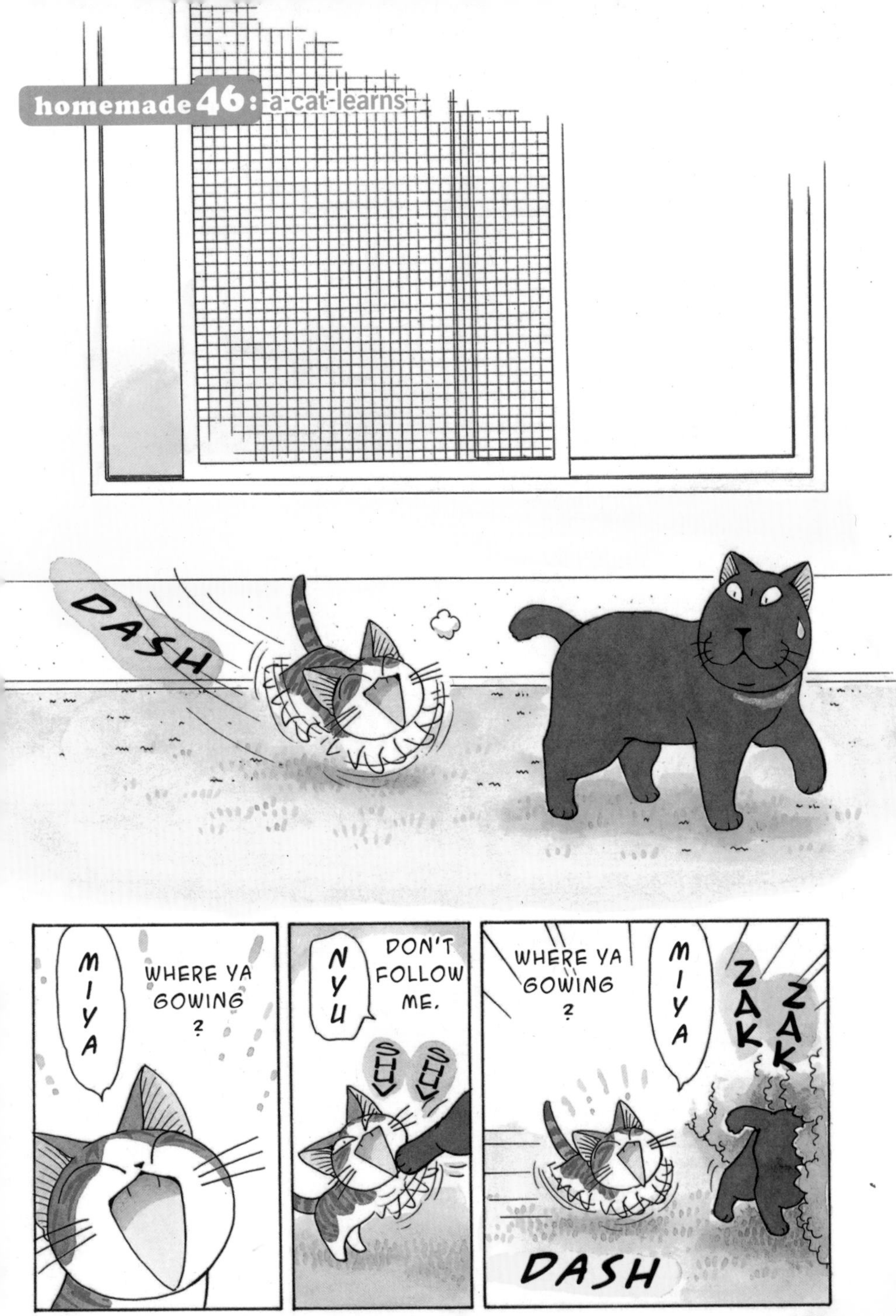
DASH
MIYA
WHERE YA GOWING ?
NYU
DON'T FOLLOW ME.
SHU
SHU
WHERE YA GOWING ?
MIYA
ZAK
ZAK
DASH

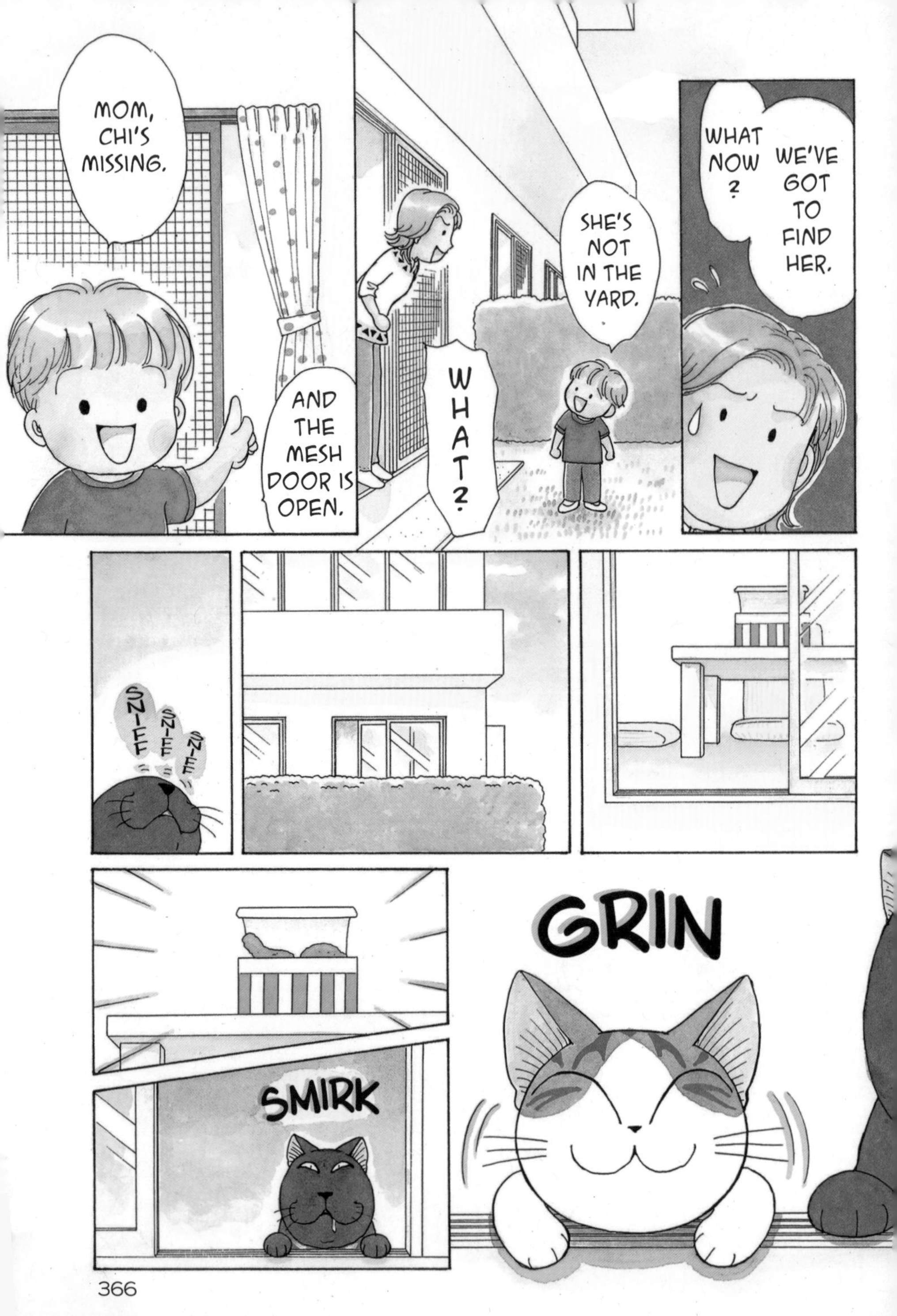
MOM, CHI'S MISSING.
AND THE MESH DOOR IS OPEN.
WHAT?
SHE'S NOT IN THE YARD.
WHAT NOW?
WE'VE GOT TO FIND HER.
SNIFF SNIFF SNIFF
SMIRK
GRIN

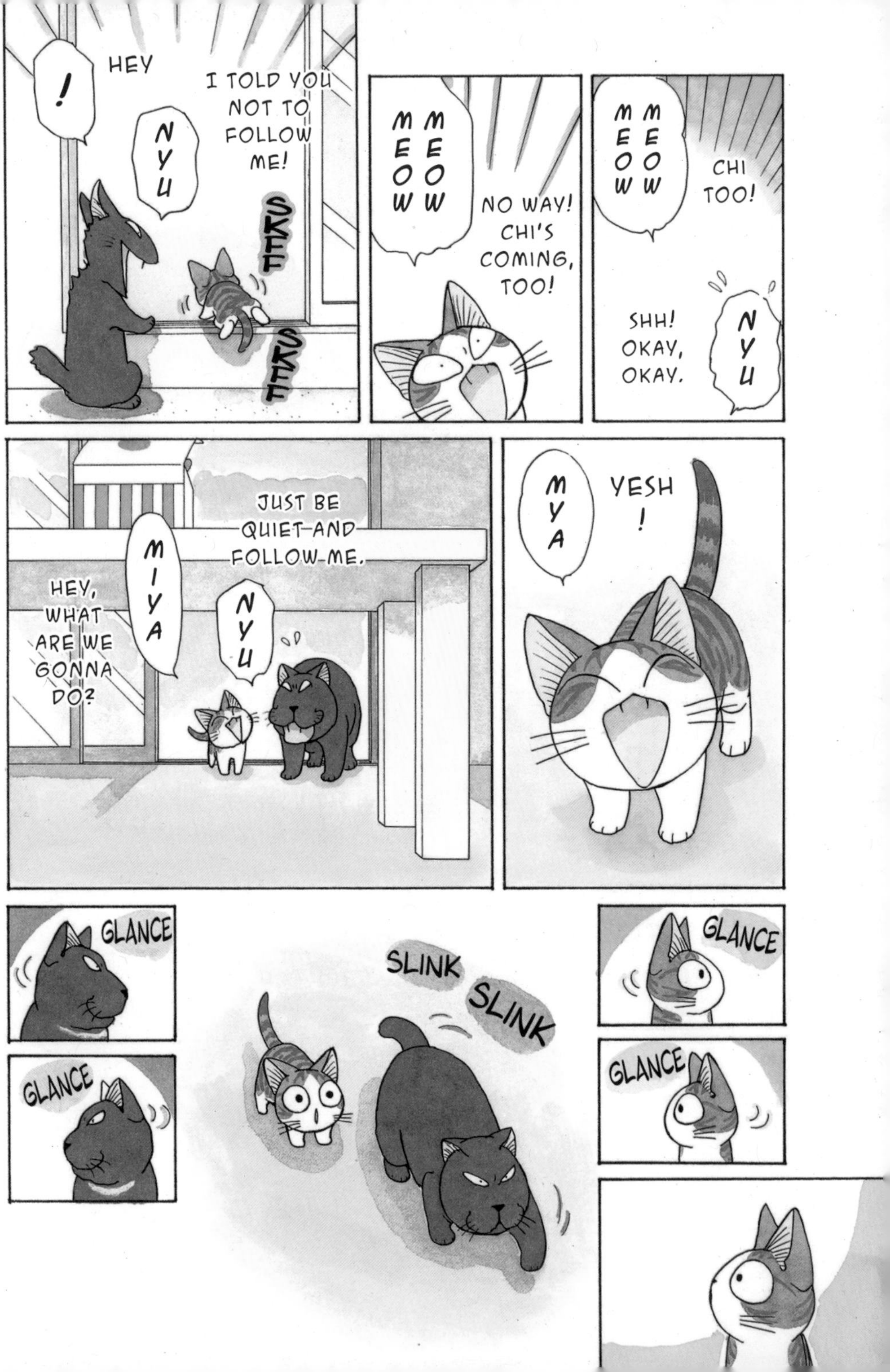
!
HEY
NYU
I TOLD YOU NOT TO FOLLOW ME!
SKFF
SKFF
MEOW MEOW
NO WAY! CHI'S COMING, TOO!
MEOW MEOW
CHI TOO!
SHH! OKAY, OKAY.
NYU
JUST BE QUIET AND FOLLOW ME.
MIYA
HEY, WHAT ARE WE GONNA DO?
NYU
MYA
YESH!
GLANCE
GLANCE
SLINK
SLINK
GLANCE
GLANCE

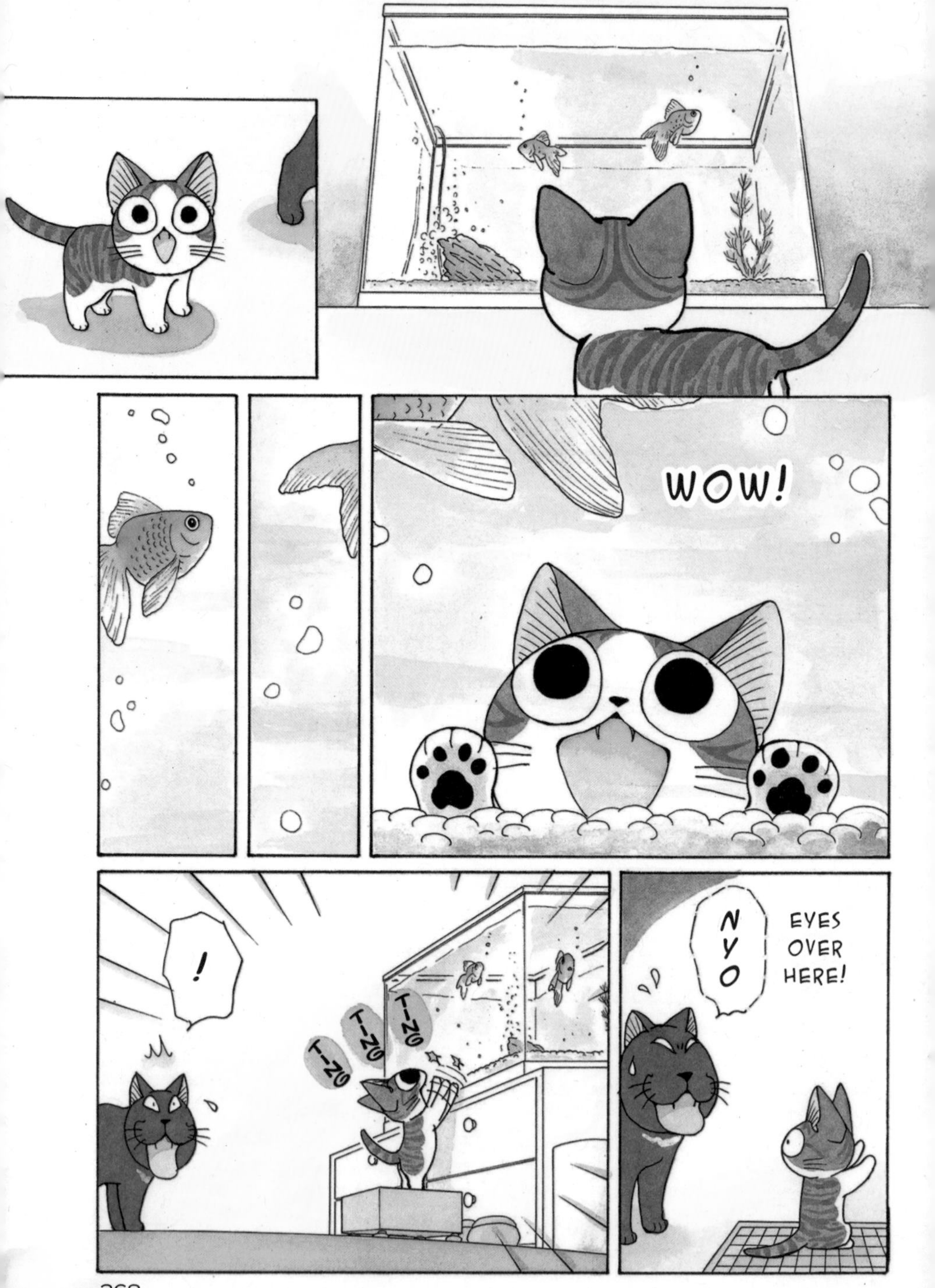
WOW!
!
T-ZING
TING
NYO
EYES OVER HERE!

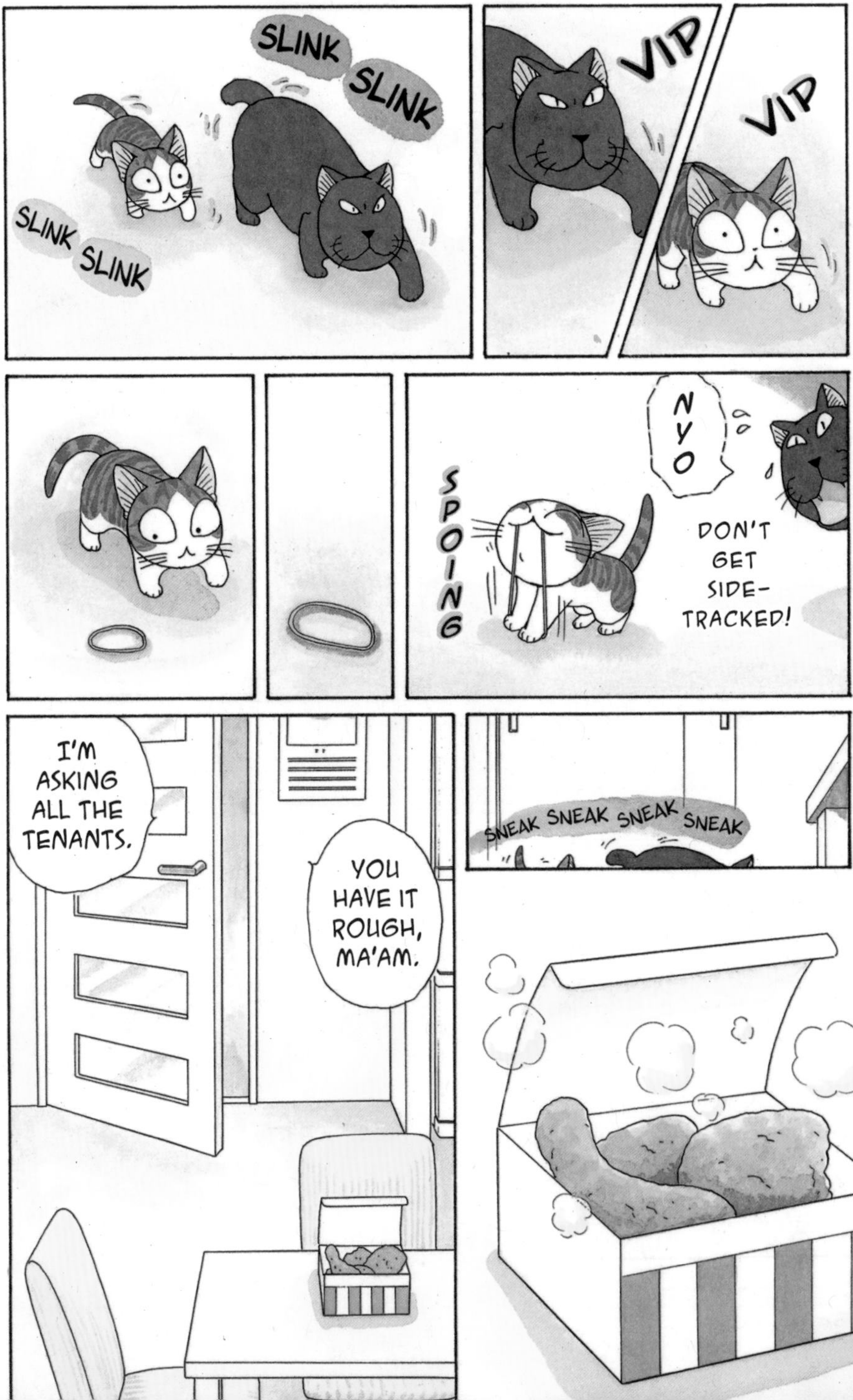
SLINK SLINK
SLINK SLINK
VIP
VIP
SPOING
NYO
DON'T GET SIDE-TRACKED!
I'M ASKING ALL THE TENANTS.
YOU HAVE IT ROUGH, MA'AM.
SNEAK SNEAK SNEAK SNEAK

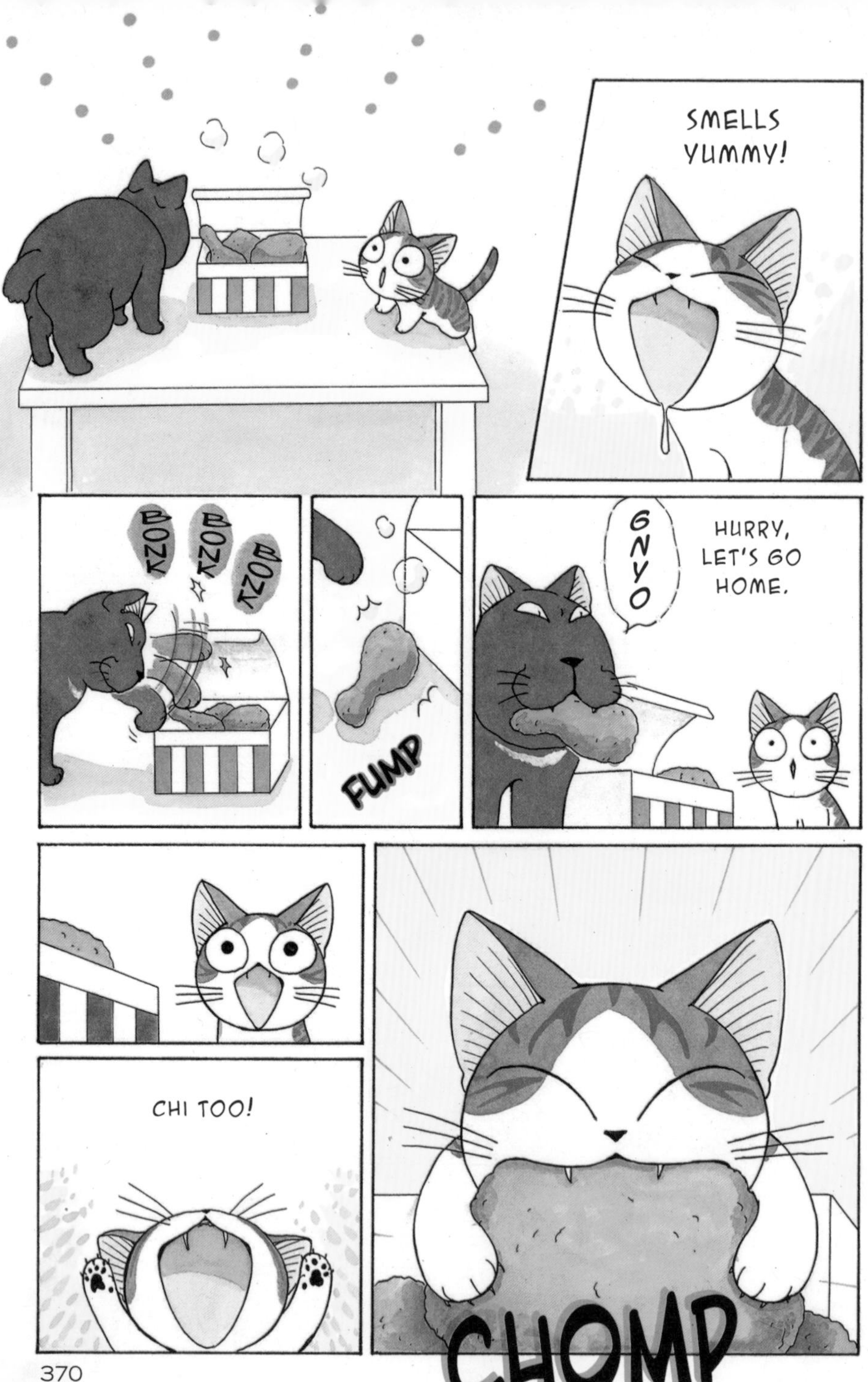
SMELLS YUMMY!
BONK
BONK
BONK
FUMP
GNYO
HURRY, LET'S GO HOME.
CHI TOO!
CHOMP

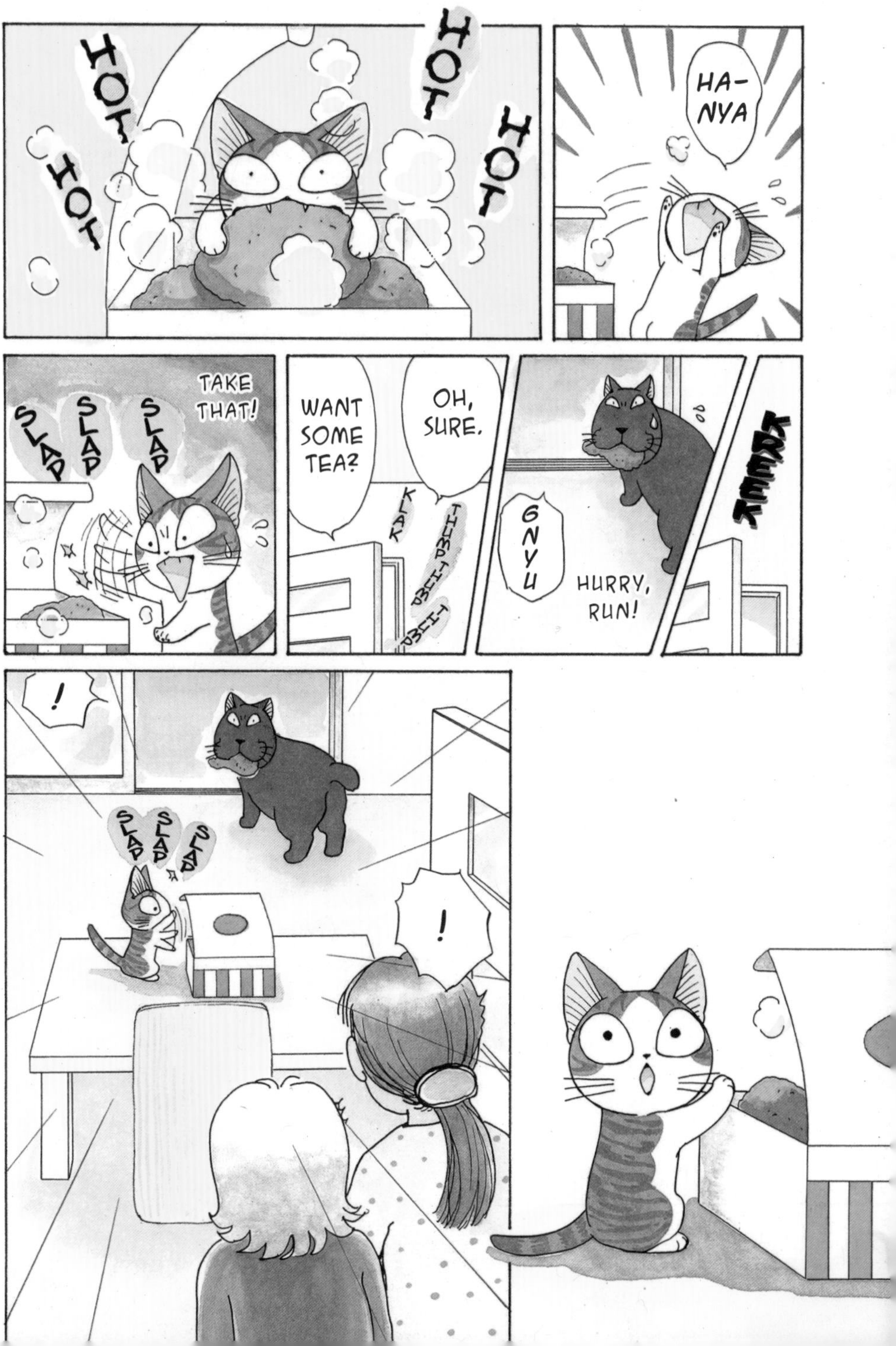
HOT
HOT
HOT
HOT
HA-NYA
SLAP
SLAP
SLAP
TAKE THAT!
WANT SOME TEA?
OH, SURE.
KLAK
GNYU
HURRY, RUN!
KREEK
!
SLAP
SLAP
SLAP
!

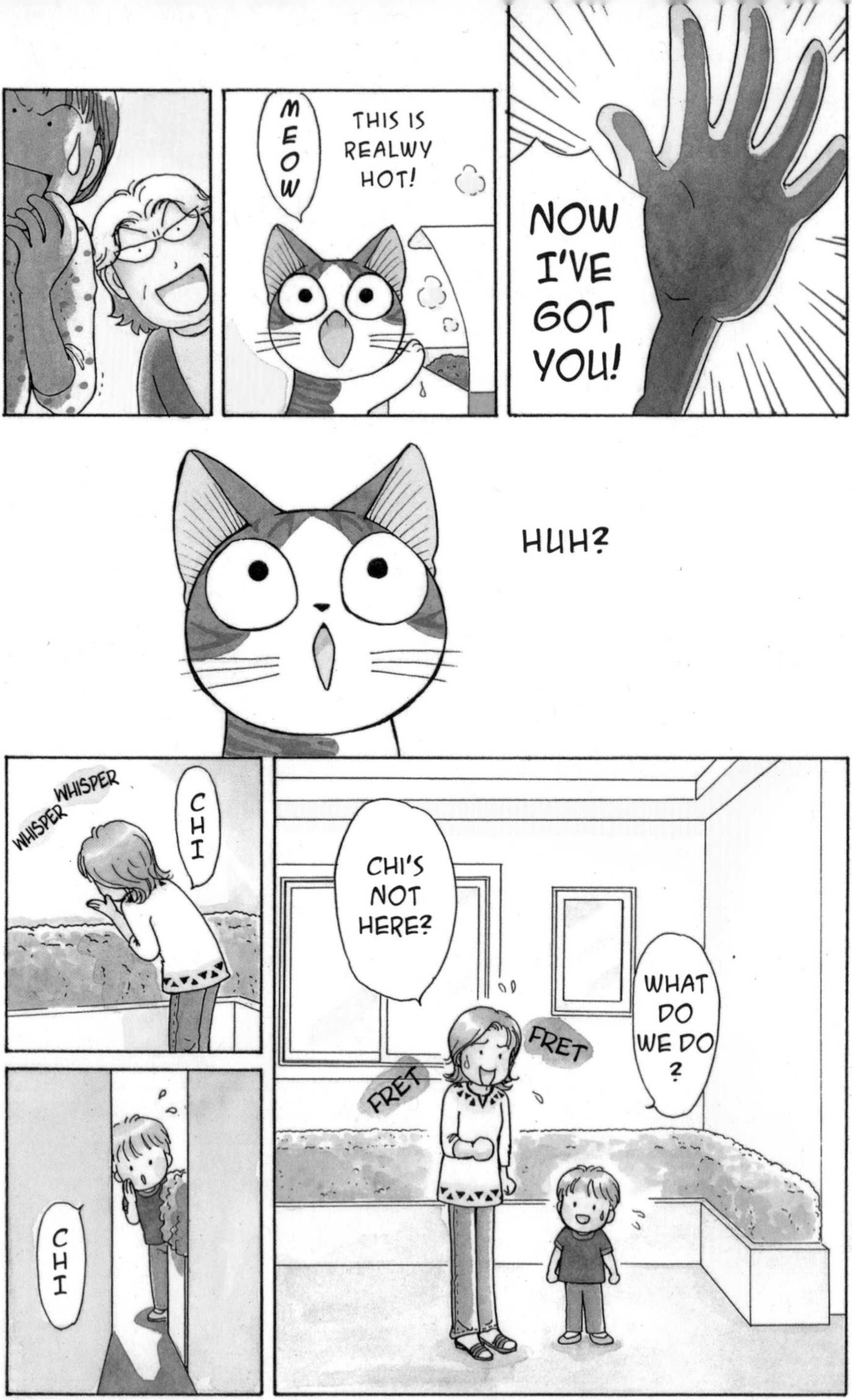
MEOW
THIS IS REALWY HOT!
NOW I'VE GOT YOU!
HUH?
WHISPER WHISPER
CHI
CHI'S NOT HERE?
FRET
FRET
WHAT DO WE DO?
CHI

the end

homemade 47: a cat is cornered

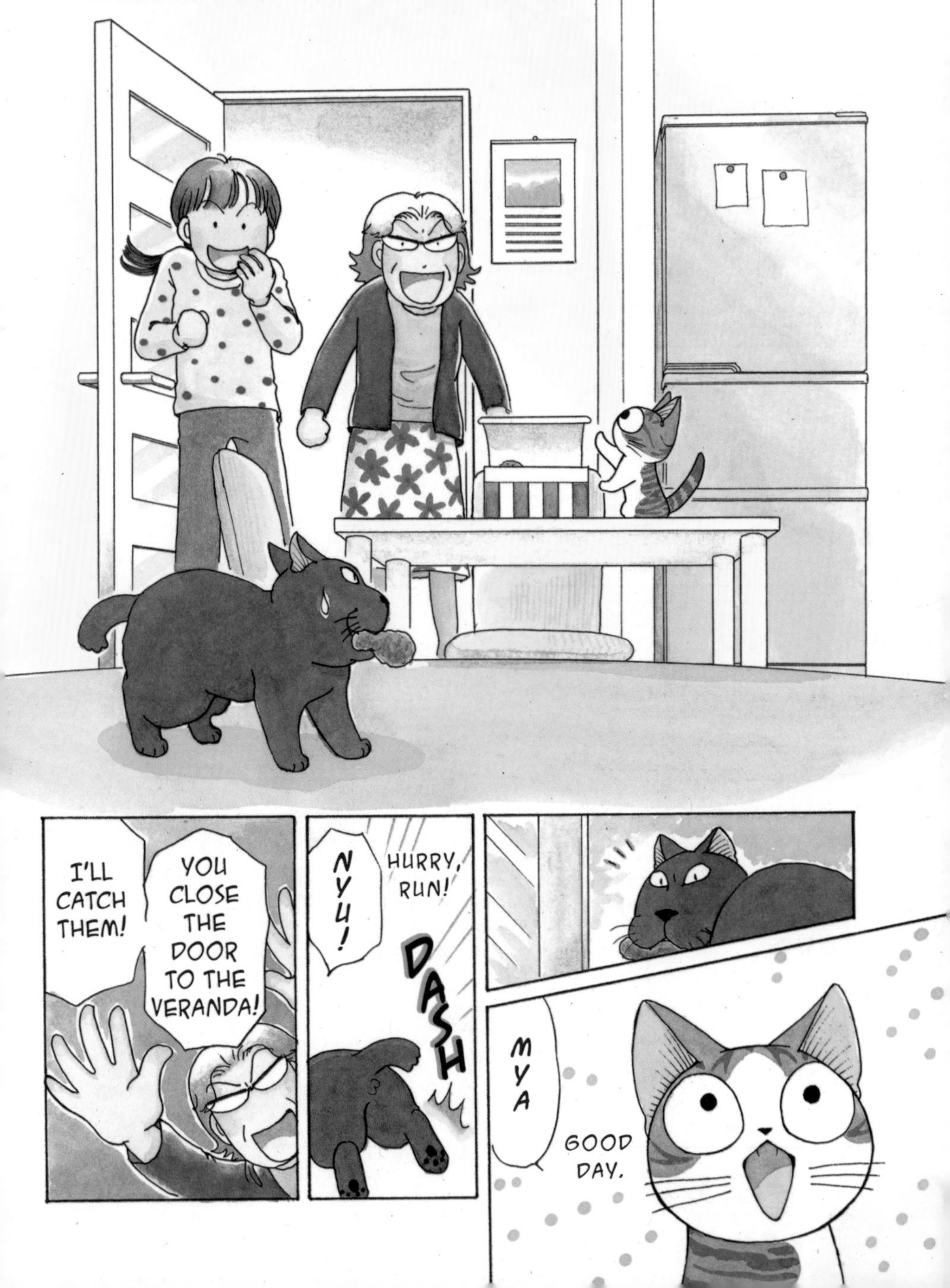
I'LL CATCH THEM!
YOU CLOSE THE DOOR TO THE VERANDA!
NYU!
HURRY, RUN!
DASH
MYA
GOOD DAY.

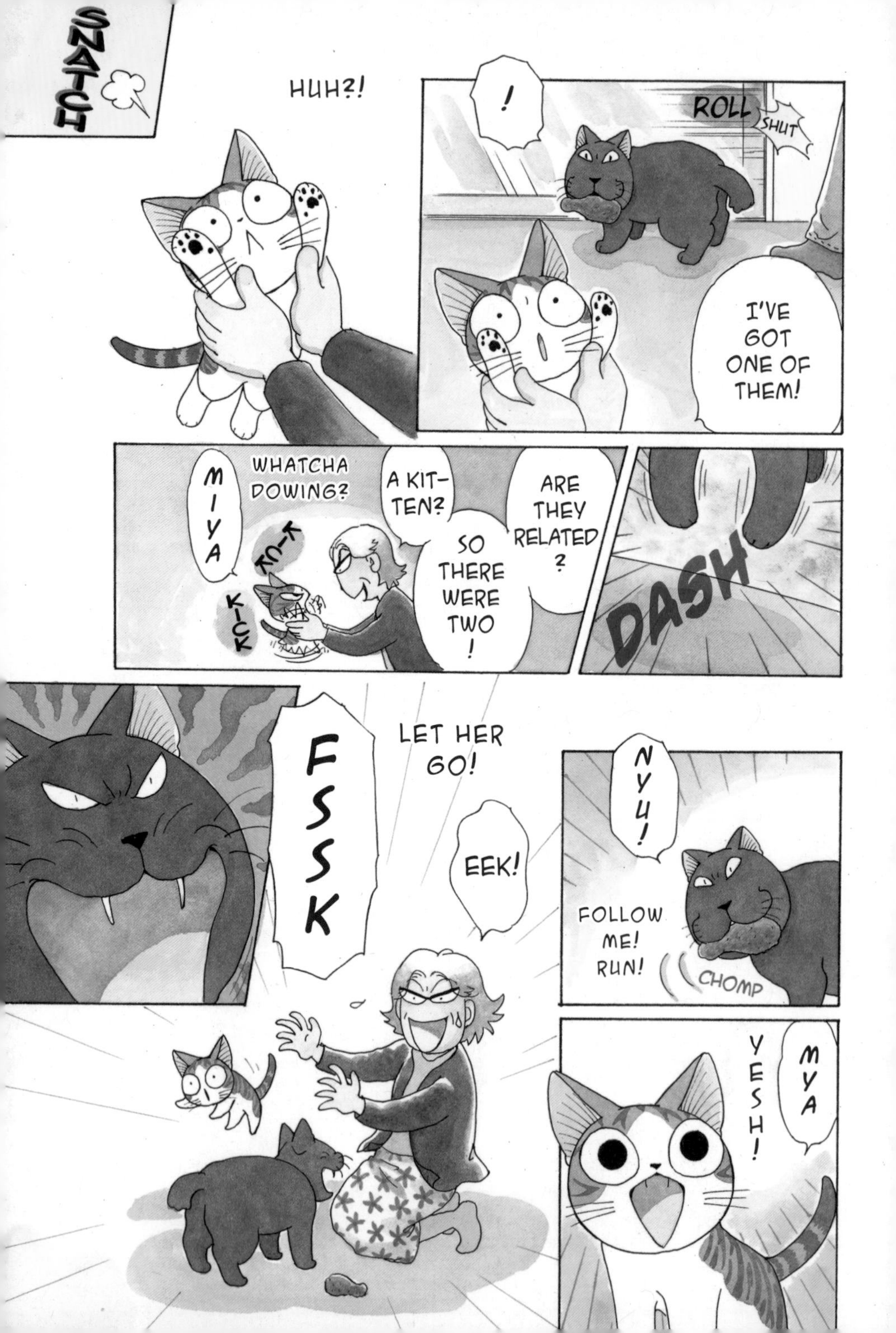
SNATCH
HUH?!
!
ROLL
SHUT
I'VE GOT ONE OF THEM!
MIYA
WHATCHA DOWING?
KICK
KICK
A KIT-TEN?
SO THERE WERE TWO!
ARE THEY RELATED?
DASH
FSSK
LET HER GO!
EEK!
NYU!
FOLLOW ME! RUN!
CHOMP
MYA
YESH!

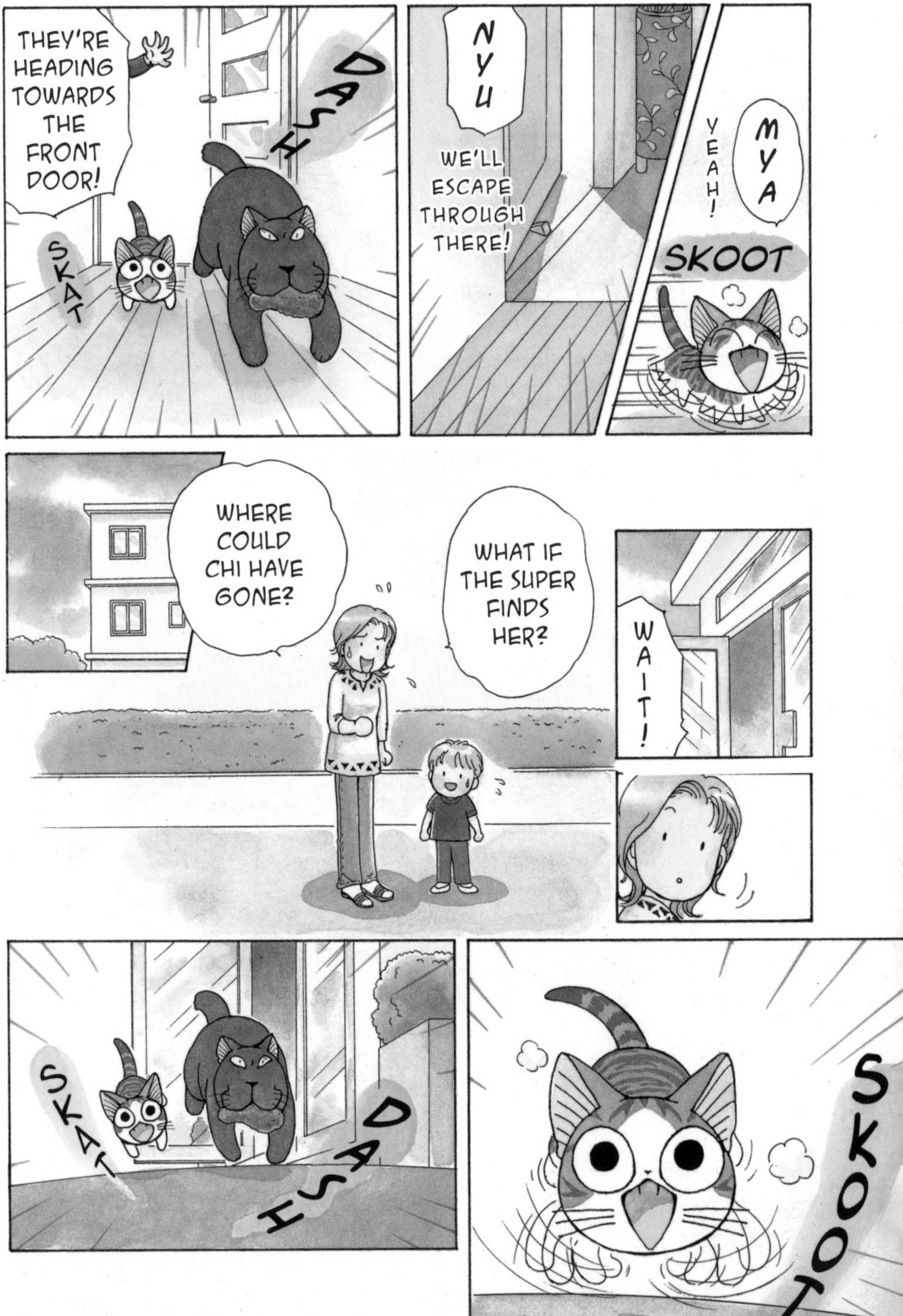
THEY'RE HEADING TOWARDS THE FRONT DOOR!
DASH
SKAT
NYU
WE'LL ESCAPE THROUGH THERE!
YEAH!
MYA
SKOOT
WHERE COULD CHI HAVE GONE?
WHAT IF THE SUPER FINDS HER?
WAIT!
SKAT
DASH
SKOOT

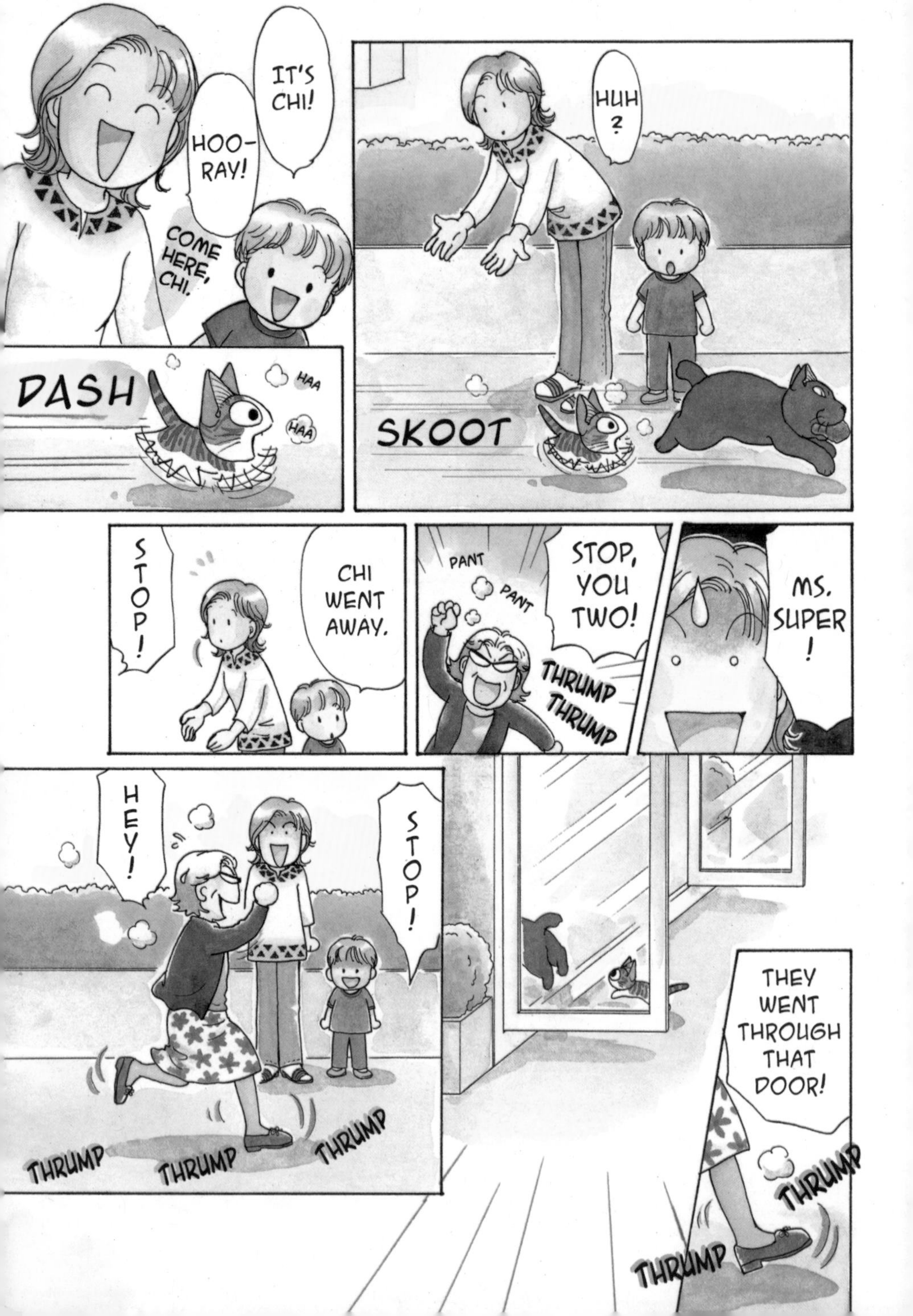
IT'S CHI!
HOO-RAY!
COME HERE, CHI.
DASH
HAA
HAA
HUH?
SKOOT
STOP!
CHI WENT AWAY.
PANT
PANT
STOP, YOU TWO!
THRUMP
THRUMP
MS. SUPER!
HEY!
STOP!
THRUMP
THRUMP
THRUMP
THEY WENT THROUGH THAT DOOR!
THRUMP
THRUMP

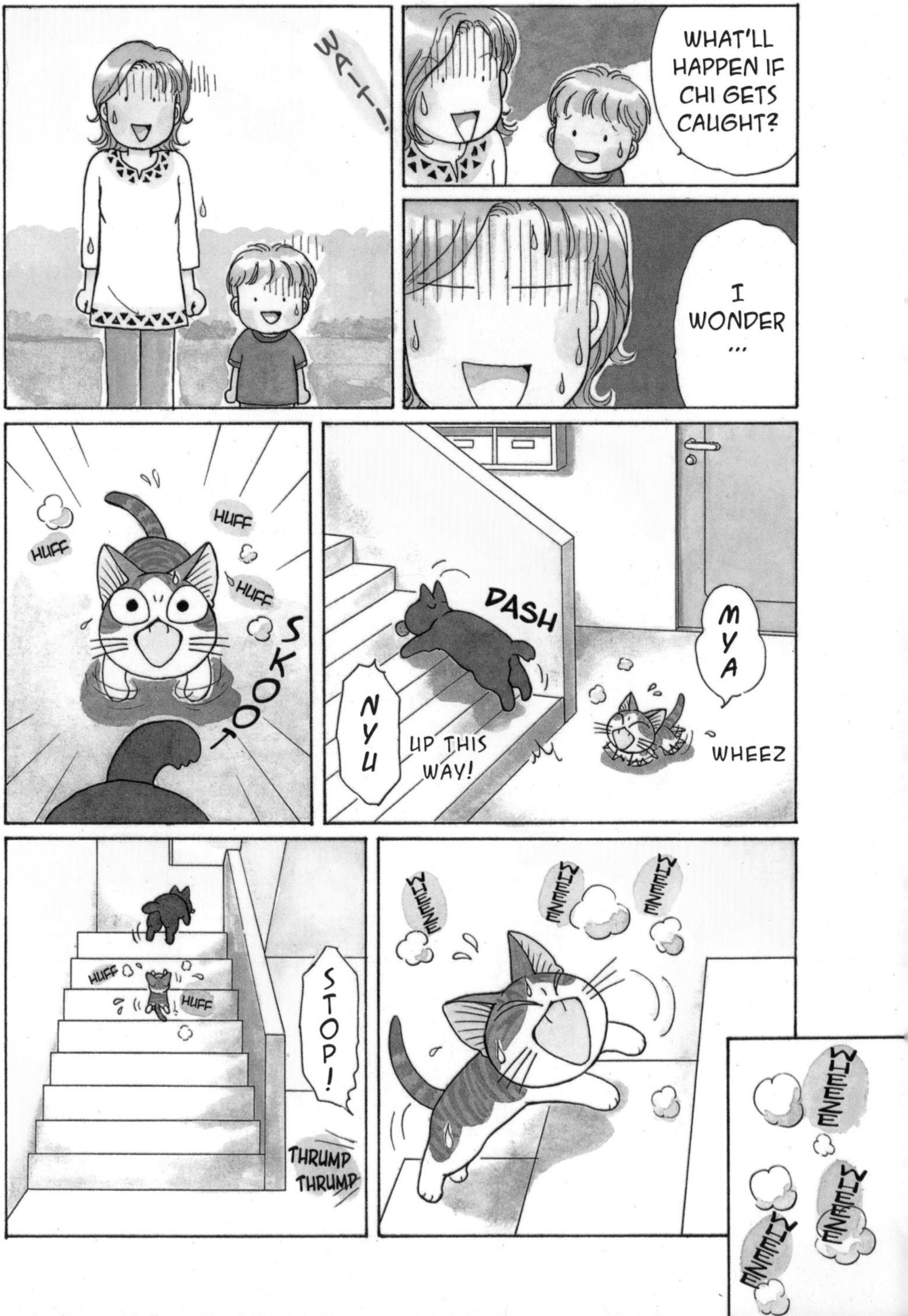
WA-I-!
WHAT'LL HAPPEN IF CHI GETS CAUGHT?
I WONDER ...
HUFF
HUFF
HUFF
SKOOOT
DASH
NYU
UP THIS WAY!
MYA
WHEEZ
HUFF
HUFF
STOP!
THRUMP THRUMP
WHEEZE
WHEENE
WHEENE
WHEENE
WHEENE
WHEENE

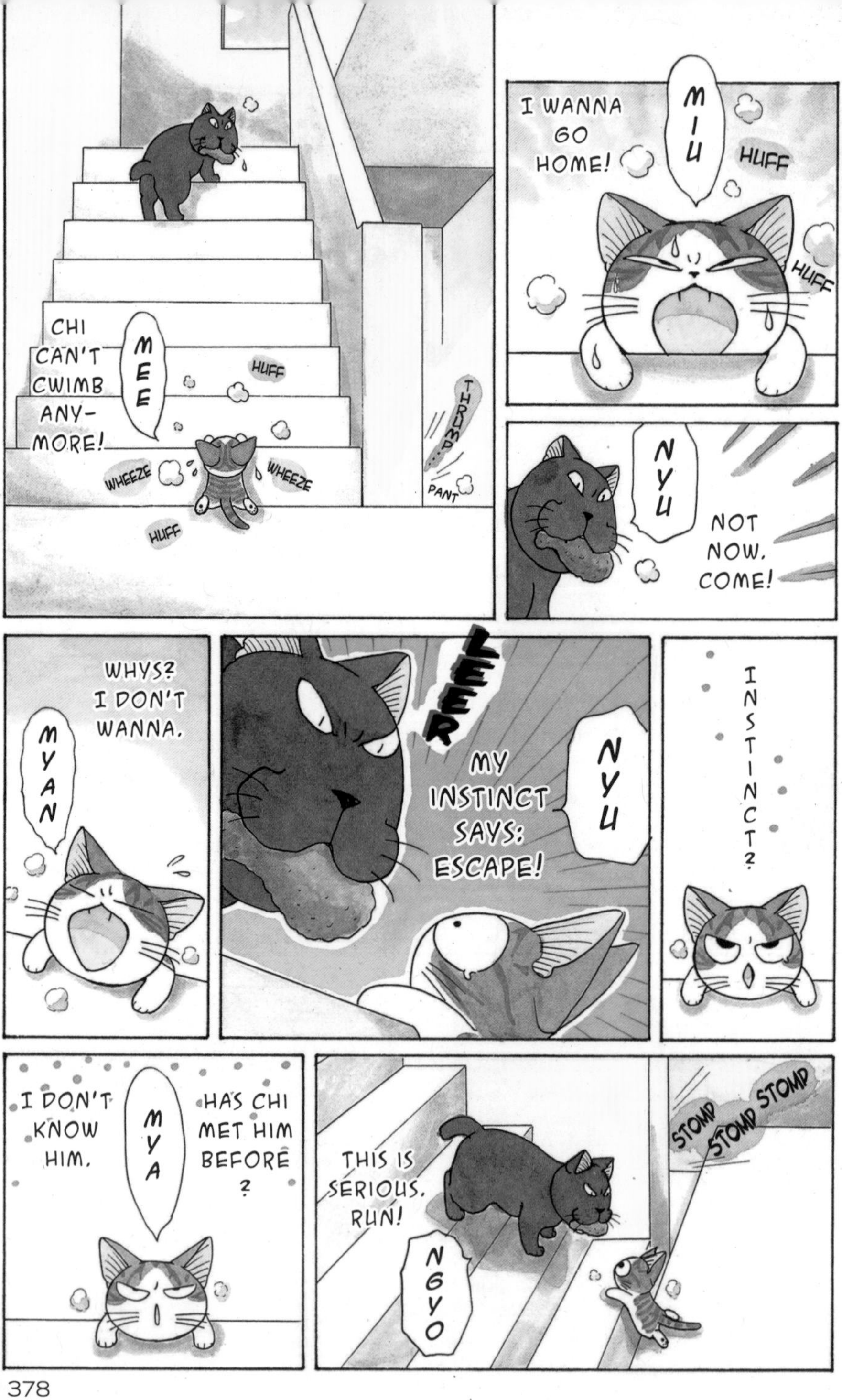
MEE
CHI CAN'T CWIMB ANY-MORE!
HUFF
WHEEZE
WHEEZE
HUFF
THRUMP
PANT
I WANNA GO HOME!
MIU
HUFF
HUFF
NYU
NOT NOW. COME!
WHYS? I DON'T WANNA.
MYAN
LEER
MY INSTINCT SAYS: ESCAPE!
NYU
INSTINCT?
I DON'T KNOW HIM.
MYA
HAS CHI MET HIM BEFORE?
THIS IS SERIOUS. RUN!
NGYO
STOMP
STOMP
STOMP

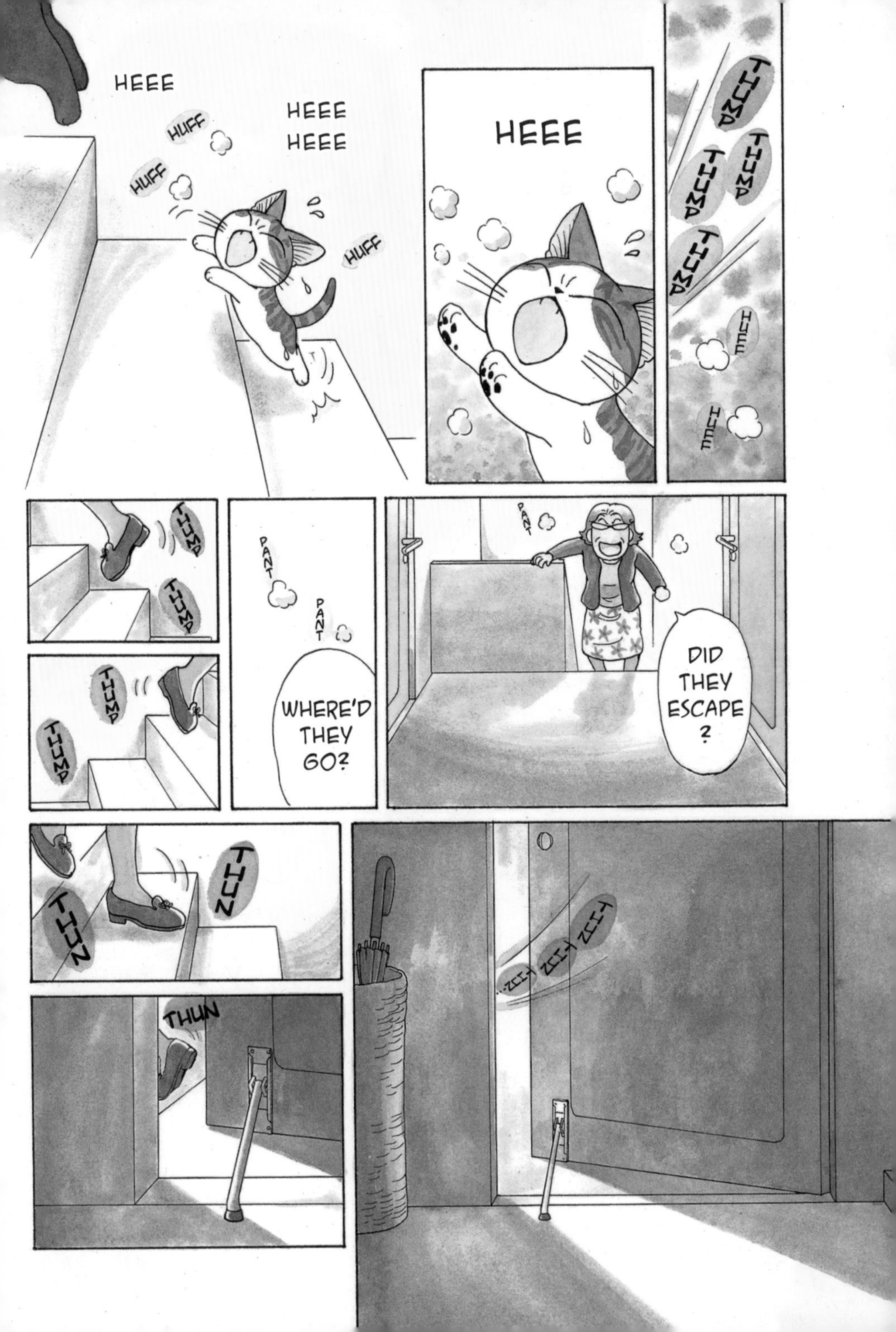

HEEE
HUFF
HUFF
HEEE
HEEE
HUFF
HEEE
THUMP
THUMP
THUMP
THUMP
HUFF
HUFF
THUMP
THUMP
PANT
PANT
WHERE'D THEY GO?
PANT
DID THEY ESCAPE?
THUMP
THUMP
THUN
THUN
TZZ TZZ TZZ TZZ...
THUN

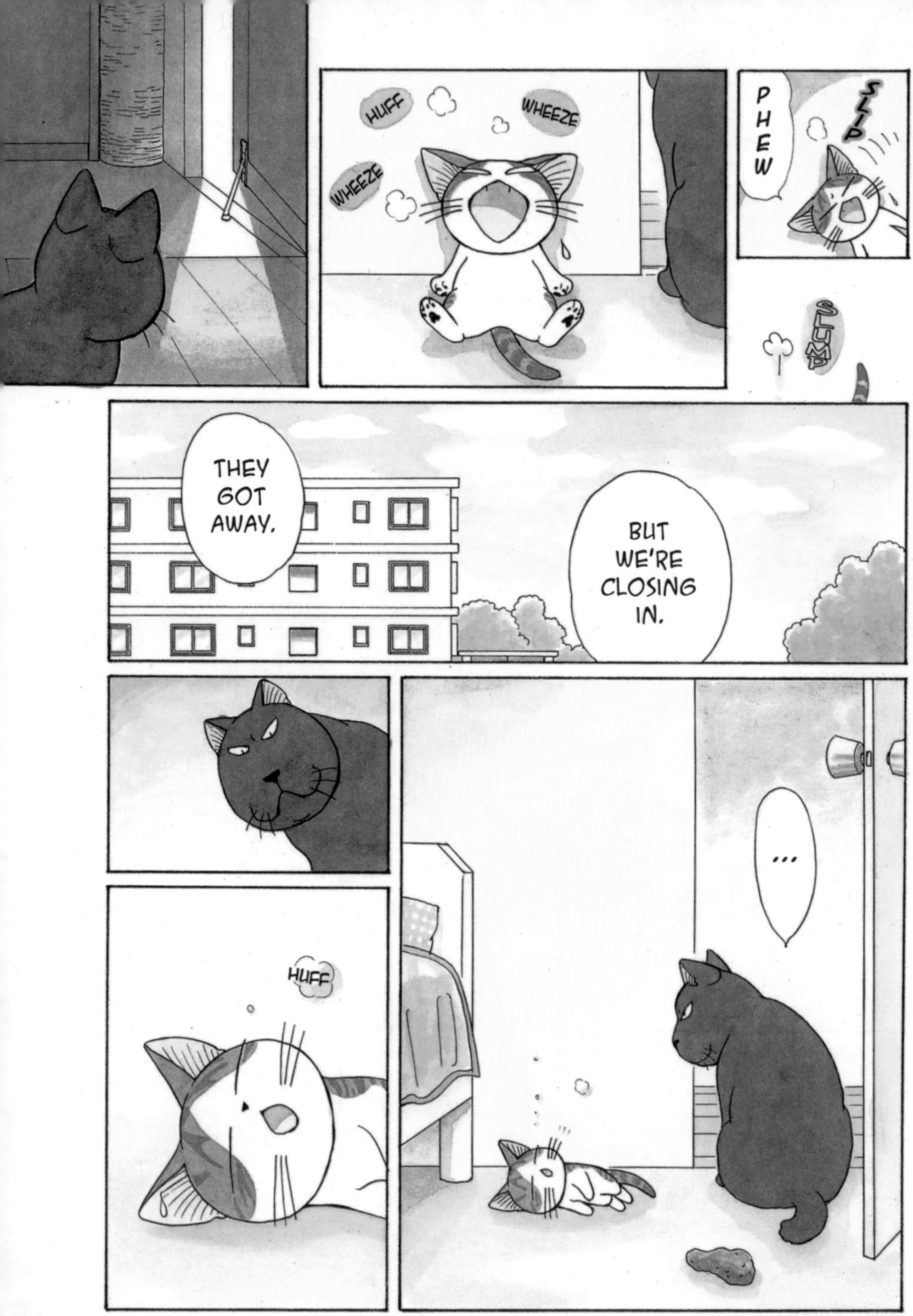
HUFF
WHEEZE
WHEEZE
PHEW
SLIP
SLUMP
THEY GOT AWAY.
BUT WE'RE CLOSING IN.
...
HUFF

the end

homemade 48: a cat studies

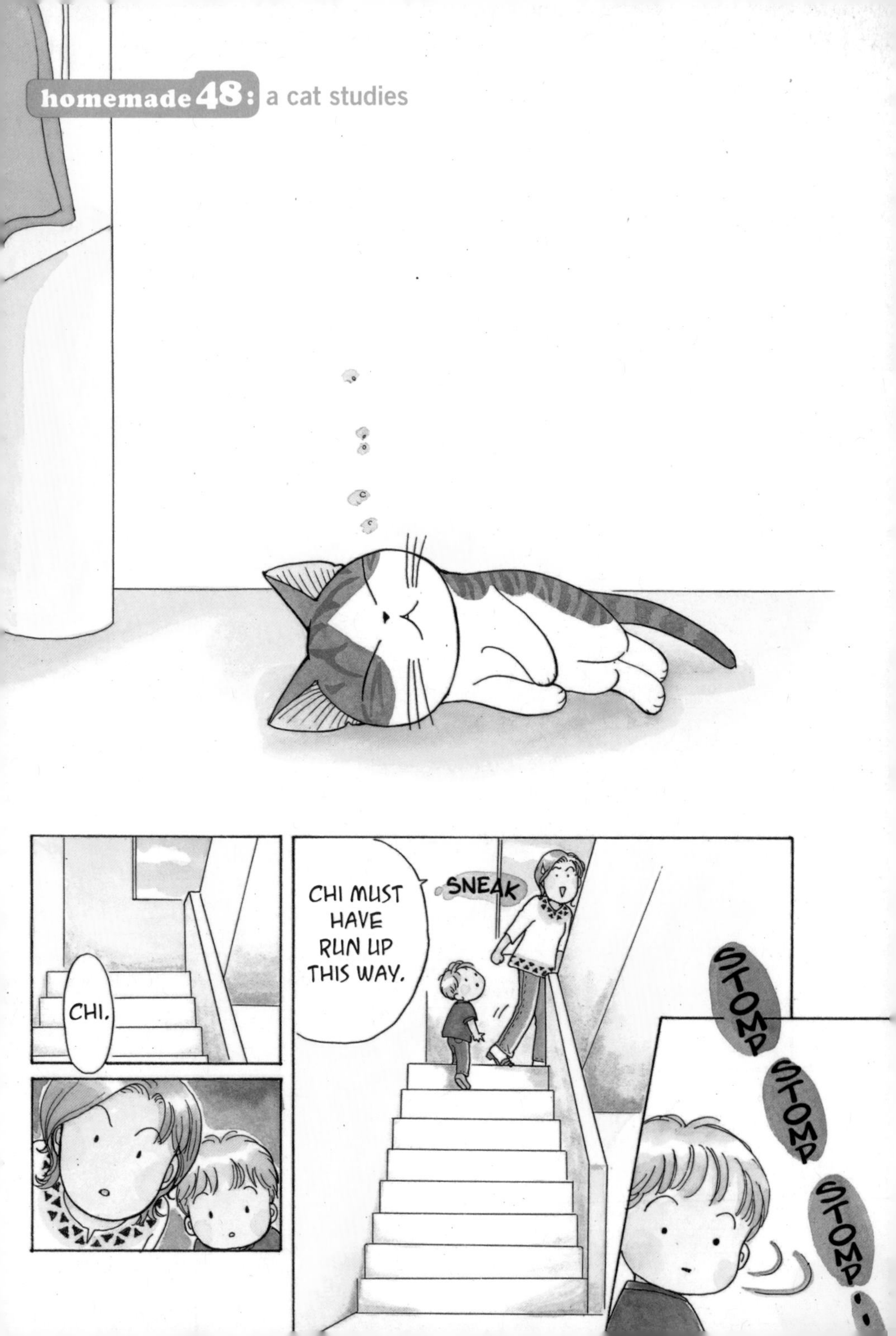
CHI.
CHI MUST HAVE RUN UP THIS WAY.
SNEAK
STOMP
STOMP
STOMP...

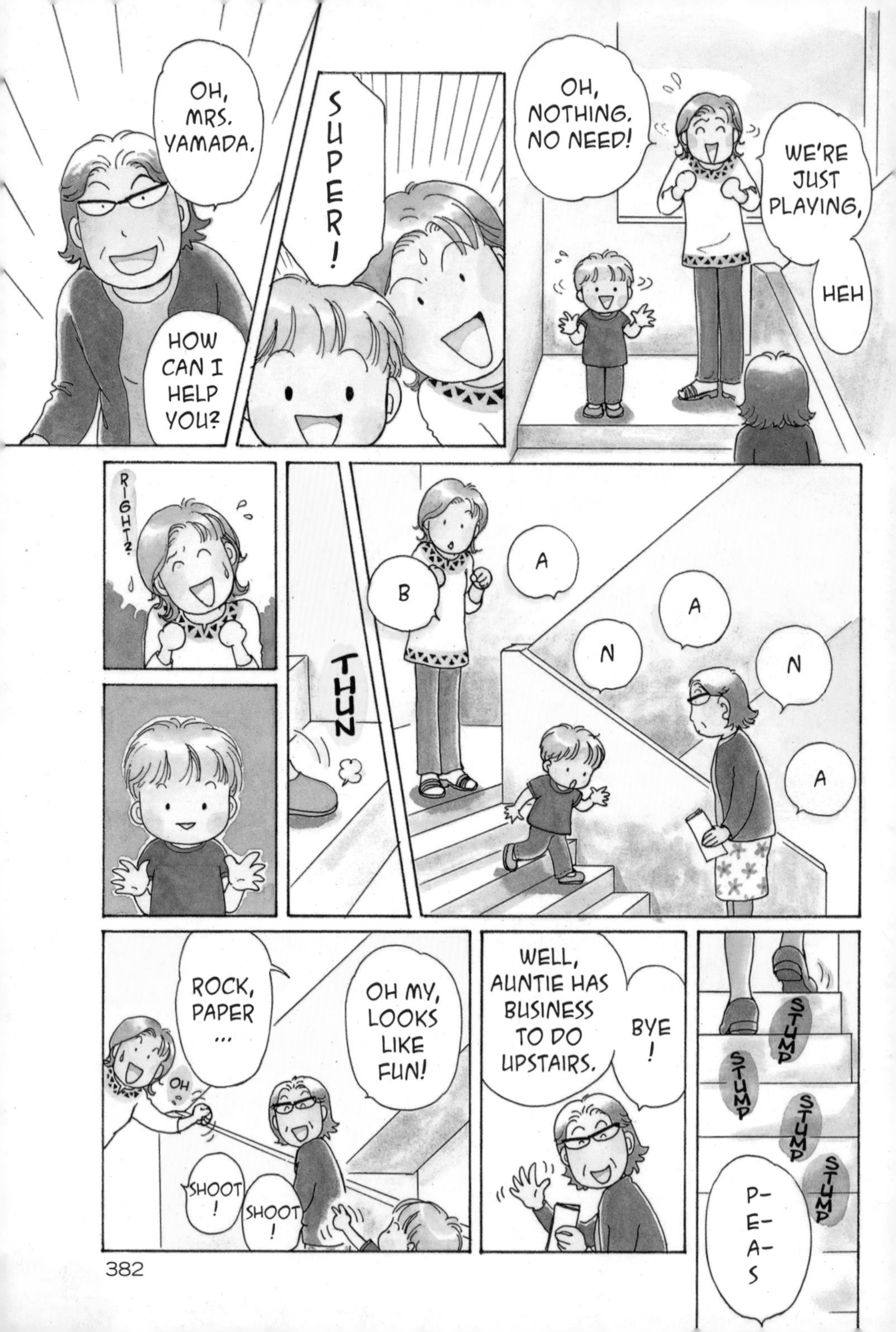
OH, MRS. YAMADA.
HOW CAN I HELP YOU?
SUPER!
OH, NOTHING. NO NEED!
WE'RE JUST PLAYING,
HEH
RIGHT?
THUN
B
A
N
A
N
A
ROCK, PAPER ...
OH
SHOOT!
SHOOT!
OH MY, LOOKS LIKE FUN!
WELL, AUNTIE HAS BUSINESS TO DO UPSTAIRS.
BYE!
STUMP
STUMP
STUMP
STUMP
P-E-A-S

C-H-O-C-O-L-A-T-E

WHAT NOW?

WE CAN'T LOOK FOR CHI.

URR...

THIS IS ALL THAT BEAR-CAT'S FAULT! CAN CHI COME BACK?!

CHI HAS TO BE UPSTAIRS, RIGHT?

FLEX

FLEX

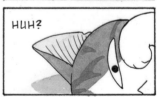

HUH?

WHERE AM I?

UNYU

YO!

ZING

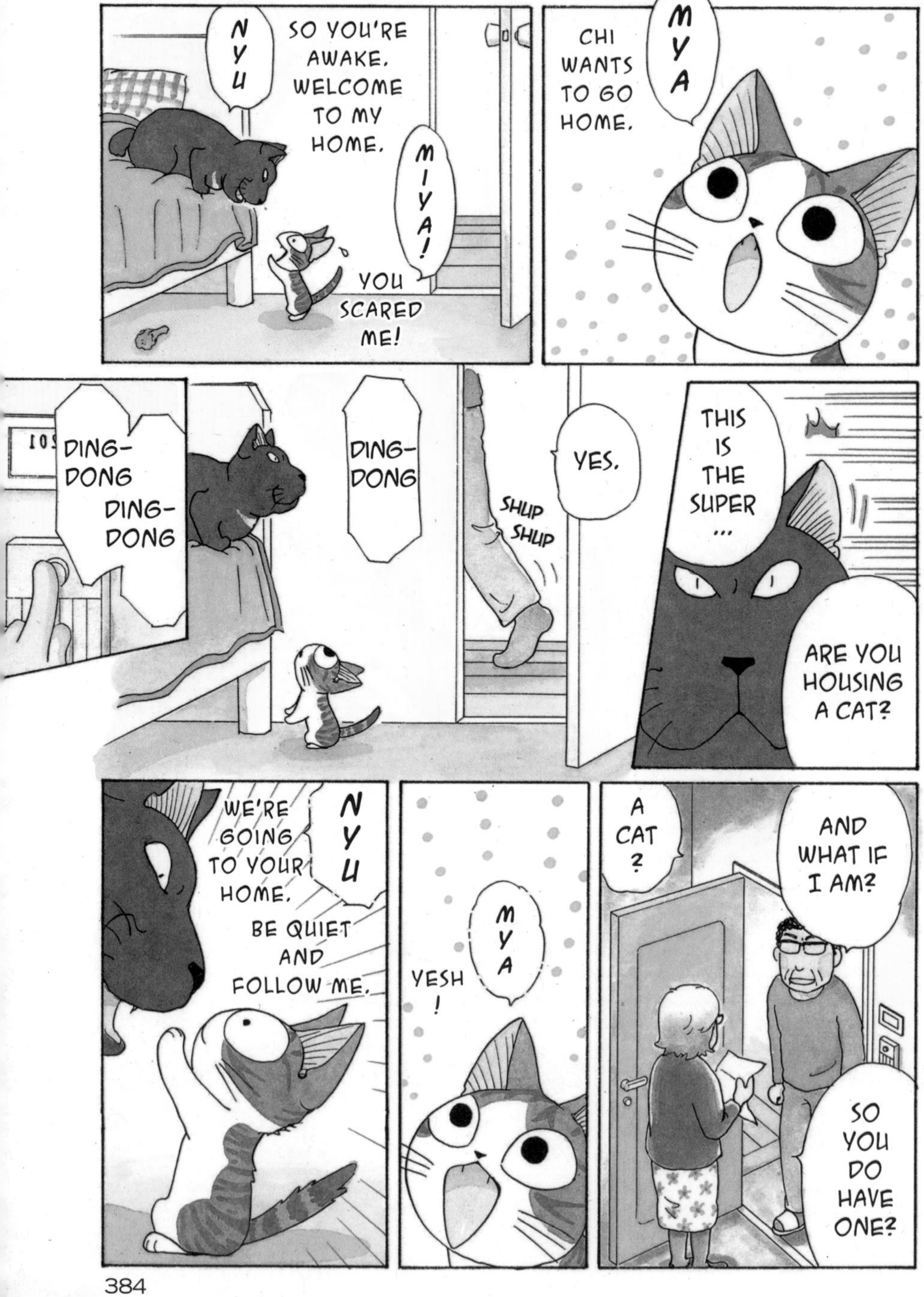
NYU
SO YOU'RE AWAKE. WELCOME TO MY HOME.
MIYA!
YOU SCARED ME!
CHI WANTS TO GO HOME.
MYA
DING-DONG DING-DONG
DING-DONG
SHUP SHUP
YES.
THIS IS THE SUPER ...
ARE YOU HOUSING A CAT?
WE'RE GOING TO YOUR HOME.
NYU
BE QUIET AND FOLLOW ME.
MYA
YESH!
A CAT?
AND WHAT IF I AM?
SO YOU DO HAVE ONE?

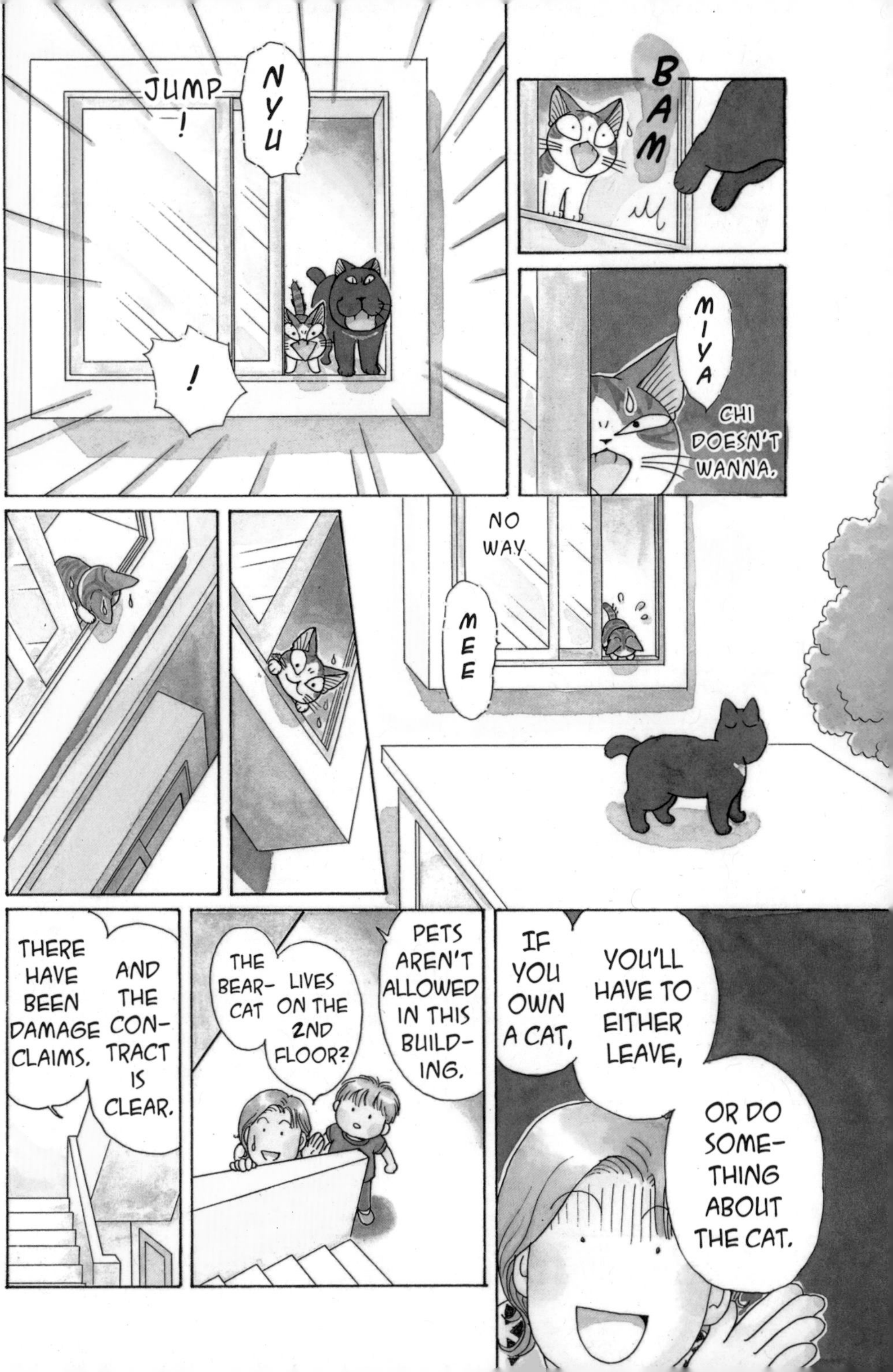
JUMP!
NYU
!
BAM
MIYA
CHI DOESN'T WANNA.
NO WAY
MEE
THERE HAVE BEEN DAMAGE CLAIMS.
AND THE CONTRACT IS CLEAR.
THE BEAR-CAT LIVES ON THE 2ND FLOOR?
PETS AREN'T ALLOWED IN THIS BUILDING.
IF YOU OWN A CAT,
YOU'LL HAVE TO EITHER LEAVE,
OR DO SOMETHING ABOUT THE CAT.

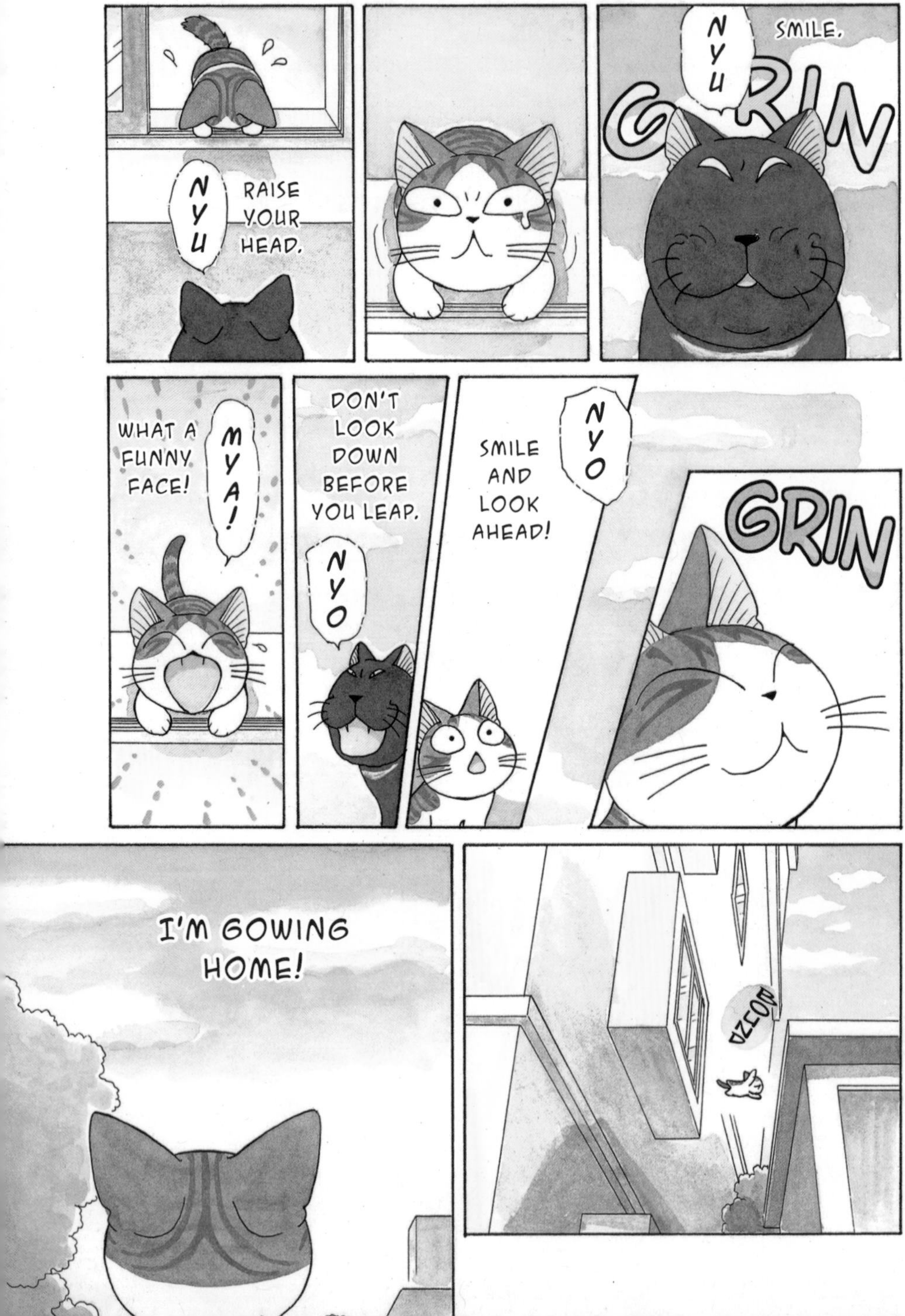
NYU
RAISE YOUR HEAD.
NYU
SMILE.
GRIN
WHAT A FUNNY FACE!
MYA!
DON'T LOOK DOWN BEFORE YOU LEAP.
NYO
SMILE AND LOOK AHEAD!
NYO
GRIN
I'M GOWING HOME!

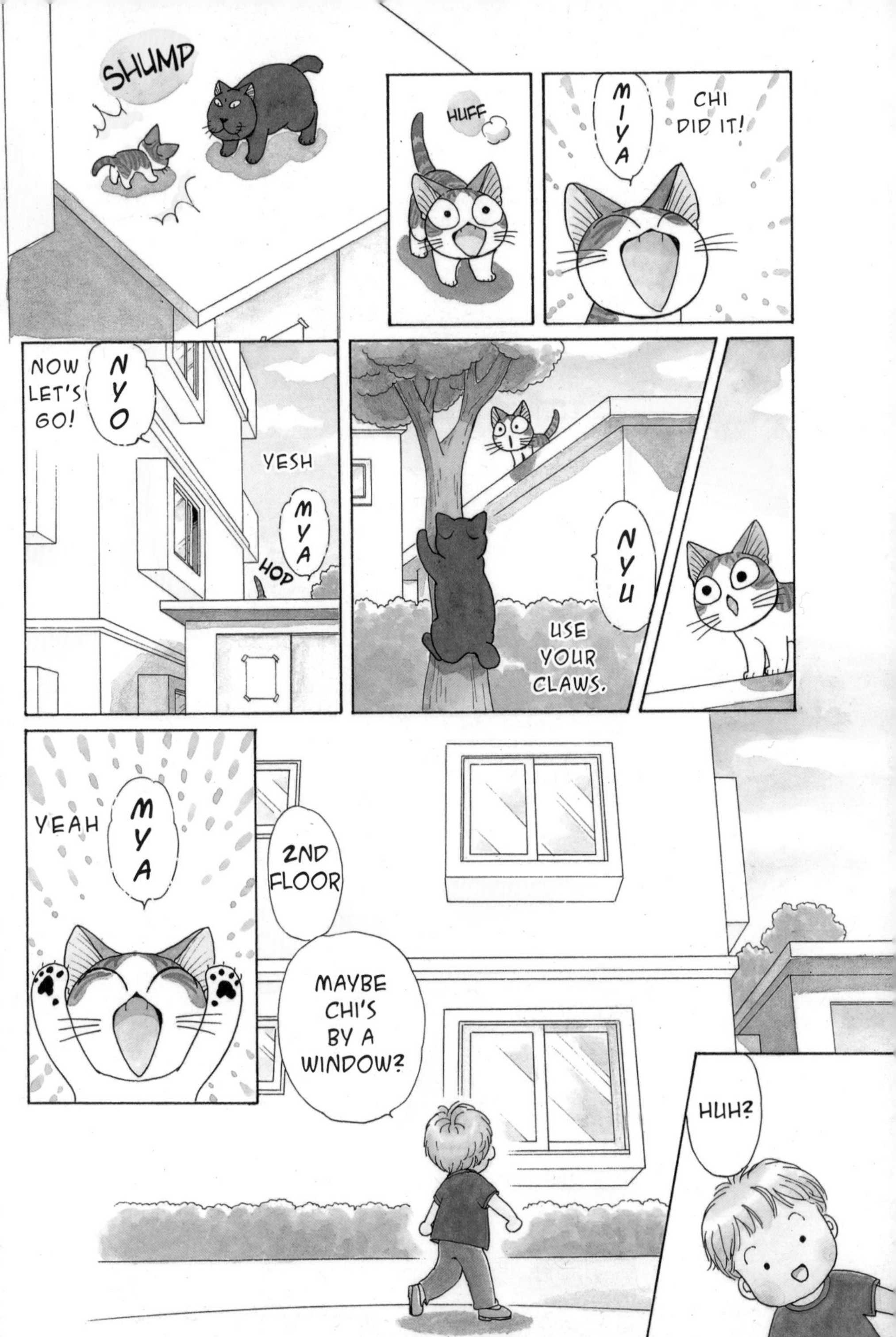
SHUMP
HUFF
MIYA
CHI DID IT!
NOW LET'S GO!
NYO
YESH
MYA
HOP
NYU
USE YOUR CLAWS.
YEAH
MYA
2ND FLOOR
MAYBE CHI'S BY A WINDOW?
HUH?

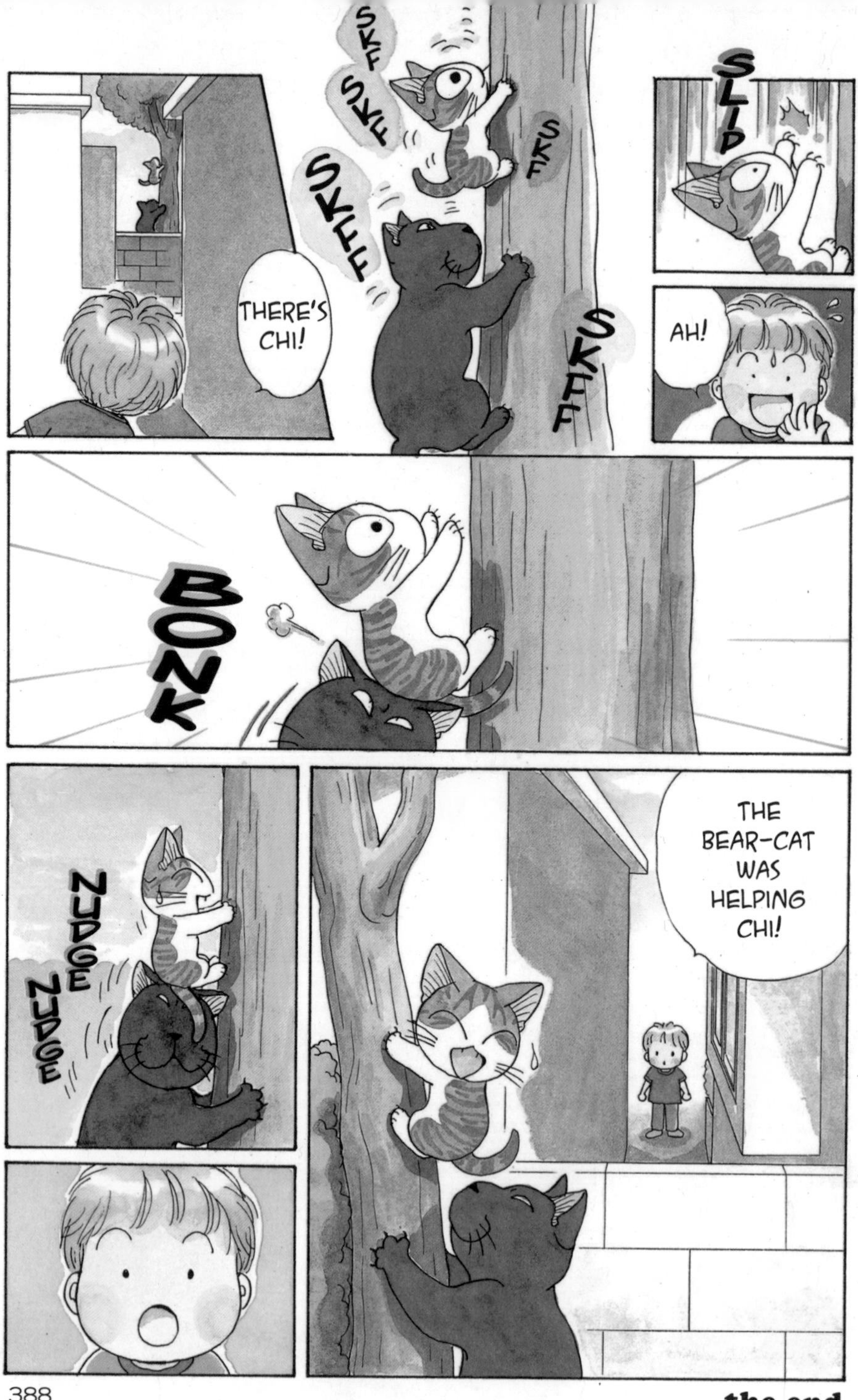
SKF
SKF
SKFF
THERE'S CHI!
SKF
SKFF
SLID
AH!
BONK
NUDGE NUDGE
THE BEAR-CAT WAS HELPING CHI!

the end

homemade 49: a cat endeavors

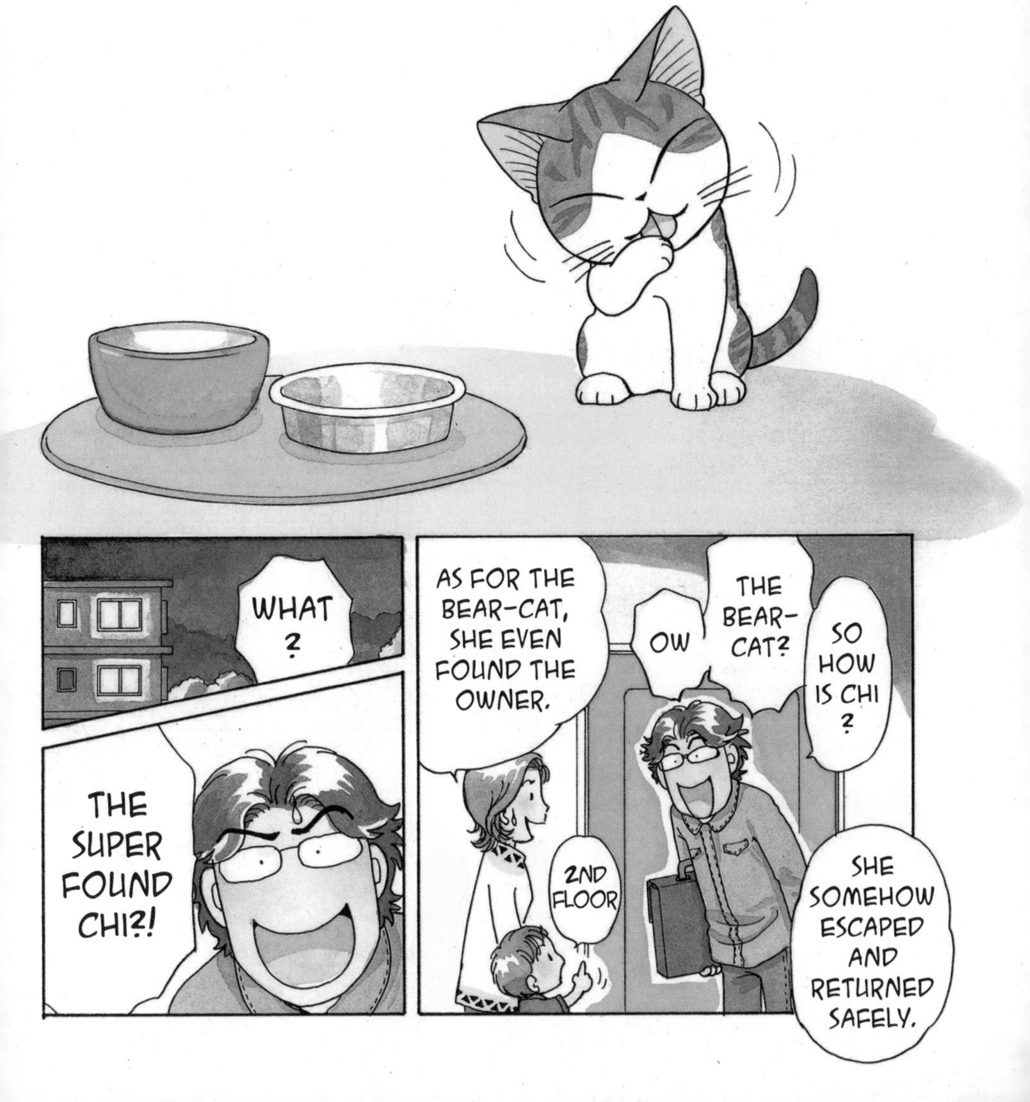
WHAT?
THE SUPER FOUND CHI?!
AS FOR THE BEAR-CAT, SHE EVEN FOUND THE OWNER.
OW
THE BEAR-CAT?
SO HOW IS CHI?
2ND FLOOR
SHE SOMEHOW ESCAPED AND RETURNED SAFELY.

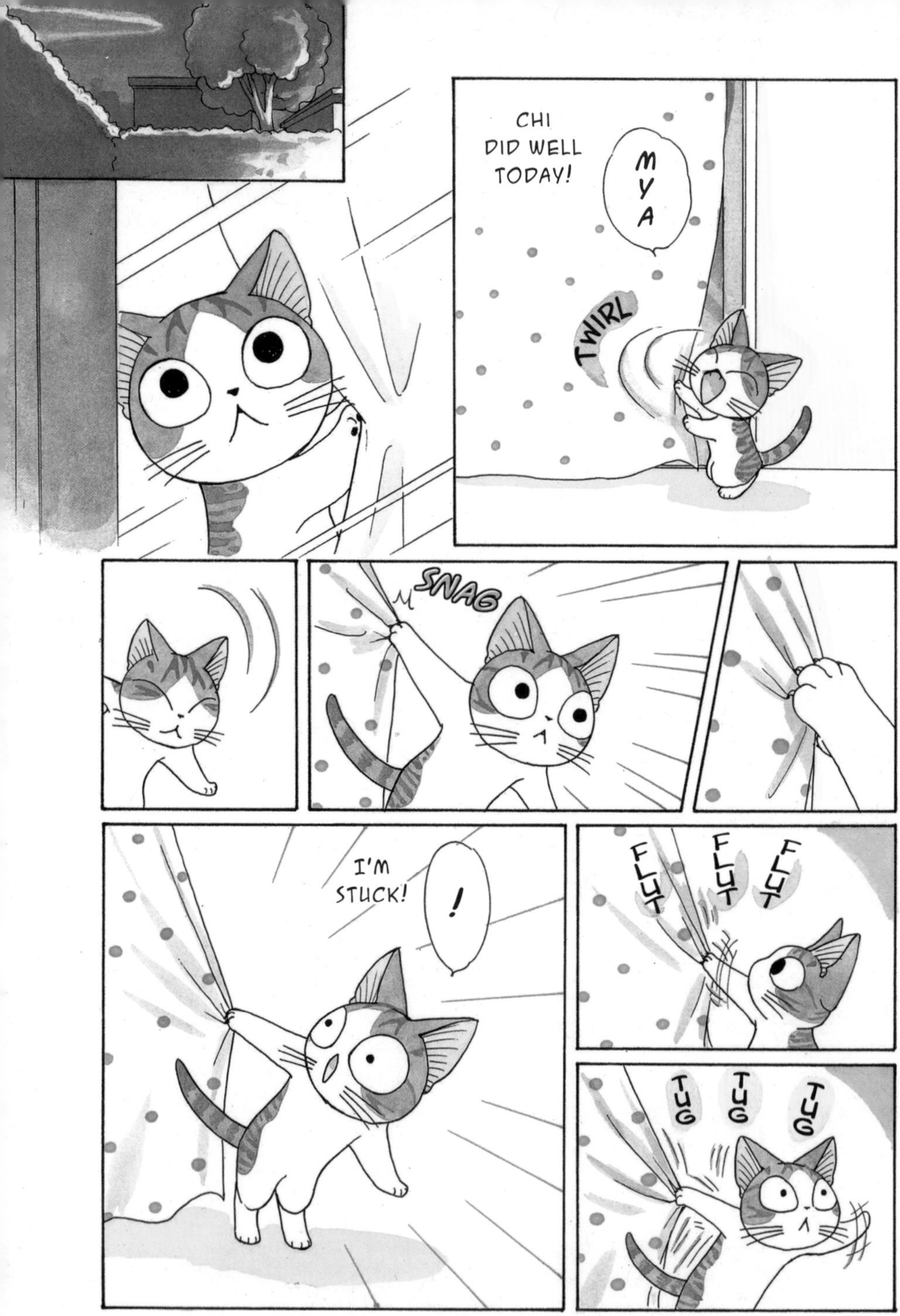
CHI DID WELL TODAY!
MYA
TWIRL
SNAG
I'M STUCK!
!
FLUT FLUT FLUT
TUG TUG TUG

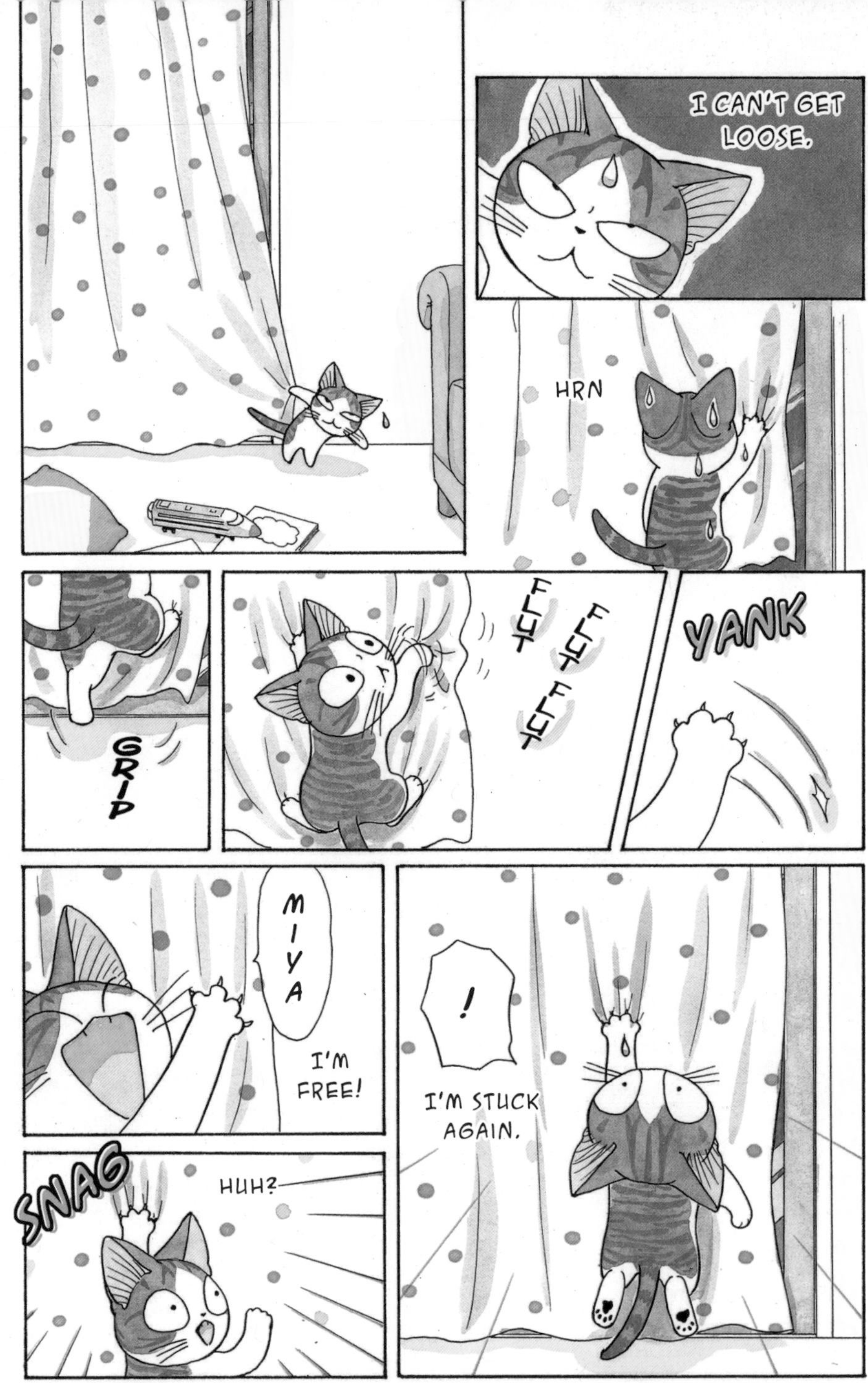
I CAN'T GET LOOSE.
HRN
GRIP
FLUT FLUT FLUT
YANK
MIYA
I'M FREE!
SNAG
HUH?
!
I'M STUCK AGAIN.

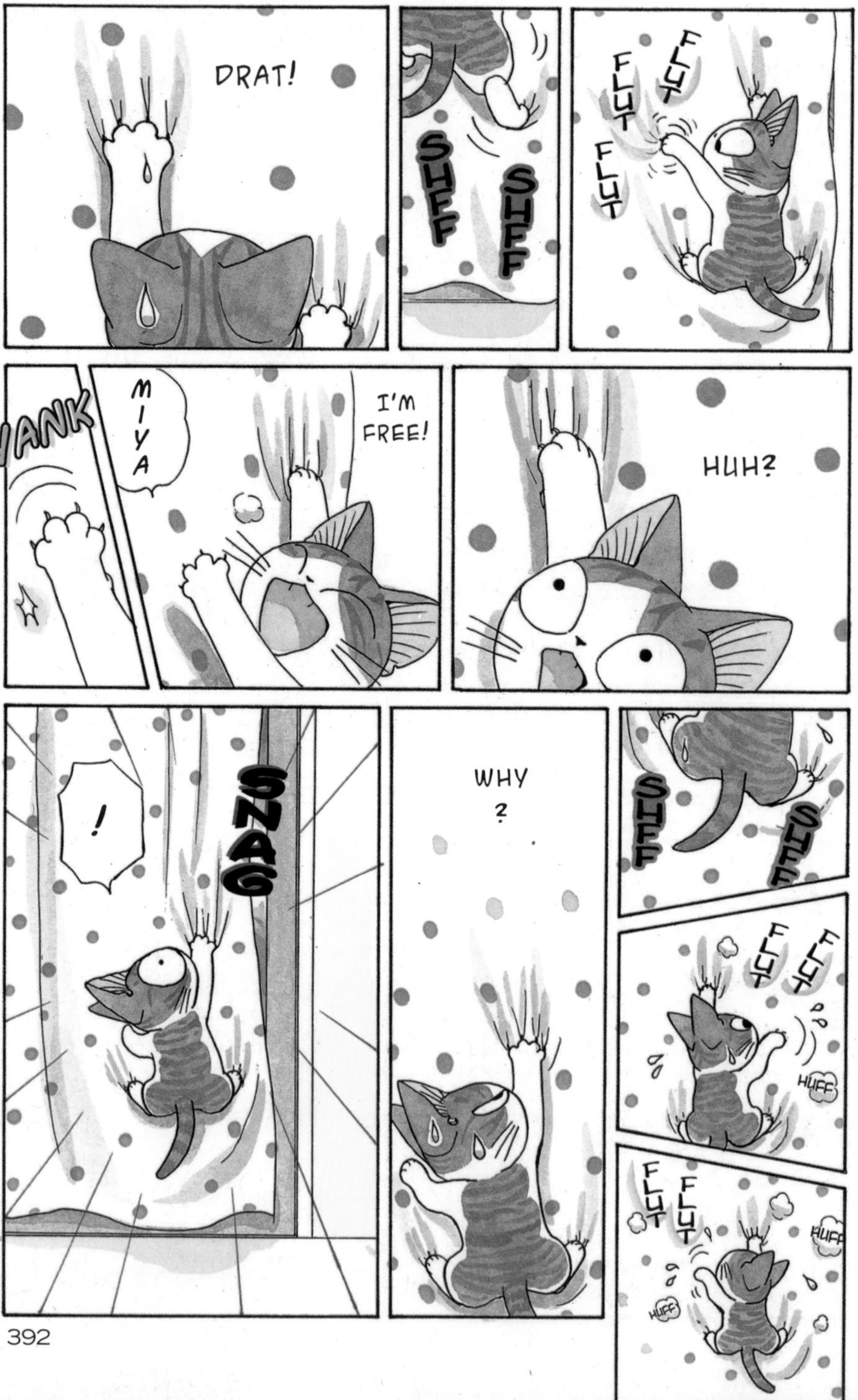
DRAT!
SHFF SHFF
FLUT FLUT FLUT
YANK
MIYA
I'M FREE!
HUH?
!
SNAG
WHY?
SHFF SHFF
FLUT FLUT
HUFF
FLUT FLUT
HUFF
HUFF

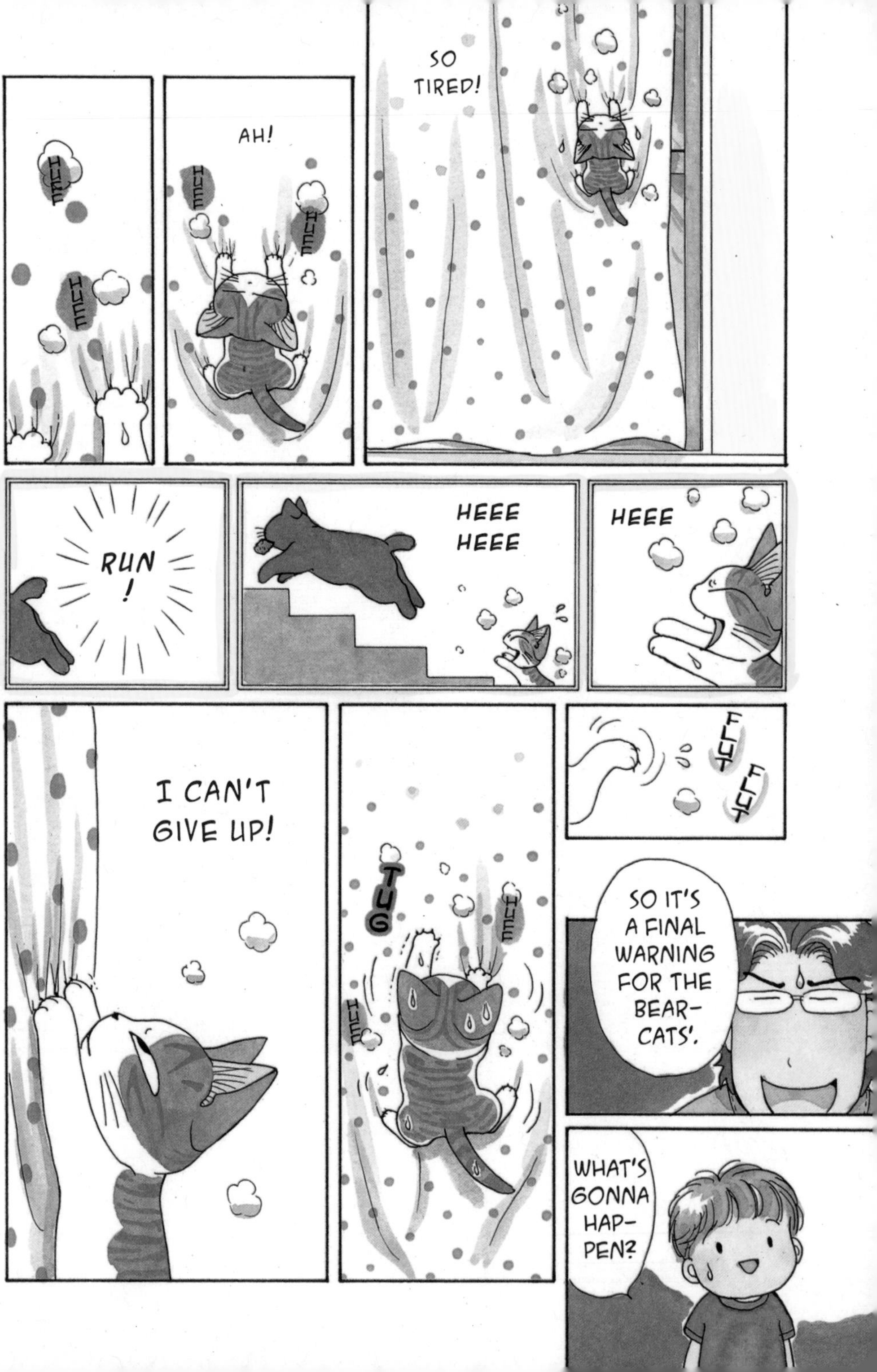
HUFF
HUFF
AH!
HUFF
HUFF
SO TIRED!
RUN!
HEEE HEEE
HEEE
I CAN'T GIVE UP!
TUG
HUFF
HUFF
FLUT
FLUT
SO IT'S A FINAL WARNING FOR THE BEAR-CATS'.
WHAT'S GONNA HAP-PEN?

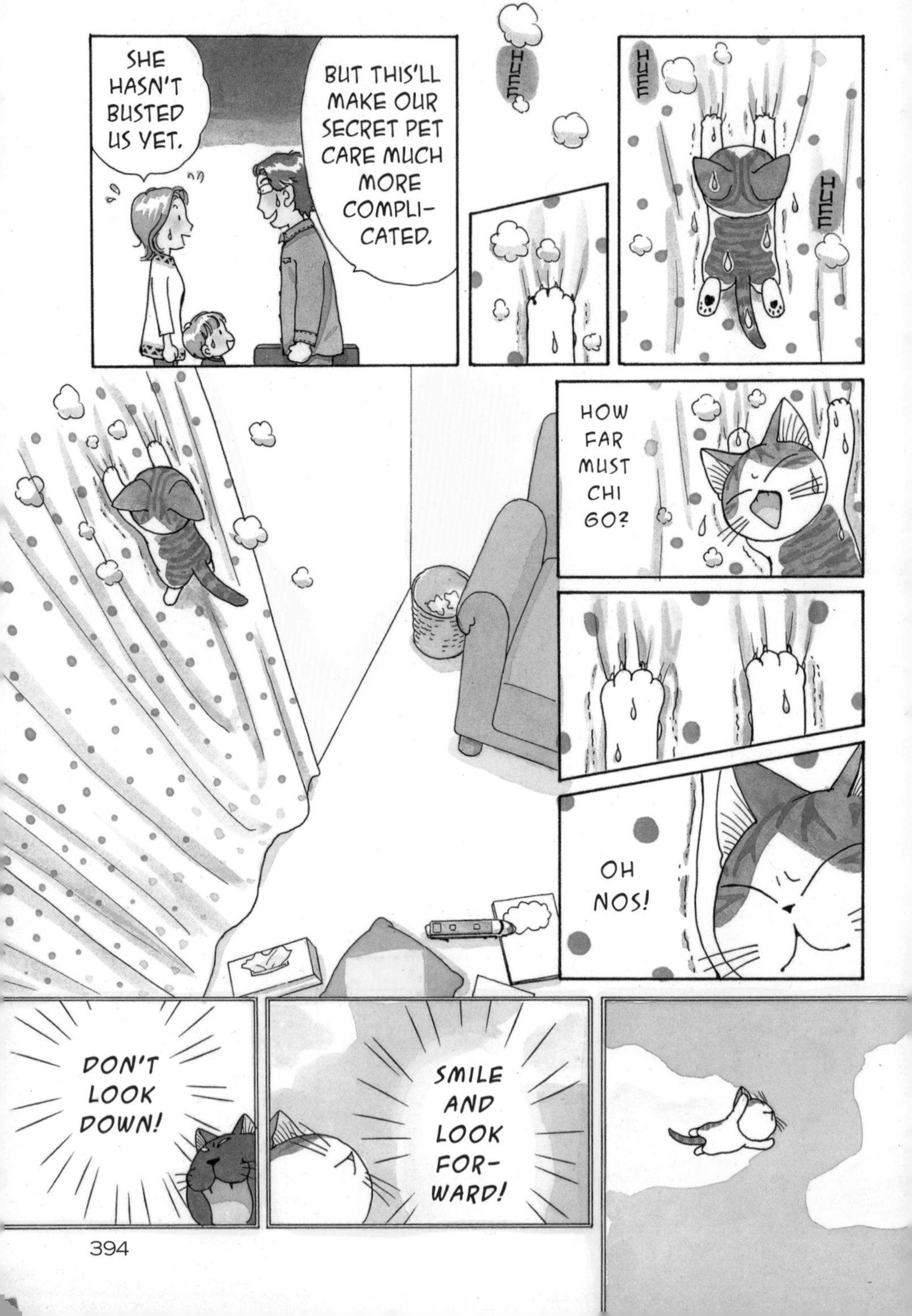
SHE HASN'T BUSTED US YET.
BUT THIS'LL MAKE OUR SECRET PET CARE MUCH MORE COMPLI- CATED.
HUFF
HUFF
HUFF
HOW FAR MUST CHI GO?
OH NOS!
DON'T LOOK DOWN!
SMILE AND LOOK FOR- WARD!

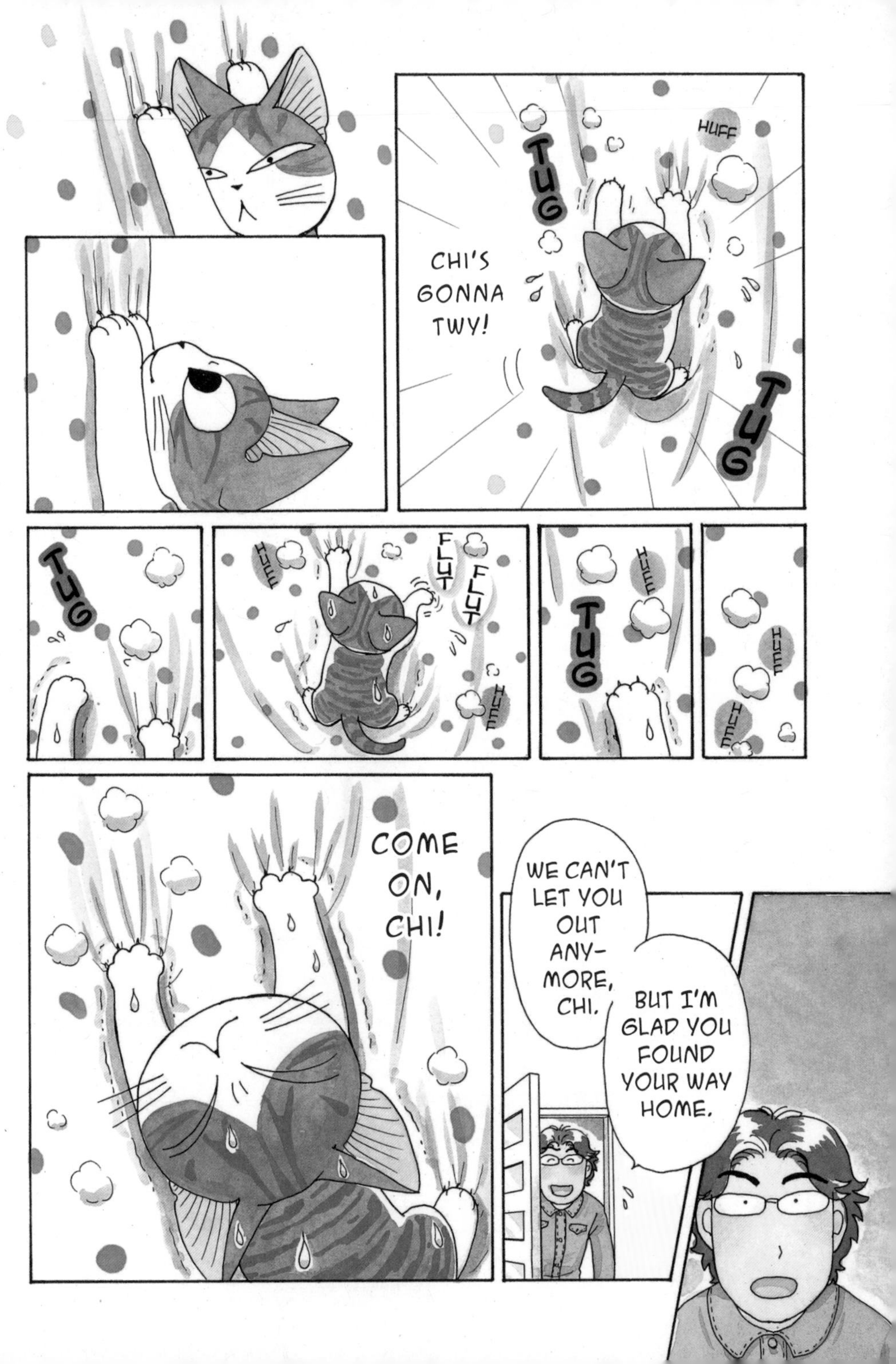
HUFF
TUG
CHI'S GONNA TWY!
TUG
TUG
HUFF
FLUT
FLUT
HUFF
HUFF
TUG
HUFF
HUFF
COME ON, CHI!
WE CAN'T LET YOU OUT ANY-MORE, CHI.
BUT I'M GLAD YOU FOUND YOUR WAY HOME.

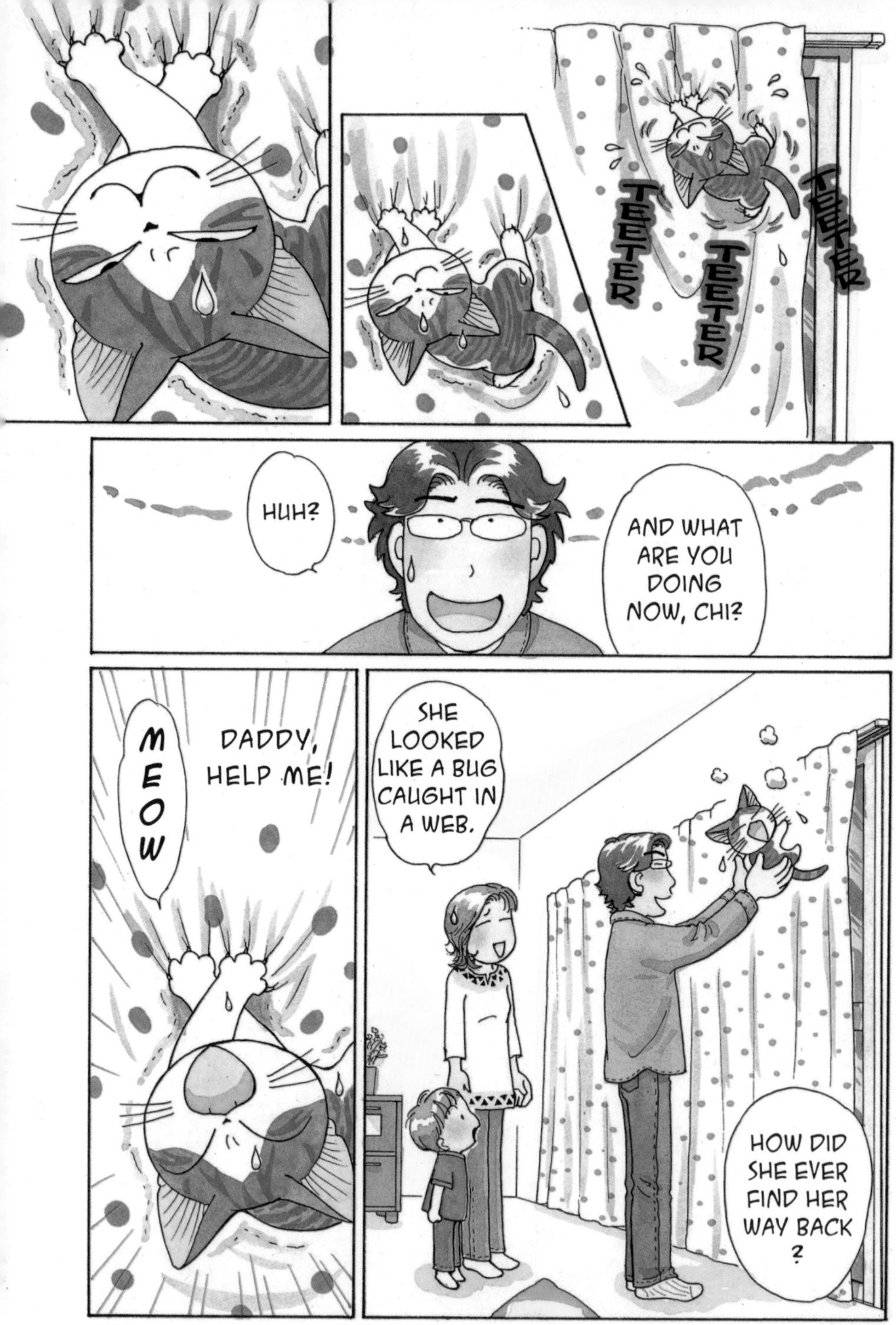
TEETER
TEETER
TEETER
HUH?
AND WHAT ARE YOU DOING NOW, CHI?
MEOW
DADDY, HELP ME!
SHE LOOKED LIKE A BUG CAUGHT IN A WEB.
HOW DID SHE EVER FIND HER WAY BACK?

the end

homemade 50: a cat yearns

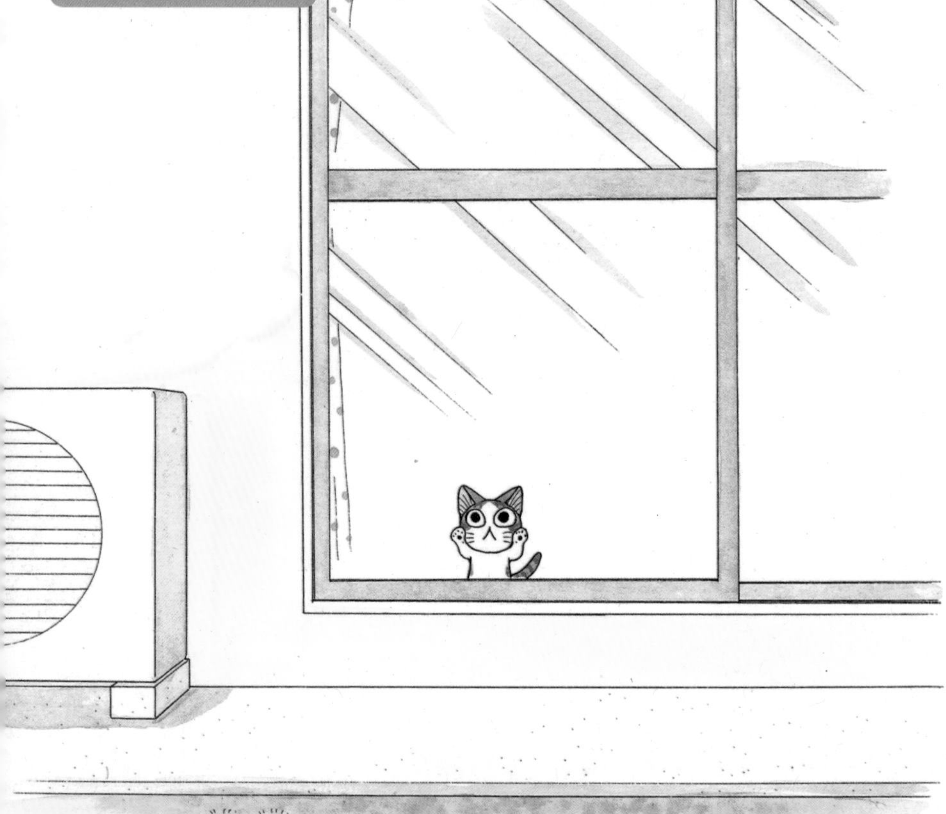

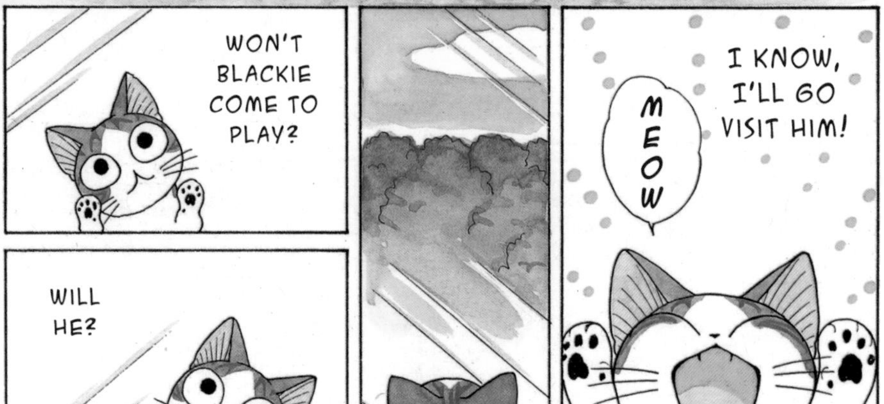
WON'T BLACKIE COME TO PLAY?
WILL HE?
MEOW
I KNOW, I'LL GO VISIT HIM!

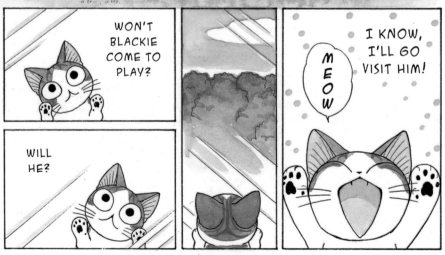

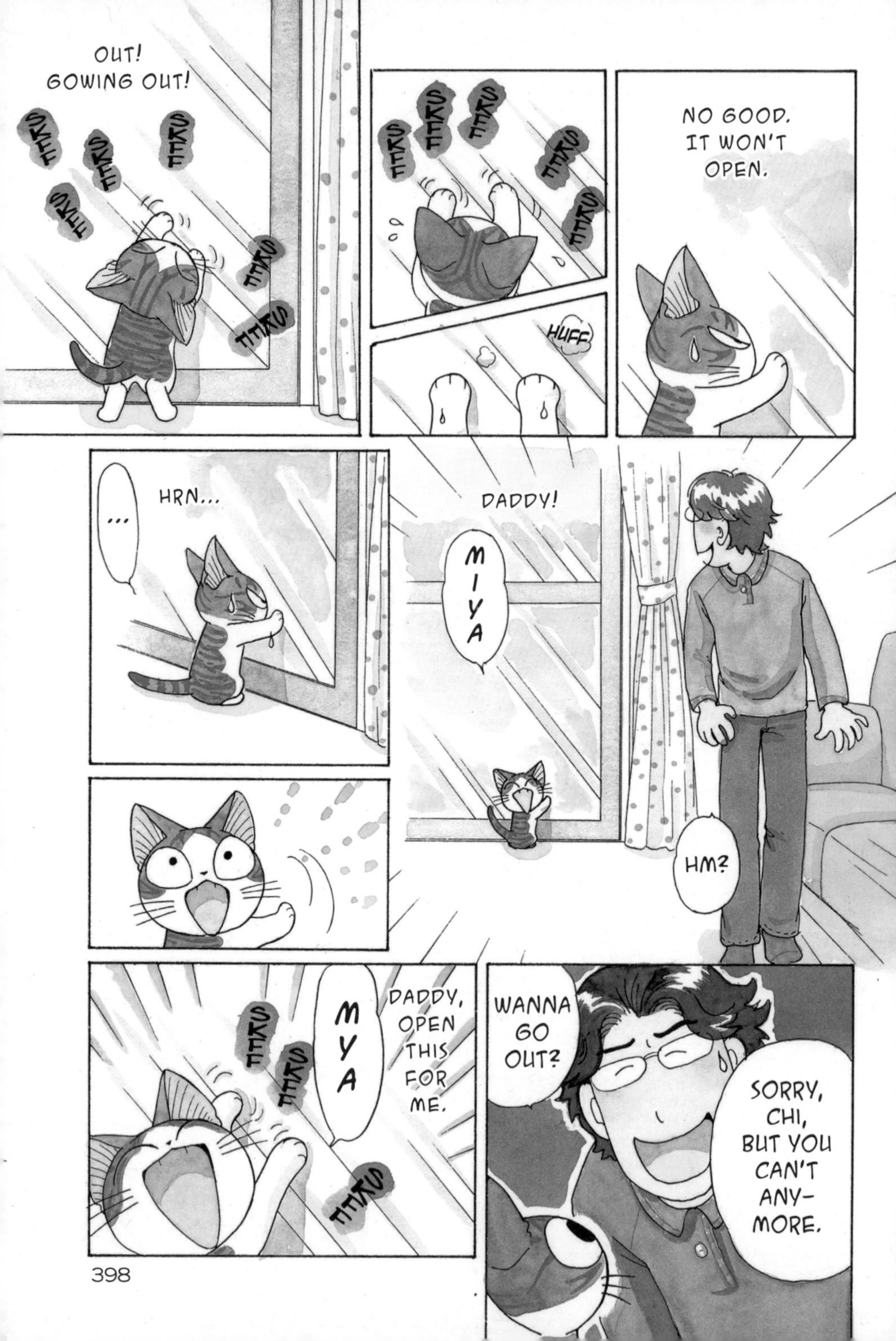
OUT! GOWING OUT!
SKFF
SKFF
SKFF
SKFF
SKFF
SKFF
SKFF
SKFF
SKFF
HUFF
NO GOOD. IT WON'T OPEN.
HRN...
...
DADDY!
MIYA
HM?
SKFF
SKFF
MYA
DADDY, OPEN THIS FOR ME.
WANNA GO OUT?
SORRY, CHI, BUT YOU CAN'T ANYMORE.

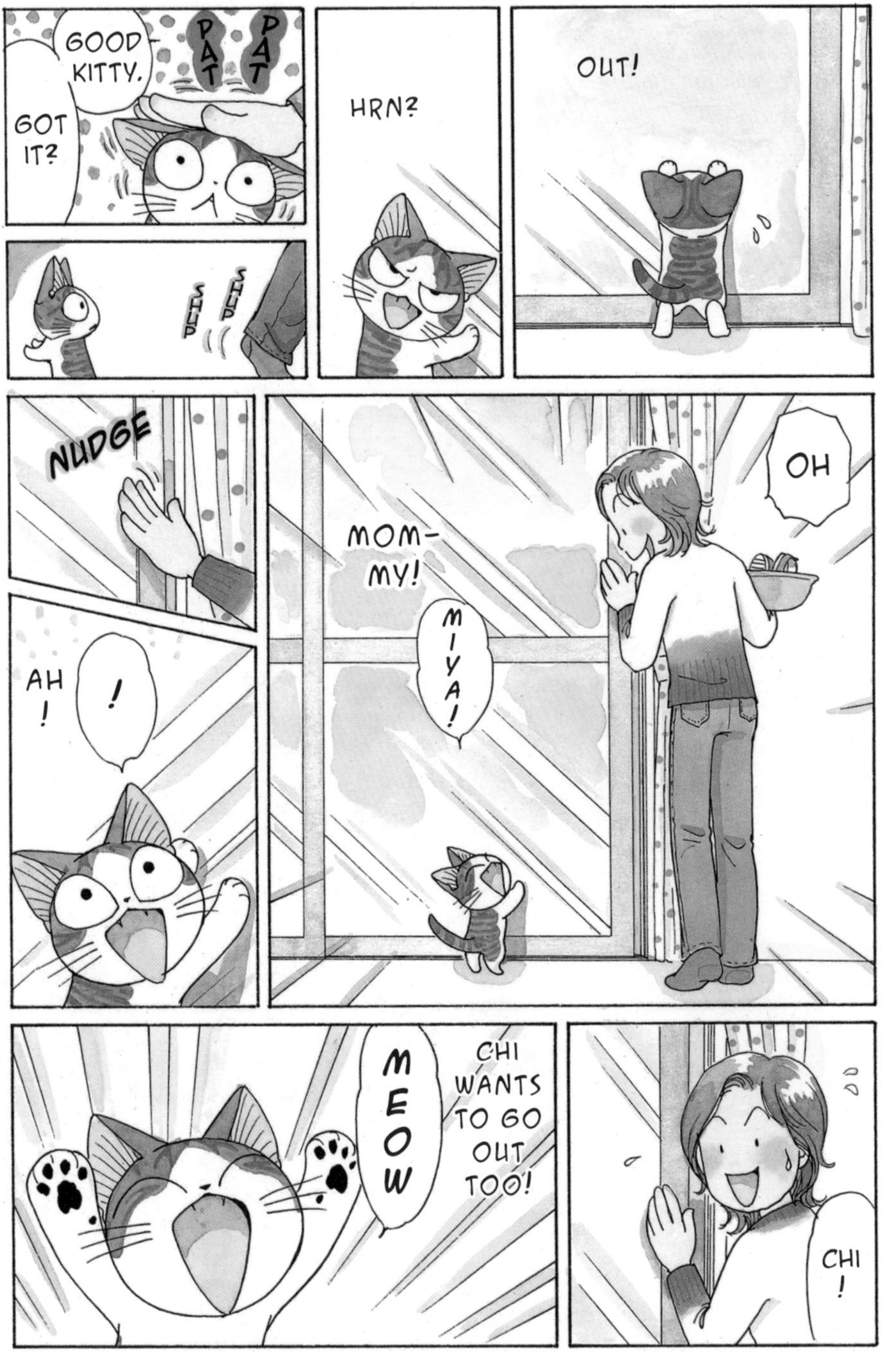
GOOD KITTY.
GOT IT?
PAT PAT
SHUP SHUP
HRN?
OUT!
NUDGE
AH!
!
MOM-MY!
MIYA!
OH
MEOW
CHI WANTS TO GO OUT TOO!
CHI!

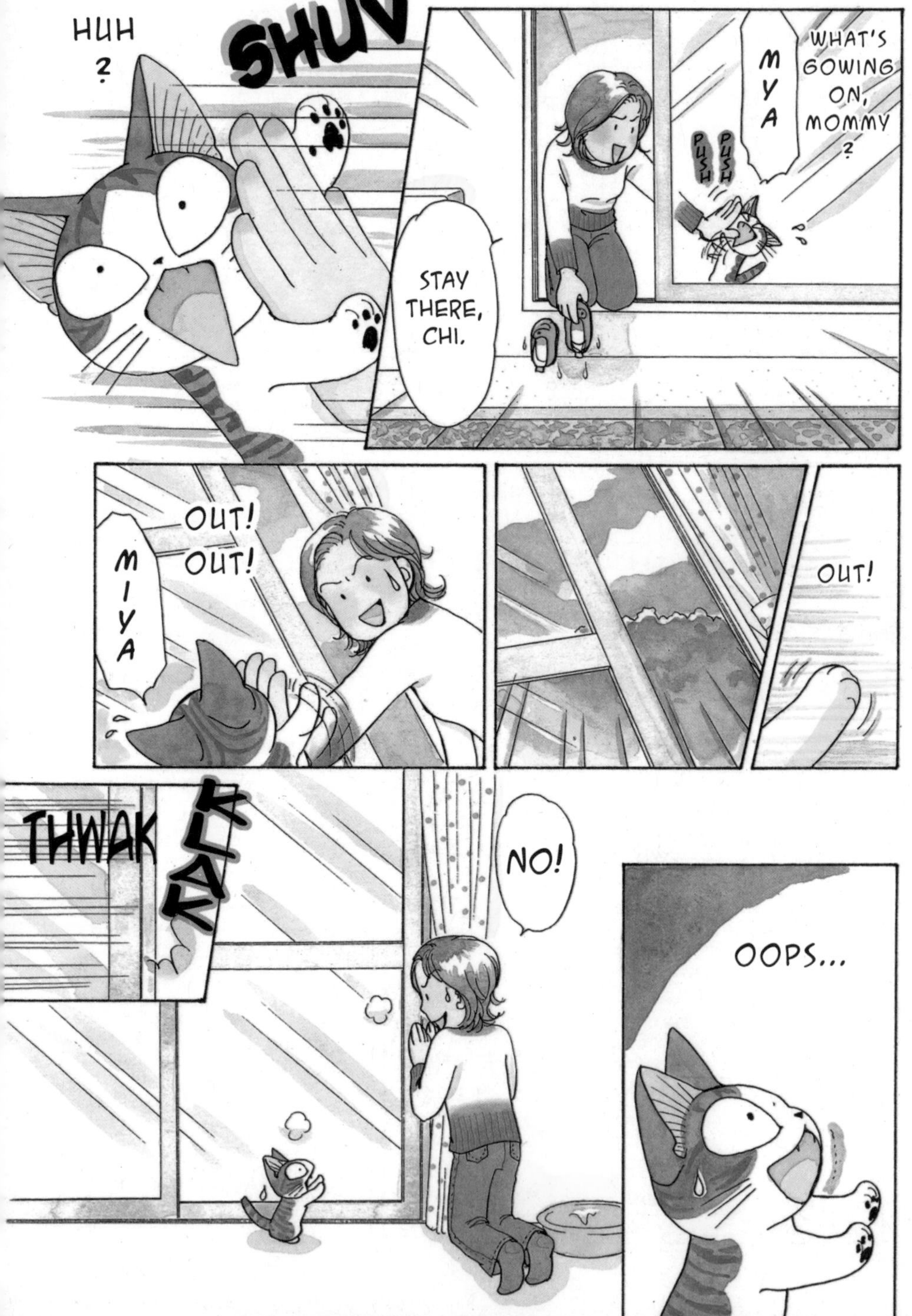
HUH ?
SHUV
MYA
WHAT'S GOWING ON, MOMMY ?
PUSH PUSH
STAY THERE, CHI.
OUT! OUT!
MIYA
OUT!
THWAK
KLAK
NO!
OOPS...

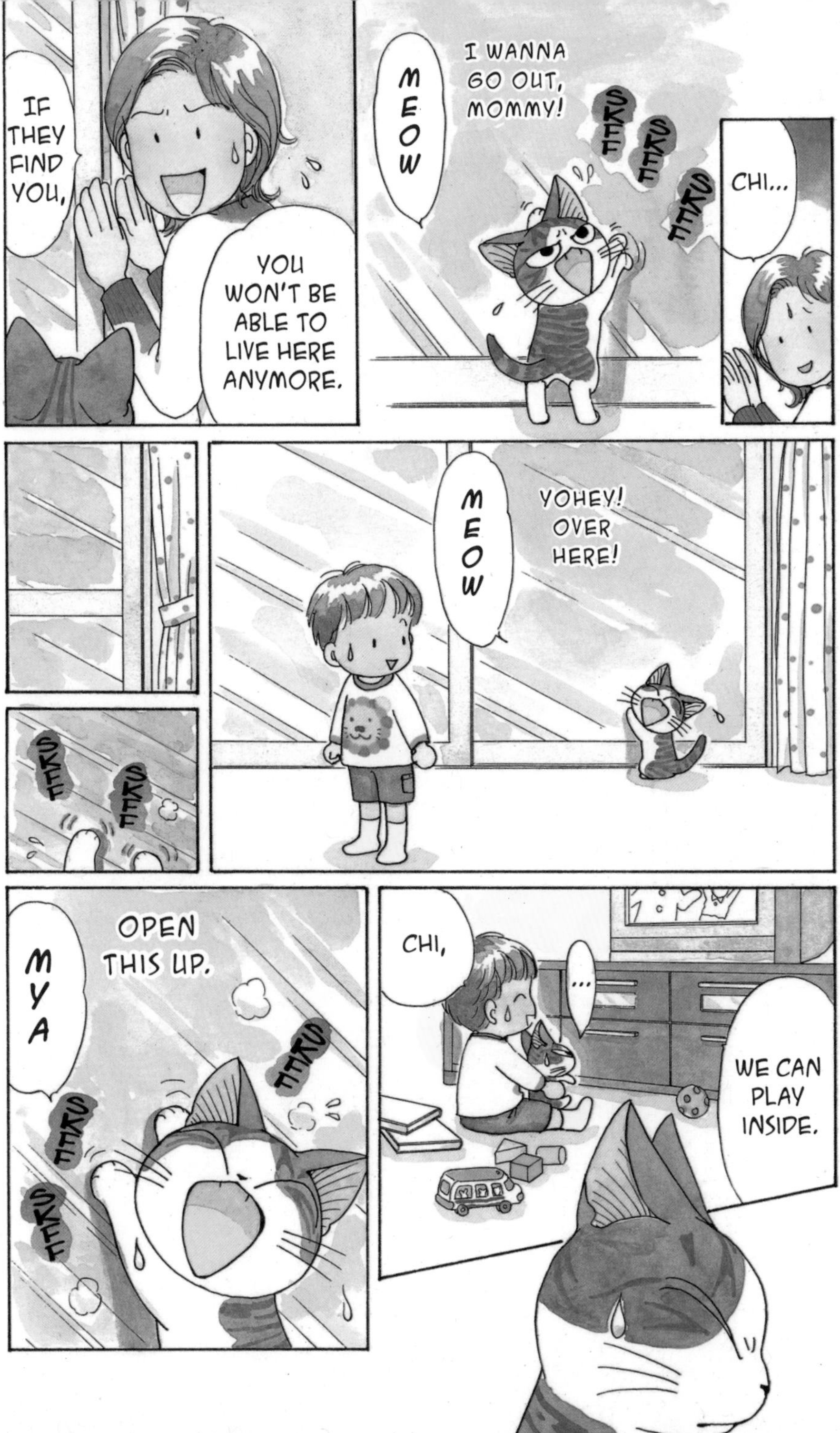
IF THEY FIND YOU,
YOU WON'T BE ABLE TO LIVE HERE ANYMORE.
MEOW
I WANNA GO OUT, MOMMY!
SKFF
SKFF
SKRITCH
CHI...
SKFF
SKFF
MEOW
YOHEY! OVER HERE!
MYA
OPEN THIS UP.
SKRITCH
SKRITCH
SKFF
CHI,
...
WE CAN PLAY INSIDE.

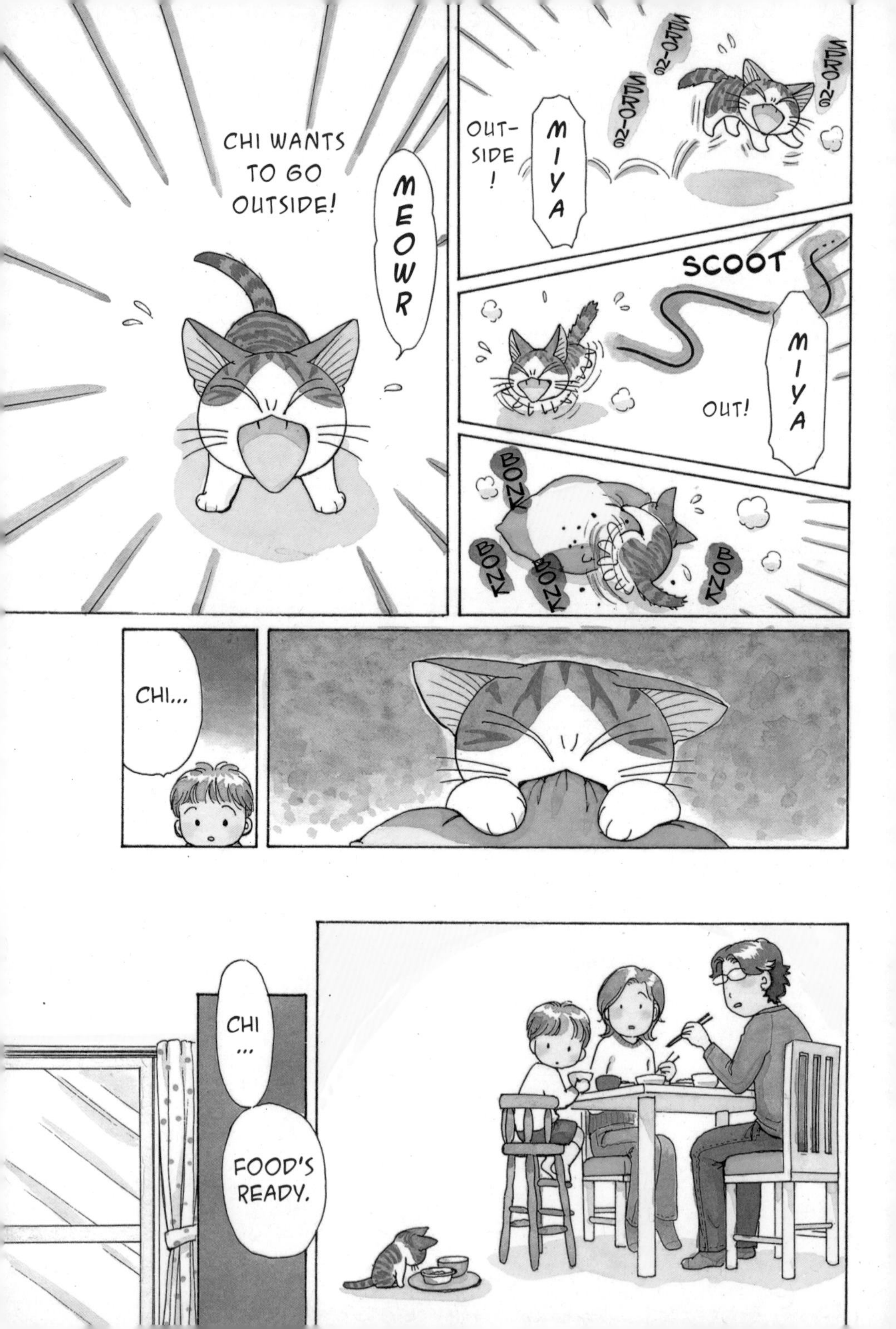
CHI WANTS TO GO OUTSIDE!
MEOWR
SPROING
SPROING
SPROING
OUT-SIDE!
MIYA
SCOOT
OUT!
MIYA
BONK
BONK
BONK
BONK
CHI...
CHI ...
FOOD'S READY.

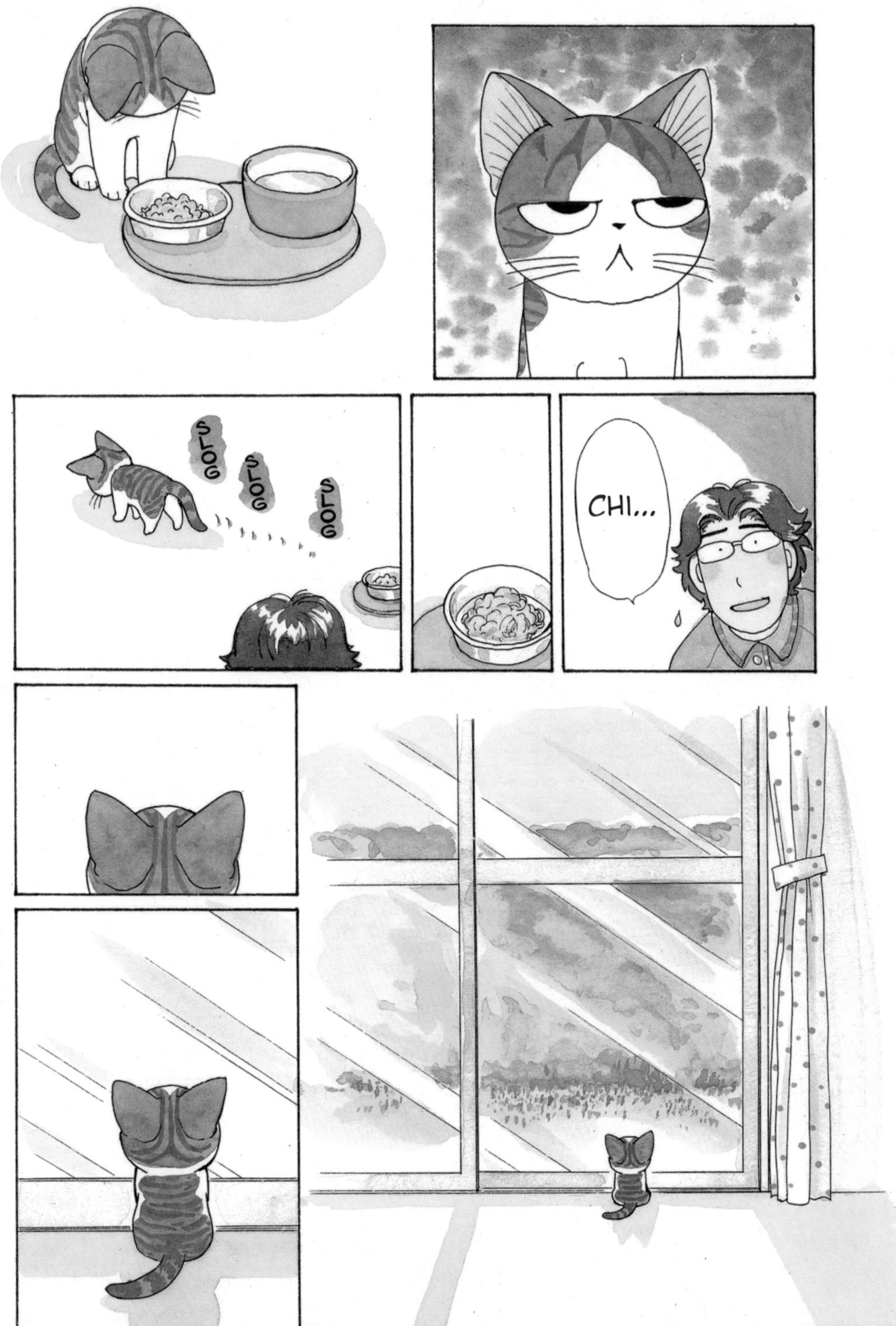
SLOG
SLOG
SLOG
CHI...

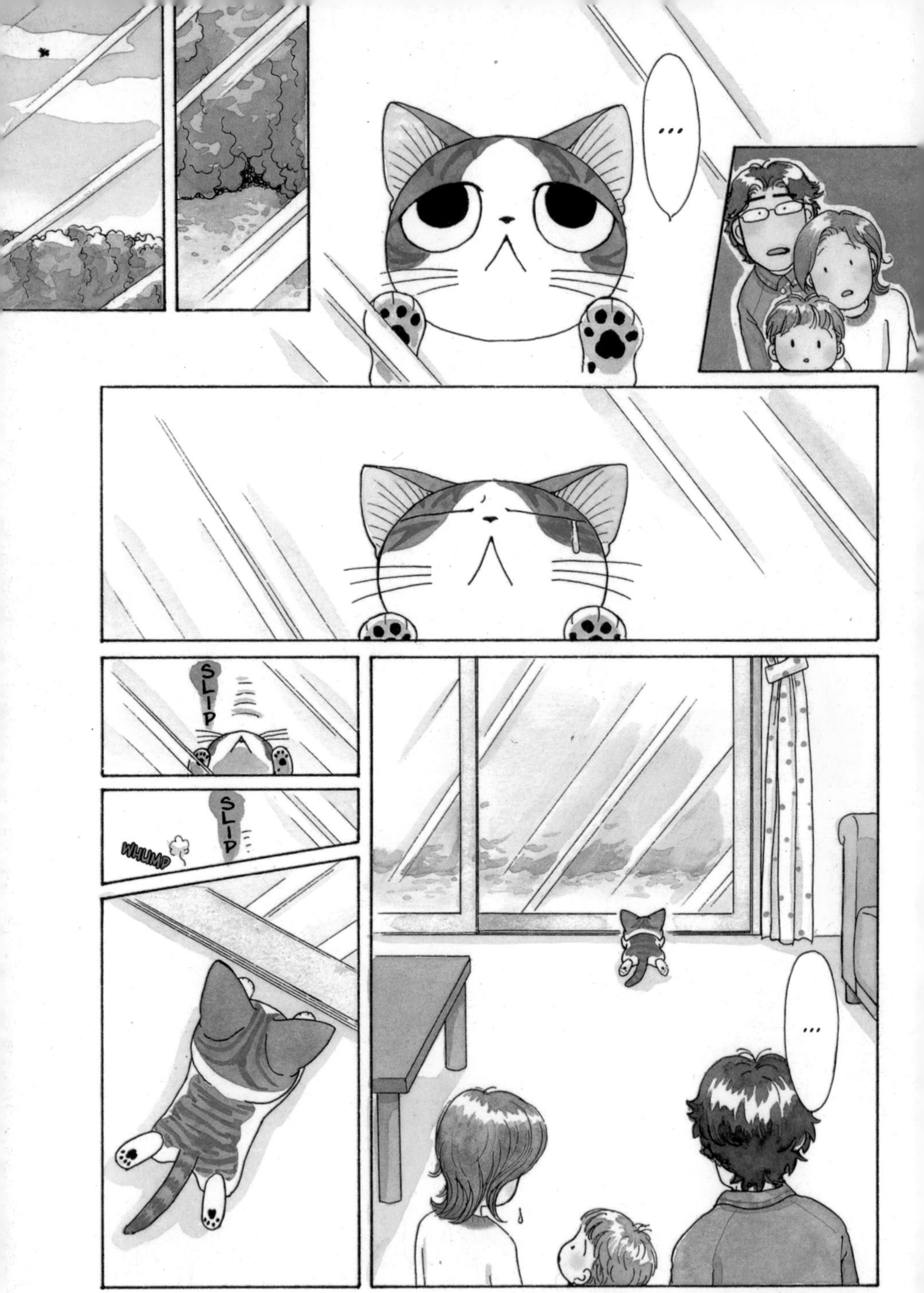
...
SLIP
SLIP
WHUMP
...

the end

homemade 51: a cat appeals

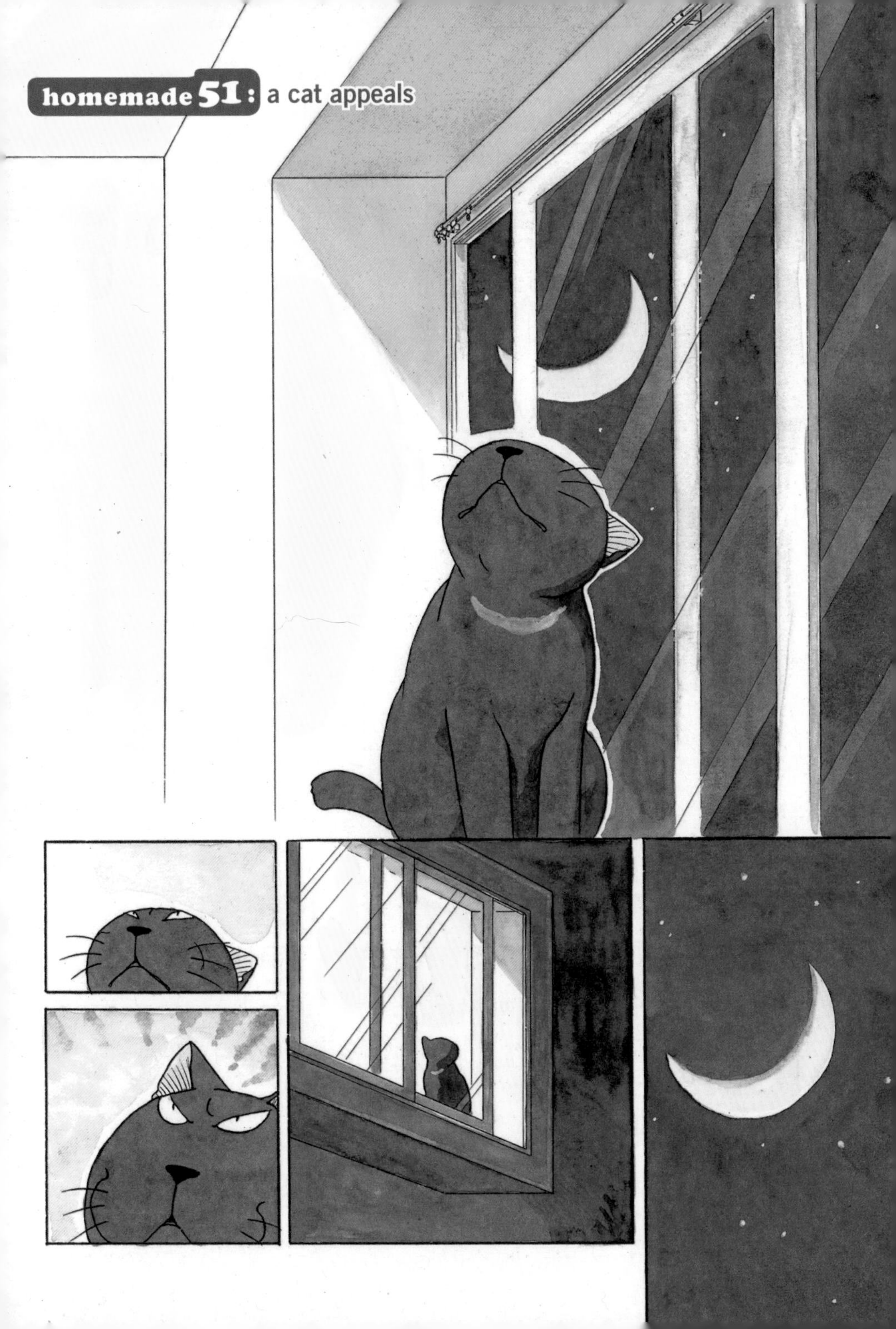

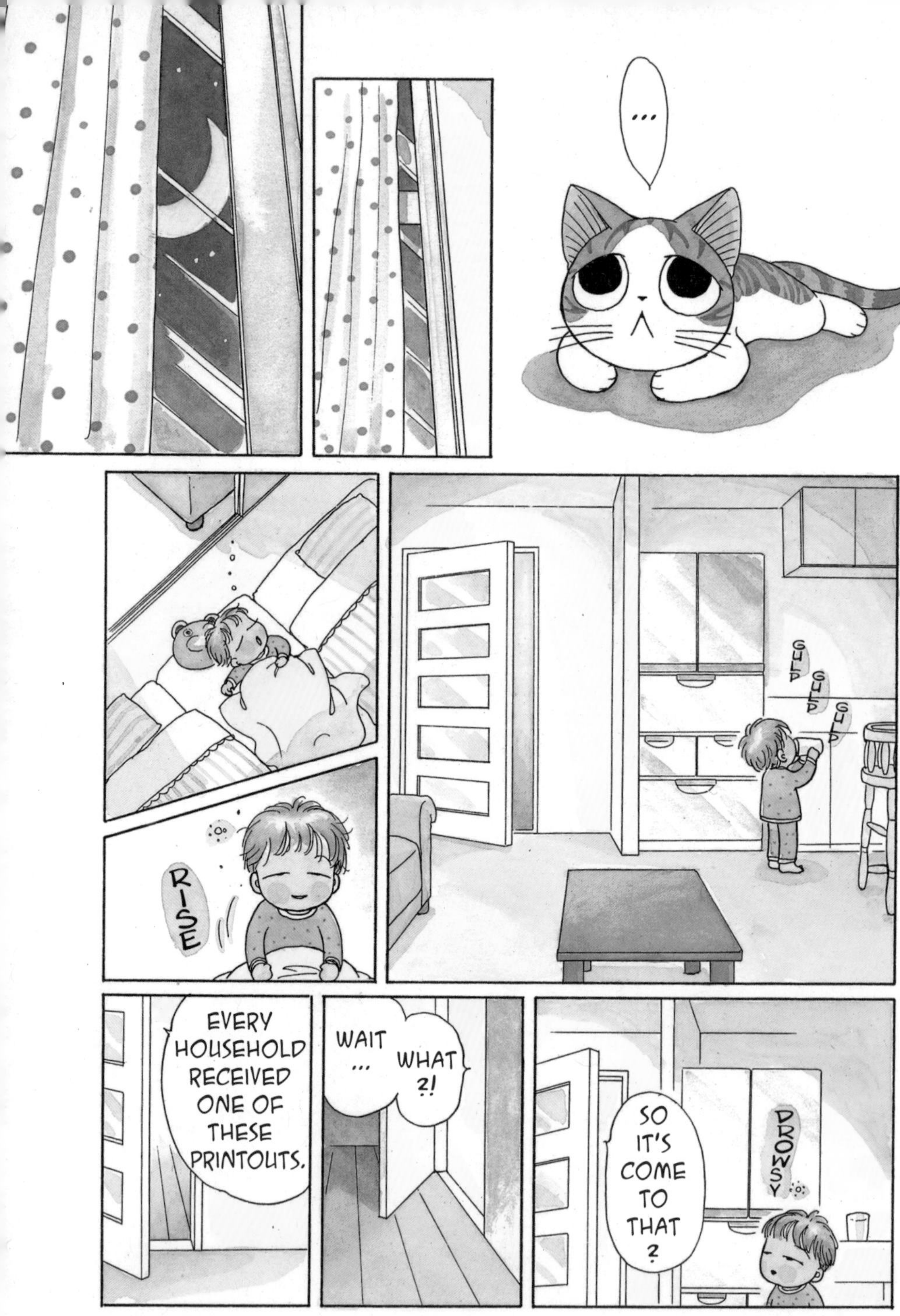
...
RISE
GULP
GULP
GULP
EVERY HOUSEHOLD RECEIVED ONE OF THESE PRINTOUTS.
WAIT ...
WHAT?!
SO IT'S COME TO THAT?
DROWSY

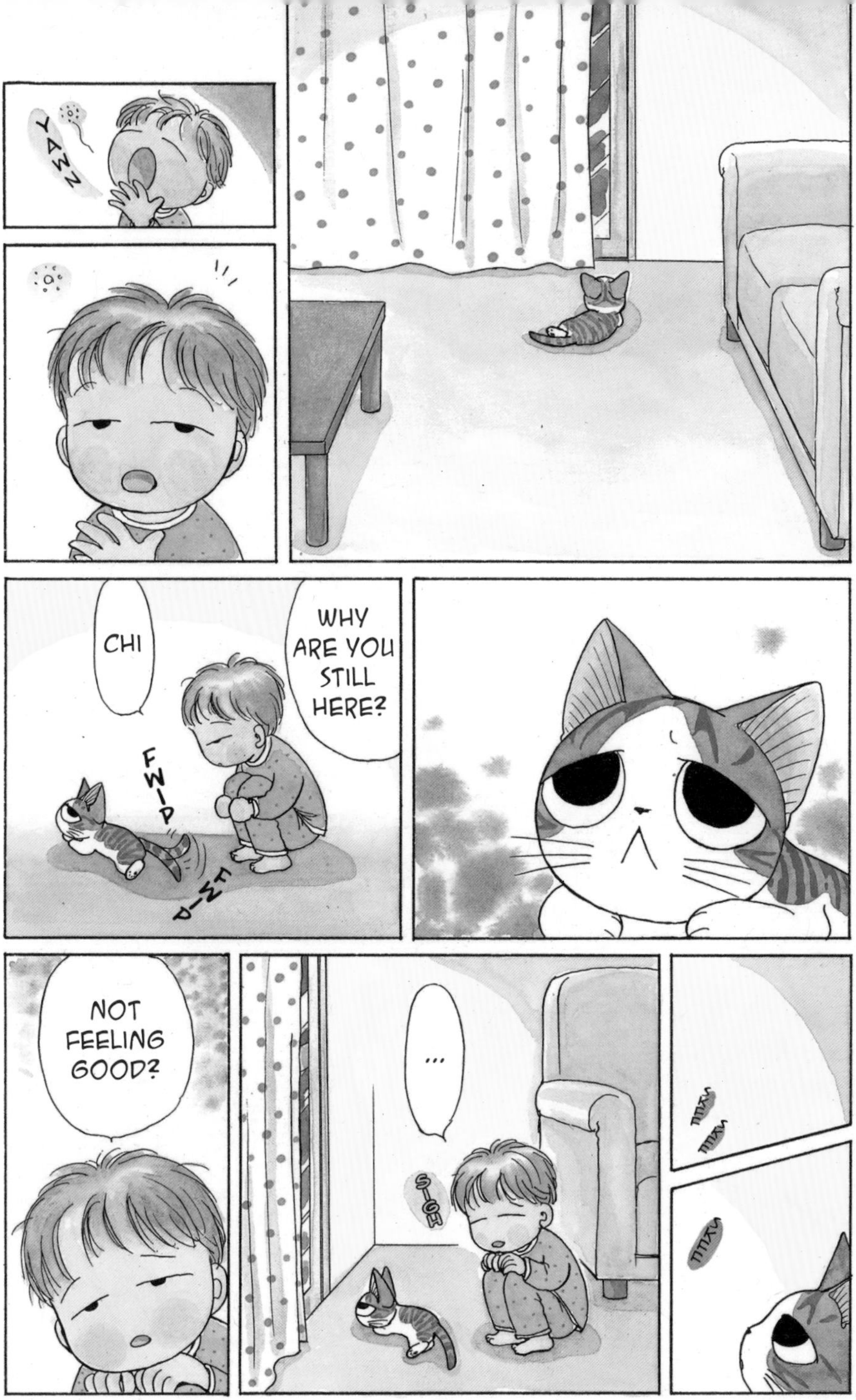
YAWN
CHI
WHY ARE YOU STILL HERE?
FWIP
FWIP
NOT FEELING GOOD?
...
SIGH

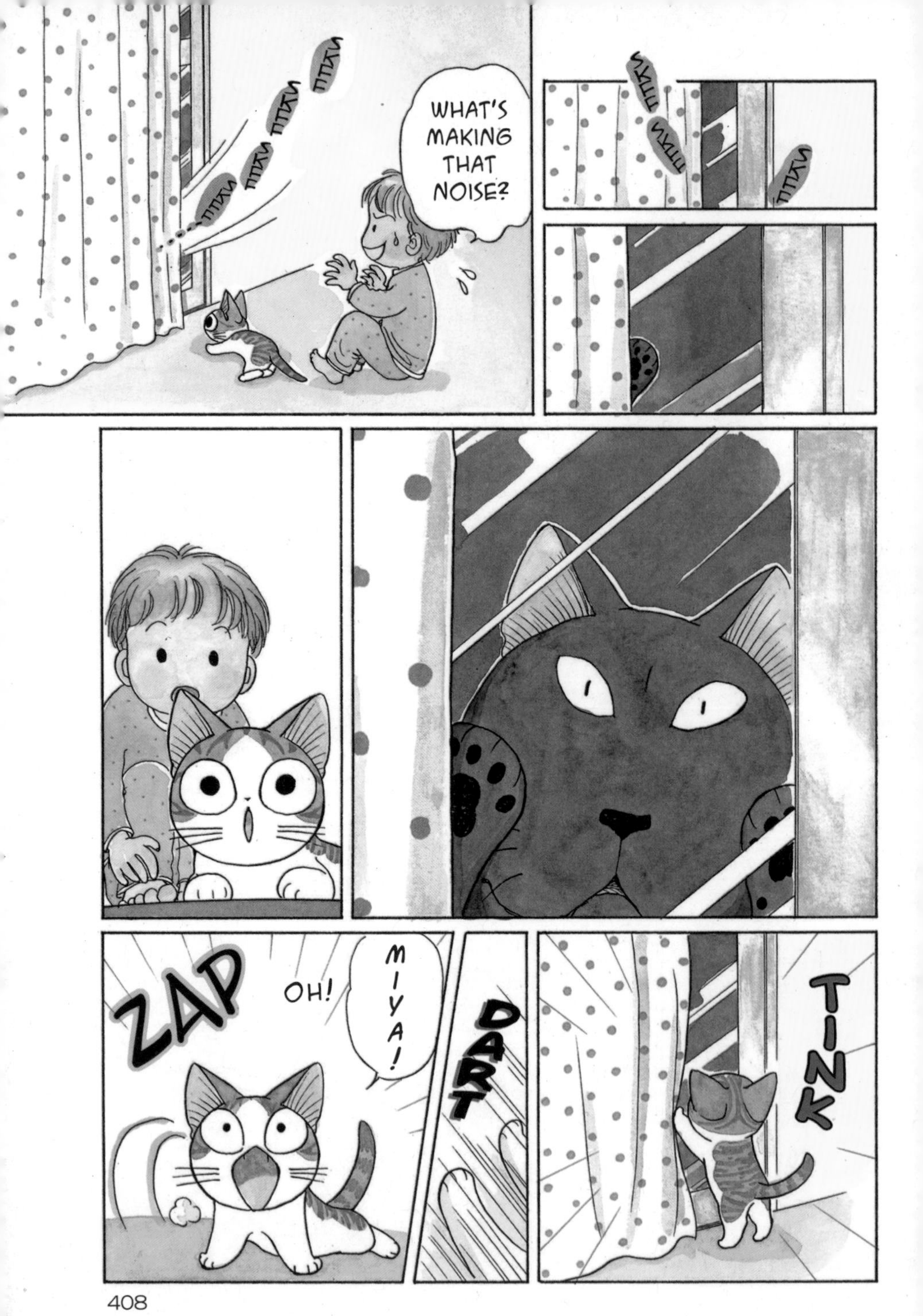
WHAT'S MAKING THAT NOISE?
ZAP
OH!
MIYA!
DART
TINK

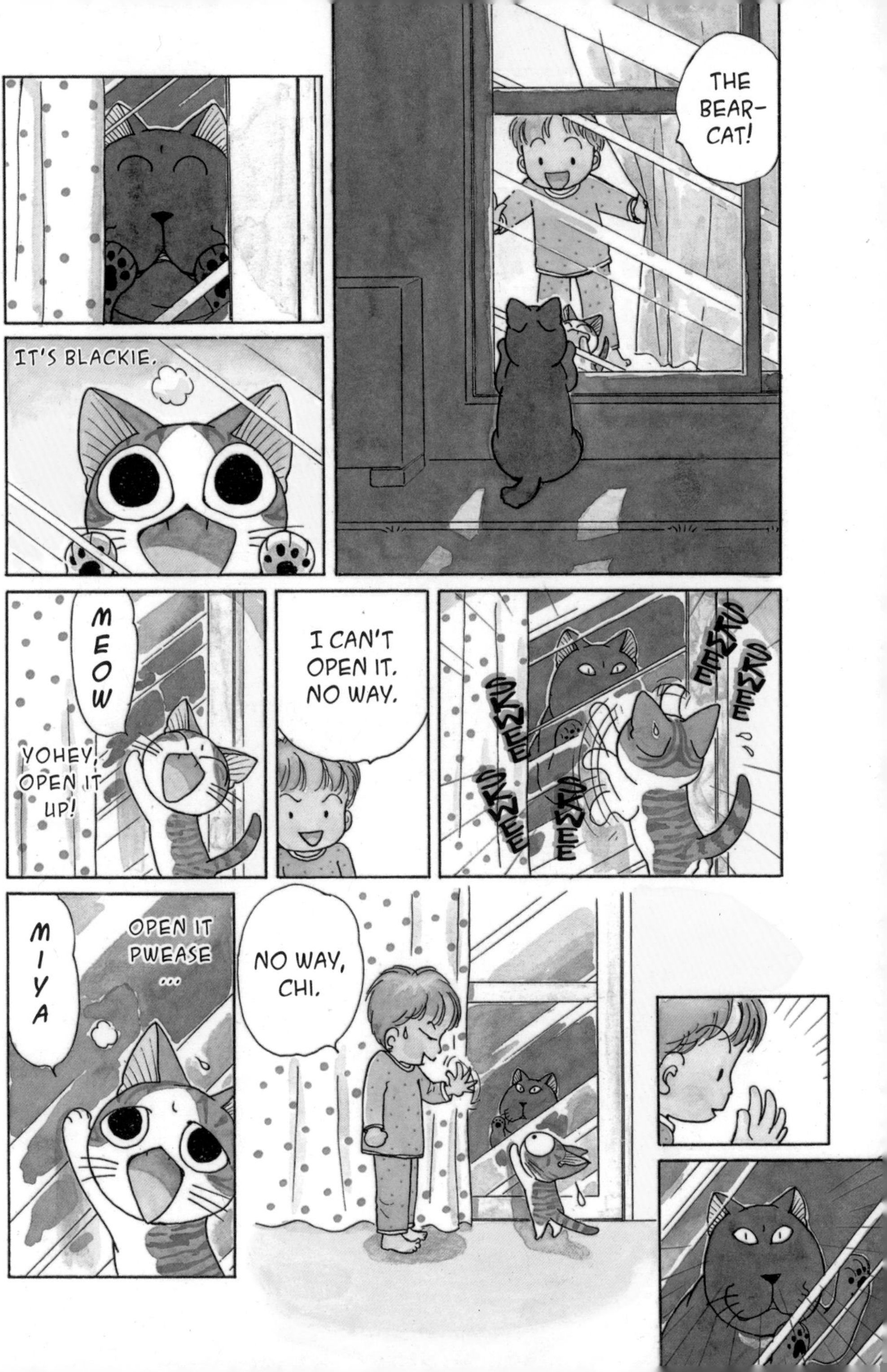
THE BEAR-CAT!
IT'S BLACKIE.
MEOW
YOHEY, OPEN IT UP!
I CAN'T OPEN IT. NO WAY.
SKWEE
SKWEE
SKWEE
SKWEE
SKWEE
MIYA
OPEN IT PWEASE ...
NO WAY, CHI.

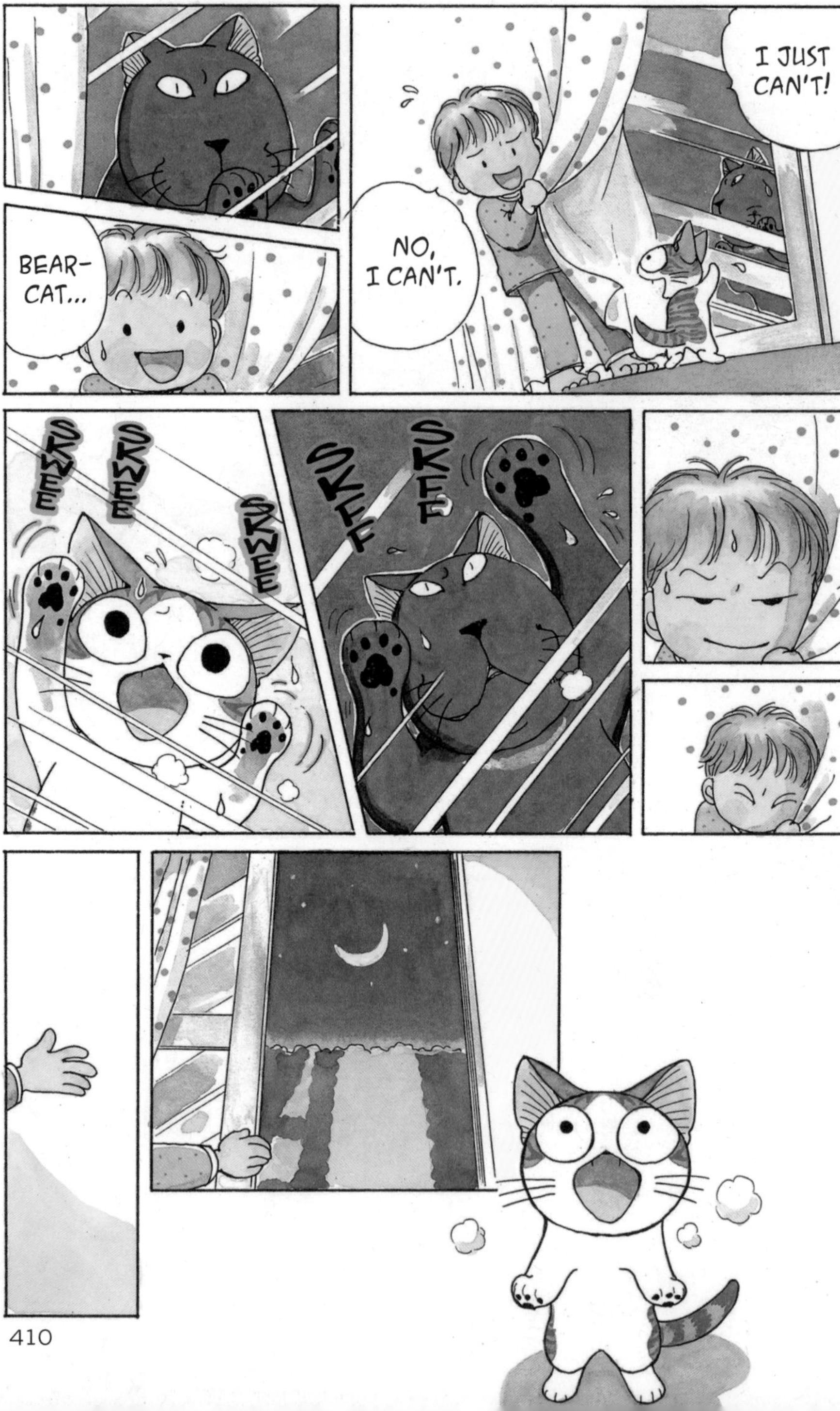
BEAR-
CAT...
NO,
I CAN'T.
I JUST
CAN'T!
SRWEE
SRWEE
SRWEE
SKFF
SKFF

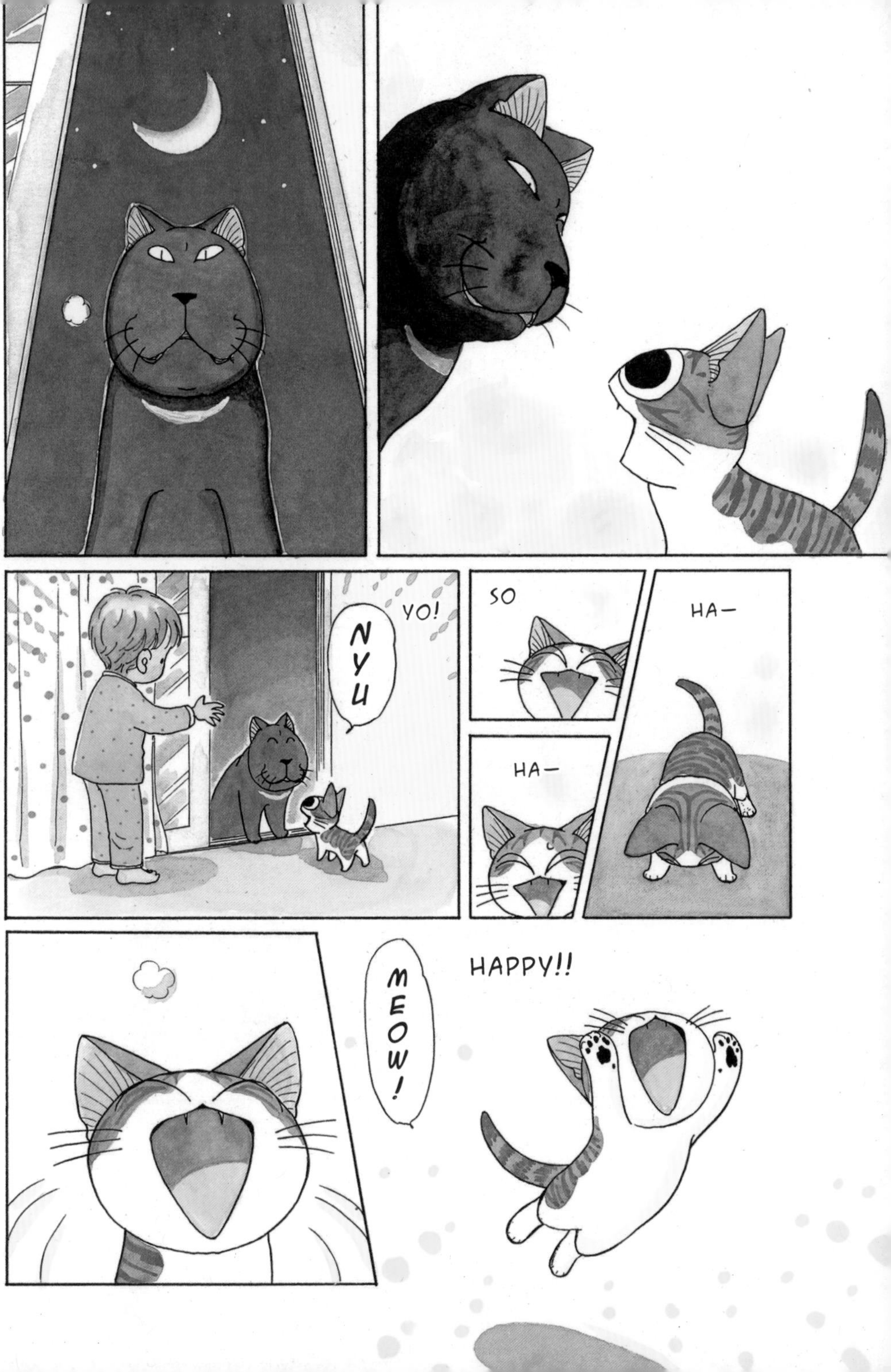
NYU
YO!
SO
HA—
HA—
MEOW!
HAPPY!!

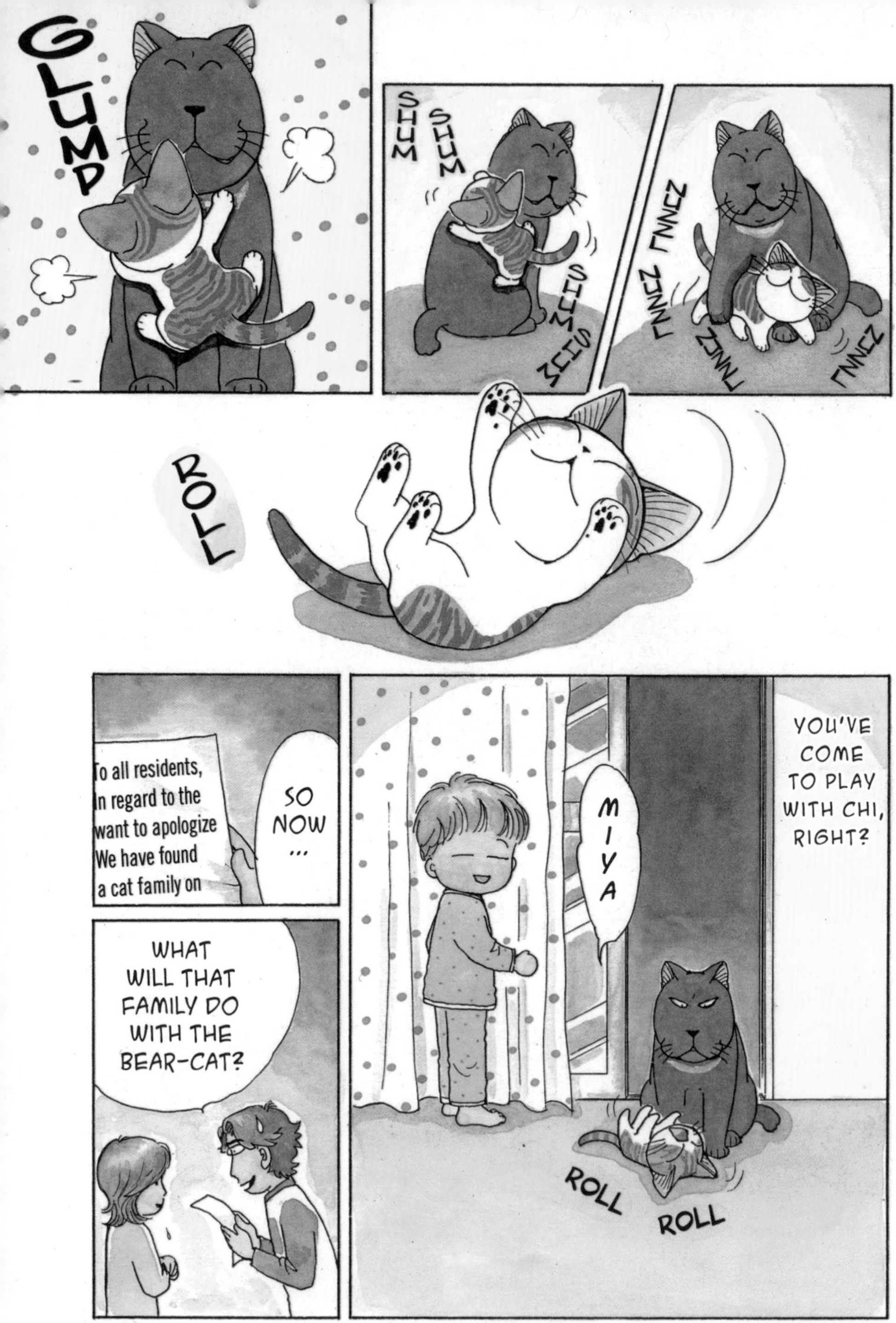
GLUMP
SHUM SHUM
SHUM SHUM
ROLL
To all residents,
In regard to the
want to apologize
We have found
a cat family on
SO NOW ...
WHAT WILL THAT FAMILY DO WITH THE BEAR-CAT?
MIYA
YOU'VE COME TO PLAY WITH CHI, RIGHT?
ROLL
ROLL

the end

homemade 52: a cat promises

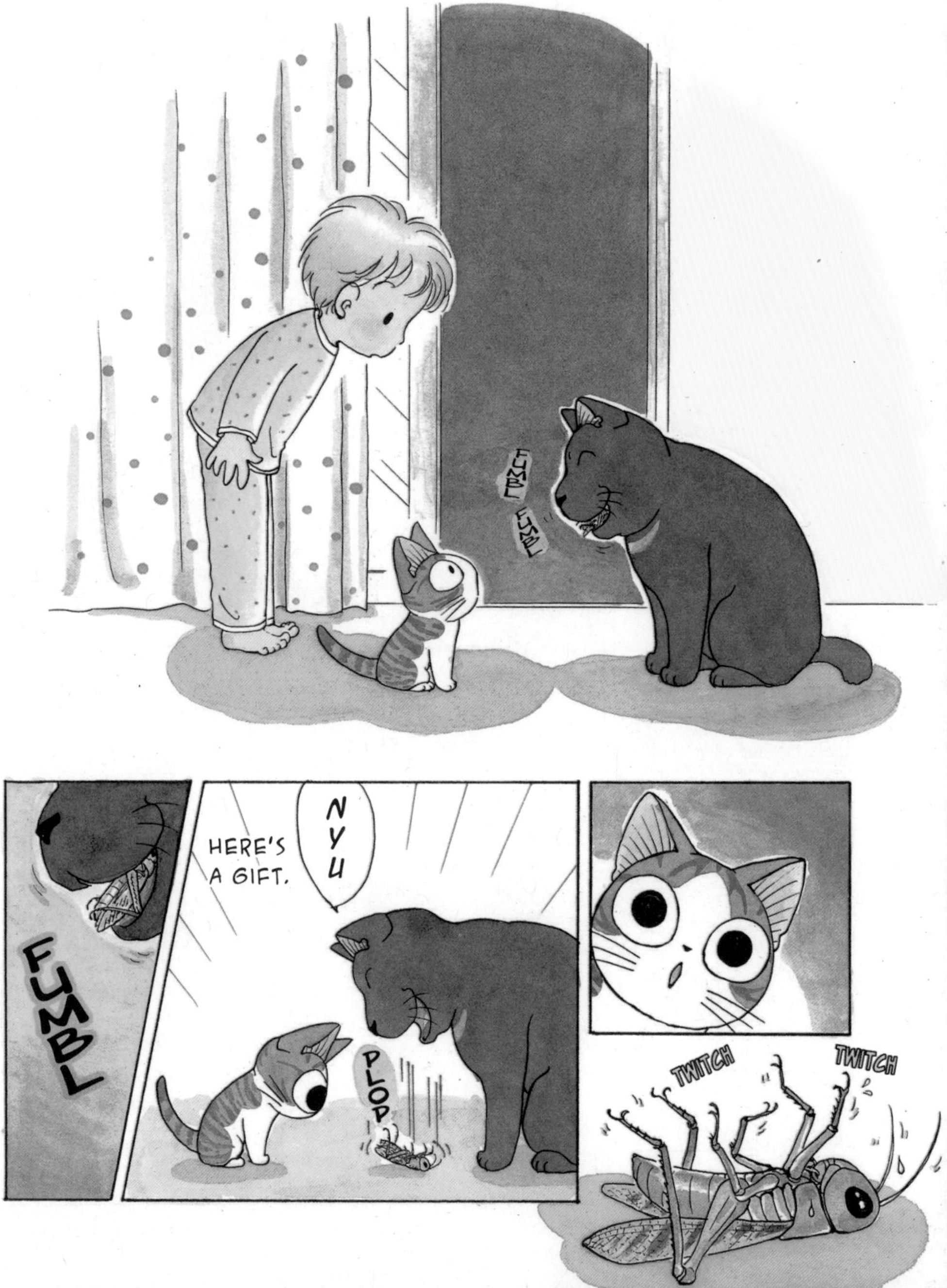
FUMBL
FUMBL
FUMBL
HERE'S A GIFT.
NYU
PLOP
TWITCH
TWITCH

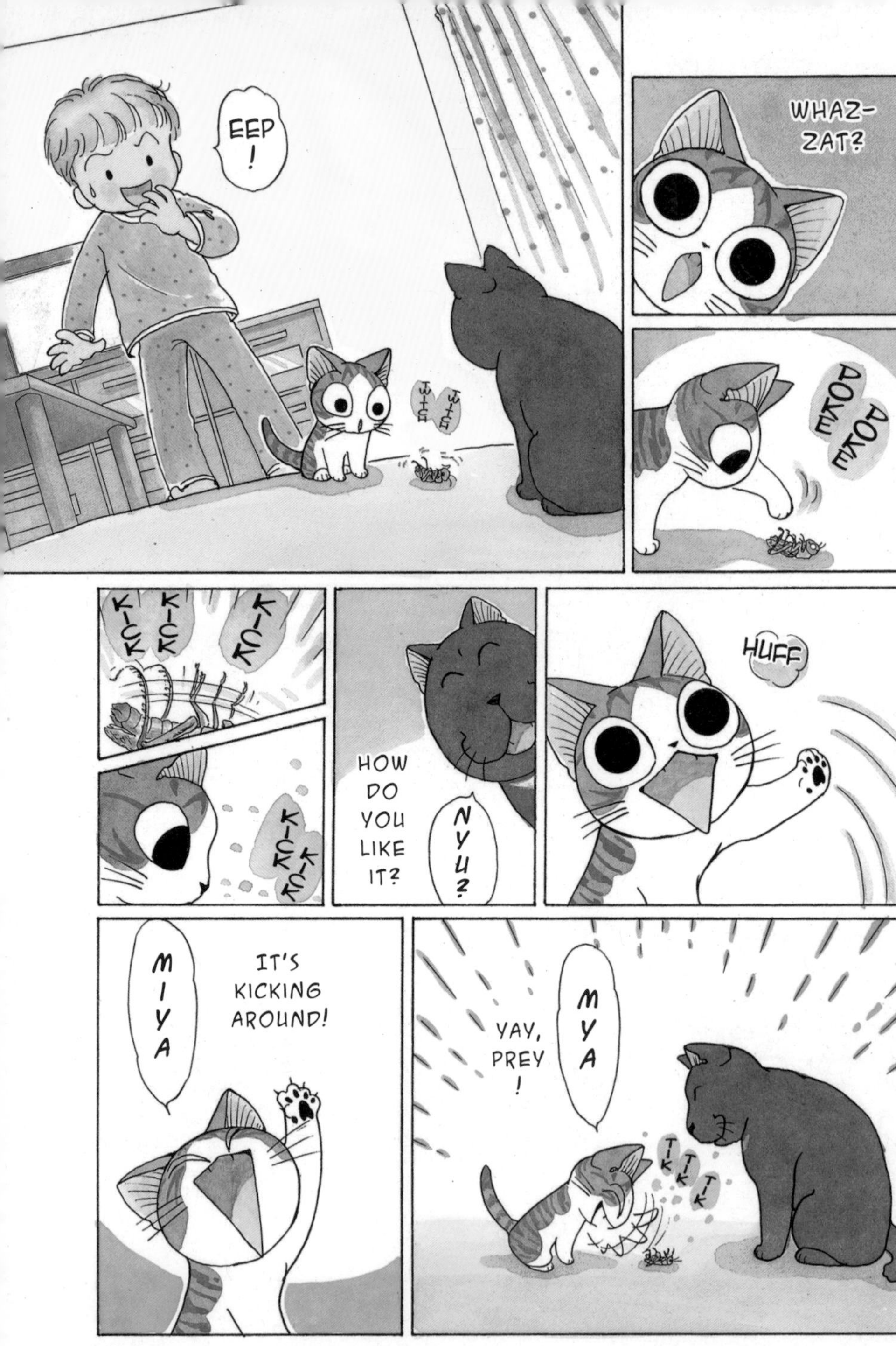

EEP!
TWITCH
TWITCH
WHAZ-ZAT?
POKE
POKE
KICK
KICK
KICK
KICK
KICK
HOW DO YOU LIKE IT?
NYU?
HUFF
MIYA
IT'S KICKING AROUND!
YAY, PREY!
MYA
TIK
TIK
TIK

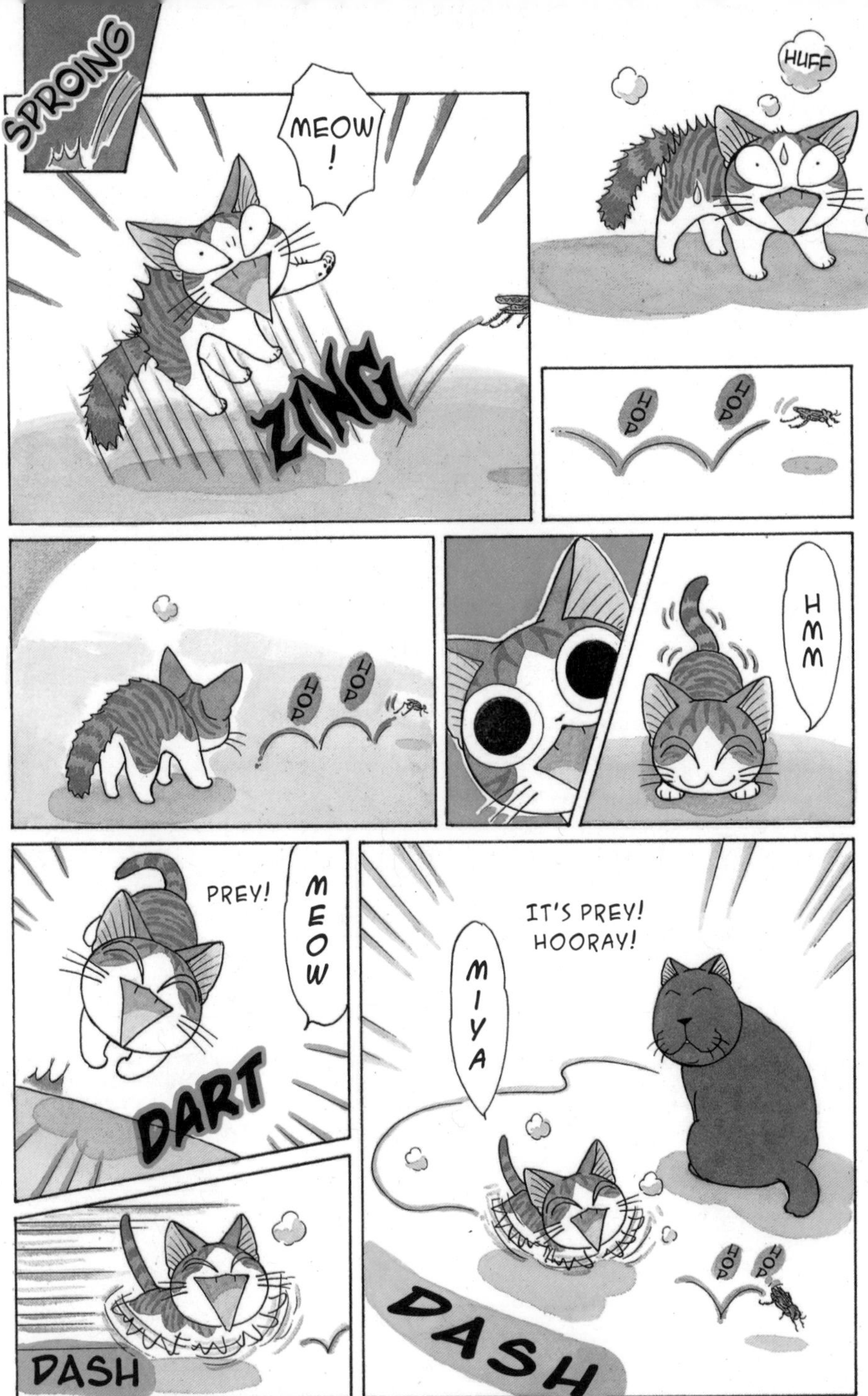
SPROING
MEOW!
ZING
HUFF
HUFF
HOP
HOP
HOP
HOP
HMM
PREY!
MEOW
DART
DASH
IT'S PREY! HOORAY!
MIYA
HOP
HOP
DASH

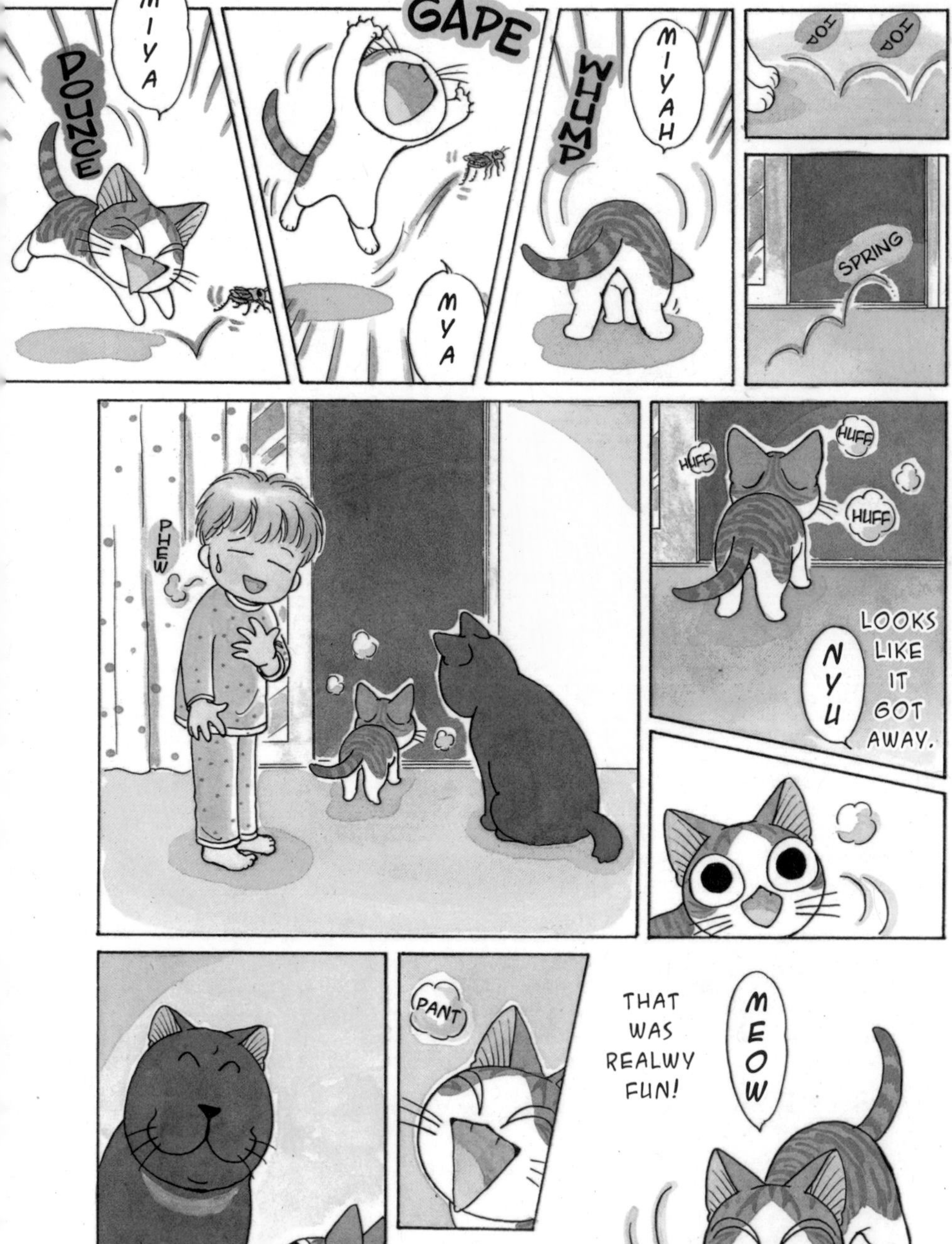
MIYA
POUNCE
GAPE
MYA
MIYAH
WHUMP
HOP
HOP
SPRING
PHEW
HUFF
HUFF
HUFF
LOOKS LIKE IT GOT AWAY.
NYU
PANT
THAT WAS REALWY FUN!
MEOW

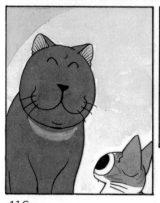

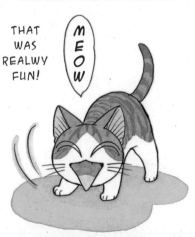

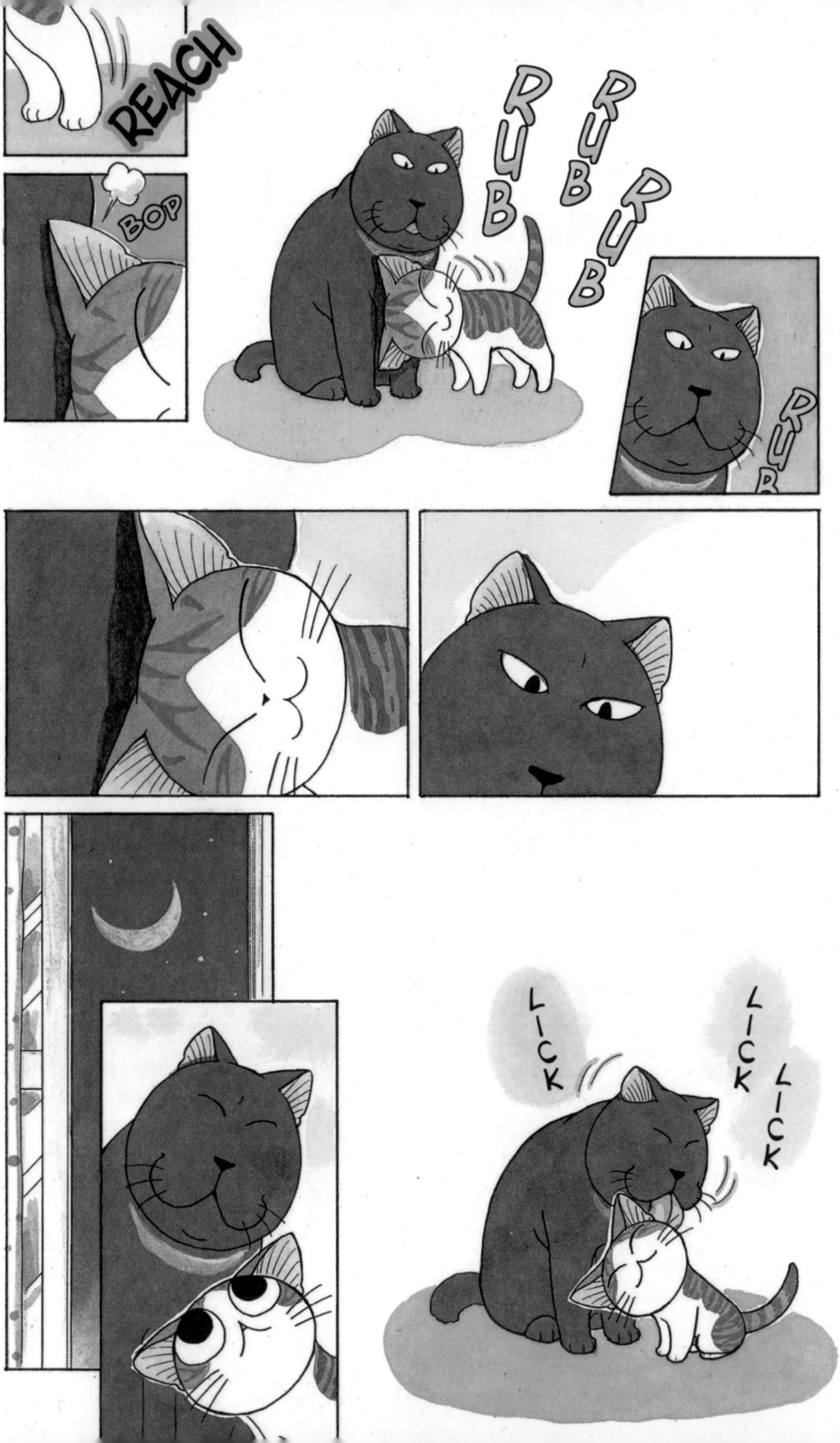
REACH
BOP
RUB
RUB
RUB
RUR
LICK
LICK
LICK

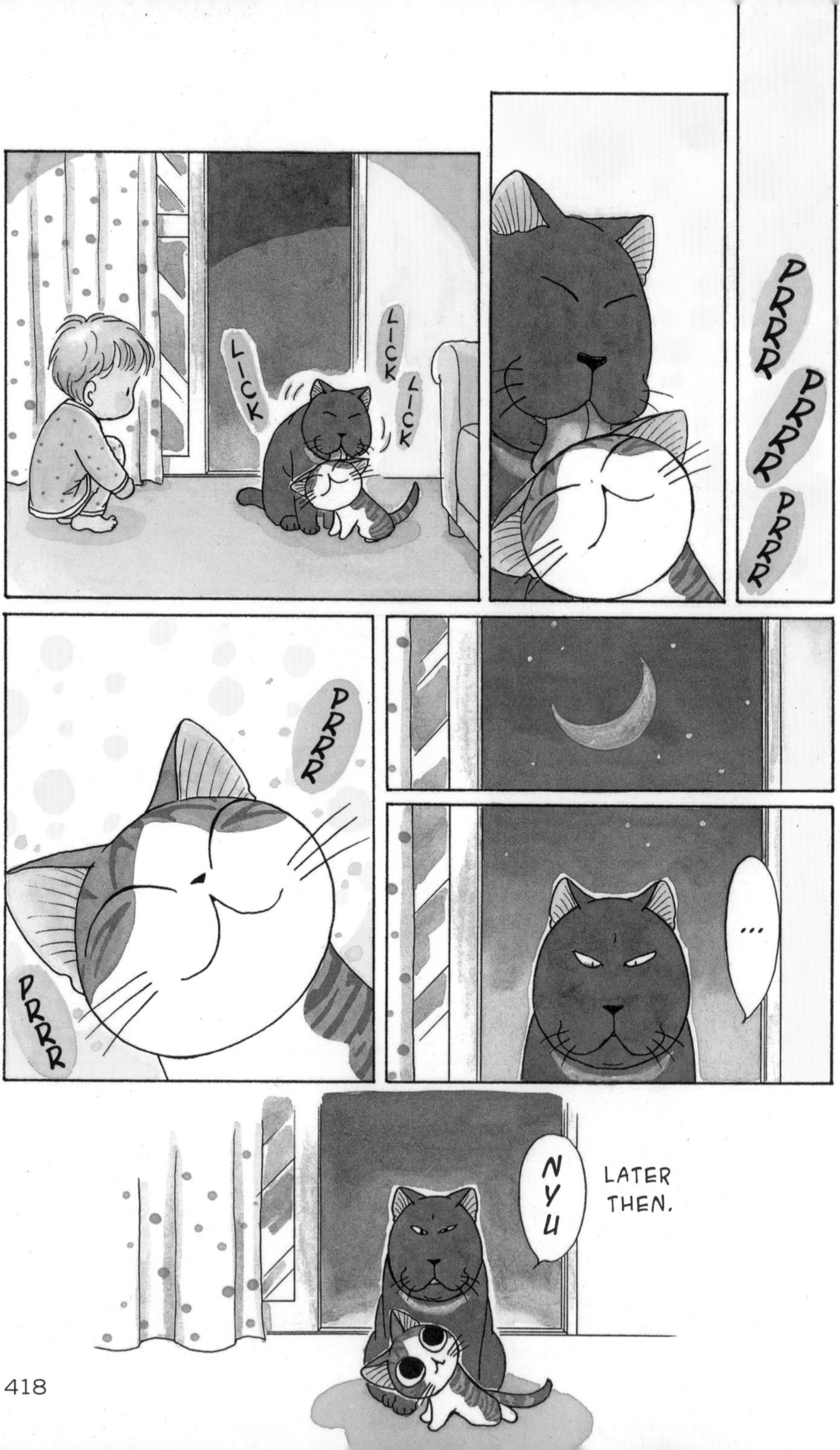
LICK
LICK
LICK
PRRR
PRRRR
PRRRR
PRRR
PRRR
...
NYU
LATER THEN.

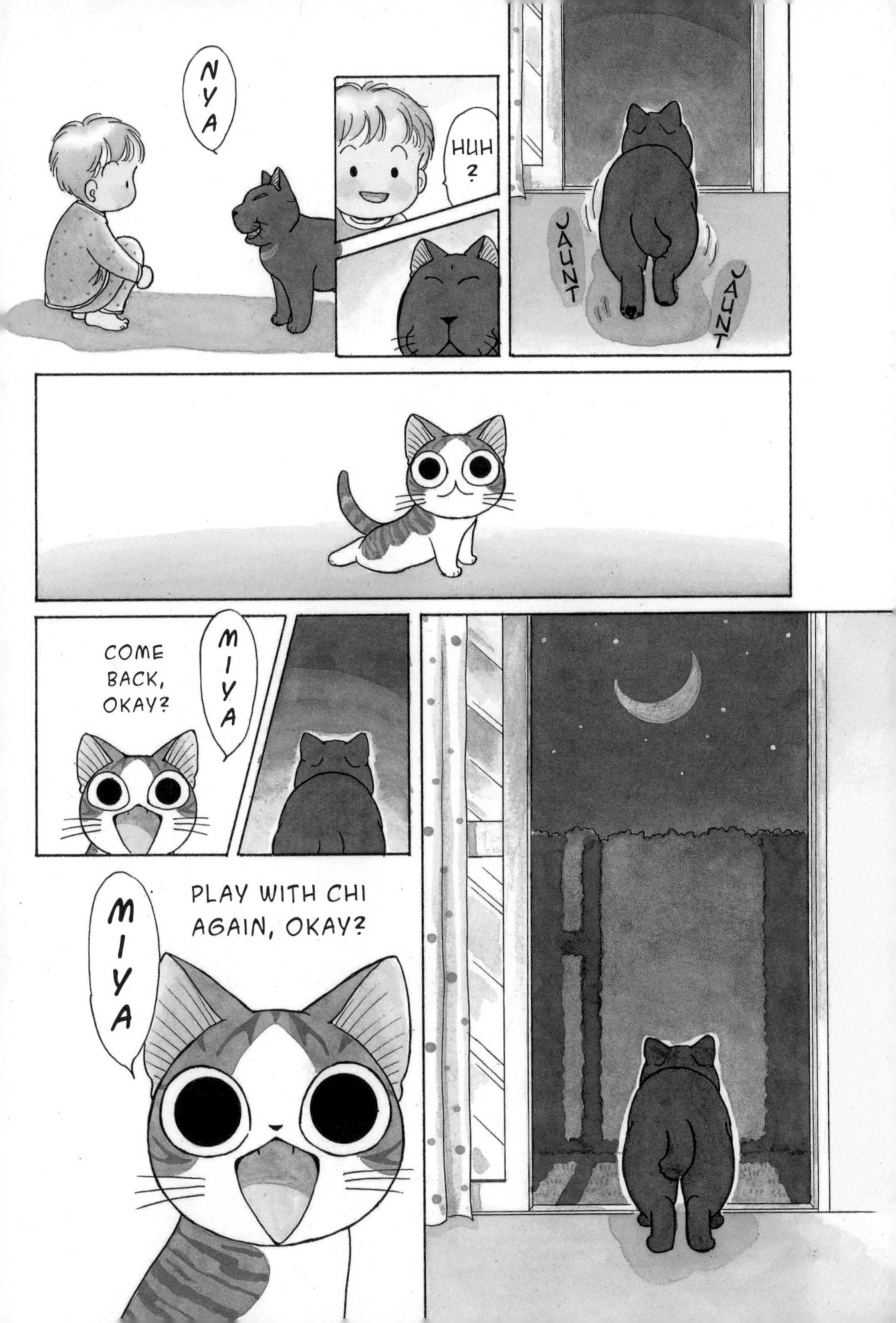
NYA
HUH?
JAUNT
JAUNT
COME BACK, OKAY?
MIYA
MIYA
PLAY WITH CHI AGAIN, OKAY?

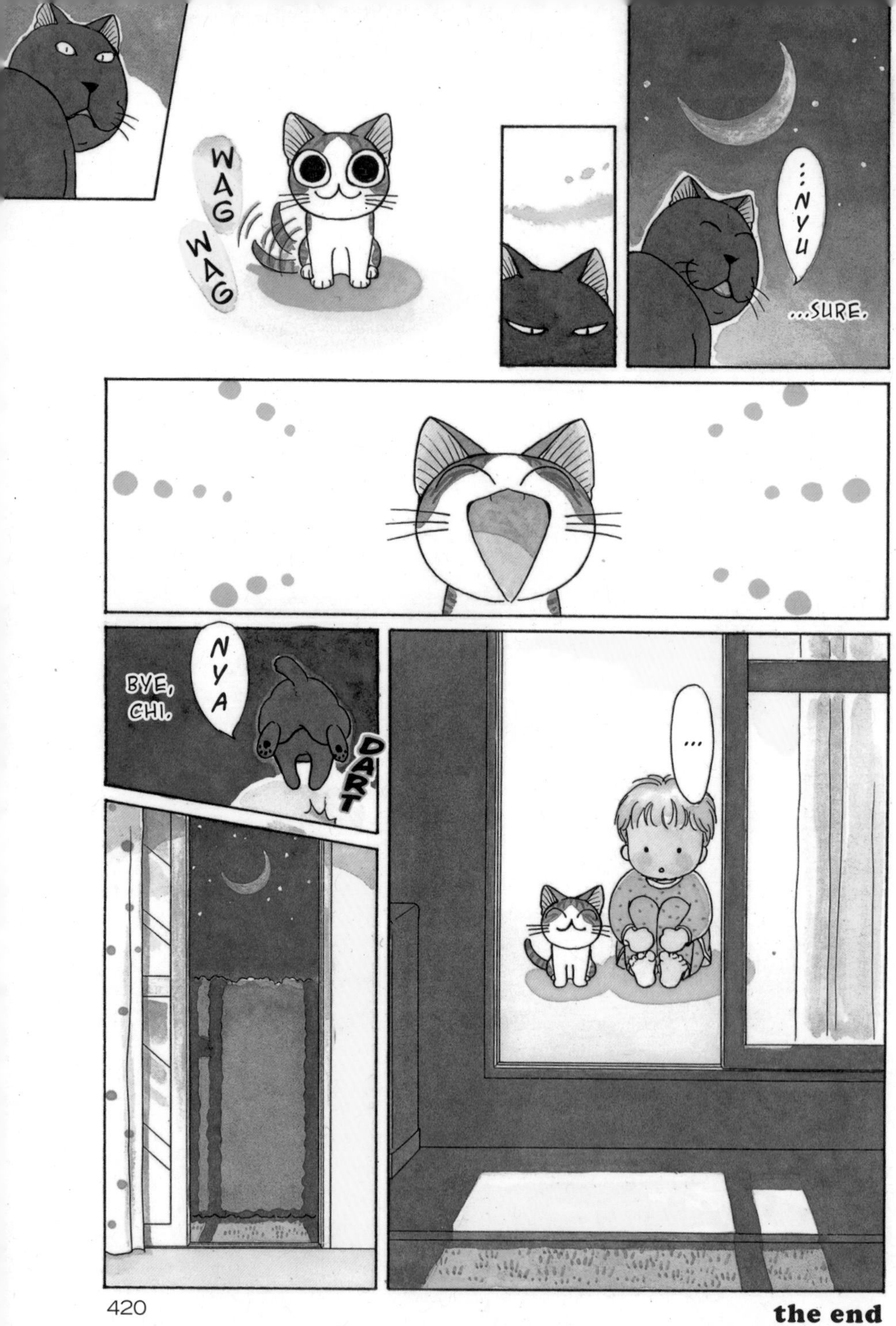
WAG
WAG
...NYU
...SURE.
NYA
BYE, CHI.
DART
...

the end

homemade 53: a cat sends off

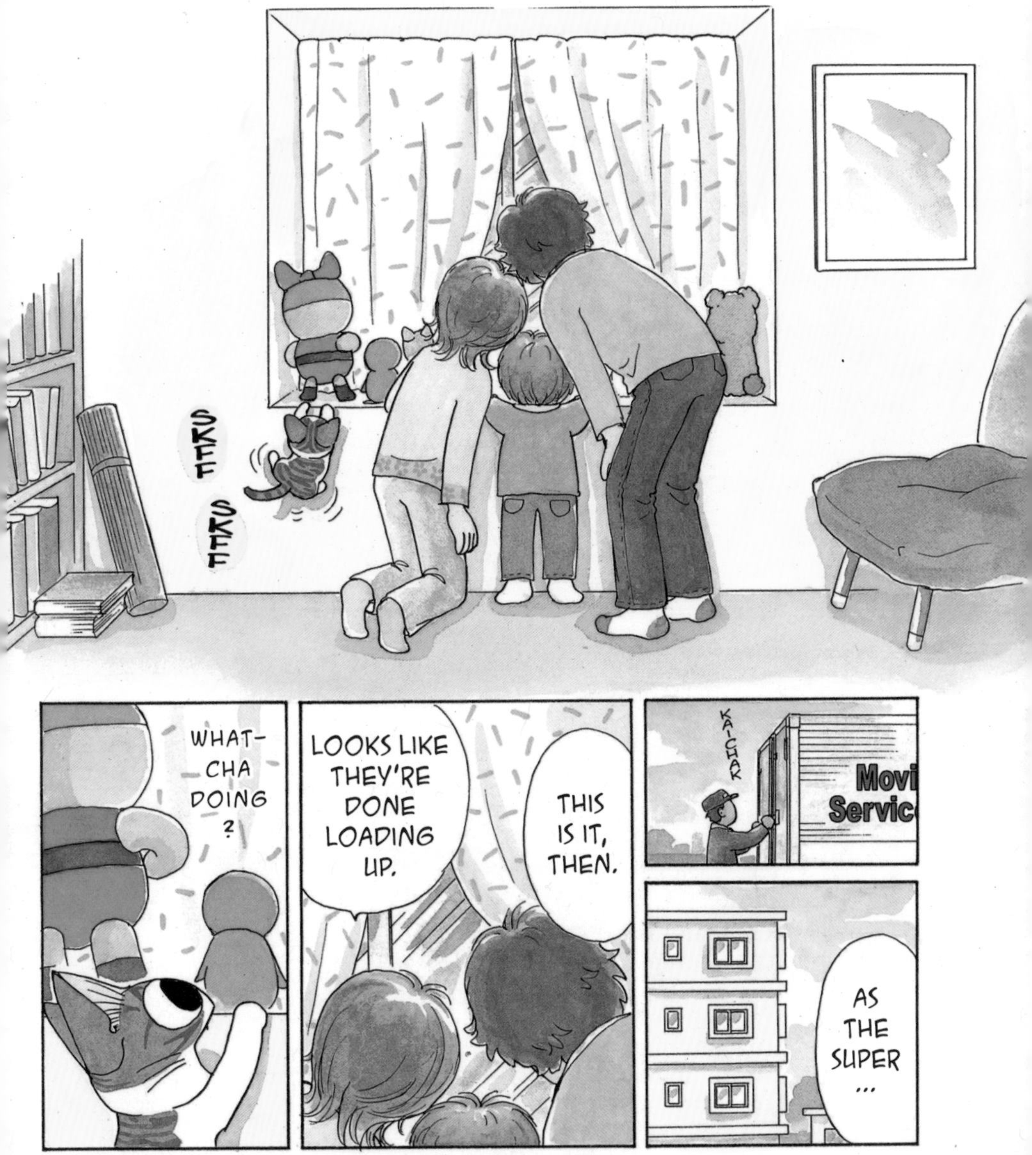
SKFF SKFF
WHAT-CHA DOING?
LOOKS LIKE THEY'RE DONE LOADING UP.
THIS IS IT, THEN.
KAICHAK
Movi
Servic
AS THE SUPER ...

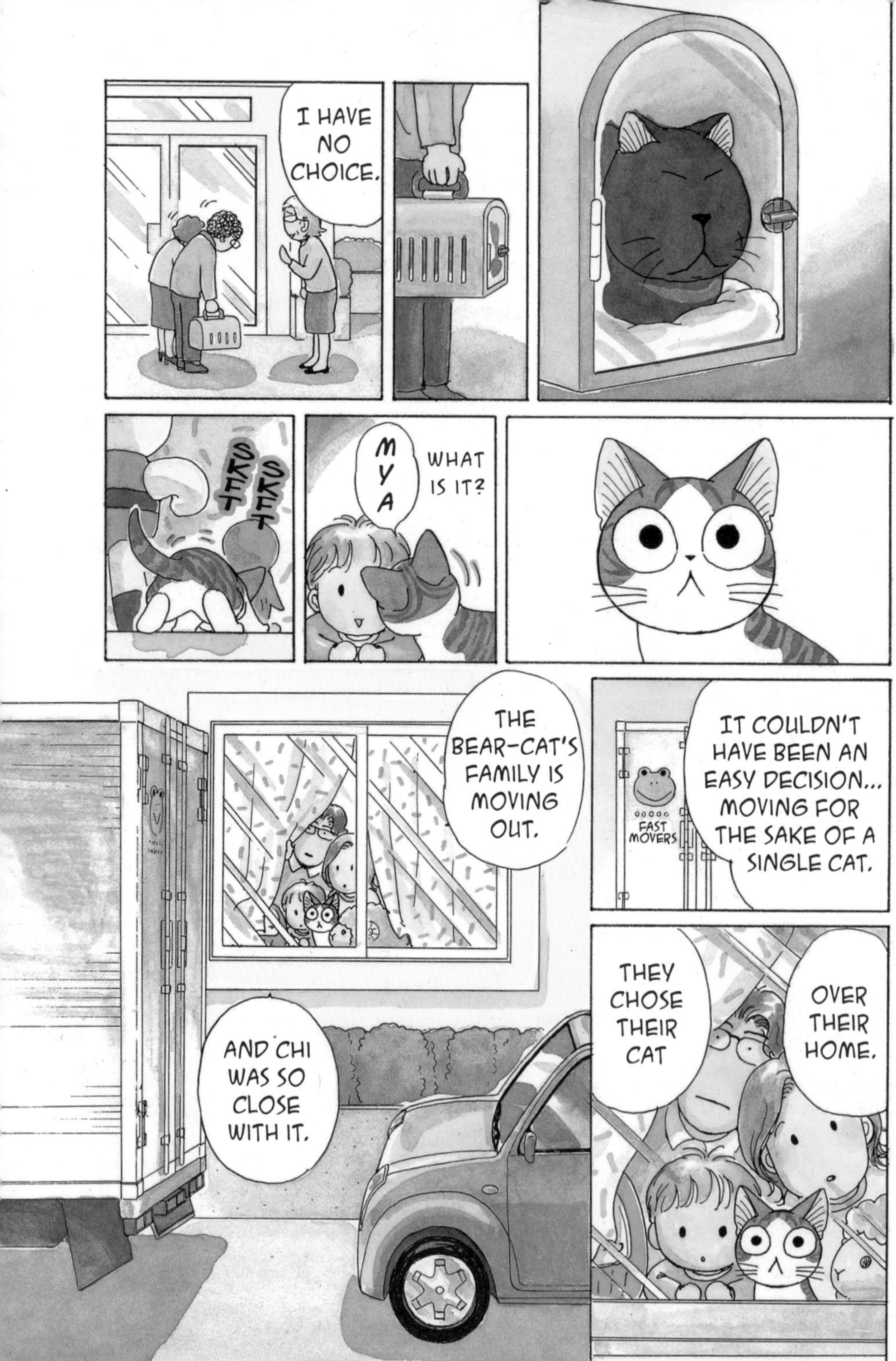
I HAVE NO CHOICE.
MYA
WHAT IS IT?
SKFT SKFT
THE BEAR-CAT'S FAMILY IS MOVING OUT.
IT COULDN'T HAVE BEEN AN EASY DECISION... MOVING FOR THE SAKE OF A SINGLE CAT.
FAST MOVERS
AND CHI WAS SO CLOSE WITH IT.
THEY CHOSE THEIR CAT
OVER THEIR HOME.

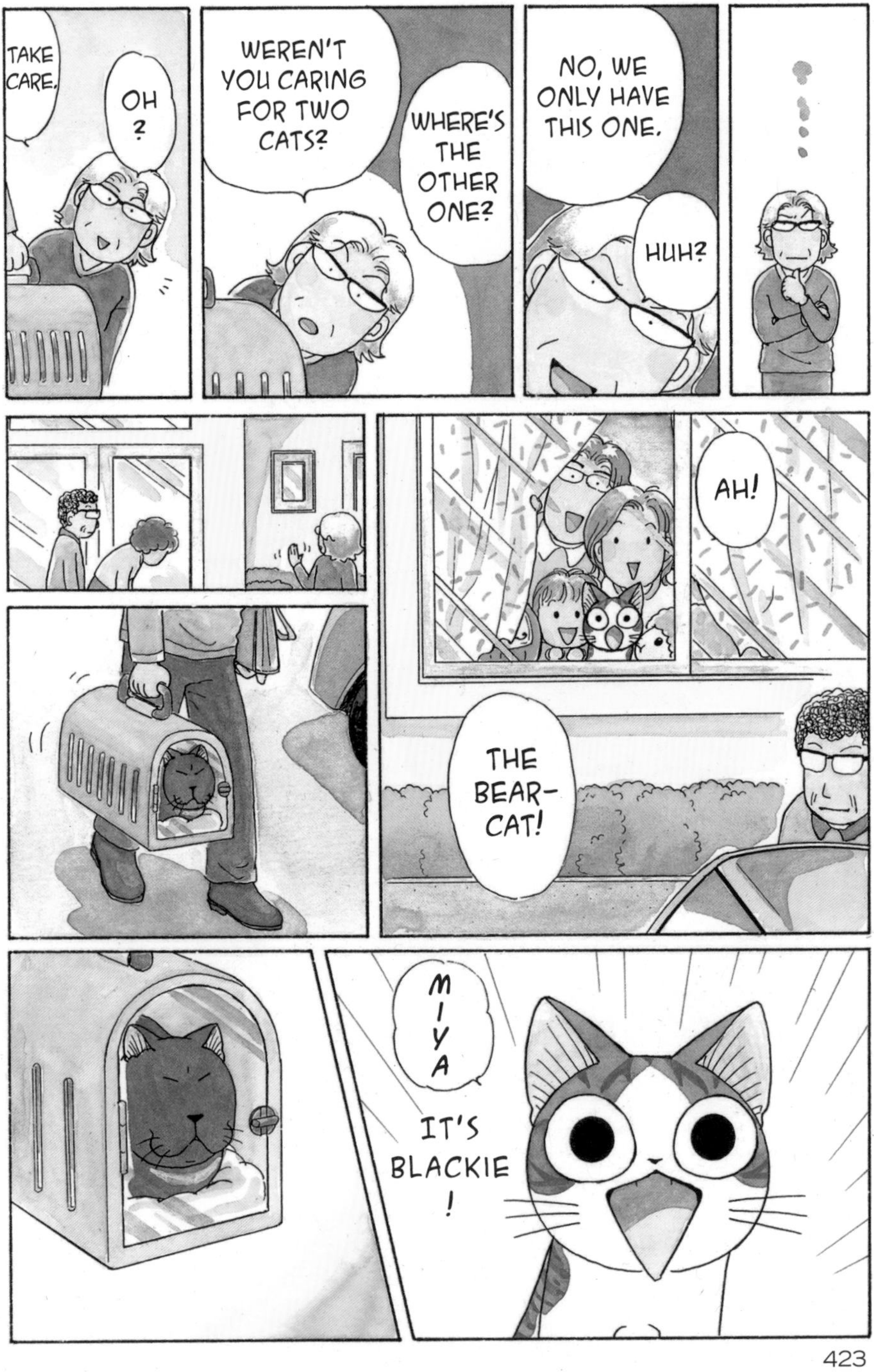
TAKE CARE.
OH?
WEREN'T YOU CARING FOR TWO CATS?
WHERE'S THE OTHER ONE?
NO, WE ONLY HAVE THIS ONE.
HUH?
AH!
THE BEAR-CAT!
MIYA
IT'S BLACKIE!

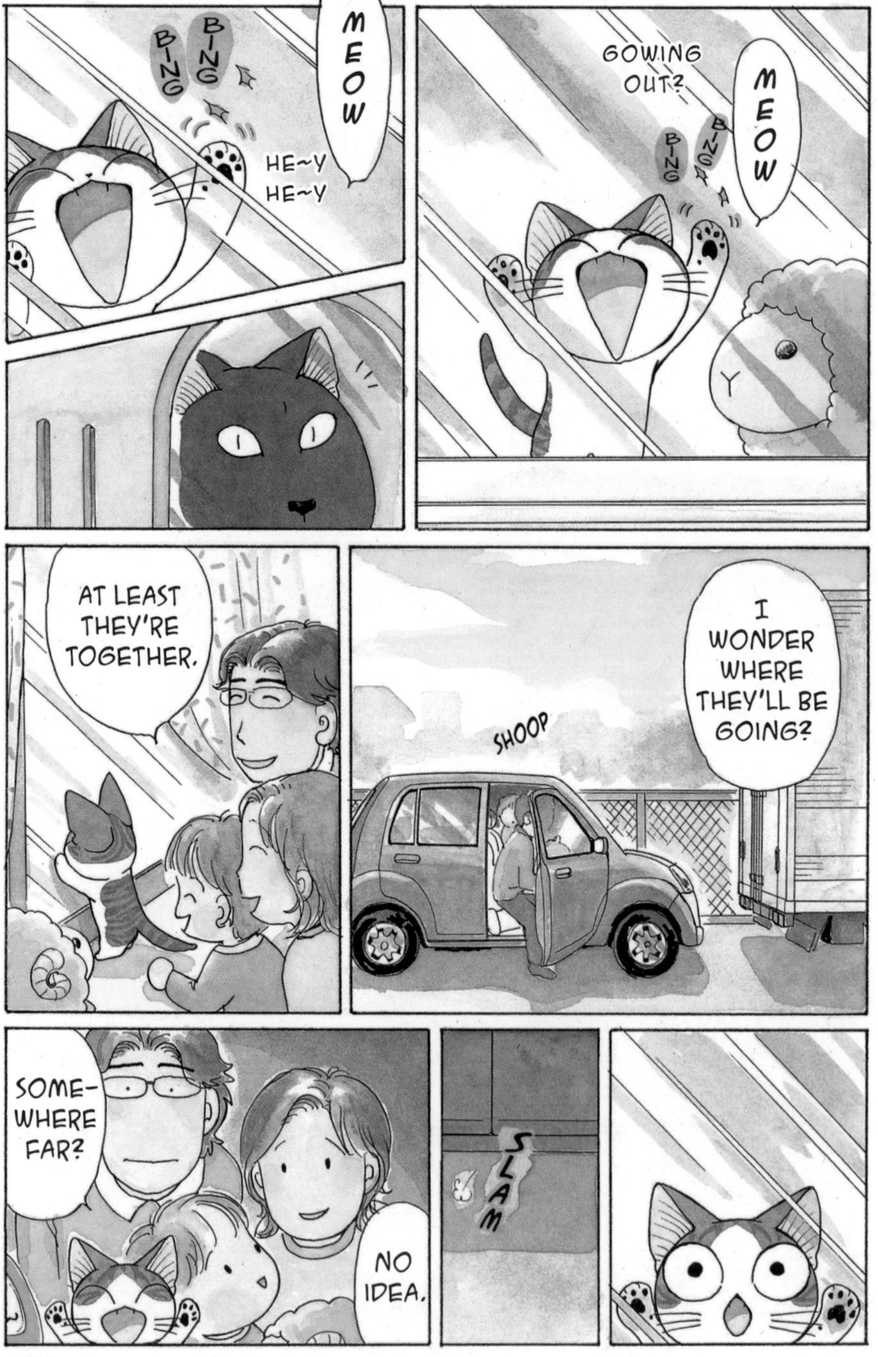
BING BING
MEOW
HE~Y HE~Y
GOWING OUT?
BING BING
MEOW
AT LEAST THEY'RE TOGETHER.
I WONDER WHERE THEY'LL BE GOING?
SHOOP
SOME-WHERE FAR?
NO IDEA.
SLAM

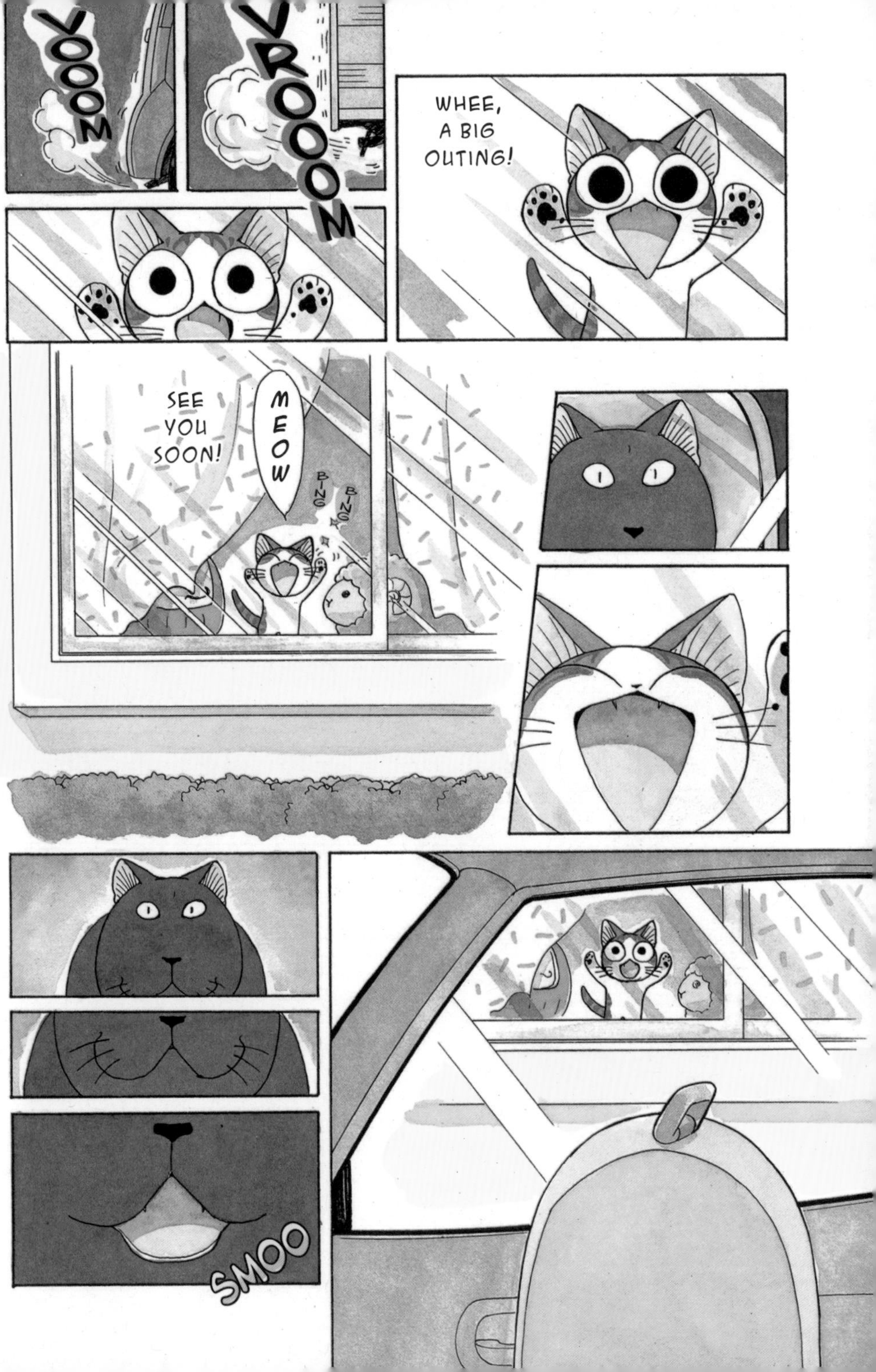
VOOOM
VROOOOM
WHEE, A BIG OUTING!
SEE YOU SOON!
MEOW
BING BING
SMOO

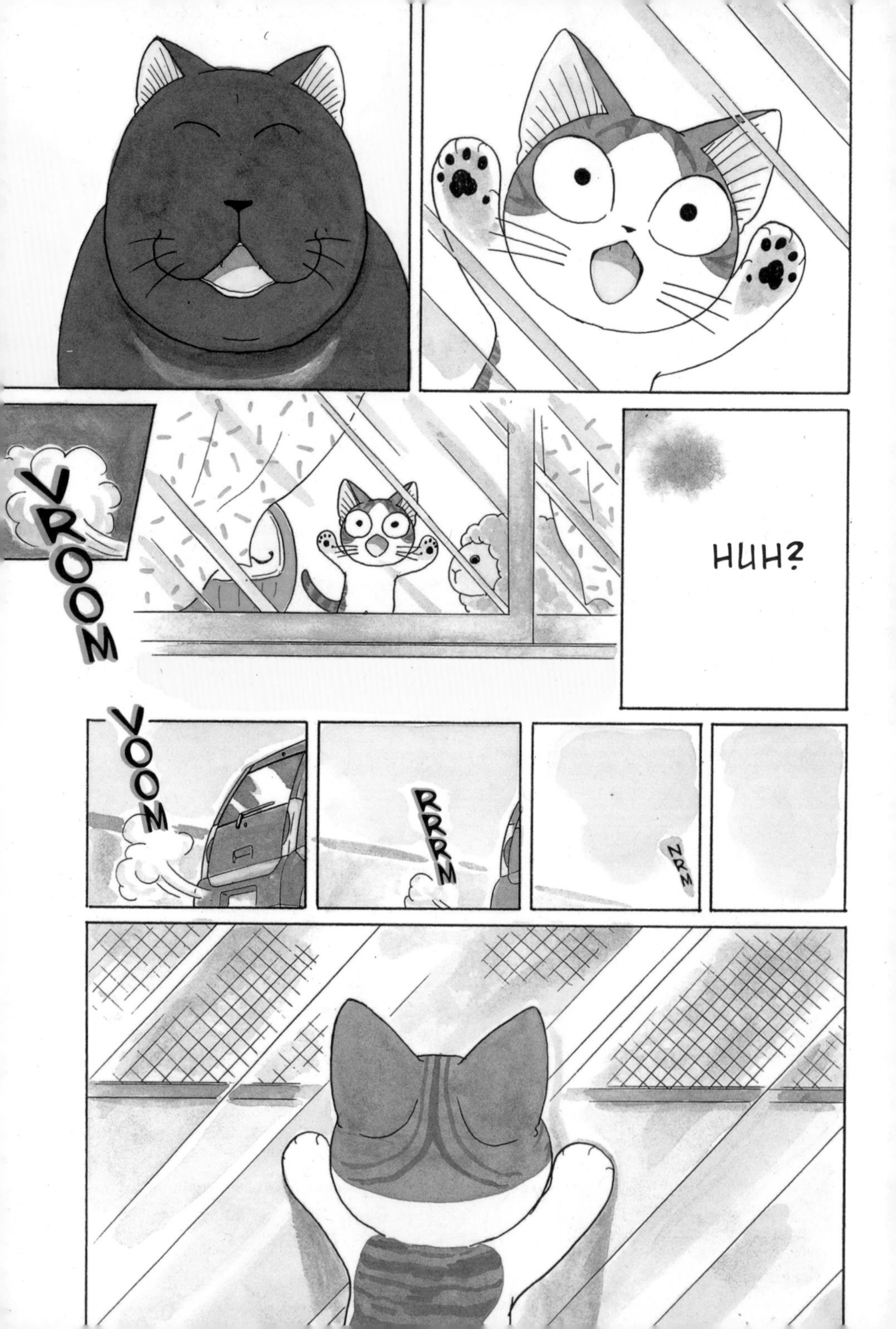
VROOM
HUH?
VOOM
RRRM
NRM

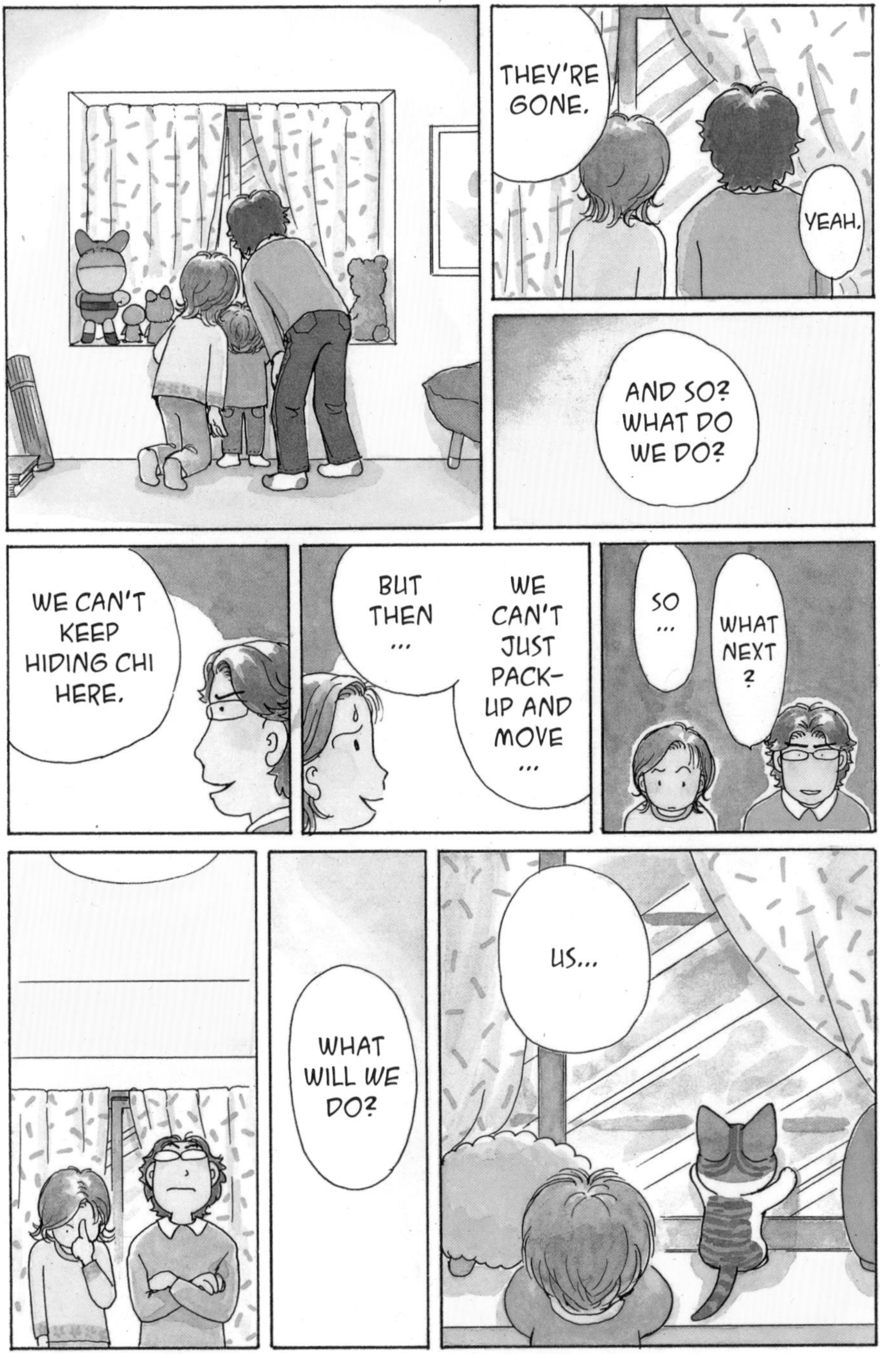
THEY'RE GONE.
YEAH.
AND SO? WHAT DO WE DO?
WE CAN'T KEEP HIDING CHI HERE.
BUT THEN ...
WE CAN'T JUST PACK-UP AND MOVE ...
SO ...
WHAT NEXT ?
WHAT WILL WE DO?
US...

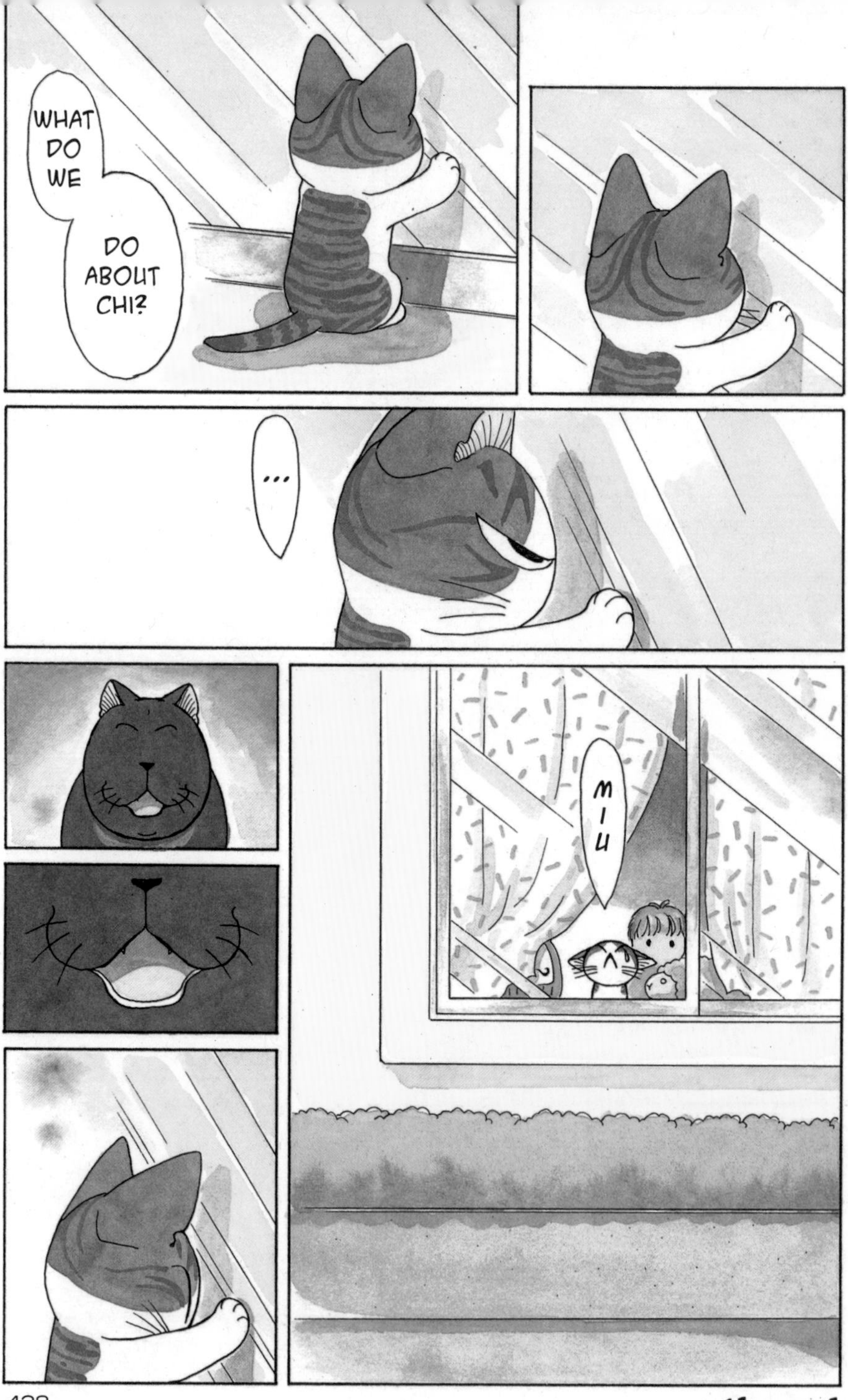
WHAT DO WE DO ABOUT CHI?
...
MIU

the end

homemade 54: a cat finds out

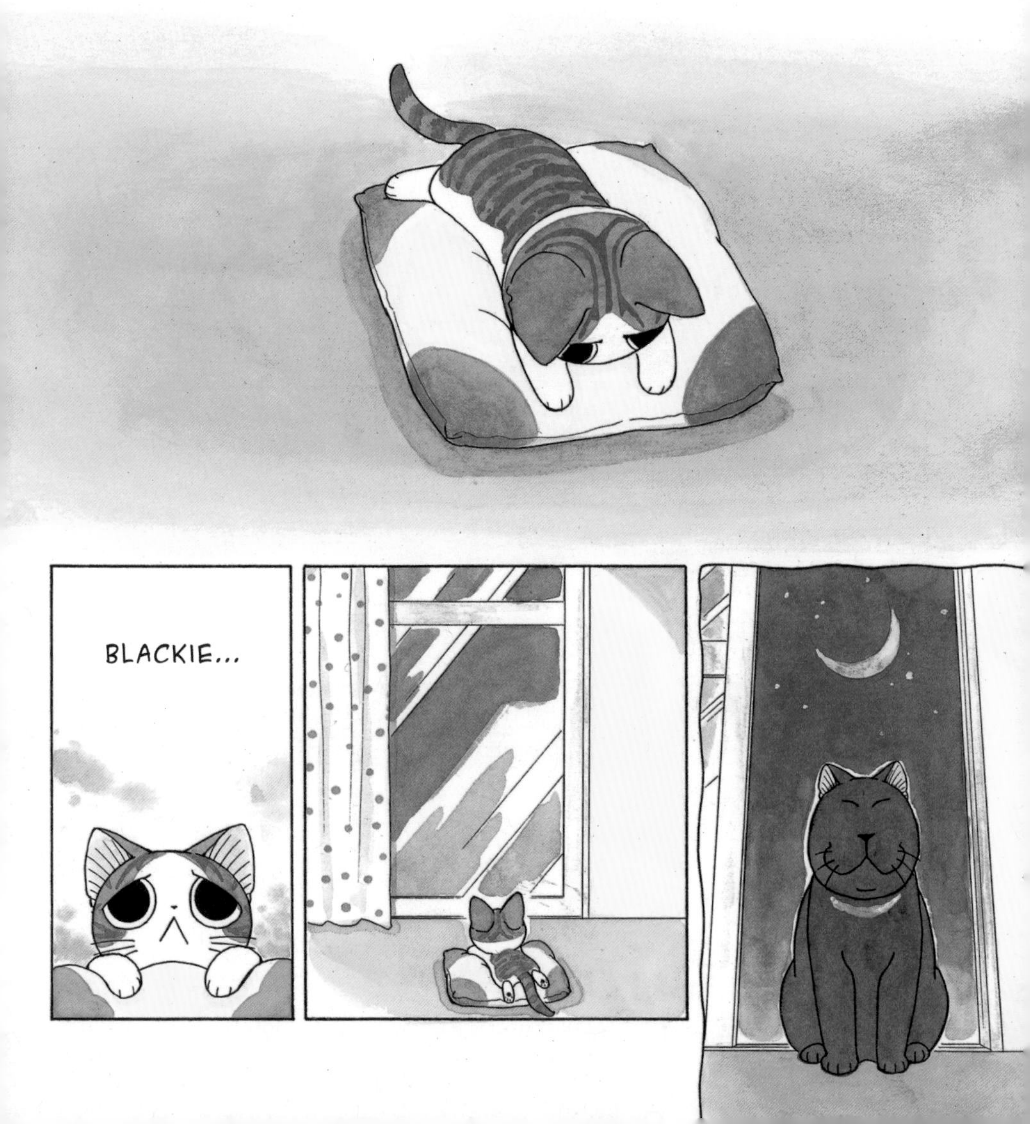
BLACKIE...

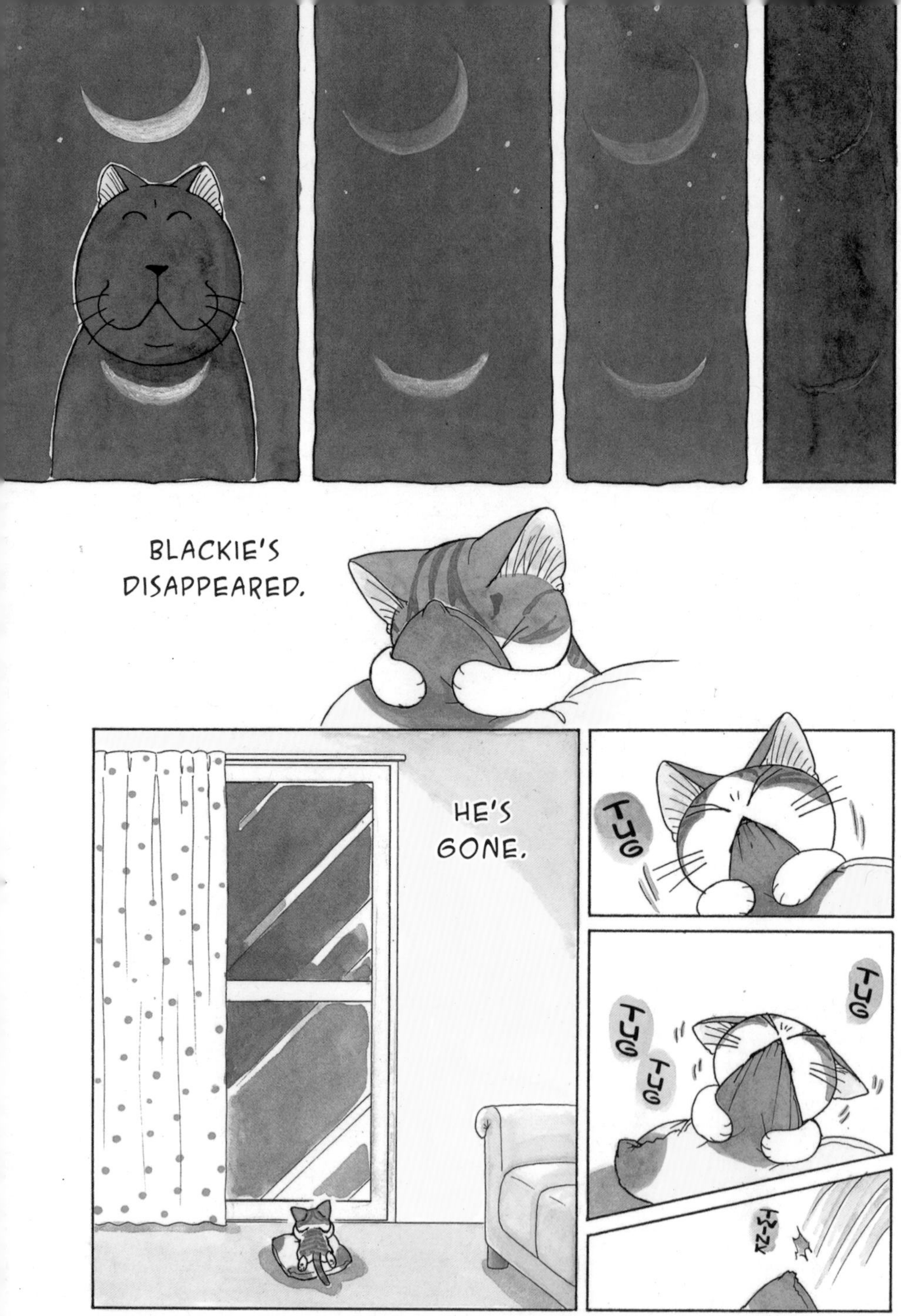
BLACKIE'S DISAPPEARED.
HE'S GONE.
TUG
TUG
TUG
TUG
TWINK

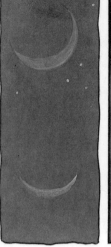

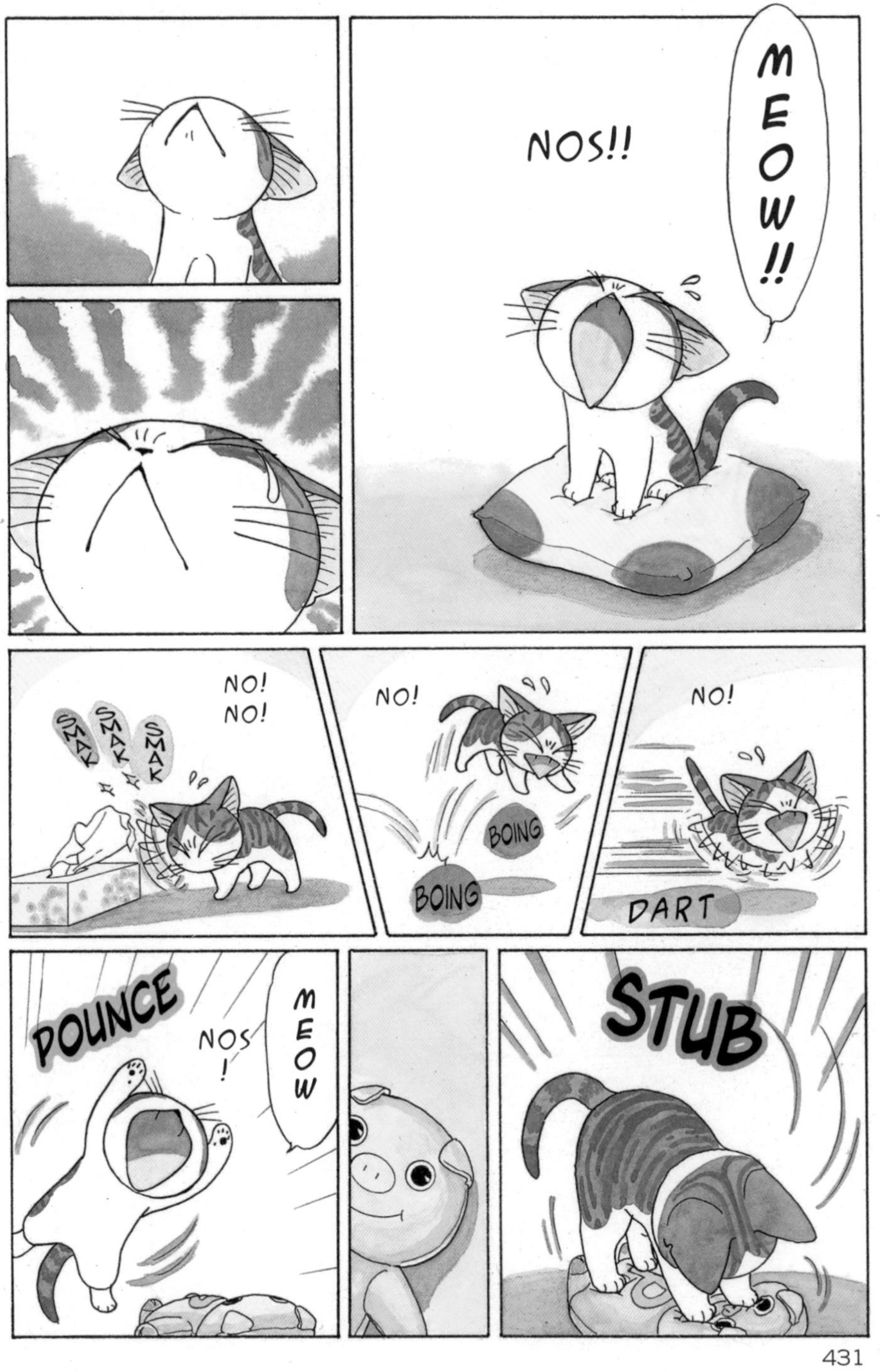
NOS!!
MEOW!!
SMAK
SMAK
SMAK
NO!
NO!
NO!
BOING
BOING
NO!
DART
POUNCE
NOS!
MEOW
STUB

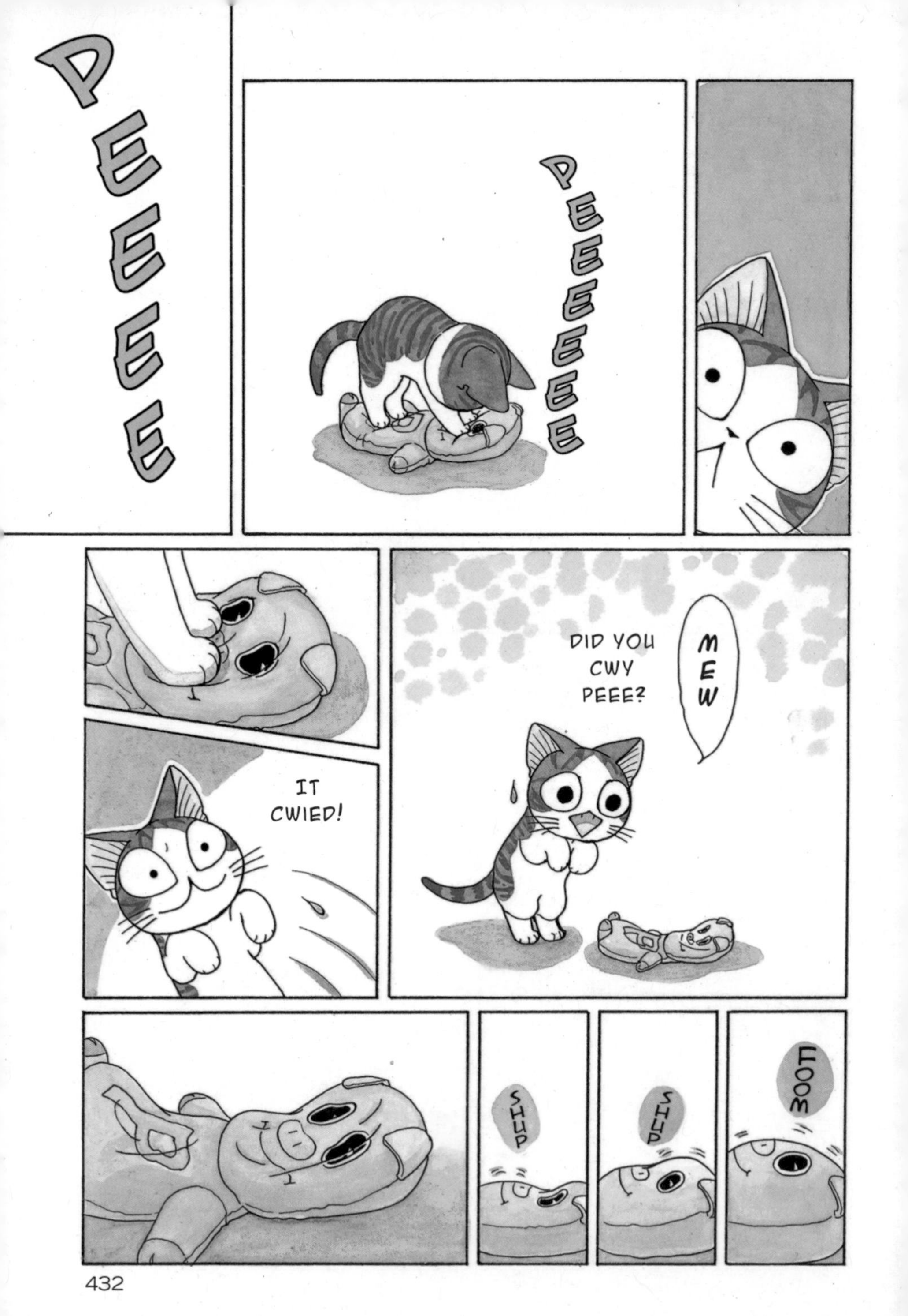
PEEEEE
PEEEEEEE
IT CWIED!
DID YOU CWY PEEE?
MEW
SHUP
SHUP
FOOM

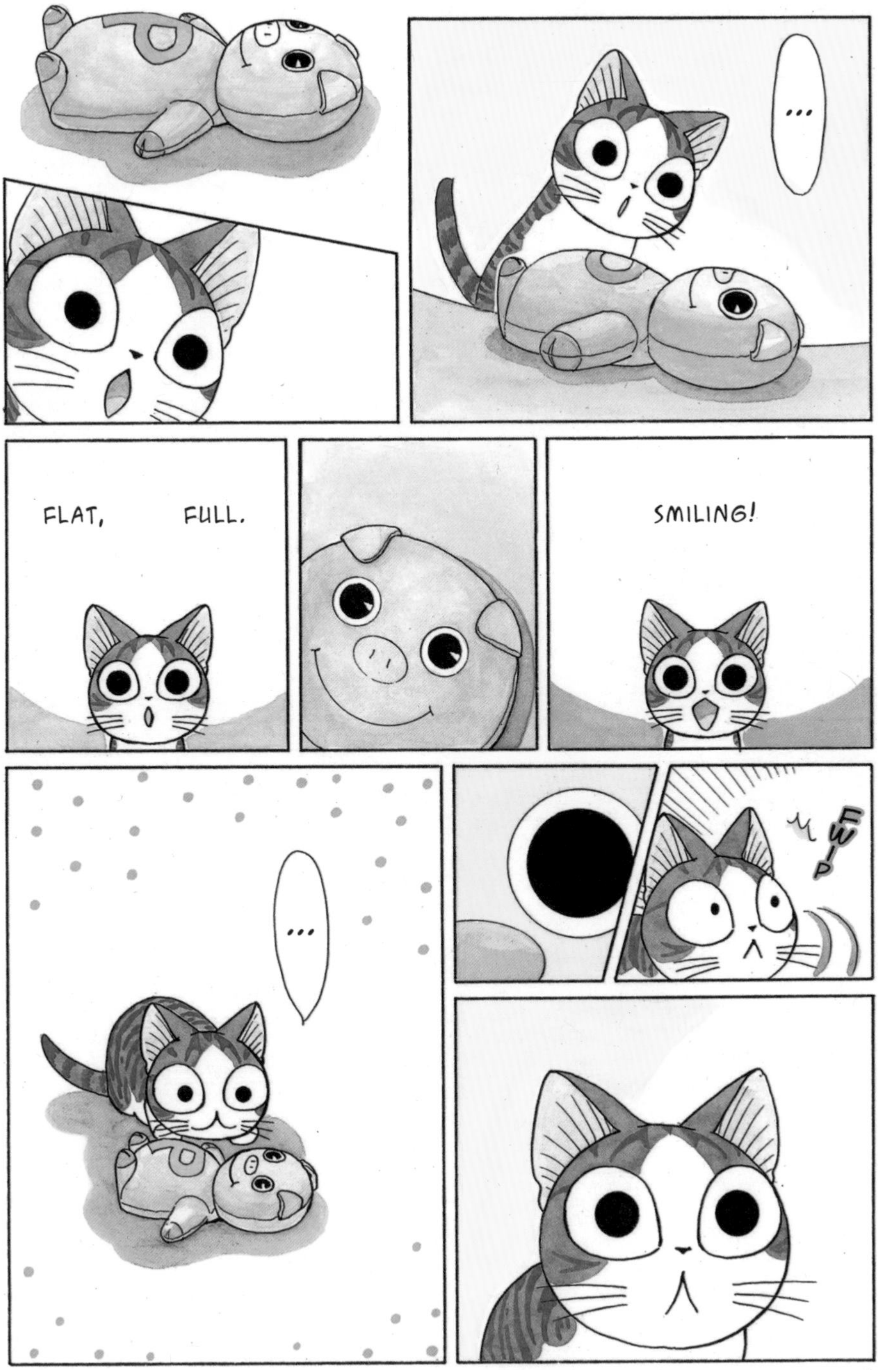
...
FLAT,
FULL.
SMILING!
...
FWIP

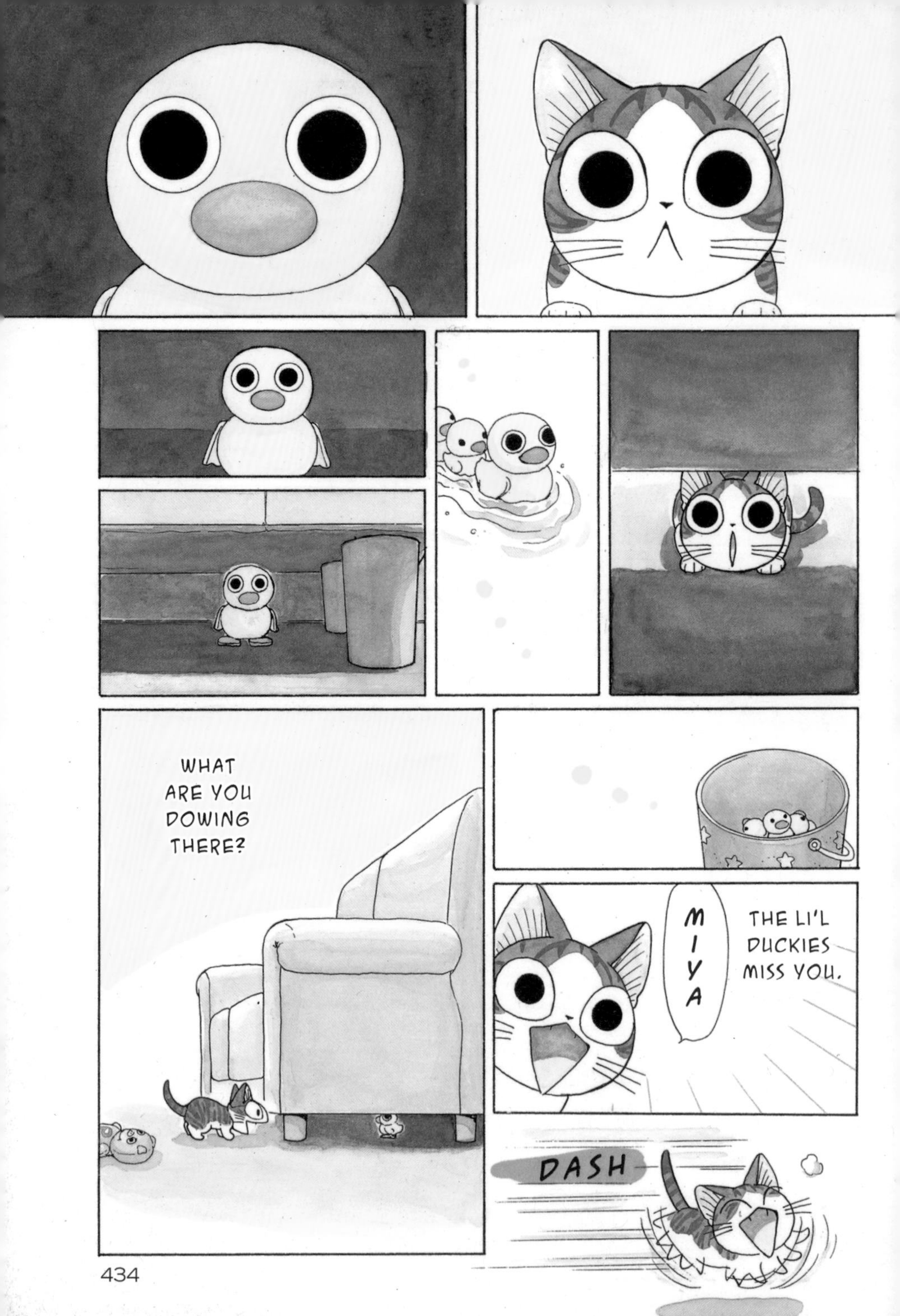
WHAT ARE YOU DOWING THERE?
MIYA
THE LI'L DUCKIES MISS YOU.
DASH

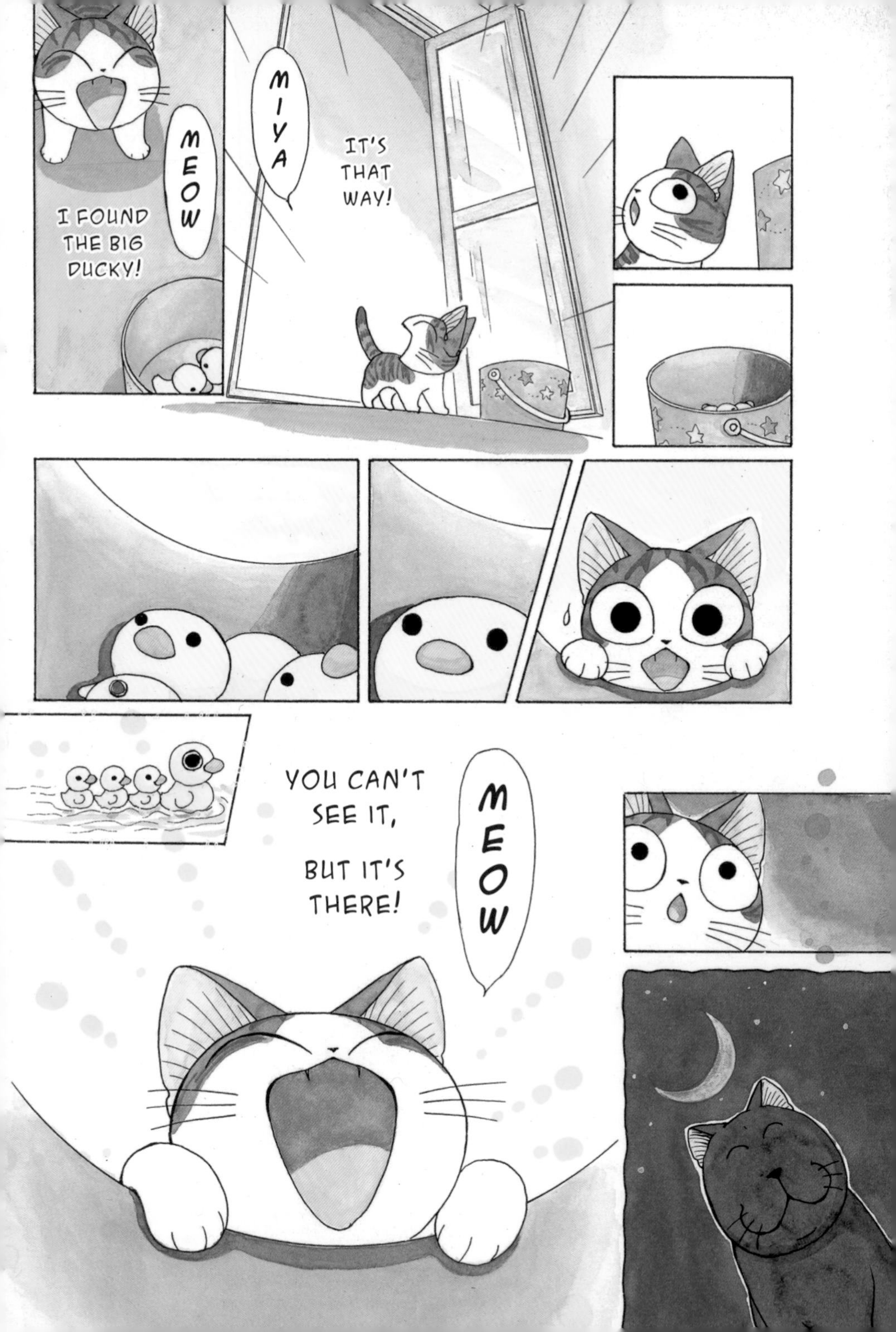
MEOW
I FOUND THE BIG DUCKY!
MIYA
IT'S THAT WAY!
YOU CAN'T SEE IT,
BUT IT'S THERE!
MEOW

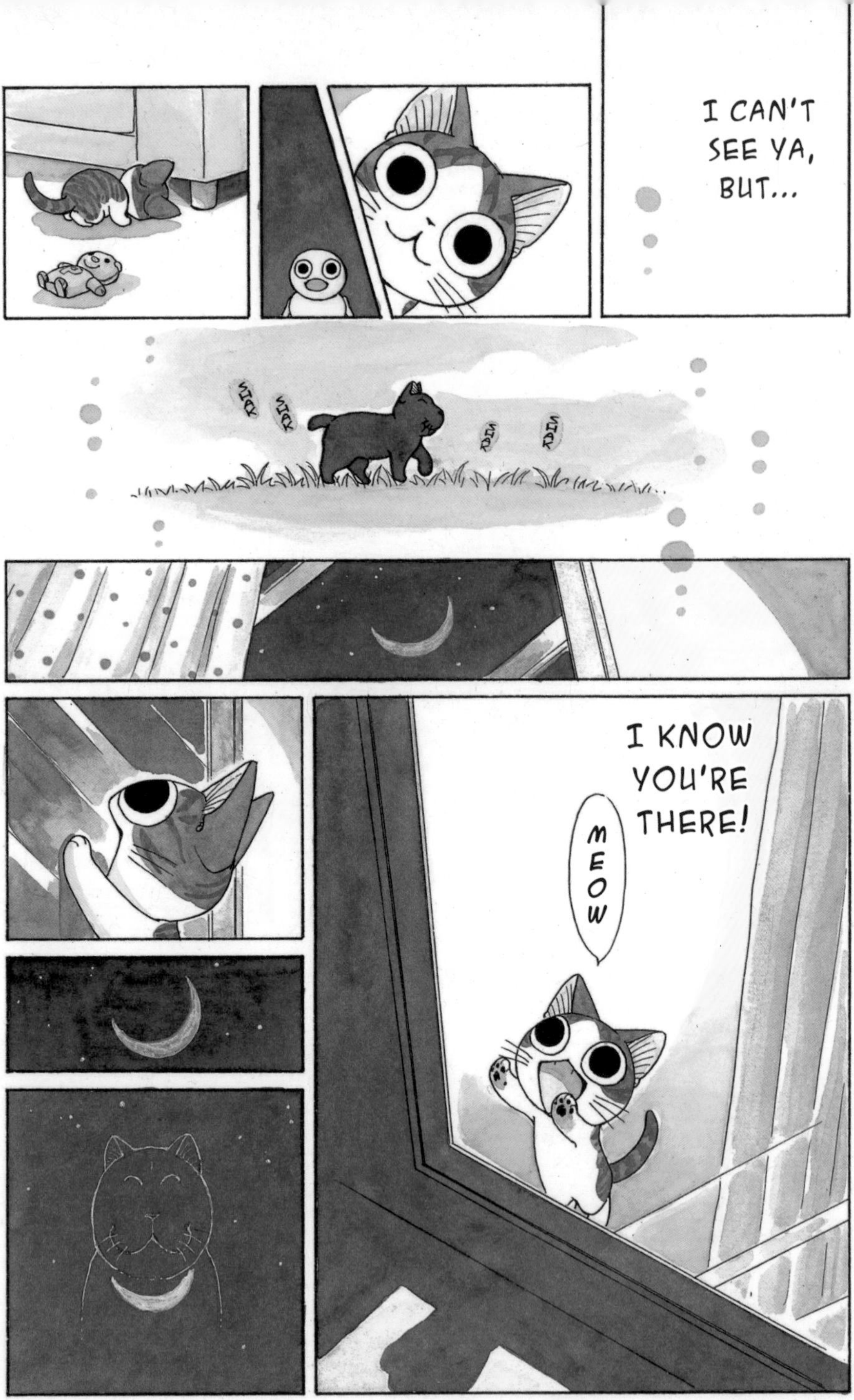
I CAN'T SEE YA, BUT...
I KNOW YOU'RE THERE!
MEOW

the end

homemade 55: a cat is taken

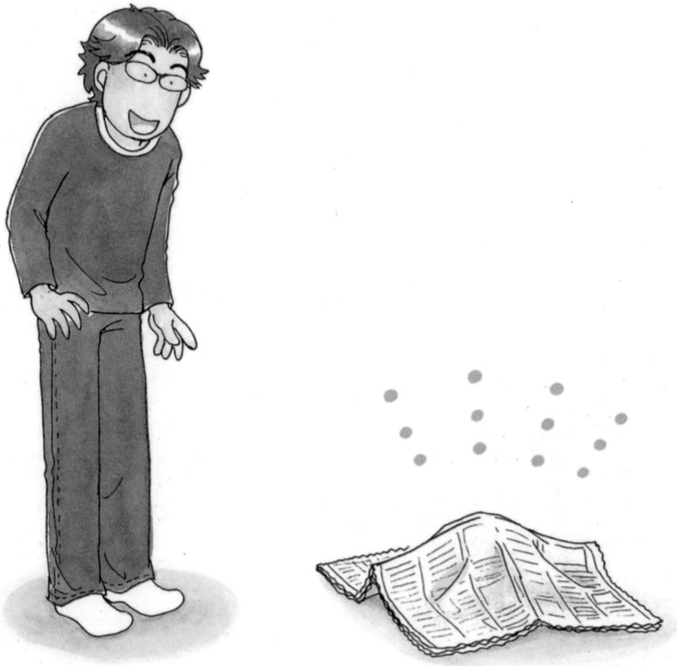

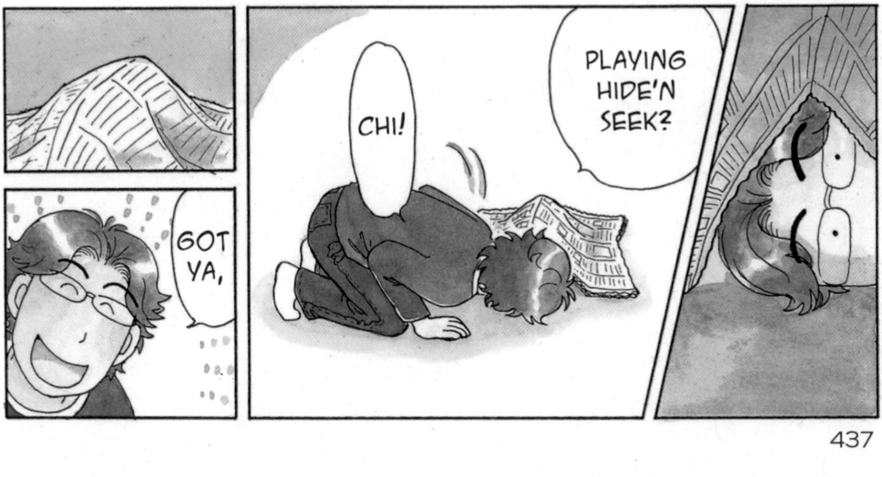
GOT YA,
CHI!
PLAYING HIDE'N SEEK?

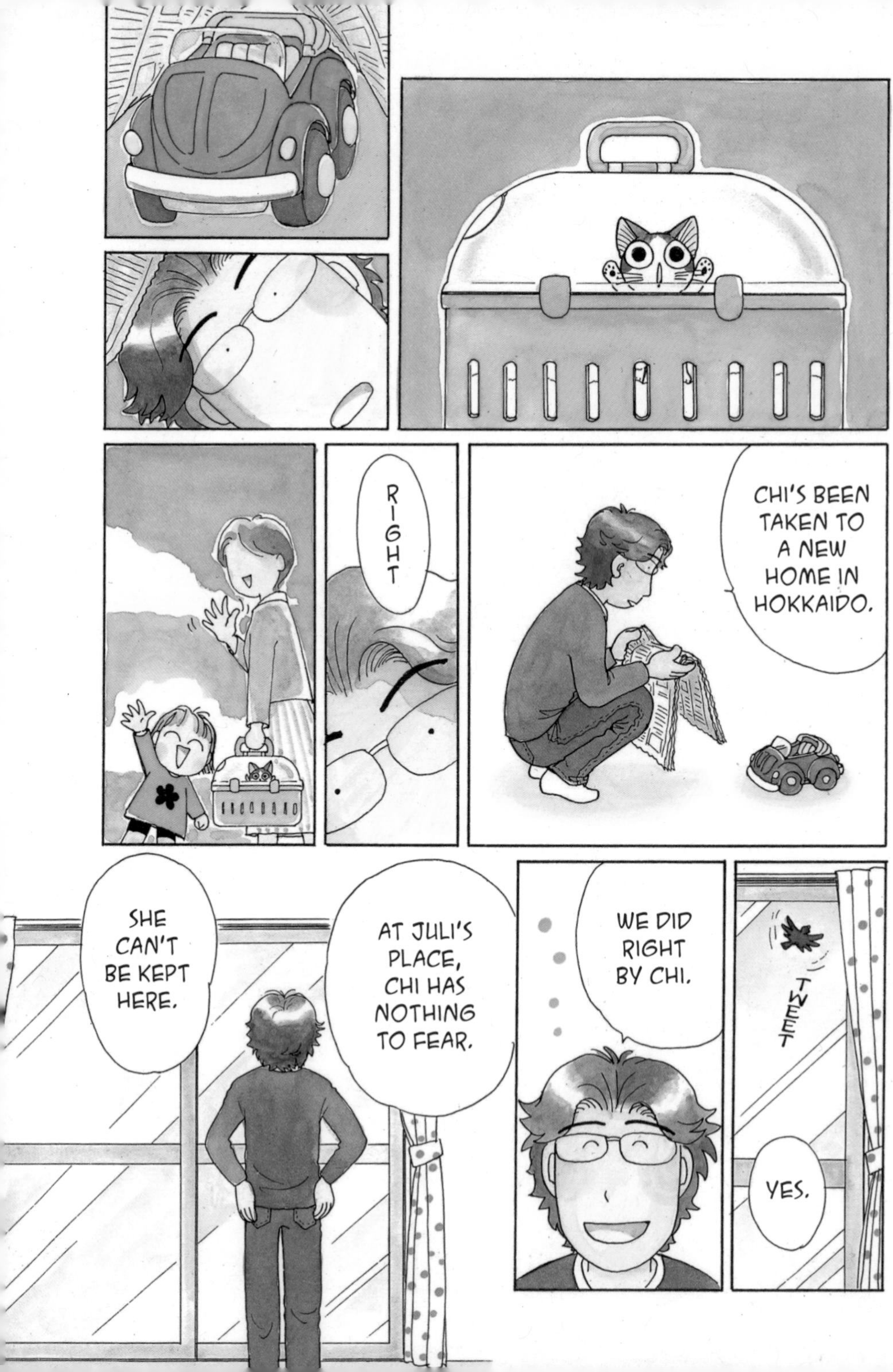
RIGHT
CHI'S BEEN TAKEN TO A NEW HOME IN HOKKAIDO.
SHE CAN'T BE KEPT HERE.
AT JULI'S PLACE, CHI HAS NOTHING TO FEAR.
WE DID RIGHT BY CHI.
TWEET
YES.

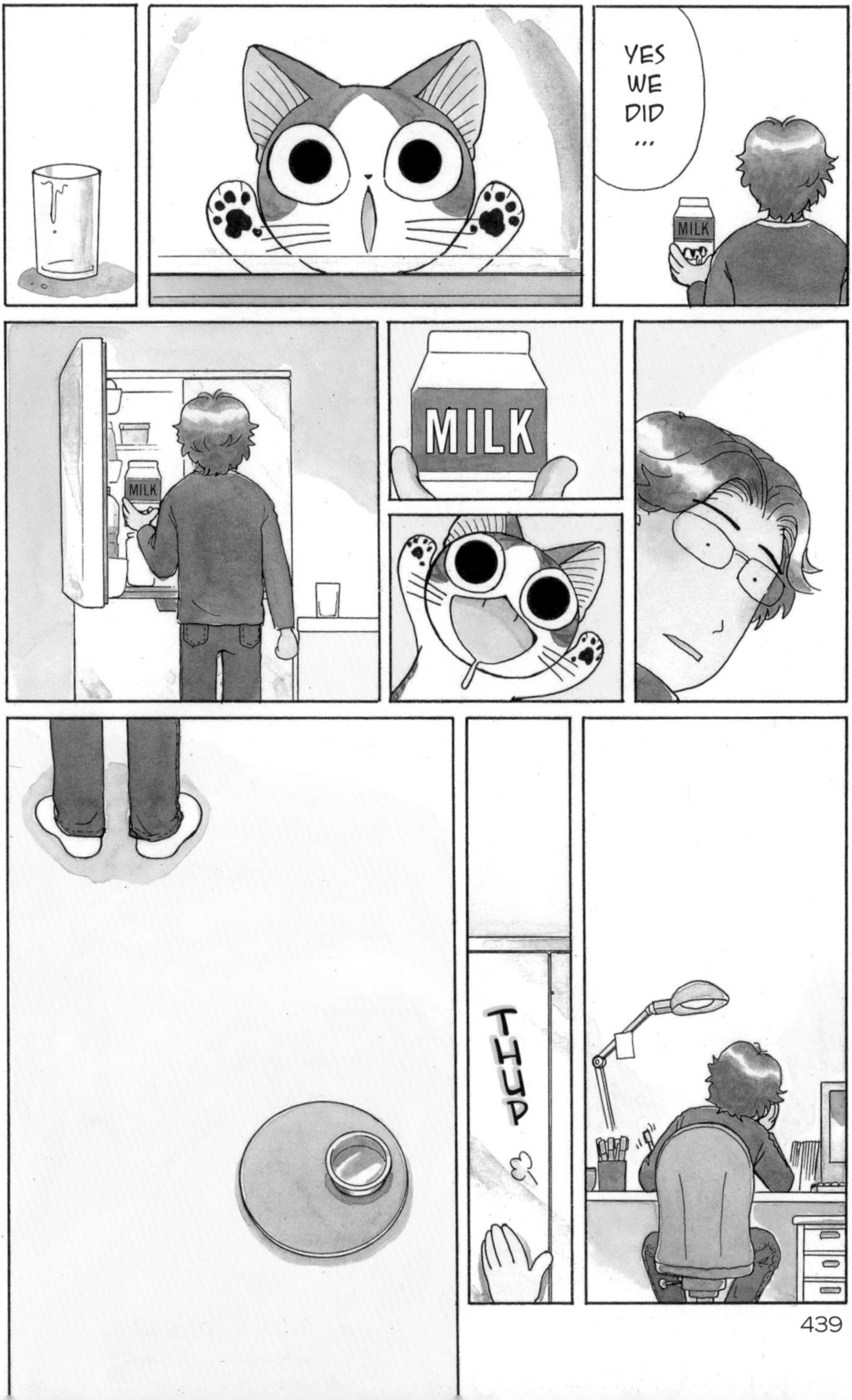
YES WE DID ...
MILK
MILK
MILK
THUP

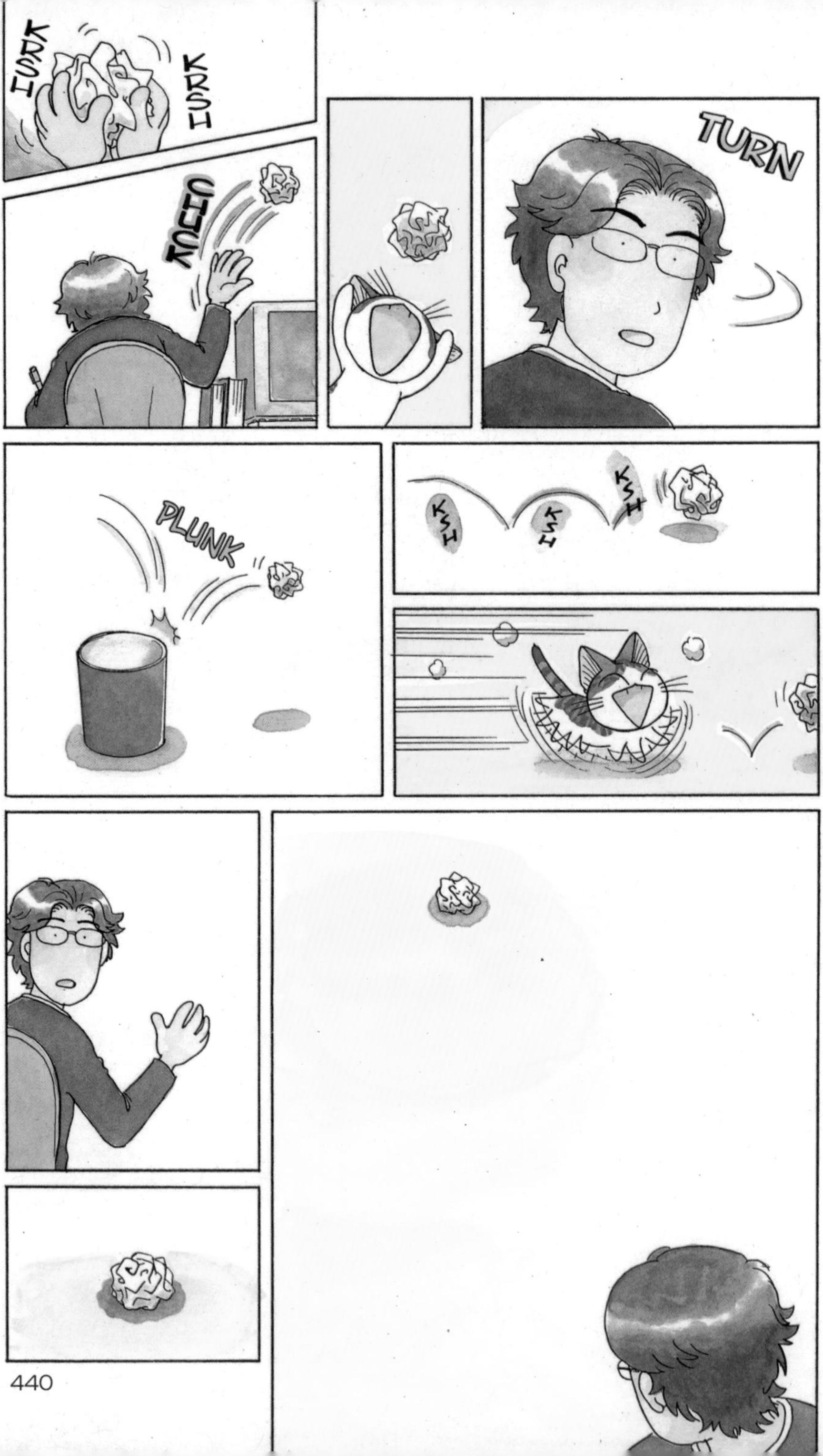
KRSH
KRSH
CHUCK
TURN
PLUNK
KSH
KSH
KSH

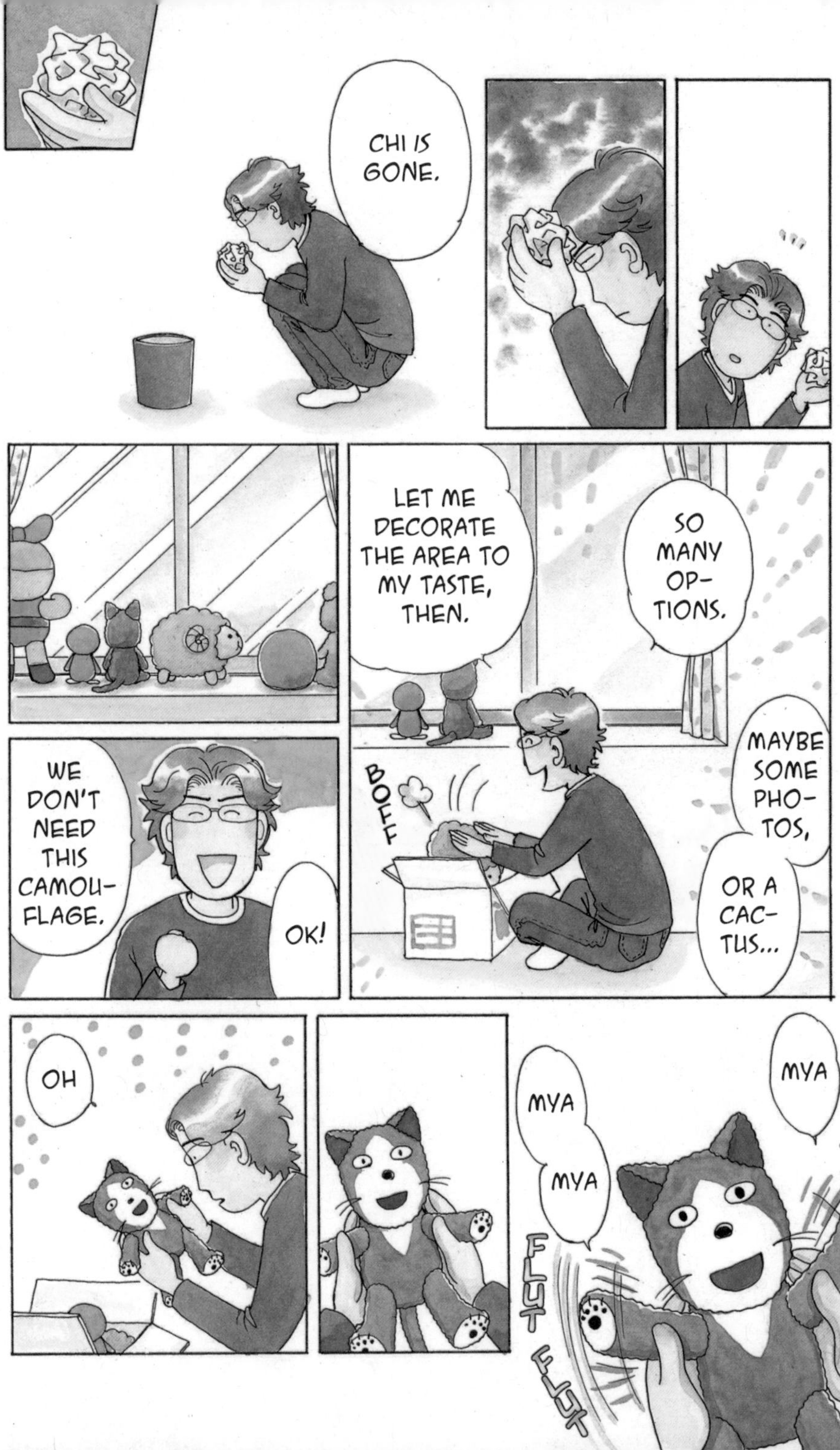

CHI IS GONE.
WE DON'T NEED THIS CAMOUFLAGE.
OK!
LET ME DECORATE THE AREA TO MY TASTE, THEN.
SO MANY OPTIONS.
BOFF
MAYBE SOME PHOTOS,
OR A CACTUS...
OH
MYA
MYA
MYA
FLUT
FLUT
FLUT

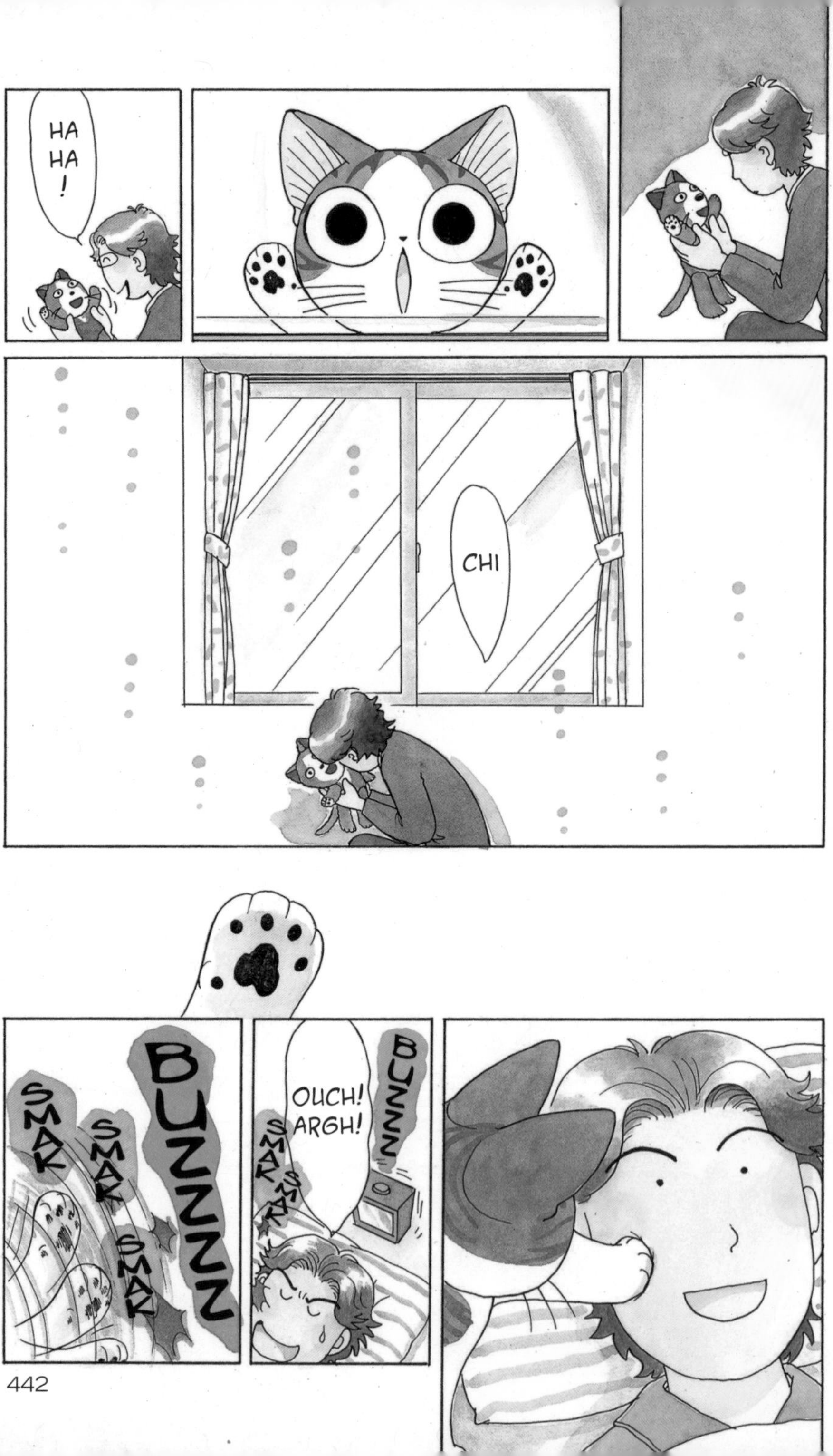
HA HA!
CHI
SMAK
SMAK
SMAK
BUZZZZ
OUCH! ARGH!
SMAK SMAK
BUZZZ

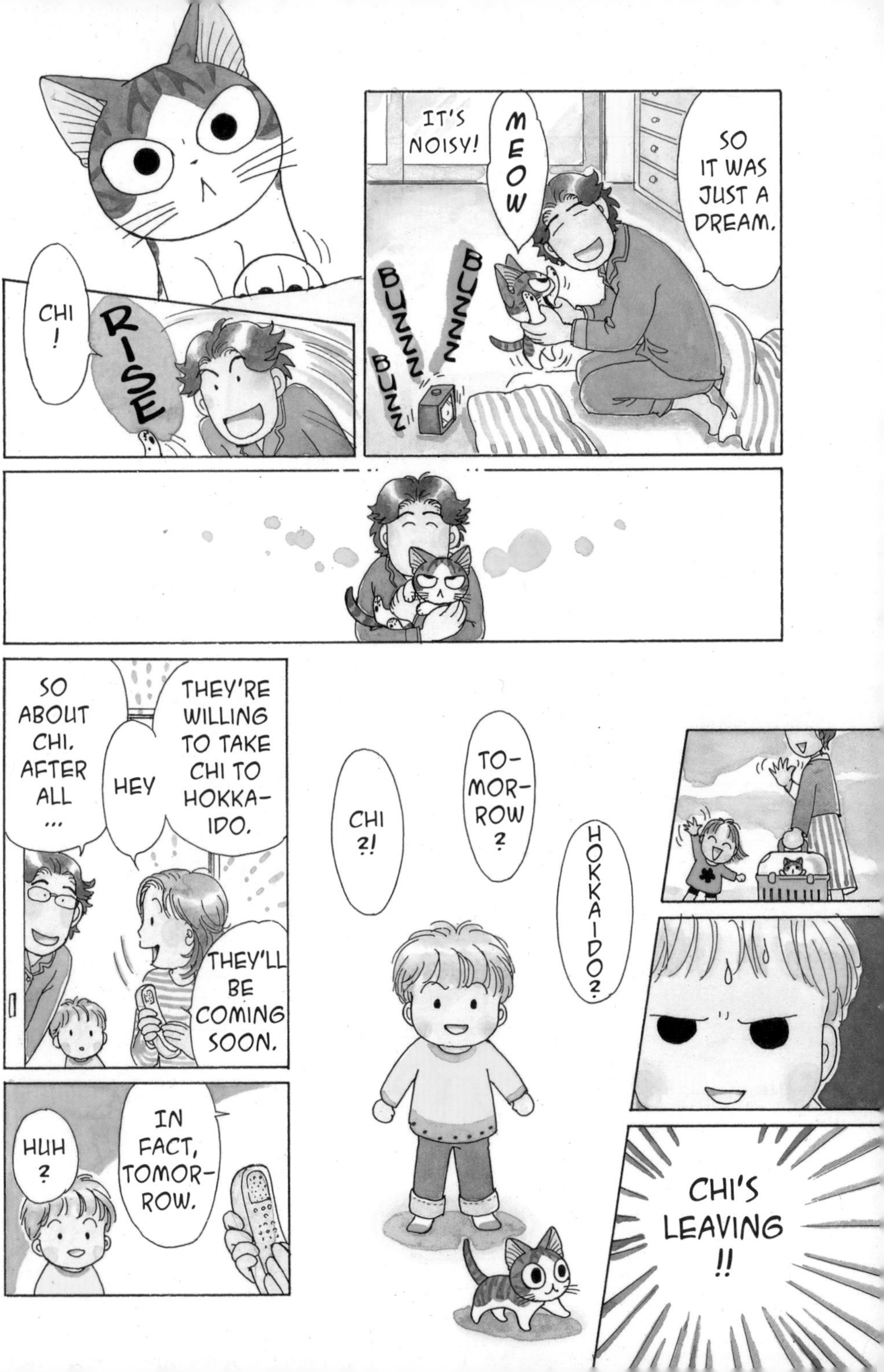
CHI!
RISE
IT'S NOISY!
MEOW
SO IT WAS JUST A DREAM.
BUZZZZ
BUZZZZ
BUZZ
SO ABOUT CHI. AFTER ALL...
HEY
THEY'RE WILLING TO TAKE CHI TO HOKKA-IDO.
THEY'LL BE COMING SOON.
HUH?
IN FACT, TOMOR-ROW.
CHI?!
TO-MOR-ROW?
HOKKAIDO?
CHI'S LEAVING!!

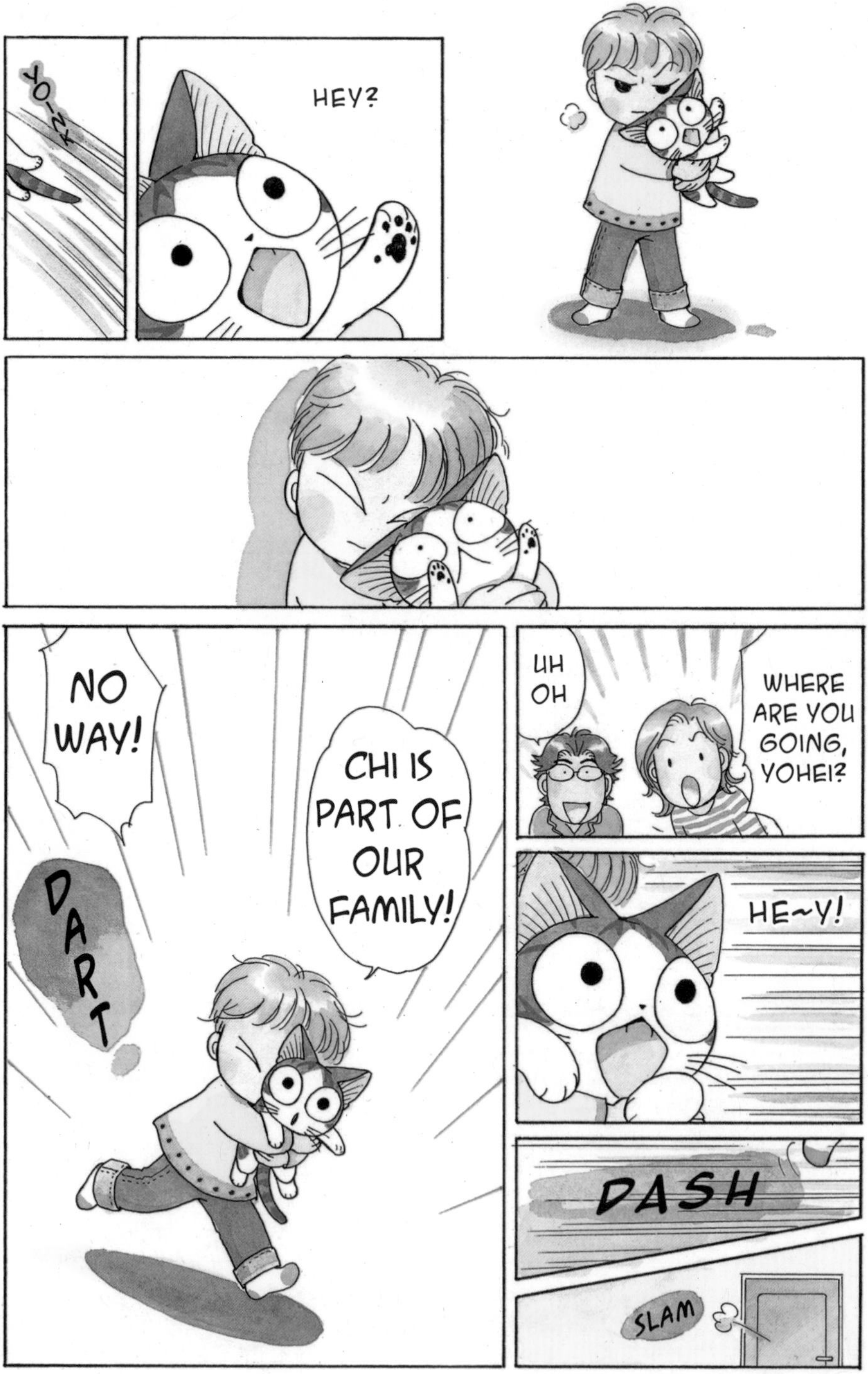
YOINK
HEY?
NO WAY!
CHI IS PART OF OUR FAMILY!
DART
UH OH
WHERE ARE YOU GOING, YOHEI?
HE~Y!
DASH
SLAM

the end

homemade 56: a cat runs away

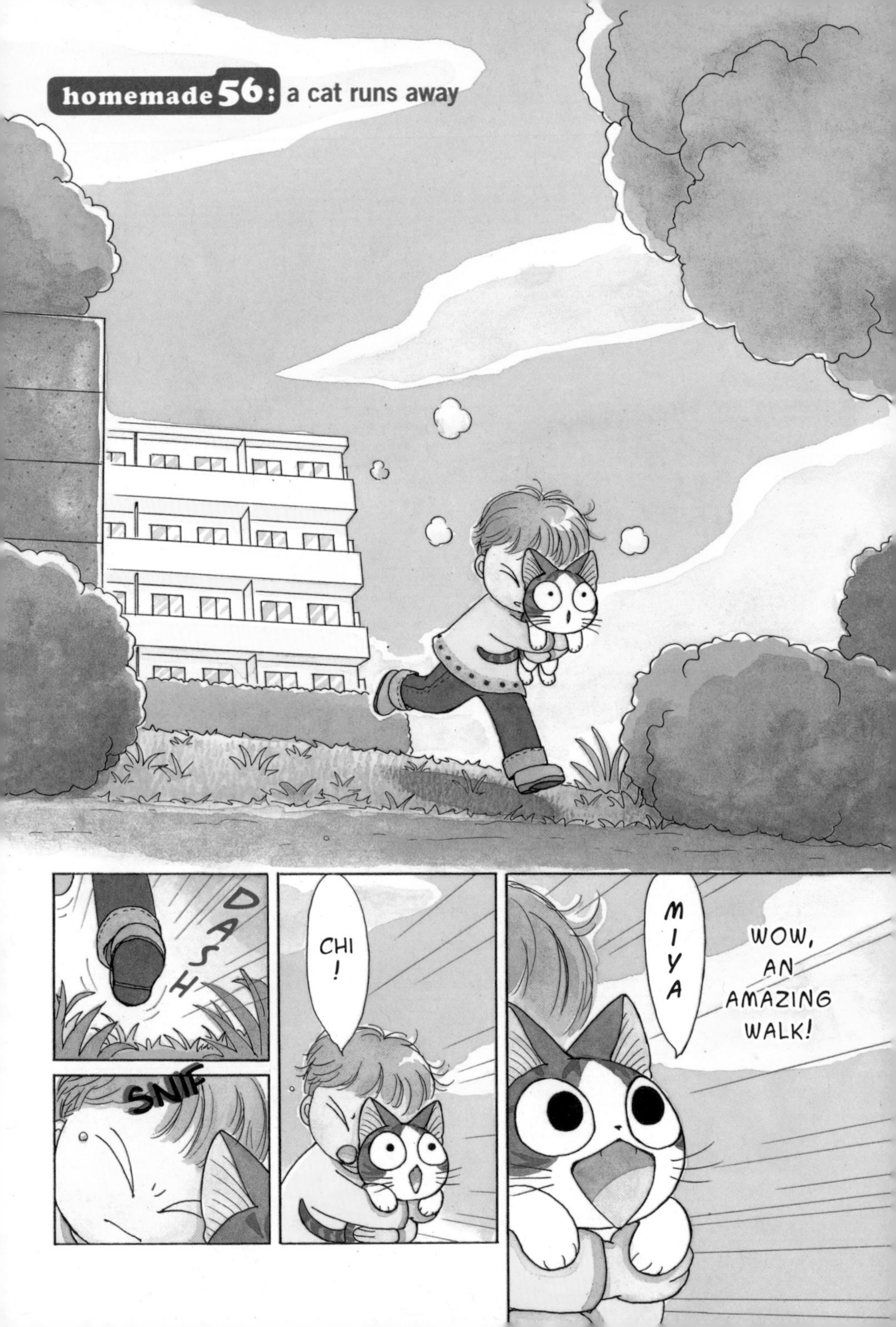
DASH
SNIF
CHI!
MIYA
WOW, AN AMAZING WALK!

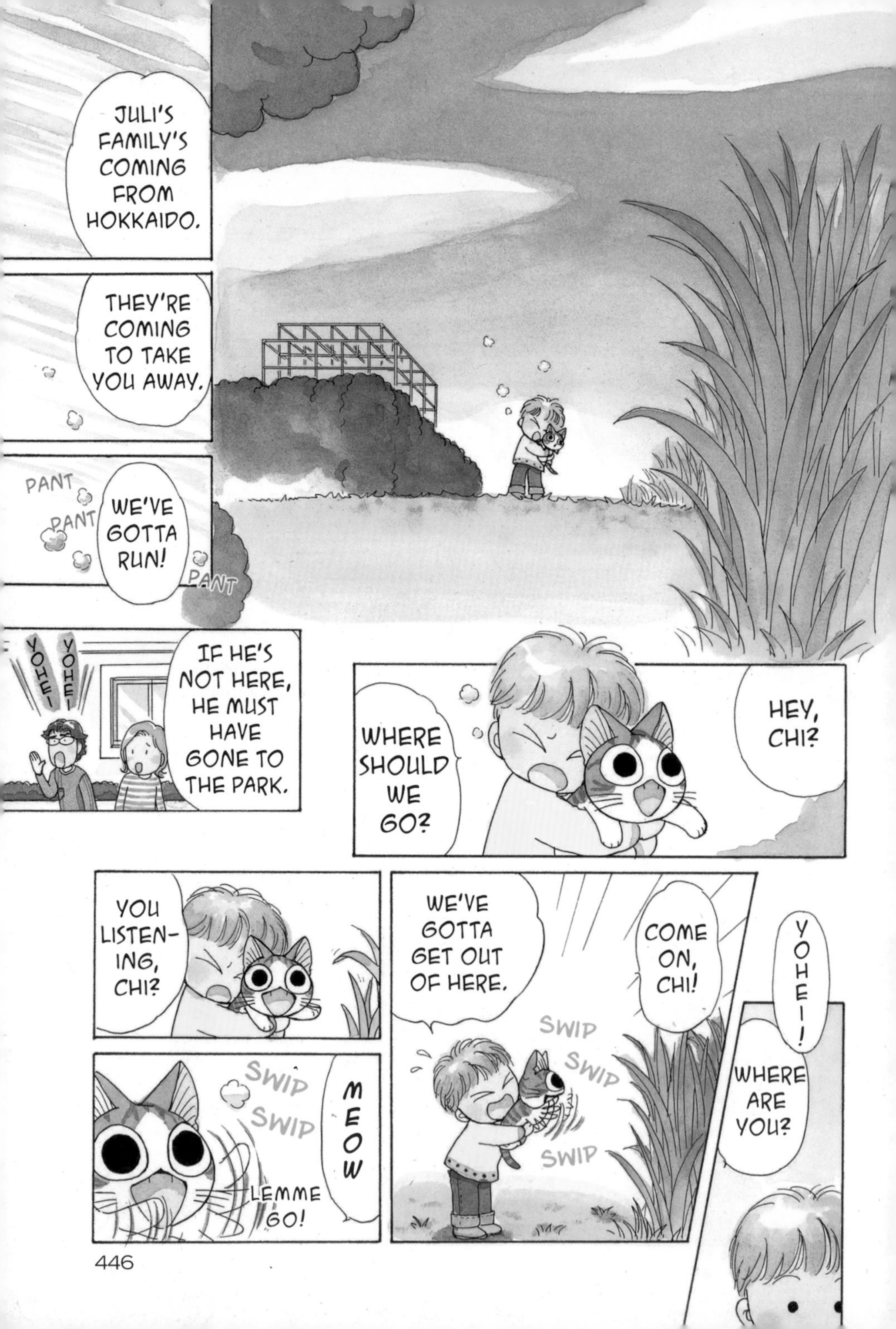

JULI'S FAMILY'S COMING FROM HOKKAIDO.
THEY'RE COMING TO TAKE YOU AWAY.
PANT PANT
WE'VE GOTTA RUN!
PANT
YOHEI YOHEI
IF HE'S NOT HERE, HE MUST HAVE GONE TO THE PARK.
HEY, CHI?
WHERE SHOULD WE GO?
YOU LISTENING, CHI?
SWIP SWIP
MEOW
LEMME GO!
WE'VE GOTTA GET OUT OF HERE.
COME ON, CHI!
SWIP SWIP SWIP
YOHEI!
WHERE ARE YOU?

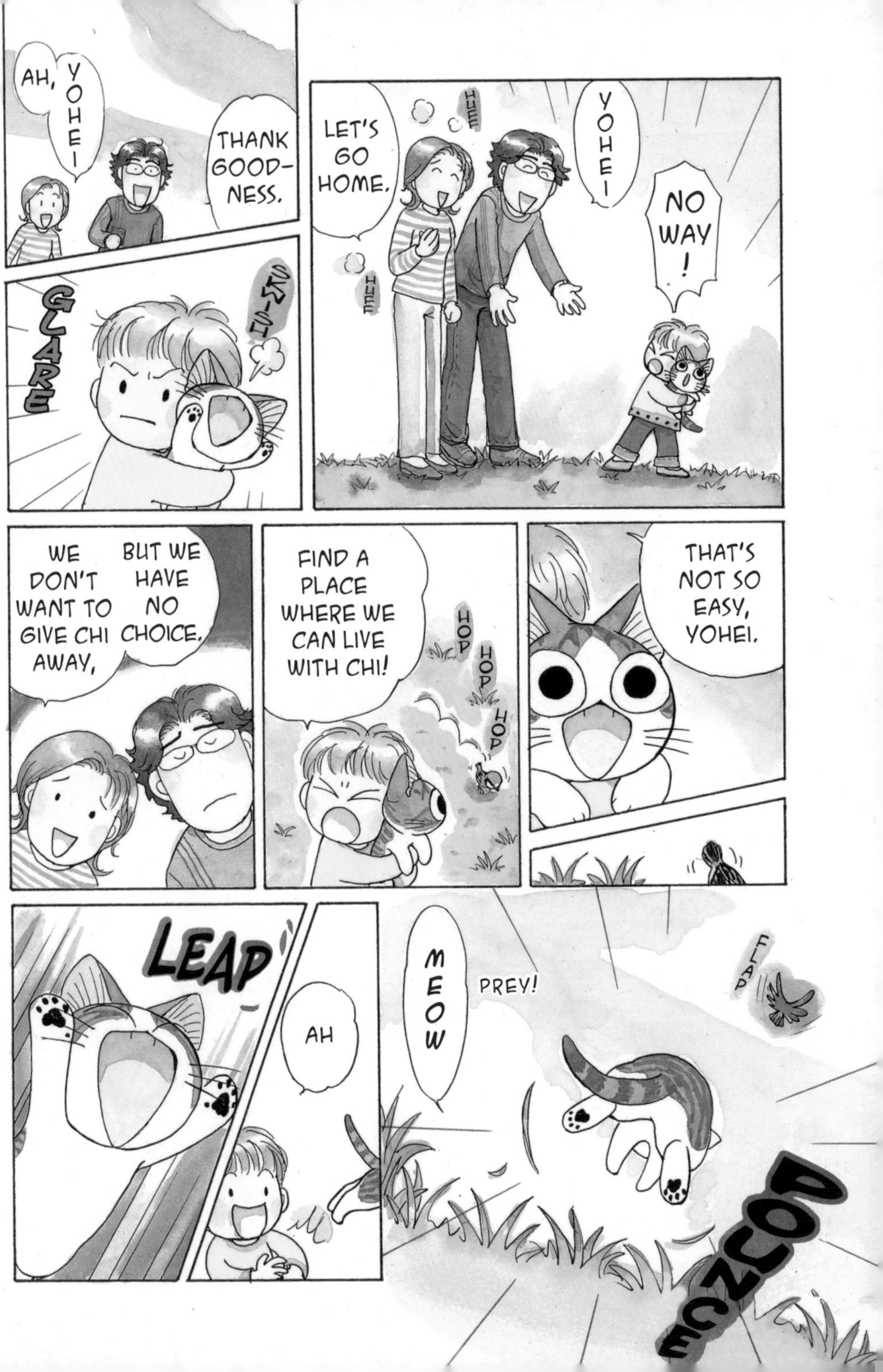
AH, YOHEI
THANK GOODNESS.
GLARE
SWISH
LET'S GO HOME.
HUFF
HUFF
YOHEI
NO WAY!
WE DON'T WANT TO GIVE CHI AWAY,
BUT WE HAVE NO CHOICE.
FIND A PLACE WHERE WE CAN LIVE WITH CHI!
HOP
HOP
HOP
HOP
THAT'S NOT SO EASY, YOHEI.
LEAP
AH
MEOW
PREY!
FLAP
POUNCE

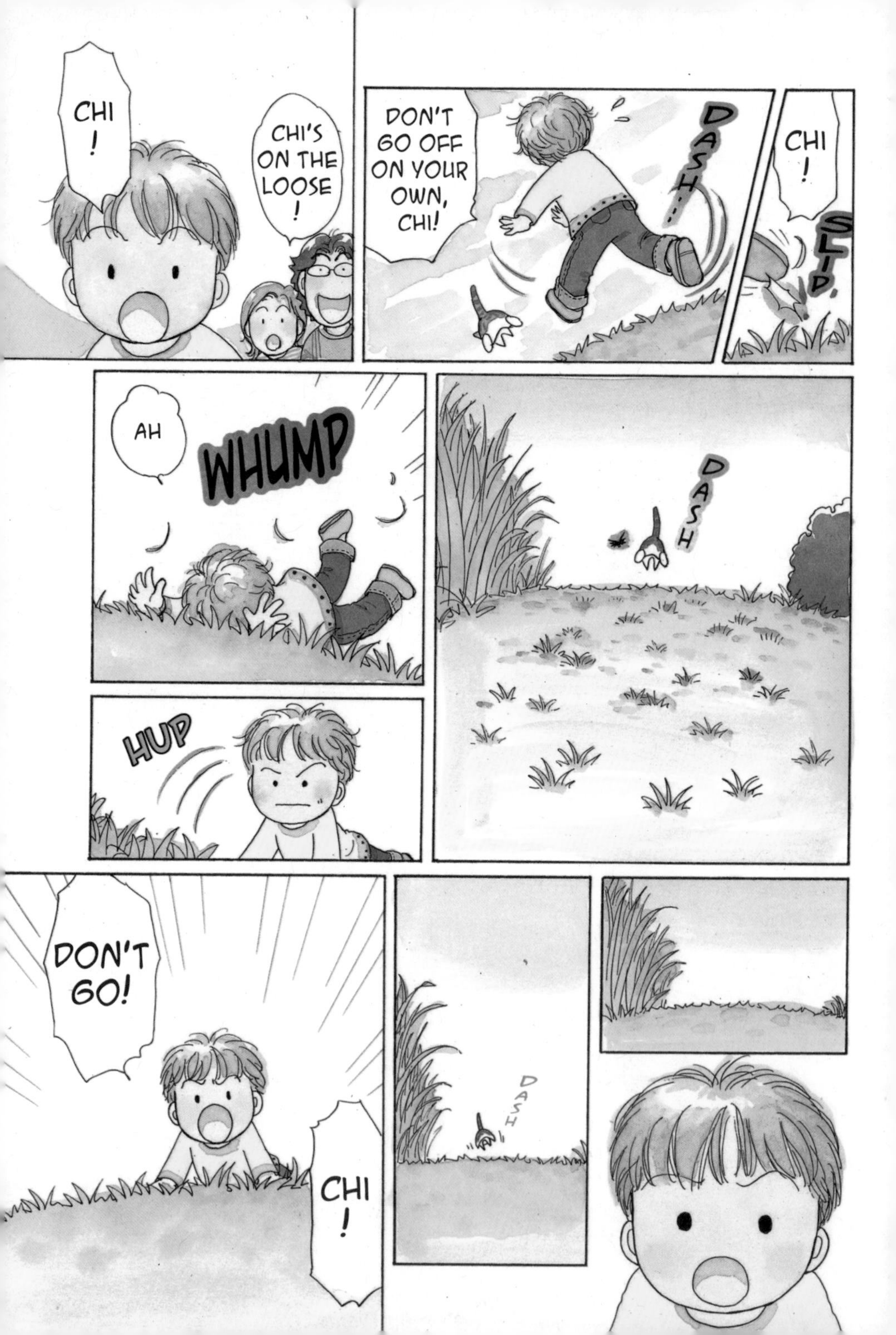
CHI!
CHI'S ON THE LOOSE!
DON'T GO OFF ON YOUR OWN, CHI!
DASH...
CHI!
SLID.
AH
WHUMP
DASH
HUP
DON'T GO!
CHI!
DASH

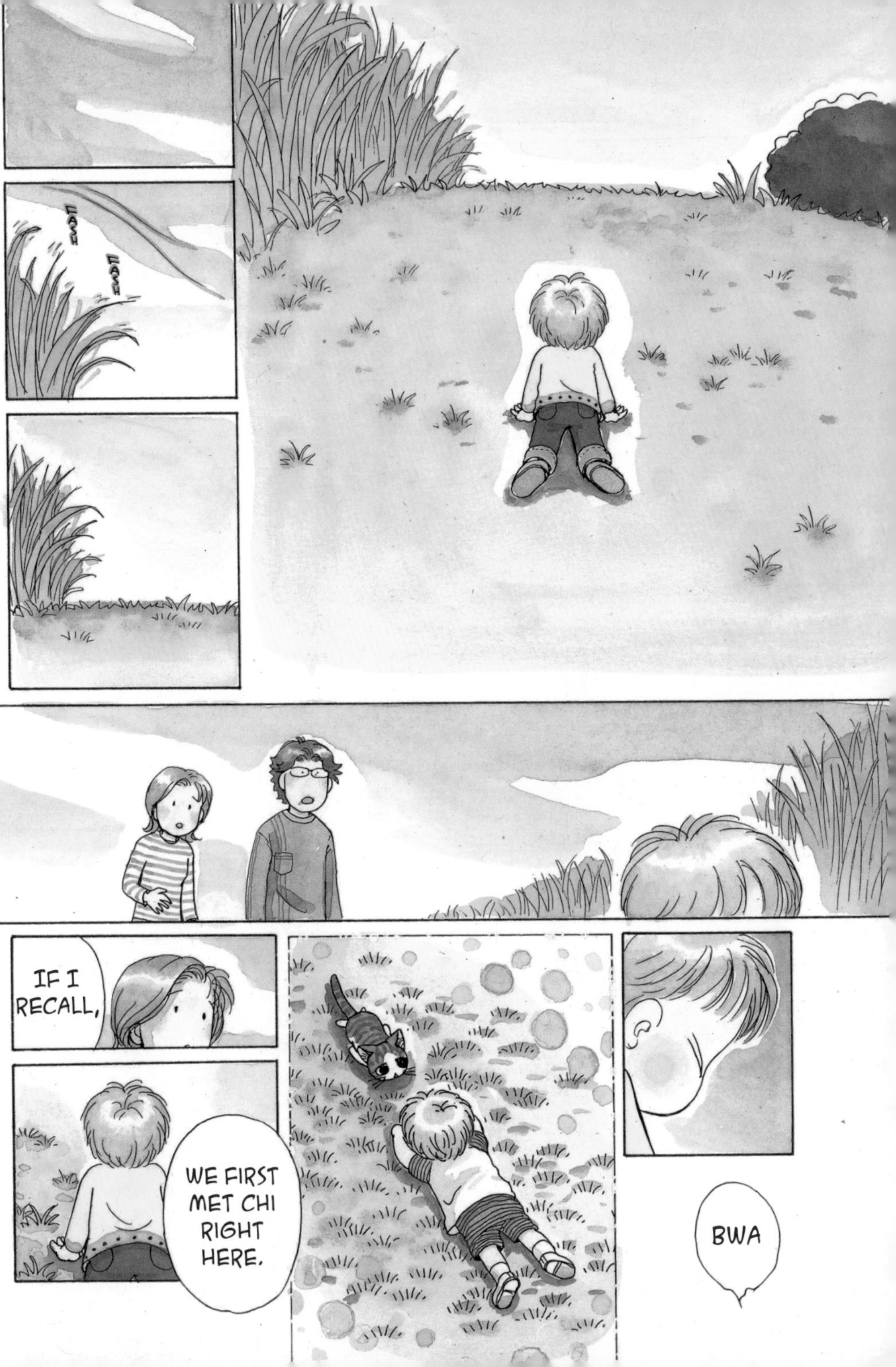
RASH
RASH
IF I RECALL,
WE FIRST MET CHI RIGHT HERE.
BWA

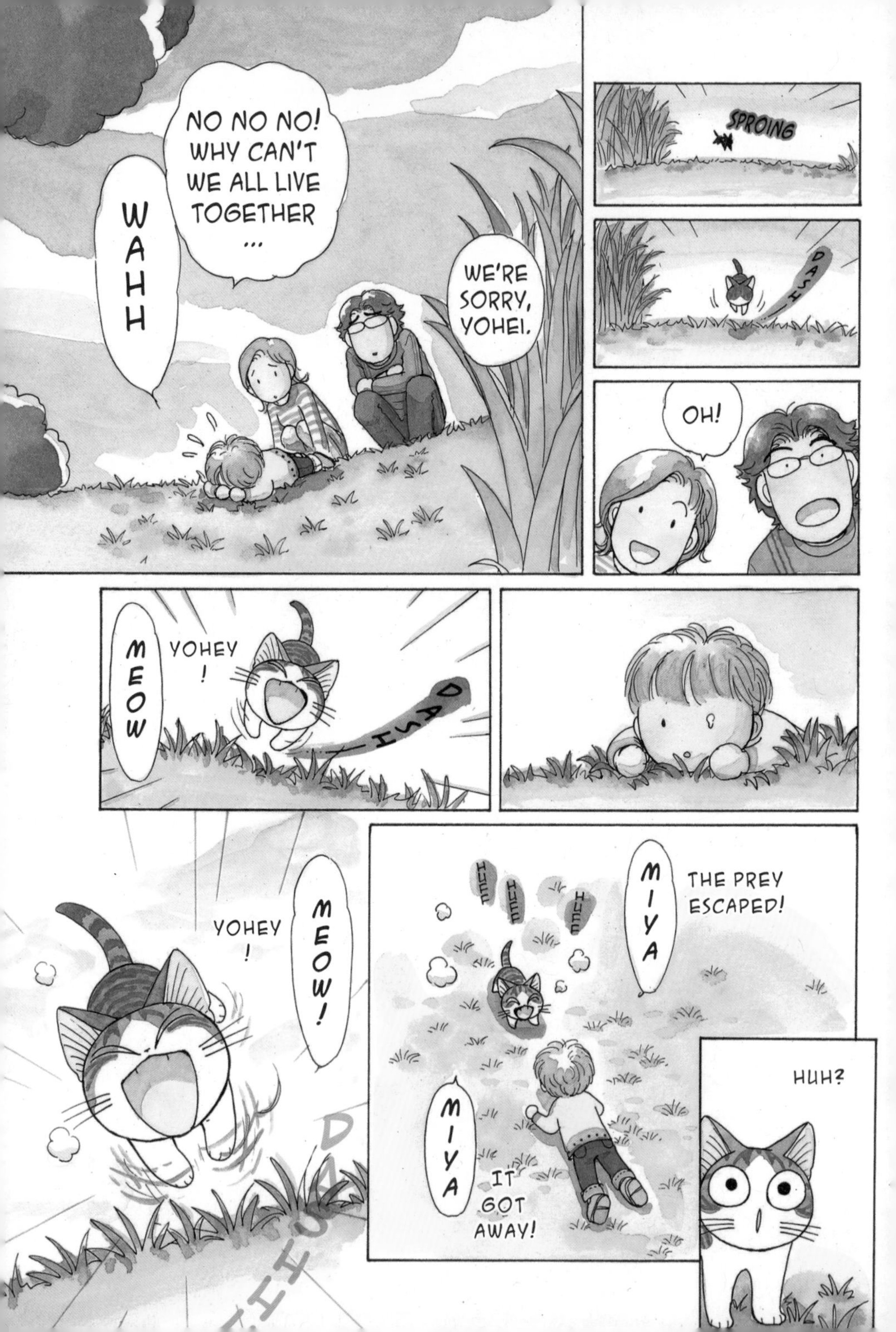
WAHH
NO NO NO! WHY CAN'T WE ALL LIVE TOGETHER ...
WE'RE SORRY, YOHEI.
SPROING
DASH
OH!
MEOW
YOHEY!
DASH
YOHEY!
MEOW!
DASH
HUFF
HUFF
HUFF
MIYA
THE PREY ESCAPED!
MIYA
IT GOT AWAY!
HUH?

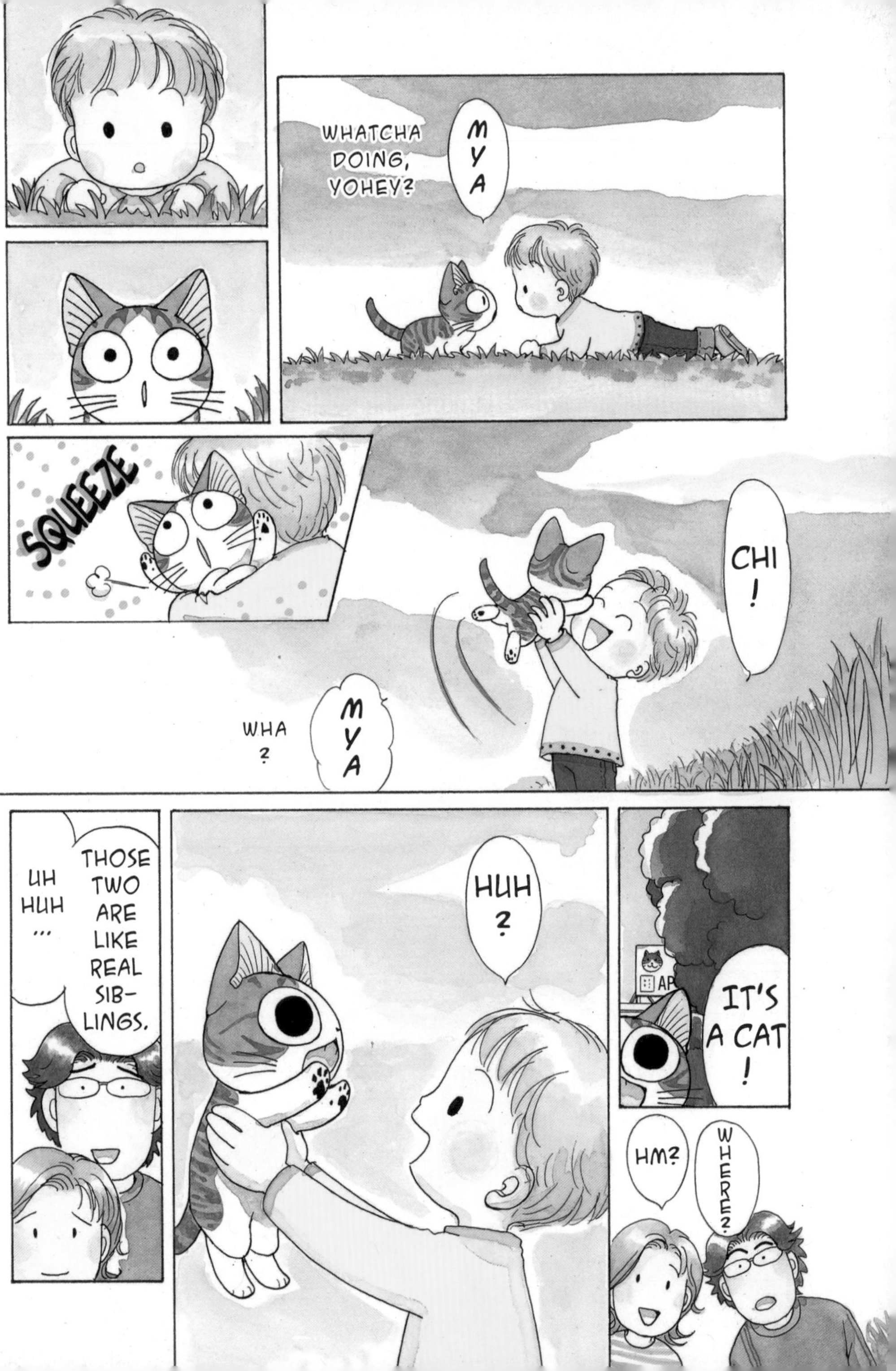
WHATCHA DOING, YOHEY?
MYA
SQUEEZE
CHI!
WHA?
MYA
THOSE TWO ARE LIKE REAL SIB-LINGS.
UH HUH...
HUH?
IT'S A CAT!
HM?
WHERE?

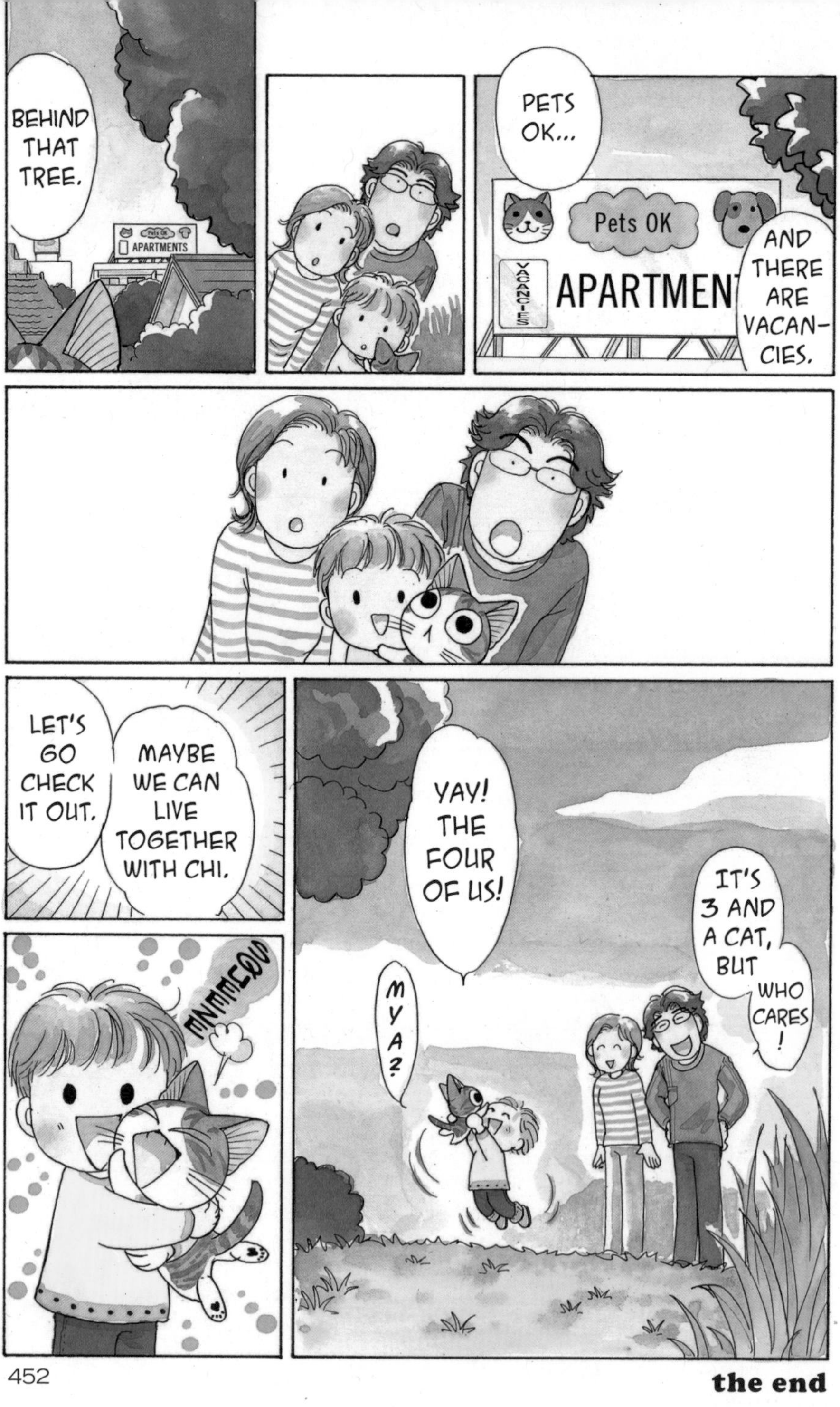
BEHIND THAT TREE.
Pets OK
APARTMENTS
PETS OK...
Pets OK
VACANCIES
APARTMENT
AND THERE ARE VACAN-CIES.
LET'S GO CHECK IT OUT.
MAYBE WE CAN LIVE TOGETHER WITH CHI.
YAY! THE FOUR OF US!
MYA?
IT'S 3 AND A CAT, BUT WHO CARES!

the end

ART BOOK
Bauhaus
DECORA

EXTRA

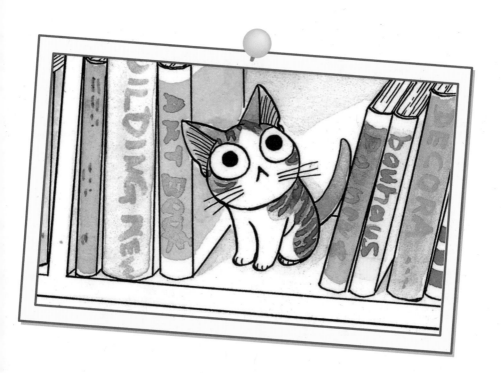

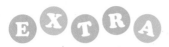

Introducing **Chi's Home Sweet Home**

A detailed look inside the Yamada family home where Chi lives!

data

4-story apartment bldg.
Room #102
670ft²

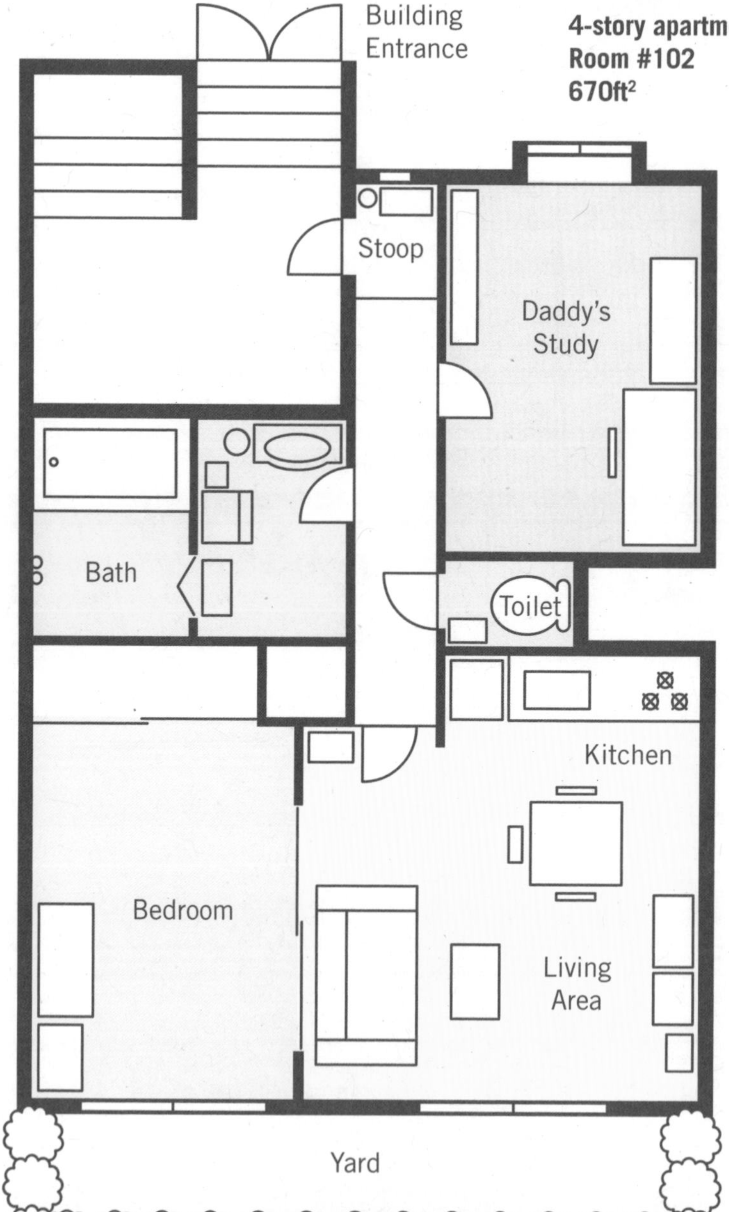
Building Entrance
Stoop
Daddy's Study
Bath
Toilet
Kitchen
Bedroom
Living Area
Yard

So how was
The Complete Chi's Sweet Home
Part 1?

This is the volume where I leave Chi,
but I bet you're wondering
what'll happen to Chi
and the Yamadas.

Well, let's find out.

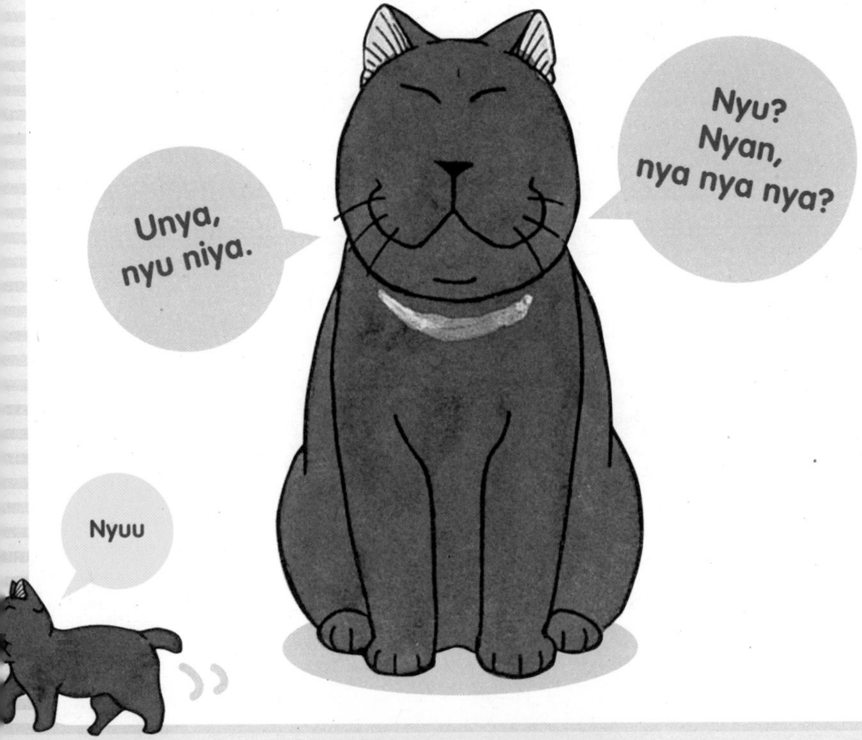
Unya,
nyu niya.
Nyu?
Nyan,
nya nya nya?
Nyuu

Chi's Sweet Home Preview

1st Event

A Big Move

Will the pet-friendly apartment building they found by chance provide a new home? What sort of place will the Yamadas and their kitten be moving into?

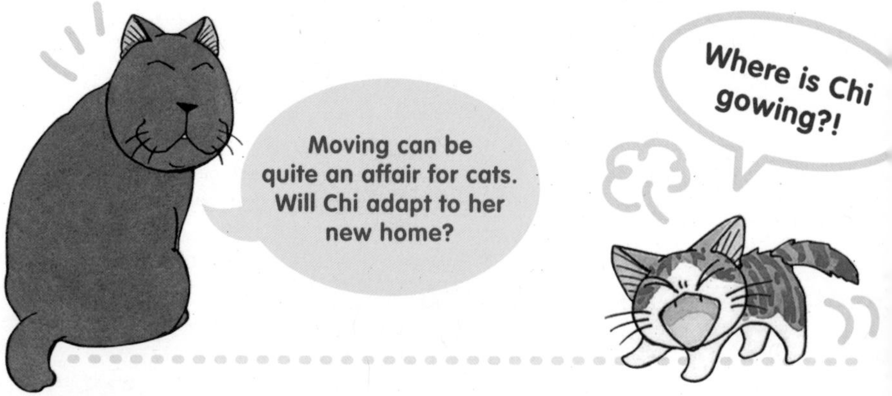
Moving can be quite an affair for cats. Will Chi adapt to her new home?
Where is Chi gowing?!

2nd Event

New Encounters?

There must be other pets living around Chi's new home. What sort of people and animals will we meet? Will Chi and Yohei be blessed with another encounter?

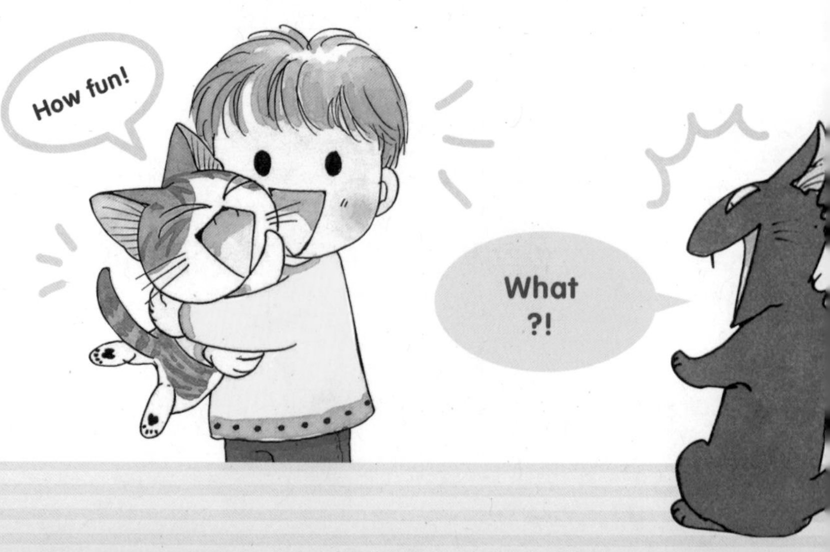
How fun!
What ?!

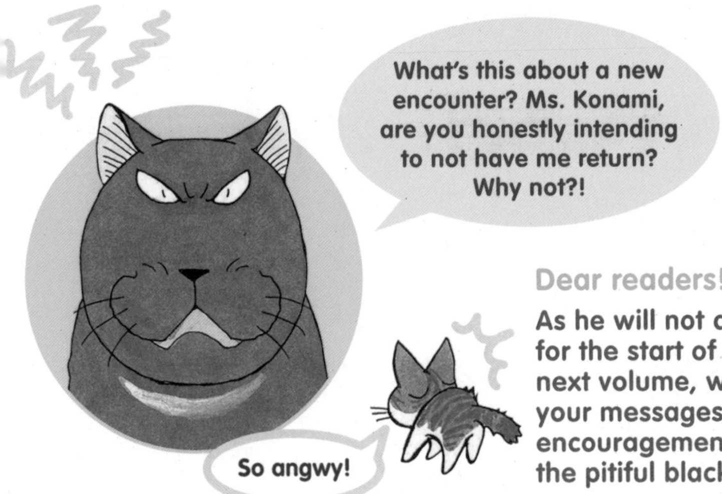
What's this about a new encounter? Ms. Konami, are you honestly intending to not have me return? Why not?!
So angwy!

Dear readers!

As he will not appear for the start of the next volume, we await your messages of encouragement for the pitiful black cat.

Please send your letters for him to our mailing address on the last page.

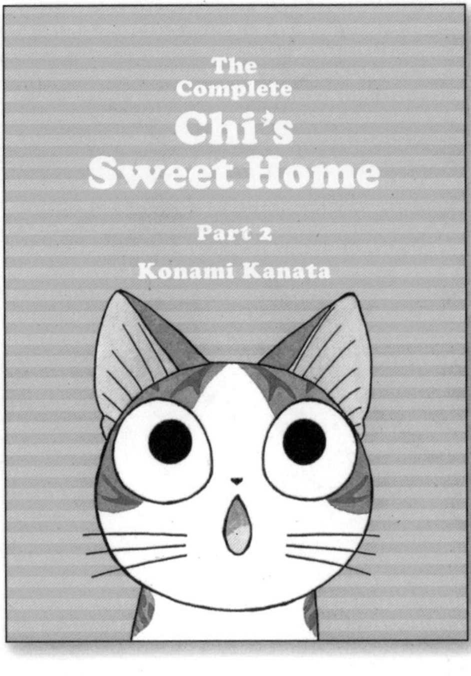
The Complete
Chi's Sweet Home
Part 2
Konami Kanata

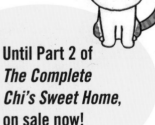

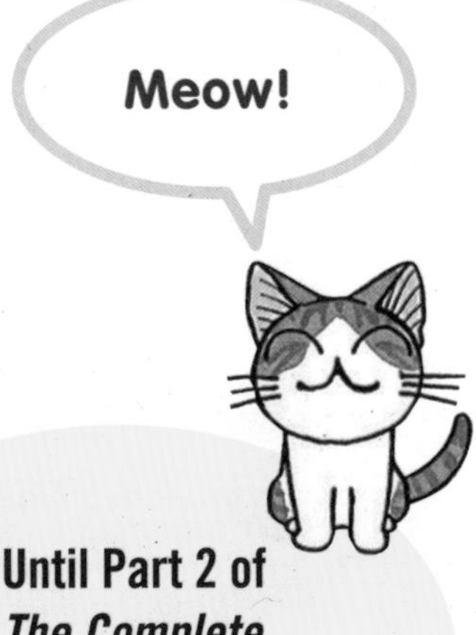
Meow!

Until Part 2 of *The Complete Chi's Sweet Home*, on sale now!

Introducing FukuFuku

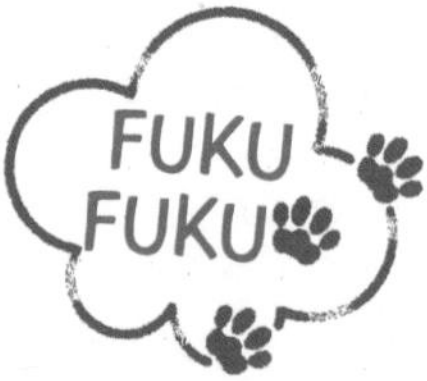
FUKU
FUKU

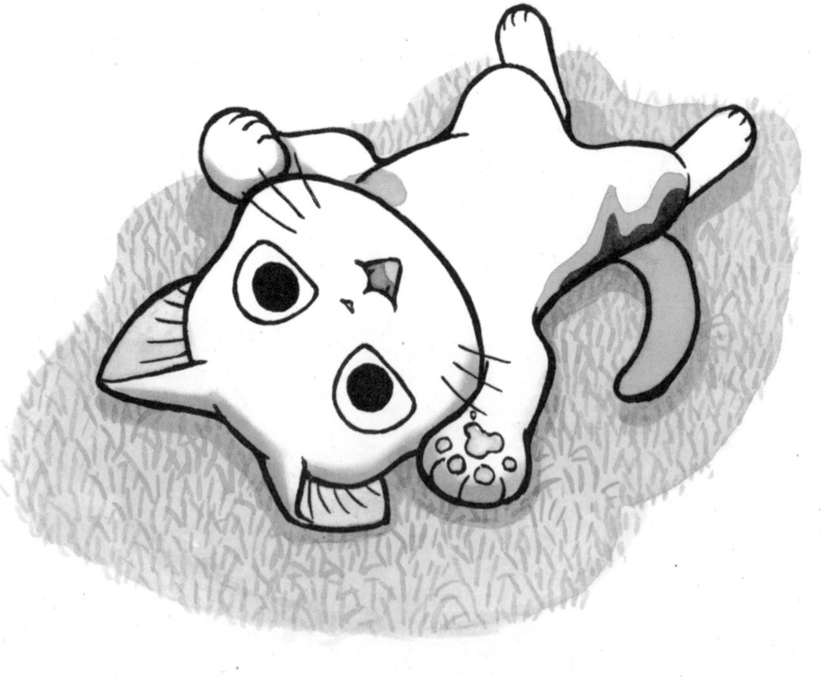

A Cat Meets FukuFuku

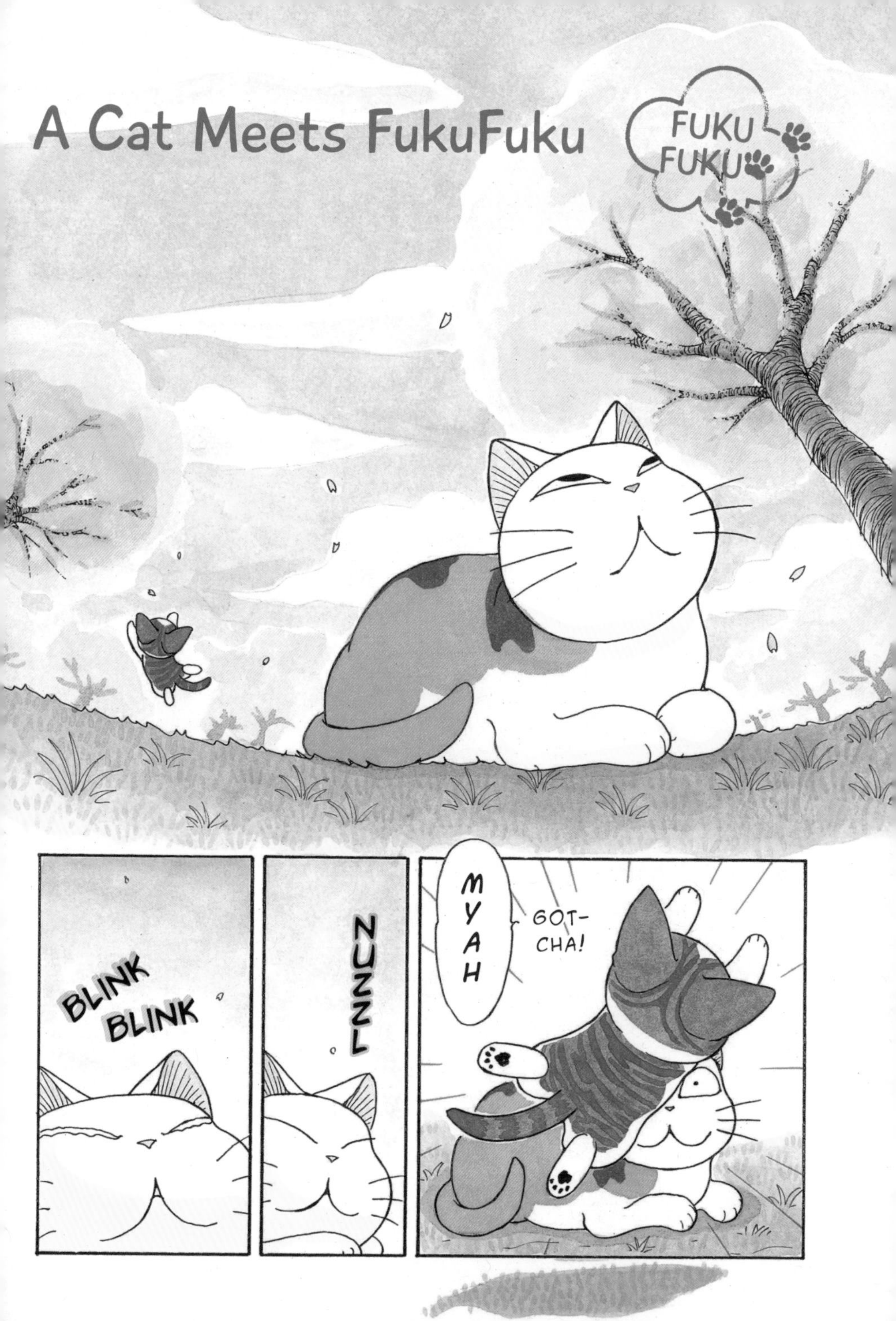
FUKU FUKU
BLINK BLINK
NUZZL
MYAH
GOT-CHA!

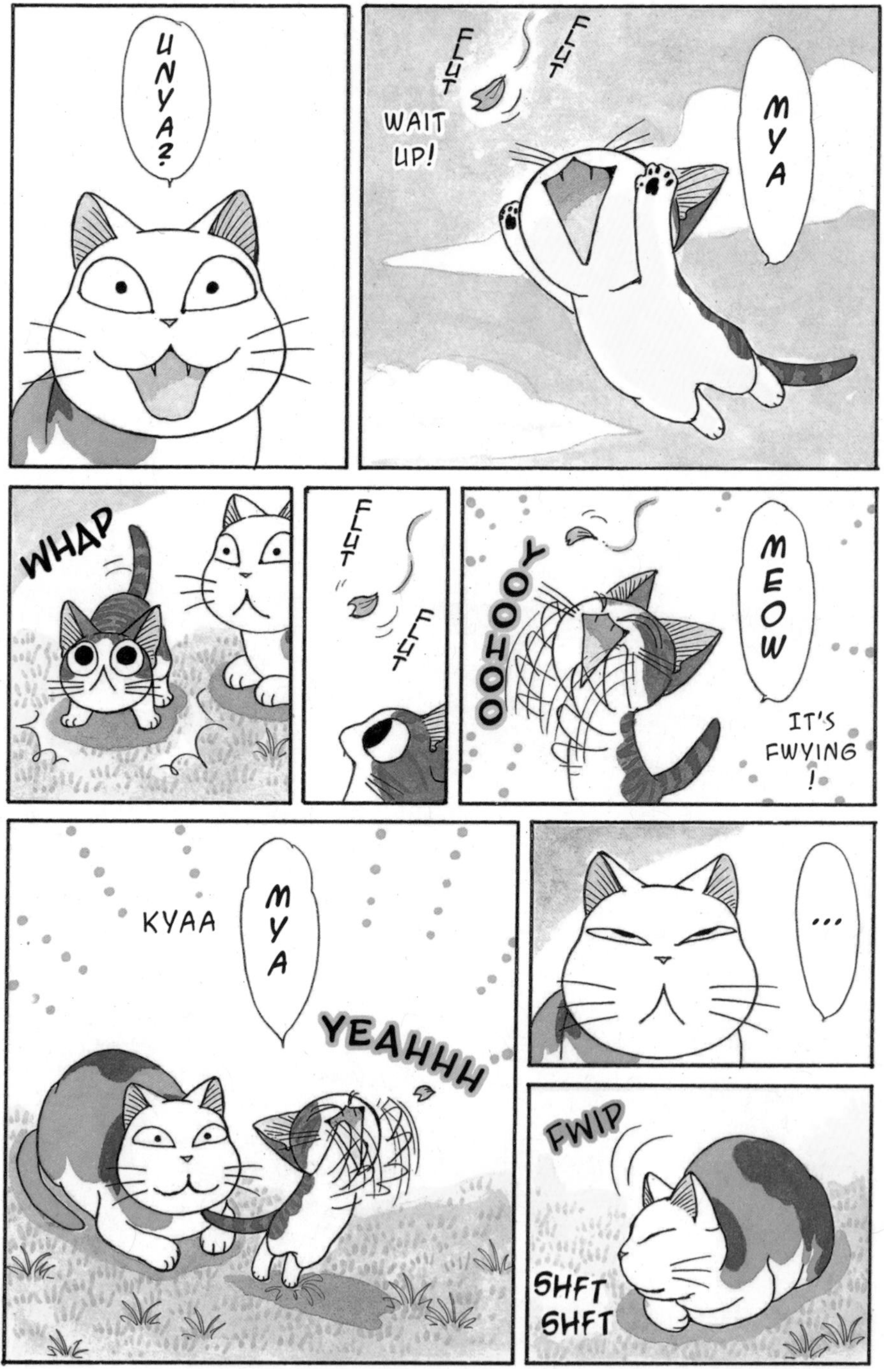

UNYA?
FLUT
FLUT
WAIT UP!
MYA
WHAP
FLUT
FLUT
YOOHOO
MEOW
IT'S FWYING!
KYAA
MYA
YEAHHH
...
FWIP
SHFT SHFT

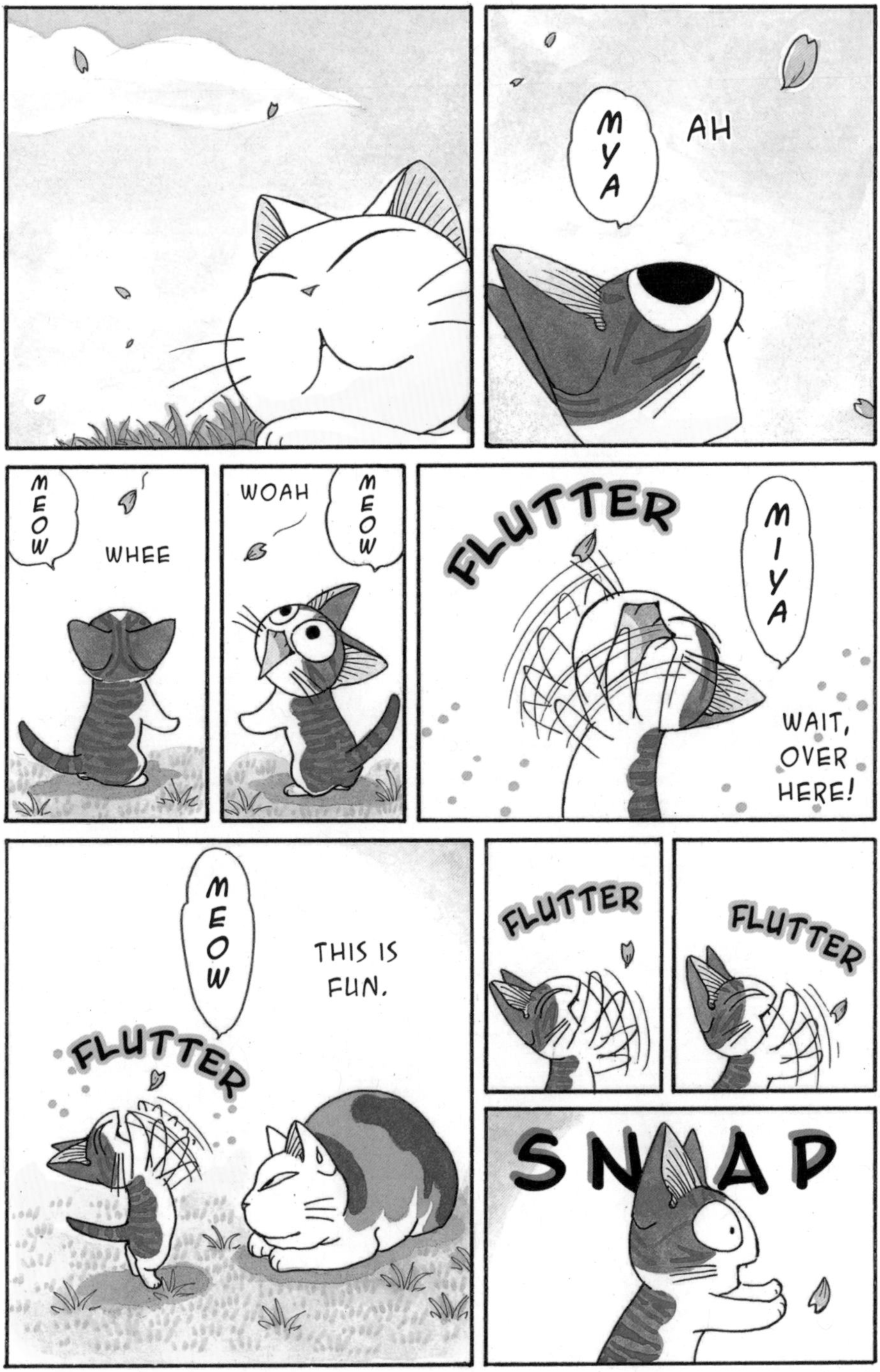
MYA
AH
MEOW
WHEE
WOAH
MEOW
FLUTTER
MIYA
WAIT, OVER HERE!
MEOW
THIS IS FUN.
FLUTTER
FLUTTER
FLUTTER
SNAP

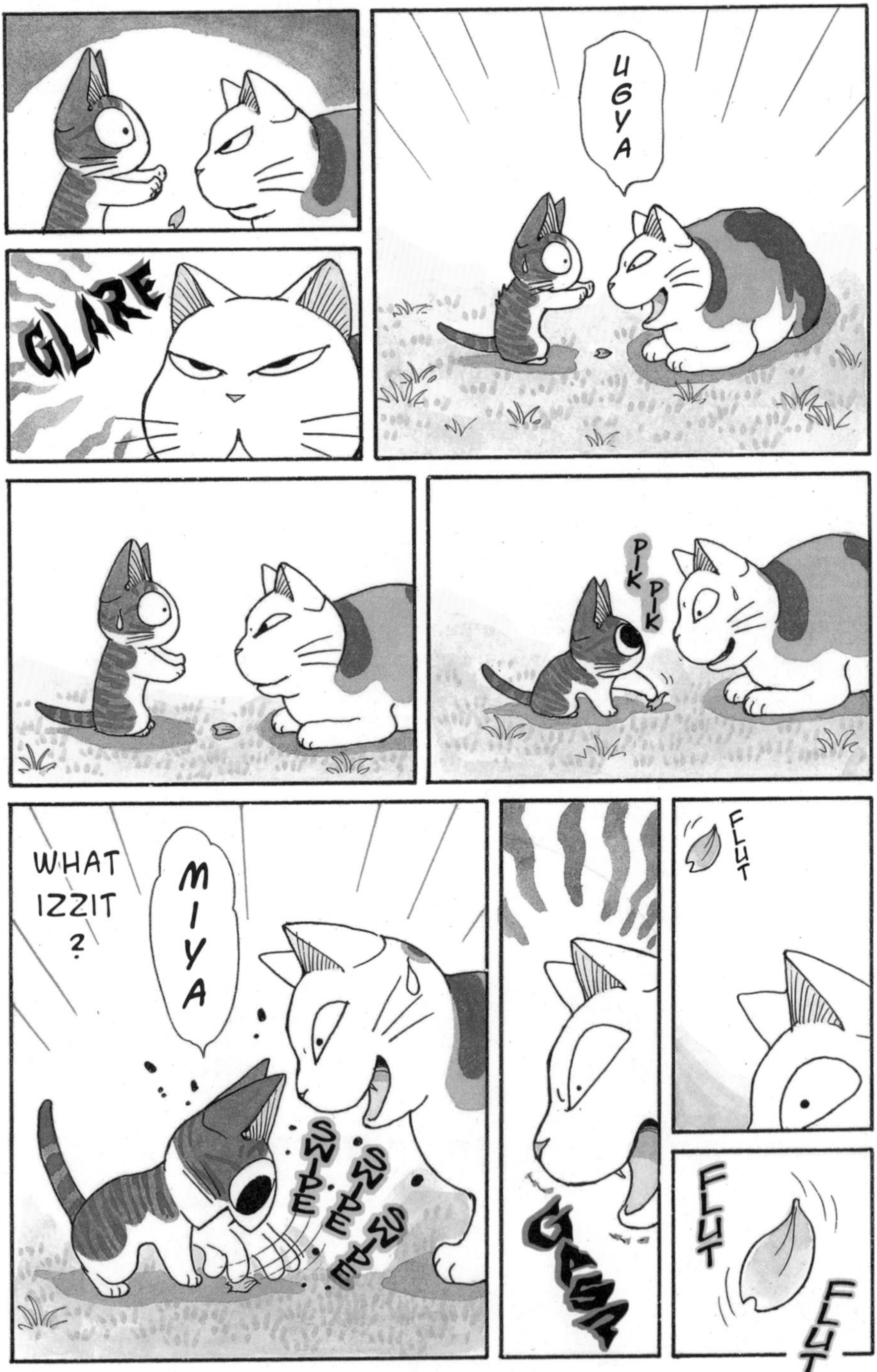
GLARE
UGYA
PIK PIK
WHAT IZZIT?
MIYA
SWIPE SWIPE SWIPE
GASA
FLUT
FLUT FLUT

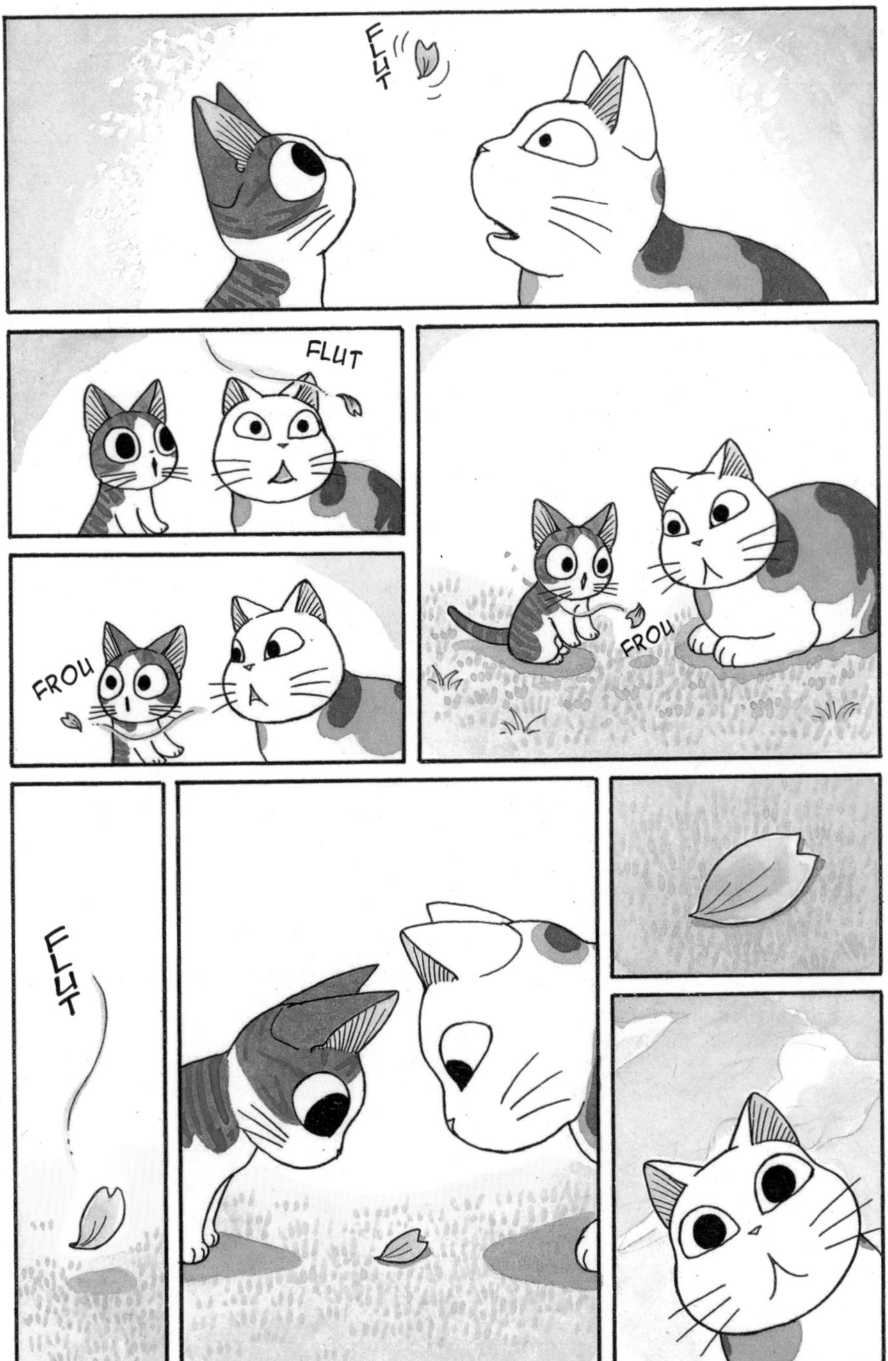
FLUT
FLUT
FROU
FROU
FLUT

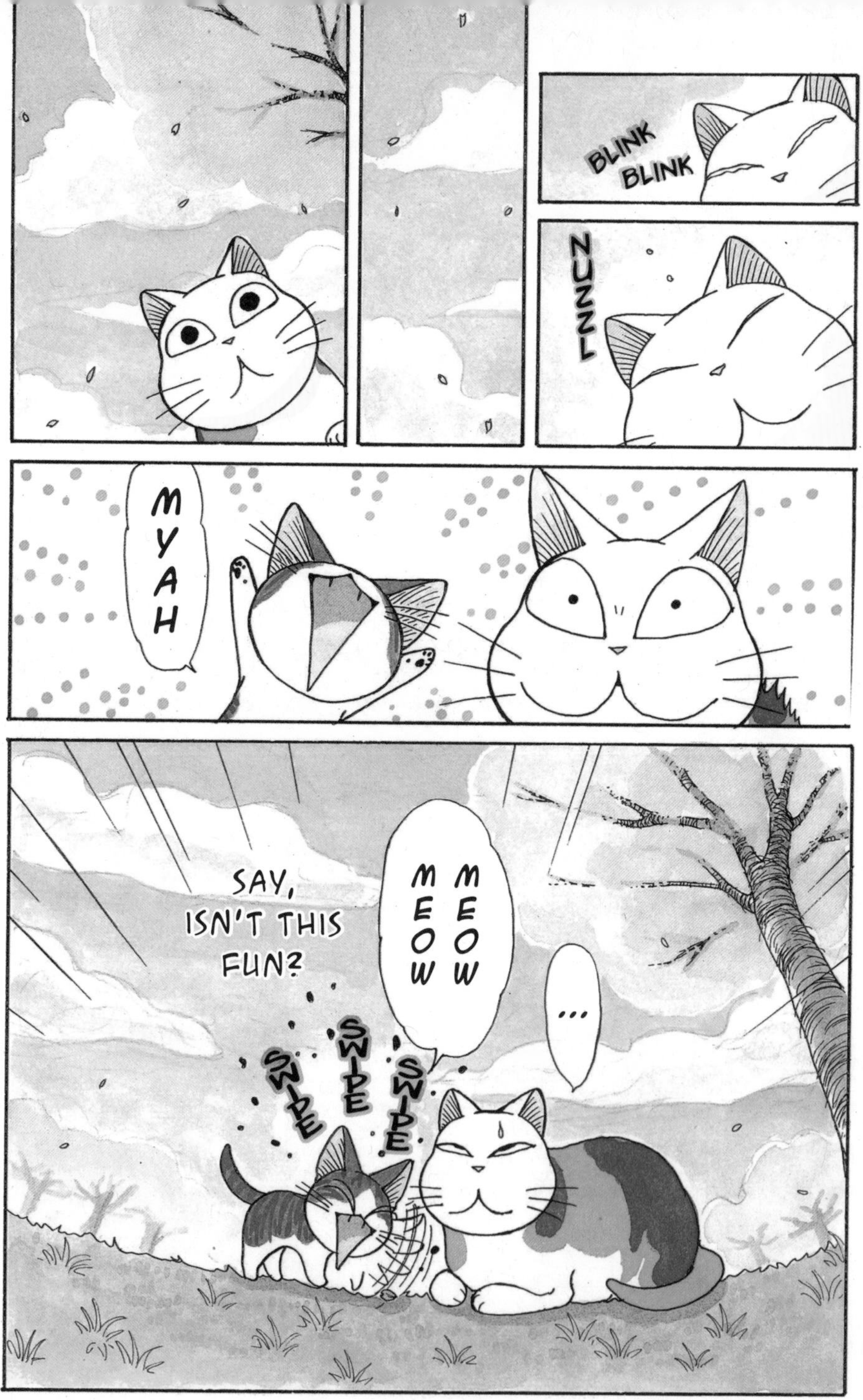
BLINK BLINK
NUZZL
MYAH
SAY, ISN'T THIS FUN?
MEOW MEOW
...
SWIPE SWIPE SWIPE

the end

Kitten FukuFuku

FUKU FUKU

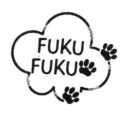

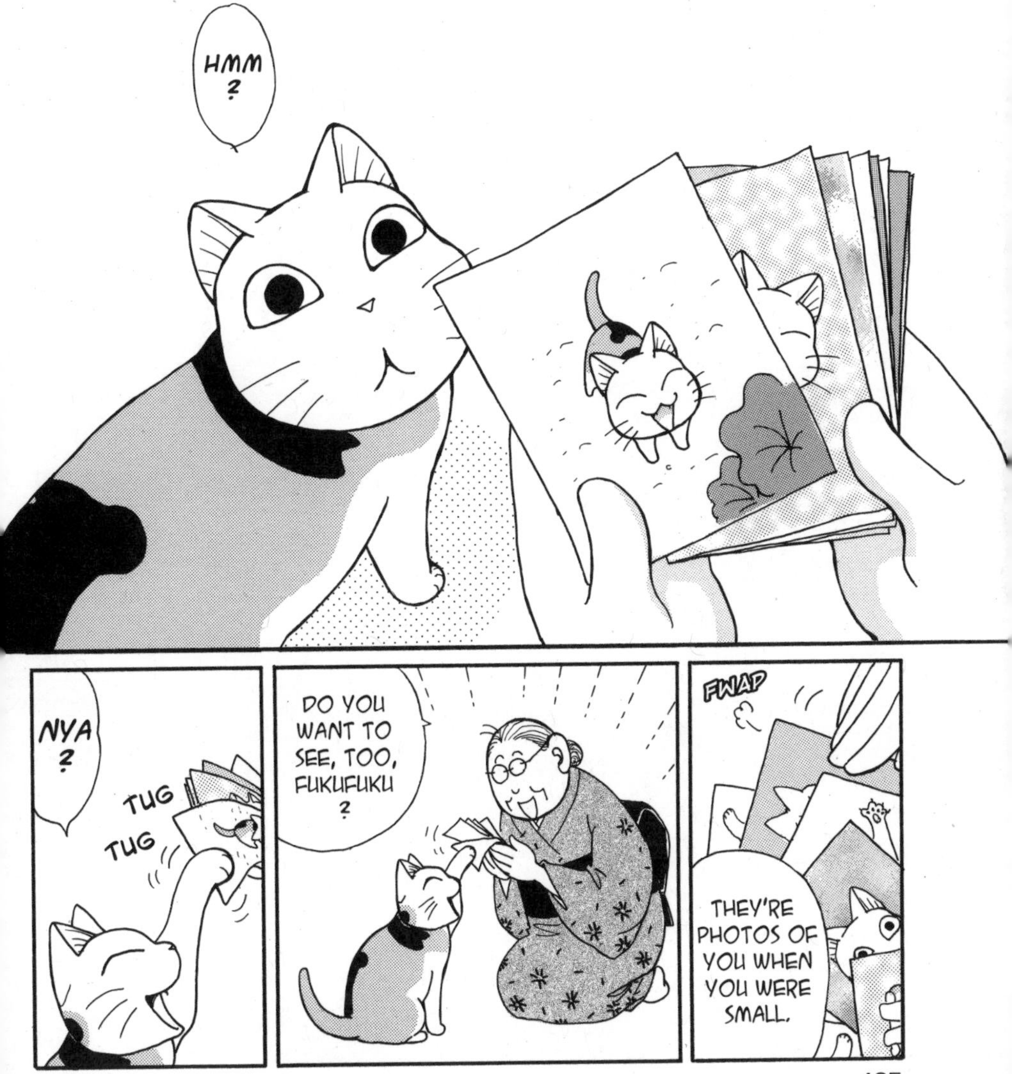
HMM ?
NYA ?
TUG TUG
DO YOU WANT TO SEE, TOO, FUKUFUKU ?
FWAP
THEY'RE PHOTOS OF YOU WHEN YOU WERE SMALL.

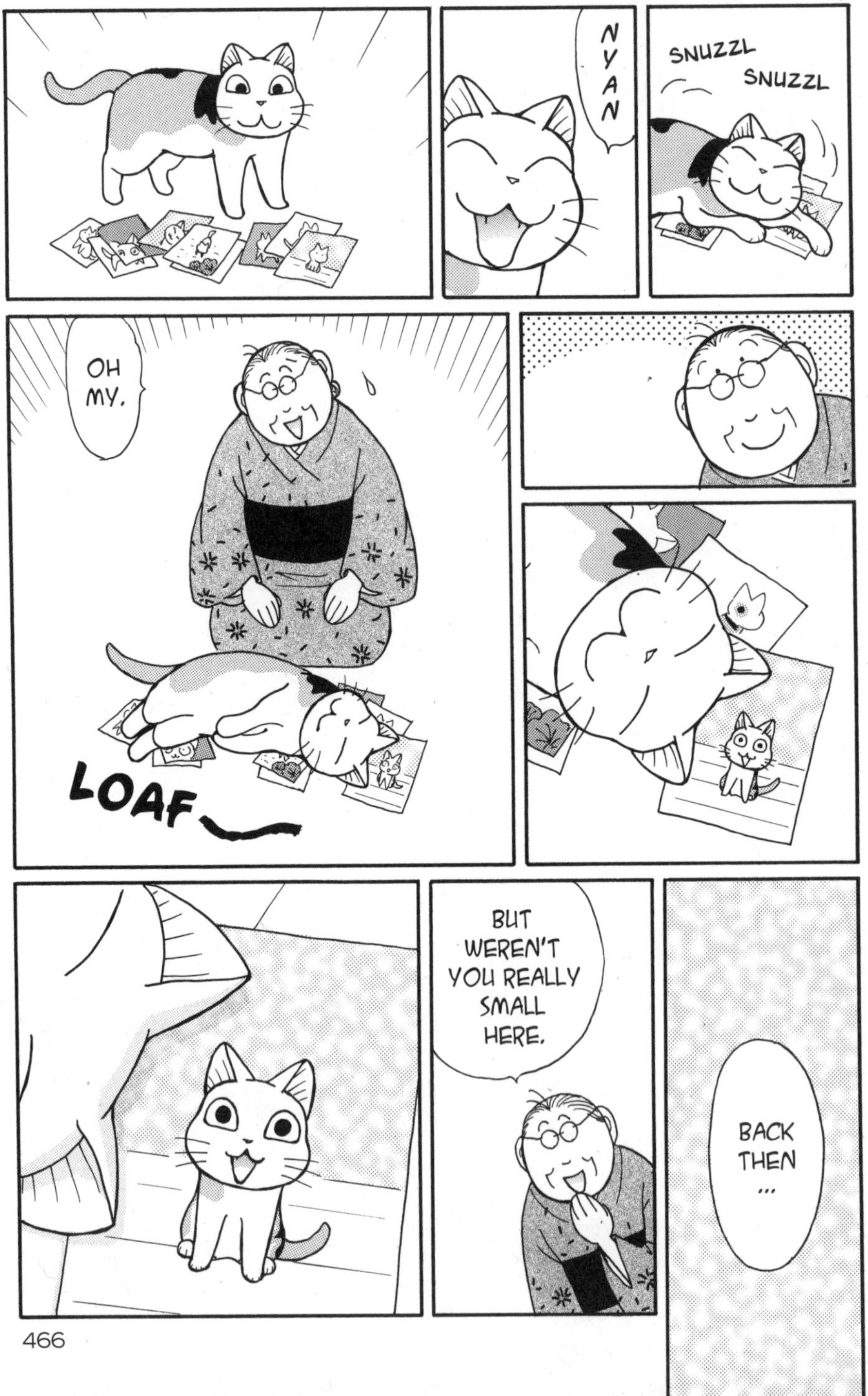
NYAN
SNUZZL SNUZZL
OH MY.
LOAF
BUT WEREN'T YOU REALLY SMALL HERE.
BACK THEN ...

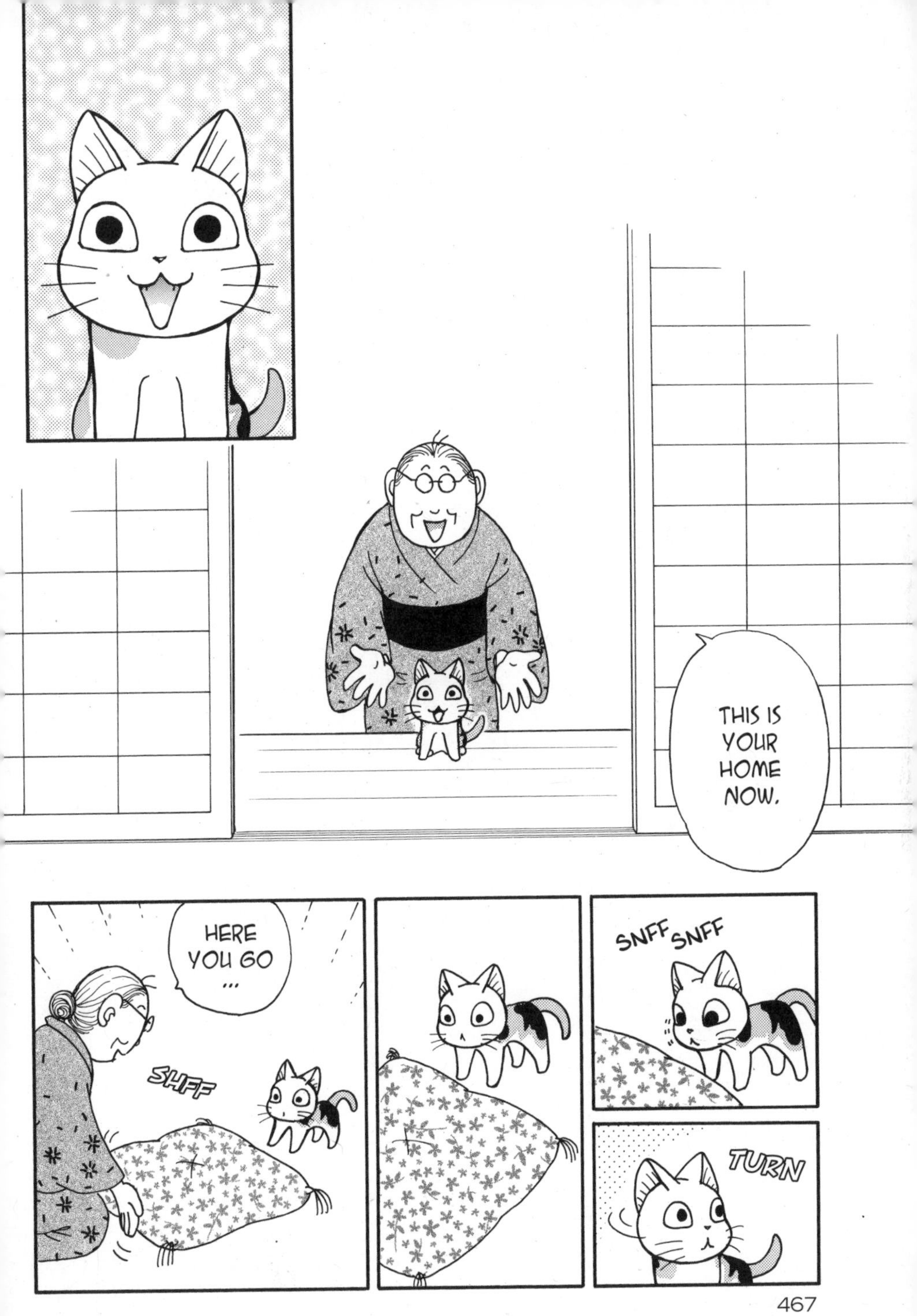
THIS IS YOUR HOME NOW.
HERE YOU GO ...
SHFF
SNFF SNFF
TURN

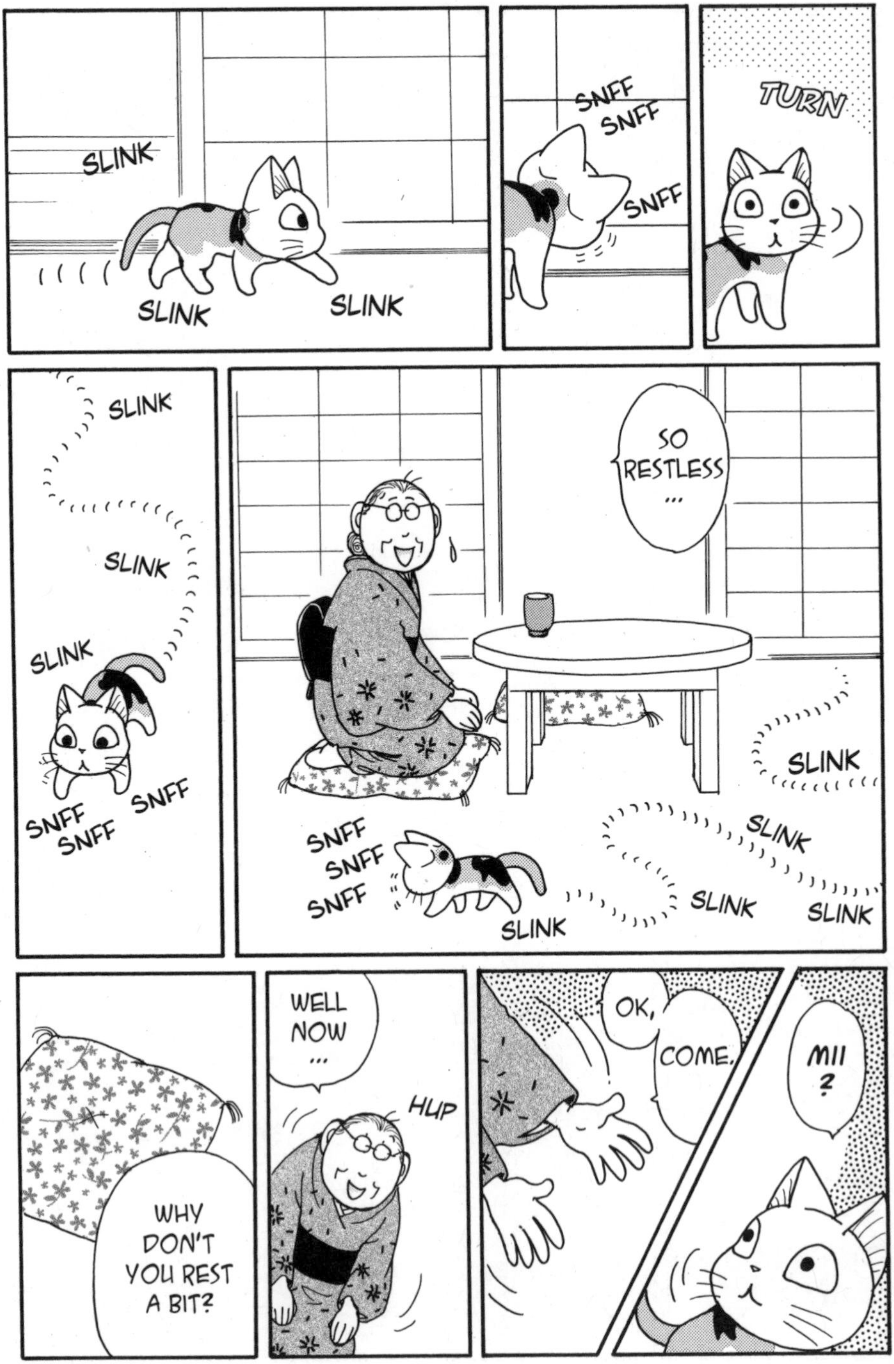
SLINK
SLINK
SLINK
SNFF
SNFF
SNFF
TURN
SLINK
SLINK
SLINK
SNFF
SNFF
SNFF
SO RESTLESS ...
SNFF
SNFF
SNFF
SLINK
SLINK
SLINK
SLINK
SLINK
WHY DON'T YOU REST A BIT?
WELL NOW ...
HUP
OK,
COME.
MII?

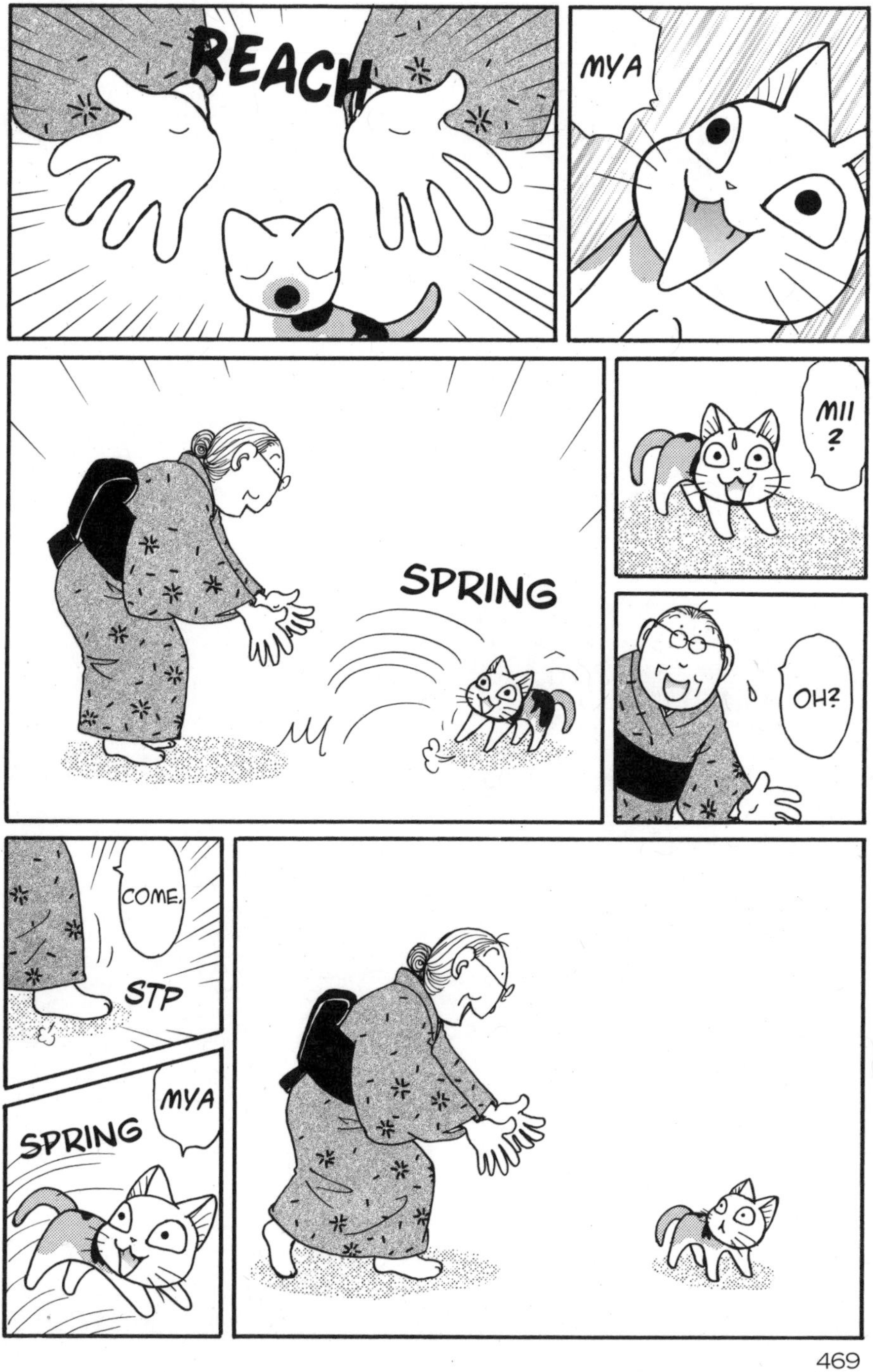
REACH
MYA
SPRING
MII ?
OH?
COME,
STP
MYA
SPRING

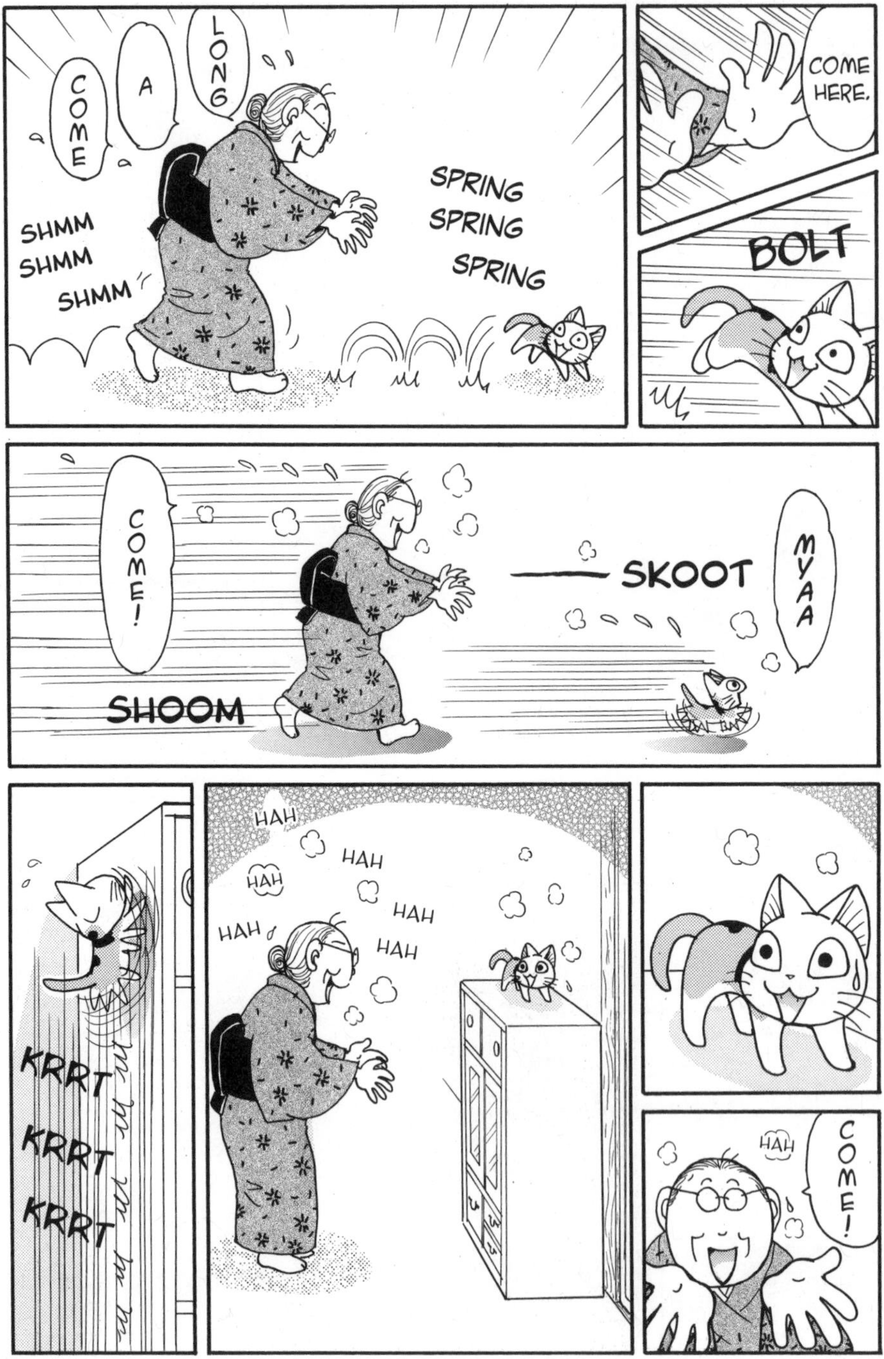
COME
A
LONG
SHMM
SHMM
SHMM
SPRING
SPRING
SPRING
COME HERE.
BOLT
COME!
SHOOM
SKOOT
MYAA
KRRT
KRRT
KRRT
HAH
HAH
HAH
HAH
HAH
HAH
HAH
COME!

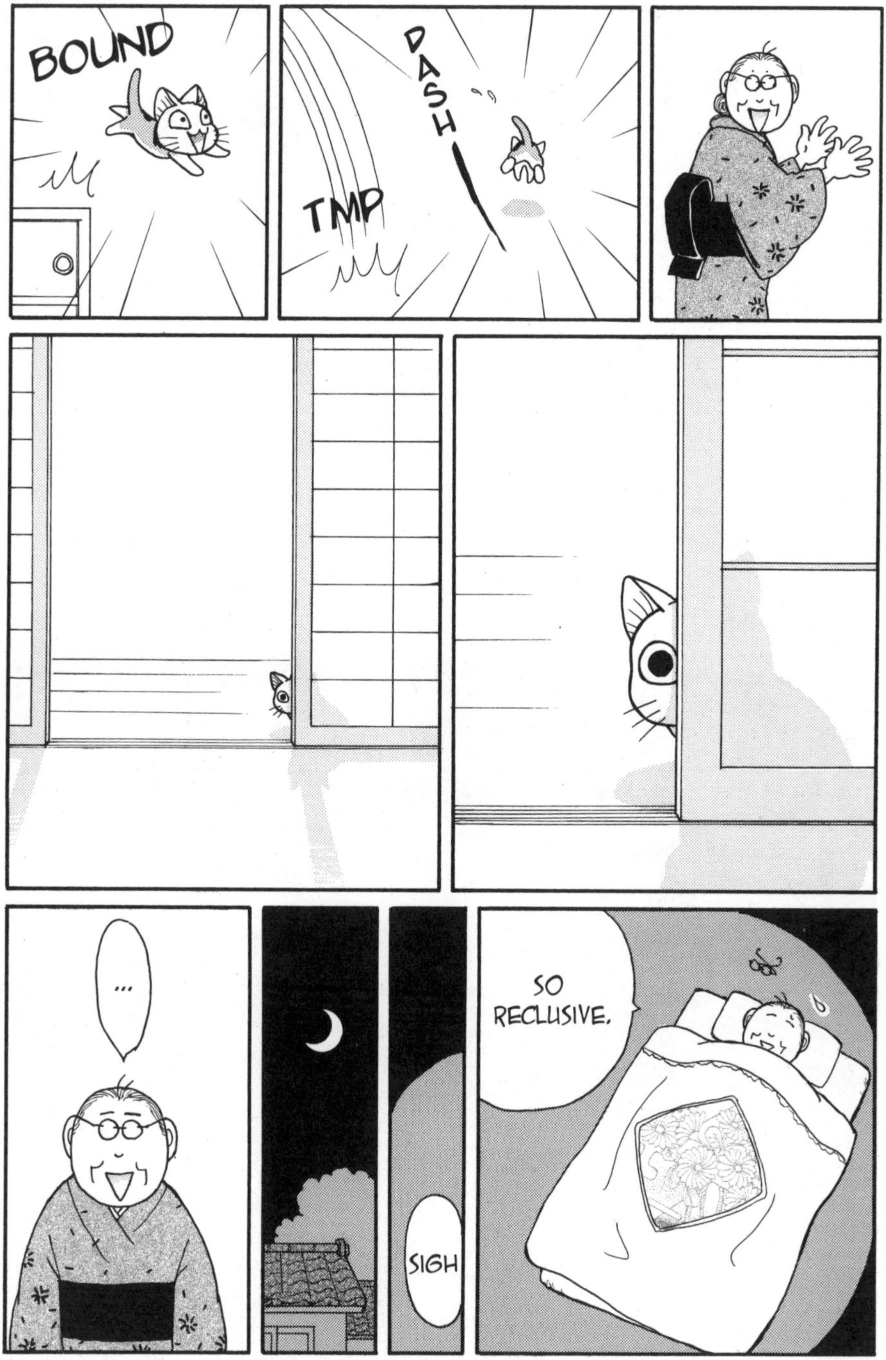
BOUND
DASH
TMP
...
SIGH
SO RECLUSIVE.

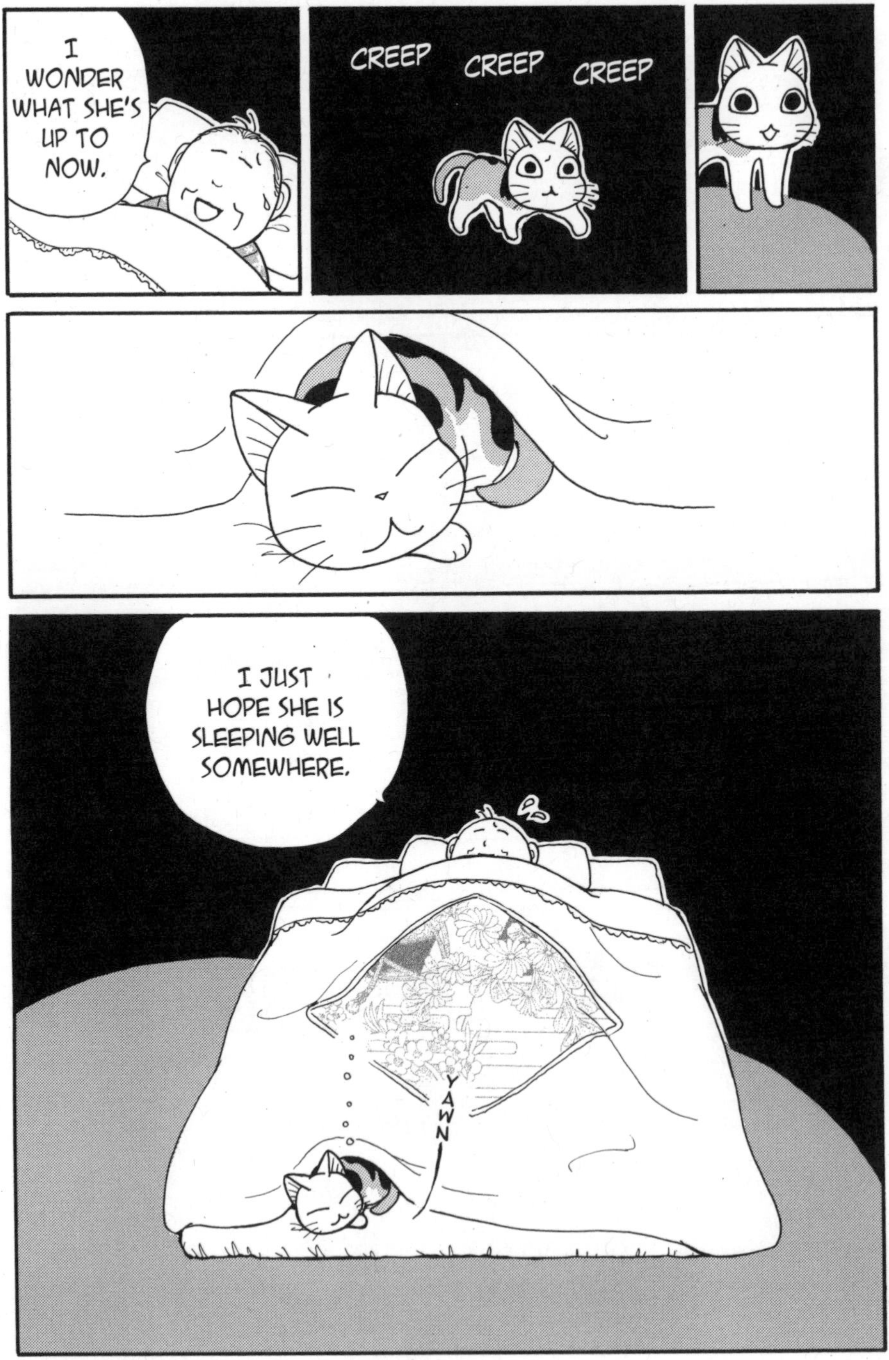
I WONDER WHAT SHE'S UP TO NOW.
CREEP CREEP CREEP
I JUST HOPE SHE IS SLEEPING WELL SOMEWHERE.
YAWN

the end

You Called?

FUKU FUKU

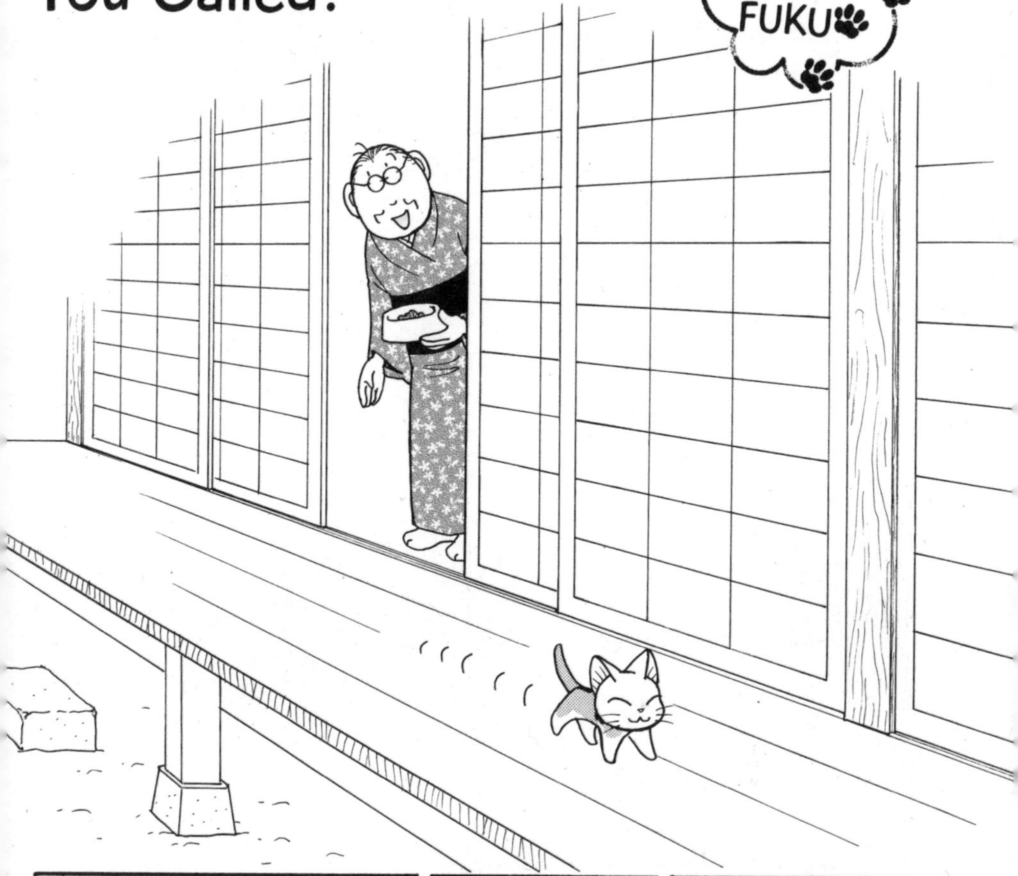

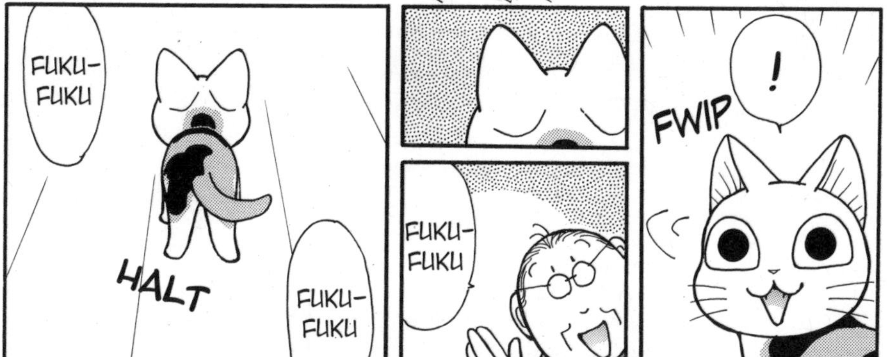
FUKU-FUKU
HALT
FUKU-FUKU
FUKU-FUKU
FWIP
!

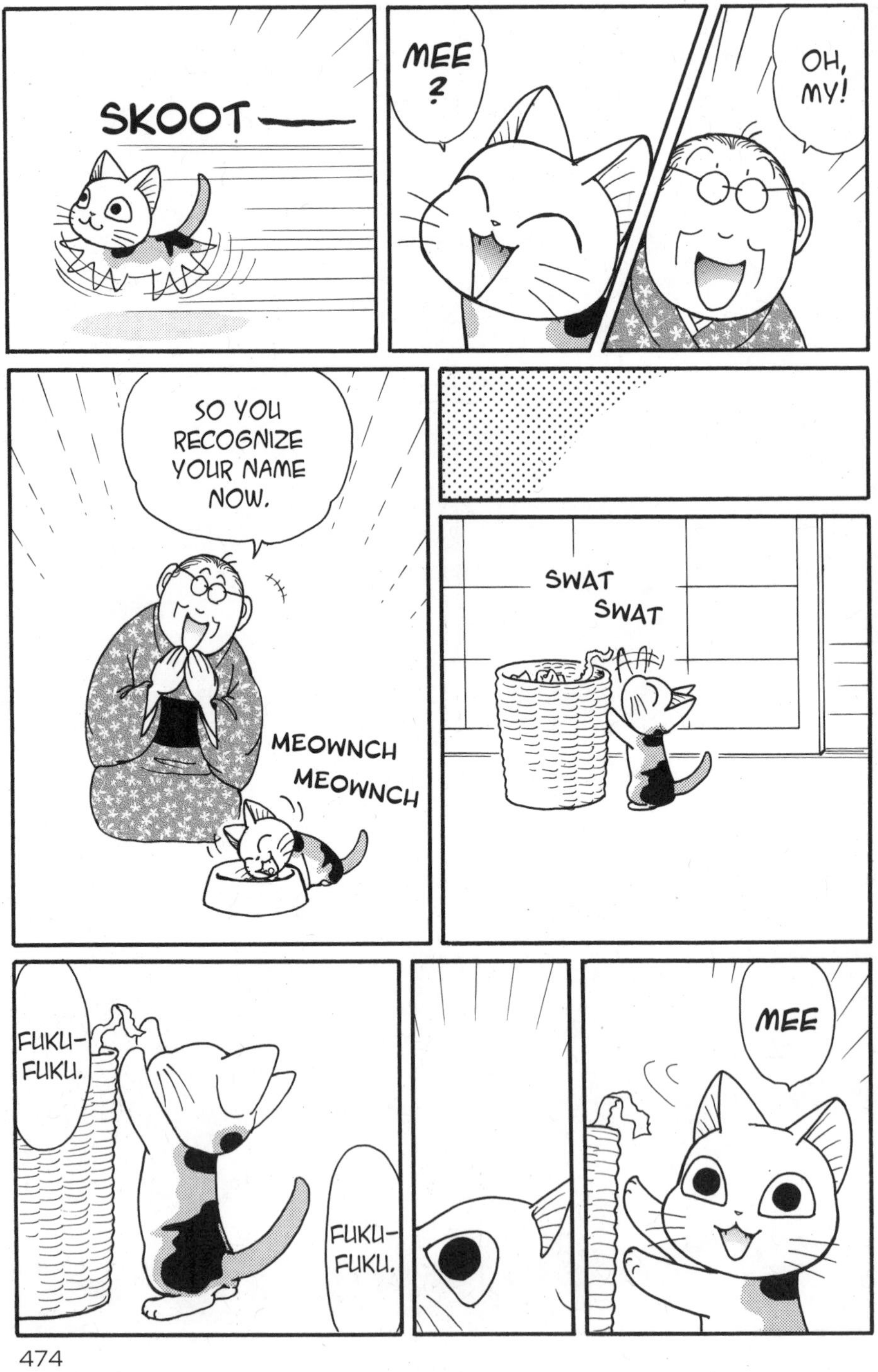
SKOOT
MEE ?
OH, MY!
SO YOU RECOGNIZE YOUR NAME NOW.
MEOWNCH MEOWNCH
SWAT SWAT
FUKU-FUKU.
FUKU-FUKU.
MEE

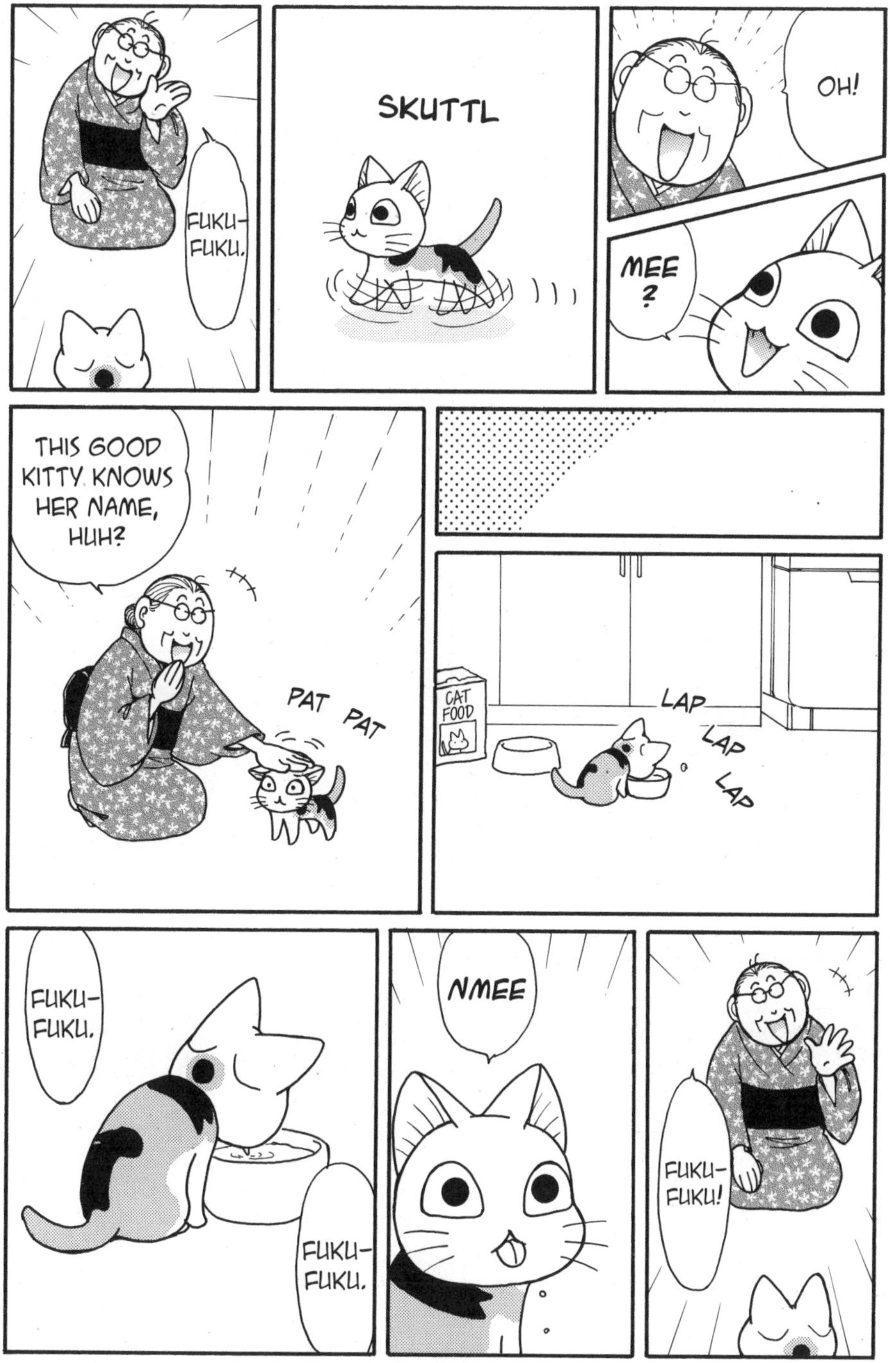
FUKU-FUKU.
SKUTTL
OH!
MEE?
THIS GOOD KITTY KNOWS HER NAME, HUH?
PAT PAT
CAT FOOD
LAP LAP LAP
FUKU-FUKU.
FUKU-FUKU.
NMEE
FUKU-FUKU!

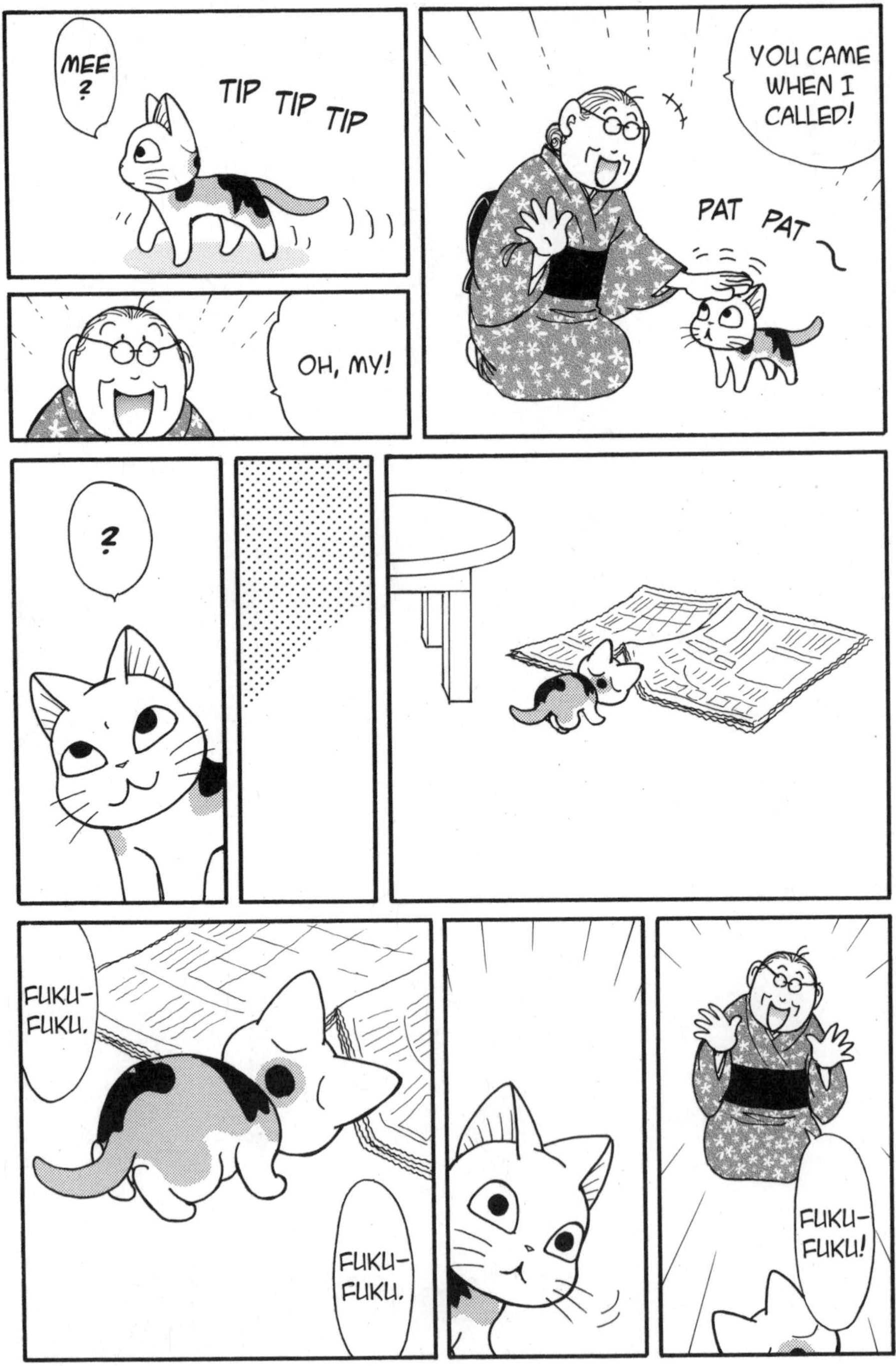
MEE ?
TIP TIP TIP
OH, MY!
YOU CAME WHEN I CALLED!
PAT PAT ~
?
FUKU-FUKU.
FUKU-FUKU.
FUKU-FUKU!

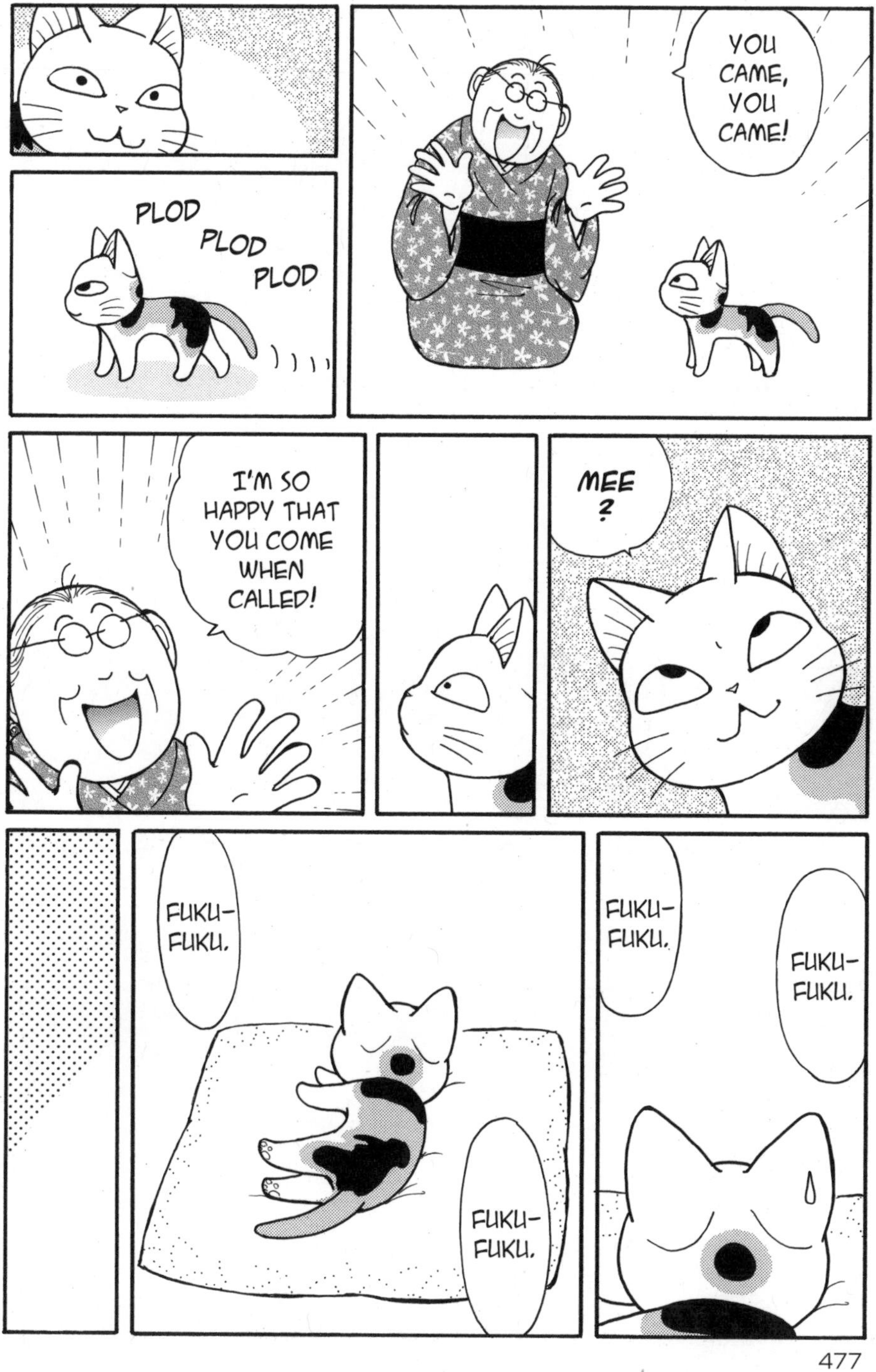
PLOD
PLOD
PLOD
YOU CAME, YOU CAME!
I'M SO HAPPY THAT YOU COME WHEN CALLED!
MEE?
FUKU-FUKU.
FUKU-FUKU.
FUKU-FUKU.
FUKU-FUKU.

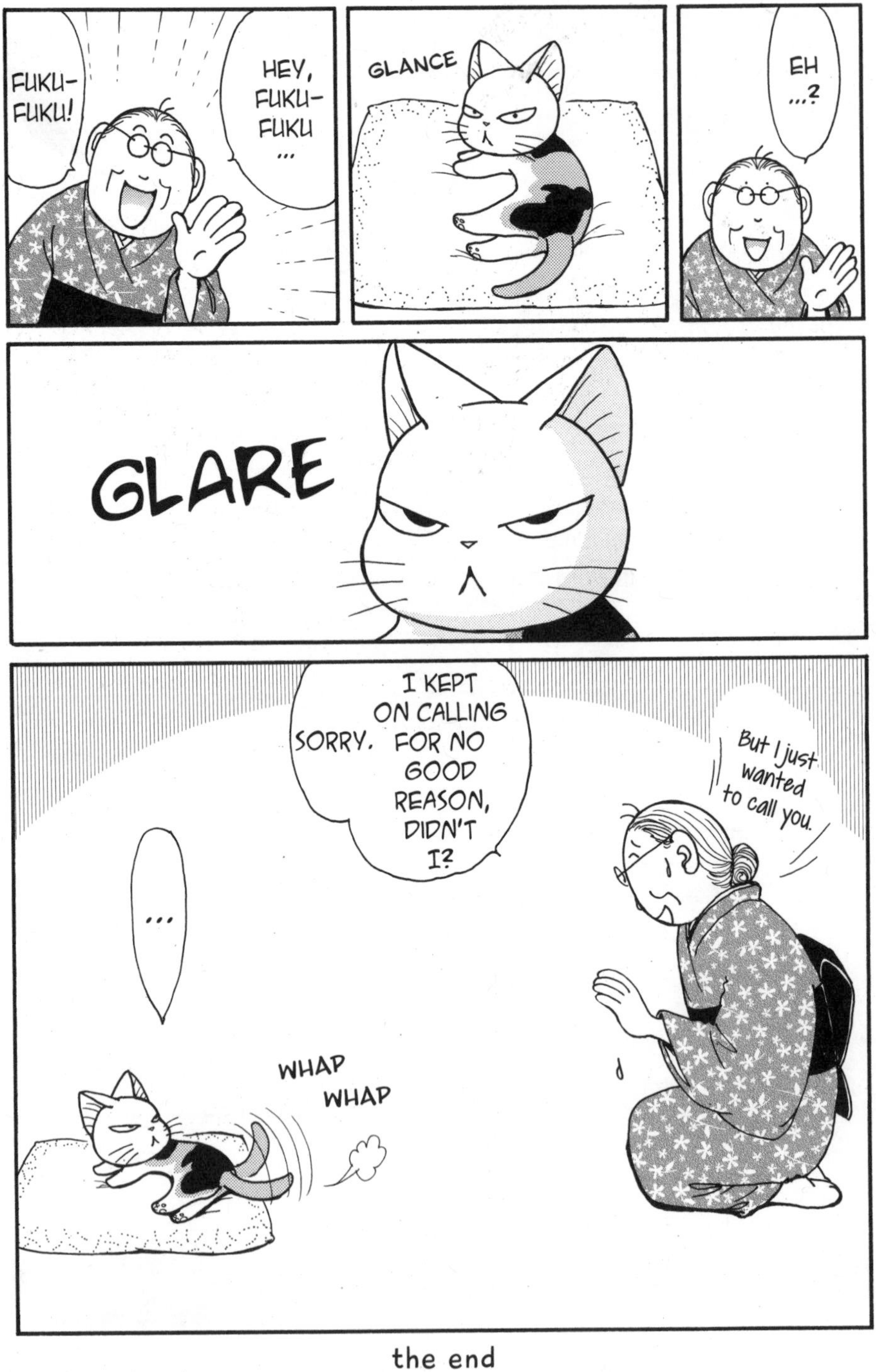
FUKU-FUKU!
HEY, FUKU-FUKU ...
GLANCE
EH ...?
GLARE
SORRY.
I KEPT ON CALLING FOR NO GOOD REASON, DIDN'T I?
But I just wanted to call you.
...
WHAP WHAP

the end

A Note on the Special Chapters

Ms. Kanata's comic career spans over three decades, with the vast majority of her works focusing on the lives of household pets. Her debut work *Petit Cat Jam-Jam*, a *shojo* (girls') comic, distinguished her as one of the best graphic storytellers for young audiences, but it was her first hit *FukuFuku Funyan* with which Ms. Kanata's cats took Japan, and eventually the world, by storm.

Premiering in women's anthology *Me* in 1988, *FukuFuku Funyan* took pet comics to new levels of recognition. While the series ran, *Me*'s editorial staff was flooded with letters from readers of all ages detailing their personal feline experiences. Cat lovers saw just how well Ms. Kanata understood and rendered feline behavior.

In 2004, *Chi's Sweet Home* started running in Kodansha's comics anthology *Morning*. Though writing for a flagship *seinen* (men's) weekly marked a bit of a departure for Ms. Kanata, it was a highly successful one. Her first feline star FukuFuku makes an appearance in the special chapter exclusive to the graphic novel edition, giving new fans of Ms. Kanata a chance to become acquainted with this other kitty idol. The first story was published in *Chi's Sweet Home volume 2*, while the two black and white stories are from Konami Kanata's latest FukuFuku series, *FukuFuku: Kitten Tales* (to be published by Vertical Comics in 2016).

A relatively plump calico, FukuFuku is notorious for her poor eyesight, grumpiness, and tendency for napping too much. Though her inter-actions with Chi are characteristic of her behavior in her own series, they only reveal a small glimpse into her history and personality. Expect to see more from FukuFuku in future installments of *The Complete Chi's Sweet Home*!

The Complete
Chi's Sweet Home, Part 1

Translation - Ed Chavez
Production - Grace Lu
Hiroko Mizuno
Glen Isip

First published in Japan in 2004, 2005, 2006 by Kodansha, Ltd., Tokyo
Publication for this English edition arranged through Kodansha, Ltd., Tokyo
English language version produced by Vertical Comics,
an imprint of Kodansha USA Publishing, LLC.

Published by Kodansha USA Publishing, LLC., New York

Originally published in Japanese as *Chiizu Suiito Houmu 1-3* by Kodansha, Ltd., 2004-2006
Chiizu Suiito Houmu first serialized in *Morning*, Kodansha, Ltd., 2004-2015

FukuFuku: Kitten Tales chapters 1 and 5 originally published in Japanese as *FukuFuku Funya~n Ko-neko da Nyan* by Kodansha, Ltd., 2014
FukuFuku Funya~n Ko-neko da Nyan first serialized in *Be Love*, Kodansha, Ltd., 2013-2015

ISBN: 978-1-942993-16-2

Manufactured in Canada

First Edition

Ninth Printing

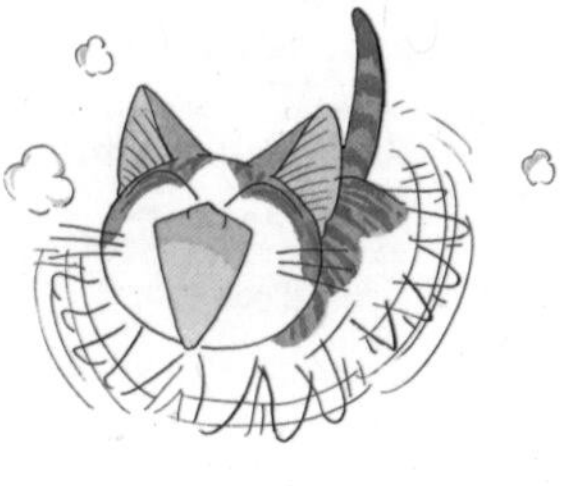

Kodansha USA Publishing, LLC.
451 Park Avenue South, 7th Floor
New York, NY 10016
www.vertical-comics.com

Special thanks to K. Kitamoto

Vertical books are distributed through Penguin-Random House Publisher Services.